Korean Studies of the Henry M. Jackson School of International Studies

James B. Palais, Editor

Korean Studies of the Henry M. Jackson
School of International Studies

Over the Mountains Are Mountains:
Korean Peasant Households and
Their Adaptations to Rapid Industrialization
by Clark W. Sorensen

Cultural Nationalism in Colonial Korea, 1920–1925
by Michael Edson Robinson

Offspring of Empire:
The Koch'ang Kims and the Colonial Origins
of Korean Capitalism, 1876–1945
by Carter J. Eckert

Confucian Statecraft and Korean Institutions:
Yu Hyŏngwŏn and the Late Chosŏn Dynasty
by James B. Palais

Confucian Statecraft and Korean Institutions

Yu Hyŏngwŏn and the Late Chosŏn Dynasty

JAMES B. PALAIS

University of Washington Press
Seattle and London

Library of Congress Cataloging-in-Publication Data
Palais, James B., 1934-
Confucian statecraft and Korean Institutions: Yu Hyŏngwŏn and the Late Chosŏn Dynasty / James B. Palais.
p. cm.—(Korean studies of the Henry M. Jackson School of International Studies)
Includes bibliographical references and index.
ISBN 0–295–97455–9
1. Yu, Hyŏng-wŏn, 1622–1673 Pan'gye surok. 2. Confucianism and state—Korea. 3. Korea—Politics and government—1392–1910. 4. Sirhak school. I. Title. II. Series.
BL1842.P33 1995 94–35259
320.9519'09'032—dc20 CIP

The paper used in this publication meets the minimum requirements of American National Standard for Information Sciences—Permanence of Paper for Printed Library Materials, ANSI Z39.48–1984. ∞

Contents

Acknowledgments

During the course of research and preparation of this manuscript I received financial aid from the National Endowment for the Humanities and the Joint Committee on Korea of the American Council of Learned Societies and Social Science Research Council. Mrs. Yun Whan Choe, the Korean librarian of the East Asia Library at the University of Washington, rendered invaluable assistance over the two decades of research involved in this project.

My greatest debt goes to the scholars listed in the bibliography of this work, in particular the growing battery of scholars in Korea who, especially since liberation from Japanese colonial rule in 1945, have made such enormous strides, not only in filling the gaps in our knowledge of Korean history, but in reinterpreting what we know of the facts. I apologize for differing with some of them on occasion, but differences in viewpoint never lessened my admiration for the quality of their work.

I benefited greatly from the comments and criticisms of a number of my colleagues at the University of Washington, including members of the History Research Group. Jack Dull was unstinting over the years in correcting numerous errors and filling embarrassing gaps in my knowledge about Chinese history. Kenneth Pyle, Clark Sorensen, Kent Guy, Kōzō Yamamura, and Susan Hanley have discussed various aspects of the work with me.

I owe thanks for many discussions of various issues to my mentor and colleague Edward Wagner and to my longtime colleague and friend Gari Ledyard. A seminar held at Harvard under Carter Eckert's sponsorship was particularly useful, especially discussions with Tu Wei-ming and Peter Bol. Conferences organized by Wm. Ted de Bary that I attended in Paris and Montreal were also enlightening.

I owe special gratitude to those who read through the manuscript and offered their kind guidance and advice: Bruce Cumings, Martina Deuchler, Michael Kalton, and Young-ho Choe. I am especially grateful to Margery Lang for the effort, care, and skill she displayed in editing such a large manuscript. Naturally, all errors and mistakes are my own.

My greatest debt is to my wife, Jane, who has shared weal and woe with me for over thirty years, and endured the annoyances of my forgetfulness, absent-mindedness, and self-absorption.

Confucian Statecraft and Korean Institutions

Yu Hyŏngwŏn and the Late Chosŏn Dynasty

0 100 200
Kilometers
Provincial Boundaries
Rivers
Cities
Russia
China
North
Hamgyŏng
Hamgyŏng Mts.
Kangnam Mts.
Kaema
Plateau
South
Hamgyŏng
North P'yŏngan
Ch'ŏngch'ŏn R.
South
P'yŏngan
Taedong R.
P'yŏngyang
Tonghae
(Eastern Sea)
Hwanghae
Kangwon
Taebaek Mts.
Han R.
Kaesŏng
Pyŏkchegwan
Kumip'o
Kangnŭng
Kanghwa
Island
Han R.
Kyŏnggi
Wŏnju
North
Ch'ungch'ŏng
Ullung
Island
Hansŏng
(Seoul)
Suwŏn
Kwangju
Ch'ungju
Iksan
South
Ch'ungch'ŏng
Poŭn
Sangju
North
Kyŏngsang
Kŭm R.
Naktong R.
Noryŏng Mts.
North
Chŏlla
Kyŏngju
Hwanghae
(Yellow Sea)
Namwŏn
South
Kyŏngsang
Pusan
Naju
Naep'o
South
Chŏlla
Tsushima
(Japan)
Chindo
Myŏngnyang
Cheju Island
Japan

Korea

Introduction

Since liberation from Japanese colonial rule in 1945 Korean historians have been waging a mighty struggle to rid themselves of the burden of Japanese colonial historiography, which decreed that for the five hundred years of the Chosŏn (Yi) dynasty (1392–1910) Korea was mired in stagnation and incapable of development and progress. In the last few years this struggle has been won because the efforts of Korean historians have shown that Korea appeared to be caught up in significant changes in its social structure, economy, and other important institutions, particularly after emerging from the disaster inflicted on the Korean people by the marauding armies of Hideyoshi Toyotomi between 1592 and 1598.

Despite the success in demonstrating that change rather than stasis is a better way of understanding the flow of history in the latter Chosŏn dynasty, the interpretation of the nature of that change has not been as successful. In crude outline the essential argument about the nature of change was that the rigid social structure of the early Chosŏn period, often described as "feudal," had been disrupted and opened to greater upward and downward social mobility, and that the primary cause of social change consisted of the growth of the market and the liberalization of the economy. Economic liberalization flowed from the increase not only in agricultural production, but also in per capita productivity and the creation of a surplus over subsistence gained through developments in agricultural technology and methods. There was, in addition, the creation of a new class of entrepreneurial farmers seeking to maximize production and wealth, expansion of the marketing of the agricultural surplus, development of handicraft industry and an increase in the division of labor, and the intrusion of private merchants into the privileges and profits of state-licensed merchant monopolies. These economic developments showed signs of a transition toward capitalism, particularly in the partial monetization of the economy after 1608, the growth of private merchant activity and the accumulation of commercial capital, the development of private enterprise in cotton textiles, ginseng cultivation, mining, pottery, and metallurgy, and increased division of labor in minting, mining, and ceramics.

These changes were allegedly accompanied by a shift from "feudal" relations between landlords and tenants and slaveholders and slaves. Commoner tenants as well as slaves were subjected to demands on their labor as well as payment of rent to a system of contractual, short-term sharecropping and hired labor. There was a rapid decline in the slave population from about one-third to less than one-tenth of the population after 1780–1800. As the line between slaves and commoners began to disappear, so too did the dividing line between the semi-aristocratic yangban and commoners dissolve as the new entrepreneurial peasants accumulated wealth and pushed their way into the upper echelons of society.

More recently, a number of scholars have been associating these developments with a virtual rise of the masses (*minjung*) and a higher level of national consciousness. In contemporary historiography the masses have become the most important factor in explaining the surge of dynamism in the late Chosŏn period and the drive toward modernity and capitalism in the economy. There is heightened awareness of Korea as an independent nation in contradistinction to the universalistic moral philosophy of Confucianism and the subordination of nationality and independence to the dependence, if not subservience, of Korea to Chinese imperial authority.

These revisionist interpretations of the history of the late Chosŏn dynasty have been consciously designed not only to prove the existence of dynamism and development, but also to counteract the previous emphasis on political history and the actions of the educated yangban class at the top of the political structure. The focus of more recent historians has been the activities of the previously neglected mass of the people, who failed to leave much of a written record of their lives because the educated elite monopolized the use of writing.

The contribution of the new Korean historiography to our understanding of Korean history has been valuable by uncovering very important, but previously unnoticed, trends in the economy. What is needed at this stage, however, is to restore some balance by examining the ideas and policies of the educated officials and statecraft writers of the time, who were attempting to analyze the problems of society and devise solutions for them. Their efforts are of invaluable aid in understanding the nature of Korean society and the changes it was experiencing in the last half of the dynasty.

YU HYŎNGWŎN'S PAN'GYE SUROK

There are a number of ways by which the current wisdom of the changes that occurred in the late Chosŏn dynasty could be studied, but it is my belief that a useful beginning could be made by analyzing what was probably the greatest piece of writing on the problems of statecraft in Korean history up to the time of its composition. That work is the *Pan'gye surok* (*A miscellaneous account of the man from Pan'gye*), written by the scholar-recluse, Yu Hyŏngwŏn, probably between 1652 and 1670. Born in 1622 to a yangban family of officials, Yu made two brief but desultory attempts at the civil service examinations, but he gave up on the prospect of an official career and chose to spend the rest of his life in scholarly contemplation and writing.

Yu's work is especially valuable for our understanding of the late Chosŏn period because he was living through the beginnings of the changes described above, and he wrote with great clarity and detail on what he perceived to be the major problems facing the country. Yu has been portrayed by contemporary historians as one of the first, if not the foremost, of a new school of scholars of Practical Learning (Sirhak) who turned their attention away from earlier concerns with Confucian ethics and metaphysics to the problems of statecraft. The first scholar to study Yu's work after liberation in 1945 was Ch'ŏn Kwan'u, who even regarded Yu's work and the Sirhak movement as a whole as reflecting the trend toward modernity and nationalism that characterized the late Chosŏn period.[1] One of the tasks of this book will be to revise that interpretation, but its ultimate goal will be to transcend the interpretation of Confucian statecraft in isolation from surrounding historical circumstance. I will discuss the nature of the major changes taking place in Korean society throughout the Chosŏn dynasty from 1392 to the conclusion of the Kanghwa Treaty in 1876 to assess the relationship between scholarly statecraft thought and historical reality and the influence that each had on the other.

CONFUCIAN STATECRAFT THOUGHT IN THE CHOSŎN PERIOD

The Chosŏn dynasty has been generally known as the age of Confucianism in Korean history, not because Confucian thought was not important in Korea prior to 1392, but because Confucianism played a secondary role to Buddhism and native modes of social and family organization. After 1392 the Neo-Confucian thought of Sung dynasty China as epitomized in the writings of Chu Hsi in the twelfth century became the basis not only of the educational curriculum and the civil service examination system, but also of ritual practice, family organization, and ethical values for an increasing percentage of Korean society. Neo-Confucian beliefs, norms, and practices may have taken two to three hundred years to permeate the lowest levels of village life, although during that time other beliefs like Buddhism, Taoism, shamanism, and geomancy were preserved, especially among the uneducated peasants. Eventually the Neo-Confucians dominated Korean society and thought even though they may not have been able to convert everyone to all their beliefs and practices.

The Neo-Confucian ideologues who participated in the founding of the Chosŏn dynasty in 1392 played an important role in carrying many features of the Confucian statecraft program into effect. Since a number of institutions were introduced or strengthened at their insistence, it was clear that the early Chosŏn period represented the zenith of the influence of Confucian statecraft ideas on practical administration. A strange development ensued thereafter, however. The influence of Confucian statecraft scholars outside the bureaucracy on public policy waned almost to the point of extinction. Since all active officials in the regular bureaucracy of the Chosŏn dynasty were certified through the civil service examinations as orthodox believers in the Neo-Confucian canon, there could be no clear accusation that the regime was failing to live up to its obligation to respect Confucian principles of governance. Active officials, however, were subjected to the debilitating effects of routinization, neglect, and even corruption as well as lingering practices and institutions carried over from the Koryŏ dynasty without Confucian rectification.

Furthermore, scholarly interest among Korean Confucians had gravitated away from the initial stress on an unsophisticated conversion of the benighted masses from Buddhism, animism, and other "barbaric" tendencies to the knowledge and practice of lives governed by Confucian ethical and social principles. The stress on tutelage of the unenlightened shifted by the sixteenth century to a more sophisticated concern with the interpretation of the abstruse metaphysics associated with fundamental cosmic principles and the rectification of the mind's proclivity for immoral, unethical, and antisocial actions. But as the major concern of Confucian scholars shifted to an inner struggle for the correct understanding of the mind's relation to pure cosmic principle, contemplation and writing on problems of statecraft faded as a subject of scholarly interest. For the Neo-Confucian ethicist, good government was simply a problem of the moral conversion of sinners to saints, to borrow a Christian phrase, not the manipulation of institutions, which was left to active officials to work out in practical affairs. To draw another analogy with the twentieth-century West, the relationship of statecraft thought to ethical metaphysics was analogous to the relationship between applied and pure science; the former was useful and practical but less respected than the latter, which dealt with fundamental truths.

For those reasons, the initiative for institutional reform came in the middle of the sixteenth century from active officials after the serious deterioration of many institutions had run its course. Those initiatives were taken by men like Yulgok (the *ho* or pen name of Yi I), Cho Hŏn, and Yu Sŏngnyŏng, who provided the impetus for others like Kim Yuk to sustain an institutional reform movement that carried over into the seventeenth century. A few scholars out of office as well then began to shift their attention to matters of statecraft and institutional reform after 1600, but it was not until 1650 or so that Yu Hyŏngwŏn embarked on an effort that would consume the rest of his scholarly life. That effort was to lay out the fundamental principles for institutional reform based on traditions hallowed by Confucian scholars and officials back to the age of antiquity in China.

Yu Hyŏngwŏn's Role

The Seventeenth-Century Situation

Unfortunately, the seventeenth-century situation contrasted markedly from the transition from the Koryŏ to Chosŏn dynasties in the late fourteenth century. The opportunity for Yu Hyŏngwŏn's message to be heard by the king and bureaucrats at court, who were already Confucian in belief and practice, was nonexistent. The channels of communication between rusticated scholars and the central bureaucrats were closed off and amateur advice on matters of statecraft was held in low esteem.

This phenomenon was not the sole fault of the exclusive right of privileged communication with the throne by regular members of the bureaucracy who had sought to block opportunities for access for nonofficials to elevate their own prestige. Fault also lay in the hereditary factionalism that had emerged in Korea after 1575 and served to further narrow access to the king. This was undoubtedly the problem with Yu himself since he was a bona fide member of the yangban Munhwa Yu clan living in Seoul. His father and grandfather had held office, he had a prestigious ancestor in Yu Kwan who associated with Cho Kwangjo's disciples in the early sixteenth century, and his mother was the daughter of a high official in the Yŏju Yi clan. His wife was from the P'ungsan Sim clan, and her father, Sim Sugyŏng, was a minister of the right – all of which should have qualified him as a social equal of officeholding yangban. Unfortunately, his father, a member of the Northerner (Pug'in) faction associated with King Kwanghaegun, suffered disaster when the Westerner faction (Sŏin) deposed the king and replaced him with King Injo in 1623. That same year his father was implicated in a plot to restore Kwanghaegun to the throne and was killed during interrogation under torture. Thereafter, the Northerners were excluded from opportunities for important bureaucratic posts.

Yu passed the *chinsa* examination, but abandoned all interest in pursuing a higher degree or an official post. He formed associations with members of factions out of power and was known by leaders of the Southerner faction (Nam'in) like Yun Hyu and Hŏ Mok, who had their heyday from 1689 to 1694, and were later purged from power for a hundred years until King Chŏngjo restored some of them to the government in the late eighteenth century. Yu spent most of his life as a recluse in the district of Puan in Chŏlla Province, where in 1652 he began work on his magnum opus, the *Pan'gye surok*. He finished it nineteen years later in 1670, only three years before his death. It is one of only three of his twenty known works that remain, the other two include his recently discovered survey history of Korea in the format used by Chu Hsi himself for China and recently compiled short fragments. He wrote treatises on Neo-Confucian metaphysics, a synopsis of Chu Hsi's writings, a Korean geography, a study of the Chinese pronunciation of Chinese characters, works on military affairs and methods, and other studies of prose and poetry, medicine and acupuncture.[2]

Some have argued that factional exclusion and the rustication of members of minority factions were, in fact, the phenomena that created the great scholars of practical affairs like Yu Hyŏngwŏn, but even if that were true, it did not serve to provide an audience for their ideas at court. The transmission of Yu's ideas was confined to his descendants, disciples, and intellectual heirs outside the bureaucracy until the middle of the eighteenth century when they began to affect some active officials who cited his proposals during the debate over the equal-service reform (*kyunyŏkpŏb*).

Yu's magnum opus, the *Pan'gye surok*, was not well known while he was alive, and it did not attract King Sukchong's interest when Pae Sanggyu recommended it to him in 1678. It was presented by No Sahyo and other scholars and degree holders to Sukchong again in 1694, but again without stirring the king's interest. It was known and admired by the statecraft scholar, Yi Ik, of the early eighteenth century and by Yi's disciple, An Chŏngbok of the late eighteenth. The text itself was made known to the court as early as 1678, and recommended to King Yŏngjo by a former royal secretary, Yang Tŭkchung, in 1741. Yŏngjo almost authorized its printing in 1750, but postponed the decision until 1769, although he permitted only three copies to be made and had them stored at the Namhan Mountain fortress and in the Historical Repository.[3] In 1770 he authorized the governor of Kyŏngsang Province to begin work on a wood-block edition. One cannot be sure from the history of its publication just how well known its contents were, and it appears that until publication of the final work in twenty-six *kwŏn* in 1770, a shorter version of only thirteen *kwŏn* lacking the chapters on Chinese sources was more widely circulated.[4]

In 1770 Yŏngjo also authorized Hong Ponghan to supervise the compilation of an encyclopedia of laws and institutions modeled after the *Wen-hsien t'ung-k'ao* of Ma Tuan-lin. This first edition contained no references to Yu's work, but King Chŏngjo, who was dissatisfied with the errors and omissions in it, authorized Yi Man'un to undertake a second enlarged edition that included statements by Yu and others known to have read his work. Although the second edition was completed in 1782, it was not published in type until 1908, which may have restricted the spread of Yu's ideas. Nevertheless, Yu's work had to have been known to the most prestigious scholar-officials at court, if not the country as a whole.[5] When the Taewongun undertook a series of reforms in the 1860s, however, Yu's ideas, and those of the statecraft writers of the eighteenth and early nineteenth centuries, were reflected in many of the policies adopted.

Therefore, the institutional reforms of the late Chosŏn dynasty got under way before Yu began writing on those questions, and an even longer lapse, three quarters of a century, occurred before his own statecraft views became known to the court and the educated public. For those reasons this book will attempt to survey the developments that were taking place before, during, and after Yu's life to compare his ideas with the reform proposals raised and solutions reached without benefit of his advice and wisdom. This exercise will not consist simply of a comparison of two unconnected bodies of thought, because Yu himself was influenced by the ideas and actions of government officials from the late sixteenth century to the end of his life in 1672. It will thus be possible to trace the direction of influence and the degree of intercommunication in the transmission of ideas, and the separation between active officials and armchair scholars on the leading institutional issues of the day.

Discussing the writings of an armchair scholar when his work was unknown to men who counted in government affairs, let alone the public at large, might appear to some as a futile, antiquarian exercise with no relevance to the understanding of real history. Some might even regard a study of an armchair Confucian writer as a waste of time with only the marginal utility of revealing the views of an single idealist. The best defense against this charge is that Yu Hyŏngwŏn did what contemporary historians and social scientists do – and what contemporary politicians cannot do – he provided a detailed study of the history of institutions from their origin and development throughout three millennia of Chinese as well as Korean history, and a lively discussion of the views of leading officials and statecraft scholars for overcoming the problems of those institutions. Whether one agrees or disagrees with Yu's own recommendations for reform, he provided what was truly an epochal and pioneering study of the institutions of his time that was far more valuable and enlightening than the usual recitation of eternal and universal Confucian moralistic verities that peppers the oft too brief and vague memorials of thousands of active officials.

Rationality and Empiricism within the Confucian Tradition

In the twentieth century, Yu, along with other members of the Sirhak or practical learning group, have been described variously by scholars as the harbingers of modernity because in their investigation of the problems of real life and the real world they seemed to presage the beginnings of a materialist rejection of Confucian moral idealism. In their use of reason and empirical observation as a means of questioning the standards of their time they seemed to threaten the solid unity of fact and value enshrined in holistic Confucian philosophy. In their awareness of Korean uniqueness and national identity they appeared to pose a threat to universal and cosmopolitan Confucian culture. In their concern for the welfare of the common man they suggested a populist attack on hereditary privilege, and in their desire for wealth and power they threatened to break the stranglehold of Confucian physiocracy and unleash the forces of production and the market.

As this study will reveal, however, these generalizations about Sirhak thought are misleading half-truths, often the product of an anachronistic misreading of the essence of Confucian statecraft in terms of modern, Western categories of positivistic science. Where rationality and empirical method is discovered, it is usually interpreted as a sign of modernity, when in fact traditional premodern or nonscientific Confucianism could be quite rational and even empirical in its approach to problem solving in the art of government. But Confucian rationality and empiricism were not based on a rigorous epistemology. Confucian thinkers could move with ease from blind dogmatic faith in the virtually holy writ of the ancient Chinese classics to a critical use of reason in attacking the anomalies of contemporary society and back again with hardly a hint of remorse over any logical contradiction.

Nevertheless, what was certainly lacking was an exaltation of reason as a criterion of knowledge higher than the bequeathed wisdom of the classics. Nor is there to be found in Yu's writings any suggestion that sense data are the only reliable sources of information or knowledge such that a new political science could be created independent of the maxims of Confucian wisdom. Yu's statecraft never separated the facts of sensual experience from the moral truths of Confucianism and never treated the facts of human society separately from the underlying cosmological principles that inhere in the universe. Yu was always a Confucian in morals and philosophy, holistic in his fusing of moral truth and empirical knowledge. Thus to separate the rational and empirical elements of his thought from the total context of his philosophical understanding of the world is to do violence to the comprehensive nature of the Confucian world view.

Yu's Historical-Mindedness

Yu Hyŏngwŏn's significance as a statecraft thinker is not to be found in the creation of new and independent theories of government and politics. He believed, as most Confucians, that the greatest wisdom was the product of the Chinese sages of antiquity and that the models of government institutions were to be found in the *san-tai* period in Chinese history, the age of the three dynasties of Hsia, Shang, and Chou. Yu did not believe it was possible to improve on the wisdom of the sages and he did not have the temerity to presume that he could attain, let alone surpass, their creative genius. The task for him was to identify and extract the fundamental principles of government theory and institutional practice as used in ancient times and adapt it to the quite different historical and social circumstances of seventeenth-century Korea. His acknowledgment of the necessity of adaptation meant, of course, that his own hopes for creating the best possible society would always be less than ideal, that Utopian aspirations would always be constrained by the contingency of existing social and historical circumstances. The fascinating aspect of his thought is to be found rather in his working out of compromise positions between the ideal and the real, revealing in the process that his realization of the impossibility of total restoration of the world of the ancient sages forced frequent pragmatic compromises.

Kim Chunsŏk in a recent study has drawn similar conclusions. He agrees that Yu was not a Restorationist despite his admiration for sage antiquity, and that he acknowledged the need to adjust principle to contemporary circumstance. Kim also held that Yu regarded almost all institutions in the period of the "later age" (*huse*) after the fall of the Chou dynasty, including the statutes of the early Chosŏn law code, the *Kyŏngguk taejŏn*, as immoral, corrupted, and deserving of reform, if not abolition. In my view, however, Kim's conclusion derives from his concentration only on Yu's land reform proposals and not consideration of other issues like military and other reforms, which reveal a surprising willingness to accept some of the early Chosŏn institutions and restore them to their pristine form. Yu's attitude toward the past and his sometimes pragmatic compromise with current reality pose a far more complex problem than Kim was willing to allow.[6]

Igi *Debate and* Sirhak*: Idealism and Materialism*

Some scholars have attempted to connect the writers of the *sirhak* group with one of the two bipolar alternatives in the philosophical debate over the primacy of either principle or material force (*igi*) in the composition of the cosmos and the human mind. Principle was defined in the Neo-Confucian lexicon as the "ought" as well as the "is" of existence, why things are both what they are and what they ought to be.[7] Material force represented the material component of all objects, but since the mind had no observable materiality, it could not have been matter in the common sense of the term. For that reason Hoyt Tillman employed "psycho-physical energy" and Wing-tsit Chan used "material force" to represent it.[8]

Although principle and psycho-physical energy (*igi*) were supposed to be inseparable parts of a duality according to Chu Hsi's formulation, Korean scholars in the sixteenth century debated whether abstract and ideal principles or the materiality of objects and the human mind really governed the operation of the human psyche and human behavior. Although almost all the sixteenth-century participants in the debate agreed on the notion that principle and psycho-physical energy were mixed together or intertwined, their disciples and descendants began to create a polarity in the debate and take sides, unfortunately mostly (but not exclusively) along the lines of the political factions that formed after 1575. For that matter, preference for psycho-physical energy had already occurred in the writings of Chang Tsai in the Sung dynasty, which was picked up by Sŏ Kyŏngdŏk (pen name, Hwadam, 1489–1546) and Na Hŭnsin (pen name, Chŏng'am, 1465–1547) in Korea in the previous century.

In any case, it was not the divergent interpretations of principle and psycho-physical energy of the two most illustrious scholar-officials of the sixteenth century – Yi Hwang (pen name, T'oegye) and Yi I (pen name, Yulgok) – who triggered the rivalry, but *the followers* (emphasis mine) and intellectual heirs of those men. The disciples of T'oegye were generally known as advocates of the primacy of principle, and those of Yulgok as proponents of psycho-physical energy. The attempt by some twentieth-century scholars to link these two alternatives to the Western dichotomy between idealism and materialism and then identify statecraft writers with material-force monism and Western materialism has not proved convincing. Yu himself was certainly no materialist, and to the end of his life he became an advocate of the supremacy of principle.

The summary of his ideas about principle and psycho-physical energy in the brief biography written by An Chŏngbok of the late eighteenth century indicates that Yu insisted strongly on the monism of fundamental cosmic and metaphysical reality and claimed that principle and psycho-physical energy were never separated from each other despite arguments of other philosophers to the contrary.[9] This idea has been further explored recently by Yi Usŏng and Kim Chunsŏk, who have studied the recently published collection of his writings on miscellaneous issues and other materials.[10] Yi found in a letter Yu wrote to Chang Tongjik at the age of thirty-seven *se* that he was inclined to favor the notion that psycho-physical energy took primacy over principle because he could not imagine how principle could even exist in the absence of psycho-physical energy since principle had no materiality to it. A decade later, however, at the age of forty-eight *se* he changed his mind and declared that both principle and psycho-physical energy existed together and were intermixed with one another, and that principle did not owe its existence to psycho-physical energy.

He rejected Yulgok's view that principle and psycho-physical energy "issued forth" or made their appearance jointly. He preferred to think of the "mind of Heaven" (*ch'ŏnsim*, the equivalent of principle in the world) as always a part of "the mind of man" (*insim*, the equivalent of the imperfect human mind beclouded by the psycho-physical energy within it) and never separated from it. But this did not mean that he automatically adopted that position because he had decided to follow T'oegye. On the contrary, he also thought that T'oegye's perception of the *igi* relationship, that "when principle emerges, psycho-physical energy follows it, and when psycho-physical energy emerges, principle rides on it" was too suggestive of dualism, connoting the possibility of separation between moral principles and the inert materiality in which it inheres.

Instead, he worked out his own formulation, that principle and psycho-physical energy were "never separated" and that principle, or moral principles, often referred to as the "mind of the Way" (*tosim*, equivalent to the mind of Heaven) was also to be found in the mind of man, which was vulnerable to human desire and corruption. Yi Usŏng suggested that he probably received some inspiration for this viewpoint from the first important statecraft scholar of the seventeenth century, Han Paekkyŏm. Han's essay on "The Four Origins and Seven Emotions" (*sadan ch'ilchŏng*), rejected Yulgok's view that moral principles in the mind (the four origins) were produced by the mind of Heaven, while the source of the seven emotions (i.e., impure feelings and desires rather than pure virtue) was the mind of man. Han's correction to this formulation was that psycho-physical energy was responsible for the emergence (of both), but that principle was to be understood as the reason why anything (i.e., psycho-physical energy) emerged or appeared in the world at all – a position that at once refuted both Yulgok's and T'oegye's positions.

Yu reinforced his preference for principle by making the conventional argument that principle was to be found in everything in the universe, but he emphasized not only things and events, but in particular the laws and institutions of the real world, which he had chosen to be the objects of his own study. He called his version of principle, "real principle" (*silli*), and the object of his study "real facts" (*silsa*). Yi Usŏng wrote that Yu's shift to a position close to principle-monism meant that his objective was now to determine what Heaven's principle (*ch'ŏlli*) was with respect to institutions, an exercise completely free from any utilitarian objective.[11]

Kim Chunsŏk expanded on Yi's analysis by pursuing Yu's formulations on what he thought was Yu's creation of a new philosophical basis for his statecraft study based on a critical evaluation of the views of Chinese and Korean scholars since Chu Hsi. Kim held that Yu did not simply follow everything written by Chu Hsi, but went back to the classics and used his own independent reason to choose among alternative formulations, a scholarly method that he applied as well to his study of institutions and laws. Kim calls the method one of "critical verification based on the citation of evidence" (*pip'anjŏg'imyŏ silchŭng [chŏn'gŏ] juŭijŏg'in hangmun t'aedo*).[12] Kim's formulation is an interesting one, and it will be kept in mind as we analyze Yu's writings on Chosŏn institutions.

Kim chose to emphasize the contribution Yu made to the establishment of a philosophical justification for the study of the real world and "real facts" (*silsa*) by introducing a new term, "real principle" (*silli*), which he defined as a monistic entity in which psycho-physical energy was included and subordinated to it. Since real principle was to him the essential feature of the universe, he stated that he would not be looking for laws of movement and action totally divorced from moral principles because those principles were an inseparable component of that world.

Yu extended his notion of real principle to all aspects of Confucian philosophical debate, in which principle was equivalent to the Great Ultimate (*t'aegŭk*), Heaven (*Ch'ŏn*) or Heaven's principle (*Ch'ŏlli*), the Way (*to*), the mind of the Way (*tosim*), human nature (*sŏng*), the four basic virtues in the human mind (*sadan*), and the idea of sincerity (*sŏng*, or being true to one's self) in the *Doctrine of the Mean*. In his formulation, however, real principle was not an equal partner with all those concepts that had been regarded as antithetical to the elements in the above list – the corruptible mind of Man (*insim*), psycho-physical energy (*ki*), the human emotions (*chŏng*), the seven emotions (*ch'il-chŏng*), and human desires. On the contrary, all of them were part of the unity that pervaded all of the world and humanity in which real principle was an irremovable part. Kim argued that the contribution of this formulation to those who came after Yu, men like Yi Ik and Tasan (Chŏng Yagyong), was that they rejected the whole *igi* debate for its fundamental misunderstanding of the unity in the cosmos and its creation of an unnecessary dualism that only reinforced factional strife.[13]

These new studies by Yi Usŏng and Kim Chunsŏk confirm my conviction that Yu's unitarian world view was based on his concept of the interconnectedness of moral principles and the mundane affairs of government and the real world, and that he was the last person one might expect would launch the separation of fact from value that supposedly marked the beginning of objective and empirical reason and empirical observation and its divorce from Christian revelation and faith in the Renaissance.[14]

THE CONFUCIAN FRAMEWORK OF STATECRAFT DEBATES

Almost all the participants in the debate over institutional reform in late Chosŏn were card-carrying believers in Confucianism, just as Yu was. Despite the current enthusiasm for Yu and other so-called *sirhak* scholars of practical learning because of the misperception that they were leading the way out of traditional Confucianism towards some form of "modernity," the dialogue was limited to Confucian alternatives alone until Christian heterodoxy intruded on the Korean scene in the late eighteenth century. And even then, the vigorous persecution of Christianity in 1791 and 1801 drove the potential for ideological disruption at the highest level of government underground, restoring the spectrum of acceptable alternatives once again to the Confucian framework.

Nonetheless, working within the Confucian framework did not mean conformity only to a single ideal or a single solution of contemporary problems. At the least, Yu's work represented a rejection of several aspects of the status quo in Chosŏn life, which most Confucian scholars and officials at the time defended as proper or rationalized as legitimate. His statecraft scholarship also marked both a resurgence of a reform movement that had begun in official circles in the late sixteenth century, and a shift to matters of statecraft and institutional reform by scholars outside the Korean capital and bureaucracy.

Whether the role of Confucian statecraft thought was to safeguard the status quo or demand change depended on the circumstances involved. In crude terms, Korean Confucian statecraft was most reformist at the beginning of the Chosŏn dynasty in the late fourteenth through mid-fifteenth centuries, again in the seventeenth and eighteenth centuries in response to the routinization of government institutions and bureaucracy, and finally after the *imsul* peasant rebellion of 1862. In between, the tide of Confucian statecraft thought reverted to a conservative mentality dedicated to the preservation of the status quo and stability.

EARLY CHOSŎN INSTITUTIONS AND THEIR DEGENERATION

Early Chosŏn Institutions

Since Yu's thought represented that second wave of reform and his writings were geared to the problems of the Chosŏn dynasty at its midpoint, and not at its creation, it is essential that the reader should understand the reasons why his reform program did not simply replicate all the proposals of the late Koryŏ reformers. For that reason, Part 1 of this book will consist of a lengthy background section consisting of three chapters devoted to the institutional makeup of the early Chosŏn dynasty (chap. 1), the deterioration of those early Chosŏn institutions up to and including the devastating effects of Hideyoshi's invasion in the 1590s (chap. 2), and the nature of the recovery and institutional reconstruction that was undertaken in the half-century prior to the beginning of Yu's two-decade long study in 1650 (chap. 3).

The description of the institutions of the early Chosŏn dynasty is essential because the essence of Yu Hyŏngwŏn's critique, based on his own Confucian perspective on institutional questions, was that the institutions adopted at the beginning of the dynasty were not fully informed by the proper Confucian spirit. Part of his reasoning for this was that those institutions were not created according to the proposals made by the most thoroughgoing Confucian reformers of the transition period (particularly land reform). The incomplete Confucianization of early Chosŏn institutions was caused either by unavoidable circumstance or by the different, nonideological perspective of the dynastic founder, Yi Sŏnggye, who was a military commander and politician rather than a philosopher or moralist.

His second reason was that the late Koryŏ Confucian ideologues were either mistaken in their confidence in certain institutions that they thought constituted essential elements of a Confucian state (like the examination system, which had been criticized by Chu Hsi and a number of other Neo-Confucian worthies), or they neglected to rectify things that they mistakenly thought were legitimate and acceptable (like inherited slavery).

The Period of Degeneration

Chapter 2 will be devoted to a discussion of the forms of degeneration and change in early Chosŏn institutions that brought both the Chosŏn dynasty and the Korean nation to the verge of destruction in the 1590s. These forms can be conveniently divided into conventional categories. In politics, the Confucian emphasis on limited monarchy, equal opportunity for all men of moral rectitude to move into the ranks of officialdom, and probity in administrative behavior was undermined by regal aspirations to tyranny, the raw political ambition of officials, favoritism, factional coalition in defense of personal interest, and backbiting calumny against political rivals. In society, reciprocity based on an exchange of loyalty and *noblesse oblige* and the bestowal of honor and prestige in accordance with moral capacity was overwhelmed by the narrower and more traditional bonds of blood and kinship that were carried over from the hoary traditions of the Silla and Koryŏ dynasties. An ever-narrowing group of yangban semiaristocrats closed off all access to their ranks by the use of inherited wealth and privilege and sharp-eyed selection of marriage partners, and an ever-increasing body of slaves were prevented by the stigma of birth from receiving the dignity due to ordinary human beings. This was possibly the most egregious anomaly in Confucian society, an hereditary aristocracy of blood and kin in the midst of a slave society (approximately 30 percent of the population) that beggared the promise of the Confucian message that only the most worthy men would lead, and only the least worthy would hold up the rear and bear the burden of support.

In military defense, an optimum system of service for all, given the conventional exemptions of yangban and slaves, a state of readiness blessed by a nationwide system of garrisons, and a high state of morale and an uncorrupted officer corps were all weakened and virtually destroyed. There had been an expansion of exemptions, replacement of duty soldiers by tax payments, a disappearance of troops from garrisons, and neglect by officers of the conditions of their garrisons and the training of their men in order to profit from support payments from the taxpayers. In civil administration, a body of reasonably honest officials and clerks and a modicum of cooperation at the village level between local officials and their clerks, the local elders and ordinary peasants had been lost. The clerks, who were shorn of their salaries by the new dynasty, began to scramble for fees and gratuities to support themselves, to accept bribes from men seeking favors, to peddle their influence, and to funnel illicit gains to their superiors in the regular bureaucracy. Cooperation disappeared as the local gentry lost their public spirit in their attempts to evade taxes and service, and reinforced their superiority as landlords and creditors at the expense of the peasantry. The communality and commonality of village life was undermined by divisions of status, wealth, and class.

In economic distribution, a reasonable system of distribution based on the secure possession of plots of land for every peasant family was lost as the ranks of the dispossessed increased, as smallholders became tenants or hired laborers of rich landlords, or as the truly distressed commended themselves to others as slaves. In taxation, a logical, tripartite system of taxes geared to a predominantly agrarian and noncommercial society in which a grain tax on land, a labor service tax on labor, and the collection in kind of special tribute products from villages was kept to the lowest possible level to guarantee subsistence to the peasant was left far behind. The tribute system was gradually replaced by private contracting arrangements and illicit market transactions, service was skewed by marked and conspicuous evasion with heavier transfers to those still in the system, and the grain tax remained too small to cover official disbursements.

In commerce and industry, a regulated system to restrict commerce and industry to the supply of necessary goods for the ruling class in the capital and bare necessities for subsistence peasants in the countryside was undermined. Private merchants had begun to break free from restrictions, engage in both wholesale and retail trade, accumulate capital, and to corner markets to make larger profits, and private artisans began to abscond from their state employers to produce goods for the market on their own.

What was the nature of this transition? It certainly represented the degeneration of the institutions created at the beginning of the dynasty, but not all such developments were negative because departures from a restricted and controlled economy could be regarded by many as favorable and progressive developments of a freer economy. Can we pin labels on it redolent of the transition from tradition to modernity, like the journey from feudalism to capitalism, from communal land to private property, from bound labor to free labor, from licensed monopolies or guilds to free merchants and free markets, from stagnation to development? There are certainly resemblances between these changes in Korea from the late fifteenth through the early seventeenth centuries that appear similar to those in the West from the eleventh through fifteenth centuries, but bedrock differences remained, impervious to facile comparison. Land was privately owned from the outset, but it lacked an independent legal system to guarantee it against predators, whether the state or influential private parties. The economic and political systems were not feudal in the classical Western sense because the centralized bureaucratic state was already in place, autonomous fiefs were not granted to military vassals, and the peasants were not bound to the land. About one-third of the labor supply was unfree, and they were chattel slaves, closer perhaps to the social system of ancient Rome than either the Western Middle Ages or early modern Europe. The smallholders, tenants, and hired laborers were legally free, but still repressed by state officials, landlords, and local magnates – and they remained that way to the end of the dynasty. The economic system did experience a loosening of the bonds and regulations imposed at the beginning of the dynasty, but the growth of the market and private merchant activity was restricted, licensed monopolies remained to the end of the dynasty alongside unlicensed or private merchants, and currency, either in metallic or paper form, *disappeared entirely from the market* just as other, presumably "progressive" developments in the economy were taking place.

Finally, class structure was not moving in the direction of freedom. Mobility there was, both upward and downward, but because the yangban class at the top through the highest civil service examination (*munkwa*) was becoming narrower, and the class of hereditary slaves were remaining in place if not growing in size until about 1780–1800, there was no corollary liberalization of society to accompany moderate economic liberalization. The state, not terribly powerful but stronger than it had been in any past dynasty, remained under the control of a class of bureaucrats educated in Neo-Confucian thought but recruited primarily from the ranks of the yangban families, not the general public.

The Disaster of the Imjin War, 1592–98

Could the Chosŏn dynasty, the political entity that prevailed over this disintegrating system, have continued indefinitely? If Chinese history were to provide the template for comparison, it would have been unlikely. There were too many things wrong in 1592 for Korean society to have continued much longer without popular rebellion. In any case, we will never know, because a *deus ex machina* in the form of the Hideyoshi war machine with a century of practice in bloody combat and armed with its new Portuguese-style muskets and cannon cut a bloody swath through the Korean countryside. If anyone had had any doubts about the health of the Chosŏn dynasty, its utter incapacity for self-defense removed those doubts forever.

Prior to the invasions only a few men of foresight could see trouble brewing from the weakness of domestic institutions and the growing threat from Japan, but most of the public was complacent. Once the invasion hit the country, however, everyone was aware that Chosŏn institutions were at fault, and that something had to be done to prevent a recurrence of disaster in the future.

What might have been called to task to atone for the disaster were some of the fundamentals of governance: the monarchy, inherited privilege and slavery, and Confucian ideology. King Sŏnjo could easily have been held responsible for failing to foresee the Japanese threat and strengthen defenses. Inherited privilege could have been identified as the reason for the incompetence of the bureaucracy and for the evasion of tax and service by the yangban. Confucianism might have been held responsible for its inability to stem the deficiency of morale, the loss of bureaucratic honesty and devotion, the loss of revenues and service, and the inefficiency of government. But because the invasion was sudden and descended on the people like a natural disaster, neither king nor monarchy, neither inherited privilege nor slavery, and neither Confucian philosophy nor Confucian statecraft were held responsible.

Leszek Kolakowski, in attempting to explain why the Communist system in Russia and East Europe did not collapse long before 1989, remarked that supposedly objective measures of decrepitude like economic inefficiency and wartime disaster were not sufficient to overthrow a regime without the mental readiness of the population for it. "As with most closed ideological systems, communism was for a long time immune to criticism, and no empirical evidence to the contrary made a difference, since the ideology could easily absorb any facts that seemed to falsify it and dismiss them as irrelevant." The same statement could be applied to Korean faith in Confucian ethics and statecraft in the seventeenth century. What chance could there have been for the overthrow of Confucianism and the institutions of bureaucratic monarchy when there was no observable challenge to its monopoly over the Korean mind at the time? There was no equivalent to the "slow but inexorable erosion of Communism as a living faith" in Chosŏn Korea in that period.[15]

Seventeenth-Century Reconstruction

Since the evidence of failure did not provoke an attack on the ideological beliefs and institutional arrangements that produced it, the survivors of the Imjin War set about searching for ways to remedy the major problems without a revolutionary abandonment of these impedimenta. Yu Hyŏngwŏn was also captive to this general mood, for he spent most of his adult lifetime in a search through the materials of his beloved tradition for solutions to institutional breakdown. He was convinced that it was not the Confucian tradition that was at fault for Korea's problems, but the misguided way that it had been applied.

In the half century before Yu Hyŏngwŏn took up his pen, change began to appear in Chosŏn institutions, some initiated by reformist officials, others as manifestations of trends beneath the surface but under way for over a century.

Some of these changes were failures. After 1598 political power was determined more than ever by factions, culminating in the successful coup against King Kwanghaegun in 1623. In the rebuilding of the military defense system, the shortage of troops was overcome, not by the enlistment of the yangban malingerers and draft dodgers, but by the incorporation of slaves into the military for the first time.

The restructuring of military defense was adversely affected by the influence of factional politics. The new divisions created after 1623 became playthings of the politicians who participated in the coup of that time, and the consequence was the weakening of national defense and eventually defeats in 1627 and 1637 at the hands of the Manchus, who in 1644 succeeded in overturning the Ming empire. After the Manchu victory in 1637, the Manchus chose not to rule directly but imposed harsh terms of tribute on the Korean economy and kept a sharp eye on the Korean military system to ensure that no major rearmament projects that might lead to an alliance with the surviving Ming restorationist armies could be pursued.

A respite was provided in the rebuilding of the economy because the destruction of land and the loss of population created a surplus of land and allowed the survivors to begin to restore their fields to annual production, but the state chose not to interfere in the system of distribution. It chose to reduce the land tax to a minimum for the benefit of reconstruction, but it allowed the return of yangban and landlords to their lands, the mobilization of private resources and capital, and the continuation of slavery and tenancy for the cultivation of large holdings.

The most striking changes took place in the economy. In the agrarian sector new techniques and methods spread and served to increase production, allowing surpluses that gradually began to be marketed. The state sought to convert tribute contracting into a system of state purchase of necessities from merchants and the market, which stimulated commerce. Officials sought to introduce metallic currency into the market to increase the speed and efficiency of exchange, and private merchants began to expand their activities beyond the restrictions of licensed merchants.

Thus, when Yu Hyŏngwŏn began to write his massive study of the problems of contemporary statecraft, Korean conditions had changed significantly from the previous century, but the Chosŏn government had by no means solved its major problems in the fifty years since the Imjin War. Yu had to decide whether the bureaucratic monarchy was functioning the way it should, whether the king had too much or too little power, and whether the right men were being recruited into government positions. He faced problems of agrarian reconstruction, land distribution, taxation, and military service. He had to decide whether the current system of landownership based on inheritance, purchase, and sale, and the use of slaves and tenants for the cultivation of estates should be maintained or changed. He had to ponder the problems caused by a largely hereditary and privileged yangban ruling class and a slave society. He had to contemplate the methods for the recreation of national defense in the face of Manchu surveillance. He had to decide whether the economic changes stemming from the *taedong* reform of the tribute system, the expansion of market and commercial activity, and the introduction of currency into the economy should be checked in favor of a return to the simpler economy of early Chosŏn times, or accepted and promoted. In general, he had to decide whether to maintain fundamental principles or adjust to changing circumstances and, devotée of Confucian statecraft wisdom as he was, he had to find a way to apply that lore to the problems of his age.

Format of the Book: Parts II–VI

This book will be divided into five sections (Parts II–VI) to deal with the major topics that Yu discussed in his *Pan'gye surok*. In each case, the presentation of Yu's ideas will be fit into the context of the previous history of the institutions involved and the development of those institutions after his death to illustrate the source of the influences on him, and the influence of his ideas on subsequent policies.

The first three parts of the book will be related to the central question of inherited status, particularly the yangban ruling class and the slaves. Part II on Social Reform will explore Yu's solution to two questions: what he regarded as a thoroughly inappropriate manner for the education and recruitment of officials that had resulted in the domination of officeholding by a closed group of yangban, and the suffering and injustice visited on a third of the population and the loss of their services to the state by the system of hereditary slavery. Part III on Land Reform will discuss Yu's conclusion that the main cause for the maldistribution of wealth was the concentration of private landed property in the hands of the yangban and landlords, and his proposals for eliminating this system and achieving an equitable redistribution of land. It will also discuss the subsequent history of land reform thought and policy to the early nineteenth century to determine whether Yu's ideas had any influence on policy, and whether they set in motion a progressive movement leading to more radical or modern solutions.

Since the allocation of service was also related to the weakness of national defense stemming from exemptions and nonregistration of yangban and slaves on the basis of inherited status and other privileges, the material in Part IV on Military Reform will discuss Yu's methods for solving this problem. Part IV will also deal with national defense in general, including strategy, tactics, weapons, and fortifications, in order to judge the flexibility and receptivity to new developments, but the section will end with coverage of developments in military organization and service from Yu's death to the end of the nineteenth century. In that period the Ch'ing peace eliminated any foreign military threat and shifted Korean attention to the financial problems relating to the support of the military. As military defense shifted away from strategy, tactics, and weapons to finance, the distribution of service and taxation once again returned to the center of attention. This meant that the inequity in the distribution of that burden based on exemptions and evasion became a serious problem that affected the lives of the mass of the population and the very viability of the dynasty. In that context, Yu's ideas were an important part of the debate over reform.

Part V will shift focus to the consideration of Yu's plan for the reform of the central bureaucracy and its mode of operation, and Part VI will treat the economic changes that were taking place in the seventeenth century, Yu's response to them, and developments that occurred through the end of the eighteenth century. The chapters in Part V will deal with agencies involved with the king and his court, the central and local government, including both regular officials and clerks, and the attempt to reinvigorate institutions of local self-government designed to assist the regular bureaucracy in controlling the villages, which remained at some distance from the district magistrates' headquarters.

Part VI will discuss the adoption of the *taedong* reform of the tribute system and Yu's adoption of that reform as a basis for proposing the complete reorganization of government finance, and Yu's support for the introduction of copper cash and his proposals to guarantee monetary stability for the future. Part VI will end with two chapters. Chapter 25 is devoted to the subsequent monetary history of Korea in the eighteenth century because it illustrates the appearance of more complex problems than Yu had imagined. Chapter 26 is a discussion of the development of commerce and industry to judge whether the late Chosŏn produced men who were really more progressive in their attitudes toward economic matters than Yu and the officials of the seventeenth century. Were these men advocates of free market activity, greater commercial or industrial production, and expanded trade who broke the conservative restraints of Confucian economic thought, or did they remain largely within the parameters of Confucian physiocracy?

The central theme of the study as a whole will be an assessment of the extent of Confucian adaptability to changing circumstances, the capacity for imaginative response to existing problems and conflicts, and the ability to seek new methods for the organization of society, government, defense, and economic affairs.

PART I

The Early Chosŏn Dynasty, 1392–1650

CHAPTER I

Confucian Statecraft in the Founding of Chosŏn

The founding of the Chosŏn dynasty was an exceptional period in the sense that Confucian scholars, officials, and ideologues were intimately involved in the political movement that led to the overthrow of the Koryŏ dynasty and establishment of the new Chosŏn dynasty under the military commander, Yi Sŏnggye. Not all Confucians (or Neo-Confucian believers in the Chinese Sung dynasty's version of Confucian doctrine) supported Yi's usurpation because some regarded it as an act of disloyalty to the Koryŏ throne, but those Neo-Confucian ideologues who did support the Chosŏn dynasty contradicted their own ethical obligation to serve the last Koryŏ ruler in the hopes of achieving the adoption of a Confucian program for the new state. For that matter, the Neo-Confucian supporters of the new dynasty did not agree on all aspects of reform for two reasons because fundamentalists thought that the new dynasty should come as close as possible to the recreation of the vaunted institutions of the ancient Chou dynasty of China, while others believed that compromises had to be struck between ancient ideals and contemporary Korean reality. Nonetheless, virtually all hoped to effect a total moral, religious, and cultural conversion of the Korean people from the evils, corruptions, and barbarities of late Koryŏ dynasty life to the refined, glorious, ordered, and ethically superior heights of a society inspired by a Neo-Confucian vision.

The vitality of the Neo-Confucian movement as a political force was fueled by the new, antagonistic attitude toward Buddhism that had originated in T'ang dynasty China in the ninth century with the anti-Buddhist polemics of Han Yü. The so-called Neo-Confucian philosophical movement of the Sung dynasty continued that spirit after 960, and the Korean Neo-Confucians of the fourteenth century adopted it in the late thirteenth and fourteenth centuries and found it quite relevant because Korea was still dominated religiously and spiritually by Buddhism and the Buddhist establishment.

Buddhism had been the paramount spiritual force in Korea since the fourth century, but because of its philosophically tolerant approach toward Confucianism, the two faiths coexisted without rancor. Confucianism was respected for its practical utility in educating officials to the methods of government and aiding in the maintenance of social order. Since the Buddhists directed their main attention toward spiritual salvation and escape from the defiling attachments of the illusory and transient real world, they were not jealous of the role that Confucians played in the world of practical rule and bureaucratic life.

When Korean Confucians became enamored of Neo-Confucian thought, they attacked Buddhism for the corruption of its monks, the submersion of the faith into materialism as a consequence of its accumulation of landed property and slaves, and more seriously, its subversion of Confucian moral values by an emphasis on individual salvation at the expense of filial obligation and family welfare. The passionate attachment to the new faith and the conviction that Neo-Confucian moral philosophy was the only acceptable fount of wisdom put an end to toleration and fueled the vehemence of the reformist spirit in general.

That passion for reform extended to the political and social realm as well. To be sure, the distaste and contempt for corruption was an obvious goad to reformist zeal, but a more crucial source of discontent stemmed from the usurpation of political power and property by private hands. Private control over resources meant the destruction of the public good to the Confucian mind, and the king, the ruler of the state, was supposed to function as the guardian of that public good.

Almost every administrative deficiency in the late Koryŏ period could be translated as a manifestation of the violation of that moral principle. The monarchy and central authority was not accorded proper respect by the private holders of power. Most of the officials were members of the hereditary yangban class who held their posts by virtue of their prestigious ancestors. Their cousins in the countryside held two-thirds of the magistrate's posts in the districts, running them as semiautonomous bailiwicks of personal power. The king was left with insufficient revenues for the central government and the national army because a succession of kings had been intimidated into granting tax-exemption privileges for most of the best land in the country. The king was unable to use the labor power of the country in the service of his own or the national interest because about one-third of the population consisted of private slaves almost totally under the control of their private masters, and the commoner peasants who served as tenants on their estates were little better off than the slaves. Even the Buddhist establishment could be regarded as another arm of the privileged Koryŏ yangban, whose sons dominated the Buddhist clergy and controlled vast monastic estates, peasant tenants, and private slaves that were likewise exempt from the taxes and labor service requirements of the central government.

To be sure, the debilitated state of the Koryŏ kingship was by no means entirely the fault of the Korean yangban. Koryŏ kings were virtual puppets under a succession of military commanders since the military coup of 1170, and after a brief exile on Kanghwa Island while the Mongols ran rampant and unopposed over Korean territory on the peninsula, they once again became pawns, this time in the hands of Mongol overlords from 1258 to 1355. During that period the military disappeared as a serious political force and the kings retained some authority, but they were able to offer little resistance against the emergence and domination of the Koryŏ state by the yangban families who dominated the central bureaucracy, the estate owners, and slaveholders.[1]

The Neo-Confucian supporters of Yi Sŏnggye proposed a program to reverse all these problems, and they did so from a feeling of moral outrage. They fully supported the creation of a bureaucratic monarchy to a level of prestige and power that surpassed anything that had been seen since the military dictatorship of Yŏn Kaesomun in the mid-seventh-century Koguryŏ dynasty. They did so not because they admired tyranny, but because they saw a more powerful king as the agent who would break the domination of hereditary yangban aristocrats of Koryŏ by requiring passage of the civil service examination as mandatory for appointment to the most prestigious offices. Once the new dynasty was in place, they expected to restrain the tendency toward arbitrary and tyrannical rule by subjecting the king to the ethical admonishments of his Confucian advisers and remonstrance officials.

Since the central bureaucracy would hence be the exclusive locus of men educated in the Neo-Confucian canon, they planned to expand central, bureaucratic control over the whole country by requiring that all district magistrates be appointed from the pool of regular officials at the capital. They also aspired to build up the defense establishment by creating a national structure of command in both the capital and the provinces, expanding the number of forts and bases throughout the country, and requiring all adult male subjects of the state except slaves to perform some service for the military. They wanted to increase the tax revenues of the king and central government, and one of them, Chŏng Tojŏn, even hoped to divest the landlords of their private property by having the new state nationalize all land and distribute subsistence grants to all peasant families.

In the economic realm they sought to counter the flourishing commercial life of the private merchants by reducing merchant activities to a minimum, taxing the merchants, and returning the excess of merchants to productive lives as primary producers of food and clothing. This, too, was based on the moral precept that merchant activity was inherently evil because it catered to the selfish desires of men for profit and wealth through the manipulation of the market, rather than through honest toil and productive enterprise.

Their practical program for the restructuring of government institutions was also accompanied by a social, cultural, and religious program. The Neo-Confucians laid out plans to replace traditional kinship and marriage practices by replacing bilateral kinship organization, occasional matrilocal marriage, and greater status and inheritance rights for women with a patrilineal kinship and inheritance system, and a reduction of the place of women by subordinating them to the male heads of household.[2] They worked to replace Buddhist funeral ritual with Confucian ceremony and ancestor worship, and they also called for the physical as well as religious obliteration of Buddhism, including the confiscation of most of its estates and slaves.

Most of these elements of the ideal Neo-Confucian statecraft program for the new dynasty, including the most radical ideals of the ideologues for land reform, can be found in the writings of Chŏng Tojŏn, one of the leading supporters of the new regime in the first decade of the Chosŏn dynasty.[3]

ACHIEVED OBJECTIVES OF THE CONFUCIAN STATECRAFT PROGRAM

General Governmental Policies

Much of the Neo-Confucian statecraft program was adopted shortly after the founding of the Chosŏn dynasty in 1392. The king was accorded more prestige and power and guaranteed more than sufficient revenue for his needs by a major increase in the volume of tax revenue. It would come from the land tax produced by a cadastral survey of all land in the kingdom and from the local product tribute tax that required payments in kind of special items from each district of the kingdom to the king or agencies of the central and local government. The king imposed labor service on the adult male population for the transport of tribute goods to the capital, the construction of roads, walls, and buildings, and service in the national army. Even the relatives of officials and yangban were required to serve in the military, although not necessarily as ordinary infantrymen. They were allowed membership in special elite units at the capital set aside in honor of the prestige of their families, but at least it represented an expansion of their requirements far beyond the late Koryŏ period.

Administrative authority was centralized in the six ministries and other agencies in the capital, and central control over every local district was expanded by replacing all local magnates (instead of about one-third of them as in the Koryŏ period) with members of the capital bureaucracy as district magistrates. Steps were also taken to create provincial governors permanently stationed in provincial capitals to coordinate control of the district magistrates, and subordinate army and navy commanders with a complement of local garrisons.

Passage of the civil service examinations was required for access to the highest posts in the bureaucracy in an attempt to create a meritocracy of talent in place of the late Koryŏ aristocracy. Since the curriculum for education in preparation for the examinations was primarily Chu Hsi's commentaries on the *Four Books* in emulation of the reforms incorporated in the early fourteenth century by the Yüan emperors, the indoctrination of all new officials and educated youth in orthodox Neo-Confucian ideas was designed to establish the basis for the gradual inculcation of those ideas and norms among the public from the top down. A school system was created from the National Academy (Sŏnggyun'gwan) and the Four Schools in the capital down to the local schools (*hyanggyo*) in the provinces to provide higher education in the Confucian curriculum. Local schools, called *sŏdang*, were run privately to provide elementary education for village youth.[4]

Economic Policy

Industry. Chŏng Tojŏn wrote only a few lines on the topic of artisans and merchants, but he did so only to stress the need for the imposition of punitive taxes on both to reduce the number of people engaged in these "lesser occupations" so that peasants would not abandon agriculture in pursuit of higher profits from commercial and industrial activity.[5] The Confucian reformers were thus not that specific about their prescriptions for an economic policy, but the policies adopted by the new government that were geared toward the control and restriction of commerce and handicrafts were generally in conformity with the conservative spirit of the Neo-Confucians.

The early Chosŏn economy was primarily agrarian, with most production coming from self-sufficient peasant families who produced grain mainly for subsistence and wove their own clothes at home. There was only a small number of professional artisans (*chang'in* or *kongjang*), who were either "good" or "base" (commoner or slave) in status. Those of good status were free and independent artisans, but most were also employed by agencies of the central government or by provincial governors or district magistrates where they were registered by those agencies as part of their labor service obligation. Officials meted out punishment if the goods they produced for the government were not up to par. When they were off official duty in government manufactories, they were free to work on their own but owed an artisan's tax to the state.

These professional artisans were engaged mainly in producing specialized ramie and silk textiles, shoes, furniture and cabinets, kitchen utensils, leather goods, tiles, paper, lacquerware, pottery, weapons, and armor and in smelting and metallurgy. The number of the artisans employed by the central government throughout the country was limited by law to about 6,600 men of which 2,800 in 130 categories were employed in the capital, and 3,800 in 27 categories in the provinces. These artisans, concentrated to a serious degree in the capital, were employed primarily to produce the goods needed to maintain the prestige of the ruling class.

In the countryside there was far less division of labor, and most artisans there were in engaged in the manufacture of weapons, agricultural tools, paper, pillows, and bedding. Most were private artisans who operated on their own and were only mobilized on occasion for government work to make necessities or tribute products for the king and court. About one-third of the provincial registered artisans were located in Kyŏngsang Province, but there were never more than a couple in each town or district. In Chŏlla Province, the towns of Chŏnju and Namwŏn, known for papermaking, only had twenty-three paperworkers each. Even the largest towns like Kyŏngju, Sangju, Andong, and Chinju only had one or two blacksmiths or metallurgists. The yamen of provincial governors and military commanders had the most artisans, about a dozen each.[6]

Most local industry at the beginning of the dynasty was in textiles – hemp, ramie, and cotton. Despite government efforts to promote the silk industry, silk weaving did not flourish, and high quality silk products were imported from China to the end of the dynasty.[7] Cotton textile production began in the mid-1290s in China, and cotton seeds were first brought to Korea around 1364, but cotton cloth did not become a major source of clothing until the 1460s. In 1469 Yang Sŏngji recommended that it be designated as an item of tribute for the three provinces in the south, and by 1516 the position of cotton as a medium of exchange became more firmly established.[8]

By the early Koryŏ dynasty, the state asserted control over salt production and granted rights to salt flats to princesses as a means of support. As royal authority waned, private magnates gained control over the salt flats, but in 1309 King Ch'ungsŏn, under the influence of Yüan dynasty methods, confiscated all salt flats in the hands of private magnates, members of royalty, and Buddhist temples. He then designated certain households along the coast as "salt households" and entrusted responsibility for salt production to them. By the end of the dynasty, however, salt production was taken over by corrupt officials, wealthy private parties, and smugglers, and the salt households either fled their lands to escape excessive levies or were driven off the salt flats by the Wakō pirates.[9]

The mining industry was also limited by the circumstances of the time. Early in the Chosŏn dynasty mining was undertaken to extract gold, silver, lead, iron, copper, and sulphur, but most activity concentrated on gold and silver to supply annual tribute to China. The sums were not large, and the government imposed a ban on specie exports and even confiscated private holdings. Even after persuading the Ming emperor to eliminate the gold and silver tribute levy in 1429, however, the Koreans refrained from expanding the mining of specie because it might have led to the reimposition of Chinese tribute demands. Since some also feared that an expansion of mining would withdraw essential labor from agriculture, mining was limited by the state to brief five- or six-day intervals or periods after a bumper crop had been harvested. Although some private mining was permitted on a small scale, there were no records of mining activities for the next century, and Korea had to rely almost exclusively on imports from Japan for its gold.[10]

There were sixty-six iron mines and seventeen smelters around the country by 1430, but regulations restricted even those mining operations to the agricultural off-season. The state used corvée labor on the iron mines as part of the tribute levy, collected an artisan tax on specialist ironworkers, and used the iron for making weapons and armor for soldiers on the frontier. Copper mining was stimulated by the decision to mint copper coins in 1423, but when the coin failed to circulate, minting was ended in 1445. King Sejong maintained copper mines to obtain material for military weapons, but the greater stimulus that might have been obtained from a free market and private demand was absent.[11]

Commerce. Commerce was also marked by tight government control and limited to the licensed shops (*sijŏn*) in the new capital at Hansŏng (Seoul) and Kaesŏng, the old capital of the Koryŏ dynasty. In 1410 King T'aejong set aside certain areas in the capital to specialize in the sale of specific products and established two agencies to control them – the Kyŏngsigam (Directorate of the Capital Markets) to regulate prices, prevent cheating, control thievery, and collect merchant taxes, and the Directorate of Sanitation (Ch'ŏngjegam) to maintain the cleanliness of the market areas. The state completed the construction of ninety-one *sijŏn* (market shops) on both sides of the streets in these areas by 1414 to provide for the needs of the capital residents. In the provinces the authorities established fixed markets on certain days of the week – usually five days a month – so that a network of markets separated by 30–40 *i* or one-day's travel and serviced by itinerant merchants and peddlers (*pobusang*) was created nation-wide, but there were no permanent markets in the countryside until *changmun* markets began to appear in Chŏlla Province after a famine in 1470.[12] Commission agents called *yŏgaek* and *kaekchu* acted as intermediaries for the sale of goods or sold goods on consignment from their warehouses, made loans, and set up grog shops and hostels for entertaining merchants and travelers for which they were paid commissions for their services.[13]

In short, government policy at the beginning of the Chosŏn dynasty was designed to control permanent markets in the new and old capitals by bringing all the permanent and large-scale merchants into a restrictive area and controlling their shops and operations, and to prevent the development of market towns with permanent shops by allowing only peddlers to handle commerce in the provinces.[14]

Since foreign trade was subjected to a number of constraints in the Chosŏn dynasty, it also failed to act as a major stimulus to economic development. Those constraints were the result of Yi Sŏnggye's decision to enroll as a tributary of the Ming emperor and accept the rules and regulations of the tributary relationship.[15]

Trade with China was legally restricted to authorized tribute missions even though some merchants were able to accompany the diplomats. Under the rubric of tribute, however, trade was conducted in the export of Korean horses and oxen in return for ramie and cotton. At first private trade with Chinese envoys visiting Korea was forbidden, but after 1442 King Sejong allowed merchants to trade ramie, hemp, sealskins, ginseng, sandalwood, alum, and pepper, for silk gauze.[16] This was a step forward toward greater foreign trade, but a very small step nonetheless. Since no free passage across the Yalu River was allowed, smuggling was the only way that trade could take place outside the legal framework, and it remained limited in scope until the seventeenth century.

Trade with Japan was also limited by restrictions imposed on the number of authorized ships that could call at authorized ports (at first two, then three after 1426 – Tongnae, Ŭngch'ŏn, and Ulsan – until the Imjin War of 1592), and by the disruption caused by the Wakō pirates through the middle of the fifteenth century. Since the Korean authorities themselves, and not the Ming overlords, imposed these limitations on the Japanese traders, it would appear that the early Chosŏn kings preferred security to any prosperity that could be gained from expanded trade.

The trade with Japan consisted primarily of imports of Japanese silver, copper, tin, sulphur, swords, sandalwood, alum, sugar, pepper, water buffalo horns, Sappan wood (for medicinal use), licorice root, and elephant tusks in return for Korean cotton cloth, rice, hemp, ramie, ginseng, floral-design pillows, sealskins, and books. Imports, which were primarily luxury items, exceeded the mainly staple exports. Trade consisted of official gifts from Japan and private trade at the three treaty ports under strict supervision by local officials, three times a month at the Japan House (Waegwan) until 1610, when it was increased to six times a month.

Yu Wŏndong has argued that the structure of foreign trade also limited the possibility for expanding that trade and stimulating the domestic economy. That structure was based on a pattern of exports of necessities under coercion from the suzerain Ming and Ch'ing emperors, and the limitation of imports to luxuries sought by the Korean ruling class, rather than a full array of consumer items for the general populace.

UNACHIEVED OBJECTIVES OF THE CONFUCIAN PROGRAM

Potential for Monarchical Despotism

The reforms carried out by the first kings of the dynasty fell far short of realizing the total program of ideologues like Chŏng Tojŏn. Before Yi Pangwŏn became King T'aejong (r. 1401–18) he manipulated the succession, first placing one of his brothers on the throne, and then inducing him to retire in his own favor. King Sejo (r. 1455–68), of course, usurped the throne from his nephew.

The Confucian bureaucrats were not able to control the revenues of the king and prevent him from treating the public exchequer as his private treasure house. Not only did they fail to control the king's treasury, but they were unable to eliminate the institution of royal tribute (*chinsang*) by which every local community could be assessed with a tribute levy over and above the regular local tribute quotas to satisfy the monarch's whims for special products. Royal tribute became one of the most onerous burdens on the peasantry because of its arbitrary and uncontrolled nature, and it was anathema to the Confucian purists who objected in principle to the satisfaction of royal desires at the cost of public good.

Obstacles to Meritocracy

The highest officials were not always chosen from among the most moral or educated of men but often they were the political and military supporters of the rulers and were indispensable to the ruler in obtaining and maintaining control over the government. The practice of appointing long lists of merit subjects (*kongsin*) in the fifteenth century was equivalent to a Korean version of the spoils system of Andrew Jackson, the granting of political position, land, and slaves to supporters to retain their loyalty. Another method used to confer prestigious titles without overloading the exchequer was to grant large numbers of *san'g-wan* positions, sinecures without salaries or prebendal grants.[17]

According to Confucian ideals the king should have been able to appoint any person of merit in the kingdom to office without respect to artificial distinctions, but once the new bureaucrats had gained power, they succeeded in drawing a new line between the regular bureaucrats and the clerks to block clerks who had not passed the highest level civil service examinations from competing with them for important posts. As a result the local *hyangni* were prevented from holding posts as district magistrates, the clerks could not be promoted to the ranks of the regular officials, and the state even ceased to pay salaries or grant prebends for the *hyangni* and clerks, leaving them to depend upon the collection of fees, gratuities, and bribes. This group of people were dubbed "the middle people" (*chung'in*) which became more restrictive and limited by birth as the dynasty progressed. This division between regular officials versus clerks and technical specialists allowed to stand for the miscellaneous technical examinations (*chap-kwa*) (or yangban and *chung'in*) was reinforced by the Confucian preference for generalists educated in the lofty moral principles of Confucian ethical texts and disdain for technical knowledge and the technicians (scribes, accountants, legal professionals, astronomists, language specialists, geomancers, etc.).[18]

Finally, the new dynasty continued the civil service examinations as the main means for recruiting men into the regular bureaucracy without ever questioning the adequacy of that institution as a vehicle for obtaining the best possible candidates. The examination system was, of course, not one of the institutions of ancient China and had first been adopted in the late sixth century in the Sui dynasty. It had also come under attack by a number of Sung dynasty scholars, including Chu Hsi himself, and yet these reservations were not taken into account. Furthermore, the Koreans added a touch of their own and made access to the examinations even narrower than in China by prohibiting the nothoi (sons of yangban by their concubines), merchants, and artisans from taking the examinations.[19] In China there was no bar to the nothoi and merchants were able to take the examinations despite the legal ban against it in the Sung dynasty. Restrictions on merchants and artisans taking examinations were lifted in the Ming and Ch'ing dynasties, and what was even more important, the sale of degrees and offices became widespread in the middle of the seventeenth century, and again during the Taiping rebellion in the mid-nineteenth century.[20]

As John Duncan has recently discovered, the percentage of the highest two ranks of central government officials recruited by the examination system in the early fifteenth century was somewhat less than the percentage for the late fourteenth-century Koryŏ dynasty (40 percent versus 60 percent) probably because of the influx of the northeastern military group into the high ranks of office after 1392, but by the end of the fifteenth century and for the rest of the dynasty over 90 percent of officials of high rank had passed the civil service examinations.[21]

Survival of the Yangban

One of the primary objectives of the Neo-Confucian reformers, to destroy hereditary aristocracy and replace it with a meritocracy based on the knowledge of the Confucian classics and Chu Hsi's commentaries, was not really achieved despite the arguments of a number of contemporary scholars that it was. The leading political and social elite in the Chosŏn dynasty were recruited for the most part from members of the late Koryŏ dynasty's upper class except for those few that were eliminated because of their loyalty to the old dynasty and resistance against the new, despite the moral liberal legislation of the new dynasty. John Duncan, who investigated the personnel of the new dynasty to trace their roots, found that the vast majority of them belonged to prestigious clans that flourished in the late Koryŏ period. These included not only the yangban but the local elite (*hyangni*), who were appointed to about two-thirds of posts of district magistrates during most of the Koryŏ dynasty.[22]

Hereditary aristocracy had a long history in Korea, reaching its height during the Silla dynasty when membership in the ruling class was determined by birth into the "bone rank" (*kolp'um*) aristocracy. Even though the bone rank system was abandoned with the Koryŏ dynasty's reestablishment of unified government in 935, the importance of inherited status as a criterion of membership in the ruling class recurred, reinforced by the retention of many members of the late Silla aristocratic families in the ruling coalition.

The Koryŏ term that later became synonymous with aristocracy in that era, yangban, originally meant only the "two files of officials (civil and military)" who lined up in front of the throne in a royal audience, that is, the regular bureaucracy of the central government. The narrow meaning of yangban as "regular officials" was retained, but by the late fourteenth century yangban was used to denote the families, relatives (including affines), ancestors, and descendants of prestigious officials as well. This broader ruling class was also referred to by the adoption of Chinese terms of ancient derivation, the *sajok* (*shih-tzu* in Chinese) or "families of the scholar-officials," or *sadaebu* (*shih-ta-fu* in Chinese), a term that could mean scholar-officials, or in Chou times (first millennium B.C.) the intermediate and lower officials of the king or feudal lords.[23]

In the last few years, a majority of scholars in South Korea have written that the founding of the Chosŏn dynasty marked the overthrow of the Koryŏ yangban aristocracy by a rising (economic) class of landowners of small and medium-sized parcels, who were also committed to Neo-Confucian ideology borrowed from Yüan China in the late thirteenth century. These men supposedly sought to create a new ruling class dominated by state bureaucrats recruited on the basis of scholarly merit in the civil service examination system.[24]

Some scholars, notably Han Yŏng'u and Yu Sŭngwŏn, argued that early Chosŏn society was divided only into two classes: the *yang'in* and *ch'ŏnmin*, or in practical terms, commoners or free men, and slaves or unfree men. The term yangban persisted, but it referred only to men who had been granted office, rank (even without office, *san'gwan*), and academic degrees including the *chinsa* and *saengwŏn* licentiate degrees as well as passers of the supreme literary and military civil service examinations (*munkwa, mukwa*), students in school (*kyosaeng*), and even soldiers (*kunsa*) who were not officials but whom Han considered as men eligible to receive an appointment to office. Other scholars like Yi Sŏngmu have acknowledged the existence of the yangban, but claimed that it only represented the elite section of the large mass of commoners, or the "men of good [status]" (*yang'in*).[25] Han argued that it was not until the sixteenth century that yangban began to emerge as a status elite after the original program of the dynastic founders broke down, and the yangban did not become a full-blown (ruling) class until the seventeenth century.

One suspects that Han was influenced by the comments of Yu Suwŏn who wrote extensively on social and economic problems of the Chosŏn dynasty in the 1730s. One of Yu's chief complaints was that increasing discrimination in favor of a hereditary aristocracy, which he referred to as either *munbŏl, sajok*, or *sadaebu*, had created a new line of demarcation between them and the *yangmin* that had not existed in the early Chosŏn period. Although hereditary aristocracy had been a feature of the T'ang, it had died out after the Sung dynasty and was not a feature of contemporary Chinese society. In post-T'ang China and fifteenth-century Korea one was either good or base in status, and the category of good people (*yangmin*) included everyone from commoners to the highest ministers of state. Officeholding supposedly did not give anyone the right to feel superior to others, but in the sixteenth century when the yangban or *sajok* became distinguished as a separate, hereditary class, the *yangmin* or commoners became a despised category, hardly different from base persons (*ch'ŏn'in*) or slaves (*nobi*) in the eyes of the yangban. The cause of it all was the inheritance of superior status from relatives who held office in the state bureaucracy. If one could find a distant officeholding relative of even fifth or sixth degree in one's family tree, one could claim membership in the *sajok* aristocracy no matter what the level of one's talent or virtue.[26]

Yu Sŭngwŏn, another recent social historian, has taken the argument of Yu Suwŏn and Han Yŏng'u to its most logical conclusion, that early Chosŏn society represented the epitome of equal opportunity for all but the slaves because it allowed anyone of *yang'in* status, defined as any one not blemished by slavery, to register as a student in official schools, take all levels of examinations, and be appointed to the highest offices of the state. The same ability existed for those who chose the military examinations and military office except that the latter carried much less prestige than the civil degrees and offices.

In addition, Yu also argued that the broadening of opportunity was matched by another process of expanding the number of people granted "good" or *yang'in* status by promoting people previously regarded as "base" in the Koryŏ period into the ranks of "commoners" or *yang'in*, and by creating a system of uniform rights and obligations available to all *yang'in* without discrimination. Yu argued that in the early fifteenth century, the basis for social stratification had, in fact, been changed from ascription to achievement because the main, if not sole, criterion for social advancement now depended on individual ability and performance in the examinations and in public office. Hence, the term yangban only meant those who had attained civil and military office, a privilege open to anyone of *yang'in* status.

Even the sons (and sometimes grandsons) of high officials who were accorded the *ŭm* (or "protection") privilege under the law that permitted them to receive appointment to office without a high degree were given that privilege only because of the achievements of their illustrious fathers, and even then, only for a maximum of one or two generations. In a paroxysm of hyperbole, Yu even argued that there was far more equality in early Chosŏn society than in most (if not all) so-called modern societies that display a pyramidal social structure.[27]

Yu Sŭngwŏn, Han Yŏng'u, Ch'oe Yŏngho, and others who support this interpretation have made the important and irrefutable point that the laws of the new dynasty did in fact specify that all *yang'in* did have the right to enter official schools, take the examinations, and hold office, in contrast to the practices of the Koryŏ dynasty, but their interpretation has been tied too closely to the written law. They did not prove their case by demonstrating that the new opportunities established by written law were met in practice, and that the door to power, prestige, and wealth was opened to a wider segment of the population, particularly those who had previously not demonstrated the possession of high office, status, education, prestige, or wealth in Korean society, than before. On the contrary, John Duncan's recent studies have refuted their contention.

The social historian Song June-ho (Song Chunho), who has written detailed studies of the yangban in the late Chosŏn period, has also argued persuasively that in the first century of the dynasty the yangban not only existed as a class in early Chosŏn, but were backed up by special privileges accorded them by the state in statute law.[28] Song felt that although the Chosŏn state never did define the standards for membership in the yangban class explicitly in law, one could deduce the existence of that class from statutory or legal privileges and government policies on a number of important questions relating to their status.

Song insisted that the yangban class after the founding of the Chosŏn dynasty had to be defined in terms of conditions that he found were essential to its existence in the seventeenth century and after because yangban status could not be confined only to individuals, but had to consist of families in which the individual was only a part. No individual could be considered a bona fide yangban without a prominent personage in his past, a proposition that Yu Sŭngwŏn specifically rejected for the early Chosŏn period.[29]

Song also used the statement of Yang Sŏngji, a prominent official in King Sejo's reign during the Yi Siae rebellion of 1467 and 1470, as an explicit verification of the existence of a yangban class of prestigious persons and families, particularly their rural members in the countryside. Yang remarked that the yangban acted as a source of social stability and protected and supported Korean kings through the ages, enabling Korean dynasties to last much longer than those in

China. Han Yŏng'u attempted to refute this assertion by arguing that Yang was only expressing an ideal condition, not a description of reality, but Yang specifically argued that if there had been a few more yangban in Hamgil (i.e., Hamgyŏng) Province, as in the south, there would have been enough loyalty to throne and court in that province to have prevented the emergence of the Yi Siae rebellion – a good indication that he was indeed thinking of the real world. Furthermore, he thought that the virtual lifeblood of the yangban (in his own time) and the very reason for their own existence was their possession of slaves, but because there were so few private slaves in the north, there was also a crucial dearth of yangban as well.[30] It was obvious that Yang thought that the yangban included people of far broader qualifications than office or academic degrees.

Song's opponents have argued that this argument was meaningless in proving the separate existence of a hereditary yangban status group because anyone, including commoners and slaves, could own slaves, but most statistical studies of the late Chosŏn dynasty, such as those by Shikata Hiroshi and Kim Yongsŏp (see chaps. 6 and 9), show that yangban almost always owned more slaves than other status groups, and sometimes in large numbers.

Song also argued that although the honor of the male line of the yangban family was the most important factor in establishing its prestige, the power and position of the families of wives and mothers were also vital to a yangban family as well, a continuation of the bilateral marriage patterns and kinship relationships of the Koryŏ period. Song found that in the seventeenth and eighteenth centuries every yangban family did its best to restrict marriage arrangements for both sons and daughters only to other yangban families, and he presumed that this pattern had to be true of the early Chosŏn period as well, but he did not demonstrate it empirically.[31]

Song held that even officeholding was not absolutely essential for the maintenance of yangban status, and it may not have conferred yangban status on a family without a previous record of prestige.[32] He also argued that obtaining the lesser literary (*chinsa*) and classics (*saengwŏn*) licentiate degrees did not confer eligibility for an official appointment but guaranteed yangban status. It was also necessary to maintain a reputation for Confucian scholarship or the conduct of Confucian rituals, and to demonstrate skill in poetry and calligraphy. Receiving merit subject status conferred by the king also contributed to the prestige of the family and helped it to maintain yangban status. While the importance of education appears to have emphasized individual accomplishment in attaining yangban status, it also appeared likely to Song that a tradition of scholarship in certain families over generations provided a de facto advantage to those over the ordinary commoner peasants.

Song also believed, contrary to Yu Sŭngwŏn, that the protection or *ŭm* privilege naturally reinforced hereditary yangban status because it allowed the king to appoint sons, grandsons, sons-in-law, younger brothers, and nephews of an official of the first and second rank to a post up to two ranks below that of the official in question. Other kinds of privileges included permission for the nothoi or sons of yangban or *sajok* by slave concubines to be admitted to membership in the Poch'unggun unit of auxiliary soldiers. They thus gained an exemption from military service required of all *yang'in* while they were attached to the unit, or were confirmed as *yang'in* or of men of "good" status after completing their tour of duty.[33]

Song also cited another privilege conferred on yangban, although it was late in coming. In 1525 their families were exempted from suffering transportation to the frontier with them if they committed a crime. The range of individuals permitted this privilege was defined in statutory law and included passers of the *munkwa* and *mukwa* examinations and their sons and grandsons, *chinsa* and *saengwŏn* degree holders, and those who had a prominent official each in both the husband and wife's "four ancestors" (*sajo*), which included their fathers, grandfathers, great-grandfathers, and spouse's father. The prominent ancestor was defined in law as any official from the first through fifth civil or military rank, including provincial governors, and district magistrates.[34]

The influence of such a prominent ancestor to confer yangban status on his descendants did not end with the generational limits defined by statute. Song June-ho found cases of local yangban in the Namwŏn area of Chŏlla Province who retained yangban status derived from eminent ancestors ten or twelve generations in the past without any further enforcement of status provided by a *munkwa* degree or the possession of government office.[35] Even though one might argue that 1525 was still too late to indicate that privileges were granted to yangban in the earliest part of the dynasty, Song also discovered in the *Kyŏngguk taejŏn* (the *Chosŏn Dynasty Law Code*, compiled in 1469 and amended later in 1474) provisions setting aside tomb-site land and prohibiting cultivation within its limits for a list of prominent persons in which nonofficials such as holders of the *chinsa* and *saengwŏn* degrees were included.[36]

Even though it was true that the broader use of the civil service examinations as the primary means for the recruitment of government officials had an indisputable effect on expanding opportunity for office, that phenomenon was restricted by the power and influence of the yangban families in society at large. That influence was expressed in two ways: by the ability of a yangban family to retain its status over many generations even without success in the civil service examinations, and the pattern of domination displayed by a relatively small number of yangban clans in the competition for the highest *munkwa* civil degree. The significance of this situation can be grasped by comparison with the Chinese Ming and Ch'ing dynasties (1368–1644–1912).

Ping-ti Ho found that in the early Ming dynasty access to the highest level of civil service examinations, the *chin-shih* examination, expanded so broadly that 40 percent of those who passed were commoners instead of scions of office or degree holders. Even though that percentage declined to 20 percent in the later Ch'ing, indicating a narrowing of opportunity for commoners, downward mobility was far more prevalent than upward mobility, and few gentry families were able to maintain success in the examinations for more than three consecutive generations.[37]

Ho's view of rapid mobility in China has, however, been severely challenged by Hilary J. Beattie's study of one county in Anhwei Province in the same period. Beattie shows that a few lineages were able to maintain their grip on status and prestige for hundreds of years because of the wealth gained from landownership and rent, and not from success in the examinations or officeholding especially because so few people in the area had achieved those goals.[38] A similar phenomenon might well have been at work in Chosŏn Korea to explain why local yangban families (often referred to as *hyangban*) were able to retain status even though their sons did not pass the examinations or hold office, as Song June-ho has argued. Nevertheless, the situation with respect to examination success and officeholding was different for Korea because the country was so small and the perpetuation of yangban domination over the examinations and high office was so prominent.

Edward W. Wagner surveyed the family backgrounds of the 14,600 passers of the *munkwa* examinations throughout the five hundred years of the dynasty and found a singular "concentration of 'examination power'" that became more prominent toward the end of the dynasty as the more successful clans "squeezed out" competing clans of lesser stature. Of the 750 clans represented among the passers of the *munkwa*, the highest level civil examination, thirty-six clans that averaged one passer every five generations produced 53 percent of the total. Perhaps as many as 80 percent of the passers had another degree-holding relative within a span of eight generations, and yet some families could not produce a passer even after ten generations. While some sublineages were enormously successful, others were not. Thus, while the examination system weakened the hereditary aspects of yangban status and precluded any possibility of the formation of a caste system on the one hand, the growing domination of a few sublineages in the competition for civil degrees preserved the maintenance of those yangban families in spite of the meritocratic potential of the examinations.[39]

Yi Sŏngmu also took exception to the view of Ch'oe Yŏngho that the early Chosŏn examination system opened opportunities for commoners (or *yang'in*) very widely. Despite the lack of legal prohibitions against them, they lacked the economic resources of the yangban families, found it difficult to obtain books, and had to study at a local elementary school (*sŏdang*) or official school (*hyanggyo*) where the facilities and teachers were inferior and the quality of the schools had declined rapidly. The sons of yangban, by contrast, were sent to private schools or educated by tutors. Commoners were also faced with obstacles in qualifying for the examinations because they had to present household registers and personal letters of guarantee and recommendation from officials in the locality and capital.

He also thought that Ch'oe was too constrained by reliance on legal regulations, and that his citation of about a dozen commoners or slaves who passed the examinations was not sufficient proof of his generalization. He argued that three of the nonyangban men who passed the examinations were private slaves of important members of royalty and high officials who had support from their masters, that the seven commoners he mentioned might have included some declassé yangban, that the cases were too small in number to prove a trend, and that some of them dated from the mid rather than early Chosŏn period. That they were cited at all in the Veritable Records (*Sillok*) probably indicated that they were exceptions to the rule. As Song June-ho has also argued, Yi insisted that family history and pedigree (*munji*) was really the basis for drawing the line between yangban and commoners.[40]

In rather rough terms, the yangban could be described as a hybrid between the contrasting ideals of meritocratic bureaucracy and hereditary aristocracy.[41] Further analysis of the pattern of examination success in the first century of the dynasty is needed to see whether it indicates a relative concentration of success in a few hereditary families or if it did provide opportunities for newcomers.

Another important contribution of Song June-ho to our understanding of the yangban was his insistence that although the yangban gained their greatest fame and honor as members of the central government bureaucracy, they generally moved out from the capital to settle in the rural villages and were primarily a rural, local, and agricultural elite. Since most of Song's evidence comes from the period after the late seventeenth century, there might be some risk in extrapolating his conclusions backward to the early Chosŏn period, but I believe it is warranted because, as Duncan has demonstrated, many of the early Chosŏn officials were carried over from prestigious families of late Koryŏ.

Song has shown that despite the importance of the *pon'gwan* (choronym or locational name) associated with the founder of a lineage, or even the sublineage designation, families were known generally, and certainly in their home regions, by the town in which their family had resided for generations.[42] He held that everyone in the village knew when the first resident of a lineage moved into the village, except in cases when that event occurred far back in the mid-to-early Koryŏ or before. As in the case of capital yangban, those in the villages maintained and reinforced their status by marrying with other yangban, passing the civil service exams, receiving a government post, earning a reputation for scholarship, virtuous behavior, or the conduct of rites. The family maintained the continuity of the family's yangban status through war and natural disaster. They also held exclusive membership in local government associations like the early Yuhyangso and were listed in the later local yangban association membership roster (*hyang'an*).[43]

In short, although the state created much broader opportunities for advancement than existed before 1392 or after the sixteenth century by allowing most categories of *yang'in* (commoners or men of "good" status) to take the examinations and be appointed to office, the yangban class was by no means a group of upwardly mobile commoner newcomers unaffected by the status of their ancestors. Birth into a yangban family still guaranteed major advantages from that family's position, wealth, political power, and prestige. It enabled individual members to receive an excellent education, pass the examinations, gain the highest positions in the state bureaucracy, and receive privileges or exemptions from certain rules of punishment and service both civil and military. They could intermarry with members of other yangban families, and support themselves in high style by incomes from landholdings, rents from tenants and slaves, government salaries and emoluments, and possibly by interest on loans as well, but not by merchant activities, at least at the beginning of the dynasty. Therefore, the radical program of some of the Neo-Confucian ideologues to replace aristocrats with bureaucrats untainted by inherited status and prestige was not achieved.

Slaves

Hereditary slavery was another crucial feature of Korean society at the end of the Koryŏ dynasty. It is highly likely that Koryŏ had been a slave society with a slave population of over 30 percent, probably since the eleventh century, if not earlier. Even though some reformers in the late fourteenth century did attempt to reduce the number of slaves by freeing commoners who had been illegally enslaved, the Neo-Confucian reformers did not make the cessation of inherited slavery or the manumission of slaves part of their reform platform. When slavery was carried over into the early Chosŏn dynasty, it did not constitute a failure to fulfill part of the Confucian reform program because it had never been part of that program.

Nonetheless, when Yu Hyŏngwŏn took up the question of hereditary slavery in his masterwork in the seventeenth century, he made clear that he felt that the neglect of this question at the beginning of the fifteenth century constituted a major omission.

Land Reform: The Kwajŏn *System*

Another major feature of the new dynasty was the system of prebendal land allotments called *kwajŏn* established to provide financial support for the king, the central government, and the ruling class. Yi Sŏnggye provided for this between 1388 and 1391, after he seized power at court and just before he established the Chosŏn dynasty. The essence of this new system was the abolition of all the tax-exempt prebends (literally, "private land" or *sajŏn*) or "special [tax-exempt] royal award land" (*pyŏlsajŏn*) that the Koryŏ kings had issued to officials and favorites over the years, most of which had been passed on hereditarily.[44] This act did not mean either that the king confiscated the privately owned lands or estates of the yangban elite, or abolished the system of prebendal grants altogether, only that the taxes granted from prebends to individuals was transferred to the central government or its district magistrates and the land so affected was immediately converted into ordinary taxable land. The taxpayer, who was the legal owner of his land, referred to most frequently as "people's land" (*minjŏn*), was now liberated from the claims of the holders of *sajŏn* prebends.[45]

On the other hand, Yi Sŏnggye created a new system of prebendal allotments in 1391 under the name of "rank lands" (*kwajŏn*), granted to all individuals with official rank (but not necessarily office).[46] Since all but a minority of incumbent, high ranking officials of the Koryŏ regime made the transition to the new Chosŏn dynasty, they retained their right to prebendal allotments but only lost control over the specific parcels of land and their owners or cultivators that they had prior to 1390.

A number of officials like Cho Chun, the drafter of the government's land reform program in 1388, Yi Haeng, and Cho In'ok, deplored the expansion of prebendal *sajŏn* throughout the country by the late Koryŏ period and its conversion into inheritable property instead of its return to the government for reassignment after the death of the recipient. Cho also criticized the proliferation of prebendal tax collectors on the land of single peasant cultivators and the collection of taxes beyond the legal limits as well as the loss of tax revenue collections by the central government.[47] His solution for this was not, however, either the nationalization of land and the rotating distribution of it to all peasants or the elimination of prebendal tax grants to individuals in principle, but rather the abolition of inheritance of prebends by the sons and later descendants of the recipients and the accumulation of prebendal holdings by single individuals. His idea of perfection was to reinstitute what he thought was the original Koryŏ system of distributing "land" only to officials, soldiers, and those performing duties for the state, and then requiring that it all be returned to the state after their deaths. The "land" he referred to, however, has generally been accepted by most scholars to mean prebends, livings, or tax allotments only rather than the land itself. As corroboration for this interpretation, we find that when Cho advocated that the provisions of the *chŏnsikwa* prebendal system of early Koryŏ be copied, he used the term, *kubunjŏn*, which under the T'ang equal-field (*kyunjŏn*) system originally meant a basic grant of land to all peasant families based on the age and sex of the family members. To Cho, however, *kubunjŏn* meant a lifetime (prebendal) grant (of tax collection rights) only for princes of the royal houses and capital officials of ranks 1 through 9 whether or not they held actual posts, for their widows with surviving children who remained faithful to them and refused to remarry after their deaths, for their orphans, and for local district and monastery officials.[48] This principle of prebendal distribution was confirmed when King Kongyang ordered the adoption of the *kwajŏn* system in 1391.[49] Furthermore, Hŏ Ŭng in the eighth lunar month of 1388 remarked that the essential element of the new system was primarily "the provision of land [i.e., prebends] to the class of officials, the *sadaebu*," not the ordinary peasantry.[50]

Even though the system of rotating prebends granted by the state to private individuals and returnable to the state at death was different from the T'ang "equal-field" system of distribution and redistribution of land to all peasants, some Koreans during the Koryŏ-Chosŏn transition period spoke of their reformed land system as if it were equivalent to the "equal field" system based on state ownership of land.[51] What they meant, however, was that the state would provide prebendal support to the class of officials (*sadaebu*) and their families and relieve the cultivators of land assigned as prebends from excessive demands by unauthorized prebendal tax collectors beyond legally authorized persons and fixed rates.

Cho Chun definitely thought of the land reform in this fashion, but he pointed out at the end of 1389 that the precedent for the *kwajŏn* system contemplated by King Kongyang was not the T'ang equal-field system, but the land reform of King Wen of Chou at the end of the second millennium B.C., specifically King Wen's expansion of the "capital province" (Kyŏnggi) for granting land or prebends (*kyujŏn* and *ch'aeji*) to his officials. King Kongyang (i.e., it was really Yi Sŏnggye, who was the man with the power behind the throne) "recently in emulation of King Wen expanded the system [territory] of Kyŏnggi and granted land to the residents and defenders of the capital to provide superior treatment for the families of the officials [*sajok*], a beautiful idea that [represented] the intent of King Wen to provide hereditary salaries for those [officials] who served him [*saja serok chi miŭi*]."

Instead of the T'ang equal-field returnable land grants for the peasantry as a whole, King Kongyang only made grants of "soldier land" (*kunjŏn*) to provide for soldiers, "a good method that the founders of the [Koryŏ] dynasty used to grant land to the selected soldiers [*sŏn'gun*]."[52] In other words, the purpose behind land reform was to provide support for the perpetuation of a class of favored individuals that would function as a ruling class, as well as support for men liable for military service in the countryside.[53] In Cho's view, land reform consisted of this combination of prebendal grants for officials from Kyŏnggi Province only and soldiers in the countryside, not to all peasants in the country.[54]

In 1388 Cho worked out a crude system of distribution based on what he thought was a total of 500,000 *kyŏl* of arable land in the country at the time, a figure somewhat less than other estimates established later. He suggested that 100,000 *kyŏl* of land be assigned to the Right Granary and an additional 30,000 *kyŏl* to the "Four Granaries" (*sago*) of the capital to pay for the expenses of the royal house (*kongsang*), 100,000 *kyŏl* to the Left Granary to pay for the salaries of officials, 100,000 *kyŏl* from Kyŏnggi Province to provide prebends for the "court officials" (*chosa*). This would leave only 170,000 *kyŏl* of land in the country for land grants for the support of soldiers, ferry stations, post-stations, shrines, and Buddhist monasteries, not to mention the salaries of local petty officials, envoys, and guests, and the costs of ordinary military expenses. This amount was insufficient to meet those needs, let alone to provide any space for granting prebends to individuals outside of Kyŏnggi.[55]

Even though heirs without rank were supposed to yield their inherited prebends at majority, they did their best to retain them prior to the *kwajŏn* reform. To provide for their legitimate needs after their prebends had been taken away by the burning of their *sajŏn* prebend certificates in 1390, in 1391 King Kongyang allocated a minimal prebend of five or ten *kyŏl* of "military or soldier land" (*kunjŏn*) from land in the provinces to heirs of prebend holders who themselves lacked a post qualifying them for a larger share (the *hallyanggwan* or idle officials).[56] Since they owed service in capital guard units in return for these minimal prebends, some have interpreted this arrangement to have meant a system of universal military service including even the most privileged status group in the country, but it was more likely that this provision was designed to provide guaranteed income for untalented descendants of prebend holders as a whole.

King Kongyang also gave special prebends called "merit subject land" (*kongsinjŏn*) and "special royal award land" (*pyŏlsajŏn*) to people in addition to whatever *kwajŏn* prebends they may have been granted, and allowed them to bequeath those grants to their heirs.[57] For the next century kings continued to grant both prebends and slave cultivators as unvarnished political rewards for those who supported them in any of the political crises that occurred.

In short, the land reform of 1390–91 contained contradictory elements: the burning of existing *sajŏn* prebendal certificates was designed to maximize taxable land for the state at the expense of the yangban class, but the establishment of new, heritable *sajŏn* as *kwajŏn* and merit subject prebends provided a new opportunity for the yangban to accumulate control over new resources at state expense. The difference between this system and that of late Koryŏ was that in the Chosŏn period the state protected itself at the outset by limiting the land over which prebends could be granted to Kyŏnggi Province alone, the province surrounding the capital, first at Kaesŏng in late Koryŏ, and later at Hansŏng or Seoul after the transfer of the capital there in the early Chosŏn period. While it expanded the territory it assigned to Kyŏnggi Province in the early Chosŏn dynasty, it did not assign all the land in that province as prebends to possessors of rank or merit subject land. A certain portion was retained as taxable land for the state, for military purposes, or for state agencies. Just after the beginning of King Taejong's reign in 1401, the territory of Kyŏnggi Province consisted of 149,300 *kyŏl* of land of which 115,340 *kyŏl* was used for prebends (84,100 *kyŏl* for *kwajŏn* rank land prebends and 31,200 for *kongsinjŏn* or merit subject prebends).[58]

The creation of this system of inheritable prebends to men of rank was far less radical and ambitious than the plan advocated by Chŏng Tojŏn, another of the chief Neo-Confucian supporters of Yi Sŏnggye and subsequently of the new dynasty. Inspired by the classical well-field model of the ancient Chou dynasty in China, Chŏng argued for a program of total nationalization of land and redistribution of land to all peasants in society as the best means to eliminate the current monopoly of wealth by the rich landlords and the landlessness and pauperization of the tenants of large landlords. Chŏng had little use even for the Han dynasty attempt to limit excessive landholding, or the T'ang equal-field system because both were only temporary systems. He objected that even the T'ang equal-field system was imperfect because instead of the classical model of state land allotments for everyone it consisted of a grant of one *kyŏng* (100 *myo*) of land for each adult male peasant, four-fifths of which was a returnable grant to the state for redistribution after the recipient's death (*kubunjŏn*), and the other one-fifth of which was permanent (*yŏng'ŏpchŏn*), with a percentage of the crop payable as *cho* to the state.

He also objected to the distribution system of the early Koryŏ period because it granted only tax revenue income (the *cho* or *chŏnjo*) to men of official rank, officials, "idle" sons of officials without posts (*han'in*), merit subjects, descendants of officials, and favored immigrants from abroad, but it did not grant or guarantee plots to the ordinary people. They were simply allowed to cultivate and "occupy" the land that they cultivated. Without any state control, those who possessed the most labor power and had the most influence occupied the most land, while those who lacked those attributes had no choice but to rent land and pay half the crop to the landlords and even more for the costs of transportation. The net result was that "the rich became richer," while the poor were forced to take to the road, pursue the debased occupations of commerce and handicrafts to make a living, or take up banditry.

Chŏng, however, was distressed when he realized that his plan never had any serious chance of adoption because it conflicted with the material interests of "the old families and hereditary lineages" (*kuga sejok*) who opposed Yi Sŏnggye's desire before he became king to carry out the ancient system of providing land grants to everyone. In short, the provisions of the *kwajŏn* system of 1390–91 to provide prebends for the royal house, civil and military officials and their unemployed sons (*hallyang*), and the soldiers and other petty officials who performed some official function for the state without guaranteeing a plot to all peasants was but a weak compromise compared with the perfection of the ancient Chou system.[59]

Furthermore, despite the arguments of many Korean scholars that Yi Sŏnggye was supported by a class of small-to-medium landowners seeking to break the power of the ruling class of large landlords, most of the leading officials of the new Chosŏn dynasty were members of clans that had long pedigrees of high status and possessed ample amounts of land and slaves.[60] They were hardly interested in promoting any reform that would have stripped them of their family's possessions.

In Kyŏnggi Province the recipient of a prebend was referred to as the "landlord" (*chŏnju*) and the peasant owner-cultivator of the prebend as the "tenant-guest" (*chŏn'gaek*). The latter was subjected to certain disabilities over and above the simple payment of a specified "tax" (*cho*) to the prebend holder in lieu of a state official. While the *cho* rate was limited to 10 percent of the crop, the owner-cultivator of the land had to provide firewood, charcoal, fodder, and transportation costs to the "landlord" (prebend holder) and his tax collection agents who collected the "tax" directly from him.[61]

Yi Kyŏngsik and a number of scholars have pointed to this aspect of the burdens of tenant-guests to indicate that the tenant-guests were still landowners, but that their ownership rights were still "immature" and had to undergo a maturation process to create a system of fully fledged "mature" property rights. Of course, the majority of landowners in all provinces outside of Kyŏnggi paid the *cho* to the district magistrate and were not subject to demands by an intermediary group of prebend holders as many of them in the exterior provinces had been in the Koryŏ period up to 1389. After 1389 these landowners were liable to transportation costs for taxes and tribute payments as part of the obligations they owed the state, but these duties could not be construed as a limitation on landownership.

The private property rights of the landowning peasants of Kyŏnggi Province were limited in other ways, however, because the state imposed restrictions on both the sale of land and the renting of land. Sharecropping was eventually permitted in 1415, and the ban on land sales was lifted in 1424 even though both practices must have existed before these dates.[62] One might deduce that the Chosŏn government must have sought to preserve the relatively small parcels held by most landowning peasants on the average by preventing the loss of peasant proprietorships through market transactions.

Since private ownership of land without the ability to alienate, sell, or rent is apparently an oxymoron, one is forced to respect the views of Yi Kyŏngsik and others who have concluded that the nature of private property under the *kwajŏn* system represented a less than complete or immature system of ownership even in the case of peasant owners of *minjŏn* in the outer provinces who were not subjected to any control or supervision by prebend holders as in Kyŏnggi Province.[63]

Military Defense and Recruitment

Chŏng Tojŏn explained what he perceived to constitute the ideal formula for military defense in the new Chosŏn state, and it was based on his perception of the militia ideal of the ancient Chou dynasty. Using ordinary peasants for soldiers had the advantage of eliminating the expense of paying for a professional force of soldiers during peacetime and the bother of rounding up recruits whenever war broke out. As in the Chou dynasty, administrative difficulty was reduced to a minimum because in peacetime the units of civil administration from the smallest cluster of households up to the largest prefectures were all placed under the central command of the minister of education (Ssu-t'u), and the peasant militia was subjected to military training during the agricultural off-seasons, while in wartime the military equivalents of those peacetime administrative divisions were simply transferred to the centralized command of the minister of war (Ssu-ma).

After the Chou dynasty no military system ever attained the perfection of earlier times, but at least the Southern and Northern Armies of the Han dynasty, and the *fu-ping* system of the T'ang dynasty, which included rotating duty soldiers from the provinces as capital guards, frontier soldiers for peripheral defense, cavalry, and marines, provided elements that were worthy of emulation. Chŏng advised that the capital guards should consist of rotating shifts of duty soldiers (*pŏnsang kyŏngjik*).[64]

Since the early Chosŏn kings did not establish a true militia system and did not provide land grants to all soldiers, let alone all peasants, they obviously had no intention of recreating the militia model of the Chou dynasty. Instead adult males liable for military service were divided into duty soldiers who rotated on and off duty and support taxpayers who paid taxes to support the on-duty soldiers. The fiction of universal service was maintained by requiring nonofficial relatives of officials and men with official rank but no posts to hold some form of military service, usually in elite guard units. In the provinces, a hierarchy of units from the provincial governors and provincial military commanders descended to individual garrisons along the coasts, the northern frontier, and at strategic locations inland.[65]

This early Chosŏn system was not necessarily insufficient for the problems of the time, especially since there were no threats of a major invasion from the continent, but it did not represent the ultimate plan proposed by Chŏng Tojŏn of universal militia service backed up by land grants to peasant soldiers.

THE TAXATION SYSTEM

The tax system of the Chosŏn dynasty represented a major breakthrough for the central government because it solved the fiscal crisis of the state that had plagued the late Koryŏ central government. By funneling more resources into the hands of the king and central bureaucracy than had been received since the early Koryŏ dynasty, it provided full funding for the royal house, official salaries, central and local government expenses, and military costs, especially for the defense of the country against the Wakō pirates.

On the other hand, since the tax system was based on principles established centuries before in both China and Korea, it reflected the relatively undeveloped state of the Korean agricultural economy. Instead of using money in the form of copper cash, silver coins, or paper bills and relying on the market for the purchase of goods needed by the state, the government relied on the collection of the land tax in bags of grain, the levying of specialized products in the form of tribute payments in kind from local communities, and the requisition of forced labor from the commoner population and from official slaves, many of which had been slaves of Buddhist temples confiscated by the state.

Uncompensated labor service, in particular, was responsible for the greatest form of state intrusion into the lives of private individuals in Chosŏn society. It was involved not only in the arduous work of transporting grain taxes and tribute items from the village to various points of collection including land and sea transportation to the capital, but also the manufacture of certain items as well. It was required as part of the expense in putting up kings as they made their way in royal progresses and hunting expeditions through the countryside, Korean and foreign traveling envoys on their way to and from the capital, and government officials on their way to new posts or in the conduct of government business. Since in many cases these requirements could be sudden, unannounced, frequent, and arbitrary, they interrupted normal village life and disrupted agricultural production.

The second source of exploitation for the peasantry under the early Chosŏn fiscal system was the expansion of bureaucratic authority in the tax collection process over the late Koryŏ period, and the increasing abuse of this authority in the arbitrary and often corrupt exaction of taxes, fees, and bribes. Although the potential for these problems existed from the beginning of the dynasty, they did not become serious until the last half of the fifteenth century as bureaucratic procedures became routinized and morale among officials suffered.

The Land Tax

After a cadastral survey was conducted in 1388, it was found that exclusive of the northern two provinces, there was a total of about 800,000 *kyŏl* of land of which 623,000 *kyŏl* was under cultivation.[66] In 1401 the territory of Kyŏnggi Province consisted of 149,300 *kyŏl* of land of which 115,340 *kyŏl* was used for prebends.[67] Efforts to expand the land under cultivation and register it for taxes continued, and by 1404 there was 922,677 *kyŏl* registered for the country exclusive of Kyŏnggi, and about 1,700,000 *kyŏl* including it, a figure close to the recorded figure of 1,619,257 *kyŏl* mentioned in the "Treatise on Geography in King Sejong's Reign" (*Sejong chiriji*, compiled 1454), the highest figure recorded for the whole dynasty.[68]

Not all fiscal problems were solved by the increase in land tax revenues. The annual grain revenue at the beginning of the dynasty was about 400,000 *sŏm*, of which 40,000 *sŏm* was used for soldiers' rations. There were problems, however, in accumulating sufficient reserves in case of emergencies. By 1403, however, the government held only about 20,000 *sŏm* in reserve for military provisions, and in 1413 it held in central and local government granaries only about 357,000 *sŏm*, and that was achieved only as a result of eliminating supernumerary officials and reducing salaries and monastic estates.[69] Despite these difficulties, however, these sums represented vast increases over revenues available to the late Koryŏ central government.

Nonetheless, the land tax was by no means the major source of revenue for the state for two reasons: Confucian norms limited the size of the tax for moral reasons, and tribute and uncompensated labor service provided the bulk of tax revenues. The volume of these latter two sources of revenue were hard to calculate because there was no common denominator for tribute and labor at the time, but the phenomenon became more obvious after the seventeenth century when the tribute taxes were converted to a rice surtax on land.

The Tribute Tax and Labor Service

When the Chosŏn dynasty was first established, peasant households had to pay local tribute in products specific to their own region to the king and royal family (*chinsang*), various bureaus of government in the capital (*kongmul*), and the Chinese emperor (*sep'ae*), and also transport these tribute goods by boat and horse, and provide entertainment costs for visiting envoys, labor service for horse guides, and attendants at funerals, and rituals. In addition, provincial governors and magistrates were also required to present tribute articles to the king and the capital in their own names, but they eventually made the peasants responsible for the goods.

Yi Sŏnggye, the founder of the dynasty, established a General Directorate for Determining Taxes (Kongbu sanjŏng-dogam), which advised him to review the tribute ledgers (*kong'an*) of the Koryŏ dynasty to reduce the tribute levied on the population.[70] Even though the Chosŏn tribute system was supposed to have been modeled on the T'ang system, it did not follow the T'ang capitation tax for tribute (*cho*², *tiao* in Chinese) because the Koreans used the term for tribute, *cho*², to mean a household tax payable in any medium, and personal tribute (*sin'gong*) paid by outside-resident official slaves (*oegŏ nobi*) to support those selected from the province for duty in the capital (*sŏnsang nobi*).

Labor service in the manufacture of tribute products was also required in addition to transportation of tribute levies. This kind of labor service involved boat construction, the mining of metals, the gathering of husks, straw, coal, and firewood, and hunting for game. Gold mining in the districts of Hwaju, Anbyŏn, and Tanch'ŏn in Hamgyŏng Province up to 1425, for example, required eighty days of labor service per year, estimated at ten times the value of one year's tribute levy. In 1470 the revised labor service law included tasks that were involved in the fabrication or transportation of tribute goods, or the entertainment of envoys involved in international tribute payments: cutting ice for the capital, gold mining, repairing buildings, constructing ranches, digging coal, cutting straw, smelting iron, tending horses, fishing, and digging tombs. Special service included wall construction, transporting rice, carrying Chinese envoys in palanquins, building new ranches, erecting tents for guests, brewing nitrate, transporting wood and stone, building dikes and ditches, finding fibrous plants, making plaster.[71]

There was no schedule of tribute levies by household for a province or even the country at large. District tribute quotas were originally set according to the amount of land in each jurisdiction, and magistrates had the authority to determine the distribution of tribute by household in their own districts. Since King T'aejo (Yi Sŏnggye) at the beginning of the dynasty prohibited peasants from moving from their home villages and assumed that the village population would never change, he forbade magistrates from adjusting tribute quotas listed in the tribute ledgers (*kong'an*) according to annual changes in population. Since people continued to move and die without respect to T'aejo's expectations, the household tribute rate could be far heavier in one district than another, and the only recourse the peasants had against an onerous tribute was to break the law and abscond. Furthermore, because the district's tribute quota was determined by the amount of land in the district, it was not possible to reduce village tribute taxes to alleviate excessive rates in any given village. Kings could issue a special dispensation to reduce tribute rates, but they rarely did so.

There was also no way for the government to return tribute if the supply exceeded demand, but the government did not hesitate to impose additional or special levies or demand payment of the next year's tribute in advance.[72] Magistrates distributed tribute levies by household according to some calculation of the amount of land it cultivated and the size of its family. The levy was assessed on the household of cultivators, not just owners. Even though tenancy had been forbidden until 1424, tenancy was practiced anyway and tenant cultivators had to pay their tribute quota in addition to half their crop in rent.

Although the details of calculating household population for tribute assessments at the beginning of the dynasty have not been preserved, it must have been similar to the method for assessing labor service. In 1392 the labor service law required that one male be furnished by a large household containing ten or more adult males, or by every two medium households with five or more adult males each, or by every three households with four or less adult males each.

In 1401 the basis of labor service was changed to a calculation of cultivated land, one adult male for every three *kyŏl* of land was adopted. The rate was reduced to one adult male for every five *kyŏl* in 1431, and finally, one adult male for every eight *kyŏl* (or six *kyŏl* if more men were needed) in 1470. In other words, some mix between the population of a household and the amount of land it cultivated (whether owners or tenants) produced a basis for household tribute assessments. The district clerks who were responsible for assessing household tribute levies used the opportunity to exploit the peasants, and the magistrates never published a written schedule of tax payments for their own districts. The tribute ledgers that set quotas of tribute items for each district were changed only after twenty or thirty years and in the interval districts were required to provide the same items even though they may have ceased their production.[73] As mentioned before, royal tribute (*chinsang*) was especially onerous because it could be levied on a monthly or even daily basis, and the peasants, particularly in Kyŏnggi Province, were subject to frequent and unrestricted demands.[74]

THE FAILURE OF PAPER MONEY AND COPPER CASH

Pre-Chosŏn History of Currency

Metallic cash as well as paper money disappeared from Korean markets by the middle of the sixteenth century, a reflection of the limitations on the volume of trade and the regression of the Korean economy to primary agricultural production in which bags of grain and bolts of cloth were the main media of exchange. This development reflected a devolution from earlier periods in Korean history in which the circulation of currency reflected a larger volume of trade and a more vigorous economy. Was this devolution, however, the result of a conscious application of part of the Neo-Confucian statecraft program at the beginning of the dynasty?

It certainly was not the result of a continuation of economic policy toward commerce and currency in previous periods. Iron was probably used as a means of exchange in raw metallic form back in the ancient Chosŏn dynasty in the third century before Christ and continued in the southern part of the Korean peninsula in the first several centuries after the birth of Christ. Gold and silver were used as media of exchange in the Eastern Okchŏ and Silla states to serve the needs of the wealthy, possibly in coin form. Chinese coins were used in Korea at least since the third or fourth centuries B.C. Coins from Han dynasty China, particularly a 5-*shu* coin dated A.D. 14 and molds for minting them, and multiple-denomination 50-cash coins as well have been discovered in the Kŭmhae region in the south and on Cheju Island. During the long period of peaceful relations with T'ang China, Chinese coins circulated in the Silla kingdom after its unification of the Korean peninsula in the late seventh century.

In the Koryŏ dynasty in the tenth century, copies of an eighth century T'ang dynasty coin were minted in Korea with a Korean inscription on the back, and at the end of that century King Sŏngjong ordered the minting of cash (most likely iron) in 996, the first state-sponsored coin in Korean history. Licensed shops were established in Kaesŏng, the Koryŏ capital, and the use of both Chinese and Korean coins flourished in the context of active trade with Sung China, the Liao and Chin dynasties in Manchuria and North China, and Japan in the tenth through the mid-thirteenth centuries.

In King Sukchong's reign an official was appointed in 1097 to oversee currency, and in 1101 a Directorate of the Mint (Chujŏn-dogam) was established. Shortly thereafter silver cash (*ŭnbyŏng*) in the form of the shape of the Korean peninsula and weighing one catty (*kŭn*, 1.1 lbs.) was minted for use in foreign trade. Counterfeiters continued, however, to reduce the value of silver currency still further by adulterating it with copper, and this drove the better government silver currency out of the market. After King Sukchong's reign (1096–1105), commerce declined and cash was replaced by grain and cloth as the main media of exchange.[75]

Commerce and trade were reduced severely by the series of Mongol invasions of Korea in the thirteenth century, but once Mongol control of Korea was established after 1259, commerce expanded under the Yüan dynasty, and 100,000 bundles of Chinese paper money including the Sung *hui-tzu* and the Yüan *pao-ch'ao* bills were imported into Koryŏ for circulation. Silver coins were minted in the late thirteenth and early fourteenth centuries but, again, adulteration with copper by counterfeiters drove silver coins from the marketplace by 1392.

Ramie cloth (*map'o*), therefore, was the dominant material used for currency in the Koryŏ period, and it was measured by the *sae*, a unit defined as eighty warp threads by Cheng Hsüan in his commentary on the funeral rituals of the classic *I-li* (*The Book of Etiquette and Ceremonial*). Cloth was generally divided into two categories of fine cloth (*sep'o*) and rough cloth (*ch'up'o*). According to the *I-li* ceremonial hats were woven from fine black threads of 30-*sae* cloth, or 2,400 warp threads, and the ceremonial court gown was woven of 15-*sae* cloth with 1,200 warp threads. In the twelfth century, however, Chu Hsi questioned these numbers since in his own time it was difficult enough to produce fine cloth of 20 *sae*, and even 15-*sae* cloth could only be woven of the finest silk.

Yi Ik, an eighteenth-century Korean scholar, however, insisted that the Koreans of the Unified Silla period had been able to weave fine cloth of 30–40 *sae* and in fact presented it to the T'ang emperors for tribute, and the *Samguk sagi* (*The History of the Three Kingdoms*) in Korea also recorded that cloth of 26 and 28 *sae* was woven for men and women of the *chin'gol* or true bone aristocracy. Nonetheless, by late Koryŏ times no cloth was woven finer than 20 *sae*, and after the establishment of the Chosŏn dynasty in 1392 fine cloth (*sep'o*) of 12 *sae* was presented as tribute to the Ming emperor or the Korean king.

The bolts of cloth used as currency had a smaller thread count and were less valuable. The standard bolt called correct cloth (*chŏngp'o*) consisted of 5 *sae* and was woven first in ramie but then replaced almost entirely by cotton by the mid-fifteenth century. Types of cloth of a cheaper grade called ordinary cloth (*sangp'o*) or rough cloth (*ch'up'o*), had lower thread counts of 2 or 3 *sae* and were about half the value of correct cloth. Because rough cloth was the cheapest, its increasing use in the market inflated the prices of commodities and drove out the more expensive correct cloth in accordance with Gresham's law.

In the last year of the Koryŏ dynasty, 1391, King Kongyang accepted Pang Saryang's recommendation that the Korean government mint copper cash, allow it to circulate with paper money, and abolish the use of rough cloth (*ch'up'o*) for currency. The office of currency was replaced by the Paper Money Treasury (Chasŏm chŏhwago), which printed paper bills valued at one *p'il* of 5 *sae* "correct cloth" (ramie cloth), or 1/30 *p'il* of cotton cloth (*myŏnp'o*), or one *mal* of rice each in the style of the Sung and Yüan notes, but the paper bills rapidly lost value (declining to one *toe* or 1/10 *mal* of rice and 1/100 *p'il* of *myŏnp'o* per bill) and only nine months later in 1392 both paper money and the Paper Money Treasury were abolished.

Nonetheless, initiative and support for the printing of paper money came from active officials in the central government who were influenced by the Chinese monetary conditions, advanced since the Sung dynasty. Yi Sŏnggye, the subsequent founder of the Chosŏn dynasty, may have been responsible for this reversal of policy for political rather than economic reasons because as virtual military dictator of the Koryŏ government in 1392 he may have been opposed to any monetary measure that would increase the financial resources of the tottering Koryŏ dynasty.

In short, Korea was more advanced in the development of commerce, trade, and monetary instruments in the Silla and Koryŏ periods than it was after the establishment of the Chosŏn dynasty in 1392. These earlier developments were obviously the product of the expansion of commerce in China prior to the Ming dynasty in the fourteenth century, and the shift away from commerce and foreign trade toward a greater concentration on agriculture after the Ming dynasty was founded in 1368.[76]

Early Chosŏn Policy

One of the intriguing features of early Chosŏn economic policy is that while the Neo-Confucian supporters of the new dynasty objected to the expansion of industry and commerce beyond the levels needed to facilitate the exchange of goods in a subsistence economy founded on agricultural production, a number of kings, with the assistance of many high officials, attempted to promote the relatively advanced use of copper cash and paper money in place of bolts of cloth and bags of grain. The anomaly between Confucian statecraft ideology and royal policy is most easily explained by the much weaker commitment to Confucian economic precepts by some kings than by the true believers among the scholars and officials. They were certainly far more appreciative of the prospect of improving the flow of revenue and the dispensation of relief during drought and famine by the relatively effortless printing of paper money or minting of copper coins.

In an era when the majority of the population was so distrustful of paper money and copper coins, the government had to find the means of supporting the value of its money by refraining from debasement, controlling counterfeiting, and regulating the money supply to prevent either excessive inflation or deflation. The most formidable obstacle to paper money was that it had very little intrinsic value and was easily worn out by use. The shortage of copper ore, the backwardness of mining technology, and the limited imports of copper from Japan were the main obstacles to providing sufficient copper cash to meet national demand. That should have eliminated the possibility of inflation and created the likelihood of deflation by increasing the value of the copper coins, but the public had lost confidence in copper coins and their value dropped below the intrinsic value of the copper in the coins. Once this occurred, the population began to melt down the coins and convert them to raw copper or copper utensils, which were worth more than the cash and could be exported abroad to pay for imports.

The use by the early Chosŏn kings of coercion and punishment to enforce the use of paper money or copper cash – even by a king like Sejong, who had a great reputation for compassion and benevolence – succeeded only in intensifying the misery and oppression of the general population. Most people were either afraid of severe financial loss by holding on to money as it depreciated rapidly in value, or were simply unable to obtain coins because they were either too expensive or too worthless, depending on the conditions at the time. It was also a violation of Confucian values by using violence just to maintain the value of the money supply.

Monetary policy in early Chosŏn began with two failed attempts to introduce paper money. In 1401 King T'aejong adopted Ha Yun's proposal to revive the printing of paper money (*chŏhwa*) and to prohibit cotton cloth as a medium of exchange to force the public to accept paper money. He created the Aid Bureau (Sasŏmsŏ) to issue the bills in 1402, but after the value of the money plummeted in value he abandoned the project after only two months and abolished the Aid Bureau in 1403.

In 1410 T'aejong tried to introduce paper money a second time to alleviate the chronic fiscal deficits, but this time he not only forbade the use of 5-*sae* cloth and the cheaper *ch'up'o* as media of exchange, but also prohibited the very weaving of 5-*sae* cloth itself, and cut up the cloth in the capital warehouses. He set the value of the new bill at one *p'il* of cloth and one *mal* of rice, and ordered that paper money be accepted in lieu of grain, beans, and cloth payments for prebendal rents under the *kwajŏn* system of 1389. Paper money was also to be used for one-third of salaries to officials, monthly taxes on merchants and artisans in the capital and peddlers in the provinces, tribute cloth taxes on persons of base status, taxes on fishing, boats, and bridges, household cloth taxes, prices for handicraft products made by artisans, and for a time redemption payments by criminals to avoid corporal punishment. He also ordered government granaries or warehouses sell rice and other commodities for paper money, or use government reserves of paper money to purchase cloth on the market.

T'aejong could hardly be faulted for any lack of determination and effort to achieve the monetization of the economy, but his methods did not succeed because merchants, wealthy individuals, and artisans ignored the order to turn in their cloth currency and continued to use it for market transactions, or left their shops in the city and traveled out to the provinces to conduct business in cloth without government interference. Ordinary peasants, however, whose holdings in cloth currency had now been declared illegal, were left without means. The government conducted house-to-house searches to eliminate the illegal possession of cloth, but the effort only had the effect of interrupting normal commerce without gaining public confidence in paper money. Miyahara Tōichi has concluded that T'aejong's paper money policy did not succeed because economic conditions were not ripe for it.[77]

After 1415 T'aejong began to consider the prospect of minting copper coins. When the value of a paper bill had dropped in value to no more than ⅓ *toe* (1 *toe* = .10 *mal*) of rice, and famine conditions exacerbated economic difficulties in 1423, Sejong authorized the minting of the *Chosŏn t'ongbo* (Chosŏn Circulating Treasure) copper cash, abolished the use of paper money, and authorized officials to buy up what was left on the market with copper cash.[78]

Managing copper cash, however, was hardly less difficult than paper money because of the shortage of copper. Only 17,107 strings of cash were produced in 1424 and 1425. At royal command the provinces remitted a total of 100,425 *kŭn* (110,468 lbs.) of copper from its warehouses to the center, and the Court for Providing Aid (Sasŏmsi) established thirty smelting ovens that produced 48,060 *kŭn* (50,666 lbs.) of copper a year. Still short of copper for coins in 1426, King Sejong melted down Buddhist bells, statues, and other implements and prohibited the use and manufacture of copper and iron utensils, to increase the supply of copper for coins.[79]

The government attempted to increase its copper imports from Japan with limited success. Between 1419 and 1428 Korea had imported only 14,820 *kŭn* of copper in official trade, and another 28,000 *kŭn* in private trade in 1428, a total of 42,820 (47,102 lbs.), still a minuscule sum compared to major shipments of 150,000 to 300,000 *kŭn* (165,000–330,000 lbs.) from Japan to Ming China in this period. The volume of Japanese copper imports did not increase, for even in the early seventeenth century after the establishment of the Tokugawa regime in Japan, the supply of Japanese copper imports averaged only about 27,000 *kŭn*/year. Obviously the difficulty at this time was the inability of the Korean economy to finance the imports. As a result copper cash only circulated in the capital at Hansŏngbu, and the supply of coins there barely reached several thousand strings to meet the demands of 100,000 residents.[80]

Despite the shortage of copper the value of coins minted in 1423 had declined to one-third their value, from one to 1/3 *toe* of rice by 1425, and to 1/13 *toe* by 1429. Ch'oe Hojin speculated that the cash supply was too large because coins from the Koryŏ period and China, along with undetermined amounts minted by counterfeiters, were also circulating along with the new official coins, but the public mistrust of the coins might be a better explanation.[81]

King Sejong ordered that taxes on shamans, merchants, artisans, and house sites in the capital be converted to cash payments, and that official slaves convert all their personal tribute payments from cloth and paper money to cash. In 1425 there were 119,630 official slaves, and each male slave had to pay an annual tribute tax of 100 *mun* of cash and each female slave 50 *mun* to the state, a total of 8,955,350 *mun* or about 9,000 strings (*kan*) of cash. Unfortunately, only 3,000 to 4,000 strings had been put into circulation at the time, far less than what slaves needed to meet their annual tribute payments, let alone other taxes and commercial transactions. Even by 1427, the total amount of cash in circulation was estimated at not more than about 12,000 strings – not enough for official slaves, artisans, merchants, shopkeepers, and shamans to pay their taxes in cash. Since the market had virtually ground to a halt because of cash insufficiency, Sejong relaxed the law in 1425 to allow cloth and other media of exchange to be used.

Likewise, the Ministry of Taxation's attempt to raise the value of cash in the market in 1426 by using price stabilization intervention tactics also failed because the ministry allocated only 20,000 strings for purchasing commodities. Finally, when a rise in rice prices following a drought forced a decline in the value of cash from 1/7 *toe* per *mun* of cash in the first lunar month of 1427 to 1/13 *toe* in 1429, and the value of cash dropped below the cost of minting a one-*mun* coin, which was 1/7 to 1/9 *toe*, no one was willing to use cash on the market, and smugglers shipped it to Japan in violation of the law. The government responded by ordering executions for the smugglers but to little avail. Then when a bumper crop in the fall of 1431 caused a precipitous fall in the price of rice, the state abandoned its attempt to regulate the value of cash (*hwamae*) by ever normal price stabilization operations altogether, probably since it held insufficient cash to buy enough rice to raise its price to normal levels.

In 1438, Sejong noticed that the supply of cash had been so depleted by the smuggling of copper abroad and the conversion of worthless cash to more valuable copper implements that the amount of copper cash in circulation was no more than one-tenth of the supply first issued. Despite this shortage, the value of the coins dropped further in 1439 to 1/14 *toe*, and occasional government sales of goods for cash only succeeded in raising the value of cash temporarily, but never higher than 1/8 *toe*. Yi Chongyŏng has concluded in his study that copper cash was doomed to failure as a currency once it dropped in value below copper's intrinsic value.[82]

Utility of Cash in Japan and China

The failure of copper cash occurred even though some Koreans were able to appreciate its utility in Japan and China. During a visit to Japan Pak Tansaeng had noticed that there was more cash than rice in circulation, and that travelers could pay for lodging and horses wherever they went. Foodsellers, tea shops, hostels, and widespread public baths all accepted payment in cash, and retail trade appeared to profit from this condition; shops in markets were better than those in Korea because merchants displayed their wares on wooden stands under the eaves of buildings, protecting foods and merchandise from dirt. Even Sejong commented ruefully in 1431 that though the Japanese lacked the benefits of a Neo-Confucian sense of propriety and ritual, they still had found a way to promote the use of cash among the population. In 1471, Sin Sŏmju also praised the flourishing markets of Japan, the prevalence of tea and pastry shops, the hustle and bustle of the markets, and the use of cash instead of rice to purchase goods and services.

Sin Sang, a visitor to Ming China in 1433, marveled at the presence of active markets in even the smallest towns while only Korea's capital had permanent markets. Cash circulated widely in China but not in Korea. When he suggested that markets be opened in at least the seats of all district magistrates to promote the use of cash, Sejong agreed, even though he realized that many would criticize the idea as promoting an increase in vagrants and idlers who would abandon their fields and flock to the marketplace in search of easy profits. He felt it was justified to violate conventional Confucian economic wisdom because it would help to alleviate population pressure on the small amount of arable land in Korea.[83]

Sejong's Attempt to Restore Paper Money and Cash

Sejong may have been depressed by his experience with copper cash, but he did not lose his determination to succeed with some form of currency, so in 1445 he tried to restore the use of paper money for the third time since 1402, and he continued to ban use of cloth for currency. He valued each new bill at fifty *mun* of cash or one *mal* of grain (in which one *mun* of cash was worth ⅕ *toe*), and he also legalized the bills previously printed in 1426 at a value of forty *mun*.

Although he banned the use of cotton cloth, he decided to allow people a choice between paper money and copper cash for paying taxes or buying goods from state warehouses. He also ordered government agencies to use paper money to pay official salaries and bureau expenses for fuel, vegetables, lighting oil, and clerical costs. To protect the money supply, he specified that any merchants guilty of exporting cash or precious jewels abroad to buy foreign goods would have their property confiscated, but later in 1447 he eased these Draconian regulations by lifting the prohibition against melting copper down to make utensils. He hoped to win popular support for paper bills and copper cash.

Although some officials felt that cash was more likely to succeed than paper money, it was cash that quickly dropped out of use. Paper money also suffered because officials, contrary to royal orders, did little to absorb paper money from the public by selling government goods, and demanded cash or even illegal cloth for taxes. By 1450 it was obvious that cloth was being used more than paper money for private transactions, and King Munjong commented that it might be a good idea to authorize capital bureaus to pay part of their expenses in cloth so that paper money might rise in value.[84]

The Decline of Paper and Copper Cash

When King Sejo came to the throne in 1455, he reversed Sejong's policy of allowing the public to choose the medium of payment by insisting on paper money and prohibiting cloth or other goods for official payments or private trade. Coercion, however, only succeeded in making people more wary of paper money, and in 1456 Sejo, recognizing that the policy was a failure, rescinded his order and returned to Sejong's policy of allowing transactions in any medium – ramie, cotton cloth, or paper bills. The exclusive use of paper money was then limited by law only to taxes on artisans, merchants, shops, and peddlers.[85]

Later King Sŏngjong in 1474 ordered the use of cloth for official slave tribute as well. Because the quantity and value of paper money had both declined severely after 1445, the taxation section of the Law Code (*Kyŏngguk taejŏn*) published in 1460 declared that the official value of one bill of paper money was to be one *toe* of rice, 1⁄10 the value (one *mal*) previously set by King Sejong. The code also declared that paper money was now the lowest grade of currency in circulation, lower than 5-*sae* (ramie?) cloth and 3-*sae* cotton cloth.

Cotton cloth, called "ordinary 5-*sae* cloth" (*sang osŭngp'o*), began to replace ramie cloth in the market, but it caused some confusion in terminology because 5-*sae* ramie cloth was ordinarly twice the value of the 2-*sae* or 3-*sae* rough (*ch'up'o*) or ordinary ramie cloth. Now 5-*sae* cotton cloth was often called rough cloth and was worth half as much as 5-*sae* ramie. Since it became difficult to assess the value of cloth, the cheaper rough cotton cloth drove 5-*sae* ramie off the market, and cotton cloth of still lesser thread count and cheaper value was made as well. The 1460 taxation code attempted to regularize the two grades of 5-*sae* and 3-*sae* cloth by ordering that all bolts be stamped on both ends with the slogan, "the seal of the Chosŏn Circulating Treasure" (*Chosŏn t'ongp'ye*). The code did not make clear whether it was distinguishing between ramie and cotton when it mentioned two grades of fineness, 5-*sae* and 3-*sae* cloth, but eventually it must have been used to assess two grades of fineness for circulating bolts of cotton cloth. Eventually cloth was debased even further by shortening the size of the bolt from the standard 35 to 30 "feet" in length, a tendency that became worse during Yŏnsan'gun's reign (1494 to 1506).[86]

After King Sŏngjong came to the throne in 1469 he attempted to revive the use of paper money by fiat to enforce its use for market transactions, redemption of punishments, half the amount of medicinal purchases, tribute levies on official slaves, and per capita taxes on artisans, merchants, and shops, but in 1472 he virtually admitted defeat by allowing official slaves, whose numbers had grown to 350,000, to pay their tribute taxes in grain – one of the most important stimulants that the government controlled for inducing the use of paper bills.

The value of paper money plummeted still further. In 1470 the value of one bill fell to 1/40 *p'il* of correct (ramie) cloth (*chŏngp'o*) and 1/20 *p'il* of ordinary (ramie) cloth (*sangp'o*), and from one *toe* of rice in 1460 to 1/30 *toe* by the end of 1473. The government suffered a great financial loss because of the decline in the value of the money it was currently holding in its treasuries.

In 1474 King Sŏngjong tried to resuscitate paper money once more rather than write off all the government's paper reserves. Between 1475 and 1480 he replaced the large and unwieldy Korean bill with a smaller one, expecting that the value of paper bills would be increased by reducing the volume of bills in circulation, but it did not become more popular, and even government officials refused to use them, leaving mountains of bills to rot in storage.[87] The Aid Bureau at the time had an accumulated reserve of 3,722,903 old bills that the public refused to accept, but only 101,078 new bills, and Sŏngjong made no attempt to print new bills because he had lost faith in the utility of paper money altogether.[88]

In 1515, King Chungjong made one more failed attempt to spend paper money, but by 1522 he had to admit that it had completely disappeared from use in recent years. As for copper cash, the *Chosŏn t'ongbo* copper coin had been minted throughout the fifteenth century, and the new Ever-Normal Circulating Treasure (*Sangp'yŏng t'ongbo*) began to replace it after 1515, but it too failed to win popular acceptance. Bolts of cotton and bags of grain remained the paramount media of exchange, but quality of the cotton cloth had also deteriorated by the early sixteenth century. By 1515 some of the rough cotton cloth (*ch'up'o*) used for currency had been debased so far below the 3-*sae* level that it had to be unwound to salvage the thread.[89]

Currency Failure: An Aspect of Overall Economic Policy

The monetary history of the fifteenth century reveals that the failure of paper and copper currency to become permanent media of exchange was not the result of a plank in the Neo-Confucian statecraft platform from the beginning of the dynasty because a number of kings and many of their high officials supported the attempt to promote those currencies even with the use of coercive legislation. Government officials contributed to the failure to circulate cash or paper money by refusing to accept it even though it was legal tender; their actions were not motivated by any ideological commitment, but by their reluctance to accept any medium of exchange that had no prospect of retaining its value.

Most twentieth-century scholars have felt that the ultimate reason for failure was the public's disinterest and the reluctance of both ordinary people and merchants to accept and trust the value of paper and copper currency in exchange for what they regarded as objects of value. The fundamental problem, however, was that the currency policy could not be disassociated from economic policy in general. Market activities and the use of cash or paper money that would be stimulated by its expansion were limited by the government's restrictive policies, and none of the early kings had a plan to expand industrial and commercial activity. It was unrealistic to expect that the attempt to introduce paper money and copper cash could have succeeded in those circumstances, and the reversion to cloth and grain as media of exchange by the beginning of the sixteenth century was but symbolic of the conservatism of overall economic policy. The kings may only have paid lip service to the Confucian notion that industry and commerce were uneconomic as well as immoral, but in devising a restrictive economic policy they fell captive to the dominant Confucian attitude that by limiting private industrial and commercial activity they ensured the maximization of the production of food and the necessities of life rather than baubles and luxuries.

CONCLUSION

The basic structure of early Chosŏn institutions had been established by the first half of the fifteenth century, but not completely in accordance with the desires of the radical Neo-Confucian ideologues of the dynastic transition. The desire of the Neo-Confucians to eliminate Buddhism and its land and slaves, weaken the political and economic autonomy of some of the Koryŏ yangban and *hyangni*, strengthen the monarchy, the state, and the bureaucracy both militarily and financially, use the civil service examinations as the main means of recruitment, and establish Neo-Confucian texts as the standard curriculum for education and the examinations was achieved. So, too, had the desire for concentrating on agricultural production at the expense of industry been achieved by limiting handicraft production to authorized artisans. Commerce had also been kept under wraps by establishing licensed shops in the capital and restricting merchant activity in the countryside to periodic markets and peddlers. While a number of kings tried to break out of an excessively conservative monetary system by introducing cash and paper money, that policy ultimately failed, but the net result was welcomed by the most conservative Neo-Confucians.

Problems emerged in the early Chosŏn structure for two reasons: the failure to solve some of the essential difficulties of the late Koryŏ period, from oversight or neglect or political opposition to the ideal reform program, and the deterioration of some institutions because of changing circumstances. The main obstacles that were carried over from late Koryŏ because the political situation prevented the adoption of the more radical aspects of the Neo-Confucian program were the continuation of the power of the yangban and the preservation of landed property. Landed property was preserved by the *kwajŏn* land reform in 1391 even before the Chosŏn dynasty was founded. The maintenance of inherited slavery was somewhat different because the reformers never considered its abolition. Its continuation, however, represented a silent affirmation of the property rights of the slaveholders. Problems that represented the deterioration of healthy institutions included the misuse of power by kings and bureaucrats, the emergence of factions, the spread of corruption among underpaid clerks, the breakdown of official schools and the deficiencies of the examination system, and the anomalies in the taxation system, especially the tribute and military and labor service systems.

CHAPTER 2

The Disintegration of the Early Chosŏn System to 1592

The system of control established at the beginning of the dynasty began to break down almost from the instant of its foundation, but not in all sectors at the same rate. This chapter will treat four major sectors of government: the political system, the growth of landlordism and tenancy, the transformation of the tribute system and its effects on commercial development, and the deterioration of military defense and the attempt to reconstitute it after the Imjin War of 1592–98.

By the time of Hideyoshi's invasions, the political leaders of the country realized that they faced a major crisis that required reform, but their responses to each situation was limited, if not dictated, by the circumstances at the time. They had to decide whether it was either possible or desirable to turn back the clock to the beginning of the dynasty, or to some other remote ideal in the Confucian tradition that the founders had failed to accomplish or whether to adapt to the flow of events and create new, more progressive institutions aimed at creating a new future.

Political Problems

The aggrandizement of royal power that accompanied the founding of the Chosŏn dynasty did not guarantee the wise and restrained utilization of that power by the early kings. Despite the elevation of Neo-Confucianism as the philosophical guide for kings and officials alike, the Chosŏn monarchy suffered from the same ills that plagued other monarchies in world history, including the violation of traditions and norms in favor of the fulfillment of personal ambition. Because Confucianism was so insistent on the importance of loyalty to the throne, and the military power of the state was so concentrated under the king, very few officials chose to challenge the legitimacy of most kings' rule, even though Confucian thought provided a moral justification for the deposition of immoral kings.

Depositions, nonetheless, did take place, sometimes justifiably, other times not, but when they did, they were as much acts of desperation by politicians as acts of moral outrage. There was just no regular, peaceful, and easy mechanism in the Confucian traditional monarchy for the replacement of immoral or incompetent kings without experiencing a political crisis, often accompanied by bloodshed and retribution, and a severe split in political loyalties. Incompetence was probably more of a problem than tyranny or immorality, because it did not constitute sufficient grounds for replacement of a king even though the exercise of his daily decision, or lack of it, wrought havoc for his people. As a result, Confucian statecraft specialists accepted what they thought was the only practical alternative, increased zeal in persuasion to wean the wayward monarch from his immoral ways, and better advice for adopting better institutions for the improvement of problems.

Usurpation and Deposition

King T'aejong's violation of the normal order of succession in 1398 and 1400 established an unfortunate tradition of political interference and manipulation that was extended when King Sejo usurped the throne in 1455 from his nephew, the legitimate King Tanjong. In tyrannical fashion he subsequently sidestepped the chain of command by ignoring the State Council and prime minister to exert direct command over the Six Ministries. The animosity generated by Sejo's usurpation poisoned the political atmosphere for the next half century and created fear among Sejo's successors at any suggestion of illegitimacy in the royal line. King Yŏnsan'gun at the turn of the century was paranoidal in his response to this problem, and he chose not only to ignore the remonstrance of his Confucian officials, but also to banish or execute those who failed to respond to his slightest whims. Insisting on his right to demand complete obedience to his royal commands, his actions passed beyond the limits of acceptability, and he was deposed by a coup d'état organized by the political survivors of his major purges.

Unfortunately, his very deposition led to the creation of a coalition of political favorites who had to be rewarded for their political acumen, and the continuation of special appointments, emoluments, and favors for the so-called merit subjects who were the beneficiaries of the Confucian spoils system. By the middle of the sixteenth century the unity of the court was again riven, this time by members of the P'ap'yŏng Yun clan who became rivals over the designation of the royal successor. The rivals were cousins, brothers of two different queens (the first and second queens of King Chungjong), and therefore uncles of the sons of those queens. When the son of the second queen acceded to the throne in 1545 as King Myŏngjong, his supporters in the so-called Little Yun faction used the opportunity to banish and execute members of the Big Yun group. They could do this because the king was a minor and his mother, Queen Munjŏng, ruled the country as regent at the time.[1] In this case, a single yangban clan created a political firestorm over the royal succession, and their internal dispute could only be resolved by the execution of their rivals – not the kind of regular succession mechanism that the Neo-Confucian founders of the dynasty had had in mind.

Hereditary Factionalism after 1575

In the next generation, the effects of political dispute were brought to an even greater evil when a contest over appointment to a key post in the Ministry of Personnel led to a split between two groups of men, known as Easterners and Westerners from the location of their homes in the capital. Officials had been prone to form personal bonds based on blood ties, marriage alliances, schoolboy friendships, and master-disciple relations, but the divisions that had been created by this pattern had not led to the permanent transmission of those connections, let alone names and symbols attached to interpersonal groups. That situation changed drastically after 1575 because the Easterners and Westerners, and the factions that stemmed from them through a number of schisms that occurred within their ranks, ushered in an hereditary factionalism that continued to the end of the dynasty.

Many officials thought that factionalism itself was the equivalent of a Confucian moral sin since every individual official was supposed to owe supreme loyalty to the king, and the organization of a group signified the elevation of the interests of the faction and its members over those of the king. The main defense of factionalism, first voiced by Ou-yang Hsiu of the Sung dynasty, was that some factions were, indeed, legitimate because they represented the forces of good who toiled in the king's true interest and performed a public service by doing battle against the factions of evil that sought to obstruct the king's will.[2]

The moral justification for the legitimacy of "good" as opposed to "bad" factions appeared rather transparent as members of each faction perceived their own to represent the forces of goodness, and all factions displayed by their actions their intent to secure exclusive access to political power and the elimination of their rivals, with the help of the reigning monarch.

King Sŏnjo (r. 1567–1608) was discomfited by the disruption caused by the struggle between the Easterner and Westerner factions, but he not only failed to stop it, he encouraged its perpetuation by switching his support from one group to another almost on whim. His legacy to subsequent generations was that the hereditary factions became involved in the problems associated with the royal succession. When Kwanghaegun (r. 1608–23) came to the throne, he was supported by members of the Great Northerner faction (an Easterner splinter faction), which used its position to eliminate its Westerner rivals, and they in turn were removed by the coup d'état led by the Westerners, who deposed Kwanghaegun and placed Injo on the throne in 1623. After a hiatus of relative quiescence, factional rivalry emerged once again after 1659 in a dispute ostensibly over the mourning ritual for a deceased king.

Yu Hyŏngwŏn, who lived through the difficult times of factional strife, found it politically and morally impossible for him either to blame the king for the misfortune, or even to raise the issue since mention of it might constitute indictment of the present king's factional favorites. Yu Hyŏngwŏn could not have helped but realize that factionalism was a pox on the body politic, but he avoided the subject altogether because as a descendant of a Northerner, he would have risked execution. I would suggest he sought to solve the problem by transcending it, by examining more fundamental issues including revising the way that men were selected for office and changing the organization of the central bureaucracy to create the possibility of a bureaucratic check on despotic and arbitrary decision-making. It was not until the eighteenth century that some statecraft writers felt secure enough to discuss the problems created by factional politics.

GROWTH OF LANDLORDISM

Changes in the Administration of Prebends

The *kwajŏn* land reform was, as we have seen, far less than what the idealistic Neo-Confucians like Chŏng Tojŏn had advocated because it provided only for a system of prebendal tax collection privileges for men granted official rank (but not necessarily office) by the king. What took place throughout most of the fifteenth century was the deterioration of this system in the struggle for control between the yangban prebend holders and the state for control of tax revenues. The net result was an apparent victory for the king and the central government and the loss of prebendal income by the yangban.

At the beginning of the dynasty the king granted power to prebend holders to collect taxes, fees, and levies from the owner-cultivators of the prebendal lands, and to administer the assessment of tax reductions on the basis of crop damage from natural disasters. The central government chafed at the sacrifice of revenue to the prebend holders and their exploitation of the peasant cultivators. After the beginning of the fifteenth century King T'aejong shifted tax collection rights from some prebend holders back to the state, and exempted Kyŏnggi peasants from certain charges. In 1417 he transferred responsibility to collect taxes on prebends to district magistrates, sent special crop assessors (Kyŏngch'agwan) to assess crop damage, and shifted one-third the area used for prebends from Kyŏnggi to the southern provinces to enable greater control over the land surrounding the capital until 1431, when he returned prebend allotments to Kyŏnggi.[3]

Nevertheless, the *chŏnju*, who continued to hold the prebends in Kyŏnggi Province and had begun to regard them as their own private property, struggled to recover the direct collection of the *cho* tax throughout King Sejong's reign to the middle of the fifteenth century.[4] On the other hand, despite the increase in the number of candidates for prebendal allotments, the kings refused to increase the amount of land granted for prebends, transferred some prebends to new aspirants by arbitrary and often unfair decision, took over some prebends to pay for military expenses, and reduced the size of the prebendal grants. In 1440 King Sejong reduced the amount of land used for prebends to individuals from 84,100 to 68,000 *kyŏl*.[5]

The government also held the lid on land granted for prebends by granting prebendal rights to waste or unreclaimed land to petitioners for prebends, which meant that they had to undergo the costs involved in reclamation. On the other hand, those who did reclaim wasteland as part of their prebendal grant also felt that they were also owners of the land as well as recipients of the *cho* tax since they had to invest their own funds in its development.[6]

In 1443 King Sejong introduced his *kongbŏp* system to increase the state's tax revenues and to ensure a more equitable and uniform method of taxation throughout the country for the benefit of the smallholding peasants. The complex set of gradations based on land fertility and climatic variations led to an increase in the assessments of the most fertile land and almost doubled the total tax revenue collected, but now that the *kwajŏn* prebends had been returned to Kyŏnggi Province, where the land was poorer than the south and the tax levels lower, those who held them there were protected against the tax increases. Prior to 1443 the land of the country had been divided into three grades of fertility, from a high of 20 *mal/kyŏl* to a low of 4 *mal/kyŏl* for the poorest land, but by the land survey of 1634 hardly any land was registered as fertile and almost all of it was taxed at the lowest rate of 4 *mal/kyŏl*, a system that had benefited the owners of the most fertile paddy lands in the southern coastal regions.[7]

Replacement of Kwajŏn *with* Chikchŏn *Prebends*

After King Sejo usurped the throne in 1455 he had to distribute more prebends to merit subjects and officials who had supported him politically but, faced with revenue problems, he decided in 1466 to abolish *kwajŏn* prebendal grants altogether. Under his new "office land" (*chikchŏn*) system, prebends were granted only to officeholders. He carried out another national survey to find the total amount of inherited prebends, reduced the average prebendal allotments for most ranks, and in 1470 turned over all tax collection responsibilities to the district magistrates, who then doled out grain allotments to incumbent officials.[8]

Certain important officials at Sejo's court took up the cause of the hereditary yangban. Yang Sŏngji complained that Sejo's measures had violated the ancient principle of maintaining a class of men on "hereditary salaries" (*serok*) and "hereditary officials" (*sesin*), for without the income from prebends, the distinction between them and the common peasants was lost, and their widows and dependent heirs were thrown into destitution. Yi Kŭkki and Ku Ch'igon also argued that hereditary prebends were necessary to encourage moral behavior, to serve as an incentive for improving moral standards of behavior, and to inculcate respect for rites and righteousness.

On the other hand, a number of important officials like Chŏng Inji, Ch'oe Hang, Sin Sukchu, and Han Myŏnghoe in the 1470s opposed the restoration of hereditary prebends. For that matter, the high officials of the late fifteenth century who possessed their own lands and estates were not that concerned about the loss of prebends, while the heirs of earlier officials who had not established successful careers were discomfited by the loss of prebendal grants.[9] Although the officials with prebends were no longer able to collect the land tax, they were still allowed to collect the traditional straw fodder fee until 1478. Nonetheless, in 1475 King Sŏngjong cut the rate of the straw fee to one-fifth of its former size, and in 1491 he ordered the district magistrates to collect the *cho* tax on monastic and shrine land directly as well.[10]

By 1484 the total amount of all types of prebendal land had fallen to about 10,000 *kyŏl* from the 115,340 *kyŏl* of rank land and merit subject land in 1400, or the 68,000 *kyŏl* in Sejong's reign (1418–50) out of the total of approximately 150,000 *kyŏl* in Kyŏnggi Province. Since only one-fifteenth of the land in Kyŏnggi was used for prebends after 1484, almost all land had been converted to private property subject to state taxes payable to magistrates or government granaries.[11]

Disappearance of Prebends

In the last quarter of the fifteenth century when the government was hard pressed for revenue, King Sŏngjong reduced the size of prebendal allotments and took over as much as half the *cho* taxes on prebends for the state, and similar measures were adopted during the reigns of Kings Chungjong and Myŏngjong to the mid-sixteenth century.[12] In 1525 the Ministry of Taxation pointed out that since the grain revenues for the three types of prebends – office land (*chikchŏn*), merit subject land (*kongsinjŏn*), and special royal award land (*pyŏlsajŏn*) – was then providing no more than 3,000–4,000 *sŏm* a year to the recipients because the assessments of land fertility had been falling continuously since 1443, the government would be better off if it abolished all these prebends and simply provided grain rations to the prebend holders instead.

Mention of office land prebends (*chikchŏn*) disappeared from court records by the mid-sixteenth century, and in 1555 and 1556 when the court was debating the food crisis created by a series of bad crops, it was mentioned that all the office land had been taken over by the state some time before. In any case, the revenue from prebends was so low that it became a negligible factor in the income of high officials. Big landlords were presumably receiving 10,000 *sŏm* in rents compared to the puny 3,000–4,000 *sŏm* from the *cho* tax at a rate of 4 *mal/kyŏl* (of which 2 *mal/kyŏl* had to be paid to the state as the *se* tax by the prebend holder).[13] What this meant was that the real contest for the control of land and revenue between the state and the landlords that had been going on since the beginning of the dynasty became more obvious now that the dispute over prebends disappeared.

Landlordism, Tenancy, Hired Labor, and Immiseration

A number of Korean scholars have interpreted the disappearance of the system of prebendal grants as a major transition from incomplete or feudal to complete or mature ownership relations in Korean history. A corollary to this theory is that the class conflict between landlords and tenants only emerged with the disappearance of the *kwajŏn* prebendal system, but this view requires some modification. Private ownership was already the foundation of land tenure under the *kwajŏn* system of 1389–91, as well as the *chŏnsikwa* system of the tenth through twelfth centuries in the early Koryŏ dynasty. Hereditary succession to *kwajŏn* and other types of prebends was superimposed on only about two-thirds of the privately owned land in Kyŏnggi Province, and the legal prohibition against the sale of land was lifted in 1424. Not much is known about the origin of the prohibition of land sales, but there is no evidence that it was associated with either nationalization of landed property and redistribution or the denial of private ownership. Possibly it was designed to keep peasant smallholders in place to guarantee the prebend recipients a constant income. Land must have been sold despite the prohibition, and after 1424 there was no legal restraint against alienation of landed property. What was more significant than maturation of ownership, since most of the land was held by private owners anyway, was the state's abandonment of any attempt to provide *extra* hereditary income for an elite that ceased to perform any function for the state. It was "extra" because such individuals already collected rents from tenants and slaves on their own private landholdings.

Furthermore, it is doubtful that landownership became more "mature" because the main deficiency in ownership was the imperfect system of protection for private ownership rights. Although kings were obliged to compensate owners for takeovers under the right of eminent domain, and aggrieved property owners could sue in the magistrates' courts to defend their property, using written deeds and official land registration documents to prove ownership, the courts and the legal system did not operate independently of government officials or the de facto influence of local magnates. If a smallholder were in a position to launch a civil suit against an illegal seizure of his property by a powerful private individual or corrupt official, he would usually avoid doing so because involvement with the magistrate, his clerks, and runners usually meant nothing but trouble, and the magistrate was vulnerable to influence from the other party in the suit. This description of the weaknesses in the legal system of the defense of property rights probably existed unchanged since the early Koryŏ dynasty, if not before that.[14]

What became noticeable by the late fifteenth century was increasing mention in the historical records of the estates (*nongjang*) accumulated by a small number of large landlords, tenancy and landlord/tenant relations, the disparity of wealth between the rich and the poor, and the failure of the state to keep up with the registration and taxation of newly reclaimed land. The assumption that all these phenomena were growing in size and amount has not been proven because of the paucity of statistical evidence, but the qualitative evidence does imply that the concentration of landownership, the increase in tenancy, and the immiseration of the peasantry were occurring in the sixteenth century.

These negative trends were matched by positive developments, such as increased production through the reclamation of land and the spread of irrigation and transplantation. By the middle of the sixteenth century almost all the arable land in the southern provinces that had not yet been had reclaimed was opened to cultivation.[15] Nevertheless, the tripling of population from about four to twelve million between 1392 and 1693 probably explains why the expansion of cultivated land and productivity from irrigation and transplantation that began in the late fifteenth century was not accompanied by higher standards of living for anyone other than large landlords. Many contemporary observers commented on growing immiseration and indebtedness by ordinary peasants, usury, and foreclosures on mortgages by creditors. This economic situation was blind to status considerations, so that even some slaves became creditors for their social superiors.[16] One commentator in 1537 noted that the commoners had lost their land, and the only ones who possessed any were the rich merchants and the families of the scholar-officials (*sajok*), that is, the yangban.[17]

As Yi Kyŏngsik has shown in his studies, landlords increased their holdings of estates by using the profits from rent for usurious lending, by selling rice and other goods like straw, willow baskets, leather, fish, salt, agricultural tools, silk, and clothing, and by manipulating rice prices on the market. They had their estate agents or managers, the *pan'in*, conduct those activities and even participate in tribute contracting (see pp. 70–75) and smuggling to maximize their profits, or act in collusion with merchants engaged in those activities.[18]

The accumulation of large holdings or estates by the landlords led to changes in the nature of the agricultural workforce. While an increasing number of commoners had ended up as slaves by the end of the fifteenth century, some by commending their lands to the landlords to escape the extra burden of military service or the military support tax, an even larger number of commoner, smallholding peasants who had lost their land either from sale or foreclosure were reduced to the status of sharecroppers. For that matter, even those private slaves who lived at some distance from the master's house and cultivated his lands for him (*oegŏ nobi*), were de facto tenant sharecroppers because they split the crop and paid what was in effect a rent as "personal tribute" (*sin'gong*).[19]

A third source of labor for the landlords was provided by hired labor (*kogong*). Hired labor existed at the beginning of the dynasty, but most of them were long-term or seasonal hired workers because there was not enough of a labor market to provide for daily wage workers (known colloquially as *mŏsŭm*). The long-term hired laborers were usually regarded as dependents of their employers, who treated them as if they were their private slaves, but they worked primarily for commoner landowners rather than for the yangban, who usually had a sufficient supply of private slaves. Their numbers began to increase in the early sixteenth century as more peasants took the road to escape famine, taxes, and military service. By the mid-sixteenth century some high officials had as many as fifty of them in their households. They generally called them *pan'in* and used them to manage estates that they began to accumulate in the northern provinces at this time.[20]

These changes in the structure of the labor force were accompanied by other signs of hardship. Impoverished peasants became more mobile as they moved out of their native villages, some moving to commercial towns or turning to banditry as the best means of earning a living. Even private slaves began to take to the road to escape oppression in the 1550s, and slaveowners began to complain that the old standards of respect had been lost.[21]

Radical Reform Proposals Ignored

A number of officials responded to this situation by harking back once again to the well-field system of the ancient Chou, which would have required the nationalization of all land and redistribution to the peasantry, or to the land limitation scheme first attempted in the Han dynasty in China, but in every instance these proposals were opposed or ignored. In 1518 Yu Ok conceded that the situation did not warrant the implemention of the Chou well-field model for granting square plots of 100 *myo* of land each to eight families who would then volunteer their labor on a ninth plot for the benefit of the state (in place of the feudal lord of the ancient Chou dynasty). He did propose consideration of the land limitation scheme of the Han dynasty or the equal-field system of the Northern Wei and T'ang dynasties to eliminate disparities of landownership and wealth.[22]

In 1519 King Chungjong rejected Ki Chun's proposal to adopt the well-field model because the land was not flat or broad enough to lay out even fields in squares. Ki responded by proposing a land limitation system, but Chŏng Sunmyŏng stymied further consideration by pointing out that a recent proposal for a 50-*kyŏl* limit was far too large to be realistic because of the population pressure in areas like Kyŏngsang Province. A more modest limit of 10 *kyŏl* was unrealistic, he continued, because that amount was beyond the reach of the ordinary peasant to obtain even in provinces like Kyŏnggi.[23] The debate ended that day without further discussion for lower limits, probably because resistance to confiscation by the larger landlords would have been too powerful to overcome.

In 1524 Nam Kon agreed that the situation at that time did not warrant the adoption of either the well-field or equal-field system, but he argued that the king was at least obliged to implement the law that required a resurvey of cultivated land every twenty years to provide for accurate taxation of land that had been brought under cultivation and exemption for that which had been abandoned. Noting that in Hwanghae Province alone a cadastral survey had not been carried out for fifty-four years, many peasants were still being dunned for taxes even though they had long since sold their land to others, while reclaimers of new land had never been registered to pay any taxes. King Chungjong agreed that whenever crop conditions improved, it would be possible to carry out a new survey, but the governor of Hwanghae and the court officials blocked the proposal, and it died without action.[24]

Despite the growth of agricultural production and productivity by the end of the sixteenth century, a crisis had developed by the maldistribution of wealth. The large landlords and slaveholders received rents from their commoner and slave tenants, while more and more of the commoner peasant population were reduced to marginal sharecroppers or hired laborers. The appearance of traditional proposals for nationalization, limitation, or even more accurate cadastral surveys were neglected because the landlords profited from the situation and prevented any serious reform until the disastrous invasion of Hideyoshi in 1592.

TRIBUTE CONTRACTING

No sooner had the system of in-kind tribute payments levied on the peasant population of the rural villages been instituted at the beginning of the dynasty than it, too, began to fall apart. It did so because the regulations governing its operation were too rigid to allow for changing circumstances, and the only way to maintain the system was to wink at the violations that began to appear. The key change in the tribute system throughout the fifteenth and sixteenth centuries can be described as its conversion to a commercial system involving the purchase and sale of goods on the market financed by fees, commissions, contracts, payoffs, and eventually by the adoption of new surtaxes. The degeneration of the tribute system was perceived by most officials and statecraft thinkers throughout these two centuries as a serious wart on the body politic. It was a corruption of the original intent of the founders to establish a regular system of taxation founded on hoary tradition and respect for law, and an illicit expansion of commercial activity by officials and petty clerks as well as private merchants, all of whom were governed by the uncontrolled pursuit of profits in trade beyond the proper limits established by a regime commited to the preservation of Confucian moral standards. What was the response of honest officials and statecraft thinkers going to be two centuries later when almost everyone agreed that the tribute system was just too corrupt to continue in its present form?

The Development of Tribute Contracting

Corruption of the system occurred early in the fifteenth century when certain districts that no longer produced tribute items asked for permission to pay rice instead. The government permitted it and temporarily allowed government agencies to purchase goods it needed on the market. In other instances, when districts were obliged to pay tribute in items they had never produced, magistrates had to send clerks or runners around to buy tribute items, and some northern districts even had to trade strategic military materials like horses, oxen, and iron to obtain furs from the Jurchen.

For ordinary tribute payments, the district magistrate would select one of his clerks to be tribute clerk (*kongni*) to transport tribute goods (*kongmul*) to a capital bureau. The bureau clerk, however, frequently rejected the tribute (*chŏmt'oe*) on the grounds of poor quality. The bureau clerk could either insist on another payment of higher quality goods, demand that the tribute clerk arrange for substitute payments at prices higher than the capital market, or pay bribes to avoid a second tax.[25]

The business of tribute contracting (*taenap*, or *pangnap*) emerged in which merchant middlemen collected rice or cloth substitute payments from district magistrates or taxpayers and used them to purchase the tribute items on the market. Kings T'aejong in 1409 and Sejong and 1420 and 1430 took action to prevent magistrates from participating in tribute contracting, but these prohibitions proved ineffective, and commoners were not prohibited from engaging in the business. In the 1440s when State Councilors Ha Yŏn, Yi Sukchu, and Chŏng Inji advised Sejong to prohibit tribute contracting, establish an open and published schedule of tribute payments in rice and cloth, and have the magistrates allocate household quotas according to the amount of land a family possessed, King Sejong failed to take any action.[26] On the contrary, as a result of Sejong's increasing devotion to Buddhism after the deaths of two of his sons and his wife between 1446 and 1448, he abandoned his attempt to uphold the original system and even decided to encourage tribute contracting by monks to help finance the construction of Buddhist temples, and he allowed them to monopolize the profits from tribute contracting between 1449 and 1457.[27]

In 1459 King Sejo also permitted tribute contracting against the letter of the law, but he sought to bring it under control. He forbade contracting arrangements against the will of the taxpayer, and he required that contractors first pay tribute goods to the capital bureau and present a receipt from the capital bureau before asking for reimbursement. This procedure was later adopted in the *Kyŏngguk taejŏn* law code of 1469, but the new restrictions were soon ignored, and tribute contracting spread beyond the monks to merchants and even yangban.

Royal relatives, high officials, and other prestigious persons began to engage more openly in the contracting business themselves by using their personal aides (*pan'in* or *pandang*) or slaves as henchmen to beat the peasants into paying higher prices. Contrary to his own laws Sejo also allowed the Office of Merit Subjects (Ch'unghunbu) and the Directorate of Buddhist Publications (Kan'gyŏngdogam) to engage in tribute contracting to support important merit subjects and publish Buddhist sutras in honor of the crown prince, who had died at the age of twenty.[28]

King Sejo's Attempt at Reform by Adaptation

Sejo, however, then had a change of heart and tried to rectify the corruption of the system by limiting tribute to existing quotas. By ordering the compilation in 1456 of the Horizontal Ledger (Hoenggan), a list of all tribute in kind and the cost of manufacturing tribute items by artisans, a task completed by King Sŏngjong in 1473, he felt that he could stop the uncontrolled demand on the taxpayer. But because the government agencies did not cut their expenditures, conformity to the Horizontal Ledger only served to guarantee annual deficits, and the government was forced either to collect the next year's tribute in advance or impose extra tribute levies. Eventually Sejo's rational attempt to cut the cost of tribute was completely frustrated by the profligate King Yŏnsan'gun (r. 1494–1506), who broke records in imposing daily demands for tribute payments.[29]

Merchants had been active in tribute contracting since the Koryŏ dynasty, but they had been overshadowed by the monks during Sejong's reign. In 1464 Yang Sŏngji proposed an entirely different solution to the problem, a method based on legalizing tribute contracting so that the state could control it. He tried to persuade King Sejo of the utility of this solution because the merchants had virtually taken control of the "miscellaneous taxes" (*chapse*), or tribute, away from the government itself, a particularly serious situation since those taxes constituted 60 percent of state income (vs. 40 percent for the land tax). He proposed that the Samsa (Financial Commission) of the Koryŏ dynasty be revived and combined with the transport commissioner (Unjŏnsa) to control and regulate tribute contracting by merchants in the hope of increasing state revenue, but Sejo refused to approve his idea.

In 1468, however, Sejo made his own adaptation to the reality of tribute contracting by instructing magistrates to set aside a certain amount of rice collected when the land tax was paid as a reserve to pay tribute contractors only after they presented a receipt for the payment of tribute goods from the Ministry of Taxation. This was the first step toward the eventual replacement of tribute by rice and cloth taxes by the end of the sixteenth century, but it could not be enforced because Sejo died three months after he issued the order. Thereafter, there were only two instances of temporary replacement of tribute with a rice or cloth tax, in 1515 and 1525, to provide relief funds. The serious replacement of tribute by a land tax was not suggested seriously until Yulgok did so in 1574, and not adopted by the king until 1594, and then only temporarily.[30]

King Yejong's Crackdown Against Corruption, 1468

When King Yejong came to the throne in 1468, he adopted the line of strict moral rectitude and immediately reversed Sejo's policies by banning substitute payments and contractual tribute altogether. However, when his uncle's slave was caught violating the law in 1470, he, too violated it by pardoning the slave.[31] The prohibition served to inhibit regular officials, yangban, and merchants from any overt illegal contracting, but it allowed clerks and official slaves to reap illicit profits by rejecting tribute items or keeping them in storage without issuing receipts to the district tribute clerks (*kongni*), a practice called *yunan*. The district tribute clerks themselves also violated laws with impunity. When they arrived in the capital they kept the goods hidden while they negotiated with merchants to sell the goods at a profit and repurchase cheaper goods to offer as tribute.

The district tribute clerks were also subject to exploitation and manipulation by the bureau clerks in the capital, who might delay acceptance of the tribute goods or reject them altogether. The district tribute clerks were then forced to store the goods until they could sell them on the market, replace them with better goods, or illegally pay substitute rice and cloth. They had to rely on a group called the masters (*chuin*) or private masters (*sajuin*), who had houses or warehouses located along the Han River where tribute ships or barges arrived, and who frequently acted as brokers or agents. These masters charged the district tribute clerks rent and storage, arranged for the tribute contracting of goods by the slave private masters of the capital bureaus, and performed other services, much like the wholesaling *kaekchu* of later times.

At the beginning of the sixteenth century, the local district tribute clerks had to borrow money at 50 percent interest to pay off the bureau clerks and slaves, replace "poor quality" tribute that had been rejected, and dun the peasants for reimbursement. By the 1540s the peasants' cost of real tribute had increased by four- or fivefold because of demands for replacement of rejected goods, costs for transport, paper, and office expenses, or forced payment of substitute rice and cloth.

Thus the chief perpetrators of tribute contracting after its "abolition" in 1468 were the low-level clerks in the bureaus (*sŏwŏn*) or warehouse clerks (*koja*), bureau masters (*chuin*), most of whom were slaves (*nobok*) or private masters of the bureaus (*sajuin*). *Nobok* and *sajuin* held their posts for life and were thoroughly familiar with the laws and procedures of government business. Tagawa Kōzō has argued that these *nobok* were so skilled in tribute contracting that they virtually became merchants in the employ of the government, and by the beginning of the sixteenth century competed with the private merchant-warehousemen or private masters (*sajuin*) for control and manipulation of the district tribute clerks. They set up their own hostels and warehouses, assumed greater risk for greater profits, and were arrested and transported to the frontier with their families more frequently. They might hold their own stockpiles of goods off the capital market until the price rose, and then sell them and depress the price so that they could repurchase them for tribute presentation at lower cost. Ultimately individual districts were placed in thrall to the capital bureau clerks and slaves, who held their posts for years and then passed them on hereditarily to their heirs.[32]

Sixteenth-Century Condemnation of Tribute Contracting

Cho Sik in the mid-sixteenth century and Cho Hŏn in 1590 accused the bureau clerks and official and private masters of monopolizing government finances, and in 1608 the Office for Dispensing Benevolence (Sŏnhyech'ŏng) created to administer the *taedŏng* system in Kyŏnggi Province summarized the situation succinctly:

> The law of the founders of the dynasty for the presenting of tribute in local products was perfect, but it developed some problems after it was in operation for a long time because it provided the opportunity for the masters [*chuin*] to make outrageous demands. Tribute goods were sent in kind to the capital, but

these clerks have been rejecting them and demanding payment in rice or cloth instead, and they have been doing it for some time. This means that the basic intent of our forefathers in founding this law has been changed into an evil practice by the private masters [*sajuin*].

The dynastic law code has prohibited tribute contracting [*pangnap*] and has prescribed that officials who engage in it will never again be appointed to office, and commoners who do so will be transported with their families to the frontier. This is indeed a severe law, but there are no greater profits to be made than those from tribute contracting. The profiteers get rice and cloth from each magistrate and make substitute payments for the tribute items, only fearing that they might have to make payment in kind. They divide the rice and cloth they have obtained, give some to the clerks and slaves of the capital bureau and have them pay it to the official. This is the way in which the original intent of the law of our forefathers has been converted into an evil perpetrated by the tribute contractors.

Of the rice and cloth collected to replace tribute items, all of it comes from the people, but 50–60 percent of it is put in the hands of the tribute contractors and 30–40 percent in the hands of the private masters [*sajuin*]. Only 10–20 percent is paid to the state treasury. There is no limit to what is taken from the people, but all of it is consumed in the lair of the profiteers.[33]

By the end of the sixteenth century, the tribute system had been converted into a new type of commerce, but not one that was fully free from governmental involvement. Almost every segment of society was involved in the trade: the peasant villagers who had to find funds to pay the district's tribute clerks, the district tribute clerks who had to pay fees to the private masters or warehousemen at the capital, the official slaves in the employ of the bureau clerks in the capital, the yangban who employed their agents and slaves to engage in the trade themselves, and the officials in charge who collected payoffs from the bureau clerks. Kings and officials could be faulted for the weakness of their commitment to maintain the legal requirements of the system and free it of all taint of commercial activity. However, since the narrow regulations and restraints imposed on private merchant activity in the beginning of the dynasty had already been violated by the emergence of unlicensed shops and active private merchants, the tribute contracting business looked like another aspect of the general economic change spreading throughout the country. What was anomalous about that economic change was that commercial activity was taking place just as more advanced forms of currency was disappearing from the Korean economy. Commercial activity along with agricultural production then suffered a severe setback from Hideyoshi's invasions, but by the mid-seventeenth century commerce regained the force it had gained a century earlier and set the stage for new economic manifestations.

What happened in the seventeenth century was partially the result of this phenomenon, the beginning of a protracted program to convert tribute altogether to a market system financed by a new tax, and that effort was led by active, pragmatic officials at court, particularly Kim Yuk. Was this kind of reform a kind of moral capitulation to the fundamental evil of the population in general, their incapacity to overcome their material desires for profit against the nobler and disinterested goal of moral cultivation and perfection? Or did it represent an awakening of a hidebound Confucian officialdom to the more progressive and liberating force of free economic activity, or a more flexible approach to reform designed to find a different method to relieve the public of the graft and corruption associated with illicit tribute contracting arrangements?

MILITARY DEBACLE: DEFEAT AND RECONSTRUCTION

The Consolidation of Military Power in Japan

There are certain events in human history that appear incomprehensible because they strike suddenly and unexpectedly, completely disrupting the standards of life that have prevailed for long periods. Such was Hideyoshi's invasion of Korea in 1592, the famous Imjin War, that, had the Koreans believed in anything like the vengeful God Jahweh, would have convinced them that they were being punished for a millennium of accumulated sins. Lacking such beliefs, however, the Koreans have been convinced ever since that they were forced to suffer, for no apparent moral or legitimate reason, a scourge of their people by the barbarous elements of a totally warlike and uncivilized people. Even though there was nothing in their recent history so heinous as to have justified the trauma and suffering that they had to undergo at Hideyoshi's hand, the failure of the Koreans at the time to foresee the tragedy and take the steps necessary to avert disaster has provided the wherewithal for almost a blanket condemnation of most of the Korean leaders of the period, save a handful of heroes who fought bravely and heroically against impossible odds.

Viewed more dispassionately, however, it is possible to see this brutal invasion as the juxtaposition of opposite trends in the histories of Japan and Korea. Although Hideyoshi's unleashing of the brutal force of his armies against the innocent people of Korea without ostensible provocation may have been tinged by the megalomania of an all-powerful military dictator intoxicated by his victories over all domestic rivals, his decision to launch an invasion of Ming China through Korea was as much the consequence of the developments under way since the mid-fifteenth century as his own will and drive.

Hideyoshi's grasp of political power over all of Japan was the consequence of a century of internecine feudal conflict after the outbreak of the Ōnin War of 1467–77. The feudal lords or daimyo of Japan had expanded their domains and military power by either defeating their rivals or incorporating them into their own forces as subordinates. This process of consolidation culminated in the career of Toyotomi Hideyoshi, a peasant who rose from the ranks in the armies of Oda Nobunaga, who overthrew the Ashikaga Shōgun in 1573. Hideyoshi finally succeeded in establishing domination by war or compromise over all the daimyo of Japan.

This political consolidation was accompanied by reforms that expanded central control over the fiscal resources of the country. In 1591 Hideyoshi completed a national cadastral survey and established a uniform land tax of two-thirds of the crop that provided regular income for the daimyo, who functioned as his chief military vassals. He subordinated the previously independent samurai, or local warriors, to the daimyo and himself by eliminating their proprietary rights over their fiefs.[34] In short, he created a powerful military force based on a decentralized, feudal structure of semiautonomous authority several times more powerful than the apparently fully centralized regime of the Chosŏn dynasty in Korea.

Lack of Defensive Preparations in Chosŏn

By contrast, the centralized power of the Chosŏn state had come unraveled by the end of the sixteenth century. Korea was weakened politically by feuding bureaucratic factions in the capital, fiscally by the corruption of the bureaucratic apparatus and the failure to maintain tax revenues by the land and tribute taxes, and militarily by the neglect of defense, the under-registration of the adult male population for service, the exemption of slaves and yangban from military duty, the lack of training, and the failure to adopt firearms.[35]

The court of King Sŏnjo failed to make any basic plan for national defense despite the threat of an invasion, and took only desultory steps to send border commissioners to the frontier and to repair some walls and moats. At the beginning of the war the Korean army used only three walled towns as bases for its operations, Pusan, Tongnae, and Kimhae, while other major towns like Sangju and Ch'ungju had no military protection at all.[36]

There were a number of signs of Korean military weakness and lack of preparation in the decades before the invasion. In 1582 Yulgok recommended the recruitment of the nothoi of yangban (*sŏŏl*) for service, permission for slaves to purchase their freedom in return for joining the army as frontier soldiers, and the creation of an army of 100,000 men, of which 20,000 would be stationed in the capital and 10,000 in each province. The last proposal was rejected by Yu Sŏngnyŏng at the time on the grounds that it would cause more damage than it would help, but he must have rued the day he uttered those words when he found himself on the Yalu River in 1592 after the Korean army had been destroyed by Hideyoshi's forces.[37]

In 1588, the provincial governor, Cho Ŭn'hol, urged that twenty abandoned strategic islands off the coast be immediately fortified and used as naval bases. In 1590 Yi Hangbok recommended stationing forces at Pusan and strategic spots such as Kyŏnnaeryang and Kogŭm Island to block any Japanese advance by sea. Kim Seryŏm warned about the likelihood of a Japanese attack in the third lunar month, and he proposed establishing two new naval bases, one in the middle of the southern coast and another on Kadŏk Island, especially to defend coastal towns like Pusan, Tongnae, Chinju, Sunch'ŏn, and Hŭngyang.[38]

Factionalism and Policy toward Japan

Only a few officials took a hard line at this time. Cho Hŏn in 1587 and 1588 attacked members of the Easterner faction like Chief State Councilor No Susin, Second State Councilor Chŏng Yugil, and Minister of Rites Yu Sŏngnyŏng for their lack of action, and demanded the installation of Westerner leaders like Chŏng Ch'ŏl and Pak Sun, and the dispatch of an armed force to Japan. King Sŏnjo, however, responded by sending Cho Hŏn into exile and appointing more Easterners to crucial posts.[39]

When the Chŏng Yŏrip rebellion broke out in 1589 in Chŏlla Province in the southwest, King Sŏnjo regarded it as an Easterner plot and carried out a purge of Easterners through 1591 that resulted in the execution or death of seventy men.[40] When the Korean diplomatic mission to Japan to assess Hideyoshi's intentions returned in 1591, however, instead of heeding the warning of the main envoy, Hwang Yun'gil, of the Westerner faction, that Hideyoshi would launch an invasion, King Sŏnjo adopted the view of Vice-Envoy Kim Sŏng'il of the Easterners, who said that Hideyoshi was not worth worrying about, and decided to take no special action to repair defensive walls and forts. Responsibility for the failure to take action in advance, therefore, rests primarily with King Sŏnjo and most of the Easterner advisers.[41]

Decline of Ming Power

Had the Ming dynasty been as virile and powerful in 1592 as it was in the previous century, the Japanese might not have dared to invade the Korean peninsula, but the Mongol tribesmen in the north, previously held in check, now launched regular raids into the interior, especially into Liao-tung in Manchuria.[42] The fiscal situation had become chaotic because of the irregular commutation of grain and labor service taxes to silver payments and the assessment of surcharges to supplement revenues. Despite the fiscal reform of Chang Chü-cheng, the grand secretary who dominated the court between 1572 and 1582, which increased tax revenues through the "single-whip system" that converted all tax payments to a single, silver-bullion payment, Ming finances and administration deteriorated after Chang's death. The Wan-li emperor became more reclusive and allowed power to gravitate into the hands of court eunuchs, who had already formed alliances with powerful bureaucrats and purged a group of orthodox Neo-Confucian reformers in 1594, in the middle of the Japanese invasion of Korea.[43]

Because the early Ming *wei-so* system of frontier defense came to an end after the Tu-mu Rebellion of 1449, the regular army deteriorated in quality. It had numbered over three million men in the early fifteenth century but was reduced to about 500,000 men in 1592, with no more than 100,000 men in the northeast region of the country. On the other hand, military organization had been reorganized successfully according to plans developed by Ch'i Chi-kuang, who fought against the Wakō in Fu-chien Province in 1563 and who published his book on military organization, the *Chi-hsiao hsin-shu*, in 1567. His text was taken over as a manual by Korean military officials during the Imjin War. Ch'i divided the infantry into five groups: musketeers, swordsmen, bowmen with fire arrows, ordinary bowmen, and spearmen, and he provided that the infantry be accompanied with cavalry and crew-served artillery units.[44] Thus, while the Ming soldiers may not have been as experienced, battle-hardened, and skillful in the use of muskets and group tactics as the Japanese, they were by no means a pushover, and the Ming army had greater numbers and direct access by land to reinforcements.

The First Phase of the Imjin War, 1592–93

In a letter Hideyoshi sent to Korea before the invasion in 1592 he revealed his plan to conquer Ming China, install the Japanese emperor in the Chinese capital, and assign his adopted son to rule over Korea, before subjugating other countries like Ryūkyū, Taiwan, and the Philippines.[45] When King Sŏnjo rejected his demands to provide safe passage for Japanese forces to China, Hideyoshi finally decided to invade Korea with a force of 281,840 men, of which the invading contingent numbered 158,700, and the initial attacking party three corps of 52,500 men, who landed near Pusan on May 23, 1592.[46] This large fighting force had been hardened by a long period of combat in Japan's internal wars, its *ashigaru* foot soldiers had been trained in the use of muskets and firearms introduced by the Portuguese to Japan in 1543, and even its peasant baggage carriers were skilled in the use of firearms, castle and fortress construction, and siege tactics against walled towns.[47]

Yu Sŏngnyŏng, the Korean chief state councilor during the invasion, praised the superior tactical organization of Japanese military units because the vanguard unit that engaged the enemy was always backed up by two units on its left and right wings to envelop the enemy, and those two wings also had two additional units behind them. In addition, these individual Japanese units were subdivided into three parts. When approaching a Korean force, the banner unit in the van divided in two to envelop the enemy, the middle unit armed with muskets would fire a volley to break up the Korean ranks, and the rear unit armed with swords would then flank the Koreans on the left and right and pursue them when they took flight, decapitating as many of them as they could. Korean units, by contrast, simply concentrated their troops in one place and moved forward, and when they saw that they were about to be surrounded by superior Japanese tactics, they usually lost heart and took flight.[48]

After Hideyoshi's forces landed at Pusan on May 23, 1592, they pushed past Korean defenses and took Seoul in three weeks. Outside of a number of naval victories the only advantage the Korean forces gained on land was to block Japanese troops from entering Chŏlla Province in the southwest. Konishi Yukinaga pushed north and occupied Pyongyang by July 23, where he halted for the winter. A second wing under Katō Kiyomasa and Nabeshima Naoshige moved into the northeast up to the Yalu and Tumen rivers.[49]

Ming forces belatedly entered the contest in January 1593 and defeated Konishi Yukinaga's men in a battle at Pyongyang on February 8, 1593. Heady with their victory at Pyongyang, the Ming commander, Li Ju-sung, rashly pursued the retreating Japanese but suffered a stinging defeat at the battle of Pyŏkchegwan on February 25–27, 1593, just north of the capital at Hansŏng (Seoul). That defeat sobered the Chinese and created an almost excessive caution and defensiveness among them for the rest of the war, but Konishi realized that the tide of battle had turned against him. He agreed on April 18, 1593, to a truce calling for the mutual withdrawal of Japanese forces from Hansŏng to the Pusan area and Ming forces to the Liao-tung area in China, and the return of two Korean princes that Katō Kiyomasa had obtained from a Korean rebel in Hamgyŏng Province.[50]

Konishi then began a period of protracted negotiations with a Chinese official, Shen Wei-ching. Sung Ying-ch'ang, the Ming military commissioner (Ching-lüeh) then in charge of affairs in Korea, was hoping that a promise to have the Ming emperor confer investiture on Hideyoshi as "King of Japan" would satisfy his desire for recognition and formal relations and bring the invasion to an end.[51]

Korean Military Performance in the First Phase

Dispatch of Field Commanders from the Capital. When word of the landing of Japanese troops first arrived at the capital in Seoul (Hansŏng) in 1592, the government followed current practice of dispatching a mobile border commander (Sunbyŏnsa), Yi Il, to take charge of troops in the south. The Ministry of War assigned him what was supposed to be three hundred crack troops from the capital as his own contingent, but he found that half the men consisted of raw recruits, clerks in their square caps, or students dressed in their hats and gowns with their examination books in hand – a motley crew of men who had spent their lives trying to evade military service. He finally left these men behind and took only sixty cavalrymen, recruiting troops on the way south.

When he arrived at Mun'gyŏng in north Kyŏngsang Province, there were no troops there to meet him. All the soldiers from the area south of Mun'gyŏng had been assembled near Taegu for several days to await his arrival but had run away when they heard that the Japanese were approaching. He pressed on to Sangju where he found but a few hundred troops whom he joined with his own men to form a small force that was soon overwhelmed by the 20,000 Japanese under Konishi Yukinaga at the battle of Sangju on May 15–16, 1592 (lunar 4.24–5).[52]

Yu Sŏngnyŏng, the chief state councilor for much of the war, later wrote that this disaster had been caused by the abandonment of the early Chosŏn *chin'-*

gwan system that placed command responsibilities in the hands of local garrison commanders. Yu blamed the scholar-officials of early Chosŏn whom he claimed had allowed the venerated institutions of the early dynasty to become moribund while they concerned themselves only with polishing their literary style or indulging in idle gossip. He believed that the new system of command was the product of the "victory strategy" (*chesŭng pangnyak*), introduced first in Chŏlla Province by Kim Sumun at the time of the Wakō pirate attack of 1555, the *ŭlmyo waebyŏn*. Under this "victory strategy," the Towŏnsu (supreme field commander), the mobile border commander (Sunbyŏnsa), the defense commander (Pang'ŏsa), and the auxiliary defense officer (Chobangjang) were sent out from the capital to assume field command over local garrison troops and district recruits.[53]

When a report of an invasion of pirates was received, all the troops in the province were immediately called out and stationed on the provincial border, but their commanders were not given the authority to move them around until the field commanders arrived. Since the latter had to travel as much as 250 miles, the trip might take three or four days while the troops were left disorganized and in exposed positions, usually on flat ground, as the enemy vanguard advanced. Then, according to Yu, when the enemy drew near, the troops would run off "like startled birds or frightened beasts." By the time the capital field commanders arrived on the scene, "the runaway soldiers were hiding in the mountains and valleys," and no men were left on reserve. Furthermore, what was supposed to be a temporary remedy for an emergency against a small force was, unfortunately, left in place until Hideyoshi's forces arrived in 1592. Yu Sŏngnyŏng insisted that this error in strategic planning could not be repeated in the future.

Yu, however, was mistaken in his facts. The author of the *chesŭng pangnyak* system in 1555 was not Kim Sumun but the then provincial army commander (Pyŏngma Chŏltosa) for North Hamgyŏng Province, none other than the same Yi Il who was dispatched to Mun'gyŏng in 1592. Yi, who had been responsible for the suppression of the Nit'anggae uprising of Jurchen people in the northeast in 1583, was appalled by the disarray in the military forces in North Hamgyŏng. He designed his *pangyak* strategy to carry out just the same kind of reform that Yu Sŏngnyŏng favored in the 1590s. He reorganized the six garrisons (*yukchin*) in the province into Five Guards (Owi) in which one district magistrate (a Pusa) was placed in charge of seven subordinate units headed by military officers, probably with jurisdiction over local districts or garrisons. Instead of waiting for the arrival of a commander sent from the capital each time there was a raid across the northern border, a practice already in place at the time, the provincial army commander would exercise field command immediately.

Another of his requests, subsequently rejected by the Border Defense Command in Seoul, was that in case of invasion from the north, troops from southern provinces would also be assigned to the various guards under command of their own district magistrates functioning as military commanders with separate military titles. The Border Defense Command at the capital refused because it wanted to maintain the principle that each province had responsibility for its own defense.[54]

Yu was also in error in dating the origin of the system of dispatching the mobile border commander and other field officers from the capital. The practice of dispatching civil officials with concurrent military command responsibilities to the provinces during emergencies had been used at the beginning of the dynasty, abandoned in the mid-fifteenth century, and then readopted with a change in the titles of such officers in 1488, long before the Japanese attack in 1555. This revival probably occurred because of the decline in effectiveness of the local *chin'gwan* garrisons, and its revival meant that the central government was assuming command responsibilities in place of the provincial army and navy commanders (Pyŏngsa, Susa) whose authority must have been reduced.

In 1555, just after the Wakō pirates were defeated, the Border Defense Command (Pibyŏnsa) realized that a system in which command over provincial or local forces was vested in capital officials was fundamentally flawed and decided to cease the dispatch of commanders from the capital and appoint the provincial governors as concurrent mobile inspectors (Sunch'alsa), the title of the fourth official down in the chain of command of capital civil officials dispatched as military commanders over armies in the field (as established in 1488). When the threat of another Japanese attack occurred in 1558, however, the government reverted to the practice of sending a supreme mobile inspector (Tosunch'alsa, the third ranking official in the 1488 chain of command) from the capital, probably because it lacked confidence in the provincial *chin'gwan* system.[55]

The mobile border commander (Sunbyŏnsa) was simply a new name created in 1558 for the old mobile inspector (Sunch'alsa), who was the assistant of the supreme mobile inspector (Tosunch'alsa). This was done to avoid confusion since in 1555 the provincial governors had been given the title of mobile inspector as a concurrency. The other two officials, the defense commander (Pang'ŏsa), and the auxiliary defense officer (Chobangjang), mentioned above were not established until 1570 when the government received reports from Tsushima that armed Japanese pirates had appeared. Kim Sumun, who had fought against the Japanese in 1555 as magistrate of Cheju (island), was merely appointed a mobile border commander in Kyŏngsang (not Chŏlla) Province in 1558.

Contrary to Yu's perception, the dispatch of commanders from the capital had been general policy since the Three Ports Uprising (*Samp'o waeran*) of Japanese residents in those ports in 1510. When generals (Taejang) or defense commanders were sent from the capital they brought a small contingent of their own troops with them. The provincial troops, both rank and file, were simply assigned to the capital commanders either as core or auxiliary units; they were not separated from their commanding officers or their units.[56]

On the other hand, at the time of the 1555 incident it had become clear that the regular soldiers assigned to garrisons were untrained for fighting, so that commanders dispatched from the capital had to recruit and mobilize whomever they could find: retired military officers, unemployed yangban (*hallyang*), slaves, or Buddhist monks. Thus, the practice of recruiting irregulars occurred about the same time as the *chesŭng pangnyak* system, but it was not an integral part of the system itself. Nonetheless, the poor state of readiness of local garrison troops coupled with the flawed system of separating commanders in the capital from local troops virtually guaranteed certain defeat at the hands of Hideyoshi's troops honed to a razor-sharp edge in the thousand battles of the sixteenth-century Japan.

Guerrilla Warfare. For the seven long months prior to the arrival of the main Ming force in Korea in January 1593, and throughout the rest of the war as well, an estimated 22,200 guerrilla soldiers compared with 84,500 regular troops harassed the Japanese throughout the line of bases and camps they set up from Pusan north to Seoul and Pyongyang.[57] Kim Myŏn operated in southeast Kyŏngsang Province; Yang Taebak, Son In'gap, and the famous Kwak Chaeu helped block the Japanese thrust into Chŏlla Province; Kim Myŏn, Chŏng Inhong, and Kim Chunmin delivered a shock to the Japanese at the second battle of Sŏngju; Chŏng Munbu helped drive the Japanese out of Hamgyŏng Province in February 1593; the monks Hyujŏng, and his disciple, Ch'ŏyŏng were active fighters, and the pugnacious scholar-official, Cho Hŏn, fought to his death at the battle of Kŭmsan. Although many guerrillas refused to obey orders from government officers and terrorized the local population, they still provided the core of resistance until the Ming armies arrived.[58]

Unfortunately there were far more villains than heroes among regular officials and ordinary soldiers who abandoned their posts and fled at the first sight of Japanese troops.[59] King Sŏnjo refrained from dismissing incompetent and cowardly officers, the Border Defense Command apparently lacked the capacity to plan strategy, and the governors and provincial magistrates were afraid to risk their necks by making proposals for action.[60]

At sea, the Korean navy under the great Yi Sunsin, initially the naval commander for Left Chŏlla Province and later supreme admiral of the fleet, outmaneuvered and outfought the Japanese wherever he found them. He won victories at seventeen of the eighteen naval battles he fought, especially ones at Yulp'o, Hansan Island, and Angolp'o from August through October 1592, and he destroyed over 400 Japanese ships in ten naval battles in December alone. His use of heavily armored turtle ships to win victory at the battle of Sach'ŏn on July 7, 1592 (5.29 lunar), was responsible for preventing the Japanese from sending their fleet up the western coast to reinforce their advance into Chŏlla.[61]

Armistice, 1593–97, and Renewal of the War

Despite their rapid advance through Korean territory in the initial phase of the war, the Japanese were by no means immune to severe losses. Supplies had to be transported by land, and in the process about one-third of the 150,000 Japanese soldiers and transport laborers in the first invasion died, mainly from exhaustion, hunger, and disease. After the retreat from Pyongyang, and later from Seoul, Hideyoshi must have realized that his original aim of conquering Ming China had little chance of success. Yet, just on the eve of an armistice agreement with the Chinese, Hideyoshi ordered the subjugation of the town of Chinju, just to the west of Pusan. The ruthless massacre of all its defenders and inhabitants – 60,000 men, women, and children – was the worst single atrocity of the war.[62]

The fighting was halted and all but 43,000 Japanese troops were withdrawn to Japan for three years between 1594 and 1597 while negotiations were conducted for a compromise. Konishi Yukinaga and Shen Wei-ching had to create a number of deceptions to keep the negotiations moving. With Shen's cooperation Konishi on February 11, 1594, forged a letter of submission from Hideyoshi to the Ming emperor that omitted mention of Hideyoshi's demands and appeared to represent a request for trade as a tributary of China to enable the dispatch of a Chinese mission to Japan.[63]

When Hideyoshi finally agreed to accept a Ming envoy at his court, King Sŏnjo, who had been opposing the negotiations from the outset, had no choice but to send Hwang Sin as the official Korean ambassador (T'ongsinsa), to follow after the Chinese to Japan.[64] The mission foundered, however, because Hideyoshi's terms for peace – amity with the Ming sealed by Hideyoshi's marriage to a Ming princess, a renewal of the tally trade, annexation of four Korean provinces, Korean hostages, and a Korean pledge to refrain from challenging Japan – were impossible for the Chinese emperor, let alone the Koreans, to consider. The negotiations came to a sudden end when Hideyoshi exploded in a paroxysm of rage when the Ming emperor's patent of investiture was read aloud to him. He found it so demeaning and insulting that he was about to order the execution of the entire Sino-Korean mission on the spot. Restrained by his underlings, however, he agreed to release the mission before he accepted the hawkish Katō Kiyomasa's request to renew the conflict. He dispatched troops back to Korea, rebuilt his forces there to 141,500 men, and then demanded the cession of the three southern provinces of Korea.[65]

In the second invasion, the Japanese navy defeated the Korean fleet at the battle of Ch'ilch'ŏllyang on Kŏje Island, which was then under the command of Wŏn Kyun because Yi Sunsin, who had been supported by the Easterner chief state councilor, Yu Sŏngnyong, had been imprisoned and demoted because of unjustified charges by the Westerner faction.[66] The Japanese then divided their forces into left and right armies, which moved into Chŏlla Province for the first time and ruthlessly carried out an extermination campaign against the inhabitants. The bloody advance was finally driven back by the Eastern Expeditionary Army of the Ming at Iksan on October 17 (9.7 lunar), 1597, a town just south of Seoul. The Japanese fleet then suffered a major defeat on October 26 at the naval battle of Myŏngnyang, and Yi Sunsin, now restored to command, was able to defeat a force of over 300 Japanese ships with only twelve of his own, therefore blocking the Japanese from further access into the Yellow Sea.[67]

Pushed back to the southern coast by Ming and Korean regular and irregular forces, the Japanese found themselves hard pressed when Hideyoshi died on September 18, 1598. Chinese and Korean forces continued their assault on Japanese positions, and Admiral Yi Sunsin was killed at the battle of Noryang on December 16–17, 1598. One week later, Japanese troops left Korea, and the invasion was brought to an end.[68]

Forts: Firming Walls and Clearing Fields

One of the tactical problems of Korean defense was the Korean military custom of relying on the mountain fort (*sansŏng*) for defense. When Hideyoshi renewed his attack in 1597, the Koreans used the tactic of "firming up the walls and clearing the countryside," which meant that the peasants were ordered to take their whole families, their belongings, and their stored grain with them into the nearest mountain fort. Any who failed to evacuate the villages was subject to arrest and execution on the grounds that they would automatically be suspected of collaboration with the Japanese, but in practice the forts were so far away that they usually buried everything in the nearby hills and waited in their villages for the Japanese to arrive.[69]

The main purpose of the tactic was to deprive the advancing Japanese army of Korean grain even though it forced much hardship on the Korean peasantry.[70] Ming commanders, however, criticized the disrepair of the walled forts in the Korean hills and urged their reconstruction, especially the forts at the crucial mountain passes at Bird's Peak (Seje or Choryŏng) and Bamboo Peak (Chungnyŏng) where a few well-armed men should have been able to block the advance of thousands. Unfortunately, these passes were not well defended in the first two years of the war, and they did not play a crucial role in the fighting at the end.[71] After the war was over the Koreans did improve the mountain fortifications, but fate played a cruel trick by changing the nature of the tactics that would be necessary in the next struggle against the Manchus.

Discrepancies in Gunpowder and Firearms

When the armies of Hideyoshi arrived on Korean shores in 1592, they were armed with Western smooth-bore muskets, superior to anything the Korean forces had at the time. Koreans had first used firearms in defending an attack by 500 Wakō ships after Ch'oe Musŏn had learned the methods of manufacture from a Chinese artisan. The court then ordered the Firearms Directorate (Hwat'ong-dogam) to take charge of manufacture.[72]

Sometime before 1578, the Korean military official, Kim Chi, had cast a new type of small-arms weapon, the *sŭng*-type gun, a piece that averaged about 55 centimeters in length with a bore 2.5 centimeters in diameter. This proved to be no match for the Western musket or fowling piece, however. The Korean government learned that the Japanese possessed the Western-style musket when a Japanese envoy, Sō Yoshitoshi, brought one as a gift in 1589, but the Koreans copied only about 170 of them. The first time the Koreans used them in battle was at Chinju in November 1592, and Yi Sunsin used some he had captured for the first time in a naval battle at Pusan.[73]

The key figure in their adoption was Yu Sŏngnyŏng, who argued for their superiority to arrows, mentioned Ch'i Chi-kuang's use of them in fighting Japanese pirates in the late sixteenth century, and cited several instances of the borrowing of superior technology by Chinese states of the past, but nothing was done to follow his advice before the outbreak of the war. Only after the invasion began did King Sŏnjo authorize the adoption of the musket.[74] One artisan who specialized in cannon at the Armory (Kun'gisi), Yi Changson, made a new type that shot a cannonball about 600 paces. It was used with great effect by Korean troops twice at Chinju and at the third battle of Kyŏngju. The Koreans also developed an explosive shell fit with iron shrapnel and a fuse.[75]

An army recruiter (Somosa), Pyŏn Ijung, was able to manufacture over 300 new "fire wagons" (*hwach'a*), each one of which had forty gun portholes that could fire at once. The Koreans also invented a catapult called a water-wheel rock cannon (*such'a sŏkp'o*) that spun around like a water wheel while shooting out stones, and the Military Training Agency began training troops in the use of "poisoned gunpowder" that the Ming commander-in-chief, Liu Ting, had sent in the last phase of the war. Kwak Sunsŏng and others studied many methods of manufacturing it.[76]

In addition to the effectively armored turtle boats that Yi Sunsin used in many of his naval battles, the Koreans did have a limited, but undeveloped, technical capacity. The search for better military techniques continued after the war. In 1601, the Ming gunpowder expert, Sun Lung, was granted a reward and kept in Korea to teach four Korean artisans the manufacture of "sea saltpetre or nitre," poisoned powder, and training in their use.[77]

Institutional Changes in Defense

The Military Training Agency, 1593. When the Ming forces arrived in Korea they immediately recognized that the Korean army was tragically behind the most advanced technological levels of the day. The Chinese general, Lo Shang-chih, recommended to Yu Sŏngnyŏng that a new unit was needed to train Korean troops in the use of muskets and other techniques of combat. As a result King Sŏnjo authorized the establishment of the Military Training Agency (Hullyŏndogam) on September 4 (8.10 lunar), 1593, but he only assigned seventy-two men to it. At the urging of Yu he later increased its contingent to 10,000 men. On the recommendation of Li Ju-sung, the king also authorized the distribution of Ch'i Chi-kuang's *Chi-hsiao hsin-shu* as a manual for the organization and training of troops in "the three skills" (*samsu*) of musketry, swordsmanship, and archery.[78]

The financing of the Military Training Agency was rather haphazard. At the outset, the soldiers were given a rice ration or salary of six *mal* per day, more to offset hunger than to provide serious support for crack troops. Because of the shortage of funds during wartime, King Sŏnjo ordered only half the men to undergo training in the capital for a tour of eighteen months and the other half to cultivate military colony lands (*tunjŏn*) attached to the agency, abandoned Buddhist temple land in Ch'ungch'ŏng Province, or land without visible resident owner-cultivators, at least until they returned to their homes. Some grain was obtained from certain colony lands by collecting taxes from peasant cultivators to offset agency expenses while the Ministry of Taxation and Military Ration Agency paid the rations of the troops.

Nonetheless, rations were still meager, less than what regular soldiers of the Five Guards were getting from the payments of their two support taxpayers. The government then divided the troops in half and assigned the inferior troops to agricultural work to increase the rations of the better troops who remained on duty. Although the government granted income from fishing weirs and salt flats to the agency, it still suffered financial difficulties, even after the war had ended.

Some of the Military Training Agency's men were semipermanent, salaried soldiers while others were support taxpayers, not necessarily assigned in any formal way to the duty troops. Since the agency was not reluctant to recruit slaves into its ranks, some déclassé yangban who either had been or were still owners of slaves ended up as support taxpayers for the slave soldiers of the agency! Because of severe losses of men from death or desertion, the agency reached a low point of 2,000 troops and 700 support taxpayers in 1603, but despite the appeal of some officials to abolish it altogether, King Sŏnjo insisted on maintaining it by cutting the salaries of his regular officials. He also prohibited private slaves from its ranks to stimulate more commoners to enlist and impoverished yangban to become support taxpayers for it.

He adopted another supplementary source of funds for troop rations in 1602 by instituting a surtax on land called the "three military skills rice tax" (*samsumi*) in the amount of one *mal* per *kyŏl* in five provinces, a practice that was approved permanently in 1606. The rate was raised slightly thereafter but reduced to one *mal* again and confined to the three southern provinces in 1634.[79] Despite the establishment of a financial base, the unit's troops had a reputation for wild and unrestrained behavior for the twenty years after they were established.[80] Overall the agency represented an extremely poor response to the challenge of creating a force of musketeers for the national army.

Yu Sŏngnyŏng's Plan for the Chin'gwan System. Even though the *chin'gwan* garrison command system of the early Chosŏn period had been rendered useless by the sixteenth century, Chief State Councilor Yu Sŏngnyŏng still thought that it ought to be restored. He admired the way it subdivided every province into regions with a main garrison (*chujin*) headed by a garrison commander called Pyŏngma chŏlchesa, which functioned as a command and control center for other garrisons and all the district towns (*ŭp*) under its jurisdiction.[81] Yu thought that the *chin'gwan* system operated with a kind of biological unity in which the troop units were bound "in a solid phalanx like the scales of a fish" and operated like the arms and legs of a human body in instantaneous response to the commands of the leader. He thought that the central provincial commander would be able to manipulate the various district units according to the tactical situation, choosing alternatively to attack the enemy frontally, pursue it from the rear, turn either of its flanks, or back up a gap created by the defeat of one of its units.

He perceived the chief advantage of this centrally commanded, strategically located system of district garrisons to be its capacity to provide a series of lines of defense no matter how many times the enemy punctured the front line or captured one of the garrisons. In discussing the advantages for checking another Japanese invasion, he outlined a possible scenario for the south: first the mobilization of as many as seventy to eighty thousand troops from commoner peasants and slaves from the districts under the command of the Tongnae garrison (near Pusan). If they were defeated, they would be backed up by the troops of the Taegu *chin'gwan* (command garrison) stationed in the middle to block the enemy's advance, with the troops of Kyŏngju and Chinju forming the left and right wings, respectively. If the Taegu troops were defeated, they would be backed up in turn by the Sangju, Ch'ŏngju (in Ch'ungch'ŏng Province), and Kyŏnggi Province garrisons (*chin'gwan*).

> The strength of the country would be like a double door or a double wall, and even though the enemy might be able to penetrate one of the layers, there would always be another one [behind it]. How would they be able in the space of a week to cut across a thousand *li* [of territory] and advance straight to the capital [as Hideyoshi's forces had done] as if they were treading on no-man's land?[82]

Although his proposal was adopted by King Sŏnjo in the winter of 1595, it was rescinded in 1598 before it could have been fully implemented or its efficacy judged.[83]

Yu also sought to remedy two other practices: stripping the countryside of troops and defensive garrisons to assemble them only on the frontier or front line, and subdividing defense forces into walled towns or garrisons too small to resist a large attacking force. He believed that Sung China had suffered defeat during the Mongol invasions of the thirteenth century because she lacked both a back-up system of internal defense and large-scale forces at the front. One Wang Li-hsin had advocated dividing local districts into four military regions called *k'un* under special military commanders (*shuai*) but the plan had not been adopted. Yu Sŏngnyŏng compared Wang's idea to the *chin'gwan* system of provincial commanders exercising command and control in a provincial hierarchy.

He also noted that Chinese commentators had contrasted the success of the Eastern Chin (317–420) with the failure of the Southern Sung (1127–1280) in defending river positions against invaders. River defense was, of course, a crucial weakness in Korea's defense against the Japanese but more from failure of the top leadership to throw their forces into blocking the Japanese advance at the Han, Imjin, and Taedong rivers.

As opposed to the Sung dynasty (960–1280), the Eastern Chin had established a *fan-chen* system of frontier garrisons that combined several civil districts in one military district with a large garrison (*ta-chen*) under a single commander. This provided unified command over a large force. The reason the Sung had not followed this earlier precedent was because they feared the build-up of regional power by commanders such as An Lu-shan of the T'ang. Thus, they abolished the *fan-chen* and kept provincial forces subdivided according to the usual civil districts, the *chün* and *hsien*. Because these units were too small and weak, the enemy picked them off one after the other.[84] The point was an important one: since Sung overreaction to the power of the military in the T'ang era had led to fragmentation of forces and weakening of the army, Yu was suggesting that a similar factor might have operated in Korea's current military weakness. Somehow, a balance had to be found between civilian control and military strength.

Ch'i Chi-kuang's System and Service for Slaves. Yu Sŏngnyŏng was also a leading advocate of Ch'i Chi-kuang's Che-chiang system of military organization, which incorporated soldiers trained in firearms and muskets into the regular army, but the key organizational principle of the system was simply to divide large forces into small units, arranged in an ascending hierarchy. The term *sog'o* (Korean pronunciation), was the label for this method of organization described in the first chapter of Ch'i Chi-kuang's *Chi-hsiao hsin-shu*, and it became the basis of Yu Sŏngnyŏng's military reorganization adopted between 1594 and 1596 by the order of King Sŏnjo.[85]

The *sog'o* system also broke the main barrier against the full mobilization of the male population for national defense by providing for the recruitment without respect to status. Men of base status, that is official or private slaves, and male nothoi of yangban (*sŏŏl*) were included in troop units alongside men of good status (*yang'in*). Their masters were compensated by the grant of either office rank or a substitute slave.[86]

On January 25, 1594, during the armistice, King Sŏnjo ordered the recruitment of all men exempted from military service (*myŏnyŏk*) and freedmen (*myŏnch'ŏn*), and formed all slaves in the capital city into companies, a policy he had refused to adopt during the suppression of rebellion in 1583.[87] After the war in 1600 and 1602 he also manumitted slaves and recruited them into the military, used male slaves employed in the palace (*naeno*) to fill military vacancies in thirteen towns, and recruited private slaves of yangban to serve as archers (*sasu*). Although he reversed this policy and returned private slaves to their masters in 1603, the *sog'o* system by which slaves were recruited into military service stayed in place for the last half of the dynasty.[88]

The new *sog'o* troops were organized into squads of 11 men, platoons or banners of 33, companies of 99, battalions of 495, and divisions of 12,375.[89] It is unclear just what the relationship was between villages and districts and *sog'o* units. In the case of Kyŏnggi Province, for example, there were five regiments (*yŏng*) for the whole province, one for the capital and four for the outlying areas. In three cases, a battalion consisted of a single district, in others, two or three districts. Even though the Central Regiment at the capital included the newly formed Military Training Agency and may have had an irregular complement of troops, we may presume that the troop strength for this province (five regiments) was equivalent to a single division. The whole system was to operate on the basis of the classical militia system: military organization would correspond to the hierarchy of villages and districts, unit commanders would be recruited from local talented men, during planting and harvest seasons the men would alternate between work and rest according to a fixed schedule, and during slack periods the men would assemble for training at the commander's (Taejang) headquarters.[90]

The organization of *sog'o* battalions for P'yŏng'an Province provides some more details about the distribution of troops by type in 1596. Each platoon had a regular complement of three squads identified by one of the three types of soldiers (*samsu*): *salsu* ("killers" or close-combat sword, pike, and spearmen), *sasu* (archers), and *p'osu* (musketeers). Of the thirty-six squads, however, only eight were musket squads, while five were close-combat swordsmen, and twenty-three were bowmen, indicating the persistence of traditional weaponry, but even the Japanese had mixed musketeers with archers and swordsmen in their units during the invasion. Despite the royal command to eliminate status distinctions, some attempt was obviously made to keep some units free of slaves entirely. Six platoons or eighteen squads – half the units of one entire battalion – had no persons of base status at all. Finally, an attempt was made at least, to combine *sog'o* organization with the restoration of the *chin'gwan* system.[91]

In certain respects, however, the new system departed from the *chin'gwan* model. Although company commanders were selected from the *myŏn* and *i* (subdistricts and administrative villages, respectively, units below the level of the central government's district magistracy), the platoon leaders and company commanders were not selected from local people. Variations from the unit quotas in the *Chi-hsiao hsin-shu* were also allowed.[92]

Yu Sŏngnyŏng realized full well that his attempt to combine the *chin'gwan* and *sog'o* systems was an unavoidable compromise with the farmer-soldier militia ideal of antiquity. In the typical fashion of practical reformers he argued that after the fall from grace that marked the destruction of the sage institutions of Chou China, the best that one could hope for was to make adaptations to the real and imperfect world because in the "later age" (*huse*) after the fall of the Chou dynasty, soldiers became distinct from peasants. Since that time, the task of the soldier was to "put forth effort to guard the people," and the task of the peasant was to "put forth [i.e., provide] grain to feed the soldier," a remark that appears to justify the system of rotating service and support taxpayers in use at the time and later advocated by Yu Hyŏngwŏn.[93]

During the Imjin War, however, it became impossible to provide rations for the soldiers even during the period of truce. Since peasants would rotate on and off duty, requiring some travel between their home villages and the place of duty, whether the capital or a garrison, their absence from home interfered with the production of grain. He found a remedy for this situation in the *Nei-cheng* (Internal Administration) chapter of the *Kuan-tzu*, according to which squad, platoon, and company officers would be recruited from the rural villages and put in charge of the peacetime training of peasant-soldiers during slack times when the men were not needed in the fields.

Yu explained that this was the basis for his *sog'o* system by which military units corresponded in size to the population inhabiting villages and districts. All the troops would be assigned to units near their homes and undergo training in their villages. During large-scale field-training exercises, all the soldiers of a regiment (*yŏng*) might be assembled in one place, or in the case of Kyŏnggi Province, all four regiments outside the capital could be assembled for inspection at the capital. Otherwise, the men would remain at home freed from the bother and expense of traveling long distances for military duty and training, and they would have sufficient time to ensure sufficient grain production.[94]

In other words, Yu Sŏngnyŏng was arguing that in a time of almost total desperation, when the nation was virtually gasping for breath, the destruction of grain reserves and production meant that an approximation of the militia *ideal* was the only *practical* method for training a provincial reserve army. The centralized, bureaucratic state was only capable of maintaining a small force of crack bowmen, swordsmen, and new musketeers in the capital under the Military Training Agency; it could not also maintain a large, permanent force of professional soldiers in the provinces. The flaw of the *chin'gwan* system of early Chosŏn was the assignment of men to posts some distance from their villages and the increase of travel and tax burdens on them, which caused many men to flee their homes and the army recruiters. He hoped to eliminate that problem by adopting the *sog'o*'s system of making a military hierarchy out of the villages, subdistricts, and districts of the countryside.[95]

No sooner was the fighting over in 1598, however, than corruption of the *sog'o* soldiers began. The Office of Censor General (Saganwŏn) complained in 1599 that the district magistrates were using the soldiers for labor service as well as military service, putting them to work as yamen helpers even during training sessions, subjecting the men to whippings and beatings, signing up all male members of families for *sog'o* service in violation of quotas, and providing none of the duty soldiers with support taxpayers.[96] Furthermore, district magistrates tired of maintaining their responsibilities as regimental and battalion commanders, turned control of the troops over to company commanders they recruited from the villages, and neglected training. Service in the *sog'o* units became so bad that the men compared it to consignment to hell.[97]

Furthermore, overall troop strength in Korea had not been built up by the government at the end of the war. Yi Sugwang, one of the first independent statecraft scholars in the seventeenth century, wrote in his *Chibong yusŏl* that although the basic quota of troops in peacetime was supposed to be 180,000 men with another 320,000 support personnel – a total of 500,000 men – after the war there were barely 60,000 men left.[98] In short, once the national crisis was over, demoralization of the troops and their commanders undermined government plans to rebuild the army.

Yu Sŏngnyong's Plan for Wall Construction. Yu Sŏngnyong also realized from observing the superiority of the Japanese in the construction and use of fortifications that a plan of major reconstruction of old and new forts had to be instituted to strengthen Korean defenses. He criticized the Korean troops because they simply piled up earth, scraps of wood, and branches instead of constructing palisade walls, and punched holes in existing walls for shooting their guns.

Yu felt that Korea did not have knowledge of the best architectural plans for wall construction, which required crenellated sections to be placed at regular intervals along a wall, proper dimensions for the height of the wall and the crenellated sections that would allow troops standing on the edge to be beyond the range of most fire from below and to have a free range of fire in shooting against an attacking enemy down below. Promontories jutting out from the main wall should be placed at intervals to allow a pattern of cross fire against an attacking force, and inner walls should be added to provide an extra dimension of protection as well. Korean walls at the time were so low that the defenders on the top were inundated by enemy shot and arrows and had to creep around on their knees to avoid being hit. Yu himself did build a wall in the Chinese style at Anju near the Yalu River, and he also recommended extensive artillery training, but Anju was never attacked, and Yu's plans were never implemented by the government.[99]

Yu Sŏngnyŏng, who might have played an important role in rebuilding national defense, was unfortunately impeached by the censorate for seizing power and forming a clique, fouling up national policy, working hand-in-glove with Shen Wei-ching, stripping men of their office warrants unjustly, and other charges in 1598 as soon as the Japanese began their retreat. Despite the defense of former Censor-General Kim Uong, he was finally dismissed and stripped of his own warrants, and the chance for significant reform was delayed.[100]

CHAPTER 3

Post-Imjin Developments in Military Defense and the Economy

The last chapter should have conveyed an inkling to most readers that the attempts to rebuild the military might not be totally successful. It was already clear by the end of the first decade of the seventeenth century that the attempt to increase the ranks of the army, arm it with a full complement of muskets and cannon, and rebuild all defensive fortifications was lagging behind expectations, but more important problems of national survival would involve nontechnical, even nonmilitary problems, such as domestic politics and foreign policy.

While attempting to deal with a new crisis from the north, the Koreans were also forced to rebuild government finances, the economy, and the welfare of the population. The struggle to achieve these objectives was protracted, but by the middle of the century, after the foreign threat had subsided, the signs of success became apparent. Success was measured not only in increased agricultural yields and taxes, and the expansion of trade, but also in the reform of the tribute system, and this new situation had an important effect on Yu Hyŏngwŏn's proposals for reform.

The Manchu Invasions

Factional Rivalry over Foreign Policy

Devastated by the Imjin War, the Korean people had only begun the long struggle to overcome the damage to population and production when they were faced by another threat of invasion, this time from the Manchus in the north. As so often occurs in human history, the Koreans attempted to apply some of the lessons they had learned in the war against Hideyoshi, but the situation had changed significantly. Some of the lessons learned were based on flawed precepts to begin with, and the ability to establish a proper policy of defense was limited by domestic political factional divisions and disagreement on the moral and practical approach to foreign policy. The results were not only tragic, they also demonstrated that national defense was not a question of military strategy and tactics alone.

King Kwanghaegun came to the throne in 1609 with the support of the Great Northern faction (*Taebuk*, a splinter group of the Easterner or *Tong'in* faction) that represented the least bellicose, if not the least courageous, response to Hideyoshi's challenge. He was opposed by the Westerner faction (*Sŏin*) that contained within its ranks some of the leading hawks during the Imjin War. Although some held office, they were in a politically vulnerable position.[1]

At the time, the main threat to Korean security shifted from Japan to the north as a result of the rise of the Manchus under Nurhaci, who had begun to take over territory from surrounding tribes in Manchuria in 1589, who ceased paying tribute to the Ming court in 1605, and who established the Later Chin dynasty, proclaimed himself emperor in 1616, and launched his first raid across the Ming frontier in 1618.[2] As the Manchus became more of a threat, the Ming court demanded aid and military reinforcements from Korea, and many Koreans, especially the Westerners, felt they had a moral as well as a strategic obligation to honor Ming requests since Ming intervention had saved Korea from destruction by Hideyoshi. On the other hand, active support for the Ming dynasty threatened to lead to a Manchu invasion of the Korean peninsula.

King Kwanghaegun sought to walk a tightrope between the Ming and Later Chin (first dynastic title of the Manchus, later changed to Ch'ing in 1636). During a famous campaign in 1619, for example, in response to a Ming request for reinforcements, he sent 13,000 Korean troops into Manchuria but instructed the two Korean commanders, Kang Hongnip and Kim Ŭngsŏ, to surrender as soon as the tide of battle appeared to shift in favor of the Manchus and then seek Manchu understanding of Korea's difficult position to forestall future military reprisals. They did so, successfully staying Manchu aggression against Korea without overly antagonizing the Ming court.[3] Nevertheless, in 1621 a Ming general, Mao Wen-lung, set up camp on an island near the Yalu estuary, and kept up pressure on Korea to join in the struggle against Nurhaci.[4]

In 1623 a few Westerner commanders of a small force of only 7,200 troops and some civil officials seized power in a coup d'état, deposed Kwanghaegun, and replaced him with Prince Nŭngyang, known to posterity as King Injo. The coup itself is known to history as the Injo Restoration (*Injo panjŏng*), a term that represents a transparent attempt to legitimize an act of treason. The Westerners who led the coup then engineered the abandonment of Kwanghaegun's cautious policy toward the Manchus.[5]

The New Divisions of the Western Political Generals

Yi Kwi, one of the Westerner leaders of the coup and a disciple of Yulgok, convinced King Injo in 1623 to convert the Military Training Agency into a permanent garrison force, support its troops with regular rations from capital granaries (instead of support taxpayers or *poin*), and use them for capital guard duty. That was the first of a series of moves to create a new military establishment, but the new system was more a product of the competing demands of political generals than a master plan for national defense. That same year the king authorized a new Royal Retinue Office (Howich'ŏng) with four of the coup leaders and two of their assistants in charge: Yi Sŏ, Kim Yu, Sin Kyŏngsin, and Yi Kwi, and their assistants, Kim Chajŏm, and Sim Kiwŏn. Since each of the four generals recruited troops on their own and treated them like their own guards, the troops of the new Howich'ong were referred to frequently as "the soldiers of the four generals [*taejang*]."

Yi Kwi then organized the Royal Division (Ŏyŏnggun, or Ŏyŏngch'ŏng) and Yi Sŏ the Anti-Manchu Division (Ch'ongyungch'ŏng), which was in fact the Kyŏnggi Province division.[6] The coup leaders overshadowed the minister of war, who was reduced in authority to the equivalent of a prominent regimental commander, and the commanders of specific regiments in the capital region maintained a semiautonomous position in the competition for resources.[7]

Even though the Westerner faction and King Injo were fully aware that the shift to a pro-Ming foreign policy increased the chances for a Manchu invasion, defense policy was stymied by the king's decision to allocate more troops to the capital region to protect the new regime against its domestic political enemies than to the northwestern frontier for defense against an invasion. In 1623, 15,000 men from the southern three provinces were sent north to join the 13,000 men already stationed along the frontier as part of a policy to build up the total northern frontier force to 50,000 men, but the force never exceeded 28,000 men because too many troops were needed in the capital. This was a minuscule force considering the 150,000 men used by Hideyoshi to invade Korea in 1592. Furthermore, the troops of the capital were even exempted from duty on the northern frontier, and the men of the whole province of Kyŏnggi (the province surrounding the capital) were reserved for duty in the capital guard units. In 1623 the king adopted Yi Kwi's suggestion to form an additional emergency royal guard unit, the Forbidden Guard Soldiers (Kŭmwigun), invested in the repair of the strategic Namhan Mountain fortress (Namhan sansŏng) just south of Seoul as the the mustering point for the troops of Kyŏnggi Province, and identified Kanghwa Island as his ultimate refuge if Manchu forces broke through the northern defense lines.

As part of the defensive strategy against the Manchus, the king planned to lead the Royal Division personally to Kaesŏng, north of Seoul, to raise the morale of the people, but he abandoned this plan when the expected Manchu invasion did not occur in 1623. Yi Kwi retained control of the Royal Division until his death in 1633, nine years after his retirement as nominal commander in 1624.[8]

The Yi Kwal Rebellion of 1624

The king's fear of a challenge to his regime was realized in 1624 when Yi Kwal, one of the discontented participants in the 1623 coup against Kwanghaegun and current vice-commander of troops in the northeast, rebelled against the government. He was able to muster 10,000 troops under his command while the king could count on only 6,000 men. Because the king was reluctant to take the 17,000 on the northwestern frontier off the front line because of the Manchu threat, Yi Kwal was able to defeat government forces in three battles and seized the capital, forcing King Injo to take refuge in Kongju. Although government forces put down the rebellion and killed Yi Kwal in less than two months, the rebellion seriously weakened defenses in the northern provinces, depleted the food and financial resources needed to supply the national army, and reduced the number of available troops for frontier defense.[9]

The rebellion only reinforced the policy to build up the capital at the expense of the defense force on the northern frontier. The Royal Division was increased from 260 to 1,000 men and put on a par with the Military Training Agency, but only half its men served on duty at any one time and its troops were not well provisioned.[10] The new 20,000-man Anti-Manchu Division (Ch'ongyunggun) for Kyŏnggi Province under Governor Yi Sŏ drew about 60 percent of the new *sog'o* soldiers created during Hideyoshi's invasions. Two thousand muskets and three thousand bows were imported from Japan for the reorganized provincial force, and the refurbished fort on Namhan Mountain was completed in 1626. Since the fort did not have a permanent force of its own, troops had to be brought in from the three southern provinces on an emergency basis.[11]

The Manchu Invasion of 1627

One might have expected the Korean court to pull in its horns after the debacle of Yi Kwal's rebellion and adopt a more conciliatory policy toward the Manchus. Unfortunately, the Westerner faction was incapable of modifying its line on foreign policy because of its strong moral convictions about the debt owed the Ming and its sense of cultural superiority over the "barbarian" Manchus. Furthermore, the operations of the Chinese general and freebooter, Mao Wen-lung, around the Yalu River region had become a nuisance to the Manchus, who, after the death of Nurhaci in 1626, were making preparations for an invasion of China proper.

Even though the Korean government was already aware by 1626 that an invasion was likely, it delayed transferring men from the southern provinces to the north and rested content with preparing a number of forts and walled towns in the northwest in P'yŏng'an Province along two anticipated invasion routes. Late in 1626 it moved only about five or six thousand additional troops to the northwest frontier before Manchu forces invaded Korea in February 1627.[12]

A split in the chain of command had developed over the choice between committing all troops to defense against the Manchus or maintaining the protective force around king and capital including the Namhan Mountain fort and the escape route to Kanghwa Island. The former policy was supported by the supreme commander (Toch'ech'alsa) of forces in the field, Chang Man, and officers under his command like Kim Yu and Kim Chajŏm, and the members of the Elder Westerner splinter faction (Nosŏ); the latter policy by the generals who dominated the royal and capital guards, Yi Kwi and Yi Sŏ, and the Young Westerners (Sosŏ).[13]

Since the king decided in favor of protecting his own regime, Yi Sŏ's Anti-Manchu Division in Kyŏnggi Province took up the defense of the Namhan fortress, and Yi Kwi's son, Yi Sibaek, led his 3,000-man force from Suwŏn to be the core of the Royal Division. The king decided to send only 2,000 men from the Anti-Manchu Division without even a full allocation of weapons to meet Chang Man's request for reinforcements on the front.

Chang Man had worked out a defensive strategy of fallback defensive command posts in a line from Anju (just south of the Ch'ŏngch'ŏng River) to Pyongyang, Hwangju, P'yŏngsan, and the Imjin River, but as soon as the Manchus overran the northernmost outpost at Anju, the commanders of other districts began to abandon their positions. Chang Man moved up to Kaesŏng to take command while King Injo moved to Kanghwa Island with his Royal Division, the Suwŏn garrison, and a contingent of the Military Training Agency troops. The king had just ordered Chang Man to defend a new line at the Imjin River and Yi Sŏ to bring troops from the southern three provinces to the Namhan fortress, when the Manchus offered peace terms. Although Chang Man wanted to continue the fight, King Injo was only too happy to accept Yi Kwi's proposal to accept Manchu terms.[14]

Not only had the Korean army failed to improve that much over its condition in 1598 in the size of its forces, the organization and training of its men, the reserves of food and equipment, the repair of defenses, and the accumulation of muskets and cannon, but the primary causes of Korean defeat in 1627 were also domestic politics and poor foreign policy rather than the state of the military. The Injo restoration of 1623 had not only led to a dangerous shift in policy toward the Manchus, it had also created an unstable political situation in which the leaders of the coup were threatened more by the divisions among them than by their former adversaries in the Great Northern faction. When one rebel, Yi Kwal, led almost one-third the troops in the north against the capital, it wrecked the possibility of maintaining a strong front against the Manchus unless a bold and rapid transfer of forces from the center and south to the north could have been carried out. The king could not do so because he was too weak to exert authority over the generals who had brought him to the throne. After Yi Kwal's coup, he needed them more than ever, and he as well as they were determined to build up the strength of the capital.

The strategic defense plan against the Manchus – a line of fallback positions situated at a series of walled towns – a strategy developed as a result of the lessons learned from the Imjin War, was static and inflexible. Whatever advantage this strategy might have possessed was vitiated by the overall shortage of troops in the area since the central government refused to move forces from the capital region or southern provinces – let alone the northeast or east – to reinforce these positions in the northwest. The fixed-position defense divided Korean forces and left them vulnerable to the Manchu invaders who could mass their 30,000-man force at will against a series of undermanned forts or walled towns. The situation called either for a reallocation of all forces for defense against the Manchus or abandonment of the anti-Manchu foreign policy, but the situation seemed to allow for neither and the result was a humiliating defeat.

The Second Manchu Invasion

Despite the 1627 peace treaty, there was no change in the dominant pro-Ming sentiment at the Korean court. The same bifurcation of command and strategy that plagued the military establishment before 1627 still hindered the creation of a unified command structure and the strengthening of the northern frontier. These drawbacks were largely the product of politics: King Injo was too dependent on the military leaders of the Restoration to assert his authority over them, and the military commanders were divided over defensive strategy and factional allegiance.

Men loyal to Yi Kwi and Yi Sŏ of the Young Westerners continued to favor defense of king and capital and controlled the Namhan fort, the Defense Command stationed at the fort, the Anti-Manchu Division of Kyŏnggi Province, and the Royal Division. They also had jurisdiction over 12,700 troops from five administrative districts assigned to the Namhan fort in case of emergency. Yi Kwi tried to build up troop strength by a more thorough and accurate registration of able-bodied males through the household tally (*hop'ae*) and household registration (*hojŏk*) systems because too many registers had been burned during fighting over the years. He also hoped to expand the network of local garrisons (*chin'gwan*) around the country (a plan favored by Yu Sŏngnyŏng), but when he attempted to strengthen the strategic town of Anju in the north, the government opted instead to concentrate on the defense of the capital region.

The Young Westerners who favored this strategy included Yi Sŏ, commander of the Anti-Manchu Command (Ch'ongyungch'ŏng) in Kyŏnggi Province and commandant of the Namhan fortress and virtual tsar of Kyŏnggi Province to his death in 1636.[15] He controlled Yi Sibang, one of Yi Kwi's sons, who was defense commander (Suŏsa) of the new permanent force at the Namhan fort, and the Defense Command (Suŏch'ŏng), and he expanded the size of the Royal Division from 1,000 men to 6,170 by 1635, but because of the rotating duty system only 1,560 men were called up for duty at any one shift, and there were only two shifts a year, of 75 days each (or 150 days per year total) during the five months when the Yalu was frozen over. On the other hand, the Military Training Agency, also located in the capital and the only unit with full-time duty troops supported by the state, was expanded from about 2,700 troops in 1627 to 5,000 in 1634. In brief, the build-up of the capital units were adequate for protection of the king against domestic rebels, but they did little to improve national defenses.

On the other side, the Elder Westerner field commanders concerned about forces on the northern frontier were led by Kim Yu, supreme commander (Toch'ech'alsa) of the Office of the Supreme Commander (Toch'ech'alsabu, or Toch'ebu for short), and Supreme Field Commander (Towŏnsu) Kim Chajŏm. Kim Yu at times blocked the plans of the Younger Westerners under his command, and the power of the Elder Westerners increased when Yi Kwi of the Young Westerners died in 1633 and Yi Sŏ, commander of the Royal Division, fell ill.[16] Yi Kwi's son, Yi Sibaek, the head of the Defense Command, was left isolated as the only Young Westerner with an important military position.[17]

Injo and his advisers, however, were united on a pro-Ming, anti-Manchu policy within the limits of their power, which meant in practice an attempt to avoid assisting the Manchus in hostilities against Ming China. When in 1631 the Later Chin (Manchus) sent a 12,000-man expedition to take over Linden Island (Tando) from Liu Hsing-cha, the successor to Mao Wen-lung, they asked the Koreans for ships and troops, but the issue was made moot when the Manchu expedition was defeated by Ming forces.

King Injo then defied two demands from the Later Chin in 1632 and 1636 for a conversion of Manchu-Korean ties from an elder-younger brother alliance that tolerated the coexistence of Ming-Koryŏ ties to a full-blown suzerain-subject relationship that would have required the Korean king to end his formal tributary tie to the Ming emperor. The king now decided to reject any future Manchu envoys or communications and promulgated a decree to all provinces to prepare for war. Unfortunately, the order fell into the hands of a Later Chin envoy just when the self-confidence of the Manchus was growing. In May 1636 the Manchus adopted the new dynastic title of Ch'ing, and the Ch'ing emperor demanded that a member of the Chosŏn royal family be sent to the Ch'ing court as a hostage along with Korean officials responsible for advocating a hostile policy toward the Manchus.

The Korean government realized that another invasion was pending but, because of the losses suffered in 1627, the area north of the Ch'ungch'ŏng River was so short of troops that some proposed abandoning it altogether. Kim Yu and Kim Chajŏm, however, insisted on establishing the first line of defense at Anju, on the south bank of the river, but it was not until 1632 that a commander was sent north to Ŭiju on the lower reaches of the Yalu River to organize the region's defense, and five months before the second Manchu invasion in 1637 the defense force at Ŭiju still consisted of only about 7,000 troops.

Neverthelesss, defense policy changed as a consequence of the decline of the Young Westerners at court. Kim Yu took over as supreme commander from Chang Man in 1629, and after 1632 he and Supreme Field Commander Kim Chajŏm began to build up the defenses of the northwest, reinforcing garrisons at five bases: Ŭiju, Anju, Pyongyang, Hwangju, and P'yŏngsan. This strategy, however, entailed the concentration of all troops in those areas at walled forts on hills or mountains nearby rather than at the district towns themselves, stripping the lowlands and the towns of defensive forces. As Yi Kung'ik described the situation in his chronology of the period, the Yŏllyŏsil kisul, the closest mountain forts were about nine miles from the main road and the farthest one or two days travel, while "the main garrisons in Hwanghae and P'yŏng'an Provinces were turned into ghost towns."[18] The Koreans were pursuing the same strategy used in the second phase of the Imjin War – "strengthening the walls and clearing the fields" – that had been criticized by some at the time. The idea behind the strategy this time was less to deny the invaders access to food and provisions than to maximize the effectiveness of inferior troop strength by concentrating them behind fortified redoubts situated at the top of strategic hills.

By February 1637, when Ming China was in disarray because of the rebellions of Li Tzu-ch'eng and Chang Hsien-chung, the Ch'ing emperor invaded Korea for the second time. Unfortunately for the Koreans, the Manchus were aware of the Korean defense strategy and the location of the mountain forts. When the invasion began, the Manchu cavalry merely skirted the forts in the hills and pressed forward to capture the major towns on the way to Seoul. Meanwhile, Korean forces locked in their mountain redoubts could only stand by and watch the Manchu armies pass.

In addition, the arrogance of Kim Chajŏm resulted in an inordinate delay in communicating news of the invasion to the capital. Just before the invasion began, a signal warning of an impending invasion was relayed from Dragon Bone Mountain (Yonggolsan) near Ŭiju to Supreme Field Commander Kim Chajŏm's headquarters at Chŏngbang in Hwanghae Province, but because Kim had been telling his subordinates for months that there was no chance that the Manchus would invade that winter, he refused to believe that the beacon signals really meant a Manchu invasion and decided against conveying the warning to the capital lest it alarm the citizens of the capital needlessly. When he received more signals on the sixth day after the initial signal warning, he interpreted it to mean that the Manchus had come to the frontier to welcome a Korean envoy, refraining again from informing Seoul. Not until the ninth day, the day of the invasion itself, did he send one officer to reconnoiter the situation to the north, and when the man reported back that the Manchus were indeed on the way, Kim wanted to chop his head off for spreading false information. He desisted when the report was confirmed and only then did he send a report to the capital. The king received word of the invasion barely two days before the first Manchu troops arrived at the capital, fourteen days after the first signal warning and only five days after they had crossed the Yalu River.[19]

The second invasion proved overwhelming; one wonders if even a better strategy or an alert and less arrogant supreme field commander would have saved the day. The initial invading army consisted of 120,000 men (70,000 Manchus, 30,000 Mongols, and 20,000 Chinese) – almost as large as Hideyoshi's invading army in 1592. Their advance was so rapid that a Manchu cavalry unit of several hundred men blocked off Injo's route of retreat to Kanghwa Island forcing him to take refuge at the Namhan fort with a contingent of only 12,000 men and insufficient rations. The fort was undermanned not only because of the short notice, but also because Kim Yu had earlier blocked a request of Yi Sibaek's father, Yi Kwi, to shift the duty assignments of soldiers from districts to the south to regions closer to the fort itself. Eventually the fort was surrounded by a Ch'ing force of 200,000 men who drove off Korean reinforcements from the southern provinces. Defense was no longer tenable, in part because most troops inside the fort refused to fight to the death against impossible odds and demanded that the officials and generals responsible for the anti-Manchu war policy be turned over to the Ch'ing emperor as he was demanding. Injo finally had to accept Ch'ing terms and signed a treaty on February 7 (1.13 lunar), 1637, just a month after the invasion began.[20]

What were the major reasons for this debacle? The stubborn and blockheaded refusal of Kim Chajŏm to pass on the alarm signal to the capital was certainly a fatal error because it prevented the king from making his escape to Kanghwa Island as planned. The failure to assign men from districts near the Namhan fort to its defense and provide it with adequate rations was serious, but by that time the king was reduced to a last-ditch effort at siege defense. Once the Manchus had closed the ring around the fort, it was only a matter of time until the defenders ran out of food. The belated and insufficient build-up of troop strength in the area north of the Ch'ungch'ŏng River and the decision to strip the lowlands along the invasion route of troops and defensive forces and move them to out-of-the-way hilltops were probably the worst of a number of blunders. This error was particularly embarrassing because the Manchus even served notice to the Koreans before the invasions that they were totally aware of Korean strategy! When the Ch'ing emperor, T'ai-tsung, sent a note to King Injo in December 1636 threatening an invasion unless his terms were met, he said:

> Your honorable country has constructed a number of forts on mountains, but we are going to follow the main road right straight to your capital. Do you think can stop us with these mountain forts? And your honorable country is depending on Kanghwa Island [as a last refuge for your king], but if we lay waste all eight of your provinces, can you make a state out of one small island? The ones who speak for your country are your Confucian officials, but do you think they can drive us off by wielding their pens?[21]

T'ai-tsung was right on a couple of counts at least. The decision to shift troops to mountain forts at the cost of building up a large, mobile army was a fatal strategy, and even if the king had been able to take refuge on Kanghwa Island, it would not have saved the country from destruction, just as it failed to do so during the Mongol invasions of the thirteenth century. Whether the failures of policy were the fault of Confucian pen-wielders is not certain because many of the decisions were made by men with military experience, not simply civil officials. The lack of a unified policy on strategic defense so divided the nation's strength that neither the northern provinces nor the capital region had enough forces to fulfill their tasks. The field commanders in the north may have been forced to concentrate their troops at mountain redoubts because they did not have enough troops to organize a conventional army on the plains, but the weaknesses of the strategy were pointed out to them in advance by the Manchus themselves! Even had those forces been used to build up the strategic walled towns in the plains along the invasion route, it is doubtful that any single point would have been able to block the advance of the initial 120,000-man Ch'ing force. What was needed in 1627 and 1637 was to move the troops from the center and south into the northern region as quickly as possible, not to leave them guarding their home districts.

Finally, Korean foreign policy at this time has to be taken into account. Hindsight enables us to see that continuation of Kwanghaegun's neutralist foreign policy could certainly have done no more harm than the Westerner anti-Manchu policy and probably would have spared Korea both invasions, but the Westerners, who had placed King Injo on the throne in 1623, were moralists who felt an unending debt to the Ming and cultural racists who held the Manchus in contempt. Since they were responsible for adopting the pro-Ming, anti-Manchu policy and were too powerful to allow the king to reverse it had he so desired, they also had the obligation to guarantee the development of a sufficient military force to back up the policy. Not only did the Yi Kwal rebellion weaken national defense, but the factional division within the Westerners prevented the possibility of a unified, let alone correct, defense policy. In that situation, the continuation of the anti-Manchu foreign policy was suicidal, guaranteed to lead to a humiliating defeat for the Korean people.

If there was a lesson to be learned for Korean students of statecraft, it was that strategy, positioning, and organization of forces have to be devised to meet the particularities of the situation, not simply copied from textbook models suited to other situations, that the sheer number of troops in the field have to be adequate for defense against an army of 120,000 men with a superior cavalry contingent, and that unity of command is a necessity. Finally, if national military strength is not suited to a hostile foreign policy, that policy should either be abandoned or time won to build up sufficient forces to prevent disaster.

Collaboration and Resistance: 1637–49

After the Manchu victory over Korea in 1637, defense policy became entangled in political disputes involving King Injo and the radical anti-Manchus and the moderates under Kim Chajŏm who favored a realistic acceptance of Manchu hegemony and some sort of accommodation with Manchu demands. There were no major changes in the composition of military divisions, but political conflict continued over the control of those divisions, and the political atmosphere was poisoned by Injo's animosity against anyone who favored compromise with the Manchus, including his own Crown Prince, Sohyŏn.

Although Ch'ing forces did not occupy Korea after the peace treaty, they were naturally concerned to prevent any serious rearmament by the Koreans. Nonetheless, King Injo undertook to rebuild the Namhan fort and fended off inquisitive Ch'ing officials by telling them that the action was justified by Japan's recent aggressive behavior, but in 1639 he was forced by the Manchus to destroy recently built cannon turrets at the fort.

The most the Korean court could do to render aid to the Ming court under these circumstances was to pass intelligence and delay Ch'ing requests for military reinforcements. Chief State Councilor Ch'oe Myŏnggil made frequent trips to Shen-yang to assuage Manchu ire, but defiance of Manchu demands proved costly and difficult. In 1640, the Manchus charged that in a campaign against Ming forces Korean infantry arrived late and Korean warships failed to fire on Ming vessels and that Korean anti-Manchu obstructionists were responsible for twelve violations of the surrender agreement of 1637. At a meeting with top Korean officials at Ŭiju on the Yalu River the Manchu authorities arrested and imprisoned Kim Sanghŏn and other well-known anti-Manchu officials, and in 1642 they arrested Ch'oe Myŏnggil for secretly conferring with Ming officials in China.[22]

Inside Korea the factional split between the Elder and Young Westerners was exacerbated by their conflicting attitudes toward Ch'ing hegemony. Kim Yu and Kim Chajŏm of the Elder Westerners advocated a realistic acceptance of Manchu hegemony, but they were opposed by other Westerners such as Yi Sibaek and his younger brother, Yi Sibang (both sons of Yi Kwi), Kim Chip, Song Siyŏl, and Song Chun'gil, and the prominent leader of the Southerner faction, Hŏ Chŏk. Yi Sibaek was favored by both the king and the anti-Manchus because during the Manchu siege of the Namhan fort only he and his troops from the Defense Command opposed the Manchu demand to surrender anti-Manchu officials.

Both sides suffered casualties in the political struggle: Kim Yu was dismissed in 1637 and later exiled, and on the other side, Yi Sibang's confidante and successor as commander of the Defense Command, Sim Kiwŏn, who favored accommodation with the Manchus, was arrested in 1644 for allegedly plotting a coup against King Injo. The official version of the plot was that he wanted to replace Injo with a minor member of the royal family, Prince Hoeŭn (the Hoeŭn'gun), but one of his collaborators testified (probably falsely) under torture to a plot that seems to have been out of character for Sim. He claimed that Sim planned to attack and kill the Manchu troop escort of Crown Prince Sohyŏn, who was due to return home from Shen-yang to observe his father-in-law's funeral, and then send their heads to the Chinese as a sign of good faith, after which Korean forces would join Ming troops against the Manchus. Injo was not to be deposed but forced into retirement as a Sangwang (Superior or Retired King) and replaced by the crown prince. One suspects that the confession may have been concocted by Sim's enemies.

Kim Chajŏm tried to eliminate his anti-Manchu rivals Yi Sibaek and Yi Sibang by having the putative anti-Manchu Sim Kiwŏn executed and justifying it by putting out the story that he had really been planning a purge of the anti-Manchu idealists – the so-called "clear stream" (*ch'ŏngnyu*) scholars.[23] He then tried to capitalize on the Byzantine intrigue surrounding the sudden death of Crown Prince Sohyŏn and his Princess Minhoe, daughter of the the state councilor, Kang Sŏkki. As a hostage in Shen-yang in Manchuria since 1637, the crown prince's residence had become the equivalent of a Korean embassy and trading center mainly because King Injo had been using chronic illness as an excuse to avoid meeting with Manchu envoys whenever they came to Korea.

After 1642 the king and the anti-Manchu officials began to suspect the crown prince of plotting with the Manchus to force his abdication. Injo's resentment was exacerbated by his own favorite concubine's hatred of Princess Minhoe and by stories of the crown prince's extravagant expenditures. After the Manchus captured the Ming capital at Beijing in 1644, the Manchu Prince Dorgon, now regent for the young Hsün-chih emperor, decided to send the crown prince back to Korea, but only two months after his return to Korea he fell ill and died so quickly that many suspected he had been poisoned at the king's direction.

The possibility of filicide was lent weight by Injo's subsequent behavior. Hinting that even filicide was condoned by Confucian moral standards in the case of a disobedient son, he ordered the torture and death of a score of palace ladies-in-waiting and servants to obtain false testimony to heinous deeds by Princess Minhoe (Minhoe-bin) and her relatives in the Kimch'ŏn Kang clan. He ordered the extermination of almost the whole family by first sending Princess Kang's four brothers into exile, then having her drink poison in 1646 on the charge that she had poisoned his food. He executed her mother and two of her brothers on false charges, and eliminated all three of her sons by Crown Prince Sohyŏn – Injo's own grandsons. He then chose his second son, Grand Prince Pongnim (Pongnim-daegun), whose wife happened to be the daughter of one of Kim Chajŏm's supporters, to be the new crown prince.

He did all this against a chorus of protests and requests for leniency from most officials. Kim Chajŏm was one of the few who defended the princess's execution, and when Ch'ing envoys appeared in 1648 to inquire about the whereabouts of Prince Sohyŏn's sons, he told them that the exiled boys had died of illness. The story was false at the time, but two of the three did die later in the year.[24] Injo's barbarity was fueled by his hatred of the Manchus and fear of domestic political conspiracy.

In the last years of his reign political power gravitated into the hands of Kim Chajŏm because he catered to Injo's fears, even though control of military forces was still split between the Royal Division under his command versus the Namhan Defense Command and Anti-Manchu Division under Yi Sibaek and Yi Sibang. Yi Sibaek also took charge of creating the new Crack Select Soldiers in 1637. Some expansion of these forces took place at this time but not for the defense of Korea. Rather, the additional troops were drawn mostly from the Royal Division commanded by Kim Chajŏm and used to provide the annual contingent of 1,000 musketeers sent to assist the Manchus in their struggle with the Ming armies.

Even though Kim had to resign from his post as commander of the Royal Division in 1643 when he was appointed chief state councilor, he maintained control over it by creating the new, concurrent post of supreme commissioner (Tojejo) for the Royal Division. Although unable to eliminate the anti-Manchu Yi Sibaek, who retained Injo's favor, Kim did succeed in marrying his grandson to Injo's daughter. When Grand Prince Pongnim ascended the throne in 1649 (posthumous title, Hyojong), Kim was able to gain control over the Defense Command at Namhan fort and the Anti-Manchu Division of Kyŏnggi Province as well.[25]

In the years from the second Manchu invasion in 1637 to Injo's death in 1649, the major army divisions, capital guards, and garrisons became the spoils of politics. The atmosphere had become even more poisoned by charges of treason and collaboration with the hated Manchus, the cruel execution of Sim Kiwŏn, the poisoning of Crown Prince Sohyŏn, and the execution of his princess and her relatives in the Kang family. While anti-Manchu sentiment burned in the hearts of many officials and scholars, they could but gnash their teeth in frustration as the Manchu hard-line policy of Emperor T'ai-tsung and Prince-Regent Dorgon kept them at heel and kept the cooperative Kim Chajŏm in a strong position at court.

Agricultural Production and Taxation

Effects of Hideyoshi's Invasions

Tax revenues and reserves were becoming a problem even before Hideyoshi's invasion of Korea in 1592. In Chungjong's reign (1506–44), the government held 2,030,000 *sŏm* in reserve, but by the time of Hideyoshi's invasion in 1592, that figure had dropped to 500,000 *sŏm*.[26] Then when the Japanese invasions occurred (1592–98), the scorched earth policy of the Japanese left the country devastated and the agricultural economy in shambles. In 1592, there were 1.5 to 1.7 million *kyŏl* of land registered, although not all of it was cultivated and taxed, but in the first survey after the war in 1601, only 300,000 *kyŏl* of cultivated, tax-paying land was found. That figure of cultivated land almost doubled to 541,000 *kyŏl* by 1611, and by the national cadastral survey of 1634, the amount of registered land (including uncultivated land but excluding P'yŏng'an Province) had increased to 1,246,310 *kyŏl*. Though recovery continued, by the eighteenth century it never increased beyond 1.45 million *kyŏl*, of which about 800,000 *kyŏl* was cultivated and tax-paying.[27] Since revenues from the land tax rate had been reduced to the lowest of the variable schedules of King Sejong's *kongbŏp* law of 1444, and the government wanted to keep taxes low to help the peasants recover from the destruction of the war, it was prevented from increasing its revenues by raising the rate.

The government, therefore, had to devise ad hoc measures to provide revenues for certain institutions and agencies instead of funding all costs from the central treasury. It used the traditional institution of military colonies (*tunjŏn*) initially to provide revenues for military units and soldiers, and it applied this model also to civilian organizations, such as "official colonies" (*kwandunjŏn*) and yamen colonies (*amun tunjŏn*) set up to support the State Council, Ministry of Taxation, and other capital agencies as well as local government officials.[28] It made special grants of tax-exempt land and prebends to the Royal Treasury (Naesusa) and the four major palaces of queens in the capital, referred to generally as the palace estates (*kungbang*).[29] Finally, it levied a host of special taxes to pay for particular needs, such as the rice tax for the "three types of soldiers" (*samsumi*) adopted during the Imjin War (1592–98) to pay for the new musketeers and other troops.

Not only did these surtaxes allow the central government an oblique means to raise the land tax, but the conversion of the tribute tax to a surtax on land (the *taedongmi*) throughout the seventeenth century eventually tripled the land tax on landowners because this *taedongmi* "surtax" was about double the size of the original land tax. As rational and beneficial as this reform was for the taxpayer in the short run in eliminating many forms of injustice in the tribute system, it boded ill in the long run because the state was unable to maintain periodic cadastral surveys and a fair distribution of the tax burden. Since influential landlords were able to keep much of their arable and reclaimed land off the tax registers, the distribution of the tax burden became more regressive with time.

Fragmentation of Landownership

From the beginning of the dynasty a gradual fragmentation of landholdings took place, but it was only revealed in 1960 by Kim Yongsŏp's study of a portion of the land registers (*yang'an*) of the mid-seventeenth and early eighteenth centuries. The interpretation of the significance of the development of fragmented landholdings has changed drastically in recent years. At first it was held by most scholars that the Imjin War had destroyed the stability of the early Chosŏn social order and increased the poverty of the peasant population in general, and eventually ended in the tragedy of the large-scale peasant rebellions of 1812, 1862, and 1894, in particular. Kim Yongsŏp, however, viewed the fragmentation of landholding in a more positive vein as causing the disintegration of early Chosŏn social barriers and opening opportunities for the rise of entrepreneurial landowners who used rational methods to increase profits and move up the rungs of the social ladder.

But is this optimistic view about the social effects of changing landholding patterns accurate, and did it transform the goals of reformist statecraft thinkers after the Imjin War? Did the reformers abandon their complaints about the maldistribution of property and wealth and their appeal for a restoration of some version of nationalization and distribution in the spirit of the well-field or equal-field systems? Did they issue a call for more freedom in the purchase and sale of land, the pursuit of wealth in the economic sphere, and greater social mobility based on equal opportunity for all?

In the mid-fifteenth century households held parcels of land measured in *kyŏl*, not really a measure of land area but a constant measure of crop yield produced by an area that varied from 2.25 to 9.0 acres, depending on the fertility of the land. By the seventeenth century the average size of land parcels had decreased so greatly that they were measured in *pu*, or hundredths of a *kyŏl* because only a minute fraction of landowners held more than one *kyŏl*'s worth of land. According to a Japanese survey in 1901, the average holding varied from 4.7 acres per family for South Chŏlla Province and 5.7 for North Kyŏngsang in the south where the land was most fertile, to 6.9 for Kyŏnggi in the central region, and to 8.7 for North P'yŏng'an, and 9.8 for South Hamgyŏng in the north where the land was least fertile and dry farming was far more extensive than rice cultivation.[30]

A land survey done in Kangwŏn Province in 1436 cited by Fukaya Toshitetsu divided landowners by the size of their holding. The highest category, "grand household" (*taeho*), included all those who owned over 50 *kyŏl*, and the average holding in that class was 80 *kyŏl* (about 400 acres at about 5 acres/*kyŏl*). By contrast, a smallholder (*soho*) was defined as one who held between 6 and 9 *kyŏl*, and the average holding in this group was 7.5 *kyŏl* (37.5 acres). The lowest category of fragmentary smallholders held 2.5 *kyŏl* on the average (12.5 acres). Kim Yongsŏp has pointed out that since Kangwŏn Province had less fertile land than the south, the pattern of distribution in the south would have been more greatly divided and the average holding smaller. He also cited other sources indicating an average holding of one *kyŏl* (5 acres) per family for the fifteenth century, but even in that case, it would have been twice as large as what Kim found in his seventeenth- and eighteenth-century examples (2.5 acres).[31]

Kim Yongsŏp conducted a study of 2,193 households listed in the *yang'an* or land registers of five districts in three provinces in the south in 1669, 1719, and 1720. The names of the heads of households in those registers were listed as *kiju*, literally "the lord (or person) who cultivates," and Kim insisted that the *kiju* had to indicate the owners of the land parcels listed in the *yang'an*, even though it was not the standard term for landowner. His main argument, that the second character of the two-character compound, *-ju*, "lord" or "master," often indicated ownership, as in the term, *chiju* (landlord, or landowner), was certainly plausible but not totally convincing since it is also possible that the *kiju* was simply the registered cultivator of the parcel, possibly with responsibility for turning over tax payments to the district magistrate. If so, the *kiju* might or might not have been the owner of the parcel, and the *yang'an* records would not be useful for determining the distribution of ownership at all.

Kim, however, insisted that his data revealed the growing fragmentation in the pattern of landownership, but even if true, there is one anomaly with his findings. It may well have been the fault of the restricted number of areas that were available to him, but the largest holdings were relatively small, and there is no sign of any of the larger holdings or estates reflected in many qualitative statements in other sources. Kim explained that a single owner could have accumulated a large estate by holding a number of small parcels in other villages or districts that would not be listed in the records he studied, but one would have expected to see some large holdings even within one district. On the other hand, if the *kiju* were cultivators rather than owners, then many of those cultivators could have been either tenants or slaves of a single owner whose name might not even be mentioned.

If, on the other hand, the *kiju* were really owners, then Kim's statistics would show that very few households held more than one *kyŏl*, most were less than .5 *kyŏl* (50 *pu*), and over half, sometimes two-thirds of the householders were below the poverty line of .25 *kyŏl* (1.25 acres on average).[32] Not only would the average holdings per family have declined considerably from the fifteenth century, but a great differentiation of ownership would have occurred within each of the three major social status categories (yangban, commoners, slaves) as well.

Fragmentation, however, did not mean the disappearance of hierarchy in the structure of ownership. According to the scheme of stratification devised by Kim Yongsŏp, the richest 10 percent of the population of these five districts owned 40 to 50 percent of the land. The next group of mid-sized landholders who constituted 15 percent of the registered *kiju* (not the population, since only male heads of households are listed, and landless laborers, whom Kim guessed must have constituted 30 percent of the male population, are not even mentioned) owned 25 percent of the land; the smallholders or "small households" (*soho*) (defined by Kim as those owning between .25 and .50 *kyŏl*/household) who constituted 20 percent of the registered *kiju* owned slightly less than 20 percent of the land; the poorest 50 to 60 percent of the *kiju* (owning less than .25 *kyŏl* per household) held only 10 to 20 percent of the land registered.[33]

Kim also claimed that the average holding of the cultivating landowners was reduced in size. According to the statistics of these five areas in the late seventeenth and early eighteenth centuries, 66 to 83 percent of the registered *kiju* in all the areas studied held either small parcels (0.25–0.50 *kyŏl*), and 43 to 68 percent held less than 0.25 *kyŏl* (1.25 acres), below the level of subsistence.[34]

Even if the *kiju* in the *yang'an* registers are not owners as Kim claimed, however, evidence from other sources is sufficient to show the progressive diminution of average holdings to the end of the dynasty. The breakdown of land ownership in 1911, for example, shows that in the southern three provinces, 55 to 63 percent of the population owned less than 0.25 *kyŏl* (1.25 acres), 81 to 85 percent owned less than 0.5 *kyŏl* (2.5 acres), while only 4.4 to 7.3 percent owned more than 1 *kyŏl* (5 acres).[35]

In the middle of the seventeenth century when Yu Hyŏngwŏn began to write his solution to the problems of land distribution and taxation, the fragmentation of private ownership had long been under way, but if Yu's testimony is to be believed, the main problem afflicting the peasants of Korea at that time was not simply the reduction of the average size of land parcels held by all cultivators, but the concentration of land in the hands of large landlords and the disparity in wealth between large landlords and slaveholders versus sharecroppers, slaves, and landless laborers.

Landownership and Social Stratification

Shikata Hiroshi, one of the first scholars to study Chosŏn society based on household registers (*hojŏk*) in the twentieth century, examined a few villages near Taegu in Kyŏngsang Province from 1690 to 1858, and the results of his research transformed the view of late Chosŏn society when he concluded that the percentage of what he defined as yangban households increased steadily from 8.3 to 65.5 percent.[36] This established the basis for the thesis of rapid upward mobility after 1600 and stimulated Kim Yongsŏp to find an economic explanation for the phenomenon.

One of the results of Kim's research, however, was that despite his search for the basis for upward mobility, he found that the economic fortunes of yangban as a whole had probably declined severely by the late seventeenth century. While the yangban *kiju* (or landowners in Kim's view) listed in the *yang'an* registers he studied were generally better off than commoners and slaves, not all of them were, and in all but one district about half or more of the yangban were below the poverty line. Some commoners held more land than some yangban, and in some districts, some slaves held more than a number of yangban and commoners.[37]

Because he demonstrated that the status hierarchy was not fully consonant with the ownership hierarchy, his findings undermined the earlier facile suppositions that all yangban were large landlords and all large landlords were yangban. Nonetheless, most of the larger landlords were yangban, and most of the yangban were the largest landlords, which is sufficient to demonstrate that by 1690, the first year of Shikata's Taegu statistics, 8 percent of the registered *kiju* in his small sample composed a rural yangban/landowning elite, and they owned most of the land in the village. Since these statistics did not reveal any of the large landed estates that one would expect from the literature, and since the *kiju* may well have included tenants of large landlords, it would be safe to assume that Kim's samples must have grossly underrepresented the concentration of land and wealth in the hands of the large landlords at the time.

The Growth of Agricultural Production

Even though the fragmentation of landholdings caused by an increase in the population presumably should have caused the immiseration of the peasantry and massive downward, rather than upward, mobility, Kim Yongsŏp saw the situation as providing opportunities to more enterprising cultivators to accumulate wealth through increased effort. Kim, Yi T'aejin, and a number of scholars have suggested that improvements in agricultural technology and techniques provided the main catalyst toward a significant increase in agricultural production and the creation of a surplus that stimulated market activity and the overall growth of the economy. The verification of this hypothesis, however, is not so easy because qualitative information about the introduction of more productive techniques has to be verified by quantitative data about the average size of crops (see chap. 9 for more discussion). Furthermore, even if a simple increase in production could be proven, that sum would have to be divided by the total population to yield an estimate of per capita national product to determine whether a surplus over consumption was being created.

The transplanting of rice from seed beds instead of direct seeding began to be practiced in parts of Kyŏngsang and South Kangwŏn provinces in the early fifteenth century, and did not spread to Chŏlla and Ch'ungch'ŏng provinces in the south until the end of the sixteenth century. The method had been banned by King T'aejong in 1414 because drought caused whole crops to be lost instead of partial losses when direct seeding was used. For the next three centuries the government continued to insist on the ban, and most officials felt that the peasants preferred transplantation only because it reduced their overall workload over direct broadcast seeding.[38] Nonetheless, transplantation began to spread quickly around the country just after the Imjin War despite the ban and seems to have reached all areas including the north at the turn of the eighteenth century, with an estimated 70 to 80 percent of rice land cultivated that way. Even the central government recognized its existence by reducing taxes for damages to transplanted crops from drought.

The main reasons for the adoption of transplanting by the cultivators was that it saved half the amount of labor in weeding and transplanting, especially when labor was used collectively, contributed to the strength of the plant by adding the nutrients of two fields rather than one, allowed bad plants to be discarded and roots to be washed during transplantation, and increased the size of the crop considerably over the direct seeding method. Even though peasants ran the risk of losing entire crops from drought, especially if the absence of rain delayed the crucial transplantation in the fourth and fifth lunar months (and some of the droughts in the late Chosŏn dynasty were disastrous), both large landowners and smallholders were zealous in adopting transplantation to increase their yields.

Kim Yongsŏp has argued that the rich, enterprising landowners, what he has called "managerial rich peasants" (*kyŏngyŏnghyŏng punong*), took the lead in pushing for the diffusion of the method because they cultivated the land themselves. The large landlords who turned the land over to tenants and simply collected rent did not. The acceptance of transplantation became so overwhelming that even the government was forced to modify its policy around 1698, when King Sukchong decided to drop the ban against transplantation in fields with a sufficient water supply.[39]

Several commentators throughout the dynasty said that transplanting saved half the work and doubled the crop, but the scholar Yi Ik, in the early eighteenth century, noted that usually the product/seed ratio of the rice crop on poor land was $^{10}/_{1}$ (ten *mal* of crop for one *mal* of seed planted on one *turak*), but reputedly as much as $^{60}/_{1}$ on the most fertile land, although he had his doubts about whether there was much land that good. In the south where transplanting was the standard, less seed was lost in planting, and the crop from a transplanted crop was 150 percent greater than one planted directly.[40]

The spread of transplanting was also accompanied by the double-cropping of rice and barley on paddy land, a new technique that had been known but hardly used in the first half of the dynasty. Double-cropping of nonrice crops like beans and millet, as well as mixed farming of secondary crops on the ridges between barley fields, had been used prior to 1600, but barley production had been limited to dry fields primarily because barley was harvested in the late fourth and early fifth lunar months, too late for beginning the direct seeding of rice. But when transplanting began, the rice was planted in seed beds and not transplanted until the fourth or fifth lunar months, which made the double-cropping of barley possible. Nonetheless, a warm climate was needed and the only area that allowed rice/barley double-cropping was in the warmest parts of the southern provinces. Double-cropping increased production and the income of large landowners and landlords, tided the poor peasant over the difficult spring season before he harvested his rice crop, and provided food for relief to the government during famine.[41]

The spread of transplantation along with greater irrigation and the double-cropping of rice and barley should have increased both production and productivity, but another factor that should be considered was the estimated loss of two million people (20 percent of the population) from the Imjin War (1592–98) and extensive destruction of crop lands. It took at least half a century to recover a large percentage of the arable land lost during the invasions, but the loss of population should have encouraged the production of a surplus by around the middle of the seventeenth century.

Even though a logical discussion of the favorable aspects of increased production and a smaller man/land ratio than before would indicate an improvement in per capita income, one could hardly discount the testimony of eyewitnesses like Yu Hyŏngwŏn to the contrary. The reason for his negative assessment of the mid-seventeenth situation undoubtedly derives from the continuation of the skewed pattern of ownership and distribution and the prevalence of slave and sharecropping cultivation that cut peasant income in half and added more to the landlords.

INDUSTRY AND COMMERCE

Emergence of Private Artisans

In the view of Yi Sangbaek, writing in 1962, the Korean economy in the seventeenth century was still what he called a natural economy, not one based on the exchange of commodities, because of the traditional government policy of the repression of commerce and industry, the cruel exactions imposed on artisans and merchants by the ruling class, the demands from China for tribute, and state restrictions on the import of goods from abroad. After the inordinate demands for gold and silver tribute by the Ming rulers had been dropped, the country had abandoned both mining and metallurgy, and because of the import of high-level silk textiles, Korean manufactures in those goods never reached the level of the Chinese. Other factors related to the lag in the development of commodity production were the extremely low level of demand for goods, the poor transportation system, and the disappearance of currency from the markets. Yi, therefore, concluded that the net result was stagnation in commercial activity.[42]

Kang Man'gil, however, has stressed a number of changes that took place in the seventeenth century. Five of the thirty bureaus (*kaksa*) of the Six Ministries were abolished, and the artisans attached to ten of them were eliminated, especially the weavers of cotton cloth and earthenware vessel potters, and these products were taken over by private artisans. The registry of artisans assigned to other bureaus ceased also, an indication that artisans were gradually moving toward a system of free and independent production. Private merchants (*sajang*) began to be mobilized by the state for the manufacture of goods for the state, particularly by Yŏnsan'gun at the turn of the sixteenth century. Furthermore, as the levels of skill among official artisans began to decline, more private merchants had to be enlisted by the state to provide items of quality, but they were still not paid wages for their services. In the countryside there were few skilled artisans, so that provincial governors, magistrates, and military commanders had to recruit private merchants to produce necessary goods.

Nevertheless, that development did not yet culminate in full-scale commodity production even by the middle of the nineteenth century because state agencies continued to use corvée labor to make goods even though they employed private artisans.[43] Monks still retained their traditional hold on papermaking, shoemaking, carpentry, and the yeast (or distillery) industry, and the *paekchŏng* outcastes were occupied mainly in butchering, leatherware, and willow basketry.[44]

Decline in Cotton and Cotton Textile Production

Cotton and cotton textiles had replaced ramie and hemp as the chief material for clothing. Trade in that commodity had increased so greatly that cotton cloth became a medium of exchange, but government taxation of cotton production inhibited its expansion, and exports of cotton cloth to Japan declined after the Imjin War because the Japanese began their own cotton production and soon became self-sufficient in it. One official, Pak Hongjun, testified in 1755 that government demands for cotton cloth had caused overcultivation of a single crop that had sapped the fertility of vast amounts of land.

Sung Jae Koh (Ko Sŭngje) has pointed out that this phenomenon was occurring as the rural economy had shifted to a general pattern of fragmented, small peasant holdings that reduced family economies to a bare subsistence. Peasants were forced to turn to cotton cultivation and weaving as the main source of subsidiary income just when it was becoming impossible to do so because the state was using cotton production to increase its taxes on land. Thus, Korea was unable to transform cotton from subsistence use to a marketable commodity as had occurred in China and Japan, but it did collect bolts of cotton cloth from support taxpayers to finance soldiers in the military.

In the eighteenth century, household and individual cloth taxes on ordinary households and military support taxpayers were levied illicitly on deceased individuals as well (the "white bones cloth levy" exactions, or *paekkol chingp'o*). The net result of the overtaxation of cotton cloth had so depleted the supply of cotton textiles that by 1866 the price of one *p'il* of cotton had reached the level of 50–60 *mal* (3.3–4.0 *sŏm*) of rice.

For that matter government policy toward cotton since King Injo's reign in the 1620s was based on dividing cotton from rice or grain cultivation so that cotton production was relegated to the hilly areas of the country. Since it was confined to the role of providing subsidiary income, it never could escape from that restraint and provide the motor force for industrial revolution as it had in Western Europe since the time of the north Italian city states.[45]

Expansion of Markets and Unlicensed Merchants

Trade expanded by the late fifteenth century as the tribute middlemen (*kong'in*) began to function as tribute contractors (substitute payments or *taenap* of required tribute).[46] When the central government began to replace the tribute system by the *taedong* reform, which legalized the state's purchase of goods directly from merchants, it stimulated greater commercial activity, a process that will be explored in detail in chapter 21.

Some time around 1637 the six licensed shops in the capital that supplied the greatest amount of goods to the state – anywhere from 70 to 100 percent of state demands for goods – were dubbed "the six shops" (*yug'ŭijŏn*). The six shops (at times expanded to seven or eight), emerged in response to tribute demands from the Manchus after the second Manchu invasion. They had the largest capital and handled general commercial goods, cotton and silver, silks, paper, ramie and cotton cloth, and fish, but specialized primarily in cotton, silk, and ramie textiles. Each of the six had about seventy employees. They also had the greatest responsibilities for meeting state needs, in return for which the state guaranteed them a monopoly over sales of their goods and the right to close down any nonlicensed shops that competed with them.

About the same time that the six shops were organized in the early seventeenth century, the peddlers (*pobusang*) were forming a kind of guild organization to afford them the advantages of mutual aid and protection against external pressures. As a result of their noble action in supplying the king with food when he was besieged in the Namhan Mountain fort by the Manchu invading force in 1637, the king granted the peddler guild monopoly sale rights over fish, salt, wooden goods, earthenware, and ironware.[47]

Yu Wŏndong has argued that an economic transformation began around the seventeenth century as merchants began to accumulate capital and use their control of money to win advantages from a central government that was facing a severe shortage in its finances. Instead of government repression of the commercial sector, the state shifted to special favors for some new merchants in the form of grants of monopoly privileges for the six shops of the capital, but this by no means signified recognition of free market principles. Furthermore, those merchants who were granted monopoly privileges also had to endure heavy burdens from the demands of the royal palace and central bureaucracy to supply goods at fixed and often uneconomic prices, and to pay bribes and kickbacks.[48]

Conclusion

By the middle of the seventeenth century Korea was just barely recovering from the shock administered by the two Manchu invasions of 1627 and 1637, the second of which imposed a heavy burden of tribute on the economy even though the effects of war from those two invasions were minor by comparison with the devastation of the Imjin War. The unhappy result of those invasions revealed only too clearly that the major defects in military service and defense had not been remedied by the reform efforts that were undertaken after 1598.

The most important method used to expand the pool of soldiers was the recruitment of slaves for military service, but little was done to incorporate the draft evaders at the top of society, the relatives of yangban officials and those of lesser status who bribed the military registrars to delete their names from the rosters. The talk of rebuilding forts and redoubts and arming the troops with muskets was not fulfilled in practice. Yu Sŏngnyŏng's idea about reorganizing domestic garrisons to create a phalanx of district units to back each other up in case of invasion was never really carried out. What had become worse was that Korean difficulties were exacerbated by factional politics, the intrusion of domestic political considerations into military strategy, and the disastrous adoption of a hostile foreign policy toward the Manchus just when they were growing to the height of their military power. King Injo, who was on the throne from 1623 to 1649, did little to stem bureaucratic factionalism because he owed his throne to the Westerner faction, and he could only mediate between splits that occurred within that faction between the Young and Elder Westerners, and between the advocates of the defense of the capital versus the northern frontier. If anything, he contributed to a poisoning of the political atmosphere by presiding over not only the possible assassination of his son, Crown Prince Sohyŏn, but also the official murder of his princess, children, and in-laws. The behavior of both king and high officials did not inspire much admiration.

In the domestic realm, the destruction of arable land and the loss of population had created tremendous hardship, but it also reduced population pressure, and the introduction of new agricultural techniques appeared to have increased yields. Nevertheless, the mode of control over land did not change because large landlords with their flocks of sharecropper and slave cultivators coexisted with smallholders tending ever smaller and barely economic tiny parcels of land. The maldistribution of land and wealth continued despite indications of surplus production overall, and the situation was exacerbated for the peasant because the new *taedong* surtax increased the nominal burden of the land tax to about three times what it had been in the sixteenth century.

The most interesting development occurred in the *taedong* reform of the tribute system because it converted in-kind tribute into a system of market purchase and sale of goods, stimulating the commercial economy, and paving the way for the introduction of copper currency (see Part 5). This represented the epitome of the reform effort in this period, based on the adoption of a rational plan put forward by reform bureaucrats like Kim Yuk to adapt an irrational tax system to a growing market. This reform was also accompanied by signs of commercial and industrial liberalization, the splitting of individual artisans from government manufactories, the formation of unlicensed merchants who began to compete with the licensed shops in the capital, and the greater exchange of commodities in the markets of the smaller towns and countryside.

The mid-seventeenth century thus offered both challenge and opportunity, the challenge to reform the sources of inequity and inequality and the opportunity to ride the wave of change that was becoming barely perceptible.

PART II
Social Reform: Yangban and Slaves: Introduction

Yu Hyŏngwŏn's magnum opus, the *Pan'gye surok*, was a monstrous treatise designed to rectify the manifold and serious problems facing Korea in the middle of the seventeenth century. Like the great Confucius himself, aspiring tutor and adviser to kings, Yu designed his masterwork as a program of policy and action for the king and sought throughout its pages to defend it as both practical as well as purely logical. Although he covered the gamut of administrative and social problems that existed in his time, he always sought to focus his attention primarily on the most fundamental problems of his society.

One of the central issues in the *Pan'gye surok* derived from the nature of the Chosŏn dynasty's structure, the fusion of a centralized bureaucratic government apparatus with a powerful tradition of inherited status in general, in particular a semiaristocratic ruling class at the top and hereditary slavery at the bottom. The principles of social and political organization under centralized bureaucracy on the one hand and hereditary aristocracy and slavery on the other were fundamentally different and often in conflict. Hereditary aristocracies valued family connections, personal ties, and inherited privilege and status, while bureaucratic states favored broadening access to political power, impersonal techniques of selection and evaluation, and a leveling of society save for the bureaucratic elite.

Yangban: The Aristocratic and Bureaucratic Traditions

As we will see, Yu was greatly upset by the domination of his society by the yangban, the group that he regarded as a hereditary aristocracy, but it would be mistaken to assume that his solution to the domination of Chosŏn society was to destroy the yangban and shift to an efficiently organized and ascetic centralized bureaucracy in which status and privilege would be abandoned in favor of pure meritocracy and absolute equality in the opportunities for advancement. Instead his goal was to attempt the recreation of the classical model of social and political organization that supposedly existed in the Chou dynasty of the first millennium B.C., a system that was embedded in feudal modes of organization but contained officials or bureaucrats in the employ of the Chou king and the various feudal lords. Even though Yu admired that ancient model, he harbored no hope of ever restoring it, but contented himself with adapting its principles to the current centralized bureaucratic mode of government organization in which the Chosŏn state was irrevocably fixed. One might add that a perfect system, either of pure feudal social and political hierarchy, or pure centralized and bureaucratic hierarchy, was impossible under these circumstances. In fact, Yu disliked many aspects of both extremes, the hereditary aspect of aristocracy, and the impersonalized, routine, excessively concentrated methods of a central bureaucracy.

These two model types of social organization were, in fact, fused together in both Chinese and Korean society at certain times, but by different means and with somewhat different consequences. In China the feudal elements of the Chou dynasty were crushed by the Ch'in dynasty unification of China in 221 B.C. Though the Former Han dynasty revived some feudal fiefs and inherited status for nobles after 206 B.C., they were obliterated with the abolition of the Three Feudatories. Even before the fall of the Later Han in A.D. 220, however, an aristocratic elite began to form, and it reached full flower during the Northern and Southern Dynasties period from the fall of the Han to the reunification under the Sui dynasty in 589.

The institutions of centralized bureaucracy were developed and expanded under the Sui and T'ang dynasties to the early ninth century, but those institutions did not result in the destruction of an aristocratic elite. Powerful families made a successful transition and continued to dominate society by adapting to new conditions, particularly the introduction of the civil service examination in 606 by Emperor Yang of the Sui dynasty. It was carried over into the T'ang (618–906) and later dynasties as a means of establishing an impersonal and objective standard for the recruitment of officials independent of the aristocratic families. The T'ang aristocrats, however, competed successfully in the examinations, winning degrees that qualified them for high bureaucratic posts. Although historians of Chinese history like to call the T'ang elite an aristocracy, it probably should be called a aristocratic/bureaucratic hybrid since the perpetuation of status depended on success in the examination system and officeholding, and not simply birth into an aristocratic family and automatic qualification for office.[1]

After the fall of the T'ang dynasty in 906 the T'ang aristocracy suffered a mortal blow to its social and political position, and under the Sung dynasty established in 960, the aristocracy as a class began to be replaced by a new social and political elite that owed its success to scholarship, examinations, and government service. This class has become known as the gentry, and although some of its members were able to maintain their status over generations, most of them did not. It was at this point that Korean social history parted company with Chinese social history, for the society of the Chosŏn dynasty was dominated by an aristocratic/bureaucratic ruling class that was similar to that of the T'ang dynasty in a number of ways, but it never made the transition from aristocracy to gentry that was achieved in Sung China.

The history of Korean social and political organization leading to the aristocratic/bureaucratic hybrid of the Chosŏn dynasty of 1392 was somewhat different, but one feature it shared with the T'ang was a shift from a more rigid experience with inherited aristocracy to a more flexible fusion of inherited privilege with meritocratic examination success. Korea had no classical age of feudalism and no cataclysmic experience to match the Ch'in unification under the mode of centralized bureaucratic organization.

Instead, Korea started with small-scale political units dominated by particular families with a strong military tradition. The Silla dynasty, one of the Three Kingdoms, began as a petty state and expanded its power and territory until it was finally able to conquer its rivals in the north and west, Koguryŏ and Paekche, with the aid of an alliance with T'ang forces, and to unify most of the territory on the peninsula. By that time Silla society was functioning under an hereditary aristocracy called the bone rank (*kolp'um*) system that lasted until the fall of Silla in 936. The adoption of certain central bureaucratic modes of organization from the early sixth century on did not interfere with the solidarity of that aristocracy.

While the bone ranks were not continued after the fall of Silla, and the succeeding Koryŏ elite was expanded to absorb local military leaders and warlords that had cooperated in Koryŏ's political victory in the dynastic struggle, the social and political leadership was dominated by important clans, including remnants of the old Silla bone-rank aristocracy, strengthened by particular bilateral marriage ties (rather than Chinese agnatic or patrilineal relations). Many of these clans sustained their positions over generations through the first two centuries of the dynasty even though a number of kings were belatedly introducing T'ang-style institutions of central bureaucracy, including the civil service examinations in 958. The examinations, however, provided only a small number of officials and by no means dominated the route to office.

These early Koryŏ clans suffered a blow when the military officials at the capital seized control of the state in a series of coups d'état after 1170, but the military did not eliminate either them or the central government; they merely kept them in place as civil officials under their control. When the Mongols began a series of invasions in the thirteenth century and finally took Koryŏ in 1270, the military leadership was removed and replaced by Mongol overlords. The Mongols kept the Koryŏ dynasty intact and the Korean kings on the throne as figureheads, but the powerful clans in the capital bureaucracy and the countryside were left in place to expand their private power at the expense of the central government. Many of their sons, however, were taking the civil service examinations as a means of gaining high office so that by the end of the fourteenth century about 40 percent of regular officials had passed the examinations.

When the Chosŏn dynasty was founded in 1392, many of the Koryŏ elite, generally referred to as yangban, made the successful transition to the new dynasty by standing for the civil service examinations. By the turn of the sixteenth century, if not earlier, the examinations became virtually the sole route to high office under a vastly strengthened central bureaucracy. Many of the old families thus retained their power and influence, but they were changed somewhat in nature because scholarly performance became a necessary means to that end. In short, they became the kind of bureaucratic/aristocratic hybrid that had been created in T'ang China. The difference was, however, that the dynasty lasted until 1910 and the yangban, or certain sublineages within that group, did not disappear and merge into the vast mass of commoners. Instead, they continued to dominate Chosŏn government and society virtually until its demise in 1910.[2]

Like the T'ang dynasty, the Chosŏn dynasty faced the problem of dealing with elements of hereditary aristocracy while it was adopting the institutions of centralized bureaucracy and reaching an accommodation with a hereditary elite, the yangban, who wanted to perpetuate its power and position despite the desire of some kings to reduce or eliminate that power. There has been considerable debate about whether the early Chosŏn government was able to do that in the fifteenth century. I believe not, but even those who do think that the old Koryŏ aristocracy was brought to heel would not question the predominance of the yangban (or its leading elements) as a privileged and hereditary aristocracy by the seventeenth century; they simply explain it as a development of a second wave of inherited privilege among the yangban following the deterioration of the more egalitarian spirit of the early fifteenth century.

Slaves and Slave Society

One significant difference between the seventeenth-century yangban and the T'ang aristocrats was that the yangban calculated their power and wealth not only in office- and landholding, but in their ownership of slaves. Not only in that century, but for many more centuries before (possibly as far back as the tenth century in the Koryŏ dynasty) Korea was a bona fide slave society with 30 or more percent of its overall population and approximately two-thirds of its capital population slaves, most of whom were under yangban masters. T'ang society had its bondsmen and a hierarchy of inferior status positions, but no one calls T'ang a slave society.

The emergence of hereditary slavery and the expansion of the slave population in the tenth century was not checked by the influence of either Buddhism or Confucianism through the end of the Koryŏ dynasty, and when the Neo-Confucian intellectual movement overwhelmed the Buddhists at the turn of the fifteenth century, it was not accompanied by any serious attacks on either slavery or slave society. By that time the power of the slaveowners and the practice of chattel slavery had been such a powerful aspect of Korean life that hardly anyone could be expected to call it into question.

It was only when the demand for manpower for military service rose sharply during the Japanese and Manchu invasions between 1592 and 1637 that the government began to relax the restraints against the manumission of slaves. Changes in the economy that were set in motion in the first two centuries of the dynasty – the expansion of agricultural production and the development of the market and a partially monetized economy – worked to disrupt the earlier social structure by permitting a few slaves, who lived at some distance from the master and functioned much like tenants, to accumulate sufficient wealth to purchase their freedom or bribe the clerks to remove their names from the registers. The general breakdown of morale and discipline made it easier for slaves to run away from their villages, but significant decline in the numbers of slaves in the population was not achieved until the middle of the eighteenth century – a century after the death of Yu Hyŏngwŏn. It was partially as a consequence of this greater sensitivity to the drawbacks of slave society in Korean society that a stimulus was provided for Yu Hyŏngwŏn to undertake the first truly serious consideration of the propriety of slavery in Korean society from a consciously Confucian perspective.

The Causes of Yangban Power: Learning from the Past

The purpose of Yu's scholarly investigations was to identify the main problem with the ruling class of his own society and to find ways of rectifying it. His individual chapters for the most part were divided in two, the first half copying out material relevant to the specific institution under discussion, usually without much comment, and the second half presenting Yu's proposals for reform, sometimes accompanied by an occasional historical reference, argument, or analogy. The introductory sections often contain material that Yu did not apply to his own reforms, but much of it did, and in any number of cases Yu simply adopted policies and plans from past Chinese dynasties or statecraft writers, or suggestions made by favored Korean officials without much change. The concluding section of most chapters included Yu's own program for reforms for contemporary Korea, the locus of his most interesting and original propositions.

The overwhelming proportion of his reference materials came from Chinese sources that were subdivided into two parts: the classics and materials covering the period of antiquity in ancient China down through the Chou dynasty, and historical references and policy statements made in the post-Chou age, the "later age" (*huse*) that was equivalent to the world after the Fall from Grace brought about by the Ch'in dynasty's destruction of classical Chou institutions.

Material from the Chou period provided models for and goals for emulation, but Yu did not believe that there was any real chance of recovering the perfection of Chou times, or even of replicating Chou institutions exactly. In fact, he thought of the entire post-Chou period as one of permanent imperfection, but with much leeway for tinkering and manipulation because any practitioner of statecraft had to adjust his classical model to current circumstances, which could be quite varied. In reading his final proposals for reform, however, one wonders in several instances whether he really succeeded in making that adjustment, and he was acutely aware of the charge that he was really a fundamentalist disguising himself as a practical and flexible thinker.

Despite the imperfect nature of the dynasties after the Chou, some of them were useful in providing lessons and examples for reform, particularly the Han dynasty, which was generally regarded as having achieved a close approximation of some Chou institutions. For that matter, even some of the more tragic and backward historical periods, like the Northern and Southern dynasties, provided a didactic example of adverse consequences that could follow from the emergence of an hereditary aristocracy.

The Sui and T'ang dynasties from 589 to 906 represented the reunification of China and reestablishment of empire with its panoply of central bureaucratic institutions, but it also represented examples of the distortions of the classical spirit that could be wrought by the operations of an impersonal, remote, top-heavy, and complex bureaucratic structure, in particular the decline in appointment, review, and promotion procedures from the Chou and even Han dynasties.

The Sung dynasty was an inspiration for Yu, not as a model for actual policy but because of its Neo-Confucian philosophers and statecraft thinkers. Although many statecraft writers and officials from the Han through the Sung harked back to the perfection of Chou dynasty institutions, it was the Sung statesmen like Wang An-shih and the Neo-Confucian thinkers like Ch'eng I, Ch'eng Hao, and Chu Hsi of the eleventh and twelfth centuries, who rediscovered antiquity. They were much like the thinkers of the Western Renaissance who rediscovered Greece and Rome, and proposed a series of ideas for the moral and institutional renovation of society. Yu was inspired by similar motives and in several cases adopted their suggestions. The main problem, however, was transcending the limitations of antiquity or Renaissance humanism, as when the heliocentric cosmos of Copernicus and Galileo overturned the Aristotelian diagram of the universe so admired by the medieval Scholastics. In the realm of statecraft it appears unlikely that Yu achieved this.

The Ming dynasty (1368–1644) played a less important role than the Sung in Yu's thought, but he was influenced by certain of its aspects. One of his favorite Chinese scholars was Ch'iu Chün, primarily because he reinforced the advice of the great Sung Neo-Confucians. He was also moved by the glowing reports of the superiority of Ming institutions by the memorials of Cho Hŏn, who had visited the Ming court prior to his tragic death during the Hideyoshi invasions in 1592. What Cho contributed that was different was praise for the practices of late sixteenth-century life in China, not simply an advertisement for idealistic schemes of Sung idealists. Other than these figures, however, Yu made no mention at all of the late Ming and early Ch'ing statecraft writers like Ku Yen-wu and Huang Tsung-hsi, and appears to have been ignorant of their work.

In summary, the Sung Neo-Confucians advertised the superiority of Chou institutions and advocated their restoration in contemporary times with adaptations to current circumstances. The Han dynasty represented the successful preservation of Chou institutions. The Northern and Southern dynasties illustrated the adverse consequences of the loss of fairness and the rise of inherited privilege, pedigree, and aristocracy. The T'ang dynasty represented the problems of bureaucracy and its deplorable influence on proper education and training and the fair selection of the best possible men for government.

YU'S METHOD AND GOALS: MODERNITY AND NATIONALISM?

One of the purposes of this book is to explore the reasons for Yu's institutional approach to the reform and recreation of the Korean ruling class, the sources of wisdom he sought in his research, and the fundamental elements necessary to a solution. The hope is that this search will yield answers not only to the definition of the optimum, if not ideal, society that Yu was trying to fashion, but also the method of his pursuit.

In the face of current views that portray Yu as the pioneer of trends leading to modernity and nationalism, it is necessary to judge whether his method contained any elements of a rationalistic and empirical pursuit of objective truth at the expense of conventional and inherited wisdom. As a member of a Confucian culture that honored the past, the ancient past in particular, did he seek to break away from the constraints of that historical impediment, or if not, did he use ancient precedent to lead the way toward a rejection of the intervening accretions of orthodox thought? In particular, did he use the reinterpretation of the classics by the Sung philosophers to break a new path of development for Confucianism or beyond Confucianism? If not, then how did he use the lessons of history in general and Korean history in particular?

Did he view history as a record of progress in the optimistic view that the recent past shows greater development than the remote past, or that the future holds greater promise than the past? Did he turn to the specific history of Korea as a source of wisdom independent from China and Chinese culture, and contribute to the foundation of a stronger sense of national consciousness than what existed before his time? And what precedents did he find important, and how did he apply them to his own social situation?

Did he challenge the fundamental moral framework of Confucian statecraft by moving toward the creation of a set of moral principles based on a Kantian analysis through a priori reason, or an emphasis on a value-free consideration of fact or practical utilitarianism separate from religious belief, and did he believe that this goal should be incorporated into his program for education? If not, then on what basis did he establish the foundation for the reform of society?

CHAPTER 4

Remolding the Ruling Class through Education and Schools

"Whatever the ancients practiced is the best, and whatever the people of later ages [*huse*] did is the worst."[1]

"If human nature [*injŏng*, lit., the feelings of the people] in the later age is frivolous and not serious, it is because the laws [*fa*] make it that way."[2]

The Ancient Model

The Institutional Approach to Moral Rectification

Yu Hyŏngwŏn was a child of the Sung in the sense that he believed not only that the laws and institutions created by the sages of Chinese antiquity were the best that could be devised by man for the governance of society, but also that these institutions could be adapted to contemporary Korean circumstance.[3] It is clear even from his own writing, however, that his optimistic belief in the efficacy of institutional reform and the adaptibility of ancient institutions was not shared by his contemporaries. The first step in the expression of this argument was to convince his readers that human nature and human behavior in contemporary times had not changed since classical times, and that the institutions of antiquity had some relevance for the present.

"People in the world commonly say that the circumstances in ancient times and the present are different. Even though they know that this opinion is wrong, still they cannot avoid being misled. If they were to look into the situation, they would understand that this opinion is in error and without foundation."[4]

Yu asserted that the root of this popular misconception about the intractability of contemporary circumstance and the irrelevance of ancient institutions could be explained by the origin and perpetuation of evil laws and systems.

"Generally speaking, the laws of the ancient people were all basically simple, and for this reason there were no evils. Laxity, carelessness, and the existence of many evils were all characteristic of the laws of the later age."[5]

Bad laws began when fawning officials catered to the whims of ambitious and avaricious rulers by changing or confusing ancient laws to satisfy a ruler's desires. As a matter of custom and tradition these laws continued into later generations. They became difficult to change because later rulers, no matter how pure in spirit and well-intentioned, lacked the learning necessary for an understanding of the superiority of ancient institutions. Even if they had the best of intentions, they were also obstructed by the advice of inferior men surrounding them. Eventually it became commonplace for people of any age to feel that the problems they faced were created by the circumstances of the recent past that were radically different from ancient times, and that mores and the nature of human feelings themselves also differed from the ancients. "But alas," he objected, "can anything be more regrettable than this [view]?"[6]

Yu's belief in the applicability of ancient models at least in principle was an inseparable part of his commitment to reform, but he also insisted that he was not simply a dogmatic fundamentalist:

> Some people say that, "No matter what the problem is the only thing you have to do is look for what's best. Why is it necessary to stick to old tracks and in every case restore what was [ancient practice]?" I would reply that it is not a case of sticking to old tracks. No matter what the case, whatever the ancients practiced is the best, and whatever the people of later ages [*huse*] did is the worst. Therefore, if we are to adopt what is best, naturally we should restore [the practices of] the ancients, and if we are to abandon what is worst, we should change what is done at the present time. . . . Mencius said: "Can you say a person understands if in governing he does not put into practice the ways of early kings?" These are truly knowledgeable words.[7]

What distinguished Yu from fellow Neo-Confucians who ascribed to the study of the Way (*tohak*) and emphasized the moral regeneration of individuals through self-rectification was that he felt that the fault with the later age of imperfection after the fall of the Chou dynasty was to be traced to imperfect laws and institutions, particularly in the realm of education and recruitment for office. "If human nature [*injŏng*] in the later age is frivolous and not serious, it is because the laws [*fa*] make it that way." The Chinese literature on the subject of recruitment was crystal clear, Yu instructed his readers. All that was needed was "an intelligent ruler to change what is evil and to restore what is good; then in what is [as little time] as it takes to turn your hand over you can make what is in decline flourish and put confusion into order."[8]

Yu's belief in the eternal capacity for moral purity by mankind signified that the dogma about the decline of humanity from the Chou to later dynasties was not equivalent to the fall from grace in Christian theology. The Confucians did not believe that a single act or a cataclysmic event like the Ch'in unification in 220 B.C. meant that mankind had irredeemably fallen into evil until the messianic appearance of a savior or the final solution of accumulated human evil on Judgment Day. Since man still retained his innate capacity for goodness, he always had the potential for recovery. Those who followed the utilitarian proclivity for reform within the Confucian tradition thought that miscast institutions could be corrected by the skills of a master social planner, who could by the study of past institutions devise better methods for approximating past glories.[9] Despite the difference in social and historical circumstance between past and present, Yu believed that "In fact there is no difference between ancient times and the present in terms of what ought to be done."[10]

Throughout his magnum opus Yu retained an unshakable, almost naïve faith in the efficacy of institutions to enable the achievement of the moral order as defined in Confucian terms. The idea that the nature and quality of institutions had moral consequences also seems on the face of it to contradict the Confucian axiom that good government depends on men, not laws, or that moral transformation rather than legal coercion is the only way to achieve social order. But Confucians had to deal with the reality of imperfect humanity and the apparent intractability of ordinary men to grasp the moral message of Confucian teaching and apply it to their daily behavior. Ideally all men were capable of moral perfection, but in actuality only a few achieved it. Because statecraft writers like Yu had to deal with the reality of human failure rather than the potential for human success, they turned to an institutional and legal approach to reform to assist the ruler in his task of the moral transformation of society.

The Moral Basis of Classical Education

Education and Government Schools. Yu's main concern with the ruling class in contemporary Korea was the domination of the hereditary yangban over the bureaucracy and society, but he found that the key to this problem was the emphasis by the rulers of the *san-tai* period of Chinese antiquity (the Hsia, Shang, and Chou dynasties) on education as the means of achieving the moral transformation (*kyohwa*) of their people. Mencius had remarked that the only thing that separated man from the beasts was education, Tung Chung-shu of the Former Han dynasty said that the ancient kings had regarded moral education as the means for perfecting customs and mores and ensuring the longevity of their reigns, and Chu Hsi had expressed the same thought in Neo-Confucian terms, that education was the means of overcoming the obstructions in the mind of psycho-physical energy:

> Generally speaking, the principles of the five ethical relationships emerge from the roots of the human mind. They are not things that can be forced on people. Men first become confused in their understanding of these principles because they are restricted by some imbalance in the material endowment of their nature or because [their inner goodness] is obscured by their immersion in material desire [*muryok*]. As a result fathers and sons are not close and loving and people are not obedient to one another. Therefore Shun [the sage emperor] gave this over to Ch'i, subsequently appointed him minister of education [Ssu-t'u], and made

> him devote himself seriously to spreading these teachings. And he saw to it that these teachings permeated [the minds of the people] thoroughly and gradually entered into their thinking so that what was upright in their Heavenly endowed natures would naturally be exposed . . . and so there was no fear that people might be lacking in a sense of shame. . . .[11]

The sages could not, however, leave education exclusively to the private devices of the people, but found it necessary to create institutions for the moral transformation of the people by appointing educational officials and staffing a school system with teachers. Emperor Shun's appointment of a Ssu-t'u thus set the precedent for the creation of institutions of education, which supposedly by the late Chou period reached a high degree of complexity and elaboration. In the Chou model as described in the *Rites of Chou* (*Chou-li*), *Book of Rites* (*Li-chi*), *History of the Han Dynasty* (*Han-shu*) and other sources, there was a hierarchy of officials each charged with both general and specific educational tasks at each level of administration and a hierarchy of schools reaching from the smallest communities in the hinterland up to the national academy (*kuo-hsüeh*, *kukhak*) or great academy (*t'ai-hsüeh*, *t'aehak*) in the capital.[12] In Yu's mind, this complete set of educational officials and schools was not only the institutional prerequisite for a successful program of moral transformation of the ordinary population, but the sine qua non of the training of the ruling class.

The Chou Curriculum: Virtue, Behavior, the Arts. Yu believed that the ancient system of education contained a core of ethical concepts with a core curriculum of books that were essential for proper moral training. Classical knowledge was divided into three major categories: virtue, behavior, and the arts (*tŏk*, *haeng*, *ye*). The *Rites of Chou* defined the six virtues as knowledge, humaneness, sagacity, righteousness, loyalty, and harmony, and a commentary on the *Book of Rites* spoke of the "seven teachings" governing the relations between people.

Knowledge of these virtues, however, was not enough; instruction in proper behavior was necessary to translate moral education into action. The *Rites of Chou* defined the six modes of behavior as filial piety, comradeship, friendship, closeness in marriage relations, responsibility, and compassion for the less fortunate. Yu emphasized the important link between knowledge and action by a reference to Chu Hsi's commentary on this section of the *Book of Rites* in which Chu referred to the oft-cited formula in *The Great Learning* (*Ta-hsüeh*) that the individual proceeds from self-cultivation to the regulation of the family, to the governance of the state, and finally to the pacification of the world.[13]

The text of and commentary on the Hsüeh-chi section of the *Book of Rites* described an arduous prolonged process of nine years of study in a national academy designed to achieve the perfection of behavior. The course of study began with the reading and understanding of classical texts. By the third year students had to be able to get along with their fellow students, by the fifth year to show respect for their teachers, by the seventh to demonstrate knowledge of the principles learned and be observed associating with other students of high moral caliber. By the ninth year, "they would know how to distinguish between the categories of things, thoroughly comprehend the principles of things, and be able to stand firmly erect without any signs of backsliding." This was called "the great achievement."[14]

The third major category of the ancient curriculum was the six arts (*ye*) defined in the *Rites of Chou* and elsewhere as rites, music, archery, charioteering, calligraphy, and calculations (or mathematics).[15] It is in this category that we would expect to find some departure from moral training and more emphasis on the practical skills necessary to the operation of government and the state. Rites, music, and archery were all extremely important dimensions of moral education and charioteering only slightly less so. Only calligraphy and mathematics were relatively free from ethical considerations, but as Peter Bol has pointed out until the emergence of the learning of the Way in the Sung dynasty, mastery of the complete corpus of culture (*mun*, *wen* in Chinese) was the mark of the educated man.[16]

Yu's stress on rites and music for moral training derived directly from the texts of the Chou period. As the Wang-chih section of the *Book of Rites* put it, "The Ssu-t'u polished the six rites in order to regulate the [human nature] of the people."[17] Ritual was important for inducing proper states of mind and attitude as well as sanctifying certain sacramental procedures, such as marriage, capping (male adult initiation), funerals, and ancestral sacrifice. Ritual performance was also stressed on certain nonsacramental occasions, such as formal meetings of guests, the local wine-drinking rite (*hyangjuŭmye*), and the archery ceremonies. The *Book of Rites*, which stressed the coercive method of inducing conformity to ethical norms, also extolled the instrumental use of rites: "Rites are the means by which one regulates [the people] and stops them from being extravagant and lying, and prevents superiors from oppressing inferiors and inferiors from usurping the prerogatives of their superiors, so that in their behavior people achieve the middle way."[18]

Music was another of the six arts that had an important moral dimension. Chu Hsi remarked that it was useful in teaching people to be harmonious and impartial. Just as the rules of harmony regulated sounds to ensure against dissonance, so would music help to calm the human tendency to aggression. "The sages created music in order to nurture the nature and the feelings, to cultivate the talents in men, and to be used in the rituals to the spirits, to harmonize those above and those below. . . ." According to the *Rites of Chou*, the grand master of music (Ssu-lo) was in charge of the operation of the National Academy (Ch'eng-chün, or Korean, Sŏnggyun), and Tung Chung-shu of the Han explained that the grand master used music to teach the sons of the nobility to "achieve the middle way and be harmonious."[19]

The mastery of ethical principles, the embodiment of those principles in one's external conduct, and skill in the performance of rites, music, archery, and the gentlemanly arts were also the main criteria for admission to the schools, promotion within the school system, and appointment to office – a clear demonstration of the crucial relationship between education, the recruitment of officials, and the formation of the ruling class. The criteria of merit were "worth" (*hyŏn*) and "ability" (*nŭng*): worth was defined as one's understanding of moral principles and overt behavior, and ability was measured by one's mastery of the six fine arts.[20]

In short, what Yu admired in education and training was the classical emphasis on moral principles and behavior, neither efficiency and practical utility, nor any attempt to find new ethical principles not firmly grounded in the classics, nor any Cartesian separation of fact from value, nor any rejection of inherited wisdom accompanied by Cartesian rational certitude, nor any measure of knowledge subject to verification either by experience, scientific observation, or testing.

Recommendation for Office and School Based on Morality

According to the *Rites of Chou* the entire population of the Chou dynasty was organized hierarchically into units of administration beginning with the basic five-family unit (*pi*) and ascending to the *hyang*, which consisted of 12,500 families. The *taebu* (officials) of the *hyang* were responsible for recommending the worthy and able, who would then be afforded honorary treatment as guests in the *hyang* or local wine-drinking rite. The *taebu* were also responsible for instructing the officials of lower level units of organization in the principles of education and governance and for recommending outstanding individuals (whether officials or commoners) for appointment or promotion. When they presented their list of recommendees to the king, he would kowtow twice in receiving it, a formal mark of the king's respect for men of moral worth and his acknowledgment of the autonomous nature of the recommendation system itself. This ceremony was followed by the *hyang* or local archery rite in order to judge the deportment of the recommended individuals.[21]

The same process would be followed for recommendation at each lower level of administration. The chief of each unit would read out the laws of government to the people, encourage virtuous behavior and the development of the liberal arts, maintain surveillance over wrongdoing, conduct sacrificial rites at the shrine, and hold archery contests at the spring and autumn rites at the local school to "rectify the position of the people according to age and teach the people filial piety and brotherly respect."[22]

At the capital selected scholars (*sŏnsa*) were recommended from the *hyang* for promotion to the National Academy, and the best were dubbed "accomplished scholars" (*chosa*). They would then be appointed to various bureaus in the capital as "advanced scholars" (*chinsa*) and placed under the charge of the minister of bureaucratic personnel (Sama, Ssu-ma), who would evaluate their capacities and recommend them to the king.[23] Fu-sheng's commentary on *The Book of History* (*Shu-ching*), the *Shang-shu ta-chüan*, also mentioned that the feudal lords recommended tribute scholars (*kongsa*) to the Son of Heaven (the king) on an annual basis. And a subcommentary by a Mr. Ch'eng noted that there was also a quota system based on the size of the feudal principality: three students a year from the largest, two from the next, and one from the smallest. This notice served as a precedent for statecraft writers of later periods who wanted to combine regional quotas with a recommendation system.[24]

The Confucian emphasis on both thought and action, or knowledge and behavior, as inseparable components of moral training meant that the ideal mode of evaluation was face-to-face observation of individuals by peers or superiors personally acquainted with the candidates. The ancient school system also provided for long-term evaluation simply by requiring years of schooling prior to appointment to office, but the schools were not the only, nor the most important, arena for the personal observation of individuals. The local community, which formed the base of both the administrative, military, and school hierarchies in the classical model, was the natural locus for initial evaluation because the community had more intimate knowledge of individual behavior than any other group. Observed behavior as the main method of evaluation required a kind of grassroots participation in the recommendation process.

Discipline and Punishment in Education

The spirit of the classical Chinese system was tough-minded, authoritarian, and punitive – close in many ways to the discredited Legalist tradition of the Ch'in dynasty. Matters involving moral principle were not open to question. The Hsüeh-chi section of the *Book of Rites* described the proper attitude of the student as one of passive acceptance of knowledge: "The young people [in the schools] just listened and did not ask questions, and as a result they learned things in the proper order." The commentary added: "The young people were never able to ask questions, or if they did ask questions, they still would not be able to understand the important elements [of the answers]. Therefore, they only listened and accepted the explanations of the teachers."[25]

Authoritarianism in learning was matched by a thoroughly punitive approach to wrongdoing and incompetence in general. The *Rites of Chou*, in describing the functions of the Ssu-t'u, listed the use of punishment at the *hyang* or local level for eight kinds of misbehavior and for misfeasance and malfeasance by educational officials. Teachers would keep thorny branches on hand for use as switches on lazy students, and if recalcitrant students and scholars failed to reform, they would be singled out by local elders and subjected to three degrees of banishment before permanent exile and exclusion from the ranks of the scholars. Students of the National Academy who failed to reform even after the king went on a three-day fast would also be banished and deprived of student status. Those feudal lords who had recommended bad students were held responsible and subjected to demotion, deprivation of rank, or confiscation of their land.[26] Even though students were ultimately subjected to punishment, every effort was taken to persuade them of their shortcomings beforehand. The ultimate punishment, however, was less physical than social – demotion from the ranks of the privileged scholar category and reduction to the rank of commoner.

Student vs. Feudal Status: The Two-track System

There was no ambiguity in the understanding of the Chou model of schools and recommendation in the minds of later scholars that the system produced a ruling class of merit and worth defined in moral terms and that this moral elite deserved to be afforded the marks and privileges of status through tax exemptions, rank, and sumptuary advantages.[27] The model was unclear or contradictory, however, about the degree to which the system of merit would interfere with the inherited privileges of the feudal order in Chou times. The *Shang-shu ta-chüan* commentary noted that in ancient times the eldest legitimate son (*chŏkcha*) usually assumed his father's office. The Wang-chih section of the *Book of Rites* described the elite as consisting of the princes, queens, legitimate sons of the high officials (*kyŏng*), middle-rank officials (*taebu*), and lower-rank officials (*wŏnsa*). A later commentator equated those of base status in society with commoners and those of noble status with the hereditary salaried families. In several instances the sons of this feudal/bureaucratic elite were called "sons of the state" (*kukcha*).[28]

One of the most interesting illustrations of the conflict between feudal inheritance and equal opportunity was afforded by the remarks of a commentator on the Wang-chih section of the *Book of Rites*, a Mr. Liu. According to him there were two routes to schools and office in the Chou. The common people were taught in the *hyang* or local schools, while the *kukcha* along with selected outstanding commoners were taught in the National Academy (Kukhak). Those students selected and promoted from the *hyang* schools, the selected scholars (*sŏnsa*), were appointed to, but could not be promoted above, regional or provincial official posts, while the advanced scholars (*chinsa*) chosen from the National Academy could be appointed to posts at court or in the central government. In other words, the distinction between sons of the nobility and high officials on the one hand and commoners on the other was maintained by separate modes of education and recruitment.

Nevertheless, some opportunity for the sons of commoners to hold high office was allowed if the Ssu-t'u recommended them for promotion from the *hyang* school to the National Academy. Once in the National Academy they were treated as equal in status to the sons of the elite and could then be recommended for promotion to high office. Another commentary on the Wang-chih also made the point that the official in charge of instruction in the National Academy (the Locheng) ranked the students only according to age and not according to the noble or base status of their fathers.[29]

This idealized model of the Chou system presumed a society in which two contradictory principles operated without conflict. Hereditary privilege and status was correct and proper for society at large and the sons of the elite rightfully gained easier access to the highest level of the educational system and high office in the bureaucracy. Yet within the school system individual students were treated as equal units and ranked at each level by age only and promoted on the basis of scholastic accomplishment and moral worth, guaranteeing some new blood in the social elite in every generation. The students in the schools constituted the lowest rung of the social stepladder in a stratified, feudal society, and student status was the only way out of commoner status, but the position of commoner students was precarious since they were under threat of expulsion and permanent relegation to commoner status.

Learning and Age as Criteria of Rank

The significance of scholarly merit and age as criteria of rank in Yu's writing is demonstrated by the importance he attached to the local wine-drinking rite, which he copied out from the *Book of Etiquette and Ceremonial* (*I-li*) and *Book of Rites*.[30] These two texts described the way that local officials (*hyang-daebu*) honored eminent local scholars by affording them special treatment as guests in the wine ritual. The main importance for Yu was the exaltation of learning and ethical behavior as more important criteria for status than the possession of official rank. Age was also the basis for ranking the assembled minor guests and visitors at the rite. Ranking men by learning and age assumed special importance if the existing society happened to be dominated by a hereditary elite, which was the case in both Chou times and contemporary Korea.[31]

Major Features of the Classical Model

To summarize the essential features of the ancient model, a system of official or public schools performed the functions of both education and recruitment for office. The king was obliged to show respect for both educational officials and schools. The goal of education in the schools was knowledge of virtue, cultivation of moral behavior, and the study of the arts. Knowledge was directly connected to moral action and behavior, and the arts included elements like ritual and archery, which were also designed to inculcate attitudes conducive to moral behavior.

Candidates for promotion within the school system and appointment to office were recommended by those best able to judge their overall behavior over the long term, not just their knowledge of objective fact or skill in useful tasks. The base of the system of education and recommendation was located in the local community where peers, elders, and teachers were best able to observe children and young men. Recommendation was also used outside the schools for obtaining men for office, and a quota system was used for recommendation of men by the feudal lords to the king according to the size of the demesne.

Appointments of officials were shared between the king and the feudal lords, so that direct central control was extremely limited. Once in office officials were subjected to triennial reviews of their performance and a grand review every nine years.

Presumably there was a two-track system of schools, one set for the commoners, the others for the feudal nobility, but an exceptional commoner might gain access to the elite National Academy. Students were subjected to severe discipline inside the schools, and if a student failed to perform adequately, he was liable to a series of punishments accompanied by an admonition to improve. If he could not do so, he was expelled from the school and returned to the lower ranks of regular society. In the feudal social order outside the schools, however, eldest sons inherited the positions of their fathers without having to pass any examination of their moral behavior. Society was bifurcated into the elite and the commoners, reflected in the two-track system of schools.

Since the purpose of the schools was to train men for office as officials in bureaucracies of the king and the feudal lords, the optimum benefit from the schools would have been the creation of a class of officials of merit, but the ruling class would have remained feudal and hereditary. The contrast between hereditary status outside the schools and egalitarian meritocracy inside was the one major contradiction in the model not fully resolved in the Chinese literature. For that matter, the duality of social and school standards remained a problem for Yu Hyŏngwŏn as he attempted to concoct a formula for his own semiaristocratic society in Korea.

THE HAN DYNASTY: RECOMMENDATION

The fall of the Chou dynasty in 221 B.C. meant a major transition to the centralized bureaucratic system of the Ch'in dynasty. Yu Hyŏngwŏn found that the most serious result of that transformation in China was that the face-to-face evaluation of individual behavior that constituted the ideal method of recruitment in the feudal system of recommendation was undermined by the rationalization and bureaucratization of selection procedures in political units of ever greater size and complexity. The more centralized and bureaucratic the government became, the more impersonal the process of evaluation. Officials in remote boards of personnel could never have intimate knowledge of the behavior or moral capacity of candidates for office from the local districts.

Yet the rulers of the Former Han dynasty were able to retain the spirit of personal evaluation of the ancient recommendation model and preserve the principle of long-term personal observation of students and officials. A number of Han emperors also allowed the few remaining feudal lords, high officials, and local magistrates to recommend worthy men for office, and the latter to appoint their own subordinates.

Both moral behavior and practical talent were used as criteria for recommendation, but by the end of the first century of the dynasty Tung Chung-shu complained that most high officials were sons and younger brothers of bureaucrats who simply worked their way up the official ladder by accumulating time-in-grade. His solution was the establishment of a National Academy staffed with the best scholars as teachers and the adoption of a system of recommendation according to which district magistrates and high-ranking officials would propose two outstanding candidates a year (*segong* or annual tribute recommendees) who would serve an apprenticeship in the imperial guards. Rewards and punishments would be meted out to recommendors to prevent a desultory approach to their responsibilities. Tung's plan, however, was a compromise with the ancient ideal: a National Academy fell short of a national school system, and the recommendation system was limited to incumbent officials and not based on local community leaders.[32]

Emperor Wu of the Former Han showed some willingness to apply other features of the ancient model. He instituted quotas of recommendees for administrative districts based on population and ordered local officials to recommend able clerks and local men of talent without quota limits. He also appointed specialists in the classics (the erudites or *po-shih kuan*, *p'aksa-gwan* in Korean) who were to teach students selected from local villages on the basis of good behavior and scholarship. After a year's study they were to be examined and appointed to office on the basis of their performance.[33]

By the end of the first century A.D. there was a decline in the quality of men recommended for office.[34] Fan Yeh, compiler of the *History of the Later Han Dynasty*, complained that strict criteria for selection were loosened and "the path to glory was opened wide," stimulating people to "falsify their reputations, embellish the facts . . ." and seek favors from the high and mighty to obtain a post. The Chou recommendation system was finally reaching its end as the major method of recruitment in China.

Nonetheless, the reputation of the Han dynasty's recruitment system waxed in subsequent centuries, probably from a nostalgic yearning for an idealized past. Shen Yüeh of the Liang dynasty (502–57) gave the Han dynasty high marks because no distinctions were drawn between the scholar-officials and commoners. "Naturally, if a man were not an official, he did not go to the capital, and if he were dismissed from his post as court minister or local magistrate, then in both cases he would return to his native village."[35] Bureaucratization in the Han, in other words, had not created the kind of urban/rural gap that characterized later dynasties and that coincided with class differentiation.

Shen also praised the Han for its extensive school system that funneled the talented into the lowest levels of the state bureaucracy as clerks or assistants to local magistrates. These men were eligible for promotion only after proving their merit by superior performance. "This was the reason why the Han dynasty reached the heights in obtaining good men for office."[36]

THE EVILS OF ARISTOCRACY

Although the Han dynasty modified many of the more Draconian aspects of Ch'in bureaucratization and centralization and preserved a few aspects of Chou administration, like the use of recommendation in recruitment, the granting of local autonomy to a few feudal lords and the district magistrates of the central administration, after the fall of the Later Han dynasty major changes were introduced into Chinese social and political organization. The most prominent was the emergence of a social aristocracy and the dominant role it played in immediate successor states to the Han in the third century, the Wei (220–65) and Chin (265–420) dynasties, and the Northern and Southern dynasties after 304. This period in Chinese history was of crucial importance to Yu Hyŏngwŏn because it enabled him to illustrate some of the major defects of aristocracy, particularly its perversion of the classical model of recruitment.

Pedigree and Aristocracy in China, 220–589

The general disruption that accompanied the fall of the Later Han transformed social conditions in the third century and interrupted the trend toward the rationalization and bureaucratization of recruitment procedures. Yu noted that even after the fall of the Later Han dynasty, Chu-ko Liang, ruler of the the Shu-Han dynasty, in 223 was able to appoint officials on the basis of talent rather than rank, and in Wei and Chin times (third century A.D.) magistrates and city officials appointed by the Ministry of Personnel (Li-pu) were allowed to hire their own subordinates on the basis of village recommendation.[37]

This perpetuation of selection by talent stemmed from the introduction of two new institutions that were established as means of official recruitment in the state of Wei (220–65). Under the nine ranks (*chiu-p'in*) established in 220, aspirants for office in local communities who passed an investigation of their merits were assigned one of nine local ranks that made them eligible for a post in the central bureaucracy.[38] A new post called the Chung-cheng was established to evaluate candidates at the local level and recommend them to the Personnel Bureau (Ssu-t'u fu) at the capital.[39] The post of Chung-cheng was created at the local level because it was felt that the Bureau of Personnel at the capital was too remote from the villages to determine the quality of candidates for office. Since many villages contained new settlers who had migrated from other areas because of political strife, the stationing of official talent scouts in the provinces was a reasonable way to deal with the effects of social dislocation. At the same time, the decentralization of recommendation approximated the ancient ideal of locating evaluation and recruitment procedures in the local community. Although the Chung-cheng was assigned to the commandery (*chün*) and not the village, he was still a lot closer to the grass roots than the capital bureaucrats. Furthermore, the assignment of rank to individuals under the nine-rank system was supposed to place a mark of status on men of virtue, fulfilling another of the ancient ideals.

Despite the noble objectives of the new institutions, as time passed the Chung-cheng eventually conferred rank without respect to an individual's moral qualities, a practice undoubtedly caused by the growth of hereditary aristocracy during the Northern and Southern dynasties (to the Sui reunification in 589). For both contemporary and later Chinese statecraft writers, what started out in the Wei dynasty as an attempt to approximate the ancient ideals of equal opportunity, recruitment according to moral worth and local community participation, ended up as the direct antithesis of those ideals.

Hsi Shen in the Chin dynasty (265–290) criticized the use of favoritism and the influence of parents, relatives, and personal connections in personnel matters, and he blamed competition for office for producing factions that distorted the truth. He tried using recommendation as a means of recruitment, but he had to use the law instead of moral exhortation to implement it.[40]

Yu found that opinion was split in the Chinese literature over the question of whether the Chung-cheng and nine-rank system were a legitimate compromise with ancient norms. Several scholars believed that the Chung-cheng system could be restored by a few adjustments. Liu I and Wei Chüan of the Chin dynasty (265–90) argued that it was not possible to restore the ancient ideal of recommendation at the village level because of social disruption and migration. Because the Chung-cheng did not have personal knowledge of the inhabitants of the villages and were influenced by rumor, unreliable opinion, gifts, and bribes, in assigning rank they failed to heed honest local opinion and failed to notice many bona fide scholars and worthy men. Wei hoped to solve this problem by using rewards and punishment and requiring new migrants to register as permanent residents in their new settlements (*t'u-tüan*) since permanent settlements and registration would create stable communities for restoring the ancient system of recommendation.[41]

Fu Hsüan of the Chin dynasty believed that the spirit of the ancient model could be retained if the Chung-cheng paid attention to "pure discussion" (*ch'ing-i*) or what might be defined as the opinions of the men of virtue, talent, and learning in the villages. Fu held that pure discussion was one of the characteristics of ancient times when sage kings had established the principles of moral transformation at court and the ordinary people in the countryside maintained feelings of righteousness in their conversations with one another, but it had been abandoned by the "defunct Ch'in" dynasty, which shifted to a reliance on law and tactics (*fa* and *shu* – the two main methods of the Legalists).[42]

Most commentators whom Yu cited, however, felt that the institutional compromises of the Wei and other states of the Northern and Southern dynasties period were too great a departure from the system of the ancients. P'ei Tsu-yeh, who lived at the turn of the sixth century, said that the local community had been lost as the proper locus for initial recommendation in the Wei and Chin (265–420) dynasties. He lauded the ancient village community, or at least his image of it, in idealistic terms:

> While a person was living at home you could observe his [capacity for] filial piety and friendship. In the sub-district and village communities [*hyangdang*] you could investigate his sincerity and trustworthiness. In his comings and goings you could see his will and righteousness. In his grief and difficulty you

> could estimate his intelligence and ability to plan. You could annoy him in order to see how he would deal with it; you could tempt him with profit in order to see how honest he was.[43]

Shen Yüeh of the Liang dynasty (502–57) argued that the classical principle of opening the opportunity for office to men of even the lowliest status had been subverted by the development of favoritism for men of status. In ancient times there were only two classes of men – the *chün-tzu* or man of superior virtue and the *hsiao-jen* or "small man" of limited moral capacity – and that because only the morally superior men were chosen for office, even fishermen, farmers, and teachers on occasion could rise from their low and humble stations in life to attain the position of prime minister.[44] When the nine-rank system was begun in the Wei, it was only intended as a temporary means for the evaluation of talent, but it resulted in hereditary class differentiation because the Chung-cheng assigned rank on the basis of existing status rather than real talent:[45]

> As time passed this tendency gradually became stronger. The gowned and capped scholars were never graded lower than second rank, and afterwards this led to the creation of a lowly commoner class. According to the system of the Chou and Han dynasties, intelligent men commanded stupid ones and people of base status were mixed together with people of high status in the formation of ranks and grades. But since the Wei and Chin dynasties, because the noble [*kuei*] commanded the base [*ch'ien*], a clear distinction was made between the scholar-officials [*shih*, *sa* in Korean] and the commoners [*shu*, *sŏ* in Korean] in terms of their grade.[46]

Fu Hsüan's (213–78, the Western Chin) analysis of what had gone wrong after the third century was based on a deterioriation in the spirit that motivated the activities of the four functional divisions of society. He endorsed the traditional concept that the essence of ancient society was based on a functional division of labor – the *shih*, farmers, artisans, and merchants – "each of which had their own occupations and different tasks to perform." As opposed to Shen Yüeh's belief that the lowliest peasant had a chance for office in classical times, Fu thought that education was justifiably restricted to the *shih*, the National Academy was established only for the sons of the *shih*, and only the talented among them were appointed to office. The farmers produced food for their support, the artisans furnished them with utensils, and the merchants exchanged goods for them.[47] Although Fu's functional division of society was not based on a feudal model, it was nonetheless bifurcated into the elite/commoner division described elsewhere for Chou society.

Then he argued that this functional differentiation was lost in the Han and Wei dynasties, and the sons of the officials neglected their classical studies and administrative duties and indulged themselves in lives of idle association and play. The farmers and artisans abandoned their basic, productive pursuits in favor of the profits to be made from commerce, and the students merely registered at the National Academy without bothering to study the ways of the ancient kings. The solution was obvious – restoration of the full functional and productive characteristics of ancient society and the return of the idle to productive jobs. All the parasitic sinecured officials, which he estimated at one-third the total population, should be sent back to the farm.[48]

P'ei Tsu-yeh (467–528, Ch'i and Liang dynasties) complained specifically of the evils of hereditary status because it contradicted the proper moral criteria of merit:

> The *Book of History* says, "People are treated as noble because they are close to the ruler; there are no people who are born into the world as nobles." This means that you should not care whether a man is a day laborer or a peddler if he can be respected for his observance of the way and righteousness, and if he is not the right kind of man, how could you select him [for office] just because he comes from a lineage of scholar-officials [*shih-tsu*, *sajok* in Korean]?[49]

He contrasted his own time with the relative social equality of the Han dynasty: "Even the sons and grandsons of famous officials were still on a par with common scholar-officials in their cotton garb. Although a distinction was made between officials and commoners, there was no major difference between the prosperous families and the plain ones." By the end of the Chin dynasty, however, aristocratic family status (*fa-yüeh*, *pŏryŏl* in Korean) was all that counted; the sons of the high and mighty looked down on the families of poor scholars and despised local magistrates [of lesser status than themselves]. "What people talked about was family line [*men-hu*, *munho* in Korean] and what they discussed had nothing to do with worth or ability. . . ." Even in his own time recommendations and appointments were only made on the basis of status (*fa*, *pŏl* in Korean).[50]

The situation P'ei complained of was continued in the Ch'i dynasty (479–502) in south China. Yu found that sons of high ranking families were given preference over lesser families for official appointments, and everyone sought marriages with influential families.[51] Official appointments were made solely on the basis of written records and genealogies of maternal as well as paternal relatives of officials because no one bothered to conduct any investigation of candidates for office. Sons of the highest ranking families were appointed to office as soon as they reached the age of twenty, and those from lower ranking families were restricted to clerk's posts and given an examination to test their skills when they reached thirty years of age. In the Southern dynasties in general the emperor conducted no interviews of any candidate in advance to determine his capacities and no agency ever reviewed the performance of officials in office. Only occasional reformers like Wang Chien recommended that local magistrates be chosen on the basis of their past records and support from local residents rather than by remote officials in the capital.[52]

In the Northern Wei (424–535) Han Hsien-tsung (ca. 471–500) complained that the only criterion for office was family pedigree (*men-ti*, *munji* in Korean) rather than worth and rectitude.

> A pedigree is merit bequeathed by a grandfather or father. How can it be of any benefit to the imperial house? If you have a man of unusual talent, even if his status is as base as a butcher, fisherman, slave, or prisoner-of-war, you still should appoint him to office. And if he has no talent, then even though he may be a son of the three empresses, you should naturally demote him to the position of runner.[53]

The Chinese commentators on the Northern and Southern dynasties provided Yu Hyŏngwŏn with a full-blown vocabulary and a well-articulated critique of aristocratic society that he adopted for use against the privileged yangban class of his own time. They also provided him with sufficient evidence to show that the use of recommendation for bureaucratic recruitment could be subverted quite readily by a society that prized inherited status. What had occurred in almost four centuries was the abandonment of recommendation, personal evaluation of candidates for office, and autonomous appointments of subordinates by magistrates, and the development of cutthroat competition in the search for office, slander against rivals rather than a yielding acknowledgment of their superiority, nepotism, and reliance on personal and familial connections, aristocratic rank, and inherited status as the basis of appointment and subsequent promotion.

Hereditary Aspects of the Korean Ruling Class

Yu Hyŏngwŏn described the yangban of his own society in virtually the same terms as the critics of the Northern and Southern dynasties of China, and in particular he focused on the importance of pedigree and the prestige accorded to high-status families:

> It is just that in our country we only respect pedigree [*munji*]. Because of the sad state of established custom we only talk about how exalted or debased a hereditary lineage [*chokse*] is; we do not inquire whether the person has cultivated proper behavior or not. As long as a person is a son or grandson of a hereditary lineage [*sebŏl*], then even though he may be inferior in talent or a worthless individual, his status is sufficient to enable him to reach the highest post of State Councilor.
>
> If a person's family happens to suffer from cold or privation, then even though he may be most virtuous and very learned, he does not qualify to be ranked among the class of scholars [*saryu*]. The reason why the Way of the age is not elevated, why men of talent have not arisen, and why laws and punishments are in confusion is all because of this. How could this have been the intention of the early kings [as the way] to embody the Way and set standards for the world?[54]

Yu acknowledged, however, that Koreans who defended the existing ascriptive social system used the argument that strict distinctions had to be made in terms of *myŏngbun*, moral obligation, a term denoting the proper social status that accrued to morally superior individuals. Nevertheless, this concept had been distorted by applying it automatically to men of high birth rather than to men of moral quality:

> The moral obligation [to recognize status distinction] [*myŏngbun*] is a natural principle of Heaven and Earth. How could one help but be strict about maintaining it? In general, however, the so-called distinctions of social status basically arise from the fact that we have grades between the noble and base, and nobility and baseness [*kwich'ŏn*] basically derives from the difference between worthiness and ignorance, and that is all there is to it.
>
> At the present time we do not distinguish whether a man is good or bad. Instead his nobility or baseness is determined exclusively in terms of how exalted the official posts and rank of his forbears were, and yet we still say that we are maintaining strict distinctions of social status.[55]

The ruling class in Korea was often referred to as yangban, but not all yangban were bona fide members of the ruling class. The term yangban signified a status designation for a core group of families with a long history of prominence and usually with advantages over others in the possession of land, wealth, and slaves, a pattern of restricted marriage with other families of like status, a strong tradition of education and scholarship, domination of the civil service examinations by a success rate far higher than average, and through it the acquisition of public office, which was source of the highest level of prestige in society (see chap. 2).

Nevertheless, since the maintenance and continuation of the families of both the ruling class and the yangban status group was dependent on periodic successful performance (in the long history of a clan) in the state's civil service examinations, the yangban could not be regarded purely as an aristocracy of birth. Many yangban families remained shut out of success in the examinations and officeholding; some of them retained yangban status nonetheless, while others lost it. Since not all members of the yangban families were able to retain wealth, land, or slaves over the generations, not all of them could necessarily be deemed rich or well-to-do even though they fought to retain their dignity and life style even in hard times. But those persons who did belong to yangban families certainly constituted the large majority of the ruling class, especially so at the highest ranks of officialdom, even though it would be foolhardy at this time to provide a specific percentage for all ranks since the research task would be enormous.

In any case, Yu was not enamored of the hereditary aspects of the ruling class (or the yangban if you prefer), and he sought to change its nature by a fundamental process of reform. He was firmly convinced that many of the members of the ruling class were not behaving in a moral fashion. They were placing their own private interests over those of the state or the public good, and since their main occupations were officeholding and scholarship, they were failing in their jobs as officials and teachers. But the important question was, would Yu's obvious displeasure with the yangban stir him to champion a position of equal opportunity based on moral capacity as resolutely as P'ei Tsu-yeh?

THE EVILS OF EXAMINATIONS

Even though north China had been overrun by the tribal "barbarians" of the area north of the Great Wall after 304, and societies of the next few centuries were dominated by aliens, military leaders, and aristocrats, bureaucratic organization had been retained throughout even though central control over the districts was weakened because of the domination of local aristocrats. When the Sui dynasty reunified all of China in 589, the power of the central bureaucracy was strengthened and its control over the periphery extended. One of the key institutions in this process was the introduction of the civil service examination in 606 to recruit officials on the basis of performance in written examinations, a method that threatened the stranglehold of the old aristocracy.

Although the aristocracy in T'ang China made a successful adaption to this challenge by standing for the examinations and passing them in large numbers, the examinations themselves introduced a completely new method of recruitment with a number of problems of its own. The examination system continued through succeeding dynasties until its abolition in 1905, and was also adopted by Koreans in the Koryŏ dynasty in 958, and strengthened in the Chosŏn dynasty after 1392, making it virtually the exclusive route to the highest positions in the state bureaucracy. It was after two and one-half centuries of experience with it that Yu focused his attention on its weaknesses, and for this task he was aided by his research into its history in China.

Tso Hsiung's Examination System in the Later Han

Yu Hyŏngwŏn's first reference to the appearance of examinations as a means of recruitment occurred fairly early in the Later Han dynasty, as a corrective to a deteriorating situation. He cited Fan Yeh (398–445) of the Sung dynasty, compiler of the *History of the Later Han Dynasty* (*Hou Han-shu*), who thought that the decline in the recommendation system in the Later Han dynasty was offset, if only for a brief time, in A.D. 132 by the reforms of Tso Hsiung, who established two types of examinations for recruiting officials, one in the classics and family law for Confucian scholars, and a written composition test for clerks. All candidates had to be a minimum of forty years of age (the age when Confucius said he was finally able to understand what the world was all about). The successful candidates were given posts as assistants to high officials to enable the latter to observe their performance.

Although Fan preferred the older system of the Former Han by which top officials selected candidates by reviewing their life histories and examining their merits, he conceded that during the decade of Tso's incumbency his reforms had been effective.[56] Tso's contemporaries like Chang Heng (ca. 126–45), however, did not fail to notice that written examinations were more likely to test one's skill with the pen than one's capacity for virtue, a complaint that was repeated frequently after the permanent adoption of the examination system in 606.[57]

Sui and T'ang: The Evils of the Examination System

The reunification of China under the Sui dynasty in the late sixth century marked the end of the Chung-cheng and *chiu-p'in* systems and the beginning of the examination system and the bureaucratization of appointment procedures.[58] Contemporary historians of China have usually seen the examination system of the Sui and T'ang dynasties as striking a serious blow at the old aristocracy because it allowed people from lower strata to move up the social ladder, and increased the power of the throne at the expense of the social elite.[59] Yu's Chinese sources did not explicitly attribute the weakening of the aristocracy to the examination system, but he might have drawn this conclusion anyway but for two important factors. The Chinese writers he studied were almost totally consumed with the flaws in the examination system rather than any benefits it might have conferred because they felt that it was as far removed from the ancient Chinese ideals of education and recruitment as the Chung-cheng system.

One of the main criticisms involved has already been mentioned, the misuse of the written word itself, which was supposed to remain a neutral instrument for conveying the moral truths of the sages. Instead, it had become the end rather than the means of education. The moralists constantly deplored the loss of moral understanding produced by excessive respect for skill in the formalistic use of language, the style of prose, or in the composition of tasteful and aesthetically pleasing poetry.

One writer of the Sui remarked that the desks of the scholars of the Southern dynasties were piled high with slips of paper devoted to lyrical meanderings on the moon, dewdrops, wind, and clouds.[60] Liu Yao acknowledged that the ancients used poetry to illustrate and enhance the emotions proper to loyalty and filial piety but criticized the exaltation of writing skill and style over moral behavior.

Liu Chih argued that in ancient times the purpose of poetry was to allow the people to communicate their feelings, even their ridicule, to their rulers, implying that grace of expression would soften the otherwise harsh and disrespectful edge of more direct prose. Now, unfortunately, style was everything, and as *The Book of History* made clear: "If you choose men on the basis of their words, they will represent themselves by their words; if you select them on the basis of their deeds, they will represent themselves on the basis of their deeds."[61]

Hsieh Ch'ien-kuan and others pointed to the total lack of utility in education.

Despite the use of policy questions in the examinations, the tests of knowledge and talent had become irrelevant to real affairs. Even military officials were selected more on their skill with the bow and arrow than on the basis of any practical ability to command men or devise strategy. Chao K'uang, a T'ang prefect, also said that "What people talk about and what they study is not what is of use. What is of use is not what is studied, and thus there are few men who can meet their responsibilities as officials."[62]

One of the most telling criticisms, however, was the charge that the examinations stressed the mastery of fact at the expense of understanding. For example, in 741 the authorities began to paste a slip of paper over a page from the classics, leaving only a single row or a few characters visible to the candidate, who had to recall the rest from memory. This ostensible improvement in objectivity, however, was attacked for encouraging rote memorization: "Those who were able to pass about a dozen of these sections knew all the difficult material in detail, but most people were as in the dark as someone facing a wall when it came to understanding the general meaning behind the regular texts."[63]

Chao K'uang thought the examination system was not merely a neutral device distorted by evil men, but an institution that even stimulated avarice, ambition, mendicant appeals for favors from high officials, and slander against fellow students because of the competitive atmosphere that had been created. "It is not that they are endowed with natures like this; it is the situation that causes them to be this way."[64] Yu Hyŏngwŏn, too, shared Chao's conviction that poor institutions were easily capable of destroying mores.

Liu Chih and Chao K'uang believed that the examination system had created a surplus of idle degree-holders waiting for appointments to fill too few posts, and that the cost of their upkeep had driven many into bankruptcy and imposed too heavy a burden in taxes and fees on the populace.[65] Liu blamed the draining of the countryside of scholars and the inundation of the capital by them on the Sui regime and regarded the old Chung-cheng officials with nostalgia.[66]

T'ang Proposals for Reform of Recruitment Procedures

Quotas. Several solutions were proposed to improve the examination system in the T'ang dynasty: quotas, decentralization of appointment powers, the revival of recommendation, or special recommendation examinations, and reform of the school system. Liu Hsiang-tao of the early seventh century proposed a quota limit of five hundred men a year for the examinations to reduce the plethora of aspirants who flocked to the examinations in the capital.[67] But Chao K'uang felt that the quota system would have a serious negative effect because incompetents would be selected just for the purpose of filling the quotas, and later on qualified men would be turned away because slots were already filled by incompetents. "Therefore scholars of no talent would reach the highest ranks while men of talent and ability would sit around and turn grey."[68]

Compromise: Recommendation Examinations. No sooner had the examination system been adopted in the T'ang period than its critics began to voice protests against it. During the reign of Emperor T'ai-tsung (r. 626–49) Ma Chou deplored the abandonment of the Han practice of judging candidates for magistrate on their skill in management because after the Ministry of Personnel had assumed responsibility for that, the quality and prestige of the magistrate had fallen.[69] In the mid-seventh century Wei Hsüan-t'ung attributed the problem to the monopoly of personnel review and recommendation by "the hands of only a few men" employed by the Ministries of Personnel and War, who were isolated in the capital from the realities of local affairs. Wei sought to reduce the responsibilities of the Ministry of Personnel and require all officials from the third to the ninth rank to recommend candidates for office.[70]

Wei also argued that not only had the examination system failed to eliminate the reliance on relationships with noble and aristocratic families and lineages (*munbŏl*) for gaining office and promotion, it had also functioned as a short-cut to regular posts for holders of honorary and irregular positions. Restoration of the Han recommendation system was the only way to obtain suitable magistrates with knowledge of ethical norms and ritual procedures.[71]

Emperor Kao-tsung did in fact ask his officials to recommend others for office, but his prime minister, Li An-chi, complained that higher officials were only recommending favorites to build their own factions (*p'eng-tang*), and many had chosen to remain silent rather than run the risk of criticism.[72] The idea was quickly abandoned, but later in the dynasty in the 790s Lu Chih argued that the only certain method to predict a man's reliability was to depend on village recommendation and recommendations by senior officials for their subordinates and provincial governors for their district magistrates. All superficial marks of character, such as "clever words, an insinuating appearance, and sycophancy" had to be discounted, and recommenders had to be held responsible for their word. His proposal, too, was not adopted.[73]

A third type of solution was a compromise between the examination and recommendation systems. Yang Kuan, an official in the Board of Rites during the reign of Emperor T'ai-tsung, proposed a recommendation examination to be called "the examination for filial and honest men." Candidates would be recommended from their native villages to the prefectural magistrates to stand for a special examination confined to knowledge of the classics and its practical policy applications. Students at the National Academy would also be recommended by their instructors and honored by participation in a wine ritual.[74] Emperor T'ai-tsung was sympathetic to Yang Kuan's idea, but he decided against it because the examination system had been in use too long to be changed.[75]

Sung Anti-Examination Sentiment

Yu cited two memorials of the great Sung reform minister, Wang An-shih, to Emperor Shen-tsung (r. 1068–86) in which Wang registered the same complaints about the adverse effects of the examination system made in the T'ang dynasty:

that fancy academic titles, degrees, and high offices were conferred on men who excelled at rote memorization, wide reading, and hack writing while the really talented died in poverty in the fields.[76] Wang ridiculed the reluctance of officials to abolish the examination system because it had been in use for so long, and he urged a return to the methods of the sages where selection of men for office originated in the local communities where education was based in local schools and local officials observed the virtue, behavior, and talent of worthy and able men recommended by the mass of the population and examined them on their knowledge and handling of affairs.[77]

Yu noted that Emperor Shen-tsung had responded to Wang by shifting the content of the examinations from literary skill to comprehension and understanding of the classics and abolished the practice of pasting paper over all but a few lines of a classic text. When the emperor personally examined *chin-shih* candidates in 1070, he also confined his questions to policy matters. Unfortunately, after Wang fell from power in 1086, "they restored the former system and examined people on the basis of *shih* and *fu* poetry."[78] Yu failed to mention, however, that Wang's plan to replace the examinations with government schools eventually failed because of Ssu-ma Kuang's opposition to his attempt to enforce conformity with his new commentaries on the classics in the school curriculum.[79]

Yu also found that Chu Hsi, the grand synthesizer of Neo-Confucian ideas in thirteenth-century Southern Sung, criticized the examination system in his own time because students paid little attention to the accumulated commentaries on the classics and simply devoted their time to memorizing only those passages that had consistently been used in past examinations. The official examiners were as much to blame because they rewarded the clever afficionados of literary legerdemain with high grades: "They want to see how skilled a person is in attaching and separating words and phrases. Once the officials in charge laud this, the examination students also adapt their studies to it and spend their whole time only trying to cut and paste phrases from the classics . . . to accord with what the examination officials want. . . ."[80] Chu praised Wang's abolition of poetical composition in the written examinations and pointed out that even the critics of Wang were less offended by this measure than by his attempt to dictate the proper interpretation of the classics.[81]

Ch'eng I, the illustrious eleventh-century Neo-Confucian predecessor of Chu Hsi, had also abhorred the examinations and the emphasis on rote memorization or skill in poetry and rhyme instead of moral knowledge. He even opposed the use of written tests in the schools because they were a poor means for judging people and stimulated personal ambition and competition.[82]

Yu was by no means thorough in his coverage of Northern Sung criticism of the examinations. He failed to mention the *Ch'ing-li* reforms of 1043–44 led by Fan Chung-yen, Han Ch'i, and Sung Ch'i, who objected to the impersonal nature of the Sung examinations such as covering the names of the candidates to eliminate favoritism because they preferred that the candidates be known and their moral character taken into consideration.[83] He also omitted mention of

Chang Tsai (1020–77), for example, but for very good reason: Chang praised hereditary principles in the selection of men and felt that the truly moral route to government was by the kin-based privilege of protection (*yin*).[84] He did, however, consider the remedies proposed for the examination system by the leading figures of the era, Wang An-shih, Chu Hsi, and Ch'eng I (see below).

Ming: Routine and Conformity in the Examinations

Yu noted, probably with regret, that Emperor T'ai-tsu of the Ming dynasty had made an abortive effort to abolish the examinations in the late fourteenth century, and that his favorite Ming writer, Ch'iu Chün, was also concerned about the way in which the original purpose of the examinations had been distorted over time.[85] Ch'iu believed that the examinations in the early Ming period were an improvement over previous dynasties because they tested candidates on the fundamental issues contained in the classics and had adopted the Yüan dynasty incorporation of Chu Hsi's commentaries on the *Four Books* as part of the required curriculum for the examinations – a policy that the Chosŏn dynasty had continued from its inception in 1392. Ch'iu thought that this stress on fundamentals left the scholar with plenty of time to study minor classics, the philosophers, and the histories.

Later on, however, examiners began to favor mastery of more obscure and arcane knowledge, and the authorities began to edit the classical texts and select phrases at random for the examinations to make things harder for the students – an obvious reference to the infamous eight-legged essay. Students had little time for questions on ancient institutions or policy matters, and examiners favored particular interpretations or commentaries to the exclusion of others. The result was to create a breed of student interested only in parroting acceptable opinions, an unfortunate tradition that soon became endemic and created a "narrow orthodoxy of mistaken beliefs."[86] While Ch'iu Chün's criticisms added nothing new to the repertoire of criticism, it added ammunition to Yu's arsenal of negative opinion that condemned the examination system as a failure in China almost since its inception.

Korea: Adverse Effects of the Examinations

From Putative Ancient Sagehood to Barbarism. Yu's discussion of the history of recruitment procedures in general in Korean history was confined to a brief, cursory addendum placed at the end of this section of his book. Part of the reason for his relative neglect was the paucity of sources on early Korean history, but a more important factor was Yu's identification with a universal, cosmopolitan Confucian culture transcending any narrow national identity, and an unashamed acknowledgment of the superiority of ancient China. His treatment of education and recruitment in Chinese history demonstrates that he was not a blind admirer of everything that had been done after the age of classical perfection was brought to an end with the Ch'in unification in 206 B.C. All subsequent dynasties only illustrated the fall from perfection, but some of them presented worthwhile attempts or proposals to recover the essence of classical institutions.

This interpretation might seem commonplace to students of premodern East Asian thought, but it takes on significance in light of recent attempts to portray the so-called Practical Learning (*sirhak*) group of seventeenth- and eighteenth-century scholars as protonationalists as well as protomodernizers. Close study of Yu's writings, however, reveals only that he was aware of the legitimate separateness and possible distinctiveness of native dynasties and customs. There is hardly a trace of national pride or any we/they nationalistic dichotomy in his thought that would produce any exaggeration of Korean accomplishments, experience, and wisdom at the expense of the universal values deriving from the Chinese, Confucian tradition. On the contrary, Yu's commitment to a transcendent, cosmopolitan culture engendered a sense of the inferiority of the Korean past and present; the past presented few models worthy of emulation, and the present in Korea represented a situation no better than the so-called later age (*huse*) of the Chinese dynastic period.

In tracing the history of recruitment in Korean history, Yu indicated clearly that there was not much worth talking about until the institution of the examination system in 958 under the Koryŏ dynasty. Although he mentioned the tale in the Chinese classic, the *Book of History*, about the culture hero, Kija (Ch'i-tzu in Chinese), a Chinese nobleman and sage adviser to the founder of the Chou dynasty who was supposedly granted a fiefdom over the state of Ancient Chosŏn (presumably on the Korean peninsula), he hardly did so with much conviction. He assumed that under his rule, "the selection of people and the appointment to office of worthy men was done by a method that was both simple and true," but he conceded that there was no evidence to substantiate it.[87]

His skepticism was not strong enough to produce a bold and unequivocal rejection of the epiphany of a sage visitor from China who brought with him a panoply of perfect institutions by which he raised the Korean peninsula to the lofty heights of the early Chou, during an era in Korean history that is now thought to mark only the bare beginnings of a shift from neolithic to bronze culture. Nonetheless, he did feel constrained to mention it since the main object of his search for models to emulate was in ancient China, not Korea. It should surprise no one, either, that he hardly deigned to mention Tan'gun, the putative progenitor of the "Korean people" first recorded by the monk, Iryŏn, in his *Samguk yusa* in the thirteenth century, belief in whose existence is taken by many contemporary Korean scholars to augur a commitment to the native tradition over Chinese culture represented by Kija.

Whatever the putative (and highly suspect) glories of Kija's rule at the end of the second millennium B.C., by the time of the Three Kingdoms period (traditional dates: from approximately the first century B.C. to A.D. 668) Korea had obviously regressed to a state hardly advanced from barbarism. "There was aggression and struggle, crudity and darkness, so that there is nothing worth talking about."[88] Yu thought it was an age dominated by warfare in which recruitment was based solely on military skill and merit in combat. It was not until the Silla dynasty during the reign of King Wŏnsŏng (r. 784–98) that a system of recruitment based on examination of knowledge of the written word (*toksŏ ch'ulsinjibŏp*) was adopted, but standards were fairly low, and only a rudimentary grasp of classical Chinese learning was required. "Anyone who could comprehend the Five Classics, Three Histories, Philosophers, and Hundred Schools was appointed to office."[89] Yu was referring to the examination established only in the Silla National Academy (T'aehak) in 788, and he concluded that it was not a major means for recruiting officials in the Silla period.

Save for his perfunctory reference to Kija, Yu was obviously ashamed by the low standards of civilization of his own people in its earliest recorded history and disdainful of the minor contributions made in the institutions of education and recruitment. It is astonishing how anyone could construe that Yu was pioneering a major rediscovery of Korean nationhood and nationality that would lead to the current exaltation of the Korean past that has exerted such powerful influence in both north and south Korea.

The Examination System in the Koryŏ Dynasty. Yu pointed out that it was not until the mid-tenth century during the Koryŏ period that Koreans adopted the examination system, but he did not extol this as an achievement of the Korean people themselves. On the contrary, it was only thanks to the advice and influence of Shuang Chi, the Chinese visitor from the Northern Chou dynasty, that King Kwangjong was inspired to push through the reform.

As we know now, it did not become an important means of recruitment until the fourteenth century, but it did contribute to the introduction of Confucian culture and supported King Kwangjong's attempt to create an institution for the royal recruitment of officials independent of inherited aristocratic status.[90] Although Yu did acknowledge that the examination system had the positive effect of raising the level of cultural accomplishment in Korea, he also condemned it for all the detrimental side effects described in the Chinese literature: excessive esteem for poetry, a preference for a frivolous and ornate writing style, and a stress on rote memorization.[91]

He noted the emergence of a brief flurry of reform at the end of the Koryŏ dynasty in the fourteenth century, but lamented its negligible consequences. He praised the proposal of Yi Chehyŏn and Pak Hyosu during the reign of King Ch'ungsuk (r. 1330–31, 1332–39), to abandon the requirement for composing *shih* and *fu* poems, and the suggestion of Yi Saek during the reign of King U (r. 1374–88) to restore the use of policy questions to the examinations, but neither of the two was adopted. Yu did admire, however, the action of the State Council in the reign of King Kongyang (r. 1389–92) for instituting regular examinations in the military arts to upgrade the quality of military officials.[92]

Yu described in rather perfunctory fashion the full institutionalization of the examination system in both civil and military specialties during his own Chosŏn dynasty, but his overall assessment of the system was negative, couched in the critical phraseology of the Sung writers.[93] Nowhere did he give credit to the examinations for weakening the exclusive power of inherited status by introducing standards of performance in passing impersonal examinations. On the contrary, he denigrated the examinations because they were the only route to office and had encouraged a mechanical approach to learning that substituted form for substance. Students learned only how to select relevant sections from the classics that would be useful in answering the examination questions, and they assembled them in composing their essays, "but with regard to the original meaning of the classics or histories, they are not concerned at all."[94]

The classics portion of the examinations was even worse because it placed a premium on memorization and induced students to devise mnemonic ditties to aid them in recollecting pertinent portions of texts. They, too, were "completely in the dark" when it came to understanding the greater meaning of the classics. Literary legerdemain was thus not an evil confined to the Sung dynasty alone, and the quality of the men obtained through the examinations, both civil and military was poor – not an unusual conclusion for a man who had himself decided to drop out of the examination rat race.[95]

Private Academies after the Sixteenth Century. Yu had also deplored the neglect and abandonment of the much of the system of official schools established early in the Chosŏn dynasty.[96] He blamed this development on the examination system because educated men had decided to turn to private elementary schools (*sŏdang*), private tutors, and private academies (*sŏwŏn*) for higher level education, not just to maintain high standards for the education of their sons, but also to prepare them for the civil service examinations that were so crucial to success in a bureaucratic career:

> Scholars with the will to learn had no choice but to build rude huts in separate, out-of-the-way places, which they used as places for study. This was the reason that the *sŏwŏn* arose. If what the state wants to teach is once restored to rectitude and the district schools [*ŭphak*] and local schools [*hyangsang*] are all repaired and restored, there will be no need for the private academies.[97]

Furthermore, the practice of establishing shrines to eminent scholars at the private academies had involved the academies in the political factionalism of the time. Originally shrines had been a good idea because they held local worthy scholars up to emulation, but in recent times the shrines had become ancestral shrines associated with specific families rather than meritorious individuals. "And when factional disputation became the custom, there were many cases where people competed to establish private academies as shrines to people who did not deserve them."[98]

The first of the private academies in Korea, the Paeg'undong *sŏwŏn*, created around 1542–43, was named after the one created by Chu Hsi and based on the regulations that Yu cited in his own work. They were designed to function as retreats to which scholars could assemble for study, discussion, and reflection, an attempt to escape from the demeaning effects of public service and politics to pursue the purer goal of moral self-cultivation. There were around a hundred of them by the mid-seventeenth century, and the biggest spurt in their growth occurred just about the time that Yu was writing his *Pan'gye surok*.[99] By Yu's time the ideal purposes of the private academies had already been sullied by partisanship, hereditary factionalism, and conversion of their purpose toward training for the examinations. He therefore concluded that the private academies were an evil consequence of the examination system, not an escape or solution to their distortion of the true purpose of education. For this reason he tended to see official schools as the solution to the examination system, not the private academies as some of the leading scholars of the Sung dynasty had. He thought this even though the official schools had failed of their purpose by the late fifteenth century.

By the mid-nineteenth century the private academies had been thoroughly politicized and became semiautonomous entities that challenged district magistrates and central authority. Although Yu's animosity toward the private academies appears less severe than the Taewongun's in the 1860s, by contributing to the critical literature on the academies, he may have laid the groundwork for the Taewongun's radical reduction of the academies in 1871.[100]

Abolition a Necessity

In searching for a solution to the evils produced by what he understood as an hereditary aristocracy Yu focused on the examination system as the key variable in both explaining and perpetuating its existence. This situation should not have been true because the inherited status of the yangban that was carried over from the Koryŏ dynasty should have been weakened considerably by the extension of the examination system in the early Chosŏn period.

For a time most Western historians of China believed that the examination system had succeeded in destroying aristocracy, but recently the prevalent view is that the examination system by itself did not eliminate hereditary aristocracy since it lasted at least three or possibly five hundred years after its adoption in the Sui in 606. In the T'ang dynasty the aristocracy did modify its behavior because its members began to participate in the civil service examinations, and by this adaptation succeeded in dominating the examinations rather than allowing the examinations to destroy it as a class.[101] In Korea as well, the adoption of the examination system had not eliminated the yangban any more than it had the aristocracy of the T'ang dynasty. Contrary to its purported intent, to create an objective and impersonal standard of recruitment irrespective of all commoners save Buddhist monks, slaves, merchants, artisans, and outcaste persons, the Korean yangban were able to circumvent the leveling proclivities of the examination system by educating their sons in preparation for the examinations.

Yu learned from his survey of the extensive critique of the examination system in Chinese history that a number of other adverse consequences had flowed from the domination of the system as the main method of recruiting officials. The most serious charge was the diversion of attention from the proper end of education – moral cultivation – to the means of education, skill in the use of words. This tendency had produced an excessive diversion into useless knowledge, poetic style, flights of rhetoric, and rote memorization, rather than useful knowledge, ethics and problems of statecraft, simple and serious writing style, and true understanding of Confucian moral principles.[102] The competitive atmosphere of the examinations had stimulated avarice and ambition, created a surplus of degree-holders and aspirants for degrees that wasted considerable human resources, and drained the countryside of scholars and potential moral leaders, are of whom flocked to the capital where the examinations were held.

Yu believed that the examination system in Korea had not only failed to inculcate proper Confucian moral standards among the men preparing for the examinations, but became one of the major tools used by the semihereditary yangban to perpetuate their own power. Consistent with his view that misguided institutions were responsible for human tragedies, he held that the failure of man (women were not central to his concept of the problem here) in living up to his inner moral capacity for goodness was not caused only by individual shortcomings, but by the examination system, which by its inherent evils had led men astray. "If we did not have the examination system," as he put it, "then even if you tried to whip people on a daily basis to force them to be frivolous and vain, you still could not make them be that way."[103] He concluded, therefore, that a plan to rectify it, or replace it with something else, was the method by which a proper elite could be obtained and true methods of education and recruitment achieved.

Reform in the Sung: Rediscovery of the Ancient Model

Utility: Wang An-shih and Chu Hsi

As we have seen above, Yu was interested in the proposals made by Chinese scholars and officials for replacing the examination system. In discussing the Sung period Yu chose to focus on the views of leading statesmen and philosophers rather than provide the kind of chronological description used for previous dynasties. Despite Wang An-shih's poor reputation in both Sung and post-Sung literature on statecraft and Yu's own objections to Wang's "green shoots" (*ch'ing-miao*) grain-loan policy, in many respects he found himself in agreement with Wang's analysis of education and recruitment, possibly because he was aware of Chu Hsi's praise for Wang's policies on education.[104]

He was undoubtedly happy to quote Wang's argument for the adoption of recommendation procedures, an improved school system, and instruction in knowledge of greater utility. Wang had praised the practice of ancient rulers in selecting only the best men to be high ministers, and then delegating responsibility to them to recommend others to staff subordinate posts, and he complained that the chief ministers of his own time were all worthless men who only recommended others of their own kind. Punishing them for faulty recommendation had proved worthless in rectifying this situation.[105]

He charged that the Sung government had neglected the prefectural and district schools and the matter of instruction in truly important subjects like rites, music, and penal law, instead of the current trend in favor of the useless explication of texts and writing style necessary for passing the examinations.[106] His definition of talent, for example, stressed expertise in civil and military affairs, and he praised the ancient kings for selecting students knowledgeable in civil and military affairs for the highest posts. By contrast, current officials had no use for these practical subjects and when on duty on the frontier or in the capital turned over responsibility to their subordinates.[107]

Wang's practicality was also reflected in his utilitarian interpretation of the purpose of archery contests in ancient times despite the traditional association of archery with the conduct of ritual and the inculcation of moral values. He wrote that when the *Book of Changes* (*I Ching*) said that "By means of skill in the bow and arrow they overawed the empire," it meant that archery was essential to the military strength of the state. Everyone practiced bowmanship at home during peacetime and used it to practice rites and music, but when they went out on military campaigns or served on border defense or the capital guards, they used it for fighting. "Since . . . the ancient rulers gave out weapons and entrusted them to people, there was nothing to be feared either domestically or in foreign affairs."[108]

Wang thus turned the usual version of the Chou model on its head: the conduct of rites was an adjunct to practice in archery, not the other way around. By extension, the strength and security of the state might well take precedence over the moral cultivation of the individual. Yet he did not separate value from fact, he merely subordinated it in some cases. As Hoyt Tillman put it, both Wang and Chu Hsi represented one of Benjamin Schwartz's polarities in Confucian thought, between the utilitarian achievement of results versus the perfection of moral character.[109]

Chu Hsi dwelled on the idea of utility more than other Sung moralists,[110] but his concept of utility contained more of a moral quotient than Wang An-shih's:

> In what was taught during the three dynasties of antiquity [*san-tai*], the arts were the very last things to be taught. Nevertheless, in everything [taught] there was practical utility [*shih-yung*]. . . . What is taught at present is not based on the actual substance [*shih*, *sil* in Korean] of moral behavior, and what is referred to as the arts are also all empty words of no utility. . . .[111]

Notice that Chu Hsi's use of the term *sil* (the *sir* of Sirhak) meant "the actual substance of moral behavior," and not the value-free practicality or utility referred to by so many twentieth-century Korean scholars. In any case, the notion of the utility of knowledge, particularly in contrast to the development of literary skill and style to no tangible purpose, exerted an influence on Yu's thought.

Ch'eng I: The Special Status of Students

While Yu's serious consideration of Wang An-shih's emphasis on practicality and utility illustrated Yu's relative openness to a variety of alternatives to the examinations, his heart was really with the Chu Hsi and the moralist wing of Chinese statecraft. He admired Ch'eng I of the eleventh century, who felt that what was needed was a return to the ancient method of personal evaluation by direct observation of the behavior and accomplishments of students, a task best left to the school headmasters and their assistants.[112]

Ch'eng I also believed that enrollment in school was the only proper means for distinguishing the class of scholars (*shih*) from the common peasantry. He extolled the practice of the ancients who sent their sons at the age of eight *sui* to grammar school (*hsiao-hsüeh*) and at the age of fifteen *sui* to the adult schools (*ta-hsüeh*). Those who failed their studies were sent back to work in the fields as peasants, and the students worked exclusively on their studies until the age of forty with the support of the state, maintaining the strict division between scholars and farmers in society.

"If someone were in school, the [the school or the state] provided for his upkeep, and if he were the son of a *shih-ta-fu* [official, *sadaebu* in Korean], then he had no fear that he would be without support. Even in the case of a son of a commoner, once he entered school, he also had to be supported."[113]

State support among the ancients was designed to guarantee economic independence for students so that they might establish the proper moral goals, but in the later age, students, encouraged to "pursue profit," often abandoned themselves to dissolute behavior. The attempt of the authorities to curtail those habits by using laws and punishments failed miserably.[114]

Echoing the complaints of the critics of the T'ang, Ch'eng I also objected to the concentration of examination candidates in the capital, who "abandoned the care of their parents and forgot the love of their flesh and blood." It was far preferable to keep them in their home villages where they could fulfill their filial duties by reducing the quotas of students at the National Academy and increasing the quotas in the prefectural and district schools. He also proposed granting outward signs of privilege and respect for outstanding scholars by establishing Halls for Respecting the Worthy and guest quarters for visiting scholars in schools.[115]

Ch'eng Hao's Plan for Schools and Recommendation

The views of Ch'eng I's brother, Ch'eng Hao, however, exerted even greater influence over Yu. Yu noted Ch'eng Hao's concern about the absence of humility and a sense of shame on the part of village scholars, the poor condition of the schools, the absence of respect for teachers, the paucity of men of talent in the state bureaucracy, and the failure of punishment and coercion to achieve moral rectification. He praised the ancient model of moral education and recruitment by recommendation, a method that was attempted in the Sung but failed because recommendation "was not based on the opinions of people in the villages."[116]

Yu admired Ch'eng Hao's *li-ming* or "courtesy appointment" plan and proposed that it be adopted for Korea. According to Ch'eng Hao's proposal, the emperor would request that his close retainers, worthy Confucian scholars throughout the country, provincial governors, and district magistrates, recommend "people who have a clear understanding of the ways of the ancient kings, are fully virtuous, and are qualified to be teachers and models for others." Once recommended, these men would be invited to court and afforded courteous treatment, provided with adequate salaries and housed in a special institute for the recruiting and training of the governing class, called the Hall for Inviting the Brave (Yen-ying-yüan).

These assembled recommended scholars would then convene on a daily basis for study and mutual reflection on "the principles of things" (*wu-li*, *mulli* in Korean) and the cultivation of such specific Confucian topics as filial piety, brotherly respect, loyalty, trust, rites, and music. The worthiest would be recommended for high official posts, the best scholars for instructors in the National Academy, and the next best for instructors in the local schools throughout the empire. All teachers would be given adequate salaries and exempted from personal labor service, but if any were found to violate Confucian norms, they would be expelled from their posts and enrolled for military service.[117]

The Chou system of village or community schools would be resurrected along with the National Academy and district schools. As in the Chou, district magistrates would show their respect for the local schools, teachers, and students by conducting the local wine-drinking rite every year and by inviting the local elders to the proceedings. The students in the local schools would then convene and recommend the most learned and virtuous scholars to be appointed to office or promoted to prefectural level schools.

Any student found deficient in his studies or behavior would be subject to dismissal, and the school instructors and officials would also be held responsible and punished. Students deemed eligible for promotion to higher level schools would be exempted, along with their families, from labor service. At the highest level, the National Academy, the worthy and able students would be recommended to the court for office. Such recommendees would be dubbed selected scholars (*hsüan-shih*, *sŏnsa* in Korean), a term used in the Wang-chih section of the *Book of Rites*, and then examined on their knowledge of the classics and their capabilities for performing administrative tasks.[118]

Students at all schools would be expected to remain in attendance for three years before being eligible for promotion from the lowest school, or one year from higher schools, with exceptions for outstanding students. Consistent with the ancient model, the goals of education and criteria of evaluation stressed the combination of knowledge and behavior: "In general the method of selecting scholars requires that all of them be straight and pure in their natures and actions, that at home they be filial and respectful of their elder brothers, have a sense of honesty, shame, and propriety, and are obedient; that they have a comprehensive knowledge of scholarly matters and are fully accomplished in the way of governance."[119]

Chu Hsi: Respect for Age

Yu Hyŏngwŏn included as part of his survey of Chu Hsi's views the texts of three documents Chu drew up for the purpose of encouraging education and moral cultivation. The first was Chu's "Posted Instructions for the White Deer Academy" (*Pai-lu t'ung shu-yüan chieh-shih*), a rather brief text that listed the five basic principles governing the five moral relationships in society and exhorted students to be loyal, control anger, repress desire, keep to their righteous duty, and eschew profit and reputation. The text ended with a restatement of the golden rule and the assertion that in ancient times the cultivation of righteousness and principle was the purpose of education.[120]

The second document was Chu Hsi's "Posted Instructions for Chang-chou" (*Chu Hsi Chang-chou pang-yü*), a set of *pao-chia* mutual responsibility group regulations governing the proper behavior of villagers on a host of everyday matters, in particular filiality and respect for elders and superiors.[121] The third document was Chu's "Emendations on the Community Compact of Mr. Lü" (*Chu Hsi tseng-sun Lü-shih hsiang-yüeh*), which stressed mutual aid and responsibility in inculcating proper moral standards in the village.[122]

What was of particular interest to Yu in these texts were those regulations that concerned the proper behavior due to elders. Chu defined six categories of age groups: the *tsun* or respected elder, defined as an individual twenty or more years older than ego; the *chang* or elder, between ten and twenty years older than ego; the *ti* or equal, less than ten years younger or older than ego; the *hsiao* or younger, between ten and twenty years younger than ego; and the *yu* or very young, more than twenty years younger than ego. The etiquette due from ego to another person in each of these categories differed with respect to paying courtesy calls on special holidays, ordinary courtesy calls, visits during travel, chance meetings on the street, making requests, welcoming people or sending them off, informal gatherings and banquets, weddings, condolence calls, and seating arrangements in village meetings or convocations. One's behavior on any occasion was to be governed by his own position in the age hierarchy relative to his guest.

The specific regulations were quite detailed, but a couple of examples will suffice to illustrate Chu's insistence on governing social relations according to hierarchical principles of respect or deference:

> If you [younger person] happen to meet a *tsun* or *chang* elder on the street and if both parties are walking, then you rush forward and bow. If the elder speaks to you, you reply. If not, you stand by the side of the road and wait until

> he has passed by and then bow and go on your way. If both parties are on horses, then if [the other party] is a *tsun* elder, you get out of his way. If a *chang* elder, you stand by your horse by the side of the road, bow, and wait for him to pass, then bow, and proceed on your way. If you are walking and the *tsun* or *chang* elder is riding a horse, then you get out of his way.[123]

In similar fashion the seating arrangements and etiquette required at village assemblies were treated with great importance. Places of honor were to be reserved for royal or imperial relatives, men with official rank, and finally men of advanced age. Regulations for the offering of wine, genuflecting, and kowtowing were equally precise and also governed by official status or age.[124]

The respect hierarchy that Chu described was by no means confined only to the single criterion of age because he included imperial relatives and men with official rank at the top of his list. Since moral worth was hardly a necessary requisite for members of the imperial family or holders of high office, Chu was obviously making his accommodation with the reality of the Sung social system.

Although Chu Hsi's emphasis on age categories as a basis for respect appear commonplace, in the context of Yu's thought, however, they take on special significance as a principle of social organization because age criteria or status posed a direct challenge to the existing Korean principle of hereditary and ascriptive social rank. This might appear strange to those who think of seventeenth-century Korea as the epitome of the Confucian social system, but from Yu's point of view contemporary Korea was a far cry from the Confucian ideal in social relations.

In summary, the Sung writers provided a number of ideas essential to Yu's own plan for the reform of the educational and recruitment systems of Chosŏn Korea. The most fundamental included the continuation of the attack on the examination system and the idea of replacing it with a system of official schools. This was accompanied by an assertion of the importance of utility in the education of youths and the selection of officials, practical utility in the case of Wang Anshih, and moral utility in the case of Chu Hsi and the Ch'eng brothers. Wang and Ch'eng Hao provided concrete plans for the establishment of official schools, but Ch'eng Hao's plan, though never adopted, had the endorsement of Chu Hsi, and provided the basis for Yu's own proposal. Finally, Chu Hsi's emphasis on the importance of age as a criterion for respect, and Ch'eng I's notion of the school as a community for scholars separate from the common herd for the training of a moral elite, both played important roles in Yu's plans for reform.

Yu's Adoption of the Sung Reform Formula

Recommendation over Examination

At the end of his essay, Yu concluded that the governments of ancient China had provided adequate economic support for students and scholars by regulating the land distribution system and maintaining low rates of taxation on scholars. It had also established schools for instruction in "rites and righteousness" (i.e., the proper moral principles), and used the local villages as the starting point for the recruiting of able men for office. The result was that all the worthwhile men in the country were chosen for office, and proper (as opposed to false or empty) customs were maintained throughout society.

During the Sui and T'ang dynasties, however, literary talent was favored over mastery of correct moral principles, and the wrong men were selected for office while the good men were "destroyed and abandoned." Since government was thus left in a state of confusion, and immoral and amoral men dominated government posts, China was overrun by barbarians.[125]

His survey of historical literature had revealed that the ancient system of education and recruitment had been undermined by several notable developments after the decline and fall of the Chou dynasty: the replacement of feudalism by central bureaucracy and the debilities of impersonal and routinized action by bureaucrats; the loss of the local village as the beginning point of personal observation and recommendation, the decline of the official school system, the development of hereditary aristocracy and the preference for pedigree and inherited status as the basis for recruitment, and the adoption of the examination system from the Sui dynasty on with its adverse effects on the content and purpose of study.

In a way Korea in the seventeenth century resembled aspects of the early T'ang dynasty when aristocratic families adapted to the new requirement that they pass examinations to hold high office. The yangban of Chosŏn had done virtually the same thing. Yu concluded, therefore, that two institutional reforms were absolutely necessary for Korea: eliminating hereditary aristocracy and abolishing the examination system. He hoped that these reforms would result in redirecting the ruling class (and some commoners as well) toward a truly moral education.

Following the lead of his Sung mentors, Yu expressed his admiration for the recommendation system because it presupposed public or mass participation (*chunggong*) in the evaluation of individuals, particularly at the village level, inhibiting the ability of aspirants to office to pursue their private ambitions. In ancient times recommendors were held responsible for assessing the true facts (*sil*) of the recommendees' behavior and accomplishments, while the examination system tested only falsities (*wi*) or the artificial and superficial aspects of human quality as expressed by literary accomplishment.

Because recommendors were held responsible for their recommendations and made liable to punishment for the misdeeds of their protégés, they had to be cautious before recommending anyone. Following the *Rites of Chou*, Yu asserted that punishment of recommendors for faulty judgment and dismissal of bad recommendees for vainglorious pursuit of private interest in office was a proper use of guilt and shame as a deterrent to future wrongdoing – "a system where by punishing one you give warning to a hundred people."[126]

Under the recommendation system things were "clear and bright," that is, the behavior of individual recommendees were exposed to public view and the selection procedures were open to all. The examinations, on the other hand, were "dark and secret" because the names of the examination candidates were obscured from the view of the examiners to maintain objectivity in grading. Furthermore, while the recommendation system was based on long-term evaluation of individual behavior both in the village and on the job as an official, the examination system reduced evaluation to the grading of tests. Examiners, as opposed to recommendors, did not have to know the people they were evaluating and the candidates only had to pass the tests; they had no need or intention of cultivating themselves.

Just as the examination system was responsible for stimulating private interest, so did the recommendation system permit the fulfillment of the public good because the mode of its operation could have no other consequence: "The system of recommendation is based on consulting the open and public opinion [*kong-gong-ji-ron*] of the local community and investigating the true facts of the daily good and bad deeds of the people. Recommendations are made openly in the light of day when everyone is assembled. . . ."[127]

Yu believed that in ancient China the main goal of the sage rulers had been the moral training of the populace by means of education; the recruitment of officials was but an adjunct to this, made easier because of the success achieved in the moral transformation of society. In later times, however, the examination system placed priority on skills necessary to the recruitment process instead of fundamental moral training, and as a result success was not achieved on either count. Yu argued that in ancient times the sages began education in both self-rectification and the governance of others (*sugi ch'iin-ji-do*) by instructing children in how to clean and sweep their rooms, entertain guests, show filial respect for their parents and elders, be loyal and true, treat friends cordially, and observe rites and music. In the education of the individual there was a proper order and sequence, the essence of which was "to begin with the cultivation of the individual self and then proceed to the transformation of the world" (from the *Great Learning*). The dogma that every person had the capacity to become a sage was based on the presupposition that all men would receive continuous moral training throughout their lives. "It is not what we speak of in recent times when we talk about skill in composition and poetry, passing the examinations, or gaining the benefit of an official's salary."[128]

Yu also believed that the administration of written examinations could easily become desultory. He objected to the routine and peremptory way the two types of special examinations called the *chŏngsi* and *alsŏng* presided over by the Korean king in person were conducted. One might presume that Yu would have admired the king's concern over the selection of able men for office, but instead he remarked that "In the *chŏngsi* and *alsŏng* examinations the king also orders the presiding official to light the candles and set a time limit for the examination. What they are examined on is no more than a matching test, and in the twinkling of an eye they decide who is to be chosen and who abandoned. That's the reason for the aphorism that even a blind man could pass the *chŏngsi* and *alsŏng* examinations."

If the king really wanted to oversee the learning process personally, what he should do is summon scholars to his court, have them recite from the classics and discuss scholarly questions, ask them about the way to govern, and use this as the means to make appointments. "He ought not to lead men into vain, frivolous, and shameless customs." On like grounds Yu also opposed holding special examinations in commemoration of felicitous events because it had nothing to do with the serious business of recruiting the best men. It was hardly better than the custom of pardoning criminals on such occasions.[129]

Yu was also unwilling to adopt the Han dynasty compromise with the ancient model of recommendation – the use of written essays on policy matters (*ch'aek*) as a means of recruitment. Yu argued that the Han practice of asking the "worthy and good" (*ch'aek hyŏllyang*) to write essays on policy was designed to solicit opinions on policy rather than examine men for posts, but it was still wrong because the practice had led to the evil of written examinations, which was sufficient reason for not adopting it. Although he conceded that writing skill might be a legitimate way to evaluate a person's scholarship, he also argued that emphasis on writing induced people to cultivate "what is external to oneself," that is, outer embellishments rather than the essence of the self. It also induced students to copy previously successful writing styles and examination essays rather than develop their own skills.

> If the court truly wants to investigate whether people are worthy or not, then for a period of several years it should look into their behavior, hear what they have to say, ask them questions and listen to their answers, [as the means by which the court] will find out everything about them. Why is it necessary to line them up in a courtyard, receive their written papers, and test them on the basis of one day's writing, after which an examination [of their merits] is made?[130]

Not even the famous special recommendation examination (*hyŏllyang-kwa*) of Cho Kwangjo and his supporters in 1518, a plan designed to adapt the recommendation system to the examination system without abolishing the latter and reminiscent of Yang Kuan's proposal in the mid-eighth century T'ang dynasty, qualified for Yu's praise.[131] Although he agreed that Cho and his literati colleagues who suffered the *kimyo* purge of 1519 had no other alternative but the recommendation examination as the optimum solution for their own time, even one of Cho's contemporaries, Yu Cho (pen name, Sŏbong), had critized the shoddy nature of this unnatural union. Yu Hyŏngwŏn argued that Cho's reform violated the Confucian principle of the rectification of names, for to retain the examination system and hope to improve it by calling it a recommendation system was doomed to failure. "Name and fact must be mutually supportive of each other, for throughout the world there has never been a case where you could borrow the name of something else and in the end be able to accomplish anything."[132]

Had Yu also had access to Edward Wagner's study of the recommendation examination by some type of time-warp commmunication, his skepticism might have been rewarded, but on a completely different basis, for Wagner asserted that "even if such was not its purpose, this examination was used to bulwark the political position of those who brought it into being."[133] Yu, however, was disturbed more by the logical contradiction involved in joining a flawed system to a perfect one than by the actual corruption of the 1518 recommendation examination by political motives.

Yu also cited a plan proposed by Yulgok to recommend scholars for enrollment in the National Academy and other schools and for recruitment as educational officials. Yulgok proposed that the recommendees come from the existing classics and literary degree-holders (*chinsa* and *saengwŏn*) and also from the *yuhak*, that amorphous group of unregistered students (and military service tax evaders?) so often discussed and condemned in the debates over the household cloth tax. Even though he did not criticize Yulgok's proposal directly, possibly because he held him in such high esteem, he could not have been enamored of the idea because it did not call for abolition of the examination system itself.[134]

Yu acknowledged that some of his contemporaries had argued that the examinations were needed to train men in the use of classical Chinese for diplomatic correspondence with Chinese officials, but he rejected this argument on the grounds that the main concern of the government should be with the facts of a situation and action to be taken rather than with words or the style of communication. Furthermore, the problem in recent times was not that Korean use of classical Chinese was insufficient to communicate ideas properly, but that literary style had become excessively ornate. On the other hand, examination candidates had butchered classical Chinese in their writing because of pressure to memorize canonical passages for the examinations. They made up colloquial expressions or lewd and humorous phrases as mnemonic devices, or cut up classical texts to form matching or parallel phrases, stripping the original text of all meaning. What was needed was a return to a straightforward style of expression in which meaning and substance took precedence over form and style. Abolition of the examination system, far from creating abysmal ignorance, would on the contrary resurrect a style of writing that would serve as the proper medium for the expression of moral ideas as well as diplomatic correspondence.[135]

In fine, Yu insisted that he could not countenance anything less than the total abolition of the examination system and its replacement with the ancient recommendation model, but, as we will see, in drawing up regulations for his plan for a new official school system he did include the use of written tests in provincial schools.[136] The superiority of the recommendation system hardly needed justification; the main problem was convincing the ruler of the state to adopt it.

Nevertheless, Yu felt that kings in his own time were desultory in recruiting men for office partially because of the routinized and perfunctory way that the rationalized, bureaucratic state was conducted. His orientation toward reform in this instance should be regarded as antirational and antibureaucratic because of his insistence on personalism and subjectivism as the proper means to the evaluation of moral behavior.[137]

Respect for Educational Officials, Teachers, Students

The essence of Yu's plan to replace the examination system was to reinstitute official schools throughout the country to educate men to better appreciation of moral wisdom and the cultivation of truly moral behavior, and then using the recommendation of superior moral individuals to promote students through the school system and eventually to select the best of them for office in the central government. If the Chosŏn school system were to become the basis for both education and recruitment, it was necessary first to improve the quality of educational officials and teachers. Yu complained that the current educational officials had long been held in low esteem because they were the products of the examination system. The so-called instructors (Kyosu) were only supernumeraries, and the post of local educational official (Hundo) was the most despised of all.

Yu pointed out that in the late sixteenth century Yulgok, in his famous "Questions and Answers at the Eastern Lake" (*Tongho mundap*), had stated that the Hundo had been reduced to such straitened circumstances that the only way they could escape starvation was by extracting fees from the students. The quality of the Hundo had to be improved by recommendation and their prestige elevated as well. Yulgok had also remarked that if a provincial governor or even a minister of the first rank happened to visit a local school, the Hundo should not rush out to greet him in obsequious fashion but remain inside the gate. The current practice of inspection by which the provincial governor examined the Hundo along with the students when he visited schools during the spring and fall also had to be eliminated because it was too degrading. The only way a teacher should be evaluated was by observation and examination of his students to see whether they had been properly educated and if they displayed the proper deportment. The governor would then recommend the best teachers for promotion and punish or dismiss the worst. The most unqualified teachers had to be eliminated as well, "those who as in former times are covetous of property, base and boorish, lacking in proper deportment, and given to drinking and fooling around with women."[138]

Yu's plan to upgrade the quality, status, and treatment of educational officials and teachers was also inspired by the views of two Chinese writers, Yü Chi of the Yüan dynasty, and his favorite, Ch'iu Chün of the Ming, both of whom complained that local teachers in their own time were of such low caliber that they had to be replaced by a state-supported search for outstanding scholars. Ch'iu urged the court to select these officials with due caution and force the population to treat them with the courtesy they deserved or suffer punishment as a consequence![139]

Yu proposed adopting Ch'eng Hao's "courtesy appointment" (*yemyŏng*) plan for recruiting eminent scholars directly into government service, one that Yulgok had also admired. Such scholars were to function in two ways: giving advice to the king and his court or functioning as teachers in government schools. He suggested that provincial governors and district magistrates be required to recommend men in their jurisdiction "who are knowledgeable in the ways of the early kings, are full of virtue, and who can act as teachers and exemplars" to be given special appointments as enlightened selected scholars (*t'ungmyŏng ch'ŏnsa*) holding ranks one-to-three on the official scale of nine. If an eminent scholar happened to hold a low rank, it was not to stand in the way of his promotion. The selected scholars would be given extremely courteous treatment wherever they traveled and when they arrived at court, they would be housed in separate quarters near the royal palace.[140]

In conformity with the ancient model the selected scholars would first be observed for a time in order to evaluate their wisdom. The king would invite them to give advice on policy matters or lectures on scholarly questions, and they would take turns attending the regular Royal Lectures and answer the king's questions on the classical text under discussion for the day. The best of them would then be appointed as teachers in the National Academy (T'aehak); the next most qualified would serve as teachers in capital, provincial, and district schools.[141]

Yu also designed similar recruitment procedures to improve the quality of prefectural and district educational officials (*kyogwan*). Local students and scholars would recommend men for this position to the provincial governor with a cover letter from the district magistrate. The only criterion for recommendation was virtuous behavior, not current status as a former official or Confucian scholar.[142]

To improve the status of official schools in general Yu also found it important to require by law that local magistrates express respect for students in the schools formally and openly. Officials on business from the capital, the governor and his assistant (Tosa), and the secret censors (Ŏsa) would all be required to pay respects to the Confucian shrine and exchange bows with the students whenever they visited the school. Provincial governors would have to visit all schools twice a year in spring and autumn. If from laziness or lack of concern they summoned the students to their own quarters instead, they would be subject to severe punishment. On the occasion of these required school visits the governor would meet with the educational officials, headmaster, and teachers, perform rites at the Confucian shrine, and conduct an examination of the students' knowledge of selected texts. Although not required by law, the governor and his assistant would also be encouraged to visit schools when off duty to lecture the students and encourage them in their work.[143]

Yu went into great detail in specifying etiquette to be used between students, officials, and guests to make sure that the proper respect hierarchy be maintained. The provincial governor and his assistant would be required to bow in response to the kowtow of the assembled students, but the headmaster and assistant headmaster would be excused from doing so, explicitly elevating them in status over the noneducational bureaucrats even though they were lower in rank. He took great care to explain the reason for this, because ostensibly it violated an ancient ritual principle of strict observation of rank:

> Basically because we are clarifying the Way and nurturing worthy men, for that reason the ritual by which we treat scholars is not done with regard to official rank or position, but superior consideration is given to the obligation of laying stress on the true Way. The reason why the educational official does not bow in reply is so that we may dignify the teacher, and the reason we dignify the teacher is in order to show respect for the true Way.[144]

This provision reflected Yu's desire to make the schools into a separate community with a hierarchy that was based on prestige and status, except that the single criterion for that status would be moral worth rather than official rank or inherited status. Yet, as we shall see in chapter 5, the principle created embarrassing conflicts with contemporary values that Yu had to resolve.

Lest this regulation be construed as indicating contempt for constituted political authority, he enjoined the educational officials of the schools from treating the local magistrates with any rudeness or disrespect.[145] He was obviously as concerned with limiting the arrogance of local yangban for district magistrates as for reversing the state's neglect of its official school system.

As part of his insistence not only on increasing the prestige of the schools and their staffs, but also of preserving the institutional autonomy of schools within the centralized bureaucratic structure, Yu expressed opposition to the king's interference in the educational and testing process. In addition to his criticism of the perfunctory way that kings conducted the special palace *chŏngsi* and *alsŏng* examinations, he insisted that the king demonstrate more respect for scholars by visiting the National Academy and "draw close to him the scholars who have knowledge and have them recite and discuss the classics and scholarship; he should ask them about the way of governance and use that as a basis for making appointments and selections."[146]

Yu noted that in ancient times when lists of recommended worthy and able men were presented to the king, "the king would kowtow twice in accepting them," tacitly hinting that the present king should do likewise. Realizing that this suggestion might subject him to charges of lese majesty, he appended a footnote stating that he would not dare, in fact, to suggest that his own king should kowtow twice; he only hoped that the king might reflect on the wisdom of the idea.[147]

In short, Yu's attitude about the role of schools in a system of centralized, bureaucratic monarchy was ambivalent. Because he deplored the decrepit condition of the state's educational system, particularly its official schools, he drew up a plan to create a system of schools sponsored and supported by the central government, but at the same time he envisioned that his new schools would be semiautonomous institutions run by scholars and morally superior men whose serious work of education and moral transformation could not be subordinated to political authority. He wanted to use the state to support Confucian education without having to acknowledge dependence on the state or king.

On the other hand, he was not happy with the private control over education by the yangban in his own time, and he probably hoped that a system of official schools would help break the power of the hereditary elite. To break yangban control over education with the aid of the state and still expect state schools to preserve school autonomy presented a formidable, if not impossible, task for the time. The control of education ultimately reflected the relative power of the central government and the yangban, and since the yangban elite had become so powerful by the seventeenth century, it was not surprising that the official school system had atrophied, and institutionalized education had gravitated to the private academies (*sŏwŏn*) and elementary schools (*sŏdang*).

Creation of an Official School System

In his "Proposals for Schools" (*Hakkyo samok*) Yu set out the details for a totally reconstituted school system extending from a new National Academy in the capital down to district schools at the township level to meet the needs of students older than fourteen *se* (12–13 years). His plans for the establishment of this system displayed his ambivalence toward the role of the state and the use of its coercive power on the one hand and local scholar-gentry initiative, spontaneity, and participation on the other. At the outset he wished the national government to establish schools based on ancient models. The capital would be the locus of a three-tiered system: the National Academy (T'aehak) which would house the selected scholars (*sŏnsa*), the Middle School (Chunghak) which would accept students promoted from the Four Schools (Sahak); and the Four Schools themselves, located at each of the four points of the compass in the capital.

This system was based on the description of the ancient school system in the *Book of Rites of Elder Tai* (*Ta-tai Li-chih*) and the T'ang system of a National Academy (T'ai-hsüeh) and Schools of the Four Gates (Ssu-men-hsüeh). Each of the Four Schools would be divided into an Inner House (Naesa) for the regular quota students (*aengnaesaeng*) and an Outer House (Oesa) for the extra-quota students (*chŭnggwangsaeng*, or *aeg'oesaeng* in the current terminology).[148]

At the provincial level the governors would establish Governors' Schools (Yŏnghak) at the provincial capitals to house students promoted from the prefectural (*chu*) and district (*hyŏn*) schools. The prefectures and districts would also have District Schools (*ŭphak*), divided into Inner and Outer Houses for regular and extra-quota students.[149]

The new system would also consolidate the Confucian shrines with the schools by locating them only in the National Academy and the Governors' Schools. The district schools would only be allowed a lesser Shrine to the Sages (Sŏngmyo), an obvious attempt to take the powerful symbols of spiritual authority away from both the private academies and the state and put them in the hands of his presumed bona fide and independent scholars operating under state control and auspices.[150] This formula was based obviously on the apparently paradoxical proposition that true scholars could have more independence operating inside a state school system than in the private academies, but Yu was obviously more worried about the pressures for conformity in academies controlled by specific political and scholarly factions.

Yu's regulations also called for the establishment of a special Peer's School (Chonghak) that would accommodate male relatives of the royal clan (*chongch'in*) who had undergone the capping ceremony initiating them into adulthood. Regulations for etiquette and ritual conduct at the Peer's School required that the students would have to demonstrate respect for school officials at all times and conform to standard rules for education and testing despite the superiority of their status as members of the royal clan.[151]

The headmasters and assistant headmasters of the schools were to be given high rank to reinforce their status, an obvious concession to the prestige attached to official rank in the real world rather than scholarly merit and ethical behavior without such formal trappings of recognition. School officials were to be selected from able scholars and teachers and function as full-time educators, rather than as concurrencies held by regular functionaries. Educational officials in the prefectures and districts were to take their families with them and be kept on duty for the full term of their office, suggesting that the current practice fell far short of this ideal.[152]

Following the recommendation of Ch'eng I of the Sung, Yu also proposed establishing a Hall for Respected and Worthy Scholars (Chŏnhyŏndang) in the National Academy, and he adopted the precedent established by Chu Hsi when he was a district magistrate for introducing the position of Visiting Scholar (Hakpin) for lower level schools.[153] He also provided full funding for the salaries of school officials, teachers, petty functionaries, and slaves, and for the expenses of the schools, and the food and upkeep of the students. Even the extra-quota students were to be provided support from official funds derived either from special school land (*hakchŏn*) or from the regular tax revenues (*kyŏngbi*) of the district magistrate. The purpose was not only to support the schools but to prevent magistrates from taking over school funds for themselves.

He hoped also to put an end to the practice of well-to-do families donating land and slaves to schools in return for obtaining student status for their sons without passing the school qualification examinations so that they could gain exemption from labor and military service taxes. He sought to do this by setting quotas of school slaves (*pogye*) and providing them with legal exemptions from taxes and military service, a temporary measure that could be eliminated once his national land system was adopted. In addition, the duties of the school slaves were to be limited to service for the school to prevent them from being exploited for private purposes by students.[154] The significance of his treatment of slaves will be discussed in more detail in chapters 5 and 6.

In summary, Yu's plan called for the establishment of a government school system extending down to the level of the district (*hyŏn*). By providing state sponsorship and supervision and budgeting all costs against state revenues or income from school land, he hoped to insure the honesty of teachers and prevent the corruption of the system by private interest. He did not, however, envision the immediate establishment by the state of schools below the district level, the smallest area under the jurisdiction of a centrally appointed magistrate. "After the [public] schools are flourishing, we will gradualy establish local *sang* and *sŏ* schools and Ward Schools [*pangsang*] in the capital."[155]

There were two reasons why he was willing to postpone the extension of the school system below the district level: the existence of certain types of schools and institutions that were already conducting elementary education, and the difficulty of mobilizing sufficient funds and manpower to carry out the project. Yu was not prepared to extend the system of official schools to the subdistrict (*hyang* in his system, *myŏn* in his own time), defined in his system as consisting of 500 families to be headed by an official called a *hyangjŏng*, who would be selected by the district magistrate from the quota and extra-quota students of the subdistrict.

He pointed out that in the capital there were six officials with the title of Instructors of the Youthful Benighted (Tongmyŏng kyogwan) who gave instruction to the youth of the city in their homes. These men were evaluated after six months on the job and, if found meritorious, were then promoted to a sixth-rank official post. Unfortunately, their homes were not located throughout the city to provide equal access to all inhabitants, they were not natives of the area and were thus out of tune with the urban population, and their rapid promotion and turnover deprived the students of continuity in education. Nevertheless, Yu felt that the system should be maintained until it were possible to establish ward schools in the capital from regular tax revenues. Service and staff personnel would be recruited from the local population and their work at the ward schools would be accepted in lieu of regular labor service. Eventually the capital ward schools would provide a model that could be extended to provincial towns as well.

As we have seen, Yu was critical of the the existing village elementary schools (*sŏdang*) as well as the private academies, but he did not call for their outright abolition because he hoped that improvement of the mores of local scholars by his program of institutional reform would eventually bring a halt to the problem. Furthermore, after his network of local schools (*hyangsang*) was established, village granaries (*sach'ang*) and village shrines (*hyangsa*) could be established as well to improve the overall condition of the villages, in accordance with precedents during the Chou and Han dynasties. Local worthies and scholars could then carry out rites at these shrines to honor local teachers (*hyang sŏnsaeng*) – an arrangement that would conform "to the intentions of the ancients."[156]

Despite his animus against the private academies he planned to encourage the continued establishment of elementary schools by private initiative below the district level but with government support and encouragement. Watanabe Manabu has argued in a recent study that even though Yu did not say so explicitly, the inspiration for these subdistrict schools was provided more by the existing elementary schools (*sŏdang*) than classical models, and it was possible that Yu may have intended only to convert these schools to his new *sang* type (see below) and add more of them. Watanabe believed that the seventeenth century was an era in which education was beginning to penetrate throughout the lowest levels of society as part of the general process of social leveling underway since Hideyoshi's invasions.[157]

What Yu did say explicitly, however, was that the proposed subdistrict schools were to be based on his understanding of the admirable ancient local schools. Citing K'ung An-kuo of the T'ang period, he pointed out that the core of the ancient system at the local level were the *suk* and *sang* schools. Every twenty-five households constituted a *yŏ* group, and at the head of the street entrance to their residential quarter was a gate with a *suk* watchtower or building where the people received instruction during their idle hours, in the early morning or at dusk when going to and returning from the fields. Men of virtue, elders, or retired officials acted as teachers. At the higher level of the *tang* unit of 500 households, there were *sang* schools for students promoted from the *yŏ* residential areas.[158]

Yu admitted that it might not be possible to reproduce this system in its entirety, but at least it could be approximated by establishing *sang* schools in the subdistrict or *hyang*, his new term for the current *myŏn*. The intitiative for the establishment of *sang* schools would come from local leaders, presumably yangban, and the district magistrate would provide financial and labor support and rewards of grain to local gentry who took a prominent role in erecting school buildings. Teachers would be recruited by recommendation from the villagers, who would select the most learned men irrespective of office or rank. Once the schools began to flourish, scholars would be attracted to serve as teachers, and they would be provided living expenses in grain by the schools. Although Yu realized that local schoolmasters had been corrupted because of the tuition payments that parents were paying to them, he was confident that compensation by the state would not whet their appetites for gain in the manner of current times because the public spirit of the new school system would overcome private interest.[159]

Despite his appeal for official financing of local schools, however, Yu opposed direct state intervention in their establishment and specifically enjoined the authorities against the use of force to achieve their ends. He believed that force would not be necessary in any case because adoption of the recommendation system for recruiting scholars and officials would stop scholars from "seeking fame and fortune and scrambling around to fulfill their ambitions."[160] The local people would turn away from selfish aims and change the purpose of education to moral cultivation. When they noticed that there was a dearth of schools, they would take the proper initiative in establishing them, and there would be no need for the government to provide material support until the local residents had taken the first steps to establish schools. The end result would be the education of all sons, an increase in the number of virtuous and talented people, and a transformation of customs and mores.[161]

There was a fundamental contradiction in Yu's attitude that explains his reluctance to carry the implications of his admiration for the public good over private interest to its logical conclusion and replace private control everywhere with state authority. Logically, he should have done so because he deplored the private academies for pursuing their private interests at the expense of the public good, but he also felt that the private sector had been forced to fill a vacuum created by the failure of the state to maintain the schools it had established at the beginning of the dynasty. He therefore sought a compromise by insisting on private initiative to establish new schools in the subdistricts while calling for state fiscal support for the subdistrict schools, state initiative and support at the district level and above, but autonomy for schools at all levels.

Why should he have thought that new, privately established schools could escape the corrupting self-interest of private founders when the private academies had not? Only because the elimination of the examination system and adoption of the recommendation system would remove private interest from education as a whole and transform the mores of the whole country. Once mores had been improved, then private acts would no longer be directed toward selfish ends and would serve the public interest. There is no way of telling whether Yu's expectations would have worked in practice since the recommendation system was never adopted by the government, but a healthy skepticism might lead one to conclude that as long as lineage solidarity remained a strong value in Korea, the new system envisioned by Yu was just as likely to become the tool of local familial and aristocratic interests as the contemporary private academies.

Two factors may have been operating in his mind. The first was his fear of the evils of bureaucratic routinization at best, corruption at worst to undermine the moral code of Confucianism because it had happened throughout both Chinese and Korean history. The second was an emotional attachment to his own yangban class that made him hestitate, at times, from the ruthlessness of his own logic – in this case, the logic of a thorough system of official education. He wanted his new social elite to retain at least the right of initiative in the local districts, and it appears that (as we will see in a number of instances) he did not expect the yangban to disappear, but rather to renew themselves.

CONCLUSION: CLASSICAL MODELS BUT NOT FUNDAMENTALISM

It was not surprising that a man born a scant quarter century after the disastrous Imjin War and a year before the coup d'état of 1623, who suffered the loss of his father from factional politics and grew up through the Yi Kwal rebellion of 1624 and the two Manchu invasions of 1627 and 1637, should think that that there was something radically wrong with the political leadership of his country. As angry as he might have been over the plight of his country, however, his Confucian education prepared him to stand back from the particularities of individual actions and events to take a longer and more fundamental view of the institutions needed to provide better leadership.

In his search for a fundamental approach to recruiting better men for government Yu was led by his Confucian education back to the classics for fundamental principles, in particular the description of the official school system and the use of recommendation based on face-to-face evaluation of the moral behavior of individuals in ancient China. It is doubtful that he derived these models by a return to the classics alone, because he also gained knowledge from the long history of denunciation of the examination system and bureaucratic routinization in recruitment from the Northern and Southern dynasties through the Ming. He was particularly influenced by the Sung thinkers, who not only stressed the superiority of classical institutions, but reminded the Chinese cultural world of the greater interest in subjects of practical utility, including military knowledge and skills, that had prevailed in the classical age but had been degraded in Sung times in particular. On this score Yu was intrigued by the utilitarian views of Wang Anshih, but not as much as by the stress on moral education by Ch'eng Hao. Despite the breadth of his learning, in his blend of morality and utility he was obviously a child of the Sung, an heir in particular to the statecraft thought of some of its reformers, both moral and utilitarian. But he was not thorough enough in his research of Sung institutions to find that in the period after Wang An-shih left office, the commitment to government schools as the sole solution to the deficiencies of the examination system waned, and Ts'ai Ching had to abandon his plan to carry out the idea in practice in 1107 because of the enormity of the opposition to it.[162] Even if Yu had been aware of these facts, I doubt that it would have deterred him in his conviction to support such a plan despite its failure in the Sung dynasty.

Did this mean that Yu was basically a fundamentalist who aimed at the literal restoration of classical institutions? No, because he insisted that it was impossible to return to the feudal setting of the classical Chou period. The conversion to centralized bureaucratic government organization had created a completely different situation, and that system was there to stay in Korea as well as in China.

On the other hand, he never entertained the notion that history represented a record of unending progress and development, or that one could look forward to unlimited opportunities in the future. Rather his concept of reform was one of returning to ancient perfection, but since it was impossible ever to achieve that goal, the best graphical representation of his future aspirations would probably have been an asymptote, a curve that might approach but never attain the limit of perfection, the outline of which was already defined in ancient texts. Yet even that degree of perfection was doubtful because his own society was so greatly flawed that he could not have believed much progress had been made since the founding of his own dynasty. On the contrary, things seemed to be worse in his own time than in the fifteenth century.

Was he a slavish admirer of China with no respect for his own country? No, because what he admired was the Confucian ideal of statecraft, particularly Sung standards in statecraft, in which perfection was located only in antiquity, the period of the sage emperors through the end of the Chou dynasty in 220 B.C. Thereafter, the chance for perfection in China, or rather, the world, was destroyed by the obliteration of a number of crucial institutions necessary to sage government.

The record of Chinese history from the Han dynasty on was one of imperfection and failure, marked by a number of noble attempts to restore the essence of ancient institutions even within the centralized bureaucratic context. The history of China was valuable to Yu for providing him information about those attempts and the more astute plans and suggestions of the brightest lights in Chinese history and statecraft thought.

Yu had no particular commitment to demonstrating or advertising the uniqueness or value, let alone superiority, of Korean culture because he judged Korean dynasties the same way that he judged Chinese dynasties: how well did they match up with the sage institutions of ancient China? On that score, he found that in Korea few attempts had been made to adopt ancient institutions until the eighth century, and even then it was a proto-examination system copied from an institution invented in the Sui dynasty in 606 and carried over into the T'ang that the government of Silla adopted to improve the training of a few officials. Since he learned from his Chinese sources that the examination system itself was flawed, he was not particularly proud either of the formal adoption of the civil-service examinations in the Koryŏ dynasty in 958, nor the intensification of their use as a means of recruitment after the founding of the Chosŏn dynasty in 1392.

Furthermore, he was all too painfully aware of the problems created in Korea by the power of inherited status throughout society. In his view, the yangban, whom he perceived as fully blown hereditary aristocrats, monopolized education, the examinations, and access to office to the exclusion of men of talent condemned to obscurity by the accident of birth. Not only had the civil-service examinations failed to open the door to office to commoners, let alone merchants, artisans, or slaves, but the official school system had also failed to provide the opportunity for education to the general public. In fact, the official schools were virtually moribund, and private academies were run by yangban factions. The conclusions he had drawn about the evil consequences of a hereditary aristocracy in his own society were only reinforced by his research into the Chinese experience in the Northern and Southern dynasties, when an aristocracy had taken over control of society. Unfortunately, the Chinese solution to the problem of aristocratic society, the creation of the examination system under centralized bureaucratic management, was as bad as hereditary aristocracy because it failed both to eliminate that aristocracy and to train men in moral standards. His own Chosŏn dynasty had, therefore, blindly adopted a system that had been fully condemned by some of the greatest thinkers in T'ang and Sung times. The only solution was to reject both the examination system and excessively centralized bureaucratic control in favor of a far better system of education and recruitment, the ancient system of official schools and recommendation.

Yu based his reforms not on any value-free study of methods that might achieve results without concern for the moral edification of the population; to the contrary, he placed heavy emphasis on the moral knowledge of traditional Confucian standards, the application of that knowledge to action to produce perfected human behavior, and the selection of those who were most adept at it for office. In fact, one could say that his main goal was to replace the current, morally imperfect, hereditary yangban with his morally instructed and perfected scholar-officials (*sadaebu*), drawn more broadly from the population at large.

CHAPTER 5

New Schools: Conservative Restraints on Radicalism

"If in some matter there should be some doubt, the students should discuss it, ask questions about it, and thus distinguish between what is right and wrong, but a student cannot simply criticize his teacher on the basis of his own opinions."[1]

"Do not read any books that have not been written by the sages, and do not look at any writings that are of no benefit."[2]

"The 'families of scholars [*sajok*]' are sons of scholars and officials [*sabu*], and they are members of that group because of their surnames and lineages [*sŏngjok*]."[3]

We have seen that Yu Hyŏngwŏn adopted the advice of the Sung masters to reestablish the essential institutional features of the ancient Chou dynasty: official schools and the recommendation of worthy men as the means to refurbish the moral capacities of the people and the excellence of its corps of bureaucratic leaders. His regulations for the actual operation of his proposed schools will tell us more about the intent and purpose of his school system, in particular the means by which he chose to assess the acquisition of moral knowledge, given his bias against written examinations, the degree of openness and freedom he would allow in the search for knowledge, and the way he would handle technical and specialized information in view of the Confucian prejudice in favor of general knowledge. Last, but not least, we will turn our attention to the way that he handled the egalitarian emphases of academic instruction in the face of strict distinctions between people based on status to assess the type of society he hoped to achieve by his educational reform.

Key Elements of Yu Hyŏngwŏn's Reform Program

Mass Education Confucian Style: The Segmented Bamboo

In proposing his plan for schools, he only called for the immediate establishment of schools to accommodate young men from the age of fifteen *se* (thirteen or fourteen years), proposing that elementary schools be established in the villages by the local gentry. He stated that his main purpose in proposing the establishment of village subdistrict (*yŏsuk*, *tangsang*) schools on private initiative was to provide for the education of the mass of the population: "Once we have established the village or neighborhood schools, then not only will the scholars be educated, but among the people of the kingdom there will be no one who is not educated."[4]

This statement, on the face of it, indicated his commitment to mass education, yet he also provided quota limits for regular students ranging from 100 students for each of the four schools in the capital down to 20 for the smallest district schools and double that number of extra-quota or irregular students (*chŭnggwangsaeng*) at each school.[5] He realized, however, that the quota limit might contradict his purpose by restricting opportunities for upward mobility for commoners, and that his purpose might better be served by at least expanding his quota for extra-quota students.[6]

In his consideration of this problem, he revealed that his professed desire for mass education by no means implied the egalitarianism of modern democratic education. He pointed out that his local or subdistrict schools were not designed to uplift the mass of the benighted peasantry by providing the equivalent of a modern college education to everyone, but rather to provide an initial demarcation point between scholars (*sa*) and the general population (*min*, the people) and a minimal level of moral education for all. He did not envision a society in which the broad mass of the peasantry would be sufficiently educated to enable any one of them to be plucked out by the king and vaulted to the commanding heights of the capital bureaucracy.

On the contrary, he portrayed his ideal society in the image of a stalk of bamboo, a vertical cylinder divided by nodes and ascending from earth to the heavens. The essence of this society was to be ranked position (*tŭngwi*), a natural feature not only of society but also of the entire cosmos.

Even though the thorough transformation of all the people through education (*kyohwa*) might be carried out throughout the kingdom, extending to "all space between Heaven and Earth," you still had to have nodal separation points (*chŏl*, the nodes of a stalk of bamboo). In fact, the bamboo-stalk society was limitless in extension but subdivided into segments, and presumably each segment would represent a stage of moral development through education and practice, not simply the current ladder of social position based on inherited status. Moving up the bamboo stalk of society would be difficult because the process of moral cultivation was arduous, possibly because the obstacle against perfection was not just man's limited capacity for knowledge and understanding, but the more serious human instinct for selfishness.

The social grades and ranks marked off by segmental dividing lines also presupposed the need for quotas (*punsu*), suggesting perhaps an overall pyramidal outline to his social bamboo stalk as well.[7] And yet his language was not unequivocal because his stratified imagery was frequently intertwined with the rhetoric of equality. Human beings, after all, shared an aspect of similitude: "What we have in common is that we are all Heaven's people [*tong si ch'ŏnmin*]." But at the same time, "There is a distinction between scholars and common people [*yu saminjibyŏl*]."

Some of his statements did appear to favor universal education: "Even though education may be widely extended, there is still the fear that there might not be enough talented people. If there are too many of them, it is not a matter of concern."

But he did not mean that all men were to be educated through the level of the National Academy, rather that it was better to have a surplus in the supply of educated men relative to the number of bureaucratic slots to make sure there was no shortage. They would simply have to wait for an opening, but it would not be right to increase the quota of officials because of a surfeit of scholars, or increase the quota of scholars because of an increase in the population.[8] Even though too many unemployed educated men might create too many discontented intellectuals, the purpose of education was to guarantee a sufficient supply of talented men for the state, not to fulfill the needs of the mass of individuals.

His quotas for schools based on his quota of bureaucratic posts and the life expectancy and average length of career of government officials was actually less than the current figures of examination candidates. He estimated that at the time there were about nine hundred civil and military regular official posts from ranks one to nine in the government bureaucracy. Assuming the average age of first appointment at forty, the average age of retirement about seventy, and deducting ten years to account for some early retirements and death in office, he estimated an average career at twenty years. He then set the quota for the number of scholars to be promoted from the highest of his new schools to office at thirty-five per annum, producing seven hundred officials over a twenty-year period. The extra two hundred slots could be filled by special recommendations made by court officials of rank three or higher, or by local magistrates.[9] In short, the masses were to be given only an elementary education, and the opportunities for higher education would be limited to quotas reflecting estimated needs for a drastically reduced central bureaucracy.

Quotas to Eliminate Regional Discrimination

Despite the criticism in the T'ang dynasty against the use of quotas because they limited opportunities for advancement (see chap. 4), Yu sympathized with the complaints of many Chinese scholars about the disparity of opportunity between the capital and the provinces and between one geographic region and another. The Chinese writers had complained that the examination system itself was responsible for this because it attracted scholars to the capital in the hope of a better chance of passing the examinations. Increased quotas for the dynastic capital to reflect the increase in population only continued to drain the countryside of talented men.[10] Yu agreed that in Korea as well current discriminatory examination quotas favored residents of the capital over the countryside and the southern agricultural heartland over the north and northwest frontier.

By changing district or regional quotas to allow more opportunities for provincial scholars, Yu hoped to offer an inducement for present residents of the capital to return to their home districts. He referred to these people as "floating guests" or wandering migrants and attributed their existence to private bias in the current recruitment process, so that "as a result the officials are all people from the capital area."[11]

Noting that discrimination against residents of the north was prevalent in Korea as well as China, he proposed the use of quotas to redress the imbalance. He cited as a precedent the Chou dynasty practice of allotting quotas of scholars that the feudal lords could recommend to the throne to vary by the size of the feudal domain, "three from a large state, two from a medium, and one from a small."[12] The recommendation system in Han times also contained graded and fixed quotas based on population, and the Han "examinations of filial and honest men" (*hsiao-lien k'ua*) provided that "one man be recommended for every 200,000 people in a given area."[13] Yu modified this by reducing the ratio to one recommendee for every 20,000 to 50,000 people. The final figure would be determined after a thorough investigation of the census registers. Pending that, officials could use the present local examination quotas.[14]

He hoped to redraw district and prefectural boundaries to conform to land area in place of the current system of grading administrative districts according to strategic location or other considerations. Under his proposed system 40,000 *kyŏng* (4 million *myo*, the Chinese *mou*) would constitute a *taebu* or *tohobu* (large prefecture), 30,000 *kyŏng* would define a *pu* (prefecture), 20,000 *kyŏng* a *kun* (large district), 10,000 *kyŏng* a *hyŏn* (district), and the quota of recommended students would vary according to these units and the population.[15] Readjusting the quota for promoted scholars to the population of his revised district boundaries would solve the problem of regional discrimination.

He also believed that the disparities in opportunities for education and recruitment could not be dissociated from the question of the distribution of wealth, which fundamentally was a problem of land distribution. At the present time the people of some regions prospered while others were on the verge of economic disaster; the breakdown of the land system and the skewing of landownership patterns had exacerbated the difference between the strong and the weak. In the face of these circumstances, even the establishment of schools and improvement of the quality of teachers would have little effect.[16]

Yu, however, was not willing to overturn the present system at a single stroke to benefit the northwest because it might impose too great a hardship on the scholars of the capital. As a temporary adjustment, he allowed that his proposed quotas for the northern frontier territories might be reduced and the capital quotas expanded to accommodate the present imbalance. After some time passed, if the capital scholars had not returned to their provincial homes in sufficient numbers, he was willing to permit a permanent extra quota for the capital. This, too, probably represents his preference for incentives over force when dealing with the scholar class.[17] Nevertheless, his objective was similar to the *t'u-tüan* (*t'odan*) policy in China during the Northern and Southern dynasties period when members of the educated elite were resettled among the villages of the countryside to provide local moral leadership and political stability.

He also expected that future disparities between the number of talented scholars in a given district and the available recommendation quotas could be rectified naturally by voluntary migration. Since the current dynastic code allowed peasants to migrate to areas of excess land, there would be reason why scholars as well might migrate to districts where quotas afforded them better opportunities for advancement. Since the in-migration of scholars might antagonize scholars already resident in such districts, he proposed punishment for any unfriendly behavior toward new scholar immigrants.

Promotion in Schools and Recruitment for Office

Face-to-Face Evaluation of Behavior and Talent

Recommendation was Yu's main method for refurbishing both schools and the government bureaucracy, one of the main lessons he had learned from the Chinese experience. It would be the means for admitting students to school and promoting them to higher schools, and for eventually recruiting them as government officials. The essence of recommendation was based on his perception of the ancient practice of face-to-face evaluation of behavior and talent.

According to his proposed regulations, a grand evaluation (*taebi*) would be conducted every third year at the same time that the household registers (*hojŏk*) were compiled. At the lowest level the district magistrate and the local school officials (*kyogwan*) would conduct an investigation to determine "the worthy and able" (*hyŏn* and *nŭng*), in which worth was defined as virtuous behavior (*tŏkhaeng*) and ability as skills in the arts (*toye*). "The standards for selection must be that the person's behavior in the village is outstanding, that in learning he understands the classics, and that in talent he is eligible to be appointed to office." To determine eligibility, the magistrate and school officials would first examine the daily records of virtuous deeds and misdemeanors recorded in the books of the Community Compact Association (*hyangyak*) and in the schools. Then they would take recommendations from people in the subdistrict and village (*hyangdang*) and rely on "public opinion" (*konggong-ji-ron*).[18]

In promoting students to the Middle School in the capital or the Governor's School in the provincial capital the elders of the subdistrict (*hyang*) and the staff of the subdistrict school would be invited to the local (*hyang*) wine-drinking ritual, treated with the courtesy due special guests, and asked to express their views on the candidates. They would be required to fill out recommendation forms that included a pledge by them to submit willingly to punishment if the candidate's qualifications turned out to be less than advertised. If a student of the

National Academy was being recommended for an official post, the recommendor would agree to acccept punishment if the candidate were subsequently found guilty of embezzlement, moral turpitude, laziness, drunkenness, crime, or injury to others.[19]

Despite his animus against examinations, Yu felt forced to rely on oral and written tests for weeding out incompetent students. Every third year (when the soon-to-be abolished examinations were held) the director of the Middle School in the capital and the provincial governor at the Governor's School would conduct an oral classics examination (*kogang*). With exceptions to be noted later, any student over the age of twenty who failed this triennial school qualification examination would be dismissed from school and enlisted for military service – a much stiffer criterion for service exemption than the tax on Select Military Officers that King Yŏngjo adopted in 1750.[20]

Furthermore, students who had been promoted to the Middle School in the capital and the Governor's School in the provincial capital would be subjected to a test on selected classics shortly after their arrival, and those who failed would be sent home. Reading examinations would be held every fifth day on the previous week's study, archery and writing tests four times a year, and a recitation examination on the classics in spring and autumn. Shoddy scholarship, poor behavior, and inferior talent would all be grounds for dismissal from school. The year after promotion the best students of the Middle School and the Governors' Schools would be recommended for promotion to the National Academy, and regulations for examination and dismissal at the National Academy would be similar to those for intermediate schools.

The last stage of the process was selection of "the worthy and able" from students at the National Academy for posts in the government bureaucracy. The criteria for selection were "correct character and behavior, honesty, deferential behavior, scholarly knowledge, and understanding of the right way of government." The recommendation procedure would be accompanied by performance of the wine-drinking rite, and the new candidates for office would then be assembled for a recitation examination at court before the high ministers, censors, and royal attendants. Those who passed would be designated advanced scholars (*chinsa*) and their names presented to the Ministry of Personnel. There would be no lists of passers issued in the manner of the current examination system.[21]

Retention of Examinations within the Schools

Yu was aware that his authorization of examinations in the schools conflicted with his condemnation of examinations elsewhere and his refusal to recognize compromises with the examination system, such as the use of policy questions in the Han dynasty fashion, or Cho Kwangjo's idea of holding special examinations of recommended scholars. He defended himself against the charge of inconsistency by specifying that only recitation examinations (*kogang*) would be allowed at the National Academy. Four times a year written examinations (*chesul*) would be conducted in the district schools, but nothing was to be feared since these written tests were designed only as a means of periodic observation of student progress and encouragement of their studies; they would be nothing like the contemporary examination system (*kwagŏ*).[22]

In drawing up sample regulations for the quarterly *chesul* tests, Yu followed the Chinese critics of poetry, excessively ornate style, and useless knowledge by instructing that questions be confined to essays on the meaning of the classics, the philosophers, histories, and matters of contemporary government policy, while the composition of poems would be abolished. Students would not line up in the school courtyard as was customary in the examination system procedure, but would be allowed to take individual questions back to their rooms in the dormitory or their homes, to compose an essay in the peace and quiet of their own quarters. The only requirement would be that the form of the essay had to be straightforward; nothing new or too embellished in style would be acceptable. The students would be encouraged to emulate the prose styles of Tung Chung-shu, Han Yü, Master Ch'eng (Ch'eng I?), or Chu Hsi, and limits were set on length to avoid wordiness. The essays were to be handed in on the day that the students were to be convened for review; the teachers would evaluate the essays and give instruction to students whose essays were not up to par. The headmaster would be forbidden from grading the essays "lest it lead to the evil of emphasizing composition style."[23]

Yu's favor for take-home essays, straightforward prose, and the discussion of papers rather than the grading of tests resembles certain theories of liberal education in the modern West, but his brand of Confucian liberalism should not be associated with respect for freedom of thought, particularly the right to express views contrary to Neo-Confucian dogma on moral or metaphysical problems. His main concern, which he shared with the Sung philosophers, was with excessive formalism, ornateness, and routine that diverted the attention of students from the moral message of classical and historical wisdom. He also argued that by restricting the use of written examinations to the district schools, he could prevent the National Academy in the capital from becoming the locus for the restoration of written examinations and the unseemly competition that was inseparable from the contemporary examination system.[24]

Yu's justification for the continued use of written examinations, however, still looks like a major contradiction in his thought. The obvious question is why he would be willing to weaken his otherwise impregnable position against examinations of all sorts? The answer is simply that the contradiction was unavoidable in a culture that regarded the written canon of Confucian wisdom as indispensable to the moral training of the individual. No matter how much stress Yu placed on the behavioral consequences of knowledge, he could not confine the evaluation of human talent merely to the observation of behavior. If men were to be educated in schools, it made some sense to require written exposition of their learning. Korean Confucians like Yu could never relegate mastery of the written word to the relatively minor role it played in a more militaristic and feudal society like Tokugawa (let alone Warring States) Japan.

Hall for Advanced Scholars

To return to a discussion of the final phases of Yu's recommendation system, those scholars selected from the National Academy for positions at court would first be assigned to a special Hall for Advanced Scholars (Chinsawŏn) for a period of training and observation. The idea was similar to one proposed by Ch'eng Hao of the Sung, although Yu claimed that the model was to be found in the Han dynasty's system of selecting scholars to serve in the San-shu and giving them posts as palace guards.[25] Yu's advanced scholars would also serve in the palace guards, subject to constant scrutiny. Any found unworthy would be dismissed, and the director and assistant director of the National Academy would be held responsible.

There would neither be fixed quotas for advanced scholars nor any assigned duties besides their shifts in the palace. They would be expected to participate in lecture discussions, rituals, and archery contests, but accuracy in shooting was only one of the marks of personal perfection, and it was subordinated to comportment. Here Yu followed the lead provided by Chu Hsi, not Wang Anshih, because he explained that the scholars would be judged on how well they "held their bodies as if they were engaged in a rite and moved as if they were reacting to [the rhythm of] music."[26]

The advanced scholars would serve on duty for a year, subject to invitations to royal audiences (*ch'odae*) where they could be exposed to lectures on the classics and learn about the way of governing, contemporary affairs, customs, and mores. All the court officials would have an opportunity to observe them in action to determine the appropriate rank of office to be assigned them in their first regular posts in the bureaucracy. Most would be given the regular rank of 9B, the lowest on the eighteen-grade scale, but the most outstanding would be assigned brevet rank of grade six or higher. Yu insisted that the only exceptions to the process of selection and advancement of candidates for office through the school system would be the occasional appointment of specially recommended persons who had experience serving in provincial posts or in the royal guards. The recommendation system would thus serve to "purify the route of advancement to office."[27]

Appointment to Office at the Age of Forty

Students in the subdistrict schools (*hyanghak*) and four schools in the capital could not be recommended for promotion until they had been in residence for three years, but the minimum residence for the Governor's School, Middle School, and National Academy would only be one year. Except in the case of outstanding individuals, no one would be eligible for government office or promotion to a court position until the age of forty. Yu attributed the idea for a forty-year age minimum to Confucius's admission in the Analects that he did not escape his own confusion until he turned forty, and the injunction in the *Book of Rites* that men at the age of forty should be appointed to office because they were strong and robust at that age.[28] Yu was aware that this provision left him open to charges of obscurantist fundamentalism particularly because the forty-year minimum might close off opportunity to younger men of talent and set an unrealistically high age requirement in an age when life expectancy was low.[29]

Yu's defense was that he was not mindlessly adopting an ancient system, and he attempted to justify it by demonstrating that any man would be convinced on the grounds of reason alone. The mode of his argument, however, was closer to a Thomistic rationalization of dogma than a Kantian attempt to prove his postulates on the basis of logic because he began by arguing that any system used by the ancients was inherently suitable and appropriate; all it took was a proper understanding of the wisdom of their measures. The ancients preferred the forty-year minimum because they understood that it took time for men to develop their intelligence and cultivate their wills before they could be properly orientated. Since he allowed for exceptional appointments of younger men, there was also no fear that the opportunity to recruit talent would really be restricted. Furthermore, the forty-year minimum would enable him to achieve a balance between the limited number of available bureaucratic posts and the pool of talent emerging from the school system. This argument was not without merit in a period when the oversupply of degree-holders created a class of potentially discontented and disruptive individuals, but it was based on an appeal to utility rather than pure reason.

Yu also argued that moral cultivation required a lifetime of unremitting effort, and young men were not to be trusted because they tended to be ambitious and careerist rather than devoted to self-cultivation. One of the reasons why dynasties of the later age declined was because they appointed excessive numbers of young men to office, a practice that led to the general degradation of mores. If the younger men knew they had no chance for office until the age of forty, they would certainly devote their early years to doing good.[30]

Yu's disclaimer is unconvincing, however, because there does not seem to be any reason why it would take forty years to prepare men for office except for Confucius's hallowed dictum. It resembles other attempts he made to disclaim charges of fundamentalist antiquarianism against him, and his mistrust of youth jibes perfectly with the stress on the primacy of age in respect relations that he copied from Chu Hsi's school regulations.

Coercion, Punishment, and Discipline

Yu was quite liberal in his use of rewards and punishments, particularly the latter, as an inducement to probity on the part of recommendors and diligence among students. These coercive reinforcements for Confucian moral objectives were an integral part of the ancient model and certainly no independent creation of his, but his readiness to use force places him firmly in the camp of the tough-minded Confucians.

He prescribed that any official who recommended a person subsequently found unworthy would be subject to dismissal from office. Mitigating circumstances could permit reduction of salary instead, but repeated violations should result in expropriating the office warrants of the guilty official and returning him to commoner status. If the official died before he could be punished, the arm of the law would be extended to him even in the grave by posthumous stripping of his office warrants (*ch'ut'al*). A strong record of recommendation, on the contrary, would be requited with special appointments, promotions, or honors, and these might also be conferred posthumously.[31]

Yu refused to allow magistrates and school officials to escape the threat of punishment by abstention. Failure to make any recommendation at all would also be grounds for dismissing magistrates and school officials. If in fact there actually was a dearth of talent in a given area, the merit ratings of the magistrates or school officials would have to be reduced. If any men of outstanding talent should then be discovered who had been overlooked, the officials concerned would be indicted for the crime of concealing talent.[32]

Yu also applied his disciplinary approach to students. Any student who had been in school for some time but failed to show improvement in his studies would be expelled, deprived of his student status with all its perquisites, and enrolled for military service. Truancy would likewise be punishable by dismissal, but in this case, Yu provided penalties to encourage reform. If a student failed to show up for class or attend spring and autumn rites, he would be reprimanded to his face after the first violation, dismissed from his seat after the second, and expelled from his dormitory or study hall after the third. He would then have to "correct his mistakes and reform himself" prior to readmittance, after which he would again be upbraided for his behavior to his face and required to make an apology. Anyone who showed no intention to attend class at all would have his name crossed off the school register and be enlisted for military service. Absence for reason of sickness had to be justified by a written excuse to the headmaster, and only students over the age of forty would be exempted from attendance requirements.[33]

School examinations were also to be accompanied by harsh penalties for poor performance. Every fifteen days students would be required to assemble at the school's Confucian shrine and pass a recitation examination graded in difficulty according to the student's capabilities. Those who failed to pass would suffer fifteen strokes of the whip.[34] The triennial examinations at the capital Four Schools and the Governors' Schools were to be taken most seriously: failure to attend or pass these examinations would result in immediate dismissal and enrollment for military service for everyone over the age of twenty. Those younger than twenty who failed would be whipped but retain student status. If a substitute took the examination in place of a regular student, both substitute and student would be dismissed and enlisted for service.[35] Finally, commuters who resided in the national or provincial capitals and missed the semimonthly recitation examinations or failed to attend school for a minimum of fifteen days in any three-month period would have to send their household slaves (!) to be flogged in their place. If their violations were more serious than this, they could personally be held responsible for criminal action.[36]

Yu's moralism hardly blinded him to the weaknesses of the human spirit, which needed something stronger than the medicine of exhortation to overcome its afflictions of laziness, ambition, or recalcitrance. He willingly turned to punishment not out of any ambivalence in his commitment to Confucian moral suasion, but because the education of men in Confucian standards and the recruitment of those men for government service was serious business. The schoolyard was not supposed to be a joyful place; it was to be a humorless, disciplined, puritanical, even grim training ground for the intense pursuit of moral perfection.

Behavior was to be strictly regulated in all particulars, no matter how minute, and Yu's description of his proposed daily regimen calls to mind the severest type of military academy or monastery. All students would rise at dawn, sweep their rooms, put their clothes on straight, and jointly call on their teacher for the morning kowtow. At dining hall the students were to sit by order of age, eating "with a strict demeanor and silently, without uttering a word."[37] Eating was not to be a pleasurable experience, and students were directed not to select food they liked to eat because it would mean they were thinking of satisfying baser tastes. At study hall they were to keep their bodies erect and sit straight, to help them concentrate their minds in striving to attain understanding of "the principles of things." They were to eschew memorization or recitation and abstain from both conversation and occasional glances toward their fellows. They were forbidden to wander away from their desks or talk to anyone else except to ask questions about their studies. Their calligraphy had to be always in the straight and square form; grass style or "reckless writing" was prohibited.

Proper respect always had to be shown to elders. During the brief recess periods after meals, they were to walk about slowly in the school gardens, looking at material objects to continue their Neo-Confucian investigation of the principle inside them (what Wang Yang-ming had such difficulty achieving). After hours they could either engage in serious discussion, practice archery, play the stringed instruments according to the proper methods or procedures, or practice their calligraphy. Playing chess or engaging in idle conversation was not to be tolerated. Selection of the proper music to play was especially serious because, like the sirens' song, the lascivious and captivating music of the streets could "incite the desires and lead one into a life of ease, and [once this happened] no one would be able to put a stop to it."[38] The music of the alleyways of his native Korea was even more base and lewd than China: "If we do not change the present music into what is correct, it would be better not to play such music at all."[39]

At the end of the day students would continue their studies in their rooms, reading by lamplight until late at night. Whatever the time of day, if a student were not able to read his books, he would have to practice "quiet sitting and preservation (or concentration) of the mind" (*chŏngjwa chonsim*).[40]

The key Confucian term for this approach to learning was "seriousness" (*kyŏng*), defined by Yu as keeping one's mind under strict control at all times, as if one were conducting a rite at an ancestral shrine or having a formal interview with one's father or ruler. If one's mind were serious on the inside, then the external manifestation would be a correct appearance in clothing and deportment, respect in all actions, and the utmost filial piety.

On the requirements of filial behavior Yu left nothing to chance, spelling out in great detail the actions required of the filial son and the norms of behavior in most social situations: choosing and associating with friends, interacting with members of the family at home, entertaining guests according to age and status, providing mutual aid to members of the village community, and demonstrating loyalty and true-heartedness toward all, especially government authorities. In school the student was to rectify and polish himself, at home or in the outside world to act in accordance with Heaven's principles and strive to abandon private desires. Moral theory always had to be carried out in action, and strict conformity with rules and procedures was required at all school rites – lining up in the proper order, kowtowing and bowing in the proper way and in the correct sequence.[41]

School regulations thus pertained to every facet of life whether in or out of school, and the most serious violations were transgressions of moral standards of behavior, more reprehensible than poor scholarship. Of a list of about two dozen reasons for disciplinary action against students, only one pertained to inattention to studies. The rest included poor deportment, mendacity, lack of sincerity toward one's father, disrespectfulness toward a teacher, insulting superiors, seeking favors from influential people, involvement in disputes and lawsuits, gambling, association with prostitutes, disruptive behavior in the local community, violation of funeral and ancestral rituals, failure to pay taxes or to obey the law. Belief in heterodox doctrines was, of course, proscribed as well. Violation of these norms would earn the student a demerit and a lowering of his seating position in class. Serious cases were to be treated by expulsion from the study hall or dormitory and suspension for a year or two. If a recalcitrant student failed to improve, he would be dismissed and enrolled for military service.[42]

Yu's puritanical disdain for any form of frivolity was also revealed in his sharp criticism of current practices of hazing successful examination passers and associating with denizens of the gay quarters. The usual practice was to lead new degree-holders "around the streets for three days of revelry" visiting singers and musicians. Congratulatory parties were held to which actors, singers, and puppeteers were invited, and established officials subjected the new degree-holders to severe hazing, "treating the newcomers as if they were animals." Yu disdained these customs as vestiges of northern barbarian (Mongol or Manchu?) influence. Furthermore, the contemporary examination celebrations were held ostensibly in honor of the successful degree-holder's father, but in fact these parties were obscene distortions of the rules of the *Book of Rites* for honoring fathers at banquets. "How could one congratulate oneself on the fact that one has been appointed to office, by setting up a party with musicians, calling it a congratulatory party, and only then claim that what you were doing was serving your father?"[43] Just as bad was the current custom of high officials forcing new appointees to hold banquets before allowing them to take their posts, or forcing newly admitted scholars in the provincial schools (*hyanggyo*) to provide food and wine or make cloth payments before being admitted to school. "All these evil practices make the blood run cold, and all ought to be abolished in the expectation that mores will change."[44]

Strictness and discipline was also an important part of the learning process. Proper respect for one's teacher required not only the performance of proper etiquette in formal meetings, but also warm trust and respectful acceptance of the teacher's instruction. "If in some matter there should be some doubt, the students should discuss it, ask questions about it, and thus distinguish between what is right and wrong, but a student cannot simply criticize his teacher on the basis of his own opinions."[45]

ATTITUDES TOWARD KNOWLEDGE

Strict Orthodoxy in the Curriculum

Yu was obviously committed to creating a school system that would be run under standards of strict discipline for both moral rectitude in daily behavior and high standards of academic performance. Nevertheless, the arduous regimen inside his schools did not necessarily signify a restrictive attitude toward the pursuit of knowledge itself, especially since he had cited the practical and utilitarian arguments of several Chinese reformers.

All doubt about the liberality of his vision and his willingness to accept the unusual and the unorthodox is removed, however, by considering his discussion of the school curriculum and the limits of knowledge. He made it quite clear that learning was to be strictly confined to acceptable texts in the orthodox canon. The student was to begin his studies with *The Small Learning* (*Hsiao-hsüeh*) and then proceed in order to *The Great Learning* (*Ta-hsüeh*), *Analects*, *Mencius*, *Doctrine of the Mean* (the above four were the *Four Books* with the standard commentary by Chu Hsi), the *Record of Things Near at Hand* (*Chin-ssu Lu*, edited by Chu Hsi and Lü Tsu-ch'ien), and the *Six Classics*. In between he was allowed to study the *Shih-chi* (*Records of the Grand Historian*, by Ssu-ma Ch'ien), and various writings of Neo-Confucian philosophers on nature and principle (*sŏngni*, *hsing-li* in Chinese). "Do not read any books that have not been written by the sages, and do not look at any writings that are of no benefit."[46]

Students had to submit for approval a list of texts that they would study for periodic recitations or written examinations, and only exceptional students or those older than thirty-five would be allowed to dispense with this requirement.[47]

Only authorized classics and other texts could be included in school libraries, and Yu urged that they be published in more quantity and distributed more widely throughout the country; noncanonical texts and frivolous works were to be kept out of the libraries.[48] There was in all this hardly a trace of the liberal approach to knowledge that one might expect of a scholar committed to any kind of breakaway from received wisdom or orthodoxy that was so typical of the Enlightenment in the West. On the contrary, the hallmark of his educational philosophy was strict conservative adherence to the Confucian classics and the conventional commentaries by Chu Hsi and the Sung school, censorship of unorthodox writings, and a ban on unacceptable books inside the schools. He was only willing to authorize his students to choose their own texts for research at the late age of thirty-five, not obviously because they would be mature enough to make wise choices, but because his solid program of indoctrination to that age would have removed all chance that individual choice might lead to a questioning, let alone refutation, of accepted wisdom.

Recitation procedure during normal study and testing sessions was also to be well ordered. Students were to take turns reciting portions of classical texts in the proper chapter order, a process that was not "to be done loosely or sloppily," but they could ask questions about obscure points in meaning.[49] Heaven forbid that they should dare to question the validity of the classics or of Confucian wisdom itself! Thus, Yu's tough-minded approach to education signified a vigorous defense of intellectual orthodoxy, which he obviously felt needed the support of a thoroughly disciplined school system as a bulwark against the corruptive influences of contemporary mores.

The Subordination of Nonmoral Knowledge

The Chinese literature on education that Yu had explored (see chap. 4) contained some emphasis on the importance of technical and useful information that could have led to a shift of priorities away from moral education toward value-free knowledge of greater utility for practical government. Even the stress on archery and charioteering in the classical curriculum introduced the potential for this kind of education. Yu mentioned that the six arts or skills (*ye*) of the classics had to be taught in the schools along with the six virtues and the six modes of behavior. Of these six skills Yu devoted some attention to calligraphy and more to archery. As mentioned above, he prohibited the use of grass writing in calligraphy examinations and sought to establish the calligraphy used in the *Hung-wu cheng-yün* as the standard form for straight characters, and the *Ku-wen yin-lü* as the standard form for seal characters.[50] One must presume that his purpose was at least to insist on the clearest and most understandable ideographic forms to eliminate the obscuration of meaning by arcane and undecipherable styles of graphic transcription.

Knowledge, Skills for the Well-rounded Generalist: Archery. Although Yu did not comment on the purposes of proper calligraphy, he did write at length on the importance of archery. In both the classical and postclassical literature on archery, there seem to have been three uses or goals of archery training. Archery was used to distinguish between scholars of equal merit, and Yu adopted this for use in promoting students to the capital and provincial schools. Archery contests were also important rituals in ancient times, and the conduct and deportment of the contestants in acting out the required procedures were judged as well. Bowmanship was also an important military skill, which Wang An-shih had stressed as a desirable weapon in the arsenal of talents of the well-rounded man. Yu was disturbed because scholars of his own time thought that archery was a skill appropriate to military officials alone. They held soldiers in low esteem and regarded archery as a baser art, but Yu insisted that skill in archery was proper for scholars as well as soldiers. It was only because "rites have been destroyed and teachings lost" that it had disappeared from the curriculum of the educated gentleman. He therefore required that all schools carry out ritual archery contests four times a year, that students use their spare time to practice, and that magistrates and school administrators conduct contests on rest days.[51]

Yu admired Ch'iu Chün of the Ming, who praised the ancient archery contests as described in the *Book of Etiquette and Ceremonial* (*I-li*) and deplored their abandonment after the fall of the Chou dynasty, except for a brief restoration during the Chin dynasty (third century A.D.). He praised Emperor T'ai-tsu of the Ming for restoring archery meets as a means of selecting scholars and establishing a detailed set of regulations governing procedure in conformity with commentaries on ceremonial practice.[52]

Yu also agreed with Wang An-shih on the need to eliminate the contemporary prejudice against military officials. He wanted to allow guard officers (*chang-gwan*) to participate in school examinations, contrary to the current prohibition:

> Originally civil and military officials could not be divided, but they were divided in two only because of the fact that when in charge of civil affairs [a man] would wear his [civilian] cap, and when in charge of military affairs, he would don his military uniform, and that was the only reason. In the later age this was lost and therefore men were not allowed to perform both civil and military functions. This kind of thing represents the worst evil of a declining age. In recent years if people regarded in name as scholars once pick up a bow or arrow, they are not allowed to enter school again. This is indeed the worst of evils.[53]

This position was close to Wang's point of view, but Yu was not advocating the greater importance of useful military skills over scholarly training in the classics and moral principles; he was merely advocating the need for eliminating the stigma against military officials and the military arts and incorporating the latter into the education of the well-rounded generalist who would eventually be entrusted with the right to govern the people for the king.

Knowledge, Skills for the Well-rounded Generalist: Law and Mathematics. Yu also felt that legal and mathematical training should be required of students in the regular school system since these specialties were important for the training of regular officials. Since mathematics was one of the six classical arts, it also should be incorporated in the curriculum of the regular schools, contrary to the present system where mathematics was taught only in the Ministries of Punishment and Personnel.

Although law had not been part of the classical curriculum, Yu believed that study of law was justifiable because the principles of law were quite close in spirit to the rites. His primary motivation, however, was not the similitude of law to rites, but his awareness that one of the main causes for the corruption of the regular bureaucracy and the misuse of power against the people was the usurpation of power by the clerks of both the capital and local districts. They obtained their power not just because they remained more-or-less permanently on the scene while magistrates (and capital officials as well) were rotated relatively frequently, but because they had become indispensable to generalist officials through their mastery of technical fields like law. Yu held that scholars should have knowledge of law and legal principles so that once they assumed magisterial posts, they would not have to entrust operation of the law to clerks.[54]

Yu's approach to the military arts, mathematics, and law were similar. They had been denigrated and neglected in Chosŏn society even though two of them had been part of the classical curriculum. By including all three subjects in the curriculum of his schools he sought to expand the education of the generalist by restoring it to the classical norm, therefore to transcend the current, narrow boundaries of education that were limited to intellectual training alone. What he certainly was not prepared to do was to elevate the knowledge of the material world, technology, and science, or practical and utilitarian action above the level of moral knowledge.

Technology and Technical Schools. Yu was certainly interested in developing practical skills of use in government beyond the military arts, mathematics, and law, but only within the context of a separate but inferior system of technical schools that conformed with current and earlier practices in both China and Korea. Although mathematics and law would be included in the curriculum for his officials-in-training in his new school system, he favored continuation, with only minor modifications, of current schools of mathematics and law as well as medicine, yin-yang, and foreign languages for specialists.[55]

Not only did he urge that talented individuals in these technical skills be sought out and given qualification examinations by district magistrates and subdistrict officials, or appointed directly to office, but he even sought to break down the current stigma against technical knowledge by insisting that even an incumbent official or Confucian scholar who possessed the requisite talents be given a concurrent post as a specialist or as a teacher of his speciality.[56] Even so, this suggestion involved encouraging yangban to engage in technical occupations, not elevating technology to the level of moral knowledge or the status of technologists to the level of the generalists trained in moral standards and classical knowledge.

This point is illustrated by his use of quotas to restrict the numbers of students in the specialist schools. His quotas for language schools included 70 in the capital and 65 in certain key districts, and 110 in the schools of medicine, astronomy, geography, law, and mathematics combined, or a grand total of 245. Only 25 new students were to be admitted after the triennial selection examination, about 100 slots fewer than what the existing law code called for.[57] These limiting quotas illustrate his belief that the number of technical experts had to be confined to the demand for them by the state. By no means was society to be allowed to pursue knowledge on its own and transform society by an unregulated pursuit of nonmoral knowledge. Technical knowledge was useful to the state, but it could not become the dominant goal of education.

It is only because of the contrast between Yu's limited admiration for technology and the current state of disdain for technical expertise and its practitioners that he appears more enlightened and liberal. He was chagrined by the current lack of care in selecting technical students and the lack of salaries for their support, and he also deplored the lack of incentives for young men to choose technical professions; the most they could hope for was a small number of sinecures (*ch'ea*). Since the only motive for choosing a technical career in his own time was to escape personal labor service, the government had to recruit specialist trainees from the provinces against their will. "Even though the numbers [of such students] is large, none of them has any talent and they are of no use." Because of the shortage of jobs or posts, too many trained technicians had to go without posts and fend for themselves to earn a living.

The government could not allow technicians to be held in such low esteem because it still had a need for them. The best solution was to reduce the number of students in the specialist schools, establish regular salaries, reduce the quotas of those selected in entrance examinations, and create enough regular bureaucratic positions to employ all the graduates. These measures would be preferable to the current forced recruitment of unwilling candidates and random filling of quotas. In addition, anyone who so desired should be allowed to take the specialist recruitment examinations instead of restricting them to students registered in the specialist schools.[58]

Technology and Technical Schools: Medicine, Astronomy, Foreign Languages. Yu insisted that royal doctors be chosen from the ablest medical specialists in the kingdom and that men skilled in medical practice and acupuncture in the provinces be recruited and examined by local officials, appointed to regular posts, given special land grants, and exempted from military cloth support taxes. He deplored the current state of medical care in Korea because the post of medical doctor in the rural districts, called medical student (*ŭisaeng*), was filled with men of base or servile status. These medical students were required to supply medicine on their own as part of their tribute obligation, and they were frequently treated by the local magistrates as if they were errand boys or official slaves, constantly in fear of the usual beatings. They were so harassed by nonmedical duties that they had no time to study or perfect their medical practice.

Yu contrasted the situation with his understanding of contemporary China in which every prefecture and district (*chou* and *hsien*) had a doctor. Yu did not insist on the immediate establishment of medical schools in the local districts. If instructions were issued to recruit men already skilled in medical practice, it would be sufficient for local needs; it would also provide an incentive for young men to turn to medicine as a respected profession with job opportunities in state service. He pointed out that the current dynastic code had established quotas for both medical and legal students (*ŭisaeng*, *yulsaeng*) in the districts, ranging from eight to sixteen depending on the size of the district, but all were of base or slave status and hardly any were literate. He also claimed that there was ancient precedent for the recruitment of doctors by the state.[59]

Yu complained that the specialists' positions in various capital agencies such as the Palace Physicians' Court (Naeŭiwŏn), the Directorate of Medicine (Chŏn'ŭigam), the Directorate of Astronomy (Kwansanggam), and the Court of Interpreters (Sayŏgwŏn) were all unranked sinecures (*ch'ea*). He suggested that both rank and salaries be provided for these officials in correspondence to their talents, and that they be subjected to a biannual review of their performance for promotion or demotion. He also drew up a detailed set of regulations for entrance examinations for students in the technical schools, specifying the technical texts to be used in the examinations for each.[60] Of course, Yu was living in an age when an educated man could lay claim to conversance with the full body of knowledge about life, but his attempt to define and impose curricula in the area of technical competence confirms his illiberal and conservative tendencies in the pursuit and instruction of knowledge.

Technology and Technical Schools: Music. Yu also castigated the pathetic situation in the Court of Music (Chang'agwŏn) in the capital. Under prevailing practice court musicians were divided by personal status into commoner musicians (*aksaeng*) and slave musicians (*akkong*), with quotas of 297 for the former and 518 for the latter. To fill quotas, people from the provinces were forced to move to the capital together with support taxpayers who were responsible for providing their upkeep. They were given examinations on their instruments, but only 2 or 3 percent were lucky enough to receive a sinecure; the rest had to perform their duties without salary and most of them ended up as runners in the Court of Music, Ministry of Rites, or other court offices, even though they retained the title of Musician. The higher officials in charge of the Court of Music had become wealthy by establishing large quotas of musicians and requiring fees (*kap'o*) from peasants liable for the duty. If the individuals owing service in the Court of Music absconded, the fee obligation would then be shifted to their relatives. Yu proposed establishing fixed quotas, providing regular salaries to the musicians, testing the candidates upon admission, and weeding out the incompetent. Unqualified musicians would be subject to corporal punishment, dismissal, and enrollment for military service.[61]

Lacunae in his Program for Technicians. In summary, Yu sought to improve the training, qualification, support, and status of the current range of the technical professions and to remove the stigma attached to technical knowledge. Yu was determined to elevate the respect for both military knowledge and skills undoubtedly because he was firmly aware of the national disasters suffered during the Japanese and Manchu invasions in the last century, but he left out any serious discussion of military technology, such as firearms, gunpowder, and shipbuilding (let alone pure science), from his section of the curriculum for the education of the new governing class. Instead he raised those issues only in his chapters on military defense.

The school curriculum for his morally aware, well-rounded candidate for office was to be based on the ancient prescription for a well-rounded education, which included archery, mathematics, and law. This approach represented an important correction to the denigration of the military and technical skills that had occurred by what Yu regarded as a distortion of classical wisdom by a misunderstanding generated within a Korean society ironically devoted to Confucian wisdom. He was not, however, able or willing to place technical knowledge on a par with moral or classical knowledge and risk a revolution in traditional Confucian priorities.

COMPROMISE BETWEEN EQUAL OPPORTUNITY AND INHERITED STATUS

From Inherited to Functional Status and Age

There is no question that the ancient Chinese model of education and recruitment that Yu admired contained egalitarian implications because the search for talent was not to be restricted by artificial restraints of birth or inherited status. Yet nowhere in his work did he ever say that his objective was the creation of a totally egalitarian society. Rather, he professed a desire to expand opportunity beyond the limits imposed on his own society by the respect for inherited status. This did not mean, however, that he opposed status categorically; on the contrary, he supported status but believed that the basis of status had to be converted primarily from inherited position to moral behavior, and within the society of the morally enlightened, to age.

Yu chose to discuss the implications of this problem by a device he used frequently, a dialogue between himself and an unidentified antagonist who functioned as a foil for Yu's subtler points of argument. In one section the antagonist attempted to refute Yu's argument for expanded opportunity because it would be destructive of the social order. He appealed to higher authority to justify his case in defense of the yangban by arguing that Chu Hsi himself had believed that the scholars represented a class of men who were entitled to elevation above the common herd, and hence should be separated from them. Since the yangban also regarded themselves as the class of scholars, the argument was tantamount to a defense of existing hereditary yangban privilege.

Chu Hsi's crucial statement was his remark on the community compact system (*hyangyak*) that if a person did not belong to the class of scholars (*saryu*), he should not be ranked with them. This statement implied that since Chu Hsi meant that *saryu* and "the families of scholars" (*sajok*) were synonymous, the *sajok*, not just individual scholars who excelled, had to be distinguished from commoners (*sŏin*).[62]

Yu, however, denied that the two terms were synonymous and accused his antagonist of misinterpreting Chu Hsi:

> What [Chu Hsi] was talking about when he spoke of "the class of scholars" did not meant the same thing as what we today call "the families of scholars." The so-called "class of scholars" means a class of scholars who are scholars because they engage in scholarly pursuits. The "families of scholars" [*sajok*] are sons of scholars and officials [*sabu*], and they are members of that group because of their surnames and lineages [*sŏngjok*]. If status were determined by the practice of righteousness, then throughout the world people would compete by diligent effort to achieve virtuous behavior, and this would be the means by which rites and mores would be perfected. But if status is determined on the basis of pedigree [*munji*], then throughout the world people would only make distinctions on the basis of family background [*munbŏl*], and this would be the reason for disputes to arise.[63]

Undoubtedly, the two terms, *saryu* and *sajok* were used rather loosely and interchangeably in Korean society at that time, but Yu insisted that Korean linguistic usage (as represented by the argument of his antagonist) represented a distortion of Chu Hsi's teachings. In no way could the superior status of scholars be used to justify superior status for families maintained over generations. "The class of scholars" was a term that denoted function (*ŏp*), not blood, and function was an attribute of an individual, not a family. The moral teachings of Chu Hsi could never justify the hereditary principle, which as we can gather from Yu's treatment of the Chinese literature, was one of the evils that plagued Chinese society from the Northern and Southern dynasties period through the T'ang.

Yu's antagonist then countered by claiming that Yu's position would have the effect of eliminating the standards for distinguishing between "the noble and base" (*kwich'ŏn*), without which inferiors would lord it over their superiors. Yu himself did not question the validity of social status distinctions and agreed that disrespectful behavior by inferiors was contrary to social harmony, but the problem for him was to establish the proper definition of nobility and baseness. Virtue was the only true criterion of nobility; people should be "divided into classes" (*pullyu*) after an investigation of their virtue, and within each class individuals were to be ranked by age. "Then the custom of respecting virtue will be bright and the principle of treating people as noble who really are noble will become even more prominent as a matter of course."[64]

Within his newly structured schools Yu had specified that the main criterion for rank order, particularly at the important ritual ceremonies, would be age instead of inherited status, with an occasional exception made in the case of truly superior talent. One other exception was that regular quota students who resided in the Inner Hall would as a group take precedence over the irregular students who were to reside in the Outer Hall for a probationary period of one year. In any case, the emphasis on age as the main criterion for status was an idea he obviously owed to Chu Hsi, among others, whose work on this subject he quoted so extensively.[65]

Since the determination of seating order at school rites was contrary to the current practice in Korea of affording higher status to yangban over commoners and legitimate sons over nothoi, Yu was at pains to defend his position in some detail. He asserted that "There is no one in the world who is born noble," implying that nobility was a matter of moral quality rather than inherited status. In ancient China when the princes of the Son of Heaven were enrolled in school, they too were ranked by age with the other students. If that were true, it made even more sense to require the same of the sons of the scholars and officials (*sadaebu*), yet in Korea the addiction to ascriptive status criteria had distorted the principles of the ancients.

Yu at this point launched another tirade against the excessive respect for pedigree (*munji*) and prestigious hereditary lineage (*chokse*) (see chap. 4). He criticized the restriction of opportunity for the highest office to the yangban, or hereditary lineages (*sebŏl*) as he called them here, even though they were "inferior in talent or worthless."[66] And he rejected the popular but specious argument that social status (*myŏngbun*) ought to be determined by birth rather than by the degree of one's moral behavior. For that reason he insisted that inherited social status could not be carried into his schools as a basis for discrimination among the students: "How much more important is it that in the local schools, which are places where people are ranked in accordance with their age and where proper morals and education are inculcated, there is even less justification for ranking people in accordance with their family lineage [*munbŏl*]."[67]

Exclusion of Slaves, Merchants, and Shamans

Since Yu lived in a country dominated by aristocratic privilege and social discrimination of various kinds, he had to confront the contradiction between the principle of equal opportunity and the fact of social discrimination. He was also a yangban himself, with a sympathy for his fellows that often expressed itself in a caution and conservatism that conflicted with the radical conclusions of his intellect. In addition, the social context of ancient China whence he derived the models for education and recruitment was feudal and hierarchical. These factors operated to impose limits on Yu's capacity for radical egalitarianism even if that had been his intent, and these limits are illustrated in his proposed regulations for the admittance of students to his revamped official schools. When he stated unequivocally, for example, that he had no intention of removing restrictions against traditional objects of discrimination, it meant that he had no idea of opening the path of opportunity for the highest levels of education and government office to all members of society: "Sons of artisans, merchants, people of the markets and wells, sons of shamans and other miscellaneous types, and official or private slaves will not be permitted to enter school."[68] These restrictions would pose no problem for understanding Yu's thought if it were not for the powerful arguments he launched elsewhere in his book against inherited slavery and for the extension of the commercial sector of the economy. But in the chapters dealing with those issues, too, he tempered radical logic with a conservative adaptation to social and traditional counterarguments.

How then did he define the class of people eligible for admittance to his proposed official schools? To what extent would it represent the creation of new and broader standards of eligibility than the existing system of private education that served to perpetuate the transmission of opportunity for education and office to a narrow (and what Wagner argued was an ever-narrowing) group of yangban?

He defined the eligible group in rather specific terms as "the sons and younger brothers of officials [*taebusa*] who have the will to learn, and [the sons and younger brothers of] outstanding commoners. . . ."[69] Obviously artisans, merchants, and slaves were conspicuous by their absence, obviating any possible claim that Yu intended to enlighten the whole population. In addition, the very phraseology separating commoners from "officials and scholars" even though both were eligible for admission, indicates Yu's perception that he was virtually joining two separate classes in his schools rather than uniting both in a broader, undifferentiated class.

In any case, once the youths of the correct status reached the age of fifteen *se*, they would be allowed to apply for admission to school. Local teachers, village elders, and even heads of families would be allowed to recommend worthy young students, and even if some aspiring young students lacked supporting recommendations, they would still be permitted to apply.[70]

This definition certainly did not represent any alteration of the existing legal situation since commoners were entitled to stand for the civil service examinations under the dynastic code. Nonetheless, Yu obviously was hoping to break the de facto stranglehold of the yangban on opportunities for education, the civil-service examinations, and officeholding, but not by extending opportunity to perhaps 30 or 40 percent of the population, the base people (*ch'ŏnmin*), most of whom were slaves, or commoners engaged in low-status occupations like commerce and industry.[71]

Yulgok had offered a similar plan except that he did not insist explicitly on the elimination of examinations or annulment of status conferred by possession of an examination degree. He had advocated recommendation and selection of outstanding classics and literary licentiates (*saengwŏn*, *chinsa* degree holders) and *yuhak* to be selected scholars (Sŏnsa) to form a pool of talent in the schools from which official appointments would be made. The existing degree-holders and *yuhak* who did not become selected scholars would continue to be registered in the Four Schools of the capital, "in accordance with old custom."[72] Their only obligation would be to attend rites at the Confucian shrines in the schools and formal visits of high officials to the schools.

Yulgok also pointed out that in his own time (late sixteenth century) there were a number of school students in the provinces (*kyosaeng*) who were, in fact, almost illiterate. Since these men were by custom listed on the registers of the district towns in the quota for scholars, it would not be feasible to strike their names from the list, but these older incompetents might be removed gradually and their slots filled by younger talented scholars. Only the extra-quota students, however, would be subject to loss of status and enrollment for military service. There was another category of scholar in the provinces called "nothos scholar" (*ŏbyu*), and Yulgok proposed examining them to test their knowledge, sending those capable of instruction to school, and eliminating the others by enrolling them for military service.[73]

Yu Hyŏngwŏn's plan went further than Yulgok's because he contemplated the total abolition of the examination system and did not discuss methods of dealing with degree-holders left over from the old system, but both men shared the ideal of confining privileged student status to men of talent and bona fide scholars and returning all others to the ranks of the commoner class. Yu appeared more ruthless than Yulgok in his willingness to eliminate the vestiges of unearned, hereditary scholar status, but neither of them envisioned an egalitarian, unstratified society. Both saw the commoner class as an intermediate stratum, from which the talented could rise first to the temporary but privileged category of registered student, and then into the ranks of the ruling class, while the drop-outs or failures would descend again to the ranks of the commoners.

This attitude was shared by many of the advocates of reform of the military service system throughout the seventeenth and eighteenth centuries, but the net result of their efforts was only the creation of the "select military officers" under the Equal Service Reform of 1750. The select military officers were a privileged group liable to a fine or tax equivalent to the ordinary *yangyŏk* tax, but by remaining exempt from actual service they were allowed to avoid a decline in social status to ranks of commoners, or "men of good status" (*yang'in*) (see chap. 14).

Vicarious Punishment of Slaves for Misdemeanors

Another manifestation of Yu's toleration for existing discrimination even inside his school system that was supposed to honor age as the only criterion of status was the leniency he allowed in the punishment of students of slaveholding families. If they were absent from school for as much as fifteen days a month, their household slaves would be beaten in the study hall as a form of vicarious punishment.[74] Obviously, the ones who did not own slaves would have to take the beating themselves, and since most of the slaveholders were yangban, Yu was obviously bowing in their direction.

This idea contradicted his previous statement about preserving schools as separate loci for egalitarian treatment, but it was consistent with his refusal to permit slaves any access at all to the school system. Slaves, however, could be used to perform the menial functions in the school including the preparation of food in the dining hall.[75] Yu's concept of progressive reform was to regularize slave service in the schools by attaching their residential land (provided in his new land distribution scheme) to the school, exempting them from taxes and military service, and providing them with regular salaries.[76] He hoped that by the eventual establishment of the *kongjŏn* (public land) system of state ownership and allotments he could insulate both the schools and the slaves from private manipulation.

He hoped also to put an end to the practice of well-to-do families donating land and slaves to schools in return for obtaining student status for their sons without their passing the school qualification examinations so that they could gain exemption from labor and military service taxes. He sought to do this by setting quotas of school slaves (*pogye*) and providing them with legal exemptions from taxes and military service, a temporary measure that could be eliminated once his national land system were adopted. In addition, the duties of the school slaves were to be limited to service for the school to prevent them from being exploited for private purposes by students.[77]

Yu was particularly distressed by the arrogant behavior of the slaves at the contemporary National Academy. So prestigious was the National Academy that the students and aspirants for examination success willingly subjected themselves to the rude and discourteous behavior of the academy slaves.

> Not only do the [academy slaves] pull people by the arm, choke them by the neck, and strip them of their coats and pants, but they also burst into homes and take away family property, the same as if they were stealing it. This is because the scholars in their pursuit of benefit have no shame. On the contrary, they regard it as an honor [to be manhandled by the academy slaves]. What kind of behavior is this . . . ?[78]

Of course, as Yu pointed out, once the examination system were abolished and replaced by a recommendation system, all reason for these practices would cease (because the National Academy would no longer ease the path to examination success). Until that time, however, the government had to enforce regulations requiring slaves to show respect for their betters.

Instead of advocating an end to the use of slave labor in the schools, he argued that if the state fulfilled its duty to provide slave labor in the schools (instead of depending on private donations), this kind of corruption would be precluded.[79] In a similar vein, his regulations prohibited students from using school slaves for private errands or from arbitrarily punishing slaves for perceived misconduct.[80]

The only modification of existing status discrimination against slaves in schools was elimination of the distinction in the titles of musicians between those of slave and commoner (i.e., base and good).[81] Since graduates of the technical schools were to be appointed to posts in the bureaucratic agency that had jurisdiction over that specialty, slaves might be eligible for such appointments, but they would not be expected to cross over to the realm of the bureaucratic generalists.[82]

In short, Yu's treatment of slaves in his regulations indicate very little sympathy for their inherited status debilities, a major contrast with his far more sympathetic attitude toward them expressed in his chapter on slavery. This might be explained in one of two ways: either he wrote the addendum on slavery after he finished his other chapters, and it represented the product of his more mature views, or because he did not envision a sudden and immediate end to slavery anyway, he felt that he had to discuss the school system with the system of slavery intact.

Acceptability of the ŭm *Privilege and Nepotism*

Yu realized that the yangban of contemporary Korean society would fear the loss of their coveted privileges and status if his new system of replacing hereditary status and influence with a moral basis for recruitment and registration in schools as the only bases for social distinction were adopted. He not only acknowledged the legitimacy of their fears, but agreed to retain the *ŭm* privilege as a sop to the discontented yangban. He justified this modification of his rules by pointing out that the early kings of antiquity had also taken cognizance of such fears and in warm, tenderhearted fashion had authorized the granting of the special "protection" privilege (*ŭmgŭp*) by which the sons of incumbent officials "were ranked by law with the class of scholars" (*saryu*), protecting them against immediate demotion to the rank of commoner.[83]

One can but surmise his motives, but it was most likely a retreat born from sympathy for his own class and his empathetic reaction to their anguish at the loss of long accepted privileges and conventions. Another sign of sympathy for his own class was reflected in a provision that smacks slightly of nepotism. In his regulations for the recommendation of young scholars to the lowest-level schools, he allowed immediate relatives, like a son or a brother, to recommend siblings, just as long as the recommendee was qualified.[84] One might have expected Yu to be more concerned about the problem of nepotism, particularly in a society that placed such a high value on family connections and loyalty.

Leniency for Yangban Flunkouts

Yu was also willing to mitigate the threat of expulsion from school by providing a probationary period to allow time for restitution:

> If at the present time we were suddenly to punish them (poor students) for this, eliminate all of them, and enlist them in the army, then not only would it lead to

> resentment, it would also provide a great way to destroy people. What we must first do is for several years have the king personally send down his bright, trustworthy, warm, and feeling instructions, promulgate a set of regulations, and make everyone aware of them so they will clearly understand what is in the king's mind. He should also encourage and uplift the people. In addition, two or three supervisors should be selected to make the rounds of the provinces to examine people and provide rewards and punishments to them. Only after this is done should we then carry out the law uniformly and without repercussion.[85]

He was also willing to provide an additional measure of leniency for yangban flunkouts. Whereas commoners who were ejected from school would be required to return all but their basic one-*kyŏng* land grant to the state (under Yu's proposed land-grant system, see chap. 8) and be enrolled for military service, bona fide sons of yangban could be enrolled in the special guard units reserved for members of their class – the Loyal and Righteous Guards (Ch'ung'ŭiwi) and the Loyal and Obedient Guards (Ch'ungsunwi), that were features of the early Chosŏn military system – and would retain two *kyŏng* of land. Even greater benefits would be afforded to eldest legitimate sons who were heirs to the family line (*sejok*) and those entitled to the protection privilege; their names would only be stricken from the school register and they would not be required to return their student land grants to the state.[86]

Privileges for Royal Princes

Princes of the royal line were also to be given ranks and awards of protected land (*ŭmjŏn*) on the basis of whether they were sons of the queen or royal concubines, and these distinctions would remain intact.[87] Furthermore, those members of the royal clan enrolled in the Peer's School who failed examinations, missed class without excuse, committed a breach of etiquette, or broke the rules of the school, would be subjected to less punishment than commoners in the other schools. Minors might be whipped, but adults on salary would only suffer salary reductions; there was no provision for reducing them to commoner status.[88]

Yu realized that his authorization of a separate Peer's School for princes of the royal blood contradicted his perception of ideal practice in ancient China where the sons of the elite, from those of the Son of Heaven and the feudal lords down to the high ministers, important officials, and scholars, all entered the National Academy to receive instruction. Furthermore, in that age the only criteria for appointment to office were worth and virtue; no one (supposedly) was favored because he was a close relative of the monarch, nor was anyone abandoned or shut out from office merely because of his blood. "They had high officials who were both relatives of officials and from [families] of different surnames."[89]

It was in the later age of moral decline, however, that the system of equal treatment of nobles and commoners was abandoned; close relatives of the emperor were honored with salaries in this period but they were not appointed to official posts, the effect of which was to create a class division between the imperial relatives and the scholar-official class (*sadaebu*). The establishment of Peers' Schools in later dynasties was thus an accommodation to this custom. Yu argued that his own provision for a separate Peer's School was nothing more than acquiescence to current conditions – another of his concessions to discriminatory practice.[90]

The Functional Definition of Status

Despite Yu's willingness to adopt modifications in his system to mollify the objections of the yangban, he refused to modify his insistence that all students in school be ranked by age no matter what their status. Since he was unwilling to call for the removal of existing marks of status distinction in society outside the school system, however, he had to work out a resolution of conflict that would emerge when diametrically opposed rules came into conflict.

Yu had his imaginary interlocutor assert that "Since it is the custom of our country that the yangban are a different class [*p'umnyu*] than nothoi [*sŏŏl*] and commoners [*sŏjok*] and cannot be mixed together in terms of age," Yu should modify his position to make some accommodation with that custom.[91] If Yu insisted on mixing yangban students with nothoi and commoners and seating them by age, he should at least be willing to seat the yangban students separately ahead of the others. And at subdistrict convocations (*hyanghoe*), the nothoi and commoners should also be seated separately, allowing only selected scholars (Sŏnsa) and court officials to sit with the yangban. Only then would it be permissible to allow promotion to higher schools or admittance to the National Academy without reference to pedigree (*munji*) and to establish seating rank in the National Academy on the basis of age alone.[92]

Yu rejected this compromise. What was true for ancient times was still true for the present. Only if the selection and dismissal of students were based solely on talent or performance, "would every man rouse himself to virtuous behavior so that the custom of respecting and yielding to others will be practiced throughout the local villages and districts, and even chronic evil practices transformed." Yu could not allow things to be done halfway because a true king could succeed in transforming mores only if he had the proper resolve not to compromise with his duty.[93]

Yu's antagonist then proposed that even if commoner selected scholars were ranked with yangban students because of their outstanding academic accomplishment, at least this practice should be restricted only to the regular quota student population in the Inner Hall. Extra-quota students on probation in the Outer Hall need not qualify for this privilege since they had not yet demonstrated their scholarly abilities.

Yu responded by appealing to an undisputed higher authority to justify his rule, claiming that Chu Hsi was the one who had explained that "ranking people by age is a universal principle throughout all the world." Assuming, however, that the yangban would not be swayed by this argument, he also set out to provide a principle of social stratification that would obviate all contrary arguments.

Yu's rule for group formation and membership was certainly not the notion that all men were to be treated equally. On the contrary, he confirmed the legitimacy of status, but based it on function or occupation (*ŏp*). If every one had the same function or occupation then every one would have the same work (*sa*), and all would deserve to be placed in the same rank. He did not say so here, but judging from his position on other points it appears that he felt that function or occupation should be the basis for defining social groups, and that respect relations or etiquette between groups should also be determined by their relative position in the status hierarchy. Yet Yu was more concerned with justifying the existence of a separate community, like his new schools, within which the rules and standards of etiquette could be separate and distinct from other groups, or the rest of society.[94]

Status Conflict: Between School and Home

This point becomes clear when we consider Yu's answer to another hypothetical problem raised by his imaginary interlocutor who asked Yu to conjure the anomalies and embarrassments that would be produced when the people of the outside world of hereditary status rubbed elbows with the denizens of his insulated ivory tower. If the sons of petty clerks were admitted to school and mixed indiscriminately with the sons of regular officials at school ceremonies, for example, then at official school rites or convocations attended by parents, the commoner-clerk fathers would come running into the school courtyard in the humble manner befitting servants while the yangban fathers, by contrast, would be comporting themselves with all the dignity and reserve that characterized their superior station in life. "How can you have this?"

In replying to this objection Yu did not deny the importance of maintaining behavioral differences in accordance with status, and he did not argue that commoner-clerk fathers of students should be afforded equal treatment with the official or yangban fathers. Instead, he recognized that commoner clerks had a different function or status than yangban but that any conflicts generated by contact between members of different functional or status groups within a setting that operated by different rules than ordinary society – that is, his schools – could be reconciled by a legitimate compartmentalization of behavior.

If the clerk-fathers had to rush into the school courtyard in demeaning fashion, it was because their lowly functions required that they observe respectful attitudes toward their legitimate superiors. Conversely, the reason why it was legitimate to rank their sons together with the sons of yangban in school was because they were both performing the same function or occupation (*ŏp*). Just because their sons were to be afforded equal treatment with the yangban sons did not give the commoner-clerk fathers the right to demand equal status with their betters. Even though the treatment of fathers and sons might appear anomalous, Yu argued, the basis for his determination of this procedure derived from a single principle – that status in society should be based on *ŏp*.[95]

Yu believed that the functional or occupational criterion for status should not conflict with the fundamental Confucian position that true manhood was determined by one's righteousness and virtue, and he argued that function or occupation had been the means for ranking people in social situations in classical antiquity, but because in the later age of moral imperfection the moral basis of status was neglected, "doubt arose over whether people who shared the same occupation should again be ranked together or not." Although he did not attempt to demonstrate why men engaged in the same occupation should also possess the same moral caliber, he contrasted it with respect based on birth: "Family lineage [*munjok*] is tied in with whether [one's forebears] prospered or suffered in life; it is not the basis for discussing the establishment of learning and the esteem for [proper] order." In other words, in Korean society hereditary yangban lineages prohibited the establishment of a proper system of status based on educational attainment and moral worth, which would have been equivalent to a functional or occupational definition of status categories.[96]

Yu adhered to his position about the legitimate, functional basis of status in the face of problematic contradictions inside immediate families. If a younger brother's function happened to be that of a scholar while his elder brother was only a commoner, then the younger brother would deserve to be afforded superior status. The contradiction between brotherly respect and functional status could be reconciled by distinguishing between the loci of action and conforming to etiquette appropriate to the particular situation. In other words, within the family setting the younger brother owed respect to his elder brother, but in a public situation their positions would be reversed. If, however, the brothers found it too difficult to reverse their roles in public, they would be permitted to avoid contact with one another to save face.[97]

Yu used the same reasoning with regard to the treatment of nothoi of yangban and princes of royal blood. Both categories would be treated as equal with other students inside the schools and ranked by age, but this did not mean that the principle of equality should be extended outside the school walls to society at large. In the family setting strict distinctions would be maintained between the legitimate and nothoi sons (*ŏmjŏksŏjibun*),[98] and in all general extracurricular seating arrangements nothoi would always be seated below the legitimate sons irrespective of age. Yu also argued that under his functional principle of status it was quite possible that a single individual might be a scholar early in his life and ranked by age among the superior scholar class, and a commoner later in life with loss of his earlier higher status.[99]

Even though Yu opposed the negative effects on Korean society by the overemphasis on inherited status, especially among the upper levels of the yangban, he did not counterpoise an egalitarian society as an alternative. Slaves, merchants, artisans, and shamans would still remain at the bottom, and even in his new schools members of the royal family and scions of yangban would be afforded a number of privileges that would assuage their fears and induce acceptance of the plan. Yet even if his systems of official schools and appointment to office through the recommendation of morally superior individuals were achieved and the yangban replaced by a new elite selected solely on the basis of superior moral behavior, his new officials and students in his new schools would possess higher status than commoners.

No matter what the nature of society outside his schools, Yu wanted to preserve status as the basis for ranking the students, but only on the basis of age. Since this would create conflicts between two systems of status, Yu had to work out methods for resolving them, either the choice of one system over the other depending on the locus of action, or avoidance of contact that would force an embarrassing choice. What Yu had done was not to replace a society of status groups with a society of atomized individuals, or reject status as a legitimate means of social stratification, but to reject inheritance as the basis for status and replace it with moral behavior for his encapsulated schools, for all of society sometime in the future.

No Fear of Social Destabilization

Few Could Overcome Psychophysical Energy. To assuage opponents of his plan to accept students of various social backgrounds into the schools and differentiate among them only on the basis of age, Yu sought to persuade them that the plan would have no serious destabilizing consequences for contemporary respect relations and social structure. To prove this point he cited the current situation in the high-level military examinations (*mukwa*) where men were tested solely on their skill in archery and horseback riding. Most of the candidates were "coarse and base people" and the successful ones were then ranked together with the members of the hereditary elite (*sajok*) and commoners in terms of their military skills. Despite this practice, he had never heard that it had resulted in disrespectful or disobedient behavior on the part of these people of inferior status. "If it is like this for people with skill and strength, then how much more so should it be for the selection of men of virtue and righteousness?"[100] In other words, equal opportunity in recruitment does and should not lead to a disruptive egalitarian ethic in social life.

A more serious and telling indication of a conservative streak in his thought, however, was his view that emphasis on moral behavior and age in the new schools would do little to overturn the current pattern of social stratification.

"Moreover, even though it were done like this, those people who would be members of 'the class of scholars [*saryu*]' would all be the sons or younger brothers of hereditary lineages [*sejok*] anyway. As for those who might rise from the commoners, *it would be lucky if there were even one or two of them*"[101] (italics added).

Yu explained that his conviction that opening up the opportunity for upward mobility on the basis of virtue or talent would not have serious destabilizing effects on society derived from two ideas. The first was his belief in the validity of the Neo-Confucian interpretation of the flaws in human nature. Even though man by nature was good (a Confucian dogma supported by many Neo-Confucians like Chu Hsi), the human mind at birth contained within it two elements, principle and psychophysical energy (*igi*). Principle was pure and good and represented natural human instincts for moral behavior as defined in Neo-Confucian terms while psychophysical energy had the effect of clouding or obscuring the principle in the mind. Even in the absence of artificial barriers against personal advancement, few men would rise from the ranks of the common man to the class of scholars and officials (even under Yu's system) because "man [at birth] is endowed with clearness or muddiness in terms of the type of psychophysical energy [*ki*] that he has."[102] He presumed that only by great effort could man return to his inborn goodness either by study or introspection (or both), and it was not to be expected that a large percentage of mankind would succeed in this effort, an argument that resonates with Thomas Metzger's portrayal of the Neo-Confucian search for fulfillment as an arduous and anxious quest for sagehood or absolute purity and oneness.[103]

The Stabilizing Effects of Family Environment. Yu's second point was a rather sophisticated argument about the effects of environment on human beings, a point of view that is redolent more of modern psychology or sociology than Confucian thought:

"In terms of what a person's residence and upbringing add to his nature, there is a vast difference between a hereditary (yangban) family and a commoner family."[104] The consequences of family background (i.e., environment) were not uniform; they could improve an individual's life chances or on the contrary contribute to laziness or lack of effort on the part of the well-to-do.

> [The elite] by relying on the vestiges of their family's [good fortune] are without fear of falling to a lower station in life. Therefore, they rest secure in their ordinary habits and do not cultivate themselves. There are few of them that rise in terms of reputation or virtue, and this is because the system makes it so.
>
> If only the good men were selected [for school or office] and the untalented were, as a matter of course, left behind, and if there were held out before a person opportunities for glory and prominence, while behind him there was the chance of falling into the mud and dirt, then of those people whose characters were firmly rooted in brightness and intelligence and who were practiced in the teachings of their fathers and brothers, who among them would not be diligent?[105]

In other words, inherited status and wealth contributed to upper class complacency, which could be remedied by introducing the classical ideal of recruitment by merit with appropriate incentives, but the result would not be leveling of the upper class but their improved performance by study and self-cultivation. Yu was concerned as much about the revitalization of the ruling class as the removal of existing barriers against the rise of a few more virtuous and talented individuals into its ranks: "It is only that if we did select men on the basis of virtuous behavior, it would be a natural condition that there would be many talented men among the hereditary lineages. But to limit opportunity to pedigree and deny it to men of talent is to confuse the teachings of the world. There could be no more serious harm than this."[106]

Yu sought to becalm the aristocratic opponents of the egalitarian implications of his plan by pointing out that the de facto advantages of wealth, status, and a family background with a scholarly tradition would have the effect of preserving the position of the yangban. His sociological intuition was impeccable: the children of the well-to-do undoubtedly did have better success as a group than their lower-class competitors, and his sociological explanation of their success is far better than any belief that yangban simply inherited their status without having to exert effort to pass the examinations.

Even though Yu's assurances may not have been heartening to certain yangban who would understandably be concerned about slipping from the ranks of the socially prominent if opportunities for education and appointment were widened, his attempt to make such concessions to the legitimacy of privilege and to assert that moral reform could be achieved without excessive disruptive social consequences to the status quo only reflects the internalized constraints on his Confucian social radicalism.

Yu's Influence on Subsequent Generations

Yu never thought that his criticism of the examination system or advocacy of government schools as the basis for a recommendation system of bureaucratic recruitment constituted innovative thinking because these ideas were derived primarily from the Chinese classics. One might criticize him for his desultory account of the history of Korean views on these issues, but he undoubtedly presumed (and correctly) that the basic points of view had already been laid out in the Chinese literature.

Insight into the influence of the two sections of his *Pan'gye surok* on schools and the examination system on thinkers of the eighteenth century may be assessed by estimating how widespread his ideas had circulated in the eighteenth century. Yi Man'un, who revised the version of the original *Munhŏnbigo* between 1770 and 1782, chose to insert three statements by Yu Hyŏngwŏn in the section on the history of bureaucratic recruitment, but he chose nothing from Yu's writing for the section on schools. The selection on recruitment contains Yu's proposal for a system of guaranteed recommendation that would keep both recommendor and recommendee honest by the threat of punishment. It also includes Yu's criticism of the routine way that kings conducted the special *chŏngsi* and *alsŏng* palace examinations, and his call for the abolition of the examination system not only for failing to obtain the best men for office, but also for wrecking public mores by encouraging competition.[107]

Yi also quoted a statement of An Chŏngbok, an intellectual heir to Yu's thought, that traced the history of recruitment in China and reflected Yu's ideas rather closely. An described the system of recommendation and selection at the village level in the Chou; the use of guaranteed recommendation in the commanderies and principates and hiring of subordinates by active officials in the regular prefectures and districts during Han times; the use of the Chung-cheng, who recommended men for office according to the nine ranks (*chiu-p'in*) in the Wei and Chin dynasties of the third century; and the adoption of the examination system in the Sui. He also praised the ancient method of recruitment because

> It cultivated [educated] men in the *sang* and *suk* [local schools], and recommended them for the higher schools, until they reached the court of the Son of Heaven. They only took scholars of virtuous behavior and talent in the arts, and in the countryside no one of any worth was left out [of the recruitment process].
>
> In Han times, even though the instruction provided in the local schools [the *sang* and *suk* of the *hyang* and *tang* local communities] was not as good as the ancient method, and even though the attainment of moral order in society was not as great as in ancient times, nevertheless the systems of guaranteed recommendation and the hiring of subordinates by officials did mean that men were selected on the basis of their actual behavior. The flourishing of men of talent and the beauty of mores during the two Han dynasties reached a level that no [dynasty] in later ages ever attained.[108]

An criticized the Northern and Southern dynasties system of recommendation because it was based on pedigree, but he allowed that it preserved something of the classical ideal because rank was (supposedly) determined on the basis of talent and behavior. With the beginning of the examination system, however, the attention of scholars shifted to the study of letters for their own sake and the use of learning for obtaining office. The result was that the bureaucracy became filled with seekers after scholarly fame and material fortune while "the men of great talent and capacity grew old and died in the caves [of remote mountains] and were never selected" – an apt description for Yu Hyŏngwŏn himself.

Ever the professional historian, An went further than Yu had by discussing the utility of examinations throughout Korean history, pointing out that prior to the adoption of the examinations (in 958), Korea had produced many great men and literary talents, Silla had unified the Three Kingdoms, and Koryŏ had reunified the Later Three Kingdoms even without benefit of the examination system. It was only King Kwangjong (in 958) who, because of his admiration for Chinese customs, mistakenly believed that the examination system was an essential part of Chinese civilization. He had no idea what the real method of recruitment was in ancient China and did not realize that the sages had never used an examination system.[109]

Criticism of the examination system and praise for schools and recommendation was, of course, not the exclusive property of Yu Hyŏngwŏn. The same encyclopedia, for example, contains a statement of Chŏng Tojŏn, one of the leading Neo-Confucian ideologues of the Koryŏ/Chosŏn transition in the late fourteenth century, citing virtually the same classical sources that Yu used to extol the classical ideal of well-rounded education in moral standards and the arts, the selection of the worthy and able, and their promotion up the ranks of a school system. Chŏng also presented a similar synopsis of developments in recruitment from the Han to the examination system of the Sui and T'ang, and the adoption of the examinations by King Kwangjong on the advice of Shuang Chi. The difference between his view and those of Yu and An, however, was that he wanted reform of the late Koryŏ examination system, not its abolition. As a follower of Yi Sŏnggye, the founder of the Chosŏn dynasty, Chŏng naturally praised him for his reforms, such as ordering the National Academy (Sŏnggyun'gwan) to examine students on the Four Books and Five Classics and the Ministry of Rites to examine candidates in poetical composition, essay writing, and policy questions, thus "providing at one stroke a system well ordered in all respects that could serve for several generations." But reformers like Yu Hyŏngwŏn in the seventeenth century and after had lost the optimistic outlook of Chŏng Tojŏn that the examination system could be restored to health by fine tuning.[110]

The encyclopedia also includes excerpts of statements by Cho Kwangjo concerning his special recommendation examination of 1519 and by Yulgok on the injustice of relying exclusively on examinations for evaluating talent, indicating that by the late eighteenth century the reform view had become widespread among the literati.[111] Reform thought obviously had some influence on King Chŏngjo, who issued a lengthy edict on the subject when he first came to the throne in 1776. Chŏngjo (or the scholar who drafted the edict for him) cited Ch'eng I to the effect that great benefits were only to be obtained by great reforms, and the one institution that cried out for reform above all else was the examination system. Possibly as a result of his reading of the encyclopedia itself (and maybe Yu's *Pan'gye surok* as well), Chŏngjo noted that the examination system was not an ancient institution but the village recommendation system was. After tracing the history of the examinations through the Ming and Chosŏn dynasties, however, he remarked (contrary to the totally negative opinion of Yu Hyŏngwŏn and others) that the examination system was not entirely without merit; it was only that it had been corrupted through long use or had failed in practice to live up to its promise. Problems in the system had to be rectified and the system adjusted to take into account the nature of the times.

He echoed the call of Yu and many others for the restoration of local recommendation, remarking that in ancient China there were two paths to office, one via the local schools run by the local scholar-officials (*hsiang shih-ta-fu*) and appointment by the Ta Ssu-t'u, and the other via the National Academy and appointment by the Ta Ssu-ma. Students were trained in the six principles of virtue, the six types of proper behavior, and the six skills of the well-rounded man, and promoted from one scholarly title to another and afforded rank and emoluments – all part of the same classical model extolled by Yu Hyŏngwŏn. Chŏngjo held that it was not necessary to reproduce antiquity in its entirety; one could also adopt the best of any age and adapt it to one's own time and place. Thus, it might not be possible to recreate the Chou, but it would be feasible to implement the principle of local recommendation, borrow the Ming practice of enclosing examination candidates in sealed rooms, utilize the Han system of the recommendation of the worthy, the good, and the filial, and adopt Chu Hsi's recommendation to examine men in annual sequence in the Classics, Four Books, Histories, and policy matters. "These [practices] would in no way do damage to the intention of the ancients and still be suitable for implementation in the present day."[112]

Despite all the pious references to antiquity and centuries of criticism of the examination system, Chŏngjo's decree did not really sound the clarion call for a radical elimination of the examination system. If the government-sponsored *Chŭngbo Munhŏnbigo* can be taken as a collection of royally approved opinion, one might conclude that Yu Hyŏngwŏn had played a significant but not exclusive role in establishing state recognition of reform ideas by the late eighteenth century, and yet this apparent victory in the realm of ideas had not brought the prospect of meaningful reform any closer to reality.

Without the prospect of abolition of the examinations, the likelihood of major financing of a totally refurbished system of government schools was hardly likely either. By the eighteenth century, the main problem in the administration of schools was no longer restoration of the defunct state schools of the early Chosŏn period, but the expansion of private academies. The main trend in educational reform was putting a rein on the private academies. Even before Yu's death certain kings were imposing limits on their quotas of students and slaves, a process that culminated in the Taewongun's bold moves between 1864 and 1871 to abolish all but forty-two academies and impose a number of other restrictions.[113]

Yu did attack the private academies for distorting the true purpose of education, and he was critical of the conversion of schools to private, political ends by the yangban. His detailed regulations for the restoration of government schools also show that he intended state schools to take over functions currently being exercised by the private academies.[114] Furthermore, his contribution to the spread of reform ideas in general probably did have some influence in the Taewongun's reform program. Although the Taewongun did not abolish the examination system, he did adopt limited versions of a number of the proposals advocated by Yu – reform of the regulations for the National Academy to improve its performance and prestige, periodic testing of academy students and suspension of those who failed to pass, adoption of a system of local recommendation of men for special provincial examinations, recommendation of men for office by incumbent officials, and abolition of all but forty-seven authorized private academies.[115]

Conclusion

The importance of Yu's essay on education and recruitment, however, is not to be measured solely by the content of his ideas on education and recruitment or its influence on thought and policy in subsequent centuries, but by what it tells us about contemporary society and the nature of his vision for an optimum society, the best society that one could achieve in the imperfect world of "the later age."

What kind of social transformation did he have in mind by his reformed system of education and recruitment? His stated goal was a stratified society based on excellence in moral behavior and talent rather than the present one dominated by inherited status, but how disruptive would such a society be to the existing social order dominated by the semihereditary yangban? When he told his yangban readers to stay calm because the admission of commoners to his new schools would neither stimulate disrespectful behavior by them nor really produce that many successful scholars from the commoner class, did he really mean it, or was he trying to lull them into complacency? He meant it because he knew that the regimen in his new schools would be so rigorous, the task of seeking true moral perfection, not just mastery of textual knowledge, would be so arduous, and the weak social, economic, and environmental background of commoner families so inferior that few would really have that much of a chance to make inroads into yangban hegemony.

Does this then call into question his commitment to the masses, to educate them all, and open the door of opportunity for them? I believe it does, because his fixed quotas of students at each level of his proposed school system was geared not to mass improvement but to ensuring better quality for a limited number of officials. When he spoke of enlightening the masses, he only had in mind the inculcation of moral standards in the peasantry by private grammar schools, but that was the last, not the first of his priorities; he even postponed their implementation into the future. He could not have envisioned education for the peasants continuing beyond the age of thirteen or fourteen at the most. Instead, he thought of education as the means for creating a moral elite that would run a paternalistic government that would act on behalf of the people.

Did he intend a leveling of the social order? Not so here because he made no mention of the abolition of inherited slavery (although he did so elsewhere) and excluded them from his schools but had them provide manual labor in his schools and take floggings in place of their yangban student masters who were too lazy to attend class.

Nor did he make any attempt to expand his schools to include the sons of artisans and merchants, let alone shamans and the flotsam and jetsam of small-town rural Korea he called the denizens of the wells and markets. Why should the artisans and merchants, who were not excluded from the examinations in China from the mid-Sung dynasty, have been excluded from the plans of a forward-minded reformer in seventeenth-century Korea if it were not for the powerful hold of habit and convention on Yu's mind?

In short, reform within the context of Yu's Confucian statecraft thought did not signify the elimination of social status, just inherited status, and primarily in the recruitment of government officials because it robbed the state of the service of the most moral and capable men in society, men who had been ignored by the examination system and left to wither in the countryside.

Within the schools he proposed a status hierarchy based on age and merit, the latter defined primarily in terms of proper behavior, secondarily as excellence in learning. But the rules of status were explicitly *not* to be extended to society at large, where they would have come into conflict with traditional modes of status discrimination, such as privilege for royal princes, rank order of legitimate brothers, maltreatment of nothoi, and the prestige afforded to sons and heirs of high officials and luminous scholars of the past.

One of the best clues to Yu's fundamental emotional commitment to the standards of his own time despite his use of the rhetoric of equal opportunity was his assurance to the yangban class that the advantages of superior environment would guarantee that their sons would not be hurt by a shift to equal treatment within his school system. Since no more than a few commoners would make it to the top anyway, what he really expected was that the goad of competition would brighten up the scions of the yangban and stir them out of their self-complacent lethargy.

Even his apparently strict rules for dismissing students from school and enrolling them for military service, dropping them down the status ladder from privileged student to commoner, was modified if the person was of the yangban class. They would be given special admonition and a probationary period, and if they did drop out, they could be signed up for special elite guard units in the capital in the manner of the early Chosŏn dynasty.

He had accurately perceived that the foundation of the yangban class in his own time had been achieved not mainly through any legal mandate of hereditary right, but by the natural advantages accruing to high officials and wealthy landlords that enabled them to hire tutors for their sons, marry with the right families, and pull strings with high officials who were all part of a restricted social network. He depicted his ideal society in the image of an infinite segmented bamboo stalk, and even though the logic of his arguments implied greater opportunity and mobility past the nodal points than existed in his own time, his contradictory limitations betrayed a fundamental commitment to the privileges of status and the legitimacy of social dividing lines.

Moving beyond the specific issue of the nature of social organization, Yu's thought about education and recruitment was characterized by ambivalence or contradiction with regard to a number of issues, produced not simply by inadequate logic or sloppy treatment of the issues, but by fundamental antinomies within Yu's own mind. Certain statements that could be construed as favoring freedom of thought, a shift toward instrumental or utilitarian knowledge over ethics, and an expansion of opportunity, mass education, and equality of treatment are in fact severely limited – in fact, often overwhelmed – by countervailing propositions. Yu's advocacy for an expansion of knowledge in the educational curriculum to include military affairs as well as the classics and moral teachings was limited by the very classical mode of thought itself, in which training in archery was perceived as a means to the cultivation of the proper seriousness and decorum in the conduct of ritual. Improvement in the teaching of technological subjects was limited by relegating them to traditional technical schools and technical professions, which were lower in status than general education and generalist bureaucrats. The imposition of quotas on such technical personnel also would have prevented the expansion of technical knowledge to the mass of the population or the overturning of the traditional priority of moral over practical knowledge.

The implied call for a general liberalization of education represented by the emphases on military and technical knowledge was contradicted by Yu's detailed description of how schools would be run, their curriculum, and the extent of their libraries. In the assessing of merits and demerits as well as the limited use of written examinations, the overwhelming focus was on behavior, producing in the individual conformity to *ye*, rites and etiquette, or the outer manifestations in behavior of the well-regulated and well-tuned character – such things as comportment, deportment, filial piety, and even serious music. The daily regimen, the liberal use of penalties and punishments, and even the threat of military service against lazy students, suggests that if Yu had had his way, he would have filled the country with military academies of moral education. The purpose of such schools was to make sure that the students received the correct message, not that their minds would be trained to free inquiry. Not only did Yu confine the curriculum to a short list of acceptable and sanitary books, he also proscribed (without defining) all heterodox, undesirable, and frivolous works.

The reason for Yu's harsh and disciplinary approach to education was undoubtedly caused by the vast departure of contemporary Korean society from the ideals represented by the sage institutions of the Chou and Yu's emotional commitment to leading, if not dragging, Korea back to some approximation of that ancient model. Since Yu himself was so certain of the verities of his own Confucian world, he could brook no expansion of the curriculum lest it misguide men's minds and lead them from the straight path. Technical and useful knowledge was good for the country, but still had to be subordinated to moral truths and limited to a subordinate class of technical experts. What Yu wanted was a struggle to return to ancient principles in a world that was not only not perfect, but could never completely be so. Though a depressing prospect for some, it did not stymie his commitment and purpose.

CHAPTER 6
Slavery: The Slow Path to Abolition

"At the present time in our country we regard slaves as chattel. Now people are all the same. How could there be a principle by which one person regards another person as his property?"[1]

"Only if a person is a slave do others make them labor, and only if a person is a slave is he made to labor for others."[2]

Slavery and Morality in World History

Throughout the history of slavery in the West the unhappy lot of the slave was often recognized and deplored, but only rarely was slavery itself attacked as contrary to social norms, ethical precepts, or religious standards. The Greek polis depended on servile or slave labor for the maintenance of its warriors and philosophers. Plato by his silence on the matter in *The Republic* implied the necessity of slavery as the labor force for his guardians or philosophers in the ideal society of his vision, and in *The Laws* he acknowledged slavery as an essential part of the existing mores of Athenian society. Aristotle, of course, went further by justifying slavery on the grounds of a natural human inequality. Since both philosophers assumed that the governing class should be restricted to men of wisdom and talent, their toleration or support for slavery was a logical reflection of their hierarchical model of society.[3]

Both Stoics and Christians who shared belief in ideas of equality, humanity, and compassion for the common man, might have provided a theoretical basis for a critique of slavery as an institution, but they did not, however, develop a strong antislavery position or social movement. The presumed equality of all men in the quest for mental peace or mystical union with the cosmos in Stoicism took precedence over any attempt to level society. As long as the ultimate objective of Christian doctrine remained salvation and bliss in the afterlife, Christians preferred to relegate social issues to the realm of Caesar and accept slavery as one of those unavoidable curses of the imperfect temporal world. Later, with the increased emphasis on original sin that came with St. Augustine and others, slavery was seen as a necessary consequence of man's fall from grace, a deserved punishment for sinfulness. After the church was recognized and legitimated by Constantine, it became part of the property and slaveholding establishment. The material interests of the church as well as the Christian slaveowners made it all the more difficult for Christians to translate Christ's message of mercy into an uncompromising attack on slavery. And Aquinas justified slavery as part of his theory of ascending stages, accepting slavery almost as part of a natural hierarchy of human types.[4]

The Reformation may have played an important role in transforming Christian attitudes toward slavery, but the results were a long time coming. The principle of predetermined salvation eliminated the efficacy of such good deeds as the manumission of slaves, but a change occurred within Protestant Christianity itself when the role of free will began to take precedence over determinism. The stress on man's individual choice in his quest for salvation and the workings of the human conscience in the practice of manumission, even as merely a demonstration of one's elect status, led some among the Quakers, and later others of other Protestant denominations and Catholics as well, to condemn slavery as a moral evil, define slaveownership and trade as sinful, and demand total abolition.[5]

It used to be thought that the credit for the disappearance of slavery in the Roman Empire as well as the anti-slave trade movement in Great Britain and the abolitionist movement in the United States in the nineteenth century should be given to the humanitarian spirit of New Testament Christianity, but while Christian belief may have ameliorated some aspects of slavery, it took eighteen hundred years before slavery became intolerable to the Christian religious conscience. Furthermore, it was not necessary for religious and philosophical antislavery positions to be developed for slavery to die out in some Western societies. Nor did the rise of antislavery sentiment necessarily lead to the abolition of slavery; in the American South and Haiti, for example, it took a civil war and a rebellion to settle the issue. Slavery disappeared gradually in the West from the late Roman Empire to the Middle Ages, not as a result of any contradiction with religious and philosophical standards, but as part of a complex economic and social process by which the mass of the free peasantry was reduced to serfdom while the servile class was escaping from chattel slavery.[6]

In fact, an antislavery position in Christianity emerged only with the modern version of slavery that came with the African slave trade, a development closely related to the economic and imperialistic expansion of the West. By the nineteenth century, slavery in the Americas was part of a world capitalist environment, an egregious contradiction to the freedom, individualism, and laissez-faire usually associated with a market economy.[7] Although those of the Fogel and Engerman school have described ante bellum slavery in the southern United States as a profitable enterprise fully compatible with capitalist rationality and profit-seeking, the anachronism of slave labor became fully apparent as industrial capitalism underwent rapid growth and the institution was destroyed by force or abandoned by consensus in one country after the other in the Western hemisphere.[8] In other words, economic and social forces appear to have played the major role wherever slavery has declined: in the late Roman Empire the influence of philosophy and religion was negligible, and in the Americas Christian attitudes were important but had to be stimulated by environmental forces. David Brion Davis, who explicitly assumed the importance of Christianity in the antislavery movement, asserted that Christian attitudes toward sin, human nature, and progress had to undergo a radical shift before antislavery sentiment could emerge. Although he associated the source of that change with naturalism, humanism, skepticism, and secular rationality without drawing a necessary causal connection to the material world, the relationship to the development of science, technology, and capitalism is inescapable.[9] Yet it appears not to have been capitalism itself that destroyed slavery, for it was a necessary concomitant of commercial cotton farming in the southern United States that supplied the raw material for British textiles. It was the support of the industrialized north for preservation of the Union against the cotton plantation system of the south – a contradiction within capitalism – that brought slavery to an end in the United States.

Despite the many differences between the nature and history of slavery in the West and East Asia, they are alike in two respects: the higher religions and philosophies proved remarkably tolerant if not supportive of slavery, and the rise and fall of the slave population occurred primarily because of changes in economy and society. In Korea the moral message of neither Buddhism nor Confucianism served to eliminate slavery, hereditary or otherwise, on its own. As in the West, when Buddhism and Confucianism became institutionalized they took on the material aspects of the leading social and economic forces of society. The Buddhist monastic estates and the Confucian academies both owned slaves.

Nevertheless, it is not that thought, belief, and attitude played no role at all. In the history of Korean slavery, Confucian attitudes were important in explaining the decline of slavery, but Confucian doctrine was not unequivocally opposed to slavery, and when some Confucian scholars and officials did attack slavery, they usually did so for economic, practical, or administrative reasons, only rarely for moral or religious ones. At times Confucians even opposed the abolition of slavery on moral grounds. Only when a number of socioeconomic, administrative, and political changes occurring in the seventeenth and eighteenth centuries established the basis for the gradual decline of slavery did some Confucian thinkers begin to reexamine some of the premises upon which slavery had been justified. Yu Hyŏngwŏn was not only one of them, but the one who initially provided the most thoroughgoing analysis of the relationship of slavery to moral standards.

SLAVES AS CHATTEL AND HUMAN BEINGS

Whatever the variations between Korean and other modes of slavery throughout the world, in one respect they were alike. Slaves could be bought and sold, given as gifts, or inherited. They conformed to the definition of chattel property and were referred to as such, even though their basic humanity was also recognized in a number of ways. Some years ago a number of scholars of slavery in China sought to demonstrate that Chinese slavery was more humane than the chattel slavery of Rome because the Chinese recognized the humanity of the slave, but the problem has been mooted by the more recent studies of Western slavery which show that all slave societies, even the ones with the most legalistic and formalistic definitions of slaves as chattel goods or inanimate objects, had to treat slaves as human beings.

Societies with slavery have varied in the degree to which they have recognized the basic humanity of slaves and the latitude or leniency afforded to slaves. Slaves in Korea usually did not have surnames except possibly in the case of recently enslaved ex-officials, an indication that the rest of society did not think it was necessary for them to be organized in familial or lineage kinship groups with an identifiable ancestry. But in the Koryŏ period, for example, marriage between slaves was recognized and slaves were listed on household registers of their masters and the localities where they resided as families or households. Although the master had the authority to sell them individually and break up the unity of their families, they usually exercised this right with domestic servants and much less so with the so-called outside resident slaves (*oegŏ nobi*) who lived at some distance from the master and maintained individual residences. Furthermore, while intermarriage between slaves and commoners was forbidden explicitly by law, the law was continually violated and the state virtually acknowledged the violation by devising a series of laws to determine the status of offspring of mixed marriages.

In law, slaves were subject to greater penalties for the commission of crimes than commoners or higher status groups, but inequality before the law in the standards of punishment is more a reflection of a hierarchic status society than it is a denial of the humanity of the slave. This is seen clearly in China during the T'ang dynasty and after when the law defined a number of intermediate non-slave and noncommoner statuses distinguished as well by intermediate treatment in the scale of punishments. In a number of ways the humanity of the slave was positively acknowledged in law. Contrary to Roman practice and in accordance with Chinese law, slaves in Korea were held individually responsible for their actions. They were also protected by law against arbitrary murder by masters as well as third parties even though the legal protections were often ignored in practice. Although there are no extant laws specifying the right of slaves to own property or defining the extent of the slaveowner's rights to his slave's property (the peculium in Roman slavery), there are many cases of slaves owning property and wealth in the form of land, cash, and even other slaves in the historical records. As Chŏn Hyŏngt'aek has shown, in the Chosŏn dynasty both private and official slaves, mostly outside resident slaves (*oegŏ nobi*), could purchase and own land and bequeath it to their sons, who inherited both his status and his obligations, but if the slave died without any heirs, the private master or official agency that owned the slave could confiscate the property. It was the lack of opportunity for the accumulation of wealth rather than any legal prohibition that probably constituted the main problem for Korean slaves, but the situation improved in the late Chosŏn period as more slaves were able to accumulate land.[10]

Yet despite the relatively liberal legal privileges of the Korean slave, Koreans from the Koryŏ period on, and probably earlier as well, described slaves as chattel property. Willingness to acknowledge the humanity of slaves in certain instances did not destroy that fundamental distinction between slaves and nonslaves common to other societies as well: the slave could be bought and sold where the nonslave could not. Nonslave is a better term to use than freeman, because other types of people in the category of base persons in Korean society were subjected to restrictions on freedom but were not bought and sold as slaves were. In the Korean situation, people used the terminology of chattel property to describe slaves, and ultimately one of the important questions in the attitude toward slavery was whether it was morally proper to treat human beings as objects of purchase and sale.[11]

Of course, many scholars prefer to avoid defining slavery simply as chattel property, or objects subject to purchase and sale. They usually stress the overwhelming power of the master in commanding or disposing of the slave, the subjugation of the slave and his physical labor to the whim of the master, or the loss of basic humanity attendant upon enslavement – Orlando Patterson's social death of the slave.[12] While the cruel and arbitrary treatment of slaves was also an important factor in the history of antislavery movements because it goaded and challenged men of humanitarian feeling, the crucial issue is the conversion from ad hoc humanitarian protest against occasional cruelty to the condemnation of slavery as an institution that robs humankind of its dignity and humanity.

KIJA AND THE ORIGINS OF SLAVERY IN KOREA

The legitimacy of slavery as an institution seems never to have been questioned in Korea because it was supposedly introduced in remote antiquity by the mythical Kija, a Chinese sage-hero who was granted ancient Chosŏn as a fief during the early Chou period, migrated there, and introduced fundamental institutions of governance. The earliest accounts simply state that Kija enacted a penal code of eight provisions, one of which provided that thieves would become the slaves of the families they had robbed.

The compiler of the prologue to the addendum on slavery in the treatise on punishments in the *Koryŏsa* (History of the Koryŏ dynasty) added a twist to Kija's law for the enslavement of thieves by claiming that it marked the origin of hereditary slavery in Korea, which he praised because it had benefited society "by ensuring a strict [distinction] between inner and outer [males and females], a [hierarchical] grading of noble and base [*kwich'ŏn*], and a [strict] practice of rites and righteousness."[13]

In the Chosŏn period the origins of slavery in Korea were commonly attributed to Kija.[14] In 1689, Chŏng T'ak argued that Kija had introduced slavery on the principle of reciprocal moral obligation, not human degradation: the relationship between slave and master was like that between ruler and subject, and slaves were neither disloyal to masters or rebels against the state.[15] In the sixteenth century an official historian of the *Veritable Records* (*Sillok*) wrote that Kija had sanctioned hereditary slavery, and it had been valuable to Korea because it eliminated any confusion in the distinction between noble and base in society.[16]

The historian probably derived his view that Kija sanctioned hereditary slavery by carelessly attributing to Kija what in fact were remarks made by the compiler of the prologue to the addendum on slavery in the treatise on punishments in the *Koryŏsa*. After describing Kija's law for the enslavement of thieves and noting that this constituted the origin of slavery in Korea, the prologue continued:

> Those slaves who were *passed on from generation to generation* [italics mine] and employed in the families of the *sajok* [scholar-officials] were called *sanobi* [private slaves]. . . . In general the existence of slaves in Korea was greatly aided by mores and teachings, which account for the strict [distinction] made between inner and outer [males and females], the [hierarchical] grading of noble and base [*kwich'ŏn*], and the [strict] practice of rites and righteousness.[17]

That it was a mistake to attribute this paragraph to Kija is indicated by the compiler of the late eighteenth-century encylopedia of Korean institutions, the *Chungbo munhŏnbigo*, who separated this portion of the text from the description of Kija's laws and specifically attributed it to Chŏng Inji, the editor-in-chief of the *Koryŏsa*.[18] Nevertheless, many Koreans by the seventeenth century must have erroneously thought that the inheritance of slave status as well as enslavement for thievery or criminal action had been sanctioned by one of the great sages of Korean antiquity.

A commentator in the *Chungbo munhŏnbigo* explained that the Koreans were a stubborn and recalcitrant people by virtue of a rough and harsh natural environment who were not given to obeying orders, no matter what the source. Kija judged that their propensity to craft and wrongdoing had to be ruled by sterner measures, and his wise use of enslavement as a mode of punishment succeeded in eliminating thievery altogether from society. Slavery was thus a fit tool for the civilizing of a barbaric people.[19]

Reform in the Koryo Period

T'aejo of Koryŏ

Another important figure in the legitimation of slavery in Korea was the founder of Koryŏ, Wang Kŏn (877–943, known posthumously as King T'aejo, r. 918–43). In 982, Ch'oe Sŭngno, a renowned Confucian scholar-official, praised T'aejo for his desire to manumit prisoners of war after the dynasty was founded in 918 even though he was unable to do so lest he antagonize his leading supporters.[20] As a spokesman for the slaveowning aristocracy he was praising T'aejo's sagacity in recognizing the legitimacy of slave property while also crediting him with a measure of compassion for the unfortunate fate of war captives. The *Koryŏsa* also praised him for redeeming over one thousand persons forced into slavery by buying them back with cloth and silk from the royal treasury.[21] Nevertheless, T'aejo made no attempt to abolish slavery, and later generations in a society that accepted slavery as legitimate merely admired T'aejo for his display of mercy.[22]

In fact, T'aejo willingly granted slaves to political rivals like Kyŏnghwŏn of later Paekche as an inducement to abandon his old loyalties and join the new regime.[23] In his last will and testament he also warned his successors against appointing official slaves to office or allowing them too much influence in the conduct of affairs because of his distrust of their loyalty.[24] He was afraid that rebels and political opponents who had been enslaved by the state as punishment would pass on their desire for vengeance to their descendants, but this limited restriction on officeholding by slaves was interpreted by later generations as a justification for hereditary slavery. In 1158 when the eunuch Chŏng Ham, a descendant of a slave who lived in T'aejo's reign, was appointed to office, a censor objected that it would be contrary to T'aejo's intent if the heirs of those disloyal to him were so honored while the scions of his loyal followers went without posts.[25]

In 1300, when King Ch'ungnyŏl attempted to block the Mongol demand that he abolish the current Korean slave laws, he explained that T'aejo's warning against manumitting slaves was the reason why severe restrictions on slave status were incorporated into Koryŏ law. He pointed out that anyone with a taint of slavery in his blood for the previous eight generations was prohibited from holding office; slave status was inherited by children even if only one of the parents were a slave; the children of manumitted slaves would remain slaves and not inherit the "good" or free status of their parents; if the master's family died out, the slaves would not be manumitted but assigned to someone of the same lineage.[26] These harsh thirteenth-century practices could not have derived simply from T'aejo's injunction against entrusting official slaves with responsibility for government affairs, but they were justified by an appeal to his legacy. T'aejo, the compassionate ruler, had been transformed into a source of legitimacy for hereditary slavery.

Ch'oe Sŭngno's Defense of Slavery

By the end of the tenth century the tension between kings and aristocrats over the control of wealth and resources that marks so much of the history of traditional Korea became prominent because of King Kwangjong's attempt to expand central power. After his death in 982, the famous Confucian scholar-official Ch'oe Sŭngno criticized some of Kwangjong's measures to bolster royal prerogative at the expense of the slaveholding interests of the high officials, landowners, and nobles. Ch'oe pictured T'aejo as a protector of the private property interests of the merit subjects and social elite because he had refrained from the manumission of enslaved war captives, even though he had tried to pry away some portion of the slave population from the slaveowners. The slaveholding elite had been satisfied for over sixty years until King Kwangjong had upset the balance in 956 by ordering an investigation of all slaves in the empire. Ch'oe took umbrage at Kwangjong's interference with slaveholding property rights even though the purpose of the investigation was not to abolish slavery, but merely to return to commoner status all persons illegally enslaved by force or foreclosure for debt. He held that the consequence of Kwangjong's action was to weaken the moral basis of slavery because he felt that the slaves lost their respect for their masters, lorded it over their superiors, and conspired and plotted their masters' downfall. He was referring to their eager participation in the rash of calumny and accusation that prevailed during Kwangjong's purges of his political enemies. Slaves were a treacherous lot, anyway, only too happy to betray their former masters for the slightest personal advantage. In other words, by Chinese legal tradition, slaves had been prohibited from accusing or testifying against their masters in any cases save treason, but Kwangjong had tolerated it as means of purging his political rivals. Ch'oe urged King Sŏngjong to stop this practice and maintain the proper distinction between masters and slaves.[27]

Ch'oe's remarks show that in the political and economic struggle between kings and aristocrats in the tenth century, even though Confucians were frequently on the side of the kings, they were never proponents of royal absolutism and their primary loyalty at that time was to the aristocracy of slaveowners, whose material interests they defended in moral terms.

The Matrilineal Succession Rule of 1039

In 1300 when the Yüan (Mongol) authorities demanded of King Ch'ungnyŏl that he limit slavery in Korea, they did not want to abolish slavery altogether, but rather to allow offspring of mixed slave/commoner marriages to be freed and given "good" or commoner status, in conformity with current Yüan dynasty practice. A matrilineal succession rule, by which offspring of mixed marriages adopted their mother's status, had in fact been decreed in 1039 in Korea, but it was ignored in practice. When King Ch'ungnyŏl opposed the Mongol request, he informed the Yüan authorities that in Korea the children of mixed marriages inherited base status if either of the parents were base, and he pointed out that the previous Yüan emperor, Shih-tsu (Qubilai), had chosen to abide by native Korean custom and laws back in 1270, when the Korean king had finally acknowledged submission to Mongol rule.[28]

Kongmin's Attempt at Reform

Despite King Ch'ungnyŏl's defense of hereditary slavery, there was still pressure on the throne to restrain the predatory slave masters from illegal enslavement of commoners. As early as 1269, special commissions were established to investigate the status of slaves for the purpose of settling disputes among slaveowners and appeals for manumission by those forced into slavery. On the other hand, some kings even condoned violations of the law by the slaveowners or competed with them to accumulate their own slaves.[29]

By the end of the Koryŏ dynasty the decline in royal power left private interests free to enslave defenseless debtors and commoner peasants. The judicial courts of the government were flooded by petitions from slaves for manumission on the grounds of illegal or unjust enslavement, and by lawsuits over ownership among family relations, a situation exacerbated by the destruction of the slave registers during the Red Turban invasions of 1361.[30] The commoner population liable for taxation and service to the state declined as more peasants were forced into slavery or commended themselves voluntarily to wealthy and powerful households to evade starvation and the depredations of the tax collector.[31]

Paradoxically, the apparent increase in the number of slaves and the deterioriation in their condition were also accompanied by a loosening of restrictions against opportunities for office and upward mobility. A number of slave revolts occurred from the late twelfth through mid-thirteenth century, more as a result of the frustration of rising expectations than as a manifestation of abject despair.[32] From the thirteenth century on slaves, ex-slaves, or descendants of slaves, some of whom were eunuchs, began to be used as confidantes of military rulers or appointed to office. After the establishment of Mongol rule, many of them served as close retainers of Korean kings who found themselves humbled and forced to compete with a number of hostile forces: Mongol emperors and officials, Korean consorts of Mongol emperors, and Korean bureaucrats allied with rivals for the throne.[33] This development, an obvious violation of the legacy of T'aejo, antagonized the Confucian bureaucrats who, as educated men trained in morality and statecraft, felt that the use of slaves and eunuchs as ministers to the king made a travesty of government.

When a reform movement began in the 1350s under the aegis of King Kongmin, the movement was compromised because the official in charge of the agency to review slave suits and petitions for manumission was the king's favorite, Sin Ton, the son of a slave woman, and a Buddhist monk to boot. The king did not want to abolish slavery altogether, just to gain greater control over the peasant population by stripping the slaveowners of illegally enslaved persons. The slaveowners, however, viewed any manumissions as an invasion of their interests, especially when the son of a slave was rendering judgment in disputes between slaveowners. Naturally, they accused him of freeing any and all slaves who petitioned. Although some Confucian scholars and bureaucrats were favorably disposed to some type of slave reform, others were afraid that wanton manumission would create a rebellious mood among the slaves, and most were firmly opposed to slaves holding office and wielding political power. The kings after Kongmin continued the process of liberating or confiscating slaves held illegally by wealthy and powerful men, but they lacked the power to solve the problem. Slaveowners continued to retain their hold over slaves and to ignore adverse court decisions.[34]

CONFUCIAN ATTITUDES TOWARD SLAVERY IN EARLY CHOSŎN

Preservation of the Patrimony

Another attempt at solving the slave question began after Yi Sŏnggye's coup d'état of 1388. The new king and his officials had to clear up a tremendous backlog of pending lawsuits over slave status and ownership. The small group of Neo-Confucians who supported Yi Sŏnggye's establishment of the Chosŏn dynasty were not in favor of slave reform. When the government closed down most Buddhist monasteries and confiscated their slaves, it did not manumit them but converted 80,000 of them to government slaves. This act initiated a significant expansion of the system of servile state labor that at its height numbered over 350,000 slaves and was not brought to an end until 1801.[35] Nothing could be more indicative of the blindness of the Confucian moral conscience to the institution of slavery than this one policy.

On the other hand, the new rules governing the inheritance of status and the division of slave property did, in fact, reflect a greater concern for Confucian ethical norms than before, but the main consequence was increased emphasis on the principle of filial piety rather than humanitarian treatment, freedom, or equality for slaves. The Confucian moral position at this time was not that hereditary slavery should be abolished, but on the contrary that its preservation was necessary to the preservation of patrimonial property, which by its bequeathal from one generation to another maintained the continuity of the family and clan. Even if an individual head of family were inclined to free slaves as an act of compassion, he had no right to do so because patrimonial rights transcended individual property rights.[36]

Just prior to the founding of Chosŏn, in 1391 and 1392, regulations were adopted for the inheritance of slaves by heirs of slaveowners that were designed to preserve the patrimony through the eldest legitimate son and the patrilineal line of succession where possible. Slaveowners were forbidden to donate slaves to Buddhist monasteries, give them away to other persons, or sell them off except in dire financial circumstances and only then with express permission from the authorities. The Slave Agency (Togwan) in 1392 proposed that when a family lacked male heirs, the husband or wife would inherit the slaves of the spouse only for their lifetime, after which the slaves would be given to the close relatives (*ponson*).[37] In other words, even if the family died out, its slaves would become part of the property of the greater lineage instead of being confiscated by the state.

New laws adopted in 1397 and 1405 that governed the inheritance of patrimonial slaves required that documents of inheritance be drawn up and certificates issued by the state prior to the decease of the family head so that after his death quarrels over slaves and family property would be eliminated. If someone died intestate, the slaves would be given to the close relatives according to the degree of relationship. The state would confiscate the slaves only if the family relationship of claimants to family slaves was not clear, or if there were no relatives to the fourth degree (cousins). In the absence of legitimate heirs, sons of concubines, even of slave women, and adopted children, whether of the same surname and lineage or not, were allowed to inherit slaves because the objective of the Confucian reformers was to preserve ancestral rites even through fictive kinship.[38] The new regulations penalized families that sold off patrimonial slaves and deprived their children or siblings from their inheritance.[39]

Emphasis was also placed on maintaining strict distinctions between good and base status (*yang/ch'ŏn*) even in the context of reform. In 1388 Cho Chun proposed that the good or base status of each household be included on the registers so that different status groups could be kept separate and distinct even while performing similar service.[40] Sudō Yoshiyuki believed that this proposal of Cho Chun's represented a Confucianization of slave law, and if he were correct, it meant that the Confucianization of slave law did not signify a humanitarian or egalitarian liberalization of those laws, but on the contrary, a moral reinforcement for patrimonial property and status distinction.[41]

Emergence of Humanitarian Attitudes

Although a sense of moral outrage at slavery as an institution appears to be lacking from most of the recommendations for slave reform, there is some evidence of the beginnings of a change in attitude in the direction of humanitarianism. In 1391 and 1392 two memorials were submitted to the throne on the question of abolishing the purchase and sale of slaves. The first was from the Office of Remonstrance (Nangsa) and the other was a set of regulations for the adjudication of slave disputes from the Directorate for Inspection of Slaves (Inmul ch'ubyŏndogam). Both deplored the sale of family slaves because it diminished the patrimonial inheritance of the family heirs, but the Office of Remonstrance also brought up the moral problem of slavery:

> Even though slaves are base, they are still Heaven's people, [and yet] we usually talk of them as chattel goods [*chaemul*] and actively buy and sell them, exchanging them for oxen and horses. Sometimes two or three slaves are paid for one horse and it still is not regarded as sufficient compensation, so that oxen and horses are deemed more important than human life. In ancient times there was a

> fire in a stable, and Confucius asked, "Has anyone been hurt?" He did not ask about the horses. This was the way the sages esteemed men over animals. How could there be any [moral] principle by which men would be exchanged for horses? The mores of the age are so benighted and confused that they naturally will produce disaster.

Despite this apparently unequivocal attack on chattel slavery as inhumane, the Office of Remonstrance only recommended that the inheritance or gift of slaves be restricted to the legitimate male line of succession or close relatives in the absence of such heirs, and that grants of slaves to Buddhist temples be forbidden.[42]

The list of regulations of 1392 also prohibited purchase and sale of slaves except when starvation or public or private indebtedness made such sales essential.[43] It was, however, preservation of the patrimony, not the welfare of the slave that was at issue here, and these regulations provided mainly for the "release and return" of slaves to their original owners if they were possessed illegally, not their manumission.[44]

In 1388 the Ministry of Justice (Chŏnbŏpsa) did ask that the enslavement of wives and children and the confiscation by the state of family property and slaves of criminals be ended because there was no precedent for either in ancient times. In 1389 the Office of Surveillance (Hŏnsa) also endorsed this opinion and urged the government to abandon enslavement as punishment to bring Korean law into greater conformity with the compassionate rule of the three ages of antiquity in China.[45] Nonetheless, neither agency called for an end to inherited slavery, and the dominant attitude at court was one of extreme caution over the manumission of slaves.

In 1392 the Slave Agency warned that if slaves were to be manumitted and they and their heirs made commoners, the release from service to their masters would breed a mentality incompatible with their station in life.[46] They would take it upon themselves to seek public office and marry women of families of good status, causing confusion in the social order. Or they might plot harm to their original masters, lose their fear of the law, and dare to bring suit in court. The agency then recommended that in the future any manumissions based on emotional considerations or meritorious achievement by the slave be confined to the slave only, and not to his male descendants.[47]

Lawsuits and Petitions

While one or two officials may have voiced an appeal on behalf of the basic humanity of the slave, the majority of bureaucrats were concerned with the more mundane problem of clearing up a tremendous backlog of petitions and suits over slaves. What this backlog of lawsuits meant was a breakdown of the solidarity of the slaveholding aristocracy itself. Powerful aristocrats used their influence against their weaker colleagues by taking away their slaves by force, seizing a greater share of inherited slaves from the family patrimony than was their due, holding pawned slaves after debts had been repaid, and retaining slaves even after a government official had ruled against them in a formal lawsuit. Unable to establish informal rules for control of slaves, the slaveowners turned to the state to intervene as judicial arbiter, but those who failed to get their way refused to honor judicial decisions and repeatedly appealed for reversals, inundating the existing judiciary and administrative apparatus and necessitating creation of temporary slave adjudication agencies. This process began in 1269 and was repeated five more times by 1391.[48]

The state responded only with temporary agencies for officials felt that disputes over slave property were best left to the private realm because slaves were so important to the yangban ruling class. In 1468, Yang Sŏngji stated that "Our country's slave law has a long history, and the *sadaebu* [scholar-officials] rely on it for their livelihood. . . . Slaves are the hand and feet of the *sa* [scholar-officials]."[49]

Unfortunately, legislation did not succeed in clearing up all pending suits and appeals of past decisions. The situation demanded the wisdom of a Solomon, and King T'aejong responded by deciding in 1413 that henceforth all disputes and appeals between slaveowners, would be settled by dividing all slaves in the possession of the two parties in half; the decision was later amended to division of just those slaves under dispute.[50] Perhaps not so wisely, however, he also opened up the opportunity for appeal of past decisions and the number of cases soon reached the astounding total of 13,000.[51]

These regulations were not welcomed by all officials or by aggrieved slaveowners, who pointed out that the decision to divide the disputed slaves in half had the effect of rewarding those who made false claims of ownership. T'aejong admitted the validity of the complaints about unfair decisions and even ruminated on the possibility of abolishing slavery altogether because slavery contributed to the subornation of officials and obstruction of justice in general.[52] In 1414 and 1415 the Ministry of Punishment proposed a plan to limit the ownership of slaves by individuals, but the limits were so high that they would not have reduced the number of slaves significantly. The formal proposal would have placed a limit of 150 slaves for royal relatives of the first (highest) rank, and 130 for officials of the first rank. Commoners would have been allowed 40 male slaves, but since there was no restriction on the number of female slaves, Yi Sugŏn estimated that a commoner could easily have possessed as many as a hundred slaves without being in violation of the law. In any case there was too much opposition to pass the law, and King T'aejong remarked that the process of divided inheritance would soon reduce the average numbers of slaves even for families that owned over a thousand. This remark indicated, however, that he was more concerned with a more balanced distribution of slaves among elite families than with manumission of the slaves themselves.[53]

Although T'aejong set 1417 as the deadline for suits and petitions over slaves, disputes continued until King Sejo ordered a new set of regulations in 1459 to settle outstanding cases. He ruled out all cases originating before 1417 and ordered disputed slaves awarded to the winner of a previous decision or to the possessor if the evidence was inconclusive.[54] After a century of active discussion and legislation on the problem of lawsuits over slaves, the commitment to property rights in slaves remained secure.

Offspring of Mixed Marriages

In the early Koryŏ period intermarriage between slaves and commoners had been forbidden altogether, but since the law could not be enforced, in 1039 the matrineal rule was adopted for the purpose of determining offspring of such illicit unions. Even this law appears to have been ignored in practice because it had to be promulgated again in 1133 and 1283. Since there is some possibility that a specific ban on the marriage of male slaves to commoner women was in effect,[55] the matrilineal law of 1039 probably pertained only to the offspring of marriages between males of good status and women of base status, ensuring that the children of such mixed marriages would inherit slave status. The purpose of the matrilineal law might then have been to increase the number of private slaves through breeding, diametrically opposite to its purpose later in the early fifteenth and late seventeenth centuries to provide a means of escape from slave status for a modest number of slaves.

In 1300 the Mongols demanded that the Koryŏ government modify current practice in the inheritance of slave status to allow offspring of mixed slave/commoner marriages to be freed and given good or commoner status in conformity with current Yüan custom.[56] King Ch'ungnyŏl, however, refused and informed the Mongol emperor that under prevailing Korean custom the offspring of mixed marriages inherited slave status if *either* of the parents were base. Even if a master chose to manumit a slave, good status would last only for the lifetime of the freed slave; his or her children and all future progeny would remain base or slave. In other words, current practice was much more restrictive than the matrilineal law of 1039.[57]

During the transition to the Chosŏn dynasty the supporters of Yi Sŏnggye's new regime believed that the proportion of slaves in society was too large and had to be cut back. Despite the occasional, and almost whimsical, wish for total abolition, the Koryŏ government in 1392 simply reaffirmed the original Koryŏ law prohibiting intermarriage between commoners and slaves altogether. The object was neither abolition nor major reduction of the slave population, but a freezing of the status quo. It was, however, impossible to enforce the ban, and it had to be promulgated again in 1401, 1405, and 1413 without much effect.[58]

No one ever suggested that slavery be limited to the existing generation of slaves or to criminals only and not their descendants. Nor did anyone propose a total reversal of late Koryŏ practice by allowing offspring to become commoners if *either* one of the parents were commoners. Thus, the only way left to reduce the number of slaves who inherited slave status was to allow the children of mixed marriages to inherit either the mother's or the father's status.

Unfortunately, either choice presented problems. The proponents of the matrilineal rule argued it was better because paternity was difficult to prove, but they failed to take into account misuse of the law to frustrate the government's objectives. Furthermore, past experience demonstrated that the matrilineal rule of 1039 could not be enforced because the aristocratic slaveowners could not countenance the prospect that their nothoi by slave concubines, and their progeny as well, would be treated as men of base status. Nor did they relish any restriction of opportunities for increasing their slaves through breeding. The real problem was whether the state had the power to enforce a law contrary to the interests of the slaveholding class.

The contribution of the Neo-Confucian moralists in the early Chosŏn period was to argue for adoption of the patrilineal rule of succession in mixed marriages. Although they used the moral argument that all children were obliged to acknowledge their fathers openly, their primary objective was probably to find a way to obtain good status for the children of their concubines. Some also believed that the patrilineal rule would be more effective in increasing the commoner population, but their opponents held that greedy slaveowners would subvert the patrilineal law by slyly marrying their male slaves to commoner women to breed more slaves for themselves. The trouble was that either law was prone to evasion.[59]

In 1397 King T'aejo showed that although he did not want to adopt an explicit law of patrilineal succession in mixed marriages, he was willing to accommodate the yangban by decreeing that their children by slave concubines "be permanently released and made good [in status]."[60] Then, in 1414 King T'aejong adopted a modified version of the patrilineal rule to avoid issuing a direct edict manumitting the sons of female slaves and men of "good" status by simply declaring that they would simply assume their father's status.[61]

At the very moment that he made this decision, however, he also made the startling announcement that there basically had been no base persons in Korea until the Koryŏ government decided to make all offspring of mixed marriages slave through the matrilineal succession law (of 1039), which only increased the slave population and reduced the number of commoners. Despite his apparent distaste for Koryŏ practice, however, he was not sufficiently moved to decree the outright abolition of slavery, presumably because he was not willing to challenge the class of slaveholders.[62]

In 1429 State Councilor Maeng Sasŏng and other high officials complained that the existing law permitted female slaves to marry commoner men but prohibited male slaves from marrying commoner women, indicating that T'aejong's patrilineal rule of 1414 was not intended to condone inter-status marriage of all types. Maeng went on to say that as a consequence of the new rule slave women were making false claims that the fathers of their children were of good status so their children could escape base status. For children to call strangers parents and vice versa (to evade the inheritance of base status) was destructive of Confucian family ethics. If the law remained in effect for a decade, the government would lose all its slaves and would have to use commoners to perform their service, and the number of lawsuits over status would exceed the capacity of the judiciary agencies. There was no need, however, to change T'aejong's patrilineal rule, which properly conformed to Confucian patriarchal standards; if slave women could only be prohibited from marrying males of good status, the important line between the good and the base could be preserved.

Inspector-General Kim Hyoson then urged the restoration of the matrilineal law because he obviously wanted to make sure that children of slave women would not become commoners, but King Sejong rejected both requests because he believed that his and Maeng's proposed reform was contrary to the intent of his royal forebears to increase the commoner population. Yet he also noted that he would rather restore the matrilineal law than prohibit female slaves from marrying commoner men.[63]

By 1432, however, Sejong changed his mind and decided to issue just such a prohibition because female slaves were changing their husbands between men of slave and commoner status, creating confusion in the determination of status, and violating the Confucian principle of treating (real) fathers with the proper respect that was owed them. He was reluctant, however, to follow Maeng Sasŏng's proposal to alter his father's patrilineal rule and return to the matrilineal succession law.[64] He eventually suggested a modified solution to allow female slaves to marry commoner males but only if they obtained an official permit (*mun'an*) in advance from the village headman as a means of preventing slave women from falsifying the status of their children's father.[65]

Nonetheless, Sejong was alarmed by the prospects of any strict and uniform adherence to the patrilineal rule. Maeng Sasŏng, who preferred the matrilineal rule to block slave women from gaining commoner status for their children by marrying commoner males, argued that if Sejong was committed to preserving the patrilineal rule, he should at least reverse T'aejong's exception that prohibited its application to the offspring of slave men and commoner women and allow those offspring to inherit their slave fathers' status. Sejong, however, refused to do it because state law already prohibited intermarriage between slave men and commoner women. When he hinted that he was prepared to add teeth to this law by prohibiting all sexual intercourse between male slaves and commoner women and punishing the violators by making official slaves of their children, his officials reminded Sejong that if he did so, he would only be encouraging slave women to continue marrying commoner men because they would rejoice at the prospect of having their children made official rather than private slaves, since the opportunity of escape from official slavery was easier. There would be too many lawbreakers to prosecute, and in less than a century, there would be no private slaves left. Better to prohibit all intercourse between commoners and slaves and turn the children of the violators over to the private slaveowners, for only then would the female slaves realize that there would be nothing to be gained by marrying commoner males.[66]

Although Sejong decided to ban the marriage of base women to good men in 1432, he made an important exception to the rule if the father were a regular civil and military official, a passer of the civil, military, or *saengwŏn* examination, a male heir of an official with the protection privilege, or an ordinary commoner who by the age of forty did not have any sons, a virtual definition of most yangban.[67] Some scholars have interpreted this act as reestablishment of the matrilineal succession rule, but Sejong did not explicitly mention the matrilineal principle. He simply tried to block slave women from gaining commoner status for their children by falsely representing the fathers of their children as commoners, but he protected the ability of yangban to maintain a harem of slave concubines and keep their nothoi offspring commoners instead of slaves. For Sejong, establishing a uniform law was less important than catering to the needs of the yangban as a class.

During the debate of the 1420s and 1430s the matrilineal rule seems to have been held in disfavor by all, but for different reasons. The Neo-Confucian officials, who felt it was anti-Confucian in spirit, preferred the patrilineal rule of T'aejong. Both T'aejong and Sejong remarked that the matrilineal rule of Koryŏ was flawed because it had contravened "Heaven's principles" by in effect creating a system of hereditary slavery. Sejong was caught between conflicting desires: he sought to allow for the expansion of the commoner population by continuing T'aejong's policy of allowing inheritance of good status in some cases of mixed marriage, but he was also persuaded by his officials that his father's patrilineal rule provided too many loopholes for mixed marriages, which threatened to undermine the clarity of social status groups, so important to the maintenance of moral order. His final solution was to outlaw intercourse or intermarriage between people of good and base status except for yangban men and their slave concubines. Since he never explicitly repealed the patrilineal succession law, the children of the latter were the only ones that could look forward to good status.

In 1468 during the reign of King Sejo a degree-holder attacked the patrilineal rule of 1414, which had never been abolished, on the issue of excessive false paternity claims, an indication that King Sejong's ban on marriages between slave women and commoner men had not worked. Although Sejo was told that the patrilineal rule had increased the commoner population and the number of men eligible for military service, while the matrilineal law might permanently increase the slave population, he was persuaded to restore the matrilineal rule because he could offset an excessive conversion of commoners to slave status by allowing individuals to purchase their children's freedom (*soksin*). As a result, the law code of 1469, the *Kyŏngguk taejŏn*, included the matrilineal law of succession for the offspring of mixed slave/commoner marriages with the exception that the offspring of officials and slave wives or concubines would be regarded as commoners (*yang*).[68]

By the sixteenth century, however, the proportion of slaves in the population appeared to be increasing because of the rise of commendation by commoners to escape onerous military and labor service burdens and the practice of slaveowners claiming ownership rights over the children of mixed commoner/slave as well as pure slave marriages, obviously to increase the number of their slaves. The household registers for Ulsan in 1609, for example, indicated that 48.6 percent of the 2,009 persons listed on the registers for a half dozen subdistricts or counties (*myŏn*) were slaves.[69]

Methods to prevent the reduction of *yang'in* or commoners had been discussed since 1515, and finally in 1543 King Chungjong decided to expand the commoner population by amending the above-mentioned rule to allow the offspring of ordinary male commoners and slave concubines to inherit commoner status. Even though this amendment was incorporated into the revised law code, the *Taejŏn husongnok* of 1543, it had little effect because it was ignored by both slaveowners and officials alike.[70]

In 1557 an official suggested that proper enforcement of the matrilineal rule could be used to ensure an increase of commoners, not slaves, but that it would take a bold king to carry it through against the private interests of the slaveowners.[71] The compiler of the *The Veritable Record of King Myŏngjong* in the next generation criticized this position severely on the grounds that under early Chosŏn law the offspring of private slaves would not be allowed to redeem themselves by purchase, "unless they were the sons and daughters of the *sadaebu* [scholar-officials]." He defended that law as justifiable not only because it had a thousand years of tradition behind it, but because it was designed to eliminate any route by which the base could become good and thus disrupt the social order.[72]

Although Kings T'aejo, T'aejong, and Sejong did attempt to prohibit intermarriage between those of good and base status, they also sought ways to permit escape from inherited slavery to prevent the loss of taxpaying commoners. On the other hand, the historian did hit upon a key goal of the early system when he noted that the opportunity for escape from inherited slavery was open only to the heirs of the *sadaebu* or yangban, for the adoption of the patrilineal rule by T'aejong and permission for purchased manumission by Sejo were both designed as means of favoring the nothoi or sons of yangban and their slave concubines.[73]

Despite the matrilineal rule of 1468, however, by the late sixteenth century a closed hereditary system of slavery had in fact become the accepted standard. As opposed to King T'aejong, however, the new view was that the matrilineal rule itself was not at fault; it was the failure to implement it faithfully. It was now argued that mere enforcement of the matrilineal rule was tantamount to a radical reform of the existing system of inherited slavery.

POST-IMJIN CHANGES IN THE TREATMENT OF SLAVES

Military service: The Sog'o *Units*

In 1298 King Ch'ungnyŏl stated that ever since ancient times the slaves of yangban never were responsible for public service or miscellaneous levies because their responsibilities were kept separate from those owed by their masters. Nevertheless, because all the men of good status had been absorbed or taken over by powerful families and no one was left to perform labor service for the state, the slaves of yangban were performing the labor service of the commoner males in their place. The king prohibited the practice.[74] In short, all private slaves were exempted from labor service during the early Koryŏ dynasty, while official slaves were subject to a variety of labor service obligations, including military service.[75]

The exemption of slaves from military service was ignored, however, in times of national emergency. In 1378 a unit of auxiliary soldiers (*p'och'unggun*) was created because of the poor condition of the regular troops (*pubyŏng*), and in the early Chosŏn period, manumitted slaves and sons of yangban officials and their slave concubines were assigned to it. The auxiliaries were expanded in 1415 to offset the shortage of commoners produced by a rise in the proportion of slaves in the population.[76]

Because Sejong banned intermarriage between men of good status and slave women in 1432, there could be no legal recruitment of offspring of such unions born after that date into the auxiliaries, but the law was not enforced. Offspring of officials and slave concubines continued to be enrolled in the auxiliaries particularly after the 1450s, and in 1456 the sons of officials and *kisaeng* (female entertainers) were admitted to the auxiliaries for the first time. Under King Sejo, other special units, the Changyongdae and Man'gangdae established in 1459 and 1462, respectively, also recruited official and private slaves, who were manumitted and made eligible for office after serving a tour of duty. These special units were abolished in 1471, however, because of complaints they allowed slaves or ex-slaves higher ranking posts than their former masters, and would confuse the status system. In addition, the miscellaneous soldiers (*chapsaekkun*), who numbered over 76,000 men in 1467, also included slaves, organized like the Koryŏ Inhogun.[77] Despite the evidence of military service by slaves, however, the vast majority of slaves did not serve except in emergencies.

This exemption from service was the reason why there was a marked trend toward commendation by commoner *yang'in* to estate owners and artisans as slaves in the late fifteenth century. They wished to escape the increased registration of men for military service that was initiated by King Sejo when he adopted the strict *hop'ae* or household tally system of registration in 1458. One such estate owner was charged with harboring 500 such concealed or commended *yang'in* in 1474, and officials complained in 1490 that there were large numbers of such commended slaves throughout the country.[78]

By the end of the sixteenth century the efforts of the early kings to expand the commoner population and reduce the number of slaves had been frustrated by the resurgent power of the slaveowners, but only because the country was at peace and enjoyed the security afforded by the protection of the Ming empire. When national security was threatened in the middle of the sixteenth century by sporadic attacks by Jurchen tribesmen along the northern frontier and pirates off the southern coast, the critical shortage of adult males of good or commoner status for military service became apparent. In 1554 and 1555 the government recruited slaves for military duty in the north and manumitted them in reward for their service, just as the Koryŏ regime had done in times of crisis. Nevertheless, because of strong opposition from owners who objected to the loss of their property and officials who opposed any weakening of the social order, the government had to backtrack and limit manumissions only to slaves who engaged in combat. The incident showed, however, how the threat of war might weaken the Korean social system.[79]

At the end of the century the Korean people had to suffer through one of the most destructive periods in their national history. The invasions of Hideyoshi (the Imjin War) and the occupation of part of the peninsula by Japanese forces lasted for almost seven years, from 1592 to 1598. The war had barely ended before a new enemy appeared on the scene. The Manchus under Nurhaci were gaining power and challenging the declining Ming, and the Koreans were caught between the two rivals. The conflict resulted in two invasions by the Manchus, in 1627 and 1637. Bitter rancor over the invasions and the severity of Manchu tribute demands kept anti-Manchu feeling at a high pitch, and in the 1650s under King Hyojong there was even talk of an armed expedition to Manchuria in reprisal. The half century of war and tension maintained pressure on the government to keep the military ranks filled.

Almost immediately after King Sŏnjo fled the capital in the spring of 1592 to avoid capture by Japanese forces, slaves and refugees attacked the Slave Agency (Changyewŏn) and Ministry of Punishment and put all the slave registers to the torch.[80] In the long run, however, the pressure on the government for expansion of the male population available for military service and taxes was more significant in weakening the restraints of the social system than isolated acts of destruction.

During the wars against Hideyoshi a number of measures were adopted that allowed the manumission of slaves in return for military service or specific acts of heroism or prowess. Manumission and appointment to office continued to be used well into the eighteenth century to reward the achievements of slave soldiers in the repression of rebellion or defense against raiders along the frontier, and another schedule of rewards was even drawn up in 1646.

In 1593 King Sŏnjo also decided to allow private as well as official slaves to stand for the military examinations, and if they passed, to be manumitted and enrolled in the royal Winged Forest Guards. Since he feared opposition by slaveowners to the loss of slaves, he provided inducements to the owners by promising them admission to the examinations, appointment to office, or increase in rank. The demand for soldiers led to the watering down of the qualifications: special red warrants (*hongp'ae*) manumitting slaves or admitting them to higher examinations were distributed to provincial officials who would supposedly hand them out to slaves after counting enemy heads. The system was easily corrupted: slaves turned in the heads of ordinary Korean vagrants or beggars who died of natural causes, and officials sold the red warrants. These measures met with stiff opposition, and some restrictions were imposed to limit the number of manumitted private slaves. The examinations were suspended once, and then dropped altogether sometime soon after the war, probably in the early seventeenth century. And yet it is likely that twenty to thirty thousand slaves gained commoner status during the period by this means.[81]

One of the most significant changes was the open recruitment of slaves into regimental units of regular commoner soldiers, but a concession was made to conventional prejudice by keeping units with slave soldiers (*sog'ogun*) separate from those with commoners alone. Slaves were also brought into the new Military Training Agency in 1593 to serve alongside yangban and commoners, but because runaway slaves were using the agency as a refuge, King Sŏnjo decided to prohibit the recruitment of private slaves for the agency in 1603. Nonetheless, private slaves remained as part of the military service system, as duty soldiers in the *sog'o* units in the provincial garrisons and *abyŏng* (ivory troops) who functioned as aides to provincial governors or military commanders, or as support taxpayers for those duty soldiers. In 1611, the minister of rites remarked that most of the commoners serving in the 200,000-man *sog'ogun* had bought their way out of service, leaving only poor commoners and slaves. In 1714 King Sukchong expanded the opportunities for both official and private slaves to substitute for commoners on military service, and by the 1720s most of the *sog'o* soldiers were slaves.[82]

Manumission by Purchase

Another important effect of the Japanese and Manchu invasions was a significant increase in the purchase of freedom by slaves. The practice, referred to as the grain contribution (*napsok*), was allowed as early as 1485 when the slave Im Pok was reluctantly allowed to purchase the freedom of his four sons for a contribution of 750 *sŏm* of grain for famine relief, but few slaves could have afforded such a large sum. In 1553, another famine year, the price for manumission had dropped to a smaller but still considerable figure, 50–100 *sŏm*, but in 1583 after the crisis had passed, the bureaucrats persuaded the king to prohibit the practice.

During Hideyoshi's invasions in 1592 slaves were able to gain exemption from service for a contribution of 100 *sŏm* and manumission from slavery for 500 *sŏm* or more, still rather expensive prices, but for the first time the state avoided compensation of the owners. Under the pressure of war the system was liberalized further; manumitted slaves could purchase rank or office as well, and officials and special fund raisers were given quotas of blank *napsok* warrants that they peddled in their districts. The practice was continued well into the 1620s and 1630s because of the government's need for revenue.

Since the freedman now became liable for taxes and commoner labor service, none but the wealthiest of slaves could have afforded the burden, and many may have slipped back into slavery.[83] Since the masters suffered the loss of the capital investment in their freed slaves and future tribute payments, in 1637 the government decided to grant the owners official rank as compensation for their loss, but the value of these rank grants soon fell because so many were given out. The government tried to limit the number of liberated slaves by raising the price of manumission from about 15 to 50 *sŏm* between the 1590s and 1670. Even though this price was a mere fraction of the 750 *sŏm* demanded in 1485, the rigid wall of discrimination had been breached by the time Yu Hyŏngwŏn was writing his essay on slavery, but the price still remained high enough to block wholesale manumission by purchase.[84]

Attitudes toward Liberalization

Liberalization of the rules for manumission were caused by necessity, for the very existence of the Korean nation was at question. It would be a mistake to think that measures loosening the lines of status demarcation were greeted with acclamation on the part of the slaveholding elite. In 1593, the famous Yu Sŏngnyŏng attacked the slaveholders for opposing the recruitment of able-bodied private slaves as *sog'o* soldiers.[85] Nevertheless, he made no humanitarian appeal to alleviate the suffering of slaves. In fact, he was probably more concerned about the excessive service requirements on a shrinking commoner population. And his proposals were not that radical: he only briefly hinted that the king might adopt the land and slave limitation proposals of the late Former Han dynasty; he did not suggest that the slavery be abolished.

Nonetheless, the national crisis forced some officials to justify the existence of slavery. During Hideyoshi's invasions Yi Hangbok argued that Heaven was responsible for the distinction between noble and base people, but it had nothing to do with human wisdom or ignorance, nor was it a characteristic of man's basic mind or nature at birth. It was connected with the tradition of social solidarity based on the relationship between men of virtue (*kunja*) and "small" or ordinary people of lesser moral capacity (*soin*). The men of virtue had the responsibility of governing, and the ordinary people had to support them, and between the two the family of man was established. This tradition endured for over a thousand years and had become thoroughly ingrained in the customs of the people and laws of the state. If any change were to be made in the slave laws, "You would have to make the sons and daughters of the *sabu* [scholar-officials] all personally take care of, support, and do the cooking [in the family] just as they do in China." In other words, the children of the aristocrats were so pampered by their slaves who did all the household labor that they would have to undergo almost total reeducation to ordinary household tasks just to discharge their filial responsibilities. The population would have to be prepared in advance lest a radical change cause more problems than it would solve.[86]

In 1597 another official, Yi Chŏng'am, also stressed the difficulty in changing long-standing custom:

> Even though Heaven's Mandate be changed [and a new dynasty established], the customs of the country cannot be changed, and the moral obligations of social status [*myŏngbun*] cannot be disrupted. Our country's method of the hereditary transmission of private slaves has endured for a long time and become the custom. Even the divine authority of T'aejo and the military might of Shih-tsu [Qubilai of the Mongol Yüan dynasty] were not able to repress or abolish it.

Furthermore, he justified slavery as if it were an essential feature of the moral hierarchy that governed society, and he complained that manumitting slaves in return for grain payments could lead to the destruction of Korean society as it was then known.[87]

The famous early seventeenth-century statecraft writer often included among the Sirhak scholars, Yi Sugwang, also complained that the Korean traditions of social status discrimination and slavery, which he claimed had begun in Silla, had been undermined by the easing of manumission through military merit and purchase. Since some ex-slaves had even been able to attain high office, the result was that slaves were looking down on the aristocracy, insulting their masters, and even commiting rebellion and murder. There was no telling what would happen in the future.[88]

Thus, while necessity had relaxed somewhat the rules of the slave system, elite opinion was generally opposed to the prospect of the erosion of status superiority and frightened by the portent of a more egalitarian society. When King Hyojong (r. 1649–59) noticed that the number of registered official slaves, which had reached 350,000 in the late fifteenth century, had dropped to only 190,000, and of these only 27,000 were available for either service or payment of "tribute" taxes to state agencies, he was determined to prevent any further deterioriation of the official slave population by establishing in 1655 a General Directorate for Slave Registration (Ch'uswae-dogam) to dispatch special slave investigators (Ch'uswaegwan) to round up the runaways and recapture the slave tribute revenue that had been lost. Much to his chagrin, the results were negligible, and most of the slaves who were ferreted out were old and weak and incapable of paying tribute to the state.[89] The attempt to rebuild the force of official slaves to provide service and taxes for the state was not discontinued, but it began to become obvious that it was more difficult to stop the loss of official slaves by coercion and punishment.

In short, officials gradually became persuaded to find some method to increase the number of commoner adult males for two reasons: to replace both the commoner males who had commoner service and the official slaves who had run away from their duties or tax obligations, purchased their freedom, or bribed their way out of registration. But this process took over a century to achieve.

Adoption of the Matrilineal Rule in 1669

In the late sixteenth century, even before the Japanese invasions, Yulgok (Yi I), who was then royal secretary, proposed reaffirmation of the matrilineal rule to counter the absorption of commoners into powerful families as their slaves and provide men for military service. His proposal, however, was blocked by an official who insisted on the moral superiority of the patrilineal succession rule.[90] Yulgok allowed that while the matrilineal law was superior, it was not being applied according to law.[91]

The scholar Cho Ik also wrote in the mid-seventeenth century of the shortage of soldiers caused by an excessively large number of slaves, which he estimated at 80 to 90 percent of the population, an obvious bit of hyperbole to lend force to his advocacy of the matrilineal rule. Nonetheless, Kim Yŏngmo has estimated that in the 1680s the slave population hovered around the 50 percent mark.[92] He blamed it on the court officials who only thought about protecting control of their own slaves, and predicted that the whole population would be converted to slavery if something were not done to reverse the situation.[93]

Song Siyŏl, the official most responsible for the adoption of the matrilineal rule in 1669 and a leader of the Westerner faction, was a student of the famous expert on ritual and Neo-Confucianism, Kim Changsaeng, who had studied with Yulgok. When Song requested adoption of the matrilineal rule to King Hyŏnjong, he gave credit to Yulgok for the idea, and he attacked the perversion of the matrilineal rule by enslaving offspring if either parent were of base status. He knew that the scholar-officials would raise a row over the loss of their slaves, yet he still insisted that the matrilineal rule would reverse the increase in the number of slaves in society.[94]

Third State Councilor Hŏ Chŏk, a leader of the rival Southerner faction, actively supported Song's proposal. It was not until after exacerbation of Westerner/Southerner animosity over the mourning rite question in 1672 that Hŏ changed his position and was able to persuade King Sukchong to annul the matrilineal rule in 1675. Thereafter the matrilineal rule became indelibly linked with the Westerners and their splinter factions, and opposition to it with the Southerner faction. It was restored in 1684 and abolished again in 1689 when the Southerners returned to power for the last time. Despite the return to power in 1694 of the Patriarch's Faction (Noron), the Westerner splinter group of Song Siyŏl disciples, King Sukchong did not reverse his earlier decision and it was not until 1730 that King Yŏngjo decisively reaffirmed the matrilineal rule.[95] What is significant about this sequence of events is that the pressures of foreign invasion did not lead to the adoption of the matrilineal rule as the means of increasing the commoner population, probably because that was done by permitting manumission either for the performance of meritorious military action or the payment of a grain contribution to the government.

Unfortunately, that measure was by no means the most radical and effective method of reform at the time because slaves had already been accepted into the *sog'o* units of the army and were performing the function of both duty soldiers and support taxpayers for the army. Since commoners began to be *formally* excluded from the *sog'ogun* after 1736, the state had obviously responded to the shortage of commoner male adults by expanding the use of private slaves to replace them. By the mid-eighteenth century slaves may have accounted for 30 percent of the soldiers in the army, approximately the same percentage of slaves in the total population.[96] To ease the tax burden on private slaves who had to pay a support tax for duty soldiers since the private slaves also owed the personal tribute tax (*sin'gong*) to their masters, the government set their tax rate at half the rate for commoner support taxpayers, but few argued that the purpose of reform was to make life easier for the slaves.[97]

Nonetheless, the main reason used to justify the adoption of the matrilineal rule first in 1669, and finally in 1730, was the argument that there were too many slaves and something had to be done to create more commoners. One might deduce that the main reason why reform policy was restricted only to liberating the future offspring of commoner mothers and permitting a minimal number of slaves to buy their own freedom was not only that the power of the slaveholding class and their domination of the government as high-ranking bureaucrats was too great to overcome, but that the reformers themselves were also members of that same slaveholding class and were reluctant to adopt any radical policy that would severely damage those class interests. Since the matrilineal law was not adopted permanently until 1731, it could not have had any serious effects on the slave population until a generation later.

Yu Hyŏngwŏn's Solutions for Slavery

Chinese Precedent

Yu Hyŏngwŏn introduced his discussion of slavery in his usual fashion by investigating classical Chinese sources on the subject, but this alone was a departure from the long tradition of beginning any treatment of Korean slavery with Kija's law code. He began with *The Rites of Chou*, which revealed to him that under the sage rule of the Chou kings the only legitimate form of slavery was the enslavement of barbarian prisoners of war and criminals and their families and who were employed by the government as official slaves. Although *The Rites of Chou* did justify slavery, it did not legitimate private slavery.[98] *"There is no case of any ordinary people who were made slaves"* [italics mine].[99]

Yu implicitly indicted the enslavement of noncriminals as private slaves and, in particular, the Korean system of hereditary slavery by which the innocent descendants of even legitimately enslaved criminals, captives, or bandits were condemned to an unwarranted servitude. He was also challenging the commonly held misinterpretation of Kija's laws that the enslavement of ordinary thieves legitimated hereditary slavery for their innocent descendants.

It certainly appears that Yu simply accepted the validity of ancient Chinese precedent rather than seeking any new standard of judgment based on the power of human reason. If he had intended by his research to produce a thorough and objective account of slavery as an institution, he might have tried to find evidence for the tolerance of inherited servitude in the Chou as well as the Han, but he either failed to discover it or suppressed it to make his case against hereditary slavery.

Yu began his treatment of the Han period by listing acts of manumission of slaves either by imperial decree or humane officials to illustrate the benign concern of the Han emperors.[100] Even though the first call for the outright abolition of slavery in Chinese history was proposed by Tung Chung-shu to Emperor Wu (ca. 140–93 B.C.), Yu did not make Tung's unequivocal appeal for total abolition the cornerstone of a radical abolitionist policy, possibly because it would been contrary to the Chou practice of enslaving criminals and war captives.[101]

In his brief discussion of the T'ang period, Yu cited materials on two issues, the T'ang system of triple pardons (*sammyŏn*) for official slaves and debt slavery.[102] Although he did not comment on these issues, we might safely deduce that his silence signified at least limited approval of the T'ang system of gradual reduction of slave status even though the T'ang system of graded manumission was probably less beneficial to slaves than the Han dynasty system, where manumitted official slaves became commoners immediately without suffering limited disabiities. Both were more liberal than the hereditary slavery of Korea.[103] Although Yu did not comment directly on cases of liberation of slaves from debt slavery that was proposed in the T'ang and Sung dynasties, he obviously approved of the policy because the enslavement of innocent commoners was contrary to a principle established in antiquity.

The Reform of Slavery in Korea

The Causes and Consequences of Slavery. Applying the lessons he learned from China, Yu argued[104] that in ancient China only those guilty of a crime were enslaved, and even in those cases the penalty was not extended to their descendants. Certainly those innocent of any crime were never enslaved, and even in the T'ang dynasty slavery was never extended to the descendants of those who had been penalized by enslavement for life.[105]

Yu was disturbed that Koreans were totally unconcerned whether or not slaves had merited their lowly status because they had committed a crime. Because the only basis for the determination of slavery was if an individual had a slave in his family tree, even men of worth and talent had been condemned to slavery without any consideration of their qualities as people.[106]

Since he believed that the hereditary aspect of Korean slavery was a departure from Chinese norms, he was naturally interested in its origin in Korea. Contrary to conventional wisdom he made no mention of Kija's law, and he was unable to find any instance of hereditary slavery in Korean history in the Three Kingdoms period (ca. the first century B.C. to A.D. 668). Slavery existed, to be sure, but enslavement occurred only as punishment for prisoners of war, criminal action, embezzlement, or robbery. He thus dated the origin of hereditary slavery at the beginning of the Koryŏ dynasty when T'aejo (Wang Kŏn) enslaved many of the opponents of his regime and gave them to his merit subjects for their private slaves.

Yu presented no positive evidence for his interpretation, but he probably deduced its origin in early Koryŏ because of the 1039 matrilineal inheritance law and the clear existence of hereditary slavery by the mid-Koryŏ period. By so doing he stripped hereditary slavery of any legitimacy conferred by a putative origin in remote antiquity, whether in China or in ancient Chosŏn under Kija's sage rule. Yu also remarked that the laws of the Koryŏ state forced people into slavery, causing an increase in the slave population to 80 or 90 percent of the population, a view that was popular in the early Chosŏn period.[107] This situation was exacerbated by *the violation of* (italics mine) the matrilineal rule of succession (*chongmobŏp* or *chongmojibŏp*) that was supposed to limit the inheritance of slave status in the case of mixed commoner-slave marriages to the children of slave mothers. Since in practice the offspring became slaves if either of the two parents were a slave, "All this means is that people are forced into slavery, and once a slave, there is no way out of it."[108]

He appears to have assumed that the law had remained on the books since 1039, albeit neglected in practice. Thus, he could not have known that the matrilineal rule itself had been severely criticized for contributing to the increase of the slave population. Yu explained that "the fault is not with the matrilineal succession law [in mixed marriages]; the error [is to be found] in the slave law [itself]; that is, the law by which slavery is [determined by] heredity [*nobi isejibŏp*]." Another factor was the onerous burden of military service, which commoners sought to avoid. Because slave status conferred exemption from military service (at least prior to 1593), many commoners often arranged marriages for their children with private slaves.[109]

Yu cited Yulgok's criticism of slavery as well as a lengthy memorial of Cho Hŏn to King Sŏnjo on his return from a mission to China in 1574 in which Cho made an invidious comparison of Korean defensive capabilities relative to China and attributed the cause of Korean weakness to slavery.[110] The reason, Cho said, why Chinese border areas were secure despite the need to defend numerous scattered towns and cities was because, contrary to contemporary Korea where slaves were exempted from military duty, the whole population, except for the scholar-officials and those engaged in farming and commerce, could be recruited as soldiers. For that matter, during the Three Kingdoms period in Korea everyone could be recruited for military service on behalf of the king because slavery had not yet become widespread.[111] In the present (Chosŏn) dynasty the increase in the slave population had left the country with barely 200,000 men on the service rosters, and of these hardly more than a thousand were fit for actual duty.[112] He presciently predicted that if the Japanese or others were to mass a force for an invasion of Korea, there would be no way to construct a defense.

He also objected to the proliferation of lawsuits over slaveownership and the depredations of the agents of slaveholders who blanketed the country looking for runaway slaves. Slavery was the main reason why lineages were divided into quarrelsome groups as they contested the inheritance of slaves, and why the district magistrates were distracted from their ordinary business by the time and trouble it took to adjudicate these cantankerous and complex cases.[113]

Humanitarianism and Equality. Yu was particularly concerned about the dehumanizing effects that slavery had on society at large. He argued that slavery brutalized not only the slaves but the slaveowners as well, who were only able to manage their slaves by whipping them. As a result the slaves had lost all sense of loyalty and all taste for diligent toil. They absconded in droves because inhumane treatment left them no redress but flight from their homes and villages.[114] Yu's concept of the brutalization of both slaves and slaveowners was a new twist on the conventional view of slavery, but by no means did he rest content with this unique view. He went further, articulating a principle of human equality nowhere to be found in the previous literature: "At the present time in our country we regard slaves as chattel. Now people are all the same [lit., people are of the same type or category]. How could there be a principle by which one person regards another person as his property?"[115]

In his view, the custom of treating slaves as chattel was absent from ancient (Chinese) society, and its existence in contemporary Korean society was an unfortunate indication of how far Korea had fallen from the glorious norms of the past.

> In ancient times when people asked how wealthy a state was, the answer was given in the number of horses [possessed]. This meant that even though the Son of Heaven and the feudal lords were responsible for governing other men, they never regarded other men as their private property [*ki chaemul*]. But as far as the customs of this country [Korea] at the present time are concerned, *if you ask a man how wealthy he is, the reply will always be made in terms of how many slaves and how much land he owns* [italics mine]. From this one can see how wrong our laws are and how sick our customs are.

The crux of the problem was that people allowed their immediate private interest to obscure their understanding and delude themselves into thinking that slavery was too hard to eliminate. Koreans were laboring under the misconception that slaves were somehow different from ordinary people, and that the ruler of the state was justified in doing them harm. Regarding slaves as a kind of subhuman had led to the cruel treatment of slaves, particularly in the process of capturing fugitives.[116]

Yu did not mean by his universal principle that "all men are the same" that all men (let alone women) were equal before the law, equal sharers in the social compact, or possessors of equal rights in the political community. Rather, he meant that all men shared a common humanity that separated them from inanimate objects or chattel. Since only chattel or things could be the property of a man, one man could not own another. Furthermore, from the standpoint of the ruler it was improper to create artificial status categories as a basis of discrimination, an argument totally at odds with the common justifications for status (*myŏngbun*) in Korean society. If Yu did not invent this idea, he certainly played an important role in popularizing it, and it was reiterated by King Sunjo in 1801 in the decree that abolished official slavery.

Unfortunately, Yu's declaration of human equality lacked a classical provenance, so he had to substitute a rather weak alternative, an ostensibly empirical statement that in China the ancients were not used to measuring their wealth in slaves as contemporary Koreans were wont to do. Even if true, this statement was certainly no proof that chattel slavery did not exist in ancient China. On the contrary, it implied that chattel slavery existed and was legitimate.

If he were looking merely for examples of the condemnation of slavery, he could have cited Wang Mang, who usurped power from the last of the Former Han emperors and established the Hsin dynasty in A.D. 9. Wang Mang had criticized the slavery of the Ch'in period in harsh terms because it locked people up in cattle pens and justified their inhumane treatment.[117] Perhaps he could not bring himself to cite a usurper as an authority on moral principle (even though Yi Ik, Yu's intellectual heir did so in the eighteenth century) and he would have preferred a pre-Ch'in source if he could have found it.

The Confucian line on slavery in Korea in the late tenth century was that it was necessary to the aristocracy, and in the early fifteenth century that it was necessary for the preservation of the patrimony. It was no easy task for Yu to find a tradition of antislavery thought in Confucian moral literature; he had no choice but to create or invent a principle of human equality. Yet it is doubtful that he really intended the immediate and total elimination of slavery from Korean society, especially since in his chapters on education and land reform slave labor was still to play an important role even after the abolition of private property and the conversion to his so-called public land system (*kongjŏn*).

The Matrilineal Succession Law

Despite his articulation of the principle of the sameness of human beings whether slave or commoner, Yu surprisingly proposed as his solution to the problem of slavery the adoption of the matrilineal rule for status inheritance by children in mixed commoner/slave marriages, the same solution that Song Siyŏl had offered in his own time.[118] What distinguished Yu from the other advocates of this method was his willingness to admit that the determination of the status of children of mixed marriages by that of the mother was really a violation of the Confucian ethical norms that he upheld.[119] On the other hand, the patrilineal succession rule was hardly better, not for moral but for practical reasons, because the difficulty in proving paternity would simply incite litigation by cunning and lawless people.

Instead, he resigned himself to the matrilineal succession law as the better choice of evils. Since a patrilineal succession law would be impractical, "it is for that reason that we have had no choice but to have things this way [i.e., strict adherence to the matrilineal succession law], and that is all."[120] Yu's practicality stands in even bolder relief when contrasted with the moralistic tone of Song Siyŏl. When Song recommended the matrilineal rule to King Hyŏnjong in 1669, he said that it represented the epitome of fairness, equity, justice, and rectitude.[121] Contrary to the view of Chŏn Hyŏngt'aek that Song and the Westerners represented the practical view of things in advocating the matrilineal law while the Sirhak scholars like Yu represented a moral approach to the problem, the essence of their positions was exactly the reverse.[122]

Yu's rejection of both the matrilineal and patrilineal rules reflects a sophistication that would have been impossible but for the experimentation with regulations governing the inheritance of status in the fifteenth century, which proved that both the patrilineal and matrilineal rules were flawed. The overriding tone of his analysis was practical acceptance of a method that he admitted was immoral from a Confucian standpoint, one of the few clear-cut statements that would indeed identify him as a scholar in the tradition of "practical learning." Yu did not conclude, however, that all offspring of mixed marriages should be free, but primarily because the times did not warrant an immediate abolition of slavery, he suggested that perhaps the abolition of slavery might have to be postponed until the appearance of a sage ruler in an age when "all institutions are rectified and all baseness is washed clean."[123]

Cessation of the Hereditary Principle

Although he was committed to the abolition of slavery in principle, he also believed that the ruling class deserved to be supported by the king as they had been in the Chinese Chou dynasty. Since he felt that a sudden abolition of slavery would be too abrupt a change of custom because it would leave not only the contemporary yangban but the members of his new class of educated moral leaders helpless and unable to care for themselves, the elimination of slavery had to be done gradually by substituting hired or wage labor for slaves. This kind of reform would also require that the ruling class become used to hired labor instead of slavery. As part of the transition the first step would be to retain the existing slaves but to set a deadline for the abolition of the hereditary transmission of slave status to the next generation by a careful program of registration of the existing slave population.[124]

Hired Labor: the Profit/Harm Calculus

Yu argued that hired labor was a justified substitute for slavery because "the custom of using hired labor and indentured servants was currently done by the scholars and officials in China and working successfully."[125] Yu admitted that the adoption of hired labor in Korea would be vexing not only because slave-owners were long accustomed to using slaves for labor and maltreating them in the process, but also because arduous labor was associated with slavery and regarded as demeaning by the commoner population. "Only if a person is a slave do others make them labor [i.e., employers of labor only seek slaves], and only if a person is a slave is he made to labor for others." Yet, despite the stigma attached to hard labor, Yu acknowledged that there were still some people who worked occasionally as hired laborers.

In any case, Yu argued that there were two ways to overcome the stigma against hard physical labor. The first was the use of legislation to effect a transformation of ingrained social custom, contrary to the conventional view that customs were impervious to transformation by law.[126] He also believed it was possible for the social elite or ruling class in society to change the manner in which it treated the lower class. If the ruling class began to show benevolence and righteousness toward their inferiors, it would lift the hereditary restrictions and excessive hardships imposed on slaves. Once this occurred, ordinary commoners would be more than willing to hire themselves out as laborers.

But how was this moral transformation in the attitude of the upper class toward slaves to take place? Not by the type of self-cultivation preached by the Neo-Confucian moralists, but by the simple device of abolishing hereditary slavery. Since legislated abolition would reduce the number of slaves in the population, the reduction of the slave population would lead gradually to the conversion of the rulers or slaveowners to benevolent and righteous treatment "as a matter of course." In effect, he did not provide a feasible explanation of why this change of attitude toward slaves should result so easily, but he was convinced that the abolition of the hereditary feature would induce many men to become hired laborers, even for their whole lives. This was a rather curious statement because the hired laborers of Hamgyŏng Province had already become laborers not only for life, but as a hereditary indentured class hardly different from slaves.[127]

Nonetheless, Yu believed that the reduction in the number of slaves would change the attitude of slaveowners, slaves, and commoners toward manual labor. It would be the objective, external conditions that would achieve the conversion of the inner mind, and not the other way around, as might be expected from a Confucian philosopher.

In an even greater departure from Confucian moral orthodoxy, Yu argued that a transformed external situation would ameliorate the external behavior of individuals not because of any influence on their innate moral capacities, but rather because of an appeal to everyone's sense of self-interest. "All men throughout the world since the most ancient times have shared the same feeling – to pursue what is profitable and avoid what is harmful. How could the present times be different from ancient times [on this score]? And how could our Eastern land [Korea] be different from China in terms of this principle?"

Once again Yu had found a principle for which there was no provenance in classical antiquity save for the Legalists, but his formula for the calculation of profit and harm was closer to Bentham's utilitarian pleasure/pain calculus than the Legalist stress on reward and punishment. To provide proof that his profit/harm model worked in practice, Yu pointed out that in China all members of the poor and lowly class were only too willing to work for wages since they were able to earn a living from it. He even extolled the benefits of wage work on the grounds of freedom of choice, language worthy of any modern free-market capitalist! "Not only do the hired laborers (in China) select their employers to work for, but the employers also select people to work for them as hired laborers." Yu had no modern concept of the labor market and its operations, but he was intrigued by the idea that wage workers and employers alike would exercise free choice and hired labor could operate without any need for the coercion and force that governed the management of slave labor in Korea.[128]

Whence did Yu derive his belief in the transforming effects of laws and institutions, the profit/harm interest orientation of human behavior, and the salutary effects of wage labor on a slave society? There is hardly any evidence that the major influence on his thinking came from his study of ancient Chinese or earlier Korean ideas or institutions, or for that matter from the writings of Yulgok and Cho Hŏn in the sixteenth century. What he shared with Yulgok, or Song Siyŏl for that matter, was merely agreement on the matrilineal rule as a means of reducing the slave population.

Although not a direct observer of the Chinese scene, he was inspired by what he had heard of economic conditions in contemporary China. He might also have been influenced by the beginnings of commercial growth in Korea even though he did not mention it, but if he had had greater knowledge about the miserable condition of hired laborers, particularly in Hamgyŏng and Chŏlla provinces, he might not have been so sanguine about the advantages of their condition over slaves. In any case, his belief that even wage labor in the mid-seventeenth century was still based on hierarchical respect, status, and coercion was quite correct.

The Social Consequences of Wage Labor

It would appear that Yu might have intended the creation of a more egalitarian society by his advocacy of the replacement of slavery by wage labor, especially since at one point he declared the virtual equality of all men as the basis for his criticism of slavery. In his description of what his future society would be like, however, he made clear that an egalitarian social order was not his goal. To begin with, his conception of his own ideal society was by no means egalitarian. Nor did he conceive of contemporary Chinese social organization, even with its use of hired rather than slave labor, as an egalitarian society. On the contrary, Chinese men of position, status, and wealth merely used their wealth to employ as many servants and laborers as they could afford without any disruption of the proprieties of social status and order.

How many hired laborers people employed was only a function of their wealth. Large landowners and high officials with large salaries could employ hundreds or thousands of hired laborers, or ordinary people might employ only a few. In any case, hired labor did not interfere with proper distinctions of social status in the homes of the high officials. And in the homes of the ordinary villagers, the employers treated the hired laborers like their own children, and people who had many sons even gave some to others to be their hired workers.

If he had had more firsthand knowledge of hired labor in Korea, rather than secondhand hearsay about China, he would have realized that hired laborers were already treated as subordinate members of a family, especially those on annual contracts like the *mŏsŭm* – let alone the so-called *sejŏn kwanha* or hereditary hired laborers in Hamgyŏng Province in the northeast who had been forced into virtual slavery by the powerful landlords there, or the hired laborers of Chŏlla and other provinces who were locked up behind walls when they were not working, as if they were in forced labor camps. By no means were slaves the only persons used to do hard and demeaning physical labor.[129]

In any case, Yu argued that the Chinese version of hired labor could be readily adapted to Korea, even after his ideal program for nationalization of property and equal distribution to peasant families had been adopted. He insisted that his own program for reform was designed to bring the hierarchy of wealth into accordance with the hierarchy of virtue and status, contrary to the existing system of hereditary property and inherited status. Otherwise, his reforms would not change any other customs and practices that were currently in use.[130]

The advantage of the hired labor system would be that it would provide for just and humane treatment of workers in the employ of the families of status and wealth, allow them the freedom of choice to remain unemployed, or if they did decide to work for wages, set limits on the term of service. Yu had never been to China, which explains why he obviously idealized labor relations there, but he believed that hired laborers in China had the choice to work or not as they wished, but once they did agree to work for a family, "they do not dare violate [the orders of the head of the family] even in the slightest, and this is because there are state laws [governing their behavior]."[131]

It is obvious that the prevailing belief among the majority of the social elite of Korea was that slavery was by no means incompatible with Confucian principles of interpersonal respect relations. Some felt that it was even consonant with, if not necessary to, the Confucian concepts of the proper distinction between noble and base and the hierarchical organization of society. Although Yu opposed slavery, it did not mean that he was committed to the principle of equality, despite his declaration that all men were "of the same kind." In fact, he insisted that social stratification could be maintained even if slavery were replaced by hired labor. While Yu's ultimate vision for the future was the disappearance of slavery and the replacement of slave with hired labor, a task that might take decades to achieve at the least, his immediate goal was only an end to inherited slavery.

The problem with his proposal to replace slaves with hired labor, however, was that according to his land distribution plan (see chap. 7) every able-bodied male would be entitled to a land grant, even slaves. And if slaves were all manumitted and hired laborers still existed, they too would qualify for a land grant. Even though he guaranteed that after his land reform was adopted there would be an increase in the number of farmers and a surplus of people available to work for the officials and scholars in his new society, logically there could not possibly be any surplus labor left because all would have been converted into smallholding peasants with a guaranteed right of cultivation.[132]

The contradiction in his plan is obvious, but Yu did not see it. Why not? Because, as we will see in chapter 7, his land grant plan was so comprehensive that there would be no landless peasants left to function as hired laborers. Even if Yu thought he could guarantee a surplus labor force of hired labor rather than slaves for his ideal *sadaebu*, was it not likely that a system of free wage labor would undermine the moral foundation of hierarchical interpersonal relations, contrary to his guarantee that it would not because it had not happened in China? In fact, in his own chapter he had his imaginary antagonist ask whether it would truly be possible to maintain proper distinctions between superiors and inferiors in his ideal society since his main objective was to provide "benevolent compassion [for the underprivileged] [*hyehyul*] without the exercise of authority to put restraints on people."[133]

When Yu put the term "benevolent compassion" in the mouth of his interlocutor, he must have been representing the antagonism of his conservative opponents toward idealistic do-gooders like himself, people who objected to social engineering on the grounds of "benevolent compassion." His egalitarian society could only be achieved if the state used force either against the slaveholders to force them to accept hired laborers as substitutes for slaves, or against hired laborers to coerce them into respectful behavior toward their employers. He must also have been charged with failing to see that a system of wage labor based on the freedom to choose whether to work for wages or not would necessarily introduce a new principle into interpersonal relations destructive of the social status quo. Yet the challenge was invalid because hired labor had been in existence since the beginning of the dynasty without affecting the superiority of the yangban or weakening the strength of slavery; in fact the employers of Hamgyŏng Province had reduced their hired laborers to virtual slaves.

When forced to defend himself against the charges of the social conservatives and assure them that his proposal was not ultimately threatening to their welfare, Yu had to abandon any pretense to sentimentality on behalf of the downtrodden (slaves and wage workers) and bare his teeth in a thinly veiled threat to wreak the vengeance of the state on any who perversely sought to disrupt the principles of proper Confucian order by using the leeway provided by the substitution of wage labor for slavery.

> To this I would reply that if rites [the Confucian norms of behavior] and laws are clear, then the difference between superiors and inferiors will be determined as a matter of course. This is the reason why the [Ming] code [provides for the punishment of] hired laborers who talk back to the head of a household or who report any crime committed by the head of a family [to the authorities]. And criminal penalties even extend to the punishment of those who talk back to or inform on the heads of families included in the group of relations who owe three months' mourning [to their deceased relatives]. If laws and teachings are like this, then there need be no concern about [wage laborers] insulting or lording it over [their superiors].

No sooner had he hinted at the threat of dire retribution in the face of recalcitrance than he retreated to his more benign posture, assuring his readers, after all, that force would really not be necessary because there was no mutually (exclusive) contradiction between treating people with benevolent compassion and maintaining status distinctions. One need not dispense with benevolent compassion as the means to maintain proper status distinctions because then, "both worthy and ignorant men will obtain their proper share in society, and superiors and inferiors will each get what he seeks. Superiors will employ [inferiors] with benevolence and compassion, while inferiors will also [serve their superiors] with loyalty and diligence."[134] This was a rather transparent appeal to utility (obtaining one's proper share) rather than an appeal to an intrinsic moral compulsion to do what was good and right, as if a utilitarian calculation of interest was the only guarantee of success.

Furthermore, he used a Chinese example to demonstrate that once Chinese laborers agreed to work for a family, they observed the proprieties. Why? Because of existing laws and teachings! In other words, teaching could instruct individuals in what they should do, law would penalize them if they failed to do it. In China, "even in the case of hired laborers who might later on become noble and prominent men, if they should happen to meet their old masters [employers], they must still treat them with the utmost respect."[135] But one could not be sure from Yu's explanation whether they did so because of conviction or fear of the cangue.

He had observed that hired laborers (*kogong*) were treated virtually as the children of the employers in farm families, and he had heard that they had been well-integrated into the family in China. In other words, what he thought of as free labor was in fact only the partially free labor of seventeenth-century Korea, workers who were still bound by real or fictive kinship bonds and obligations. It was thus quite logical for him to presume that the replacement of slaves by this mode of labor would not destroy contemporary principles of social organization.

Having sheathed the sword of retribution, Yu went further and even asserted that the use of force would be counterproductive as well as unnecessary. In Korea, where the reality of master/slave relations had been deplorable because of the whipping and beating of slaves by their masters, the slaves not only failed to learn obedience, but lost completely any feelings of loyalty for them, which is why so many of them ran away.[136]

Of course, Yu's willingness to use law and coercion to win conformity to social norms was consistent with his belief in the utility of laws and institutions to control and guide human behavior, and his liberal use of punishment to maintain discipline in the schools, a reflection of the amalgam between Confucian and Legalist principles achieved in China at least as early as the Han dynasty.

Although Yu Hyŏngwŏn was one of the first and most vociferous critics of the brutality of the Korean system of slavery, and his hope to see it abolished was undoubtedly genuine, he was reluctant to advocate any sudden action that might disrupt the sensibilities of the slaveholders or disturb the idea of social order that he felt was so essential. For that reason he had to find a method to ensure the gradual replacement of slavery, and he did so by settling on the matrilineal succession law in mixed marriages and the gradual introduction of hired labor, but he was so concerned lest hired labor weaken proper principles of social hierarchy that he was willing to threaten the use of law, force, and punishment as the ultimate guarantor of those social principles. This willingness to use the mailed fist only underscored the force of social order even in the minds of the most radical critics of seventeenth-century Korean society. For Yu's objective was not the destruction of social order itself, but the reconstitution of social order on the basis of more valid principles derived from classical, Chou dynasty practices.

The Debate over Hired Labor in the Twentieth Century

Recent studies of hired labor in the Chosŏn dynasty have become embroiled in a major controversy. One group of scholars have seen hired labor as wage labor in the Marxian sense, people who have lost their land, property, and the means of production and have been forced to sell the only thing they have left, their labor power. The leading proponent of this point of view was Kim Yongsŏp, who argued that the development of agricultural production was stimulated by a new class of peasant entrepreneurs who were able to accumulate a surplus over subsistence, began to sell their agricultural products on the market rather than consume them, accumulate a surplus for reinvestment, and use their capital to buy up the land of the impoverished smallholders.[137] Kim's student, Ch'oe Chun'o, applied this schema to hired labor and argued that the annual (*mŏsŭm*) or seasonal hired labor of the early Chosŏn period in which the worker received room and board but no wages changed in character and became a daily laborer who received wages in the form of a grain ration, usually 3 *toe* per day (9 *mal* a month) and 1 *chŏn* or .1 *yang* per day of cash. The ranks of these hired laborers increased in number as the enterpreneurial rich peasants took over the land of impoverished small holders and drove them into vagrancy, where they roamed the countryside looking for work, assembling near some of the larger towns in labor markets. By the middle of the nineteenth century the countryside was filled with these wage laborers who were prime for two potential consequences as Korean agriculture moved toward commercial capitalism. They could be employed by large landowners who were presumed to be shifting from tenancy to more efficient and less costly production by using itinerant wage workers or they could join the mobs of discontented rural proletarians with their rising sense of class consciousness and who were ready to rise up in rebellion at the slightest provocation.[138]

As part of this general interpretation Kang Man'gil has also argued that when Yu Hyŏngwŏn suggested replacing slaves with hired laborers, he was on the same track as the current trend by which the system of required labor service was shifting to a system of hired (or wage) labor.[139] The main thesis of Kang's article on hired labor was that it marked the positive development of the Chosŏn economy since the sixteenth century, but Yu's own observations about hired labor indicate that he was inspired not so much by the use of hired labor in Korea but by China, where physical labor was not regarded as demeaning and the hiring of labor was a common practice.

By contrast, Pak Sŏngsu criticized the slavelike treatment of hired laborers in Hamgyŏng and Chŏlla provinces, but he was not the only contemporary scholar who took a less than sanguine view of the progressive consequences of hired labor. In his investigation of hired labor in the late Chosŏn period around Taegu (Kyŏngsang Province) from 1705 to 1858 Han Yŏngguk called into serious question the idea that hired labor in late Chosŏn necessarily pointed the way to the development of free wage labor. He also questioned Kim Yongsŏp's thesis about the development of capitalistic management methods by "managerial" or entrepreneurial landowners (the ones who spawned the use of wage labor over tenancy as a more efficient mode of production) as based only on conjecture, not solid fact.[140]

He found that the number of registered hired laborers in both the urban and rural districts almost disappeared between 1825 and 1858, and that the percentage of households of hired laborers in the total population of his sample also dropped from 8.5 percent to 0.2 percent. On the other hand the number of households hiring laborers inside the town of Taegu increased from 12.3 percent to 21.2 percent.[141] The ratio of commoners to slaves in the registered population of hired laborers dropped from about 25 percent to almost zero by 1825 even though the slave population as a whole had almost disappeared. Since almost all the outside-resident slaves and male domestic slaves had run away from their masters, only a population of old slave women were left to act both as domestic slaves and hired laborers. Han concluded that it was impossible that these female slave hired workers could in any way have represented annual or seasonal hired labor; they could only have been a kind of servile servant population who worked without wages just to survive.[142] One of the reasons that they survived as laborers was because the commoner and male slave hired laborers usually ran away from their employers.[143]

Contrary to the argument of Kim Yongsŏp that the chief employers of hired labor should have been commoners, especially the entrepreneurial types, most of the employers in Han's sample in and around Taegu were *chung'in* or petty clerks and official slaves![144] Furthermore, while Ch'oe Chun'o believed that short-term day labor represented the culmination of a progressive process that left the peasant with nothing but his labor power to sell and no other guarantee of support for a season or a year, Han cited a few sources in 1783 when the Korean court was about to adopt the Chinese law governing long-term labor contracts for five years or more showing that short-term migrant labor had always been the main type of hired labor in the dynasty, not the end-point or culmination of what Ch'oe termed the "commoditization" of labor.[145] Ch'oe also included the process by which immiserated and starving people in times of famine begged the well-to-do to hire them on and provide room and board as one of the progressive developments taking place. Han, however, regarded this as a backward form of labor because room and board, not wages, was the main form of compensation, not to mention hired laborers who had no choice but to indenture themselves to employers for life just to stay alive and as such were subject to the same kind of abusive treatment and harsh punishment meted out to slaves.[146]

The weakness of Han's study was that the evidence he used was limited to the household registers. Ch'oe Chun'o cited the appearance of *koji* contracted labor in the mid-eighteenth century as another sign of progress. This form of labor was also the product of desperate circumstances, in which peasants on the verge of starvation in the winter months would enter into a contract with an employer and take an advance payment in cash or grain with a promise to work for the lowest possible wages on his fields in the spring and summer. Employers could get ten men to contract as laborers in the winter for only 1 *yang* or string of cash (.1 *yang* per man to do transplanting, weeding, and harvesting for this "wage"). On the other hand Ch'oe cited evidence that some landowners were offering higher than usual wages to attract *koji* laborers, particularly around larger towns.[147]

So the kind of labor that Han described as the last refuge of the desperate, Ch'oe Chun'o treated as part of the development of the free labor market and rational, capitalist business practice by entrepreneurial rich peasants. Unfortunately, the ability to choose between these two interpretations is not aided that much by studies of the rural sector in Europe. While Fernand Braudel pointed out that itinerant rural wage labor was very much a part of a Europe plodding slowly toward the burgeoning of industrial capitalism in late eighteenth century England, that phenomenon was as much a feature of the fourteenth century as the mid-eighteenth.[148] Georges Duby pushed the replacement of forced labor by wage work back to the twelfth century in France and England.[149] In other words, since the conversion from forced labor in Korea in the form of both slavery (as opposed to serfdom in Europe) and corvée service began to weaken in the sixteenth century, the labor market in nineteenth-century Korea was undoubtedly far behind the northern Italian city-states of the quattrocento that developed a major international export market in textiles, developed sophisticated monetary instruments like bills of exchange and double-entry bookkeeping, established worldwide contacts for the sale of products in international markets, and accumulated the fabulous wealth that spawned the Renaissance. As a rough sort of comparison Braudel noted that in Tudor England (sixteenth century) one-half to two-thirds of all households received a part of their income in wages, while Han Yŏngguk pointed out that only about 8 percent of the households in his sample in 1858 were listed under a hired worker as head of the household with one hired laborer in each such household.[150]

In short, while Yu Hyŏngwŏn's proposal to substitute hired labor for slavery represented an advance in freedom over the slavery of Korea, it was limited by his commitment to Confucian moral standards and respect for obedience and hierarchy within the family. Despite the progressive historians like Kim Yongsŏp who would like to portray the advances made in the Korean economy at this time as only a shade behind Western Europe, Yu's conservative expectations about the subordination of hired labor to employers as a matter of propriety and respect continued to prevail despite his discussion of the beauties of free choice.

Yu's Influence on the Eighteenth Century

There were a number of major developments in the slave system that occurred in the next century: the permanent adoption of the matrilineal rule for inheritance of status in mixed marriages in 1731, a conversion of labor service for official slaves to substitute tribute payments, a reduction in the tribute payments for official slaves to the same rate paid by commoner support taxpayers in the labor service tax system, a decline in the percentage of private slaves beginning in the late eighteenth century and their replacement by commoner tenants and hired laborers, and finally the abolition of official slavery in 1801 by the royal decree of King Sunjo. These changes were accompanied by – many would argue, caused by – shifts in economic circumstances such as a presumed increase in surplus agricultural production, the accumulation of wealth by entrepreneurial peasants of all status categories, and the growth of the market. Unfortunately, the assertions about the increased wealth of outside-resident slave cultivators and peasant commoners as the main factor in the decrease of private slavery through the purchase of manumission or bribery of slave registrars has not been proven by any detailed microeconomic studies. What is a more compelling explanation is the indisputable rise in the number of runaway slaves, a phenomenon that is not necessarily caused by an increase in wealth by those slaves.[151] Because of the high opportunity cost – and also futility – of searching for and recovering runaways, especially when turning over the cultivation of surplus land to commoner peasant sharecroppers cost the landlord-slaveowners very little, it becomes even less important to insist on a revolutionary increase in individual peasant income to explain the decline of slavery. Furthermore, while the matrilineal rule of 1731 may have contributed to the reduction of the slave population, it had not had that effect in the previous eight centuries of its history.

Despite the decline in the percentage of the slave population, hereditary slavery remained intact as a legal principle and social custom to the end of the nineteenth century. The purpose of this chapter is to explore the possible influence of Yu's ideas on attitudes and policies toward slavery in the century after his death.

The Matrilineal Rule of 1731

Yu had argued in favor of adopting the matrilineal succession rule in mixed marriages as a means of gradually reducing the slave population even though he objected to it in principle because it recognized the legitimacy of inherited slavery for children of slaves. The matrilineal rule was adopted in 1669 without Yu's influence, but its effects in the decade after its adoption did not indicate that the confidence that Yu or Song Siyŏl had in it as a means of increasing the commoner population was warranted. On the one hand, it appeared that as much as 60 percent of slave marriages at this time were with commoner spouses, but the slaveowners took steps to reduce the impact on the number of slaves they owned by the matrilineal law.[152] In 1678, when the law was rescinded by King Sukchong, Minister of Punishments Yi Wŏnjŏng stated that the owners of male slaves who married women of good status were falsely calling their commoner wives their own family slaves (*panno*) so that their sons (and daughters as well) could remain base in status and retain exemption from labor service.[153] He estimated that no more than 10 to 20 percent were accurately registered. "What originally was supposed to be a means for expanding the number of commoners, had in fact become the means for extending chicanery and falsification." Furthermore, there had been an increase in the number of lawsuits between masters over ownership because slaves were falsifying the birth dates of their children. It was at this time that Hŏ Chŏk, the Southerner faction leader, claimed that although he had been sympathetic to Song Siyŏl's advocacy of the matrilineal rule in 1669, he now saw the need to rescind the matrilineal law because of these problems in its administration. Although Hŏ's opposition has been attributed to an intensification of factional animosity, he certainly had reason for doubting the effectiveness of the law and may have changed his mind for rational rather than political reasons.[154]

The Westerners replaced the Southerners in power in 1680 and immediately thereafter Song, as chief state councilor, proposed restoration of the matrilineal rule to expand the commoner population, but King Sukchong did not agree until 1684. In 1689, after Sukchong carried out a great purge of Westerners, removed Yulgok's tablet from the Confucian shrine, and executed Song, Mok Naesŏn (leader of the Southerner faction) obtained King Sukchong's approval to rescind the matrilineal rule. Like Hŏ Chŏk and some of the fifteenth century opponents of the matrilineal rule, he complained that the rule had produced too many lawsuits over ownership of slave children, and he advised Sukchong to copy King Sŏnjo's method of allowing private slaves to buy their way out of slavery (*napsok*).[155] For that matter, even though the Westerner splinter group loyal to Song Siyŏl's memory (the Patriarch's Faction [*Noron*]), returned to power in 1694, the king ignored a half dozen proposals between 1697 and 1714 to restore the matrilineal rule, undoubtedly because the effects of that law had been so disappointing.

Nevertheless, Hiraki Makoto has written that the issue had become thoroughly politicized by this time: the Westerners took the side of the state by adopting the matrilineal rule and relaxing status restrictions on slaves to secure more commoners for military service, while the Southerners defended the interests of the slaveowners. Other scholars like Chŏn Hyŏngt'aek have carried the argument further by linking it to the philosophical positions of the two major factions. The Westerners supposedly followed the lead of Yulgok's practical and this-worldly orientation toward problems, while the Southerners preferred abstract speculation on ethics, spiritual cultivation, and the cosmos in the tradition of T'oegye (Yi Hwang) and his disciples Yu Sŏngnyŏng and Kim Sŏng'il. They supposedly supported the social status quo and the master/slave relationship by investing it with moral significance.

This factional explanation of attitudes for and against the matrilineal rule is far too simplistic. The Southerner leader, Mok Naesŏn, for example, favored abolition of the matrilineal rule because it was not as effective as manumission by purchase, not because he was opposed to liberalization of manumission procedures in principle. For that matter, the utility as well as the ethical propriety of the matrilineal rule had always been a legitimate subject of debate for all parties. The rule had always been found wanting in practice, and even Yu Hyŏngwŏn (a Northerner by hereditary affiliation with friends and followers among eighteenth-century Southerners), who opposed it in principle, still favored it as the best available alternative to releasing some slaves from servitude.[156]

No matter how ineffective the matrilineal law may have been in reducing the slave population, its rescission left the state without any means for checking its growth. Hiraki has pointed out that the creation of new military units throughout the seventeenth century increased the demand for soldiers, and by 1730 there was also a growing shortage of commoner males because too many were commending themselves to powerful families to escape service obligations. It was the pressure of these circumstances that explains King Yŏngjo's decision to adopt the matrilineal rule again in 1731. When the idea was first broached in 1730 by Third State Councilor Cho Munmyŏng, a Westerner who appealed to the positions of Yulgok and Song Siyŏl in favor of the rule, Yŏngjo first rejected it on the grounds that it could be easily corrupted or evaded.

A few months later, in 1731, a secret censor from Kyŏnggi Province reported to Yŏngjo that commoner peasants had been commending themselves as slaves and local officials were shifting their commoner tax and service burdens to relatives and neighbors. Cho argued that the abolition of the matrilineal rule in 1689 only benefited the scholar-officials (*sadaebu*) who wanted their sons by slave concubines to be able to inherit their father's good status, and if the 1669 matrilineal law had not been abolished, there would have been an additional several hundred thousand more commoners by that time. It was then that Yŏngjo changed his mind and agreed to adopt the matrilineal rule despite his earlier reservations because in the struggle for the control of manpower the pendulum of fortune had once again swung too far to the side of the slaveowners.[157] Hiraki Makoto was unable to give credit to the influence of Yu Hyŏngwŏn or other rusticated scholars on King Yŏngjo in 1731, but he did feel that they undoubtedly contributed to a favorable climate of opinion for the matrilineal rule.[158]

Decline in the Eighteenth-Century Slave Population?

It is not entirely clear, however, whether the matrilineal law of 1731 deserves the credit for reducing the the size of the slave population after 1760 or so. Some scholars have assigned more importance to other trends such as the adoption of the *taedong* tribute reform that stimulated the growth of commerce and provided opportunities for slaves to become tribute merchants. Kim Yongsŏp has argued that because of the expansion of double cropping, transplantation, and irrigation facilities, there must have been an increase in agricultural production that may have provided enterprising slave cultivators with sufficient surpluses to buy their way out of slavery (*napsok*).[159]

In 1718 the government first allowed official slaves to buy good or commoner status by paying a lump sum equal to the total value of all tribute due the state from that time to the slave's retirement from service and tribute obligations at the age of sixty-five. The government lost nothing by such a transaction – in fact, it may have even gained if the manumitted slave was then required to perform service and pay taxes due from ordinary commoners. There is some evidence that private as well as official slaves were able to purchase their release from slavery or bribe petty clerks to falsify their status on the population registers. Some wealthy slaves also gained freedom by purchasing other slaves as substitutes for themselves, leaving only the poor in the ranks of slaves.

Changes in the military service system provide another possible factor in the decrease of the official slaves. Because of a shortage in the number of peasants of good status for the military ranks the government began to recruit official slaves to fill the vacant slots, and then to hire commoners to take their place in government bureaus. Once slaves and commoners were allowed into the same military units, the difference in status between them was narrowed considerably. Furthermore, to reduce the double burdens placed on slaves by adding on military service to their personal slave tribute and service obligations, the government began to release them from base status and servitude if they passed examinations for talent in the military arts, a measure that Yu Hyŏngwŏn had recommended. Slaves soon took advantage of this opportunity to gain manumission by bribing officials to give them passing marks.[160]

The most important route to freedom, however, was simply running away and hiding from the slave registrars. There was a decline in the rate of recapture of runaway slaves, and increasing laxity in the registration of slaves by district magistrates, particularly outside-resident slaves, but private masters frequently sent slave catchers out to roam around the provinces, ignoring the sixty-year statute of limitations on the recapture of runaways.[161]

Outside resident slaves were classified as base or slave in status and legally the property of their masters, but in fact they functioned as semiautonomous tenants. Some of the slaveowners may have tolerated their gradual conversion to good status as long as they continued to pay their rents, an interpretation suggested by the transformation of official slaves from providers of labor to the equivalent of tribute or rent-payers.

Of course, the shift in status did not occur in one direction only. Many commoners took on base status as a means of evading commoner tax and service requirements as well. But the more rigid demarcations of status that characterized the early part of the dynasty began to decline, as reflected in the number of complaints registered about the disrespectful behavior of slaves toward their masters and betters. One official remarked in 1761 that official female slaves could hardly be distinguished from commoner women since most of them lived in the villages with their own families.[162]

Thus a number of factors besides the matrilineal rule could explain why the number of slaves in the population was declining and the line of demarcation between commoners and slaves weakening, and the evidence on the effectiveness of the matrilineal rule is mixed at best. There were some reports that sons of mixed marriages who should have been liberated by the matrilineal rule were still being charged for slave tribute and other payments. On the other hand, there was such a marked reduction of official slaves that there was a shortage of those who owed special service as soldiers or post-station workers. Policy makers were reluctant, however, to substitute commoner hired labor (as Yu Hyŏngwŏn had suggested), so they occasionally required children of such slave workers or soldiers to acquire both the status and occupation of their fathers, contrary to the matrilineal rule. This was made obligatory for post-station slave workers in 1791. In fact, during one discussion at court over the shortage of official and post-station slaves in 1761, Chief State Councilor Hong Ponghan, who was appalled by what he felt was a violation of respect for status (*myŏngbun*) brought on by the wholesale liberation of slaves under the matrilineal rule, argued for its abolition. Only when he was reminded by a colleague that he was arguing against a long-standing policy of his own Patriarch's faction, did he come to his senses and drop his objections.

As Chŏn Hyŏngt'aek has pointed out, even though the matrilineal rule had been adopted to produce more commoners for labor service, it was again modified or ignored to secure an adequate number of male slaves for traditional low-status occupations. Nevertheless, in Chŏn's view, the matrilineal rule acted as an incentive for intermarriage because it offered an escape from slavery, reduced the gap between slaves and commoners, and began the trend toward the abolition of slavery.[163]

On the other hand, Ellen Kim found that 6 percent of the slaves of the Sunch'ŏn Kim lineage in the Myodong subdistrict (*myŏn*) of Taegu area listed in the household register were children of commoner mothers born after 1731, a violation of the matrilineal rule that should have authorized commoner status for them. She concluded that although the lineage was not ignoring the law, it was not complying with it completely.[164] The matrilineal rule may have achieved its intended purpose by the end of the eighteenth century, but it is hard to understand why, given its past ineffectiveness, unless other factors were at work as well.

At least we know now that for whatever reasons the slave population declined sharply in the late eighteenth century, but not as sharply as the great pioneer in the study of social change, Shikata Hiroshi, indicated. Shikata's article in 1938 presented population tables for a cluster of villages in the Taegu area of Kyŏngsang Province in four time periods: 1690, 1729–32, 1783–89, and 1858.[165] Of approximately 3,000 households in each of the four periods, Shikata showed that the percentage of slave households in the total household population dropped from 37.1 percent in 1690, to 26.6 percent in 1729–32, to 5.0 percent in 1783–89, and finally to 1.5 percent in 1858. The population figures, however, differed considerably from the household statistics. While the slave population decreased in the first three periods from 44.6 percent to 33.3 percent to 16.5, in the last period, 1858, it rose to 31.7 percent (or 4,189 slaves of a total of 13,195 persons), but they were divided into only 44 registered households.[166] Shikata explained the general reduction of slaves as the result of the desire for upward mobility, and the small number of slave households in 1858 by the absorption of slaves into the households of the masters and problems created by false registration.[167] The slave population figure for 1858, however, leads one to wonder whether the slave population at the end of the dynasty was really as low as has been advertised by those who choose to focus only on the number of slave households, such as Kim Yŏngmo, who found that the slave population dropped in the Taegu area from 47.9 percent to 13.0 percent between 1684 and 1867.[168]

Chŏng Sŏkchong's study of population statistics in one of the subdistricts near Ulsan (Nongso-myŏn) from 1729 to 1867 demonstrated that the outside-resident slaves (*oegŏ nobi*) virtually disappeared from sight by the end of that period, but the service slaves (*solgŏ nobi*)[169] remained in slightly larger numbers. The percentage of slave households to total households dropped from 13.9 percent in 1729 to 2.0 percent in 1765 to 0.56 percent in 1867. These households represented a slave population of about 1,208 in 1729 that dropped to 466 in 1867. Of these the number of outside-resident slaves decreased from 9.2 percent in 1729 to 0.3 percent in 1867, but the domestic slaves decreased only from 21.8

percent in 1729 to 14.4 percent in 1867. The main reason for the decline in the number of slaves was that about 50 percent or more in each of the four years recorded had run away. The number who were manumitted by purchase, died, or were sold by the owner was negligible.[170]

Ellen Kim's study of the Sunch'ŏn Pak lineage's slaveholdings in Myodong shows that the lineage members residing there reached a peak of 889 in 1744, and declined to 255 in 1786, after the direct descendant of the lineage, who owned over 55 percent of the total number of slaves of that lineage in Myodong, moved away and was no longer recorded on the household register. Even without the largest slaveholder in the lineage, the slaves owned by the Sunch'ŏn Pak in Myodong increased to 365 in 1846 and to an unusually high 660 in 1858. The number of lineage slaves in Myodong dropped severely to the 30s in the 1870s, but yet every household in the Sunch'ŏn Pak lineage owned at least one slave, indicating a much greater persistence of private slavery than the studies of Shikata and others indicated.[171]

Scholarly Critiques of Slavery

Even though Yu Hyŏngwŏn's recommendation on behalf of the matrilineal rule did not influence its adoption by the government in 1669, his unpublished work was circulated to a few and exerted an effect on some scholars in the eighteenth century. At the same time a critical attitude toward slavery became more widespread in that period than in the seventeenth century as part of a general trend in thought.

Yi Ik (pen name, Sŏngho). The eighteenth-century statecraft scholar Yi Ik (1681–1763), who admired Yu Hyŏngwŏn's work and deplored its neglect by scholars, once singled out Yulgok and Yu as the only two men who really understood the essence of government affairs since the founding of the Chosŏn dynasty. Like Yu, Yi also was forced into a life of scholarship because his father, a member of the Southerner (Nam'in) faction, was exiled, and his brother was executed for treason in 1695 when he complained about King Sukchong's favorite consort, Lady Chang. In fact, one could argue that the factional discrimination against the Southerners had virtually forced some of their brighter members into a life of scholarship and activated their concern with the injustices of Korean society.

Yi wrote a brief essay on slavery that stressed many key points raised by Yu: the absence of any precedent for the Korean slave law in ancient times anywhere in the world, the hereditary system that condemned a hundred generations of descent from one slave to lives of suffering, the effects of the matrilineal rule, not as a panacea, but as the means for perpetuating endless hardship on relatives through the female line, the loss of human talent and ability that might otherwise serve society's ends, and the harsh labor conditions of slaves in private families.[172] Instead of advocating immediate abolition Yi accepted the view that slavery could not be eliminated and proposed only that purchase and sale be prohibited.

He also quoted Wang Mang on the perversity of penning up people in slave markets like animals (a statement Yu had either overlooked or omitted from his study) and argued that a prohibition of purchase and sale would put an end to this, limit the accumulation of slaves by slaveowners, force the idle rich to do some work themselves, and prevent the current practice of false enslavement of innocent country bumpkins by people who forged documents of purchase. If, Yi conceded, some purchase and sale had to be allowed, then a time limit should be placed on the terms of servitude and the requirements of service forced on the slaves' heirs. Furthermore, no family should be allowed to own more than one hundred slaves (a far from stringent encumbrance on the slaveholding class, and approximately what had been proposed in 1414–15 under King T'aejong); all the rest would be converted to men of good status. He said his goal was to approximate contemporary Chinese laws on slavery.[173]

It seems safe to say that Yi Ik shared Yu's animus against slavery and echoed his call for an end to inherited slavery, but he was somewhat more reluctant to advocate an immediate and total abolition of slavery than Yu.

Yu Suwŏn. Yu Suwŏn was another eighteenth-century statecraft writer who wrote a book on statecraft, *Usŏ*, between 1729 and 1737, with extensive comments on slavery. Like Yu Hyŏngwŏn he was a member of the Munhwa Yu clan but politically aligned with the Disciple's Faction (Soron). Although a critic of hereditary slavery, his position on slavery was less radical than Yu Hyŏngwŏn's. He deplored the Koryŏ practice of re-enslaving freedmen who either offended their former masters or got involved in a dispute with their former master's relatives, and he criticized the Koryŏ rule that forced the descendants of manumitted slaves to revert to slave status and prohibited descendants of slaves through the eighth generation from holding office. He also opposed discrimination against the nothoi of yangban and slave concubines.

He remarked that even though slavery itself may have been legitimized by Kija's law, Kija never specified the re-enslavement of redeemed or manumitted slaves or any ban on officeholding by the descendants of slaves. He cited the *Book of History* (*Shu-ching*) to the effect that punishments should not be extended to one's heirs, and quoted a statement in the *Tso-chüan* that family members were not to be [implicated in the crimes] of criminals. In contrast to the benevolent laws of the sage kings of yore, in Korea offspring of merchants and artisans as well as slaves were prohibited from officeholding, and slaves were treated with particularly cruel laws and never allowed to rise to good status.[174]

Like Yu he criticized the dependency of the yangban aristocracy on slave labor and explained that the reason why private slaves were not subject to state taxes in Korea (i.e., up to the institution of military service for them in 1593) was because of the Koryŏ custom of prohibiting the scholar-official class (*sajok*, i.e., yangban) from earning a living as merchants or artisans, whose offspring were in any case prohibited from holding office. Since scholar-officials were not supposed to work for a living, the state provided them with land grants varying in amount according to rank.[175] But he thought that this system had degenerated into an illicit takeover of public land (*kongjŏn*) as well as the land of ordinary peasants by the scholar-officials and the great and powerful. Even though the state in late Koryŏ sought to eliminate or reduce large estates by confiscating their land and granting prebends in Kyŏnggi Province to the scholar-officials under the *kwajŏn* system, it also permitted the scholar-official class to keep their hereditary slaves "as their private property" because they were their sole means of livelihood and support.

He concluded that the Chosŏn government was worse than Koryŏ in its respect for and exaltation of the hereditary aristocratic families (*munbŏl*), who refused to work as artisans or merchants or till the soil as peasants even if the only alternative was starvation, because such work stamped one as a commoner and involved loss of face and status. They were even more dependent on their hereditary slaves for service and economic support than their counterparts in the Koryŏ period. The state thus put these private slaves of the aristocrats outside the realm of its jurisdiction and left them completely untouched. As yangban became even more impoverished, it was even less likely that the government would levy personal service (*sinyŏk*) on private slaves.[176]

Yu Suwŏn regarded this as a perverse system. Like other opponents of slavery, he often asserted the equality of all subjects of the king and the basic humanity of the slave. For example, he remarked that, "Even though slaves are base, they are still human beings [*illyu*], so how could you permit them to be returned to slavery once they have been permitted to purchase [good status, i.e., freedom]?"[177] Or,

> Even though slaves have masters, they are in fact all the people of the state, but the state regards them as people beyond the pale [i.e., incapable of moral instruction and civilization], and [for that reason the state] has never required any labor service of them or levied a single coin [of tax on them], leaving their masters to do with them what they will, never daring to lay a hand on them. This is the reason why the evil [burden] of commoner labor service [is so bad]. . . . The state regards all its people as the same and loves them all equally. How could there be a principle according to which the state would not levy [taxes or service] on private slaves but only do so on people of good status (*yangmin*)?[178]

For the 1720s his statement about the exemption of private slaves from taxation was obviously untrue because slaves had already become a major component of the *sog'o* troop units and the *abyŏng* military aides to high provincial officials. His statements about equality, however, did not mean that he wanted all slaves be freed. They were in fact to be taxed, and at a rate different from commoners as well. In the case of public or official slaves, he urged the adoption of a uniform cash levy on both, and a reduction of the personal tribute levy on official slaves. In answering the charge that this would reduce state revenues unacceptably, he argued that there were so many official slaves that if those currently unregistered were all accurately recorded, rate reduction would not reduce revenues. Current practice, however, involved the short-sighted pursuit of immediate profit by squeezing official slaves for all they were worth. This tactic only forced the official slaves into tax evasion, which was the real cause of reduced revenues. The Western Han dynasty had in fact released official slaves and made them commoners and the ancients had also feared impoverishing their slaves and granted them lenient treatment. It might not not be possible to go this far, but at least the state could aim for equal and fair treatment and taxation.[179] Whether or not Yu Suwŏn's opinion actually influenced many officials at the time, he virtually predicted the trends that would take place by the end of the eighteenth century, the reduction of support taxpayer burdens on private slaves to the same level as commoners.

He also praised King Sejong's ruling that private slaves would be made official slaves if their masters were guilty of arbitrary murder, cruel punishment, or immoderate tribute impositions. It was regrettable that later generations had neglected this law, for it would serve to prevent excessive tribute levies on private slaves. Nevertheless, he felt that, as in China, the slave should be punished more severely than people of good status for the same crimes, or that commoners who committed a violation against a slave be punished a degree less than if they had done so against other commoners.

He favored more lenient manumission procedures and hoped to prevent the corrupt custom of forcing slaves who had purchased commoner status to purchase it again by proposing the issuance of official certificates as proof of manumission. He also supported the matrilineal rule by asking that offspring of women of good status not be allowed to adopt their father's status.[180]

Yu Suwŏn's analysis of the economic dependency of the yangban slaveowning class on its slaves was similar to Yu Hyŏngwŏn's acknowledgment of the need of the yangban for a work force. Where the two men differed was in their hopes for the future. Yu Hyŏngwŏn felt that the use of hired labor would eliminate the economic necessity for slaves and his future land-grant system would ensure their livelihoods along with the rest of the population. Yu Suwŏn, however, was more concerned about maintaining tribute revenues not only by equalizing burdens on official slaves and commoners, but also by levying government tribute on private slaves as well. He preferred to make the state an exploiter of slave labor and production along with the private slaveowners rather than an agent for the liberation of slaves.

An understanding of Yu Suwŏn's attitude toward slaves, however, only comes with a full appreciation of his feelings about contemporary society in general. He felt that while a clear line of separation had not been drawn at the beginning of the Chosŏn dynasty between the ruling class and the commoners, that line had become quite strong by the seventeenth century, and the ruling class, which he referred to as either *munbŏl, sajok,* or *sadaebu*, had turned into a hereditary aristocracy (see part 1). Yu also felt that the yangban of his time were unique in treating their own class of good persons or commoners as if they were slaves, a point of view that may have been somewhat closer to the mark than his opinion that the yangban had only emerged as a distinct social class in the late sixteenth and early seventeenth centuries. In his eyes it was the decline of the commoner class to the level of despised persons that was the most serious problem of the day, not the rise of slaves to the level of commoners.

This attitude emerges clearly in his comparison of contemporary Chinese and Korean status systems. He pointed out that some Koreans were under the delusion that because the Chinese did not discriminate in favor of hereditary aristocratic status (*munbŏl*), they therefore allowed slaves and the basest of persons to rise to become high officials and treated them without discrimination (*myŏngbun*). This was mistaken, however, because even though the Chinese paid no special favor to the descendants of officials, "when it comes to slaves and lowly base persons, the severity of their respect for status distinction [*myŏngbun*] is on a par with our country; it is doubly strict. So how can you say that China does not take the requirements of social status [*myŏngbun*] seriously?"[181]

Yu Suwŏn was not a conservative defender of the status quo against change or reform. On the contrary, he was a critic of hereditary slavery and oppressive taxation of slaves, but his sympathies for the sufferings of slaves did not encompass a desire for the abolition of slavery or elimination of status-based society. Reform for him also meant a return to equal opportunity for all men of good status and reestablishment of a firm line between them and base persons or slaves. For that matter, he was not a supporter of land reform like Yu Hyŏngwŏn, and he was critical of the more egalitarian aims of the early Chosŏn reformers like Chŏng Tojŏn and Cho Chun.[182]

Living in a more commercialized age than Yu Hyŏngwŏn, he favored increased specialization of function among the population and more commercial and industrial activity. He also devoted some space to the problem of wage labor in the economy, but he did not see it as the wave of the future or the substitute for the main force of agricultural workers, let alone the other standard occupations. Nevertheless, his discussion of the matter yields some important insights into the role of wage labor at the time and even the nature of Yu Hyŏngwŏn's concept of the phenomenon in the previous century.

Yu Suwŏn took as his model for the division of labor in contemporary society the nine categories of occupations listed in *The Rites of Chou*. The eighth category were the *sin* and *ch'ŏp* or male and female base persons, respectively. Yu Suwŏn defined this type as equivalent to the male and female slaves (*nobi*), hired laborers (*kogong*), and household servants (*kach'uk*) of contemporary Korea. The *kogong* were the hired laborers that Yu Hyŏngwŏn planned to use to replace slave labor in Korean society. It may seem odd, however, that Yu Suwŏn should adopt the ancient Chou conception of wage labor as similar in kind to slave labor since he was living in a period when the difference between the two should have been obvious. Although he did distinguish wage labor from slave labor, he still regarded the *kogong* as similar to private slaves.

Since Pak Sŏngsu also found that hired laborers in mid-Chosŏn were by no means the free wage labor of the capitalist West, and that those in the northeast had been reduced to inherited indentured servants, Yu Suwŏn's version of hired labor may well be an accurate picture of the hired labor that Yu Hyŏngwŏn had in mind in the previous century. Yu Hyŏngwŏn's argument that the substitution of these *kogong* hired laborers for slaves would not disrupt the norms of respect and status within the family was, therefore, by no means outlandish.

As for wage labor in the sense of workers free to move around and sell their labor in the open market, Yu Suwŏn defined *The Rites of Chou*'s ninth category of occupations as the equivalent of contemporary wage labor. This type was defined in that text as "idle people without regular occupations" (*hanmin musangjik*), in contrast to the other eight categories of various types of cultivators, merchants, artisans, and slaves and *kogong* hired workers who did have regular occupations. These people "moved [from one place to another] in doing their work; they were workers who were hired." Yu remarked that there were plenty of these people in contemporary Korea in both urban and rural settings. They were sometimes employed by the state for building walls, or by villagers for building dikes and sluices, maintaining agricultural fields, building houses, and odd jobs. He pointed out that Koreans of his time looked upon them as useless objects whereas sage rulers of the past (i.e., the Chinese Chou dynasty) had put them to use, moving them from place to place to fill in for temporary shortages of labor around the empire. Thus, he thought of wage laborers as a kind of lumpenproletariat of itinerants, vagrants, beggars, or idlers whom he sought to put to work in a more organized and rational way to increase the efficiency of labor utilization and production in society as a whole. Wage labor was to perform those miscellaneous tasks not taken into account by the traditional occupational categories referred to as the regular occupations (*sangjik*).

Ostensibly these itinerant wage workers could not take the place of the regular cultivators, merchants, and artisans, let alone displace all official and private slaves as Yu Hyŏngwŏn had proposed. But Yu Suwŏn did argue that their labor was less costly and more efficient than that of slaves or regular hired laborers. "Thus [these itinerant wage workers] can finish in a few days what it takes regular hired laborers [*kogong*] a month to do, or for a few coins they can take the place of ten slaves, and you will not have to pay the costs of food and clothing for slaves or regular hired laborers."[183]

He appears to have had a clearer idea of the difference between bound and unbound wage labor and a better understanding of the potential challenge of wage labor to slavery than Yu Hyŏngwŏn, undoubtedly because of the greater development of the market over the past century. And yet he was probably less committed to the abolition of slavery than Yu, and he did not see wage labor as the exclusive mode of labor as Yu had. While in some respects more advanced in his thinking than Yu, he was less radical in his antislavery attitude.

Official Slaves: From Labor Service to Tribute Payments

A significant change in the nature of official slaves and their obligations to the state took place in the eighteenth century. Early in the history of the dynasty official slaves were divided into those who performed direct labor, called either "service slaves" (*ibyŏk nobi*) or "slaves selected and sent up [to the capital]" (*sŏnsang nobi*), and those who remained in their villages and simply remitted tribute payments to the government, called either "tribute-paying slaves" (*napkong nobi*) or "outside resident slaves" (*oegŏ nobi*). By the middle of the eighteenth century, the select-service slaves almost completely disappeared, converting the vast majority of official slaves to the tribute-paying type – even including the select-service slaves of the capital. The first case of official slaves paying tribute to the state in lieu of service occurred in 1654, and the example was expanded in 1707. When official slaves were held responsible for support payments for a commoner soldier, two were assigned in place of one commoner support taxpayer because their tax rate was half the rate for commoners, in compensation for their personal tribute (*sinyŏk*) paid to their private masters.[184] Chŏn Hyŏngt'aek has argued that a major transition was taking place from labor rent to hired labor in the performance of menial tasks for the central government.[185] This trend covered both slaves and commoners, and it also had the effect of weakening the foundation of the traditional system of official slavery, rendering the cumbersome system of personal service superfluous. What Yu Hyŏngwŏn had done in the mid-seventeenth century was not to set the process in motion, but to notice the general trend to hired labor in a number of areas, a process that Yu Suwŏn discussed in far greater sophistication in the 1730s.

The conversion of the mode of official slave obligations was accompanied by a radical reduction in the number of official slaves. At the end of the Koryŏ dynasty there had only been about 20,000 government slaves, but the number increased overnight to about 100,000 by the state's confiscation of the slaves of Buddhist temples and monasteries. By the late fifteenth century the maximum of 350,000 official slaves was reached, but as indicated above by 1655 the number of registered official slaves was reduced to 190,000, but only 27,000 were able to perform duty or pay tribute taxes.[186] By 1755 there were only 5,574 royal treasury and royal relative palace slaves (*naenobi*) and 30,617 capital bureau slaves (*sinobi*), or a total of 36,191.[187] For some unexplained reason, however, there seems to have been a sudden increase right after this time, because when most official slaves were manumitted in 1801, there were about 60,000 of them. Yet even that number was only about one-sixth of the maximum reached in the late fifteenth century.

Originally the tribute levy on slaves was 2 *p'il* of cloth for male slaves and 1.5 *p'il* for female. The rate was reduced to 1.5 and 1 *p'il* respectively by the late seventeenth century to alleviate the burden on the official slaves, but when the decline in the number of tribute-paying official slaves reduced government revenues, the central government bureaus dispatched slave registrars (Ch'uswaeg-wan) to the provinces to maintain rosters of tribute-paying slaves despite the failure of their activities to increase the number of official slaves in 1655. Since they were charged with raising revenue rather than obtaining justice for the slaves or ensuring accuracy in reporting, they demanded payments in excess of the legal quotas as well as gratuities and transportation fees, continued to list runaways and "bleached bones" (i.e., Gogol's dead souls) on the books, and demanded payment from the relatives and neighbors of runaways.

King Yŏngjo tried to stem the corruption by shifting some of the responsibility for registering slaves from the slave registrars to local magistrates in 1735, but without much effect. He then adopted a provincial quota system (*pich'ongbŏp*) in 1745 in some provinces for official slaves attached to central government bureaus (slaves of the royal treasury were left under the jurisdiction of the registrars). By setting a fixed quota for a province it was hoped that this would eliminate the pressure on the provincial authorities to falsify registrations to raise revenue. Since each district's slave tribute would be determined by the ratio between its slave population and the total for the province, it was assumed that the real number of slaves and runaways could be truthfully reported without penalty. The system was extended to two other provinces in 1764, and finally to the whole country in 1778 when all registrars were abolished. Meanwhile, in 1755 Yŏngjo reduced the slave tribute rate by an additional one-half *p'il* per person, a measure modeled after his reform of the commoner service system in 1750. The government sacrificed revenue to alleviate the burdens on the tribute slaves, but the continuing shortages of funds must have convinced an increasing number of officials that the system of state slaves and tribute payments was becoming uneconomical and obsolete.[188]

Nevertheless, the system did not function as it was supposed to because magistrates were lax and clerks took bribes to falsify the records.[189] In 1778, the very year that the quota system was extended to the whole country, the governor of Chŏlla reported that the quota system resulted in forced exactions from neighbors and relatives and false registration of the deceased. Furthermore, there was no reduction of the category of royally granted slaves (*sap'ae nobi*) given to individuals by the king from the capital bureau slaves (*sinobi*). While Yŏngjo cannot be blamed for the shortcomings of the quota system, he never intended to abolish official slavery, merely to eliminate corruption and maintain the flow of revenue from slave tribute.[190]

Then in 1774 Yŏngjo adopted a recommendation by Kim Ŭngsun to abolish the tribute of official female slaves employed in government agencies and post-stations, and female shamans (*mudang*). He wanted to eliminate tribute levies on private female slaves as well, but they were not included in the final edict. The motive for the reform appears to have been a new awareness that levying tribute on female slaves was improper. Yŏngjo had a scholar read through the section on Kija from *The Comprehensive Mirror of The Eastern Land* (*T'ong-guk t'onggam*) to affirm that slavery had begun in Korea only as a means of preventing thievery. Since the levying of tribute on female slaves had begun sometime afterward, he asked whether it would be appropriate or correct for him to abolish tribute on both official and private female slaves? Wŏn Inson agreed it would be correct, not only because Kija never approved it, but also because tribute levies on female slaves was not even a part of the *tsu-yung-tiao* triple tax system (of the T'ang dynasty); it had to be abolished because it was practiced nowhere else in the world besides Korea. Others agreed that abolishing female slave tribute was correct and proper but objected that it would encourage female slaves to keep their children off the slave registers thereby reducing the official slave population even more, and that the loss in revenue could not be made up from other sources. Wŏn rejoined that any losses in the official slave population could be made up by tightening the opportunities for manumission by purchase, and restricting the freedom of movement of slaves.

When Yŏngjo also suggested removing tribute levies from female post-station slaves as well because they were really not guilty of any crime, most of the high councilors objected. They insisted that requiring post-station female slaves to pay tribute was not a violation of fundamental principle because they only paid tribute when off duty, while the capital bureau female slaves performed actual service. Besides, their tribute was essential to the maintenance and operation of the post-stations and their horses! And when Yŏngjo proposed eliminating tribute cloth levies on female shamans as well, his officials pointed out that this levy was designed to deter shamanism rather than punish criminals.

In the final version of the decree, Yŏngjo confined the abolition of female slave tribute to official slaves, leaving private female slaves unaffected. The result of the law was that henceforth only male official slaves paid tribute at the rate of one *p'il* of cloth, the same rate as the commoner peasant cloth levy in lieu of service. Nonetheless, any positive results of the reform were probably offset by official corruption, in particular the practice of arbitrary levies on relatives and neighbors.[191]

By insisting on a close reading of classical sources Yŏngjo had found justification for eliminating female slave tribute by discovering that Kija's slave regulation had allowed enslavement only for thieves or criminals, not the transmission of slave status hereditarily. Even though no mention was made of Yu Hyŏngwŏn's ideas in the court discussion of the issue (Yu had little use for Kija's laws as justification for slavery anyway), Yŏngjo's approach was in keeping with the spirit of Yu's use of classical sources. He did not, however, follow Yu's lead by calling into question hereditary slavery as a whole.

Although most of Yŏngjo's officials were opposed to the reform because they feared the loss of revenue, they nonetheless confirmed that Yŏngjo's decision was in accord with the principle of the rectification of names (*chŏngmyŏng*). In other words, abolition of female slave tribute was in no way a violation of what was written about Kija or classical antiquity, of what the meaning of the name *slave* denoted. In short, the reform was inspired by a subtle change in attitude, a shift from blind acceptance to a questioning of tradition and custom that Yu Hyŏngwŏn had helped set in motion.

By the last two decades of the eighteenth century, the system of official slavery was in disarray despite the reduction of tribute rates, abolition of the special slave registrars, and adoption of the provincial quota system. Official slaves were supposed to be living and registered in their home villages in the countryside and liable for service or tribute payments, but many had run away. When the officials shifted the burdens to neighbors and relatives, that forced more peasants out of their villages.[192] Something had to be done to stop the oppression of these people, stem the tide of migration, secure the stability of the villages, and guarantee the funding of the government's needs.

Spread of Yu's Influence

The Munhŏnbigo Revised, 1782. It was in the midst of these difficulties that the 1782 revision of the *Munhŏnbigo*, the encyclopedia of important institutions, was completed by Yi Man'un, who cited Yu's ideas on slavery in two places. The first was inserted by Yi as a fitting commentary to the matrilineal rule of 1039 in the Koryŏ dynasty. Here Yu had said that it was bestial to have a rule that one's mother rather than father would determine a child's status, but because it had unfortunately become the national custom to treat persons of base status like animals anyway, and the patrilineal rule would only lead to endless lawsuits, there was no better alternative than the matrilineal rule. In any case, Yu said, the problem was not the matrilineal rule; it was the slave law itself. For even after the matrilineal rule was adopted, children of women of good status were still forced to adopt their father's base status. "This is a law that is no law, the only purpose of which is to force people into base [status]. Of all unjust laws it is the worst."[193]

It is not clear why Yi Man'un chose this part of Yu's writings to put in the encyclopedia since the matrilineal law had been permanently adopted in 1731. Maybe he was trying to highlight its defects rather than its advantages because several of the Yu's negative assessments had actually taken place.

Yi Man'un's second citation of Yu's ideas on slavery was his indictment of hereditary slavery on the grounds that there was no precedent for it in ancient times. Under Korean law, by contrast, guilt or innocence was not even at issue because base or slave status was inherited.[194] Even though Yi did not highlight Yu's main source for this view, the *Rites of Chou*, Yu's refutation of any classical justification for hereditary slavery must have contributed to the growth of a critical attitude toward habitually accepted ideas and prepared the ground for the liberalization of Korean slave laws. Possibly it influenced King Yŏngjo to reread the text of Kija's slave law in a critical light. Unfortunately, Yu's novel views about the equality of men and the use of hired labor were not included in the *Munhŏnbigo*, but some of the leading scholars and officials must have been familiar with them (as the following section shows), even though the text of the revised *Munhŏnbigo* was not printed in type until 1908.

An Chŏngbok. The same 1782 revision of the *Munhŏnbigo* also included a brief synposis of An Chŏngbok's account of the history of slavery and his own condemnation of the institution, culled from An's multivolume survey of Korean history, the *Tongsa kangmok* (Major and Minor Points about the History of

Korea), written between 1756 and 1758 in the style of Chu Hsi's *T'ung-chien kang-mu*.[195] An had learned of Yu Hyŏngwŏn's work from his mentor, Yi Ik, and even though the *Munhŏnbigo* synopsis did not acknowledge the great debt that An owed to Yu on the question of slavery, in the *Tongsa kangmok* itself An cited most of Yu's major ideas and proposals on slavery from the *Pan'gye surok*. It was, in fact, after a lengthy quote of Yu's condemnation of hereditary chattel slavery that An chose to place the most important statement of his own views.

> I note that hereditary slavery in our country is truly something that the government of a true king could not stand. How could it be that once a person is entered on the slave registers, [his descendants] can not escape slavery for a hundred generations? There were slaves in ancient times and all of them had been confiscated [enslaved by the state] because of thievery or banditry or were pirate and brigands among the four barbarians who were captured, but the penalty did not extend to their heirs, only to [the guilty parties] themselves. How could there have been a law like that in our country?
>
> Some say that the slave law began with Kija, but how could they take an evil practice like hereditary servitude and mix it together with the rule of a sage who had benevolent compassion for the people? Even though there is no clear statement in the histories, I have found the origin of this evil practice beginning in the Three Kingdoms period. During the Three Kingdoms the nobles and great officials held power hereditarily, and of the three, Silla was the worst. *The History of the T'ang Dynasty* (*T'ang-shu*) says that the chief ministers of Silla had permanent salaries and 3,000 slaves, from which we can tell how prestigious and powerful they were. The poor and destitute, those without any means of support, perhaps sold themselves into slavery or commended themselves to the powerful so that their descendants suckled [at the breast of their masters] and were employed [as slaves] in service. In addition war captives were confiscated as slaves, were not able to purchase their freedom or obtain their release, and served generation after generation without cease. This is how bad this evil became.
>
> When Koryŏ unified the country many of the enemies and rebels who were conquered as war captives were given to the merit subjects to be their slaves or assigned to the various official yamen. Thus, both private and public slaves existed in name, and almost the whole population of the country ended up on the private and public slave registers. There could have been no worse law than this. The kings should have reformed or rectified it, but they did not have the time to do so.[196]

An thus pushed back the origins of hereditary slavery from early Koryŏ to the Three Kingdoms, but like Yu he criticized the policies of early Koryŏ for exacerbating slavery in Korea. While Yu had neglected discussion of Kija, An raised Kija's slave law directly and stated his belief that hereditary servitude was incompatible with sagehood. Since An had occupied the post of adviser and tutor to King Chŏngjo when he had been crown prince (prior to his accession to the throne in 1776), it is quite possible that this last statement formed the link between Yu's neglect of the Kija slave law and King Yŏngjo's order to his official in 1774 to investigate the classics to find whether Kija had ever authorized tribute payments for female slaves, and King Sunjo's decree of 1801, which rejected Kija's slave law as a legitimate basis for hereditary slavery.[197]

An was as ambivalent as Yu on the prospects for slave reform because both admitted the power of social custom and were reluctant to risk the social disruption that would result from immediate abolition. Although his own ruminations on the question demonstrated his debt to Yu (italicized in the following quote), his own solution was different.

> Some have asked: "What should be done to rectify it?" Some have said: "Let's just follow the ancient way and *only enslave those guilty of crime.* Let's just *adopt the Chinese system and employ hired labor.*" Others have said that "[Korean hereditary slavery] has been in practice for such a long time that [Korean customs] are not the same [as those in China]. This was the reason that the Yüan people were not able to abolish [the Korean slave laws] even though they wanted to do so."
>
> Some have said: *"If the laws are changed, then the situation will change. If the situation changes, then customs will follow along and change."* If you can find the right way [of doing things] and put it into practice, then why is it not possible that what was used in ancient times would not work in the present? Why would not something that [worked] in China be adopted in our country? The reason why the Yüan were not able to abolish [our slave laws] even though they wanted to do so was because the power rested with us, but how would the hereditary aristocrats and great clans been pleased [with the loss of their slaves] and gone along with it?
>
> That is why the elimination of this evil must pass through a great change, for only after there is no difference between noble and base to speak of can a true king make his appearance and bring [slavery] under control. If, prior to the abolition [of slavery], you only take the rather petty measure of investigating and judging each and every case [of possible improper enslavement], this will not be the right way to do things, and social order will be completely destroyed, and the habit of [slaves] lording it over their superiors will prevail just as described in the histories.[198]

An felt that heroic or courageous leadership could not possibly overcome the resistance or inertia of social forces. When he wrote that a great transformation had to take place, he meant that society itself had to change to the point where distinctions of social status diminished in importance before slavery could be abolished. Until it did, it would be harmful to tamper with existing practice even by the otherwise apparently laudable attempt to manumit illegally enslaved persons because it would let slaves think that they were the equals, if not superiors, of their masters.

Yu Hyŏngwŏn had also shied from suggesting immediate and total abolition and proposed instead the gradual method of the matrilineal rule for virtually the same reason if the cessation of hereditary slavery could not be mandated for the next generation, but as An astutely observed by a choice quote from Yu's *Pan'-gye surok*, Yu did believe that legislation by a bold king could transform society. An was much more conservative, and confirmation of this appears in a comment he made on the Koryŏ law adopted in 987 to return freed slaves to base status (see the discussion of Yu Suwŏn's ideas, above). The royal decree stated that "The longer that manumitted slaves have become good people [commoners], the more likely it is that they will treat their former masters with contempt. If any of them should insult their former masters or challenge the master's relatives, return them to slavery and servitude."

An appended his own commentary on this decree:

> For a manumitted ex-slave to hold his former master in contempt is something that ought to be dealt with severely by clear laws. Even though a person has been liberated from slavery and made a good person [commoner], there can not be any changing of names [i.e., positions, respect relations] between slave and master. It was all right to put him [the disrespectful freedman] in awe and fear [of punishment], but it was going too far to return him to slavery."[199]

While opposing the reenslavement of manumitted slaves, Yu still expected them to treat their former masters with respect, an attitude common to the slaveowning class of most slave societies. It did not matter whether An was talking about a few freed slaves in a slave society, or the mass of freed slaves after a possible abolition of slavery. In either case, he presumed that hierarchical status and respect relations would be maintained in society even after slaves were freed. Ex-slaves were not to get the mistaken idea they were as good as anyone else.

The attitudes of most Korean statecraft reformers were similar in one respect: caught between contradictory feelings, their aspirations for reform of an obvious evil were ultimately checked by attachments to members of their own class; they feared the potential of social chaos in a situation of unlimited opportunity and mobility. Their advertised arguments for liberation and freedom from bondage disguised a more fundamental elitism and status-consciousness.

Thus An shared Yu's ambivalence but not necessarily other aspects of Yu's interpretations of and solutions for slavery. Although An cited Yu's reluctant endorsement of the matrilineal rule as the means for the eventual elimination of slavery, he himself did not endorse it, let alone Yu's appeal for ending hereditary slavery in the current generation.[200] He also chose not to emphasize Yu's dictum about the equality of all men in their aspect as human beings as opposed to chattel, and he appears to have rejected the idea that the use of hired labor could successfully replace slave labor, on the grounds that Chinese customs were not adaptable to Korean circumstance.

Given the developments in the commercial economy in the century since Yu wrote, this argument should have made even more sense in An's time, but An was more pessimistic than Yu in his expectations for reform and more bound to the social status quo. It would therefore be mistaken to presume, as many modern students of the Practical Learning (Sirhak) movement usually do, that the eighteenth century heirs of Yu Hyŏngwŏn carried Yu's ideas to even more radical and progressive heights.

Abolition of Official Slaves

King Chŏngjo Alleviates Discrimination. After King Chŏngjo came to the throne in 1776, some officials began to argue that the difficulties of life for official slaves stemmed from the stigma attached to slave status. Since both commoners and official slaves were alike in paying cloth tribute to the state, if the stigma of slavery or baseness could be removed simply by changing their title from slave to commoner, they would cease running away, and government revenues would be replenished. Between 1784 and 1796 there was a total of eight requests for the outright abolition of official slavery based on this logic.[201] It is hard to imagine anyone blithely remarking in the seventeenth century that the only difference between commoners and official slaves was an unfortunate sense of social stigma, which could be eliminated simply by ceasing to call slaves slaves anymore.

Naturally, these proposals to abolish official slaves were opposed by conservatives who feared that it would stimulate private slaves to rebel against their masters and disrupt traditionally accepted standards of social status. The advocates of reform, however, defended their position by pointing out that Kija's slave law, the primary legitimating symbol of slavery in Korea, was limited in its application to thieves and robbers and did not justify hereditary slavery. Hence, the abolition of hereditary official slavery would not do violence to social status distinctions.[202] This interpretation represented the culmination of a trend set in motion by Yulgok and Yu Hyŏngwŏn in the late sixteenth and mid-seventeenth centuries even though Yu himself neglected the Kija story and preferred to rely mainly on *The Rites of Chou*.

King Chŏngjo, however, was still bound by tradition despite his sympathy for the plight of the official slaves. In 1791 he praised his grandfather, Yŏngjo, for his reforms but remarked that it was not possible to dispense with the label of slave, because slavery had been in use in Korea for over a thousand years, since the sage Kija. If you stopped calling official slaves *slaves*, then private slaves would want the same thing, and the whole system of status distinction (*myŏngbun*) would be destroyed. Nevertheless, he brought up a number of alternatives for discussion, such as allowing slaves with military talent to purchase good status or stand for the military examinations, changing their title from slave to auxiliary soldier and allowing them to form special units intermediate in status between the units composed of (the sons of) petty officials and slaves, or even manumitting them in return for a lump sum payment of the total amount of tribute due between their current age and their age of retirement.[203] Even though the large capital required would have limited the opportunity to only a few, this discussion presaged a significant liberalization of the rules for escaping the burdens of slavery.

Chŏngjo went still further in 1797 when he approved a proposal to drop all terminological distinctions between good and base (slave) status troops among the provincial *samsu* (the three types of soldiers of the Military Training Agency) to remove the social stigma from military service and increase the number of recruits. Hiraki marked this as an epochal decision, for up to that time slaves had to receive an exemption from slavery before they could become commoners, and now they became commoners without having to pass through that process.

Several suggestions were also made that official slaves be called support or service personnel instead of slaves, in effect converting official slavery into some form of obligatory service for commoners. This was not exactly the plan that Yu Hyŏngwŏn had proposed, which was to convert all slaves into hired laborers, but at least Chŏngjo presided over the partial elimination of status distinctions even though he had declared it was against his principles to do so.[204]

King Sunjo's Abolition Order of 1801. In 1801, half a year after Chŏngjo's death, King Sunjo ordered the abolition of most but not all official slaves (*naesi nobi*): those of the Royal Treasury, palace estates of royal relatives (*kungbang*), and the capital bureaus of the regular bureaucracy. The records of 66,067 slaves were burned, but official slaves attached to the Ministries of Works and War, the offices of provincial governors and district magistrates (*kwannobi*), the nationwide post-stations, and of course, private slaves, were not affected by the edict. The edict also had no effect on the reduction of criminals to slave status in the future. Liberation only affected tribute-paying official slaves listed on the slave registers, but of these probably all but a few thousand were liberated by the decree.[205]

Since Sunjo was a minor acting under the instruction of the dowager regent, King Yŏngjo's second queen, Chŏngsun,[206] and most high officials were members of the Patriarch's and *pyŏkp'a* factions who were sympathetic with the idea of abolishing most official slaves, he obviously does not deserve credit for the decision.[207] The instruction to the people (*yun'ŭm*) issued in his name shortly after the abolition indicated an important shift in the officially sanctioned attitude of the throne toward slavery. Chŏngjo had taken several steps to liberalize the means of escape from slavery but was reluctant to condemn status distinction in principle. Sunjo's edict, on the other hand, claimed he was motivated by one of the principles for the governance of a state in the *Doctrine of the Mean* that the ruler was responsible for "treating his people as [his own] children." What this meant was that it was improper for the ruler in governing his people to discriminate against one group in favor of another. The king should "not distinguish between the noble and base, those close to him or distant, but treat them all equally as his babes. How is it in conformity with the principle of regarding all as brothers [*tongp'o*] to label [some of the people] male or female slaves [*nobi*] and divide them up and separate them [from the rest of the population]?"

While difficult to pinpoint the origin of this idea, it was close to one of the arguments made by Yu in the mid-seventeenth century. Yu's main appeal for eventual abolition was based on the idea of the equality of man in its nonchattel aspect, and he had remarked upon the need for a virtuous ruler to treat his subjects without discrimination. Sunjo's declaration of the equal status of all subjects and criticism of the principle of status distinction was a shift from Chŏngjo's views, and yet still limited in its application, for it was not extended to private slaves, who constituted the vast majority of the slave population.

Another issue had to be cleared up before the justification for abolition was complete – the meaning of the precedent of Kija's slave law. Sunjo's decree stated that people mistakenly believed that the holding of slaves by the Royal Treasury and administrative offices of the capital had originated with Kija. The decree explained that Kija had indeed granted instruction to the people of the Eastern Land (*Tongguk*, i.e., Korea), in eight categories. These eight instructions were in fact the eight divisions of kingly administration that were part of the "great plan" (*hongbŏm*) that Kija had imparted to the first emperor of the Chou dynasty. One of the eight categories of governance was the management of crime and rebellion by the Ssu-k'ou (the Chou minister of punishments). Unfortunately, the Koreans (the people of the Eastern Land) were stupid and mistook minor regulations for Kija's eight major categories of governance. Thus they thought that the law that provided that thieves would become the slaves of their victim was one of the eight major categories when, in fact, it was but a minor regulation that evolved from the exercise of the police power by the Ssu-k'ou.

Sunjo's decree also stated that the regulation for the enslavement of thieves should have been entirely consistent with the principle of the *Doctrine of the Mean* that the ruler was obliged to treat all his subjects equally. But contrary to this intent,

> Slavery [in Korea] in recent times is more reflective of an age of decline because officials impose great burdens on slaves, and ordinary people treat them as extremely base. Their lineages and communities are kept separate [from the rest of the population], they have to live in separate villages or areas, and for their whole lives neither sex is capable of legitimate marriage. How could Kija ever have been called a sage if he [devised] a system like this?

To the contrary, the decree continued, Kija was known for advising the ruler to make the people happy, eliminate cruel treatment of the helpless and unprotected, and act as the father and mother of all the people. Slavery was thus not an institution that could have been created by Kija.

The decree also cited the reforms of previous kings, the reduction of slave tribute by both Kings Sukchong and Yŏngjo, the latter's abolition of the slave registrars (Ch'uswaegwan), and Chŏngjo's intention to abolish government slavery frustrated by his officials who failed to respond to his wishes. At present, the decree concluded, the grievances of the slaves reached to the heavens; the wind and rain had been put out of order and the ripening of the crops obstructed – all because slavery had not yet been abolished. Sunjo's prime task was thus to carry out the intent of previous kings to abolish [official] slavery.[208]

Sunjo's decree did not adopt Yu Hyŏngwŏn's approach to the origin and legitimacy of slavery because Yu ignored the Kija slave law altogether. It was obviously a blatant bit of sophistry invented by a clever government scholar under orders to reinterpret the Kija story, and yet the argument could not have been accepted by a sufficient number of educated scholar-officials unless the ground under the Kija myth had been weakened by scholars like Yu over a century before.

Sunjo also had to deal with the revenue shortage created by the abolition decree. He originally ordered that the slave tribute payments to be lost by the abolition order would be made up by substitute payments and taxes from other sources, but there was only about three-quarters of the total of 80,000 *yang* of annual tribute cash available to offset the tribute due from the official slaves. Some arrangements were made for substitute payments for slaves of the various palace establishments as well. Since the official slave system already operated on the basis of tribute levies on slaves instead of actual service, it is possible that the abolition of official slavery meant in fact that the expenses of the central and local government offices and the various princely palaces would be henceforth paid out of general revenues or even specific funds. These funds would be used to purchase required materials, and the labor service could be performed either by hiring labor or requiring the labor service of ordinary commoners – an arrangement approximating Yu Hyŏngwŏn's proposals.[209]

The history of the eighteenth century shows a gradual trend in the reduction of the slave population produced by the growth of commerce, the conversion of service obligations to payments in cloth and cash, and increased movement and fluidity across village boundaries and previously rigid status lines. Ideas were undoubtedly influential in affecting these processes, and contemporary scholars have conceded that Yu Hyŏngwŏn and other rusticated scholars in the Southerner tradition, particularly those living in the Kiho region of Kyŏnggi and Ch'ungch'ŏng provinces, played an important role in the shift.[210]

CONCLUSION

In 1601, in the aftermath of Hideyoshi's invasions, one desperate official did in fact call for the abolition of slavery to increase the size of the army, but once the excitement born of crisis had died down, it became infinitely more difficult for scholar-officials to challenge the interests of their own class and the traditions of a millennium.[211] Nevertheless, changing social and economic circumstances in the sixteenth and seventeenth centuries weakened the boundaries between slaves and commoners and permitted more opportunities for escape from slavery. These changing circumstances also produced a new awareness on the part of Yu Hyŏngwŏn, who called into question traditionally accepted views about slavery, and proposed methods for the gradual reduction of slave inheritance, eventual elimination of the hereditary principle, and ultimately, the ending of slavery for all save criminals. Even though he did articulate a theory of human equality and perspicaciously intuited the possibility of the replacement of slave with hired labor, he was reluctant to call for immediate abolition because of his commitment to the economic needs of the ruling class, and he understood hired labor in the context of Confucian subordination and hierarchical respect relations between inferiors and superiors.

He laid the groundwork for open challenges to traditionally accepted attitudes toward slavery in the eighteenth century and the abolition of most official slaves in 1801. The leading eighteenth-century scholarly theoreticians of slavery shared Yu's ambivalence: they sought an alleviation of the burdens and injustices imposed on slaves without, by so doing, causing the destruction of the basis of status and hierarchy in Korean society. Nevertheless, they contributed to an atmosphere in which the virtual abolition of official slavery became possible. The reduction of the private slave population also occurred at the same time, but it was less the product of the transformation of the attitudes of the private and official slaveowners than the inability of those parties to stem the flight of the slaves from their villages and the slave rosters. When indirect methods were adopted to alleviate the burdens on the slaves by reducing their tax burdens to the level of commoners, the possession and upkeep of slaves no longer became economical, and slaves were replaced by commoners.[212]

Despite the significant reduction of both official and private slaves, total abolition was not possible until after the opening of Korea to the outside world in 1876 because many yangban families continued to possess one or two slaves in domestic service and enslavement as a form of punishment was still acceptable to even the most "liberal" Confucian reformers. Hereditary slavery was not abolished until 1886, and slavery itself not until the *kabo* reforms of a Japanese-sponsored cabinet in 1894. Even when Kojong abolished hereditary slavery in 1886, he went no further because he was obliged to maintain the standards of proper status discrimination (*myŏngbun*).[213] Yu Hyŏngwŏn had relied on the wisdom of classical China and Confucian statecraft and the practical example of hired labor to help open the door to new attitudes toward slavery, but the social milieu was too restricted to allow for legislated abolition of private slaves. Nonetheless, he made a significant contribution to a severe reduction in the percentage of slaves in the population to around 5 percent by providing a moral basis for manumission of the innocent and the end of an 800-year era of slave society in Korean history.

Did the reduction of slavery to negligible limits mean either an improvement in the fortunes of the peasantry or a sign that Korea was progressing to a higher level of human freedom or economic development? Certainly the removal of the social stigma, legal discrimination, personal tribute, and susceptibility to physical punishment by masters and others that accompanied slavery must have provided great relief to the slaves. The loosening of the restrictive economic ties of the early Chosŏn period and the growth of commercial activity must also have contributed to the relaxation of rigid rules of status distinction. But since many more slaves ended up as tenants or landless laborers than as rich landowners, the liberated ones may not have found themselves any wealthier than before. More likely, they became part of the broth that made the nineteenth century the most rebellious century in Korean history.

Nor did the escape from slavery necessarily mean automatic progress to a more advanced economic or political system. Barry Hindess and Paul Q. Hirst have recently pointed out that slavery has existed in a number of different political forms, and that, contrary to a number of Korean historians who have believed that slavery ought to be found between the ancient and feudal modes of production (which it does not in Korea, to their grief), it does not constitute in itself a distinct mode of production in the Marxist sense, let alone one that necessarily follows the ancient mode of production and precedes the feudal. They believe that slavery has been found in a variety of modes of production and political systems, and they think, and I agree, that "The character of a slave system is dominated by the social structure in which it exists and not vice versa."[214]

The mode of production in the early Chosŏn dynasty could be described as an agricultural economy based on private property, by which surplus profits were extracted by landlords from tenant rental fees while the smallholders engaged in subsistence production. Commerce and handicraft industry played a very small subsidiary role in the economy. The pattern for the late Chosŏn dynasty was modified by introducing a small increase in profits from a modest increase in agricultural wage labor, commercial agriculture, handicrafts, and trade. Slavery was part of that mode of production, but it was not the main cause of that mode's coming into existence, and its reduction to negligibility did not result in its disappearance.

PART II

Social Reform: Yangban and Slaves: Conclusion

One of the major goals of Yu Hyŏngwŏn's work was to rectify the distortion of his vision of an ideal Confucian society wrought by the effects of inherited status. By the time he reached adulthood in the mid-seventeenth century he realized that he was living in the midst of a slave society dominated by a hereditary yangban ruling class, particularly disheartening to him since both those phenomena were foreign both to the ideal society of ancient China and the reality of contemporary Chinese social life in which hereditary aristocrats had long since been replaced by a relatively mobile class of gentry or literati, merchant families had access to the civil service examinations, and slaves represented only a marginal fraction of the population.

He lived at a time when an important transformation in Korean society was taking place along several fronts. In the economic sector private commercial activity was expanding and knocking on the door of the system of state control and licensed monopolies. The system of taxation was shifting away from tribute and forced labor service to an expanded land tax that financed market purchases of goods by the king and government and the hiring of workers to perform government services. The rigid separation of social status groups was showing signs of weakness, particularly at the lower levels as slaves began to abscond from their home villages to escape the exactions of their private and official masters, and commoners sought to evade taxes and service by moving up the social ladder by purchasing titles and cheapened status. These processes had an effect on Yu by stimulating his concern for the reform of the adverse consequences of inherited status in Korean society. He could not help but realize that the yangban of his own time had failed to protect Chosŏn Korea from foreign invasion and the deterioration of domestic institutions, and that hereditary slavery had robbed the state of its control over manpower and the slaves of their dignity as human beings.

While he showed important signs of adaptability to current changes, particularly in advocating the use of hired labor and praising the advantages of free choice over coercion in the labor process, he did not seek to extend the logic of current changes to the distant future by using rational efficiency, free choice, and practical knowledge as the sole basis for the reform of society. On the contrary, he returned to the traditional sources of wisdom of his highly Confucianized society, the Chinese classics and the giants of Neo-Confucian intellectual and statecraft thought and policy in the Sung dynasty.

His social vision consisted of the transformation of the hereditary yangban to an ethical elite ruling over a country of commoner peasants with a marginal number of merchants, artisans, and slaves, and the abolition of hereditary slavery by converting them to commoner smallholders, tenants, or hired laborers free of the exploitation and degradation of servility. He did not mean to cast off Confucian norms and values in a time of utmost adversity, but rather to reconfirm them in new institutions, inculcate them in the new elite, and make Chosŏn Korea a truly moral society.

Although his ideas became widely known by the end of the eighteenth century, it is difficult to argue that he transformed the way of thinking of the government leaders or the public, especially since scholars who counted themselves his intellectual heirs and disciples thought his proposals for slave reform were too radical. Nor were most of the educated yangban whether in or out of office ready to jettison the privileges of their class, or scuttle the examination system that had provided them entré to the highest levels of government power.

Some contemporary scholars think that Yu and other members of the so-called school of practical learning were responsible for aiding and abetting the positive changes that took place in the seventeenth and eighteenth centuries, and it is true that Yu's rationale for bringing hereditary slavery to an end probably had some influence on the decision to abolish official slavery in 1801, if not the final adoption of the matrilineal succession law for mixed commoner/slave marriages in 1730. But it was neither the intellectual arguments nor the development of entrepreneurial peasants that best explain the rapid decline in the slave population after the late eighteenth century; it was the action of the slaves themselves, who took advantage of a demoralized and corrupted bureaucracy that lost the will to round up the runaways and "voted with their feet" by running away in large numbers. No matter how enterprising or capitalistic some of the outside-resident slaves may have been, as some scholars have argued, very few were able to buy their way out of slavery because the cost was prohibitive.

The exclusivity of yangban domination in Korean society was also challenged by late Chosŏn social trends as more and more people bought titles, evaded taxes and service, and falsely registered themselves as students and scholars. Many have taken this phenomenon to indicate rapid upward mobility spawned by a new class of entrepreneurial rich peasants, but the facts reveal a narrowing of the core of yangban families that were able to dominate the examinations and the upper levels of the central bureaucracy, and very few newcomers from the peasantry. The examination system remained intact, the official school system was not reestablished, and the private academies were corrupted by the accumulation of estates and the growing connection with political factions. It was not until the crisis of the mid-nineteenth century caused by the combination of domestic rebellion and the threat of foreign invasion by the Western powers in the 1860s that a serious attempt was made to reorder the governing group, but the reforms achieved were led by a slightly different group in composition. They were still all bona fide yangban and the structure of power was not really changed until the loss of national independence in 1910.

Yu Hyŏngwŏn represented the voice of Confucian conscience, ignored and unsung for fifty years or more, who reminded the Korean people that they were not living up to Confucian ideals of the well-run state, that they were not allowing people of talent to crack the barriers against advancement to office, and that they were using a slave labor force to do too much of the work of society. If these deficiencies could be eliminated, Korea would be able to increase agricultural production to support the population, improve the circulation of goods for the benefit of all, and raise revenues for defense against foreign enemies, all the while maintaining the ethical principles and standards of the Confucian canon.

PART III

Land Reform

Introduction

Living in the aftermath of the Japanese and Manchu invasions of 1592–98, 1627, and 1637, Yu Hyŏngwŏn was well aware of the suffering that was caused not only by the loss of life and the destruction of property and cultivated land by the ravages of war, but also the skewed distribution of privately owned arable land in an economy that was still overwhelmingly agrarian, despite the beginnings of a development toward a more active market. The trend toward greater concentration in landholdings by a few was fueled by the loss of land by marginal peasants from bankruptcy and the commending of land by destitute peasants. The latter became private slaves of large landlords in return for protection from state taxation and labor service, a trend that was already prominent by the mid-sixteenth century. Therefore, the task of any reformer included both the expansion of cultivated land and agricultural production and the restoration of a base of economic support for the peasant population, whether commoners or slaves.

Land and agricultural production was not only the major source of wealth in Korean society, it was also becoming an important source of taxation as the early Chosŏn taxation system based on the tripartite division between the land tax, local product tribute in kind, and labor service was shifting by the seventeenth-century conversion of tribute taxes in kind to a surtax on land (the *taedong* law). Later, labor and military service was replaced by cloth tax payments in lieu of those services by support taxpayers (*poin*) and by revenues from the *taedong* rice surtax. Even the tax rate on land had increased because of these reforms. The nominal tax rate was still within the range of acceptability, but the burden on taxpaying landowners, and by extension their commoner and slave tenants, was increased by the fees, gratuities, and bribes exacted by the plethora of unsalaried yamen runners, and clerks in the district yamen or granaries and capital financial ministries.

One means of lightening the land tax and the tax burden on the landowners and peasants in general might have been the exploitation of commercial taxes, but this would have required a fundamental shift in the physiocratic bent of Confucian economic thought that emphasized the primacy of agricultural production and the necessity to begin any meaningful institutional reform with the redistribution of land. Would Yu Hyŏngwŏn have enough flexibility and foresight to appreciate the capacity of the nonagricultural commercial and industrial sector of the economy to generate greater wealth and to tax that wealth to reduce the burden on the peasants?

Traditional Confucian thought did stress the need to encourage agricultural production, but not for the purpose of promoting surpluses above and beyond the requirements of reproduction and the payment of a tithe to the state. The goal was to provide subsistence for the common peasant and taxes for the support of the ruling class. On the other hand, idealistic Confucian reform also entailed the redistribution of wealth through the redistribution of land or its use. Land redistribution was, therefore, regarded by Confucian statecraft reformers as a powerful tool in the hands of reformers for the modification, if not radical reorganization, of the structure of society.

There was no doubt in Yu's mind that some kind of land reform was an absolute necessity to restore the dynasty to health, but it was one thing to discuss reform in the abstract, and another to contemplate the reaction that might ensue from any radical plan to shift landed property from the rich to the poor, especially when a plan for land reform risked the possibility of antagonizing the ruling yangban whose support and leadership might be needed to maintain order and stability in society.

Since redistributive land reform had been discussed for almost two millennia in both China and Korea with a general record of failure since the equal-field system of the T'ang dynasty and the *chŏnsikwa* system of the early Koryŏ dynasty (which was erroneously perceived by Koreans in the seventeenth century as a copy of the T'ang equal-field system), how would Yu avoid the charges of his more pragmatic critics that radical reform was chimerical and unfeasible? Since we have seen that Yu intended to reform society by transforming the basis for the recruitment of officials and the ruling class in general through educational and school reform, did he also plan to reinforce this goal by restructuring the distribution of wealth to favor his new ruling class?

He had expressed hope that hereditary slavery could be abolished in the next generation and existing slaves reduced in number by replacing them with hired labor, so did he also plan to take those slaves into account in his plan for land reform, and if so, could he do it without creating serious contradictions?

In short, did Yu consider the distribution of wealth and property as seriously as he did the moral goals of recruiting a more ethical ruling class and abolishing hereditary slavery? What method did he use to reconcile the distribution of wealth with his moral goals? And did that method represent a departure from Confucian dogma to a more rational and practical selection of policy alternatives?

CHAPTER 7
Land Reform: Compromises with the Well-Field Model

"If the great root is in confusion, in all other matters there will be nothing that is not done incorrectly."[1]

"If we could in accordance with present circumstances take into consideration the intention of the ancients and put it into practice, we would have a method . . . and if changes were adapted to present-day circumstances, then all people would obtain what [they require] and all plans would turn out well. Even though you would not delineate the shape of a well-field, the essence of the well-field system would still be contained in it."[2]

Land Reform and the Maldistribution of Wealth

Yu Hyŏngwŏn lived in a society that had represented an intolerable departure from classical ideals because its ruling class was dominated by the semihereditary yangban and more than a third of its ruled class consisted of hereditary slaves. He prescribed formulas for redressing these problems by proposing the creation of a new ruling class through strict standards of education and the recruitment of officials by the evaluation of individual moral behavior, and yet he did not desire this process to remove or eliminate the existing yangban. He wanted only to force them to reform their ways while allowing some opportunity for upward mobility for those few of lesser status capable of moral perfection.

He also suggested a gradual method for achieving the abolition of slaves by the immediate prohibition of the transmission of slave status to one's heirs, the adoption of the matrilineal rule for mixed commoner/slave marriages, and the replacement of slaves by hired laborers. This gradual approach was designed to buffer the economic and cultural shock that the yangban slaveowners might otherwise suffer if a royal decree was issued to abolish slavery instantaneously.

In between yangban and slaves in the Chosŏn social status system were the commoners, the people of good status (*yang'in*). The vast majority of *yang'in* were peasant cultivators differentiated into a small number of landlords and a far greater number of smallholders, tenants, and landless hired laborers who were burdened with heavy shares of taxes and service requirements (both labor and military) and whose levels of livelihood were reduced to a bare minimum at best. Since the economy was overwhelmingly agrarian, the distribution of land and the social relationships of people involved in agricultural production was crucial to the distribution of wealth throughout society.

Yu Hyŏngwŏn's initial chapter in his *Pan'gye surok* was a study of the system of land tenure because he had concluded on the basis of his statecraft studies of Chinese and Korean institutional history that it was the key to the solution of all problems of state and society. Land was the primary factor in determining income and wealth in a society in which agriculture was the dominant mode of production, and land reform would rectify not only the problem of the maldistribution of land among the people, but the unfair levies of grain taxes and labor and military service as well.

Private Property

Yu concluded unequivocally that the primary cause of the maldistribution of land was the institution of private property. Whether he arrived at this conclusion from his own observation of contemporary Korean circumstance or not cannot be confirmed, but he based most of his argument on earlier Chinese critics of private property. The core argument of that literature, which Yu accepted without question, was that the perfect system of land tenure had been the well-field system of the Chou dynasty in which all peasant families were guaranteed equal plots of land to cultivate with a minimum of taxation. That taxation consisted of shared labor on the lord's plot. Since there was no private ownership under the Chou feudal system, the peasant families retained only rights of use or cultivation of their plots.[3]

Whatever the ambiguities of the Chou or well-field system, most traditional Chinese scholars agreed that Shang Yang (Lord Shang) of the Ch'in state abolished the well-field system and opened the door to the evils of private property.[4] There is a minor dispute in the Chinese literature over just what Lord Shang did. The language of the *Shih-chi* states that "He opened up the *ch'ŏn* and *maek*," which most commentators have taken to mean that he destroyed the land boundaries around the well-fields. Tu Yu in the *T'ung-tien* (early ninth century) disagreed; he believed that Shang Yang had created a new system based on the *ch'ŏn* and *maek* boundaries that resulted in temporary increases in production but also led to inequitable distribution of land. He conceded that after the fall of the Ch'in, this *ch'ŏnmaek* system was also abolished.[5] Chu Hsi (twelfth century, Sung dynasty), however, argued that Shang Yang was only advocating fuller utilization of land by opening it up to cultivation to maximize agricultural production. Like Tu Yu he thought that the well-fields continued through the Ch'in dynasty to the Han, but he did acknowledge that private property began under Lord Shang in the preunification Ch'in period.[6]

Tung Chung-shu of the Former Han dynasty condemned the heinous destruction of the well-fields and pointed out that the purchase and sale of land enabled a few individuals to accumulate large amounts of land (*kyŏmbyŏng*) while the mass of poor peasants were left with hardly enough land to "stand an awl on."[7] In other words, the replacement of the well-field system with private property was even more destructive of Chou standards than the Ch'in abolition of the Chou system of education and recruitment on the basis of moral standards because the Han regime at least sought to maintain those institutions. But in Yu's view, during the Han dynasty and after there was no attempt to restore the well-field system. "In the later age [*huse*] there were those who wanted to allow private land [*sajŏn*, obviously private ownership here] and permit the purchase and sale [of land] and yet establish controls over it by limiting [the amount that could be owned], but this was lacking in the correct principle."[8]

Yu also cited the argument of Hsün Yüeh of the Later Han dynasty that because private property allowed landlords to charge tenant cultivators exorbitant rents, it had subverted the benevolent intention of the Han dynasty rulers to reduce tax burdens on the peasant population. Although the legal land tax in his own time was only 1 percent of the crop, a mere fraction of the ancient tithe, the large landlords were collecting over half the crop from the peasant cultivators as rent (literally, *pu*), while the officials were only collecting one part in a hundred for taxes (*se*). "Although the benevolence of the [Later Han] officials is superior to that of the three dynasties of antiquity [*san-tai*], the tyrannical exactions of the great and powerful are worse than the fallen Ch'in dynasty."[9]

Hsün Yüeh also castigated landownership in pejorative terms, what he called "exclusive control over land" (*chŏn ki-ji*). In his opinion, even though the feudal lords in the Spring and Autumn period of the Chou dynasty were granted fiefs, they were not given exclusive control over them (*chŏnbong*), and the officials were likewise not given exclusive control over land (*chŏnji*). That is, feudal lords had neither the right to sell or dispose of their fiefs. By Later Han times, however, private owners occupied as much as several hundred or several thousand *kyŏng* of land, surpassing even the princes and marquises (*wanghu*), because of the system of purchase and sale and the failure of the former Han to establish limits on landownership.[10]

Yu also noted that Tu Yu, compiler of the *T'ung-tien* in the early ninth century, pointed out that Han dynasty rulers failed in their attempt to maintain surveillance over cultivated land by investigations of hidden or unregistered land because investigation and survey depended on the probity of an army of clerks for proper implementation, and the clerks were not to be trusted. Even the severe punishments used by Shen Pu-hai and Shang Yang of the Ch'in dynasty could not have rectified this difficulty because the fundamental problem was the existence of private property and the exclusive control by landlords over land, which had been avoided in the Chou dynasty.[11]

In discussing the complex plan to limit the maximum size of private landholdings put forward by Lin Hsün (fl. 1127–30) of the Sung dynasty, Yu noted that although Chu Hsi and Lü Tsu-ch'ien also praised Lin's plan, it was too far a departure from the well-field model because it allowed for the temporary purchase and sale of land.[12] In similar fashion Yu also noted approvingly the remarks of the late Koryŏ land reformers Cho Chun and Yi Haeng that the *chŏnsikwa* system of early Koryŏ, which Yu had thought was a replica of the T'ang equal-field system based on state ownership of land, was undermined by the conversion of public land to private ownership.[13] In short, when Yu summarized his main conclusions from his research, he wrote that private landownership was the main feature of the post-Chou age of decline: "In the later age the land system broke down and there was private occupation of land without limit, so that there were problems in all affairs and everything was contrary to this [the perfection of ancient China]."[14]

THE CHOU WELL-FIELD MODEL

The Nine-squares: The Lord's and the Peasants' Plots

Private ownership was thus the antithesis of the well-field model, but an investigation of its content is necessary for an understanding of the principles Yu derived from it. He began his *Pan'gye surok* with a paean of praise to the beauties of the well-field system in its time:

> In ancient times the well-field system reached the limit [of perfection]. The laying out of land boundaries [*kyŏnggye*] was all rectified, all affairs were completed, and all the people had a firm basis for steady occupations [*hang'ŏp*]. In military affairs there were no problems attendant on finding and recruiting men for service [*suhwa*]. Among the noble and base [in society], there was no one who did not have his proper job [*chik*]. For this reason men's minds were firmly established and the customs of the people were harmonious. This was why things were firmly established and maintained for several hundreds and thousands of years in ancient times. The fact that rites and music flourished was because of this root and foundation.[15]

Even as described in classical sources like the *Mencius* and *The Rites of Chou*, however, the well-field system was not the sole method of land tenure and distribution during the Chou; its use was purportedly confined to fiefs assigned to those feudal nobles (*kyŏng* and *taebu*) in the service of the Chou king or the chief vassals of the king who ruled over the feudal states of the period. There are several descriptions of the well-field system in classical sources, but the most important one is in the *Mencius*, which states that farmland under the control of certain feudal lords was divided into squares of 900 *myo* in area, defined in terms of a specific number of square feet, and each of these squares was further subdivided into nine equal squares of 100 *myo* each. Eight peasant families occupied eight of the nine squares, which they cultivated for themselves. The ninth square, located in the center and called *kongjŏn* (public land, or the lord's field) was cultivated by pooling the labor from the surrounding eight families and the produce from this square went to the lord of the land. The peasants paid no land tax on their own land but were required to perform labor service on the lord's land to cultivate the crop for him.[16]

Mencius was famous for insisting on the obligation of a virtuous ruler to provide for the economic security and well-being of the general population, and he lauded the well-field model because it provided enough land to peasant families for a standard of living somewhat higher than mere subsistence by guaranteeing a uniform sized plot. Although the Chinese word *kyun*, often translated as equality, and the phrase *kyunmin*, making the people equal, was frequently used to describe the principle involved in the distribution of equally sized plots of land to peasant families, there are some problems involved in interpreting the essence of the well-field system as one of equal distribution.[17]

The only aspect of the system that was absolutely equal was the 100 *myo* (or one *kyŏng*) plot. Since the number of people in a given household could vary and productivity could depend on land fertility, labor, fertilizer and other inputs, a fixed and uniform plot of land to peasant families would not necessarily guarantee complete equality of income on a per capita basis. It is obvious, however, that the disparities of income among families could never be too great under such a system, so that relative equity was obviously one of its perceived goals. Equity or fairness defined as a guarantee of income above subsistence is probably what he meant by the term *kyun*. Nevertheless, it must be kept in mind that although absolute equality of per capita or even familial income was not an indispensable principle of the well-field system, the idea of a fixed plot of land of uniform area defined in terms of a number of square feet was in fact regarded by Yu and a number of his Chinese sources as absolutely essential to a successful adaptation of the well-field system. It was of special importance to Yu because Koreans were not using a standard linear foot or constant unit of area as part of their land survey technique in the seventeenth century.

The concept of a fixed plot of land of uniform size was also related to another classical term, *kyŏnggye*, or the establishment and regulation of land boundaries. Yu believed that one of the reasons why the well-field system was superior to any that followed it was that the fixed squares of land were bounded by ridges and dikes in such fashion as to leave an indelible imprint on the soil, impervious to the forces of time and change. Any land reform unaccompanied by the laying out of these land boundaries was doomed to failure.

It might well appear that flexibility on the question of income equality and distribution but rigidity on the matter of the permanently fixed, uniform plots of land surrounded by physical boundaries signifies a reversal of proper priorities and a rather simplistic literalism with regard to the sanctity of the classical literature and the models of Chinese antiquity. The idea of the fixed, bounded plot, however, was less a matter of dogmatism than a conclusion derived from a concern for the difficulties of administration associated with the assessment and regulation of taxation and military service.

The image of the fixed square permanently embossed in the landscape provided an important symbol of stability and security in contrast to Yu's perception of the utter chaos of private land relations in which the host of private transactions between individuals proved impossible to control. The freedom associated with a private market in land opened opportunities for the greedy, wealthy, and powerful to obtain large holdings and create severe divisions between the rich and the poor, landlords and tenants, and large owners and small cultivators. Yu and his Chinese authorities also admired the image of the fixed plot because it connoted a simplicity and ease of administration that was necessary to prevent administrative manipulation and corruption and the subversion of state control by private interests.

*The 100-*myo *Plot*

Yu was so obsessively attached to the specific dimensions of the individual plot, the unit area of 100 *myo* equivalent to one *kyŏng*, that he was charged with the sin of archaic literalism or dogmatism, but he defended himself by arguing that his preference for these dimensions was the product of his own independent study of its feasibility.

> The reason why I now choose 100 *myo* is not because I want to copy the ancients. I calculated the labor power of the people and I estimated productivity. I compared it with the fertility of the land and the population and also compared the old with the new [situation]. . . . Only after making my calculations did I realize that the method used by the ancient sages [was good for] ten thousand generations and could not be changed.[18]

In his survey of Chinese dynastic history through the T'ang, he carefully recorded total population and acreage statistics to calculate average per capita holdings as a basis for judging the optimum size of a familial land grant.

He might also have chosen the 70 *myo* unit if he had so desired because Mencius referred to this size as the standard during the Shang (Yin) dynasty, and it was also the standard area supposedly utilized by the sage Kija in the Pyongyang area of northern Korea after he arrived from China with the title of marquis of Chosŏn, a title granted by Wu-wang of the early Chou. Yu's attention was brought to this system by Han Paekkyŏm's (1550–1613) essay, *Kijŏn tosŏl* (*The Land System of Kija, with Illustrations and Explanations*). Han had personally visited the Pyongyang area to investigate the putative archaeological remains of Kija's model of a square divided into four equal parts of 70 *myo* each in area. Even though this grid was different from the well-field pattern, it was also by

Yu's admission "a system devised by the ancient sages."[19] The details of Yu's reasoning on the question of the 100-*myo* plot will be taken up later and it remains to be seen whether his choice represents the triumph of reason or tradition.

Yu did not insist on the literal adoption of the nine-square layout of the *Mencius*, possibly because the classical literature left room for variation on this matter. In addition to Kija's four-square configuration, the *History of the Han Dynasty* (*Han-shu*) by Pan Ku and the Kung-yang version of the *Spring and Autumn Annals* (*Ch'un-ch'iu*) stated that the well-field unit had nine squares of 100 *myo* each (a total of 900 *myo*) and eight families but there was no central *kongjŏn* or lord's field. Instead, each of the eight families possessed its own plot of 100 *myo* and an additional 10 *myo* of *kongjŏn*, the produce from which was used to pay the tax. The combination of private plots and public lands totaled 880 *myo*, and an additional 20 *myo* was set aside for house sites for the peasants.[20] While two descriptions in the classical literature agreed on the 100-*myo* unit for the private land (*sajŏn*) of the peasant households, they differed on the pattern of configuration. Yu, therefore, insisted on the 100-*myo* unit but not on the nine-square pattern, and he claimed nonetheless that rationality and utility were the basis for his selections.

It was also Yu's conviction that a land unit of fixed size had to be the basis of any system of taxation and military service, but the inspiration for this idea could not have come from a literal interpretation of the well-field system alone. The standards for the land tax and military service that Yu favored were more generalized features of ancient Chinese institutions. Classical literature on the land tax is ambiguous and contradictory; there were two basic concepts or models that derived from ancient practice. One was the idea that the ideal tax rate on agricultural production was one-ninth of the crop, derived from the well-field model in which the *kongjŏn* or central plot was one-ninth the area of the 900-*myo* unit. The other standard was the tithe or collection of one-tenth of the crop, a rate in use on fields not organized under the well-field system during the Chou.[21] The tithe became the preferred rate in the Chinese literature because the *Mencius* contains the statement that it was the main principle of taxation for all dynasties of the *san-tai* period despite differences in basic land units and methods of land tenure. The Kung-yang commentary on the *Spring and Autumn Annals* also praised the tithe as the optimum tax, not on the principle that the lower the tax the better, but because the tithe struck the proper balance between the needs of the peasantry and the requirements of the state. More than a one-tenth tax would be too oppressive, and less than one-tenth would mean that the state's revenues needs were too low for a civilized country that needed funds to conduct proper sacrificial rites.[22] As is well known, the tithe was believed to be the ideal tax rate for a virtuous ruler throughout post-Chou Chinese history, a dogma that derived not from the well-field model itself, but from other statements in the classical literature about the sage institutions of antiquity.

Ch'aeji *(Fiefs of the Feudal Vassals) and the* Sadaebu

It would be a mistake to think that the well-field system only represented a scheme for the equitable (if not equal) distribution of wealth for the whole population because the eight families who were guaranteed uniform 100-*myo* plots were all peasants, and provisions for the Chou ruling class were somewhat different. Yu subscribed wholeheartedly to the Mencian dictum that society should be divided between the rulers and the ruled. The rulers were those who worked with their minds, governed those who worked with their hands, and were entitled to support from them. Mencius's ideal ruling class was of course a moral elite (not the real feudal elite), and he referred to them as men of superior virtue or moral capacity (*kunja*), as opposed to "the men of the fields" (*yain*), or the ordinary farmers who tilled the land and provided military service. The well-field model, therefore, also guaranteed financial support for the ruling class.

In the various classical descriptions of the Chou system, the well-fields were not characterized as ubiquitous. They were supposedly employed outside the capital or ducal domain in areas called *tobi* which were the loci of the *ch'aeŭp* or *ch'aeji*, the fiefs of feudal vassals usually referred to as "the feudal lords" (*chehu*), subdivided into dukes, marquises, viscounts, counts, and barons. But they were also called the *sadaebu* or *taebu*, which included *kong*, *kyŏng*, *taebu*, and *sa*, which corresponded respectively to ducal petty feudal rulers, high ministers, officials, and retainers or knights. The distinction between the two sets of terms is not altogether clear and there was considerable overlap in terminology, but in general *taebu* or *sadaebu* connoted some form of service in the bureaucracies of the Chou king or the ducal rulers. These terms seem also to have referred to a hierarchy of feudal families who possessed the status qualifications to hold posts of certain rank in the service of the lord, something in the manner of the hierarchical divisions within the samurai class in late Tokugawa Japan. *Sadaebu* thus indicated the Chou ruling class defined simultaneously in terms of moral quality, officeholding, and feudal status. Although elite social status and officeholding overlapped, they were supposed to remain distinct in concept and terminology, and also in the mode of support and remuneration due each category.[23]

The *chehu* or feudal lords also were supposed to have controlled lands farther out from the capital or ducal domain in more autonomous fashion than the *ch'aeji*, but Yu believed that the *ch'aeŭp* (or *ch'aeji*) were the prime means of support for the *taebu* while incumbent officials (*sija*) were entitled instead to "hereditary salaries" (*serok*).[24] Since this distinction only makes sense if the *taebu* are conceived of as something different from incumbent officials, the terms *taebu* or *taebusa* (or *sadaebu*) must have designated a social elite eligible for official service but not necessarily performing that service or holding posts at any given time. Since Yu also remarked that the *ch'aeji* in ancient times "combined overlordship over its people" (*kyŏm chu ki inmin*), suggesting political autonomy over it by a feudal vassal, it must have resembled a fief even if the provision of knights or military service were not a reciprocal obligation attached to it.[25] In short, the *ch'aeji* was simply designed to support the *taebu* as a class on the grounds that the ruling class or the superior men in society could not be allowed to till the fields like the common "men of the fields."

Yu argued that in "the later age" (*huse*) (i.e., the post-Chou period of centralized bureaucracy) there was no constancy in the appointment or dismissal of officials and no equivalent to the Chou system of economic support for the *sadaebu*. He warned that simply restoring well fields without providing for the support of the *taebu* or *sadaebu* would be inappropriate because any of them who might be dismissed from office "would not have the means for gaining a living." The only way to have a complete restitution of the well-field system would be to restore the granting of fiefs (*ponggŏn*).

Since Yu did not expect that *ponggŏn* feudalism in general or the *ch'aeji* (i.e., well-field system) in particular could literally be restored in his own time, he intended only that the spirit of the system should be preserved by the adaptation of the idea that a *taebu* ruling class somehow transcends the narrow functional definition of incumbent officeholding (and for that matter the simple reciprocal or contractual definition of a class that performs service in return for fiefs) and is entitled to guarantees by the state of a standard of living superior to the commoner peasant. The justification for this was both moral and ascriptive: the *taebu* were presumed to be *kunja* or morally superior men (Mencius), and a ruling class deserved superior status and privileges. As we will see later, however, Yu's concept of privilege by ascription or status was limited by an equally powerful commitment to standards of performance, merit, and function, so that he felt constrained to work out a compromise between the two ideals.

The terms *taebu* and *sadaebu* were also used in post-Chou bureaucratic times in China to distiguish civil bureaucrats from soldiers in the Han, aristocrats from commoners in the Northern and Southern dynasties, and degree-holders and scholars from petty officials, farmers, merchants, and artisans in the Sung and after. The term *sadaebu* was used in the Chosŏn period not only to mean scholar-officials in general, but the semihereditary yangban as well, but Yu also used *sadaebu* for his own idealized moral elite, and on occasion *yangban* as a pejorative label for the contemporary Korean ruling class. The model for Yu's ruling class was thus the *sadaebu* of the Chou, who were allowed to avoid the ardors of agriculture or commerce and enjoyed the support of the peasants who contributed labor on the "lord's plot" in their fiefs (*ch'aeji* or *ch'aeŭp*). When the Chou political and social system was destroyed in the Ch'in unification, the elimination of the *ch'aeŭp* and well-fields left the *taebu* as a class without proper economic support. They were forced to rely on their salaries as state functionaries, a comparatively risky and insecure situation.[26]

To summarize our discussion thus far, Yu Hyŏngwŏn identified certain essential principles and features of the well-field or ancient system of land distribution that could be adapted to a centralized-bureaucratic situation. These included the laying out of fixed land boundaries to create unit plots of standard dimension, adoption of the 100-*myo* unit (a specific number of square feet of standard and uniform length), the use of this unit as a basis for land distribution, taxation, and military (or labor) service, the adoption of the tithe as the ideal land tax, and the use of this system to provide not only relatively equitable income somewhat above subsistence for the peasant families but also superior income for a *sadaebu* ruling class. The *sadaebu* would correspond to a ruling class, and officials in the service of the state would represent a segment of that class, entitled to extra salary allotments from the government in return for service. These principles represented a blending of traditional fundamentalism with a rationalistic and empirical methodology in adapting the principles or models to contemporary circumstance, a combination of egalitarian and hierarchical ideas of relative equality for the peasantry but stratification for society as a whole. It would achieve a proper balance between the public interests of the state and the private interests of the ruling class and laboring peasants.

THE HAN LIMITED-FIELD PROPOSALS

For those who conceded the impossibility of restoring the well-field system, two types of reforms were proposed – the limitation of property holdings (limited-field system), and nationalization of land and redistribution to peasants under the equal-field system. The former was proposed in the Han dynasty, and the latter was born in the late fifth century in the Northern Wei and carried over in subsequent dynasties into the T'ang period.

Tung Chung-shu of the Former Han recommended that the imposition of limits on land privately occupied (*han min myŏngjŏn*) was the closest approximation possible to the well-field system because "it would block the path for the accumulation of excess land" (*kyŏmbyŏng*).[27] Tung's plan was not adopted, but a second attempt at a land limitation system occurred during the reign of Emperor Ai (6 B.C. – A.D. 1) toward the end of the Former Han dynasty when Shih Tan's recommendation to set limits on private holdings was adopted. According to the sources the emperor established a single limit of 30 *kyŏng* (3,000 *myo*) on private landholdings, but a graded series of limits on the number of slaves that the nobles could own. Provisions were included for confiscation (of land and slaves) of violators of the law. The system was abandoned because it "conflicted with recent practice," that is, the interests of the land and slaveowners of the time.[28]

Some contemporary scholars hold the view that since the 30-*kyŏng* limit was too large to represent a serious attempt at land limitation, it was nothing more than a sumptuary regulation to limit the ostentatious display of wealth. Others take the view that since there were graded limits of slaveownership established, lower grades for landholding must have been stipulated as well, but were simply omitted from the historical record.[29] Nonetheless, it appears obvious that the Chinese commentators Yu cited believed that the 30-*kyŏng* limit was a serious attempt to impose restrictions on private ownership. Yu, for example, cited Chu Hsi's cryptic paraphrase of both the Tung Chung-shu recommendation and

Emperor Ai's decree: "The emperor decreed limits on the possession of land (*myŏngjŏn*) by the people [but] it really was not carried out,"[30] as if it were not simply a statement of fact but as a cry of anguish, no doubt because of Chu Hsi's conscious emulation of the laconic and didactic style of the *Spring and Autumn Annals*.[31] He also quoted Tu Yu's lament on Tung's land limitation proposal:

> It was a great pity that they did not really carry out the imperial edict to limit the amount of land the people could possess [*han min myŏngjŏn*)]. It was only that they did not know how to regulate the limiting [of landholding]. If they had taken land as the basis [of distribution and taxation], rectified the land boundaries, and in accordance with [the number of?] people graded the land received [from the state, *suin kwa su*], thereby equalizing taxes and military service requirements, then even if it had not been the well-field system [that they adopted], in fact they would have obtained the spirit [lit., the intent] of the well-field system. Once this system had been established, they could have ensured that a hundred generations would have lived without problems.[32]

As we will see, however, despite Yu's admiration for the limited-field concept, he did not regard it as optimum because it represented a compromise with private property.

THE EQUAL-FIELD SYSTEM

China: Northern Wei through T'ang

Yu regarded the equal-field system of the fifth to eighth centuries in China as a close approximation of the well-field system because it purportedly eliminated private property, nationalized ownership of land, distributed it on an equitable or relatively equal basis to the peasantry in return for tax and service obligations, and provided for the support of officials.[33] Nevertheless, the equal-field system could not be taken as an ideal model because it had not endured, and its flaws had to be remedied if a perfected system of *kongjŏn* (public land) were to be created. Even though the equal-field system was one of public or national ownership, the perceived cause of its eventual failure was related to the problem of private property. The historical description of the system revealed that it had degenerated not once, but several times into private property relations.

Yu's historical account included a brief treatment of the equal-field system as it supposedly functioned after its inception in the Northern Wei dynasty in 486, in the subsequent Northern Ch'i, Sui, and T'ang dynasties in China, and in the early Koryŏ dynasty in Korea.[34] The various Chinese systems had certain features in common. Land was divided up and allotted to individuals with the amounts varying according to sex, age, occupation, and sometimes status (commoner or slave). This per capita grant, called the *k'ou-fen-t'ien* (per capita share land) and *lu-t'ien* (open or treeless lowland fields) in Chinese (*kubunjŏn* and *nojŏn* in Korean) could not be privately owned, inherited, or bequeathed. It was granted when the individual came of age (fifteen or twenty, depending on the dynasty), and most of it was to be returned when the individual attained an age exempting him from military or labor service obligations (usually sixty years of age). If a recipient died before this time, the grant was to be returned to the state for redistribution to someone else, with certain provisions for transfer to widows and minor children. The individual (and his household) who received the *k'ou-fen-t'ien* grant was also the subject of taxation, so that in addition to a land tax (*tsu* in Chinese, *cho* in Korean) able-bodied adult males were required to perform so many days of national labor service as well as military service, and the household was obliged to pay a household tax (*tsu*) equivalent to local tribute.

Each individual also received a smaller amount of land in the form of permanent tenure (*yung-yeh-t'ien* in Chinese, *yŏng'ŏpchŏn* in Korean) and housesite land. He was required to plant mulberry trees on the *yung-yeh-t'ien*, which did not have to be returned to the state. It could be bequeathed to heirs and within limits sold or otherwise disposed of.

Officials were granted either office land (*chih-fen-t'ien* in Chinese, *chikpunjŏn* in Korean), or *yung-yeh-t'ien* or both, depending on the dynasty. Office land was allotted from so-called public land (*kung-t'ien* in Chinese, *kongjŏn* in Korean), which did not refer to the nationally owned land distributed to individuals either temporarily or permanently (i.e., the *k'ou-fen-t'ien* or *yung-yeh-t'ien*), but to lands under the control of the state or the district magistrate that was not subject to distribution. For example, in the Northern Ch'i land in the capital province surrounding the imperial capital was set aside as *kung-t'ien* during the reign of Emperor Wu-ch'eng (561–565) and allotted to men with official rank.[35]

It is, of course, possible that these *kung-t'ien* (*kongjŏn*) allotments were prebendal tax collection rights on land that was distributed to individual peasants under the temporary allotment system. In the Northern Wei *kung-t'ien* in local districts was allotted to provincial officials and magistrates in amounts descending from fifteen to six *kyŏng* depending on the rank of the official. It is not clear whether these were separate lands or prebendal tax rights over *k'ou-fen-t'ien*.[36] The description of the T'ang system states that officials of rank six and below could fill their quota of *yung-yeh-t'ien* from *kung-t'ien* that had been returned (to the state) in their local areas or from areas where there was a surplus of land. In the latter case officials were prohibited by law from selling this office land (*chih-fen-t'ien*) when leaving their posts.[37]

One source on the Northern Wei and Northern Ch'i dynasties noted that irregularities in the administration of the office and imperial award land grants subverted the equal-field system and led to the expansion of private holdings. In the Wei dynasty "office land was granted to people without regard to whether they were noble or base in status," and Emperor Hsüan-wu began to make imperial land grants in perpetuity and to tolerate purchase and sale of land. In the

Northern Ch'i after the *wu-p'ing* era (570–576), "irregular imperial grants were made to the nobility and female relatives (of the imperial house) and favored families without any restraint . . ." and arable lands along rivers or foothills was taken over by powerful households, "while the common people could not obtain even a clod of earth."[38]

Emperor Wen of the Sui made large grants of hereditary land (*yung-yeh-t'ien*) to princes and nobles from 30 to 100 *kyŏng* in size and in addition provided office land to capital and provincial officials.[39] This practice was continued in the T'ang dynasty, and as Yu's text noted, "Hereditary land [*yŏng'ŏpchŏn*] was all handed down to sons and grandsons and was not included within the limits of land that was taken back and given out [*susu chi han*]."[40] Of course, these official hereditary holdings were subject to limitations by law. Officials dismissed from office or guilty of some crime were required to return their hereditary holdings to the state.[41] Nevertheless, the toleration of even limited forms of private ownership by nobles, merit subjects, and high officials must have been perceived by Yu as a major cause of the return to private landholding. This point must be deduced from Yu's overall position because *yung-yeh-t'ien* and *chih-fen-t'ien* grants were not specifically identified by Yu or his sources on the T'ang as the major problem. He did, however, mention them in his discussion of the etiology of the failure of the Koryŏ dynasty land system. As will be seen in the description of his own system, however, he was strongly opposed to private ownership in any form and made no provision for any equivalent of the *yung-yeh-t'ien* of the T'ang system.

In addition to the toleration of the permanent holding, the equal-field system seemed to allow loopholes in the handling of the rotating returnable *k'ou-fen-t'ien* grants that also opened the door to private ownership. During the Northern Wei the law allowed individuals with surplus land to sell the surplus to those lacking a full share even though an individual was not supposed to accumulate more than what the law allowed him.[42]

Excess population pressure on available land for *k'ou-fen* grants was to be alleviated by freedom of movement and the expectation that people would naturally migrate into areas of low population density. If this did not work to equalize man/land ratios throughout the country, it was always possible to reduce the size of the per capita grant in areas of overpopulation.[43] In the Northern Ch'i the law prohibited the purchase or sale of land, but the account in the *Kuan-tung feng-su chüan* by Sung Hsiao-wang indicates that in fact the rich and powerful accumulated vast holdings at the expense of the poor peasant.[44] One of the reasons for this was that the state was unable to enforce the prohibition against the alienation of the temporary *k'ou-fen-t'ien* allotment. The law provided punishment for those who held land in excess of the *k'ou-fen-t'ien* limits and encouraged private citizens to inform on their neighbors by a promise that they would receive the confiscated land of the guilty as a reward. This led to the practice of false accusation and the expropriation of *k'ou-fen* lands from their rightful possessors. In addition, enforcement of the prohibition against purchase and sale was inefficient, and the peasants in fact sold off their allotments either to alleviate indebtedness or to pay off the land and household taxes. The toleration of purchase and sale even allowed slaves to accumulate greater holdings than commoner peasants.[45]

Although the *k'ou-fen-t'ien* allotment system was reinstituted in the Sui and T'ang, population density continued to be a problem, which the government offset by grants of reduced size. T'ang law also permitted peasants willing to move from overpopulated to underpopulated areas to sell their *k'ou-fen* allotments; like the Northern Wei, the purchaser could not buy more than he was legally entitled to, and all sales had to be approved by the authorities.[46] Otherwise the property would be confiscated by the officials.

Yu ended his discussion of the equal-field system in China with the remarks of Tu Yu and Ma Tuan-lin. Tu Yu (*T'ung-tien*) noted that by the middle of the eighth century the equal-field system had broken down completely and the problem of land accumulation and large holdings was worse than the late first century B.C. during the Former Han dynasty.[47] Ma Tuan-lin (compiler of the *Wen-hsien t'ung-k'ao*) identified the method of taxation as the major cause of the failure of the equal-field system. Instead of using land as the basis of taxation, which he claimed was the principle used in the Hsia, Shang, and Chou dynasties of antiquity, the governments of the Northern and Southern dynasties and T'ang used households or individuals as the subject of taxation. In the *san-tai* period land was granted to people without household or capitation taxes; in the Former and Later Han dynasties there were no land grants but light household taxes were begun; in the period from the Northern Wei through the T'ang, household taxes were levied supposedly in return for land grants but governments were unable to guarantee regular land grants while the burden of household taxes increased to oppressive levels.[48]

Yu Hyŏngwŏn expanded at length on Ma's interpretation. The main fault of the equal-field system was "registering adult males to establish labor service and calculating population in order to divide up and grant land."[49] The authorities should have surveyed the land to establish correct land boundaries. Because they did not, it was easy for individuals to encroach on the land of others. Regulations were also too complex, which made it difficult to administer the system. Complex regulations required complex record-keeping to maintain accuracy and fairness, but it was difficult to keep accurate records and ensure that the agricultural population would remain fixed and stationary. Written records could not keep up with the migratory shifts in the population, and a system of land grants based on population offered no flexibiity for dealing with this problem. As a result, there were too many inaccuracies in the records and too many cases of underregistration.[50]

Furthermore, a system of capitation or household taxes produced a particularly egregious form of corruption and oppression. If certain individuals fled the village or died, the officials would make up the lost tax revenues or military service obligations by increasing the assessments on neighboring households. The increased burdens only acted as a stimulus for more out-migration, leading to another round of increased allocations on the remaining population. It was a vicious cycle that could only end in the downfall of the dynasty itself.[51] The only antidote to this problem was to use land units as the basis for calculating and assessing taxes and military service.

> Generally speaking people can not live without land and land can not be cultivated without people. But land is something that is all fixed in place and does not move from one place to another. People [on the contrary] may either move or stay at rest, live or die; they do not always do the same thing. This is the reason why if you base [taxation] on the land and clarify the shares of landholding, then [provisions pertaining to] the people will be contained in it, and as a matter of course everything will work out equitably. . . .[52]
>
> If taxation were based on land, then even though the harvest was bad and the people abandoned the land and absconded, someone else would probably take over the cultivation of the land in his place, so how could you have this kind of problem (of taxing neighbors)? In general, if you do not levy taxes on land, then you can not avoid the problem of shifting service requirements to neighboring families. . . . You must rectify the land boundaries and base taxation and military service requirements on the land.[53]

The establishment of physical boundaries around fixed units of land area and the use of these units as the means of assessing tax and labor service were two of the most important principles that Yu and others supposedly obtained from the objective examination of the well-field system of antiquity, but in fact these conclusions derived more from the perception of the weaknesses of the equal-field system of the Chinese Northern and Southern dynasties and T'ang than from the deduction of principles from the well-field system in vacuo. Instead of concluding that the failure of the equal-field system proved that egalitarian distribution was unworkable because it was contrary to the acquisitive nature of man or because it required too high a level of probity and honesty from ordinary bureaucrats, people like Ma Tuan-lin and Yu Hyŏngwŏn preferred to believe that the equal-field system failed because it did not conform in every respect to the well-field model. And since fixed land boundaries and the idea of reciprocal tax obligations in return for land grants appeared to be features of the well-field system, they thus seized on these factors as the most important variables. As a result Yu idealized them and turned them into immutable principles of land organization, which he claimed could be discovered only by empirical investigation of the facts, and not by a priori reasoning.

> This is not just a matter of circumstance; it is also a principle of Heaven [*ch'ŏlli*]. It is like the principle governing the transition from rest to movement. The sages completely abided by Heaven's [i.e., natural] principles, and that is why their institutions were all like this. They first had to begin with the form that

> existed before doing anything. The reason why their systems were well regulated was all due to this intention. That is why in discussing learning it is said: "The extension of knowledge depends on the investigation of things"; it is not said you extend your knowledge and then investigate things.[54]

Yu thus claimed that his deductions (and those of Ma Tuan-lin and others) were based on empirical investigation of circumstance, but in fact Yu did not conduct an exhaustive analysis of the reality of the Chou well-field system by a collation and comparison of all facts available from that era, whether in tomb, vessel, monument inscriptions, or written documents. His conclusions on the principles of the well-field were obtained by a simple process of elimination. The equal-field system failed because certain elements of the well-field system were not included in it; those key elements of the well-field system left out of the equal-field system were thus indispensable for the successful operation of any system of national ownership and distribution.

The Koryŏ Land System

Yu Hyŏngwŏn believed that the land system of the early Koryŏ dynasty in Korea, from the early tenth through the late twelfth centuries, was a copy of the T'ang equal-field system. Contemporary scholars, however, have rejected this view because of important anomalies and contradictions between the early Koryŏ land system and the T'ang equal-field regulations.[55] Descriptions of the early Koryŏ land grant system, for example, do not indicate that fixed land allotments of uniform size were granted to all peasant cultivators or that the basic land grant to the peasant was the main building block of the system as a whole. The early Koryŏ *chŏnsikwa* system was, in fact, a graded system of land grants to men of rank with or without office or service obligations. Functionaries who did receive land grants included local clerks in magistrates' yamen and ordinary soldiers as well as regular officials of the central government. Since neither clerks nor soldiers were rewarded by land or prebendal grants in the late Koryŏ or early Chosŏn dynasties, it was natural for scholars of that period to assume that the early Koryŏ grants of land to soldiers and yamen clerks and runners meant that everyone in society was provided with a land grant and that the only difference from the T'ang equal-field system was in the use of terminology. Hence, instead of the *k'ou-fen-t'ien* or *lu-t'ien* (per capita mouth-share land or the treeless open land) of the Northern Wei through T'ang, the smallest and most basic grant under the Koryŏ system seemed to be the *kunjŏn* or soldier's land. Put another way, in the T'ang dynasty the peasant received a per capita share of land, and in return he owed military service, but in the Koryŏ system it appeared that the individual performed military service in return for which he was granted a piece of land. This interpretation would help to explain why *kubunjŏn* or "mouth-share land" in the Koryŏ system did not refer to the basic peasant grant (i.e., the T'ang *k'ou-fen-t'ien*), but had a restricted and specialized meaning –

it referred only to land retained by retired functionaries or the widows of deceased functionaries.[56]

Nevertheless, Yu described the early Koryŏ system as if it were copied from the T'ang equal-field system, an interpretation he borrowed from the *History of the Koryŏ Dynasty* (*Koryŏsa*), which said that King T'aejo, the founder of Koryŏ, "divided up the land and gave it to the officials and people."[57] At the end of the fourteenth century, the famous advocate of land reform, Cho Chun, portrayed the achievements of T'aejo as equivalent to the founders of the Chou dynasty because the early Koryŏ land system was based on two fundamental well-field principles, the rectification of land boundaries and equity (*kyun*) of distribution.

> Kings Wen and Wu and the Duke of Chou [of the early Chou] used the well-field system to nurture the people and for that reason the Chou dynasty lasted over eight hundred years, whereas the Ch'in dynasty destroyed the well-field system and fell after only two generations. T'aejo [of Koryŏ] unified the Samhan [i.e., Korea] and established land [allotments] and regulated the officials, granting land in accordance with rank [*p'um*]. If a person died, his land was taken back. If he was a *pubyŏng* [soldier], at the age of twenty he received land, and at the age of sixty he returned it. In the case of the *sadaebu* who received land, if they committed a crime, their land was taken back. Every person took care of himself and did not dare break the law. Rites and righteousness flourished and customs and mores were beautiful. The soldiers of the guard units and the clerks of the prefectures, districts, ferry stations and post-stations were each supported with land grants. They were settled on the land and were secure in their occupations, and because the state was rich and powerful, even though the Liao and Chin dynasties kept a hungry eye on the world and were situated next to our borders, they did not dare swallow us up because T'aejo had divided up the land of the Samhan and shared with his officials and people in the enjoyment of its benefits, the enhancement of their livelihoods, and the resolution of their minds, creating the original spirit that would enable the state to last for a thousand or ten thousand generations.[58]

Cho Chun's idealization of the early Koryŏ land system and his hagiographic account of T'aejo's accomplishments were undoubtedly designed to provide a sense of sharp contrast with the problems of late Koryŏ land arrangements, but Yu Hyŏngwŏn accepted his views as factual and accurate. Yu's own brief account was but a synopsis of Cho Chun's exposition and the *Koryŏsa* account:

> The Koryŏ land system was in general modeled after the T'ang system. They made a total [survey] of the amount of cultivated land and divided it into categories in accordance with its fertility. From the civil and military officials down to the regular soldiers [*pubyŏng*] and the unemployed scions of merit subjects [or off-duty military reservists? *han'in*], everyone's qualifications were determined by rank [*kwa*] and each was given a land grant. If a person died, his share

> was returned to the government. Even a *pubyŏng* regular soldier first received a land grant when he attained the age of twenty, and when he reached the age of sixty, he returned it. If a man had sons and grandsons or close relatives, then his land was transferred to an adult male [*chŏng*] [on his death]. . . .[59]

Had Yu been more perspicacious, he might have emphasized important differences between the early Koryŏ and T'ang equal-field systems, especially since the basis of land grants in early Koryŏ was either officeholding or some other criterion of personal status that differentiated a natural aristocracy from the common peasantry (or slaves). Yu mentioned, for example, the *yŏkpunjŏn* land grants instituted by T'aejo in 940 that were "given to all the court officials and military men at the time, irrespective of their official rank. People were observed for their character and behavior, whether it was good or bad, and whether their merit and effort was great or small, and they were given this land in grades." He also stated that the first *chŏnsikwa* regulations of 976 provided land grants that "did not depend on the official's rank, but was determined on the basis of personal quality [*inp'um*]."[60]

One might surmise that the early Koryŏ system, if it actually functioned as described, served to provide support for an ascriptive, hereditary aristocracy (albeit somewhat more attenuated than the Silla bone-rank aristocracy) rather than the elite of merit and virtue as described in the sources. Yu, however, probably perceived *inp'um* not as an indication of inherited status, but as a mark of virtue and hence roughly equivalent to the well-field principle that the *sadaebu* as a class deserved some mode of support by the state whether or not their members held office as individuals. Later revisions in the *chŏnsikwa* system, as copied by Yu from the *Koryŏsa*, showed that *inp'um* was discarded as a criterion for land grants and replaced by position in the civil and military bureaucratic hierarchy (*munmu yangban*).[61]

Yu's sources on the putative early Koryŏ version of the equal-field system also described and analyzed its breakdown. A careful reading of these sections reveals interesting differences in viewpoint. While there was general agreement that the equal-field model degenerated into private ownership with the accumulation of large holdings by certain individuals and families, the causes for this were attributed variously to foreign intervention, flaws or deficiencies in the original system, or the corruption of an originally perfect system by domestic forces impinging on the model from without the system itself. The laconic explanation of the *Koryŏsa* compilers attributed the breakdown to a combination of domestic politics and the Mongol intervention:

> After the reigns of Ŭijong and Myŏngjong [the period of military dictatorship and Ch'oe family hegemony, ca. 1170–1270] the powerful and deceitful ran government affairs as they pleased. The barbarian Yüan were not reluctant to make exactions and demands, and there were all kinds of taxes so that the population declined by the day. By the time of the fall of the dynasty virtue was lost and the

> land and population statistics were not clearly known. The grades of farmland and woodland [*chŏnsikwa*] were abandoned and became private land [*sajŏn*],[62] and the influential families and hereditary clans [*sejok*] competed with one another to accumulate large holdings [*kyŏmbyŏng*]. Their landholdings were so great that they extended across the *ch'ŏn* and *maek* embankments [i.e., the terms used to allude to Shang Yang's reform that expanded the land boundaries beyond the 100 *myo* unit of the well fields] and [their holdings were so large that] they had to use mountains and rivers to mark the borders of their lands. The common people [*yangmin*] were all absorbed into their huge houses and as a result the state gradually fell into decline.[63]

This paragraph, of course, mentioned several of the shibboleths of the well-field idealists – private property, hereditary clans that were the antithesis of an ideal *sadaebu* elite whose status was founded on virtue, and the conversion of the peasantry from ordinary taxpayers supporting the state to the minions of an aristocracy.

The analysis of Yi Chehyŏn, the famous fourteenth-century Neo-Confucian scholar, differed in significant ways from this statement and from the opinion of Cho Chun. To begin with, in contrast to Cho Chun's apotheosis of the early Koryŏ land settlement, Yi emphasized the incomplete and flawed nature of land relations in the tenth century. He noted how T'aejo was faced with a chaotic situation inherited from the late Silla dynasty and the disruptive rule of the successor state of T'aebong (founded by Kungye, under whom T'aejo or Wang Kŏn first served). Lacking sufficient time for a more thoroughgoing and complete land reform, T'aejo was only able to establish a system for the grant of *kubun* land allotments.[64] King Kyŏngjong (r. 975–981) improved on T'aejo's system somewhat by establishing the *chŏnsikwa* graded allotments of farmland and woodland. "Even though the system had some crude and rough elements, it contained within it the intention of the ancients for establishing a system of hereditary salary provisions [*serok*]."[65] This comment indicates that Yi perceived correctly that the main feature of the *chŏnsikwa* allotments was the provision of support to officials rather than the guarantee of a basic plot to all peasants. In other words, the *chŏnsikwa* system accomplished only half the objectives of the well-field model, omitting provision of a basic land grant to commoner peasant families. Furthermore, Yi argued that the *chŏnsikwa* system departed from well-field or Chou principles in the method of taxation as well.

"As for such methods as the one-ninth 'aid' [*chu*] or the one-tenth tax [*pu*], which were the means by which [the ancients] provided superior treatment for the men of superior virtue [*kunja*] and distinguished them from the small men [*soin*, ordinary people, the equivalent of Mencius's *yain* or 'men of the fields'], there was no mention of this at all."[66]

Other sources in the *Koryŏsa* on early Koryŏ taxation were not in agreement on this problem. An early Koryŏ source, for example, stated that the *cho* tax rate on public land (*kongjŏn*) was set in 992 at a rate of one-fourth the crop.[67]

On the other hand, a late Koryŏ official, Paek Munbo, noted in 1362 that the Koryŏ dynasty did in fact adopt the tithe of the Han dynasty. Yu remarked that "At present I note that in Koryŏ times the tax laws underwent several changes over time, but because the *Koryŏsa* does not record these clearly, at present I can not discuss them in detail. However, if you look at the memorial of Paek Munbo, it would appear that only at the beginning of the dynasty did they regard the tithe as standard."[68] Yu thus doubted that the early Koryŏ government had been able to live up to the ideal of the well-field model.

Finally, Yi Chehyŏn also pointed to another major deficiency of the tenth-century system, failure to establish clear boundaries – in other words, failure to mark out fixed units of land area with ridges and dikes. "What a pity that the officials at the time did not conduct a study of [the ancient] laws and systems on the basis of what Mencius said. . . ."[69] Had this key principle of the well-field system been adopted, it would have ensured the longevity and success of the land system. "If the land boundaries are rectified, then with regard to dividing up the land and regulating salaries, one can sit by [and do nothing] and everything will be determined [correctly]."[70]

In brief, Yi Chehyŏn argued that the incomplete and imperfect nature of the early Koryŏ land system was responsible for its ultimate failure. Similar to Ma Tuan-lin's critique of the T'ang equal fields, Yi held that the early Koryŏ kings and ministers had failed to adopt crucial elements of the well-field system, specifically, the rectification of land boundaries, the distribution of basic land parcels to the peasantry, and the use of the tithe for taxation.

Yi's negative and critical analysis of the early Koryŏ system, however, had positive implications for Yu Hyŏngwŏn, just as the criticisms of the T'ang equal-field system had positive implications for the Sung statecraft writers.[71] It held out the promise that attainment of the well-field ideal was still possible, even in the post-Chou centralized bureaucratic age, if only all essential elements of the well-field model were incorporated into a contemporary land reform scheme.

Cho Chun, as mentioned before, began his analysis on the premise that the early Koryŏ land system was a close approximation to the well-field ideal, but one suspects that his idealization of early Koryŏ was only done to highlight the deficiencies of late Koryŏ policies. The most egregious of these was the practice of government grants to a variety of people who did not perform actual service for the state, such as the *han'in* or "idle people" who were scions of merit subjects, or officials who did not hold incumbencies, descendants of officials or merit subjects entitled to office appointments because of the status of their forebears (*kong'ŭm*), immigrant foreigners who joined Koryŏ military forces and received land grants as a reward or inducement, or examination passers who were given special land grants. Because government officials failed to maintain the bothersome task of proper registration, the state lost control over land, and government land grants were passed on illicitly to descendants or otherwise ended up in private hands.

> Men who were not in the ranks of the soldiers still dared to receive soldier's land [*kunjŏn*]. Fathers concealed their holdings and privately gave them to their sons. Sons hid and stole the land and did not return it to the government. Once the law of the founding fathers was destroyed, then the gates for the accumulation of large holdings [*kyŏmbyŏng*] were opened. . . . The land which our founding fathers so justly divided up and granted has become the private property of individual families or persons.[72]

According to Cho Chun the reciprocal feature of the equal-field system of the early Koryŏ was lost by the conversion of public land to private ownership. Regular officials and soldiers in the state armies were both entitled to land grants under this system because of the service they performed, but not after the conversion of land grants to private ownership.

> There are some persons who never once leave their homes to serve as officials at court, never once put their foot forward to serve in the army, yet they wear fancy clothes and eat fine food, and they sit around and enjoy the benefits [that accrue to officials and regular soldiers]. On the contrary, the officials who serve on duty guarding [the king] day and night and the soldiers who fight hard in a hundred battles do not get even one *myo*'s worth of land to cultivate to provide for their fathers, mothers, wives, and sons. How can they be encouraged to be loyal and righteous and meet their responsibilities for earning merit in what they do?[73]

Private ownership of land was also a cause for the loss of public spirit and a stimulus to avarice and unseemly competition. The time of the officials was taken up in investigating and adjudicating claims and counterclaims over title to land as the whole population competed to increase its holdings.

"If sons do not get what they want in seeking one *myo*'s worth of land from their fathers and mothers, this on the contrary gives rise to feelings of resentment. It is even worse when brothers are involved. This is because the existence of private land [*sajŏn*] has caused people to fall from moral behavior to the behavior of animals."[74]

Cho Chun's disdain for private property was echoed by the censor, Yi Haeng, who was also a leading advocate for land reform in the 1380s. Yi Haeng summed up the critique of landownership in one pithy paragraph: "It is due to the evil of private land [*sajŏn*] that the wealthy and powerful families accumulate large landed property, that the state has nothing for its expenses, that tax burdens have doubled, that the people are fallen and distressed, that the strong devour the weak, that disputes and lawsuits are prolific and numerous, that flesh and blood suspect one another, and that customs and mores have been destroyed."[75]

Yi also echoed a point that had been made in the Chinese literature on land reform about the bad effects on the ruling class of the destruction of the well-field system of the Chou – that the loss or absence of a system of state land grants to the *sajok* or families of scholars made them totally dependent on salaries received for incumbent service as officials, and hence removed a secure and stable basis of livelihood. On the contrary, "If the scholars [*sa*] who have no jobs are given land, they will be enabled to cultivate it, and if those with posts are given salaries in place of [the income they would earn] from cultivation, their means of living can be continued."[76]

Almost every point made by Cho Chun and Yi Haeng in their description of the early Koryŏ land system has been rejected by contemporary twentieth-century scholars. It is no longer believed that land in early Koryŏ was owned by the state and distributed to peasants in the mode of the T'ang equal-field system, or that all commoner peasants served in the army under a militia system of rotating tours of duty. On the contrary, the early Koryŏ *chŏnsikwa* system is now seen as a system of fictional grants of land, that is, prebends, to a broad variety of individuals, some of whom possessed only title or rank, and others who were officeholders or functionaries of the state, including soldiers. Grantees were allowed to transfer or bequeath their grants to close relatives as long as the heirs qualified under the regulations of the state. Not all peasants received land grants, and even those that did may have only received a fictional grant for military service, confirming private land they already owned or possessed. Similarly, the land grants or prebends to high officials may have only been a fictional device limiting or legitimizing private estates already held.[77] Yu Hyŏngwŏn, however, took as literal truth the statements of the compilers of the *Koryŏsa* and the late Koryŏ land reformers about the existence of state ownership and equitable distribution in early Koryŏ.

Yu Hyŏngwŏn's study of the equal-field system as it functioned in China and Korea was perceived in terms of a uniform pattern and logic. Although he showed some sympathy for Cho Chun's view that the early Koryŏ system was close to perfection, in the end he perceived both the T'ang and Koryŏ equal-field systems as initially flawed and containing the seeds of their own destruction. As he put it in the introduction to his own plan for land reform:

> The equal-field system of the T'ang period also came close to the intention of the ancients. The Koryŏ dynasty used it in order to produce wealth and strength, but the system did not make land the chief [subject]. It took people as the basis [for distribution and taxation] and therefore registered able-bodied males and granted them land in grades of many categories. When land was granted, there was always the problem of too many people and too little land, or vice versa. After the land was granted there was also the problem of having an initial surplus but shortages later on, or of having initial shortage and surplus later on.
>
> According to the ancient law, land was taken as the base. Taxes were paid on the basis of land. Since the people resided on the land, they set the land boundaries straight. Since [taxes were based on] what each man collected [in harvest], there were no evils. The T'ang and Koryŏ systems took men as the basis [for

> distribution and taxation] and granted land to able-bodied males. Therefore, you had the problem of an unequal balance between the number of people and the amount of land. Even though this appears to be close [to the ancient or well-field system], in fact it was not the same as the ancient system.[78]

Yu's evaluation of the weaknesses of the equal-field system formed the background to his analysis of the essential elements of the well-field system, and he assumed that the equal-field system had failed because it had not incorporated all elements of the well-field model.

SUNG DYNASTY OPINION ON LAND REFORM

The Sung era (tenth through thirteenth centuries) was naturally important to Koreans in the seventeenth century because Sung scholars and statesmen produced a number of ideas about the problems of land and tax reform as well as their contribution to Neo-Confucian moral philosophy. The central issue in their statecraft thought was whether the well-field system could ever be restored, and if not, what alternatives were possible?

The Feasibility of a Well-Field Restoration

Yu traced the history of the debate over the feasibility of restoring the well-field system in the age of centralized bureaucracy. He noted that after the establishment of private property in the unified Ch'in dynasty, the well-field system was held up as a model for reform, but few believed it could be restored. Hsün Yüeh of the Later Han dynasty preferred the adoption of the well-field system but pointed out practical difficulties in its application. He felt that it was best suited to a high man/land ratio, but during the middle of a dynastic period population density was higher and private property rights were firmly entrenched and difficult to abolish. Although it was politically more feasible to attempt a well-field restoration at the beginning of a dynasty when there was a low population and a lot of available land, it was not really needed at such times because there was plenty of land for everyone and not much pressure for redistribution. He expressed regret that Emperor Kuang-wu had failed to abolish the purchase and sale of land to prevent the accumulation of excess property in later times when he founded the Later Han dynasty in A.D. 25. Yet he still believed that at least *the principles* of the well-field system could be adapted to the centralized state: "Even though institutions in ancient times were different from the present and the advantages and disadvantages differ in accordance with the time, still in terms of their grand outline and major principles, they are one and the same."[79]

The famous poet-statesman Po Chü-i of the T'ang dynasty agreed generally with Hsün Yüeh's point when he suggested that although the Ch'in *ch'ŏnmaek* system was more suitable when population was low and land in excess, in a time of population surplus and land shortage the well-field system was more appropriate. Yu commented that this was a shallow opinion based on Po's failure to conduct a thorough study of the ancient system.[80] Yu probably meant either that the term *ch'ŏnmaek* did not represent a new system at all, as Chu Hsi had pointed out in the twelfth century, or that since it was a system of private property, it was an unsuitable substitute for the well-field system at any time.

Yu also copied out Tu Yu's (T'ang dynasty) opening statement in his survey of land systems in China in the *T'ung-tien*, which lauded the well fields and the hierarchy of local communities (*pi* and *ryŏ*) of the sages because they perceived that land was the basis of agricultural production and that settling the people on the land would guarantee continuous production and ensure equitable distribution of labor service requirements through an accurate census of the population.[81]

A recent study by Sudō Yoshiyuki has revealed that by the Sung dynasty a large majority of scholars and statesmen felt that a literal restoration of the well-field system was impossible if not undesirable, even though most of them were in favor of some kind of reform. The great philosopher Ch'eng Hao, for example, was a gradualist willing to settle for either the well-field or limited-field system. Ou-yang Hsiu proposed limiting the land the rich already owned but giving them free rein on the reclamation of wasteland. Su Hsün thought that you needed flat land to lay out the well-field grid and that it would take a century to do it. Wei Hsiang and Ch'en Liang agreed that the task was too difficult, and that a gradual approximation, possibly a limited-field scheme, was the best that could be hoped for.[82]

Sudō also showed that the most forceful and optimistic advocate of a restoration of the well-field system of antiquity was Chang Tsai of the Northern Sung, even after the T'ang equal-field system had collapsed. Chang believed that a well-field restoration would naturally be welcomed by the majority of the peasant population and opposed only by the minority of landlords. Although he admitted that the well fields were ensconced in a feudal context in Chou times, he also had hopes that enough elements of feudalism could be revived to make the well-field system viable. He was confident that the adoption of the system depended only on the will and resolution of the ruler and that the use of force would not be necessary. Private ownership would be disallowed and the needs of the officials would be met by fiefs of no more than fifty *li*. His assumption that the landlords would be willing to give up their land for the benefit of the people without coercion was, however, condemned for its naïveté by most other Sung scholars and statesmen.[83]

Chang's optimism was reiterated by Ch'en Fu of the late Southern Sung, who thought that the well-field system was adaptable to any age as long as a sufficient lead time of three to seven years was provided to ease the pain to the landlords from the confiscation of their land. In addition to Chang Tsai, Ch'en cited Chu Hsi as an authority on the feasibility of restoring the well-field system, even though Chu had expressed reservations about its feasibility.[84]

Yu Hyŏngwŏn omitted an evaluation of the history of land reform and confined his attention to the theoretical discussion of Sung scholars and statesmen.

He cited Ch'eng Hao's memorial to Emperor Shen-tsung (r. 1068–86) that praised the well fields of ancient times for ensuring equitable land distribution, lauded the efforts of the T'ang rulers for granting land allotments to individuals (i.e., the *k'ou-fen* grants), and chided the Sung rulers for failing even to attempt the T'ang adaptation of the well-field to save the peasantry from penury.

Yu noted that Fan Tsu-yü extolled the well-field system for "repressing the wealthy" to eliminate the differences between the rich and the poor, and that Lin Hsün had recommended an adaptation of the well-field system to Emperor Kao-tsung of the Southern Sung (r. 1127–31) as an antidote to conditions of economic chaos.[85]

The more optimistic supporters of the well fields agreed that the landlords would provide the stiffest opposition to any seizure of their property. Ch'eng I warned that care should be taken to prevent popular resentment against the institution of a well-field system (that is, against confiscation of private land), but success could be achieved by the use of correct methods. Chang Tsai agreed that thorough discussion in advance and careful implementation would be needed to ensure cooperation and prevent opposition, but there was no substitute for the well-field system. Lü Ta-lin agreed that "The most difficult thing to do is first to seize the land of the wealthy people forthwith," but he was confident that "with the use of skill and proper tactics, this could be carried out without having to punish a single person."[86]

Land-Limitation Plans

Most Sung reformers who rejected the Utopian possibilities of a literal well-field restoration and opposed outright confiscation, however, favored some form of a limited-field plan in the fashion of Tung Chung-shu and Shih Tan of the Former Han dynasty, and Sudō Yoshiyuki has provided a convenient summary of these views. Li Kou of the mid-eleventh century deplored the monopolization of fertile land by the rich, their use of tenants as cultivators, and their lack of interest in reclaiming marginal land. He favored limiting the occupation of land but not limiting the reclamation of marginal or wasteland.[87]

Su Hsün was a gradualist who believed that literal restoration of the Chou well-field system was impossible because it would take several hundred years to recreate the waterway system associated with it. Since the thirty *kyŏng* limit of the Han could not be adopted so easily either, the only solution was a gradual program of limitation. No land would be confiscated, but subdivision of landed property among heirs over the generations would eventually yield an egalitarian pattern of landownership tantamount to a well-field system.

Ch'en Shen-yu optimistically believed that if the families of officials were provided their "hereditary salaries" (*serok*), they could be induced to give their surplus land to the state voluntarily, and landlords would not resent confiscation if limits on ownership were large enough. Wei Hsiang called his own plan an equal-field system, but in fact he proposed limits on land that could be owned and prohibition of purchases above the limit. Like Li Kou, he hoped to force people back into agriculture by prohibiting commerce. Liu Yen wanted to combine a program of limited fields with the Northern Sung square-field system (*fang-t'ien, pangjŏn* in Korean) of accurate registration and progressive taxation (so-called tax equalization).

Yang Chien also sought to achieve the well-field ideal by the use of a land limitation plan that would establish a liberal quota and allow landlords to sell but not buy land. After a generation or two had passed and the average holding had been reduced in size, the state could set new, lower, limits on ownership. Since landowners could be counted on to alienate their property either through sale or division among heirs, the eventual equalization of landownership would be assured.[88]

Although Yu had not surveyed all the Sung proposals for land limitation thoroughly, he did cite a number of views that represented land limitation plans. Fan Tsu-yü, who assisted Ssu-ma Kuang in compiling the *Tzu-chih t'ung-chien* and later opposed Wang An-shih's "new laws," remarked that even though the rulers of later states were not able to restore the system of antiquity, they were at least able to place limits on the possession of land (*chŏmjŏn yu han*) to enable the poor to sustain themselves.[89]

Yu quoted at great length the land limitation plan of Lin Hsün of the early Southern Sung (after 1126), the most complex system of all the Sung writers. Lin sought to guarantee a basic plot of 50 *myo* of land to each peasant or peasant family, but he opposed the use of force and confiscation of land from large owners. He worked out a compromise with the status quo in the following fashion. He divided the population into three categories: "good farmers" (*yangnong*) who owned more than 50 *myo*, "secondary farmers" (*ch'anong*) who owned less than 50 *myo*, and landless peasants, vagrants, "lazy people," and those engaged in minor occupations. Fifty *myo* of the land of the "good farmers" would be set aside as their "regular fields" (*chŏngjŏn*). Land held in excess of this amount would not be confiscated; instead the landless peasants would be recruited to cultivate it as "attached peasants" (*yenong*). Similarly "secondary farmers" who owned less than 50 *myo* of their own would be allowed to cultivate the surplus lands of the "good farmers" up to the limit of 50 *myo*, to fill in their basic land allotment. In addition, the "good farmers" would not be allowed to use their wealth to purchase more land than they currently owned.[90]

Lin did not specify whether the attached landless peasants or secondary smallholder peasants who were to cultivate the surplus lands of the "good farmers" would pay rent to the latter, but one can presume that this was the object of the plan. This situation was designed to be a temporary arrangement, combining a limitation on the ability of wealthy landowners to increase their holdings and a system of state-enforced tenancy and serfdom (which has been documented for the Sung period) to guarantee a minimum plot of 50 *myo* for cultivation purposes to the tenants and serfs. Lin believed that through the process of division of property among sons, the surplus lands of the "good farmers" would eventually be reduced to the 50 *myo* plot.

"If a 'good farmer' does not want to sell his surplus land, he should wait for his sons and grandsons to grow up and then divide it [among them]. The officials will not seize their property and earn their resentment. They should be given some leeway, and then naturally things will hit the mark by themselves in a good system."[91]

Yu cited Ch'en Liang who praised Lin's plan and assured his readers that "It is only necessary to have a brave and dauntless ruler who can especially stand up and adopt [his plan] to carry out a grand reform. . . ."[92] Yu also referred to the praise of Chu Hsi and Lü Tsu-ch'ien for Lin's ideas, but ultimately he concluded that Lin's plan departed from the well-field model in two respects:

"What a pity [Lin's proposals] were not studied and put into practice. The only problem with what he says is that he does not take rectification of land boundaries [*chŏng kyŏnggye*] as the first order of business. He prefers to allow purchase and sale of land temporarily so that you would still have obstruction and problems that would prevent the complete implementation [of a well-field model]."[93]

Yu's opposition to toleration of purchase and sale appears to reflect his animus against private property, but it did not necessarily indicate his support for confiscation of land from the landlord class as a means of achieving the well-field ideal. Yu, however, did address this question directly in the discussion of his own land reform program, which will be taken up later.

The land limitation plans that Yu selected for discussion shared certain points in common. Though directed toward the limitation of private property, all were governed by a fear or dislike of confiscation. Although land limitation itself presupposed the preservation of private property, there was no bias against state intervention and regulation at the expense of private right. It was assumed that the skillful creation of an institutional structure would lead gradually to a relatively equal distribution of land and tax burdens. Although it might take generations to achieve the desired end, the gradual transition would preclude any political opposition to be expected by a sudden imposition of an egalitarian model accompanied by confiscation.

Chu Hsi: Pessimism about Land Limitation

By the same token Yu omitted treatment of Chu Hsi's pessimistic views about the limited-land plan. Chu believed in the historical existence of the well-field system, held Shang Yang of the Ch'in responsible for introducing private property as a means of maximizing production, praised the equal-field system of the T'ang as a close approximation of the well-field ideal, and criticized Yang Yen of the late T'ang for dismantling the early T'ang tax system and replacing it with the double tax. Chu Hsi praised Lin Hsün's limited-field scheme to one of his disciples because it was based primarily on an arrangement of land boundaries and areas and secondarily on population, and in 1191 and 1235 he attempted rectifications of land boundaries in two separate districts on the basis of Lin's proposals. But as Sudō Yoshiyuki has argued, his overall attitude toward the prospects for land limitation proposals was pessimistic and critical.

One of the reasons for his pessimism was his admiration of the view of Hsün Yüeh of the Later Han that idealistic plans for nationalization and distribution of land could only be accomplished at the beginning of a new dynasty when the government had full control over land and the ratio of available land to population was large enough to allow a system of distribution. In the middle of a dynasty, by contrast, the interests of the landlords had become too entrenched to permit the confiscatory policies necessary for redistribution. Therefore, although he had admired Lin Hsün's emphasis on the rectification of land boundaries, he criticized Su Hsün's land limitation scheme for being frivolous. His skepticism was doubtless reinforced by the difficulties of implementing reform in his own era: given Emperor Hsiao-tsung's failure to institute a *pao-cheng* mutual surveillance and guarantee system in 1170, he felt that the prospects for land reform based on confiscation or limitation of ownership were poor.[94]

Although Yu's *Pan'gye surok* includes a lengthy section from Chu Hsi's *Opinions on the Well Fields* (*Ching-t'ien lei-shuo*), the quotation consists mainly of a collage of opinions from earlier sources, including the view of Hsün Yüeh of the Later Han and a brief reference to Emperor Shih-tsung of the Later Chou (r. 944–60), who did his best to adopt an equal-field system based on his reading of ancient texts. Other than these, Yu did not include any explicit statements by Chu Hsi on the adaptability of the well-field system to current times or on the feasibility of large-scale confiscation.[95] Either Yu missed Chu Hsi's skepticism, chose to ignore it, or concluded that Chu's attitude did not preclude the possibility of a limited-field adaption of the well-field model. As for other Sung figures Yu quoted, such as the Ch'eng brothers, Chang Tsai, and Lü Ta-lin, all appeared to have agreed that the adoption of the well-field model was necessary, but none offered a concrete plan to prevent or suppress landlord opposition to the confiscation of land.

*The 100-*myo *Land Unit*

A matter of slightly less significance, and yet one that attracted much attention in the Sung, was the question of whether the 100-*myo* unit of the well-field system was feasible in the Sung. Ch'eng Hao defended the well-field model against two counterarguments: that there was not enough land available in his own time to provide a 100-*myo* allotment to everyone, and that 100 *myo* in Chou times was equivalent to only 41 *myo* in Sung times, an amount insufficient to provide enough food for a family of nine people. Ch'eng responded that only six out of every ten people would really qualify for land allotments anyhow; the rest were either the elderly or children, so that 100 *myo* would be adequate, given the actual age distribution of the average family. If the farmers were diligent in their work, they would be able to overcome the problem of relatively small land allotments, and, in any case, the custom of mutual aid and relief in the villages would serve to prevent starvation.[96]

Another argument used to denigrate the well-field model was that it required broad flat plains to lay out squares of 100 *myo*. Yu, however, cited a discussion among the Ch'eng brothers and Chang Tsai in which all three agreed that the problem of irregular topography could be solved by the use of mathematics to calculate fractional areas. In places with hills or rivers a farm family could be granted 100 *myo* by allocation of several smaller units.[97]

Lin Hsün, of course, did not hold to the 100-*myo* plot. He favored the 50-*myo* unit, which was not sanctified anywhere in the classical literature, but he reached his conclusion by adopting 100 *myo* as a basic or standard unit of allotment and then calculating actual man/land ratios and production figures in his own time. He concluded that the optimum situation would consist of a 100-*myo* unit cultivated by two *pu* (male farmers or farm families). Production would vary from 50–100 piculs (*sŏm*) each, which would be more than sufficient to support their families. The average plot per farmer or farm family would then work out to 50 *myo*. In addition, Lin calculated the tax yield that would be produced by a tax rate of 10 percent, and the amount of land to be set aside for homes and schools.[98] Lin's technique was identical to the method proposed by the Ch'eng brothers and Chang Tsai, even though he failed to support the literal interpretation of the well-field 100-*myo* unit.

One other element of the well-field model was mentioned briefly by the Sung writers – the establishment of units of land area fixed in the landscape by means of elevated ridges, the so-called rectification or establishment of land boundaries (*kyŏnggye*). Chang Tsai, for example, noted that fixed boundaries were necessary if there were to be any hope of creating a lasting system in the face of the subversive effects on a well-field land system by the depredations of tyrannical rulers and corrupt officials of later periods. He argued that contrary to the conventional wisdom that the destruction of land boundaries on the well-field system took place in a relatively brief period of time in the Ch'in state (by Shang Yang), in fact it was a protracted process.[99] Yu Hyŏngwŏn's criticism of Lin Hsün, that he failed to provide for the creation of fixed boundaries in his program of land reform, was undoubtedly derived from Chang Tsai's views.

Defense of Rich Landlords: Wang An-shih and Yeh Shih

Not all Sung writers and statesmen agreed with the optimistic forecasts of the proponents of land limitation. Some of them, including ardent reformers rather than conservative defenders of property, made powerful arguments for the positive contributions made to society by the rich landlords, but Yu did not include any of these arguments in his survey of Sung thought.

Wang An-shih in the late eleventh century, possibly the most well-advertised reformer in Chinese history, opposed confiscation of land from the rich for redistribution to the poor and landless not simply because of fear of political opposition – he certainly did enough to invade the privileges of the rich in many other ways – but because of what he deemed as the indispensable role played by the landlords in the local, agrarian economy. Since the Sung government lacked a full fleet of agricultural promotion officials (what we might call an agricultural extension service), the landlords functioned to preserve dikes and waterways, encourage planting and harvesting, and provide seed and food to the peasants during the cultivation season.[100]

A more assertive defense of the role of the rich landlord was put forward by Yeh Shih of the Southern Sung, not because he was totally oblivious to the sufferings of the poor, the injustice of unequal tenure and tenancy, or the corruption of the bureaucracy, but because he was thoroughly skeptical of well-field Utopianism. In his view, for all the talk of restoring the well fields of the Chou or "repressing the rich" (by confiscating their land), neither had been done since the founding of the Northern Sung, and for good reason. Even if the Sung had been able to gain total control of all land in the empire, the well fields could never be restored even if the sage kings Wen and Wu and the Duke of Chou were around to administer the system because the system was too complex to work. In ancient times emperors had only small states to govern and could leave the fiefs to the feudal lords; in the Sung the officials of the central bureaucracy had responsibility for the whole empire but were unable to perform their duties because of the frequent rotation of magistrates. For that matter, even in the Chou period it had not been possible to adopt the well-field system everywhere. The well fields were inseparable both from the feudal system and the complex system of ditches and dikes of Chou times and the former could not survive the demise of the latter. The problem for contemporary times was thus not a literal restoration of the well-field system but the elimination of poverty.

The other popularly advertised means to this end was the "suppression of the rich," that is stopping the accumulation of land by confiscation and redistribution to the poor. The ruler would have to be fully secure politically to carry this out; otherwise he would be inundated by protests and suits by the rich landlords and forced to devote all his time to adjudicating such cases. Furthermore, since the Sung government had lost the power and ability to support the common peasant, the rich landlords were indispensable to the agrarian and peasant economy. It was the rich who rented land to the peasants, loaned them what they needed to plant the fields and get through the planting and harvesting seasons, provided them with relief during famine, or employed them as slaves, artisans, and entertainers. The rich supported the people for the emperor and paid the lion's share of public taxes. To be sure, they profited from their activities, but what they got out of the system was equivalent to what they put into it. Officials should therefore not attempt to control or restrict their accumulation of land; they should only admonish them to reform their ways.

In the end Yeh believed there was nothing that could be done to put land in the hands of the poor, and yet some kind of system could be devised so that after a decade or so there would be no extremes of wealth or poverty and the concentration of land in the hands of a few would come to an end. But he failed to make clear just what the nature of this system would be.[101] In the spectrum of reformist thought in the Sung, Yeh Shih appears to represent the opposite pole from Chang Tsai – pessimistic on the possibility of restoring the well fields, favorable to the landlords, and optimistic about their capacity for moral improvement. Yu's omission of his ideas, as well as the views of Wang An-shih on the contribution of rich landlords, probably indicates that Yu's own prejudices biased his selection of Sung views on reform.

Cadastral Surveys and Progressive Taxation

Despite Yu's neglect of the subject, any discussion of land reform in the Sung should not be confined to the theoretical expositions of scholars because Sung emperors and statesmen did make repeated attempts to rectify inequities in the distribution of land and the land tax. These measures pale by comparison only with the equal-field system of the previous era, for they were restricted in type either to some mode of efficient cadastral survey and registration under the square-field model or some variant of land limitation usually imposed on the families of officials. Unfortunately, Yu Hyŏngwŏn failed to include a discussion of these practical reforms in his account.

The square-field system that was adopted in the Northern Sung in the era of Wang An-shih between 1072 and 1085 and reinstituted under Ts'ai Ching's sponsorship between 1104 and 1120 was a combination of two principles of organization used intermittently since the late T'ang and Five Dynasties period in the early tenth century. One of these principles, usually referred to as an equal-tax system (*chün-shui fa*), was nothing more than progressive taxation based on accurate and periodic land registration and a variable tax rate graded according to the fertility of the land.

The other principle was the laying out of boundary lines around cultivated land in square or grid patterns. This was first attempted in the square fields established along the northern frontier after 986 to provide food rations to soldiers stationed there and to establish bases to interdict the advance of the Khitan invaders. These military colonies were abandoned after the peace treaty with the Khitan in 1004, but the two principles of organization were combined in 1044 with the creation of the thousand-paced square fields (*ch'ien-pu fang-t'ien*). As before, land was laid out in squares and tax rates were graded according to the fertility of the land, but in place of the previous system of self-reporting, officials were now put in charge of surveying property and assessing taxes. It was attempted only in a few districts and soon abandoned, but it established the model for the system adopted by Wang An-shih.

When Emperor Shen-tsung died and Wang fell from power in 1085, the succeeding administration abolished the system and destroyed both the land survey records and land boundary markers. The system was devoured by the fury of the northern landlords who were the main target of the system – it had not been applied to south China or Ssu-ch'üan. In its reincarnation under Ts'ai Ching from 1104 to 1120, the system ceased to benefit the smallholders for whom it was designed because of irregular and inaccurate assessments.[102]

The Southern Sung Limited-Field System

An attempt was also made in the Southern Sung period to adopt a version of the limited-field system. As early as 1022 in the Northern Sung an imperial decree had limited the estates of officials to thirty *kyŏng* and of clerks to fifteen, but the order was abandoned almost immediately afterward.[103] In 1172 under Emperor Hsiao-tsung of the Southern Sung there was a revision of the laws governing the exemption of officials from labor service. Prior to this time officials were exempted from labor service (and land taxes?) levied on units of land area from a high of 100 *kyŏng* for first rank officials to 10 *kyŏng* for ninth rank officials. Land held in excess of those limits were to be subject to ordinary taxes and service required of commoner households; it was not to be confiscated by the state as called for by some advocates of a limited-field system. The reform of 1172 only reduced the limits to a range of 50 to 5 *kyŏng*. A century later Sun Meng-kuan complained that the Sung statutes limiting the tax exemptions of families of officials had lapsed; if they were only enforced, it would be possible to curtail the accumulation of landholdings even without forcing members of these official families to perform labor service.

In 1263 Emperor Li-tsung responded by ordering a land limitation scheme to be tried out in six districts in the province surrounding the capital. Families of officials were limited to a theoretical maximum of 50 to 5 *kyŏng* of land depending on rank, and commoners were limited to 5 *kyŏng*. The law, however, did not call for the state to confiscate all amounts over the limit and no provision was made for distribution of land to the poor. Instead the authorities were empowered to purchase only one-third the surplus, which was then converted to public land (*kung-t'ien*, *kongjŏn* in Korean) cultivated by tenancy or subcontracting. The income from this public land was then used to pay for military provisions so that the previous system of forced requisitions could be eliminated. In subsequent revisions of the law, the limit for commoners was reduced to 200 and 100 *myo*. As Sudō Yoshiyuki pointed out, however, this late Southern Sung *kung-t'ien* system was but a pale shadow of Shih Tan's proposal in the late Former Han dynasty, which called for a limit of 30 *kyŏng* and confiscation of all surplus land.[104]

What the history of reform in the Northern and Southern Sung reveals is that the power of the landlords precluded any possibility of a centralized, imperial bureaucracy nationalizing all land, confiscating surpluses over fixed limits, or even carrying out a successful program of registration and progressive tax assessment. Wang An-shih's square-field system was dismantled by a regime sympathetic to landlords. Ts'ai Ching's attempted restoration of the square-field system was undermined by a corrupt bureaucracy acting in collusion with landlords and tax-cheaters. Emperor Li-tsung's public field system was conservatively conceived from the outset, in terms of the limits imposed on land, the penalties for retaining surpluses, and the area of its implementation. If Yu Hyŏngwŏn had paid as much attention to the failure of these attempts at land limitation as to the theoretical plans of the scholars, it might have dampened his idealism.

Yu's Treatment of the Sung

In summary, the Sung discussion of models of land reform stressed the importance of adopting some method that would guarantee equitable distribution of land to the peasants. Almost everyone agreed that the well-field model represented perfection, but only a few like Chang Tsai thought it could be restored. Among the rest, opinions were divided on whether reform necessitated confiscation of land from private owners and the creation of a system of public ownership or distribution, or required a compromise with existing private property and landlord/tenant relations to ensure a minimum of equitable distribution until natural tendencies like the division of property among sons would achieve the desired result over time. Similarly, there were different points of view over the question of the inviolability of the 100-*myo* plot; some favored it and others were willing to adjust the size. The latter position placed priority on mathematical estimates of optimum size based on land area, population, and productivity, and in this respect introduced a new element of empirical and rational analysis into the literature of land systems. Last, some Sung thinkers stressed the importance of the fixed plot, marked by physical boundaries, as indispensable to guaranteeing the longevity of any major system of land reform.

Yu on the Spirit of the Well-field System

Yu began his *Pan'gye surok* with a recitation of the evils that resulted from the abolition of the well-field system, a dismal picture that covered every dynasty after the Ch'in and Korean dynasties as well.

> Taxation and service was not regulated and there was no equality between rich and poor. Because of the accumulation of large landholdings [*kyŏmbyŏng*] and the search for profit, the "good people" [*yangmin*] lost their places [*silso*]. It was easy to delete households and population [from the tax and census registers]. Lawsuits proliferated. No distinctions were made between the noble and base in society [*kwich'ŏn mu pyŏlbun*]. Quotas were not clear, and because of this powerful households found it easy to act willfully. Morality and virtue did not

flourish, bribery was the easy thing to do, and there was no foresight in the administration of punishments. The minds of the people were unsettled and customs were crude.

In general there was no one who could again take charge of the affairs of the world. People in charge of the state in this later age merely delayed for time, and there was no reign that lasted as long as the Three Dynasties of antiquity [*san-tai*]. From time to time there were sage rulers and good advisers who were good at government affairs, but the effects of their rule did not last for long, and the reason for this was that there was no basis for the essential core of the world [*ch'ŏnha taech'e*]. It was like a case of a man who builds a room; if he does not build it straight on the foundation . . . , then it topples over.[105]

Yu was not arguing here for the reproduction of the well-field system in toto, just the creation of a structure of government that could restore society as a whole to order, and he presumed that the reform of the land system based on principles embodied in the well-field system was critical to this end.

Even though there might be a ruler who wants to govern [well], if he does not rectify the land system, then the production of the people can never be stabilized, taxes can never be equalized, [the numbers of] households and population can never be made clear, the rank and file of the army can never be put in order, lawsuits can never be stopped, punishments can never be reduced, bribery can never be eliminated, and mores can never be restored to health. There has never been a person who can govern and teach [the people] in a situation like this.

What is the reason for a situation like this? Land is the great root of the realm. Once the root is established, all things will follow along and there is nothing that will not be done correctly. If the great root is in confusion, in all other matters there will be nothing that is not done incorrectly.[106]

It then followed that the well-field system provided the model for rectification of the land system, and the essential features of the well-field system could be reduced to a few necessary principles. The first of these was the concept of *kongjŏn*, which was transformed from the lord's field of the Chou feudalism to the concept of public or national ownership of land in the post-Chou age of central bureaucracy. The lord's square in Mencius's description of the well-field pattern was called *kongjŏn*, but in later periods the term underwent a change in meaning and became public, national, or state land. Yu not only used the term in this sense, but also argued that the principle of state or national ownership of land was inherent in the meaning of the term in the Chou well-field context.[107] By so doing Yu borrowed the convention that conferred legitimacy on public ownership in the era of centralized bureaucracy, thereby enabling the state to issue land grants and demand the return of land from grantees after their eligibility had run out to secure a system of equal or equitable distribution of land to peasant families. In addition, the well-field system also entailed the use of land units of constant size marked by fixed boundaries as the basis for both distribution and taxation, and these bounded squares provided a powerful symbol of stability and constancy.

The well-field system also included the principle of using publicly owned land for providing stable economic support, not simply for incumbent officials, but also for a *sadaebu* type of ruling class that transcended the narrow definition of officeholding. In the well-field system this was done by the *ch'aeji*, a cross between a prebend and a fief, but in the later age of centralized bureaucracy, another device had to be found to approximate this principle.[108]

As mentioned in the previous chapter, Yu believed that the equal-field system of the T'ang and Koryŏ [*sic*] had succeeded in approximating the well-field model by replacing private ownership with a public ownership or *kongjŏn* system and by providing plots of equal (or relatively equivalent) size to the peasant cultivators and their families. It failed, he added, because the use of individuals or able-bodied adult males as the criteria of land grants, taxation, and military service broke down under the pressure of population movement, and the natural tendency of bureaucrats toward corruption and maladministration permitted the reappearance of private property. Similarly, the intent of the limited-field concept to check the growth of private estates was admirable, but the system was flawed because it tolerated the existence of private property, thereby violating the requirement that some form of *kongjŏn* or public ownership of land was necessary.[109] If the defects of the equal-field and limited-field models could be overcome, then the essence of the well-field model could be transposed to a post-feudal centralized, bureaucratic environment.

Yu did not intend to recreate the total Chou historical context, let alone the well-field system in every feature, because the feudal age belonged to an irretrievable past. For example, one objection to the use of the well-field model was that it required broad expanses of flat land to lay out nine-square grids, but he argued that this kind of fundamentalist literalism was misguided and unnecessary. A system of equal plots of land could readily be adapted to terrain like Korea's, where alluvial plains were interrupted with hills and rocky outcroppings, a point that he had learned from the Ch'eng brothers and Chang Tsai.[110] A literal restoration of the well-field system was not necessary, only a successful adaptation of the essence of the well-field model to his own time.

> If we could in accordance with present circumstances take into consideration the intention of the ancients and put it into practice, we would have a method. With regard to the shape of the land, it would not be necessary to have broad (and flat) fields, and the system would still be all right. It would not be necessary to set up the lord's fields [*kongjŏn*], and we could still tithe the land. It would not be necessary to establish *ch'aeji* [prebend/fiefs for the *sadaebu*], and [yet] every one [among the *sadaebu*] would still obtain support.
>
> If it were in accordance with the principles of nature [*chayŏn ji ri*] and if changes were adapted to present-day circumstances, then all people would

obtain what [they require] and all plans would turn out well. Even though you would not delineate the shape of a well-field, the essence of the well-field system would still be contained in it. And you also would not have to worry about the difficulties of the T'ang and Koryŏ dynasties. If it were most fair [*kong*] and correct, it could be put into practice for a long time. If it were most simple and confined to essentials, there is no place where it would not be appropriate.[111]

CHAPTER 8

Redistributing Wealth through Land Reform

"If [land] is publicly [owned], the people will have regular production, the minds of the people will be settled, moral transformation can be accomplished, mores and customs can be good, and in all things there will be nothing in which each person does not obtain his share. If [land] is privately [owned], everything will be contrary to this."[1]

"The implementation of this law will not involve officials taking away land from the people!"[2]

FUNDAMENTAL PRINCIPLES OF LAND REFORM

Public over Private Property

Yu Hyŏngwŏn believed firmly that the principles of the well-field system could not be adapted to his own time unless private property were abolished and land tenure and distribution carried out in the context of public ownership. He defended his *kongjŏn* or public land system and contrasted it with the defects of *sajŏn* or privately owned land in the form of a dialogue with his anonymous adversary, that ghostly figure who pursued Yu throughout his book to carp at his proposals and to provide him with a foil for the elaboration of his arguments.[3]

In laying out the details of his *kongjŏn* system Yu had argued that it was the best way to achieve equality and adequacy of income for the peasant cultivator, sufficient economic support for a *sadaebu* elite, and wealth and power for the state. Private property, by contrast, had produced a situation where "at the present time only 10 percent of the population possess large amounts of land while 80 to 90 percent of the population has no land at all!"[4] The abolition of private property was essential to the achievement of his goals:

> If [land] is publicly [owned], the people will have regular production, the minds of the people will be settled, moral transformation can be accomplished, mores and customs can be good, and in all things there will be nothing in which each

person does not obtain his share. If [land] is privately [owned], everything will be contrary to this and that is all there is to it. Moreover, if this method [of public ownership] is carried out, then food will be as common as water and fire. How could you have [the same] situation that exists in the present age?[5]

The argument was both moral and utilitarian: a system of public ownership would not only provide the economic foundation for the moral transformation of the populace, it would also increase production and wealth for the state as a whole.

Yu's adversary, however, charged that the abolition of private property was impractical, unworkable, and dangerous, and that the *kongjŏn* system contained serious flaws.

When this method is first implemented, the wealthy will not escape difficulty. At the present time the [rich] people live in idleness, do not study, and are without virtue, and the wealthy people in the village who have fields that extend in breadth beyond natural boundaries and are lined up one after the other, definitely exceed what is due them. These people have long become accustomed to wealth. If all of a sudden this were to be taken away from them, it would be too difficult for human nature to bear. We should treat them with leniency.[6]

Since the landowners were too jealous of their private lands to give them up without a struggle, to soften opposition to confiscation, large landowners ought to be allowed to purchase sinecures or honorary posts that would include extra land grants and exemptions from military service.[7]

Yu replied that this problem did indeed require some adjustment, but it would not be necessary to provide sinecures with temporary land grants and military service exemptions because his method for nationalizing land would not be based on the use of force!

The implementation of this law *will not involve officials taking away land from the people!* [emphasis mine] The [authorities] will calculate the [number of people and the amount of land] and divide up and grant [land to them]. Each of the people will naturally hope to receive [land], and the wealthy will naturally divide up [their land] among their sons and slaves [à la Lin Hsün]. Nothing more will be done than to establish a nominal requirement for military service [*ipho ch'ulbyŏng*] and that is all. Accordingly if a [wealthy] household worth 1,000 gold [units] has its property reduced, in the end it will definitely be better off than the poor people are now.[8]

In other words, the rich would not feel the pain of confiscation because they would simply transfer title to land to their sons, relatives, and slaves, who would be the ones who would end up performing military service, not the old wealthy families. Yu's position here was only slightly more radical than the formula of

Lin Hsün of the Southern Sung, who counted on the division of property among heirs and a limited-field plan as the means for a gradual transition toward equality of landownership. Lin tolerated private ownership but Yu ruled it out.

Could Yu have possibly believed that wealthy landowners would have regarded confiscation as little more than a slight modification of existing land relations? Was this simply a case of naïveté or a rationalization forced by his basic unwillingness to use force against the landowning class? In fact, how much chance was there that a *kongjŏn* system could be achieved without confiscation?

Yu refused to accept the suggestion that landowners be compensated with sinecures on the grounds that it would continue to stimulate competition among the people for accumulating property. Creating special considerations for certain people would also be contrary to the method of the sages for establishing institutions designed to benefit the public at large. If a total system such as his plan for nationalization and redistribution were adopted, "then every man will obtain his place and rest secure in his share. It will not be necessary to twist the law in order to benefit [certain] people."[9]

As we will see, however, Yu's ideal social system contained a number of regulations supporting inequalities. He could only have meant here that landowners were not entitled to special privileges just because they owned land or were wealthy.

The adversary then switched to a different tack. Although he agreed that private property had led to the accumulation of large holdings by the rich and the pauperization of the mass of the peasantry, because of the attachment of private owners to their land, land reform could only be achieved by recognizing private ownership and limiting the size of holdings as in the Han dynasty. "Those who have too much land will be permitted to sell it off, and those who have too little will [obtain] sufficient amounts by buying it."[10]

Yu, however, rejected this statement of the ideas of Tung Chung-shu, Su Hsün, Lin Hsün, and others on both practical and moral grounds. Yu's practical argument was that government officials would not be able to keep up with the changes in population and ownership of land under a system of free purchase and sale, and "the corruption and deceit [by those seeking to avoid registration] will be too bothersome."[11] This point was obviously reminiscent of the fears of Tu Yu in the *T'ung-tien*. Under a system of national ownership, however, the officials would be able to lay the foundation for accurate record keeping at the outset by rectifying land boundaries and registering households and adult males liable for military service despite shifts in population.[12]

Practicality was not the only consideration, however. Yu also believed that a land limitation system could not work because private property itself provided the opportunity and stimulus for man's greed: driven by avarice, man would find a way around the law and not even the use of punishment would ensure compliance with a land limitation system. In fact, to set limits on landholdings and fix penalties for violations while allowing the people to continue to engage in purchase and sale would be tantamount to entrapment, and if and when the implementation of punishments became lax "in the slightest, the law will be ignored."[13]

Yu's third objection to a limited land system arose from his concern that private ownership caused the division of families and the weakening of family and village solidarity, and jeopardized the economic well-being of the ruling class. Yu's imaginary adversary argued that a public land system would force fathers and sons to live apart from one another because once a son attained majority, Yu's land allotment system would require that the son be given his own separate parcel of land. If all the available land near the village had been used up already in land grants, the son would have to be assigned a parcel in a distant village.

Yu responded that, to the contrary, private ownership was more likely to cause the separation of close kin than a public land system. The reason why Shang Yang of the Ch'in dynasty abolished the well-field system, Yu asserted, was because "he hated the fact that fathers, sons, and elder and younger brothers of the people were living in the same place," and he sought to divide them up. Yu did not explain why, but we may surmise that family solidarity may have interfered with the Ch'in state's ability to control individuals and to move cultivators freely from overpopulated districts to underpopulated ones to maximize agricultural production. In any case, Yu argued that the legacy of Shang Yang was carried over into the later age of centralized bureaucracy, "making it easy for fathers and sons to be separated from one another and scattered about."[14] Yu implied that since the abolition of the well-field system signified the end of public land and the beginning of private property, it was private land that caused the break-up of the family unit, a "phenomenon that was definitely not a matter of concern under a public land system."[15] Yu's argument may seem strange to a modern, Western audience long used to thinking of industrialized urbanism as the proper setting for the fractured family, but evidently even in a traditional Korean village real families failed to live up to an ideal of solidarity, and Yu attributed the cause to private property.

Yu asserted he could prove his point by considering what took place in his own time. If a man had many sons, the only means available to him to provide them with land was to buy land wherever he could find it. If land was not available nearby, he had to purchase it in a distant place. Furthermore, if someone died and no longer utilized his land, the owner or heirs were under no obligation to sell it to anyone else. Under a public land system, however, the law would require the transfer of the land of a deceased person to another individual. Or if the owners of land under a system of private property did choose to sell the land of a deceased member of the family, anyone who needed the land would have to have sufficient capital to purchase it. Under a public land system need, not money, would qualify one for a land grant. Yu concluded: "Therefore, under which of the two systems would it be easier to cause fathers and sons to live in different places – under a system of public land or a system of private land?"[16]

Certain apparent anomalies are revealed by consideration of Yu's remarks on this question. Is it not strange after all that a Confucian like Yu who was so committed to family solidarity should have argued that state ownership and bureaucratic control, and not private ownership under the control of the paterfamilias, was the best means of achieving the family unity? Is it not also anomalous that the Confucian paragon of evil, Shang Yang, the early Legalist architect of the all-powerful centralized state, should have been responsible not for the nationalization of private property but the *creation of private property*? In Yu's thinking, the centralized state may be good or bad depending on what it did; its proper role was to be the agent for the achievement of familial good and village solidarity rather than either the maximization of state power (Chinese Legalism) or the freedom of the individual (Western liberalism and capitalism). Yu's concept of the state bears only slight resemblance to the modern welfare state insofar as he approved of state intervention in society to achieve the moral goal of equitable economic distribution that individual men could not achieve on their own.

There is some doubt, however, whether Yu's concern about keeping fathers and sons in the same village community was simply a matter of village solidarity. In another section of the debate he raised the question again, but in what appears as a Freudian slip, he revealed that he was specifically concerned about the scions of elite households.

> [Under a *kongjŏn* or public landownership system], if a father is an official [*taebu*] and his son a scholar [*sa*], then even though the rank [by which they would be entitled to land grants of different sizes] might be different, there will be nothing to obstruct their receipt of land. But if a system of private land is in operation and there is no way for them to receive land from the officials, their families will have to purchase land for their sons in advance, and those sons of officials who are not yet officials themselves will be forced to sell off their surplus land [*yŏjŏn*].[17]

In other words, Yu was concerned about guaranteeing a stable income for the families of the *sadaebu* in place of the insecurities posed by total reliance on officeholding (especially because of the limited number of posts and the dangers of factional politics) or the purchase of private land in the open market. By no means were his sympathies confined to the lower orders of society.

Having disposed of the idea of limiting landownership, Yu turned his attention next to the possibility of limiting sharecropping and rent. His adversary suggested that in place of Yu's public ownership plan, a law should be promulgated requiring large landowners to rent out all land that they could not cultivate themselves to sharecroppers at a rental rate no higher than 20 percent of the crop, with taxes to be paid by the landlord out of his share – a plan reminiscent of Lin Hsün's proposal. "If done like this, then peasants with labor [power] will be able to support their labor, and those who do not cultivate their land themselves will have no way to profit from excess land, . . . and the evil of accumulating surplus land [*kyŏmbyŏng*] will naturally die out."[18]

Yu found the idea of government-controlled sharecropping no more congenial than limited ownership because it was still based on private property and unrestricted private transactions. Magistrates would not be able to control such a system, and the landowners would rely on deceit and fraud to get around the restrictions. He, therefore, insisted that regulated tenancy would not be as good as a land limitation system.[19]

Yu also argued that sharecropping was intrinsically flawed because it inhibited productivity – at the present time the large landowners had excessive amounts of land and insufficient labor to cultivate it, while the landless peasants were vagrants who did not engage in cultivation. The result was that there was much uncultivated wasteland around the country. This problem had been solved by sharecropping by which the landless vagrants exchanged their labor for land that they rented from the large landowners, but sharecropping was faulty because

> those who have no land and who temporarily cultivate the land of others every year find it difficult to regard as regular the possession of that which is not their own. Therefore, they also do not give a thought to proper fertilization, and that is why a lot of land is not fertilized. If my method is adopted, there will be no wasteland and all the land will be diligently worked. If you calculate all the production from the land [under my system], then compared to the present not only will it be doubled, but year after year, forever, you will have constant production that is double [what it is at present]. How then would it be that foodstuff would not be [as plentiful and common] as water and fire?[20]

Yu conceded here that sharecropping was not an illogical way to share land and labor, but that tenants had less incentive to make labor and fertilizer inputs on rented land than on their own private holdings. It would seem that logical consistency would have required Yu to advocate the retention of private property in a land reform program to increase the incentives for maximizing production. But as we have seen, Yu rejected private property in any form because he was much more interested in achieving the moral goal of an equitable distribution of wealth in society (i.e., a decent income for the peasantry if not equality with the ruling class) than in maximizing production. Yet to persuade his opponents, he argued that public ownership was a better means to stimulate incentive than private ownership because tenancy had robbed the tenants of any real hope of maximizing their income.

This contradiction can be explained, but not fully resolved, by considering Yu's understanding of the nature of his one-*kyŏng* family plot in his *kongjŏn* or public field system and its roots in the so-called private fields of the well-field system. In the well-field system peasants were supposed to have had their own private fields that they cultivated in addition to the lord's public field. Although these private fields were not privately "owned," they were private enough to guarantee a sense of attachment on the part of the peasants so that they would be motivated to devote time and effort in cultivation.

Yu probably felt that the recipient of a state-granted plot would have a greater incentive to produce than the sharecropper who had no sense of attachment to the land at all. The concept of the family plot was essentially different from modern Communist systems of collectives or state farms, which more ruthlessly dissociated the peasant cultivators from the land. Nonetheless, Yu's position was fundamentally contradictory because he supposed that public ownership of land would both eliminate greed and stimulate labor and other inputs. Most modern economists would assume that the advantage of private ownership of land was based on the incentive provided by the opportunity to maximize wealth, which to a Confucian or any other kind of moralist should be tantamount to greed.

Yu obviously did not think through the logical implications of his argument. He must have assumed that by some mystical mechanism the incentive to produce engendered by granting a plot to a family would reach its natural limit once subsistence had been achieved and that the desire for greater wealth would be satiated and assuaged, or that it would stimulate greater production but prevent endless maximization of wealth by forbidding purchase of surplus land.

Economic Security for the Sadaebu *Elite*

Yu's final reason for opposing sharecropping or tenancy was that it could not ensure economic security for an ideal *sadaebu* elite because it would require their nonofficial members to engage in agricultural labor as the only way to earn a living.

> If you do not restore regulations for the nurturing of scholars and just want to do it like this [i.e., just have a system of regulated tenancy], then the *taebu* [officials], those eligible for office who do not have posts, and their sons and descendants who are local Confucian scholars, down to the clerks who work for the officials, and their orphaned children and widows will all lose what they rely on for support. These are the people who do not want to accumulate large amounts of land and who do not want to seek profit, but this method [tenancy regulation] would destroy altogether the purpose behind making distinctions between the superior man of virtue [*kunja*] and the man of the fields [*yain*]. It will only allow those who carry their rakes and hoes in their hands [i.e., peasants] to obtain food, while the officials and scholars [*taebusa*] will have no way to take care of themselves. Indeed, this is not the way things ought to be done in the world.[21]

Lest his reader miss the *locus classicus* of the reference to the *kunja/yain* distinction, Yu referred him in a footnote to Confucius and Mencius, the latter of whom distinguished between those who worked with their minds and those who worked with their hands. In fact, Yu chose this spot as the place to issue his clearest statement about the necessity for a class of officials and scholars set apart from the common herd: "For truly if the court has no hereditary officials [*sesin*] and the country is poor in itinerant scholars, how would this be of any benefit to the people or the state?"[22]

As if this were not clear enough, he expanded on the theme in a footnote:

> In the final analysis you must have a scholar-official [class] [*taebusa*], and that is all there is to it. Those who are noble [*kwija*] can not suddenly become men who grow crops. If those who do not engage in cultivation find it difficult to feed themselves, this is bad. If the officials [*taebu*] have salaries and you allow the scholars [*sa*] to seek emoluments by advancing in competition, and the corrupt clerks devote themselves to seeking bribes, then not only will you produce a situation like what exists at present, but the way of [knowing] shame [i.e., having a proper sense of ethics] will be lost and fraud and thievery will become customary.[23]

This is an important passage that requires some explication. By hereditary officials (*sesin*), Yu did not mean that access to official posts in the state bureaucracy should be locked up by a hereditary aristocracy. Yu was talking about a class of morally superior men who had to be freed from the demeaning aspects of grubbing for a living by manual labor in the fields as peasants, by engaging in bribery and extortion as clerks, by competing in the examination system with other scholars for degrees and posts, or presumably by vying for profits in the marketplace. As he made clear in his discussion of education and recruitment, he was prepared to allow men of the scholar-official class who failed to maintain standards of virtue and scholarship to be flushed out of the ruling class (albeit with some leeway for them to reform their ways), but until they demonstrated their incapacity, they were entitled to support by the state, which could only be ensured by a system of public ownership and distribution.

Guaranteed Peasant Subsistence

To be sure, Yu was also concerned with the livelihood of the peasantry, which had been undermined by private property.

> Moreover . . . once you fail to set limits to the land, then you can not in the end equalize poverty and wealth. Also, if you do not distribute [taxes and military service] on the basis of land, then those who escape labor [and military] service will increase in numbers and become vagrants. In general, if you do not restore a system of public ownership of land [*kongjŏn*], then in making laws for all matters, not one of them will be done right.[24]

His goal was stability of income for the producing peasant, not necessarily absolute equality of income. An approximation of equality would be sufficient. For example, his adversary remarked that equality of income could not be achieved under Yu's proposed land grant system because some land was rice paddy land and some dry bean fields and the rates of productivity varied between them. Yu replied that this was not a matter for concern because even after the nationalization of land the people would be granted the leeway to make private exchanges of different types of land or enter into private agreements to swap labor for land as long as it was confined to the village. "Among relatives and neighbors naturally there could be mutual adjustment in accordance with the circumstances."[25] Even though some would end up with all dry land and others with all paddy land, the situation would still be equitable and certainly preferable to present circumstances where large numbers of peasants had no land at all. In any case, the northern part of the country consisted mostly of dry fields while the southern part was mostly paddy land. Nationalization would not change this situation and the peasants could work out minor problems through mutual agreement.[26]

Obviously Yu was willing to tolerate the private exchange of land within the context of a public ownership system because the abolition of private property would sanitize the private transaction, converting it from a mechanism for the satisfaction of greed and desire into a simple means for the cooperative exchange of goods and services. Once society was rid of the profit motive, social solidarity would operate to ensure harmonious relations in the village community.

Yu, of course, felt constrained to demonstrate that his system of distribution would guarantee equality of income to the peasant cultivator and his family. He had to show not only that each family would get the same sized plot but also that there was sufficient land in the country to guarantee a grant to everyone, and he went to great lengths to present the mathematical evidence for this. In addition, in his debate with his adversary he responded directly to the charge that the *kongjŏn* system would result in unequal distribution in places with high population density or a high man/land ratio, a popular argument against the feasibility of restoring the well fields by the more practical reformers of Chinese history (see chap. 5).

He began his defense with a patently nonempirical statement of blind faith.

> In the creative and transforming power of nature [*ch'ŏnji chohwa*] there is no such principle [i.e., where nature would allow for disparities of a local or regional nature between people and land]. The relationship between living beings and land is similar to the relationship between fish and water [lit., the way man is born on the land is like the way fish are born in the water]. I have never heard of a case where there were too many fish and not enough water to sustain them.[27]

He made this statement only by way of introduction, however, for his main point was that minor inequalities or discrepancies that might result from an imperfect system of public ownership and distribution were as nothing compared to the major inequalities that plagued the system of private property.

> Should we be unconcerned about the fact that at present one man may monopolize control over large areas of land [*kyŏmbyŏng*] while the mass of the people

> have no land at all, [or should we] be concerned over the fact that after land is equally distributed to all the people [under my *kongjŏn* system] there might be a few people left over [who do not get a sufficient share]? . . . It is only that in the case of public land, [tenure and distribution] is fair [*kong*] and equal [*kyun*], but in the case of private land, it is private [*sa*] and skewed [*p'yŏn*].[28]

And, he continued, only a public land system could guarantee constant production for everyone, the necessary material foundation for moral transformation.[29]

Rejection of More Practical Administrative Reforms

Overwhelmed by Yu's Socratic skill in destroying the case for either land limitation or regulated tenancy, Yu's adversary had to concede that public ownership might indeed be the best system. Nevertheless, if it proved too difficult to carry out right away because of potential opposition, it might be better to adopt as an interim measure a major cadastral survey of the land and the use of a tally system of registration (*hop'ae*) (to identify people for labor or military service).[30] Yu was not disposed favorably to this method either because "it would require constant bother and easily lead to corruption . . . and the results obtained would be shallower and of shorter duration."[31] Land parcels might be recorded on the registers, but land boundaries would not be clearly established on the land itself. Adopting a tally system would be as troublesome as confiscation but without any effect. There would be no correlation between land and people or between the distribution of land and the distribution of tax and labor or military service. Under a tally system people would seek to avoid registration to evade service obligations, but under his public ownership and distribution scheme they would not avoid registration because it would guarantee them a land grant. The common people would thus have every reason to obey the law.[32]

Weights and Measures

Yu's plan for land reform also included a small treatise on the need for standardization of weights and measures not only because he had proposed replacing the *kyŏl-bu* system based on a constant unit of crop volume by a unit of area based on linear measurement, but because one of the major causes of peasant exploitation was the manipulation of weights and measures by tax clerks to extort higher payments. He believed that a return to the simplicity and standardization of ancient standards could solve many of the problems of contemporary Korean society.

Yu realized that the superiority of a system of standardized weights and measures for the whole nation had been clearly elucidated in *The Book of History* (*Shu-ching*). The sage Emperor Shun had seen to it that all the pitch-pipes, linear and volume measures, and balances all conformed to standards whenever he went on hunting expeditions throughout his empire. The policy of maintaining standard measures was followed later, from the Hsia through Chou dynasties. Even Lord Shang in the Ch'in state that eventually unified China saw fit to standardize weights and measures even though he made no attempt to preserve the specifications of the ancients. After the fall of the Chou, the Former Han dynasty maintained its own sets of standards in copper and bamboo, but unity was lost after the fall of the dynasty and problems were created by the existence of different standards of weight and measure. Yu believed that the key to restoring those standards was to cast weights and measures primarily in copper, store them in the palace, and distribute copies to the provinces.[33]

Yu himself defensively asserted that he was not a rigid fundamentalist in deriving certain ideas for land reform from classical models, but rather that he based his proposals on what we today would call the use of both reason and empirical investigation. He pointed out that in the seventeenth century Koreans were used to subdividing the basic unit of grain volume, the *sŏm* (*sŏk* in Sino-Korean pronunciation, *shih* in Chinese), into 15 *mal* (*tu* in Sino-Korean pronunciation), but he preferred to use a scheme based on the decimal system. He proposed that the term *kok* (*hu* in Chinese) would replace the *sŏm* and would consist of 10 *mal* instead of the fifteen in a *sŏm*, and he justified this substitution on the basis of the ease of calculation in a decimal system. Since the *kok* had not been used for *sŏm* in ancient China and began only in the nefarious Ch'in dynasty, one might conclude that Yu was opting for rationality over historical legitimacy.[34]

Yu has also become famous for his plan to eliminate the Korean *kyŏl-bu* system and replace it with the Chinese *kyŏng-myo* units of areal measurement. The *kyŏng* and *myo* were units of land area (100 *myo* = 1 *kyŏng*) based on a standard linear foot, but the *kyŏl* and *pu* were by Yu's time terms for land area based on a standard unit of grain volume produced by different areas of land depending on the fertility of the land. He pointed out that his contemporaries were reluctant to abandon the *kyŏl-bu* system because they mistakenly believed it had originated in the Samhan period (ca. the third century B.C. to the fourth century A.D. in the southern part of the peninsula), but he had discovered that the term *kyŏl* could not have been in use even by the early Koryŏ period because the term *kyŏng* was still in use in the reign of King T'aejo, the founder of Koryŏ (r. 918–943), and the cadastral survey of 949 determined grades of land on the basis of a standard linear foot and standard units of area with variable tax rates to adjust for differences in productivity, suggesting that the *kyŏng-mu* system was still in use. If a *kyŏl-bu* system had been in use, a progressive tax system would have functioned by keeping the tax rate constant and varying the size of the *kyŏl* and *pu* according to the fertility of the land. Yu concluded that the *kyŏl-bu* system must have been established relatively late in the middle of the Koryŏ period, certainly not by the ancient Chinese sages, and even if it had been established in the Samhan period, that was certainly not the essence of sage wisdom: "We should only be discussing whether [the *kyŏl-bu* system] is proper or not. What difference does it make if it began in the Samhan period?"[35]

Yu believed that the *kyŏng-mu* system was easier to implement, less susceptible to corruption, and more likely to ensure fair and progressive taxation. He reported that at the beginning of the Chosŏn dynasty the *kyŏl* was defined as equivalent to 57 Chinese *myo* (8.64 acres at 6.6 *myo* per acre?), and taxes were kept uniform by calculating production from six grades of land in a bumper crop year. The standard difference in productivity between each of the six grades was 12 *sŏm*, and the taxes were levied at a standard rate of 1/20 or 5 percent of the crop (see table 1).

TABLE 1
RICE PRODUCTION AND TAX BY GRADE

Grade	Rice Production		Tax
(land)	(unhulled) (*sŏm*)	(hulled) (*sŏm*)	
1	80	40	30 *mal* (2 *sŏm*)
2	68	38	25 *mal* 5 *toe**
3	56	28	21 *mal*
4	44	22	16 *mal* 5 *toe*
5	32	16	12 *mal*
6	20	10	7 *mal* 5 *toe*

* One *toe* equals .1 *mal*.

Later in the dynasty the government adopted a system of six specific grades of *kyŏl*, each with a different area. The *kyŏl* was defined as a square consisting of 100 "feet" of length on each side, but to provide for six different sizes of *kyŏl* there had to be six different standards, linear "feet" defined in units of the "Chou foot." Yu listed the lengths of the six standard "feet" and gave the equivalent area of the six *kyŏl* in terms of the Chinese *myo* (1/100 *kyŏng*) at the time.[36] Note that grade 1 land was 4.22 times more productive than the lowest, grade 6 (see table 2).

TABLE 2
RELATION OF FERTILITY AND SIZE OF FIELDS

Grade of *kyŏl*	Area in *myo*	Ratio (*x*/grade 1)
1	36	—
2	44.7 *pun*	1.24
3	54.2 *pun*	1.51
4	69	1.92
5	95	2.64
6	152	4.22

Yu also summarized the difference between the two systems as follows: "Under the *kyŏng* method of measurement the area of the land is the same but there are grades of tax in accordance with the fertility of the land. Under the *kyŏl* system the taxes are all the same, but the *kyŏl* varies in accordance with the fertility of the land."[37]

Yu felt that by using the *kyŏng-mu* system of measurement there was no fear that cultivated land might be hidden from the eye of the tax registrar, even though some mistakes in accounting or bookkeeping might be made if the officials did not maintain surveillance. Under the *kyŏl* system, however, while the tax account ledgers might be easier to keep because the amount of tax was easy to grasp, it would be far more difficult to maintain surveillance over false registration or illegal exemption of land. Because of the complexity of the varying *kyŏl* units, it was impossible for ordinary people to comprehend the method of registration and check the deceit and falsification of the local clerks. "This is why there is no place that does not have the evils of bribery, improper requests, illicit exemptions, and fraud, and in the end taxes are not levied equitably." Because the grades of *kyŏl* were supposed to be determined on the basis of an estimate of uniform production per *kyŏl*, false or erroneous registration required a massive effort to correct because changing the grade of a *kyŏl* of land meant either increasing or decreasing the land area assigned to it, which then required a total resurvey and resetting of boundaries of all other land parcels in the area.[38]

Yu compared the *kyŏng* and *kyŏl* systems to the traditional Confucian dichotomies of essence and function (*ch'e/yong*), root and branch (*pon/mal*): "If you calculate the total by making clear the root, then the numbers will all be before your eyes and the function [or practical utility, *yong*] will reside in it. If you hold on to the branch and apply it to the matter of drawing land boundaries, then the basic land will be in confusion and there will be no way to investigate and rectify it."[39]

He felt that the complexity was so great that even a sage would not be able to rectify the inequalities present in even one *myŏn* (a subdistrict or county), let alone correct the situation for the entire nation. "How much less so considering that there are thousands or ten thousands of [land units] in a *myŏn*, and the officials in charge are not necessarily sages?"[40]

Yu believed that if men were left to themselves, greed, competition, profit-seeking, and confusion would produce gross inequality in the distribution of wealth. Wealth and poverty were not simply the fault of the land system; they were also caused by the diligence or laziness of men, unanticipated natural disasters, or the luck of the natural fertility of the land. The sage's task was "nothing more than making equal [*che*] what can be made equal and striving to do what can be done right," but in the absence of sages, Koreans could replace the *kyŏl* with the *kyŏng* as a means of "making the people equal [*kyunmin*]."[41] Yu suggested that even if contemporary Koreans failed to restore the ancient well-field system in its ancient form, they could at least settle for the adoption of the *kyŏng-myo* method of linear measurment.[42] And he cited Chu Hsi's treatise on the rectification of land boundaries (*Kyŏnggyejang*) to show that Chu had made the same argument: "Thus in China, even though they did not carry out the well-field system [in post-Chou times], they still determined land area in paces [*po*] and *myo* and had nine classifications for tax purposes. We may criticize Korea for not reaching [the heights achieved by] China since ancient times in various matters."[43]

He even extolled the land system of contemporary Tokugawa Japan described in Kang Hang's *Kanyangnok* as superior to contemporary Korean methods: "Even though Japan has vulgar barbarians throughout its islands, they are still able to fix boundaries when making measurements of land and keep the statistics of land and population clear. Could a country known for its respect for rites and righteousness [Korea] not do as well as an island of barbarians?"[44] If Yu had been either a fundamentalist or a nationalist, he would not have made invidious comparisons of Chosŏn Korea with post-Chou China or contemporary Japan.

Was Yu, however, correct in his belief that the inequalities and injustices of the Korean land-tax system were the fault of the *kyŏl-bu* system of measurement? Kim Yongsŏp, the leading scholar of land tenure relations in the late Chosŏn period, thought that the regulations for the grading of land was in fact the key to the state of both state revenues and the peasant agricultural economy, but he has assigned responsibility for the failure to implement these regulations to the irregular and arbitrary decisions of clerks and petty officials in deciding which of the six categories of *kyŏl* was to be chosen to register a specific parcel of land, and what was worse, failure to register the lands of the more influential persons in a community at all. He found that land was hardly ever registered in the highest two grades of *kyŏl* in the three districts he studied, and he assumed that the more prestigious owners were able to register their land in lower categories than the fertility of their land warranted, while the land of the poor peasants was registered in higher categories than they deserved. Furthermore, land surveys that were supposed to be carried out at a national level every twenty years were often neglected. In the seventeenth century, land surveys were carried out in 1601, 1634, 1663, 1665, and 1668–69, and even then sometimes only in a few provinces, but thereafter only in 1719–20 and in the late 1860s under the Taewongun's regime.

In the early nineteenth century Tasan (Chŏng Yagyong) complained bitterly about the failure to carry out a cadastral survey for some time, and in the mid-nineteenth century Yi Kyugyŏng listed twenty different illegalities and distortions in the survey of land that were unrelated to the type of measurement used. He complained primarily of bias in favor of the wealthy, a lack of compassion by the clerks, an excessively mechanical method of establishing boundaries and quotas, putting fallow land on the tax registers and preventing anyone from reclaiming it, relying on the word of the clerks no matter how valid the grievance of the peasant, failure to conduct personal inspections of the land or reduce taxes under famine conditions. He concluded that it would have been better to dispense with surveys altogether.[45]

In short, Kim concluded that as rational and enlightened as Yu's proposal for conversion of land measurement to a decimal system may have been, it was probably far less important than the power relations in the villages and the laxity of administration by clerks. Nonetheless, as we will see in the next chapter, both Tasan and Sŏ Yugu, scholars whom Kim also regarded as the most progressive writers on the land question in the early nineteenth century, also advocated the idea of replacing the *kyŏl-bu* system of measurement with the *kyŏng-mu* system, and both attempted to use the well-field model as a basis for their proposals for the gradual reform of the land system.

Royal Leadership and Popular Obedience

Yu had now come to the point where he had demolished every alternative to the abolition of private property and the nationalization of land, his *kongjŏn* system. A *kongjŏn* system might be as difficult to implement at first, not only because of the problem of confiscation and redistribution, but also because Yu had assumed that the task of redefining land boundaries with the proper dikes and ridges would take about six or seven years to complete.[46] Nevertheless, in addition to achieving the same objective as a survey and census, it would also "equalize and make uniform the rich and the poor," thus gaining the willing compliance of the mass of the people. Once fixed in place a *kongjŏn* system would provide the kind of constancy that was lacking in life itself: "Human beings are sometimes active and sometimes at rest; they live and they die, so that things are never the same. It is not like land which once fixed never changes."[47] Installing a *kongjŏn* system would require a "single great effort that would result in perpetual ease [*illo yŏng'il*]."[48] Since it was a system that would produce the most conformity, simplicity, and security, there was no reason it could not be carried out. And because it had been deemed by sage kings of yore not only as the best, but the only possible system to ensure good government, all that was needed was an enlightened ruler to carry it out:

> When [sage] emperors and kings ruled the states of the world, they had no other method than this. If [the rulers] of the later age in the end were not able to carry it out, in the last analysis it only meant that there was no hope for good government. If a brave and intelligent ruler were boldly to implement it, there would be no difference between ancient times and the present, no difference between the civilized and barbarian [*hwa-i*]. In essence, there would be no reason why it could not be carried out.[49]

But what if the great landowners held fast to their private lands and refused to conform willingly to confiscation? Would Yu then say, as he had with regard to slavery, that the custom of private property was too firmly entrenched to be eliminated at one fell swoop? Would he relegate public ownership to an indefinite future and seek a compromise with existing circumstances on the grounds of practicality? By no means, was his reply, because adoption of the *kongjŏn* system would depend ultimately on the character of the ruler and his ministers.

If we had a king lacking in bright virtue and ministers who all pursued their own personal benefit and profit, then not only would there be no hope whatsoever that this matter could be accomplished, it would even be difficult to preserve the very altars of the state. But if in fact we had a ruler of bright virtue on the throne and ministers who devoted their minds to the benefit of the country, they could do it and manage it and all the people would gladly conform to it with a sincere mind.[50]

Although a few deceitful people might violate the law to profit themselves, most of the people would not join with them in causing trouble. Those few who did would be punished. "I have never heard of a case where humane government was practiced in utmost sincerity [by a ruler of true virtue] where there were people who caused trouble."[51]

We must pause to take note of Yu's insistence on the need for strong royal leadership. Despite Yu's commitment to an institutional approach to reform and his call for the creation of a morally superior *sadaebu* ruling class, the above passages reveal a fundamental Confucian moral faith in the transforming power of the man of virtue that is reflected even in current Korean attitudes in both north and south Korea about the positive and dynamic role of the supreme leader in carrying out economic, social, and political development.[52] This is one of the reasons why Yu's thinking was different from the late Ming and early Ch'ing statecraft writers like Huang Tsung-hsi and Ku Yen-wu, who were more concerned about the problem of imperial despotism or the abuse of power by a ruler. Yu, by contrast, sensed the lack of leadership in his own time and was not fearful of the excesses of despotism.

His emphasis on personal leadership, however, should remind us of the danger of oversimplified interpretations of Korean Confucian political thought. Yu's ideal system was, after all, a combination of elements that might appear contradictory. His ideal state was to consist of classes and institutions that would limit arbitrary despotism, and yet the king was to be a true and forceful leader, not merely a puppet in the hands of a hereditary ruling class.

Yu ended his argument with a theme that repeatedly appears in his writing – an almost Manichaean dichotomy between the dictates of moral principle and the desires and compulsions of an imperfect humanity, expressed in the Neo-Confucian language of the opposition between Heavenly principle (or natural principle) and human desire (*ch'ŏlli* and *inyok*).

In all things of the world, there are only two poles worth considering [*yangdan*] – Heavenly principle and human desire. From the minutest [aspects] of one's single mind to the most distant affairs of the world, everything is governed by one rule. If man preserves Heavenly principle, then human desire will retreat by itself. If he heeds it, he will have good fortune, and every thing will turn out to his advantage. Has anyone ever seen a case where a man preserved Heavenly principle and it caused him harm? What the sages held to be the main thing was

> always principle, and that alone. Where principle was to be found, even though [sage rulers] had to exert the utmost effort to chastise, put to death, attack, and punish [the wrongdoers], they never shrank from it.[53]

And then he provided several examples from Chinese (not Korean!) history to illustrate the difference between resolute leadership and vacillation:

> Emperor Shun's chastising of the four evil ones, King Wen's [of Chou] destruction of fifty states, King Hsüan's [of Chou?] attack against the dog barbarians – all of these are examples of this. It is like a situation where you are lacking a main [goal], where you are half up and half down, afraid of both head and tail. If you are concerned lest the wily and deceitful be resentful, you will not be able to drive the "small men" [men of small virtue] from your midst. If you fear that corrupt clerks might rise up in anger, you will not be able to put a stop to bribery. If you think accommodation and appeasement [*insun kosik*] is the way to run a country, then you would have to acknowledge that Te-tsung of the T'ang's permitting [his generals or regional commanders?] to launch attacks on their own authority was the right policy while Hsien-tsung's bold extermination of rebel [provincial governors?] was a mistaken policy; or that Kao-tsung of the Sung's concluding peace with the [Khitan] enemy was correct, while the righteous desire of his worthy ministers to recover lost territory [in north China] was wrong. Considered from this standpoint, in terms of which [behavior or policy] was right or wrong, which ensured security for the country or endangered it, which would lead to its prosperity and which to its destruction – even though each of the [above] cases is different, the principle is the same [*kisasu kiriil ya*].[54]

The single principle that Yu was thinking of was that a ruler never shrinks from danger in pursuit of a righteous cause, even if it means war against a superior or feared enemy. Perhaps, however, there were other considerations in his mind, particularly in his choice of the contrast between Hsien-tsung's repression of rebels and Te-tsung's toleration of provincial autonomy during the eighth century T'ang period. Hsien-tsung was, after all, one of the best examples in Chinese history of a restorationist king who sought to stem the tide of dynastic decline and assert the power of the throne against the independent power of the provincial governors.[55] Yu was not concerned about provincial autonomy in Korea because that was not a problem, but he was arguing for assertive royal leadership against the private power of the landowning class. The king and the central government would have to provide the power – even the use of military force if necessary – to carry out confiscation if the landowners proved too stubborn. The dauntless resolve of a righteous king could carry the day against the recalcitrant, and lest anyone attempt an anachronistic portrayal of Yu as an early Korean democrat, his admiration for the authoritarian leader was complemented by his regard for the Korean people's capacity for obedient compliance.

> How much the more so [should a righteous king be able to enforce confiscation and enactment of a *kongjŏn* system] when you consider that our people are the type that when you give them orders, they do it, and when you give them guidance, they follow, [let alone the fact that] both great and small, the noble and the base will each obtain his proper share and should [be as happy] as someone plucked out of a state of abject destitution and put in the lap of luxury. The only thing I am concerned about is that the king might not be able to cast off his own private [desires] and keep bright the virtue of his single mind. As for the possibility that rich men might stir up rebellion, it is not something that I worry about.[56]

State Ownership and Distribution by Class and Status

Since Yu Hyŏngwŏn intended to use land reform as the means for the creation of a new society, his ideas can be analyzed in terms of the social class and status groups to be affected by institutional reform. These include the two major components of the lower class of agricultural producers, the commoner or free peasant cultivators and slaves, and the elements of the ruling class such as scholars, officials, members of the royal family, descendants of merit subjects and high officials, nothoi of the upper class, and petty functionaries (an intermediate group that belonged to the upper class in function and to the lower class in status). A third group of merchants, artisans, shamans, actors and performers, and other occupational groups of the nonagrarian and urban economy will be discussed in later chapters. Here we will confine our attention to the agricultural producers and the members of the ruling class.

Commoner Peasant Cultivators

As far as the commoner peasant cultivator was concerned, Yu's reform program constituted a subtle compromise. While he accepted the view that the reproduction of the well-field system was impossible in the age of centralized bureaucracy, he rejected the pessimistic and pragmatic wing of the Chinese land reformers from Tung Chung-shu and Hsün Yüeh of the Han through Lin Hsün and Chu Hsi of the Sung, who claimed that expropriation of land from landlords in the middle of a dynasty was a virtual impossibility and that some compromise with private ownership in the form of a limited-field system had to be made. According to Yu's plan, the state would nationalize all land and issue a plot of one *kyŏng* (or 100 *myo*) to each farmer (*pu*) or farm family. The land tax would be assessed on the land with adjustments for fertility and productivity to achieve a rate close to the ideal tax of 10 percent of the crop. These one-*kyŏng* land units would form the basis for military service requirements for the peasant cultivators. The farmer would not own the land that he received; he would simply "occupy and receive [*chŏmsu*]" one *kyŏng* as a basic allotment.[57]

When a male farmer reached the age of twenty, he would receive his land grant from the state, although in the case of families with many sons, fractional grants might be issued at the age of sixteen. The basic one-*kyŏng* allotment would provide support for a standard extended family, consisting of the farmer, his wife and children, and his parents. Since Yu assumed that the number of household members would vary from five to eight, he was obviously not concerned to create a system of perfect per capita income equality.

Each peasant would have the responsibility of finding a suitable empty plot of land and petitioning the district magistrate to receive his land grant. If the petitioner chose a piece of wasteland, the magistrate would conduct a survey and lay out the boundaries around the one *kyŏng* area and draw up a new register. If more than one individual applied for the same piece of land, the magistrate would have to make a decision along certain guidelines. Assuming that officials might be competing with commoner peasants for the same piece of land, preference had to be given to those with the highest rank; otherwise priority would be afforded to the largest families. If family size were equal, the family with the poorest land would get preference.[58]

If the recipient died, his land would be returned to the state unless he had an heir who was qualified to receive his father's grant in full, or a widow who was entitled to retain a fraction of the original grant for her support, termed *kubunjŏn,* in the style of the early Koryŏ land system. Each farmer was to receive a grant only in the district where he lived. If a person of higher status was authorized to move, he had to receive a signed document from his district magistrate and register with the new magistrate before a land grant would be authorized.[59]

Yu claimed that he had selected the one-*kyŏng* or 100-*myo* unit of land as the basic grant for all peasant families in his system on the grounds of rational calculation rather than fundamentalist literalism because the standard, fixed plot of one *kyŏng* or 100 *myo* in ancient China kept the area of land under cultivation constant and free of confusion.[60] But if it were not fundamentalist literalism that attracted him to the idea of a fixed plot, he appears to have been obsessed with the sense of permanence and security conveyed by the concept of a square etched out of the landscape by means of ridges and dikes, a pattern that he derived from *The Rites of Chou*. He copied out its description of the network of waterways, pathways, and roads that accompanied the well fields and then commented that even if it were not possible to reproduce the classical model in exact form, it was essential to surround the squares with ridges, sluices, paths, and wide roads of specific dimensions. Every fall the district magistrate and a special commissioner would have to make the rounds to investigate these facilities to inspect maintenance, "enforce the law and make punishments of those who failed to keep the law."[61]

He anticipated that the project of redrawing the land boundaries and constructing the earthworks and sluices would take six or seven years. Nevertheless, nationalization and redistribution of land could be done right away, and he was certain that the peasants would observe the boundaries without trespassing against their neighbors, even prior to the completion of the earthworks. After redistribution, the land registers and a standard survey foot would be kept on hand in the *myŏn* or subdistrict office for everyone to see.[62]

Contrary to the early Koryŏ *chŏnsikwa* system, which allocated the woodland surrounding the cultivated fields of the villages to the men of rank and office to provide fuel for heating, Yu reserved such land as commons (*kong*) for animal husbandry and woodcutting. These wood and grazing lands were not to be divided up for occupancy by individuals for their own profit because it would lead to trespass, forcible seizure, and lawsuits, and it would interfere with the fundamental task of setting fixed boundaries for agricultural land. "The *sikwa* [grades of woodland] in Koryŏ times were indeed not the intention of the ancients."[63]

Yu's attitude toward the fishing weirs, salt flats, and marshlands of the coast that had been taken over by the palace estates of royal relatives (the *kungbang*) was similar: he wanted to liberate all of it for the use of the common peasantry either as commons or as individually possessed and taxable specialty land. Fruit and special purpose trees were handled differently, however. Yu proposed that peasants be encouraged to plant trees for fruit, papermaking, varnish, and mulberry on nonarable hilly land, and he allowed such land to be bequeathed to heirs as private property, a minor departure from his general rule of public ownership.[64]

In summary, Yu's land reform would have affected contemporary Korean society in a number of profound ways. Every peasant of commoner status would have been guaranteed a plot of land to occupy and cultivate for his lifetime and a kind of social security plot for his widow and children after his death. Private property together with tenancy and agricultural wage labor would have been eliminated. Cultivation would have been conducted in terms of the family unit so that the contemporary rural pattern of villages composed of clusters of households would have been retained. Woodland, fishing weirs, salt flats, and marshland would have been taken away from private owners and converted to common use for fuel gathering, pasture, or other uses. The guaranteed land grant would also have functioned to resettle wandering peasants on the land and in villages to ensure social, economic, and political stability.

By using one *kyŏng* of land as the basis for assessing taxes and service, changes in the population or migration could not be used as an excuse for the transfer of military support cloth taxes or service to relatives or neighbors, nor would failure to keep up with the census registers allow clerks and magistrates to distribute military service and support taxes unequally or unfairly. Increased benefits would accrue to the state through more tax revenues and more men for military service, and more equity would be secured for the peasant cultivators through reduced per capita tax burdens and a larger manpower pool for military service.

Yu's plan also contained two features that were distinctive components of the early Koryŏ *chŏnsikwa* system: provision for transfer of land allotments to close relatives and the use of the term *kubunjŏn* for residual grants to widows and retired soldiers. It could be argued that this reflected a Korean bias toward family inheritance of property as occurred in early Koryŏ, but Yu unequivocally departed from the *chŏnsikwa* system in two ways. He explicitly provided for land grants to commoner peasants in the fashion of the Chinese equal-field system, and he specifically ruled out the allocation of woodland to officials and declared it to be commons (*kong*) for the peasants. Yu was willing to use the *chŏnsikwa* system as a model because he thought of it as a replica of the T'ang system, but he was not a simple-minded copier of early Koryŏ institutions.

Slaves

Private slaves in the seventeenth century consisted of two components: domestic servants, and those who tilled the land of their masters as tenants, living either in rooms in the master's quarters or in their own homes at some remove from the master's house – wherever the family's scattered parcels of property happened to be located, sometimes in faraway districts. Total manumission of slaves would, of course, have converted all of them to commoners, making them eligible for Yu's standard one-*kyŏng* grant. Since Yu could not bring himself to adopt such a radical position, he sought to work out a compromise by which slavery would be retained and yet slaves could be guaranteed basic land grants and required to perform military service for the state. Nonetheless he required a levy of military service on private slaves that was twice as heavy as commoners (see chap. 10).[65]

Each official slave who was either subject to service for officials (*kwalli noye*) or holders of specific posts (*yuyŏkcha*) would receive a land grant that would be returned to the state at the age of sixty when he retired from his post, and his widow would be entitled to a support grant or *kubunjŏn*.[66] He did not specify the size of a land grant for official slaves with posts, but it was undoubtedly supposed to serve as remuneration for service.

Yu did not make clear whether he expected private slaves, who would now be the recipients of a land grant, to continue to pay sharecropping rent in the form of personal tribute to their masters in addition to a tithe to the state, but judging from the overall context of his discussion he probably did. It is hard, therefore, to see how private outside resident slaves would have been better off under his new system.

Yu admitted that a "true king" ought to abolish hereditary slavery (*nobi seji-bŏp*), but circumstances prevented it.

> Until it is abolished, we have no choice but to grant them land [*sujŏn*], which will make things easier for them than before. The reason, however, that they will be unable to avoid excessive burdens is because this is the way things are. There is nothing that we can do about it. In making plans for the present, we only ought to carry out equitably the matrilineal slave succession law [*chongmobŏp*] so that the problem of an excessive slave population will disappear and the system of the early kings can can accordingly be restored.[67]

Since the matrilineal slave succession law was designed only to reduce the number of slave offspring of mixed commoner/slave marriages, at best a small fraction of total slave marriages, Yu could not have expected that private slaves would benefit too soon from his land reform plan.

Even though slavery was, of course, not part of the well-field system, and hereditary slavery in particular was not justified by either classical or historical models, or for that matter by logic or moral precept, Yu could not bring himself to insist on total manumission because he ostensibly was sympathetic to the yangban's need for a labor force. He may also have been intimidated by the potential resistance of the slaveowning class to any attempt by the state to deprive them of a major component of its work force. Although Yu's sentiments for eventual manumission probably represented a minority, liberal, and humanitarian position for his time, the details of his land reform plan indicate that in the long transition to manumission he sought to allow the state to gain a measure of control over private slaves by legitimizing a double burden on private slaves in particular, their enrollment for military service or military support taxes while they continued to pay personal tribute or rent to their masters. Furthermore, household slaves would evidently not have been affected at all by the proposed regulations.

The only curious point is why he would have felt that manumission of all slaves would have posed a lesser threat to stability than the abolition of all private landed property, especially since almost all his Chinese sources save for Chang Tsai, Ch'en Fu, and perhaps Ch'eng I of the Sung dynasty (see chap. 7) argued to the contrary. Perhaps because Korea in the seventeenth century was still a slave society and the Korean penchant for the hereditary transmission of status in the Chosŏn period was more powerful than anything in Chinese life since the end of the T'ang dynasty, Yu was far more reluctant to challenge slavery than the concept of private property in land.

Kang Chinch'ŏl, the historian of Koryŏ land relations, once suggested that the milestones of historical development in Korea should be judged by shifts in the mode of labor relations, from personal subjugation to contractual obligation, more than by the development of the modern, Western notion of private property.[68] If so, then even though landlord/tenant relations had already undergone significant development for a period of at least a thousand years and slavery in the seventeenth century was not quite the main or dominant mode of productive labor, still it played a greater role in Korea than in the rest of East Asia at the time.

On the other hand, the contradiction between Yu's boldness toward landlords and pusillanimity towards slaveowners cannot be so easily explained as a weakness in Korean consciousness toward landed property. The general trend in recent scholarship on the land question in Korea has been to push back the origins of private property and emphasize its strength in land tenure relations. The Korean landlords of the seventeenth century wanted to keep their property and Yu knew it, but his moral outrage against private ownership as a stimulus to greed and human desire fueled by the instructions of the classics and the ethical statesmen and scholars of the past meant that he could brook no compromise with it. Slavery was wrong, but he could have perceived it as but an extreme case of social hierarchy, which in principle was acceptable. Judging from trends of thought among reformers after Yu's death, Yu appears to have been the exception because almost all abandoned the idea of confiscation of private property as a chimerical fancy.

Sadaebu: *Scholars and Officials*

Yu's system of land grants was not confined to the class of cultivating peasants, whether commoners or slaves, for he also provided that "every one who performs a function or service [*chigyŏk*] [for the state]" would receive additional land grants over and above the basic one-*kyŏng* peasant allotment, scaled in accordance with the importance of the function. Service or officeholding would also carry with it exemption from military service.[69] Yu defined function or service in much broader terms than existing practice because he included clerks, runners, and petty officials in this category, people who received no official support in the seventeenth century and were forced to make ends meet by collecting fees or taking bribes.

In his plan petty clerks and runners employed in the bureaus of the central government at the capital would receive salaries but no land grants; clerks and runners in the provinces serving in magistrates' yamen and other agencies would be alloted salary land (*nokchŏn*) only. Minor local officials such as messengers, guards, keepers of grazing lands, ferrymen, tomb, forest, and shrine guards would receive one *kyŏng* of land. All petty officials would be exempted from military service or the payment of cloth support taxes.[70] Yu justified exemption for officeholders, no matter how menial the occupation, in terms of ancient precedent.[71] In the case of petty officials, however, land or salary grants and exemption from military duty were tied strictly to service; these men were not to be part of the *sadaebu*, Yu's ideal ruling class.

The lowest category of Yu's ideal ruling class was to consist of the *sa* or scholars, but contrary to the current loose custom of allowing sons of yangban to claim scholarly status as *yuhak* whether they merited it or not, Yu sought to restrict the claim, with some exceptions, to students registered in schools. This plan depended, of course, on the successful establishment of an extensive school system, described in chapter 5. Students classified as extra-quota students residing in the outer dormitories of the schools would receive a land grant of two *kyŏng*, and regular students in the inner dormitories would receive four *kyŏng*.

The *taebu* or regular officials of the central bureaucracy would receive grants ranging from six to twelve *kyŏng* depending on the rank associated with their official post.[72] This scheme of providing a scale of extra land grants (i.e., greater than the one-*kyŏng* allotment to the commoner peasant) was Yu's solution to the problem of guaranteeing economic support to the *sadaebu* or ruling class. These extra land grants were to perform the function of the feudal *ch'aeji* of the Chou period, which meant that they were not perceived as compensation for office-holding as such, but for membership in the ruling class. Officeholding was to be rewarded by salaries: "As for those on duty as officials [*sija*], if they are on duty [*si*], they will receive salaries [*surok*]."[73]

It therefore followed that even though an official might resign or be dismissed from office, his land grant would not be taken away by the state. "Except in the case of officials who have violated regulations and morality, or embezzled funds, or surrendered to the enemy, or committed other serious crimes, do not confiscate their land."[74] Therefore, even though Yu defined his system of graded land grants in terms of functional reciprocity for service performed for the state, in fact he thought of the ruling *sadaebu* class as transcending the functional definition of status.

Nevertheless, Yu was aware of the differences between his system of providing support for the *sadaebu* and the *ch'aeji* of the well-field system. Under the well-field system every peasant was supposed to have received a grant of 100 *myo* (i.e., one *kyŏng*), but the families of the *taebusa* (i.e., *sadaebu*)[75] received both *ch'aeji* and hereditary salary lands (*serokchŏn*) (if they held office). According to Yu the recipients of the *ch'aeji* and salary lands in the Chou system were only entitled to collect public taxes (*kongse*) from these lands and nothing more; that is, they were prebends. He remarked that this system was superior because it did not require any changes in the standard land allotment; no addition in the size of the land grant had to be made to compensate the *sadaebu*.

Furthermore, since military service was based on a land unit of constant size, there were no problems associated with the need to keep accurate records of the movement of adult males eligible for service, but in the later age of centralized bureaucracy the recruitment of officials by the central government and their promotion and dismissal was irregular, implying that the *sadaebu* had much less security and could never tell whether they would be promoted or dismissed from office at the whim of the ruler. Conditions under centralized, bureaucratic rule did not allow for the enactment of a system of prebendal allotments (*siksejibŏp*), which would have provided stable income to a *sadaebu* class and made them less than totally dependent on the salaries granted them by the central government for officeholding.

Why then did Yu not adopt the use of the prebend into his own system as the means for providing stable economic support to the families of the *sadaebu* elite, especially to those who might not be incumbent officeholders? One of the main reasons was that he conceived of the prebendal system as part and parcel of feudalism (*ponggŏn*), and if prebends were introduced into a system of centralized bureaucracy, it would have the adverse effect of producing an undesirable aristocracy of hereditary official families, like the hereditary ministers (*segyŏng*) of the Spring and Autumn period of the Chou. Who knows if Yu was not using a classical allusion to make an oblique criticism of his own dynasty, for the *kwajŏn* system of the early Chosŏn period had provided prebends to men of rank (with or without office) and it had resulted, or more accurately, reinforced, the dominance of a semihereditary official class, the yangban. Yu, therefore, explicitly stated that he was combining the *kongjŏn* or public ownership aspect of the well-field system with the graded land allotments of the limited-field (*hanjŏngbŏp*) system "according to which people who are Confucian scholars [*yusa*] or higher [in rank and status] will be granted additional amounts of land [over the base grant of 100 *myo* or 1 *kyŏng*] and will be exempted from military service."[76]

Yu's provision of extra land allotments to the *sadaebu*, however, violated one of the principles of the well-field system, which was that the state granted land only to peasants because they cultivated the land and contributed to agricultural production. How then could Yu justify land grants to noncultivators, or as his imaginary partner in debate in the *Pan'gye surok* put the question: "Is it justifiable to provide extra land grants to those who are scholars or officials since they are not engaged in agriculture?"[77]

Yu replied that scholars and officials had to be supported some way, but there were only three choices: land grants, salaries, and prebends. The grant of land to scholars and officials (in amounts greater than the commoner peasant allotment) was the most appropriate method because the land could be cultivated by their *solchŏng*. *Solchŏng* is a term defined by the dictionary as dependents or family members, but we may pause to ask what group Yu was referring to.[78] Since all commoner adult peasants and *sadaebu* would qualify for land grants, and since in any case Yu was opposed to tenancy, it is hard to imagine any adult males of the elite or commoner class who would have been available to work the excess land grants of the *sadaebu* under the terms of Yu's system. For that matter, it is hard to find any room for the landless hired laborers he planned to use to replace slaves unless he envisioned a rather lengthy transition period prior to the enactment of his land reform program or the abolition of hereditary slavery.

As for private slaves, remember that Yu put the idea of granting land to slaves in the conditional tense, and even in that case confined the grant of land to the outside resident slaves (*oegŏ nobi*). The only category of people that would have been available to serve as cultivators of the *sadaebu* land grants were private slaves. In other words, Yu argued that the grant of larger allotments to the *sadaebu* was the only proper and feasible method of approximating the *ch'aeji* prebendal model of ancient China because the *sadaebu* would be able to use their private slaves to cultivate the land!

As we might expect, therefore, Yu took this into account in drawing up a sample format for registration of cultivators under his proposed system. The land of commoner peasants would thus be registered in their own names, and they would be designated either as a cavalryman (*kibyŏng*) or infantryman (*pobyŏng*) depending on their military service assignment. In the case of the *sadaebu* elite, however, the name of their slave cultivator would be included in the land register after the name of the scholar, official, or royal prince. The purpose was to spare them the embarrassment of being listed in a land register along with common peasants!

"Some say that if all the *sadaebu* have to write their names in the land registers, it will bother them. I say that land registers are as important as household registers [*hojŏk*]; they are material necessary for later investigation and they have to be clear. . . . In accordance with present regulations, just have them write in the name of their household slave."[79] In other words, contrary to Yu's expressed sentiments against slavery, slavery was necessary to the operation of his own system of land reform!

If Yu had abolished slavery (in his system) at the same time that he ruled out tenancy, the only alternatives he would have had left to provide for the support of the *sadaebu* would have been either prebends (the right to collect taxes from certain lands) or salaries paid from general tax revenues. Yu, of course, explicitly ruled out both salaries and prebends as the means of supporting a *sadaebu* elite. Salaries were improper because an immutable principle of ancient government was that salaries could only be provided to those who performed service for the state as officials.

Prebends were a more difficult problem because, as Yu admitted, under the well-field system the *sadaebu* did receive *ch'aeji* for their families; they only received salaries if they held office. He had to concede that in principle it would be proper to grant prebends (*sikch'ae* or *sikse*) to scholars and officials because these had been used in ancient times. In fact, he stated that if some future government were to adopt this method, it would also be proper to permit some degree of inheritance to ensure that the families of scholars and officials who did not hold office would not suffer from poverty.

Furthermore, if a prebendal system were used, Confucian scholars and men with official rank from 7A to 9B (in a scale from 1A to 9B) would be entitled to retain the prebend only for their own lifetime (irrespective of officeholding). If the recipient had no male heirs, his widow should be entitled to half the prebend until she died. Men with official rank higher than grade 7A, with their sons, would retain the prebend for their lifetimes, and prebends of officials of the highest ministerial rank (the *taebu* and *kyŏng*), which probably referred to officials of the first two or three ranks, would be retained through the generation of the grandsons or great-grandsons.[80]

Although Yu conceded that prebends were justified and permissible in principle and theory, they would be undesirable because "most of the taxable land (*sejŏn*) in the country would end up in the hands of the families of the *sadaebu* and the state would not have enough to meet its expenses."[81] In other words, in an age of centralized bureaucracy, the financial requirements of the state could not be satisfied by a system that was originally designed to fit a feudal, decentralized mode of government.

Furthermore, there was a fundamental difference between the *sadaebu* of a feudal system and the *sadaebu* of a centralized bureaucratic system. The *sadaebu* in feudal antiquity were granted either *ch'aeŭp* or *sikse* (prebends), but their powers or rights were not limited to the collection of tax revenues from these grants; "they were also in charge of the governance of the people on their land, or they entrusted [control over the people] to their stewards [*kiin*]." Yu noted that these agents or stewards were public servants subject to state control, probably lords of minor territorial or political units who were absorbed into larger states or fiefs.[82] Yu probably meant that in a feudal polity the grant of *ch'aeŭp* and *sikse* was justifiable because the grantees had responsibility for governing the population of their domain and were under the control of the central authorities, arrangements that were totally at odds with a centralized bureaucratic system.

Nevertheless, *ch'aeŭp* and *sikse* prebends were correct in one sense: they represented a feudal mode of land tenure the intention of which was to underline the proper distinction between the rulers and the ruled, the *sadaebu* elite and the peasant cultivators. Paraphrasing Mencius, Yu stated that the payment of taxes and tribute (*ch'ulse* and *kongsang*) was the responsibility of "the men of the fields [*yain*]; studying the [moral] Way, performing official duties, and consuming taxes [*sikse*] was the job of the scholars [*sa*] and the men of superior virtue [*kunja*]."[83] Using a land system to maintain this difference of status and function in society was "a universal principle and also the intention of the ancients." But in feudal times it was done by granting fiefs (*ponggŏn*). Yu subsumed both the *ch'aeŭp* and *sikse* types of grant within the general category of *ponggŏn* (granting of fiefs), implying also that feudal relations were a thing of the past and never to be restored. One could only *adapt* ideal feudal principles to a centralized bureaucratic present.[84]

In the centralized bureaucratic age, however, the nature of the relationship between the *sadaebu* and the peasant cultivators was different. Since in bureaucratic times the *sadaebu* had no source of income but official salaries, they were forced to rely on their own devices for a living when out of office. In fact, it would appear that things had to be this way if the ruler or central government were to have a free hand in recruiting its officials and in adhering to strict standards of merit and performance. "Even though the *taebu* of the later age who did not hold office differed from the common people in terms of their houses and residences, they were [otherwise] the same as the men of the fields [*yain*]. How much more so in the case of the scholars [*sa*] who never served in office? This is the reason why the prebendal grant [*sikse*] method was not fully implemented even though it appears to be the intention of the ancients."[85] In other words, the rulers of centralized bureaucratic regimes destroyed the proper status barrier between common peasant and scholar-official and had no desire to provide prebends to a feudal nobility.

Yu acknowledged, however, that even in the age of the centralized bureaucratic state there had been times when rulers did issue prebendal grants, such as a grant of half the land tax (*cho*) on people's land (*minjŏn*) (i.e., land privately occupied or owned by individuals, whether landlords or small proprietors), but experience showed that this method caused more problems than it cured.[86] Under a system of centralized control prebends would not be concentrated in a single place as in the case of a fief in a feudal system, but "small parcels of land set aside for prebendal grants [*siksejiji*] would be spread around several thousand places and assigned to thousands of individuals."[87] Prebends would cause administrative difficulties in keeping track of changes in allotments and in maintaining control over peasant requests for tax alleviation or exemption because of yearly variations in crop damage from natural causes. This would result in inequities in the real assessment of tax burdens and a de facto increase in the tax levies on the commoner peasant. "This is the greatest harm that could befall the country; it would be better not to carry out a land reform at all," Yu concluded.[88] Thus the adaptation of a limited-field method of graded allotments to the scholars and officials was the best possible adjustment to an age of centralized bureaucracy, for "the gist of the well-field system is all contained within it."[89]

It is almost impossible to avoid a certain cynicism in judging Yu's arguments. If Yu feared that prebends to men of status would end up as their private property, how could he be so sanguine that granting extra allotments to *sadaebu* and allowing them to retain their slaves as their private cultivators would not also result in the creation of private estates cultivated by slave labor?

Yu's self-perception of his overall plan was that it was an eclectic combination of two models: the *kongjŏn* system based on the principles of public ownership and equal distribution of land and service contained in the well-field model, and the *hanjŏn* (limited-field) system of allowing larger holdings of land for the ruling class than for the commoner peasant. As in earlier limited-field schemes, there was a system of graded quotas corresponding to rank or office. Yu's eclecticism, however, meant that his type of limited-field scheme was different from the proposals of the Han or Sung scholars and statesmen. He did not propose his graded quotas as a compromise with private property or as a transitional means to the achievement of a system of relatively equivalent private plots or an equal-field sytem of public ownership. On the contrary, he envisioned an immediate nationalization of private property followed by redistribution to peasants and *sadaebu*.

What he meant by a limited-field system was that the *sadaebu*, as opposed to the peasantry, would have larger allotments of returnable, nonprivate land and could bequeath them to heirs only if they qualified under the law as scholars or officials, and according to strict generational limits according to rank. His limited fields were not a compromise with private property as in the plan of Lin Hsün; they were a compromise with elite status.

Princes and Merit Subjects

No sooner had Yu finished his criticism of the use of prebends to support the *sadaebu* elite, than he turned around and justified their use for members of the royal family and merit subjects. He stipulated that princes and princesses of both queens and royal concubines were to receive two modes of support. In the first instance they would be granted a basic land allotment of twelve or ten *kyŏng* that was not to become private property but would be "land to be occupied and received [by them]" temporarily just like the basic land grant to the peasants.

As in the case of the larger land allotments to the *sadaebu*, land taxes would be paid to the state but no military service would be required.[90]

In addition to this basic, returnable grant, princes and princesses would also be entitled to a prebendal grant called *sasejŏn*, "land from which taxes are granted by the throne." These grants were to be measured in terms of grain production, from 500 *kok* (where in this case he defined one *kok* as equivalent to one *sŏm*, *sŏk* in Sino-Korean pronunciation, or 15 *mal* or *tu* in Sino-Korean, not the 10 *tu* of his new measurement system)[91] for a *taegun* or grand prince down to 100 *kok* for the daughter of a crown prince by a concubine (*hyŏnju*).[92] Yu specified that the recipients would be entitled to receive only tax revenues from people's land (*minjŏn*), which in his scheme meant the basic land grants awarded to the peasantry and cultivated by them. Accordingly, people's land would be subject to military service requirements because the land itself was granted to the peasants and not to members of the royal house. Local magistrates would take responsibility for assessment of crop damage and temporary tax reductions. The taxes on the people's land would be paid directly to the local magistrate's granary, and the granary would issue in its place stored grain to the designated recipients.[93]

Yu also indicated that these *sase* prebends would be used for rewarding merit subjects so designated by the king, but he left out of his regulations any program for gradations based on degrees of merit. He also stipulated that the royal prebendal grants could be inherited by sons and grandsons; the eldest son of the legitimate wife would receive an extra third, obviously to support ancestral sacrifice, when the prebend was divided up among all the sons.[94]

Yu, of course, realized the necessity to provide justification for a system of double grants to royal relatives and merit subjects – both land grants and prebends. He defended the use of regular land grants to princes on the grounds that "it is an ancient principle that the *taebu* do not engage in agriculture; how then could the household of a prince engage in agriculture?" Certainly if scholars and officials were entitled to land grants, so too were princes.[95] But why did he insist on providing prebends as well?

Yu answered this question in the context of a debate with his hypothetical adversary, who complained that Yu's system was too complicated and too detailed (*tadan*) and objected that there was no need to grant princes and merit subjects both land and prebends; either one or the other would be sufficient. The antagonist offered two alternate plans each with its own set of tax and military service requirements and exemptions. To understand the terms of the debate and Yu's reasons for rejecting his adversary's propositions, it is necessary to review the relationship between the type of grants and tax and military service obligations that Yu proposed in his own system.

As we have seen thus far, Yu offered three kinds of grants based on the position or status of the recipient. Commoner peasant cultivators were to get a land grant (*sujŏn*), pay the land tax (*napse*), and provide military service (*ch'ulbyŏng*). The *sadaebu* (scholars and officials, or more accurately the class of families that produced scholars and officials) would also receive land grants (albeit in larger sizes than the commoner peasant), pay the land tax to the magistrates, but be exempted from military service (*myŏnbyŏng*). Finally, princes and other royal relatives and merit subjects would receive both land grants (*sujŏn*) and prebends (*sasejŏn*). On the land grants they would be required to pay the land tax to the magistrate but would be exempted from military service, just as in the case of the land grants to the *sadaebu.* On the prebends they would collect the tax income themselves (*sikki seip*), which was equivalent to a land tax exemption (*myŏnse*) in the sense that they would pay the land tax to themselves rather than to the magistrate, but military service would be levied on the land grants. Since prebends entitled them to collect the land tax revenue from *minjŏn* or people's land, which referred to the regular land grant (*sujŏn*) to the commoner peasant cultivator, military service would be required of the commoner peasant cultivator, not the princes or merit subjects themselves. There was no inconsistency here because by the terms of Yu's system, land taxes and military service were not levied on individual recipients but were tied to and determined by the nature of the land grant. The above discussion is summarized in table 3:

TABLE 3
MILITARY SERVICE AND LAND/PREBEND GRANTS

Recipient	Type of Grant	Land Tax	Mil. Service
Commoner peasant	land	yes	yes
Sadaebu	land	yes	no (exempt)
Princes and	land	yes	no
merit subjects	prebend	no[1]	yes[2]

[1] Recipient receives equivalent of land tax from magistrate, i.e., tax exemption.
[2] But the owner of the land, not the prebend holder, owes military service.

Yu asserted that although his proposal to provide princes and merit subjects with both land grants and prebends appeared complicated and haphazard, it was not only simple, fair, and equitable, but was also governed by a consistent logic that determined "the relationship between [the type of] land and the type of exemptions, whether exemption from military service or from the land tax." This meant that exemption from military service was inseparably associated with land grants to men of superior status, such as princes and merit subjects. Land grants were also necessary because without them the princes and merit subjects would have difficulty in obtaining land for gravesites for their parents. Since a land grant, by Yu's arbitrary definition, could not be associated with exemption from the land tax, however, the additional award of a prebend, defined by Yu as a land tax exemption, was the only justifiable way to provide the princes and merit subjects with land tax income.[96]

Yu's adversary, by contrast, preferred the choice of either land grants or prebends. He pointed out that in the case of land grants, since princes and merit subjects already received salaries, it would be sufficient simply to give them additional land grants in decreasing amounts (scaled according to blood relationship or distance from reigning kings or merit subject ancestors), exempt them from the land tax, and allow their retainers (*pangdang*) to perform military service in their stead. The land grants could be inherited by their descendants in decreasing amounts until the time that this inherited tax-exempt land might be less than the heir was entitled to by virtue of his own rank and position. At that time the heir would receive an additional (taxable) land grant according to Yu's regular rules of land grants to *sadaebu* to bring his allotment up to the appropriate size. Notice, however, that the tax and service obligations associated with this plan violated Yu's rules (see table 4).

TABLE 4
YU'S PLAN VERSUS LAND GRANTS ONLY

Recipient	Type of Grant	Land Tax	Military Service
Yu's plan:			
Sadaebu	land	yes	no
Prince, or merit subject	prebend	no	yes (by cultivator)
Adversary's plan:			
All the above	land (only)	no	yes (by retainers)

Yu objected to this plan because it violated his sense of equity: "Military service is assessed on the basis of the amount of land, whereas the land tax is assessed on the basis of the quality of the land. If in the case of princes and merit subjects you hold the taxes constant, there will be inequalities in the exemptions from military service; if you hold military service constant, there will be inequalities in the exemptions from the land tax."[97]

Yu explained this by arguing that if his adversary's plan were adopted, heirs of princes and merit subjects in succeeding generations would receive decreasing amounts of tax-exempt princely land (because of the division of inheritance) while they received increasing amounts of taxable land to match their actual rank, a system that would be too cumbersome to administer effectively.[98]

Yu's adversary then suggested that instead of land grants, the princes and merit subjects might simply be given prebends (*sase*) or tax collection rights over people's land (*minjŏn*), and that the cultivators be required to provide military service in accordance with (Yu's) regulations. The adversary also suggested that these prebends should be retained by the eldest legitimate son, and not divided up among all the other sons (of princes, princesses, or merit subjects) until the fifth generation in the case of descendants of royalty, when their royal status ended. At that time tax collection rights (prebends) would be taken back by the state, and afterwards each royal prince would only receive regular (taxable) land grants (*sujŏn*).

Yu remarked that this plan seemed to be all right because it was close to the ancient system; that is, it was similar to the *ch'aeji* arrangements of the Chou. But under the terms of the *ch'aeji*, the recipient also had overlordship over the people who resided on the *ch'aeji*, implying by this that political autonomy was an important power that benefited the recipient. In contemporary times, however, prebends did not carry with them any exemption from military service, so that while they might appear to benefit the recipient, in fact they caused him more harm than good.[99] In brief, Yu took the position that land grants and prebends each contained drawbacks from the standpoint of the recipient that could only be offset by using both in combination. Land grants, under his plan at least, would confer the benefit of exemption from military service but would entail payment of the land tax; prebends conferred the benefit of exemption from the land tax (i.e., by allowing the recipient to collect the tax in lieu of the state) but entailed military service. By granting princes and merit subjects both land and prebends, they would be able to receive the benefits of military service exemptions from the one and tax income from the other.

We may well ask, however, what the purpose of all this convoluted reasoning was? On what basis did Yu claim that land grants had to be associated with land tax payments and exemption from military service, and that prebends had to be associated with the reverse formula? Yu argued that there was a logic that governed the type of obligation associated with the type of land, and he also insisted on creating as consistent, uniform, and equitable a system as possible. Logical consistency would certainly appear to be an advanced and desirable basis for legislation, but it is not evident to the Western reader why Yu's rules were any more logical than his adversary's proposals.

The answer to this problem is to be found in the basis for Yu's rule making. He was not simply attempting to create a logical and consistent system of rules based on an à priori and rational elimination of internal contradiction, for if that were the case, the range of possible options would have been far wider than what he was willing to allow. On the contrary, he was attempting to discover what the consistent principles of land tenure and organization of ancient Chinese institutions were, and once he had done so, he insisted that they be adhered to.

Because there were rules or principles governing the type of tax obligations associated with land and principles governing the proper means of providing economic support and status distinction to various strata of the ruling class, Yu had to fit these two sets of rules together in a way that the requirements of both sets would be satisfied without contradiction. The result seems to have been a kind of rule-bound rigidity that was antithetical to the spirit of practicality and utility that some modern scholars claim was a hallmark of the Practical Learning (Sirhak) movement of this period.

Another important problem in interpreting Yu's regulations for *sadaebu*, princes, and merit subjects is to determine and define his objectives in social terms. This is a difficult task because of contradictory evidence. On the one hand, he was obviously dissatisfied with a functional definition of an ideal ruling class. A ruling class had to be something more than the collectivity of incumbent officials because it had to include educated and morally cultivated men who would provide a pool of leadership, not only as officials but also as leaders of the community and guides for the common people. A ruling class consisting only of officials would rule out economic support for the nonofficial scholarly, moral, and community leaders who were part of a true *sadaebu* class. It had to have some ascriptive qualities over and above the narrow functional and utilitarian definition of service for the state.

On the other hand, ascriptive characteristics could not be carried to extremes lest they result in the formation of a hereditary status elite that was completely dissociated from true virtue and functional merit. Yu hoped that a proper balance could be struck by imposing limitations on the economic support to be provided to princes and merit subjects (and *sadaebu* as well). He remarked, for example, that the *sase* or prebendal grant was a vestige of the ancient feudal system of *yŏlt'o*,[100] a type of fief granted from conquered territory or confiscated land, but that in adapting this model to the present, care had to be taken to limit the number of generations that the prebend could be inherited. If the state failed to take back the prebend from the original recipient (upon his death?) and allowed his descendants to inherit it without any generational limit, the state would soon run out of land.

Yu noted that the few feudal nobles tolerated in the Han and Chin dynasties (third century A.D.) were not permitted to have hereditary holdings or prebends for the most part. Even in the case of exceptions, inheritance was limited for one or two generations, and at times the prebend might even be confiscated for cause. Since ad hoc confiscation was more appropriate to a feudal age than a centralized bureaucratic one and would do harm to both upper and lower classes alike, Yu felt that it would be preferable to set up a system of prebends for princes and merit subjects regulated by law and designed to accommodate private and public interests alike.[101]

Yu also argued that prebends (*sase*) were preferable to the practice of outright grants of private land by the throne (*sajŏn*) to princes and merit subjects that could be inherited without interference by the heirs of the recipients. "Once this path were opened, there would be no way to rectify later evils. The destruction of the Koryŏ land system came about because of this."[102] In other words, royal land grants to princes and merit subjects were too dangerous because it opened the door to the hereditary transfer of land to descendants and weakened the state's control over land and taxes.

Yu did not comment directly in this section on the problems of his own dynasty created by the land grants to merit subjects in the fifteenth and sixteenth centuries. Yi Sangbaek, for example, attributed the failure of the early Chosŏn land settlement to the excessive granting of hereditary merit subject lands, and Edward Wagner showed how the political domination of the merit subjects remained a problem through the fifteenth century to the purge of 1519.[103] Yu did, however, discuss a major problem of the seventeenth century, the palace estates (*kungbang*) of the princes and princesses, located usually along the coast in southern provinces. Not only royal relatives but central government agencies and influential magnates as well were allowed by the throne to petition to take over control of fishing weirs, salt flats, and marshland along the coast, a process called *ch'ŏlsu ib'an*. These lands were run as estates by stewards called *kamgwan* or *tojang* who tyrannized the local fishermen and salt manufacturers. Local big shots had even taken to legitimizing arbitrary seizures of land by the use of these palace estate certificates of registration (*ib'an*).

Furthermore, palace families in the capital were entitled to grants of woodland to supply fuel. Yu proposed to eliminate both the fishing weirs and salt flats of the palace estates and capital bureaus and the woodlands assigned to royal relatives. The weirs and salt flats would be turned over to the common people to earn a living and the woodland would be turned into commons for fuel gathering and pasture. Yu's recommendation probably had an effect on the Taewongun, who perceived the palace estates to be a major source of corruption and loss of state revenue and finally took over their tax-exempt lands between 1866 and 1868.[104] Yu's proposed reforms appear on balance to have aimed at a significant reduction of the economic advantages of the estates of the merit subjects, princes, and princesses, even though he was willing to provide them with both land grants and prebends.

Yu seems to have been unwilling to adopt a ruthless, functional definition of power, privilege, and status that would have led him to strip all the idle or unemployed nobles and scholar-officials of their perquisites. On the contrary, his approach was to acknowledge status but limit its propensity to perpetuate itself over generations, to prevent the creation of hereditary aristocracy. Contrary to commoners the sons of the sadaebu would be able to retain their father's land grants for three years before the officials would make a determination whether to take back the land or transfer it to some one else. Young or orphaned sons of scholars would be entitled to receive all their father's land grant, and sons of officials would be entitled to four *kyŏng*. When they reached the age of twenty, they would be given the allotment equivalent to their own position or function. But if the sons of scholars and officials failed to keep up with their studies by the time they reached the age of twenty and were unable to gain admittance to school, their land grant would be reduced to the one kyŏng given to commoners.[105] This was Yu's attempt to strike a compromise between functional and ascriptive criteria for the *sadaebu*.

Yu also established regulations for allowing but limiting the inheritance of status by descendants of kings, merit subjects, and high officials. He set the number of generations that could inherit land grants, prebends, eligibility for appointment to office, and membership in special capital guard units. He used four types of terms for these categories. *Sejok* or "hereditary eldest legitimate sons" was defined as including the eldest legitimate son and grandson of regular wives (*chŏkchang-jason*) of princes (*wangja*) and merit subjects (*kongsin*). The term "son and grandson" must have meant all descendants of kings, not just the first two generations, because Yu's regulations stipulated that eldest sons would inherit their status and privileges in perpetuity. The eldest legitimate son of each generation descended from a reigning king and a merit subject would retain *sejok* status.

The other legitimate sons of kings would be included in a different category called *ch'in* (lit., "having a royal parent"). All those in the category of *kukka tanmun*, or blood relationship of the lowest of the five Chinese degrees of mourning (five months), would retain this status. This would include relatives of four generations in each direction from a living king.[106] It would also include any one who had to observe one year's mourning or more for the wife of a crown prince.[107]

A third category was called *ŭm*, or protection, indicating residual privileges inherited by heirs of merit subjects or high officials. This category included three subcategories: eldest legitimate sons, grandsons, and great grandsons (i.e., three generations) of regular wives of merit subjects and officials of rank 2A or higher; legitimate sons and eldest sons of the regular wives of officials of *tangsang* rank or above (ranks 3A to 1A); and sons of *tangha* officials (i.e., some 3A but mainly 3B to 6B) including sons of certain special officials like chiefs of directorates (*chegam*), vice commanders of guard units, state councilors, officials of the six ministries and the censorate, royal chamberlains (*sijong*), officials in the National Academy (Sŏnggyun'gwan) of rank 6 or higher, governor's assistants (*tosa*), district magistrates, and provincial educational officials. For sons of these *tangha* officials to inherit *ŭm* status, their fathers would have to have held office for three inspection periods (three years each) (*samgo*) or a total of nine years.[108]

Yu pointed out that under current law governing inheritance of the *ŭm* privilege, sons, sons-in-law, younger brothers, and nephews were eligible to inherit certain privileges, but in fact only the most talented among them were given the right. He was not sure whether this was right or wrong, but at least with regard to the inheritance of the regular land grant (*sujŏn*) in his own system, it did not seem appropriate to allow all family members to inherit the *sabu* (i.e., *sadaebu*) land allotment of an ancestor who reached high office. In the Sung dynasty brothers were not allowed to inherit the *ŭm* privilege, and the system of *serok* or hereditary salaries of ancient China were limited to the *sejok* category (eldest legitimate sons only) and did not extend to the other sons, let alone younger brothers and nephews. In any case, Yu sought to exclude younger brothers and nephews from the *ŭm* privilege.

Furthermore, under the current system of selecting only the talented for the *ŭm* privilege, it was possible that a younger brother might qualify for a land grant in place of a living elder brother. This appeared inappropriate to Yu, probably because it contradicted age and generational respect rules.[109] Yu obviously regarded contemporary Korean practice as idiosyncratic, a failure of Koreans to understand and fully conform to the principles governing the definition of privileged status and royal blood line that could be deduced from the Chinese historical record. As in his treatment of the relationship between types of land and types of tax exemption, Yu believed that the principles governing the *ch'in* royal relationship and *ŭm* residual privilege contained an inner logic. This attitude is revealed in a brief discussion Yu conducted with his imaginary adversary.

The adversary charged that Yu's formulas governing the generational limits for the inheritance of royal blood status and *ŭm* privileges were inconsistent and discriminated against the descendants of merit subjects and high officials. He conceded that according to principle a strict distinction had to be made between rulers and their relatives (*kun*) and subjects or officials (*sin*), but like the head and feet of the human body, both were part of the same organism.[110] For example, even though princes received ten times the salary of an official, there were cases where officials (*taebusa*) also received large salaries. Furthermore, in ancient times important officials were given extremely generous treatment by the throne. Now, in establishing his regulations for members of the royal family on the one hand and descendants of officials and merit subjects on the other, Yu was not consistent; he wanted to eliminate brothers of high officials from inheritance of the *ŭm* privilege but he was willing to allow retention of *ch'in* or royal blood relations even to the remotest degree of mourning – even to the fourth generation of descent from queens or fourth cousins of queens. This was a violation of ancient principles.

Yu's rebuttal was based on a logical analysis of his perception of operative rules. He asserted that a single principle governed both eligibility for *ŭm* status and the state's general treatment of members of the royal family. That was the reason that the *ŭm* privilege for heirs of high officials and merit subjects and for members of the royal family did not run out until the fourth generation (*hyŏnson*), but in both cases there should be no provision to extend those privileges to collateral lines. The determination of *ch'in* relationship, however, was a separate problem altogether; it pertained only to relatives of kings, and there was no principle by which the state could confer *ch'in* status on a subject or official.[111] Nor should the rules pertaining to *ch'in* status be used to determine inheritance of the *ŭm* privilege; it was not necessary to be consistent or uniform in dealing with two separate categories.

Nothoi: Sons of Concubines (sŏŏl)

Yu was clearly interested in improving the status and opportunities of nothoi. According to his rules anyone inheriting the *ŭm* privilege from an illustrious ancestor, or any member of royalty designated as possessing the proper degree of relationship to a king (*ch'in*) would be given a two-*kyŏng* basic land grant in accordance with the grant allowed a regular student of an inner dormitory of a school (*naesasaeng*). A *sŏŏl* or nothoi (of a yangban or Yu's *sadaebu*) would also be entitled to the same treatment. Sons of the concubines of officials and degree-holders would also be entitled to membership in the Loyal and Obedient Guards along with legitimate sons.[112] He defined the general rule as follows: "If a nothoi is a scholar, he should be treated as a scholar; if he is a member of the Loyal and Righteous Guards or the Loyal and Obedient Guards, then he is entitled to treatment as a member of those guards."[113]

Nevertheless, Yu did not mean by this that a rule of absolute equality between legitimate sons and nothoi had to be followed, or that any form of distinction or discrimination was improper. He remarked that the law of the dynasty stated that nothoi were ineligible to receive the *ŭm* privilege from illustrious forbears, but people were of two minds about how nothoi should be treated. Some thought that current laws had to be strictly observed and nothoi excluded from the *ŭm* privilege; others believed that it was improper to make any kind of distinction between legitimate sons and nothoi (*chŏk/sŏ*).[114] Yu felt that both extremes were wrong: the rules governing the qualification for the *ŭm* privilege to descendants had to be uniform (that is, applied to both legitimate sons and nothoi), but there was no reason why gradations or distinctions could not be made in the case of nothoi. In one of his headnotes he stated that nothoi of the royal family, for example, were given lesser noble titles than legitimate princes, so that distinctions could also be made in conferring *ch'in* or royal relative status on nothoi. Students in schools, however, had to be admitted solely in terms of their scholarly ability and not pedigree (*munji*) or degree of noble or base status (*kwich'ŏn*).

Furthermore, since membership in the elite guard units should not be connected with possession of the *ŭm* privilege, he rejected a suggestion that one way to draw a proper distinction between legitimate sons and nothoi who were both entitled to the *ŭm* privilege would be to deprive nothoi of the opportunity for membership in the elite guards. He insisted that inheritance of the *ŭm* privilege should be determined by its own set of rules; the elite guards was simply an office or post that had nothing to do with the *ŭm* privilege.[115]

In summary, Yu's position on nothoi or merit subjects and high officials was cautious and moderate. He believed that they were entitled to the *ŭm* privilege on the basis of their fathers' accomplishments, membership in the elite guard units in the capital, admission to schools on the basis of their scholarly talent, and allotment of a land grant of two *kyŏng* if they had the *ŭm* privilege (but not double awards for both the *ŭm* privilege and student status).[116] He conceded that it was proper to reduce the eligible rank or grade for nothoi in some instances, but he only provided a single example – the degree of *ch'in* royal blood relationship in determining the ranks of royal relatives.

The problem of nothoi was, of course, one of the outstanding examples of customary Korean social discrimination based on inherited or ascriptive characteristics. Whether the practice should be regarded as a manifestation of Korean proclivities embedded in the deep structure of their minds and attitudes, the product of the political circumstances involved in the founding of the Chosŏn dynasty in 1392 as Yi Sangbaek argued, or an attempt by the early Chosŏn ruling class to narrow access to the top of society as Yi Sŏngmu suggested, it would appear that Yu Hyŏngwŏn thought of the practice as an illustration of a local custom rather than as an ideal principle found in or derivable from ancient Chinese models.

Although he found contemporary discrimination against nothoi excessive and sought to remove some of the restrictions on them, he could not state a satisfactory general principle justifying equal treatment once he had conceded the propriety of discrimination. The choice, therefore, was not between equality and discrimination, but the proper degree and type of discrimination for which there were no clear guidelines.

CONCLUSION

It is quite clear that Yu was adamantly opposed to the private ownership of land but not necessarily private property in general, especially because he was willing to countenance the continuation of slavery for at least fifty to a hundred years. He was also reluctant to advocate the use of force to confiscate land from the landlords and proposed a number of scenarios by which the landlords might be willing to permit the division of their property by their heirs. But when forced to confront the prospects of indefinite postponement of his plan for the redistribution of land, he had to admit that he was willing to authorize the use of force against them. How then does one explain the apparent contradiction between his readiness to compromise with slavery and other modes of discrimination and special privilege, and his unyielding opposition to the private ownership of land?

In the first place, it should be obvious that he was a social engineer and a social planner who felt strongly that private landownership would be an insurmountable obstacle to the achievement of a perfect society. The existence of private ownership presupposed a society of individual choice, where people would be free to move from one place to another, or to exchange land for money or goods. Constant movement in an open society made it too difficult for government authorities to keep accurate records of land and population to ensure fair and equitable assessment of taxes and military service. The open society presupposed flux and change, which was uncontrollable. Land, however, was tangible and provided the opportunity for fixity and stability in a world of change, but it could not perform that function if private individuals controlled it for their own purposes. In other words, the planned, controlled, and regular distribution of land was the means by which the state could create an ideal society.

In the second place, private property was morally corrupting because it stimulated man's propensity for avarice and self-interest. No matter how equitable a system of distribution or taxation, if private property were tolerated, it would drive men to neglect, avoid, or totally transform any ideal system of distribution so that the division between the rich and the poor would be recreated just as it had in both the late T'ang and late Koryŏ periods. Private property was associated with private desire and the dark side of man's nature, whereas a system of public ownership of land was in full conjunction with the spirit of a true moral order. Thus for a combination of utilitarian and moral reasons, private ownership of land had to be abolished.

Status distinction, privilege, and discrimination was a different matter altogether. While true that Yu sought to create an ideal society to replace his own, he did not seek to replace hierarchy with equality as the fundamental principle of social organization; he sought rather to change the basis upon which social hierarchy rested. He would replace birth, heredity, and private wealth with virtue, learning, and achievement as the criteria for social distinction – but not altogether, because the Confucian tradition allowed for fine marks of distinction on the basis of age or blood relationship. In a sense, therefore, nothoi of yangban and slaves were for him problems of degree, not kind; some of the grosser injustices associated with these statuses should naturally be eliminated. Korean discrimination might be worse than Chinese, but it could be ameliorated and made acceptable.

Yu, however, did not simply tolerate social discrimination; he accepted it as legitimate, justified by the classical division between the rulers and ruled, the *kunja* and *yain*. For this reason he was excessively tolerant of some of its grosser forms and blind to its potential consequences. Despite his talk of the abolition of hereditary slavery or the eventual manumission of slaves, his excessively complex set of rules precluded any form of extra support to the *sadaebu* elite but the grant of extra land allotments, and there was no group of cultivators other than the private slaves of the existing yangban available to work these lands. Even if they were to be converted from slaves to hired laborers, as he suggested, they would still be acting as fully obedient employees in the manner of social inferiors. Since the prospects for the manumission of slaves was so far in the future, for the immediate present he made slavery *necessary* for the cultivation of his *sadaebu* ruling class, most of whom he presumed would be drawn from the ranks of the current yangban.

Yu also proposed using hired labor to replace slaves, and some scholars have indicated that this suggestion indicated that Yu was following the progressive trend from forced to free labor that accompanied the expansion of the market and commerce in the seventeenth century. But his land reform would have been diametrically opposed to this trend because it would have returned all landless laborers and vagrants to the land and guaranteed them their subsistence by granting them a piece of land to cultivate. Though he spoke of the advantages of free choice or free contracts between the laborer and his employer, his land reform program was so inclusive that it would have left little room for free labor to operate except in a very limited way.

The public ownership of land or a *kongjŏn* system was absolutely essential to Yu as the means for the creation of a society in which two objectives would be secured. The first was relative equality of income and fairness in taxation for the peasant cultivator. The second was economic control by the state to free the families of scholars and officials from the uncertainties of a market economy or from the arbitrary aspects of bureaucratic recruitment. Yu's animus was directed against the existing yangban elite, composed of landlords who accumulated their holdings out of a base desire for wealth and bureaucrats who gained office through a misdirected examination system or by personal, familial, or factional connection and patronage. Just as private land provided the economic foundation for a yangban class devoted to its private interests, so would public land provide the economic foundation for a *sadaebu* moral elite that would devote its efforts to the public interest. Kim Yongsŏp's "managerial" or entrepreneurial rich peasant must have been anathema to Yu, the representative of selfish greed rather than progress.

What, in short, was the nature of the social structure to be after the adoption of Yu's *kongjŏn* system, and how would it differ from contemporary Korean society? In answering this question we will omit discussion of the nonagrarian, urban, and commercial sectors of the economy and society, which will be treated in subsequent chapters. In certain respects the new society would be similar to the old. The ruling class would consist of a nobility of royal relatives and an elite of officials and scholars supported either by salaries, prebends, or the labor power of their slave cultivators. Certain hereditary rights for the descendants of merit subjects and officials and certain types of discrimination against nothoi would continue, although in the first case generational limits on inheritance would be tightened, and in the second case more opportunities would be allowed. Petty officials would continue to function as an intermediary class or status group, not members of the *sadaebu* elite and yet entitled to emoluments and privileges in return for service to the state, an improvement over their present condition and reminiscent of the features of the *chŏnsikwa* system of early Koryŏ.

Peasants would be given economic security in terms of cultivation rights over land but subjected to more thorough and rigorous methods of registration for military service and support taxes. Slaves would not only continue to provide labor for their princely or scholar-official masters by working on their large-sized land grants, but they would be indispensable to the economic support of his new *sadaebu* ruling class as the only available labor force to cultivate their land.

It is clear that this social system would have been differentiated only partially in terms of function or utility. Yu's program of land grants to the *sadaebu* were designed to support a class of men for at least a couple of generations, not to compensate functionaries for their service. Limited hereditary privileges would have been extended to royalty, and through the *ŭm* privilege to descendants of merit subjects and high officials; hereditary discrimination would continue to function in terms of nothoi and slaves. In fine, the customary distinctions of social status of contemporary Korean society would be carried over in large measure to the new society.

Essentially there were two reasons for this. Because Yu sought a workable formula, one that would not cause rebellion and resistance, he obviously felt that the outright abolition of slavery was politically impossible and the importance attached to status was too great to be challenged directly. In the second place, his conception of the ideal well-field model justified a definition of the ruling class in ascriptive terms, and Confucian social thought in general accepted distinction and discrimination in principle as legitimate.

Nonetheless the new system would have differed from the old in certain important ways. The *sadaebu* elite of the new system would have permitted greater mobility both downward and upward on the basis of scholarship and performance. The abolition of private landownership would have eliminated the landed base of the contemporary hereditary yangban aristocracy and transformed the commoner peasant into a limited proprietor, holding only the right of possession or cultivation over a family plot. This would have entailed the disappearance of the private smallholder, the sharecropper, and the landless laborer – except for the slaves whom he suggested might be converted to hired laborers. This suggestion, of course, contradicted his basic provisions to provide a land allotment to slaves as well, so if they were to be manumitted by making them hired laborers, they would have to give up the land allotment they would have received as slaves. In any case, by granting the slave a plot to cultivate (and legitimizing his duty of performing military service for the state), Yu would have weakened the slaveholder's control (but not necessarily improved the slave's lot).

Yu obviously yielded a great deal to the customary Korean respect for social status, particularly with regard to slavery, but this caution did not carry over to his treatment of private landownership, which he insisted had to be abolished totally. If he thought that private ownership was less important to the yangban than slaveholding or that its abolition would not result in political opposition and rebellion, he was sadly mistaken. Private property was maintained intact until the decade after Korea's liberation from Japanese colonial rule in 1945.

CHAPTER 9
Late Chosŏn Land Reform Proposals

Was There a Legacy to Yu's Land Reform Plan?

Most students of the Practical Learning movement (Sirhak) of the late Chosŏn dynasty have assumed a continuous development of radical and progressive reform ideas stimulated in part by the writings of Yu Hyŏngwŏn, but that kind of assumption may be unwarranted unless verified by a consideration of the leading proposals for land reform that were put forward after Yu's death. The record we have considered thus far on attitudes toward education, recruitment, and slavery in previous chapters by no means demonstrates that statecraft thought after Yu's death was necessarily more radical or progressive than his.

Yet what is meant by radical or progressive in the area of land reform, and does radicalism indicate progressivism? In East Asian statecraft thought the most radical solution to land distribution was already defined by the well-field system of the Chou dynasty, the essence of which was public ownership and fair, if not equal, division of property to the peasantry. Since the ideal model was in remote antiquity, radical reformers had no need to base their vision for Utopia on an unremittent process of progressive development.

Yu conceded, as the majority of Chinese statecraft writers had over the centuries, that the well-field system could not be restored in its pristine state, but how much of the original vision did he sacrifice? Not much, because his notion of a limited-land system did not mean abandoning the principle of public ownership and fairly equivalent land grants to the peasantry, only establishing limits on land grants to the new *sadaebu*. Where then was the possibility of a more radical goal of reform if it were not a ruthless determination to strip the current ruling class of its land? And since Yu had already specified that if all else failed, a bold and willful ruler should use force to carry out the confiscation of privately owned land, one could even say that Yu came within a hair's breadth of coopting the most radical program possible, leaving space only for a still more radical egalitarianism in which the ruling class would be stripped completely of any aspects of ascription and hereditary status.

If, on the other hand, progress means a tendency toward modernity, as Ch'ŏn Kwan'u has suggested, then what other model of modernity has there been except the path trodden by those nations on the way to modern industrial capitalism, particularly the model of the development of England, the first industrial nation in the world? If that becomes the criterion for modernity, then Yu's program for the abolition of private property, egalitarian state-regulated distribution of land for the subsistence of the peasantry, and support of a monolithic bureaucracy are all items that are contrary to the developments achieved by England, the first nation to embark on a successful program of industrial capitalism. England's "development" toward capitalism was marked in the rural sector by a long transition from the feudal demesne to the private ownership of land, accompanied by the enclosure of fields for sheepherding, dairying, and cattle-breeding from 1300 to 1800, the expulsion of the peasantry to the towns and the disappearance of the small owner-farmer, the development of market forces and commercial agriculture by entrepreneurial leaseholders or tenant-farmers producing wool to meet the new demand for textiles in what was really a regional, if not world, market.[1] In that scenario the equal distribution of land to the peasantry was totally irrelevant to, if not obstructive of, the forces needed to free labor and capital for new forms of investment and manufacture.

State control of the economy was more characteristic of the age of absolutism in France after 1466 and particularly under Colbert in the seventeenth century, in Spain from the sixteenth century when it monopolized specie imports from its empire in the New World through the eighteenth century, and in Germany under Frederick the Great in Prussia and Austria under Joseph II in the eighteenth century, when governments sought to maximize wealth at the expense of their national rivals by export promotion and import restriction. While some scholars grant that state control of the economy had dynamic qualities in the stimulation of production and trade and that concern for the balance of trade and protectionism was important for the maintenance of infant industries, most prefer to think that mercantilism interfered with the full flowering of capitalism, which required an international free-market trading system to thrive and flourish.[2]

Only after England had led the way by carrying out the industrial revolution did some of the late developing nations, like Germany and Japan in the late nineteenth century, take an active role in accumulating capital, directing it toward industrial investment, and creating the basis for a modern industrial economy. And when those governments did so, they cared more about industrial growth than the equality of distribution. In Japan, for example, the state had been more interested in extracting savings from the agrarian sector to invest in urban industry, and by the 1930s a growing number of peasants were left to fend for themselves as dependent and defenseless tenants.[3]

The problem with state or bureaucratic control of a rural economy dominated by a landlord class was that it maintained the status quo based on gross inequality in the distribution of wealth. As Barrington Moore, Jr., has argued, some agrarian nations like Russia and China came into the twentieth century dominated by nonprogressive landlords who exploited their landholdings and peasant tenants and laborers for their own consumption rather than for investment in commercial and industrial ventures. They were backed up by rigid bureaucratic governments, either native or colonial, that supported them with the coercive powers of the state, exacerbated the crisis of the peasantry, and drove their nations toward peasant-based revolutions.[4] Whether Moore's schematic explanation suffers too much from reductionist oversimplification or not, it retains immense importance as an illustration of what momentous political consequences can result from the failure of agrarian regimes, particularly those with a centralized bureaucratic tradition, to solve the problem of the maldistribution of wealth. Many of these peasant-based revolutions began with promises for land reform guaranteeing a plot of land for every peasant family, but the purpose of these promises was not only to redistribute wealth to the impoverished peasantry, but to attract support for a political revolution. And after a political revolution was carried out, promises of proprietorship for peasants often ended up as a program of confiscation and collective ownership, as in Stalin's and Mao's collectivization campaigns after 1928 and 1955, respectively. In other words, neglect of the problem of distribution in a rural economy has political consequences, and political leaders who are able to take the lead in advocating a program for land redistribution can succeed in overthrowing the political order by appealing to a desperate peasantry in a period of crisis.

How is this relevant to the Korean experience? It is important to know what the direction of change in the rural sector was. Was it toward the creation of capitalist commercial agriculture in accompaniment with the expansion of trade and industry that tended toward a solution of rural immiseration by increased production and a shift of population from rural to urban areas. Or was it the continuation of a fundamental nonprogressive domination by a small class of landlords of a fragmented class of minute petty proprietors, tenants, and hired laborers pushed to the margins of subsistence?

It is my contention that although certain aspects of capitalism in a nascent stage were present in the rural economy, the latter view is the best way to understand what took place. Not only was this deterioration of distribution characteristic of the Chosŏn dynasty, but the severity of landlord/tenant relations in particular was maintained by the policies of the Japanese colonial regime after 1920 and even exacerbated by the world depression in the decade after 1929.

In his massive and penetrating study of the origins of the Korean War, Bruce Cumings has shown how the distributive problem was left hanging in mid-air even after Korea's liberation from Japanese colonial rule in 1945, but the amazing denouement of centuries of difficulty was that within a few years a solution was achieved.[5] Divided by the physical, ideological, and political split between the Korean Communists in the north and the anti-Communist landlords in the south, and supported on each side by the Soviet Union and China and the United States and its allies, both North and South Korea adopted solutions that restrained private property rights. The North, in emulation of precedents set in

China, simply abolished private ownership and began by distributing the land to peasant families, but after 1955 it began to reorganize petty proprietors into collective farms. The South, pressured by its challenge from the North, preserved private property but set limits on landownership during the Korean War in a land reform program somewhat similar to that carried out in Japan after the end of World War II. Landlord domination of Korea simply came to an end in both North and South Korea.

Whether that momentous conclusion to a centuries-old system of economic control was produced by extraneous factors such as the influence of the Communist victory in China, the United States's defeat of Japan, or the Cold War confrontation on a world-wide level, inside Korea the discontent over the maldistribution of land and wealth was crucial to the political fate of the two Koreas.

What, then, occurred in thought and action on land reform in the Chosŏn dynasty, particularly in the period after Yu's death in 1672? Was there a continuation of his vision for the redistribution of land and wealth, or a rejection of it, and if the latter, did it mean development of any kind, toward more radical egalitarianism among statecraft scholars and officials, greater development of private ownership and productive forces, or continued deterioration of land ownership and distribution?

LAND TENURE CONDITIONS: PROGRESS OR DETERIORATION?

Fragmentation and Tenancy

Conditions in the nature of land tenure changed gradually in the late seventeenth century, and in many ways for the better, but by the mid-nineteenth century an agrarian crisis founded on maldistribution of landownership, wealth, and taxation had reached epic proportions. Kim Yongsŏp, on the other hand, has attempted to show the beginning of a long-term increase in productivity gained from the spread of irrigation, transplantation, and the use of fertilizer, the growth of markets, and the development of commercial agriculture. These developments enabled enterprising peasants to use more rational and profit-driven management techniques to accumulate wealth, lend out grain and cash to others, and increase their holdings through purchase or foreclosure on mortgages. Unfortunately, the denouement of this story of progress did not lead to a transition to commercial agriculture for the whole economy, let alone the creation of a dominant industrial and commercial sector. Instead, it ended with the entrepreneurs in the lower status orders using their wealth to buy office titles in return for contributions to the government (*napsok*), or if they were slaves, to purchase "good" or commoner status (i.e., manumission from slavery) by the same means. Although social climbing was not unusual for bourgeois entrepreneurs who sought to buy their way into the English or Spanish aristocracies or the Japanese samurai class, one might have expected capitalistic farmers to have utilized their wealth to reinvest their profits either in commercial agriculture, or better still, nonagricultural industrial enterprise, to gain even larger profits.[6] But there is little solid evidence to indicate this kind of development until the 1920s.[7]

On the other hand, the position of many small peasant proprietors was weakening. Since the beginning of the dynasty the average size of the small-peasant plot was declining, and under the pressure of taxes, bribes, and famine many holders of small plots were forced to mortgage their land to the wealthy or sell it to the landlords and become tenants or day laborers.

Kim Yongsŏp, a pioneer in the study of land tenure and agriculture in the Chosŏn dynasty, wrote a series of articles based on land registers (*yang'an*) in which he used the registration of *kiju* (lit., master of cultivation). According to this formula the wealthiest landowners in the villages he studied owned on the average only about 1 *kyŏl* (2.2 acres of the most fertile land or 18 acres of the least fertile land), while most of the *kiju* owned less than .5 *kyŏl*, and the majority of those about .25 *kyŏl*. He used these figures to support his interpretation that the average holding had declined significantly from the average of 5 *kyŏl* per peasant family in the early fifteenth century, a process that he described as fragmentation.

Unfortunately, since his villages showed no signs of large landlords, he had to explain the absence of evidence to demonstrate the accumulation of land lost by small peasant proprietors to the hands of large landlords by arguing that those large landlords must have owned parcels in other villages not included in his documents, that the "estate" of large landlords consisted of separated and scattered pieces. In addition, his figures showed that slave "owners" of land (i.e., *kiju*) often owned more than some commoners and even some impoverished yangban, supporting his argument about the emergence of a new class of entrepreneurial peasants among all status groups that led to an overturning of the old status order.[8]

Kim's arguments have been weakened to some extent by the work of Pak Nouk, who found that the term *kiju* did not indicate ownership at all. He demonstrated this by showing that the "land" of a runaway official female slave, Kim Idŏk, had been "recorded and turned over" to her "master," the Royal Treasury (Naesusa). Even though she was the registered "master of cultivation" (*kiju*), it was impossible for her to be the real owner of that particular parcel. In addition, Kim also showed that the land register usually juxtaposed *ki* with *chin*, meaning "cultivated" or "fallow," respectively. Kim's findings called into question Kim Yongsŏp's use of *yang'an* data to define in quantitative terms the average size of the land owned by the yangban, commoners, and slaves in the late Chosŏn period.[9]

Despite this damage to Kim Yongsŏp's conclusions, other kinds of qualitative evidence indicate that he may have been on the right track in several respects. While the *yang'an* records may have hidden the actual extent of real landholdings by the wealthiest landlords and exaggerated the amount of land owned by commoners and slaves, most of the ordinary peasants were either reduced to the ownership of small parcels, partial tenancy, outright tenancy, or work as seasonal, settled, or migrant laborers who worked either for room and board or a small wage. In the late eighteenth century, for example, Pak Chiwŏn thought that only 10 to 20 percent of the peasants owned their own land, and Yi Kyugyŏng reported that only 10 percent of the land in a village was owned by smallholders. Kim Yongsŏp himself discovered that in the Kobu region of Chŏlla Province, 60 percent of the land was rented and 40 percent of the peasants were tenants in the early eighteenth century, but a century later, 5 percent were landlords, 25 percent were owner-cultivators, and 70 percent were either full or part-tenants. The number of full tenants had increased from 25 percent to 40 percent in that interval, and over half rented only slightly more than .1 *kyŏl* per person.[10]

Tenancy, by itself, does not necessarily indicate backwardness or poverty, but as an indication of development one would at least expect something approaching the emergence of an equivalent of the capitalist tenant-farmers of England who leased large amounts of land, employed wage laborers, and profited from the sale of surplus products on the market.[11] Unfortunately, most of the evidence indicates a pattern of minute parcels of rented land cultivated by tenant families just eking out a bare living.[12]

Earlier in the dynasty, when most land was held by owners who held larger parcels on the average of 5 *kyŏl*, the labor was done either by the family or by slaves, but as the holdings of the rich peasants grew larger and transplantation requiring much larger amounts of labor spread around the country, peasants had to turn to hired labor to supply the need. The poor peasants who lacked the capital to hire workers or to afford the oxen and tools needed to increase production either borrowed what they needed or donated their own labor as compensation, losing time on their own fields. Kim believed that the need for capital was also increased by the shift to nightsoil fertilization, which spread widely only in the eighteenth century.[13]

There is little doubt that the increase in tenancy was accompanied by harsher conditions for tenants in general as the landlords tried to increase their rents and the return on their investment. Landlords also shifted the mode of rent from sharecropping (*t'ajak* or *t'ajo*) to fixed rent (*tojo*) to guarantee at least a secure and stable rental income, and they added other kinds of charges to increase their income, such as taking over reservoirs for irrigation and levying a water tax on the tenants.

Landlords began to require that tenants pay the land tax as well. In fact, in the early eighteenth century the land tax had become an even more important segment of national tax revenues because the tribute tax had been converted from payment of goods in kind to a surtax on land (the *taedongmi*) throughout the seventeenth century. Since the government failed to maintain accurate registration of cultivated and taxable land (a cadastral survey was not carried out between the 1680s and 1717), that omission favored the wealthy landlords and shifted a greater percentage of the tax quotas to the backs of the smallholders. As a result of these developments Kim Yongsŏp concluded that the accumulation of wealth through tenancy by rich landlords had widened the gap between rich and poor.[14]

The impoverishment of the less industrious peasant or landless tenants could have been a necessary but unfortunate consequence of progressive developments in land tenure relations, a by-product of the concentration of landownership in the midst of a shift to market-oriented agricultural production by a small number of enterprising landlords. Except for the growth in cotton and cotton textile exports that financed copper imports for the minting of metallic cash in the late seventeenth and eighteenth centuries, and the growth of some exports of ginseng, there is little evidence of a significant growth in an external market for agricultural products or any great growth of the urban population. Nor is there sufficient evidence to indicate that there was any great shift away from agriculture to industry or that the cotton and homespun cotton textile industry was assuming a significant proportion of the economy. Failing proof of any major shift away from agriculture and consumption to industry and commercially marketed products, the pattern of increased concentration of landholding and deteriorating conditions of tenant tenure would seem to demonstrate an increase in peasant discontent, if not the immiseration of the majority of peasants.

"Managerial Peasants" as a Cause of Social Mobility

As pointed out before, Kim Yongsŏp followed the lead provided by Shikata Hiroshi, who in his early studies of population and status pointed out that in the few villages he examined near Taegu in Kyŏngsang Province from 1690 to 1858 the household population fluctuated only slightly, but the percentage of what he defined as yangban households increased steadily from 8.3 to 65.5 percent, the percentage of commoner households increased slightly from 51.1 to 59.9 percent between 1690 and 1789 but then declined sharply to 32.8 percent by 1858, and the percentage of slave households began at 40.6 percent, declined sharply to 5.4 percent by 1783–89, and then still more to 1.7 percent by 1858. Kim accepted the validity of Shikata's findings almost without question, and then sought to find the economic reasons for these social changes.

He attributed the rise in the number and percentage of yangban in the population to the new opportunities for the private accumulation of economic wealth, and the accumulation of surpluses by the range of middle peasants (presumably owning from 0.5-1.0 *kyŏl*) per household originally.[15] In conclusion, he argued that a "managerial" or entrepreneurial type of landowner was the core of this drive for upward social mobility. His managerial landowner, however, was a hypothetical figure, not one based on an empirical examination of the account books of even a single such landowner to calculate the degree of rationality used to cut costs. Such cutting of costs was possibly through employing more efficient wage labor over sharecropping tenancy arrangements, by increasing the inputs of fertilizer, experimenting with more productive varieties of seed, maximizing profits by aiming at sales of surplus on the market, or reinvesting those profits either in agricultural production or in nonagricultural industries.

One of Kim's conclusions was that the economic fortunes of yangban as a whole had probably declined severely by the late seventeenth century. Unfortunately, the validity of his quantitative evidence on the distribution of landownership by status was weakened considerably because he assumed that the *kiju* were all landowners when an unknown portion could easily have been tenant cultivators. Based on this questionable evidence he concluded that the yangban *kiju* were generally better off than commoners and slaves, but not all of them were, and in all but one district about half or more of the yangban were below the poverty line (ownership of .25 *kyŏl*). Some commoners held more land than some yangban, and in some districts, some slaves held more than a number of yangban and commoners.[16] Unfortunately, the *yang'an* data do not reveal the extent of the holdings of large landlords, undoubtedly because they were disguised by registration in the names of their slaves and tenants. Nevertheless, even though it may not be possible to rely on Kim's quantitative calculations, his general conclusions about the decline of many yangban to subsistence levels, or even below, and the general fragmentation of landholdings by the peasantry was undoubtedly true.

Kim has written that the evidence from his studies showed a trend that became more prominent by the end of the dynasty: greater opportunities for the accumulation of wealth by the lower commoner and slave status groups in Korean society until eventually commoners bought yangban titles and flooded the yangban ranks, and slaves bought their freedom or ran away from their homes and gained liberation in that manner. This conclusion, however, is open to some question. It is hard to believe Shikata's finding that the number of bona fide yangban increased from 8 to 65 percent of the population, especially since the more cautious analysis of Kim Yŏngmo has shown that the greatest increase came in the group he portrayed as quasi-yangban and Song June-ho has rejected the idea that some people in the *yang'an* registered as *yuhak* or *p'umgwan* were really members of bona fide yangban families.[17] One has to presume that what was really taking place was the purchase of rank without office from the government or false registration by the bribery of local clerks. In short, Shikata Hiroshi grossly overcounted the yangban population, and Kim Yŏngsŏp accepted his conclusions without question.

By Song June-ho's definition of yangban status, the purchase of a title, or even appointment to a regular post, would not automatically elevate one from the ranks of the commoners to the yangban because bona fide yangban families almost always had to have an illustrious ancestor in their background. Furthermore, since passing the civil service examinations was the main criterion for obtaining high office and the status that accompanied it, Wagner's studies have shown that the influx of new families into the ranks of degree-holders and the highest ranking officials not only remained small to the end of the dynasty, but the opportunity for the admission of new families to their ranks decreased over time.[18]

What about the relationship between the still narrow pool of yangban degree-holders and officeholders to the possession of land and wealth? It is obvious that many members of yangban families were not able either to pass the examinations or gain office, and it would appear that many of them were reduced to difficult economic circumstances and eventually lost status, their descendants showing up on the military registers as soldiers or support taxpayers. Yet it is unrealistic to expect that the *yang'an* registers of *kiju* provide a satisfying description of the pattern of landownership since the large estate owners and landlords described in the work of Yi Kyŏngsik and many others simply do not appear, and one would have to conclude that the yangban were exclusively dependent on official salaries and bribes, but not landed property, whether inherited or purchased.

What about the pattern of inheritance? The Chosŏn dynasty law code suggests that property was divided among the sons in the latter Chosŏn period, with only an extra portion of about one-fifth the total granted to the eldest son, who had responsibility for conducting ancestral sacrifice to the father.[19] One might therefore expect a perpetual reduction of large inheritances by this mechanism, countering any trend toward the accumulation of gigantic estates.[20]

On the other hand, if it were held that large landlords disappeared from Chosŏn society after the Imjin War, it would be almost impossible to understand the concern of statecraft thinkers about the concentration of land in the hands of the landlord class. There is no reason to deny the coexistence of fragmented holdings and large estates, and large estates probably consisted of a collection of scattered small plots cultivated by both slaves and commoner tenants before 1780, and primarily commoner tenants after that date. If this pattern is correct, then by the mid-nineteenth century the landlords remained in possession of a large percentage of national wealth, while the smallholding peasants and tenants were the victims of immiseration.

Productivity

Kim Yongsŏp, Yi T'aejin, and other scholars have also assumed that an increase in agricultural productivity generated by improvements in technique and technology coupled with the emergence of enterprising peasants created surpluses that allowed upward social mobility in late Chosŏn. Direct evidence about the presumption of increased productivity would be desirable, but the available statistics are somewhat ambiguous. The wide variation in the fertility of the land throughout the country makes an estimate of average production per acre complex. From the beginning of the dynasty to 1430 the land tax was based on the division of land into three grades of fertility, but in 1430 it was pointed out that only 0.1 to 0.2 percent of the land in Kyŏngsang and Chŏlla provinces really qualified as the best land, and only 1 to 2 percent of the land met the standards for medium productivity. Since the other 98 percent of the land was graded at the lowest level of fertility, it would probably make more sense to concentrate on productivity of the poorest or lowest two grades of land in estimating average productivity for the nation.

Unfortunately, the estimates we have for productivity in early Chosŏn are based on a measure of the crop harvested relative to the amount of seed planted on the most fertile coastal paddy land in those two provinces, not the least fertile land. For fertile land 1-2 *mal* of seed yielded a dozen *sŏm* (i.e., 180 *mal*) of grain, a yield/seed ratio of 90/1 or 180/1, a higher estimate than Yi Ik made of 60/1 for the early eighteenth century, while in the upland dry fields of Kyŏnggi and Kangwŏn provinces, 1-2 *sŏm* (15–30 *mal*) of seed yielded 5–6 *sŏm* (75–90 *mal*) of crop, a crop/seed ratio that varied from a low of 2.5/1 to a high of 6/1, somewhat lower than Yi Ik's estimate of 10/1.[21] This yield/seed ratio on dry land was closer to Braudel's estimate of wheat yields for Europe from the fifteenth through eighteenth centuries, but luckily for the Koreans, rice, grown primarily in the southern three provinces, was the staple crop where yields were much higher.

Another estimate of production was based on the yield per *kyŏl*, but unfortunately the area of one *kyŏl* varied from 2.2 to 9 acres depending on the fertility of the land – a less than ideal measure for a modern statistician. One estimate of the average production of rice per *kyŏl* in the late Koryŏ period in the 1380s was 45 *sŏm*, and in 1446 the Chŏnje sangjŏngso (Bureau for the Determination of the Land System) reported that the average yield on 1 *kyŏl* of land was 53.3 *sŏm* (799.5 *mal*), but these two estimates were only for the most fertile land in the country. Kim Chaejin discounted this high a yield for estimating average productivity and concluded that the average yield must have been 20 *sŏm/kyŏl*.[22] In fact, in 1445 during the debate over the *kongbŏp* tax reform, Ha Yŏn estimated that the most productive land yielded 50 to 60 *sŏm/kyŏl* while the least productive produced only 20 to 30 *sŏm/kyŏl*, so that the average yield must have been 40 *sŏm/kyŏl*, but this is a numerical average only and did not weight the calculation by any estimate of the percentage of land in the best and worst categories. Of the six categories of *kyŏl* established in 1445, the highest and lowest two ranks of fertility existed only rarely; most land was graded as third or fourth grade.[23] On this basis, the average yield should have been closer to 25 to 30 than 40 *sŏm/kyŏl*. Kim Chaejin's estimate of 20 *sŏm/kyŏl* could easily have been correct except that the statistical basis for an exact estimate is lacking.

In the early seventeenth century after Hideyoshi's invasion had laid waste the land, Cho Ik estimated the yield/seed ratio of agricultural land at 18.75 to 20/1 (750/40 or 600/30 *mal*) for the most fertile land under the most favorable weather conditions, 10 to 11.25/1 for land of medium fertility under average weather conditions, and 5 to 7.5/1 for the poorest land during the worst weather conditions – a serious *decline* from the yield/seed standards of the mid-fifteenth century!

On the other hand, the estimate of productivity per *kyŏl* was from 10 to 50 *sŏm/kyŏl*, while the production from fields of average fertility under average weather conditions was 20 to 30 *sŏm/kyŏl* – figures that were not that different from the early Chosŏn period. Since the tax rate was 4 *mal/kyŏl* on the poorest land, and 6 *mal/kyŏl* on average land, the tax rate on average land was from 1.7 to 2.7 percent of the crop on land of poor and medium fertility (6 *mal*/350 *mal* – 4 *mal*/150 *mal*), indicating that the tax rate had dropped considerably from the beginning of the dynasty, reflecting the pathetic agricultural conditions after the invasions and the government's desire to reduce taxation to a minimum to aid the subsistence of the peasant population.[24]

As mentioned above, in the early eighteenth century Yi Ik wrote that the yield/seed ratio for rice on the worst land was no more than $^{10}/_{1}$. Although he thought the ratio on the best land might be as high as $^{60}/_{1}$, he doubted if that were so. His overall estimate, therefore, did not indicate a major rise in productivity in the century after the Imjin War. Tasan (Chŏng Yagyong) in the early nineteenth century estimated that the yield/seed ratio on the best paddy land was $^{100}/_{1}$ and $^{20}/_{1}$ for the worst, but he also estimated the yield per *kyŏl* at 800 *mal* for the best land, 600 *mal* for land of moderate fertility, and 400 *mal* for the least fertile, or 40, 30, and 20 *sŏm/kyŏl* by his calculations.[25] This latter set of figures indicated that the yield on the best land may have declined slightly while the worst land may have produced two times more than it had at the beginning of the dynasty.

Tasan also made estimates for the yield/seed ratio in the Chŏlla Province breadbasket area, but they did not indicate any increase in productivity over the previous century! He estimated that for Chŏlla Province 1 *kyŏl* of the most fertile paddy land was equivalent to 20 *majigi* (*turak* in Sino-Korean pronunciation, the amount of land on which 20 *mal* could be planted as seed) while the poorest land was equivalent to 40 *majigi*. Thus the yield from 1 *kyŏl* (or 20 *majigi*) of prime paddy was 1,200 *mal* or 60 *sŏm* by Tasan's calculations, a yield/seed ratio of $^{60}/_{1}$, while the yield on the poorest land (40 *majigi*) was 400 *mal* or 20 *sŏm* and a ratio of $^{10}/_{1}$. Thus, in Chŏlla the yield/seed ratio was almost identical to Yi Ik's estimate a century before, while the per *kyŏl* product on the most fertile land was higher than other provinces, but not higher than the best land in the early Chosŏn period.[26]

A ratio of ten grains for every seed sown, let alone sixty, was of course significantly larger than the average low yields from wheat cultivation in Europe from the fifteenth through the eighteenth centuries. Fernand Braudel estimated the average yield/seed ratio at no more than $^{5}/_{1}$ and sometimes less, with one grain deducted for the next season's planting, and an average yield per hectare at 7.5 hectolitres or about 17.6 bushels per hectare or 7.16 bushels per acre.[27]

The Japanese were the first to introduce modern measurements into the study of Korean agriculture, and Hoon K. Lee's study of Korean agriculture in 1936 based on Japanese colonial government statistics showed an average yield for all varieties of rice at 17.17 bushels per acre from 1911 to 1915, while Hishimoto Chōji found in 1938 a slightly lower rice yield per acre at the beginning of the colonial period in 1910 of 15.55 bushels (38.1 bushels/ha, or 0.473 metric tons/acre).[28] This figure could have been smaller in the mid-nineteenth century or earlier, but in any case it was about double the average wheat production per acre in Europe through the eighteenth century, indicating, as Braudel pointed out for the rice culture of East Asia in general, that Korean agricultural productivity was far in advance of Europe. Nevertheless, despite the Korean evidence of higher ratios of production on the most fertile land in Korea that would have yielded a total product six times greater than Europe, or about 45 bushels/acre, the average production figures that Hishimoto and Hoon K. Lee discovered just about matched the productivity of the least fertile land, undoubtedly because the vast majority of land in Korea was at the lowest level of fertility.

Crude though these calculations may be, they call into question much of the recent Korean literature about improvements in agricultural productivity. There is little question that the extension of irrigation, transplantation, and double cropping in the south must have improved average yields over what they were at the beginning of the Chosŏn dynasty, but Hishimoto held Korean production standards at the end of the dynasty in relatively low esteem and took pride in the accomplishments of the Japanese colonial administration in raising acreage productivity in only eight years (by 1917) to 20 bushels/acre, a figure just slightly less than the extrapolated estimate for Japanese acreage production around 1880.[29]

Pre-Meiji Japan would provide a better comparison for Korean rice productivity than with the wheat culture of pre-modern Europe, especially since so much has been written about the economic advances made in Tokugawa Japan prior to the Meiji Restoration in 1868. Unfortunately, the figures for agricultural productivity have been mired in dispute since James Nakamura rejected government statistics, claiming they had underreported actual production. He proposed an extremely high productivity rate of 84.6 bushels per hectare of paddy or 34.5 bushels/acre for the years 1878–82, a figure 2.2 times greater than Hishimoto's estimate for Korea in 1910.[30] Nakamura was attempting to argue that the pre-modern expansion of agricultural productivity in Japan actually fueled the industrial development of Japan in the Meiji period by mobilizing savings for investment in industry. The other two, more modest, estimates for rice yields in Japan in this period were 25.1 bushels/acre (61.4 bushels/ha) and 26.9 bushels/acre (66 bushels/ha), and the last estimate is the conclusion of a more recent study designed to modify Nakamura's claims.[31] In summary, Hishimoto's figure of 15.55 bushels/acre for Korean productivity about 1910 was about 58 percent of this most recent revised figure for Japanese productivity for 1880, and it is possible that the average yield on Korean paddy may have been still lower in that year. For that matter the estimate of yield in the Kamakura period in Japan (1191–1333) was 22.5 bushels/acre, still a higher percentage than Korean production in 1910.[32]

On the other hand, productivity in Korea in 1910 appears to have about the same as China in 1400 in the early Ming dynasty. Although estimating the average yield of rice (unhulled) per acre for the pre-twentieth century era is quite difficult because the figures either represent yields on the best quality land, or the quality is not specified. Francesca Bray found citations of productivity for the period from 1050 to 1700 indicating a range from 3.1 to 21.6 bushels/acre.[33] Medium quality land in Shanghai in 1511 yielded 9.27 bushels/acre, and the yield in good years in Canton in the late seventeenth century was 11.8 bushels/acre.[34] If Dwight Perkins's calculations of average yields for China are converted to bushels per acre, the amount would be 15.29 bushels/acre for 1400, 22.33 bushels/acre for 1770, and 26.73 bushels/acre for 1850.[35] Perkins calculated yields in the twentieth century at 242 catties/*shih mou* for 1933, and 274 catties/*shih mou* for 1957, or 26.62 and 30.14 bushels/acre. The bushels/acre figure of 27 bushels for 1850 is close to double Korea's output, and 30 for 1933 is still ahead of Korea's at that time.[36]

By the mid-1920s Korean productivity had risen beyond the 15.5 bushels/acre of 1910. Hoon K. Lee found an average rice yield in the 1921–25 period of 18.81 bushels per acre, a time when about half the rice crop was planted in improved varieties of seed introduced after 1910, while Hishimoto Chōji reported rice productivity in 1918 at 20 bushels/acre.[37]

In summary, the average productivity of the rice crop in Korea in 1910 was significantly less than Japan or China, but this measure does not take into account total food production.

The Growth of Population and Per-capita Productivity

Estimating the national population for the pre-twentieth century period is fraught with difficulty because of the unreliability of traditional government statistics in the Chosŏn period. Demographers agree that the figures for the number of persons in the traditional records cannot be accepted, and Tony Michell's demographic study has been based on statistics for households multiplied by a crude estimate that includes a guess about a uniform level of underreporting. In any case, he has written that the Korean population grew steadily from about 4.4 million people at the beginning of the dynasty to about 9.8 million just prior to Hideyoshi's invasions in 1592, an average growth of 0.61 percent a year for the 200-year period. It then dropped by as much as 20 percent or 2 million during the Imjin War, and did not reattain the 1592 level until about 1650. The population continued to increase to 12.3 million by 1693, when a famine from 1693 to 1695 caused another severe drop to 10.2 million. Recovery occurred by about 1717 and further growth continued to 13.6 million by 1732. Several population crises occurred thereafter in the eighteenth century, which interrupted short-term trends toward population increase. The population achieved 14 million by 1810 before the crisis of 1812–13, when it dropped to 12.4 million by 1816. Thereafter the population fluctuated between 12.2 and 12.7 million to 1876, a million less than the eighteenth century.[38]

Kim Yongsŏp, Yi Chunyŏng, and Michell have argued that the production of rice and barley, even millet and beans, increased after the Imjin War of 1592–98 because of the expansion of wet rice cultivation and transplantation on paddy land, the sudden expansion of irrigation through the construction of reservoirs and poulders, double cropping, particularly of rice and barley on paddy fields, and the introduction of new crops like red peppers, gourds, and tobacco. Transplanting spread everywhere except the northern provinces by 1674, and the increase in production allowed a growth of population (from 9.8 to 12.3 million according to Michell), but also greater vulnerability to drought and disease, leading to a leveling of population by the eighteenth century, and a slight decline in the nineteenth.

If one were to look for parallels to this Korean experience, the closest one might be what Bray has described as the Green Revolution begun in the Sung dynasty in which production was increased by land reclamation, irrigation, water control, multiple-cropping, commercial agriculture, regional specialization, and the development of the silk and tea industries. There was also the expansion of production through migration into central and southwest China in the eighteenth-century Ch'ing dynasty, after which "population growth overtook agricultural production," leading to rural impoverishment.[39]

One of the main differences between China and Korea, however, was that the increase in agricultural production and the greater development of the commercial economy in the Ch'ing as well as Sung periods, was followed by a rapid increase in population, whereas the Korean population appears to have leveled off after 1693 and subsequently fluctuated between ten and twelve and one-half million, somewhat similar to the stabilization of the Japanese population at thirty-five million in the late Tokugawa period.

We will see in part 6 how the development of copper currency in the late seventeenth century and later undoubtedly indicated the expansion of surplus product that was sold on the market. On the other hand, that surplus production was not great enough to create the accumulation of sufficient capital to fuel a take-off phase for rapid economic growth, let alone sustain the continuation of population growth in the eighteenth and nineteenth centuries, if Michell's population figures are to be believed. At the current stage of our knowledge, it would be safer to disclaim some of the arguments about the magnitude of the advance in production and productivity.

Nineteenth-Century Peasant Rebellion

The nineteenth century was a period of serious peasant rebellion: the Hong Kyŏngnae rebellion of 1812, the Imsul rebellion of 1862, and the peasant uprising of 1894 that accompanied the revolt of the Tonghak religious movement in search of religious toleration. While maldistribution of landownership and onerous conditions of tenancy were important contributing factors in these revolts, they were not the only ones. Unfair distribution of the tax burden and the corrupt behavior of magistrates and clerks contributed to discontent as well.

Even though the core area of the 1862 rebellion was a section of Chŏlla Province that had a long history of tenant disputes, the rebels directed their attacks against the government and its officials rather than the landlords. Although government investigators were not necessarily the most objective analysts of the rebellion, their opinions are the only records we have, and they identified the major causes of rebellion as the absence of adequate credit, usurious interest rates, and the regressive and oppressive cloth support tax for duty soldiers as well as improprieties in the registration and taxation of land.

There is no doubt, however, that the skewing of landownership patterns and the deterioration of landlord/tenant relations had contributed to an agrarian crisis that resulted in a major peasant rebellion. That denouement would tend to place the Korean agrarian economy in the same boat with Ch'ing dynasty China, which despite a greater degree of commercialization and monetization of the economy than in Chosŏn Korea, ended up with the massive T'aip'ing Rebellion in the mid-nineteenth century that reflected the income distribution crisis of that society. While it is certainly possible that nineteenth- century rebellion in Korea could have been the consequence of the frustration of higher expectations from a more prosperous peasantry rather than lower levels of income, it is far more likely that the growth of landlordism, tenancy, usury, and indebtedness were products of the deterioration of the system of distribution of both wealth and land.

Having described the history of the Korean economy to the end of the nineteenth century, let us turn back to the response of the statecraft successors to Yu Hyŏngwŏn to the problems of the agrarian economy and their proposals for reform. Did they perceive a better or more progressive route out of the agrarian crisis; did they transcend or surpass the solutions that Yu had to offer?

YI IK (SŎNGHO)

Yi Ik, one of Yu Hyŏngwŏn's leading early eighteenth-century admirers, was particularly sensitive to Yu's discussion of land reform because he himself was a landlord and slaveowner who by the 1740s was losing most of his land and slaves.[40] Yi was certainly not one to admire the adverse results of concentrated landownership, nor portray it as the signs of economic development. On the contrary, he shared Yu's view that in principle land ought to be owned by the state, and that all land was public land (*kongjŏn*) or the king's land (*wangjŏn*) as Wang Mang had declared at the end of the Former Han dynasty. Both men recognized the existence of private property in land but not anything like a natural right to its ownership by private parties. Yi was far more interested in fair distribution than in maximization of profits. He criticized the large landlords who were causing the bankruptcy of small peasants through debt, and he argued that the state had every right to take over their land and redistribute it to poor peasants, since the landlord was really only borrowing the use of land from the king. He repeated Yu's call for "setting the land boundaries straight," by which he meant the necessity for full and accurate registration of all arable land.[41]

Although Yi sympathized with poor peasants, he also agreed with Yu that the *kunja* or men of virtue were entitled to support from the *soin*, the small men, or ordinary peasantry. He parted company from Yu, however, on the question of attempting an approximation of the well-field ideal in land relations because the method of agriculture had changed too much since late Chou times.

He imagined that in the Chou in the upland areas the fields were all dry and the boundaries were set by sluices and ditches and the plants on the dikes drew off the water from the ditches, an impractical arrangement for modern wet-rice agriculture in Korea. Furthermore, well-fields could only have been laid out in the plains and divided up by embankments that served as walkways, but water stagnated in the fields, and eventually the wind and rain broke down the embankments. Thus, recreating the ancient methods of agriculture as well as the raised embankments was almost impossible.[42]

Yi Ik also shrank from both Yu Hyŏngwŏn's plan for total nationalization and redistribution and any coerced confiscation of excessive landholdings. He argued that although some might think that force would be necessary to get the large landlords to divest themselves of some of their property, if force were used, "it would destroy the law." No owner should be forced to sell land against his will, and no peasant with insufficient holdings should be allowed to importune a large landlord to sell his land to him. Instead, each individual would be recognized as having rights to 100 *myo* or 1 *kyŏng* of permanent land (*yŏng'ŏpchŏn*), in emulation of Lin Hsün of the Sung dynasty, who proposed a limit of 50 *myo* of permanent land and argued that 50 *myo* was sufficient because 41 *myo* at that time was equivalent to 100 *myo* or 1 *kyŏng* in the Chou period. The only prohibition that Yi attached to this permanent land was a ban on the sale of any part of it. Sales would only be permitted of land owned above the 1-*kyŏng* permanent land parcel to prevent a poor peasant from selling his last remaining plot to pay a debt, protecting him from the overwhelming monetary power of the rich who had enough wealth to buy all the land they wanted from the poor.

Yi thought that through the normal practice of subdivision of property among male heirs, within a few generations the surplus landholdings of the rich would be reduced as a matter of course, but this was a mild, cautious, and probably worthless method of land redistribution for the benefit of the poor and landless peasants. Despite Yi's sympathy for the plight of the poor peasants, he was even more limited than Yu had been by his consideration for the sensitivities of the yangban landlords.[43] But this did not mean that he favored free market capitalism and profit maximization as the solution to the distribution crisis; on the contrary he advocated realistic means of limiting property ownership and preventing free purchase and sale to protect the smallholders from the loss of their land.

Han Woo-keun in his extensive study of Yi Ik has pointed out that Sŏ Myŏngsin actually recommended a limited-field system to King Yŏngjo in 1740 because restoration of the well-field system was impossible, but Yŏngjo rejected it because he did not think it would be possible to confiscate all land over the limit established by the state and grant it to poor peasants, especially since the large landlords included the *sadaebu* (i.e., yangban). In other words, Yŏngjo shrank from even a land-limitation program, let alone total confiscation, because he feared a direct challenge to the interests of yangban![44] But does this mean that King Yŏngjo defended landlord interests because he thought private ownership of land represented a progressive force in Korean society, or that he feared the threat to political stability posed by a discontented landlord class? I would prefer the latter. Had either Yu or Yi been alive, they certainly would not have applauded King Yŏngjo for defending the interests of the landlord as the harbinger of free market enterprise and the engine of greater production; rather they would have grieved mightily over the lost opportunity for fair distribution.

Although Yi agreed with Yu's argument that the *kyŏng-myo* system of areal measurement was more rational and better than the Korean *kyŏl-bu* system based on a constant crop volume, he still remained convinced that if the Korean system were well used, it would not obstruct attempts at land reform. He felt it was more important to achieve complete registration of all land and readjust the grades of tax to the fertility of the land, providing that any owner who disagreed with the tax assessment should be allowed to petition the authorities for a reconsideration of his tax. Since he felt that since the land tax was graded officially at a 4:1 ratio of productivity between the most and least fertile land, there was lttle to complain about.[45]

For that matter, Yi Ik also argued that the tax rate was not the main problem for the peasantry because the complex system of graded taxation of King Sejong in the mid-fifteenth century had been so difficult to maintain that the authorities had in fact abandoned the higher rates for a uniform tax of 4 *mal* of hulled rice per *kyŏl*, closer to one-thirtieth the crop rather than one-tenth. Even though the total taxes on land had been increased from 4 *mal/kyŏl* to about 20 *mal/kyŏl* by the addition of 12 *mal/kyŏl* for the *taedongmi* surtax to take the place of in-kind tribute, and a little extra for the *samsumi* to pay for the support of the new troops of the Military Training Directorate (Hullyŏn-dogam), that was still only 5 percent of his estimate of 400 *mal* of hulled rice (or 1,000 *mal* of unhulled rice) per *kyŏl*.

If one were to calculate the land tax using a more liberal estimate of 40 *mal/kyŏl*, the tax rate would still only be 10 percent of the crop, the classical ideal of the perfect tax rate. The main problem for most peasants, therefore, was the 50 percent sharecropping rent paid by tenants. Any reduction of the tax rate would only benefit the landlord, and the landlords, in his estimation, only represented 10 or 20 percent of the rural population.

The real problem was the small size of peasant holdings, which were were less than 1 *kyŏl* of land, whatever its grade, and only 10 or 20 percent of peasants owned or even rented that amount. Elsewhere he estimated the crop of a tenant who cultivated 1 *kyŏl* at 360 *mal* (24 *sŏm*) on dry land and 320 *mal* (21.3 *sŏm*) on wet rice land, somewhat less than the 400 *mal/kyŏl* (26.7 *sŏm/kyŏl*) estimate he used in discussing the land tax, leaving him with after-rent income of 160 to 180 *mal*. Since the average family consisted of five or six persons, their consumption needs would require 230 *mal* of income a year, a monthly consumption rate of approximately 3 *mal* per month – a fairly conservative estimate since Yi's previous estimate for monthly subsistence for rank 7–9 officials was 6 *mal*. Yi's message, in short, was that tenancy had pushed the tenant cultivator of even a relatively ample 1 *kyŏl* of land below the subsistence level.

Furthermore, the plight of some tenants had increased because they now had to pay the land tax and supply their own seed.[46]

In short, Yi was undoubtedly inspired by Yu's *Pan'gye surok*, but it did not mean that he was bound by the obligations of discipleship to parrot Yu's belief in the advantages of state confiscation of private property in mechanical fashion. If anything Yi's proposal was more conservative than Yu's because he refrained from using force or coercion to limit maximum holdings and achieve redistribution. He proposed allowing tenants to buy more land not because he believed that private ownership was the foundation of incentives for profit maximization and increased production, but rather the most feasible and practical means for rectification of the maldistribution of wealth.

KING CHŎNGJO'S REQUEST FOR ADVICE, 1797–98

In the face of a series of crop disasters in 1792, 1794, 1797, and 1798, King Chŏngjo put out a number of requests for recommendations for solving the problems of the land system as a whole. In 1797 and 1798 sixty-nine memorials were submitted in response to that request, and although most memorials were from scholars from the countryside and only a few high officials dared to risk their careers by making serious suggestions, the respondents included some of the leading reform thinkers of the day, including Pak Chiwŏn, Sŏ Yugu, and Tasan. Almost all of them adopted what amounted to Yi Ik's position: that the well-field system could not be restored, but that some form of limited land tenure was by far the next best remedy. By that time majority reform opinion had virtually abandoned any notion of a literal resuscitation of the well-field model, but while the Border Defense Command signified its admiration for the limitation of landownership, it rejected even that as impractical.

Kim Yongsŏp has pointed out that these proponents of a limited-land system suggested liberal limits that were far too high to be effective because they were afraid that more restrictive limits would provoke active resistance by landowners and landlords. One man recommended a limit of 10 *kyŏl* of land (i.e., from 24.5 acres for first-grade *kyŏl* to 100 acres for sixth grade), another proposed a limit of 150 *turak* (i.e., *majigi*) equivalent to 18.4 acres of first grade *kyŏl*.

Early in 1799 King Chŏngjo agreed that land limitation was hardly practical, especially because it had not succeeded in China either; in the 1,600 years since the end of the Han dynasty a land limitation or distribution system had only been practiced for two hundred years. Emperor Hsiao-wen of the Northern Wei had instituted the equal-field system (in 485), but in his view only with respect to land already possessed by the people, and Emperor T'ai-tsung of the T'ang had modeled his *kubunjŏn* rotating land grants and permanent grants (*seŏpchŏn*) on the Northern Wei model, but by the *ying-hui* era (650–56) the land had already been taken over by large landlords. He thought that it would be impossible for any land distribution scheme to work in Korea because a grant of 1 *kyŏl* for each farmer would have required 6,360,000 *kyŏl* for distribution even if all civil and military officials were left out. He confessed that he had been trying to work out a solution for some form of redistribution or limitation since he ascended the throne in 1776, but he been unable to do so.

In 1795 he commented that if he could only restore the office-land (*chikchŏn*) system (in actuality prebendal grants to incumbent officials only) adopted by King Sejo in 1466 and then extend it by granting land to the scholars and commoners, the Chosŏn dynasty would deserve ranking as the fourth sage dynasty along with the Hsia, Shang, and Chou of Chinese antiquity. In any case, he took no steps to implement it.[47]

The government also rejected two other plans, one to force wealthy landlords to rent some of their land to poor or landless peasants, and another to grant ownership rights to landless peasants who reclaimed unused land to protect them against the return of the original owner who had the legal right to stake a claim to the property. While none of the officials at court was willing to overturn this legal protection of ownership, Chŏngjo ruminated that it might be possible to grant a cultivation right to the squatter.

King Chŏngjo was willing to accept a proposal for a three-year tax exemption for reclaimed land since such a law was already on the books but had been neglected by local clerks. He was not willing, however, to extend the tax exemption to five or ten years because he could not afford to forfeit the revenue for so long. Even the idea of a three-year tax exemption for slash-and-burn cultivation in the hills was rejected because the law provided for taxation of any cultivation of this type; only the appeal to prohibit illegal exactions by the clerks received a positive response from government officials. The government showed little enthusiasm for the recommendation to recruit landless vagrants, settle them in sparsely populated regions, and grant state support for the purchase of tools, oxen, and irrigation ditches. The Border Defense Command even rejected a request to carry out a nationwide cadastral survey to prevent the continuation of tax collections on land that was no longer arable, or to clarify boundaries to prevent disputes and lawsuits over trespass violations or illegal seizures of land, preferring simply to order magistrates to inspect crops or conduct partial surveys. No order was made to carry out a long overdue national survey.[48]

In short, what was ostensibly King Chŏngjo's ambitious attempt to consider all the possibilities of reform ended in dismal failure. The most radical proposal, land limitation, was a puerile attenuation of Yu Hyŏngwŏn's more ambitious program, but even far less ambitious suggestions than these were fully stymied by the king's ministers, who were obviously unwilling to countenance any weakening of landlord prerogatives.

TASAN (CHŎNG YAGYONG)

The Early Land Reform Plan

While little excitement was to be expected from the court, one of the greatest statecraft thinkers at the turn of the nineteenth century, Tasan (pen name of Chŏng Yagyong), was willing to challenge the status quo, at least in his writings. Kim Yongsŏp has recently shown that Tasan changed his thinking on land reform after his exile in 1801. His first programmatic thoughts on the land question written sometime between 1793 and 1800 stated not only that the literal replication of the Chou well-field system would be impossible, but also that the limited-field system of the Han dynasty and the Northern Wei or T'ang equal-field system would not work either because Korean topography was broken up by hills and cultivation was primarily wet-rice agriculture, in contrast to the flat land and dry farming that characterized the Chou period. To adopt the well-field system would have meant the abandonment of irrigated wet-field rice cultivation or the reclamation of upland regions for farming, the kind of criticism that Yi Ik had made. Yu, on the other hand, believed that the differences between wet and dry agriculture could be ignored when instituting a program of national ownership and redistribution.[49]

To achieve full and adequate registration of land to avoid the injustice that had been wrought by underregistration or omission of cultivated land by the local clerks, Tasan followed the recommendations of Yu Chib'il, governor of Hwanghae Province in 1708, and Sin Wan in 1709, for adoption of the "square land" (*pangjŏn*) system of Chang Tsai in the Sung dynasty, and the use of the fish-scale registers (*ŏrindo*) to list all land parcels with accompanying maps of their location to prevent false registration and omission.[50]

Otherwise, Tasan concentrated his attention on technological improvement, seed selection, fertilization, weeding, better tools, labor saving, and borrowing Chinese techniques. He obtained his knowledge from agricultural texts and the reports of Koreans who had returned from China, and he wanted to publish technical manuals and distribute them to the rural areas for the peasants, promote the spread of irrigation by building dams, poulders, and reservoirs, and introduce water wheels for moving water around the fields. He hoped to raise the status and prestige of the peasant to the level of the scholars, merchants, and artisans, and encourage them to increase production and productivity.[51] His interest in technology and productivity might well be understood as a "modern" shift to increasing general wealth and welfare, except that he would have had to grasp some understanding of the need to transcend the traditional Physiocratic approach to legitimate production.

Tasan's early skepticism about the obstructions to reproducing the well-field system did not mean, however, that he was committed to the maintenance of private property. On the contrary, he called for a system of state ownership and the eradication of private ownership and the purchase and sale of land, positions that were similar to those of Yu Hyŏngwŏn. He created a scheme based on the communal ownership of land and distribution of wealth and the limitation of the land tax to an optimum of one-tenth or one-ninth the crop under his community land (*yŏjŏn*) proposal.[52]

He argued that a national program for the redistribution of land was certainly feasible: if the 800,000 *kyŏl* of land in the country (as registered in 1769) were divided among the population of 8 million (possibly an underestimate by as much as 4 million according to Tony Michell), then each household, which he felt should consist of an extended family of about 10 persons (a rather large family), could receive an allotment of 1 *kyŏl* of land, a probable area of 8.6 acres (see chap. 8) that may have been close to the approximately 7–9 acres of grade 5 or 6 land in Korea, but more than double the average holding in the late eighteenth century calculated by Kim Yongsŏp in his studies.

Tasan argued that this would be far better than the current skewed distribution of ownership, whereby rich families like the Ch'oe family in Kyŏngsang Province or the Wang family in Chŏlla had no less than 400 *kyŏl* of land and income of 10,000 *sŏm* of grain while the rest of the population was either landless or eking out their lives in penury. On the other hand, since Tasan may have underestimated the real population by 3 or 4 million and posited an unrealistic household size of 10 persons/household, the population/land ratio may have been far too great for his plan to succeed, unless, of course, the actual area of arable land was far greater than the official cadastral survey information.

Kim Yongsŏp has argued that Tasan had been stimulated to a more radical position by his observation of the stripping of small plots from independent peasants by land barons, the growth of tenancy and hired labor, and the skewed distribution of land among peasant proprietors. He felt it was perverse for the ruler of a state to tolerate present conditions in land tenure especially because it was his responsibility to ensure an equitable distribution of wealth.

Despite his optimistic estimate of the possibility of distributing 1 *kyŏl* of land to each household, Tasan was still worried that the Korean population might be too large for the redistribution of land to everyone. Since he did think that the equal-field system of the Northern Wei had failed because it had forced the distribution of land to the whole population, he suggested that the problem of surplus population could be solved by allowing those men interested in commerce and handicrafts to shift to those occupations freely, reducing the demand for land grants – a significant departure from Yu Hyŏngwŏn's belief that a land grant of 50 *myo* (half a peasant allotment) had to be provided to artisans and merchants because their incomes from these occupations might not be sufficient to sustain their families. Living in an age when the use of cash and market activities had developed beyond what existed during Yu's time, Tasan was convinced that merchants and artisans could make adequate livings on their own, and he was willing to limit land grants only to those farmers willing to cultivate the land with perseverance and diligence.[53] Although he justified this position by a slight reinterpretation of classical thought, insisting that the ancient Chinese sages had always intended to limit grants only to willing and able tillers of the soil and had thus allowed others to function as artisans and merchants, his instincts definitely marked a departure from the fundamentalist Physiocracy of traditional Confucian thought.

Like Yu Hyŏngwŏn Tasan also argued that the equal-field system of the Northern Wei and T'ang dynasties was too difficult to operate because it required constant revision in the distribution of land as people died and children became adults. Furthermore, that system did not provide for variations in land grants to take into account differences of fertility. Although he did not take solace, as Yu did, in overcoming the complexity of population movement and other forms of change by insisting on fixing land boundaries in embossed squares to create a stable and unchanging basis for land distribution and taxation, he did conclude that the limited-field system would not work because it would be impossible to prevent people from buying and selling land on their own, especially if they bought land in the name of other people, and state ownership was the only possible formula for successful redistribution.[54]

Tasan stressed the importance of the community in sharing the ownership of land and the work associated with production, and he believed that the optimum community (*yŏ*, named after one of the putative communities in the Chou era) should consist of about thirty families. The crop produced by a community working on land owned by the state but granted to individual households would be turned over to the head of the thirty-family unit called the *yŏjang*, who would then allocate after-tax shares of the crop to the families on the basis of work performed by family members. Individual peasants were to be remunerated at the rate of 4 *toe* (.4 *mal*, or 10.4 *mal* for a 26-day month?, 124.8 *mal* or 8.32 *sŏm*/year) for every day of labor. Agricultural tools, however, could be owned privately by individuals. Taxes would be fixed for each community based on a constant rate of 10 percent of the crop and a one-time assessment of the fertility of its land and a calculation of the community's average tax yield over the past.

Possibly Tasan's greatest departure from Yu Hyŏngwŏn's plan was to eliminate land grants altogether (let alone extra-large ones) for the scholars and officials, and provide only salaries for the support of incumbent officials. He felt that since they did not work the land, they were entitled neither to land grants nor to a share of the harvest, but on the other hand nothoi of yangban (*sŏŏl*) would be eligible for a land grant under his system because he hoped to convert them from idle and despised members of the elite into productive members of society.[55] Tasan had little use for the yangban in his own time because they exploited the common peasants, acted with arrogance toward their inferiors, and spent lives of total idleness.[56] Although he acknowledged that in ancient times a legitimate distinction had been made between the *sa* (scholars) and the peasants or agriculturalists (*nong*), the *sa* of contemporary Korea did not deserve support from the public coffers because they did not serve at court, engage in agriculture, or perform any labor service for the country. He prescribed that under his system all the *sa* not employed in office were either to open up new lands for cultivation, or study the improvement of agricultural technology, animal husbandry, irrigation, and tools to help the peasants. Only those men who did engage in these useful scholarly pursuits would be entitled to adequate compensation for their labors, and only the most able people were to be appointed to office, but he defined ability as administrative talent, not moral superiority.[57]

When he relegated commerce and industry to secondary status under his *yŏjŏn* system, he hardly differed from Yu Hyŏngwŏn, Yi Ik, or most other commentators save for Yu Suwŏn in the early eighteenth century, but in his later years when he proposed the gradual adoption of elements of the well-field system to Korea, he provided for a larger role for at least commercial agricultural production and the use of the market.[58]

Yu Hyŏngwŏn had derogated the threat of a possible rebellion by the landlords against confiscation of land by contending that a courageous king could overcome all opposition by displaying resolution and determination. Tasan also maintained, like Yi Ik, that all land belonged to the king anyway, and that the emergence of private ownership of land after the Chou dynasty had deprived the emperor of his ability to improve the income of the common people, but he failed to provide a method by which the government of the time could confiscate private land from the landlords and yangban without risking serious resistance. In any case, Kim Yongsŏp was right when he wrote that there was no political support to defend confiscation or to support the interests of the dispossessed peasants, but it is difficult to say that Tasan's thinking on land reform represented either a more radical or more developed mode of thought than Yu, since both based their plans on national ownership without dealing adequately with the problem of confiscation. Tasan's major contribution was his willingness in his early plan to allow individuals to pursue commerce and industry at will to reduce the farming population, and to reduce the status and prestige of scholars and intellectuals to the equivalent of clerks.[59]

The Later Land Reform Plan

Nonetheless, during his almost twenty years in exile, Tasan modified his animus against private property and shifted to a piecemeal and gradual adoption of well-field principles on the grounds that the well-field system had not been adopted in all parts of the realm, even in Chou times. He recommended that the state use cash in its treasuries to purchase land from private owners and convert it to publicly held land. The fund for this purpose could be expanded by donations from officials or wealthy landowners, entrepreneurial activities run by officials, government takeover of mines, and public reclamation of unused land and the use of one-ninth of it as public land (*kongjŏn*) in emulation of the Chou well-field model.

Since it was a violation of propriety for a king to buy land, recruit cultivators, and then demand that they pay half the crop under a sharecropping system, Tasan also suggested that the state take over land already under its control, like the palace estates granted to princes and princesses (*kungbangjŏn*) or the colony lands (*tunjŏn*) controlled by civil and military officials, and convert them to well-field lands with a one-ninth tax rate from the cultivators. This measure would also eliminate the loss of revenue caused by the extortion and embezzlements of the palace estate stewards (*tojang*).

The capital guards could even be given leave from their duties and allowed to cultivate the military colonies in the vicinity of the capital, and the lands under the control of magistrates for yamen expenses, clerks' salaries, post station costs, grazing lands, ferry stations, and hostels could be converted to well-field principles as well. Even if it were not possible to convert all odd-shaped fields in the hills to well-field dimensions, the government could still use the fish-scale registers to record cultivated land accurately.[60]

Under this revised plan the cultivators would possess eight of the individual plots and manage them independently, a combination of public ownership and private control that Yu Hyŏngwŏn had made clear was a main feature of the Chou system. Nevertheless, Tasan added a new feature to the classical scheme by dividing the types of work involved in agriculture into six specialties: grain, fruit, vegetables, cotton, forestry, and animal husbandry (in addition to commerce and nonagricultural artisanry). Each man had to specialize in one of these occupations and would not be allowed to change. Tasan allowed these specialists to volunteer to perform their tasks in specific locations without much limitation on the amount of land they were allowed to use, primarily to raise the income of the commune through the sale of their products in the domestic market and to China.

Although Tasan insisted that the sages of antiquity had required this professionalization of occupation, Kim Yongsŏp claimed that his argument was really a distortion of the classics to justify improvement in the quality and efficiency of work in Korea, and that he was inspired to do so because he had been influenced by the growing differentiation of labor and the sale of commodity products in the market that had been taking place in a number of areas.[61]

Like his earlier, more radical *yŏjŏn* plan, Tasan also insisted that the distribution of either land or income be limited to the peasants according to the labor power (i.e., productivity) of the family rather than the individual. Now he defined the optimal family as eight individuals (instead of his previous ten), five or six of whom would be able to work the land, and this family, called the "basic farmer [family]" (*wŏnbu*), would receive a 100-*myo* grant. "Other males" (*yŏbu*) would only receive an allocation of 25 *myo*, but he meant by this term primarily a conjugal family of husband and wife and possibly minor children, and not simply unmarried or elderly single males.

He appears to have borrowed Yu Hyŏngwŏn's definition of 100 *myo* as a parcel upon which could be planted 40 *mal* of seed, 40 *turak* (*majigi,* colloquially) or 8,000 *p'yŏng* (6.5 acres at 1,224 *p'yŏng*/acre), and he calculated the yield from that area as varying from 600 to 4,000 *mal* of millet, compared to Yu's estimate of 1,600 *mal* of unhulled or 800 *mal* of hulled rice. The plot of a conjugal family, 25 *myo*, would have been about 10 *turak* or 1.6 acres. He also mentioned that 100 *myo* in Chŏlla Province (he was exiled in Kangjin) was equivalent to 1 *kyŏl* of poor land (or .5 *kyŏl* of medium land).

He arranged for the assignment of parcels on the basis of the capacity and productivity of the peasant. The best farmers and those with the most labor would be awarded the most fertile land because in the daily world of experience landlords always rented their best land to tenants with the most labor power and oxen of their own. To do otherwise would have reduced the size of the product. Granting land to peasants just to provide relief from poverty was unjustifiable because in ancient times the government did not grant land to the sick and the widowed; they simply provided for them through community relief. The tax rate would be limited because the peasants would pool their labor on the one parcel of public land (*kongjŏn*) first, an equivalent of a one-ninth tax since the eight heads of households in a well-field would presumably only be spending one-ninth their time on that plot.[62]

Since the introduction of the well-fields would take place incrementally, he also provided that in those areas where they could not be adopted the magistrate might try to distribute rental land more evenly by ensuring that each tenant might cultivate the equivalent of two parcels of land (50 *myo* at 25 *myo* per parcel), and soldiers on colony land might also be given one or two parcels as well on a 50 percent sharecropping basis. Larger amounts could be allowed for newly reclaimed land.[63]

Tasan placed more emphasis in his revised scheme on raising production rather than on equal distribution of property because he felt it was quixotic to imagine that the latter could ever be totally accomplished, and he hoped that justice could be achieved at least by reducing the tax to a consistent 10 percent of the crop. He also warned that the government should not increase its taxes on the community as its prosperity increased lest it stifle the prospect of future growth.

He favored hiring labor to cultivate commercial products or to till the land in place of duty soldiers, especially given the increasing number of landless peasants that had been driven off the land by the land grabbing of rich landlords. He even hoped to hire slaves (*tongbok*) for this purpose, presumably the slaves owned by peasants that Tasan expected would be brought with families of basic peasant households (*wŏnbu*) to cultivate their 100-*myo* parcels. Since Tasan calculated his basic household at eight persons, four more than one might expect for a normal average, and he also estimated the number of workers at five or six, the remainder probably included slaves, or hired slaves, and unmarried males in addition to other family members, a calculation that Yu Hyŏngwŏn also made in calculating family size.

In Yu Hyŏngwŏn's plan the use of slaves, especially for the cultivation of the land of the officials, was intended to be temporary because he hoped that slavery would eventually die out, but Tasan expressed no compunction about using slaves to raise production. Kim Yongsŏp has argued that Tasan's willingness to hire slaves indicated that he was more interested in borrowing the rational methods of rich peasants in the early nineteenth century to maximize production than in freeing the slaves or creating a system of perfect equality of income – a far more progressive idea than the pattern illustrated in his earlier essay on land (*chŏllon*).

Kim argued that by raising production, improving methods, stressing specialization, and favoring the most productive peasants, Tasan hoped to transform society by elevating the wealth, status, and prestige of the peasant class as a whole. He even proposed that district magistrates conduct an investigation to find peasants of the greatest ability in agriculture once every twenty years and recommend them for office either in the central government or in the local district. Kim concluded that in his later, more mature writing, Tasan must have planned to revolutionize society by expanding the number of rich peasants and educating the poor peasants in more rational methods of production, thus breaking the stranglehold on society by those few landlords and rich peasants who had become successful in recent years.[64]

Kim's argument is a curious one, as if the justification of slavery on rational, capitalistic grounds is more deserving of praise than Yu's condemnation of hereditary slavery as a violation of Confucian moral standards. On the other hand, Kim was correct in showing how Tasan's standards of reform shifted in the last part of his life in the early nineteenth century from exclusively moral criteria to arguments based on greater productivity, efficiency, and utility.

A few years ago Pak Chonggŭn praised Tasan for his concern for a more equitable distribution of wealth and his confidence in the "masses," but he criticized him for his inability to perceive the necessity to mobilize the revolutionary power of the masses to carry out a social revolution, let alone the creation of a new economic order based on capitalism or industrial production. Although Pak charged that Tasan's revolutionary method was "backward" because he aimed for gradual progressivism based on the king's authority rather than the power of mass action, it is anachronistic to expect that any of the Chosŏn dynasty statecraft reformers could have had any notion that the uneducated peasant masses possessed the potential for a revolutionary transformation of society. The Confucian reformers did, however, have a strong sense of economic equity and a powerful distaste for the maldistribution of wealth in Chosŏn society.

The evolution of Tasan's proposals on land reform does illustrate a shift from an ancient model of national ownership and equal distribution similar to Yu's plan, to an acceptance of private property with greater efficiency and productivity. The development of this mode of thought can not be attributed to the logical fruition of Yu's ideas, but to Tasan's observation of prevailing practices in farm management in the early nineteenth century, stimulated no doubt by King Chŏngjo's abject failure to seize the initiative for a land reform program in the 1790s.

Sŏ Yugu

According to Kim Yongsŏp, another representative of the new tide of rational planning and efficiency in agricultural production was the scholar-statesman, SŏYugu, son of a family of experts in agricultural methods, who authored a number of texts on the subject. In his later writings, presumably around 1820, Sŏ set forth a new program for the gradual elimination of landless peasants and tenancy and the creation of a more collective form of agriculture.[65]

Like Tasan's second plan, Sŏ's program did not involve a massive confiscation of private property from the landlords and rich peasants because he feared that they might rebel against the government. Instead, he believed that expansion of the military and civilian colony lands (*tunjŏn* or *kwandunjŏn*) that had been created to support soldiers on the frontier or pay for expenses of magistrates' yamen and some offices in the capital would provide the basis for the creation of state farms. He recommended that the state use its own capital to buy land for the creation of colonies of about 400–800 *kyŏng* (400,000–800,000 *myo*, or 147.2–294.4 acres at 0.0368 acres per *myo,* according to Sŏ's definition, see below) of land each and to absorb excess landless peasants by recruiting them for labor on the colony lands. The mode of management of the colonies would be reorganized to emulate the methods of successful peasants by using capital to invest in tools, fertilizer, irrigation projects, and advanced methods of production.

Sŏ planned to organize the colonies internally in emulation of the well-field system, dividing them into units of 10 *kyŏng* laid out in perfect squares, surveying the land and recording it in detail according to the fish-scale registers, and marking the major subdivisions by sluices and waterways. Like Yu Hyŏngwŏn, he also wanted to replace the *kyŏl-bu* method of calculation and measurement with the *kyŏng-myo* system of the Chinese, adopt a "survey foot" defined as 6 "Chou feet" and use it as the basis for measuring a *myo* (i.e., 100 square "feet"). The *kyŏng*, or 100 *myo*, in contemporary terms would have been equivalent to 4,444 *p'yŏng* or 3.68 acres, and the 10 *kyŏng* subunit would have been 36.8 acres (i.e., 0.0368 acres/*myo*).[66]

Each of these 10-*kyŏng* squares would be staffed by five peasant households, provided with tools, four oxen, and two carts. The state would own the land and provide the tools and equipment, and the peasants would cultivate the land jointly and receive wages (probably double the current rate on the market), food, and housing in compensation for their work. Kim Yongsŏp pointed out that the system was similar to Tasan's early *yŏjŏn* system, except that in Tasan's system the peasant would work as an individual and would receive compensation based on an exact calculation of his work time.

Sŏ also prescribed that the land would be plowed by two oxen pulling a double plow rather than the usual method of a single ox pulling two plows, to ensure deeper plowing and more efficient utilization of the land. The method of transplantation in wet-rice cultivation in Kyŏngsang Province and the three-furrow crop rotation practiced on dry fields in Hwanghae and Pyŏng'an provinces would also be used. Peasants from those areas would be recruited for membership in the colonies to instruct others in those methods.

For the colonies to be established on the outskirts of Seoul, the men from these provinces would be brought to the capital with their wives and children as part of their rotating duty in the capital guard divisions. Sŏ assumed that these peasants were probably already existing on the margin of subsistence and would have been happy to move to the capital voluntarily, especially considering the generous wage inducement. The other cultivators on these capital colonies would consist of the available unemployed and landless farmers or wage workers in the capital who had migrated there recently. Sŏ hoped that by this method of recruitment, the best methods of cultivation could be spread throughout the country as a whole.[67]

In addition, the management of the state farms (or colonies) was to be recruited from people who had the most skill in managing agriculture and handling wage labor. Those people would be selected to become agricultural managers (*chŏnnonggwan*) on the colony-estates. Sŏ expected that these managers would transfer the most advanced and productive methods developed over the years by the most successful landlords to these state farms, and eventually become prime candidates for the posts of district magistrates. As Kim Yongsŏp argued, Sŏ did not reject the existing landlord system itself, but planned to have the state adopt its methods to increase production on the state farms, expand the state-farm system of collective cultivation and wage labor, and solve the evils of landlessness and unemployment that had virtually accompanied the "enclosure" of land by the enterprising landlords.

In addition to the four colonies he planned to create around the capital, he also wanted a network of others established in the colonies, some in conjunction with military defense garrisons and command centers. Along the southern coasts he hoped to establish official colonies (*kwandun*) of 5,000 *kyŏng* in every key defensive district and 3,000 *kyŏng* in every garrison town, but these colonies would function by renting out land to tenants rather than using hired labor and direct management by the local officials or commanders.

In addition, civilian colonies (*mindun*) would be established and organized along the lines of the well-field model, but under the control of the people themselves rather than officials. They would pay a tithe to the magistrate, half of which would be used for the support of the colony chief and the other for emergency reserves. The colonists would be exempted from military service but would pay the cloth-support tax for duty troops. Aware of the danger of rebellion by landlords if the state tried to confiscate land for establishing these well-field colonies, he proposed simply that they only be created on unused land by the reclamation efforts of peasants, but they would be managed either by an official or by a commoner, not by a landlord. Any private individual who raised capital, bought tools, and recruited peasants to work on reclaimed land who wanted to become the agricultural manager of such an estate would be granted the land by the government and appointed to that post. He presumed that such individuals should be able to create colonies anywhere from 200 to 2,000 *kyŏng* in size.

Presumably, the managers would thus not be the expert agriculturalists recruited for agricultural managers on the colonies close to the capital, but rich peasants or venture entrepreneurial farmers who invested their own capital in reclamation. Sŏ naturally presumed that these rural entrepreneurs would have been willing to give up their own wealth and independence to become a managerial functionary on a state farm!

Thus, by capitalizing on the supposed desires of all rich peasants to attain some kind of office, the state would be able to coopt the rich peasants into the effort to put an end to the landlord-tenant system and work toward the collectivization of agriculture, but it would be done by the adoption of a capitalist mode of production and managerial management techniques worked out by capitalistic farmers. Kim Yongsŏp believed that even though Sŏ Yugu shared the goals of previous reformers in taking land away from large landlords and redistributing it to peasants in one fashion or another, the others all thought that the confiscation of land could only be carried out by a revolution. So's formula differed from all previous reformers because it was based on a realistic acceptance of the world as it was, promotion of production, and absorption of the rich peasants and landlords into the new system rather than their destruction.[68]

CONCLUSION

It is difficult to see, however, how Sŏ's plan was any more realistic than those of previous reformers except that he was willing to recognize the supreme power of private landownership but disarm it by publicly announcing his capitulation to it. Once the landlords were disarmed he could then seek to undermine their domination by working around the edges of the system. Continuing the tradition of attachment to the well-field model by most reformers, he proposed a system of state farms run by enlightened bureaucratic managers who would be devoted to the incorporation of the most advanced methods of cultivation. His intention was to surround the landlords with examples of superior collective organization as a new strategy for the gradual but inevitable replacement of private property.

What was significant about Tasan's second plan and Sŏ Yugu's military colony plan was that both seem to be products of the failure of King Chŏngjo and other kings to even attempt a beginning of land reform led by the center, for without royal support there were virtually no prospects for any plans based on confiscation of land from private landowners. Since all reformers were either scholars or officials who had been educated in the standards of bureaucratic organization and were members of the yangban class themselves, they could envision no leadership for reform coming from any other place but the pinnacle of the bureaucratic hierarchy, the king. The concept of popular sovereignty, or the legitimate political role of the uneducated peasant masses, simply did not exist at the time.

What took place after 1801, therefore, was the continuation, not development, of the supreme ideal of the well-field collective model, but an unmistakable retreat in the face of landlord power on the part of kings as well as reformers. Forced to accept this reality, Tasan and Sŏ Yugu sought to work out schemes to create the possibility of establishing collective organization without challenging the landlords directly, a scheme that would succeed by lulling them into passivity or overwhelming them by the superior efficiency and productivity of their proposed systems.

I doubt that these tactics were any more realistic than Yu Hyŏngwŏn's if only because they were ignored until the Imsul rebellion of 1862 shocked the government into serious consideration of the economic causes of the rebellion. And the response to the crisis of 1862 did not indicate that the government was willing to challenge private property by instituting state ownership of land, redistribution, and collective agriculture.

PART III

Land Reform: Conclusion

Yu's Legacy

The most interesting aspect of Yu Hyŏngwŏn's discussion of land tenure was his attempt to solve the problem of the maldistribution of land and wealth by seeking to balance the conflicting demands of the various parties to the debate: the commoner peasant's desire for land, the slave's desire for manumission, the ruling class's demand for a higher level of income than the commoners and the maintenance of a labor force at their service, and the state's need for fiscal security and adequate revenue. His solution was an attempt to adapt classical and historical models to contemporary Korea by combining elements from both the well-field and limited-land systems, but his radical and egalitarian propensities toward confiscation, state ownership, and redistribution were restrained by his desire to retain a special place for the ruling class, albeit a new class recruited by principles of moral behavior rather than the contemporary yangban who represented a combination of inherited privilege and achievement in the civil-service examinations. He grappled with the curse of hereditary slavery and courageously called for an end to the inheritance of slave status, but in his more sober moments he was forced to compromise and even accepted it and incorporated it into his calculations for the immediate future. Yet in many ways his philosophical objection to slavery was more humane than those who followed him in the eighteenth century, a period when the slave population even began to decline. He also argued for a more rational adoption of standards of measurement for a better system of cadastral survey, tax reduction (the classical tithe), and a fairer and more efficient tax system.

He never felt that he was creating anything new, simply adopting the methods of classical China and adaptations in later dynasties to eliminate some of the anomalies that had developed in recent Korean history, and he perceived of himself as a transmitter of Confucian wisdom, much the same role that Confucius himself had played. His ideas became known by the early eighteenth century and had an effect on a number of scholars and officials, but even his intellectual disciples like Yi Ik did not necessarily subscribe to all elements of his plan.

The Challenge to Private Property

Yi Ik thought that Yu's plan to induce a courageous king to confiscate all private property to redistribute land on a rotating basis to the peasantry had no chance of success in contemporary Korea, and almost all other scholars and statesmen of that time shared that view. Tasan was one exception. In his first *yŏjŏn* plan he did propose a far more radical scheme of distribution, for in his proposition rewards were based on the amount of work contributed to production, as well as the ruthless elimination of the class of scholars for the special forms of remuneration such as those contrived by Yu Hyŏngwŏn.

Nonetheless, Tasan was forced by the pressures of real life – either the prospect of his imminent execution during the repression of Catholics in 1801 or the observations he made during the years of exile – to modify his views and work out a solution that accepted the reality of private property. The futility of top-down radical reform instituted and led by the king was better illustrated by King Chŏngjo's failure to formulate any kind of substantial land reform program despite an extensive search for advice in the 1790s.

The curious aspect of this history of debate over land reform was that the classical model of public ownership and relatively fair (if not totally equal) distribution of land was accorded public respect by almost everyone, no matter what their private interests were. Since private property was never extolled as the proper ideal for the distribution of land because it was always stigmatized by its association with private interest and greed, public ownership and egalitarian distribution schemes were never denounced as either heretical or subversive. Nonetheless, all serious statecraft writers, including Yu Hyŏngwŏn himself, were aware that any attempt at confiscation would lead not only to resistance by landlords, but to possible rebellion by them against the king and state. Since few officials were willing to advocate that dangerous path, especially since so many of them were landlords themselves, no king and precious few scholars were willing to challenge the landlords on their own.

The result was a curious anomaly: the dominant principle of land tenure in reality – private ownership – was never, and could never be, articulated either as a legitimate legal or moral principle by anyone in Korean society. Certainly there were very few who, like Wang An-shih, had the courage to openly extol the positive contributions to the agrarian economy of the landowners. Nevertheless, the debate over land reform after Yu's death focused on the question of whether one should challenge the private landowners and landlords or acquiesce to their interests.

This chapter has traced the history of the debate over land reform in the eighteenth and nineteenth centuries in a brief and possibly too cursory manner, but this abbreviated treatment was sufficient to show that in both thought and action, reformist scholars as well as officials and kings were forced to make concessions to the dominant power of the landlords and the sanctity of private landownership, if not capitulate to it altogether. The only exception was Tasan's first plan for collective ownership, but even he was forced to commit apostasy – for his political and economic as well as his religious beliefs.

Yet retreat and accommodation did not mean that reformers abandoned their ideal; they still sought to work toward the well-field ideal of state ownership, collective organization, and egalitarian redistribution by devising some method that would overcome landlord interests without challenging them directly. Whether they emphasized rational management and productivity as part of their plan, as Tasan and Sŏ Yugu did, or Yi Ik did not, was beside the point, because the telos of their plans was not the supposed goal of free market capitalism, the liberation of the individual from state control, the defense of private property and private profit, but rather the apotheosis of state control of private interests in favor of the public welfare and the achievement of a more equitable distribution of land and wealth. In short, their ultimate goal remained the same as that of Yu Hyŏngwŏn, except that they were forced to admit that no king was likely to appear who would summon the resolve to strip the landlords of their property. And they did not dare advocate a political plan to overthrow the dynasty to carry out their objectives as another Neo-Confucian, Chŏng Tojŏn, had done at the end of the Koryŏ dynasty.

The Ruling Class

Yu Hyŏngwŏn sought to create a system of land distribution by which the ruling class of his society, defined as a select group of eminently moral men, would be provided support by the state in proportion to their official ranks or scholarly positions, which would ideally correspond directly to their moral capacities. His purpose in eliminating purchase and sale and private ownership was to eliminate the possibility that contingency or chance could play any role in the distribution of wealth and income. Those reformers who lived after him, by compromising with his goal of nationalizing all landed property, generally modified Yu's vision to create a perfect system of distribution according to moral capacity by yielding to the reality of private ownership. Their goals were far more modest, simply the limitation of ownership to provide some land for the ordinary peasant smallholder, landless tenant, or laborer.

The most significant development in thought about the nature of the ruling class after Yu's time was probably Tasan's first plan to shift the pattern of distribution from either rank or office, or from Yu's criteria of moral capacity, to new criteria of efficiency and productivity – which is one of the reasons why Kim Yongsŏp labeled Tasan a more progressive thinker than his predecessors. Keep in mind, however, that his progressivism would have to be based on the view that efficiency and productivity were more important because they contribute to the growth of material life rather than than to the maintenance of traditional Confucian moral standards. And it is quite possible that Tasan adopted this position at the turn of the nineteenth century because he was either a Christian (or a reluctant Christian apostate) who had abandoned his unquestioning allegiance to Confucian moral principles, and was thus looking for different (even alien) ideals.

SLAVERY

Yu Hyŏngwŏn was one of many scholars and statesmen in the seventeenth century who attacked the system of slavery in Korean society, but although he agreed with others on the instrumental value of reducing slavery to increase the pool of adult males available for military service and taxation, he was also the only one to attack hereditary slavery on moral grounds as a violation of norms established in classical China. His recommendation for adoption of the matrilineal rule to determine the status of offspring in mixed marriages was debated by court officials from 1669 to 1730 without knowledge of his ideas, and finally adopted permanently in the end. Another partial victory was won in 1801 when King Sunjo manumitted most of the official slaves.

Furthermore, for whatever reasons, the slave population appears to have plummeted precipitously after 1780, primarily because outside-resident slaves and male slaves in general simply ran away, and it was cheaper to replace them with tenants and hired laborers than pay for the cost of an army of slave-catchers. Whatever the reasons, most would agree that the decline of slavery was a sign of progress, but there was no development of an abolitionist movement to outlaw slavery altogether. Nor can much credit can be given to Yu's statecraft successors because none of them led any serious movement to abolish hereditary, private slavery as a matter of moral principle, and even the most astute thinkers like Tasan merely considered hiring slaves for labor to meet ad hoc labor shortages. Even Yu himself provided land for slaves in his land reform scheme on the assumption that slaves would be around for a long time.

RATIONAL STANDARDS OF MEASUREMENT (THE KYŎNG)

One of the most fundamental reforms that Yu proposed was replacing the *kyŏl-bu* system of assessment with the linear *kyŏng-mu* system copied from ancient China, and this idea was picked up readily by a number of his successors. Yu should therefore be credited with transmitting an important way of rationalizing the measurement system, but unfortunately, the government never attempted to adopt it.

The primary problem was not simply the technical question of easy measurement, but the inequalities of ownership stemming from the market in landed property, the dispossession of smallholders, and the deterioriation of terms of tenancy in the last part of the dynasty. Yu was convinced that the adoption of more rational methods of measurement were bound to solve far more serious problems, but I doubt that it was true.

PROGRESS: TECHNOLOGY AND COMMERCIAL AGRICULTURE

In recent years, many Korean scholars have revised the criteria for judging radicalism and progressivism in the thought of statecraft writers by replacing egalitarian distribution with what they have perceived to have been aspects of modern capitalism, particularly the emphasis on rationality, efficient management, technology, the use of wage labor and tenancy to cut costs and maximize profits, greater production, and the development of commodities for sale on the market. The motivation for this new shift in interpretation is especially obvious to the outside observer: the desire to demonstrate that in thought as well as action, Koreans had demonstrated a capacity to trod the same path as the West in developing the sprouts of capitalism without the need for outside tutelage. Kim Yongsŏp, for example, argued that both Tasan and Sŏ Yugu had been able to develop unique plans for reform by their own thought and intiative, not simply by borrowing ideas from abroad. They did it by striking a compromise with traditional historical-mindedness and the learning of the Han and Sung dynasties to break with and transcend the tradition established by Chu Hsi. They developed realistic reform proposals that might be adopted by the government to reform both agricultural methods and society and "overcome the feudal socioeconomic order founded on social status and landlord-tenant relations."[1]

Kim was right: Tasan and Sŏ Yugu's land reform proposals did incorporate some elements of rational, capitalistic farming seen in the modern world, they were more sensitive to the potential effects of the market on rural production and income, and their ideas were derivative of what they observed had been taking place in their own society, but their vision for the future did not include the replacement of agriculture as the primary mode of production by industrial production or commercial activity. In fact, even some of the Confucian Physiocrats were interested in increasing agricultural production, and as we will see even Yu Hyŏngwŏn conceded that the role of merchants was useful because it circulated goods from the place of production to places of shortage. Tasan and Sŏ did carry this mode of thought another stage further than Yu Hyŏngwŏn had, but they did not become spokesman for the supremacy of commerce and industry even though Tasan's fascination with technology might have carried him or others after him along that route. As it turned out, no matter how practical or progressive their proposals might have been, no regime adopted them as policy in the nineteenth century. As far as their ultimate objectives were concerned, however, far from advocating the superiority of private property, private initiative, and the free market, they sought throughout to reinforce state control, public ownership, collective production, and egalitarian redistribution wherever possible – the same goals that Yu had advocated in the seventeenth century.

Even though certain features of the late Chosŏn economy could be identified as features of a system moving toward capitalistic agriculture – land accumulation, tenancy, and hired labor – it is difficult to demonstrate a serious rise in agricultural productivity by comparison with Japan, let alone per capita productivity that was probably stymied by population growth by the end of the seventeenth century. On the contrary, by the end of the Chosŏn dynasty those same phenomena had also produced severe anomalies in the distribution of wealth and much suffering by the poorest peasants. Whatever developments had taken place in commerce and industry, it was not sufficient to absorb surplus labor in any new factory towns and raise the overall standard of living by providing a peaceful, alternate economic exit from the pressures of agrarianism. By the middle of the nineteenth century the only way out of this situation was massive peasant rebellion, but that rebellion was still crushed by the superior forces of the ailing dynasty. While the rebellion at least stimulated a mild reform movement under the Taewongun in the 1860s, the yearnings of the mid-Chosŏn reformers for public ownership and redistribution was neither achieved nor attempted. Disaster was postponed for a couple of decades until the same scenario was repeated again in the Tonghak Rebellions of 1894–95, and Yu Hyŏngwŏn and his successors in the Confucian reform movement remained outcasts in the wilderness, appealing to their vision of a more ideal distribution of landed wealth.

PART IV

Military Reform

INTRODUCTION

Yu Hyŏngwŏn began writing his *Pan'gye surok* around 1650, thirteen years after the humiliating Manchu invasion of 1637. The situation in the middle of the seventeenth century had changed significantly since the circumstances existing just prior to Hideyoshi's invasion of Korea in 1592. For the next two hundred years the threat of foreign invasion would decline significantly, but the risk of domestic rebellion would increase. After the Yi Kwal rebellion of 1624, Kim Ik attempted a coup d'état against King Hyojong in 1651, and members of the Disciple's Faction rose up in rebellion against King Yŏngjo in 1728. In the nineteenth century, Hong Kyŏngnae led a rebellion in the northwest in 1812, and the largest domestic rebellion of the dynasty broke out in the south and elsewhere in 1862. Because sufficient force was needed to defend the throne against these domestic threats, there was a change in thinking among kings and government officials about the optimum deployment of divisions throughout the country.

Significant changes had also taken place in the nature of the Chosŏn military system as well. The Five Guard system of the early Chosŏn system had been abandoned and replaced by the Five Military Divisions created since 1592 and most of the new units were controlled by political generals who used them as a basis of power for themselves and their factional associates. After 1659, political factionalism became more intense, creating a greater potential for domestic trouble and maintaining the necessity for adequate military forces, thereby reducing the benefits that international peace should have brought to the body politic.

The late Ming method of troop organization based on the incorporation and integration of musketeer squads with archers and spearmen had spread throughout the army and the need for cannon, gunpowder, ammunition, and fortifications increased. These requirements, in addition to the addition of new units and divisions, created a greater financial burden than in earlier times.

After the Imjin War of 1592–98, slaves were brought into the national army for the first time on a regular basis. In fact, slave soldiers became an unavoidable necessity since the evasion of service among adult males of commoner or good status (*yang'in*) had spread, reducing the basis for the recruitment of both rotating duty soldiers and their support taxpayers. These developments exacerbated the inequities and inequalities in the distribution of service and tax burdens that had existed prior to the Imjin War and had created hardship for both slaves and commoner peasants, who had to supply soldiers for the national army and pay for their support while on duty.

Military finance, in fact, remained based on the early Chosŏn system of assigning adult males as support taxpayers for duty soldiers, but the expansion of military costs continued to increase. Officials began to consider ways to reduce troop quotas and tax rates, as well as placing military finance on a different basis. This idea was stimulated by economic developments that had led to greater production, the spread of markets, and the beginning of the circulation of metallic currency, which, as we will discuss later, had precipitated a complete reformation of the system of tribute taxation. Nevertheless, the discussion of these measures of reform were obstructed and delayed for years by the various conservative forces that resisted change.

The next five chapters will be devoted to an exploration of Yu Hyŏngwŏn's detailed study of the military problems of his time and his proposals for reform, but the objective is to go beyond an analysis limited to Yu's thought. Instead, his ideas will be placed in the context of his age, especially the complex and protracted debate among active officials over military issues that began before he began work on his magnum opus and continued long past his death. That debate continued even past the time when his writings on military problems were brought to the attention of king and court in 1750. The purpose of this extensive treatment will be to show whether his approach to military problems represents a new and different approach to institutional reform that could be labeled practical, pragmatic, innovative, or in any sense "modern."

One of the tests of practicality, as opposed to traditional Confucian dogmatism, fundamentalism, or rigidity, would be the degree to which he was able to adjust his principles, be they Confucian or otherwise, to the changed circumstances of the time. For example, if he was able to identify the most serious problems plaguing military service and organization, did he seek to adapt to changes and establish better modes of dealing with problems than did the body of active officials? Did he represent a progressive force as opposed to the conservative tendencies of officialdom? Was he able to sense the economic changes taking place and use them as a basis for new thinking on military service and finance? Did he appreciate the importance of new military technology and push for the extension of new techniques throughout the armed forces?

Was his capacity for outrage over the drawbacks, inequality, and injustice contained in the Chosŏn systems of education, inherited social status, and land distribution and taxation sustained in his treatment of the military system? If not necessarily new or modern, was he a force for liberation from the accumulated restrictions and disabilities of the past? Finally, did he convey a legacy to the next generation, or next century, that stimulated the reform efforts of that age, or if not, can he be regarded as an unsung and tragic prophet ruefully ignored by lesser men in positions of political power, an example of a tragic flaw in the incapacity of a Confucian dynasty to appreciate one of its more astute institutional thinkers?

CHAPTER 10

The Royal Division Model: Rotating Duty Soldiers and Support Taxpayers

To provide some background for the context of the mid-seventeenth century, we must consider military and political developments that had occurred since the Imjin War. The lessons learned from that war had, unfortunately, not stimulated a self-strengthening effort sufficient to insulate the country against a challenge from a different direction. Not only did politics interfere with the strategies adopted to block the thrust of the Manchus, but the problems of defense had been exacerbated by the challenge of the Yi Kwal rebellion of 1624 to the throne and the necessity to provide for both the defense of the capital as well as the northern frontier. After capitulation for the second time to the Manchus in 1637, Korean kings and officials were enraged by their humiliation at the hands of the Manchus and yearned to rebuild their armies to take vengeance, but they were limited in their freedom to do so by the sharp and suspicious eyes of the Manchu overlords.

Problems of Hyojong's Military Expansion Policies

When Grand Prince Pongnim, the second son of King Injo and recently designated successor to his deceased elder brother, Prince Sohyŏn, ascended the throne as King Hyojong in 1649 he succeeded to a court that was dominated almost exclusively by members of the Westerner faction but split between moderates under Kim Chajŏm who advocated accommodation with Manchu overlordship, and a contingent of anti-Manchus that included Yi Sibaek and his younger brother, Yi Sibang, as well as Kim Chip, Song Siyŏl, Song Chun'gil, and the prominent leader of the Southerner faction, Hŏ Chŏk. Kim Chajŏm had been able to maintain his position even though King Injo was anti-Manchu because he supported him in the vindictive execution of Crown Prince Sohyŏn's wife, sons (Injo's own grandsons), and family, all of whom he suspected of treasonous sympathy with the Manchus.

King Hyojong, however, who had spent a decade as a hostage in Manchuria nurturing his hatred for the Manchus in silence, immediately set about replacing Kim Chajŏm and his leading cohorts with anti-Manchu officials. Isolated politically, Kim turned to the Ch'ing court for aid, informing it secretly through Manchu language interpreters of Hyojong's purge of Manchu sympathizers and neglect of strict use of Ch'ing year periods in dating books and documents.

The Manchu Prince Dorgon, a hardliner on Korean policy, had become regent in 1643. He directed the campaigns to capture Beijing, destroy the army of Li Tzu-ch'eng in 1644, and complete the conquest of south China in 1646. When Hyojong asked Manchu permission in 1649 to rebuild forts and walls against a possible Japanese attack, Prince Dorgon suspected his motives and sent a mission to investigate the purge of Kim's faction. Korean officials succeeded in putting them off by explaining that military decisions were made collectively by the Border Defense Command (Piguk or Pibyŏnsa) rather than any anti-Manchu clique, and that Kim had been dismissed only because he happened to be chief royal physician at the time that King Injo died. No sooner did they depart, however, than Kim was exiled.

After the Ch'ing envoys returned home, however, Dorgon had the Hsün-chih emperor send a letter to the Korean king citing direct testimony from Korean provincial officials interviewed by the Manchu envoys to refute Hyojong's contention of a Japanese threat that warranted reconstruction of fortifications in the south, mobilization of troops, and the laying up of weapons. The emperor suggested that the Koreans were in fact preparing for war with Ch'ing China and that in such circumstances he had no choice but to "make preparations," which was tantamount to a threat of invasion.[1]

When Prince Dorgon died in 1650, Hyojong's government was allowed some respite from Manchu suspicions, but Kim Chajŏm's so-called Fallen Party (Naktang) faction was placed in jeopardy. His son, Kim Ik, attempted a military coup in 1651 by using the soldiers of Suwŏn district and the Defense Command (Suŏch'ŏng) at the Namhan fort, with the objective of placing Prince Sungsŏn (Sungsŏn'gun) on the throne and eliminating his father's anti-Manchu rivals: the Original Faction (Wŏndang) of Wŏn Tup'yo and the Mountain Faction (Sandang) of Kim Chip, Song Siyŏl, and Song Chun'gil. But the latter succeeded in orchestrating the execution of Kim and his son and removing all pro-Manchu officials from crucial military command positions like provincial army and navy commanders in Kyŏnggi and Kyŏngsang provinces, the magistrate of Kwangju who commanded the Namhan fort, and the commander of the anti-Manchu division stationed in Kyŏnggi Province.[2]

Nevertheless, the death of Prince Dorgon did not mean that King Hyojong would be able to carry out a major military build-up in anticipation of renewed hostilities with the Manchus. The court and country were still under the sharp surveillance of Ch'ing authorities who arrived in Korea on both official and unofficial business one or more times a month. Hyojong was able to soothe Manchu suspicions at the time, but any effort too ambitious or visible to rearm the nation would risk discovery and reprisal. Because the country was also pressed financially both because of poor crop conditions and the costs of putting up frequent

Ch'ing envoys, Hyojong had to abandon plans for rapid replacement of worn-out weapons. Recruitment and training of troops were hampered by the same problems described by Yu Hyŏngwŏn in his book (see later), training and firing practice had to be conducted out of sight of Ch'ing envoys, and grain rations had to be diverted to famine relief. In short, initial attempts to rebuild the military between 1649 and 1651 were almost completely frustrated.[3]

Even assuming a successful rearmament policy, Korean forces would have had no chance at all against the Manchus after the conquest of China because the Manchus then had access to the manpower of all her conquered territories. Loyalty to the Ming was an admirable sentiment, but the obligation had been removed for all practical purpose by Ming capitulation. Continuing discussion at court of rearming to attack the Manchus was understandable as an act of catharsis, but it was hardly practical. Since there were no threats of attack from Japan or elsewhere, Hyojong's "attack the North" (*pukpŏl*) policy might be deemed, in that situation, a needless burden imposed on the Korean people.

Despite Manchu surveillance, Hyojong was determined to pursue his military expansion policy, but he had to face a number of problems that had plagued the military system for years. He was less interested, however, in reform than in expansion of his army and its training. As a result, when Minister of War Pak Sŏ made five recommendations for reform early in 1652, he did not respond positively to all requests. To prevent unsalaried commanders of local naval garrisons from dunning marines (*sugun*) for payments of cloth and forcing them to abandon their homes to evade the levies, he suggested that the government provide these officers with stipends. To remove the difficulty imposed on peasants living inland from serving as marines at coastal duty stations, he asked that their duties be switched to coastal residents instead. To prevent peasants from running away from home and commending themselves to powerful landlords to escape military registration, he recommended that local officials should register everyone wherever they happened to reside (rather than at their original domicile), punish landlords for hiding peasants from registration, prohibit unauthorized migration and movement by peasants from their villages, compile accurate household registers (*hojŏk*), and issue household tallies (*hop'ae*) as a basis for assessing service. To stop the high runaway rate by both commoners and government service slaves who were trying to escape military duty and the practice of officials shifting their service obligations to neighbors and relatives, or seizing the land and houses of the runaways and selling them off, Pak Sŏ requested that Hyojong make several changes. He asked Hyojong to guarantee the return of the property of runaways, cancel their delinquent cloth taxes and criminal charges for service or tax evasion, and exempt the current year's personal service (or slave tribute), as an inducement for them to return home and register for service.[4]

The Border Defense Command recommended that in Ch'ungch'ŏng and Chŏlla provinces various funds be taken to provide monthly salaries for coastal naval garrison commanders to alleviate the situation of marines, but opposed transferring the locus of their duty because the service duties for marines (*sugun*, *chusa*) had become a hereditary practice that had been incorporated into the dynastic law code. It refused to adopt Pak Sŏ's recommendation to return land to runaway commoners and slaves because the law already authorized sale of the land of runaways to meet delinquent taxes, but allowed that if they returned home, they could buy back their land and houses at a price.

As disappointing as this response was, King Hyojong's decision was even more depressing. He rejected the proposals to repair cannon for naval vessels, switch assignments of peasants for naval duty, and provide naval base commanders with salaries to prevent their fleecing the naval soldiers. The only incentive he was willing to allow for resettling runaways was reduction of the current year's personal service obligation. He did not approve returning land or homes to them, with or without compensation to the current owners or occupants.[5]

Resettling runaways and vagrants was, of course, related to the fundamental problem of maintaining troop levels up to quota, but it was next to impossible for the king to remedy this problem. In addition to the disruption left over from the last invasion and famine conditions, an epidemic had left the military registers filled with the names of men who had either died or run away. The law code required registration on a triennial basis, but because of the disruption caused by the recent invasions, King Injo had agreed in 1648 to extend the interval between registration to five years. In 1653, one official reported that in P'yŏng'an Province only 30,000 men were available for duty out of a quota of 70,000, and Minister of War Wŏn Tup'yo remarked that there were only 150,000 men on the national military registers, 250,000 less than before the Imjin War of 1592! King Hyojong was forced to postpone registration for another five years, because of the anticipated hardship a sudden imposition of additional military service obligations would impose on a peasant population already suffering from famine and disease.[6]

A fillip of sorts was provided to Hyojong's ambition to rearm the nation when the Manchus requested the dispatch of a hundred Korean musketeers as reinforcements for the Ch'ing campaign against the Russians in Manchuria in 1654. The creditable performance of the Korean troops in the field earned Manchu gratitude, and their perception of trouble from the Russians enabled the Korean court to begin open discussion of the defense of its northern frontier for the first time since 1636. Hyojong was even emboldened to conduct a personal inspection of the troops of the Military Training Agency and the Royal Division, despite objections from some officials fearful of Manchu retaliation.[7]

Hoping to improve the sorry military situation in the provincial garrisons, King Hyojong planned to adopt a proposal of Pak Sŏ in 1652 to restore the older system of appointing civil district magistrates concurrent Yŏngjang or garrison commanders of specific garrisons in the provinces. After a two-year delay because of Kim Yuk's opposition, Hyojong accepted Wŏn Tup'yo's proposal to select able military officials (instead of civil magistrates who had neglected their military duties) to hold the post of Yŏngjang in charge of the sixteen Yŏng (command centers) in the southern provinces and make the rounds of all the districts under their jurisdiction to supervise training in military skills. He guaranteed them a tour of duty of twenty-four months to prevent interruption of their work, promoted those with demonstrated military capabilities, and dismissed a number of military officials who had neglected their duties. In one case in 1655 he executed a military officer who objected to a sudden military inspection on the grounds it was a violation of military regulations.[8] He also established a Military Academy (Nŭngmaach'ŏng) in 1655 at the recommendation of Yi Sibaek to train young officers truly able to command men in battle situations.[9]

King Hyojong also succeeded in providing financial support and tax exemptions to slave troops of *sog'o* units despite the opposition of some of his officials. In 1654, he ordered the payment of travel expenses for official and private slaves from Kyŏngsang Province service in the Royal Division, but instead of financing this from the state treasury, he levied a support tax of 7 *mal* of rice on over 28,000 other slaves who had no military service obligations. He ignored Kim Yuk's protest that the extra tax to finance this would be too oppressive for slaves already overburdened with obligations.

In 1656 he stepped up the training and inspection of all *sog'o* troops in the three southern provinces in shooting firearms but allowed as compensation an exemption from the land tax on one-half *kyŏl* of their holdings and other types of labor service requirements.[10] This was a decent arrangement, but he had to postpone the decision until 1657 when a number of high civil officials including Song Siyŏl and Kim Yuk protested the special tax exemption because it would cost the state too much lost revenue even though only 20,000 *kyŏl* of land of a total of 500,000 *kyŏl* in the southern three provinces would be exempted. After eventually winning over the chief and second state councilors to his side he ordered the land tax exemption.[11]

Hyojong's performance on this question was mixed. The extra tax on slaves to finance the travel for some on military duty was not that beneficial for the slaves, but the reduction in their land tax was. In any case, his primary objective was not to alleviate slave service, but to get the most he could from the slaves and improve their training as soldiers. Overall, Hyojong made some progress in improving the military, but he was limited by Manchu suspicions and his own reluctance to engineer more positive systemic reforms.

YU'S ANALYSIS OF MILITARY WEAKNESSES

Despite the creation of new military units, the army still suffered from a chronic shortage of troops because of under-registration of eligible adult males, exemption from duty of the yangban, and the loss of population from the effects of war, but the problem was not limited to these factors alone. Because more and more commoners sought to evade service by whatever means they could find, the government found it difficult to maintain the number of duty soldiers and support taxpayers (*poin*).

The post-Imjin situation, however, differed markedly from the pre-Imjin period because private and official slaves had been brought into the military service system, primarily by membership in the new, *sog'o*, units, to compensate for the reduction of available commoner adult males. State exploitation of slaves for service created two new problems: competition with the slaveowners for the labor power of their human property, and increasing burdens on the slaves themselves, who were now asked to perform service for the state along with their obligations to their masters.

The system of service continued, for the most part, to be based on a bifurcation between rotating duty soldiers and taxpaying support personnel, but corruption in the military cloth support tax meant that officials and clerks were using the tax as a device to increase both revenues and graft, and there was a growing trend toward the neglect of actual service in favor of tax payments. As a result, there were not sufficient funds to support those men who did show up for duty or provide special equipment to them, and the peasant support taxpayers were subjected to oppressive taxes far beyond the legal limits.

Yu Hyŏngwŏn approached the problem of reform for the military the same way he did for other questions, by returning to classical sources. Here he found that the ideal model for a military system was to be found in the militia system that accompanied the well-field system of Chou China. He defined the nature of that system and traced the attempts to approximate it in post-Chou Chinese history.

Since the militia system as well as the well-field system was now part of an irretrievable past, the problem for Yu was to decide how much of the classical model of militia organization could be restored and adapted to seventeenth-century Korean life to restore the Korean military system to health.

Troop Shortages, Poor Training, Corruption

No one was more aware of the deficiencies of the current system of military service than Yu Hyŏngwŏn. The military rosters were worthless pieces of paper, most of the troops remained untrained, and the system of military service itself had been converted to a separate system of taxation based on the payment of cloth, ostensibly for the support of duty troops that no longer existed.

> Even garrisons of a thousand soldiers in fact did not have a single man on duty, while the men who were assigned as soldiers [to the garrison] worried day and night over whether they could manage the cloth tax payments, and did not know a thing about shooting an arrow or riding a horse. All types of soldiers, including the infantry, ended up as names [on the rolls] of cloth taxpayers. Even the so-called cavalrymen only paid a cloth tax; not one of them had a horse.
>
> The training of troops, the instruction of soldiers, the guarding of the country, and defense against insults [from other countries] are hardly worth mentioning, while tens of thousands of innocent people have been forced to endure the agonies of flood and fire. Really what kind of a thing is this?[12]

Since the situation in the mid-seventeenth century had changed so little from the late sixteenth century, Yu found it profitable to quote at length from the leading critic of the military system at that time, Yulgok. Yulgok remarked that the conversion of duty soldiers to cloth taxpayers was probably the fundamental weakness of the system itself, not only because it reduced the number of real soldiers, but increased tax burdens on the adult commoners and their families:

> Even though paying cloth is more convenient than performing military service, they [the families of men liable for military service] still find this hard to do. For this reason, if they have to perform military service a couple of times, their families become impoverished and unable to support themselves and begin to take flight one after the other. And in the next year when an inspection is made of the military registers and people are forced to assume military duty, their whole clan in the village is forced to assume military service. And then when the whole clan absconds, the burden is placed on the relatives of the relatives. The calamity spreads like weeds so that there is no end to it; in the future it will get to the point where the people will have no seed [children?] left over.[13]

In a memorial to King Sŏnjo around 1575 Yulgok blamed the corruption of military service on an evil coalition of interest between the garrison commanders and the duty soldiers:

> These types [of officers] only know how to fleece their troops in order to benefit themselves. What else would they be concerned about? The soldiers, who find long tours of duty on guard burdensome and voluntarily pay cloth to avoid military service, are only too happy to go along with them [the commanders]. Those who do stay in the garrisons are forced to perform duties they find hard to bear and are made responsible for paying for costs they find difficult to manage. It is like being fried and simmered in the flames of their own fat.
>
> People are not wood and stone, so who would not look out for his own welfare [in these circumstances]? And when they see other people avoiding military service and resting at ease in their own homes, there is no one who would not long for [this too] and also emulate this behavior. If too many people avoid military service and the garrisons and redoubts become empty [of soldiers], this will induce the people who live nearby [the garrisons] to borrow other people's names and have substitutes checked off whenever inspections are made to ferret out corruption. The only thing that officials who make the rounds on inspection actually do is inspect the numbers. Does any one of them check to see if the numbers are true or false?[14]

Obviously, commoners did not have to attain yangban status to evade military duty, and officials were only concerned with maintaining troop quotas on paper, not on guaranteeing that the barracks would be filled with troops.[15]

Yu described a similar situation for his own time. Not only were the garrisons empty of soldiers, but even those on duty were affected by the general corruption and subjected to exploitation by clerks of the Ministry of War or garrisons. These clerks would falsify attendance certificates in advance to make it look like the soldiers had been AWOL, and then use this to collect cloth payments from them as a penalty. After the men did show up for service, they might take bribes in return for assigning them lighter duty, or collect payments or fines on the grounds the men were late for duty or had faulty equipment. Meanwhile, they allowed their relatives and men from influential families to pay cloth taxes for the purpose of hiring a substitute without ever finding a substitute to serve. "Guard posts with a contingent of twenty men were left with only seven or eight, and the soldiers who did serve on rotation were left with heavy burdens."[16]

He condemned the practice of excusing duty soldiers from service and collecting tax payments from them instead (*panggun sup'o*). He did not know just when the practice had begun, but he was aware that the government had felt that funds could be saved by sending duty soldiers back home to the farm during peacetime rather than support them on tours of duty. The problem was that the practice was excessive: not only was the Ministry of War guilty of releasing guard soldiers and runners from service in return for tax payments, but the situation in provincial garrisons was even worse.

The practice had commercialized military service by converting it into a source of revenue and income. The military officials had taken to discussing garrisons in terms of their revenue income instead of their military capability. Thus, a frontier garrison of a hundred men was referred to as "a 200 *p'il*-a-month-post" (since the tax payment per soldier, in lieu of service, was 2 *p'il* per person). In making appointments personnel officers used this criterion in deciding whether to reward or penalize officials. The spirits of the officers appointed to command garrisons either rose or fell according to the prospective income of the post, and their friends offered either congratulations or condolences based on the prospective income. Provincial military commanders and garrison commanders "treated [the soldiers] as sources of income for the extravagant spending of their wives and concubines or to raise funds to bribe influential people," while the officials at the Ministry of War used the revenues to pay the costs of banquets and entertainments for their friends and superiors.[17]

Peasants in the villages were happy to go into debt at usurious rates of interest to obtain the funds for cloth taxes that would gain them relief from actual duty. When they did serve at places like provincial military commanders' yamen at great distance from their homes, they were required to transport all the heavy goods that the commanding officer required as well as pay fees and bribes to the yamen clerks. If soldiers chose to run away to evade service, their taxes were distributed among their relatives and neighbors in the usual fashion, driving these people out of their villages as well.

In their eagerness for collecting taxes, the officials were registering babes at the breast for military service and collecting cloth payments from their parents.

> Moreover, at the present time when a son is born to a family of the people, even before he is weaned, he is registered for military service and his name is counted for the purpose of collecting the cloth tax. If a commoner family has three or four children, then what one family has to pay in cloth taxes for a year comes to over 100 *p'il* of standard cloth. Even before the child has grown up, he becomes a vagabond, and even though the court has issued orders that [the officials] should wait for a boy to attain majority before he is registered for military service, this [order] has generally become a dead letter, and I have not seen one case where this law has been followed. Although this may be the fault of the magistrates, if we did not have this business of using soldiers for the purpose of collecting cloth payments, how would this evil exist?[18]

Yu claimed that in his own time military service itself had virtually been converted into a cloth tax payment, a condition that was to become even more prominent in the next two centuries: "If someone is called a soldier, it means that he is a cloth taxpayer. This has long been the custom, so that the name, "soldier," has come to mean cotton cloth [*myŏnp'o*]. If you call someone an infantryman [*pobyŏng*], everyone thinks of it as a name for cloth; they do not realize it is a term for soldier."[19]

Furthermore, just as in Yulgok's time, provincial military commanders and garrison officers spent the cloth fees "on luxuries for their wives and concubines, or for the bribes they pay to powerful people. . . . The income is used completely for the expenses of gifts and favors for friends, wine, food, banquets and music."[20]

The number of men available for service was also reduced by laxity and corruption in the registration system. Yulgok had also pointed out that since the regulation requiring registration of eligible males every six years had not been observed, in 1553 King Myŏngjong ordered a special registration to discover all the draft evaders. Unfortunately, the registrars were so anxious to fill the rolls that they registered everyone and everything in sight, not only beggars and vagrants, but chickens and dogs as well. In short, the registers were worthless, and twenty years later, the shortage of troops was just as bad.

The reduction in the number of troops on duty at garrisons and forts was also matched by a low level of military training for the duty soldiers, and if mobilized in an emergency, they would be a poor match for regular or professional soldiers.

> This is the reason why even though you have in name a garrison that is supposed to have a thousand men in it, in fact there is not even one man there. And those who actually are soldiers spend day and night worrying about the difficulty of meeting their cloth payments; they do not know anything about archery or riding horses . . . The so-called cavalrymen also only pay cloth; there is not one man of them who has a horse.[21]

As corrupted as the system of military finance by support taxpayers had become, the troops of new units formed during and after the Imjin War, like the slave *sog'ogun* and the Special Cavalry of the Military Training Agency (Pyŏltae), had no support personnel at all and insufficient resources to buy equipment or horses.[22] Even the regular duty soldiers were hard pressed to pay for their own equipment because cloth support tax payments were not supposed to cover equipment needs.

Yu cited the testimony of Cho Hŏn after his return from China in 1574 in which he commented that the Ming dynasty government provided to regular duty soldiers five extra personnel (*yŏjŏng*, or extra adult males), silver for buying a horse, food (or cash), cloth rations, and all equipment including armor, bows, arrows, spears, and swords.

> In our dynasty [by contrast], the soldiers only have one or two support taxpayers [*poin*], and they are unable to provide for their horses, equipment, and weapons, for everyone has to provide his own items. At times when inspections are conducted, everyone commonly borrows equipment from someone else, and if they cannot do so, they pay a few *mal* of rice to the clerks. By this means, what does not exist is treated as if it did. . . . It is the custom of our country that we make [the soldiers] responsible for providing their own food and drink. There is not a place where this evil does not prevail, but it is even worse for soldiers. . . . Without even waiting for the commanding officers to make extortionate demands, [the soldiers] are forced to make payments to subordinate officers. . . . The [soldiers] have to sell off their land and bankrupt their families, and still it is not enough. Only after we have first abolished this evil will the problems of the soldiers be somewhat relieved.[23]

Assignment of soldiers to duty stations at some distance from their home villages made life difficult for them because of transportation costs and separation from their families. Yu Hyŏngwŏn recommended abolishing the use of cavalry from Hwanghae Province (along the western coast, southwest of Pyongyang) for duty on the northern frontier. He pointed out that although in T'ang China the amount of service owed varied with the distance of the soldier's home from his military duty station, Korea was relatively small in area, so that "each man can be assigned for duty near his home."[24]

Furthermore, the common practice of using soldiers to perform the duties of clerks, runners, and slaves only interfered with the military training and capabilities of the troops. Yu remarked that this was a "an extremely bad practice that had originated in recent times." It had a systemic cause, however. Duty as servants and runners (*pogye*, literally servants and servile persons) was forced on people as part of their personal labor service requirement (*sinyŏk*). Because they received no salaries or rations for this duty, they ran away, leaving officials with no choice but to use soldiers in their place. The solution was twofold: provide adequate salaries to these petty clerks and runners, and prohibit the use of soldiers as runners or slaves.[25]

Yu's description of the corruption of the system of cloth support taxes was even more tragic because it was not new; it was certainly a continuation, if not exacerbation, of the situation that had left the Korean garrisons empty of real troops when Hideyoshi's men first landed on Korean shores in 1592. Kings Kwanghaegun, Injo, and Hyojong had failed to correct the situation.

Military Service for Slaves

The exclusion of slaves from military service prior to Hideyoshi's invasions was probably the major reason for the shortage of eligible male recruits prior to 1592. That problem had been remedied to some extent by the enlistment of private slaves in special *sog'ogun* units that originally mixed both slaves and commoners together, but that solution was resisted by the slaveowners who sought to regain exclusive control over the labor power of their slaves. The state, however, was not willing to give up its military service requirement for slaves. They had become essential for filling the ranks following the decrease in the number of commoner adult males eligible for service because of the corruption of the military registration and service system.

Yu noted that prior to Hideyoshi's invasions the number of regular duty soldiers plus support personnel was not quite 400,000, of which 180,000 men were regular duty soldiers, both cavalry and infantry, but when the Japanese landed at Pusan in 1592, most of the regular troops scattered to the winds.[26] Yi Sugwang's *Chibong yusŏl* of 1614 recorded pre-Hideyoshi troop strength at less than the 200,000 men registered under King Kongmin of Koryŏ in the 1360s, and Yi attributed the cause to "too many *sajok* [families of scholar-officials, i.e., yangban], idlers and vagrants, and too few people liable for service."[27]

Yu Hyŏngwŏn found that according to the records of the Ministry of War the number of registered males of "good" or commoner status in 1660 consisted of only 66,702 regular infantry and cavalry duty soldiers and 132,160 support taxpayers, a grand total of 183,258 men.[28] In addition, there were 161,929 *sog'ogun* soldiers, 47 percent of the total number of males in the army.[29] Since *sog'o* units combined slaves and commoners, one could not conclude that all these troops were slaves in 1660, but the percentage of slaves in the armed forces must have been considerable, probably more than the 30 percent in the general population, because commoners had been evading association with slaves in the *sog'o* units. A recent estimate of the percentage of slave duty soldiers and support taxpayers (*poin*) in some select units in the late eighteenth century was that about 25–30 percent of those units consisted of private slaves, most of whom were outside resident slaves who paid support taxes in lieu of duty.[30]

Yu could not have advocated a return to the early Chosŏn practice of exempting them from duty without drastically weakening the national defense, but he might well have called for immediate abolition of slavery, for manumitted slaves or freedmen would have become eligible for military service. He declined to do so not only because he was reluctant to deprive the yangban of its workforce, but also because slaves had become indispensable to the maintenance of adequate troop quotas for the nation, and he did not want to challenge the slave-owners directly.

DEGENERATION OF THE FARMER/SOLDIER MILITIA IDEAL

The Chou Model

It has already been pointed out how the well-field model of the Chou period provided the basis for Yu's conception of the basic organization of an ideal society. This model provided a military as well as a civil dimension. In conjunction with the temporary assignment of arable land to peasant families, those families were required to undergo military training and function as soldiers in wartime – the farmer/soldier militia mode of military service.

The militia model meant that the amount of time spent on duty in peacetime would be reduced to a minimum, and never so burdensome as to bankrupt the peasant. Military training would be conducted in the agricultural off-season so that it would not interfere with production and the subsistence of the peasant family. Since all adult males were obliged to serve on duty themselves, there would be no need for a standing army of professional soldiers or a system of taxation to support that army, both of which were conventionally understood to be features of China in her age of decline or later age (*huse*) after the ideal systems of the Chou were destroyed.

Another basic principle of the well-field model and the militia ideal was village organization and community solidarity. The smallest unit of civil life, whether the well-field with its eight families, or alternate systems of seven or five families, also served as the basis for the organization of squads and companies.[31] The eight-family unit and the village as well were marked by their cohesiveness, mutual aid and concern, familiarity, and intimacy. Cheng Hsüan, the Later Han dynasty commentator on the *Rites of Chou*, praised the advantages of troop units recruited from men of the same communities because of mutual aid and relief, and ease of recognition of clothing and voice when in combat.[32] Yu mentioned Duke Huan's reorganization of the Ch'i dynasty's military system at the suggestion of Kuan-tzu (during the Chou period), as recorded in the *Kuo-yü*. This system was also based on the five-man squad and the village militia, in which the solidarity of the village soldiers was described in effusive terms:

> Therefore, the men of the squads protected one another, and the families loved one another. When they were young children, they lived in the same place, and when they grew up, they went around together. When they performed the ancestral rites, they shared their happiness with one another, and when there was a death or funeral, they commiserated with one another. They had the same con-

> cern for calamity and happiness. When they were living at home, they shared he same joys, and when they were going around [together], they knew of one another's activities.
>
> For this reason, during night battles they would hear the sounds of their voices, and it was sufficient to prevent their being confused. During daytime battles, they could see one another, and it was sufficient to [enable them] to recognize one another. Their joy was such that it was enough for them to die for one another. For this reason, they were strong on defense and victorious on the attack. Trained like this, a force of thirty thousand men in crossing the land was used to chastise those who did not obey [lit. "lacked the proper way"] and to protect the Chou house. Eventually they [the Ch'i] became the hegemon of the world.[33]

Ch'iu Chün, Yu's favorite Ming dynasty commentator, also praised the advantages of the village militia. It was not necessary to recruit more men than needed for service because sons could take the place of their fathers who might die in battle. Since the militia fed themselves from their own crops, there were no costs in providing them with salaries. And because they were disbanded after the fighting was over, there was no need to keep them stationed in garrisons, and no political threat from commanders who might have control over them and use them to seize power.[34]

The Han Military Service System

The conventional evaluation of the nature of the Former Han dynasty military service system differed considerably from the generally negative view of the Han land tenure system. While the twin evils of private property and landlordism were reputed to have made their appearance in the Han, the Han military service system was supposed to have preserved the Chou militia ideal and carried it over into the period of centralized, bureaucratic empire. Yu's account of the Han military system repeats the well-known description of its division into capital and local forces, the main feature of which was that service was both universal and rotating. The imperial or palace guards (Southern Army or *Nan-chün*) and capital guards (Northern Army or *Pei-chün*) were staffed by peasants recruited from the countryside and the capital provinces, respectively, and both capital guards and frontier defenders rotated on and off duty, and when off duty the rotating soldiers would return to their farms.[35]

Even though the system of tours or shifts of duty appears to have been a necessary feature of universal service, peasants obligated supposedly for their annual quota of a month's duty in the capital guards or three days on the frontier could buy substitutes with cash payments. Ma Tuan-lin criticized the system because it meant that one hired soldier would end up substituting for a hundred men, leaving the garrisons bereft of troops.[36] Obviously Yu had found a precedent for the problem that emerged in Korea in the Chosŏn period: the replacement of duty soldiers by payments, but in cloth rather than cash.

The T'ang fu-ping *System*

Yu did not bother to trace the decline of the Han system of universal military service, but he obviously regarded it as a fact familiar to his readers. Almost from the time that Emperor Wu of the Former Han began his large-scale conquests in the late second century B.C. the militia ideal began to break down; by the time of the Northern and Southern dynasties from the third through sixth centuries A.D., aristocrats and warlords controlled their own private soldiers.[37] The *fu-ping* system, the organization of military service that complemented the equal-field system of land distribution, originated in A.D. 486 in the Northern Wei dynasty, a dynasty run by the non-Chinese T'o-pa people. It represented an attempt to return to the militia model of the Chou.[38]

Yu's description of the *fu-ping* system relied heavily on *The New History of the T'ang Dynasty* (*Hsin T'ang-shu*) written by the famous tenth-century Sung scholar-statesman Ou-yang Hsiu. After the T'ang military reorganization of A.D. 636 there were ten circuits (*tao*) in the empire with 634 *fu* or *che-ch'ung-fu* (564 according to a different source) under a commandant called a *tu-wei*. At the height of the system there was a total of 500,000–600,000 *fu-ping* militiamen and no fewer than 80,000 capital guards.[39]

Ou-yang Hsiu was particularly enamored of the institutional advantages of the *fu-ping* system because he deplored what he portrayed as a shift from virtue to brute force as the main determinant in the rise and fall of states since the Warring States period in the late Chou (fifth-fourth centuries B.C.). Of the military systems of all the dynasties of conquest since the Chou dynasty, the only one worthy of emulation was the *fu-ping* system of the T'ang because it was based on, but not fully consonant with, the militia ideal associated with the Chou well-field system.[40]

Ou-yang Hsiu also admired the distribution of *che-ch'ung-fu* garrisons around the provinces, and the delegation of registration, training, logistical, and command functions to their commandants (*tu-wei*). After it ceased to function, the official, Li Pi, lauded its organizational advantages and urged its restoration to Emperor Te-tsung (r. 780–805) because the *tu-wei* had done such an efficient job of training the militia during the agricultural slack season and helping the district magistrate in calling up soldiers during emergencies. The proximity of the peasants to regional garrisons meant that they did not have to waste precious time in traveling to distant posts, and the dismissal of militia soldiers from duty after a war obviated their use as a base of political pawns by their commanders.[41]

Another T'ang commentator, Tu Mu, also admired this feature because it would have prevented the anti-dynastic regional rebellions of Han Hsin, Ching-pu, and the Seven Feudatories of the Han, and An Lu-shan of the T'ang dynasties, and also the usurpations by commanders of capital guards like Wang Mang, Tung Cho, Ts'ao Ts'ao, or Ssu-ma Yen of the Han and Wei. In short, the *fu-ping* militia system would have obviated the problems that were created by excessive centralization or decentralization of military authority.[42]

Yu Hyŏngwŏn was, however, somewhat more skeptical of the effectiveness of the *fu-ping* system itself because it was not an exact replica of the Chou militia ideal, nor was it strictly enforced even in the reigns of Emperor Kao-tsung (r. 649–683) and Empress Wu (r. 690–705). The troops were shifted on and off duty without consideration of the planting and harvesting season as would be required for a militia system, and the soldiers on guard duty absconded and hid from the authorities. Contrary to regulations, the soldiers were not exempted from miscellaneous labor service, and the common peasants were impoverished by the demands of military and labor service. Furthermore, by the reign of Hsüan-tsung (r. 713–756) the size of the army had been severely reduced.

Nonetheless, Yu shared the opinion of Ou-yang Hsiu that the *fu-ping* militia system was infinitely superior to what replaced it: long-term, professional soldiers (*chang-tsung*, *changjong* in Korean) established by Chang Yüeh in 723.[43] The problem with the professional soldiers was that they did not contribute to their own expenses and had to be supported by the population. Since their numbers expanded (there were soon 120,000 of them), they represented an enormous cost to the state and the peasant taxpayers. The source of evil, therefore, was the destruction of militia service and the "separation of farmers from soldiers" in the military service system.[44]

Sung Military Organization

Yu wasted little space in describing the Sung system of military organization other than to list briefly the three types of troops in that period.[45] Yu omitted from his account what must have been common knowledge, that the Northern Sung government (founded 960) sought to prevent the recurrence of the military power of the late T'ang military governors by rotating commanders and concentrating the largest military force in the capital, where it could be controlled from the center. Unfortunately, these measures probably contributed to weakening the defensive posture of the country somewhat in the face of the aggressive attacks by the Khitan and Jurchen people in the northeast. The Northern Sung lost North China in 1126, and eventually was completely overrun by the Mongols in 1282.

Yu used as his chief source on the military problems of the Sung the opinions of the famous eleventh-century Sung poet and official, Su Shih, a protege of Ou-yang Hsiu and opponent of the "new laws" of Wang An-shih. Su felt the *fu-ping* militia system was superior to both the Han and Sung military systems because it was economical and would have effectively prevented the concentration of power in large garrisons or armies. Su complained about the heavy costs associated with a professional standing army of several hundred thousand men in the capital, including the transport of vast amounts of grain from the Huai and Yangtze river basins to the capital, and the dispatch of capital armies to trouble spots in the provinces. He also deplored the lack of experience in combat and training among officers and men, and shortages in rations and provisions for the permanent soldiers.[46] Yu Hyŏngwŏn agreed with Ou-yang Hsiu and Su Shih and concluded that the cessation of militia service and its replacement by professional soldiers since the early eighth century had created serious problems of military defense for China through the Ming dynasty.[47]

The Modern Critique of the fu-ping *System*

The enthusiasm of institutional reformers like Ou-yang Hsiu and Yu Hyŏngwŏn for the *fu-ping* militia system is to be explained in part by their unfamiliarity with the defects of that system in actual operation. Hamaguchi Shigekuni, who has recently studied the *fu-ping* system, admired it because it was more economical than the cost of maintaining a large standing army, and it raised the status and prestige of soldiers by requiring that recruitment be limited only to men of "good" status as opposed to vagrants and criminals.[48] On the other hand, it proved deficient in building national strength because the *che-ch'ung-fu* were established in only 90 of the 320 prefectures (*chou*) in the ten circuits (*tao*) of the empire, and two-thirds of these were located in the nineteen districts around the capitals at Ch'ang-an and Lo-yang to defend against rebellions against the throne, a problem similar to what occurred in Korea in the 1620s and 1630s.[49]

Equal distribution of military service burdens among the commoner peasant population could not have been achieved either because many categories of persons were exempted from service. These included slaves and persons of base or inferior status, guest and vagrant households not registered as commoners, most merchants and artisans who were registered as commoners but who did not receive land grants, Buddhist and Taoist monks, all functionaries of the state from regular officials to lowly clerks, close relatives of high officials, imperial nobles, merit subjects, and those commoner peasants who lived in districts where *che-ch'ung-fu* were not located.[50]

Hamaguchi also believed that not all commoners were required to serve during peacetime, and when they were called up, only one of every three adult males was required to serve. Nor were the men called up annually. Rather a recruitment was held once every three years to fill vacancies. The amount of service performed varied with the distance of one's residence from the place of service. Men who lived close to the place of service would be required to serve twice a year for a month each time, while those at the greatest distance might serve one tour of two months every eighteen-month interval. An adult male would be liable for service from the age of twenty-one to fifty-nine, and during that interval he had to serve one three-year term on frontier guard duty.[51] Since these limitations on the principle of universal service and the types of legal exemptions were typical of military service in Chosŏn, Yu Hyŏngwŏn might not have been as enthusiastic about the *fu-ping* system had he known of them. Nonetheless, Yu as well as most traditional commentators conceded that the *fu-ping* system was at best an approximation of the well-field ideal.

Ming Military Organization

Yu relied on a single source for his description of the Ming military system, Ch'iu Chün, who served as an official in the late fifteenth and early sixteenth centuries. This system, like that of the Sung, was based on the recruitment of soldiers from the general population to form a standing army. The imperial and capital soldiers were organized into a number of guard (*wei*) units that were also under the jurisdiction of a Five Armies Command (Wu-chün tu-tu-fu) that might use them on expeditions outside the capital. In addition, over 500 *wei* were also located throughout the empire.

Although Chiu praised this *wei-so* system for at least establishing quotas for the provincial and district garrisons, he also reported that the actual number of soldiers on duty barely averaged half the quota and recruiters were unable to enlist sufficient troops in the districts. Men were still evading service by changing their names, getting clerks to falsify the military rosters, illicitly dividing their families to avoid registration, or hiding from the registrars.[52] Although Yu Hyŏngwŏn appended no comment to these remarks, he must have felt that the late fifteenth-century Ming military system had produced problems similar to those in seventeenth-century Korea. As we will see, what Yu admired most about the Ming military system was the *sog'o* mode of organization developed by Ch'i Chi-kuang, not other aspects of the Ming armies.

The Koryŏ Military System

Yu's account of past military systems concluded with a brief treatment of Korea, but it was limited only to the Koryŏ dynasty (918–1392). His interpretation was based on the biased view of the Neo-Confucian compilers of *The History of the Koryŏ Dynasty* (*Koryŏsa*) in the fifteenth century that the early Koryŏ military system was a copy of the admirable *fu-ping* system of the T'ang, but that it began to deteriorate at the beginning of the twelfth century and fell into total disorganization after the military coup of 1170. King Kongmin's attempt to restore it in the fourteenth century (r. 1351–74) ended in failure. In short, Korea also suffered from problems in its military system after the abandonment of the militia system.

Yu repeated the *Koryŏsa* account that in early Koryŏ all males were liable for military service at the age of twenty, given land grants, exempted from military duty at the age of sixty, and organized according to the *fu* and *wei* (guards) of the T'ang.[53] According to more recent scholarship in the twentieth century this account has been discounted; most scholars no longer believe that a version of either the *fu-ping* or equal-field systems were adopted at the time. Rather, military service was probably limited to military families, and the state granted soldiers, along with other civil functionaries of the state, prebendal rather than land grants in exchange for their service.[54]

Nonetheless, the *Koryŏsa* account, which Yu cited, explained that the *fu-ping* system lasted supposedly until the establishment of the *Pyŏlmuban* or special military unit during the reign of Sukchong (r. 1095–1105). Although this measure was only a temporary reorganization adopted as part of the campaign against the Eastern Jurchen, it was significant because it abandoned the various status exemptions of early Koryŏ and required almost everyone in society, from officials without posts, clerks, merchants, slaves, and Buddhist monks, to serve in the army. While this modification might appear more admirable to some twentieth-century observers because it was more egalitarian in its distribution of service, it was deplored by the status-conscious compilers of the *Koryŏsa* (as opposed to Hamaguchi) who associated status discrimination with the admirable features of the *fu-ping* system. They also deplored the destruction of the system when military commanders usurped political power in 1170 and converted the troops of the national army into private soldiers under their own personal control. This, they believed, left the government virtually with no armies of its own to defend the country against the Mongol invaders after the 1230s.

Again the status-conscious compilers of the *Koryŏsa* were offended by the government's desperate scramble to find troops by ignoring all the customary taboos against mixing the higher and lower orders of society in the armed forces.

> They might recruit men from the capital without regard to whether they were noble or base in status. They might inspect the civil and military officials without posts, the *paekchŏng* [men of intermediate status between commoners and base persons], or the clerks and select them for service. Or they might take the house servants [i.e., slaves] of officials of the fourth rank or higher, or recruit people on the basis of the size of their families. Thus the condition of the state was destitute until the time when the dynasty actually fell.[55]

The compilers of the *Koryŏsa*, in other words, believed that maintaining necessary status distinctions by excluding men of lower status, particularly slaves, from military service was a necessary feature of the *fu-ping* system. Although Hamaguchi asserted that in fact this was so, this feature had never been advertised by *fu-ping* admirers like Ou-yang Hsiu or Su Shih, nor praised as part of the militia system in the classics. The power of Korean custom had apparently emphasized a view of the essential nature of the Chinese *fu-ping* system that conformed to Korean practice and prejudice.

Yu also cited the *Koryŏsa*'s decription of the frustrated attempt of King Kongmin (r. 1351–74) to reinstate some version of the T'ang *pubyŏng* (*fu-ping* in Chinese) system.[56] In emulation of what he thought was the essence of that system, Kongmin ordered in 1356 that the state grant seventeen *kyŏl* of land as a *chŏkchŏng* (full quota land grant to an adult able-bodied male liable for military service). Modern scholars have pointed out, however, that the seventeen-*kyŏl chŏkchŏng* could not have qualified as the equivalent of an equal-field type of land grant for all peasants because there was not enough land in the country to supply such a large allotment to all adult males. It must have been a land grant (or prebend) conferred only on duty soldiers. Its resemblance to a *fu-ping* system, therefore, would be restricted to the rotation of these men between their duty posts and their farms, not the requirements that *all* adult males were militiamen, nor that *every* militiaman was guaranteed a state land grant.[57]

Kongmin gave a Koryŏ twist to the measure by stating that the military households (*kunho*) who were to receive the seventeen-*kyŏl* grant were to be established by hereditary succession (*yŏn'ip*), "and if [their land grants] were taken away by force by anyone else, they will be permitted to report it to the authorities who will give it back to them."[58] What this shows is that Kongmin's conception of the T'ang and early Koryŏ systems consisted of a grant of land to a soldier, to be inherited by his male successors (preferentially by primogeniture) along with his military service obligation. Although male heirs of equal-field peasants in the T'ang system might have been eligible to take over their father's land grant, the land grant was defined as a returnable grant to peasants, not soldiers. Since Yu Hyŏngwŏn raised no objection here, it is likely that he accepted the notion of hereditary land grants to "soldier families" as part of the T'ang equal-field system when in fact it was a distinct feature of early Koryŏ society marked by stronger tendencies toward hereditary aristocracy and status than in T'ang China.

King Kongmin also reiterated the lesson learned from Chinese history about the costly burden of permanent soldiers. He complained that in his own time the large number of soldiers and officers guarding the palace imposed a heavy fiscal burden on the country. Finally, despite his concern to recreate a militia, he was unwilling to allow men of low status to infiltrate the command structure.

"Thus, the system of our forefathers has become an empty thing and the resources of the country are wasted on salaries [of a permanent standing army]. The men who consume the salaries of the five officers in charge of the forty-two battalions [*tobu*] . . . are either young and weak youths or artisans, slaves and underlings. How could this have been the intention of our forefathers?"[59]

Yu's Admiration for the Militia Model

Yu omitted any serious discussion of the 250-year history of his own dynasty in presenting the history of military systems in Korean history; he discussed the weaknesses of the contemporary system mainly in the context of discussing issues for reform. The main point of his background discussion was to gather description and opinion on the militia model of the Chou and its *fu-ping* approximation in the T'ang dynasty to illustrate their superiority over long-term, professional soldiers. Having established the decline from perfection since the abandonment of the militia system in both countries, he obviously felt that it was not necessary to go into too much detail in describing inadequate military systems. As in so many other categories, he was more interested in deriving wisdom and models from the Chinese experience because so many Korean institutions had been borrowed from China. The wisdom of China on military affairs was already clearly established in the Chinese literature; it was not something that had to be derived by arduous empirical investigation of raw data or by imaginative deduction from a body of evidence.

Practical Reform

What possible remedies could there be to a system of military service that left the state short of soldiers, oppressed the commoner peasants with impossible taxes, and exploited slaves by adding military service to their normal duties? Reducing the size of the army could alleviate the tax burden on the support taxpayers, but it also would have weakened national defense. Lowering the tax rate might also benefit the taxpayers, but it would reduce income for the armed forces. If, on the contrary, it were decided to increase the number of duty soldiers, the additional troops would increase the tax burden. In either case, it was impossible to tolerate the substitution of active duty troops for cloth payments or the imposition of illegal or unauthorized charges on the support taxpayers.

What about the conventional wisdom in the Chinese literature on professional, long-term duty soldiers? After all, was there anything intrinsically wrong with a system of trained and paid professional soldiers supported by tax revenues paid into a general fund? It might even be regarded as superior to a militia of part-time soldiers who would have to be mobilized and given additional training whenever an emergency arose, and it would certainly be better than the Chosŏn system in which even the duty soldiers served only a fraction of the year on duty, if duty soldiers existed at all. But to advocate this position, it would require the courage of a man willing to repudiate the teachings of men he acknowledged as his masters.

Or maybe there was something wrong with the way the current system had been operated that allowed it to be corrupted. Was there a key to the success of the system that had been neglected or ignored? Was it Confucianism itself and its disdain for the military ethic, military education, and the martial figure?

If remedies to these problems were not acceptable, there was always the classical ideal of a farmer/soldier militia system based on the well-field or equal-field models. Since Yu had already insisted on reinstituting an approximation of the well- and equal-field systems, why not advocate the institution of its military counterpart as well, the militia system, and recreate the vaunted village solidarity that underlay it?

Recruitment by Land Area and Village Solidarity

Yu had placed great emphasis on the need for a fixed square of land embossed into the landscape with a border of ridges to provide a firm and unchanging basis for land grants to the peasantry. He derived this idea from the well-field model, and he was also convinced that his embossed square could become the basis for his military system as well. He stated unequivocally that "In general, requirements of able-bodied adult males for service as soldiers will be based on land [allotments]," and he referred to this principle of military service by the four-character slogan, *kyejŏn ch'ulbyŏng*, "furnishing soldiers by measuring [the amount of] land."[60] What Yu meant by this was that for each fixed area of land a certain number of men would be required to meet military service obligations.

Yu clearly attributed the inspiration for his scheme to the standards of antiquity, in which the recruitment of men for service was conducted in the village, the strength of the militia system was based on the village community, and the village community was in turn the lowest rung of a civil/military hierarchy of residential communities units (the *pi*, *yŏ*, *chŏk*, and *tang* organization). Members of these units protected and succored one another, shared both work and leisure time, gave consolation at funerals, and shared in the joy of felicitous occasions. Thus, on the battlefield they could maintain order in the ranks day or night simply by recognizing faces or the sounds of voices. It was this system that guaranteed that "they were always firm in defense and assured of victory in attack." It was this system that enabled Duke Huan of Ch'i to become hegemon over all his rivals in Chou China.

Conversely, the loss of solidarity in the ranks was intimately associated with the destruction of the well-field land distribution scheme of antiquity, for once the well fields were destroyed, then the rulers of later ages (*huse*) filled the ranks of the army "only by conducting an investigation of individual adult men, and enrolling them for service as they were found." In other words, dissociating military service from land meant soldiers were treated as interchangeable individuals, not members of tightly knit village communities. As Yu put it, "Within the same district, men from the eastern subdistrict were mixed in with those from the western; in a province, men from the south were mixed in with those from the north. Even though they were said to belong to the same squad or platoon, the actual situation was that they did not support or recognize one another or trust each other's thoughts and feelings."

It was the loss of community solidarity pursuant to the destruction of the well-field system, therefore, that corrupted the military service system and induced men to evade service by running away from their villages, hiding from the registrars, or paying bribes to evade registration. And it was the loss of community solidarity that explains why their neighbors "covered the tracks of the runaways and tolerated corruption."[61]

It was this hope to recapture the bond between community solidarity and military organization that led him to emphasize the necessity of land reform as the only way to eliminate the corruption that was a necessary consequence of the process of investigation and registration of individual adult males for military service. It would be impossible, for example, to establish a system of truly universal service in which all adult males except for those serving as court officials, passers of the highest civil and military examinations, students in school, and men employed in the Inner (Palace) Forbidden Guards (Naegŭmwi), would be enrolled for military service as long as the practice of individual registration was in effect.

The reason was because everyone in society, "from soldiers and local gentry up to the noblemen at court, from the lowliest clerks and district magistrates to the generalissimo of the armies in the field, everyone had their own private interests." To have a system of individual registration where the registrar would have to make a decision on each individual "opened the path to corruption," and created the circumstances for "the evil of requesting favors and paying bribes to spread throughout the world."[62] The only way to eliminate the system of individual registration was to carry out land reform, shifting the basis of registration from individuals to unit areas of land, thus eliminating the opportunity for negotiation on each person's status or situation. Yu was emphatic on the absolute necessity of land reform for rectification of military service:

> Once the land system is carried out, then the grand framework of things will be established, and everything will work out as a matter of course and very easily. But if land reform is not carried out, there will be great confusion in the grand outline of things, and everything will be contrary and difficult to achieve. What hardship could there be [from land reform] that would be a reason for not doing it? Outside of this method, I know of no other way of [bringing the military service system] under control.[63]

Unfortunately, he did not say what should be done if land reform could not be carried out. Radical land reform and redistribution was so central to his plan for military service that one wonders whether he intended any of his proposals to be considered separately from his land allotment scheme. As we will see later on, some of his proposals for reform of the military service system were, in fact, divorced from his land reform program by his admirers, but this was a disservice to the logic of his views. Furthermore, he was not consistent in his idealism. As mentioned in previous chapters, he believed that radical land reform was not a Utopian pipe dream, but a distinct possibility once a resolute king could be persuaded of its advantages.

Unfortunately, slavery was also an important component of the current Chosŏn dynasty system of military service, and slavery was not part and parcel of the well-field model. Despite his opposition to it, Yu was willing to tolerate it for the time being because it was so firmly entrenched in Korean social practice; it could only be eliminated by subtle and gradual methods.

Nonetheless, his flexibility on slavery did not shake his conviction that land reform was both necessary and possible, and military service could not be rectified without it. Thus, he provided that "Once the land system is carried out, organize all soldiers – regular cavalry and infantry and the *sog'o* (slave) soldiers – into squads and platoons on the basis of villages."[64]

According to Yu's basic plan for military service, each man (of good status; for slaves and others see following section) would receive 100 *myo*, equivalent to 1 *kyŏng*, of land; each unit of 4 *kyŏng* (defined as a *chŏn*) would furnish 1 adult male for service as either a cavalryman (*kibyŏng*), infantryman (*pobyŏng*), or marine (*sugun*).[65] In light of Yu's admiration for the ideal of militia service associated with the well-field system and his stipulation that squads and platoons of all types of soldiers should be organized on the basis of village communities, it seems strange that he would have bothered to set a quota, or even a limit, of a certain number of men for each four-*kyŏng* unit of land to be liable for military service. Why did he not simply state that all adult males would serve in the army, rotating on and off duty in fulfillment of the principles of farmer-soldier service?

The answer is simple but disconcerting, for it turns out that he was not proposing a militia system in strict terms at all, but a continuation and modification of the system adopted at the beginning of the Chosŏn dynasty and still in use for most soldiers in the seventeenth century. In short, he fused two different principles of recruitment and service in his reform proposal, one based on the selection of a specified number of men per basic unit of land area, the other a division of servicemen between rotating duty soldiers and support taxpayers based on current Chosŏn dynasty practice. As in current practice, not all men liable for military service would be duty soldiers, and for that matter, the method of recruiting soldiers according to a quota per unit of land area had also been tried in the early Chosŏn dynasty in the fifteenth century. It did not necessarily signify a perfect militia system, but Yu claimed that it was derived from the militia model. But why would Yu have chosen to use the system of rotating duty soldiers and support taxpayers when by his own admission it had become thoroughly corrupted?

The Royal Division Model

One of the most important lessons Yu learned from his study of the history of military systems in China was that the abandonment of the militia system led to what was called the separation of soldiers from farmers. What this meant was that the economical benefits of the militia system by which the peasant paid for his own costs by the produce of his agricultural labor was lost, and the costs of the professional, salaried soldiers became a heavy burden on the state and the taxpaying peasants, with dire consequences:

> I note that the greatest harm that there is is to divide [the people] into soldiers and peasants. If you have too little to provide for the soldiers, they will not have enough to be of any use. And if you give them too much, then the first thing that will happen is that the people will be oppressed, after which the state will be

> destroyed. This will be an inevitable result of the situation, and the pros and cons can clearly be seen [in China's experience] from the T'ang and Sung dynasties on.[66]

The military system of Yu's time in the Chosŏn dynasty only had a small contingent of permanent, professional, and salaried soldiers in it, primarily the Military Training Agency first established in 1593 during the Imjin War and a few other units. Otherwise, adult males were divided into rotating duty soldiers and support taxpayers. The soldiers did not serve permanently on duty as professionals, but rotated on and off duty according to the number of shifts or groups of men (*pŏn*) assigned to a given unit by law. Since they returned to their farms during the long, off-duty intervals, they were true militiamen, but the support-taxpayers were not because they had no regular duty shifts.

A unit's quota might be defined as consisting of 1,000 men of which only 100 had to be on duty at any one time. Since there would be 10 shifts (*pŏn*) of 100 men each, and their term of service might be set at 2 months, each soldier and each shift would only be called up for duty every 20 months. The government could and did vary the number of men per shift, the number of shifts in a given unit, and the length of a tour of duty, lengthening or contracting the tour of service and the interval between tours. In addition, each duty soldier would be assigned support taxpayers whose tax payments would cover the uniforms and rations of the soldier while on duty. If a soldier were assigned by law 3 support taxpayers, a unit of 1,000 soldiers would thus have an additional 3,000 support personnel associated with it, and the total military service quota for that unit would be defined as 4,000 men.[67]

Despite Yu's criticism of the corruptions of this system, he did not bother to justify his choice, but one might surmise that he did not regard the Chosŏn division between duty soldiers and support taxpayers as a transgression of the normative admonition against creating separate categories of peasants and (professional) soldiers probably because the duty soldiers in the Chosŏn system were not paid salaries by the state. Since duty soldiers were supported by their support taxpayers (*poin*), theoretically the whole system was self-supporting and not a burden on the state treasury. Of course, from the standpoint of the support taxpayer, the tax he paid for the upkeep of the soldier was imposed by the state according to rates set by the state, and if he paid that tax to a garrison commander or the Ministry of War instead of the soldier himself, the tax certainly looked like a state tax. In other words, the notion that the whole system was self-supporting was a fiction, but an important fiction that justified the system in moral terms.

Another surprising feature of his essay on military service reform is that he provided no theoretical justification for retaining the current system. There was nothing in his historical coverage of the Chinese experience that resembled the current Korean system, and even his brief treatment of military service in the Koryŏ period emphasized the superiority of the *fu-ping* modification of the militia model over what followed it. Judging, however, from the regulations adopted in King Hyojong's reign in 1651 for the reform of the Royal Division (Ŏyŏnggun), it would appear that Yu's ideas derived in large part from the organization of that unit. In other words, the achievements of active officials at the time when he first began writing his masterwork provided him with the inspiration for his ideas, not the wisdom of China – with the exception of two elements that he may have derived from the classical militia model: village assessment of service and tying service to units of land area.

The Royal Division was first established during the Yi Kwal rebellion of 1624 with a membership of 4,000 volunteers recruited on the basis of examinations in musketry, archery, and brute physical strength (presumably for training as swordsmen or spearmen); official and private slaves were allowed to join the unit as well as commoners. At the outset the soldiers were evidently provided rations from the Ministry of Taxation and not by assigned support taxpayers. They were put on duty only for a four-month period from the fifteenth day of the tenth lunar month to the fifteenth day of the second lunar month to provide an extra contingent during the months that the Yalu and other rivers were frozen over, no doubt in anticipation of an invasion from the north.

The regiment had 6,170 men assigned to it in 1635, but was disbanded and then reconstituted. By 1649, when King Hyojong came to the throne, it had 12,000 duty soldiers, but the quality of the unit had deteriorated considerably, primarily because the burden of service on its soldiers had become lighter than that in other units, and unqualified men were attracted to it as a means of evading more onerous service. Hyojong appointed the experienced military official, Yi Wan, to get rid of the dead weight.

Hyojong carried out the reconstitution of the unit despite the opposition of Kim Yuk, who felt that it was an unwise allocation of tax resources during a period of acute financial shortage.[68] In the sixth lunar month of 1651 he increased the number of duty soldiers to 21,000 and created a new system of finance for the regiment based on the support taxpayer system. Each duty soldier was provided three support taxpayers. The number of shifts was not specified, but 1,000 men went on duty for a tour of two months at a time. Presumably there were twenty-one shifts and an interval forty-two months between shifts. Of the three support taxpayers, one would be responsible for making cloth tax payments to the soldier at his duty station for his equipment expenses while on duty, and the other two would remit their tax payments to a treasury located along the Han River in the capital. Support taxpayers living inland in hilly regions would pay two *p'il* of cloth per year, and those living in the lowlands along the coast would pay twelve *mal* of rice. The capital granary would dispense rations to the duty soldiers, thus relieving the Ministry of Taxation of all responsibility for providing rations or funds for the Royal Division.[69] The main contribution to military finance was that the administration of cloth and grain tax collections and disbursements would be shifted from a civilian agency to the capital treasury associated exclusively with the Royal Division, presumably on the expectation that this separation of funds would preserve the fiction of the self-supporting nature of the unit.

In delineating the details of his own program Yu Hyŏngwŏn made quite clear that he intended to maintain a distinct separation of men liable for military duty and those responsible for support tax payments for the soldiers: "The support personnel may be examined for talent, and if any of them passes, he may be permitted to become a soldier. If there are crimes involving duty soldiers having too many support personnel or collecting too much from them, then the person on military service will be punished and dropped down to become a support person."[70]

He also stipulated that when a soldier ran away or died, his place might be taken by an heir or a support taxpayer, indicating that in normal circumstances soldiers and support taxpayers were neither equal nor interchangeable.[71] Obviously, if Yu had chosen to adopt a militia system in which all adult peasants were potential or actual soldiers, there would have been no need for regulations defining duty soldiers and support persons as separate entities.

Of the four peasant recipients of land for each 100 *myo* in a village, only the strongest and healthiest would be designated "the main householder" (*chuho*) or household head (*hosu*) and act as the duty soldier. The other three would be support taxpayers (*po*).[72] The support taxpayers, presumably other members of an individual family, would be required to pay either 12 *mal* of rice or 2 *p'il* of cotton cloth a year to support the main householder (*chuho*), that is, the family of the regular duty soldier. Of the three support persons, one would pay either rice or cloth directly to the place where the soldier served on duty. In the case of infantrymen (*pobyŏng*), only the man singled out for military service would serve either at the capital, a provincial commander's headquarters, or a frontier garrison.[73]

One of Yu's main objectives was to extend the Royal Division model of rotating duty soldiers and support taxpayers to all military units. He complained that new types of soldiers like the *sog'o* troops established in 1594 and the Special Cavalry of the Military Training Agency created in 1669 had never been assigned support taxpayers.[74]

He also hoped to remedy the main weakness of the current system, the acceptance of cloth tax payments in lieu of service from duty soldiers. He insisted that all the duty soldiers must remain soldiers and not be converted to cloth taxpayers, and all duty soldiers had to be supported by the assignment of support taxpayers. Since the regular infantrymen and cavalrymen, who were nominally duty soldiers backed up by support taxpayers, were in fact paying a fee or tax instead of serving, he insisted on adoption of a regulation to prohibit this practice: "With regard to all types of soldiers, completely stop collecting the [substitute] cloth payment [in lieu of service] [the *kap'o*], and for all of them provide cloth."[75] Any commanders of army or navy garrisons found guilty of releasing even a single soldier from duty to collect a cloth tax from him would be indicted under the laws against embezzlement. For that matter, the same ordinance would be applied to any provincial army or navy commander or local garrison commander who extorted funds from any duty soldier to pay for their miscellaneous expenses or transport costs.

This last regulation was punctuated with a quotation from the venerated Cho Kwangjo, the great Remonstrator of 1515. Cho, a man extolled in the conventional literature as a hero of the moral purists (the *sarimp'a*) at the turn of the sixteenth century, provided an admonishment to King Chungjong that had nothing at all to do with moral leadership, exhortation, or persuasion. On the contrary, he criticized King Sŏngjong's (r. 1469–94) policy of leniency toward embezzlement because it had only opened the door to bribery and corruption. If King Chungjong would only "punish any such transgressions, no matter how minor, and prohibit all violators from holding office at court, the concern among officials [over the prospect of a ruined career if caught violating a regulation] would keep them straight and honest."[76]

In other words, the reason why the moralist Yu Hyŏngwŏn believed that he could retain the current military system and reform it was derived from a dictum handed down by Cho Kwangjo, a good exemplar of muscular Confucianism, that severe punishment of recalcitrant officials could prevent the perversion of institutional rules and procedures. The reliance on Legalist methods of coercion to reinforce the institutions of Confucian states was by no means an exception to practical statecraft thinking among officials, but Yu's masterwork was devoted to the notion that superior institutions derived from classical models based on moral suasion could provide the way to achieve the reform of contemporary institutions. This departure by Yu from the moral and institutional solution to problems was by no means an isolated instance, and it shakes one's confidence in Yu's commitment to his own method.

But why should royal interdictions and prohibitions have had any effect under his system when they did not in the past two centuries? There was little evidence that they would with the current body of officials, but Yu hoped to train a new body of officials, men who would represent the cream of the crop of moral men. Undoubtedly his new moral men would not need to be coerced by the threat of punishment.

Taxpayer Support for Long-term Soldiers and Clerks

One of Yu's greatest concerns was the excessive costs associated with professional, long-term soldiers, but instead of advocating their replacement with militia, he sought to convert the method of finance for all service whether in the capital guards or provincial garrisons to the support taxpayer system. Ostensibly, this should not have been that serious a problem because the only military units that consisted of professional soldiers were the Military Training Agency, and possibly the Special Cavalry of the Military Training Agency (Hullyŏnbyŏltae or Pyŏltae), and *sog'o* soldiers in the provinces. But he was also concerned about men in nonmilitary posts who had to perform labor service for eunuchs, the Court of Interpreters (Sayŏgwŏn), Directorate of Medicine (Chŏn'ŭigam), Directorate of Astronomy (Kwangsanggam), and the Office of Benefiting the People (Hyeminsŏ). He wanted to convert all such service personnel, whether petty officials and clerks, or specialists like scribes, accountants, doctors, legal specialists, veterinarians, musicians of classical or popular music, post-station clerks, and artisans, from salaries to payments from support taxpayers.[77] In short, his desire for a more rational and economic policy of government finance was more powerful in guiding his thinking about the reform of the military service system than the wisdom he had accumulated about the Chinese and Korean military systems alone.

Maintaining Accurate Records

Yu was confident that he could reestablish the integrity of a support taxpayer system, eliminate the illicit registration of children, old men, and deceased persons, and ensure that duty soldiers would be kept distinctly separate from taxpayers by maintaining accurate records. In addition to land registers there had to be detailed military records kept with the name, age, distinguishing marks, and residence of all men liable for military service. Copies would be sent to the Ministry of War, provincial governor's yamen, and local garrison. Annual changes would be recorded by pasting stickers onto the register, and these would be incorporated in more permanent fashion when the triennial cadastral survey would be conducted. All soldiers, or males liable for service, would wear tallies on their belts recording their names, type of service, military unit, and land grant parcel, in accordance with the format in Ch'i Chi-kuang's *Chi-hsiao hsin-shu*.[78]

Ch'i Chi-kuang's registration system was obviously no less susceptible to falsification and corruption than the existing one, but Yu probably believed that since land area was the basis for assessing service and not his proposed military registers, there would be no incentive to falsify the registers – a questionable deduction.

One Type of Service per Man

Yu further specified that each man would be restricted to only one type of military service obligation, in contrast to current practice where almost every man had anywhere from two to as many as four types of service to perform. Some had to pay cloth taxes and were obliged to serve as *sog'o* troops as well, or serve in the Special Cavalry and supply his own weapons and horse, or perform some kind of long-term service as a runner in a magistrate's yamen.[79]

Regular duty soldiers (*chŏnggun*) – but not their support taxpayers – would be exempted from all miscellaneous service (*chabyŏk*) assessed at the local level, and the civil bureaus at the capital were to be prohibited from assigning soldiers to civilian service duties as runners and guards. The latter practice was particularly annoying because the law provided quotas of slaves to civil agencies for these functions. The bureaus had recruited soldiers to perform slave service functions because a shortage of slave workers had developed in recent years. Bureau slaves maltreated by officials and destitute because of the lack of regular rations or salaries had been running away in droves. Yu argued that all soldiers could easily be returned to their primary function simply by providing adequate compensation to the bureau slaves.[80]

Guaranteeing Support for the Duty Soldier

Yu felt that the current Royal Division soldiers provided a good model for his principle that the duties of soldiers should be confined to their basic tasks. Even though he proposed to do away with the Royal Division itself, he approved that its troops had only been required to stand guard duty and undergo training and had never been used for service in lieu of slaves in the capital bureaus.[81] He admired the Royal Division for another reason as well; it provided a model for proper operation of the support taxpayer system by limiting the duties of the support person to the payment of tax, and by guaranteeing that duty soldiers would be provided with a rice ration during their tour of duty.

The problem with the current support tax system was that the duty soldiers were not always able to obtain their full support allotment because some of their assigned support personnel were too poor to make payment. Or the soldier might squander his allotment even before he showed up for duty. In either case, the soldier would be so poor and hungry that he had to borrow from usurers while on duty. After returning home, he had to sell off all his land and oxen to repay principle and interest double the value of the original loan. Thus, under the old system, "all the rotating duty soldiers were beggars and hardly seemed human."[82]

In the Royal Division, however, two of the three support taxpayers were designated to provide a cloth or rice support payment per year, not to the soldier himself but to the soldier's duty station whether in the capital or provinces. The unit or base would then pay monthly rations to the soldier to ensure steady rations while on duty. The other support taxpayer would be responsible for paying for the materiel and equipment costs of the soldier.

Yu reversed the proportion: under his system only one support taxpayer would pay twelve *mal* of rice per year to the capital granary, while the other two support persons would pay a cloth tax to the soldier directly for his equipment costs. Yu anticipated that one support taxpayer's rice payment would not only be sufficient to provide rations for soldiers who would serve on duty only once in a year and a half under his system, but that there would also be a surplus over the soldier's consumption that could be used to pay for rewards and banquets for soldiers who performed well in the military skill contests.

Yu felt that this system could be run without corruption if there were detailed inspection procedures for each phase of the operation. Thus, when the support taxpayer paid rice to the capital, the local magistrate would be required to go personally to the dock where the rice was to be loaded on a transport ship. If the rice were to be converted to cloth, clerks would be designated to supervise the collection. Likewise, if the reception point were in the capital, the granary officials would ask agents from the Ministry of War to oversee the collection; if in a provincial military base, the district magistrates would monitor the collection. The same procedure would be observed when rice rations were paid to duty troops every month.[83] Yu summarized the advantages of the Royal Division's system of rotating service and support taxation by quoting what he had heard from the soldiers and common people in the streets:

> "Of all the soldiers in Chosŏn, it's only the men of the Royal Division who have been able to escape the hell [of military service] and gain a glimpse of the sun in the sky." What makes Royal Division service so much better than the rest? Nothing more than the fact that the soldiers received rice rations when on duty and the support taxpayers only had to make their rice payments and were not required to perform double and triple service as *sog'o* soldiers and the like.[84]

It should be clear that part of the reason why Yu was willing to retain the support taxpayer system is that he believed that it was already functioning smoothly in one of the capital divisions. All that needed to be done, therefore, was to extend the model of the Royal Division to all military units.

Weaknesses of the Royal Division as a Model

Increased Fiscal Burden. Unfortunately, reform of the military service system was more complex than Yu imagined. Not only was his faith in detailed regulations to ensure probity and honesty in the administration of tax funds rather naïve, but what was even more important, he failed to take fully into account problems involved in the actual operation of the Royal Division and the military system as a whole.

For example, Yu was either unaware of or neglected the debate that took place when the Royal Division was expanded from 12,000 to 21,000 duty soldiers and reorganized under the support tax system in 1651. This measure was bitterly opposed by the then Second State Councilor Kim Yuk, author of the *taedong* tribute reform and proponent of the expansion of metallic currency in the economy. Kim, who was at the same time one of the most progressive and yet fiscally conservative statesmen of the century, remarked that when the Royal Division was first created in 1624, it was not intended to be a permanent palace guard, only a temporary unit to operate in the provinces. It was only when the "bandit ministers" (i.e., the political generals of the 1620s) got hold of it that they were able to expand it by unrestricted recruitment to 40,000 men.[85]

Kim argued that a number of problems developed in association with the division: there was never a full complement of troops on duty in the ranks, special tax exemptions for its soldiers led to a reduction of tax revenues, and unemployed relatives of yangban (*hanjŏng*) who were not really serving on duty were provided with support taxpayers. The net result was that "for the last four or five years there has been no way to provide for the financial expenditures of the regiment. [Those supposed to be on duty] have been spending long days in idleness and leisure . . . and they have become soldiers that are very hard to control."

Kim saw nothing but trouble coming from an expansion of their numbers. To slap a support tax on peasants to increase the rice ration for an expanded quota of soldiers by a couple of *mal*, and to require that the men actually show up for duty in the capital would only earn their resentment.

He was undoubtedly considering that expansion of the Royal Division from 12,000 to 21,000 soldiers meant an increase of 9,000 troops plus the creation of 63,000 new support taxpayers.[86] Even though remittances from support taxpayers were not supposed to impose an additional burden on the taxpaying public because they were designed to replace ordinary tax payments, Kim Yuk still viewed the conversion of the Royal Division's finances to a support taxpayer system as a shocking tax increase.

Furthermore, the additional men that would be recruited for service would mostly be vagabonds from the hills, like "wild horses that have never been bridled." If they had any skill at all, it was as bandits and robbers. There was nothing but harm to be anticipated by bringing such men into the capital as guards. Kim's suggestion was that if you had to recruit them for service at all, it would be better to assign them to units in their home provinces, grant them tax-exemption privileges and support taxpayers in accordance with standard regulations, provide them with a special, prestigious title and somewhat favorable treatment, and subject them to normal training and instruction. That way, it would not be necessary to go through the bother of accumulating a grain reserve for their rations or set up rotating tours of duty in the capital, and the country would still have a reserve force of men to use in an invasion or emergency.

He also complained about expanding military forces during a time of hardship and famine. He predicted that the order to recruit more men for the regiment would create a greater demand for rations and resources than could be met by the support and grain-remittance procedures of the support-taxpayer system, particularly since grain and cloth had to be transported by ship from support taxpayers in some provinces. The increase in soldiers would thus impose demands on the Ministry of Taxation for support, contrary to Yu's theory of the independence of the support taxpayer system from the state treasury.[87] Although Kim Yuk's objections may well have represented the viewpoint of a conservative, tight-fisted fiscal expert who was not committed to King Hyojong's policy of taking revenge on the Manchus, his criticism at least reveals that the expansion of the Royal Division and the use of support taxpayers as a means of finance was a mixed blessing at best.

Difficulty of Enforcing Rules: Old-Age Exemption Fees. Yu's faith that his rules of administrative procedure would be followed to the letter seems strange when some of the simplest rules of the military service system were not being followed in his own time. Take, for example, the rule that all adult males were to be excused from military service at the age of sixty. Yu himself had discovered that currently men past retirement age either found it impossible to obtain their old-age exemption, had to pay a gratuity of thirty *p'il* of cloth to obtain it, or even if they did, found themselves enrolled as beacon station soldiers beyond their retirement date. The gratuities were so onerous in some cases that the men preferred to stay on service rather than pay them. In the worst case, even death did not provide relief from oppression, for the clerks collected a death gratuity in cloth (*mulgo injŏng p'o*) amounting to twenty to thirty *p'il* (ten to fifteen times the current seventeenth-century annual military cloth level) for the trouble of filling out the death certificate.

The plight of the widows and surviving relatives was particularly poignant:

> I once saw a case in a village where a soldier died and his father wanted to take care of the death gratuity. He rushed around from one direction to the other for over a year but was not able to make plans for the funeral, and because his wife was not able to pay the fee, she was made a prisoner and locked up in jail. [When I saw her there], her hair was a mess and she was crying in distress. It was so pitiful I can't bear to talk about it.[88]

What was Yu's solution to this rather blatant violation of the law? He simply insisted that after his land grant system was implemented, there had to be strict observance of the regulation that ended military service when an able-bodied adult male reached the age of sixty or became seriously ill, at which time the soldier's land grant would be returned to the state. He provided no reason to expect that officials in the future would be any more willing to forego the profits of extortion and squeeze than at present.

Difficulty of Enforcing Rules: Training for Off-duty Regular Soldiers. Another drawback of the support system was the difficulty in regulating training for off-duty regular soldiers. Since the system restricted service to only one fraction of the number of adult males who served on duty for only one or two months in a period that could range from several months to four years, the off-duty men might be neglected altogether and left untrained. Conversely, they could also be exploited by local officials for nonmilitary duties. Yu hoped to solve this problem by requiring that during the sixteen-month interval between shifts, off-duty infantrymen take military skill examinations once a month in their home district and assemble at the regional command garrison (*chin'gwan*) twice a year in the spring and fall for training camp. To provide them with some respite from local training sessions, they would be given two months of leave both prior to and after the completion of their two-month tour of duty.[89]

Yu admitted that this system might impose a heavy burden on the corps of regular soldiers, but it was still an improvement over current conditions where both duty soldiers (infantry and cavalry) and support taxpayers had to double up as provincial *sog'o* soldiers subject to examination and inspection once every ten-day week in addition to serving tours of duty or paying cloth taxes. Although it might be easier for the regular soldiers if they were left alone for the rest of the year after serving their two-month shift, they would lose their military skills without constant training. He advertised his solution as the middle way between the extremes of excessive exploitation and underutilization.[90]

Exclusion of Cavalry from Rotating Service. Yu also decided that for the six southern provinces, the cavalry would train at home but, in contrast to the infantry, would be excluded altogether from rotating service arrangements mainly because the cost to the cavalrymen for maintaining their horses had been too expensive. Instead, they would stand for the bi-monthly shooting examinations in their home district and the spring and autumn general muster and bivouac training at the regional command centers (*chin'gwan*), in accordance with regulations governing the Special Cavalry Unit of the Military Training Agency (Pyŏltae) established in 1669. He justified his plan by arguing that cavalry on rotating service in the capital would not be needed because he planned to retain the horse platoons (*madae*) already on duty in the capital.

He also preferred not to assign them to the provincial military commander's headquarters (Pyŏngyŏng) in the provinces as well because that kind of system had already been proved a failure in the early Chosŏn period. The cost to the duty cavalryman of maintaining his horse at his duty station had been so great that all cavalrymen had taken to renting or substituting horses despite laws against it, so that in no time none of them had his own. Since it was ridiculous to treat men as criminals for regulations impossible to observe, it was better to dispense with rotating cavalry in the provinces altogether.

In case of a real crisis, cavalrymen could be rounded up with the *sog'o* slave soldiers, who also were to train in their home districts as a reserve force. The only exception would be in the northern two frontier provinces, where cavalry could serve on rotation with infantry and be provided horse fodder by the provincial officials, who would have sufficient funds because the land tax was to be kept on reserve in those provinces and not remitted to the capital. For that matter, even in the south, rotating service for cavalry might be instituted any time there was a serious crisis, but it was far better to eliminate rotating duty during peacetime to avoid the cost of having to provide extra support taxpayers for expensive cavalry.[91]

Excluding the cavalry from rotating service assignments indicated a serious weakness in the system of finance through support taxpayers. When the evidence available indicated to Yu that the financial support from these taxpayers had not met the costs associated with keeping military horses, he chose to eliminate the system rather than increase the number of support personnel for cavalrymen.

His solution appeared to reflect the prejudice of a cost-cutting civilian with an ingrained bias against the military despite all his protestations to the contrary, particularly because he insisted on retaining rotating service for cavalry along the northern frontier, where the threat of war was the greatest. Furthermore, it suggested that if he had no confidence in the financial capacity of the support taxpayer system to support cavalry, why was he so confident that it could provide adequately for infantry, particularly when the evidence of corruption in its operation in his own time was so overwhelming?

He also felt that Sung systems of providing for combat horses were not good solutions. Under the "household horse system" (*hu-ma-fa*) of the Sung, still in use in the Ming period, the government abolished state-run ranches and either provided one state horse to any family that volunteered to accept and care for them, or provided funds for a family to buy a horse on the market. The (*pao-ma-fa*) system divided households into groups of ten and either held the household or a particular cluster of households (*pao* or *she*) responsible for paying compensation if a horse under its care happened to get sick or die.[92] He obviously felt that this arrangement imposed too heavy a burden on the individual household.

Easing the Burden of Military Support Taxes

Varying Tours of Duty and Nonduty Intervals. Yu felt that it was possible to regulate burdens on ordinary infantrymen of good status by adjusting provisions for the number of shifts, length of service, time intervals between service, and location of duty posts. Infantrymen, for example, would be divided into eight groups or shifts serving on duty for two months at a time. Presumably, the interval between service would be sixteen months.

To reduce the burdens of travel and the transport of support payments, in all cases men would be assigned to units closest to their homes. Yu noted that in T'ang China, distances were so vast that the government established a system of grades of hardship (each 500 *li* of travel constituted a grade) to standardize the travel burdens on soldiers. Since Yu decided that these grades would not be necessary in a country as small as Korea, he reduced travel burdens to a minimum by dividing all regular infantrymen into eight shifts and reducing their service to sixteen-month intervals. In the few cases where soldiers might have to travel to a post between 500 and 1,000 *i* (125–250 miles) from their homes, their burdens could be alleviated by dividing them into ten shifts (rather than eight) and extending the interval between service to twenty months.

In accordance with the principle of village solidarity, all companies from a given district would serve as a unit rather than individual companies or platoons disassociated from their districts and companies. The only exception would be if a frontier garrison lacked a full complement of troops, then it would be able to draw on soldiers from another district.[93]

Yu also proposed reducing the burden on current soldiers in two other ways. Currently rotating duty soldiers who served at the headquarters of the provincial army commander (the Pyŏngyŏng) had to serve tours of one month. By increasing the term of duty to two months, Yu was in effect doubling the time interval between tours of duty. He also proposed setting a quota limit on the number of troops assigned to provincial army commanders' headquarters, perhaps as few as 600 but no more than 1,000 in the southern provinces for any one shift, with higher quotas for the northern and northwestern provinces according to the need.[94]

Discrimination Against Men of Low Status. Despite Yu's arduous attempt to work out flexible arrangements so that the burden of service would not fall too heavily on any one type of soldier, his regulations in fact provided for differential rates that would easily lead to evasion in practice. By varying the number of men to be provided for military service based on both the type of service and the status of the soldiers involved, he was departing from his supposed egalitarian ideal.[95] Thus the service obligation for men of good status in the cavalry and infantry was assessed at the lowest rate – one man for every four *kyŏng* of land (or one duty soldier for every four heads of household). Grain transport workers (*chojol*) were recruited on the basis of one man for every three *kyŏng*, sailors (*subu*) and slave soldiers (*sog'ogun*) at the rate of one man for every two *kyŏng*, and a number of other types such as able oarsmen, beacon station soldiers, attendants, flag bearers, drummers, herdsmen, and tomb guards at the rate of one man for every one *kyŏng* of land. In other words, the service burden was four times heavier for men in the last category than regular soldiers of good status.

Able oarsmen were also to be recruited from among both official and private slaves living close to coastal naval bases, and they were not to be provided with support taxpayers as other commoner soldiers were. If the men earned their living as fishermen, however, land could not be used as a basis of recruitment, and the rate of service for both commoners and slaves was to be one oarsman for every two fishermen. Tomb guards were to be recruited from slaves as well as commoners, and both would enjoy exemption from the land tax as compensation.[96]

Yu's use of a variety of land/service ratios, tantamount to a variety of military service tax rates, was less a method for equalizing service burdens or rates than it was a means of discrimination based on status and prestige levels.

Reduction of Tax Rates. Yu also believed that he could reduce the burden on support taxpayers by reducing the amount of tax each would have to pay. Under his reform regulations the musketeers and horse soldiers on duty in capital guard units, for example, would receive eight *p'il* of cloth, two from each of four support personnel residing in the provinces. Yu declared that he was thus reducing the tax rate on support taxpayers from the current three *p'il* to two, but increasing the number of support taxpayers from three to four.[97]

As the history of the military service and tax system was to demonstrate after Yu's death, the attempt to alleviate tax burdens on support taxpayers by reducing higher rates to two *p'il* was doomed to failure for two reasons. The rate had to be sufficiently low that people would not consider it too onerous and attempt to evade it, and it had to be uniform so that there would be no opportunities for evaders to sign up for lower service rates. In Yu's own time, there were some rates lower than two *p'il* so that a two-*p'il* rate constituted a tax raise for some taxpayers, and in the century after his death two *p'il* came to be regarded as a high rate, inducing tax evaders to find officials who would sign them up, whether legally or illegally, for lower-rate service. Although Yu's plan is to be admired for its intent, his rate was still too high and his toleration of differential rates of service failed to establish a uniform standard for either service or tax.[98]

Furthermore, he had to face the question of a revenue shortage that would be produced by reducing the per capita tax rate on support taxpayers. He did this by increasing the number of support personnel for each duty soldier. Again, as subsequent experience would show, this tactic merely shifted tax burdens, it did not reduce them. The tactic was also based on the presumption of an available supply of untaxed or idle males to fill expanded quotas, but that presumption was unjustified. Increasing the number of support taxpayers only increased the pressure on magistrates to sign up more people for taxes.

Yu can be defended on this point, however, since his whole scheme of service was based on the nationalization of land and distribution of plots to all peasants, guaranteeing sufficient livelihoods to all. But without major land reform, the most difficult of all programs to implement, his remedies were not likely to produce either uniformity or true reduction of tax burdens on the male population.

Rejection of the Land Tax to Finance the Military

Since Yu argued elsewhere that all state finances should preferably be paid for from general state funds for expenses (*kukka kyŏngbi*), he raised the question whether it might not make more sense to use the land tax as a basis for providing funds to soldiers rather than the support taxpayer system, especially since the recruitment system was based on units of land. In fact, one might have expected Yu to adopt this idea for several reasons. He was an admirer of Kim Yuk's *taedong* reform that had converted the whole system of in-kind tribute payments to a surtax on land. He had already argued that land or land area should be the basis for assessing military service, and he had suggested having one of the support taxpayers pay a rice tax directly to the soldier's base or duty station to make sure each soldier actually received his food ration instead of squandering his support payments in advance of service. Furthermore, in the three-quarters of a century from his death to the adoption of the equal service reform of 1750, a number of reform advocates were to propose the complete conversion of military support taxes to a levy on land because they felt it would represent a fairer distribution of tax burdens than the highly regressive military support cloth tax system.

Nevertheless, his response to this proposition was that the land tax revenues were already fully committed to paying official salaries and could be decimated by a bad crop year or famine. Thus it was essential to keep the financing of the army separate from general revenue and assign support taxpayers to a specific duty soldier. He did not explain, however, how peasants suffering from famine would be any more able to pay military support taxes than the land tax. As a creature of the mid-seventeenth century, he was tied to the tradition of a support system of finance for soldiers and still confident that it could be run without corruption if only the proper administrative arrangements were found. In fact, in 1750, his opposition to the land surtax as a substitute for the support system was cited by one participant in the debate over the equal service reform.[99]

Yu was, however, willing to use some revenues from land for military purposes, but only to defray certain logistical costs of the military establishment. Instead of adding a surtax to the existing land tax, he proposed using the usufruct from specially designated military expense land (*kunjajŏn*). Yu designed this as part of his plan to rationalize finance in general, for military units had evidently been raising funds for expenses by exploiting fishing weirs, salt flats, and iron smelters in territories under their jurisdiction. These revenues were used for weapons repair, construction, banquets held after the annual spring and fall maneuvers, and special banquets to honor the winners of skill examinations. These post-maneuver banquets in particular were to be costly affairs, financed at the rate of fifty *mal* per man, equivalent to the annual grain levy on four support persons. The costs would be deducted from the district's account of funds derived from these lands.

Funds for the repair of weapons for both capital and provincial soldiers were also to be paid for from military expense land revenues. For example, in the case of the Military Training Agency a couple of land parcels in Kyŏnggi Province would be set aside to defray weapons repair costs and the expected revenue would be fixed at 2,400 *kok* (24,000 *mal* at 10 *mal* per *kok*) for approximately 2,000 capital soldiers. The land was not to be administered or taxes collected by an agency supervisor, probably to prevent the agency from gaining its own independent revenue base, but would be handled by the regular district magistrate as one type of special tax-exempt land.

By funding weapons repair and banquets for the Military Training Agency in this way Yu hoped not only to abolish the arbitrary use of the fishing weirs, salt flats, and smelters, but also to remove the financing of these needs completely from all independent revenue-raising, commercial, and industrial activities run by the Military Training Agency that involved employing ships, collecting taxes, releasing soldiers for nonmilitary work, and hiring commoners as workers. "The only thing that the agency should be in charge of are troops. . . . When it comes to collecting taxes, naturally we have appropriate bureaus to do that; it is not work to be done by the agency." It is hard to understand why he should have opposed in principle the collection of taxes by a military unit since his support taxpayer program already provided that part of the taxes paid by support personnel for individual duty soldiers would be "collected" in grain by the base or duty station of the soldier, and part by the family of the soldier in his village.

It is also unclear why he would allow land taxes to be used only for military expenses of units and not for the rations and equipment of soldiers. Setting aside military expense land (*kunjajŏn*) certainly suited the tradition of separate military colony lands in Korea, but the use of grain income from these lands was hardly different in type than the use of a grain tax to finance military costs. One can hardly help but conclude that his respect for the support taxpayer system and his rule excluding the use of the land tax for overall support of the military was nothing but the product of a rigid commitment to what he viewed as an inviolable classical norm and artificially compartmentalized thinking on financial questions.

Furthermore, he was not entirely consistent in respecting his normative categories, for he also stipulated that in unusual circumstances, if revenues from the military expense lands were insufficient to pay the costs of banquets, they could be defrayed by the use of funds in the ever-normal relief and loan granaries, or interest charges (*mogok*) on state-sponsored grain loans (*hwanja*) until the time that the grain loan system was abolished. The latter point was later used by his intellectual heir, Kwŏn Chŏk, as a means of financing a different kind of scheme to finance military service in 1750 (see chap. 12).

To the objection that holding costly banquets to reward winners of skill examinations was an extravagance, Yu replied that large expenditures were not a problem as long as "in all cases there is a source from which [expenditures] will come, and in each case it can be paid for."[100] It may have been true that Yu budgeted every item of expenditure by identifying a source of funds, but he was certainly willing to use a variety of forms of revenue for military expenses. There was thus no logical reason why he should have insisted on the inviolability of the rule that land tax revenues should not be used to support the military. Why could he have not showed the same flexibility that Kim Yuk did when he violated the customary rule that tribute taxes had to be treated separately from all other taxes and replace them by a surtax on land, or the agricultural product from land?

HEREDITARY FEATURES IN YU'S MILITARY SERVICE SYSTEM

The Replacement of Duty Soldiers

Yu's preference for the contemporary Korean rotating service and support taxpayer system over the classical militia ideal was not the only example of his departure from classical fundamentalism. His specific regulations for the replacement of runaway or deceased soldiers were influenced by Korean tradition as well. "If [a soldier] dies or runs away, the next person who receives his land will take his place. Or you might choose one man from among the support [taxpayer] personnel and make him the main householder, and make the one who receives the land grant in the [deceased] man's place a support person."[101]

This provision had nothing to do with any well-field militia system that would have allowed any commoner to replace another. Instead, it was close to the early Koryŏ *chŏnsikwa* model that allowed for inheritance of supposedly returnable land grants by relatives, suggesting a system of inherited occupations and military service rather than a true militia. In one footnote describing the way the land grant of a deceased or runaway soldier was to be "returned" to the government, Yu stated that

> If a person has sons, grandsons, or close relatives [*ch'inch'ŏk*], he may transfer his land [to them] and pass on his responsibilities [to them]. If he has no sons or grandsons and wants to keep his land and drop down to the [position of] support taxpayer, then allow him to do so. After a person reaches the age of seventy, grant him *kubunjŏn* [mouth-share land, i.e., retirement land] in the amount of twenty *myo*. He will return the leftover portion [of eighty *myo*]. On this twenty *myo* of land he will also pay a support rice tax of one-fifth [the crop]. After he dies, all his land will be given to a substitute serviceman.[102]

These regulations and, in particular, the misuse of the T'ang term for the basic equal-field allotment, *kubunjŏn*, to mean a small retirement grant were all features of the early Koryŏ *chŏnsikwa* system. Yu also noted that the same regulations would also apply to clerks and runners who had service obligations. Thus, what Yu really had in mind was some variant of the *chŏnsikwa* system, which contained provisions for hereditary occupations, military service obligations, and land grants subject to state approval.

Privileged Exemption from Military Service

Yu's respect for hereditary privilege was also manifest in the selections he made for privileged exemption from military duty itself. His list included all officials (*taebusa*), those who passed selection examinations (*chesŏn*), close relatives of the royal family (*yuch'in*), those who inherited the right to office without examination (the *ŭm* privilege) because of the high rank of their fathers or ancestors, clerks and runners, and "in general everyone who has a post or service [*yujigyŏkcha*]."[103]

Yu thus exempted the elite of his ideal society from military service, but as a group it was somewhat less hereditary and aristocratic than that of seventeenth-century Korean society because exemption of descendants of nobility and high ranking officials under the *ŭm* privilege was far more limited than the open-ended, de facto exemptions and evasions of military service by yangban at the time. And the exemption of clerks and runners probably provided more status and protection to commoner and low-class functionaries than they enjoyed in the seventeenth century. In fact, this exemption also is reflective of the early Koryŏ *chŏnsikwa* system. Not that early Koryŏ society was egalitarian; it was just that the early Koryŏ local gentry and soldiers had more status than they did five or six hundred years later. On the other hand, the pattern of exemptions also support previous findings that Yu's egalitarian proclivities were always modified by a degree of respect for status and traditional discrimination.

Inner [Palace] Forbidden Guards: Excluded Social Categories

As will be explained later, Yu made special plans to retain the Inner [Palace] Forbidden Guards (Naegŭmwi) at a reduced quota of 200 men.[104] Although he planned to recruit members of this unit by special military examinations, he also excluded from participation in these examinations the following categories: the sons of artisans, merchants, [the denizens of] the wells and marketplaces [of the cities], shamans and other miscellaneous occupations, all official and private slaves, criminals subject to punishments of transportation or worse penalties, officials dismissed and sent home under some onus of malfeasance, and all unregistered individuals. Candidates would also need a guarantee from two men, either a court official or degree-holder living in the countryside, or a local petty official or functionary in the community compact association (*hyangyak*), to affirm that the man had always been righteous in action and never committed a crime or violated a regulation of the local oath association.[105]

If the examination system was such a terrible institution (as Yu had argued elsewhere), however, why preserve it at all, and if at all, why restrict its use to the king's bodyguard? King T'aejong founded the Inner [Palace] Forbidden Guards in 1407 as one of several royal guard units designed to augment his power. Although he recruited them primarily on the basis of military talent, he did not require them to pass the higher military examination (*mukwa*) because he was more interested in their political loyalty than their skills. He also rejected the attempt of civil officials to impose pedigree and status qualifications on these guards, and he continued to give preference to the sons of local gentry from the royal family's home province of Hamgil (Hamgyŏng) rather than young yangban from the capital. Later in the century, Jurchen tribesmen in the north were also recruited into the guards, no doubt because they were more reliable than the sons of the politicized and contentious officials in the capital.

It was only after T'aejong's death that the Ministry of War bureaucrats were able to introduce military skill examinations in archery as a criterion for recruitment. Although the emphasis on military talent continued into the 1430s, skill examinations were tempered with calculations of time-in-grade as a basis for promotion. King Sejong also allowed recruitment of sons of yangban officials of middle or lower rank into the Inner [Palace] Forbidden Guards.

King Sejo, who usurped the throne from his nephew, King Tanjong, and sought to strengthen his bodyguard against disgruntled loyalists, detached the Inner [Palace] Forbidden Guards from the Five Guard organization in 1457 and had it report directly to him. Abolished during the Imjin War, it was restored in 1601 and joined with the Concurrent Royal Stables and Winged Forest Guards to be one of three royal bodyguard units. Its troops were permanent, salaried soldiers. By the late fifteenth century, administration of the military admission examinations became lax and in 1507, an official complained that the quality of the guard had fallen off and most of its men were sons of commoners.[106]

Since the Inner [Palace] Forbidden Guards were a manifestation of the desire of strong kings like T'aejong and Sejo to strengthen royal power at the expense of yangban, bureaucrats, and political opponents, a reduction of the royal guard and the adoption of impersonal examinations to govern recruitment such as Yu Hyŏngwŏn proposed represented a bureaucratic attempt to impose limits on the king.[107] If he were interested only in merit and equality, he would not have included the current restrictions against merchants, artisans, shamans, and slaves. His purpose was obviously to allow only the elite of his new society, one that was only slightly less exclusive and hereditary than contemporary Korea, into his new royal bodyguard. He did the same thing when he opted to retain the Loyal and Righteous Guards (Ch'ung'ŭiwi) and the Loyal and Obedient Guards (Ch'ungsunwi), albeit combined into a single unit.[108]

In the fifteenth century the main purpose of these two guards was to provide jobs and salaries for sons of kings, princes, merit subjects, and higher civil and military officials at a time when all adult males were supposed to perform military service for the state. Even though these special elite units were designed to bolster the authority of kings like T'aejong and Sejong in the early fifteenth century by providing guaranteed jobs for their political supporters and leading officials, as time passed, they were viewed as a refuge for the lazy and incompetent sons of the yangban. For example, in 1445, when King Sejong founded the Loyal and Obedient Guards, a number of officials complained that so many sons of the elite were abandoning their studies to sign up for the elite guards to find an easier path to office than the civil service examinations that the National Academy had been virtually emptied of students.

For his reformed system Yu defined the Loyal and Righteous Guards as consisting of princes and sons and grandsons of merit subjects (*kongsin*), and the Loyal and Obedient Guards as sons of ranked officials and select officers who either could not get into a school or had been dismissed from school. They were to supply their own horses and serve on shifts of duty in the capital for two months at a time. They would receive special benefits in the form of extra land grants (two *kyŏng*) and two support taxpayers as well as rations while on duty, and if they passed the monthly training tests in first place five times, they would be appointed to office. When at home off duty, they would have to attend spring and autumn field training. Nothoi (of yangban) would be allowed into the unit as a means of eliminating one form of discrimination from contemporary society, but the special guard units were themselves a form of discrimination in favor of a narrow elite.[109]

He did rule out all other special guard units, such as the Loyal Assistant Guards (Ch'ungch'anwi), the Royal Relative Guards (Chokch'inwi), and the Jurchen Quelling Guards (Chŏngnowi), primarily to eliminate superfluous units and inequalities in duty requirements. Furthermore, the Jurchen Quelling Guards, which were not even listed in the dynastic law code of 1474, had become a haven for men seeking to evade military service. The origin of these guards stemmed from two abortive attempts in 1457 and 1480 to form a guard unit of "idle" men from well-to-do families who had evaded service. The two abortive units were called the Tiger Wing Guards (Hoigwi) and the Jurchen Pacifying Guards (P'yŏngnowi). Then the Jurchen Quelling Guards (Chŏngnowi) were established in 1512 just after the Three Port Uprising (*samp'o waeran*) of Japanese residents in Korea in 1510, as part of a plan to build up defenses in the north against a possible invasion. Examinations were held to recruit 1,000 sons of ranked officials unregistered for military service (*hallyang*) into the Jurchen Quelling Guards, which was assigned to the Concurrent Royal Stable (Kyŏmsabok). As an inducement to enlistment, the best of the new recruits were allowed to transfer into the Concurrent Royal Stable and Winged Forest Guards, but only after first serving in the new unit. By 1513, however, complaints were already being made that the Jurchen Quelling Guards was tantamount to a sinecure for young yangban seeking to avoid military service.[110]

By proposing the abolition of the Jurchen Quelling Guards, Yu was eliminating one opportunity for sons of yangban to evade or lessen service, but he contradicted this purpose by tolerating the existence of the Loyal and Righteous or Loyal and Obedient Guards, probably to assuage potential opponents within the current yangban class and to provide them some benefits of rank and status. He also hoped to impose a check on the king by creating a royal bodyguard consisting of the Inner [Palace] Forbidden Guards recruited by examination and the special Loyal Guards recruited from the elite. In other words, these units would have greater loyalty to their own elite class than to the king, a principle he could not articulate clearly and directly without risk of lèse-majesté.

Military Service for Slaves

The best example of Yu's modification of the egalitarian well-field ideal in the face of contemporary Korean social reality is to be found in his handling of slaves in his military service reforms. As discussed previously, there could possibly be no starker contrast than that between Yu's explicit distaste for the institution of slavery in theory and his various accommodations to slavery in practice. In this chapter as well, he spared nothing in condemning the injustice of the institution. It was all right, Yu remarked, to enslave individuals for the commission of a crime, but it was unjust for this punishment to extend to their innocent descendants. Slaves were just as much "Heaven's people" as anyone else, and yet their masters who might be ignorant and base persons inferior to their own slaves in moral worth and talent were empowered to use their labor and even determine whether they lived or died. "How could this be the way of justice in the world?" he implored.

To be sure, he proposed solutions for slavery, but all were gradual.[111] Yu thus had to provide for some modification in the ideal system of universal commoner service during the period of transition. He retained the current category of *sog'o-gun* or *sog'o* soldiers, which by the mid-seventeenth century had included a large component of slaves, but he had to defend this policy against the opponents of change. He called these opponents obscurantists "who only thought of their own private interest and gave no consideration to the needs of the country."[112]

He argued that slaves had to be taken from the clutches of their masters to help in the defense of the nation and alleviate the burdens on the commoner peasants. The problem for Korea was that it was a small country with a small population to begin with, made smaller still by its social system.

> [Our country] is divided into yangban and commoners [*sang'in*], and there is difference between the noble and base. The so-called private slaves [*sach'ŏn*] are multiplying in numbers by the day and month and are counted in the thousands and ten thousands. Not one of them has military service while the men of good status [*yangmin*] are burdened with such heavy taxes that they cannot make ends meet and have gradually been driven into running away from their homes. Everywhere people have ended up [as slaves] of private families, [the heads of] which are treated like the dukes and marquises of ancient China while the state has no people left of its own. This was the reason that worthy statesmen of the past wanted to institute laws to limit the amount of land and the number of slaves [that private families could own]. Their ideas were really far-reaching.[113]

Yu pointed out that earlier in Korean history, when slavery was less of a problem, smaller states than Chosŏn had been able to mobilize larger armies. Back in the Three Kingdoms period, when Koguryŏ was left alone in the northwest to face the armies of the Chinese Sui and T'ang dynasties (ca. 612–68), she was able to muster several tens of thousands of soldiers in her walled fortresses and towns and raise an army of 150,000 troops to relieve the town of Ansi. In the Koryŏ period when the famous generals Yun Kwan and Kang Kamch'an fought off the Jurchen and Khitan, both of them had armies of 200,000 men behind them. In the Chosŏn period, by contrast, the country had never been able to muster a force larger than about 10,000 men, "a situation [that was the product] of accumulated decline and dire weakness that did not come about overnight."[114]

Back in the 1590s, when Korea was facing the crisis of invading Japanese armies, it made no sense at all to say that "old customs cannot be changed and the feelings of the people [against slave participation in the army] cannot be violated." This is why King Sŏnjo not only insisted that people learn how to shoot muskets, he also enrolled "those private slaves who lived in different residences from their masters in the ranks [with them] and named them *sog'ogun*."[115] It was even less possible to ignore slaves in seventeenth-century Chosŏn than before because now slaves were 80 to 90 percent of the total population. "If you abandoned the slaves [from one's calculation of military service], there would be no people in the country left."[116] Even though this statement was punctuated with exaggerations (there were more than 10,000 men in the army, and the slave population was closer to 30 than 80 percent), the point here is that Yu was unabashed in his willingness to sacrifice the welfare of the slaves to alleviate the burden on commoners.

Even though Yu was advocating the necessity to enroll slaves for military service, he was not willing to tolerate the admixture of slaves and commoners in the *sog'o* units, as they had been since the Imjin War. Pandering, no doubt, to the sensitivities of social conservatives, he explicitly stated that the *sog'ogun* of his system would consist *exclusively* of official and private slaves.[117] He instructed that caution be exercised against allowing public or private slaves into the ranks with soldiers of good status. Such a policy would only result in what Yu euphemistically called "obstruction to affairs both public and private and harm done by people transgressing their station in life confusing the system." In other words, mixing slaves with commoners would weaken if not destroy legitimate status distinctions and tear apart the social fabric, if not bring on rebellion. This kind of social mixing could not be attempted prior to the abolition of the slave law itself. Yu apparently tried to achieve this by ordering that the *sog'o* slave soldiers would not serve on rotating shifts of duty but would remain in their home districts and undergo training there.[118]

This provision may have been one of the most unrealistic and impractical of all Yu's propositions, for slaves were so numerous and such an important source of troops for both capital and provincial rotating service units that relegating them to the duties of a home militia would probably have decimated some of the main garrisons and increased the pressure placed on officials for recruiting adult males of good status. He made the proposal because it was important to him to cater to the status sensibilities of yangban and commoners even if it affected the strength of the army.

He also provided somewhat less beneficial terms of service for them than for soldiers of good or commoner status. As mentioned above one slave soldier would have to serve for every two *kyŏng* of land (i.e., one of every two slave household heads), double the rate of recruitment on commoner peasants. One would be the main householder and duty soldier, the other the support person. That meant that the slave soldier on duty would have only one support taxpayer while the infantrymen and cavalrymen of good status would have three. Slave soldiers would have to provide their own clothing and horses, but the government would furnish muskets, saddles, and other equipment for the horses, and armor and helmets when on expedition.[119]

Yu was willing to provide some benefits for them by continuing the current law that allowed total exemption from the personal tribute or slave tax (*sin'gong*) that an official slave had to pay to the government, and a reduction by one *p'il* of cloth of the tribute that a private slave (owed his master?). Nonetheless, their burdens were still heavier than peasants of good status who were independent owner-cultivators because slaves owed personal tribute to state agencies or private masters. On the other hand, they may have been no worse off than commoner tenants whose rental payments were probably equivalent to the slave's personal tribute.

Although mid-seventeenth century conditions were far different from the period of crisis during the Japanese invasions, Yu's position was a retreat from the greater toleration of slaves in the 1590s, despite a more explicit and doctrinaire attack on slavery in principle than anything seen in the previous generation. He realized that under his scheme, private slaves would still have a harder burden of service to bear than men of good status, but such inequality would also have to persist as long and until slavery were abolished. "If you cannot abolish slavery, and you also have no choice but to require military service from those who are recipients of [state] land grants, then even though you make [the burden of service on slaves] somewhat lighter than it was before, there is still no way to avoid [having slaves] bear a heavier burden [than men of good status]. The situation makes it that way, and there is nothing you can do about it."[120]

He pointed out that he could have taken the position that slaves should neither receive land nor be required to perform military service, which in fact had been the law at the beginning of the Chosŏn dynasty. The result, however, was a gradual increase in the slave population and creation of a severe shortage in the number of men available for military service. It was this crisis that was solved by the creation of the *sog'o* soldiers and the recruitment of slaves for military service during the Imjin War.

Furthermore, there was also a law in the Koryŏ dynasty that forbade the granting of land to persons of base status (slaves), "but not only was that wrong, it could not be carried out." Yu remarked that most slaves in the Koryŏ period were domestic servants who lived in the household of the master, but there were also the so-called "outside resident" slaves as well who actually cultivated parcels of land at some remove from the master's house. In other words, it was not possible to prohibit slaves from possessing or owning land in fact, and once this were acknowledged, it was legitimate to expect them to perform military service. So much the better if a land-grant system, such as Yu advocated, provided slaves economic support in exchange for their military service.

Yu actually considered the possibility of allowing a slave to assume the role of one of the three support personnel of a soldier of good status and receive a one *kyŏng* land grant, but he was willing to allow this only in exceptional circumstances. "With regard to the duty household and support persons of commoners and slaves, there is a proper way to deal with them according to their type."[121]

He was also willing to allow that slaves who passed examinations for military skills be exempted from base status (*myŏnch'ŏn*) or manumitted. If they were private slaves, however, the owners would be compensated by the grant of an official slave as a substitute or payment of twenty *p'il* of cloth.[122] This regulation was, of course, consistent with his policy of easing the rules of manumission to promote the gradual disappearance of slavery, but it was hardly an aggressive abolitionist tactic to allow a few slaves with outstanding military talents to be manumitted with considerable compensation by the state to their masters. What had been taking place since the Imjin War, the sale of exemption or manumission certificates to slaves who had the money to pay the price, was far more effective in reducing the number of slaves, even though the motives involved were far less noble.

Finally, Yu understood that requiring military service of slaves as *sog'o* soldiers was also an imposition on the property rights of the slaveowners, but he considered this a small price for them to pay. He defended a law already in force at the time, that slaveowners would be prohibited from seizing their slaves on their own authority and removing them from service as *sog'o* soldiers.[123] In the short term, Yu was more concerned about utilizing slaves for state service simply because they constituted too great a percentage of both the current duty soldiers and the population at large to ignore. As indicated previously, he estimated that there were about 162,000 *sog'ogun* (mostly slaves?) compared to 67,000 regular soldiers (*chŏnggun*) and their 132,160 support taxpayers of commoner status in 1660.[124] Nonetheless, they had to be segregated from soldiers of good status and kept at home as a reserve force.

CONCLUSION

In his usual fashion Yu Hyŏngwŏn began his study of the reform of military institutions by considering classical and historical literature that revealed that the model institution to be emulated was the militia system of the ancient Chou that was associated with the well-field method of land distribution. The essence of this model was the training of ordinary peasants during peacetime and their recruitment in the army during wartime, and the organization of those peasants into military units organized around villages to maintain high morale, cooperation, and solidarity. The system also reduced the cost of supporting the military by having peasant soldiers provide their own rations and supplies as self-sufficient farmers.

After the Chou dynasty fell the closest approximation to its militia system occurred with the institution of the *fu-ping* system in the Northern Wei that was carried over into the early T'ang dynasty. It purportedly obviated the need for a standing army of professional soldiers supported by tax revenues, and it eliminated the political threat to the state posed by commanders of long-term soldiers either on the frontier or in the capital – problems faced in China from the eighth-century T'ang through Ming dynasties and Korea in the Koryŏ dynasty.

When the time came for Yu to apply the lessons learned from scholarship to the problems of military service in his own time, however, he confined his use of the militia model to three principles: the assignment of military service according to units of land area, the organization of low-level organization based on village units and community solidarity, and the rotation of duty soldiers back to the farm during the intervals between tours of duty. He believed that the existing system that required the assignment of military service on the basis of head counts of the adult male population was doomed to failure, but otherwise he adopted the model of organization used in the Royal Division established in 1651 as the basis for his plan for reform.

The Royal Division model represented a continuation of the division of all men liable for military service into rotating duty soldiers and support taxpayers. Even though that system had been corrupted over the past two centuries by the illegal exemption of duty soldiers, the inadequate financial support for duty soldiers, and excessive taxation of support taxpayers, he believed that those problems had been overcome in the Royal Division of the seventeenth century and could be rectified in other units by strict enforcement of laws requiring all duty soldiers to serve on duty, by punishing all commanders and clerks who exempted them illegally in return for cloth payments or taxes, and by limiting taxes paid by the support taxpayers to published schedules.

Unfortunately, he was only able to believe that the Royal Division had succeeded in overcoming these problems because he was largely unaware of the problems that the Royal Division had experienced. His assumption that he could reduce overall taxation rates and individual burdens on support taxpayers had already been questioned in court discussion by fiscal conservatives like Kim Yuk.

He thought he could manipulate the rules of the game to lessen individual burdens of service on the duty soldier without reducing necessary quotas for national defense by increasing the number of groups of duty soldiers for each unit and the time intervals between the tours of duty, and by increasing the number of support taxpayers that would support the duty soldier. And he sought to reduce taxes on the support taxpayer by reducing the tax rate. Unfortunately, both were doomed to failure, although Yu should not be held totally responsible for not seeing it. Expanding the interval between tours of duty meant that the duty soldiers might lose the edge in training during the long layoffs if local training in the districts were not maintained up to par. The reduction of tax rates did not offset the increase in the number of support taxpayers per duty soldier that he prescribed, and his supposed low tax rate was in fact higher than the lowest possible rate at the time. Yu was already out of date on the rate, and thus miscalculated the true cost of supporting his army.

Yu advertised his plan of military service as one that avoided the pitfall of long-term service, because only one of every four peasants would have to serve as a soldier while the rest paid taxes, and the duty soldier would return home after his two-month tour of duty and not be called up again for a year and a half at the least. Unfortunately, the long term of inactivity between tours of duty created the likelihood of the loss of military skills by the duty soldiers, a problem that no military professional could have willingly condoned, and Yu's solution to provide interim, off-duty training appears woefully inadequate.

Yu appears to have thought that financing soldiers by support taxpayers assigned to rotating service soldiers was better than drawing revenues from state treasuries to support long-term, professional soldiers simply because it made the military system self-supporting and no longer a concern of the fiscal authorities, but this was nothing more than an exercise in self-delusion. The support persons were still paying a tax established by the state to the granaries of military units (as well as to duty soldiers) at a rate set by the state. Excluding the burden of military finance from the civilian Ministry of Taxation may have made it less susceptible to embezzlement by civil officials and clerks, but it did not eliminate the possibility of corruption by the garrison commanders and officials in charge of the military treasuries.

Yu objected strongly to the use of ordinary grain taxes to finance military service from the central government's treasury mainly for the doctrinaire reason that grain-tax financing was a symbol of high-cost standing armies. He was willing to propose a modification of the existing system because he thought of it as self-financing.

If he had believed in the priority of military strength and a well-trained army no matter what the cost, he would have been far more flexible in determining the mode of finance for the military. Since the traditional three separate categories of land, tribute, and personal service had already been modified by the *taedong* reform of the tribute tax based on a conversion of tribute to a surtax on land, *a proposal that he himself had admired*, he could have adopted a newer system of finance based on taxes from a variety of sources to finance the military. He could have included a grain or other surtax on land, or God forbid, a tax on real estate, net worth of individuals or families, or commercial transactions. He did not do so because all those alternatives were considered illegitimate, unorthodox, or taboo; they were not part of the accepted wisdom on the modes of taxation.

One suspects that Yu really had not worked out in advance just what kind of army was needed in Korea in the late 1660s, because what his plan provided for was a small force of duty troops, a slightly larger force of reserve, off-duty soldiers, a still larger number of provincial slave reservists, and a very large force of poorly trained support taxpayers. A rational budget-planner at heart, he was more interested in keeping costs under control than in building a large army. He would have been a more consistent cost-cutter if he had, in fact, insisted on creating a militia system in conformity with the well-field model. He chose instead to retain the contemporary Korean rotating duty and support taxpayer system despite its past dismal performance.

Although he claimed, and probably believed, that he was advocating an egalitarian well-field ideal in the distribution of military service and tax responsibilities, his plan was modified in serious ways by contemporary social prejudices and status criteria. He allowed for inheritance of vacant duty soldier positions in conformity with the rules of the early Koryŏ *chŏnsikwa* system, which contained within it certain features of hereditary service, occupation, and tenure that contradicted the fundamental principle of returnable grants and rotating, universal, militia service. Finally, despite his theoretical opposition to slavery, he would have legalized their military service, doubled their burdens relative to commoner peasants of good status, and kept them segregated from commoners in the ranks. In other words, the influence of heredity, aristocracy, and status still exerted a significant influence over a scholar who thought he was doing his best to eliminate those features of Korean society.

CHAPTER 11

The Debate over the Military Training Agency, 1651–82

Since Yu Hyŏngwŏn believed that a large force of permanent, professional, salaried soldiers was a threat to the financial stability of the state because it imposed a heavy burden on state treasuries, he proposed to convert all military units to the supposedly independent and self-financing rotating duty soldier/support taxpayer system described in chapter 10. This meant that he had to change the method of service and the financing of the Military Training Agency. At the time it consisted of between six and seven thousand permanent or long-term duty troops, funded by the Ministry of Taxation or the Military Ration Agency (Kunhyangch'ŏng) in combination with peasant support taxpayers in the countryside. This method of finance differed from the rotating duty soldiers funded exclusively by tax payments from the supporting taxpayers (*poin*) of the Royal Division and other units.

As we have seen from Yu Hyŏngwŏn's treatment of specialized royal guard units, however, despite the traditional wisdom that permanent troops financed by the state treasury were a threat to the security of the state, he did not believe that long-term service was necessarily or totally bad; it was the failure to hold down the number of salaried soldiers that led to difficulties. He illustrated his point by discussing the Military Training Agency's musketeers stationed in the capital on a permanent basis. He pointed out that even though there were already rotating service troops (*pŏnsang-ji-gun*) on duty (in the agency) in the capital during the Imjin War, the situation required the presence of at least some permanent soldiers in the capital. In his opinion, the number of these permanent capital troops and the corresponding burden on support taxpayers had not been too great because the capital soldiers were under the close supervision of able civil commissioners (Chejo) of the agency like Yu Sŏngnyŏng, Yi Hangbok, and Yi Wŏn'ik. Of course, Yu gave far too much credit to these men for the low numbers of Military Training Agency troops; the real reason was death, desertion, decreased production and tax revenues during the war, and the stigma attached to serving side-by-side with slaves in the same unit.

In any case, Yu pointed out that during the reign of King Injo after 1623 an inordinate expansion in the troops of the agency as well as other capital divisions occurred. After Injo appointed leaders of the coup against King Kwanghaegun to the position of commander (Taejang) of the capital guard divisions, the chief ministers of state at the time, who did not want to be bothered handling military affairs, turned control of the capital guards over to them. Originally the capital guard divisions were filled only with residents of the capital, but these divisional commanders began to increase the size of their units by recruiting peasants from the remote provinces to build up the units under their control. The men so conscripted had to "leave their parents and abandon their land," as Yu put it, because long-term service meant permanent residence in the capital.

In the case of those capital soldiers financed by support personnel, the government raised the cloth support tax from two to three *p'il*, and Military Training Agency officers also began to sign up extra support personnel without authorization from higher authority, even at times excusing soldiers from their rotating shifts of duty to collect substitute payments (*kap'o*) from them instead. In other words, the expansion of the agency was caused by the unauthorized partial conversion of the unit to a support taxpayer system that Yu had adopted as the basis of his reorganization plan.

Furthermore, the treatment of the soldiers recently added to the agency by its commanders was by no means gentle. They would not allow the district magistrates to grant exemptions to old soldiers of the Military Training agency when they reached retirement age and find substitutes for them. Instead, "they had them dragged by the hair all the way to the agency's main base in the capital to go on duty. And the commanders gave free rein to the clerks of the agency to demand bribes from the men."[1]

The problems of the agency, however, were not confined to the actions of its commanders. Yu was particularly critical of the behavior of its musketeers and horse soldiers in the capital because they had turned to hanging around the capital marketplaces trying to make as much money as they could. Almost all the troops had, in fact, gone into business and competed with established merchants. Some of them persuaded their commanders to obtain special exemptions from commercial taxes for them. In general, Yu condemned most of them for being extremely "idle, lazy, and arrogant."[2]

Nonetheless, Yu was willing to retain the Military Training Agency because of its important troop-training functions, but only if reforms were made in its operations. To bring it under the control of civil officials and prevent political appointments, he stipulated that all officers from division commander (Taejang) to battalion commander (P'ach'ong) be appointed on the basis of recommendations from the Ministry of War. The two main staff officers under the divisional commander in charge of military affairs and infantry, respectively (the Chunggun and Ch'onch'ong), who were currently appointed by the commander himself, would be recommended only after consultation between the Ministry of War and the State Council.

Finally, he proposed a total conversion of the agency's system of finance to the support taxpayer system. All the agency's musketeers (*p'osu*) and cavalry (*madae*) would be recruited from residents of districts near the capital, and men previously assigned from more distant regions would then be converted to support taxpayers. Support taxes would replace the rations or salaries previously paid by the central government's treasury and financed by military colonies or the *samsumi* surtax. The support personnel under his new system would pay either twelve *mal* of grain or two *p'il* of cloth a year. As mentioned in the previous chapter, this represented a rate reduction from the current three *p'il* to two on support taxpayers but an increase in the number of support taxpayers from three to four.[3]

DEBATE OVER THE MTA AND SUPPORT TAXPAYERS

Yu's plan for reconstruction of the Military Training Agency was hardly a radical departure from current thinking, for the financial problems associated with the agency had been under discussion at least since the 1650s when King Hyojong was pressing for an increase in the size of the agency as part of his military expansion program. In 1657, when Yi Wan, commander of the agency, told him that the agency only had a force of 5,650 men, he forthwith ordered an increase of troops to 10,000 men. His over-all plan was to create a capital guard of 30,000 men since the Royal Division had been raised to 20,000 and the Forbidden Guards from 600 to 1,000.

He was opposed this time not only by the fiscal conservative, Kim Yuk, but by some of the most ardent supporters of his plan to build up the army for an invasion of Manchuria, including Song Siyŏl and Song Chun'gil. Their objection was based on the hardship that the expansion would cause the common peasants suffering from a series of bad harvests, especially since the agency's soldiers were permanent troops supported by the Ministry of Taxation's grain stores in addition to payment from support taxpayers. They argued that instead of imposing service and support tax burdens on the peasantry, the king should be distributing military grain rations to relieve the starving, or at least postpone the order until the following harvest.

Although forced to retreat from his goal, in 1658 Hyojong insisted on at least a thousand-man increase in the Military Training Agency. Because of the difficulty of finding men without service assignments to recruit, he hoped to solve that difficulty by promoting support taxpayers to duty soldiers (*sŭngho*), and transferring tribute rice paid by (official?) slaves to the government to the military granaries. The first of these measures provided only temporary relief at best, because for every man promoted to duty soldier, another had to be found to take his place as a support taxpayer, and if not, then the tax burden was increased on the rest to make up the difference.[4]

When he was forced to suspend the required rotation of troops from the southern provinces to the capital in the fall of 1659 because of famine conditions there, he still sought to maintain troop quotas by using tally and five-family mutual surveillance (*oga chakt'ong*) systems to reduce the number of deserters. Increasing soldiers and the supply of military rations proved impossible in the midst of famine, and he was not able to attain the 10,000-man quota by the time of his death that year.[5]

In King Hyŏnjong's reign, in 1662, Yi Wan proposed a method of financing Military Training Agency musketeers by almost the same plan that Yu had recommended in his writings. Since the agency already had 19,690 support taxpayers (four for each of the approximately 1,500 cavalrymen, and three for each of the 4,100 infantrymen), he proposed to recruit an additional 9,000 support taxpayers to pay for the costs of the musketeers. The additional taxpayers would enable the tax rate to be reduced from the burdensome three *p'il*/taxpayer to two *p'il.*

Because it was too difficult a task for the agency to carry out the investigation and recruitment of new support taxpayers, Yi Wan suggested an incentive system by which the current support taxpayers would recruit new ones. Each pair of support taxpayers would be granted a reduction of his current rate from three to two *p'il* if they could recruit another adult male to sign on as a support taxpayer. He assumed that it would take five or six years for this incentive system to produce the additional 9,000 taxpayers. Hyŏnjong approved the plan, subsequently referred to as "combining support taxpayers" (*pyŏngbo*, *happo*) or "marginal support taxpayers" (*malbo*).[6]

Yi Wan's recommendation shows that by 1661 the support-taxpayer system already played an important role in the financing of the Military Training Agency in addition to revenues from the *samsu* land surtax and military colony lands, but that it was by no means a panacea. The high tax rate was stimulating tax evasion and financial shortage. His plan was also testimony to the helplessness of the central government in ferreting out runaways or unregistered men to put on the military tax rolls. Why, for example, would anyone not currently paying taxes be willing to sign up for a two-*p'il* rate? And if the plan attracted taxpayers already paying higher rates for other duty soldiers, it would only reduce revenues in another sector.

According to a notice in the *Daily Record of the Grand Secretariat* (*Sŭngjŏngwŏn ilgi*), in the first lunar month of 1669, Song Siyŏl in a court discussion with King Hyŏnjong praised the system by which the Royal Division was organized and proposed that the Military Training Agency's troops be abolished by attrition.[7] According to another source, the *Revised Veritable Record of King Hyŏnjong* (*Hyŏnjong kaesu sillok*), Song praised both the Military Training Agency and the Crack Select Soldiers but suggested not only that the agency be eliminated by attrition, but that it should be reorganized along the lines of both the Crack Select Soldiers and Royal Division.[8]

Song pointed out that paying rations for the 7,000 troops of the Military Training Agency imposed too heavy a burden on the national treasury. The unit had not been a fundamental part of the dynasty's military system as created by the founding kings, and the only reason King Sŏnjo created it was because he needed some men to share "weal and woe during the difficulties [of the Imjin War]."

He meant for its troops to be special or auxiliary posts (*pyŏlkunjik*) and provided them with salaries, but he did not intend that each soldier who died be replaced, because maintaining troops on permanent salary would only have been a waste of funds.[9] But since at this time the agency's troops were financed in part by support taxpayers, Song's point seems to have been that the agency itself was a superfluous addition to the capital garrison.

The Crack Select Soldiers were first established around 1638 as a force of 1,100 men of whom only 148 served on duty at any time. Both the Military Training Agency and the Ministry of War appear to have exercised jurisdiction over the new unit at the outset. The duty force was increased to 200 in 1663, but in 1668 it was converted into a major guard unit, called the Crack Select Agency (Chŏngch'och'ŏng) under the Ministry of War, and expanded to 19,391 men in forty companies of 111 men each. Of this number, 4,440 were regular soldiers who were divided into eight groups of five companies (111 men per company or 555 men) that rotated on and off duty. The remaining 14,911 were support taxpayers; 4,400 were equipment support persons (*chabo*) who provided the costs of equipment for the duty soldier, and the other 10,511 paid rice or cloth taxes for the rations and clothing of the troops. The Minister of War not being in total command of the unit meant that it could not yet be an independent source of power for that official, but it established a precedent for providing a supposed civil official with logistical responsibility for troops that he could command.[10]

Ch'a Munsŏp has remarked in a recent study that the Crack Select Soldiers were established as a means of reducing the cost of troops by using rotating duty soldiers and support taxpayers. Since both the Royal Division and the Crack Select Soldiers were financed by support taxpayers, Song Siyŏl was really proposing a return to the Five Guards system of the early Chosŏn period as the best means of getting away from permanent, salaried soldiers. Not only was Yu Hyŏngwŏn also in agreement with the restoration of the Five Guards system, but his plan for the conversion of all divisions into a combination of rotating duty soldiers and support taxpayers was almost identical to Song's plan, except that he would have retained the Military Training Agency as a separate unit, while Song would have fused it with the Crack Select Soldiers.

THE SPECIAL CAVALRY UNIT OF THE MTA

On March 5, 1669, a very illuminating discussion of Song's recommendations was held at court by Hyŏnjong and his leading officials. At this conference, the most fundamental assumptions of both Song and Yu Hyŏngwŏn about the superiority of rotating duty soldiers and support taxpayers over long-term professional, salaried soldiers were attacked by the current commander of the Military Training Agency, Yi Wan. This discussion began when King Hyŏnjong mentioned that he did not want to eliminate the Military Training Agency altogether as Song had proposed. He preferred to eliminate the elderly soldiers and retain functions that could not be performed elsewhere, but otherwise convert its organization to the one used in the Royal Division. Although it is unlikely that Hyŏnjong had even heard of Yu Hyŏngwŏn or his views on this question, his position was identical to Yu's.

Financial Weaknesses in the Royal Division Model

King Hyŏnjong first asked Yi Wan his views, expecting his support since he had been responsible for creating the Royal Division in the first place. Yi Wan, however, responded negatively. He said that when he had taken over the Military Training Agency, Song Siyŏl had told him that he should replace deceased soldiers and runaways (in the agency ranks) not with capital soldiers (*kyŏnggun*) but rather with provincial soldiers (*hyanggun*). The vast majority of the 6,000 musketeers of the agency were provincial soldiers who had to sell off their land and homes before moving to the capital to serve on duty. When discharged from service, they had no place to return to. In other words, the permanent troops could not be abolished because it would cause them too much hardship.

Furthermore, he had had plenty of trouble even filling the ranks of the agency. Seven years before the late Wŏn Tup'yo had told him that you could only be sure of getting one of every two men you signed to show up for service. It had taken him five years to fill the ranks, and after seven years of arduous recruiting, he still had only 8,000 men. Since it was so difficult to find men in the provinces willing to serve in the capital, the only way to solve the problem was by "opening the path" to obtaining soldiers, no doubt a euphemistic expression for eliminating the exemptions allowed certain kinds of men.[11]

Set back by Yi Wan's objections, Hyŏnjong then asked how much grain was available for the Royal Division, an important question if the troops of the Military Training Agency were to be converted completely to a rotating duty and support taxpayer system, but Yu Hyŏgyŏn, the current commander of the Royal Division, gave him the startling news that the support taxpayer method was by no means a secure method of finance!

He replied that when Yi Wan had been in charge of the division, he had been able to accumulate a two- or three-year reserve, but it had all been depleted more recently by its expenditure for famine relief. Yi himself remarked that under his own command, he was able to provide rations for the thousand men that served on duty at any one time and accumulate a reserve of 2,000 *sŏm* of grain, but now the regiment "had nothing in hand" even though it had 60,000 support taxpayers backing up the full complement of 20,000 rotating duty soldiers.

Hyŏnjong and others insisted that something had to be done to maintain a force of capital soldiers. Second State Councilor Hŏ Chŏk then suggested that since it was so difficult to replace vacancies in the Military Training Agency, an entirely new unit of rotating duty soldiers ought to be created to maintain an adequate number of troops in the capital with additional financing by grain rations from the Ministry of Taxation. Yu Hyŏgyŏn objected to allowing any reduction in a unit like the Military Training Agency because it would leave gaps in its ranks, and Hyŏnjong now expressed his desire to preserve the Military Training Agency by transferring 10,000 men from other units to it.

Hŏ Chŏk supported the king, reminding him that the reason why Song Siyŏl had proposed reducing the agency by attrition was because he believed that financial support for its soldiers had depleted the state's reserves, but he opposed the idea on the grounds that elimination of the agency would cause more serious problems than its retention. Hŏ, however, was less concerned with finance than with the lack of order and discipline in the agency, a problem that could be solved just by getting the right people to lead it.

Min Chŏngjung and Hyŏnjong also chimed in that "you just have to have capital soldiers." Hŏ Chŏk later said that in easy times, you could muster a force of 20,000 men, but in hard times, you could get no more than a thousand. Yu Hyŏgyŏn noted his concern that there were only 6,000 Military Agency soldiers in the capital (down 2,000 from the number Yi Wan had been able to recruit?), who in wartime would have to leave the capital with the supreme field commander (Towŏnsu) dispatched to command the armies in the field, leaving a force of only 3,000 soldiers as the king's personal retinue.[12]

Yi Wan brought the discussion back to reality by again calling into question the feasibility of the support taxpayer system of finance. He did not believe that the Royal Division model constituted an efficient way of paying for soldiers through support taxpayers because it was almost impossible to find new men not already encumbered by service or tax obligations. He reminded Hyŏnjong that to provide for a force of only 1,000 men on duty at any one time (*sangbŏn*) in the Royal Division, it was necessary to sign up 20,000 "heads of households [*hosu*]" to serve as rotating soldiers and another 60,000 men to act as support taxpayers, a task extremely difficult to achieve in current circumstances. When the discussion turned to the problem of retaining the Military Training Agency, Yi Wan again remarked that the system of rotating duty soldiers and support taxpayers was flawed as a system of finance because you either had to find 8,000 men to support every 1,000 troops on duty or have the Ministry of Taxation make up the shortage in rations.[13]

Off-duty Rotating Duty Soldiers Lose Their Edge

Spokesmen for retention of the agency became more vigorous in their arguments as they realized that the reform suggested by Song Siyŏl would sacrifice military strength at the capital for proposed savings of questionable value. Hyŏnjong said that the best troops he had were those of the agency, and Hŏ Chŏk argued that long-term service was better than the rotating service system because it ensured that the troops would always be in a state of readiness! To be sure, when rotating duty soldiers were called up from the provinces for short-term duty, they were trained night and day and "left no time to rest," but they soon lost their edge after they returned home. Yi Wan agreed, and Yu Hyŏgyŏn added that the time it took to get men back into fighting shape depended on the skills of the battalion commanders and platoon leaders. Good ones could do the job in one or two days, otherwise it could take as much as ten days. This discussion called into question Yu Hyŏngwŏn's assumption that the level of troop training and skill under a rotating service system could be maintained by periodic training sessions while the troops were off duty at home.

The Annual Selection of Unregistered Men

Several officials expressed the view that a major reason for the shortage of possible recruits was that too many men, both yangban and those posing as students in schools or military officials (*kun'gwan*) had illicitly gained exemption from military service. These views reinforced Yi Wan's point about the difficulty of finding new men for service, given the restraints of the existing social system. The government had not neglected the problem entirely because it regularly sent out agents to enroll men who had escaped registration by one means or another, but these periodic registration campaigns could be quite severe and caused the public justification for complaint. Ch'oe Husang, for example, pointed out later that day that one of the main grievances of the common people in the countryside was "the annual selection" (*sech'o*) or recruitment of unregistered adult men (*hanjŏng*) which resulted not in an honest enlistment of draft dodgers but the illegal signing up of "children, youths, and babes in swaddling clothes." He complained that the fundamental cause of this registration campaign was not evasion of service but the excessively high ratio of three support taxpayers (*pongjok*) for every duty soldier in the Military Training Agency, Royal Division, and Robust Select Soldiers (Changch'o), a ratio that was double the peacetime ratio. This point is important because Yu Hyŏngwŏn had himself adopted a three-to-one ratio to provide support for the duty soldiers in his reformed system, not fully appreciating the pressure this increased ratio of support taxpayers to duty soldiers would put on the commoner population. In any case, Ch'oe did not elicit much of a reaction from King Hyŏnjong, who brushed off his complaints about the evils associated with the registration process as a minor issue.[14]

During the court conference Hyŏnjong had asked his officials to determine the number of unregistered "idle adult males" (*hanjŏng*) available throughout the country in order to judge the feasibility of recruiting new soldiers on the basis of the rotating service and support taxpayer system. The next month Hŏ Chŏk reported that there were 54,000 *hanjŏng* in the country, of which about 43,890 could not be considered for service because they already held office or other (nonmilitary?) service obligations or were official or private slaves. One wonders why those who had official posts or other service obligations should have been registered as *hanjŏng* in the first place unless the term itself really meant some thing like "all those unregistered for military service," with or without a legitimate reason, rather than idle scions of yangban families. It is also clear, from the above statement, that despite the importance of the *sog'o* slave soldiers to the overall military picture, at this time no one wanted to assign slaves or *sog'o* soldiers to important capital guard units like the Military Training Agency – an attitude reflected in Yu Hyŏngwŏn's assignment of *sog'o* soldiers exclusively to be duty at home as a provincial reserve force.

In any case, of the remaining 10,110 men, residents of P'yŏng'an and Hamgyŏng provinces had to be excluded because they were needed for frontier defense. This left only 6,665 unregistered men available for service. That only 6,665 of 54,000 *hanjŏng* could be used to increase the capital guard forces supported Yi Wan's view on the question; it also attests to the restrictions imposed by status privilege and discrimination on the state's ability to muster a national army.

Recruits of Unregistered Men to a New Unit

Since there were not enough men to replace the Military Training Agency, it was decided to add these new *hanjŏng* recruits to the agency as a new and separate unit. Following the proposal made by Song Siyŏl and Hyŏnjong himself to adopt the system of the Royal Division, Hŏ Chŏk recommended that the 6,665 men be divided into thirteen groups of 512 men.[15] The 512-man group would be divided into 127 rotating service soldiers (*hosu* or "household heads") and 381 support taxpayers (*pongjok*) at the rate of three per soldier.[16] These figures can be translated in the following way: of the 6,656 men in the Special Unit of the Military Training Agency, 4,953 would be support taxpayers and 1,651 rotating duty soldiers, of whom only 127 would serve at any one time. Hŏ also recommended another investigation of over 4,700 men, whose status as either good or base (slave) had not been indicated in the provincial records, to see if more *hanjŏng* could not be obtained for service.

The result of the investigation for "idle males" confirmed Yi Wan's point about the difficulty of finding recruits. As opposed to the 1,000-man duty force and 20,000 rotating service soldiers of the Royal Division, or the 6,000-man Military Training Agency, the supply of *hanjŏng* allowed for an increase of a mere 127 soldiers on actual duty, or a pool of 1,651 rotating duty soldiers. As Yi Wan pointed out, replacing the entire roster of permanent Military Training Agency troops with rotating service soldiers – one of the key recommendations of Yu Hyŏngwŏn – was impossible.

Hyŏnjong adopted Hŏ Chŏk's recommendations with only minor modifications. He instructed that of those *hanjŏng* discovered in the search for suitable soldiers, youths younger than fifteen and men older than sixty be assigned duty as support taxpayers, and that the healthy adults who were assigned rotating duty would each be responsible for signing up their own support taxpayers. Then after enough men were recruited for a regiment, some consideration might be given to "making adjustments among the old soldiers," an oblique reference either to Song Siyŏl's proposal to eliminate the agency through attrition, or more likely, to Hŏ Chŏk's earlier suggestion about recruiting new soldiers to replace the troops of the old Military Training Agency.[17] Furthermore, new troops who showed up at the capital before they were able to find support taxpayers would still be paid rations on a temporary basis by the Ministry of Taxation.[18]

Later in the year Hŏ Chŏk reported that the recruitment of new soldiers for the Military Training Agency was going well because the men had heard that the new soldiers would be organized along the lines of the Royal Division. In fact, the reputation of the agency was so bad that Hŏ recommended changing the name. At Yu Hyŏgyŏn's suggestion, the title, Special Unit of the Military Training Agency (Hullyŏn-byŏltae) was chosen.[19]

Part of the reason why recruitment for the special unit was successful was because the new commander of the agency, Yu Hyŏgyŏn, was personally dispatching his own aides to the countryside to conduct an unauthorized investigation of unregistered males (*hanjŏng*) who were evading service. They sent back secret lists of such men, and the agency then dispatched formal notification to the district magistrates where the men lived to investigate whether they had service obligations or not. Obviously, yangban tax evaders were the ones who suffered most from this tactic, and they made their discontent known to the authorities, for the Office of Censor-General (Saganwŏn) impeached Yu for his illicit methods and demanded his punishment. Hyŏnjong, however, rejected the request.[20]

Hyŏnjong's final decision, therefore, was to create the new Special Unit of the Military Training Agency and staff it with rotating soldiers and support taxpayers rather than permanent, salaried soldiers, with the expectation that the salaried soldiers of the agency might be reduced as men were signed up for the special unit. This policy was essentially Hŏ Chŏk's modification of Song Siyŏl's recommendation for immediate abolition of the agency, but it was a very modest reform limited by the paltry number of *hanjŏng* that could be found to recruit for the new unit, yielding only 127 duty soldiers at any given time.

The historian of the *Sillok* who penned his opinion some years later remarked that everyone at court agreed with men like Yi Tanha and Song Siyŏl who wanted to eliminate the Military Training Agency because of its high cost and the low quality of its troops. Hyŏnjong, however, was opposed to abolishing an old unit and was only too happy to establish a new one because his primary concern was building up military strength.[21]

The assessment was correct, but it only covers part of the story. King Hyŏnjong's policy was quite close to Yu Hyŏngwŏn's thinking on the question: retain the Military Training Agency because it was essential for training soldiers in the most advanced methods of weaponry and organization in use in Ming China (even though those methods were not sufficient to save China from the Manchu conquest of 1644), but convert the system of financing the agency by replacing tax support from the Ministry of Taxation with support taxpayers from the commoner population. The only difference was that when Hyŏnjong realized that it was not possible for him to find enough adult males to register as rotating duty soldiers and support taxpayers, he created a special unit based on that formula only as large as the number of unregistered males he was able to find. Whether this beginning would eventually succeed in saving the Military Training Agency and convert it to an "independent" support-taxpayer system of finance would depend on how it was administered. But in spirit, the king had worked out a solution quite close to Yu Hyŏngwŏn's recommendation without benefit of direct advice from him!

Thanks to the efforts of Yu Hyŏgyŏn, the commander of the agency, much progress was made to achieve this solution. Not only was the number of special unit troops increased, but vacancies in the basic quota of Military Training Agency continued to be filled with men financed by support taxpayers instead of allocations from the Ministry of Taxation. One of the compilers of *The Veritable Record of King Hyŏnjong* noted that by 1671 alone Yu was able to expand the special unit from 7,000 to 13,700 men. He divided them into 4 regiments, suspended tours of duty during summer and fall, and required 10 companies, or a total of 1,370 men, to serve on duty during winter and spring. Each duty soldier had 3 support taxpayers, or a total of 41,000 men for the whole unit. In addition, the 6,000 men of the Military Training Agency itself each had 4 support taxpayers, or a total of 24,000, an increase of almost 5,000 over the 1669 figure.[22]

The Analysis of Song Siyŏl, 1670

Weaknesses of the Military Training Agency. Some time in late 1670 or early 1671, Song Siyŏl, who was resting at home during this period and evading repeated requests from the king to attend court on the grounds of illness, drafted a memorial that he apparently never submitted. The memorial contains a full discussion of the problems of the Military Training Agency and an evaluation of the results of the decision to establish the special unit in 1669. Song again expressed his "deep concern" over the agency and advocated its abolition on three grounds: it was too costly and acted as a drain on the state treasury, and the soldiers were "lazy," worthless, arrogant, and out of control; in fact, they posed a serious threat of a coup d'état.

Song argued that the financial burden on the state treasury to support the agency's six-to-seven thousand permanent duty soldiers was equivalent to the cost of a wartime army. The agency troops spent their time hanging around the marketplace, never training, and barely able to stand the rigors of a hard run. When they did have to march out on a royal progress as part of the retinue, they were so out of condition that after only five or six miles they were "wheezing like a pitch pipe and sweating like an overturned clam, falling down on the ground from exhaustion one after the other, some even dying." Troops like these would be of no use in wartime, "which is why Chu Hsi wanted the imperial guards to be divided into rotating shifts of duty. When off duty they could return to their home districts to feed themselves, and they would never be allowed to sit around at their ease."[23]

Song claimed that the agency soldiers had been terrorizing the residents of

Seoul; they committed robbery in broad daylight and no one dared stop them; some even joined gangs and became part of the capital underworld. Their arrogance and brazenness was virtually unlimited. Song told of an incident that occurred when he and Hŏ Chŏk were on the king's flagship on a return from a royal progress. An escort ship under Hŏ's command was taken over by the agency's soldiers without authorization. Hŏ personally told them to stop, but they paid no attention to him even though he happened to be a high ranking *taesin* official and also concurrent assistant commissioner (Chejo) of the Military Training Agency itself. It was only when he asked Yi Wan (commander of the agency?) to order them to return the boat that they did so, and even then, Yi made no attempt to punish them. Later, at court, when Song was about to tell the story to the king, Hŏ Chŏk stopped him in his tracks by flashing a fearful glance in his direction.

Song was really concerned about the possibility of a coup against the throne by soldiers of the Military Training Agency because it had happened before. Could it be possible, he asked, that "His Majesty is the only one who has not heard about the incident in the fourth month of 1627?" At that time a soldier of the Military Training Agency, Kim Yejŏng, held a secret meeting with 200 agency troops behind a Buddhist temple. They set up an altar, wrote out a declaration to Heaven, killed a chicken to make a blood oath of brotherhood, and prepared to attack the palace. Before they could carry out their plans Kim got roaring drunk and stabbed one of his own party. Fearing that the victim would take revenge by reporting his role in the conspiracy to the authorities, he tried to save his own neck at the expense of his fellow conspirators by reporting the plot to the agency commander. The conspirators were arrested and executed, but Kim Yejŏng obtained a pardon from King Injo. Song remarked that the reason the agency troops were able to get this far in their conspiracy was because they were thoroughly familiar with weaknesses in the palace guard arrangements, knew all the nooks and crannies in the walls, and formed close ties with the officials of the palace administration to gain information about everything that went on in the royal quarters.[24] Song concluded that for all the above reasons the agency had to be phased out by attrition, a process that would take seven or eight years. Then all troops in the capital would be under the command of two generals (presumably the Five Guards and the Royal Division?) just like the Northern and Southern Armies (capital and imperial guards, respectively) of the Han dynasty.

Failure to Reduce the MTA by Attrition. Song noted that, as a matter of fact, King Hyŏnjong had confirmed his ideas by ordering the selection of new men to staff the special unit of the Military Training Agency, but the men in charge of recruitment had not fulfilled their charge. Instead of reducing the agency by attrition, they had allowed it to remain at full strength so that the new troops of the special unit were just an additional source of harassment to the people of the capital. "Even though in name the old system has been changed, in fact, whereas at first we had one [unit] that was impossible to bear, now we have two of them."[25] But this statement does not reflect accurately the king's fundamental intention, which was *not* to eliminate the agency through attrition, but simply to begin a slow conversion of its method of finance to support taxpayers.

Song also complained that official registrars were also supposed to be weeding out all men falsely registered as support taxpayers and signing them up for service in the special unit, but corrupt clerks were taking bribes from the wealthy and prominent families and exempting them from service, leaving only the poor and unfit to be registered for duty. Song claimed he had personally witnessed what was going on because he was then living at his country home. The whole process of finding and registering men for the special unit had created "more angry cursing" by the people than before. Finally, he uttered the same plaint that Yi Wan had the year before about the shortage of men available for a new unit.

"You only have a limited number of adult males in the country, but at present not only have we selected quite a few for the special unit, we have also continued to fill the original quota [of the Military Training Agency] as well. And in addition to this, we have recruited more men for the regular cavalry, infantry and other categories. How is it possible for the provinces to fill these quotas?"[26] The basic problem, in his view, was not that the special unit was such a bad idea, it was just that the government was too quick to implement it. Deliberation in the adoption of reform was essential to its success, a lesson learned from Sung China. Chu Hsi's village granary system for cheap relief loans to peasants had proved successful when in fact it was nothing more than a copy of Wang An-shih's "green shoots" system. But where Wang had put his plan into effect with undue haste, Chu Hsi had done so with due attention to the advantages. People in charge of implementing the special unit recruitment, however, handled it in slipshod fashion and ignored the resentment of the common people simply because they felt it had not been their idea in the first place.[27] Yet despite Song's complaints about the corruption of the registrars, the real point of his critique was that the system of finance by support taxpayers made necessary the recruitment of *more* men than those currently on the rolls as permanent, salaried soldiers.

1671: Fiscal Crisis: Demand for Troop Reduction

The effort to expand the number of troops in the capital and support taxpayers in the countryside was made more difficult by famine conditions. It only increased the burdens on the starving peasantry. In the late spring of 1671, the Office of the Censor-General criticized the poor administration of relief and the drain on resources caused by the unnecessarily large number of the king's personal guards. They noted that even though the addition of more than 4,000 new rotating service cavalrymen to the military service rosters when the Crack Select Agency was established in 1668 had not increased the total number of duty soldiers since these had been taken from the existing pool of available troops, the collection of cloth payments by magistrates caused no end of difficulty for peasant support taxpayers. Despite the extraction of additional revenue, there was not enough to provide for the new duty soldiers, so that the

Crack Select Agency had to borrow rice from the Royal Division to make ends meet. The censors remarked that there was currently no national crisis that would warrant depletion of military grain reserves just to support a new unit like the Crack Select Soldiers, but if the king was reluctant to abolish it, at least he could suspend all tours of duty at the capital for these troops until the next crop came in, and eliminate the excessive number of personal aides of its officers.

The censors also charged that too much edible grain from the Ministry of War was being consumed as horse fodder for the cavalry of the Forbidden Soldiers (Kŭmgun), the special or temporary guard units (Pyŏlkunjik), the Military Training Agency, and the Royal Division. They proposed that the horses could be let out to pasture for the next five months until the fall harvest, allowing the transfer of 5,000 *sŏm* to provide relief for several thousand starving people.[28]

The next month, Yi Wan, transferred to the post of commander of the Defense Command (Suŏsa), made a strong argument for a sharp reduction of military expenditures in the face of the worst famine in a century, exacerbated by the recent damage to the seed for the "double wheat [*yangmaek*]" crop, which meant the loss of the expected crop at harvest time. If miscellaneous labor service were demanded of the people while they were trying to get the harvest in, there would be no telling how many people would die, and if military cloth taxes were demanded on schedule from the tens of thousands of soldiers and support taxpayers enrolled in the Military Training Agency and Royal Division, it would cause them great hardship. These taxes should be canceled or reduced.

A censorate official, Yi Tanha, reported that since two-thirds (!) of the government's total annual expenditure of 120,000 *sŏm* of grain, or 80,000 *sŏm*, was allocated for the support of soldiers, the king's guard should be cut by 3,000 men. Yi Wan, who had opposed the conversion of the Military Training Agency to rotating soldiers and support taxpayers, now asked that the Crack Select Soldiers (who were also organized in that fashion) be eliminated entirely if the state had any chance of saving itself from destruction. He claimed that the Ministry of War's entire reserve of support tax revenues was spent on the Crack Select Soldiers, leaving it without resources in case of emergency.

Yi explained that the Crack Select Soldiers had imposed an intolerable burden on the state's resources because its ranks had been filled with *sog'o* soldiers from the provinces who had previously been self-supporting but now had to be supported by the state treasury. He also complained about the financial drain caused by an excessive number of salaried troops in the Military Training Agency. Because of the current revenue crisis he advised that the king choose between abolishing the Crack Select Agency altogether, reducing its size by attrition, or cutting its quota of troops. King Hyŏnjong responded by authorizing the elimination of "superfluous and miscellaneous" soldiers.[29]

The next month top officials and the Office of the Inspector General (Sahŏnbu) recommended eliminating one regiment (*pu*) of the Military Training Agency, temporarily suspending the rotating shifts of duty of the Special Cavalry Unit (Pyŏltae) of the Military Training Agency, and abolishing the post of Supreme

Commissioner (Tojejo) of the Crack Select Soldiers and shifting responsibility for it to the Ministry of War. Chief State Councilor Hŏ Chŏk affirmed what Song Siyŏl had criticized in his unsubmitted memorial of 1670, that despite the promise to replace the old soldiers of the Military Training Agency as new soldiers were added to the special unit of that agency, there had been no reduction in their numbers. He insisted that it be reduced in size.

Hyŏnjong explained that he was only waiting until the duty soldiers of the new special unit arrived in the capital before he would allow reductions in the Military Training Agency, after which he would permanently cut one of the agency's four regiments (*pu*). Given the current fiscal crisis, however, he ordered the one-regiment reduction to take place immediately, allowing those soldiers to be dismissed to fill vacancies in the other three regiments.

Yu Hyŏgyŏn then proposed that the Front Regiment be eliminated, and that 592 of its 1,081 men be transferred to fill up the other current vacancies and replace elderly soldiers about to retire in the other three regiments. After suggesting a number of other arrangements, he estimated the net saving at 13 officers and 877 men, but no instructions were ever issued to allow further reduction by attrition, as Song Siyŏl had proposed two years before. The net savings would have been 10,000 *sŏm* of rice and 200 *tong* of cloth annually. The cut in rice expenditures alone would have been equivalent to one-eighth or 13 percent of the annual military grain budget of 80,000 *sŏm*, a significant amount but still not enough to solve the country's financial problems.[30]

Hyŏnjong also suspended all army and marine bivouac training in every province, tours of inspection and testing by provincial army commanders and major garrison commanders, the collection of monthly levies of weapons and grain for troop rations, and school examinations of students until after the fall harvest, and forbade the annual recruitment drive (*sech'o*) to fill vacancies in the troop ranks.

Third Minister of Rites Kim Man'gi then rose to express his displeasure at the failure of the court to achieve any meaningful cuts in military expenditures. Since cutting one regiment of the Military Training Agency was hardly meaningful, the king ought simply to eliminate both the Crack Select Soldiers and the special unit of the Military Training Agency. Kim's idea was welcomed by State Councilors Chŏng Ch'ihwa, Hŏ Chŏk, and Kim Suhang, and Hŏ remarked that everyone knew that these two units were causing the destruction of the country. Hyŏnjong, however, failed to respond, indicating his reluctance to part with his newly created guard units and the Military Training Agency.[31]

1681: The Forbidden Guard Division and Factional Politics

Reemergence of Factional Strife: Rites Debate of 1659

The denouement of the debate over the merits of permanent, salaried soldiers versus rotating duty soldiers and support taxpayers and the fate of the Military Training Agency occurred a decade after Yu Hyŏngwŏn's death. In that interval factional strife began to reappear once again in court politics after a long hiatus of inactivity. After the death of Prince Dorgon in 1650 had allowed King Hyojong to purge Kim Chajŏm's faction from the political scene, the contest between Westerner splinter factions was reduced, but factional strife reemerged with the death of King Hyojong and ascension of his son, King Hyŏnjong, in 1659.

The Southerner faction had played an important part in the fight against Hideyoshi and suffered along with the Westerners when the Great Northern faction was in power during King Kwanghaegun's reign (1608–23). They were allowed back in the government after the Westerners seized power in 1623, and in the reigns of Kings Injo and Hyojong worked alongside their Westerner colleagues without much rancor. The situation changed, however, because of the so-called mourning rite controversy (*yesŏng*), which arose when the Westerner faction under the leadership of Song Siyŏl took the position that Dowager Cho (or Dowager Chaŭi), King Injo's second queen, owed a lesser degree of mourning to the deceased King Hyojong than what one might ordinarily expect because Hyojong had not been the eldest legitimate son of King Injo.

Even though Song was an ardent defender of Chu Hsi orthodoxy in philosophical matters and based his argument on his interpretation of the *I-li*, an ancient Chinese ritual text, his position logically threatened the legitimacy of the deceased Hyojong, and by extension to his son Hyŏnjong. The Southerners, led on this issue by the scholar Yun Hyu and the official Hŏ Mok, insisted that Hyojong be treated as a fully fledged heir of Injo and a legitimate king, and that Dowager Cho owed a higher degree of mourning than what Song prescribed. By so doing, they threatened the king's confidence in the Westerner faction as the most loyal supporters of the throne.

King Hyojong's legitimacy was a particularly sensitive issue because he had come to the throne only after Crown Prince Sohyŏn had been poisoned, his princess and in-laws executed or exiled, and two of his three sons killed – all with King Injo's assent or complicity. Nonetheless, in 1659 King Hyŏnjong adopted the Westerner position on the degree of mourning and did not purge any Southerners over the matter. In fact, he even appointed one of their leaders, Hŏ Chŏk, to the State Council.[32]

Southerners Control of the Military Training Agency, 1669

Even by 1669, when disposition of the Military Training Agency was being debated, rivalry between Westerners and Southerners still remained latent. When the Westerner leader, Song Siyŏl, proposed reduction of the Military Training Agency by attrition, his leading opponent was the Westerner and then commander of the agency, Yi Wan, while his leading defenders were Southerner officials like Second State Councilor Hŏ Chŏk and commander of the Royal Division Yu Hyŏgyŏn. But Southerners then gained control over important capital units when Hŏ Chŏk engineered Yu Hyŏgyŏn's replacement of Yi Wan as commander of the agency and Yi Yŏbal's appointment as commander of the Royal Division.

Yu Hyŏgyŏn was also put in charge of the new special unit of the Military Training Agency (Hullyŏn-byŏltae) established in 1669. The core of the unit consisted of troops who had served under Yu in the Royal Division. These were the men Yu sent out to the villages as secret recruiters to inform on so-called idle adult males (*hanjŏng*) who had evaded military service, and when he was severely criticized by the yangban for this action, it was only because of Hyŏnjong's protection that he escaped impeachment. Yu was also responsible for expanding the Military Training Agency from five to six thousand men, contrary to the intent of Song Siyŏl to eliminate it by attrition. Thus, the agency and its special unit became the basis of the Southerners in the military establishment by 1674, the year of the second mourning rites controversy.[33]

Crack Select Soldiers and the Rites Issue of 1674

Tension between the two factions was exacerbated when Hyojong's queen, Queen Insŏn of the Tŏksu Chang clan, died in 1674, and the degree of mourning that Dowager Cho had to observe for her was debated again. The debate was conducted along the same lines as before, but this time Hyŏnjong rejected Song Siyŏl's argument and chose the longer mourning. He had obviously become sensitized to the question of his own legitimacy in the intervening years, but he still took no action against the Westerners.

Nonetheless, the stage was then set for the first in a series of bloody purges that marked King Sukchong's reign (r. 1674–1720). After Hyŏnjong's death later in 1674, King Sukchong quickly indicted all officials – mostly Westerners – who argued for the lesser degree of mourning in 1659, stripped Song Siyŏl of his office warrants, and sent him into exile. As a result the Southerner faction found itself in power.[34]

Sukchong's Purge of Southerners, 1680

When Sukchong came to the throne in 1674 the Southerners were in a stronger position than ever before, but they still did not monopolize all military units. They controlled the Military Training Agency and the Royal Division, but Westerners Kim Man'gi and Kim Sŏkchu had charge of the Anti-Manchu Division and the Defense Command at the Namhan fort, respectively, as well as influence over the Crack Select Soldiers (Chŏngch'ogun) attached to the Ministry of War.[35]

The minister of war had become concurrent commander of the Crack Select Soldiers, which had been increased to 6,250 men in 1668, as well as 700 Forbidden Soldiers (Kŭmgun), and since other, lower officials of the Ministry of War had no connection with the Crack Select Soldiers, they were almost like his personal troops. Since the Crack Select Soldiers and the Forbidden Soldiers formed the left and right flanks of the king's retinue on progresses, these units were very close to the throne, equal in importance to the Military Training Agency and Royal Division.[36] From 1663 to 1673 all the ministers of war had been members of the Westerner faction, but the minister of war under Sukchong was Kim Sŏkchu, one of the few Westerners allowed to remain after the king shifted his favor to the Southerners. He did so, in part, because Kim was related to Hyŏnjong's queen and never got along with Song Siyŏl.[37]

One of the men who entered the government after Sukchong became king was Yun Hyu, a rusticated scholar-official originally affiliated with the Small Northerner (Sobuk) faction who had gone into retirement in protest over the capitulation to the Manchus back in 1636. He came out of retirement only because he believed the times were ripe for revenge against the Manchus because the Wu San-kuei rebellion in China (1674) had weakened the Ch'ing regime. He had originally been on friendly terms with both Westerners and Southerners, but he sided with the latter on the rites controversy and became friendly with some hard-line anti-Westerner Southerners like Hŏ Mok. In 1676, his party began to push for war with the Manchus and restoration of the Office of the Supreme Commander (Toch'ech'alsabu, or Toch'ebu), a post that only existed when the country was preparing for or in the midst of war and required a supreme command headquarters. It had been dropped during Hyŏnjong's reign.

Even though the moderate (on foreign policy) Southerner, Hŏ Chŏk, differed with Yun Hyu and Hŏ Mok on political issues, he supported their attempt to restore the supreme commander's headquarters and sympathized with their desire to send an expedition into Manchuria, but he obstructed or opposed concrete measures designed to carry it out. Despite Hŏ Chŏk's caution, both he and Yun Hyu realized the political importance of gaining control over a revived supreme commander's headquarters, but Hŏ did not trust Yun and sought to gain power himself. Yun Hyu supposedly anticipated that once the supreme commander's headquarters was revived and hostilities with the Manchus commenced, Hŏ would be appointed supreme commander and sent out to the field in command of the troops and he, Yun, would be appointed vice-commander and remain behind in charge of the capital forces, giving him de facto control over the government.[38]

Yun Hyu's plans were stymied by Hŏ Chŏk, who in 1676 had his own followers appointed to command positions. Hŏ and Yu Hyŏgyŏn, commander of the Military Training Agency, decided to make Kaesŏng the locus for the supreme commander's headquarters, built up the Taehŭng mountain fort in the vicinity, and expanded the military colony lands in the area. They established a new recruitment examination for soldiers, called the *mankwa*, and moved troops from the Military Training Agency and the Royal Division to the Taehŭng fort. The post of vice-commander that Yun Hyu hoped to get was never filled.[39]

Then Ho Chŏk also tried to persuade King Sukchong to place all the capital guard units, especially the Military Training Agency and Royal Division, as well as troops of five provinces, under the jurisdiction of the supreme commander's headquarters, giving him total control of the military, but Westerner Kim Sŏkchu convinced Sukchong not to do so. Hŏ Chŏk's very success in monopolizing the restored supreme commander's headquarters and other capital divisions had alerted King Sukchong to the political threat Hŏ posed to the throne itself.[40]

Then in 1677, Kim Sŏkchu, the minister of war, influenced the king to agree to the abolition of the supreme commander's headquarters on the grounds it was too costly. The only way he could achieve agreement to this in the face of Southerner opposition was to accept reductions of the Crack Select Soldiers under his own command from 5,000 to 3,000 men and the Special Cavalry Unit of the Military Training Agency from 13,700 to 10,000 men. The compromise agreement evidently did not last because at the request of the Southerners Sukchong reestablished the supreme command headquarters under Hŏ Chŏk's command late in 1678. Just when the Southerners had apparently secured their dominant position for good, in 1679 Sukchong sent them into shock when he also appointed Kim Sŏkchu – not the Southerner, Yun Hyu – to the post of vice-supreme commander to keep Hŏ in check.[41]

The previous year Kim had been appointed commander of the Royal Division concurrently with his post as inspector-general (Taesahŏn). Now his appointment as vice-supreme commander was the harbinger of disaster for the Southerners, for early in 1680 Sukchong purged Southerners from command of most key military units. Yu Hyŏgyŏn, who had been commander of the Military Training Agency for years, was dismissed from his current post as minister of public works, simply on the grounds that "your old muscles must be worn out after twenty long years of service as a guards commander through three reigns." Sukchong appointed his own father-in-law, Kim Man'gi, commander of the Military Training Agency, and Kim's son, Kim Ikhun, to the post of magistrate of Kwangju with control over the Namhan fort. The latter was a Westerner who had been shuffled out to the northern frontier when the Southerners gained power. Since the post of commander of the Defense Command (i.e., Kyŏnggi Division) was also transferred to another official and Kim Sŏkchu was already commander of the Royal Division, the Westerners were now in command of the key military posts around the capital.[42]

The Westerners under Kim Sŏkchu were now in a position to take more serious action against their Southerner rivals. Kim set the wheels of a purge in motion by calling to the king's attention suspicious training exercises of six companies of the Ich'ŏn Military Colony troops attached to the Taehŭng mountain fort. Then, in the sixth lunar month, the so-called *Sambok* plot was reported to the throne. The illegitimate son of Hŏ Chŏk, Hŏ Kyun, was accused of conspiring with the three grandsons of King Injo to put one of them, Prince Poksŏn (the Poksŏn'gun), on the throne by mobilizing the troops of the Taehŭng fort near Kaesŏng, the headquarters of the supreme commander. The conspirators had supposedly even brought their troops to the capital for action in the third month when the king suddenly ordered the transfer or dismissal of the top Southerner military commanders, and in the wake of this action they had no choice but to disband their forces.

A censor reminded the king that the Southerners had tried to use the supreme commander's headquarters to control all military forces, and he pointed out that when Yu Hyŏgyŏn had been commander of the Military Training Agency, he had issued orders on his own authority to expand his control of military forces. Hŏ Chŏk and Yun Hyu were implicated mainly because their previous attempts to gain control over military units appeared suspicious, and both were executed on the grounds of failing to inform the king of everything they knew about the plot. The government was purged of Southerners, and the military units the Southerners had done so much to create or expand ended up in the hands of their Westerner enemies.[43]

The Forbidden Guard Division, 1681

In 1681, a year after a conspiracy trial and purge had brought the Westerner faction back into power, Song Siyŏl, restored to court as a sinecured minister-without-portfolio (Ch'ungch'ubu Yŏngsa), revived his pet project to pare back the Military Training Agency and aimed his guns at the agency's special unit as well. He instructed King Sukchong, as he had Hyŏnjong, that permanent soldiers imposed a heavy cost on the state.

> The Military Training Agency and its Special Unit have become plagued with problems. I once read a statement of Chu Hsi's that in ancient times, the soldiers were all out in the countryside and were only provided rations by the state when the army was on a campaign. The only reason that the army was permanently fed by the state during the Sung dynasty was because they were constantly at war.
>
> At the present time the cost of rations for the musketeers of the Military Training Agency comes to 80,000 *sŏm* [of grain per annum], while the cost of salaries for court officials is no more than 40,000 *sŏm*. Furthermore, musketeers were not part of the old military system established by the founders of the dynasty; they were established only after 1592 by the recommendation of Yu Sŏngnyŏng [a Southerner!]. I hear that before 1592, after the government paid officials their salaries, it ordinarily had 300,000 *sŏm* left over [in the treasury], and yet in those days they still said that state finances were impoverished. Nowadays how could we even hope to have a balance of 300,000 *sŏm*?

Song's remarks illustrates three major points of policy: a civil official's objection that two-thirds of the national grain expenditures were devoted to the cost of the Military Training Agency, that muskets were not that important for military defense and were not justified by precedents established at the beginning of the dynasty, and that the agency had been created by the most prestigious member of the Southerner faction. For a disciple of Yulgok to degrade military strength and the most advanced infantry weapon of the time must have meant that times had changed, and indeed they had. Although Song was still smarting from the humiliation suffered at the hands of the Manchus, the state was facing a fiscal crisis, and relations between the Westerners and Southerners had become hostile.

As he had done a decade earlier, Song proposed that the Military Training Agency be reduced by attrition. Any musketeer that wanted to return to the countryside should be allowed to do so, and any vacancies due to death or desertion could be replaced by rotating duty soldiers of the Royal Division. Eventually the agency and Royal Division would be run the same way and would function like the Northern and Southern Armies of the Han dynasty.

Song then launched into a very questionable argument, that the rotating duty system of the Royal Division was preferable not just because it was more economical, but also because its troops were in a far better state of readiness – more so than the professional soldiers of the agency:

> The soldiers of the Royal Division live in their village where they practice and work at their skills, but the musketeers [of the capital] just take their ease and sit around at home. Once when I accompanied the king on a royal progress to Onch'on, I saw how the soldiers of the Royal Division were able to run quickly back and forth while all the troops of the Military Training Agency had fallen out of ranks and flopped down exhausted by the side of the road.

Song then recounted that King Hyŏnjong had decided to justify a reduction of 1,000 musketeers in the agency by transferring a very large number of ivory soldiers (*abyŏng*) – aides of high military officers – from the provinces to the Royal Division, but the agency's commander in that period, the now purged Southerner, Yu Hyŏgyŏn, failed to carry out reductions.[44]

Ultimately, Song's recommendations were ignored by both Kim Sŏkchu and King Sukchong despite the dominant position of the Westerner faction at court. In 1682, Kim only proposed reducing the permanent troops of the Military Training Agency by 707 men, from 5,707 to 5,000, and transferring them to the category of rotating duty soldiers of the Special Cavalry Unit of the agency. He also recommended fusing the 13,949 soldiers of the Special Cavalry Unit of the agency and the 3,773 soldiers of the Crack Select Soldiers into a single Forbidden Guard Division. One might surmise that now that Kim, himself, was in control of the government and army, there was no need to disband an important military unit.

After certain adjustments were made, the new Forbidden Guard Division was designed to have 14,098 rotating duty soldiers in 105 companies. Each soldier was assigned three support taxpayers, which yielded a total of 42,294, but in actuality a number of other miscellaneous types of soldiers and their support taxpayers were to be attached to the Forbidden Guard Division, more than doubling its number to 90,000 duty soldiers and taxpayers. Some of these additional troops were to be called the Forbidden Guard Special Unit (Kŭmwi pyŏltae) to serve alongside the regular Forbidden Soldiers (Kŭmgun).[45]

The final regulations, however, provided for a somewhat smaller force: a pool of 12,700 regular, rotating-duty soldiers (exclusive of special troops, clerks, and officers) organized into 100 companies of 127 men each, with 5 companies in each of 20 battalions, and 5 battalions in each of 4 regiments. Ten companies or 1,270 men were to serve at any one time for a two-month period; half that number during the four months of the year when agricultural work was heaviest. Although figures for total support personnel are not available, one might deduce that since each soldier was assigned 3 support taxpayers, there should have been an additional 38,100 taxpayers, for a combined total of at least 50,000 men, 60,000 if miscellaneous types of soldiers are included.[46]

Certain measures were taken to cut costs, such as reducing the Military Training Agency by 707 men and shifting them to the new Forbidden Guard Division, where presumably some of them might liberate rotating soldiers to be converted to support taxpayers. By tightening up the organization of the rotating troops, about 3,600 of them were converted to support taxpayer status, alleviating the pressure for registering new men for this purpose.

Nonetheless, the numbers of the Special Cavalry Unit of the agency and the Crack Select Soldiers and their support taxpayers had almost doubled in number between 1669 and 1671 even though the purpose of those two units was to reduce costs and tax burdens on the peasantry. At the same time the Military Training Agency was supposed to be reduced as the new rotating service soldiers were created. The new Forbidden Guard Division retained most of the expanded rotating service soldiers and support taxpayers while retaining a 5,000-man Military Training Agency of permanent, salaried troops – contrary to the recommendations of Song Siyŏl, who wanted to phase out the agency's permanent salaried soldiers. Officials at court were aware of this and the issue was debated yet another time.

Second State Councilor Min Chŏngjung noted that the only justification for the expansion of the Special Cavalry Unit of the agency was the supposition that the salaried soldiers of the Military Training Agency would be reduced. Fusing the Special Cavalry Unit with the Crack Select Soldiers to create a new division would eliminate whatever hope there was for the abolition of the Military Training Agency. In addition, the troops of the agency were of no value and there were already so many separate divisions and units in the Korean military, that unity of command had been fractured.

Minister of War Kim Sŏkchu, who proposed the formation of the Forbidden Guard Division in the first place, defended his idea along the same lines as Yi Wan's argument over a decade before. He agreed with the idea of replacing long-term salaried soldiers with the Special Cavalry Unit troops who were financed by their own support taxpayers, but since such a radical change could not be carried out overnight, his recommendation to shift about 700 agency troops to the special unit would garner an annual savings of 6,780 *sŏm* of grain and 127 *tong* of cloth for the Ministry of Taxation.

He argued that replacing all the Military Training Agency's troops would also be too expensive because it would require replacing them with a pool of 30,000 rotating duty soldiers divided into six groups of of 5,563 men on two-month shifts, and 90,000 support taxpayers – altogether 120,000 soldiers and taxpayers combined. Given the hardship in finding unregistered adult males (*hanjŏng*), this was simply an impossible task.

He also had a completely different view about the talents and characteristics of the agency soldiers. He remarked that because its musketeers grew up around the king's capital guards, they were far better than the provincial soldiers; they were quick, nimble, bright and intelligent, kept their appearance in trim, and were ready to serve at any time. For that matter, he shared the departed King Hyŏnjong's conviction that the Military Training Agency should never be totally eliminated.[47]

In any case, after 1680 Kim Sŏkchu was able to concentrate control over the military in a way that Hŏ Chŏk only dreamed of. He was appointed commissioner of the new Forbidden Guards from 1682 to 1684, and held the posts of commander of the Military Training Agency, and concurrent commandant of the Taehŭng fort near Kaesŏng.[48] Even after he was promoted to third state councilor and could no longer command the Forbidden Guards, Sukchong made Kim a special palace guard officer so he could have some troops under his command. A few days before his death he received the unprecedented concurrent appointments as commander of the Forbidden Guards and minister of war.

Sukchong's motive for approving the formation of the Forbidden Guard Division in 1682 is important because it reveals what the aims of policy on troop quotas and military organization were at the time. After Kim Sŏkchu's death in 1684, when an official proposed abolishing the new Forbidden Guard Division, Sukchong angrily rejected the proposal and made a surprising revelation of his reason for establishing it. He reminded his officials that when Hŏ Kyun's *Sambok* conspiracy was uncovered in 1680, Kim Sŏkchu, who was then minister of war, had no troops under his command to check such political threats to the throne. He claimed that was the reason he had made the minister of war concurrent commander of the Forbidden Guards in 1682, but as Yi T'aejin has pointed out, it was Kim Sŏkchu that Sukchong wanted to provide with a personal command, not simply any minister of war.[49] Kim Sŏkchu needed the extra power after 1680 because of his rivalry with other members of the Westerner faction. For that matter, even after the Westerners split into the extreme anti-Southerner Patriarch's Faction (Noron) and the moderate Disciple's Faction (Soron) in 1683, the dispute over control of military forces took place within the Patriarch's Faction, primarily among those related by marriage to queens.[50]

After Sukchong came to the throne in 1674, Kim Sŏkchu was able to gain influence through his connections as a consort relative, but when Sukchong's queen, the daughter of Kim Man'gi, died in 1680, she was replaced by a second queen of the Min family, Queen Inhyŏn. Her father, Min Yujung, and paternal uncle, Min Chŏngjung, began to oppose the control of the military exercised by Kim Sŏkchu and Kim Ikhun. All four men were members of the Patriarch's Faction, but that was not enough to keep them together. The need for new units and maintenance of the status quo in troop strength, if not an increase in troop quotas, was motivated by domestic political considerations – no longer because of the threat of foreign invasion or emotional schemes to take revenge on the Manchus.[51]

The Anti-Manchu Division and Defense Command, 1681–90

The Westerners also sought to build up their control of two other important units in the capital region. The Anti-Manchu Division of Kyŏnggi Province and the Defense Command stationed at the Namhan fort had long been under the control of Westerner officials, even before 1680. Yi T'aejin has called them "the last bastion that the Westerners had in their competition with the Southerners until Sukchong's reign."[52] Both forces underwent a gradual change in their composition throughout most of the seventeenth century, mainly by the accretion of a separate capital garrison staffed by different categories of rotating duty soldiers. These included the Standard Bearers (*P'yohagun*) and ivory soldiers (*abyŏng*) or personal troops of ordinary civil and military officials as well as unit commanders. Some were used to cultivate military colony lands (*tunjŏn*) of the Anti-Manchu Division almost like slaves. Others included flag bearers or honor guardsmen of great strength or prowess. In other words, many of the troops of the capital garrisons of the Anti-Manchu Division and Defense Command functioned as the personal bodyguards of their political commanders.

By Sukchong's succession in 1674, the Anti-Manchu Division had a miminum force of 20,000 men drawn from Kyŏnggi Province organized and divided into five divisional headquarters (the *oyŏng* system). In 1687, the number of divisional headquarters was reduced to three, and remained that way until a major reorganization was undertaken in 1704.[53]

When the commander was at the headquarters in the capital, the provincial troops of the Defense Command were controlled by the vice-commander, a post held concurrently by the magistrate of Kwangju (Kwangju-buyun). In 1681, Min Yujung, Kim Sŏkchu's rival in the Patriarch's Faction, asked that the capital headquarters be abolished because it placed the commander of the Defense Command at some distance from his troops in the province, and in 1683 Song Siyŏl backed the idea because the capital headquarters imposed an extra and unnecessary burden of service and taxation on peasants who were being dunned constantly by two commanders instead of one. Since almost all the leading Westerner officials at court supported the recommendation, Sukchong abolished both the capital headquarters and the post of commander (Suŏsa). The magistrate of Kwangju was upgraded to a Yusu (special mayor) and given exclusive jurisdiction over the Defense Command.

The original system of a separate commander stationed in the capital was restored in 1690, a year after the Southerners returned to power, on the grounds that the troop quota of the unit had been allowed to shrink and military capability had become lax. Judging from reports of discontent among the thousand or so troops stationed at the Namhan fort after the reorganization of 1690, however, it appears that the Southerner regime was trying to break up the control of the Westerners over the troops by bringing in a new staff to the fort. At the same time, the magistrate of Kwangju was given command over an independent Defense Regiment (Pang'ŏyŏng) stationed in his town, probably for the purpose of strengthening Southerner political control over the capital region.[54]

The complex controversies surrounding the composition, size, and control of the various guard units and divisions around the capital, in particular, soon became part of the political disputes that emerged among factions, not only among the established hereditary factions, but within them as well. In some cases, these internal splits became formal as rivals announced their reorganization into new factions, but in other cases they remained informal. Economy, efficiency, and rationalization in the reorganization of the military were given second place to gaining political control over military units and expanding their size in competition with rival politicians.

CONCLUSION

Since Yu Hyŏngwŏn sought to reorganize all military units on the basis of rotating duty soldiers and support taxpayers, he was determined to eliminate any permanent salaried soldiers that drained resources from the state treasury, like the core contingent of the Military Training Agency. But, since the Military Training Agency with its core constituency of musketeers and its advanced weaponry and mode of organization was so important for defense, he hoped to preserve it at little cost to the state by converting it to a rotating duty soldier and support taxpayer system of service and finance. Not only could the national budget crisis be solved by this means, but an economical adjustment of tours or shifts of duty and rational adjustment of tax rates on the support taxpayers would enable reduction of the tax burden on individual support taxpayers. In short, Yu's plan for military reform combined selective use of aspects of the classical militia principle at the local level combined with a rational readjustment of the traditional military system to save state expenditures, reduce taxes on peasants, create an equitable distribution of service for the duty soldiers, and retain what was supposed to be the most advanced technical unit of the army, the Military Training Agency.

Coincidentally, just at the end of Yu's life, between 1669 and his death in 1672, the court engaged in a serious debate on the question of military reform, and people like Song Siyŏl and King Hyŏnjong himself also believed that the permanent duty soldiers of the capital divisions could profitably be replaced by rotating duty soldiers and support taxpayers. Other officials, like Yu Hyŏgyŏn, the commander of the Military Training Agency, and again, King Hyŏnjong, shared Yu Hyŏngwŏn's view that the agency itself should be preserved at all costs because it represented the most modern of military units and could be saved by financing it through support taxpayers rather than the state treasury. These men shared Yu's views even though they undoubtedly had never met him nor heard of his ideas.

The court discussion, however, revealed that the presumptions of Yu and the king were naïve and unrealistic because there were so few adult males of commoner status, let along idle, unregistered yangban, who could be called upon to fill the slots for 90,000 rotating duty soldiers or support taxpayers that would be needed to replace the 6 to 7 thousand permanent soldiers of the Military Training Agency. The supply of men had been reduced by exemptions for yangban and other means of evasion used by commoners, and many of the high officials like Yu Hyŏgyŏn sought to register these evaders and enlist them for service. It was not just intellectuals divorced from responsibility like Yu Hyŏngwŏn who were capable of perceiving the rot that had pervaded the military system because of yangban privilege, but awareness and occasional individual action was not enough to remedy the problem. By the seventeenth century evasion had become a way of life for too many men, a right expected by many, not a violation of a limited few. Therefore, what Yu thought would be very easy – to enroll more men as support taxpayers – was, in fact, very difficult if not impossible.

Furthermore, several court officials revealed that the troops of the Military Training Agency were not that good; in fact they were a plague on the capital population because they were in poor physical condition, neglected their training to engage in business in competition with the merchants, swaggered around intimidating civilians, sometimes joined with thieves, and posed the threat of a military coup against the king himself. Neither Yu Hyŏngwŏn nor King Hyŏnjong himself was deterred by these drawbacks, for both men were determined to preserve the agency, and the king succeeded in doing so no matter what the cost.

After King Hyŏnjong's death, the final decision on the Military Agency was taken by Minister of War Kim Sŏkchu, the most powerful official at the time because King Sukchong had chosen to concentrate control of the major military units in his hands. Kim decided to preserve the agency and combine the Special Cavalry Unit of the agency with the Crack Select Soldiers in the new Forbidden Guard Division as a means of securing his own control and the domination of his Westerner faction as well, for political power replaced national defense or economic reduction of cost as the primary determinant of military policy.

Yu's plan to increase the number of support taxpayers for every category of duty servicemen, not just the Military Training Agency, was adopted by the court, but instead of alleviating the tax burdens on the commoner population, it actually increased them. As time passed, more rotating duty soldiers were authorized for new units, and for each new man on actual duty, eight to ten more were needed to form a group or pool for each tour, and each of these required three support taxpayers on the average. Since not enough men could be found, the local officials had to use tricks to justify the levying of increased taxes, which meant imposing extra taxes on families by registering animals, babies, and the elderly, the same kinds of predatious oppression that had been visited on the peasants a century before.

Finally, the system of rotating duty soldiers created a serious flaw in maintaining the crucial sharpness and readiness necessary for troops and troop units. They lost their edge and some of their skills during long periods when they were off duty, and the system of local training was insufficient to solve this problem. The only thing that saved the country from another potential disaster was that there were no longer any major military threats to the nation: the Japanese pulled in their horns and abandoned their agressive ways after 1636, and the Manchus established firm control over China after 1644, and removed the threat of invasion from barbarians in the north or northeast.

Yu Hyŏngwŏn did have a partial solution to one of the main defects of his proposal – finding a sufficient number of adult males to replace the permanent soldiers of the Military Training Agency – by reducing overall troop quotas in the capital guards and provincial forces (see chap. 13) and drastically curtailing exemptions of men from service on the grounds of yangban status or corruption. He spelled out provisions to achieve this in his chapters on education, recruitment, and land distribution, but few active officials wanted to eliminate yangban privilege and put an end to illicit exemptions. As a result some officials sought to solve the problem by abandoning the very concept of military finance through support taxpayers and shifting to a different source of tax revenues – a method that Yu abjured because it did not conform to traditional ways of supporting troops in Korea.

CHAPTER 12

The Search for Alternative Modes of Military Finance

The idea of cutting military costs by shifting to rotating duty soldiers and support taxpayers failed for a number of reasons. The government found itself increasing the demands on the peasantry in its search for more support taxpayers, a problem exacerbated by its inability to curtail its penchant for expanding the number of troop units and soldiers. The state's need for revenues also contributed to this phenomenon by allowing adult males to purchase exemptions (*napsok*) to become service-exempt *yuhak* or *kun'gwan*, or to obtain a place in the Loyal or Righteous Guards. (*Yuhak* was a term originally meaning student or scholar who had not passed one of the state examinations, then denoting a living student rather than a deceased *haksaeng*, and finally a student of yangban or *sajok* status not necessarily registered in school; *kun'gwan* was a military aide to an official.) As the pressure for more revenue increased, the state kept lowering the price for these benefits. Even though it sought to limit these measures to emergencies, recurrent famine prevented it from suspending them indefinitely, and in 1661 the government again permitted purchase of service-exemption privileges because of famine and need for contributions.[1]

These legal reductions in the number of available adult males only exaggerated the pressures on military finance by expanding the quotas of duty soldiers and support taxpayers. Available statistics reveal that the number of men registered for either mode of service increased greatly in the next century.

The crisis in military finance had, of course, not been created in 1681. It had been a problem since the beginning of recovery after the Imjin War, and a number of officials had sought ways either of reducing the number of men required for duty and support taxes, expanding the tax base by forcing those exempted from service to register, or shifting the mode of military taxation away from adult males to some other tax base. These movements culminated in a major debate over restructuring the military tax base in 1681 and 1682, a debate that is particularly interesting because it was founded on principles that Yu Hyŏngwŏn had rejected.

PROBLEMS OF SUPPORT-TAXPAYER FINANCE

Expansion of Men Registered for Military Service

Despite several attempts to reduce soldiers and support taxpayers, the total number appears to have risen. One reckoning made by An Chŏngbok some time after 1746 concluded that there was a total of 1,083,784 soldiers and support taxpayers of all types of service in the country.[2] According to this account, the Five Military Divisions located in or near the capital had the numbers of soldiers and support taxpayers shown in table 5:[3]

TABLE 5
MILITARY AND SUPPORT PERSONNEL, BY DIVISION

Unit	Soldiers	Support Taxpayers	Total
Mil. Trg. Agency	6,316	41,099	47,415
Forbidden Guard Div.	20,505	67,546	88,051
Royal Division	25,938	74,089	100,020
Defense Command	29,360		29,360
Anti-Manchu Division	22,463	2,468	24,931
TOTAL	104,582	185,202	289,777

The total figure of 289,777 reflects the 10 percent cut made in troop and taxpayer quotas of the five military divisions made in 1704, but there were additional categories and numbers that had not existed in 1704. An recorded, for example, 323,117 men attached to the Ministry of War,[4] 51,499 soldiers and support taxpayers of military officers (*kun'gwan*) and forbidden soldiers (*kŭmgun*), and aides and miscellaneous types assigned to government agencies (Yuch'ŏng chapsaek).[5] These categories add up to 374,616, and if we combine them with the soldiers and support taxpayers of the five military divisions, then the total number of soldiers and taxpayers assigned to capital divisions, guards, ministries, and bureaus should have been a whopping 664,393 men. Naturally, the vast majority were taxpayers residing in the six provinces whose *yangyŏk* taxes were remitted to the capital.

In addition, there were 217,998 regular cavalrymen and infantrymen and their support taxpayers assigned to duty in the provinces, of which 112,857 were stationed in local areas for guard duty (*yubang*) and 105,141 paid support cloth taxes during on rotation. There were also 45,793 soldiers and support taxpayers assigned to beacon stations throughout the country, and 41,438 marines and their officers, of which 13,657 were "oarsmen" and 27,781 "fighting troops," all of whom paid cloth for the hiring of substitutes. The other major categories of provincial soldiers and taxpayers were, first, the 20,486 soldiers assigned to local garrisons and forts (*chinbo*), of which 7,305 were local troops and 13,181 were recruited soldiers (*moipkun*); second, the 141,922 ivory soldiers (*abyŏng*, personal aides) attached to the headquarters of the provincial governors, of which 17,045 were support taxpayers and military officers (*kun'gwan*). Thus, the total of soldiers, sailors, marines, and their support taxpayers of good status (as opposed to base or slave) that served in the provinces was 426,745 men.

Finally, there were the soldiers and taxpayers of base status, primarily the *sog'o-gun* in all provinces, totaling 191,786 men, of which 3,762 were officers, 26,520 were horse soldiers (*magun*), 111,895 were infantry, and 49,609 were miscellaneous (reserve) soldiers (*chapsaekkun*). The other category of slave servicemen were the 69,350 post-station workers, who were not soldiers but were included nonetheless in An's service statistics. An Chŏngbok also noted that he was not including *sog'o* soldiers formed into platoons in the northern provinces.[6]

An's figure of one million soldiers and support taxpayers is confirmed in at least one place by the offhand statement of Second State Councilor Cho Hyŏnmyŏng in 1751, who was trying to defend the 50 percent tax cut on support taxpayers enacted the year before by King Yŏngjo. He was arguing that even though there were some problems involved in the substitute taxes adopted to make up for the loss in revenue, one could never expect perfection in reform, and the situation was still better than when "over" one million men (or 1.2 million to use the a rule of thumb for estimating the size of "over") were paying the two-*p'il* cloth tax.[7]

The well-known memorial of Hong Kyehŭi in 1752 claimed that because of various types of tax exemptions, only about 120,000 households were paying the cloth taxes that were due from "500,000 *yangyŏk*," which presumably means taxes due from 500,000 adult males.[8] One can only speculate how to reconcile this figure with the one million mentioned in An Chŏngbok's statistics, but if one deducted the *sog'o* and post-station slave servicemen, the figure would be reduced to about 750,000. It may also be justifiable to deduct the rotating duty soldiers and a variety of miscellaneous troops as well, which might leave about 500,000 support taxpayers.

The lack of statistical accuracy in these estimates makes it difficult to compare eighteenth with seventeenth century quotas, but some figures exist to enable a rough comparison. In 1640, for example, the Border Defense Command estimated a total of 401,390 men listed on the military rosters for all eight provinces, of which 101,914 were soldiers organized into regular military units (*p'yŏn'o-gun*) and 299,476 were miscellaneous soldiers (*chapsaekkun*). These appear commensurate with the approximately 400,000 soldiers estimated for the pre-Imjin (1592) period. But these 1640 figures only represented numbers on ledgers, for eight years later the same office reported that 251,613 of this number could not be located at all![9]

Ledger quotas may have borne little relation to reality, but there are other indications of high or increasing levels of troop and taxpayer quotas. For example, the number of men registered for "extra-quota service" (*aeg'oeyŏk*, as opposed to regular quota service, or *aengnaeyŏk*), must have been relatively small prior to 1650, but by 1699 there were 10,000 of them.[10] Perhaps a better measure was the quota of soldiers and support taxpayers combined located in six of the eight provinces and assigned to the Five Military Divisions (Ogunyŏng) that defended the capital region in 1704. According to a Reform Bureau (Ijŏngch'ŏng) investigation, the total came to 307,926 men distributed as shown in table 6:

TABLE 6
TROOPS OF THE FIVE MILITARY DIVISIONS (OGUNYŎNG), 1704

Unit	Quota
Military Training Agency	49,816
Royal Division	106,270
Forbidden Guard Division	91,696
General Army	21,021
Defense Command (Namhan Fort)	39,123
TOTAL	307,926

SOURCE: *Kagyŏng Ijŏngch'ŏng-dŭngnok, Ogunmun kaegunje pyŏnt'ong chŏrmok* [Reform Bureau record of the divisions: Reform bill for the reorganized Five Military Divisions], cited in Chŏng Yŏnsik, "Yangyŏk kyunilhwa," p. 155 n.130.

This figure is close to the 290,000 recorded by An Chŏngbok for the mid-eighteenth century. An's figure is less because of the approximately 10 percent quota reduction enacted in 1704. The pre-reduction figure should be compared with the period prior to the 1627 Manchu invasion to get the sharpest contrast, for at that time the Military Training Agency had only about 6,000 permanent, salaried soldiers and few support taxpayers, and the Defense Command and Forbidden Guard Division, and its earlier components, the Special Cavalry Unit of the Military Training Agency and the Crack Select Soldiers, had yet to be created. And when the Crack Select Soldiers were first established in 1638, there were only 1,100 rotating soldiers, with another 3,000 taxpayers. The Royal Division had only been increased in size in 1652, and consisted of a much smaller number of a few thousand permanent and rotating soldiers in the 1620s.[11] Keep in mind that most of the 307,296 men in 1704 were taxpayers, probably about three-fourths of them (230,000), and that of the remainder of rotating soldiers only one of eight or ten (depending on the number of shifts or groups into which they were divided) were actually on duty at any one time. Compare this total with Yu Hyŏngwŏn's proposal for a total capital guard force, which would have required only 70,000 men: a restored Five Guards of 12,500 men (plus 37,500 support personnel, or a total of 50,000), and a Military Training Agency of about 20,000, that is, about 5,000 rotating soldiers and 15,000 support taxpayers. Since Yu favored dividing rotating soldiers into eight shifts, only 2,187 would have been on duty at any one time, in addition to about 200 royal bodyguards, and a number of gate and wall guards and capital police.

Reducing Soldier and Support Taxpayer Quotas

Every administration from Kings Hyŏnjong through Yŏngjo (1650–1776) was aware of the problem of high quotas and sought to do something about it. The process of reducing quotas was begun even while the total was expanding, and the first cuts were made in 1650. Subsequently reductions were ordered in the 10,000 extra-quota service soldiers in 1669 and in three of the capital Military Divisions in 1682. The most ambitious attempt at quota reduction, however, did not occur until 1704.

TAXING SCHOLARS AND YANGBAN: 1626–59

King Injo: Enroll School Failures for Service, 1626

There were two methods advocated throughout the entire last half of the Chosŏn dynasty to provide adequate funding for the military. The first departed from the support-taxpayer system of military finance altogether by substituting a different type of tax on a different subject than adult males. Proposals in this category included a cloth levy on household units called the "household cloth" (*hop'o*), a capitation tax in cash called the "mouth [i.e., head] cash" (*kujŏn*) tax proposals, and a surtax on land of either cloth or cash (*kyŏlp'o, kyŏlchŏn*). The second method retained the support-taxpayer system of finance but attempted to expand the tax base by including men who had been left out of the military service requirement, either by legal exemption, claim of superior status privilege, or corrupt falsification of status. This method was considered because previous attempts to round up tax evaders or the tax-exempt had not been successful.[12]

Back in 1626 King Injo had ordered that all students who failed their periodic qualification examinations be dismissed from school and signed up immediately for military service. Injo and some officials – no less than Yu Hyŏngwŏn a generation later – were appalled that not only sons of yangban but anyone able to gain entrance to a school felt that they were too prestigious or exalted for military service. He even had to point out that since the dynastic code already provided that students who failed their tests were supposed to become soldiers, he was really only affirming existing law.

Within six months, however, he was forced to rescind the order because of the fierce opposition of a number of officials who complained that military service had by then become so demeaning that the sons of yangban could not bear the loss of status that would accompany enrollment for service. He was finally forced to accept the compromise solution of Yi Sŏ, who proposed collection of cloth taxes from students who failed their tests for a period of three years as a penalty. As Ch'oe Yŏngho pointed out in his study of this question, it was about this time that government schools in the capital and provinces no longer functioned as centers of study for bona fide students and scholars of the elite class, but rather tax shelters for the sons of commoners and peasants seeking a means of evading service. The inability of Injo to enforce his will in 1626 shows that the system of the fifteenth century had already moved off the stage of history.[13]

The "cloth tax on men of leisure," or "Confucian scholar cloth tax" (*yup'o*), represented an attempt to place a permanent tax on the class of scholars without requiring that they perform military service, either as duty soldiers or a support taxpayers. By eliminating the stigma attached to military service, it was hoped that the yangban would consent to the new tax. At the same time, the idea of taxing scholars or yangban without requiring military service represented an acknowledgment that the military service system had already gone a long way toward becoming more of a tax than a service system.

Yu Hyŏngwŏn, on the other hand, wanted to return to the early Chosŏn Five Guards system according to which most of the scions of the yangban – more narrowly defined as a class of scholars, officials, and those with limited hereditary privileges – would be brought back into the military service system itself. In that respect he wanted to turn the clock back, while the other proposals – taxes on persons, households, or land – were all based on unequivocal acceptance of the need to finance the military by any revenue source available, not just the formula of rotating duty soldiers and specific support taxpayers assigned theoretically to each duty soldier. Yu was still partially bound to the mentality of the T'ang dynasty by which adult men were expected to perform actual labor service for the state in addition to the payment of a land tax and tribute in whatever unique local products were produced. As we will see later, Yu was willing to abandon the traditional formula for tribute taxes, but he was unwilling to show equal flexibility in dealing with military finance. Although some officials attempted to justify the use of per capita, household, and land taxes for raising revenues for military purposes by citing (or twisting) historical precedent, they really were adapting to a new trend in national finance that involved breaking away from the old rigid category of labor service toward a more flexible use of available revenues.

Kim Yuk and a Tax on Yangban, 1653

Kim Yuk, Third State Councilor in 1653, had his own ideas about how to solve the problems of military defense and financial shortage. He also endorsed the idea that the quality of troops took precedence over numbers, and proposed that the royal guard (Military Training Agency?) quota be set at 5,000 men and that all old and ill troops be eliminated from the unit and replaced with able men. To solve the problem of the large number of peasants who had run away from their villages to escape the burdens of military service and support taxes, he proposed that vagrants or illegal migrants be rounded up and settled permanently on state colonies (*tunjŏn*); the taxes they would pay would then be used for military food rations.

He also identified the special exemption privileges of the elite as the major cause of the insufficiency of funds for military defense. He proposed, therefore, that men who had no official posts, including sons or younger brothers of high officials and scholars as well as commoners, should be required to pay an annual cloth tax of one *p'il* from the age of twenty (i.e., twenty *se*). This proposal went beyond King Injo's attempt in 1626 to impose a fine on school students who failed their qualifying tests because it was aimed at the host of elite tax and service evaders who did not even bother to claim a student exemption. By recognizing that military service was more of a tax than service problem, Kim had also adjusted his thinking to real circumstances. His proposal sparked a debate that was to last for the next two centuries – the imposition of a military cloth tax on yangban households. It was not to be adopted, however, until the era of reform under the Taewongun in 1870. Note also that the one *p'il* rate was half that proposed by Yu Hyŏngwŏn. At this time, however, King Hyojong merely noted that there had been a recent increase in military registration, obviating the need for Kim's proposal. As Ch'a Munsŏp pointed out in his study of this period, the king and the ruling class had no interest in reducing their tax-exemption privileges.[14]

Yu Kye's Yangban Tax Proposal, 1659

The suggestion to impose the military cloth levy on the yangban ruling elite was raised again in 1659, when the country was suffering from a third year of famine and the pressure on state finances to provide both relief and funds for military defense was particularly acute. Assistant Vice-Minister (Ch'amji) of the Ministry of War Yu Kye told Hyojong that it was unfair that the military cloth levies (*kunp'o*), alone of all types of taxes, had not yet been reduced to provide relief to the peasants. It was the most onerous of all taxes, the worst evil in the kingdom since its "poison" had been extended to the neighbors and relatives of runaway peasants.

> If something is not done immediately to change it, within a few years there will be no adult males of good status [*yangjŏng*] left in the whole country. Even if you have worthless military registers with a million names on them, it will only [represent] an accumulation of rage and resentment [by those illegally registered] without at all providing hope [for a full complement of troops] on the day when a crisis occurs.[15]

He proposed eliminating from the military tax rosters the deceased, aged, and young, who did not belong on them in the first place, and cutting the rate in half to one *p'il* of cloth for support taxpayers of regular soldiers. The loss of revenue occasioned by this reduction would be made up by imposing the cloth levy on the sons and younger brothers of the *sadaebu* (officials and scholars, i.e., yangban).

Yu Kye also pointed out that the discriminatory exemption of yangban from military service or payment of the cloth support taxes was a product of the middle period of the dynasty, and not an institution created by the founders.

> During the age of the fathers of the dynasty, the sons and younger brothers of branch lines of the *sadaebu* [i.e., the *jisŏ*, all male relatives except for the eldest sons and heirs] were immediately upon birth regarded as adult males [*namjŏng*]. There was no distinction made between noble and base [*kwich'ŏn*, in this case yangban vs. commoners since slaves were not allowed to serve at this time], and each of them was assigned to a guard unit. By this means the will of the people was settled and service obligations among the people made equal.
>
> But in the last several generations, the country's laws and customs have become lax and people think only of benefiting themselves. The descendants of the scholar-officials have never again had their names listed on the guard rosters. And it is not only the [bona fide] scholar-officials [*sabu*] for whom that it is true, for even in the case of the impoverished branch lines of [yangban] living in remote villages, there are none of them who do not regard it as a mark of great shame to have their names put on the guard rosters. Thus, today the so-called guardsmen are all from the ranks of the various types of base status, a thorough controversion of the old system of our forefathers.
>
> We have a country small in area and population. Even if we used the labor force of everyone in the entire country to provide support for the soldiers, we probably would still not have enough. How much worse is the situation when we make further distinctions among those few people that we do have so that 80 or 90 percent of the people live a life of ease and idleness while the rest of the people of good status [*yangmin*] are left alone to bear the burden of military service. Confucius once said: "Do not be concerned about how little [people have], but do be concerned lest they be treated unequally; do not be concerned about how poor people are, but do be concerned lest they be discontent."[16]

Yu Kye also remarked that inequality in the distribution of military obligations among adult males was the main source of discontent in the minds of the people. Everyone with an opinion on the question believed that the way to reform the military registration system was to assign all the "silk-clad and hatted ones" (officials or yangban) to military units as at the beginning of the dynasty. Nevertheless, he acknowledged that if they were suddenly to be returned to the military rolls after over a century of exemption from military duty and idleness, they were bound to be both shocked and resentful. It was, therefore, not possible to return to a system of universal military service for men of all statuses, but a compromise of sorts could be achieved.

Since what the yangban hated most was the stigma attached to military service by having their names listed on the military registers, the problem could be solved simply by "allowing" all those types of privileged persons currently exempted from military service to pay one *p'il* of cloth (per year) between the time of marriage and the age of sixty. He listed the current types of exempted individuals as follows: regular court officials, ex-officeholders, *saengwŏn* and *chinsa* degree-holders, *yuhak*, men with office rank but no post (*p'umgwan*), those eligible to take the *kwagŏ* highest civil service examination, and nothoi sons of yangban given special permission to take the examinations. In consideration of their "voluntary" payment of the one-*p'il* cloth levy the government would exempt them permanently from any future attempts at military registration and assignment to guard units. On the other hand, nothoi of yangban who were not given permission to take the examinations, extra-quota school students (*aeg'oe kyosaeng*), and the male descendants of regular soldiers (*chŏnggun*) (i.e., commoner peasants or men of good status with regular military service obligations) would be forbidden from making cloth payments in lieu of service.

To allay the anger of the yangban class at the prospect of a new tax and stave off any possible uprising against the throne, the king would be obliged to instruct them that he could not permit a situation in which one part of the people were allowed to enjoy ease and idle luxury while the men of good status alone (*yangjŏng*) had to bear all the burdens and hardships of military service. He would also have to make clear that the purpose of such a reform would be not to increase the number of men liable for service but to ensure equal distribution of the burdens of service, not to increase the wealth of the state, but to save the nation from military disaster, and not to invade the interests of the scholar-official families (*sajok*), but in fact to allow them permanent exemption from actual military service. Thus, Yu Kye concluded that the promise of permanent, legal exemption from the military rosters should provide sufficient incentive for the scions of the yangban to make a one-*p'il* tax payment while those who at present were making illicit, low-rate payments to escape higher rates would be prohibited from doing so. "Then, in the name of a service-exemption, we would be able to gain the real goal of equalizing [the burden] of military service." In addition, it would become possible to cut the cloth tax rate for ordinary support taxpayers by half.

On the other hand, such a radical reform could not be adopted right away because impoverished yangban (*sajok*) as well as commoner peasants were currently suffering from famine, but the measure could be implemented after the next harvest. By severing taxation from service Yu Kye was abandoning the hoary tradition of the T'ang. Not only was this an adaptation to yangban status sensibilities, it also represented a progressive move toward a more flexible system of military finance. Hyojong replied that Yu Kye's proposal was certainly out of the ordinary and to be admired, and he turned it over to his high officials for deliberation.[17]

A few days later Hyojong held discussions with his chief ministers on the question. Chief State Councilor Sim Chiwŏn opposed the plan because imposing a cloth tax on the *sajok* was unprecedented and was bound to create resentment and hardship, but Hyojong asked why the resentment and hardship of the poor peasants who were forced to run away from their homes because of military service were any less to be feared than that of the *sajok*. "If you want to do something, you cannot talk about the resentment and hardship [that might be suffered by] some [a minority of privileged?] people."

Second State Councilor Wŏn Tup'yo remarked that the suffering of the soldiers and people had never been worse than at the present time. If reform were not carried out at a time like this, when could you ever do it? But Sim replied with a strong defense of elite interests: "What maintains our country is the power of the *sadaebu*. If we now were to suddenly do something that has never been done before and impose a cloth tax on them just the same as that on commoners [*sŏin*], would their resentment not indeed be great?"

There was an alternative, however. The government could collect a cloth payment from all regular officials, the amount to vary by rank, and if this were not sufficient, additional funds could be obtained from the reserves of the provincial governors and army and navy commanders' yamens.

A number of other officials were either opposed or reticent. Some proposed using the household tally system (*hop'ae*) or the five-family mutual responsibility and surveillance system (*oga chakt'ong*) as a better means of ensuring full and accurate registration of all eligible males for military service and taxes. Song Siyŏl, then minister of personnel, remarked that he had previously discussed Yu Kye's ideas with him and felt that a bill of particulars should first be drawn up for consideration before final decision was made.

Even Yu Kye retreated somewhat from his first position in the face of the open criticism. He told the king that in any case the imposition of a tax on the yangban families was not something that could be done by force. The king would have to make clear just what the purpose of the law was to be, but if any of the yangban were not willing to make cloth payments, they definitely should not be forced to do so. Cloth payments were only to be voluntary, but since such payments would be compensated by exemption from all future military service, the yangban who refused to make payments after the law was passed would regret it in the future when the government might require them to serve on military duty and be listed on the military registers. He was still convinced, however, that his proposal provided the perfect solution: by having those living in idleness and luxury pay cloth, the arms-bearing soldiers would be absolved from any payment of cloth levies. In the end, however, Hyojong concluded that the proposal was too serious to adopt so suddenly.[18]

Eliminating Slave Evasion and the Matrilineal Rule, 1655

Hyojong showed less aversion, however, to taking action against slaves discovered paying less than their due. When, for example, Minister of Taxation Yi Sibang reported in 1655 that only 27,000 of the 190,000 government slaves registered with capital agencies were actually paying tribute, Hyojong expressed indignation:

> Some time ago, the Chief of the Bureau of Royal Relatives [Yŏngdollyŏng], Kim Yuk, wanted to collect cloth taxes from the idle [yangban] and vagrants, but this would really be hard to do even though I, too, wanted to do it. But how could we help but collect the full tribute due from the 190,000 [official] slaves in order to pay for military needs? Wouldn't one's blood run cold at the prospect of the government not doing what it ought to do while the strength of the country is waning every day? Set up a Directorate [*togam*] to handle it.[19]

Hyojong forthwith established the Directorate for Investigation of Slave Status (*Nobi ch'uswae-dogam*) to make sure that all persons falsely claiming good or commoner status be returned to slave status, making them liable for cloth tribute payments to the state. Now that slaves were also required to perform military service, it was more important to return those who had escaped it and register them for military duty or support tax payments than to allow them freedom.

Hyojong then set forth the special rules for deciding individual cases, but he also permitted some exceptions to the law. If the grandfather of a person claiming good status had passed the *kwamok* (highest civil service examination), *saengwŏn* or *chinsa* (classics or literary licentiate) examinations (and therefore been granted good status), the law limited elevation to good status to the grandfather; it was not to be passed hereditarily to his descendants including the claimant. On the other hand, if the claimant's father and he (as grandson) had on the basis of the grandfather's accomplishment illicitly claimed good status, he would not be returned to slave status if he obtained a special royal pardon for his criminal evasion of duty. In other words, Hyojong sought to exercise leniency by making exceptions to the rule exempting only a single generation from slave status by passing examinations.

If one's father had passed the *kwamok*, *saengwŏn*, or *chinsa* examinations and a son illicitly claimed inheritance of good status, or if a son or grandson had himself passed either the military, *saengwŏn*, or *chinsa* examinations, but his father and grandfather had illicitly and falsely claimed good status while never passing these examinations themselves, then such persons would be allowed to pay a fine without being returned to slave status. (Women would be treated the same as men under these regulations.) Furthermore, anyone descended from a slave who had passed these examinations three or more generations earlier would also be allowed retention of status on payment of a fine, but only if the person volunteered the information to the authorities. If, however, a person in this situation failed to make confession and was either reported by another or discovered by official investigation, his name would then be returned to the slave registers.

Hyojong himself pointed out the contradictory goals of this measure. On the one hand, he said he was trying to make up for the failure of the government over the last century to maintain accurate slave registration and rectify the many cases of falsification of status by those who should have been slaves. On the other hand, since the dynasty had long shown respect for those who passed the civil and military examinations, he had to give consideration to the passers of examinations (and their descendants) who would be shocked if suddenly returned to the slave registers. Flexibility was the proper way of the virtuous ruler, and he preferred to lose a few official slaves rather than force some deserving types to suffer the hardships of a life of vagrancy and worry. In other words, even though some slaves may have used the examinations to escape slavery (whether taken legally or not, with or without royal permission) and their descendants utilized inherited prestige to avoid reverting to slave status, an investigation into the status of degree holders might well have involved offending legitimate yangban families, thus weakening the loyalty of the ruling class to the regime. Furthermore, as Ch'a Munsŏp astutely observed, the king was more interested in raising extra revenue for the defense of Kanghwa Island than in restoring the social order to an earlier ideal.[20]

If, however, he had been single-mindedly devoted to national self-strengthening, he would have been thinking about abolishing slavery altogether and making everyone liable for military service or cloth taxes. As it was, his failure to act on the proposal for imposing military cloth taxes on the yangban as well as his desire to return some men to slavery while allowing others descended from degree-holders to retain status and exemptions only demonstrates his reluctance to pose a frontal challenge to the privileged yangban aristocracy.

THE DEBATE OVER A YANGBAN AND SCHOLAR TAX, 1674

One month before Hyŏnjong died, in the midst of the debate over the mourning question, the Office of the Inspector General (Sahŏnbu) again raised the issue of reforming the military support tax system (*sinyŏk*). Hŏ Chŏk, the Southerner sinecured minister-without-portfolio at the time, reported that one Yi Yut'ae had submitted a private memorial in which he called for a one-*p'il* cloth tax on yangban as well as commoners, an idea which Hŏ said he too had proposed in Hyojong's reign. Yu Hyŏgyŏn, a fellow Southerner, raised a number of objections to the idea. He suggested that any innovation caused consternation among the people, just as the adoption of the household tally system (*hop'ae*) prior to the Manchu invasion of 1627 had led to more panic in the streets that the invasion itself. Furthermore, oppressive taxation was a result of the shortage of registered adult males of *commoner* (!) status caused by various forms of evasion, the chief of which was posing as students (*kyosaeng*). He noted that certain districts like Chunghwa in South P'yŏng'an, Andong in Kyŏngsang, and Namwŏn in Chŏlla had over a thousand each. The private academies were recruiting large numbers of common peasants and accepting runaways as supposed students, gaining for them permanent exemptions from miscellaneous labor service (as well as military support taxes).[21]

A few days later, Chief State Councilor Kim Suhŭng reported that a conference of ministers had concluded that it was in fact possible to devise a new "personal cloth tax" (*sinp'o*) to be imposed on previously untaxed men, but the scope of the new tax was to be kept conservatively small. The ministers decided to exclude passers of the intermediate level *chinsa* and *saengwŏn* (literary and classics) examinations from the law, and only included the *yuhak* or general category of student, not necessarily registered in a school, or lower types. They also incorporated into the draft law the proposal of Yu Kye in 1659 that these previously exempt students would only be required to pay one *p'il* in cloth and not be registered for military duty.

Second State Councilor Chŏng Ch'ihwa responded that this kind of individual or per capita levy was not as good as a household cloth tax (*hop'o*). If individual males were taxed, then families with large numbers of adult males would have to bear a heavy burden. Kim Suhŭng, on the other hand, believed that it would be easier for people to evade registration for a household tax than for a per capita tax. Chŏng replied that this could be avoided and a household cloth tax successfully adopted if the families of the highest officials set a model for others by paying the tax and advertising their compliance with the law.

King Hyŏnjong gave some indication of where his sentiments lay when he asked which of the two methods was more likely to yield the larger revenue. Kim replied that the personal tax (*sinp'o*) would yield far more than a household cloth tax. Royal Secretary Yun Sim raised the point that so many persons had been able to evade registration under the normal census (household registration system or *hojŏk*) that the initiation of a per capita cloth tax would inevitably result in the discovery of many unregistered persons, obviously requiring large scale punishment, but Minister of War Kim Man'gi retorted that men so discovered could be excused from criminal punishment, and Hyŏnjong agreed with him.[22]

Although Hyŏnjong's appetite was whetted by the prospect of more revenue, he did not have the heart to prevail against the spokesman of yangban-scholar class interests. A few days later Inspector-General (Taesahŏn) Kang Paengnyŏn argued (erroneously) that the state had been showing favor to the scholar class for three hundred years by exempting them from military service. If this policy were changed overnight and the scholars lumped together with ordinary peasants on the cloth tax rolls, there would be tremendous opposition to it.

Kim Suhŭng then reversed his opinion, claiming that the imposition of a per capita tax would be too onerous in families that had five to ten adult males. The plight of the poor scholar families living in remote areas was particularly disheartening. They might call themselves yangban, but they could hardly scrape together enough to support a scholar in the family. If a new cloth tax were imposed on them, they would not be able to pay it, and they would end up in jail for violating the tax law. He had heard so many criticisms since the law was first broached that he was certain it would have to be rescinded soon after adoption. Hence, it was better not to implement it at all.

When Hyŏnjong turned to other officials for advice, most, including Kim

Sŏkchu, soon to become the dominant figure at court at the end of the decade, expressed negative views. Minister of Taxation Min Yujung proposed carrying out the usual thorough investigation of tax evaders among school students, military officers (*kun'gwan*) attached to various yamen, and other types of unregistered idlers, and Kim Suhŭng supported him. He also recommended binding men to the village by the five-family mutual responsibility system (*ogat'ong*) according to which the chief of each five-family group (the *t'ongjang*) would be responsible for paying the cloth taxes due from the group as a whole.[23]

Even though the mourning ritual debate was at its height at the time, the defeat of this measure cannot be attributed to factionalism. The 1674 debate followed the same lines as the discussion fifteen years before except that the initial proposal to tax only the *yuhak* was far less ambitious than Yu Kye's. The handful of reformers willing to intrude on yangban and scholar interests were simply overwhelmed by the defenders of privilege, and it was obvious from the testimony of Kim Suhŭng that the officials at court must have been besieged by complaints from the scholar class around the country. As he remarked, every poor family with a single student, no matter how poor and how thin the line of descent from yangban ancestors, identified with the most exalted yangban families when it came to defending the exemption from military registration, service, and taxation. Kim Suhŭng's watered-down version of a yangban tax would have merely imposed a one-*p'il* levy on only a restricted category of students, the *yuhak*, without requiring them to register as soldiers or support taxpayers. All the illicit students in state schools or private academies, the idle degree-holders, and hosts of other types would have been untouched by the provision, and yet the opposition was so stout that even this proposal was abandoned. The prospects for squeezing an extra farthing from the yangban-scholar tax evaders for military costs appeared to be receding. A scant two years after Yu Hyŏngwŏn's death, the debate over the one-*p'il* scholar tax made Yu's proposal for a return to yangban military service appear both radical and anachronistic.

In the last twenty years of Yu Hyŏngwŏn's life, four active officials – Kim Yuk, Yu Kye, Pak Sedang, and Hŏ Chŏk – all made proposals that would have imposed taxes on some or all of the yangban class. Their purpose was similar to that of Yu Hyŏngwŏn only in that they all sought to expand the tax base, but they differed from him in two ways: they wanted a one-*p'il*, not a two-*p'il*, tax rate on all support taxpayers of good status, and they wanted to impose a tax on yangban or unqualified students and the like without bringing them back into the system of military service itself. On the tax rate, they had a far better idea of what was needed to reduce the burden on the commoner peasantry, and in proposing an expanded tax base rather than a reversion to labor service, they were more in tune with the times.

Furthermore, their plans were not informed by his, nor his by theirs, and it was some combination of their ideas rather than his that formed the basis for the protracted debate that lasted from this time into the next century, even past the equal service reform of 1750. In other words, reform-minded officials did not need the inspiration of reclusive scholars to propose ideas for change because they both derived inspiration from similar sources: the environment of the seventeenth century, and an inclination to rectify faulty institutions that was part of an intellectual tradition shared by all. In addition, their ideas were more advanced or progressive in the sense that they had adapted to a changing economic and fiscal environment where Yu's thought was closer in some respects to that of the fifteenth century. When Yu Hyŏngwŏn's ideas were finally broached at court in 1750, right in the midst of the debate over reform of the military service system, we have certain proof that contact between the recluse world of the scholar and that of the active official was finally made. But by that time, the world had changed considerably.

DEFEAT OF THE HOUSEHOLD CLOTH TAX, 1681–82

Yun Ido Opposes Household Cloth Tax, 1680

Despite the failure of reform in 1674, the debate over expanding the tax base was revived again in 1680, but this time over the household cloth tax, which was based on the fundamental proposition that the financing of the military by support taxpayers tied to duty soldiers ought to be shifted to a more flexible and dependable source of tax revenues. The idea ran into difficulty from the outset, however. Third Minister of Taxation Yun Ido remarked that the household cloth tax (*hop'o*) would not produce sufficient revenue because it would exclude official and private slaves, while a capitation tax would be harder to bear for poor families with several adult males. Based on his own recent experience in the south where he found evasion of military support taxes to be ubiquitous, he believed that dispatching registrars to sign up the shirkers would be the quickest way to eliminate double and triple taxation of registered males.[24]

What is interesting about Yun Ido's criticism is that it focused on fiscal calculation – the amount of revenue to be produced and the burden on individual families – not on the legitimacy of taxation divorced from adult males, of whatever status. Although his opposition to both household and capitation taxes was ostensibly based on concern for peasant welfare, others reacted defensively against possible inroads into yangban privilege.

Yi Tanha Opposes Equality in Taxation, 1681

In 1681, after Sukchong came to the throne, Yi Tanha, then inspector-general (Taesahŏn), spoke out against any household cloth tax that would be levied on all families from the highest state officials down through commoners and base persons or slaves, and he provided a philosophical justification for discrimination and against equality. He said the idea had been abandoned in 1674 because the whole country was up in arms over it and court opinion was too sharply divided. Nonetheless, its advocates believed it was the best way to achieve equality in the distribution of taxes and sweep away all the problems associated with illegal and forced taxation of children, the aged, dead souls, and the neighbors and relatives of runaways. What they failed to take into account, however, was that difference, not equality, was a principle of nature and that differential and discriminatory treatment of people was justified and proper: "It is in the nature of material objects that they are not all alike, that they differ from one another in ten thousand ways – the noble from the base, the thick from the thin, the large from the small, the light from the heavy – and that everything is this way."

He then extended his concept of the pattern of nature and material objects by affirming distinction and hierarchy as the basis of Confucian moral standards:

> This [the existence of real differences among all things] was the reason why the sage kings in governing the states of the world necessarily did so on the basis of the inequality of the nature of things. They honored the noble and treated the base with disdain, provided generous treatment for the deserving and meager benefits for the undeserving; they did the same [in distinguishing between] the great and small, important [heavy] and unimportant [light], seeing to it that each should obtain his own place and not dare transgress his role [*pun*] in life.
>
> It might be possible that if such a nondiscriminatory household cloth tax were adopted, court officials might willingly comply with it to aid their country in a time of danger, but "if you talk about the scholars who spend their whole lives in arduous study, would it not indeed be grievous to make them pay the same cloth tax as those who have never read a single word?[25]

He justified his view with a classical attribution to Mencius, who he claimed once rejected the idea that large and small straw sandals should be sold for the same price. He was probably misquoting Mencius because the only statement in the book of *Mencius* close to this citation is a reference to a scholar named Lung, who once said that a sandalmaker asked to make shoes for people without knowing their specific sizes would never make any as large as a basket; he would make them all more or less the same size "because all men's feet are like one another" (literally, "the feet of the world are the same"). The rest of this section in the *Mencius*, however, is not a defense of innate difference but the opposite – an assertion of the equal and uniform capacity of all men for moral principle and righteous behavior. Mencius made his point by raising a problem that later plagued the English empiricists: the seeming constancy and uniformity of perceptions of material objects shared by all human beings. For Confucians, however, the problem was the human capacity for moral behavior, not the real existence of objects nor the capacity to know of them. Mencius's point was that because human beings appear to share not only the same perceptions of, but also tastes and preferences for, the objects of the senses, the uniform capacity of human minds for moral perfection should not be lacking. As Mencius stated in the section preceding the remarks on shoes, "Thus all things which are the same in kind are like to one another; why should we doubt in regard to man as if he were a solitary exception to this? The sage and we are the same in kind."[26] In other words, the Confucian tradition contained within it a moral and philosophical justification for a certain degree of human similitude, if not perfect equality, that had to be adapted to the more advertised principles of distinction and hierarchy. This idea in Mencius also formed the basis for Yu Hyŏngwŏn's arguments against slavery, but it was evidently distorted or misquoted by Yi Tanha to justify natural inequality, a kind of Freudian slip produced by an aristocratic environment.

Yi's alternative to the household cloth tax was a large-scale registration to put the military rosters in order, but even that measure had to be put off because of current famine conditions. In the meantime he suggested returning to the early Chosŏn Five Guard system, which required all sons of officials to be assigned first to elite guard units like the Loyal Aide and Loyal Obedient Guards in the capital before taking the civil-service examinations or holding office. Then the elite guardsmen who were students of literary affairs might be enrolled in the National Academy and Four Schools (*sahak*) in the capital and the government schools in the provinces (*hyanggyo*), and the students of military affairs could be assigned to the Inner Forbidden Guards (Naegŭmwi) or other units. All the rest, who did not qualify as legitimate students, would be required to stand duty as a rotating service soldier or pay the military support tax. The additional revenues would help to reduce the depletion of state resources by Guard soldiers, reduce the number of untaxed idlers, and fill the service ranks.

What is really significant about Yi Tanha's position on this problem was that he was both an opponent of a household cloth tax because it would have been imposed on yangban households, and an advocate of a return to the Five Guard system of military service, which would have required greater yangban participation as servicemen. His ideas only differed from Yu Hyŏngwŏn's plan in certain details. For example, he did not mention examination passers and degree holders, who presumably would retain their exemptions from military service. Yu would have abolished the examination system and made performance in school the main criterion for service exemption. On the other hand, it is significant that both Yu and Yi harked back to the early Chosŏn system that both believed required service of all but elite guard membership for the privileged few. It suggests that Yu's supposed egalitarianism was but a hair's breadth separated from Yi's respect for hierarchy because both men approved a return to the Five Guards system that required yangban unemployed as officials or not in school to stand for special service in elite guard units. This coincidence was not happenstance, because both had a very strong respect for difference and hierarchy, as long as it was based on moral criteria.

Furthermore, both Yu and Yi Tanha opposed the equal (if not progressive) tax scheme geared to current demands for independent financing. Yi justified his opposition because he felt it would tax yangban or scholar families on an equal basis with commoners, Yu because it would have departed too much from traditional principles of actual labor service and the militia idea.

As for the provincial soldiers (of good or commoner status), Yi recommended granting them land tax exemptions (*kŭppok*) and providing support taxpayers to ensure funds for emergencies and continuous training – his way of providing equivalent consideration to those of lower status than the sons of the yangban. Accumulation of grain reserves could be left to the voluntary action of the rich in the countryside, who would be encouraged to establish their own village granaries (*sach'ang*). This was the essence of his program for a restoration (*chunghŭng*) of the dynasty's fortunes.

Yi also referred to Sŏng Hŏn of the fifteenth century, who had recommended the establishment of a General Directorate To Eliminate Evils (Hyŏkp'ye-dogam) to revive laws of the dynastic founders that had either fallen out of use or had become corrupted over time, carry out a population census and a survey of total production, and use these as a base for creating an "equal" or fair tax system. Yi argued that a grand directorate was not essential; a Reform Bureau (Hyŏkp'yech'ŏng) attached to the Border Defense Command staffed by concurrent officials would be sufficient. But it should set about finding real adult males to put in the military registers in place of all the children and dead souls listed there, reduce the size and weight of the cloth bolts required for tax payments, reduce the number of soldiers in the capital guards, provide support for provincial soldiers, put the national accounts on a pay-as-you-go basis (*yang'ip wich'ul*, i.e., adjusting expenditures to revenue), and stimulate savings by both the state and private parties to build a reserve defense fund. Despite the frustrating record of reform in the past, Yi believed this could be done if the government just made a beginning. "If today we take care of one of these matters, and tomorrow issue another order, then in one or two years the state will come close to achieving it."[27]

Yi Samyŏng: Household Cloth Tax on all Statuses

Later in the year, however, Second Minister of War Yi Samyŏng made the most vigorous case to date for adoption of a household cloth system, but he did it on the basis of a mathematical calculation of income and expenditure in association with certain dogmatic and traditional views about the nature of a household tax system. To counter earlier criticism that a household tax would produce insufficient revenue to replace the taxes collected from existing support taxpayers, he cited tax and census statistics. He estimated total expenses for the capital and provinces at about two to three hundred thousand *p'il* per year (which compared to statistics of a later period seems to be only *half* of what they should have been), and total population as recorded in the census of 1678 (*muo* year) at approximately 1.2 million households (6 million people if one assumes an average of 5 persons/household, only half the population estimate of Tony Michell). Excluding 420,000 or so households of official and private slaves, the unfit and sick, beggars and others who could not be expected to pay a military cloth support tax, he estimated a total of 720,000 potential taxpaying households.[28] He took the T'ang dynasty labor service system as a model, not to justify the militia ideal of service but the household tax system! In accordance with T'ang practice he divided households into two categories: a family of eight persons (both men and women) would be a "complete household" (*wanho*) and pay two *p'il* of cloth a year (in spring and fall), and a family with less than eight members would be a "weak household" (*yakho*) and pay only one *p'il* in the fall. The tax could be payable in whatever the special local product of an area might be, cotton, silk, ramie, hemp, even silver or copper cash – a reflection of his adaptation to a changing economic situation with greater exchange of goods on the market and more use of cash. He estimated total revenue in bolts of cloth at eight to nine hundred thousand *p'il*, an amount sufficient to pay for both the costs of all types of personal service (*sinyŏk*, i.e., support taxes) as well as the costs of supporting soldiers in the local districts.

He defended his proposal on the grounds that its principles and effects would be in close conformity with ancient ideals:

> The reason why this system would be the closest thing to [the methods of] antiquity is only because the powerful families would not dare to be the only ones to evade taxation, while the households of lower status [*haho*] would not have to bear an excessively heavy tax burden. The amount of tax collected would be kept small; the service required of the people would be made equal; the regulations would be kept simple, and the method of collection would be kept distant [not require close supervision and constant dunning by officials?].
>
> [According to ancient principles], anyone who has land should pay the land tax [*se*], and anyone who has a household should pay the cloth tax [*p'o*]. Thus the people would have a fixed amount of labor service taxes, and the state would have a regular sum of revenue for its ordinary expenses. There would be a surplus of "idle adult males" [*hanjŏng*], and a doubling of the number of fighting men as a natural consequence. The service tax burden on the people would be reduced, and there would be sufficient funds for state finance.[29]

He rejected the popular view that levying a household labor or military service tax on the families of men with offices and posts would eliminate the necessary distinction between men of moral virtue (*kunja*) and "the men of the fields" (*yain*). Why is it, he asked, that there should be any difference between the operation of a service or household tax and that of a land tax? Under current law, if the chief state councilor owned land, he still owed a land tax, and there could be no special exemption from it on the basis of the status of the landowner.

No matter what Yi Samyŏng said, he was not really a conservative, historical-minded idealist trying to restore an archaic system in new circumstances. He was clearly using his view of T'ang institutions to persuade his colleagues by twisting T'ang principles out of shape. He did this by ignoring the requirement for actual service by adult males in the T'ang system and talking instead about household taxes. In the thinking of Yu Hyŏngwŏn and Yi Tanha, for example, the essence of both the early Chosŏn and T'ang systems was service by all but for a few minor exceptions. In pressing for a household tax levied in any current product or in cash, Yi Samyŏng was really trying to liberate the military finance system from old categories.

Critics also opposed the household cloth tax on the grounds that the vast majority of taxpaying households were so poor or destitute that the tax collectors would have to use the whip and stick to obtain payment, forcing large numbers of people to take flight from their villages. But Yi insisted that it would cause no undue distress to assess a cloth tax by counting the number of persons in a household exclusive of the young and elderly. It was simply a matter of bias for people to claim that an annual one-*p'il* per household tax was too heavy compared to the cruel exactions of the current system. "Any resentment against a household cloth system would still be far preferable to the current personal service tax [*sinyŏk*]."

He also mentioned two other objections by critics. The first was that there were currently far more slaves than commoners of good status (*yangmin*) in the country. If slaves were excluded from the household cloth tax calculations, then the tax burdens on them would be too light, but if they were included, they would end up with a double service levy (i.e., one to the state and the other to the master). The other objection was that under a household cloth system, the young, adult males would be made duty soldiers in the ranks while the youths and elderly would be the only ones left to pay support taxes, creating double tax burdens on families. Yi countered these arguments by claiming the critics just misunderstood the basic idea behind the household cloth system. For example, in P'yŏng'an Province (the place where the system was first to be tried out), there were 170,000 households of which official and private slaves in combination counted for about 30,000 (only 17.6 percent). If you extended these figures to the nation as a whole, and reduced the total taxpaying households by an equivalent percentage of slaves, the net sum of 700,000 taxpaying households should easily provide 500,000 p'il of support cloth tax revenue. Of course, even if it could be assumed that the census statistics for P'yŏng'an were accurate, the percentage of slaves in the population was undoubtedly much higher in the central and southern regions of the country.

Yi claimed that the purpose of the household cloth system was not simply to alleviate the burdens of commoners of good status (*yangmin*), but also to provide enough men to serve in the armed forces, especially since the dissolution of the early Five Guards system meant that the only troops left capable of fighting were the rotating duty soldiers (*hosu* or heads of household who served on duty) of the Royal Division, Crack Select Soldiers, and Special Cavalry Unit of the Military Training Agency (i.e., prior to unification of the last two in the Forbidden Guard Division later that year), and the [7,500] musketeers of the Military Training Agency – a total of something over 30,000 men. In addition, there were around 200,000 *sog'o* (slave) soldiers, and another 200,000 members of the Anti-Manchu Division (stationed in Kyŏnggi Province), the Defense Command (at the Namhan fort near Seoul), the ivory soldiers, and the so-called new select soldiers (*sinsŏn*) in each province. Unfortunately, these last 400,000 were only untrained local militia (*t'odan*) that could not be counted on in an emergency.

If a household cloth tax were instituted, the men who would be paying the new tax would be the current "idle adult males" who were neither serving nor paying support taxes, not the "household heads [*hosu*]" who were rotating duty soldiers. According to his investigation of the military registers of all yamen and in all provinces but the northern two, there were close to 500,000 infantry and cavalry duty soldiers and their support taxpayers listed on the rolls, plus over 80,000 Royal Division and 100,000 Royal Select Soldiers and Special Cavalry Unit Soldiers (of the Military Training Agency) combined, making an additional sum of over 300,000 (why not 180,000?) rotating duty soldiers and support taxpayers.[30]

If you selected from this total the 40,000 troops who have undergone training plus another 80,000 support taxpayers who could become crack troops, you would have a fighting force of 120,000. Then a couple of firearms soldiers (*hwabyŏng*) could be added to each platoon (*tae*), and the force (of 120,000 plus) divided into twelve groups for rotating duty (10,000 per group?), and assigned to the three commanders (*taejang*, of the Royal Division, Royal Select Soldiers, and Special Cavalry Unit of the Military Training Agency. Each group would consist of 6,000 men (not 10,000?), 3,000 of which would serve on duty at the above three divisional headquarters undergoing training for two months, and then switch assignments. The other 3,000 would serve in the southern six provinces at the provincial governors' or military commanders' headquarters for a tour of two months of guard duty, and then return home. (We might also assume that if twelve shifts served for two-month shifts, there would be an interval of twenty-four months between shifts.) The whole system of rotating shifts was based on the Forbidden Guard (Kŭmgun) system of the Sung dynasty. Thus 40,000 men could be trained every year (six shifts of 6,000 men each), and within three years, the whole 120,000 would be fully trained. All musketeers would also become crack shots.

He also provided figures to justify the program. He estimated the cost in grain of supporting rotating soldiers at 500,000 *sŏm*, to be paid for by converting all household cloth taxes remitted by sea or river to the capital to grain. To meet the room and board expenses of troops serving in the provinces, which he estimated at not more than 120,000 *p'il*, he recommended that household cloth tax revenue could be paid to the Office of Dispensing Benevolence (Sŏnhyech'ŏng), the agency that handled *taedong* tribute grain surtax payments, which would then order its branches in the provinces to convert *taedong* cotton taxes in the hilly or dry-farming regions of the country to rice to be paid to the provincial governors' and military commanders' yamen. In short, he believed that if the system were carried out properly, there would be no need for additional taxes on the people and all costs of the state for its troops would be met. Sukchong welcomed the plan, congratulated Yi Samyŏng on his obvious concern for the welfare of his country, and ordered the Border Defense Command to conduct detailed discussion of the proposal.[31]

Yi Samyŏng's household cloth system would have eliminated totally the system of support taxpayers assigned to individual rotating duty soldiers. Instead, all households would have paid a tax to a fund that would then finance a core of 120,000 soldiers who would not be full-time professionals, but would rotate on and off duty as before. The key to the system, of course, was not simply the reduction of the tax rate by taxing households instead of individuals, but extending the tax base by including previously exempt yangban families and tax evaders. Although his system still suffered from the same drawbacks associated with rotating service (the long intervals between two-month tours of duty would dull the skills of the soldiers), the plan would have reduced the number of men liable for actual military service.

The key issue, however, is that his plan would have totally and radically destroyed the principles that governed the older system by creating an independent and flexible system of both finance and service. Funds could be raised by taxing households, or by any other means, and service could be thought of as a problem of finding a small number of men and training them to a high standard of performance. Both precepts were contrary to the fundamentals of the militia ideal and the requirements of personal labor service, which required all adult males (no matter how awkward and hapless) to serve, and finances to be based on specific support taxpayers assigned to servicemen. The household tax proposal in all its ramifications (not just the idea of taxing yangban) represented an adaptation to current circumstances and a violation of classical principles.

Rebuttal of Yi Samyŏng's Household Tax Plan

The challenge posed to the privileged social elite by Yi Samyŏng's plan was recognized immediately. The next day three low-level officials in the Office of Inspector-General – Yun Pan, Kim Sejŏng, and Yi Sebaek – said that it was impossible to adopt such a major reform in the midst of a series of natural disasters and famine. Not only was the system entirely different from anything ever done in the three-hundred-year history of the dynasty, but the levying of a tax on households would only increase the amazement and consternation of the people. They demanded rescission of the order to test the system in P'yŏng'an Province. "Supposing [the people of] this province really do like the system? Would the other provinces that do not want to adopt it also be forced to do so just because the people of P'yŏng'an like it?"

What this statement showed was that even if there were to be popular support for the household tax, rather than the consternation they predicted, they would still oppose it because it was too threatening to their own class interests. Sukchong rejected their protest on the grounds that the court had already given due deliberation to the question, and the decision to test the household tax in P'yŏng'an was not simply the product of a couple of officials.[32]

Royal Secretary Song Kwangyŏn also called into question Yi Samyŏng's calculations. He claimed that Yi's proposal for 6,000 duty soldiers serving on rotation, half in the capital and half in the provinces, was the same as the existing system of the Royal Division, but without the tax income from support taxpayers. Did Yi really think that the costs of the equipment of duty soldiers, their travel expenses, and their room and board while in the capital could be provided for just by the household cloth tax revenue? You could not really abolish the support taxpayers of the provincial garrisons and the frontier duty troops (*ippangjigun*) because the revenue from the household cloth tax would only be enough to provide the out-of-pocket expenses of garrison commanders during peacetime, let alone wartime. Yi Samyŏng's estimate that annual military costs were no more than two to three hundred thousand *p'il* while the revenue to be expected from the household cloth tax would come to over one million *p'il*, was just not to be believed. To cap it off, the tax resembled all those last-ditch schemes of Chinese dynasties to save themselves from ruin. "The per capita cash tax was a product of the evil government of the Ch'in dynasty; the two-*p'il* silk tax was a legacy of Emperor Wu of the Wei dynasty, all features of an age of decline. Even the Chou system of levying taxes on households was only some kind of twisted reading of the *Chou-kuan* [*Chou-li*, or *Rites of Chou*]." Despite Song's criticism of Yi's underestimate of expenditures being undoubtedly correct, Sukchong rebuffed his criticism and later transferred some of the officials of the Office of Inspector-General who had opposed the household cloth tax in P'yŏng'an.[33]

Court Debate over Household Cloth Tax, 1682

Sukchong's apparent decisiveness was undermined, however, by a rising tide of protest, which culminated in a major debate in the first lunar month of 1682. Chief State Councilor Kim Suhang, a supporter of the household tax, acknowledged that court ministers were divided over the issue, but he had heard that a majority of the people of the Western Route (i.e., both Hwanghae and P'yong'an) actually wanted the household cloth system. He had recommended that the Border Defense Command draw up a bill of particulars and a special official be appointed to administer the new system, but the high ministers were afraid to take responsibility. He even admitted he was reluctant to make a final recommendation on his own. The *Sillok* historian also noted that the top state councilors, Kim Suhang and Min Chŏngjung, who favored the household cloth tax, were opposed by Third State Councilor Yi Sangjik, who was staying away from court on grounds of illness.[34]

Opposition of Kim Suhŭng. A few days later, the sinecured Kim Suhŭng proposed that the household cloth tax be dropped. He pointed out that Yu Kye had been the first to raise the issue in 1659, but nothing had come of it because the Border Defense Command officials were hopelessly split. Of course, it is important to point out that what Yu Kye was advocating in 1659 was a cloth tax on yangban or leisured men, not a household tax proposal, indicating that what Kim Suhŭng was opposed to was any kind of tax on yangban, whether individuals or households. Then he said that when the issue was raised again in 1674, there had been so much irreponsible and angry shouting that he (as chief state councilor at the time) asked King Hyŏnjong to end the debate. Now that the matter had come up for the third time, it was again causing a big hullabaloo. "It would be hard enough to satisfy people's feelings in instituting a major reform even if you had a good law that was totally without fault. How much harder is it in this case of this law where the advantages and disadvantages cannot be known?" But Sukchong ignored him and ordered the Border Defense Command to continue its discussion.[35]

A few days later Second State Councilor Min Chŏngjung insisted that more discussion was needed. "If you were to cut off debate just because an issue was controversial, how would we ever be able to accomplish anything? Furthermore, the *taedong* reform of the tribute system, carried out throughout the century, had been just as controversial as the household cloth tax, and it was adopted even though there was much about it that both the *sajok* (yangban) and common people did not like."[36]

There were repeated attempts throughout the month to rescind the order to apply the system to P'yŏng'an. The Office of Inspector-General stated that the people there did not really want the household cloth system and the times were not ripe for it, and he recommended the arrest and trial of the governor and provincial army commander for throwing the whole province into an uproar by failing to take into consideration the feelings of the people or the situation at the time. Sukchong, however, said that the purpose of the new law was to benefit the people and create equality in military service burdens. He accused the censors of contentiousness and said that all the wrangling at court and confusion in the streets over the issue was the fault of young men like them who stubbornly held on to their own views without any consideration of affairs of state.[37]

Yi Sehwa's Defense. P'yŏng'an Provincial Army Commander Yi Sehwa then defended himself against the inspectorate in a lengthy memorial. He was clearly in favor of doing something about eradicating the evils associated with the military service system because he thought that it was the most difficult burden both the commoners and slaves of the province had to bear. Since cloth taxes on commoners were currently assessed on the individual, the more persons in a family the greater the tax burden. Since in slave families, women as well as men were counted for cloth tax purposes, a husband-wife nuclear family had to pay four *p'il* (two *p'il* each), and some families of six owed twelve *p'il*. The military support taxes kept the people mired in poverty: "Men till the fields but they cannot eat; women weave cloth but they have no clothes to wear." Ultimately, they had no alternative but to sell their family property, leave the village, and become vagrants. Once this happened, it set in motion the vicious cycle of transferring tax obligations from the departed to the remaining, the neighbors and relatives in the village, who were subjected to "the whip and stick" of the tax collectors. The situation was exacerbated by tax evaders who posed as students of literary and military affairs. The so-called *yuhak*, or nondegreed scholars, were young, robust men who never cracked a book nor shot an arrow. They were worthless for fighting and never paid a foot of cloth or a measure of grain in support taxes, thus leaving the entire burden of supporting the military establishment to the poorest "lower households" (*haho*).

Yi pointed out that the standard methods of making adjustments to distribute service more equally (*kyunyŏk*) were doomed to failure. In years of famine, for example, the annual investigations to fill empty slots in the military rosters (*sech'o*) were suspended, and officials would search out runaways and offer reductions in their cloth tax assessments to induce them to return and pay taxes. These were all good ideas, but several years of famine had forced the authorities to suspend the registration of adult men for service or taxes, and there was no one left to serve. So many had run away or died that reduction of tax rates had become standard practice, but that left the military system short of revenue. Officials in the province then ordered that all relatives of runaway or deceased soldiers and slaves to the fourth degree (including uncles, first cousins, and nephews) would henceforth pay the military cloth levy, offsetting whatever benefit might have been conferred the previous year by cutting the tax rate. The standard temporary remedies were thus no more useful than "pouring a cup of water on a cartful of burning wood; you would be better off doing nothing at all rather than adopting a temporary measure that cannot be continued."

That brought Yi to an evaluation of the household cloth system. He acknowledged that the measure was adopted out of necessity even though everyone knew it was full of difficulties, but the grand purpose of the system was definitely to "make service equal" (*kyunyŏk*). The problem was that opinion was divided between that of Yi Samyŏng and his critics in the censorate. Yi Samyŏng had given two reasons for the law: that a tax on all households including officials, yangban, and scholars was justified because even the highest ministers of state were already paying the land tax as landowners, and there was no justification for excluding from the military service taxes only the families of the *sabu* (scholar-officials). The critics, on the other hand, held that it was wrong to institute such a radical and unprecedented reform in a period of famine.

Yi Sehwa felt that in view of these two extreme and contrary opinions, there was no reason why the alternatives could not be studied at leisure, and tried out or not as seen fit. He opposed a sudden and rash adoption of a system that was bound to destroy social harmony, but he did not oppose the household cloth tax in principle. He reminded Sukchong that both he and the governor had been asked to submit their written opinions on the household cloth proposal when it was under debate at court in 1681. The governor had, in fact, indicated a preference for simultaneously eliminating the per capita levy on slaves (i.e., women as well as men) and adopting the household cloth system. Yi Sehwa had also approved of the household cloth system, on condition that the two-*p'il* tax on soldiers (i.e., men liable for military service) be eliminated and that the household cloth levy (presumably two *p'il*) be paid only by the one man in a family who was to be treated as if he were a soldier (here referred to as *wŏnho*, or basic householder); the other adult male dependents in the family (*solchŏng*) would only pay half the rate (one *p'il*). This refinement would have increased revenues over Yi Samyŏng's estimate, and if there were still shortages of revenue, they could be made up by cloth taxes collected from currently "idle" males or other types. Yi said he was certain that any slaves or commoners liable for military service would approve his proposal.

He also pointed out that at the same time the court ordered the household cloth system adopted in his province, it had also ordered a weeding out of phony official school students (*kyosaeng*) and military officers (*kun'gwan*) by special examinations, an order which threw all the "idle and leisured" tax evaders into a fit because they knew that enrollment for service would hit them in the pocketbook. But when the order to implement the household cloth tax came down, they changed their minds because they realized that it would be cheaper for their families, as households, to pay the household cloth levy than for them as individuals (now signed up on the military tax rosters) to pay the per capita two-*p'il* tax under the current system. They may also have derived some solace in that the families of ministers and regular officials would also be paying the tax. Thus, Yi concluded, the enthusiasm of the scholar-official class for the household cloth system may have been less than commoners and slaves, but their attitude was nonetheless positive.

> This means that all the court officials, military degree-holders, literary and classics licentiates [*saengwŏn* and *chinsa*], men with rank but no office [*p'umgwan*], and passers of the preliminary examination [leading to the highest civil examination (*kwagŏ*)] fear that their sons, grandsons, brothers and family members might not only be eliminated from the official schools or the [ranks of the Military Officers] by failing the literary and archery examinations, they might also be subject to the exactions levied on neighbors and relatives [to make up shortages in military support tax revenues]. So even though their desire [for the household cloth tax] may not be as great as the slaves and the [commoner] soldiers, one might deduce that there would be more of them who would want it than not.

His feeling was that the only ones really to oppose the new law would be the unscrupulous types who spent all their time devising ways to evade taxes anyway. Yi was sure that none of the people of the province wanted continuation of the present problems of the military service and tax system: levying the tax on both male and female slaves, requiring a two-*p'il* payment from every adult male of good status liable for military service, continuing to entrust responsibility for examining school students and testing military officers in archery (to their own superiors?), and only collecting cloth taxes from households that ordinarily did not have the service obligation. If the new law were adopted, everything would depend on the how well provisions of the law were drawn up. Both he and the governor had recommended earlier that the law should be applied not only to P'yŏng'an, but also to the hilly regions of South Hamgyŏng and Hwanghae. He also wondered whether it was possible that he and the governor were the only supporters of reform?[38]

Yi Sehwa's remarks are truly valuable because they represent a practical approach to military service reform from the mouth of a working military official, and they demonstrate a practical willingness to attempt new and radical measures according to the criterion of what would work rather than what was ideologically acceptable. His argument was that the household cloth tax was practically feasible and would be accepted by yangban because they would prefer it to worse alternatives like a massive registration program. The capacity for adaptation to changing circumstances and the willingness to adopt new solutions to old problems was by no means confined to idealistic, scholarly recluses.

Eight in Favor, Six Opposed: Sukchong Capitulates! Sukchong praised Yi Sehwa's remarks, but the very next day his chief state councilor Kim Suhang called for more study. He said the household cloth should not be promulgated immediately, but recommended that advocates on both sides of the question be calm and moderate their emotions, and criticized the king for his excessive behavior in punishing protesting censors. Sukchong said it would have been all right if the censors had only given their opinion on the issue, but they "overturned right and wrong" by demanding that the governor of P'yŏng'an be punished for criminal action.[39]

A few days later a censor in the inspector-general's office, Yi Ŏn'gang, requested cancellation of the household cloth system in P'yŏng'an. Admitting his knowledge was based on hearsay, nonetheless he claimed that he was more in tune with the sentiments of the yangban in P'yŏng'an Province than Yi Sehwa was. He believed that the only people in the province who wanted the system were the soldiers who sought a reduction in their service taxes. "There is no reason why any of the ordinary people who do not have military service would actually want to pay a cloth tax." Since the same logic applied to all eight provinces, there was no reason even to test the system out in P'yŏng'an. The minister of personnel later remarked that everyone was opposed to the household cloth tax, and the only court official to support it or the capitation cloth tax this day was none other than Yi Samyŏng, recently promoted to second minister of personnel.

Sukchong finally showed signs of weakening and summoned a major court conference. He told his officials that in the face of criticism a decision had to be made either to retain the household cloth system or do something about the worthless military registers. If both those alternatives were rejected, some other means had to be found to solve the military tax problem. Chief State Councilor Kim

Suhang supported the idea of testing the household cloth system in one area. There was simply no other way to find out whether it would be beneficial or not, and if it proved faulty, he would willingly change his mind. Two supporters of the tax rebutted the criticism that the cloth tax should not be imposed in a famine year by pointing out that it could be collected after the fall harvest, or instituted in subsequent years after better harvests. Yi Samyŏng noted that it was understandable that the commoners would resent having to pay several *p'il* of tax under the current system, but he could not understand why the scholar-officials (*sajok*) would object to paying only one *p'il*. He also said that the household cloth tax would reduce existing evils and was less of a problem than carrying out a major registration campaign. Kim Suhang agreed with him that the people detested even the annual supplementary registration investigations and would be sure to oppose a major one. One could not predict that the household cloth tax would be fault-free, but at least it would be no worse than the current system.

Many others, however, opposed the system. The sinecured Kim Suhŭng rejected both the household cloth and a major registration campaign and supported a suggestion to cut the quota of troops instead. Another semiretired minister, Chŏng Ch'ihwa, supported this idea by asking for reductions in the superfluous Special Cavalry Unit of the Military Training Agency established by the recently executed Southerner, Yu Hyŏgyŏn. Third State Councilor Min Chŏngjung remarked that all empty slots in the military registers caused by deaths and runaways could be filled by that means, and Censor-General Yu Hŏn asked for the abolition of the Crack Select Soldiers as well. He thought that troop reduction to save expenses was preferable to a major registration effort. He agreed with other officials who asked for a weeding out of unqualified students and military officers by special testing, but he preferred to fine those who failed their tests rather than require them to serve as soldiers.

Indeed, several compromisers were heard from as well. The censor, O Toil, approved the household cloth tax but opposed adopting it in a famine year. He did recommend its adoption after a few years of bumper crops, and its application to the capital rather than P'yŏng'an. He opposed cutting the capital guard units because they were "established agencies." Several other officials agreed with testing the tax in the capital region first, for if the people saw that the high officials were willing to pay the tax, they would not be able to raise any objections to it. Even the censor Yi Sebaek, who had opposed Yi Samyŏng and requested rescission of the order to test it in P'yŏng'an, said that there was no better alternative, and that it could be adopted after an economic recovery. In short, while only four officials (Yi Samyŏng, Kim Suhang, Min Chŏngjung, and Hwang Yun) supported immediate adoption of the household cloth plan, four others accepted the basic idea and suggested postponement until the return of good crops. Eight officials might be counted among its supporters, while about six were opposed to it outright. It is by no means certain, as Chŏng Manjo has written, that the vast majority of those in attendance were opposed.[40] In fact, if the household tax is regarded as the most progressive proposal then under discussion, there was a considerable body of opinion present throughout the bureaucratic hierarchy that was more progressive, at least on this question, than Yu Hyŏngwŏn.

Although opinion was obviously divided, Sukchong still had more than enough support to make a favorable decision, including two of his three top state councilors. The opposition had taken its toll, however. Now, even though he reiterated his preference for the household cloth system over all other alternatives, he agreed to postpone it until crop conditions improved in a few years, and then he would adopt it in the capital area first. He asked for discussion of a bill for a major registration effort instead, and appears to have also ended the experiment in P'yŏng'an Province. The decision did not bring the debate over the household cloth tax to an end, but it probably scotched the best chance it had for adoption until 1750. It also laid the groundwork for the decision to combine the Special Cavalry Unit of the Military Training Agency and the Crack Select Soldiers into the new Forbidden Guard Division later that year, in conjunction with attempts to reduce troop quotas.[41]

VARIABLE AND LOW-RATE MILITARY CLOTH TAXES

After the attempt to institute the household cloth tax on all families irrespective of status, the attention of reformers shifted back to administrative measures like reductions in the number of duty soldiers and in the tax rates for support taxpayers. The first of these has been treated above, but the second has yet to be discussed.

Even before 1682 both civil and military officials had occasionally reduced tax rates for support taxpayers, but they did not do it specifically to alleviate the burden on those taxpayers. They did it to solve the shortage of adult males in the ranks of their own units by offering a lower tax rate than normal to draw men away from other districts or units. While this stratagem succeeded in solving their problems, it was bound to leave vacancies in the units the new recruits left behind. This practice was called low-rate (*hŏryŏk*) service, and it was initiated by officials on their own authority (referred to as *samosok*) – not with the approval of the central government. But, as with so many practices, the central government tolerated the practice because it had become so common and even openly acknowledged a distinction between regular quota (*aegnaeyŏk*) and extra-quota service taxes (*aeg'oeyŏk*), defined as tax payments outside the control of the central government.

Regular quota support taxes were levied at rates of two or three *p'il*, but extra-quota support taxes at two or one *p'il*. Officials even began to devise new types of service at the lower one-*p'il* rate to attract peasants seeking a way to reduce their taxes. By 1699 there were an estimated 10,000 of these extra-quota support taxpayers. The method was used by all kinds of officials at central and provincial levels. Peasant demand was so great for low-rate service that officials or commanders of some units often issued blank warrants without informing the district magistrates.[42]

The benefits of rate reduction (i.e., getting two support taxpayers to find a third to reduce their rate from three to two *p'il* per person, in the 1660s and after) were, however, offset by raising the standard bolt of cloth from six *sŭngp'o* to nine, equivalent to a cash raise from five to seven *yang* (40 percent). Rate reduction to two *p'il* by itself did not eliminate rate variation because of the continuing practice of illicit recruitment of men at the one-*p'il* rate by individual officials. In 1689, Sukchong prohibited direct recruitment (*chikchŏng*) by officials of men for extra-quota, low-rate service (*aeg'oe samosok*), but his order was probably not followed strictly since other investigations were conducted in 1695 and 1699 to reduce the 10,000 men then registered for extra-quota service.[43] Sukchong's order probably had the effect of *raising* rates by cancelling much of the low one-*p'il* rate service.

The significance of the development of this low-rate system of taxation to attract support taxpayers into affiliation with certain units was to drive the de facto rate down and decrease the total revenue that the state as a whole might expect. It also made Yu Hyŏngwŏn's proposal for a reduction of the tax rate from three to two *p'il* per taxpayer a totally unrealistic rate because it actually represented a tax increase, not a reduction.

CONCLUSION

The Chosŏn government was not particularly successful in solving the problem of finance for its military establishment, but the discussion in government circles over various plans for reform provides an interesting basis of comparison with Yu Hyŏngwŏn's scheme to introduce a more equitable and efficient system of finance. Both Yu and the practical reformers in office were convinced that something had to be done to reduce the number of men exempted from either service or payment of the military support tax, whether they were yangban, relatives of yangban, or commoners.

The most significant difference between Yu and the active officials, however, was that Yu wanted to retain the existing system of support taxpayers assigned to rotating duty soldiers, while some of the reformers in government service like Yi Samyŏng boldly insisted on a more flexible approach of utilizing other objects of taxation beyond adult male support taxpayers tied to duty soldiers. By imposing a uniform tax on all households no matter what the status of the head of the household, Yi argued that sufficient revenue could be raised to support the national armed forces, and that the distribution of taxes among the population would be far fairer (though not perfectly equal on all households) than the status quo. The key to its success would have been the expansion of the tax base by including yangban relatives and tax shirkers, adding them to the pool of taxpayers, and using the tax receipts to support duty soldiers without necessarily enrolling them for military service.

Eight of fourteen officials who expressed clear views during the debate of 1682 favored the measure, as did King Sukchong, which indicated that an influential segment of the high officials were willing to take action that would cause pain to their fellow yangban. That King Sukchong was eventually persuaded by the conservative defenders of the status quo to postpone a decision – which meant permanent abandonment of the idea during his lifetime – was a disappointing display of leadership, but it also indicates that he was at least willing to consider a more flexible response to the institutional problem of military finances than Yu Hyŏngwŏn.

It was not that Yu was not capable of radical thought, for he ostensibly sought to eliminate all forms of illicit exemption from military service by requiring most men – except for a limited number defined as officeholders, students in good standing, and a limited number of royal relatives and noblemen – to serve in the military in some form, but his main justification for this solution was that it was based on his idealized vision of military service when the Chosŏn dynasty was founded. The principles by which it had been organized had been corrupted, but it should be retained and restored to its original, pristine purity by which all service evaders, yangban or otherwise, would be returned to some form of military duty no matter what the political repercussions might be.

Practical statesmen like Yi Samyŏng, who realized that demanding military service or support taxes from yangban and others who had for so long held that duty as demeaning to their status and prestige would be virtually impossible, or might even provoke rebellion, concluded that the yangban and other service evaders could be brought into the system simply as taxpayers, particularly since no stigma had ever been attached to the payment of land taxes by yangban landowners. This was a solution that Yu abjured, on the grounds that using land taxes to support the military was a violation of principle, by which he probably meant the traditional precedent of treating military service separately from other modes of taxation and requiring the registration of adult males to serve as support taxpayers if not rotating duty soldiers.

The curious thing about Yu's attitude on the question of military taxation was that his views were so similar to the leading opponent of the household cloth tax in 1681, the inspector-general, Yi Tanha. Like Yu, Yi also wanted to restore the early Chosŏn system to its original purity by requiring yangban without office to serve in elite guard units, and by retaining rotating duty soldiers in combination with support taxpayers as the only legitimate mode of military finance. But he justified his view by appealing to the overriding principle of *difference*, not equality, in the operation of nature as a whole, not just human life, and the legitimacy of discrimination in the determination of tax burdens. It was appalling to him that yangban could be subjected to the same tax as commoners (even though he was not disturbed by the imposition of the land tax on them as well as commoners or slaves) or slaves because yangban were obviously superior to either of them.

Was this, therefore, just a case of anomalous coincidence, where two men of completely different philosophies end up advocating the same position in practice? No, because Yu believed essentially in the legitimacy of difference as well

– despite his occasional defense of equality – except that he would not have approved of status (let alone inherited status) as a justification for discrimination between yangban versus the lower social orders. For him, superiority had to be rewarded, but only in the case of the moral quality of those men who deserved to be officials or officials-in-training in the schools because they had proved themselves (under his reformed system of education and recruitment) by a lifetime of observation by their peers or superiors. Once education and recruitment on the basis of moral behavior could be achieved, and hereditary transmission of both advantage and servile status eliminated, then an equitable system of service and taxation could be achieved, reinforced by assignment of military service obligations based on quotas of adult males per constant unit of acreage. Since, however, he was willing to consider arrangements for the transition during which slavery and military service for slaves would remain in force, he probably was willing to tolerate yangban exemption from military service, but to require that their male relatives unemployed in state service serve in special guard units.

Yu's plan was somewhat different from that of Yi Tanha, but equality of tax burden or equal distribution on all families without any distinction as to rank or status was not the essential task for him. As a result he had nothing to contribute in his writing to the main proposal for reform of military taxation that lasted into the next century, and beyond, for that matter, to 1870 – the household cloth tax and its imposition on yangban households. His unwillingness to compromise with the traditional formula for support taxpayers made him irrelevant to the small band of pragmatic reformers who continued to campaign for military taxes (or service) for the yangban.

CHAPTER 13

Military Reorganization, Weapons, and Walls

This chapter will cover three topics related to military affairs in Yu's writings: the reorganization of the military structure, including the positioning of units and the distribution of power between the capital, the countryside, and the frontier; the strengthening of technical capabilities in weapons and modes of defense construction like walls and moats; the insistence on shifting Confucian education from civil matters exclusively to a balance between civil and military training. These ideas were related to three serious weaknesses in the Korean defense establishment. The first includes the poor organization of existing units, the excessive number of troops in the capital, and the strategically disadvantageous placement of provincial garrisons. The second relates to the technological backwardness of the Korean military compared to its neighbors, China and Japan, and the third refers to the low level of preparedness and low morale of Confucian-trained officials and military leaders of the past century.

As in most other cases, Yu took an approach toward these three matters on the basis of his own strong commitment to Confucian norms and values and the wisdom of the Chinese tradition, but the question is whether the solutions provided by that tradition provided much hope for successful reform.

Principles of Reorganization

Elimination of the New Capital Units

In a footnote to his list of the types of soldiers he would retain in a reformed military system, Yu categorized military units in existence in the mid-seventeenth century in two ways: the old system (*kuje*), which consisted of those units established from the beginning of the dynasty to the Imjin War (1392–1592) and described in the existing law codes, and the new system (*sinje*), which included those units established after 1592. He saw his main task as paring down superfluous units and creating a simpler organization, but he chose to do it by restoring the fundamental organization of the early Chosŏn period rather than by creating a totally new system. He retained only certain elements of the new system: the Military Training Agency (Togam, or Hullyŏn-dogam) and the capital soldiers (*kyŏngbyŏng*), which included the capital musketeers (*p'osu*) and horse platoons (*madae*), and finally, the *sog'ogun*, to be composed in his system exclusively of official and private slaves (not mixed with commoners as in contemporary practice). All other troop units established since the Imjin Wars, such as the Royal Division – the model for his reformed duty soldier/support taxpayer system of service – the Crack Select Soldiers (Chŏngch'ogun), the New Select Soldiers (Sinsŏn'gun), the Special Musketeers (Pyŏlp'osu), and the Special Cavalry (Pyŏltae) of the Military Training Agency, were to be abolished. The Royal Division was established in 1624, abolished, reestablished, and reorganized and expanded in size in 1651. The Crack Select Soldiers were created some time between 1638 and 1649, expanded and put under the Crack Select Agency (Chŏngch'och'ŏng) in 1668. The Special Cavalry Unit was established in 1669, and then combined in 1682 after Yu's death with the Crack Select Soldiers to form the Forbidden Guard Division (Kumwiyŏng).[1]

Yu did say that these units could not be abolished right away because at the current time there was a surfeit of military examination passers (*ch'ulsin*), who obviously needed employment as officers in the above units. So he suggested the units be eliminated by attrition, another indication of his trepidation at the possibility of reactionary anger by members of his own class.

He also wanted to eliminate a number of types of soldiers who were not organized into discrete units but attached in small numbers to civil bureaus or military units and headquarters. These included the military students (*muhak*), archers (*sabu*), officers' personal aides known as the ivory soldiers (*abyŏng*), soldiers conscripted directly by base and unit commanders or civil officials (*mogun*), and support slaves (*pono*). Although he intended to restore the military system of early Chosŏn, he specifically ruled out the miscellaneous units of that era as well.[2] In short, Yu intended to reduce the number of duty soldiers overall and confine the types of soldiers to five categories: regular cavalry and infantry, *sog'o* slave soldiers, marines (*sugun*), and able-oarsmen. His goals was to rationalize and simplify military organization and cut its cost.

Yu did not include the Defense Command stationed at the Namhan fort just outside Seoul in the list of units to be dropped, possibly because that unit was intimately involved in the politics and foreign policy of King Hyojong. Hyojong's build-up of the Namhan fort and the Defense Command associated with it after 1649 involved important issues of politics, strategy, and even weapons policy. He had appointed Yi Sibang, hawkish anti-Manchu rival of the late accommodationist Kim Chajŏm, commander of the Defense Command in 1651, and then carried out the reassignment of troops to it and the Namhan fort that had been requested by Yi's father, Yi Kwi, and blocked by Kim Yu in years past. Since the troops assigned to the fort from Taegu and Andong had not been able to reach the fort before the Manchus did in the invasion of 1637, Yi Sibang recommended that almost all the soldiers from Ch'ungch'ŏng and Kyŏngsang provinces assigned to the post be replaced by men from Kyŏnggi Province.

This measure certainly made rational sense, but building up the Namhan fort was of little practical value if the aim of Hyojong's policy was to attack Manchuria. One suspects that despite the rhetoric of Hyojong and his anti-Manchu supporters at the time, the purpose of the Namhan fort was twofold: a last place of refuge for a beleaguered king holding out against a third Manchu invasion, or a command center for a king under siege by his domestic political enemies.[3]

Defense of the Capital

Restoration of the Five Guard System. Yu wanted to reorganize the royal and capital guards because he was concerned about the inefficiency of the units and the financial drain on the state treasury by an excessively large force of capital guards, some of whom were permanent, salaried soldiers. He learned from Chinese experience that long-term troops on salary tended to increase in number and impose a serious tax burden on the state. Emperor T'ai-tsung of the T'ang began with an imperial guard of only one hundred cavalrymen, but by the late seventh century under Empress Wu it had grown to a thousand, and by the turn of the eighth century, ten thousand. Then they became permanent long-term imperial guards, but the T'ang court was no longer able to control them, they were unable to repress rebellion, and the dynasty fell. The situation could be controlled by wise rulers if they took care to set quotas on permanent, or long-term capital troops in particular.

The number of capital guards had to be determined by the amount of available resources. If there were sufficient tax revenues to pay for ten thousand troops, then the limit should be set at four or five thousand to ensure a surplus of funds. Since Korea was much smaller than China, a force of one or two thousand permanent, capital soldiers would be more than enough. Since duty soldiers had to be provided enough support to make them effective, it would not pay simply to cut their support. The only acceptable method was to cut the number of troops to provide tax relief for the support taxpayers.[4]

Yu proposed a plan to divide the capital forces into a capital guard and a small number of royal guards and specialized units like gate guards, patrols, and police. To achieve this he wanted to abolish the Royal Division and restore the Five Guard (Owi) system of the early Chosŏn period. All soldiers of the Five Guards as well as those of the Military Training Agency would be organized under the system of rotating service and support taxpayers currently in use in the Royal Division. Yu claimed that the two organizations (Five Guards and Military Training Agency) would complement each other like the inner and outer lining of a coat (i.e., guarding the areas inside and outside the walls of the capital) in conformity with the Northern and Southern Armies (Nan-pei chün) of the Han dynasty. This arrangement would solve two problems at once: it would prevent an excess of troops at the capital while ensuring that the soldiers the state did have could really be of some use in combat.[5]

The earlier Five Guard system, which had command and defense responsibilities for each of the provinces, proved worthless when Hideyoshi invaded Korea, but it was not removed from the military table of organization and apparently retained vestigial functions in the defense of the capital. After the Injo Restoration of 1623, new guard divisions were created with responsibilities that overlapped and replaced the functions of the older Five Guards, which apparently were not legally abolished.[6] Yu's restored Five Guards, as opposed to the earlier version, were to be responsible only for capital defense, to pare down the politicized capital divisions of the period after the Injo Restoration. He also wanted to eliminate the current Five Guards Directorate (Owi toch'ongbu) that exercised overall control over the Five Guards because there was no precedent for it in ancient times, and instead to direct each of the Five Guards to report directly to the Ministry of War.[7]

One of his objectives was to achieve a balance between civilian control and military necessity, a point illustrated by his remedies for the problems of command at the capital. He complained that the guard commanders (*wijang*) of the current Five Guards (Owi) at the capital had no fixed assignment to any particular unit and were merely given a command whenever they checked in for duty. For that matter, a few days after they reported, they might be transferred again to another command. Even the rank-and-file soldiers of the palace gate guards (*kammun*) and the capital constabulary (*sunwi*) were only given duty assignments daily at dusk and then suddenly transferred to another post a few days later. There was no familiarity between commanders and troops and no continuity in the commanders, not only when on guard duty, but in military training and on bivouac exercises.

He described the situation as one of utter confusion caused by the inordinate fear of military domination by the civil officials. Just as the Sung government had overreacted to the excessive political power of the late T'ang regional commanders, so the early Chosŏn authorities had sought to prevent a recurrence of the excessive power of the military in late Koryŏ by rotating commanding officers. He conceded that the concern was justified, but not at the expense of national defense. A confused system was worse than no system at all. "If one day there were to be a sudden and unexpected problem [invasion], then how would we be equipped to defend against it?" His solution was to assign commanders and officers to specific guard units with exclusive control over their units.[8]

Fully consistent with his abhorrence of permanent, salaried soldiers, Yu stipulated that the troops of the Five Guards would be divided into groups or shifts and serve on rotation for two-month tours of duty. All would be recruited from districts adjacent to the capital and each soldier would have a basic assignment (*wŏnjong*) to one of the capital guards to promote solidarity and identification with their units. In fact, all soldiers from a given civil district would be assigned as a group to one of the Five Guard units in the capital and would not be transferred from one unit to another except for unusual circumstances.[9]

The total force of the capital contingent of the revived Five Guards would consist of 12,500 men, five 2,500-man regiments of five 500-man battalions for each of the Five Guards. Yu did not say just how many troops would serve on each shift and for how long, but if they were organized into eight shifts or groups for two months of service as ordinary infantrymen were supposed to be, then 1,562 men would be in the capital at any one time.

Yu's regulations for duty, however, prescribed a force of one battalion or less from each of the Five Guards to serve for three-day shifts inside the palace grounds. This would require more than 1,562 men to be stationed in the capital because there were 2,500 men in five battalions. Even if each battalion were under strength, about 300 men each, you would need a reserve force of at least another 1,562 men to relieve those on duty after their three-day stint. Yu may have intended the soldiers to return home after their three-day tour, but this would have required a lot of traveling back and forth, once a week or so. It would appear that Yu did not really work out the logistics of his program in sufficient detail, and he may well have underestimated the number of troops required and the cost of the system.[10]

Yu's system of assigning peasants living in districts near the capital to the same unit in the capital guards was designed not only to use village cohesion as the basis for solidarity inside military organizations – a principle derived from the classical militia ideal – but also to eliminate the use of city dwellers for guard duty, the equivalent of modern-day city slickers. He was familiar with the sorry reputation of the the troops of the Military Training Agency, and he blamed it on their long-term service in the capital and the corrupting influence on their behavior by their association with sharpsters and slick traders in the big city. Yu mentioned that Ch'i Chi-kuang of the Ming had, in fact, warned against this: "The worst people you could recruit [for service] are the slippery people from the marketplaces and wells; and the second worst people you could recruit are the wily and tricky people. The best you can use are only the old and true people from the villages and fields, and the second best you can recruit are veterans."

Yu punctuated this advice with his own endorsement: "Ch'i Chi-kuang really knew what he was talking about, didn't he?" The capital guards were filled with these crafty city folk who spent all their time scheming to make money, lazily neglecting their duties, becoming more arrogant and undisciplined, and fighting with the city residents until both sides hated each other with a passion.[11] By confining the area for the recruitment of the capital guards to the vicinity of the capital, Yu had in mind the hardy peasants of Kyŏnggi Province, possibly a product of an anti-urban bias shared by most rusticated scholars.

Gate Guards and Night Patrol. In addition to the Five Guards, Kŭm'o night patrol, and the gate guards, Yu made special plans to retain the Inner Palace Guards (Naegŭmwi) as well, but he insisted on reducing its quota. He pointed out that at the beginning of the dynasty the *Kyŏngguk taejŏn* code of 1469 called for only 190 Forbidden Guards, but the number had grown to 600 by his own time. If you counted the troops of the Concurrent Royal Stables (Kyŏmsabok) and Winged Forest Guards (Urimwi) in addition (the troops of all three were referred to as the Forbidden Soldiers or Kŭmgun), the number of royal guards was really closer to 1,000 men.[12]

King Hyojong continued to press for expansion of the capital guard force toward the end of the 1650s despite the increasing tide of protest from officials. Between 1651 and 1655, he reorganized the Forbidden Soldiers (Kŭmgun, his personal guard), converted them all to cavalry, an increased their numbers from 600 to 1,000 men.

Yu felt that 200 men would be more than enough, especially since Emperor T'ai-tsung of the T'ang only had 100 cavalry for his personal guard, and there would be a large contingent of rotating duty soldiers from the Five Guards on duty as well. The troops of the Forbidden Soldiers would be divided into three shifts that would rotate on and off duty, and they would be furnished horses and a standard salary by the government. As permanent, salaried soldiers, they constituted one of the rare exceptions to his preference for a support-taxpayer finance system, but he felt that costs could be kept under control by limiting the number. If he had known that the actual number of Inner Forbidden Guards in 1407 was somewhere between sixty and ninety, he might have called for an even lower quota.[13]

One significant aspect of Yu's plan for the Inner Forbidden Guards was his elaborate set of regulations for recruitment examinations in both military skills and classical learning. Even though Yu called elsewhere for the total abolition of the current civil and military examinations, in existence continuously in Korea since 958, he allowed for military examinations along the same lines as the current *mukwa* or highest military degree examination only in the case of this small royal bodyguard.

In addition to tests of archery and musketry, the candidates would be examined every three years on civil classics like The Four Books, military classics, and Yu's favorite *Chi-hsiao hsin-shu* by Ch'i Chi-kuang. He claimed that his intention was to create the well-rounded man, skilled in both the civil and military arts in emulation of the classical ideal, who "while at home could act as an official to look after the people of the local communities, and when out on a military campaign could lead the army in defense against the enemy." In other words, proper education would create the ideal *sa* or scholar-soldier who would all engage in "true learning" (Sirhak). "Those who do not learn [the double path of the well-rounded man] would not be allowed to become officers, while those who concentrated exclusively on a specific skill like archery, running, or riding horses would be relegated to the role of ordinary soldier. How could you take these kinds of men and put them in a position to command others?"[14]

Even though he disdained the creation of the military examination system in the reign of Empress Wu of the T'ang as the work of an evil genius, deplored its adoption in the late fourteenth century in Korea by King Kongyang, and ordered its abolition in his new society, nevertheless he adopted many of its administrative features, such as the triennial interval between tests, the division into preliminary and final examinations, and quotas for each province. In the initial examination 500 would be taken, and 50 in the final, compared to the quota of 190 and 28, respectively, in the current military examinations.

Although the Five Guards in the capital might all be mobilized in time of war, their normal duties were to be confined to specific guard responsibilities and they would not be asked to act as police for the capital as well. Yu wanted to create a separate capital constabulary (*sun'gyŏng kunsa*) consisting of four special battalions to patrol the capital at night and guard the palace and capital gates – the Kŭm'o, Kammun, Sŏngmun, and Igwi battalions. Nighttime patrol of the capital was currently performed in a haphazard way. The Ministry of War appointed patrol officers (*sunjang*) from unemployed high-ranking (*tangsanggwan*) officials every three nights, and borrowed troops from the Five Guards to go on patrol. Yu believed that night patrol was so important to the security of the capital that a separate agency staffed with its own officers and troops was a necessity. He intended to restore the Kŭm'o Guards, which had performed that function in the beginning of the dynasty, and specified that all its soldiers would be recruited from men living in the neighborhood of the capital.[15] Every night the Kŭm'o battalion would furnish from 200 to 400 patrol troops. Some would be assigned to the existing network of police boxes (*p'o*) at intervals of three *i* (three quarters of a mile) with a staff of five constables and one commanding officer, much like the system used in the colonial era and present-day south Korea. The rest would go on patrol throughout the city in squads of five or ten men.[16]

Yu believed it was extremely important to maintain strict distinctions between the duties of each unit to eliminate confusion and keep command and responsibility clear. He strongly opposed using soldiers of the Military Training Agency for night patrol and police functions, insisting that its troops should be limited in number and restricted to guarding the exterior of the palace walls and performing special duty inside the walls, supplementing the rotating soldiers of the Five Guards, whose main task would be interior palace patrol.[17]

Yu's main complaints about the current way the capital guard was organized indicate a number of serious deficiences in his own time. He observed that the troops were poorly educated and lacked training as soldiers. They were inadequate for their duties as guardians of the king and palace, night watchmen, and constables. The units functioned like the personal battalions of their commanders because the government had allowed them to recruit their soldiers directly from the countryside. Troops trained for field battle were used for tasks for which they were not adequately trained. The overlap of responsibility was too confusing, and there were no restraints on the number of constables and guards.

No Capital Guard Services for Remote Provinces

Another part of Yu's military reorganization plan called for the assignment of peasants in provinces more distant from the capital to provincial army commander's headquarters or frontier garrisons to eliminate one of the anomalies of the early Chosŏn Five Guard system. In the fifteenth century soldiers from all parts of the country were assigned to one of the Five Guards in the capital, but since the troops from P'yŏng'an and Hamgyŏng provinces in the north were kept in those provinces for permanent frontier defense, they were excused from rotating service in the capital, and the two guard units to which they were assigned were left without a troop contingent. His plan limited the source of supply for the capital guards to districts surrounding the capital. This arrangement would ensure reduction of travel expenses, ease of mobilization, a sense of solidarity among the troops, and familiarity between commanders and soldiers.[18]

Yu realized that his system of military service organization and assignments differed from the *fu-ping* system that accompanied the T'ang equal-field allotment system, and he felt under some constraint to justify the differences. Under the *fu-ping* organization, local militia troops were assigned to various *fu* or *che-ch'ung-fu* located in the provinces, and the *fu* were in turn placed under the command structure of the sixteen capital guard units. Although his plan to adopt the *chin'gwan* system of provincial garrisons organized hierarchically with a number of superior command garrisons in each province might be compared to the T'ang *fu*, nonetheless these provincial troops were not to be placed under the command of the capital guards. He specifically stated that there was no need to copy the T'ang *fu-ping* system exactly because every system of military organization devised after the destruction of the well-field system was at best a makeshift adaptation to the circumstances of any given period. They were not worth discussing because once the unity of farmer and soldier in the well-field militia had been broken, there was no way to put it back together again.

The T'ang equal-field system was the best of the makeshift programs of a "later age" of decline, but what made it superior was its granting of land in combination with assigning military service to the grantee (*kŭpchŏn chŏngbyŏng*), not the creation of *fu* attached to the capital guards (*wei*). He believed that his plan did approximate the well-field system in one respect: assigning troops to units in close proximity to their villages. In the Chou the soldiers of districts near the capital were attached directly to the capital chief military official, the Ssu-ma (Sama in Korean), while peasant-soldiers of the remote outer regions were assigned to the chief regional officials or military commanders. This was a principle that should not be changed no matter what the terminology used to distinguish territorial units.[19]

Assignment of Troops Near their Homes

To eliminate long-distance travel by soldiers to their duty stations, Yu specified that the capital guards were to be filled only by peasants living in the Kyŏnggi area around the capital, and the soldiers of the provinces would serve in garrisons closest to their homes. The boundaries of the nation were, of course, the first line of defense, and in view of the two Manchu invasions of 1627 and 1637, the Yalu River area was obviously the area of greatest concern. Yu believed it was much better to move people to frontiers and settle them there permanently to provide a defensive force against invaders rather than move large central or capital armies from the interior to the border only when invasions occurred. He cited the testimony of a number of Chinese statesmen and generals to justify the adoption of this plan for Korea.

Ch'ao Ts'o of the Former Han, in advocating this policy in the mid-second century B.C. as a defense against the Hu barbarians, argued that permanent residents would be familiar with the terrain and would fight to the death against the Hu barbarians to save their families and relatives. Lu Chih of the late eighth-century T'ang period complained that troops sent from mid-China to the remote frontier were unhappy and lonely; only those born on the frontier would fight willingly.[20]

Since soldiers in the provinces would be serving in units closest to their homes, it was necessary to improve the organization, location, and disposition of provincial forces, and spell out in detail the assignments and responsibilities of each level of provincial defense, from the village and district to the larger military bases and garrisons. Yu noted that in his own time many of the provincial army commanders' headquarters were located on the periphery of provincial territory rather than in a central district town. Probably for this reason, the commanders served on temporary duty without their families. Yu wanted to relocate the sites of the headquarters and lengthen the tour of duty allowing dependents to live with the commander. He also complained that the coastal garrisons were simply scattered around without relation to topography or strategic planning, that some were too far inland or in remote places, and should be relocated near populated areas.

Furthermore, as a late fourteenth-century governor of Chŏlla Province, Chŏn Noksaeng, had once pointed out, eighteen special bases had been established in the province as a consequence of Wakō raids, but the garrison commanders tended to act as independent satraps, recruiting men as soldiers on their own and then using them for personal gain. The garrison commanders became self-appointed tax collectors and their soldiers were their agents. The Inhogun special forces raised at that time to resist the pirates ended up as oppressors of the people. Chŏn asked that the bases be abolished.

Yu remarked that a similar situation prevailed in his own time. Even though the garrison commanders (*chinjang*) could not be totally abolished, the garrisons could be put under the jurisdiction of the district magistrates. He also proposed eliminating superfluous garrisons, relocating the remainder, and putting their commanders on long-term duty with their families. This reform would reduce arbitrary taxation and rationalize strategic defense.[21]

Concentration of Frontier Forces

Yu Hyŏngwŏn cited a number of Chinese sources to justify an argument against the excessive fragmentation of military forces on the Korean frontier. Ou-yang Hsiu of the Sung, for example, had complained that in his own time frontier forces were too finely subdivided into small, walled-town garrisons, and strategic defensive positions were staffed by only a few soldiers. He argued that these small garrisons were too weak to defend against a concentrated force of invaders.[22]

Ch'iu Chün made virtually the same remarks for the Ming. In the early Ming dynasty (during the Hung-wu and Yung-lo eras, 1368–98, 1402–24), the troops on the frontier were able to defend a border that was much longer than in Sung times because troops were concentrated in a few strategic places. By the Cheng-t'ung era (1436–49), however, the mistake was made of dividing up frontier troops into a number of small redoubts, repeating the mistake warned against by Ou-yang Hsiu of the Sung.[23]

Weaknesses of the Chin'gwan System

Yu also believed that a hierarchical organization of provincial bases backed up by local troops under district magistrates was also necessary. His thinking on this question was heavily influenced by Yu Sŏngnyŏng's proposal offered initially in 1591 just prior to Hideyoshi's invasion, and with greater force in 1594 during the period of armistice, to establish a phalanx of local garrisons that would enable multilayered lines of defense against an invading enemy.[24]

The essence of the system was decentralized command and responsibility. Commanders would be given authority to train their troops in peacetime, and in wartime to organize the troops, form them into units, and defend the territory under their charge. The area under the jurisdiction of the *chin'gwan* would consist of several civil districts so that it could mobilize a force sufficiently large to resist an invader.[25] Yet one wonders how efficacious this plan would have been had it been tried against Hideyoshi. Hideyoshi's initial landing force at Pusan in 1592 was 18,000 troops, but five days later there were 40,000 Japanese on Korean soil, and by the end of the next month, 156,000.[26] It is doubtful that even a large garrison under the *chin'gwan* system could have held out against such superior numbers without the assistance of divisions of mobile reserve forces.

Both Yu Sŏngnyŏng and Yu Hyŏngwŏn probably misunderstood the true nature of the *chin'gwan* system adopted under Sejo in the mid-fifteenth century. Although this system established a hierarchy of command in three tiers of garrisons and called for distribution of army bases in the interior and naval bases along the coast, the fundamental principle of organization was that the civil district magistrate would assume military responsibilities for the defense of his own walled town. On paper, one could draw a diagram that might suggest the capacity of large inland bases to mobilize the troops of the subordinate garrisons under their command, but in fact the troops of each inland garrison were drawn from the peasants residing in the district, and each district walled town was still vulnerable to attack by concentrated, superior forces.

Furthermore, the *chin'gwan* system deteriorated before it was tested, and it may be that the seeds of that deterioriation were found within the system itself. Since district magistrates were civil officials who at best were more interested in tax collection than military training and defense, they began to reduce troop strength to collect substitute cloth payments, and they neglected the periodic training of the peasant soldiers. Because the country was not subjected to major inland invasions, the internal army garrisons in the district walled towns were neglected or ceased to function. Then when Japanese raids along the coast began to increase in frequency after 1500, the coastal towns, garrisons, and naval bases had to bear the brunt of the attack, and attention was shifted to the build-up of naval garrisons.

Another flaw of the *chin'gwan* system was that the bases and chains of command of the army and navy were kept so distinct that cooperation between the services was impossible during wartime. Even in emergencies, provincial army commanders could not mobilize marines assigned to the coastal bases and the provincial naval commanders could not command soldiers assigned to army garrisons. Thus when the naval bases were attacked by Japanese pirates and raiders, the only way to adjust to the new situation was to increase troop strength in the coastal bases by shifting the permanent assignments of peasant infantrymen at inland garrisons to duty at the naval bases, stripping those inner army bases of their troop strength. It was only after the the *Samp'o waeran* uprising of Japanese residents at the Three Ports in 1510 that some attempt was made to allow interservice command, primarily by allowing provincial army commanders concurrent jurisdiction over marines or naval garrisons.[27] In other words, contrary to Yu Sŏngnyŏng's idealistic image of the solid phalanx of rear garrisons and defense lines backing up the front line of coastal garrisons, the actual experience with Japanese attacks in the late fifteenth century demonstrated that the *chin'gwan* system was at first too rigid and static and did not allow the mobile and flexible transfer of troops from inland areas to points of vulnerability along the coast.

Even after the government decided to drain the inland areas of troops by reassigning them to the coastal garrisons and naval bases, laxity in the administration of the naval bases led to a shift in naval defense strategy. At first each naval base maintained a force of marines on permanent duty on men-of-war, trained constantly and kept on alert so that the first line of defense against a naval attack would be a fleet of ships at sea. Because commanders of naval bases failed to maintain the ships and men in a constant state of readiness, however, after 1484 the government decided to begin construction of more formidable forts and redoubts at the naval bases to provide land-based defense against attack from sea. Because it was recognized that it was no longer possible to maintain a fleet at sea, the effect of the shift in strategy was to convert naval bases into land or army bases, and soon the marines were replaced by land troops. Since the system of inland army bases had already fallen into desuetude, by the beginning of the sixteenth century the country was defended by a thin line of coastal army bases – both the original front line of patrolling vessels and the rear echelon of inland garrisons had atrophied or disappeared.

In short, the *chin'gwan* system was fundamentally flawed because it was a static system of fragmented and small political and military units incapable of responding quickly to coastal attacks concentrated at certain points. Its chief merit had nothing to do with national defense; it was primarily a device for repressing small-scale domestic rebellion. As soon as the Japanese pirate raids along the coast began in the late fifteenth century, the weaknesses of *chin'gwan* organization were revealed and changes – not all of which were particularly effective – had to be introduced.[28]

For that matter, the *chesŭng pangnyak* strategy may not have been such a bad remedy for the static, inflexible, and decentralized nature of the earlier *chin'gwan* system. It was based on the idea of immediate mobilization of larger scale forces than could be mustered by magistrates of district towns or even larger *chin'gwan* that supervised several district towns. By directing that troops from a number of areas immediately proceed to command centers, the system provided, theoretically at least, a sufficiently large force to meet an invader. Yu Sŏngnyŏng objected to the staging areas in 1592 being camps in open fields rather than fully fortified garrisons, but if troop quality had been high and the forces had not been forced to wait until commanders arrived from the capital, such forces might have had the advantage of mobility over the *chin'gwan* fortresses. In any case, it was better than the dysfunctional *chin'gwan* system.

Yu Hyŏngwŏn's adoption of Yu Sŏngnyŏng's proposal for the establishment of larger military bases with a larger complement of troops was at least a reasonable attempt to remedy the problem of scattered and undermanned local military bases. How far Yu Hyŏngwŏn had come from the early Chosŏn fear of independent military power is shown by his proposal to put the provincial Chŏltosa (Army Commander) in charge of all the garrisons (*chin'gwan*) of a province, which he estimated would vary from two to six depending on the province. The term was the same as the Chieh-tu-shih (Regional Commander) of T'ang China, a symbol of regional military usurpation in China ever since the An Lu-shan rebellion in the eighth century.

Yu, however, did not think of the Chŏltosa, or provincial army commander, as an officer with exclusive jurisdiction over military, let alone civil, affairs. To be sure, during peacetime he would take charge of training, and during wartime he would lead the troops to battle while the provincial governor remained at his post to continue supervision over general affairs. But if the Chŏltosa were killed in combat, the governor would then assume command of the army and the various commanders. This arrangement was another illustration of Yu's belief that too strict a separation of military and civil responsibilities was contrary to the classical lesson of the Chou era that all officials were to have both civil and military capabilities.[29]

The provincial command garrisons, the *chin'gwan*, would be headed by garrison commanders called Chŏlchesa (equivalent to the Ying-chiang in Ch'i Chi-kuang's system). This commander would also have concurrent civil jurisdiction over the district or county seat where his garrison was located (under the title of Chinsa), and the magistrates of other towns subordinated to his command would be given lower ranking military titles. The Chŏlchesa could command any number of subordinate district units, depending on how the final details of organization were worked out. These subordinate units would be commanded by the district magistrate, who would supervise the battalion commanders. The rest of the organization down to the squad would, of course, be based on the *sog'o* system of organization.

The advantages of this organization were its regularity and simplicity. Yu conceded that the actual number of troops in any district might not allow for perfect adherence to the quotas of his various troops units, but this could be solved by a little flexibility in assigning extra personnel to units of neighboring villages. It would still be less of a problem than

> at the present time when the names of [various types of soldiers] is so numerous and the soldiers of each of the administrative districts are all divided up among so many different categories, and each category has a different commander. . . . The soldiers might be in one district and the officers in another, and many of the officers and men do not know each other's faces. The one in charge of the soldiers is the magistrate but the one who commands them [in the field] is the officer; the one who instructs them and reviews them in peacetime is the magistrate, but the one who leads them into difficulty and commands them in combat is the officer. When someone earns merit or commits a crime, should we hold the magistrate or the officer responsible? There could not be any greater confusion in the military system than this.[30]

Yu's critique here is again based on his well-field bias rather than any sound principle of military organization. Modern armies are based on the principle of professionalism, and it is presumed that the command structure consists of a professional officer corps rather than civilian magistrates. Yu sought to clarify command and responsibility, but he wanted neither a thoroughly professional army led by army officers alone nor a permanent army of trained soldiers. He preferred his duty soldiers to serve only for a couple of months at a time with idle intervals of over a year, and he provided for the inclusion of the provincial governor and district magistrate at certain levels of the military system in accordance with his well-field militia principles.

Sog'o Organization: Centralized Command

Yu Hyŏngwŏn claimed that he admired Ch'i Chi-kuang's system of organization because it was in tune with the hierarchy of military units recorded in the *Rites of Chou*. Even though the size of a state's forces would vary with its population – the Son of Heaven had six armies while the smallest feudal state had only one – the system of organization would be the same for all. It was also not necessary to be too literal in the adoption of the quotas: "Whether you are dealing in units of tens, hundreds, thousands, or ten thousands, they all follow the same principle and are just multiples of one another and that is all. . . . The military systems of both ancient and modern times in neither case stick [too closely] to fixed quotas."[31] The basic principle of this organization was to create a fixed order, simplify training, and concentrate responsibility in the hands of the unit commander.

Yu Sŏngnyŏng had specified regulations governing the recruitment of officers for the battalion or company commanders that were not fully consistent with the well-field ideal that civilian leaders and magistrates would automatically assume military responsibilities in the military chain of command during wartime. Following his view, Yu Hyŏngwŏn also recommended that these posts be filled by a selection process based on a certain degree of military talent rather than simply giving incumbent magistrates command. The battalion commanders were to be selected from men who had previously been local officials (*hyanggwan*), or were currently dormitory students (*naesasaeng*) in Yu's proposed academy at the capital, or were currently company commanders with exceptional ability. They would command the company commanders, supervise training, and lead the regiment during the spring and autumn bivouac exercises. Yu obviously intended these battalion commanders to be chosen without discrimination from both civil and military officials, assuming the cultivation of an elite skilled in the martial as well as the literary arts.

He did, however, allow for company commanders to be selected on some grounds of heredity or status as well as talent, restrictions that were not included in Yu Sŏngnyŏng's original *sog'o* system. In addition to the pool of men who passed military selection examinations (the *musŏn*) and students of the outer dormitories exempted from military service, he also allowed recruitment of descendants of high officials, royal relatives, and merit subjects, and talented members of the elite capital units, the Loyal and Righteous Guards and Loyal and Obedient Guards. But these company commanders were to be watched constantly to eliminate the incompetent. They were to remain with their men both on training and tours of duty, test the troops in archery, and maintain discipline by reward and punishment. They would be required to pass periodic archery shoots and written examinations and if found wanting, they would be subjected to punishment along with the magistrate of their home town who recommended them. Yu purposely designed a strict disciplinary system based on praise and blame, complaining that at present all such disciplinary rules were a dead letter.[32]

Another type of official, the Kip'aegwan (Officer of the Banner and Tally), was to act as liaison between the commander of the main provincial garrison and the subordinate garrisons (*chin'gwan*). They already existed but Yu complained that they were uniformly men of inferior quality. Yu wanted to station them at each garrison and have them examined on the four military classics and the writings of Ch'i Chi-kuang.[33]

At the same time superfluous officials left over from the old system, the Tohundo, were to be abolished, not only useless ones with no duties, but also the garrison commanders or Yŏngjang created in recent years who only duplicated the work of the provincial military commanders and the magistrates of garrison towns. In fact these Yŏngjang had taken over the job of making rounds of inspection previously done by the Provincial Military Commander, who now sat around in idleness doing nothing but attending parties and banquets. Another superfluous post, that of Chunggun (middle officer or governor's military aide) stationed at the governor's yamen, was also to be abolished.[34]

Yu also called for elimination of the personal aides or soldiers called ivory soldiers (*abyŏng*) assigned not only to military officers but to civil yamen as well. Only the provincial governor should be allowed a quota of anywhere from one to three hundred of them, and their positions were to be filled by the *sog'o* (slave?) soldiers attached to the district town in which the governor's office was located. The ivory soldiers were to be trained like the *sog'o* troops and not simply used as cloth taxpayers according to current practice. There was no need for them in other yamen at all, and they had never been part of the early Chosŏn military system.[35] In addition, the permanent military police (*kullo*) stationed at military headquarters could be replaced by runners (*saryŏng*).[36]

Finally, Yu hoped to eliminate corruption in the provincial garrisons by providing regular salaries to the commanders. Like the clerks and runners in provincial and district civil yamen, the provincial army and navy commanders in charge of garrisons (*chinjang*) were not provided with regular salaries. Yu felt that this was the main cause of the common practice among garrison commanders of discharging soldiers on duty in return for payment of a cloth tax instead, "a practice that has become so bad that it cannot be abolished." Since civilian clerks and runners at these garrisons were also not given salaries, the commanders were using troops to perform their functions, at some reduction of the number of trained soldiers available for defense. The solution to this was to provide quotas of regular salaried clerks so that the soldiers performing their duties could be returned to military service.[37]

Troop Training

Yu also endorsed Yu Sŏngnyŏng's praise of Ch'i Chi-kuang's *sog'o* organization as a remedy for the almost total confusion among Korean troops during Hideyoshi's invasion. Yu Sŏngnyŏng had described Korean troops in the following fashion:

> Basically they do not know anything about fighting, and they have no units such as platoons, squads, banners, or companies to which they are attached. They are in confusion and without order, make a big racket and run around in chaos, not knowing what to do with their hands, feet, ears, or eyes. And then all of a sudden

> these men are placed in the midst of arrows and stones where they have to fight to the death and give their all in the fight to gain a victory over the enemy. Is this not indeed difficult [for them to do]?[38]

The inadequacies of military training were as serious as backward technology. Yu Sŏngnyŏng, of course, had criticized the lack of training among troops during the Imjin Wars and blamed it on the practice of excusing men from duty in return for cloth payments. He also mentioned the laxity of the officers in calling the roll during training sessions, and the general disorganization in the ranks:

> In particular, our military system is not in good condition and the standards of order are in a state of confusion. Our weapons and tools are not 'sharpened' [in good repair], our ranks are not well ordered, and our pledges [? *yaksok*] are not clear. Our soldiers do not hear the beat of the metal drums with their ears nor distinguish the colors of the [unit] banners with their eyes. They do not know what it means to sit [in wait] or to stand, to attack or to thrust. And when all of a sudden they do meet with a powerful enemy, the officers do not know their troops, nor the troops their officers, and they are broken up like clods of earth and smashed like tiles.[39]

He cited Cho Hŏn, who had also criticized the absence of regular training exercises, the lack of organization and discipline during training sessions after his return from his trip to China:

> The ranks of the troops are not clear and the banners drums are not in order, and anyone who observed them would think that they only look like little children at play. If it is like this in peacetime, what could we do during wartime? Even though we have regulations requiring soldiers on duty to train in shooting and take military examinations, the officials in charge of training only receive a piece of paper [affidavit?] from the absentees [who receive] absolutely no training in the methods of shooting the bow and arrow. . . . [In China, by contrast], the men engage in military training every day, so that there is no concern about the state of the army.[40]

Yu Hyŏngwŏn, writing almost a century later, also felt that the regulations for training of both duty and off-duty soldiers and periodic testing of their skills was lax and that the country lacked a reserve guard, obviously a problem derivative of the substitution of cloth taxes for service and training. As we will see, his concerns were reflected in his extensive proposals for the training of all kinds of troops on a regular basis. The officers were even more of a problem, for they were not selected on the basis of skill or ability.[41]

Duty Assignments

His most serious concern, however, was for problems of organization, particularly those that resulted from irrational planning and thinking. Marines (*sugun*), for example, were recruited from soldiers who lived inland, even in the mountains, rather than along the seacoast, while the able-bodied males of the seacoast were recruited for duty as infantrymen. Yulgok had attempted to remedy this problem when governor of Hwanghae Province prior to the Japanese invasions, but his reform was rescinded by his successor.[42] Yu felt that it had become difficult to solve this problem because military assignments had become hereditary, as had so many other things in Chosŏn society.

"The practice of hereditary performance of military duties is basically a bad law. Even though these tasks have become hereditary, in fact there is no reason why they cannot be changed. It is only that the people in charge of affairs see the harm done to the state and people but treat it cursorily and have not yet done anything about it."[43]

Yu also discussed irrationalities in the disposition of warships, the assignment of troops to ships and garrisons, the lack of territorial jurisdiction of naval garrison commanders, poor staffing of warning beacon stations, and the absence of a reserve national guard to defend cities and towns.[44]

Naval Reorganization

Yu also found the organization of the navy and its garrisons and ships confused and irregular. Under the pre-Hideyoshi system, marines (*sugun*) were under the command of the naval garrison commander (*sujinjang*). The district civil magistrates had the responsibility of recruiting men for service but they neglected their responsibilities. The number of warships and quotas of naval soldiers were determined for each garrison, but after the Imjin War, the quotas of ships were increased on an ad hoc basis and assigned to seacoast district towns without any specific plan. Yu hoped to rationalize the system by limiting the assignment of ships to naval garrisons alone and abolishing those under the jurisdiction of civil magistrates. Evidently he believed that naval expertise was not within the capacity of even his ideal, well-rounded officials.[45]

Like the army organization, the naval command structure would be arranged in hierarchical fashion. The largest command would be the Regional Naval Headquarters (T'ongjeyŏng) with seven warships (including one armored turtle-boat) and 2,100 marines and able-oarsmen, of which either 105 or 210 men would be on duty during windy or calm days, respectively. The Provincial Naval Commander's Headquarters (Susayŏng) would have five ships (including one turtle-boat) and 1,500 men, and the lowest naval garrison, the Manhojin, would have two warships, 300 marines and 300 able oarsmen, with 150 serving on duty at any time. The Manhojin flotilla was to consist of two warships (*chŏnsŏn*), two armored ships (*pangp'aesŏn*), two troopships (*pyŏngsŏn*), and four patrol boats (*sahusŏn*). The warship was a masted brig of war with a crew of 80 boatmen and oarsmen, and 77 musketeers (*p'osu*) and archers (*sasu*). He listed a total of 12,500 marines for naval garrisons for the southern provinces, leaving the northwest to future determination.[46] Although the hierarchic system of quotas appears rather simple in conception, it constituted a major reform since the complement of ships, troops, and sailors in some places in the existing system bore no relation to the strategic importance of the location.

Yu was hard pressed to devise a solution for recruiting a full complement of marines and oarsmen because he estimated that no more than 10 percent of the existing quotas were actually filled, and there were hardly enough sailors to run the ships during training periods. He was reluctant to authorize the use of private slaves for marines, probably because they were either domestic servants or cultivators unused to fighting at sea. He also insisted on adhering to the principle of recruiting naval personnel from the inhabitants of seacoast towns. He solved the problem by suggesting that men of good status be used as naval soldiers, while slaves and men without land grants would be oarsmen. Contrary to current practice, marines would have support personnel to provide them with monthly grain rations like land troops, and the soldiers would be divided into shifts that rotated on and off duty. He stipulated periodic testing of skill, elimination of frequent transfers, and punishment for commanders who exempted men from duty in return for cloth payments.

Someone must have suggested to him that since it would be impossible to guarantee that naval commanders in distant locations would not release their men in return for cloth payments, it would be preferable to reduce the duties of the marines, use them as servants and runners of the garrison commanders, and save funds by reducing the number of their support personnel. But he was adamant in insisting on providing rations and preventing exemptions and subsitute cloth tax payments, the two major reasons in his view why the naval garrisons were lacking full complements of personnel in his own time.

> If people are exempted from military service and [soldiers] have their grain and cloth rations cut off, then the people living in the areas near the garrisons will gradually leave the area, and within a decade all the garrisons will become desolated. After a long period of time goes by, all the posts of the border [coastal] commanders will be held in low esteem, and they will be regarded as no more important than the present day village constables.[47]

Furthermore, he called for the cessation of the practice of using garrison naval soldiers and personnel for transporting local products like bamboo and wood to capital headquarters. Instead, all such items would be handled by the new *taedong* system by which district towns remitted grain surtaxes to the capital for the purchase of such items.[48]

Unfortunately, the tragic aspect of his criticism of the Chosŏn navy in his own day was that it indicated a continuation of the same deficiencies that had weakened Korean forces before Hideyoshi's invasions over a half-century before.

WEAPONS AND TECHNOLOGY

Muskets

Yu Sŏngnyŏng's Praise of Foreign Methods. Yu Hyŏngwŏn was inspired by Yu Sŏngnyŏng's argument for the importance of weapons and technology. He was also disturbed about deficiencies in conventional technology, such as poor workmanship in bows, arrows, spears, and armor, shortages of warships, cavalry horses, carts and chariots, poor construction of walls and ramparts, and poorly maintained beacon warning post-station systems.[49] He also cited Yu Sŏngnyŏng's criticism of the inferior and backward equipment of Korean troops during the Imjin War and mentioned that he was among the first to record awareness of the superiority of the musket to the bow and arrow, especially in its range, a lesson learned from bitter experience. "When [our] soldiers are lined up against the enemy ranks, our arrows do not reach the enemy while their musket balls rain down upon us."[50]

Majority opinion during the invasions was opposed to the adoption of the musket or fowling piece because Korean customs were different from foreigners and muskets were believed to be either unsuitable to Korea or of no value in warfare. Yu Sŏngnyŏng urged the court to overcome its prejudice against newfangled things, just as other nations, present and past, had gained an advantage by responding quickly to the superior techniques of their enemies.

> If you think the world is divided into geographical regions, that the talents and skills of each are different, and that those of one region cannot be understood by another, then how do you explain how [in the Chou period in China] the armored soldiers of the state of Wu learned from the state of Ch'u her method of fighting on chariots and in the end was able to subjugate Ch'u?
>
> Even if one does not talk about examples from remote antiquity, in recent times in China they did not have muskets [either]; they first learned about them from the Wakō pirates in Che-chiang Province. Ch'i Chi-kuang trained troops in their use for several years until they became one of the skills of the Chinese, who subsequently used them to defeat the Japanese.[51]

He developed his argument on the superiority of the musket to a general theory of the importance of adaptation and progress:

> If you look at it from this [point of view], there is not that much difference in human nature [among different peoples]; it is just that their customs are different. I have never heard it said that something could not be accomplished just

> because of custom. They say that the silk-clad gentry and the people in the streets all consider the musketeers [*p'osu*] and "killers" [*salsu*: close-combat sword, pike, and spearmen] [introduced into Korea during the Imjin Wars] as something laughable, and this is really so. It is human nature [for people] to get used to what is easy, and for people to become chronically used to repetitious habits.
>
> In this time of crisis we prefer to use the inferior views of former days to disparage and criticize [new] and creative opinions. All sorts of worthless views are floating around and a ruckus is stirred up in the capital and provinces. A hundred means are used to obstruct things. Meanwhile, people who are [supposed to have] some knowledge of things, on the contrary, beat the drum and stir up waves to increase their influence [against change]. Is this right?[52]

His forceful advocacy of the adoption of the advanced technology of foreigners would have stood the Koreans in good stead in the nineteenth century, when the elite of that era found it so difficult to appreciate the value of gunboats and cannons. By the middle of the next century, however, Koreans were still finding it difficult to make much progress in the manufacture and use of firearms as a primary military weapon.

Hyojong's Policy on Muskets and Ammunition. King Hyojong (r. 1649–59) was quite interested in the technological aspect of military defense during his reign, in particular the manufacture of weapons and the construction of walls and moats. Fowling pieces or muskets had become a primary weapon after Hideyoshi's invasions and there were two sources of supply for both muskets and cannon by Hyojong's time – a monthly production quota levied on the province, and the production of armories, such as the Special Armory (Pyŏlchoch'ŏng) of the Weapons Bureau (Kun'gisi) and the manufactories attached to special units like the Military Training Agency and Defense Command responsible for the protection of the Namhan fort.

Despite Hyojong's ardor for more weapons, however, his plans were obstructed by financial shortages and competing uses for metal. In 1649, 1650, and 1652 the monthly quotas of muskets for one or more provinces was canceled because of economic hardship or because copper and iron were diverted for use as metallic currency. In 1654, when the Ch'ing court demanded Korean musketeers to help fight the Russians, Hyojong wanted to increase allocations of funds for weapons construction, but famine conditions prevented it. The result was a severe shortage of weapons for the troops. As one official reported that year, of the 1,500 troops assigned to the Defense Command of the Namhan fort from ten surrounding districts, 300 had no muskets, and in 1655 about half the 2,000 men from Kangwŏn Province assigned to the same unit were without firearms. A shortage of bullets only compounded the difficulty.[53]

In 1654, the method of financing the manufacture of muskets and bullets by a provincial quota system was readopted. Large districts had to pay the cost for 2 muskets, 8 *kŭn* of gunpowder, and 400 rounds of ammunition every month while the smallest district only had to furnish 1 musket, 4 *kŭn* of gunpowder, and 200 rounds every six months. The annual production quota financed by this province was probably around 250 weapons. But the districts were not given the responsibility for the actual manufacture of this material, just paying for it. The funds were to be accumulated by a grain tax on land, and then when the *taedong* system of substituting a grain surtax for the local products tribute tax was adopted in the seventeenth century on a piecemeal basis, these revenues were used to pay for the monthly district weapons quota. In Hyojong's reign, the *taedong* system had not been extended to the whole country, so allocation of grain from the *taedongmi* or *taedong* rice revenue to pay for weapons was only applied to Ch'ungch'ŏng and Kyŏnggi provinces. Thus the quotas of guns, gunpowder, and bullets were converted into grain price equivalents.

At first, district magistrates received allocations of grain from the *taedong* rice revenues and then remitted them to the Weapons Bureau (Kun'gisi) as payment for the production of the material. Later, in King Sukchong's reign (r. 1674–1720) the rice was shipped to the Sangp'yŏngch'ŏng (Ever-Normal Bureau), which in turn paid the Weapons Bureau for muskets and the tribute middlemen (*kong'in*) of the Samgun'mun (Three Armies Office) for the ammunition. In those areas where the *taedong* rice tax was not collected, grain was collected as a weapons tax in accordance with the material resources of the district overall.[54]

It is hard to estimate the total number of muskets in use in the mid-1650s, but in 1656 one decree called for the production of 1,600 muskets each for the governor's and provincial military commanders' yamen in Kyŏngsang and Chŏlla provinces – a total of 6,400 muskets for the two provinces – which does not sound like a large number unless some troops were already equipped with weapons. If the production quota per province was about 250 a year for six of the eight provinces, one might expect annual production of 1,500 pieces, really not enough to supply more than a fraction of the total force of infantry. Even this number might be too large considering that production was frequently suspended for lack of funds or to reduce tax burdens on the population during famine conditions.

On the other hand, the demand for muskets may have been limited by King Hyojong's own hesitancy about the superiority of firearms. When Yi Wan, commander of the Royal Division, complained that the armed forces were relying too heavily on musketeers because a sudden rainstorm could drench the powder supplies and silence the army's muskets, instead of demanding that all commanders make sure that the men keep their powder dry, or that more tarpaulins be made to cover the powder, Hyojong ordered that the number of bowmen of the Defense Command at Namhan be increased to half the force.[55]

Even though the Ch'ing court asked directly for Korean musketeers to be sent as reinforcements in the fighting against the Russians in 1654 and 1658, the constant fear of discovery by the Manchu authorities also inhibited the production of guns. Muskets were even kept locked up except for actual training sessions in North Hamgyŏng Province in the northeast. Furthermore, the quality of Korean weapons was not up to the standard of Japanese muskets. When the Ch'ing court demanded 100 muskets from Korea in 1657, the government scoured the country for Japanese muskets but found only 60 good enough to send; of all the Korean guns available, only 30 were accurate enough to pass muster.[56]

Yu Hyŏngwŏn was very much in favor of the use of firearms, and he included testing in the shooting of fowling pieces or muskets (*choch'ong*) in his proposed major military skill examinations for soldiers of the capital guard, citing Ch'i Chi-kuang's *Chi-hsiao hsin-shu* as a precedent. He also stipulated the exact amounts of these fowling pieces, rounds of lead musket balls, and gunpowder for each military garrison or civil district.[57]

Yet his quotas do not indicate that he imagined that the fowling piece or musket would become the standard weapon for all footsoldiers in the army. A strategic prefecture (Taebu or Tohobu), for example, would only have 24 of them with 4,800 rounds of ammunition (200 per musket), while the smallest civil district (*hyŏn*) would have but 6 muskets and 1,200 rounds.[58] Since there were only about 330 districts in the whole country, Yu could not have envisioned more than a total of four to five thousand muskets for local units.

Assuming that King Hyojong in 1656 ordered 6,400 muskets to be made for the governors and provincial army commanders in the two southern provinces and was having about 1,500 muskets manufactured each year in the late 1650s, Yu's quota represented only about three or four year's production at that level. One must conclude that he expected spears, swords, bows and arrows to remain the main types of small arms for a national army of about 220,000 men, let alone 400,000 support personnel functioning as a reserve militia.

Cannon

Hyojong was even more concerned with the manufacture of cannon than muskets. There is no evidence that Hyojong ordered the casting of cannon after his accession in 1649 until the end of 1652, when he told his officials he wanted to improve the quality of Korean cannon by melting down all the copper or brass cannon used on ships of the southern fleet and convert them to wrought iron (*suktong*) because the brass cannon had frequently broken apart on firing. This was opposed in early 1653 by Pak Sŏ, his minister of war, on the grounds that brass cannon had long been in use and if they broke apart (or exploded?), it was more the fault of inattentive officers than the guns themselves. Furthermore, conversion would impose too heavy an economic burden on the people, the quality of workmanship would not be good, and the state lacked the financial resources to do it; if it had to be done, it would be better to wait until the next bumper harvest. Hyojong refused to be put off and said that even if wrought iron (*suktong*) cannon could not be made, at least they could be converted to (pig) iron, and he countered with the suggestion that funds could be raised by selling off the brass cannon. Pak later agreed to casting cannon in both both pig iron (*such'ŏl*) and copper (brass) and testing both for comparison.[59] At the urging of Yi Wan and his successor as commander of the Royal Division, Yu Hyŏgyŏn, Hyojong also created a new 510-man unit of cannoneers called the Special Destruction Corps (Pyŏlp'ajin), consisting of 470 powdermakers and 114 ivory soldiers.[60]

Financial shortage, of course, imposed a check on Hyojong's ambition to increase the number of cannon available, and the minister of taxation, concurrently responsible for military logistics (as concurrent commissioner or Chejo in the Quartermaster Bureau, Kunjagam) frequently opposed the minister of war, who also acted as a concurrent commissioner in the Weapons Bureau (Kun'gisi). At the beginning of 1654, for example, Minister of War Wŏn Tup'yo requested that the supplies of copper at Tongnae be sent to the capital for the casting of Pullyanggi (Fou-lang-chi, i.e., Portuguese or simply, Western-style) cannon, but he was opposed by Minister of Taxation Yi Sibang, who asked for all metal left over after 142 weapons were made for use in making metal utensils. When Hyojong decided, however, to devote the copper to gun manufacture, Yi protested that the metal had been purchased with land tax revenues collected by his ministry and that the king had already promised the metal to his department. Even though one might expect Yi Sibang to give priority to military uses of metal since he was also commander of the Defense Command stationed at the Namhan fort, in this case he was wearing his civil finance minister's cap and defending his bureaucratic bailiwick. Eventually Hyojong retreated and agreed to assign some of the copper to the Ministry of Taxation.[61]

Another hindrance to cannon casting was the competition for copper for the minting of cash as a medium of exchange, a favorite project of Kim Yuk, one of the leading economic experts of the day and father of the *taedong* tribute tax reform. He requested the use of copper for minting cash in 1651 and the governor of Chŏlla did so in 1656. As Ch'a Munsŏp has pointed out, probably because of the demand for copper for currency, evidence of the casting of cannon is scarcely to be found after 1657.[62]

One might conclude, however, that the lack of surplus production on a national level, and the corresponding shortage of tax revenues combined with a lack of metal ore production in Korea itself, obstructed any policy of large-scale musket and cannon manufacture. This sorry situation prevailed during the reign of one of Korea's most aggressive kings, so there was plenty of room for improvement, but Yu Hyŏngwŏn mentioned nary a word on cannons, confining his remarks primarily to muskets. This omission was a singular defect for someone who insisted on building up a better defense system and admired Yu Sŏngnyŏng's appeal to cast off custom and borrow the superior military technology of foreigners.

Gunpowder

Yu also neglected the problem of gunpowder and its manufacture, a serious component of the national capacity in firearms. King Hyojong had promoted the manufacture of gunpowder to supply his muskets and cannons. He established a

Nitrate Bureau (Yŏnsoch'ŏng) in 1650, but its facilities and operation were less than adequate; the nitrates were often left outside in the rain and lost their potency. As mentioned above, gunpowder production was financed initially by a gunpowder tribute levy, to be paid in kind, imposed on local districts according to their size, but after the adoption of the *taedong* land surtax, the government was supposed to purchase gunpowder on the market with surtax revenues. Evidently, Hyojong was reluctant to apply the new system to gunpowder manufacture. After 1653 Ch'ungch'ŏng Province, one of the first provinces to institute the *taedong* system, did become a major location for the manufacture of gunpowder from nitrates, but the government continued to allocate gunpowder quotas to each district. The entire province of Kyŏngsang was forbidden from purchasing gunpowder from any other province to fulfill the government quotas. That is, the government insisted that each district take responsibility for manufacturing its own quota, like the backyard furnaces of Mao's Great Leap Forward. This system imposed a heavy burden for those districts unskilled in its manufacture and undoubtedly increased the cost of production because the people had to scurry around gathering wood for fuel, axes, and cauldrons for boiling and refining the ore. One official recommended in 1654 that districts that did not usually manufacture gunpowder simply be allowed to purchase it on the market.

Nevertheless, Hyojong wanted to make Ch'ungch'ŏng the base for gunpowder production, not only because it was close to the capital, but also because he was afraid that the manufacturing techniques would be leaked to Japan if its production were allowed in Kyŏngsang Province in the southeast. He also feared that if it were produced in the northern provinces, the Manchus might become suspicious of Korean intentions. While the fear of Manchu discovery had in fact led to a complete cessation of nitrate manufacture in the north, unauthorized, private nitrate and gunpowder production had already developed in Kyŏngsang in the south, so much so that both items circulated on the open market. In 1654 the commander of the Defense Command even bought his supply on the market there.

Manufacture of these substances required iron for boiling cauldrons, which sometimes broke apart if allowed to cool. The government encouraged iron mining, particularly in the rich veins of the hills near Ŭlsan. On the other hand, little progress was made in solving the problem of the shortage of supply of sulfur needed for converting nitrates to gunpowder. China was now cut off since the Koreans were afraid of arousing Manchu suspicions, and Japan was left as the only source of supply.[63] Again, King Hyojong and many of the active officials at the time were obviously more aware of the problems involved in increasing gunpowder supplies than Yu Hyŏngwŏn, but their efforts had not been successful.

Walls and Forts

Hyojong was also interested in building up walls, fortresses, and fortifications – one of the concerns of Yu Hyŏngwŏn as well – but Hyojong was subjected to a number of constraints of which Yu was apparently unaware. Since almost everyone at court was concerned lest the Manchus discover any major military preparations, even Hyojong deemed it impossible to begin a program of fortification in the northern provinces. He preferred a policy similar to the strategy adopted prior to the second Manchu invasion of 1637, to concentrate on defense of strategic locations around the capital. Thus, he pushed hard for construction of redoubts and fortifications along the coast of Kanghwa Island and wanted to move people there on a permanent basis, even supporting the idea of using men from Chŏlla and assigning the governor of that province to the defense of the island. He also wanted to build a string of forts from Hwanghae Province through Kyŏnggi and Ch'ungch'ŏng, even to and including Chŏlla Province, with Kanghwa Island as the linchpin and the Namhan fort south of Seoul as another major base.

He was opposed not only by the economic specialist Kim Yuk, then minister of the left, but the other two highest civil officials of the time as well. Kim's objections were that the economic situation was too bad to warrant the extra burdens on peasants close to starvation, and that winning the minds of the people was more important than building walls and moats. The debate continued through the late 1650s but progress was slowed by these objections.[64]

Yu Hyŏngwŏn was, like King Hyojong, most interested in the building of defensive walls and moats, probably because of the inadequacy of existing ramparts to check the advance of the Japanese and Manchus over the previous seventy years. Like a variety of other subjects, he was inspired by classical wisdom as well as contemporary experience, and the Chinese classics taught that the methods involved in wall construction had a moral as well as technical component. Good rulers were obliged to build strong walls and deep moats for the protection of their own people. The *Rites of Chou* recorded the existence of a special official (the Chang-ku) to supervise this kind of work, and another (Ssu-hsien) in charge of maps to ascertain the most strategic spots for the construction of defensive fortifications. The *Book of Changes* described strategic forts, the *Book of Poetry* and the *Mencius* praised the rulers who constructed them. Mencius even commented that rulers who failed to build forts in the strategic, precipitous places in the realm would eventually be chased out or destroyed. The dimension of walls was even preserved in classical accounts and commentaries, and the length was graded according to the ranks of the feudal nobles of Chou times.

Another important feature of ancient wall construction were provisions for scheduling the work at just the right time of year. The *Tso-chuan* commentary and the commentary of Hu An-kuo (of the Sung period) on the *Spring and Autumn Annals* both stressed this point; the former noting that construction was to start when the Dragon Star appeared in the heavens and be completed when the sun reached the zenith. Besides the obvious symbolic significance of adjusting human actions to the rhythms of the heavens, the aspiring sage ruler had to make sure that compulsory labor service did not take peasants away from planting, harvesting, and other fundamental tasks of production and livelihood. Rulers of some of the feudal states of Chou times were also described as planning all aspects of construction in minute detail, including distances of travel for workers, food and provisions, limits on the use of materials, and the setting of deadlines for labor – all of which were designed to prevent construction projects from becoming the means for the exploitation of the workers.

Defensive walls became almost a symbol of sage rule, not simply a practical means of defense. Shih Huang-ti, that evil first emperor of the Ch'in dynasty, destroyed all the walls of the late Chou feudal states when he unified the empire in order to subjugate them to Ch'in control. But after the fall of the Ch'in, Emperor Kao-tsu of the Han ordered wall construction in each district (*hsien*). As one commentator remarked: "One can see from this which of the two was broader in foresight and which of the two [dynasties] would last the longest." Ch'iu Chün of Ming times described the two acts almost in moral terms: Ch'in Shih-huang-ti destroyed the walls because he regarded the people of the empire as his enemies and was only concerned that defensive preparations might become a threat to his security, but "Kao-tsu, on the other hand, regarded the officials and people of the empire as one family and was only afraid they might not have places in which to defend themselves against the enemy. He was afraid that perhaps he might have to attend the funerals of people who had lost their lives. This spirit marks the difference between public and private [interest] and is the dividing point between the preservation and loss [of a kingdom]."[65]

For a more recent example of ancient principles in action, Yu cited the action of Emperor Shih-tsung of the Later Chou, who in 955 ordered expansion of the walls of district towns but took pains to keep labor to a minimum and scheduled the work for the winter slack season.[66]

In applying the lessons of antiquity Yu showed a tendency for excessive literalism, just as he did in insisting on the 100-*myo* unit for his land distribution system. He was careful to lay out the dimensions of territories and walls of the various feudal nobles of Chou times and insisted that the principles of establishing a hierarchy of dimensions for the thickness and circumference of walls be followed in contemporary Korea. He adjusted his classical literalism to the contemporary situation, however, by stipulating that the varying sizes of contemporary defensive walls be determined in accordance with the size of the area and amount of population to be defended. Classical wisdom seemed a reasonable remedy for the contemporary Korean situation because not only were current walls in bad repair, missing altogether, or located at some distance from where the people lived, but also in some cases they were usually too "narrow" or small in circumference, encompassing only one or two small villages. A balance had to be struck between areas and populations too small or too large for adequate defense.

Like his arguments for adjusting the rigidities of well-field dimensions to the mountainous topography of Korea by using fractional grants, he urged that fixed quotas of area and population be ignored in certain cases if district towns happened to be located in a valley or mountain pass. "What we ought to do is take into account the intent of the ancients and require that [the system of walls] does not go against what is proper in terms of the lay of the land."[67] Yu took to heart the classical admonition about limiting construction work so it would not interfere with the livehood of the peasantry, although he allowed for the use of land-grant peasants on miscellaneous labor service and hired laborers at any time for minor repairs and small jobs.

For major construction work, however, the whole adult male population, including both regular soldiers and support taxpayers, were to be mobilized. Yu deemed this an appropriate way to use soldiers during peacetime, but he also provided that they be compensated for every thirty days of labor by exempting them from one shift of duty (two months) and the archery examination; cavalry and *sog'o* soldiers would be excused from one year's training and archery examinations for every fifteen days of construction labor.

Contrary to current conditions under which workers were not exempted from other duties, were not given rations, and were subject to demands for bribes, under the new system officials would also pay the workers a ten-day week's worth of rice or three *mal* and hold a celebration banquet. Payment of the workers could be provided from a percentage of the grain transport rice that would be retained in their home districts and by the use of the regular grain payments from support taxpayers. If the support taxpayer lived at some distance from the construction site, the government would work out arrangements for substituting local grain to prevent the burden of shipment over long distances. Officials were to take the distance of the soldier or peasant from the work site and the exact amount of labor needed into consideration and assign men from districts near the site in limited numbers. Work assignments were to be made clear and schedules of work laid out in advance; the workers were not to be rushed, and if the job were not completed by the seasonal time limit, completion was to be put off to the next season. Yu was, indeed, following the teachings of the classics that sage rulers worked out rules for construction in fine detail to make sure that these public works would not become a source of oppression.[68]

He was not sure that high quality construction could be maintained without spelling out every detail of the work procedure and maintaining strict military discipline because Korean work habits were notoriously bad.

> The people of our country are lazy and lax by nature. They are always careless in everything they do and they dissemble, so that the construction of walls and moats is very shoddy. . . . Since the custom of the people has been slipshod, and this has been the case for a very long time, it is very difficult to enlighten them just with the use of words alone. You must first build a wall in accordance with my system in one place, and then have [people in] other places see what has been done and adopt the [same] method.

The men would proceed to the workplace under the command of their local commanding officers, a method not only convenient "but also the way in which the ancients carried out tasks that combined [the work] of large numbers of people. . . ." All such work units were to be coordinated in a military chain of command: every five men under a squad leader, with larger units of thirty, a hundred, five hundred, or a thousand. The unit commanders would be held responsible for the quality of the work; if a wall crumbled within a decade, they were to indicted for criminal negligence.[69]

Yu's concern lest the people be overly burdened with compulsory labor service was confined to the limits outlined by classical texts. The dicta against excessive corvée requirements were motivated not only by his desire not to interfere with agricultural labor during crucial planting and harvesting seasons, but also to bring the labor of peasants or soldiers under the iron discipline of a military regime, and although he was willing to countenance the eventual replacement of private slaves with hired labor, he did not envision a liberal wage market for the construction of defensive walls.

Yu's lack of faith in the technological skills of Korean construction workers doubtless explains why he went to such great detail in recording the dimensions of walls and their slope, the depth of moats, the amount of earth to be moved, the type of cement, the positioning and height of cannon and archery turrets, and the daily work per laborer as recorded in certain Chinese sources as Tu Yu's *T'ung-tien*, and Ch'i Chi-kuang's *Chi-hsiao hsin-shu*. Of course, he adjusted the Chinese figures to Korean conditions, pointing out for example that it took 6,000 monk-soldiers eleven days to repair a wall 2,000 paces long. He calculated the per capita labor requirement at six men for every two paces of wall length, or in the case of new construction of strong and long-lasting walls, twelve men working thirty days to complete two paces of length.

These calculations were his solution to the sorry state of wall construction in Korea where men were frequently called out for ten-day weeks of work but the walls crumbled soon after they were built or repaired. The one case of good work he could think of was the Namhan mountain fort (Namhan sansŏng, south of the Han River), but it was a job that took three years to complete, and on the way half the work had to be redone. "Therefore in fact what should take one year of construction work actually wastes three years' time, it is said."[70]

Following Ch'i Chi-kuang and Yu Sŏngnyŏng, Yu's instructions were particularly detailed on the shape of cannon and archery turrets and ribbed promontories jutting out from the walls.[71] He was obviously eager to adopt both the new cannon and the new kinds of defensive walls that could both resist their impact and provide secure pods for the lobbing of cannonballs on an attacking enemy. Yu Sŏngnyŏng had pointed out in his ten "Essentials of Military Strategy" (*Chŏnsu kiŭi*) that the Korean people were really unskilled in the location and construction of walls; they just followed the shape of the mountains and mountain paths. The turrets on the top of the walls were too low to provide cover for the troops at the top who had to crouch or lie down just to move back and forth. The spaces allowed for small arms fire were too wide because they allowed enemy troops scaling the wall to gain easy access. There was also infrequent use of jutting promontories to provide crossfire or a field of vision to the base of the wall, or the use of peepholes along the base as recently introduced into China. The Chinese also used special cannon emplacements in the moats outside the walls that were particularly effective. These also had yet to be adopted in Korean wall construction. Yu also recorded in his "Precautions Against Attack" (*Chingbirok*) that he had devised his own wall architecture and dimensions one day during Hideyoshi's invasions while sitting on the banks of the Ch'ŏngch'ŏn River near Anju. He proposed constructing gun holes and turrets separated by six to seven hundred paces with a pile of cannon balls stacked by the big guns "like chicken eggs."

"Then when the enemy approaches the walls, he will be hit by a cross fire from the guns. Not to speak of men and horses, even metal and stone could not escape being pulverized by this. . . . All you would have to do is to have several dozen men man the gun turrets and the enemy would not dare draw near."[72]

Yu Hyŏngwŏn recorded, however, that despite the wisdom of Yu Sŏngnyŏng's plan for a field of cannon fire, the government failed to adopt it, not only during the invasions but even to his own time. Just as Ch'i Chi-kuang had been beleaguered by conservatives in Ming China who felt that his new methods of wall and turret construction were newfangled and outlandish, so too did Yu Sŏngnyŏng have to buck the resistance of traditionalists.[73]

Yi Hyŏngsŏk in his magnum opus on the Imjin War commented that Yu Hyŏngwŏn's essay on wall construction was particularly valuable because it emphasized not only the proper construction of mountain forts (*sansŏng*) which were so popular in Korean defensive strategy, but because his advocacy of wall construction around the district towns in the plains rectified one of the major Korean strategic deficiencies during Hideyoshi's invasions. At that time the main defensive policy used in the face of the superior advancing Japanese forces was to "strengthen the walls and clear the countryside," which did not refer simply to clearing the wet and dry fields of all peasants, food, and property and bringing them inside the walls of the district towns, but to moving the entire population and their property to the mountain forts located at remote distances from the villages of the peasants. Because of the general reluctance to move to such quarters, the peasants either neglected to move, failed to maintain the mountain forts in good repair, or delayed their movement to the mountain forts to the last possible minute. The result in most instances was that the advancing Japanese forces were soon upon the villagers before they could seek shelter, and they were forced to flee to the hills and remote valleys and live in hiding without adequate shelter. Even when the policy was followed, it meant that the Korean military commanders abandoned the lowlands and the towns, for the mountain forts, leaving the Japanese unopposed access to the towns and the main travel route from Pusan through Hansŏng (Seoul), Kaesŏng, and Pyongyang.[74]

Finally, Yu appears to have been unaware of the main constraints against wall and fort construction in the 1650s. One of the main restrictions was the poor economy and opposition by Kim Yuk to the debilitating effects of King Hyojong's vast reconstruction plans. Kim's main argument, that demanding labor service from starving peasants was a cruel injustice, was similar to the Confucian admonition that Yu had advertised in his own writing, about refraining from demanding labor from the peasants during the planting and harvesting seasons. This Confucian spirit of concern for the hardships of the peasant operated in Yu's mind as well, but since there was no class of professional construction workers to be hired for wall construction, there was no alternative but to extract that labor from the peasants. In any case, needs of the state for better forts and walls had still not been satisfied by the time of Yu's death.

Warships

In his coverage of the history of military affairs in Korea, Yu stated that Korean governments had lacked both fleets of warships and sufficient naval soldiers until the late Koryŏ period. He quoted the memorial of U Hyŏnbo during King Kongmin's reign (r. 1351–74) who proposed warship construction as a means of countering raids of Japanese pirates at the time.[75] As previously noted, he himself proposed quotas of warships and funds for their construction and repair. He remarked that present regulations only called for a single warship, armored ship, troopship and two patrol boats for each coastal garrison and district town; several places had no armored ships at all. Prefectural-level naval garrisons (Ch'ŏmsajin) had only two warships; provincial naval headquarters (Suyŏng) had only three and one turtle boat; and regional naval headquarters (T'onggwan or T'ongjesa) had but four warships, two special warships, and two turtle boats, without enough crew to run the ships. He suggesting doubling the quotas at each garrison and specified the number of naval soldiers and oarsmen to be stationed at each base. He wanted to have ships built (replaced?) every six years and repairs every three years. He calculated the cost of a warship at 450 *kok* (4,500 *mal* or 300 *sŏm* of rice according to current units of measurement, equivalent to about the military grain tax to be paid by 38 support taxpayers every year). Since the old ship could be sold for 90 *kok*, the net cost would only be 360 *kok*. He estimated the cost of repairing a warship at 150 *kok* (100 *sŏm*) and made similar calculations for smaller ships: 90 *kok* for armored vessels, 45 for troopships, 15 for reconnaissance vessels. Repair and construction was to be based on a set of deadlines, and the funds were to come from regular revenues, not ad hoc levies. The costs of masts, oars, and sails were to be paid for from a rice levy to pay these specific costs (*kami*), one-third of which would be converted to cash, probably for paying wages to artisans.[76]

What these plans reveal is a desire to create a strong naval fleet based on the existing level of maritime technology, but no special interest in developing technology through research. His system of finance for the cost of ship construction was also based on a grain surtax, a more flexible stratagem than his method of support for soldiers and sailors. Given the traditional neglect of naval affairs, this was still a significant step forward in strategic thinking.

Military Education and the Totally Mobilized Population

One of the major themes of twentieth-century observers of the Chosŏn dynasty particularly during the difficult years of the Hideyoshi and Manchu invasions from 1592 to 1637 has been the conclusion that the weakness of the Korean military was largely the product of the Confucian emphasis on literary culture and civil officials at the expense of military affairs and training. Had it not been for this deleterious influence of Confucian education and morality, a more efficient, dedicated, and patriotic officialdom would never have allowed national defense to deteriorate.

Chosŏn dynasty reformers in the seventeenth century, however, were not willing to admit that the main cause of military weakness was Confucian education and values. On the contrary, men like Yu Hyŏngwŏn were convinced that the flawed men of their dynasty had misconstrued the true Confucian message in a number of ways by overemphasizing literary culture at the expense of the proper balance between civic pursuits and military training that was the hallmark of the classical age.

In his discussion of the role of the provincial governor and provincial military commander, for example, Yu wanted to remove the distinction between civil and military affairs. His application of this principle was not confined merely to the commanding officers of the province, but also to the district magistrates, the general population, and even the nature of knowledge and training. He believed that once a distinction was made between soldiers and people, the fundamental unity and solidarity of classical times was destroyed beyond repair. Then in peacetime the soldiers became oppressors of the people and the cultivated scholars who received no military training were no different from "delicate and tender women and children" when they had to fight. Under the ancient Chou system the commanders of units in the military chain of command during wartime would become officials in charge of the districts in the civil hierarchy during peacetime. The ideal type of leader, the *sa* (*shih* in Chinese, a term that meant warrior elite in the Chou, but changed to scholar or scholar-official by the late Chou and Han), engaged in what Yu called Practical Learning (Sirhak), which was required before they could become garrison commanders.

Since the term Sirhak has been applied by most twentieth-century scholars to the entire corpus of Yu Hyŏngwŏn's writing, it would be of some interest to see what he himself meant by the term in one of the few times he used it. In this case he meant the Chou ideal of broad and catholic learning extending to the military arts as well as classical literature and history. He contrasted it with narrow and specialized learning that appeared after the deplorable division of general knowledge into parts, a trend that accompanied the disappearance of the liberally educated generalists of Chou times and the rise of the narrow military and literary specialists of the post-Chou era.

"In later ages letters became the occupation of people who used pen and ink and became the cutters and polishers [of their own natures], while [those knowledgeable in] military affairs ended up consisting of archers and boisterous wild men only. This was because the selection of men was not in accordance with the proper way."[77]

Yu also approved as well of one feature of Han dynasty local administration, which provided that the magistrate be held responsible for military command functions during wartime and that he be provided an aide (like the *tu-wei* in the Han) who would assist him in military affairs and also take care of civil administration when the magistrate (i.e. the *t'ai-shou* of the commandery or *chün*) was in the field with the troops, or on occasion take the magistrate's place as commander when necessary.[78] Yu hoped by this plan to ensure that the district magistrates would fulfill their responsibility to defend their districts, contrary to their past record.

> In the wars that have occurred off and on in our country the district magistrates have all abandoned the defense of their territories without authorization. They have either run off into the hills or taken refuge along the seacoast. This has been the situation throughout all the prefectures and districts of the eight provinces. If it is a province you're talking about, then the whole province is left without anyone in charge; if a district town, then the whole district has been left without anyone in charge. Because of this once they hear that the enemy is coming, without waiting for the enemy to spread around, the whole country becomes an empty wasteland and the government has no one to whom it can issue orders. The fighting troops have nothing to fear or avoid; they just make it their business to take flight and scatter. Enemy bandit cavalry in groups of [only] three or four men roam all over the eight provinces and plunder the country at will, and there is no one who can say anything about it. . . . We should post clear laws to the effect that in wartime each district magistrate will defend his walled town to the death and not leave it. Anyone who does abandon a town should be punished by law without mercy; only then can we avoid this concern.[79]

It would not take a military specialist to note that magistrates of small towns with small populations might not have a sufficient force to resist large units of a well-trained invading army. Yu himself realized that 80 or 90 percent of the districts were in fact very small with sparse populations and defensive walls that a goat could jump over in a single bound. He conceded that "If you hold a man responsible for something he is not able to do and then follow this up by killing him, isn't this close to killing an innocent man?" But he thought he could solve the problem by reorganizing the whole layout of provincial districts and combining small districts into decent-sized ones, each with a walled town of sufficient strength to resist attack.[80] The idea, like many others, may have come from Yulgok, and it explains why he devoted such a large part of his book to a complete plan for administrative reorganization and the methods of constructing strong walls.[81]

If, however, education and organization were not sufficient to bring about the appearance of the perfect magistrate, talented in both civil and military affairs, then recourse could be had to rewards and punishment:

> The magistrates will also realize that the people's affairs and the country's affairs are their own concern, and they will not act in such desultory fashion, lying around lazily eating and drinking as they do at present, just paying vague attention to their responsibilities. If we can really make each of the district towns defensible and restore the military colonies [*tun*] so that they will be within eyeshot of one another, the whole country will become strong. Even if we unfortunately should incur another incursion such as the Imjin [1592] and Pyŏngja [1637] invasions, how would the country be so instantaneously thrown into shock and confusion? And even though our military commanders might suffer defeat in the fighting, the enemy would indeed not dare to take us lightly and run around the country plundering it as if it were an unpopulated land.[82]

What Yu was really thinking of was a totally mobilized population. While the regular soldiers were out on the front "chasing the enemy in running battles," the districts might well be depleted of regular troops. In that case, the numerous support personnel, almost triple the number of regular soldiers by Yu's own plan, would be available for village and town defense. In fact, the dual combination of regular troops fighting pitched battles and home militia defending walled towns was for Yu the warp and woof of military strategy, a fulfillment of the Chou militia ideal adapted to contemporary Korean circumstance. What that meant was that even though the male population was divided between rotating duty soldiers and support taxpayers, a program of training in the villages would prepare the support personnel to take up arms in an emergency. "Regarding regular soldiers and support personnel, basically it is the people you train to be soldiers and soldiers who defend the people, and in wartime you use both."[83]

The idea of total war in which all civilians are subjected to the terrors of war and rigors of combat is something that is, unfortunately, not foreign to the twentieth century. It was a lesson learned well from Korea's unfortunate experiences during the Imjin War. Yu was sensitive enough to realize that the reorganization of the national army, the use of reason in the placement of garrisons, and better training methods for soldiers were still not sufficient to create a strong nation from one so weak in the recent past. It required the revamping of education to produce civil servants with military training and the ability to convert the whole population into a fighting force in an instant. Only with this transformation of the whole population would his system of rotating duty soldiers and support taxpayers work effectively in case of war.

Nevertheless, total transformation of contemporary ethics and mores is not the easiest of tasks no matter what the society or the period. The shouts of warning from a country scholar in a remote village were not to be heard in the capital in his own time, and even a century later after he became well known, his admonitions had little effect on transforming the military system and solving its problems.

CONCLUSION

In many ways Yu Hyŏngwŏn was not a rigid or dogmatic fundamentalist in his approach to military reform. It would be better to say that he sought compromises – between the ideal of antiquity and the circumstances of contemporary Korea, between the need for fiscal restraint and the need for a strong defense, and between central civilian political control and decentralized military force and authority. It is not clear, however, that his compromises yielded fully satisfying solutions to the problems of military organization at the time.

His plans were not simply the product of rational calculation because he depended heavily on institutions of the early Chosŏn period and traditional Korean practice. His preference for the Five Guards and the rotating service and support taxpayer system happened to constitute the methods of organization, service, and finance in operation at the beginning of the dynasty. For that matter, his retention of certain elite guard units to protect the sons of the elite against the loss of status that might ensue from duty alongside commoners also reproduced rules in effect in the early Chosŏn period that were social compromises with principles of efficiency, rationality, merit, and equality. His strict separation of slave from commoner soldiers and relocating all slaves in the *sog'o* units was not, however, based on any precedent since there were no slaves in the army in any numbers until the Imjin War, but then they had been combined with commoners in the *sog'o* units. His reform represented a retention but separation of slave military service, a double retreat from his professed ideal of abolition.

His almost visceral dislike for permanent, salaried soldiers was argued on the grounds of financial rationality, but it was really more a product of a bias learned from Confucian scholars of the past, both Chinese and Korean, and his own prejudice against the crude behavior of the Military Training Agency troops in his own time. Although neither a blind fundamentalist nor a literal admirer of antiquity or early Chosŏn, he retained a basic reverence for antiquity reinforced by a somewhat idealized vision of early Chosŏn institutions and respect (or fear) of upsetting long-standing social practices in his own time.

His scheme for the reorganization of palace and capital guard forces was not simply an antiquarian scheme for the restoration of early Chosŏn institutions, it was also a reaction to a situation that prevailed throughout the seventeenth century. Outside of a brief reference to the political guard commanders of the 1620s and their tendency to increase their forces, he refrained from any detailed discussion of the relationship between foreign policy and domestic politics to the capital guards. Nevertheless, his appreciation of the matter is implicit in his formula for reform: limiting the entire guard force to about 2,000 men, eliminating all new units created since 1592 save for the Military Training Agency, and then converting the mode of organization and finance of that agency. The reduction of forces in the capital was an admirable goal, but it would have required other measures that were quite difficult to achieve at that time: the elimination of politics from the capital guards, reduction of the capital guards relative to provincial military forces, and unification and centralization of authority in the hands of the king and the regular bureaucracy.

He planned to strengthen provincial and regional forces by adopting the *chin'g-wan* or regional garrison or command center with jurisdiction over a number of administrative districts to provide the double-door phalanx of defense against invading forces proposed by Yu Sŏngnyŏng. He hoped to reconstitute land and sea forces alike on the basis of Ch'i Chi-kuang's *sog'o* system of an ascending hierarchy of units located in the most strategic places possible, to combine civil and military responsibilities by correlating low-level troop units with civil districts and bring civil magistrates into the chain of command of provincial forces, and to retain the existing, Korean *sog'o* troop units, but exclusively constituted of slaves, as some kind of national guard that would train at home.

His plan for the deployment of forces in the provinces owed much to Yu Sŏngnyŏng's hierarchical system of strategic garrisons overseeing civil districts as subordinate units of military organization. Even though the system looked on paper as if it filled the countryside with soldiers, it would not really have been effective against foreign invaders who could concentrate their forces at will. The major flaw in his system was that he placed more faith in defensive warfare and fixed positions than in mobility and flexibility.

The strategy was not completely based on militia organization and yet called for a significant role for district magistrates in the military at the lower end of provincial organization, but were they ready and equipped to meet the task? By his own admission, the civil magistrate of his own time had to be converted by a thorough reorganization of education to become a generalist of the classical type, skilled in the military as well as the liberal and civil arts. This was not such an easy task in an era of Neo-Confucian ideology and civilian domination. The idea was good, the chance for achieving it slim.

Yu also urged the production and distribution of muskets and other weapons and favored the construction of defensive walls and fortifications. An admirer of the most advanced military technology available at the time and a supporter of Yu Sŏngnyŏng's radical call to depart from convention to adopt more advanced foreign techniques, he was not, however, a radical advocate of open-ended technological development. He appears to have been content with the weapon mix of smooth-bore muskets, bows and arrows, and swords and spears that characterized the partial shift toward firearms made in the 1590s, and he made no plans to convert all the troops to musket bearers, no doubt because neither Japanese nor Ming forces consisted exclusively of musketeers. His practical considerations about walls and defensive fortifications was also informed heavily by moral criteria associated with the ancient Chou and confined to a defensive technology applicable to the age before firearms and cannon, the last of which he neglected even to discuss. And he was not aware of the financial constraints placed on government by periodic famine conditions in his own time and the severity of Manchu surveillance against the slightest hint of rearmament.

Unfortunately, he did not discuss the political and foreign policy assumptions upon which his program was based. Certain questions must be kept in mind, however. Could reduction in the numbers of capital guards, elimination of specific guard divisions, and centralization of command in king and civil bureaucracy be adopted or achieved in the context of the foreign policy or political context of the century? After his death, the threat from the Manchus declined, but the contest between political factions at home intensified, and control of the major central divisions became a part of the power struggle.

Despite these drawbacks, Yu represented a positive view of the capacity of the Confucian tradition to sponsor reform of a military system plagued with problems. Rather than abandon the Confucian tradition or condemn it for engendering national weakness, he sought wisdom in the classics and histories and argued that flexible adaptation to contemporary circumstances, including the borrowing of foreign technology, could save Korea from destruction. But despite his interest in technology he really believed that the transformation of man was the key to the reform of any problem, including military defense.

He recognized the neglect of military education and military training in the recent Chosŏn dynasty, but he attributed that to the loss of an earlier part of the classical tradition, the well-balanced man of civic and military virtue and accomplishment and the well-balanced society of village peasants that combined cultivation with military service. He believed that these defects could be remedied by changing the content of education and training and mobilizing the entire population for war. Perhaps this aspect of his program was more fundamental than his practical admonitions on structural reorganization and weapons, but these would have been enormous tasks to achieve. The body of incumbent officials were not ready to take these measures seriously.

CHAPTER 14

The Military Service System, 1682–1870

Yi Samyŏng and others who proposed the use of some other form of taxation to finance the military besides the support taxpayers tied to duty soldiers – particularly the use of capitation, household, or land taxes – were arguing for an abandonment of the militia ideal and adoption of a new principle of finance: the separation of finance from service. Those who opposed these plans were not just defenders of the interests of the tax-exempt yangban and tax evaders of lesser status; they were also locked into rigid categorical thinking on the way military service systems should work. This conservatism was not, however, only a conservatism of doctrine, it was also a conservative reaction to changing economic circumstances because the development of production, market exchange, and the use of currency together with the expansion of population and the fiscal requirements of the state necessitated a better method of finance for the military system. Some reformers in the bureaucracy conceived of this initially as merely a problem of slapping a tax on the yangban or the tax-evaders, but this was only a limited and partial solution. Those who had a greater perspective realized that the best and most comprehensive way to expand the tax base was by liberating finance from the old formula of adult male support taxpayers of good status (*yangjŏng*, *poin*) for rotating duty soldiers, and shifting to the use of general revenues raised in any way that seemed feasible.

Conservatism of Yu Hyŏngwŏn's Military Finance Plan

The way in which soldiers were to be financed may even have been more fundamental than the debate over extending taxes to yangban, even though that was also of crucial importance. It enables us to see that the household cloth tax, which was the favorite version of an independent revenue source, was opposed by some not necessarily or only because it would have taxed the yangban, but primarily because it was too close to the stigmatized separation of soldiers and the peasants deemed responsible for a standing army and heavy taxes.

If one regards the development of the market and a cash and exchange economy as progress from a more ancient to a more modern mode of economic life, then the household tax represented a flexible and progressive response to changing circumstances. Had the governing class in Korea at that time been even more progressive than they were, they might have considered not only taxing nonagricultural industry, commerce, and trade, but even stimulating those areas of activity as a means of building the wealth of state and society at large, but it was not capable of adopting that point of view.

Yu Hyŏngwŏn clearly belongs in the conservative camp on this issue at least. Even though in other respects he was open to change and expressed admiration for Kim Yuk's *taedong* tribute reform, which was a progressive adaptation of the tribute tax system to developing market conditions, he was not prepared for any change that would violate the principle of universal military service and the militia model. Although he recognized that the separation of rotating duty soldiers from support-taxpayers was not fully a militia system, the rotation of duty soldiers presupposed preservation of the principle of returning the troops to their farms for prolonged intervals between duty assignments, which was close enough to the principle of the self-financing of soldiers and the militia ideal to suit his sensibilities. While he did not discuss the household cloth tax, he did oppose the use of a land tax for financing the military except where justified by historical precedent, such as the use of military colony land – a system, by the way, that was based on the direct use of soldier labor on land rather than the taxation of privately owned land. As we will see, when his name was first introduced at court in 1750 during the debate over reform of the military service system, his leading intellectual disciple at the time, Kwŏn Chŏk, acting as a virtual self-appointed spokesman for Yu, vigorously opposed the household cloth tax, a position that was quite consistent with Yu's theoretical stance on the proper form of military finance.

What Yu had regarded as a corruption or deterioration of the early Chosŏn system of rotating duty soldiers because of the growth of illegal substitution of cloth payments for actual service, might also be regarded as an institutional shift that required a flexible response by divorcing the fiscal support for duty soldiers from adult males of good or commoner status to more general sources of revenue. The real irony of the situation was that just at the time that military service was becoming more of a tax than a service problem, the number of men who were able to gain *de iure* and *de facto* exemption from payment of the cloth tax was increasing. This was accompanied by a long trend toward the debasement of military service that had to be the product of Korea's most intense period of Confucian learning. Scholars and students regarded the listing of one's name on a military roster, even though it entailed no more than the payment of a cloth tax, as disastrous to one's status. It was no longer a question of evasion by a narrow elite of yangban progeny – large numbers of commoners were using every device imaginable to escape military service registration, possibly gaining a step or two on the ladder of prestige as well as avoiding the onerous burden of tax payments. The country could not afford the luxury of such a large number of tax-exempt individuals, a group that far surpassed what anyone would define as a hereditary yangban class even under the broadest definition.

The main task, therefore, was not simply forcing yangban, or hereditary aristocrats, back into a system of service in elite guard units, but requiring the majority of the population to pay its fair share of taxes for the support of the military establishment. But this was resisted because developing a broader fiscal base for military finance would have violated the classical principles that Yu Hyŏngwŏn and some other active officials held dear – the injunctions against separating farmers from soldiers or requiring the payment of taxes to support permanent duty soldiers.

FACTIONAL POLITICS AND THE THREAT OF REBELLION

Another problem that affected the capacity for reform of the military system was the military challenge that faced Korea at the time. The threat of foreign invasion had waned considerably by the end of the seventeenth century. Japan had withdrawn largely within herself and the powerful Ch'ing dynasty had secured Korea from other predators from the north and had moderated its tribute demands. These positive developments, however, did not eliminate the need for a military force because factional politics became more brutal and violent after 1689. King Sukchong himself was largely responsible for the exacerbation of political disputation, but he still felt the need to maintain a more-than-adequate force of troops especially around the capital to protect himself against potential usurpers.

After Sukchong postponed major reform in the military service system in 1682, no changes were made for twenty years until the same problems came up for debate at court in 1704. In the interim, however, two major changes occurred in politics: in 1689 Sukchong shifted his favor from the Westerners to the Southerners, and in 1694 he suddenly reversed his position, discharged his Southerner government and replaced them wholesale with Westerners. These political reversals were related to alignments of officials behind candidates to the throne, which usually involved support for one of the king's consorts and their male issue. King Sukchong was the major cause of the problem because his devotion to his wives and favorite concubines was short-lived, and every time he shifted his favor, he demanded full support from all members of his court. Those unlucky groups or factions of officials that failed to comply with Sukchong's wishes on these matters were condemned to political disaster in the form of a purge of all their members, sometimes accompanied by a rash of executions.

In the 1680s Yun Chŭng, one of the followers of Song Siyŏl, split from the Westerners because he could not stand Song's overbearing arrogance. The group that followed him became known as the Disciple's Faction (Soron) while Song and the other Westerners were called the Patriarch's Faction (Noron). The Disciples opposed the demand of the Patriarchs for severe punishment of their Southerner rivals, but the dispute became moot when the Westerner splinter groups fell foul of the king's wishes over the choice of a crown prince.

The Westerners had favored Sukchong's first queen, who had died in 1680. The next year Sukchong chose the daughter of Min Yujung to be his second queen, Queen Inhyŏn, but when she failed to produce an heir, Sukchong shifted his favor to Lady Chang, who gave birth to a son in 1688. Angered over Westerner criticism of his desire to make the boy crown prince in 1689, Sukchong replaced Westerner officials with Southerners and deposed Queen Inhyŏn. Now it was the turn of the Southerners to seek vengeance, and the primary casualties were Song Siyŏl and Kim Suhang, both of whom were forced to drink poison.

In 1694, when the Southerners discovered that the Westerners were conspiring to restore Queen Inhyŏn, they thought the opportunity for a grand purge of all Westerners had finally arrived. But for reasons that are still obscure, Sukchong suddenly turned the tables on them, purged the Southerners instead, and brought Westerners, mainly of the Disciple's Faction, back into office. The Southerners remained out of important office for the next century.

After the Westerners returned to power, however, there was only a brief respite before factional struggle resumed, again over the designation of a crown prince. When the restored Queen Inhyŏn died in 1701, someone reported that her death had been caused by the secret voodoo ceremonies of Lady Chang, the mother of the crown prince. Sukchong's affections for her must have waned, for he not only failed to defend her honor but forced her to take poison in expiation of her evil practices. The Disciples now had their chance to make the same mistake that the Patriarchs had in 1689; they took the side of Lady Chang and her son, the crown prince. Sukchong did not hesitate to punish their insensitivity to his wishes by dismissing them from office, leaving the Patriarchs in control of the court. This was the political situation when Sukchong established a Reform Bureau to reconsider the question of military reform.[1]

THE MILITARY REFORMS OF 1704

Aborted Plan to Return to the Five Guard System

The boundaries of possible reform were defined at the outset of the discussion by the leading members of the Reform Bureau, Yi Yu, Min Chinhu, and Yi Inyŏp, who dismissed the idea of replacing support taxpayers with household (*hop'o*) or capitation (*kujŏn*) taxes out of hand because of the persistence of famine for several years. Instead they recommended the reduction of troop quotas by eliminating one of the royal or capital guard divisions.

Like Yu Hyŏngwŏn, Third State Councilor Sin Wan wanted to eliminate all new military divisions created after 1593 and return to the Five Guard system of early Chosŏn because it was (supposedly) based on the ancient farmer/soldier militia principle as opposed to permanent, salaried soldiers. The inspiration for the idea derived not from Yu but from Song Siyŏl's attack on the Military Training Agency in 1669. Yi Yu of the Reform Bureau recommended shifting the rotating duty troops of the Forbidden Guard Division back to the agency and eliminating the agency's permanent soldiers by attrition as Song had suggested decades earlier. When Minister of Taxation Kim Ch'angjip, a prominent Patriarch, endorsed the idea, Sukchong agreed.

Abolishing any one of the Five Military Divisions proved almost as difficult a task as adopting the household cloth tax.[2] A month after the king had made his decision, a number of officials led by Censor-general (Taesagan) Yi Kŏnmyŏng of the Patriarchs protested that the times were too precarious to permit disbandment of the most essential divisions in the capital for the purpose of reorganization, no doubt because of the disruption caused by the purge of the Disciple's Faction in 1701. Yi felt that the Royal and Forbidden Guard Divisions were indispensable because they were ideal approximations of the *fu-ping* of the T'ang dynasty and were properly financed through the assignment of support taxpayers to duty soldiers, even though the T'ang *fu-ping* were supposed to be manned by militia soldiers. He preferred the immediate abolition of the Military Training Agency but was willing to compromise by reducing it by half. When other officials opposed any major reorganization, Sukchong reluctantly withdrew his initial decision to abolish the new divisions created since the Imjin War.[3] The only alternative was an across-the-board reduction of all divisions and military units and fixed limits for all the service-exempt military officers (*kun'gwan*) and school students (*kyosaeng*) in the provinces whose numbers had long since far surpassed earlier quotas. All agreed, however, this kind of reform could only be temporary and marginal in its effect.[4]

The commanders of the the Five Military Divisions of the capital region and the civil officials associated with them (as concurrent appointees), had an interest in their perpetuation if only to maintain collection of tax revenues. Sending a division of capital troops back to the countryside or reassigning thousands more support taxpayers to different units would have created unnerving dislocations if only by breaking old networks. In a society where personal contact was so important, people may have felt comfortable knowing what to expect in the way of bribes, extortion, and gratuities from army officers, clerks, and officials they had been dealing with for years. Eliminating such established institutions was hardly easy, something that a recluse scholar like Yu Hyŏngwŏn never had the opportunity to find out because he was never in a position of power. He was unaware of the practical problems that could be caused by abolishing four of the five military divisions, paring back the capital guards from about 300,000 to 70,000, reassigning the 230,000 men, and breaking the networks of attachments of so many thousands of people. Furthermore, the king could not risk weakening the existing divisions while the transfers of troops to new units took place.

Yi Yu's recommendation for cuts in all units rather than the elimination of any single one became the basis for the major troop reduction of 1704. A net reduction of 35,365 from the total of 307,926 soldiers and support taxpayers of the Five Military Divisions amounted to an 11.5 percent service or tax cut. The Military Training Agency's 49,816 troops and taxpayers (of which only about 5,000 could have been permanent, salaried soldiers) was only reduced by 787 men, while the biggest cut of 19,317 was sustained by the Royal Division, bringing it from 106,270 to 86,953 men.[5]

*The Uniform two-*p'il *Support Tax Rate*

Reduction of troop quotas was accompanied by an attempt to establish a uniform and equal tax rate on all support taxpayers of two *p'il* per person per annum. This goal required two operations: reducing the highest three-*p'il* tax rate to two *p'il* for support taxpayers not only for frontier cavalrymen, but also for civilian forms of labor service such as grain transport sailors, tile and pottery workers, musicians, and artisans. The rate for support taxpayers for marines had been reduced to two *p'il* ever since the adoption of the method of "combining" a third taxpayer was adopted in 1665, but now the third taxpayer was to remit his payment to the Border Defense Command in the capital.

Although some one-*p'il* rates were confirmed by the reform, as in the case of support taxpayers for the Jurchen Quelling Guards (Chŏngnowi) and fishermen, some types of illicit low-rate (usually one-*p'il*) service were eliminated, particularly in the case of men attached to the Namhan fort. Since abolishing the one-*p'il* rate would result in a doubling of the tax rate on the individuals involved, creating a uniform (or "equal") tax seems to have been the objective, rather than simply reducing all tax rates. Orders were also sent out to the provinces to commands and garrisons at all levels to set the rate for support taxpayers for all forms of commoner service (*yangyŏk*) at two *p'il*. In addition, the government set fixed tax quotas for specific units and categories of support taxes to eliminate arbitrary and excessive levies by commanders and officials, defined a forty-foot length of six *sŭngmok* cloth as the standard bolt to be paid by regular cavalry and infantry support taxpayers, and established cash and grain conversion rates (to be adjusted for price fluctuations). The standardization of both cotton and ramie cloth was more strictly defined by weave count as well, to eliminate manipulation of cloth payments by corrupt clerks.[6]

The decision in 1704 to retain a system primarily organized around support taxpayers in conjunction with a uniform two-*p'il* tax rate were both elements in Yu Hyŏngwŏn's reform proposals. Even though other parts of Yu's reform proposals were not adopted at this time, the adoption of the two-*p'il* rate at least provides an opportunity to test the validity of Yu's argument that it would provide relief to the support taxpayer.

A Cloth Fine on Dismissed Students

Finally, the Reform Bureau issued regulations imposing a fine on students who were dismissed from school by failing their school examinations, an amelioration of a stricter measure adopted back in 1626 but ignored in the interim. The regulations explained that up to the present time students of this type had been acting in collusion with school authorities to keep their name on the school registers as extra-quota students to evade military service or support taxes. Past proposals to enroll school dropouts for *yangyŏk* military service and tax obligations had never been adopted because the yangban relatives of the drop-outs could not stand the stigma attached to military service. When some actually were enrolled for service, they went to the greatest expense to evade it, or would feign illness or unfitness, sign up illicitly for low-rate service taxes, or even run away. These practices that "damaged customs and mores" had to be reformed, but for fear of the anger and resentment that would result from too thorough a housecleaning of all student service evaders, the Reform Bureau adopted some lenient modifications in the new law.

Quota students as well as extra-quota students were now to be examined for their scholarly performance, but those who failed would be kept on the school registers and only required to pay a fine. Paying a fine would presumably not stigmatize them because they would not be required to serve either as duty soldiers or support taxpayers, and it was already an accepted practice for regular officials to pay fines in expiation of wrongdoing or for any revelation of ignorance at Royal Lecture sessions or other court audiences.

The inspiration for these methods was attributed to Chang Yu, who at the time of the Manchu invasions suggested that school dropouts be given the special title of military student (*muhak*) so that they could have a second chance if they failed a qualification examination. Only if they failed the second one were they to be enrolled for military service. The regulations also cited Kim Yuk's statement that even though enrolling school dropouts for service was the law of the founders of the dynasty, some modification was called for in the early seventeenth century. Both quota and extra-quota students had to be subdivided into the scholar-official families (*sajok*) and "those of somewhat lower status." If the less prestigious students failed their examinations, they would immediately be enrolled for service, but the scions of scholar-official families would only be assessed a fine. The reason for the modifications proposed by Chang Yu and Kim Yuk were motivated by their consideration of "the situation at the time and their desire to make plans in accordance with the people's feelings."

The *Sillok* historian, writing of these events in the 1720s, pointed out that even though the regulations of 1704 called for biannual testing, the examinations to qualify school students were later reduced to once a year. Otherwise, students who failed the examination were placed on a special list and assessed a fine of two *p'il*, the same as the standard cloth tax rate on support taxpayers. Failure to take the test, hiring substitutes to do it, refusal to pay the fine, or collusion with school clerks to evade it would result in immediate enrollment for military service. The new regulations were also extended to students in private academies and shrines, and the annual qualifying tests were to be given to all men from the age of fifteen to fifty. In the northern and northwestern coastal provinces and regions, students would be given a special dispensation: they would have to fail the test three straight times before having to pay a fine.[7]

This measure for the fining of unqualified students, with discriminatory penalties based on status, probably represented the limit of acceptable reform at that time designed to expand the tax base to include the tax-exempt elite. It was certainly a far cry from the universal household or capitation taxes that would have dissociated finance from service in a way unacceptable to the conservative defenders of militia theory. Nevertheless, a fine on some of the unqualified high-status students in lieu of service was a slight move in the direction of financing the military by taxes on people not part of the military service system.

Sukchong and his government could go no further because of the obvious fear of offending the yangban, which might easily shift its support to another claimant to the throne if its interests were encroached upon. The power of this privileged elite had to be taken into account by all reformers, who were forced to devise compromises with radical egalitarianism sufficient to induce conformity to reform legislation and prevent any radical political reaction.

Rationalization of Marine Duty and Organization

The reform law of 1704 also contained some regulations pertaining to marines (*sugun*) that are interesting because they were so similar to the ideas of Yu Hyŏngwŏn a half century before, and illustrate again the point that reform plans based on rational reorganization were not the exclusive prerogative of rusticated scholars alone. The very first regulation pointed out that under current rules peasants living in inland regions with no experience at sea were enrolled as marines. Instead of serving, however, they merely paid the cloth tax, and the funds were used to hire substitutes from residents of the region around the naval base. The new law provided that henceforth any resident of the coast or area near the base who did not have a service assignment, whether of noble or base status, would be required to perform service as a marine, according to the regulations governing *sog'o* soldiers (i.e., units with both commoner and slave members but primarily the latter). Regarding slave marines, the law noted that even though official slaves also had to pay tribute to a government agency, and private slaves to their masters, no master would be allowed to seize and remove his private slave from marine service.[8]

The reforms of 1704 also included a rational reorganization of military units to create more regularity and uniformity.[9] The Reform Bureau tried to concentrate capital forces in three major units: the Military Training Agency, the Royal Division, and the Forbidden Guard Division. Since the minister of war, however, continued to hold the post of commander (Taejang) of the Forbidden Guard Division as well as the Forbidden Soldiers, the problem of duplication of forces was not entirely eliminated until the Forbidden Guard Division was given its own commander during King Yŏngjo's reign. At that time, the minister of war was made Taesama (grand controller of horse, a name borrowed from the Chinese Chou period), and given formal control over all three units.[10]

Similarities with Yu Hyŏngwŏn's Plan

What is particularly striking about the reform measures of 1704 is how many of the measures were similar to the reform program of Yu Hyŏngwŏn. Yu had proposed the elimination of permanent, salaried soldiers and the conversion of all service to rotating duty soldiers backed up by support taxpayers paying rates that might vary but in most cases would be two *p'il* of cloth. He would have reduced the capital guards to 17,500 rotating service soldiers (12,500 Five Guard soldiers and about 5,000 Military Training Agency soldiers) and presumably another 52,500 support taxpayers, or a total of 70,000. The 1704 reform program was far less ambitious, but still it achieved an 11.5 percent cut in the over 300,000 rotating soldiers and support taxpayers of the Five Military Divisions. Two key features of his program – troop reduction and establishment of a uniform tax rate of two *p'il* per support taxpayer – were adopted in 1704.

By returning to regulations of the early Chosŏn, Yu would have left out of military service and tax obligations only registered students in school; sons of scholar-official families would be required to serve, albeit in elite guard units. He would have rationalized the marines and naval system by bringing then into the ordinary rotating service and support tax system and shifted responsibility for marine (and sailor) service to residents of coastal areas. Finally, he would have retained the use of slave soldiers (*sog'ogun*) as a local reserve, but paying a rate double that of commoner support taxpayers.

Under the regulations of 1704 sons of yangban who failed annual school qualifying examinations were not returned to service but were required to pay fines equivalent to the commoner support tax rate. Several of his ideas for rationalization of naval and marine service such as reallocating service from the inland to the coastal population, and setting quotas for ships and crew happened to be adopted at this time. For that matter, the treatment of slave support taxpayers (at least for marines) by assessing the same rate of support tax as that paid by commoners was better than what Yu had in mind. The only matter not taken care of was the abolition of permanent soldiers of the Military Training Agency, but so many officials had pointed out over the years that there was so little to be saved anyway because of the large number of rotating duty soldiers and support taxpayers that would have to be found to replace them that it was hardly worth the effort. Even the program of rationalizing the organization of the Five Military Divisions by creating uniform and balanced units to eliminate both confusion and inequality in the treatment of soldiers could be regarded as similar in spirit if not detail to Yu Hyŏngwŏn's thinking.

In other words, without reference to or knowledge of Yu Hyŏngwŏn's ideas, the program of 1704 shared some of the goals and solutions put forward by that recluse philosopher of practical learning. But what did that mean, especially since the 1704 reforms were not the most radical program possible? That the officials of the time were only slightly less radical than he, or conversely that he was only slightly less conservative than they?

THE REFORMS OF 1711

Capitation Tax on Yangban Blocked

A 10 percent quota reduction of the capital divisions and the half-hearted attempt at a uniform two-*p'il* tax rate did not succeed in eliminating the pressures on a shrinking population of taxpayers to bear the costs of the whole military establishment. The quota reduction was only temporary in its effect because enrollment of support taxpayers continued almost without interruption to the middle of the eighteenth century. At the same time, tax evaders were still signing up for lower, one *p'il* service or escaping registration and taxation altogether. The registration of extra-quota students in government schools was also becoming a particularly egregious form of evasion.

In 1711, Yi Imyŏng, one of the four Patriarchs executed later in 1722, a supporter of Prince Yŏn'ing (later King Yŏngjo) for the throne, and heir to a tradition of practical statecraft in the Westerner faction that could be traced back through Song Siyŏl to Yulgok, made the strongest argument to date for a per capita tax on all adults (women as well as men) to provide a better and fairer financial base of support for the military system than the current support-taxpayer system. He cited as a precedent for this proposal the cash capitation tax used in the Former Han dynasty, but he added the proviso that because of the cash shortage in Korea at that time, cloth would be used instead. Although he would have benefited the slaveowners by exempting slaves (contrary to Yu Hyŏngwŏn's plan), only a limited number of high officials and their eldest sons would have been exempted from the tax. Although he did not say so explicitly, Yi's capitation tax would have separated military finance from military service by including women as persons to be counted as subjects for the tax and by not requiring the yangban taxpayers to enroll either as duty soldiers or support-taxpayers.

Six months later, after Sukchong had rejected Yi's proposal and made his final decision on policy, Pak Kwŏn, the assistant vice-mayor of Seoul and previously an advocate of the household cloth tax, offered his own amendment of Yi Imyŏng's capitation cloth tax proposal by lowering the rate on men and women of good status and taxing slaves at half the rate of commoners. He naïvely believed that lowering the tax rate would eliminate the resistance of yangban to the proposal. Both he and Yi, by the way, placed a lighter burden on slaves than Yu Hyŏngwŏn had proposed.

Pak clearly stood against inherited privilege as he articulated his belief in equality as the fundamental principle of taxation. "It is clear," he said, "that in taxing the people, one should be concerned about inequality and should not vary taxes according to whether some people are noble and others base," and he truly believed that the T'ang *tiao* or household cash tax did not exclude men of high status.[11] Since active officials like Yi Imyŏng and Pak Kwŏn perceived the T'ang and Sung tax systems as more egalitarian than those of mid-Chosŏn Korea and were willing to cite them as precedents for making inroads into the tax-exempt privileges of the yangban, they were participants in a shared discourse with so-called practical scholars like Yu Hyŏngwŏn. Nonetheless, like the advocates of the household cloth tax in 1682, their notion of equality did not extend to the question of military service for yangban, just the ability to levy a supposedly status-neutral cash tax on all persons.

Yu Ponghwi also advocated that a tax-rate reduction from the current rate of two *p'il* per adult male be reduced to one *p'il* as a means of lessening yangban resistance to their payment of a new tax, but backed by a national census to provide information to calculate total revenues. Minister of Rites Cho T'aegu preferred simply to strengthen the system of investigation and registration of tax evaders, including irregular or extra-quota school students.

Although Yi Imyŏng believed in the legitimacy of financing the military by a general capitation tax, he noted his opposition to the household cloth tax because it would be susceptible to corruption and could not be fine-tuned to take into account variations in the number of persons per household. He astutely observed that a registration campaign such as Cho T'aegu suggested would not work because past history had proved it was impossible to find and register enough untaxed adult males. He also argued that a household tax would still be opposed by yangban even if the rate were reduced to one *p'il*/household, and it would not yield enough revenue. It is hard to understand, however, why Yi believed that yangban would be any less opposed to a capitation than a household tax.[12]

Enrollment of Failed Students for Military Service

Discussion of major systemic reforms such as the household or capitation taxes had almost become ritualistic because Sukchong showed no signs of reversing his decision in 1682 to reject the household cloth tax, and the capitation tax on yangban was only marginally different in nature. In this instance he expressed favor for investigating and registering extra-quota students for military service (instead of simply fining them) and for punishing incompetent magistrates – a more radical challenge to yangban privilege than the fine on failed students of 1704.

The final set of regulations adopted at the end of 1711 closed loopholes in administrative procedure and delegated responsibility to village officials and local yangban under the village responsibility system for registration and paper work governing runaways and deceased soldiers. Qualification tests for school students and low-level military officers were required, and those who failed were to be enrolled forthwith for military taxes, without any mitigating measures to ease the pain – a second attempt at the measure King Injo had adopted in 1626 and rescinded six months later. Quotas were also set for students of private academies as well as government schools.

The legislation of 1711 was not a bold and comprehensive new program of military taxation, it was designed to remedy administrative defects at the point of contact with the population, a problem that was of no less consequence than the mode of taxation itself. But if this approach were to fail, what alternatives would be left?[13]

Sukchong shut the door on visionary reforms and for the remainder of his reign trod a declining path to more mundane solutions – first to quota and tax rate reductions and fines on students who failed qualifying examinations in 1704, and then to the village responsibility system and enrollment of failed students for military service in 1711. These reforms were by no means unimportant or shoddy in conception. All the problems of evasion and corruption of the tax system were laid out in great detail in the context of the debates, and the combination of solutions certainly represented the best administrative thinking possible. But the true test of these reforms would be in their effects.

Fortunately, this question has been studied, to some extent in the earlier work of Ch'a Munsŏp, but more recently by Chŏng Yŏnsik. Their evidence convincingly demonstrates that the reforms hardly slowed the decline of the military service system, its corruption by officials and tax evaders alike, and the redistribution of taxes to an ever narrower base of poor taxpayers. The authorities had to continue with periodic investigations to find and register adult males to fill vacancies on the rolls caused by death, desertion, and evasion.

THE FAILURE OF MILITARY REFORM, 1704–50

*Failure of the Uniform Two-*p'il *Rate and the Land Surtax*

The government was not able to establish a uniform two-*p'il* rate except for *yangyŏk* service in the capital because unit commanders continued to offer illicit low one-*p'il* rate service on their own, and where illicit rate reduction did occur, it reduced revenue that had to be made up in some other fashion. Even in 1704, substitute payments from other revenue sources like grain loan interest were authorized to compensate for the loss of revenue from rate reduction on support taxpayers for marines. In short, the failure to produce a uniform two-*p'il* rate for all support taxpayers meant the continuation of an unequal and unfair tax system, declining revenues, and total evasion.[14]

In 1714 Inspector-General Song Sanggi made a suggestion that indicated that King Sukchong's order in 1704 to enroll all failed students for military service had proved totally ineffective in filling the military registers. He argued that because the adult male population was far less than the military service and tax quota in many districts, the government should revive the old formula of combining a tax cut to one *p'il* with an additional one-*p'il* tax on all "leisured households," including families of court officials, local influentials of rank (*t'op'um*), school students, and military officers. The idea was rejected, but the proposal contained two of the basic elements adopted in the 1750 equal service system.[15]

As time passed more people came to the realization that the two-*p'il* rate was too high to eliminate tax evasion by illicit, lower-rate service. In 1721 the Patriarch Second State Councilor Yi Kŏnmyŏng made an important proposal to combine rate reduction to one *p'il* with another kind of supplementary revenue measure, a surtax on land to be tried out in a few select districts at first. The idea was almost adopted by King Kyŏngjong, but was dropped when Yi was arrested and exiled the next month.[16]

Restoration of the Matrilineal Rule, 1730

No further action was proposed for the next sixteen years until Third State Councilor Cho Munmyŏng in 1730 requested restoration of the matrilineal succession rule in mixed slave-commoner marriages to expand the population of adult males of good status and alleviate the service tax burdens on the commoner population. He pointed out that the inheritance of slave status had never existed in China but conceded it could not simply be abolished in Korea because it had been in use for such a long time. There was, however, absolutely no justification for children of mixed marriages to adopt their father's status, a specious argument since it had been so ordered under King T'aejong's reign. Because of this rule, a number of men who should have been of good status (*yangjŏng*) had been converted into slaves.

Although the matrilineal succession rule had been adopted at Song Siyŏl's suggestion in 1669, it had not been followed, and was later rescinded for the second time in 1689. That meant that for forty-one years no attempt had been made to reinstate the matrilineal law because of conservative opposition to any loss of private slaves by the slaveowners. A number of officials supported Cho's recommendation at this time, but because Yŏngjo was concerned lest this rule stimulate slaves to turn against their masters, he dismissed Cho's proposal as "empty" armchair talk.[17] Obviously, the king was no liberal sympathizer for the plight of the slaves.

Nonetheless, he changed his mind a few months later when the secret censor for Kyŏnggi Province, Kim Sangsŏng, reported that the illegal extortion of military service taxes from neighbors and relatives was as bad as ever. Yŏngjo immediately approved Kim's recommendation for adoption of the matrilineal succession rule and ordered that it apply to all children born that year.[18] The successful though belated achievement of the matrilineal rule, which happened to be one of Yu Hyŏngwŏn's favorite ideas, was another example of shared discourse among scholars and officials throughout this period. It is one of several of Yu's ideas that actually became law even without the direct knowledge of his views by active officials, but the matrilineal rule could not offer an immediate solution to the problem of military taxation because sons of mothers of good status in mixed marriages were too few in number to cause a sudden increase in the taxable male population. Its short term effects were negligible, but it might have contributed to the more noticeable decline in the slave population around 1800.

Rate and Troop Reduction, 1732–34

When debate over military tax reform was resumed in 1733, Pak Munsu took the lead in defending status-based exemption from military taxes, and King Yŏngjo agreed with him, probably because after the *imsin* rebellion of 1728 by the Disciple's Faction and local yangban, he was not likely to approve any solution that involved an additional tax on yangban. He was willing, however, to consider Kim Sangsŏng's idea of using land tax revenue to offset the costs of rate reduction, and he suggested himself that taxes on newly reclaimed land might be used for this purpose, but after a protracted debate in 1734, he decided to take no action.[19] In 1732 he did scale back troop quotas for the civil bureaus in the capital and the Five Military Divisions to 1699 levels, and made an attempt to eliminate unessential service in 1734, but the results of these efforts were negligible.[20]

In 1742 King Yŏngjo established another Commoner Service Investigation Bureau (Yangyŏk sajŏngch'ŏng) and sent commissioners out to the provinces to accumulate information on the operations of the military support tax system. Publication of all statistics was finished in 1748.[21] The figures indicated that the legislation of the previous fifty years had hardly affected the advertised flaws and evils in the system.[22] The only immediate effect of the survey was a minor reduction of troop quotas.

THE EQUAL-SERVICE REFORM, 1750–52

Opposition to Major Overhaul

A hundred years of controversy culminated in the equal service system (*kyunyŏkpŏp*) established first in 1750 and modified in 1752. Furthermore, for the first time in the history of the debate the ideas of Yu Hyŏngwŏn were recommended to the throne by State Councilor Kwŏn Chŏk. Despite the apparent openness of the debate, however, the denouement might have been predicted by anyone familiar with the history of decisions made since 1682, when the opportunity for adopting the household cloth tax was passed by. Thereafter, radical proposals were eschewed in favor of more practical measures like registration and investigation campaigns, quota reduction, and rate uniformity at two *p'il* per support taxpayer.

When the debate began, however, it appeared that Yŏngjo had convinced himself that the time had come to adopt the household cloth tax, and his minister of taxation, Pak Munsu, who had opposed it in 1733, also came around and supported it as well, with the proviso that a cash tax be imposed instead of a cloth tax. Since not every official at court opposed the idea of a household tax, the prospects for a departure from the early Chosŏn system of support-taxpayer finance seemed good.

Nevertheless, some criticized the household tax for being fiscally unsound, for if the rate were set high enough to ensure sufficient revenue, it would be too heavy a burden on taxpayers; if it were set low enough to alleviate their burdens, it would not yield sufficient revenue. Others also attacked it for being unequal because a uniform tax would impose a heavier burden on families with more adult males.[23]

The core issue, however, was the imposition of the tax on yangban households, and on this point several officials claimed that the yangban could not stand the imposition of a new tax or tolerate the social stigma attached to military service. Since Yŏngjo had already rejected a direct tax on leisured males (*yup'o*), most of whom were yangban, the only reason he tolerated discussion of the household cloth or cash tax systems at this time was because he must have believed initially at least that neither one was too threatening to yangban interests. He was dissuaded from this notion from the arguments of men like Yi Chongsŏng, who insisted that yangban were poorer than anyone else and could not afford even the lowest of suggested rates for a household cash tax. Yi's mournful lament for the plight of the poor scholar was also accompanied by an intimidating hint of the potential of another yangban-led rebellion.[24]

Kwŏn Chŏk, Intellectual Disciple of Yu Hyŏngwŏn

The first evidence of any direct influence of the ideas of Yu Hyŏngwŏn at court over military policy occurred when State Councilor (Uch'amch'an) Kwŏn Chŏk submitted a lengthy memorial to the crown prince (the Sado seja), sitting that time as acting head of state. Kwŏn was effusive in his praise for Yu's *Pan'gye surok*, touting it as the best book of statecraft since the Three Ages of antiquity. He noted that it was based on the laws and systems of the *Rites of Chou* and should be used as a source of methods by any monarch "who wants to carry out the humane rule of a true king." He asked the crown prince to approve a request he had made many times before, that it be printed by the governor of Chŏlla Province and distributed throughout the kingdom. Although the text was not carved into wood blocks and printed until 1770, Kwŏn's remarks attest the popularity of the hand-copied text in 1750: "Though the man has already died, his writings are still preserved in the families of the scholar-officials [*sadaebu*] in the capital, many of whom have it ready at their side."

It was indicative of the tenor of Yu's ideas that Kwŏn took the side of the opposition against both the land-cloth and household-cash proposals. The first is less surprising than the second because even though Yu had favored the use of the *taedong* surtax on land to replace tribute in kind, he had unequivocally opposed the idea of land surtax to replace the *yangyŏk* support cloth tax because there were already too many taxes imposed on land. Kwŏn also argued that adding an additional cloth tax on land (*kyŏlp'o*) would only drive the peasants from the land and reduce both acreage under cultivation and tax revenue, forcing the government to increase the tax rate in the future to make up for revenue shortages. Kwŏn also betrayed a rather conservative fear of a cash economy because peasants would suffer additional burdens if they had to exchange rice for cloth or cash on the open market to meet their tax obligations. He also believed that the time was not ripe for any innovative laws because of the low state of morals and the easily excitable nature of the people of the time, hardly an attitude one would expect from a follower of Yu Hyŏngwŏn.

Since he did share Yu's belief in the legitimacy of support-taxpayer financing of the military and the need for a balanced budget based on a calculation of revenue and expenditure, he attempted to work out a solution based on a careful calculation of tax rates, revenues, and expenditures. He pointed out that annual expenditures of cloth tax revenues had increased over the past, from 604,000 *p'il* prior to the service tax reform of *imsul* year (1682), to 633,708 *p'il* at the present time. Of this total, 456,543 *p'il* was paid in by support taxpayers attached to the Five Military Divisions of the capital region, and another 46,116 *p'il* by the taxpayers attached to the civilian capital bureaus (subtotal, 502,659 *p'il*), all of which was tax revenue at the two-p'il rate. In addition, the taxpayers paid .5 *p'il* as transport fee, and this total levy of 2.5 *p'il* was in fact the heaviest rate then in use.

His estimate of provincial expenditures (i.e., income as well) is shown in table 7.

TABLE 7
KWŎN CHŎK'S ESTIMATE
OF PROVINCIAL MILITARY EXPENDITURES

Province	Amount (in *p'il*)
Kyŏngsang	43,012
Chŏlla	46,207
Ch'ungch'ŏng	15,952
Kyŏnggi	3,664
Hwanghae	22,214
TOTAL	131,049

SOURCE: SJW 58:141a-143a; *Yŏngjo sillok* 71:24b-25a, same date.

He noted that these provincial taxes consisted of the one-*p'il*-rate tax that was also exempted from transportation fees, the lightest type of *yangyŏk* in the country. The combined total of capital and provincial expenditures of 633,708 *p'il* was 29,708 *p'il,* or about 5 percent, higher than the pre-1682 figure. Although the size of the increase appeared small, it was in fact large because it had been expected that expenditures would *decrease* after the reform of that year.

He believed there were only two sources of supplemental revenue: (1) profits from special nonagricultural production such as fishing and salt production along the coast, and silver and iron mining in the interior, and (2) the capital fund of the goverment's grain-loan system (*hwanja*) accumulated in granaries throughout the country. If the king took over these resources, he could finance the total abolition of the two-*p'il* military support tax "as easily as turning over his hand." Unfortunately, because there were not sufficient resources on hand to carry out an immediate and total abolition, it was preferable to cut the tax rate in half to one *p'il*. Kwŏn had obviously abandoned Yu Hyŏngwŏn's two-*p'il* tax rate because the history of the period since his death in 1673 had proved the weakness of that position.

Kwŏn's economic thinking had obviously progressed beyond the level of Yu Hyŏngwŏn because he abandoned the idea that the financing for duty soldiers had to be provided exclusively by cloth or grain taxes from the support taxpayers (*poin*). Instead, he argued for the utilization of supplementary mining as well as fishing and salt revenue and proposed substituting cash revenue for the reduction in cloth taxes. He estimated the amount that would be needed after the tax cut to maintain the Five Military Divisions and civilian capital bureaus at 502,659 *yang* of cash (half the original revenue of 502,659 *p'il* or 1,005,318 *yang* of cash). He predicted that revenue from the taxation of fish, salt, iron, and silver would be sufficient to offset it, but without presenting a detailed statistical breakdown of revenues. He then estimated the revenue shortage in the countryside from a one-*p'il* tax cut at 60,314 *p'il*, which, converted to cash at the rate of two *yang* per *p'il,* would be equivalent to 110,628 *yang*.

He claimed that his proposal to offset this deficit was based on the militia model extolled by Yu Hyŏngwŏn, but in fact it appears to have been based on the replacement of support-taxpayer taxes with another form of revenue in a form that was far less progressive than some of his other suggestions. He wanted the state to buy up a restricted amount of land and become the landlord for peasants who would become tenants of the state, a tactic he referred to as a "supporting land" system (*yangjŏn*). The leading military headquarters in a province (those of the governor and provincial army and navy commanders) would be authorized to buy land offered by ordinary landowners for sale on the market, lease it to tenant cultivators either on a fifty/fifty sharecropping arrangement or according to fixed, lower-rate, longer term leaseholds (*toji*), and use the rental income for military expenses. He asserted that this method would benefit both public and private interests simultaneously, encourage the people to engage in primary production, substitute for the current cloth tax exactions, provide for regular tribute payments (out of income) without any reduction in revenue, and operate according to the principles of the ancient militia system, where "agriculture is used to support [*yang*] soldiers and soldiers do no harm to agriculture, what could be called a complete policy."

Financing of the purchase of land from private owners would be provided by the grain loan funds currently stored in granaries that were currently either rotting away or being used for forced loans on people who did not even want them at interest rates so heavy that they were tantamount to a surtax. By using these grain loan funds to fund state-tenancy one could convert a source of one evil into a cure for another. Of the 1,540,000 *sŏm* of grain loan funds in P'yŏng'an and over 2,000,000 *sŏm* in Kyŏngsang provinces, he proposed allocating 500,000 *sŏm* in each province, convertible to cash at one *yang/sŏm* to provide a cash fund of one million *yang* to finance the purchase of land. The estimated annual rental income from the lease of this land would be 120,628 *yang* of cash (12 percent return on invested capital) which would be distributed to the specific military headquarters of governors and provincial army and navy commanders in every province. This income would offset the 110,628 *yang* revenue reduction from a tax cut, and during a three-year transition period until rental income flowed into government coffers, interest on grain-loan funds from the provincial government offices in Ch'ungch'ŏng and Chŏlla could be used to finance military costs. In addition, budget balancing could be aided by reducing expenditures or by transferring cash from other sources.

He countered any possible objection to cannibalizing grain loan funds and eliminating the current source of rural credit and relief by arguing that the peasants would benefit more from obtaining land as state tenants than obtaining loans under current conditions. He defended the use of land for supporting soldiers because of the precedent of military colony lands (*tunjŏn*), an argument that Yu (along with many others) had made. And he also justified the use of nonagricultural production by citing the unsuccessful recommendations of the late Yi Minsŏ and Min Chinwŏn, who had previously advocated using fish, salt, and mining income exclusively for support of the military.

He then turned to the question of military organization. At the beginning of the dynasty when the Five Guard system was in use, the system was good, but the troops themselves were not so good, which is why it was necessary to create new military divisions during and after the Imjin War. Then the situation changed to one in which the troops were in good condition but the system had deteriorated. He said he would rather have good troops than a good system, but the Five Military Divisions of the post-1592 era was a bad system because their support was not grounded in peasant production like the farmer/soldier militia (of antiquity) but relied instead on onerous taxes collected from peasants of good status (*yangmin*) – a curious remark from a disciple of Yu since Yu had favored retention of the support taxpayer system of military finance (and hoped eventually to convert all slaves to men of good status).

Yu Hyŏngwŏn had only wanted to retain a reorganized Military Training Agency without permanent soldiers but otherwise replace the rest of the Five Military Divisions with the Five Guards. Kwŏn did not advocate reestablishment of the Five Guards, but he was in general agreement with Yu's preference for support taxpayers. He did complain, however, that the main problem with the Royal Division and Forbidden Guard Division was that their rotating duty soldiers (*hosu* or household heads) had been required to pay their own support along with their support taxpayers (*poin*), imposing an unbearable burden on them. There were about 30,000 men involved in this, and he expected that a gradual reform of the situation could be achieved, but not evidently by abolishing the units themselves. The Military Training Agency, however, was another story. Because its soldiers were not peasants but professional soldiers, they were a curse on the commoner peasants (*yangmin*) who annually had to supply 5,000 *sŏm* of rice and 70,000 *p'il* of cloth in support taxes, all of which had to be forced from peasants who did not have the means to pay. The problem derived from the failure to base the Five Military Division system on the fundamental principle of preventing "mutual harm between farming and military service" when its units were first established in the seventeenth century.

This slogan, of course, referred to the presumed complementarity of agricultural production and military service under the classical militia system. Kwŏn said that when the Military Training Agency was first established (in 1593), there was no time to provide a regular source of income and support for the unit, so the government created the temporary *samsuryang* or "three types of soldiers rice surtax" on land in the southern three provinces. What then happened was that later generations respected and preserved as an honored institution what the creators of the agency had only intended as a temporary measure. By contrast, his proposal to use the profits from salt and fishing and to use grain loan funds to rent land for the support of soldiers (*pyŏngjŏn*) was based on the fundamental (and classical) proposition that no military system should do harm to agriculture or be a burden on peasant producers.

Kwŏn then turned his attention to the problem of the palace estates (*kungbang* or *kungga*) established by kings for the support of princes and princesses. Since the end of Sŏnjo's reign in the late sixteenth century, an increasing number had been given special royal grants of land in the countryside for their support, but because the fields had been laid waste by Hideyoshi's invasion, there was not enough land to fill the quota of the land grant. In effect, they had been given blank warrants (*kongp'ae*) without any real income, and in compensation they were awarded tax revenues from fishing and salt manufacture along the coast. Although this arrangement was only supposed to be a temporary adjustment, at the present time palace estates had a full quota of land grants and also retained and increased their monopoly over income from the production of the sea. "The catch of each fishing net and pole is in every case assigned [to some palace estate], and the [profits] of the great deep all ends up in their nets. How could this have been the basic intention of Sŏnjo's court?"

The poor fishermen on the other hand, had to bear a half-dozen taxes on each catch in addition to those owed to the palace estates: taxes owed to local magistrates, to owners (of fishing weirs?) who held certificates (*ib'an*) from the government, to bureaucratic offices of the capital, and to the provincial governor and army and navy commanders. Kwŏn insisted that all these extra levies be abolished and that peasants living along the coast only be required to pay taxes authorized by the state.

Kwŏn also urged the crown prince to use what he heard were vast reserves of rice, beans, and other grains in the capital granaries to make up any shortages in required (military) expenditures by selling it off for cash. He referred to this as "doing injury to those on top in order to benefit those below," a standard paraphrase of the Mencian injunction to virtuous kings to reduce their expenditures to alleviate tax burdens on the peasants. In this case he cited the words of the grand duke (T'ai-kung, Lü Shang) of early Chou China, who when asked by King Wen how to govern a state well, responded that the fortunes of a state depended on whether the king distributed wealth to the people or confined its use to a narrow elite. He described four different situations in descending order: "The way of a true king was to make the people rich, but the way of a hegemon was to make his petty officials [*sa*] rich, and the way of a ruler barely able to keep his kingdom was to make his middle-rank officials [*taebu*] rich, and the way of a ruler about to lose his kingdom was to make [his own] granaries rich."[25] As one might expect, Kwŏn not only asked that surpluses be spent to enable tax reduction, he also recommended cutbacks in unnecessary regular officials and clerks in the capital bureaus, slave employees, and special military petty officers in the Royal Treasury (Naesusa), and abolition of the hiring of soldiers by private families.

Although Kwŏn was not advocating Yu Hyŏngwŏn's plan for total nationalization of land by confiscation of private property, he did criticize current violations of the law that restricted royal grants of land to private individuals (*sajŏn*) to four generations of descent from the original recipient, and prebendal grants under royal warrant (*sap'ae*) to the recipient only. He had heard that all such grantees were retaining their control over these royal grants and converting them to family property in perpetuity, in contravention of the will of the founders of the dynasty. If it were allowed to continue, the amount of land controlled by the state would shrink to a plot 100 *i* on each side. He cited a story in the *Shih-chi* of Ssu-ma Ch'ien that Emperor T'ang of remote antiquity only granted fictive fiefs to his nobles, preferring to give them bolts of silk instead of land. "If T'ang with the whole world at his disposal was as sparing of land as this, how much more so should a small country [like ours]? If granting tax revenue to private individuals is regarded as something commonplace, it will produce the evils associated with an age of decline."

What had to be done was to confiscate all parcels of land held beyond the legal time or generational limit, expand land under state control and the tax revenues therefrom, and use them to defray the expenses usually paid for by support tax cloth assigned to the capital bureaus.

Kwŏn ended his long memorial by reminding the crown prince that the key to good government was frugality and concern for the people. The king had to set an example of modest consumption and impose sumptuary regulations all the way down the social ladder.[26]

Kwŏn Chŏk's memorial provides convincing circumstantial evidence that Yu Hyŏngwŏn's *Pan'gye surok* was widely known and read in leading scholar-official circles at the time and that the ideas of this pioneer of Practical Learning statecraft studies were by no means confined to a small audience of recluse outcastes. It also allows us to see how the seventeenth-century ideas of Yu were adapted to eighteenth-century circumstances. Kwŏn brought one new and original idea to the debate over reform of the military tax system: his proposal for state-sponsored purchase and distribution of land to landless peasants, but as tenanted plots rather than as conditioned, returnable grants. The inspiration for this idea must have come from Yu Hyŏngwŏn's work, even though what Yu wanted was a far more radical policy of confiscation, nationalization, and distribution along the lines of the T'ang equal-field system. Yu could envisage no other way to achieve it but to persuade a reigning king to assert his will, ignore the counterforces of private property and private interest, and resolutely create the Utopian order by fiat.

Kwŏn, on the other hand, produced a more practical remedy: exploitation of the grain-loan capital fund to engage in a limited program of land redistribution by buying land on the open market, renting or leasing it to landless peasants, and using rental income to finance soldiers. This was not really the parroting of Yu's traditional talk about a farmer/soldier militia, but the fulfillment of Yu's injunction to adapt principles of governance gleaned from one's study of the classics and history to contemporary circumstance. Yu meant by the slogan to base military service on agriculture that peasants should be given land grants by the state, in return for which they would serve on duty as a true militia. Kwŏn adapted this to mean that any plan for financing the military should not result in the accumulation of taxes on peasants but should, on the contrary, be combined with some sort of program for enhancing peasant agricultural production and income. Mutual support between agriculural and military affairs, between farmers and soldiers was what Kwŏn perceived as a fundamental principle of governance extracted from the ancient militia ideal.

Kwŏn's opposition to the use of a surtax on land to finance the military and his proposal to transfer control of nonagricultural income from palace estates to the government for this purpose were derivative from Yu's views on these questions. Yu had objected to a surtax on land to defray military costs, but approved the use of specially designated "military expense land" (*kunjajŏn*). More to the point, Yu justified the idea because military units had already been using certain sorts of revenue from fishing weirs, salt flats, and iron smelters to finance banquets, weapons repair, and construction. He also hoped to abolish all types of private control over these sources of wealth. Kwŏn also shared Yu's bias against the permanent, salaried soldiers of the Military Training Agency, but he differed with Yu by arguing for retention of the Five Military Divisions, no doubt because their elimination had proved so difficult, but also because he could appreciate military and political reasons for special divisions surrounding the capital.

Perhaps of more importance than agreement on specific issues was the matter of a shared mode of thought, in particular a rational approach to budget balancing by calculation of expenditures and an educated estimate of potential revenue. Although his estimates of supplementary income from fishing, salt, silver, and iron taxes and from rental income from leased lands fell short of the kind of accurate ledger-balancing that Yu seemed to hold dear, the spirit was similar.

It may be somewhat disconcerting, however, that Yu's intellectual disciple, Kwŏn, should have argued against the most radical proposal for military taxation reform since Yu's own time, the household cash tax. Unfortunately, although Kwŏn explained his opposition to the land cloth (*kyŏlp'o*) proposal in some detail, about the household cash tax he merely said that there was no need to repeat arguments made by others.[27] One might presume that Kwŏn must have shared the general hostility to the household tax because it would have been levied on yangban households. But how could a disciple of Yu Hyŏngwŏn fail to support an egalitarian and status-blind tax measure like the household cash tax? Even though Yu was not totally egalitarian, he still advocated bringing most of the yangban back into a military service system in the manner of the elite units of the Five Guard system.

The explanation must be sought elsewhere. Kwŏn shared with Yu a prejudice in favor of retaining the system of support taxpayers and a bias against the separation of military finance from adult males deemed categorically appropriate to perform national military service functions. Since he was proposing a cut of the support tax rate to one *p'il*, he worked out a scheme to raise other kinds of revenue, something that Yu Hyŏngwŏn had not envisioned, but he must have been heir to Yu's penchant for categorical thinking and his association between a mode of taxation and an object of taxation, or between a mode of taxation and a use for the revenue so obtained. He only departed from Yu on the matter of the two-*p'il* rate because it had been proved ineffective.

Kwŏn's opposition to both land and household taxes probably derived from Yu Hyŏngwŏn's general respect for traditional categories of taxation and service. Although his proposal for state-sponsored sharecropping grants to tenants would in fact have used land rent to support soldiers, Kwŏn did not deem it a violation of the militia ideal because he focused on the reciprocity involved between a state grant and a return payment by the grantee. Men like Yu and Kwŏn ruled out programs that did violence to a fundamental principle of taxation in a precommercial economy, one that extolled the idea of service in the form of labor.

The Reform Debate of 1750

In the summer of 1750 the governor of Kyŏnggi, Yu Pongmyŏng, wrote a lengthy memorial on the reform of the system of military taxation, but he was deeply pessimistic about the prospects of a successful reform because of the low state of mores at the time. He recommended only the adoption of the precedent previously set in P'yŏng'an Province of cutting the two-*p'il* rate to one *p'il* because it removed the incentive for commanders to sign up adult males for low-rate, one-*p'il* service. He felt that the experiment had worked in P'yŏng'an because the people had never complained about rate reduction, and the proposal was fiscally feasible as long as the government eliminated unnecessary expenditures and imposed a one-*p'il* tax on all the currently tax-exempt types like the extraquota students, district military officers, and banner and tally officers (*kip'aeg-*

wan). To salve their feelings, he proposed calling them cloth taxpaying military officers (*sup'o kun'gwan*) instead of ordinary soldiers or support taxpayers.[28]

A few days later Yŏngjo told his officials that even though he had been told that a one-*p'il* tax cut would be a great blessing, he would always have regrets if he were not able to abolish the military support taxes completely. Chief State Councilor Cho Hyŏnmyŏng, however, then told him that even if he ordered the abolition of the two-*p'il* support tax, it would be impossible to abolish the rotating duty soldiers of the Royal Division and Forbidden Guard Division. Since the cost of their equipment was so great, if the king chose to abolish the two-*p'il* rate, he would soon run out of funds and be forced to reinstate at least a one-*p'il* tax on support taxpayers to provide for their expenses. Rather than do that, it would be better simply to cut the current rate to one *p'il*. Yŏngjo then remarked that Cho's words had put him at ease, indicating that his resolve to abolish cloth taxes on support taxpayers was not that strong to begin with. Probably he had reached a turning point in his own mind, setting the stage for his final decision.

The *Sillok* historian who recorded these events in the next generation, however, was incensed by Cho's remarks and inserted his own opinion into the text that Cho was only deceiving Yŏngjo (into abandoning total elimination of the two-*p'il* tax):

> [Every time any proposal was raised,] not to mention the household and land [cloth tax propositions], they always wanted to use revenues from salt and fishing to replace revenues from the support cloth taxes, so why was it only the rotating duty soldiers for whom substitute taxes could not be found, and why was it necessary to have a personal cloth support tax only for them? He only wanted to make his words sound good and put the king's mind at ease in order to achieve his own desires.

The historian was making an excellent point: why did Cho Hyŏnmyŏng think that the only legitimate source of funds for rotating duty soldiers was adult male support taxpayers of good status? Why could he not see that soldiers could logically be supported by revenues collected from any source? The historian's anger at Cho may not have been justified. Although it was possible that Cho was merely using any argument available to block a new tax on yangban, he was obviously limited by the same categorical thinking shared by Yu Hyŏngwŏn and his intellectual disciple, Kwŏn Chŏk. This was the reluctance to sever any time-honored relationship between a particular mode of tax and its objective, or between the peasant rotating duty soldier and the peasant support taxpayer characteristic of the mode of labor dues.[29]

The gist of the debate held at court in the seventh lunar month, however, did not focus on the propriety of abandoning reliance on support-taxpayer finance, but on whether the funds generated from a household cash tax imposed on all families irrespective of status offset the loss resulting from reduction or abolition of the military support tax. To do this, the rate would have to be set so high that it would constitute a new form of oppression on taxpayers. Conversely, if it were set so low as to guarantee a light tax on the population, it would not raise enough revenue to meet expenses. In short, the point had been reached where the minimum tax rate on households necessary to match the loss in revenue from a tax cut on adult males appeared to be too high for the king to accept, at least according to the information he was getting from his fiscal experts. In addition, there was powerful opposition to any status-blind tax on the household that would include the yangban.[30]

Yŏngjo held a second public meeting outside the Honghwamun in which he declared his sincere concern for the people and his desire to consult public opinion. He also declared that when he had been crown prince (in the early 1720s) he had favored adoption of the household cash tax even though the argument had been made at the time that any tax that was levied on slave householders as well as others would be destructive of proper social status (*myŏngbun*). He believed in the principle that anyone with a household ought to pay a household tax, and that the long suffering of the *yangmin* (men with good status) had to be alleviated by adoption of an equal service system. He even stated that cutting the tax rate to one *p'il* would constitute a betrayal of popular wishes. Most of the officials in attendance, however, opposed imposition of a household tax on yangban primarily because it really meant an additional tax even though it was supposed to replace an onerous tax, and hence was a violation of the Confucian norm to reduce taxes to a minimum.[31]

Censor-General (Sagwan) Yun Kwangch'an also opposed the household cloth tax and when Yŏngjo asked him what other means were available to make up the loss from a one-*p'il* tax cut, he replied that King T'aejong of the early fifteenth century had not adopted a household tax because it did not conform to the principle of rectification of names, that is, it was not the appropriate category for military support taxes. The *Sillok* historian took umbrage at this statement: he castigated the officials of the time for their lack of new ideas except for Censor Yun's proposal to eliminate the Royal Treasury, and criticized Chŏng Ingnyang and the other high officials for failing to support the idea. Of course, writing a quarter century after the fact, he knew full well that the opportunity for major institutional reform had been missed in 1750, and he chose this spot to record one of his most serious objections to the progress of the court discussions: "Equal service was just a matter of knocking down something in the East and building it up in the West [robbing Peter to pay Paul], taking something away from the root and adding it to the branch. There was a major reform in name, but there was none in fact, and in the space of an instant the evils it produced were tremendous."[32]

One additional point remains to be made about the conference this day – the role of Kwŏn Chŏk, the admirer of Yu Hyŏngwŏn. The previous day Kwŏn had not attended court but he was praised by Chief State Councilor Cho Hyŏnmyŏng because he had bothered to write a lengthy and valuable memorial even though he was eighty years of age and in declining health. Yŏngjo, however, replied that "His policies have a lot of mistakes, but in this matter I value each man expressing his own views, and so this is also good [that he did so]." The reason why Yŏngjo had been unimpressed by Kwŏn's argument should be clear. Kwŏn opposed either a household or land tax because he represented Yu Hyŏngwŏn's archaic or classical mode of reform, one that stressed adherence to traditional categories of taxation, including something equivalent to actual labor dues from men.

When called upon to express his views while in court the next day, he replied that he had already said everything he had to say in his written memorial, but since he had not seen any action taken as a result of it, he was convinced the royal secretariat had thrown it into the wastebasket. He had taken the trouble to rouse himself from his bed and go to the palace gate to listen to the king's discussion with the crowd, and he had been discomfited by what he heard "the people" say. Their support for the household cash tax distressed him because it was too bad for words. While the *yangyŏk* system might be equivalent to "an illness suffered by one person, the household cash tax would be the edema of ten thousand."

Yŏngjo on the other hand said he had been committed to a household cloth tax since his Heir Apparency in the 1720s; he belonged to a more progressive mode of thought that was open to more flexible taxation based on new economic circumstances. That alone, however, was not sufficient to induce him to adopt one of the new taxes because he had to be convinced that it would do more good than harm. But this brief exchange demonstrates that Yŏngjo's favor for reform was not really informed by Yu Hyŏngwŏn's ideas even though they had been recommended to him in indirect form by Kwŏn Chŏk. Kwŏn's contribution (or Yu's influence through Kwŏn), if any, was a negative one – opposition to a household or land tax. But he was not the only one opposed to them, and there were a number of other arguments used against them in addition to his, the most important being a defense of yangban privilege, distaste for new and additional taxes, and insufficient revenue to offset a cut in the military cloth tax. Kwŏn did not necessarily intend to defend yangban privilege, but his arguments had that effect. Most of the men who favored some version of a general tax to finance the military were either active officials or members of the Patriarch's faction who were more responsive to environmental changes than the recluse scholars with their classical learning. But in any case, it was the mode of thought that was more important than factional affiliation.[33]

Later in the day, Yŏngjo also remarked that he had been upset when the Confucian scholars at the palace gate had said that a household tax would be nothing more than an "additional tax." Kim Chaero reminded him of Yi Chongsŏng's statement that he would be better off losing the support of the people than the scholar-officials (*sadaebu*), and he suggested a one-*p'il* cut supplemented by a tax on the *yŏjŏng* or "extra adult males," presumably untaxed and unregistered evaders.

Finally, Yŏngjo remarked that he was determined not to be known as a king who imposed an additional tax burden not only on the people, but on their descendants in perpetuity, so some other method besides the household or land tax even as supplements to a partial tax cut had to be found. He declared that if any shortages in revenue resulted from it, he would meet the deficit by cutting his own consumption.[34]

Yŏngjo then made a formal announcement of his decision to cut the *yangyŏk* rate in half. He explained why he had decided to reject all other alternatives. The per capita cash tax (*kujŏn*) would be destructive of respect for social status distinctions (*myŏngbun*) because it would be levied on both masters and slaves (!) within the same family. A cloth tax on land (*kyŏlp'o*) would be tantamount to an additional tax since there were already regular taxes assessed on land. Even though the household cloth tax appeared to be the best system, people were sure to be disturbed if the current tax were cut by one *p'il* and household taxes were levied to make up the difference. "[If I retain the current] military cloth tax, half the country will be angry, but [if I adopt the] household cash tax, the whole country will be. The minds of the people should be settled, not stirred up."

But what he was really thinking was that if he adopted the household cloth tax, a significant minority of privileged yangban and successful tax evaders would be upset and might organize a repeat performance of the *imsin* rebellion of 1728, whereas retention of the current cloth tax on adult males of good status only with a 50 percent rate cut might create a fiscal crisis, but it would alleviate the immediate suffering of the peasantry and buy off the yangban. In other words, Yŏngjo's abandonment of the household cloth tax was as much a product of his own reluctance to antagonize yangban interests as the overt opposition of court officials and capital scholars.

The practical learning view, as represented by Kwŏn Chŏk, the disciple of Yu Hyŏngwŏn's thought, was no help, for both household and land taxes were ruled out of order by the more archaic approach to reform. Land reform, even in his watered-down version, and return of yangban to actual physical service in military units, were so outmoded and unacceptable that nobody wanted to hear of them.

Shifting his attention to ways of cutting costs by abolishing troop units, Yŏngjo concluded that the threat of domestic rebellion virtually prevented any major reordering of the Five Military Divisions established after 1592. He remarked that the Military Training Agency, the unit most frequently criticized because of the expense of permanent, salaried soldiers, was not the only flawed institution in the military establishment. By this he meant that as a unit with a contingent of permanent soldiers on duty in the capital, he could at least count on them for support in case of a domestic political crisis. By contrast, he pointed out that neither the Forbidden Guard Division nor the Royal Division were useful in any major emergency because their force consisted of provincial troops (*hyanggun*) who served on duty on rotation (!*pace* Yu Hyŏngwŏn and Song Siyŏl). But it was not the quality of their performance as rotating duty soldiers that bothered him, but their political dependability. During the *imsin* rebellion of 1728, he noted, a special messenger had to be sent to order them to report to the capital for fear that they might be won over to the rebel cause. "If we had established capital soldiers, then how could we have had this problem?"

In this last instance, Yŏngjo was voicing the same proposal made by Yu Hyŏngwŏn, that after restoration of the Five Guard System (in conjunction with a reorganized Military Training Agency), the Five Guards in the capital would recruit their troops from men living in the capital region, and not from the provinces. On the other hand, Yu had nothing but admiration for rotating duty soldiers, he just opposed assigning them to units too far from their home villages. In the end, Yŏngjo could not bring himself to order the abolition of any of the existing capital divisions, concluding that while it might be a good idea to get rid of some border garrison commanders (*pyŏngjang*), the (Five) Divisions had been around too long.

At the end of the day Yŏngjo issued his formal decree cutting the tax rate to one *p'il*, eliminating dependent payments to provincial governors and to the commanders of the Defense Command and Anti-Manchu Division, and reducing expenditures of the agency of national relief and the Office of Benefiting the People (Hyeminsŏ) by combining it with the Directorate of Medicine (Chŏn'ŭigam) in a single office. He issued another decree later in the day, cutting his own food ration by 200 *sŏm* and that of the crown prince by 100, and transferring the funds to the Office of Dispensing Benevolence as a demonstration of his unselfish concern for the people. He ordered reduction of annual tribute offerings of delicacies to the royal kitchen, and his officials responded by volunteering to cut their own salaries. By now he was fully caught up in the game of making a public display of Confucian frugality.[35]

Not mentioned by the king at this time, but a crucial element in the measures adopted to supplement lost revenue was his adoption of a one-*p'il* levy on students who failed school examinations. Although designed as a revenue measure to offset losses from the cut in the tax rate, this measure was subsequently to give rise to a vocal protest movement.

Hong Kyehŭi's Memorial on Equal Service, 1752

In 1752, Minister of War Hong Kyehŭi presented a long memorial to the crown prince that introduced a document called "The True Facts of Equal Service" (*Kyunyŏk sasil ch'aekcha*), which began by tracing the history of the military service system from the beginning of the dynasty. He stated his commitment to two propositions that were also fundamental to the thinking of Yu Hyŏngwŏn – the militia ideal and the Five Guards system of early Chosŏn – and he traced the process by which those two ideals had been adulterated since the fifteenth century.

> In Yin and Chou times [in ancient China] they used land as the basis for furnishing soldiers, and soldiers were dependent on agriculture [or soldiers were depen-

> dent on peasants], but in the later age [*huse*], soldiers and agriculture [or soldiers and peasants] were divided, the system of the early [sage] kings was destroyed. The Five Guards system of our dynasty was in fact modeled after the *fu-ping* system [of T'ang China, according to which] soldiers rotated on and off duty, and being a soldier did no damage to agriculture. In the interval [between planting and harvesting?] they would engage in the construction of walls or service on the frontier. Because the court was deeply concerned over the difficulty that cavalrymen and infantrymen had in having to carry their food rations with them over long distances [in reporting to duty from their homes], they allowed them to pay cloth and hire substitutes. The was the origin of the system of the cloth tax.
>
> At the beginning of our dynasty the system of personal service [*sinyŏk*] was very strict, and everyone, from the sons of the highest lords and officials down to the common people, had a service assignment. Those who had the protection [*ŭm*] privilege were enrolled in the Loyal and Obedient Guards or the Loyal Assistant Guards. Those who did not have the protection privilege were regular soldiers [*chŏngbyŏng*] or armored soldiers [*kapsa*]. Thus the will of the people was settled, and the service required from the people was distributed equally.
>
> Since that time the way of the world has been such that law and order has gradually disintegrated and the sons and younger brothers of the officials [*sabu*] no longer have their names listed on the rosters of the various guards. Even the local gentry with rank titles [*hyangp'um*] and the relatives [of officials] who are cold and destitute have also styled themselves yangban in order to evade personal service. The result has been that military service has fallen exclusively on the poor people who are tired, weak, and have nothing to rely on.

Hong believed that the cloth tax system had its origin in the substitution of a cloth payment in lieu of service accompanied by a shift in the subject of service from all adult males, no matter what the status of the individual, to only men of good (*yang*) status, but as more men succeeded in escaping military service, the definition of *yang* became narrower and was applied eventually only to men unable to acquire yangban status or de facto exemptions from service. Hong also claimed that there were currently only 120,000 households available to pay the taxes due for support of duty troops, a figure that had risen from 300,000 households in 1682 to 500,000, and he listed a half-dozen measures adopted to make up for the shortage in revenue produced by Yŏngjo's decision to cut the military cloth tax rate in half.

These measures included a version of the fine or levy on students who failed qualifying examinations. Instead of registering them for military service and taxation like other commoners, each province conducted a "capital examination" and the top student was granted a degree, the second student a chance to proceed to the regular civil service (*hoesi*) examination, and the next five an exemption from the current year's cloth taxes. All the rest had to pay a one-*p'il* levy, but were designated specially selected military officers (*sŏnmu kun'gwan*).

The fifth measure was referred to as allocations (*punjŏng*) that provincial governors, and provincial army and navy commanders were required to raise any way they could and pay to the central government to offset the loss of revenue from the one-*p'il* tax cut. As Ch'a Munsŏp has pointed out, the two-*mal* rice tax on land (*kyŏlmi*) was dropped, as one might have expected, and replaced with the vague provincial allotments (*punjŏng*), which allowed provincial officials carte blanche in raising funds, and may have done more to offset the benefits of the tax cut than any other item.[36]

Hong had reported the hue and cry raised in the provinces over the one-*p'il* levy on the specially selected military officers after 1750. At the time Yŏngjo denied that he had intended the measure to be construed in any way as a "tax on the leisured" (*yup'o*) or a household cash tax. He had only placed a levy on them because he wanted to reduce the excessive tax burden borne by commoner men of good status, which had been caused not by the men of leisure themselves, but by the corruption of the district magistrates over the years! He hoped to gloss the issue of taxing yangban by calling it something other than a tax – a tactic that had been tried as far back as 1626. He probably did believe, however, that yangban should be preserved from a military service tax, not only because he was afraid of a yangban-led rebellion, but because he also supported the idea of a status-based society.[37]

After listening to a raft of complaints about his new taxes designed to make up for lost revenue, Yŏngjo promulgated the order for the "rice surtax on land" (*kyŏlmi*) in the ninth month of 1751.[38] He ordered a surtax of two *mal* of grain or five *chŏn* of cash per *kyŏl* of land in six provinces (exclusive of the northern two), and he estimated the total revenue, calculated in terms of cash, at about 320,000 *yang* for an average crop year.[39] In addition, he also set the terms for the use of grain loan interest (*hoerok*), and then conceded that the fine on student dropouts designated specially selected military officers was necessary to replace revenue lost by the tax cut on peasants of good status.

CONCLUSION

The denouement of the equal-service debate produced a couple of ironic situations. In his first public meeting outside the palace in 1750 Yŏngjo had declared that he had given thoughtful consideration to a special tax on idle yangban (*yup'o*) but had decided to rule it out. He asked the people to decide between a surtax on land or a nondiscriminatory household tax on people of all statuses. Shortly thereafter he announced he had rejected all those alternatives in favor of a tax cut, but in a desperate search for funds by 1752, Yŏngjo ended up by imposing a tax on idle yangban and a surtax on land, in addition to creating a number of other new taxes. He had rejected a household tax because of the objections of the defenders of yangban privilege against either military service *or* taxes, but the special levy on school dropouts (specially selected military officers) was only a thinly disguised tax on yangban. The protest raised over this measure probably dissipated any good will the king had earned from the yangban class by passing over the household tax. The contradiction in his policy was produced by the balance between his own inner respect for the dignity of yangban-scholar families and fear of yangban discontent and his desperate need for substitute revenues to maintain basic military costs. He really appears to have convinced himself that a fine on school dropouts was not really a tax on yangban, and since only 24,000 men were involved, he did not expect the protest that soon emerged.

He had also ruled out a land surtax because he was opposed to levying "additional" taxes on land in principle, but he ended up doing so anyway because of the fiscal crisis produced by the tax cut. Thus, a portion of the tax relief provided to the peasant of good status by the service tax cut was taken away by the surcharge on land.

Pak Kwangsŏng in his recent study concluded, as had some officials at the time, that the whole equal service reform merely involved moving tax revenues and resources around from one source to another without solving the fundamental problem of the military service and tax system. Of course, that problem was the narrowness of the tax base caused by exemptions based on status and evasion.[40]

Aftermath of the Equal Service Reform

The equal service reform of 1750 did, after all, cut the tax rate on men of good status in half, and for that reason provided an immediate benefit to that class. By the end of 1753, a small surplus in the revenues of the Equal Service Bureau even permitted a small reduction in the land cash surtax. But by 1754 corruption was beginning again in a number of areas. In 1764 Chief State Councilor Hong Ponghan complained that in the last decade the financial situation had become progressively worse, and by the 1780s fish, salt, and boat taxes were becoming onerous and forcing coastal residents into bankruptcy. Despite provisions for review and reassessment of taxes on boats, fishing weirs, and salt flats, quotas were not changed and became permanent charges imposed on the descendants of seventeenth-century producers, or their neighbors and relatives, right through the 1850s. The substitute taxes established to compensate for the tax cut of 1750 became themselves new sources of corruption in taxation.

There was some alleviation of the evils associated with *yangyŏk* service and taxation but only until the late 1750s. Not only did the equal-service reform of 1750 fail to extend the tax base to include yangban and quasi-yangban tax evaders in any serious way, it did not deal directly with the problem of administrative corruption and inefficiency in the registration of commoners of good status for military taxes. Even the fines levied on the specially select military officers did not succeed in expanding the tax base to yangban because ordinary commoners began to use this as a route for evading service itself, fulfilling the prediction of Pak Munsu in 1752. There was thus no reason to expect that the evils of commendation, false registration, and evasion would be solved in the long run.

In fact, a number of new problems were added to the old ones. By King

Chŏngjo's reign in the late 1770s, men were still evading service by registering with government schools or private academies as students or school officials or getting registered as *yuhak* without respect to their scholarly qualifications. The rich and influential were signing up for low-rate service if they could not escape taxes altogether, and some tax evaders were able to register with local gentry associations (*hyang'an*) by donating money to their support. Men were beginning to form associations called *kye* according to function or occupation (like local clerks, local gentry, military officers, even official slaves) to protect themselves against military taxes (a practice called *kyebang*). Sometimes a whole village (*kyebangch'on*) would sign up with an official for low-rate service to reduce the tax burden collectively. To maintain tax quotas officials were continuing to pile up taxes on the remaining members of the village, the "neighbors and relatives." And officials of various types continued to recruit additional men for service or tax payments under an almost infinite variety of titles.

Writing in the early nineteenth century, Chŏng Yagyong (pen name, Tasan), noted that in 1750 presumably 500,000 men of good status were paying four *yang* of cash (the cash equivalent of the two-*p'il* cloth rate), or a total of 2,000,000 *yang* in revenue to the state. Even though the rate was cut in half, by the turn of the century the number of cloth taxpayers had in fact increased to something over two million people, four times his estimate of the number in 1750, and double the highest estimate of the actual total of taxpayers in other sources. Although the rate was supposedly reduced to two *yang*, the total revenue had doubled to 4,000,000 *yang* by his estimate. "If you consider that the benefit of a 50 percent tax cut resulted in a doubling of the taxes collected by the local districts, can you say that this country has laws?"[41]

Even though the number of taxpayers was increasing, military service quotas established in 1750 that were supposed to be revised periodically in accordance with changes in population became fixed quantities distributed among rural districts, without any respect whatsoever to the adult male population or the number of men actually available for tax payments. For that matter, Kim Yŏngsŏp found that district military support taxes quotas were established as a factor of government costs or requirements rather than simply as a function of the adult male population even before 1750. This development led to some fascinating adjustments. In 1790 some magistrates in the Hwanghae and P'yong'an areas had begun levying household taxes as the only fair and feasible way to distribute the tax burden, but the central government refused to adopt the method for the entire country, primarily because King Chŏngjo treated the equal-service legislation as an ironclad legacy from his grandfather that could or should not be amended. Some villages began paying the quotas collectively on their own, in the fashion of the village-responsibility system the government attempted to adopt in the early eighteenth century, distributing the burden equitably among households, including in some instances yangban as well as commoners. They did this by forming military cloth tax associations, donating land to be used for paying the village's military tax quota, contributing to funds used for that purpose, or paying the village's quota collectively. These measures were taken as a defensive reaction on the part of some villages rather than as a positive policy advanced by the government, but on the other hand these village cloth-tax associations appeared to have included yangban members of local society. By no means, however, were all yangban households throughout the country required to pay the military service tax.[42]

Failure to solve the fundamental problems of military service taxes contributed to the *imsul* rebellion of 1862, and that rebellion finally stimulated the Taewongun in 1870 to issue a private order to all yangban households to pay the military cloth tax in the name of their household slaves.[43] By the middle of the nineteenth century, military service had been converted mainly to a tax system rather than a labor service system with the unfortunate consequence that when Western and Japanese gunboats appeared off Korean shores, the armed forces were too weak to defend the nation. Despite the changes that had taken place, those who had succeeded in evading or gaining exemption from military taxes were able to defend their privileges against the interests of the state. The yangban and the official spokesmen for yangban interests put up an impregnable barrier against kings and reformers, but the ever-expanding pool of tax-exempt men had gone far beyond any narrow group of hereditary yangban aristocrats. That is why Kim Yŏngsŏp found that in Yŏngch'ŏn district of Kyŏngsang Province in 1792 only 15 percent of the households were paying service taxes.[44]

PART IV

Military Reform: Conclusion

Kang Man'gil has written recently that there were two types of reform plans advocated by scholars of so-called Practical Learning in the seventeenth and eighteenth century for the reform of the military service system. The first involved the farmer/soldier militia ideal and the other a per capita cash tax based on a system of tax support for soldiers that was not tied to a land grant system. Kim Yongsŏp also called attention to the difference between a corvée or labor tax and taxation of goods, production, or money, arguing that labor service was a medieval feature of Korean society rendered obsolete by the development of commerce and currency and the household cloth tax. He also pointed out that discrimination based on status and the exemption of yangban from military service and taxation was another of the medieval categories of taxation as well.[1]

Both Kang and Kim have thus drawn attention to an important distinction in the way men conceived of military service and its role in a taxation system in this period. Although they held that there were two approaches to military service reform, neither was the product of traditional scholars alone, but of a cross-fertilization of ideas between active officials and scholars. This can easily be seen in Yu Hyŏngwŏn's borrowing of the ideas of Yulgok (Yi I) and Yu Sŏngnyŏng on military affairs in particular. Yet it was also Yu Hyŏngwŏn who in the mid-seventeenth century derived his main inspiration for the reform of military service from the classical and archaic militia model of antiquity in which men were obligated to perform service for the state. And it was a number of active officials rather than Practical Learning scholars who accepted the transformation of the earlier military service obligation into a system of taxation and sought to reform it as such instead of returning to a personal service or militia system. What then took place in the eighteenth century was that the reform proposals of the active officials of the seventeenth century worked their way into the consciousness of the statecraft scholars so that classical models and archaic concepts of physical labor service competed side-by-side with more contemporary ideas about taxation and expansion of the tax base (rather than service) into the protected realm of the yangban.

When Yu wrote that he abhorred the idea of long-term, professional soldiers on permanent salary like those of the contemporary Military Training Agency, he was merely repeating the wisdom of his Chinese sources. As Ou-yang Hsiu of the Sung period had pointed out in his discussion of the T'ang military system, an army of professional soldiers was a permanent drain on the treasury and a potential political threat to the regime. Yu agreed, but he also believed that the combination of rotating duty soldiers and support taxpayers that had been in effect since the Koryŏ period was tantamount to the militia system subject only to slight adaptation to Korean circumstance.

The support system was in use during Yu's lifetime with some of the capital divisions, and it was adopted as the main mode of service and finance for the Forbidden Guard Division (Kŭmwiyŏng) established in 1682, a decade after Yu's death. Yu and others perceived its main advantage to be that it created an independent financial base for each division and supposedly eliminated the burden on the state treasury for funding permanent soldiers. Not only recluses like Yu, but active officials like Song Siyŏl, also believed that the few thousand salaried soldiers of the Military Training Agency were the main reason for the high cost of the seventeenth-century military establishment, and if only these men could be replaced by rotating soldiers backed up by their own support taxpayers, military costs could be cut and heavy taxes on the peasantry reduced.

They were almost totally mistaken because they refused to see that support taxpayers in the traditional system of Korea were in fact taxpayers and not militia soldiers. They failed to see that the peasant's total tax bill was not reduced one whit by having him make his payments to the duty soldier rather than to the district magistrate. Furthermore, the support taxpayer system was also flawed because treating military service as a tax rather than required days of training and service contributed to the general weakening of military defense. Even though the militia model may have been impossible to achieve or even impractical for a country needing a standing army of trained troops, at least it placed emphasis on the need for providing partial training for the whole male population. The support system, by contrast, already represented a transition from service to tax payments, and it was too easy in times of fiscal crisis to turn to it as a source of additional revenue. Inklings of this weakness were already present even by Yu's death in 1672. Furthermore, even Yu himself acknowledged that support personnel were paying *taxes* (!) rather than simply providing equipment or rations to duty soldiers because he also proposed setting a fair *tax rate* for them. Unfortunately, his proposed two-*p'il* tax rate was anachronistic at the time he suggested it because active officials were already pointing out that it was too high and induced many officials to sign up tax evaders for service at the lower, one-*p'il* rate.

It was certainly no secret to anyone at the time that the main reason why the financial support system for the military was in such terrible condition in the seventeenth and eighteenth centuries was because the tax base was shrinking as both bona fide yangban and commoner tax shirkers successfully gained exemption from tax payments. Yu's solution to this problem was to advocate the recreation of early Chosŏn institutions, which would require the return of yangban not just to taxation but to real military service, albeit in prestigious guard units. The difference between Yu and the active officials who sought reform, however, was that Yu believed it was possible to turn the clock back to the early fifteenth century. The others hardly raised the issue because they realized that by the early seventeenth century members of prestigious families had come to believe so firmly that their high status entailed exemption from military service, and that service itself demeaned one's personal and family dignity so much that service for them was out of the question. In this sense, Yu's approach was at once more radical, more idealistic, and more anachronistic.

Officials like Kim Yuk, Yu Kye, Yi Kŏnmyŏng, Yi Imyŏng, Pak Munsu, and others who proposed ideas like a fine on school dropouts, a tax on idle and leisured men, or a capitation or household tax levied on the yangban elite as well as the lower orders of society shared a different orientation toward reform than Yu Hyŏngwŏn. They no longer believed universal service was necessary for a fair tax system, and they were willing to separate the question of finance from service – even though most were not willing to challenge accepted dogma by calling for a completely professional national army. They were thus far more practical than Yu because they were willing to accept reality, and they could be deemed more progressive by recognizing that the increase in commerce and the use of money had rendered the system of personal service obsolete. And those who wanted to tax the yangban rather than press them into service were hardly less radical than Yu in their desire for a fair and equitable distribution of taxes.

Yu showed only a limited capacity to adapt to the changes underway in the seventeenth century. He saw the wisdom of Kim Yuk's *taedong* reform and the conversion of tribute in kind to a surtax on land, but he could not conceive of anything but support taxpayers and rotating duty soldiers as the proper mode of financing the military. Although he did approve the use of production from land for military finance, it was only within the context of an institution sanctioned in historical lore – military colony land (*tunjŏn*). He could not, therefore, approve a land surtax for that purpose. Even though he did not comment on the household or capitation taxes, his disciple Kwŏn Chŏk did oppose the household tax in 1750, advocating instead a new plan for state purchase of land to be rented to landless peasants and the rental income used for military finance. This was justified in his mind because of the vague connection in classical principle between some kind of land grant and reciprocal military service.

EIGHTEENTH-CENTURY SCHOLARS ON MILITARY REFORM

A comparison of Yu's ideas with those of some scholars who supposedly inherited the tradition of Practical Learning from Yu demonstrates that they tended to inherit their classical orientation from him but their practical proposals from the debates among active officials waged over the previous century. The problem is made complex, however, because the eighteenth-century statecraft scholars by no means treated the ideas of their predecessors as if they were unassailable dogma.

Yi Ik (Sŏngho)

One of the most prominent of the next generation was Yi Ik (pen name, Sŏngho), who in one respect came even closer to the classical ideal on military service than Yu because he insisted that physical labor was the only proper mode of fulfilling the service obligation. "Labor service means personal service because in wartime, the one thing you cannot dispense with is physical labor."[2] Although he conceded that the practice of substituting cloth payments for service was understandable because of the desire of individual servicemen to escape the onerous burdens of traveling back and forth to their duty stations, providing rations, and doing patrol duty, he insisted that substitute cloth taxes violated the basic purpose of what a soldier was supposed to be. The only solution was to abolish cloth payments altogether and return to rotating service.[3]

On the other hand, Yi Ik could see what Yu Hyŏngwŏn could not, that the system of support taxpayers was by no means sanctioned by the classics, and he advocated that all the support taxpayers of the Forbidden Guard and Royal Divisions should be abolished or converted to soldiers. He felt that it was bad enough to use support taxpayers to provide cloth or grain to duty soldiers, but even more absurd to have support taxpayers for soldiers who were off duty. He contradicted Yu again when he argued that the proper way to finance soldiers was by the use of the land tax, based on what he called the classical precedent of "making the land tax responsible for supporting soldiers. I have never heard that [men liable for military service] had to pay additional rice for troop rations." Yi was right in saying that the support tax method of finance had no classical justification, and he was more flexible than Yu in arguing for a land tax to finance the military, but he was hardly on firm ground in arguing for a classical precedent for a military land tax.[4]

On the other hand, as Han Woo-keun has pointed out, Yi Ik was less radical in his treatment of the yangban than Yu because he felt that it was no longer possible to reestablish the Five Guards system or the principle of service for all men, including scions of the scholar-official class, that supposedly prevailed in the early Chosŏn period. He took this position partially because of the classical requirement that support of a class of scholar-officials (*sa*) was necessary even though it might conflict with the state's need for soldiers. Yu Hyŏngwŏn shared this view, but he also believed that in classical times military knowledge and skill was part of the education and training of the well-rounded scholar-gentleman and some form of service was required of the social elite. He also felt that the Five Guards system of early Chosŏn had incorporated these classical principles.

Yi Ik, by contrast, argued that the population had grown so large by his time that had it not been for the reduction of the men of good status to no more than a tenth of the population by tax evasion and corruption, there would be more than enough men to fill the military rosters without having to recruit yangban. It was the shift from service to cloth taxes that had driven the commoners to commend themselves to others as slaves or to take the tonsure and become Buddhist monks, thus reducing the number of men available for service. His solution was to require that private slaves as well as commoners of good status be obliged to perform military service, except that they be mixed together without distinction (as opposed to Yu who wanted them to serve, but in separate units from other status categories). To prevent their oppression by their own masters, the state would relieve them of paying personal slave tribute to their masters, presumably while on duty. Thus, both commoners and slaves would serve as soldiers, and the only distinction made would be between those serving at duty stations close to home or far away. If the former, they would be given two support men to provide equipment or the cost of equipment; if the latter, three. Of course, he was reintroducing support taxpayers into his reform plan even though he earlier condemned them as illegitimate. The point to be stressed here, however, is that like Yu, Yi Ik was willing to use slaves as the main means for alleviating the service burden on commoners of good status even though he deplored slavery in principle. The main reason was that he was not willing to reimpose service on the scholar-official (or yangban) class, an attitude similar to the reforming bureaucrats of the eighteenth century who only wanted to tax the yangban, not enroll them for service.

But he differed from most of them because he also opposed the use of the household cloth tax, ostensibly for the reason that it would be susceptible to corruption by officials and clerks. He agreed that it might produce a surplus in revenue, but the new funds would only be spent wastefully. But the most important reason was tucked away in his list of complaints: "It will be very wrong to subject the most exalted and respected high officials and ministers to the payment of a tax on an equal basis with the common people because it will overturn the legitimate order of society (*ch'et'ong*)!" If there were such a thing as a Practical Learning tradition, it was not necessarily producing more socially radical or economically progressive thinkers in the eighteenth century.[5]

Where regular officials differed from Yu in their grasp of the situation was that after the third quarter of the seventeenth century they forgot about the quality of the army and focused mainly on tax revenue. Yu was still a creature of the mid-seventeenth century who was born a couple of decades after Hideyoshi and lived through the Manchu invasions. He took the matter of a strong national defense seriously and gave as much space in his writing to weapons, fort construction, defensive strategy, and troop training as tax payments and finance. But his successors in the next century grappled with military "service" primarily as a burdensome and oppressive tax system. They accepted exemptions from military duty for yangban and other so-called irregular students and military officers and the like as a fact of life that could hardly be redressed, but they hoped to bring them into the financial system as taxpayers – an attitude that could be described as a pragmatic adaptation to reality.

Yu Suwŏn (Usŏ)

After Yi Ik, other statecraft scholars of the eighteenth century who took up the problems of military service incorporated the proposals and orientations of active officials into their writings. Yu Suwŏn, writing in the late 1730s, rejected the idea of a land allotment scheme such as the one Yu Hyŏngwŏn called for because it was an historical anachronism, a system that could only succeed within the context of a feudal (*ponggŏn*) environment. He was definitely a practical statecraft writer willing to deal with the contemporary situation, but he also criticized not only the support taxpayer system and the levying of cloth taxes on adult males but the household cloth tax as well. He did so, however, because he felt both were regressive taxes, not because he was opposed to imposing a tax on all status groups including yangban. He wanted to base all revenue on two taxes only: a land tax and an "equal service rice tax" levied on households divided into three categories based on wealth rather than family size. As a mid-eighteenth century statecraft thinker, his writings not only discussed a number of proposals in which military finance was treated separately from labor service or the militia ideal, he also advocated a program of finance based on rational criteria for equitable taxation of property, production, and wealth.[6]

An Chŏngbok, Yi Kyugyŏng, Tasan

In like fashion, An Chŏngbok, in his discussion of the *yangyŏk* system, cited the ideas of Yu Kye, Kim Yuk, Song Siyŏl, Song Chun'gil, Kim Sŏkchu, Nam Kuman, and other active officials and their discussion of taxation (rather than strictly service) alternatives, without, by the way, bothering to mention the views of Yu Hyŏngwŏn on this question.[7] Yi Kyugyŏng thought that the capitation tax imposed on all status categories was the best method of taxation, and even argued that it would provide the means for achieving something akin to the personal service of the T'ang, the rice capitation tax of the Chin, or the adult-male cash tax of the Sung dynasties in China.[8]

And Tasan (Chŏng Yagyong), writing in the early nineteenth century, discussed the history not only of alternate tax proposals but also the equal service reform of 1750 and the rather sorry results of that reform. As he put it, how could a reform that cut the tax rate in half end up with people in his own time paying twice what they used to pay in taxes? Like Yi Ik, he also believed that collecting a cloth tax had no classical sanction, but his views on solutions differed from statecraft writers of earlier periods because he had become aware of collective methods used by villagers on their own for distributing village tax quotas more equitably among village residents. In fact, he appears to have favored either a capitation or household tax of some sort, but pointed out that it was only necessary for the government to encourage the spontaneous formation of village collective tax associations (*kunp'ogye*) or the establishment of funds or lands (*yŏkkunjŏn* or *kunbojijŏn*) in villages for the purpose of paying the village's tax quota. Although famous for his radical *yŏjŏn* program for national ownership and egalitarian land distribution that was certainly inspired by classical models, his ideas about military service derived from two sources: the previous debate over various tax alternatives and his own observation of popular adjustments to the evils in the country's service system.[9]

Yangban Power

While Yu Hyŏngwŏn wanted to bring the yangban and commoner service evaders back into service, the reformers of the next century wanted to impose some sort of tax on them. The best that could be done, however, in the package of reforms referred to as the equal-service system of 1750–52 was a fine on 24,500 of their number who could not devote enough time and effort to pass what must have been an extremely easy qualifying test for registration in school. This was the measure that King Yŏngjo, a professed advocate of a household tax on yangban as well as commoners, was barely able to achieve in 1750. Why so? Why such a feeble conclusion to over a century of debate? Was it because the eighteenth century officials were weak and cowardly compared to the resolute and determined scholars of principle like Yu Hyŏngwŏn?

Hardly. The best answer is to be found in two problems – the power of the yangban and their representatives in the bureaucracy, and the weakness of the bureaucracy itself as an efficient instrument of central authority. What made the interests of the yangban so formidable was that their opponents and critics – kings seeking to maximize their power and reformers seeking a more equitable distribution of wealth and tax burdens – were limited and restrained in their contest with the yangban. Kings were fearful of the political threat posed by discontented yangban, not simply as leaders of mass rebellion, but as supporters of palace coup d'états. Even supposedly resolute monarchs like Yŏngjo believed in the image of yangban as a class of educated men deserving of respect even though he knew full well that claims for tax-exemption based on status privilege were being put forward by simple tax evaders, not necessarily heirs of the great scholars and officials of past generations.

Just as Yŏngjo was limited by his own feelings from a direct challenge to the prestige and privilege of the yangban, so too were scholarly reformers like Yu Hyŏngwŏn limited in their radicalism by natural sympathies for their fellows. No matter how deflated the coin of yangban status had become because of the constant striving of lower orders for higher prestige and privilege, the rock bed of that status was still deemed to be knowledge and mastery of the Confucian canon. For that reason, even reformers like Yu who spoke the language of classical egalitarian radicalism, could not bring themselves to demand a total and ruthless leveling of the existing social order. That is why Yu argued at times for the preservation, at least for the time being, of the slave servants of the yangban until such time that they could get used to the idea of doing some manual labor and cleaning up after themselves, or why he proposed a system of schools as a means of producing a truly qualified and educated elite that would deserve the kind of status and privilege currently enjoyed by heirs of former officials by hereditary claim rather than scholarly achievement. It was not until exemption from military service and taxation had become so widespread that it probably lost its utility as a means of conferring meaningful status that the people in the villages began to divide up tax quotas among themselves on an equitable basis without respect to the status of their households, and this development did not occur until the end of the eighteenth century.

Those officials of the seventeenth and eighteenth centuries who advocated expansion of the tax base and extension of taxes to yangban were certainly no less radical in their challenge to the social status quo than scholars like Yu Hyŏngwŏn, but they inherited their ideas from the active officials of the seventeenth century, not from Yu Hyŏngwŏn. And when the household cloth tax was finally adopted by the Taewongun in the mid-nineteenth century, he was following in the footsteps of the practical, bureaucratic reformers of the seventeenth and eighteenth century more than Yu Hyŏngwŏn or any separate tradition of Practical Learning scholarship that was the exclusive preserve of scholars.

THE SHARED DIALOGUE BETWEEN OFFICIALS AND SCHOLARS

On other points as well, such as the organization of military forces, military strategy in the face of invasion, the disposition of garrison forces, the construction of walls, and the adoption of advanced military technology, Yu's ideas were either derivative of those of active officials like Yulgok (Yi I) and Yu Sŏngnyŏng, or were no more rational, empirical, progressive, or advanced than ideas held by a number of active officials. Reclusive scholars had no monopoly on rationality, practicality, or reform. In fact, Yu ignored totally two areas that were absolutely essential to the overall aspect of military defense in the seventeenth century – domestic politics and diplomacy. His proposals for troop cuts and military reorganization treated those subjects in a vacuum, but in real life the control and disposition of forces was as much a product of political considerations as national defense. The continual turmoil in the political realm – the coup d'état in 1623 that led to the reign of King Injo, the Yi Kwal rebellion of 1624, the suspicious poisoning of Crown Prince Sohyŏn and the shaky legitimacy of King Hyojong and his heirs, the purges of King Sukchong, the murders of Patriarchs and Disciples in the 1720s, and the radical Disciple *imsin* rebellion of 1728 – meant that the defense of the capital and the political control of the Five Military Divisions in the capital region (along with provincial garrisons) would require a high level of troops and a concentration of forces around the king. The first functioned to drain the tax resources of the state, the second to weaken the nation in the face of foreign threat. These were crucial problems, but they were not discussed in Yu's magnum opus.

For that matter, he never raised the whole question of the wisdom of a hostile, anti-Manchu policy in the context of the Manchu conquest of China. His strategy for national defense reflected a kind of static, Maginot-line mentality that was inappropriate for more mobile Manchu forces, and ultimately one could argue that a circumspect foreign policy would have been more useful than the double-door phalanx of defensive garrisons he borrowed from Yu Sŏngnyŏng. In short, the so-called Practical Learners had no monopoly on sagacity. Statecraft was shared by both active officials and retired scholars, and one needs to understand the interplay of ideas between the realm of the contemplative and the active. The study of Practical Learning statecraft divorced from the real world is the kind of useless intellectual exercise that has to be abandoned.

PART V

Reform of Government Organization: Introduction

Since Yu Hyŏngwŏn had a lengthy and comprehensive agenda for the reform of seventeenth-century institutions, it should be no surprise that he devoted considerable attention to the structure and operation of the centralized bureaucratic system of mid-Chosŏn Korea. Not only did the bureaucracy function as the agency for the implementation of royal commands, but it was responsible in large part for the maintenance of order and the stability of the regime in power, according to how efficiently and honestly it was able to carry out its duties. Implementing royal commands went far beyond the diurnal transmission of daily decrees to include the functions of advising the king, presenting proposals, and solving problems. These tasks were mainly the functions of administrative agencies at the capital, which devised its own plans or funneled ideas from the lower levels of the bureaucracy to the king, and then worked in conjunction with him to determine policy. Most Confucians believed that success or failure in initiating successful reform plans at this policy-making level depended on the quality of the king and the officials he chose to staff these supreme administrative agencies. For a scholar like Yu, however, who was committed to analyzing the defects in existing institutions, it was also essential to correct the organization and mode of operation of government agencies.

Yu divided his discussion of matters pertaining to government organization and operations into several parts. He devised structural changes, including the rational reorganization of agencies to eliminate waste and create better efficiency and he discussed rules and regulations pertaining to the handling of bureaucratic personnel, including terms of office and procedures for the review of performance. He also wrote a separate chapter on rites as opposed to laws as a means of inducing conformity to regular procedures in ceremonies, commitment to specific moral values, and limitations on arbitrary, ostentatious, and profligate habits of expenditure. In addition, he worked out measures for local control as well as structural rearrangement of local institutions. These measures included a discussion of the administration of price stabilization, relief, and loan granaries for the benefit of the peasantry in the villages, and the draft of a set of regulations for semiautonomous community compacts designed to supplement the powers of the district magistrate in achieving conformity with the requirements of the national government.

CHAPTER 15

The King and His Court

"So extreme had the majesty of the throne become that the officials trembled with fear. That we still lie prostrate [before the king] is also a custom bequeathed to us from the reign of the deposed king [Yŏnsan'gun]."[1]

Reducing Expenditures by the Throne

Loyalty to the ruler was one of the articles of faith of the Confucian creed, and yet most idealistic Confucians viewed the arbitrary exercise of power by the monarch as a threat to good government. Yu Hyŏngwŏn accepted without question the traditional legitimacy of the kings of Chosŏn, which ruled out any discussion of the means of replacing incompetent monarchs, and he never once mentioned that any of the kings of the dynasty should be deposed.

Short of questioning the king's legitimacy, however, there were a number of measures that Yu as a Confucian statecraft thinker sought to use to block the potential for despotism and tyranny by the ruler. Yu's treatment of this issue involved three main areas. The first was control of expenditures by the king on himself, his relatives and favorites, and ultimately, the exchequer, particularly the Royal Treasury, which operated independently from the Ministry of Taxation. It also included decisions about the prerogatives of the king to conduct his supposedly private affairs, such as conducting marriages, funerals, banquets and appointing lists of men to be afforded rewards for political loyalty – his merit subjects. All these were budgetary matters, but they were all relevant to the question of balancing royal prerogative against bureaucratic rights.

The second area of his concern was the use of the king in a symbolic way to inculcate respect for certain Confucian values, and the third concern involved the distribution of authority in running the bureaucracy and conducting daily affairs of state. The last of these was related to the proper distribution of power between the supposedly absolute monarch and his loyal and obedient officials in conducting the daily affairs of government.

Nobility

Princes. As a fiscal conservative, Yu Hyŏngwŏn was naturally concerned about any inordinate expenditure of public funds, particularly on the king and any of his relatives. He was, therefore, particularly anxious about the perquisites granted to princes of the blood, and he sought to reduce the costs involved by limiting the emoluments paid to them. Under current rules, descendants of kings retained their status and privileges as members of the royal family for four generations, but Yu sought to curtail the costs to the public treasury by revamping noble titles (*pongch'aek*) associated with royal princes by introducing qualifications based on knowledge of the classics and Confucian moral standards. Any prince, down to the great-grandsons of deceased kings, would be eligible for the grant of a noble title if at the age of twenty years (Korean-style, where the baby was one year of age at the date of birth and two years of age at the next New Year's day) he could demonstrate mastery of one classic, the *Small Learning* (*Sohak*; *Hsiao-hsüeh* in Chinese), and the *Four Books* of Chu Hsi's tradition. If he failed to pass the examination by the age of thirty, he might then be awarded a royal title but at only one-half the ordinary salary. The prince of the incumbent king might receive his title at the age of sixteen, but he, too, would be subject to a half-salary cut after the age of twenty if he failed to demonstrate familiarity with the texts. The object of this proposal had two objectives: reducing the cost of supporting princes of the blood and indoctrinating all the royal princes in the Confucian canon.

Another device Yu proposed was to assign noble rank to the princes according to the position of their mothers. This procedure would limit the highest rank and emoluments only to a select few of the total body of princes. He did this by drawing distinctions between the eldest son of the legitimate wife (the queen in the case of the reigning king), other sons of the legitimate wives, and sons of other royal or princely concubines, who in the royal harem would not be regarded as concubines but as consorts of lesser rank than the queen. Thus, the eldest son of a legitimate wife (including the queen) would be given rank 1A, and his eldest son 2A, while other sons would be given a title of rank 1B, and secondary grandsons would receive rank 2B, and on down the line through the fourth generation of descent from a king. Only when the line of noble blood ran out in four generations would all future royal descendants be allowed to enter service in the king's regime.[2]

Yu's distinction between the eldest son of the legitimate wife (or queen) (*chŏkchangja*) and all other sons of legitimate wives (*sŏja*) was similar to Song Siyŏl's argument in 1659, that the deceased King Hyojong (r. 1649–59) deserved to be mourned as a secondary son (*sŏja*) rather than the eldest legitimate son of a previous king because as Grand Prince Pongnim, he had inherited the throne only after Crown Prince Sohyŏn had been poisoned (or murdered). Yu shared with Song the view that the traditional Korean use of the term *sŏja* to mean nothoi by concubines was contrary to the Chinese definition that the term indicated secondary sons of legitimate wives (i.e., all but the eldest son). Yu, however, also recognized that both usages prevailed in Korean practice: "In ancient times [in China] the name, *chŏk*, only referred to the eldest son of the legitimate wife [*chŏkchangja*], while the other sons were referred to as *sŏ*. In addition we [Koreans] have also referred to the sons of wives [*ch'ŏ*] as *chŏk* but the sons of concubines [*ch'ŏp*] as *sŏ* [nothoi]."[3] In other words, the use of the term *sŏ* in two ways in Korea had to be retained as the basis for the assignment of noble titles.[4]

Curiously, Song Siyŏl was eventually forced to take poison because his definition of King Hyojong as the *sŏja* of his father, King Injo, in the Chinese or classical sense of the term meant that all who mourned for him owed a lesser degree of mourning than that required for the eldest son of King Injo, the deceased (possibly murdered) Crown Prince Sohyŏn (Sohyŏn seja). For one thing, many Koreans were offended at Song's using *sŏja* for a king since Koreans had been using the term to mean the nothos of a slave concubine. In the second place, the Southerner faction demanded Song's death because his ruthless logic had impugned the legitimacy of King Hyojong by defining him as something less than the legitimate successor of a king. Had Yu lived to 1689, he might have shared Song's fate, but the purpose of his argument was not to determine the mourning period for a member of the royal house, but to establish a method of ranking royal princes to reduce the expense of supporting them.

Even though Yu adopted Song's position that the term *sŏ* did not mean the nothoi or son of a concubine in the manner of colloquial Korean parlance, he did take cognizance of Korea's traditional discrimination against sons of concubines, because he did drop the sons of royal or princely concubines (or palace ladies) one degree below the sons of legitimate royal and princely queens and princesses. His ground for doing so was not because the mother was good or base (commoner or slave) in status, but because she was a concubine or secondary wife (*ch'ŏp*), a status lower than the main wife (*ch'ŏ*). In other words, he retained the principle of discrimination but tried to remove the stigma associated with inherited slavery.

Otherwise, if distinctions were made because of the mother's status (i.e., slave as opposed to commoner status), "it would do damage to the Way [that should be maintained] between father and sons," by which he noted that it would reduce the respect that sons owed to their fathers and poison the feelings of harmony between half-brothers. For those reasons he preferred to eliminate all discussion of the family pedigree (*munji*) of the mother, high or low.[5] Although he hoped to eliminate the stigma attached to inherited slavery in the case of royal or princely concubines, at the same time he also incorporated, and thus legitimized, the unique Chosŏn prejudice against concubines and their sons, the nothoi.

Yu made clear that the reason for his division of princes into three categories was to reduce expenditures when he cited Chu Hsi's reference to the financial problem created by the support of large numbers of princes. He also mentioned that in the Han dynasty the emperor granted land to imperial sons and declared them "kings" or princes (*wang*), but only one of the sons of the kings, the eldest legitimate son, was allowed to succeed to the title of prince. All the rest, referred to as *sŏja*, were only granted the title of marquis (*hu*), and only the eldest legitimate son was allowed to inherit his title. The rest of the sons were not given noble ranks, and after several generations the descendants of imperial descendants for the most part ended up in the ranks of commoners (*sŏin*).[6] Naturally restricting the pool of princes who could be appointed to prestigious titles limited the number of those enjoying large emoluments from the state treasury.

In Korea, Confucian opponents of discrimination against the nothoi of the yangban class had been protesting the injustice of this practice continuously since the beginning of the dynasty.[7] Yu, however, had no intention of abolishing the category of nothos as a position of lower status than the sons of wives. He certainly was not interested in abolishing all types of distinctions to create a thoroughly egalitarian society, and one might suspect that even though he wanted to remove the stigma of inherited slavery from royal concubines, he was probably concerned about preserving the supremacy of yangban daughters who married into the royal line over those women who needed no special documents from their family relations to gain admission to the royal harem.

Yu was not willing to allow his formula for noble rank to stand without some kind of explanation because he realized that there was no classical precedent in ancient China. In feudal China in the age of Chou, the process of granting a fief (*feng-chien*; *ponggŏn* in Korean) meant that noble ranks granted by rulers of states could pass on their title and rank without any generational decline in rank for hundreds of generations. Since feudalism had disappeared after the Ch'in unification of China, the rulers of the bureaucratic era in post-Chou China modified that rule by limiting the inheritance of royal blood to four generations (*ch'injin*) and dropping the noble title and rank by each generation.

Yu even made an exception for the son of the last descendant of a grand lord (Taegun), who would be allowed to continue his royal relationship by another generation if he qualified as a Confucian student (*yusaeng*) – an obvious compromise with his desire to cut costs because of his preference for converting royalty to Confucian philosophy. Otherwise, he borrowed this Chinese precedent with modification for the prejudice against concubines to limit the ranks and costs of the royal princes.

Merit Subjects. Yu drew up specific regulations for handling merit subjects (*kongsin*) as well. Merit subjects were an especially serious problem in the fifteenth century because kings frequently used this special award to honor political supporters and loyalists. Because merit subjects, whether of major or minor status, were granted prebends, slaves, and important posts, independent scholars opposed them because they had gained high office for political reasons, particularly after King Sejo's usurpation from King Tanjong in the mid-fifteenth century.

After King Yŏnsan'gun was purged in 1506, the new government under King Chungjong rewarded the leaders of the coup who had put him on the throne by proclaiming 117 major and 200 minor merit subjects in 1506. The censorate then attacked the long list of merit subjects because too many low-ranking and undeserved men were appointed or promoted in rank or granted awards in land and slaves. Cho Kwangjo led a movement in 1519 to convene a special recommendation examination to allow chances for worthy scholars to transcend the bottlenecks against advancements caused by the monopoly of officeholding by merit subjects, but in the end he and his friends were purged by the king and high officials, who feared their challenge to the regime.[8]

Despite his sympathy for Cho Kwangjo, Yu Hyŏngwŏn could not bring himself to any major diminution of the merit subjects in the mid-seventeenth century. He grouped the merit subjects with the nobility, such as the princes and sons-in-law of the throne, limited the amount of support allowed, and only refused to allow lists of minor merit subjects appointed in the fifteenth century. He permitted the eldest son and grandson to inherit merit subject status down to rank 2B, and reinstated compensation for them by granting ancient *sig'ŭp* or prebends in certain towns. He also sought to rework titles to conform to the Chou feudal pattern of the five grades of noble titles, from duke to baron.

To reduce the ostentatious display of merit subject status, he prohibited the printing of "merit subject" titles on their calling cards, and the devising of excessively long titles that had been used in Sung and Koryŏ times – what Yu called a phemonenon of a fin-de-siècle age of darkness and decline. The number of servants had to be limited to a range of one-to-seven retainers and servants for royalty of noble rank, and the merit subjects might only use clerks attached to the Office of Royalty and Rectitude and personal servants limited to a maximum of a half-dozen men at rank six, or two men at rank two. The principle governing this rule was that ancient standards only allowed servants and runners for rulers of states and for princesses married to feudal lords who might also have a fief because there was no reason to have special servants dissociated from public responsibility. But since feudalism had disappeared, the recipients of these feudal titles were not given office and their titles had nothing to do with political rule because royal relations were prohibited from holding posts.

In ancient feudal times any royal relatives who had not performed a meritorious deed was simply not given an office, relegating them to the ranks of the commoners (*sŏin*; *shu-jen* in Chinese). Their only reponsibility was to help out during funerals, recommend men of quality for appointment to office, attend court and congratulatory celebrations, and serve on tours. They paid most of the costs of their retainers and received no official payments.[9] In short, Yu tried to limit the perquisites and costs of supporting merit subjects ostensibly as a means of cutting public expenditures, but also to restrict the king's ability to convey wealth, honor, and power on his personal favorites.

Funerals: Frugality

Yu set out a program of regulations for government-sponsored funerals aimed primarily at reducing the debilitating expenses involved in burials and the oppressive levying of uncompensated labor service on ordinary peasants. Since the precedents he sought for these regulations were also taken from classic examples, his proposal for reform did not mean that he wanted to eliminate any of the religious or pietistic ceremonies of ancestor worship. On the contrary, he opposed the suggestion that the expenses for state funerals for royal relatives could be reduced greatly if the number of eligible relatives be cut back to only the highest ranks or closest relatives because the king was obliged to provide gifts and pay for sacrificial rites for all royal relatives. By the same token, he expanded the realm of individuals warranting state support for funerals and sacrifice from royal relatives and officials from the first and second ranks to the *tangsang* category. That category included some third-rank officials and officials on a mission abroad to a foreign nation to symbolize the close relations between the king and his highest ministers. In other words, while demanding cost-cutting and frugality in expenses for royal relatives, he was not averse to adding a few extra members of the bureaucratic class for state-supported funerals.

He did insist that the cost of these funerals and the burden imposed on commoners for the labor required in conducting the funeral and building the burial tombs had to be limited. Instead of the traditional practice of commandeering uncompensated labor, officials in charge of funerals were henceforth to be required to hire all labor needed. A bureau in the capital would work out the itinerary for the funeral route, designate the post-stations and passes along that route, list the authorized expenses, have them posted at each station, and transfer a copy to the district magistrates involved. Those hired to build tombs might be recruited from a locality, but only for three days, and all were to be compensated for their work. Any provincial governor or district magistrate who recruited unpaid labor on his own would receive one hundred strokes and sent to the frontier as an ordinary duty soldier on the line. Any magistrate who found he could do the work with less labor but collected a substitute cloth fee from the workers for his own profit, or any noble family who received payments from the state for funeral expenses and demanded uncompensated labor from district magistrates in addition would be indicted for criminal action. The number of tomb construction workers was to be limited according to the status of the deceased, and all compensation was to be paid from public funds.

One of the more onerous forms of local labor was bearing the biers of deceased yangban or scholars or those who had connections with officials to their graves. Yu estimated that the peasants of Kyŏnggi Province, where more funerals of nobility and high officials took place than anywhere else, had to perform this duty as coffins passed through their district five or six times a month. They had to proceed to the road in advance and pay for their own food during the several days it took for the bier to arrive in their town. As they transported the bier to the next district boundary, they had to suffer the whipping of the overseers, who pressed them to move more quickly. Even though state laws provided for oxen to drag the funeral carts, the magistrates ignored this regulation, or they required local inhabitants, instead of the relatives of the deceased, to bear the cost of the oxen.

Altogether, as many as a thousand men from Kyŏnggi Province might be allocated for the labor of transporting a bier to the place of burial. The clerks dispatched to each district to supervise the work would quarter themselves in peasants' homes and demand that the peasants either perform work for them or pay cloth fees of as much as thirty to forty *p'il* of cloth. Those too poor to pay had to work days or even weeks for these clerks. For that matter the costs of ritual utensils was divided up among the districts along the funeral route as well as labor service. Even the gravediggers often had to leave their homes for several days to do the work at a gravesite some distance from their villages.

Yu claimed that labor service for funerals was worse than the land tax, a burden equivalent to an emergency levy in time of war. He suggested banning the use of human labor for bearing biers and replacing it either by horse-drawn vehicles or by cooperative labor from the neighbors of the deceased. He was sure that the wording of the *Li-chi* clearly described horse-drawn carts instead of manual portage of coffins and biers, standard limits on the use of human labor, and community cooperation in the conduct of funerals.

Yu also prescribed that soldiers who happened to die during guard duty on the frontier were also entitled to immediate temporary burial by the members of the man's unit, and state-assisted transportation of the corpse back to his home village. He felt that this kind of assistance was necessary because a number of soldiers had died from the cold on the northern border and their corpses were simply dragged to the side of the road and left as carrion for dogs and pigs, "a sight so pitiful that I cannot bear to look at it." Some poor soldiers on duty in the capital away from their provincial homes had died from the cold as well, but nothing had been done to transport their bodies back home either and "the high ministers of state and all the officials see them with their own eyes and look upon it as if it were an ordinary matter without giving it a thought, a sign that government has failed [to do its duty]." Yu charged that if there were no relatives available to take the body home, the state had the responsibility for providing permanent interment and the captain of the man's unit should lead the troops in accompanying the funeral bier and offering wine and drink in the burial rite.

Royal tombs and burial areas in general were to be protected by law from cultivation or the grazing of animals, and the dimension of the forbidden territory should vary with the prestige and rank of the individual. Yu also wanted to limit the indiscriminate use of arable and grazing land because Sŏ Kyŏngdŏk (d. 1546) had complained that people had been locating new grave sites at places deemed lucky by the geomancers, which sometimes required that old graves be disinterred and the bones removed to different places.[10]

Although Yu concerned himself with reducing the labor service associated with state-supported funerals, and not just limiting the expenditures for royalty, his primary object here was to limit the king's power to requisition funds and labor for funeral expenses.

Banquets: Regulation of Costs and Ritual Propriety

Banquets for officials were an important part of the ritual regulations for the civilized state in Korea, but Yu sought to limit the cost by restricting attendance at the spring and autumn banquets to officials and by arranging payment for all expenses by the state. Yu insisted that the government conserve on the food served and the utensils used, restricting the number of servings, the dishes used, and the cups of wine poured according to the rank of the official. Even the size of the cups should be standardized and distributed to all provinces to be used as models for the manufacture of more cups in the provinces. Every official in attendance at the banquet had to follow rigid procedure governing the number of bows made and the number of times ascending and descending the steps to the dais. Any individual who violated the limits on food and utensils was to be led out of the hall by the sergeant-at-arms and subjected to impeachment for a criminal act even though, as Yu asserted, the whole point of the banquet and the rules was to "harmonize the relationship between ruler and subject."

The "harmony" was evidently to be established by the threat of force, and the music played at the banquet had to conform to ancient Chinese court music, not the popular women's music that currently flourished. Flowers were not be displayed in vases or eaten by the guests, and the popular foot-high oil-and-honey pastries were to be ruled out; only those four inches on each side were to be allowed. The king was to be granted fifteen pieces to consume, while the lowest ranking officials could only eat six. Banquets had to be governed by these strict regulations "to instruct people in respect and frugality, and to display mutual compassion and benevolence; only then could you eliminate the evils of a declining age."

Yu was again somewhat more liberal in tolerating a few extra banquets for officials. He prescribed banquets to honor the dispatch of provincial governors and military commanders, envoys to China and Japan, or commissioners on domestic missions. Banquets were to be held to receive messengers with formal letters from the provinces to the king, even though these banquets had been discontinued for a long time because they had encouraged profligate spending by both the participants and the government. Nonetheless, because ancient rulers had held such banquets for their officials and artisans to promote moral standards and not simply as an excuse for enjoyment or for receiving the praise and adulation of their subjects, they had to be held in Korea as well. Yu assumed, however, that extravagant expenditures could be brought under control by restricting consumption, and that the banquets might also be suspended if the harvest was poor.

Furthermore, a number of unnecessary banquets had been held in Korea, particularly those hosted by the State Council and Six Ministries, and the agencies in charge of merit subjects, royal relatives, and the sons-in-law of kings (the Ch'unghunbu, the Chongch'inbu, and the Ŭibinbu). These were unjustified because there was no such example either in ancient times or in the T'ang dynasty of subjects holding banquets in honor of their ruler or in repayment of his great favor. In the Han dynasty, however, Emperor Kao (Kao-tsu) held a banquet where officials and a few feudal lords offered him their congratulations, and in the Sung at the banquets in spring and autumn in honor of the emperor's birthday and the sacrifices to Heaven and Earth, officials toasted the emperor's long life and the emperor granted them flowers in return.

Yu, however, thought that these practices were "like playing games, completely contrary to the utmost respect with which rites were treated by the men of ancient times." For Koreans to continue banquets held by official agencies in honor of the king would also be tantamount to presumptuous acts ill-fitting the place of subjects, a mistake in the conduct of rites, and an excuse for profligate spending. The only purpose of banquets in ancient China was for "the ruler to get his officials to give all their efforts and exhaust all their abilities in performing their tasks for the country, and only for that reason did he [the ruler] provide them with food and drink in order to encourage them."[11]

Abolish the Royal Treasury: Bureaucratic Control

Financial policy under the king's regime had led only to rapid expansion of funds controlled by agencies under the king's command. The most powerful agency of royal finance was the Royal Treasury (Naesusa), but Yu reasoned that since the king had lawful title to all property available in the kingdom, there was no need for a royal treasury at all. Because the only justification for its existence was to store small amounts temporarily, Yu invoked the ancient rule that the ruler of a small state was entitled only to ten times the income for a prime minister, and a separate Royal Treasury was totally unnecessary for this purpose. Once it were abolished, its slaves could be reallocated to capital bureaus and provincial yamen, or assigned as tribute payers to other agencies. Lands owned by the Royal Treasury could be used to provide allotments to peasants, and its slaves could be used for assignment to princes or princesses. (One can't help but notice that Yu called for reassigning official slaves to other agencies rather than manumitting them, as one might expect!)

Yu cited Nam Hyoon, who in King Sŏngjong's reign (fifteenth century) praised the deposed King Tanjong for having reduced his royal expenditures, an example of frugality abandoned by the expansion of Royal Treasury income under Sŏngjong. The expenditures of the Royal Treasury rose because of the frequent trips of its staff to local districts, the maintenance of private warehouses in the capital, and the rotting of excess grain storage in ocean-going transport terminals. In the worst cases, the "agrarian huts of the main palace" (*pon'gung nongsa*) were taken over by the king as his private property and used for funding Buddhist and lewd rites.

Yulgok urged King Sŏnjo in the sixteenth century to turn over all funds in the King's Treasury (Naet'ang) because it was wrong for him to maintain his own private treasury. The king had access to the nation's production, granaries, and state treasuries anyway, and he was obliged to limit his expenditures. Yu sought to prove his contention that the king had no right to maintain his own separate treasury by arguing that had the Royal Treasury been the only locus of funds left for state purposes in a time of crisis, the king would have had no choice but to turn them over to the responsible agencies of state, anyway.[12]

Yu also sought to curtail other methods for providing food and provision for kings in similar fashion. The Royal Cuisine Office (Saongwŏn) had already been given funds for the purchase of pheasants so that the earlier system of maintaining 8,000 falconers (*ŭnggun*) and supporting them by collecting cloth payments from peasants could be abolished and the peasants returned to regular military service.[13] Abolishing falconers would establish a precedent for eliminating a number of offices for obtaining material goods directly by replacing it with purchases of goods on the market (see the discussion of the reform of the tribute system, later). Yu recommended abolishing one special office for supplying the costs of guest expenses (the *Sajaegam*) simply by purchasing firewood and coal from the tribute middlemen (*kongmul chuin*). He felt that even when palace agencies had sufficient reserves to provide these goods without buying them, during periods of shortage the large population of the capital would be willing to offer these products for sale to the palace.[14]

Yu's was a voice in the wilderness when it came to curtailing the king's prerogative to dispose of funds for his own purposes, and the problem was not solved until the Kabo reform of 1894. His attitude was born of the frugality typical of most Confucians, but he also wanted to constrain royal authority and bring it under the restriction of a more rational process of governance, which signified bureaucratic oversight over royal profligacy.

The King as Symbol

The King's Personal Plot: Encouragement of Agriculture

One of the most important rituals in Yu's catalogue was the ancient tradition of the ruler's ceremonious cultivation of his own plot (*chŏkchŏn*; *chi-t'ien* in Chinese) primarily because it was an important symbol of the Physiocratic tradition in Chinese and Confucian thought. He began by tracing the origin of respect for agriculture by rulers to the Duke of Chou and King Wen of Chou. He then described the ceremonies first conducted at the beginning of the reign of King Hsüan (827–782 B.C.) at the time of the first planting of crops in the spring when the positive force of yang was flowing through the earth to assist the earth in conveying the vital forces that would cause crops to grow. Ceremonies of purification were held and officials fasted prior to King Hsüan's personal cultivation of his personal plot of land (*chŏkchŏn*), and a toast of wine and offerings of food to the god of the earth were made that same day. The king then made tours of the kingdom at weeding and harvesting time to ensure that the peasants were diligent in their labors, and he devoted his attention exclusively to agriculture during three of the four seasons, and only in the winter would he concentrate on military training. The tradition was continued by dukes and other feudal lords later in the Chou, and Emperor Wen of the Former Han in 178 B.C. performed the same ceremony.

Yu's concerns extended beyond the symbolic cultivation of a plot by the king to practical methods for increasing crop yield. He cited Chao Ts'o's remarks to Emperor Wen that agricultural production was essential to provide the surpluses that were needed to stave off the tragedy of flood or drought that would result in poverty and starvation. Hardship gave rise to corruption and heterodox beliefs because peasants could not be expected to maintain moral standards in the face of starvation. Poverty occurred because not enough people stayed on the land and devoted their time to agriculture, and the reason why many had abandoned agriculture was because they were afflicted by the vicissitudes of onerous agricultural work, the vagaries of nature, and the depredations of the tax collectors, clerks, and creditors. The only way out of these troubles was for the emperor to concentrate on raising agricultural production. In other words, the ruler's ritual cultivation was intended to symbolize his commitment to maintaining agricultural production and to eliminating official malfeasance in the care and nurturing of the peasant producers.

Emperor Ching of the Han dynasty (r. 156–140 B.C.) also personally cultivated his small plot (*chi-t'ien*) and his empress personally raised her silkworms on her mulberry leaves, and both performed rites at the ancestral shrine in honor of primary production. In the last year of his reign (87 B.C.) Emperor Wu issued a statement deploring his own past excessive attention to warfare, and declared that he had then to concentrate on agricultural production. He appointed Chao Kuo to be grain commissioner, and Chao instituted a crop rotation system (*tai-t'ien*) based on raising three furrows in a one-*mou* field, using oxen for plowing, and cultivating two of the furrows per year by "weeding and pushing the mounds of earth down around the roots." By this means crop production was doubled over normal methods of cultivation.[15]

Yu commented that the Chinese system of furrows and rotating cultivation had to be the reason for far higher productivity in contemporary Manchuria around the Liao River than in Korea. He recommended that Koreans make their hoes and plowshares narrower and smaller, dig furrows, plant the seeds in them, and pull out the weeds on the ridges to nurture the sprouts.

Stressing the importance of agricultural production would obviously be important in any preindustrial economy, but Yu felt that the religious significance of the king's act of personal cultivation was necessary to stimulate the peasants to work harder and adopt more advanced methods. After the Chou dynasty in China emperors only conducted this rite intermittently, and in the T'ang, Sung, and later dynasties, the rite lost its meaning because emperors only used the ceremony as an excuse for a pleasure trip or party. Yu therefore urged not only that parties and drinking be abandoned at such times, but that all other business not related to agriculture, such as praising the emperor, pardoning criminals, and appointing men to office, had to be abandoned. In addition to his own act of cultivation, the ruler had to encourage provincial governors and district magistrates to lead their subordinate officials to cultivate plots of earth as well.[16]

He prescribed that a *chŏkchŏn* ritual plot of one *kyŏng* be established next to the district shrine to the gods of earth and agriculture (*sajiktan*). Under his new system the peasants who cultivated this plot would pay one-ninth of the crop (in the well-field tradition) to support the rite performed at this altar and would be exempted from payment of the land and cloth support taxes. The king would personally cultivate his plot of land in the the spring in accordance with the ritual in the *Li-chi*, but not necessarily in the first lunar month of that season as that text described, but in the second lunar month when land was actually cultivated in Korea. He would ride a wooden cart with a plow on its side and lead his court officials to the eastern suburbs and personally turn over the earth, and then conduct sacrificial rites at the Altar of Earth and Grain (*sajik*), the Ancestral Shrine of the Royal Lineage (Chongmyo), and the shrines to mountains and rivers. The queen would also lead the palace ladies out to a field and plant seed, and the king would follow the Chou regulations for the number of times he was obliged to wield the hoe. Wine and music would be forbidden at the ceremonies, and the government would pay for the oxen and all implements used so that the peasants would never be burdened by the cost.[17]

The importance Yu placed on the ruler's ritual act of cultivation indicates a full commitment to his belief in agriculture as the main source of wealth and welfare. Had he been more aware of nonagricultural industry and commerce as equal, if not superior, methods of producing wealth and prosperity, he might have created new icons for worship, but his pantheon of religious symbols was still rather strictly confined to classical possibilities.

There is no question but that Yu placed high priority on the symbolic and ritualistic roles of the king in conducting ceremonies to set a normative model for the population, but it did not necessarily extend to his role as the chief executive.

Respect for the Aged

Since respect for age was a major feature of Yu's proposed regulations for community compacts, it was not surprising that he also called for an annual celebration of a rite dedicated to the care of the aged in the fall. The king would conduct this ceremony when he made his annual visit to the National Academy where he would grant gifts of food to men in their eighties and nineties. The precedent for the ceremony, of course, came from Chinese antiquity. According to the *Li-chi* the sage Emperor Shun donned his simple and unadorned *sim'ŭi* ceremonial garment in conducting rites in honor of the ages, and the commentator Kung Ying-ta remarked that Shun performed four separate ceremonies that were supposedly continued throughout the Hsia, Shang, and Chou dynasties as well. The *Li-chi* also recorded that the elderly were honored in the National Academy and lesser schools in the capital.

Yu also traced evidence of observance of these ceremonies in the Han dynasty, the Northern Wei in the late fifth century, and the Later Chou in the mid-sixth century. Yu described the conduct of the rite in the Later Chou as an attempt to replicate Chou practice, particularly the care taken by the emperor to demonstrate his own humility and respect for the aged by cutting their meat for them, presenting them their wine cups, and asking their advice.[18]

Yu conceded that it might not be possible to hold this rite every year, but he urged that the king at least could order the Ministry of Rites to grant food to the elderly. At present an annual banquet for the elderly (*yangnoyŏn*) was held to honor all men over the age of eighty no matter what their status, and elderly women were feted in a banquet in the queen's inner quarters. Yu thought that these ceremonies were inappropriate because they were less formal and serious than the august ritual of Chou times. Furthermore, there were too many elderly people in the country to entertain all of them. It would be better to invite only those of them who were virtuous.

The purpose behind the ritual was not simply to provide food to the elderly, but for the king to demonstrate by his conduct his respect and deference to the elderly much as a child would behave toward an elder. By this means the king would encourage people to be filial toward their parents and respectful toward their elder brothers, and to refrain from using their own strength to oppress the weak.[19]

THE KING AS CHIEF EXECUTIVE

Samgong: Three Moral Advisers to the King

When the Chou dynasty was founded at the end of the second millennium B.C., a fully articulated model of government was supposedly established, although its description in the *Book of History* and *Rites of Chou* do not match each other exactly. According to the *Book of History*, the ruler was assisted first of all by three advisers, the San-kung, chosen for their virtue and skill in understanding yin and yang (the complementary negative and positive forces of the cosmos) and the transformations of nature so that they could regulate the laws and help the ruler govern the empire. They in turn were assisted by three subordinates, the San-ku. Since the *Rites of Chou*, however, did not mention these six officials but did include in its table of organization a couple of officials with similar titles who were subordinates of one of the lesser ministers, a Sung dynasty commentator, Ts'ai Ch'en, believed that the *Rites of Chou* must have been compiled by a sage and was entitled to as much respect as the *Book of History*. The *Rites of Chou* supposedly represented the regulations for officials that the duke planned to install, but he died before he could set pen to paper.[20]

The six ministers decribed in the *Book of History* included a prime minister (Ch'ung-tsai) in charge of all other officials, and ministers of education (Ssu-t'u), rites (Tsung-po), war (Ssu-ma), punishments (Ssu-k'ou), and economy (Ssu-kung). Yu also quoted the commentary of Hu An-kuo of the Sung dynasty, who wrote that if no one of suitable virtue was found to serve as one of the San-kung, one of the six ministers could be promoted to the post as a concurrency, and any of the San-kung could also be asked to serve as prime minister, the best example of which was the Duke of Chou (Chou-kung) himself.[21] This point of view was opposed by Chu Hsi in Sung times, who insisted on the necessity of separating the San-kung from the six ministers because their task was devoted solely to instructing the ruler on the fundamental principles of government itself, not the administration of specific tasks.[22]

The *Rites of Chou*, on the other hand, described a more complex bureaucratic system than the laconic account in the *Book of History*, and yet it too was organized at the top under six ministers. Although the titles of these ministers were different, a commentator of the Han period, Cheng Ssu-neng, equated them with the six ministers in the *Book of History*. These were the officers of heaven (prime minister), earth (education), spring (rites), summer (war), fall (punishments), and winter (economy). In addition, each of these officials had six separate codes of law covering their responsibilities and those of their sixty subordinates.[23]

Yu's sources on the Sung dynasty, Ma Tuan-lin's *Wen-hsien t'ung-k'ao* and the treatise on government organization in the *History of the Sung Dynasty* (*Sung-shih*) stated that the Three Teachers (San-shih) in the Sung dynasty had been designed to function as the equivalents of the San-kung of the Chou, but unfortunately the posts were often left vacant. This implied that the emperor lacked the kind of impersonal advice on fundamental moral principles of governance that would prevent him from pursuing his own interests at the expense of the public good.[24]

In discussing his own plan for the reform of the Chosŏn bureaucratic structure at the capital, Yu insisted on the establishment of the three advisers to the king (Samgong) like the San-kung of the Chou, but he ignored Chu Hsi's injunction that they be kept separate from functional ministers. Instead, he allowed that other high ministers could hold them as concurrencies and that their three assistants (San-ku) could be dispensed with, as had occurred in the T'ang system. But the three advisers to the crown prince were absolutely essential. The essence of this proposal was the notion that kings and crown princes needed to be surrounded by moral exemplars and tutors to ensure that they would behave in acceptable fashion, uphold morals, and observe the proprieties. The Samgong were to be chosen more for their own moral rectitude than for their qualities as efficient administrators or specialized experts.

State Council and Prime Minister: Bureaucratic Autonomy

Prime Minister. Yu's most important recommendation, however, was for the establishment of a State Council (Ŭijŏngbu) of five senior and three lower ranking officials, headed by a single councilor (Ŭijŏng), that would supervise not only the Six Ministries but the whole bureaucracy. The State Council had been created in 1400 by King Chŏngjong to replace the supreme deliberative council carried over from the Koryŏ dynasty, the Top'yŏng'ŭisasa, and Yu pointed out that there had been considerable debate since the founding of the Chosŏn dynasty in 1392 whether supreme responsibility should be vested in one or three state councilors. He, himself, had decided on the basis of his study of the Chinese situation that a single prime minister (Sŭngsang; Ch'eng-hsiang in Chinese) was the correct way. In fact, in one place he referred to his State Council as the Prime Minister's Office (Sangbu). His councilor or prime minister would, along with the next two councilors, also function concurrently as the Samgong, or the three virtuous advisers to the king in the Chou fashion.[25]

Yu observed that in Chou times in China the elevation of a single prime minister to take overall charge of government affairs was indispensable to a good system of government, and he cited two commentaries that praised the practice in both the Ch'in and Han dynasties of frequently leaving the same man in the office of prime minister (Ch'eng-hsiang) for long periods, even for life. Chung Chang-t'ung of the Later Han, for example, believed that this was the reason for the success that the Former Han dynasty enjoyed: "Generally speaking, when you appoint one man, he has exclusive charge over government affairs, but when you appoint several men, they rely on one another [i.e., share responsibility]. When government is in the exclusive charge [of one man], it is harmonious, but when [several men] rely on one another, there are violations and perversions."[26]

Fan Yeh, author of the *History of the Later Han* (*Hou Han-shu*), described the advantages of a single prime minister in terms of the Taoist-Legalist ideal state, where affairs are so well regulated that the ruler hardly has to lift a finger:

> The kings of ancient times only appointed a single prime minister to govern the empire. This was the reason why government orders emanated from a single place and there was a place to exert control over [the rest of] the government. The prime minister was able to carry out his responsibilities, and the ruler was able to attain the right Way [of ruling]. [The ruler] kept himself modest and respectful and did nothing [*wu-wei*], yet the empire was well governed.[27]

Yu found that the treatise on government organization in *The History of the T'ang Dynasty* (*T'ang-shu*) criticized the operation of the T'ang system because the responsibilities that should have been vested in a single prime minister were shared by two men, the two leading officials of two of the Three Departments (San-sheng). What was worse, from Emperor T'ai-tsung's reign (r. 626–49) on, lesser officials like a minister of personnel, or the head of the Department of Secret Documents, were also summoned to participate as councilors in the highest level deliberations of state. In the mid-seventh century another adulteration was added when new titles were created for lower officials to justify their temporary assumption of the duties of a prime minister.

Hu An-kuo of the Sung also deplored this situation in the T'ang era and emphasized the need for a single prime minister. The initial motivation behind the use of two officials to function as counselors to the emperor was to allow some debate and correction of possible errors in the advice of a prime minister, and yet that device had not prevented the emergence of dictatorial officials like Li Lin-fu, Yang Kuo-chung, and Yüan Tsai.[28]

Hu's idea of the prime minister was not one who concerned himself with detail or bothered to sign all the casebooks of documents involved in routine business. He viewed the task of the prime minister as if he were one of the three San-kung of ancient Chou times, discussing the proper Way of government (i.e., matters of principle and larger policy issues) with the ruler, encouraging the ruler to righteous behavior, expanding the search for outstanding men of talent for the bureaucracy, consulting the opinions of the people far and wide, and finding out problems that were concealed from the ruler's view.[29]

Usurpation of the Roles of the Prime Minister and State Council. Yu Hyŏngwŏn was not only a forceful advocate of the views of Chung Chang-t'ung, Fan Yeh, and Hu An-kuo for establishing a supreme prime minister, he also insisted on the restoration of the State Council to its legitimate place at the pinnacle of the Chosŏn dynasty bureaucracy. The State Council had been displaced by the Border Defense Command (Pibyŏnsa) that had been created by King Myŏngjong in 1555 to oversee defense of the southern coast against the Wakō pirates. Although Yu had elsewhere recommended abolition of the Border Defense Command, he did not mention it directly in his chapter on the bureaucracy, but he obviously believed that the Border Defense Command was analogous to the Bureau of Military Affairs of the Sung dynasty, a national defense council that had usurped the proper role of a civilian deliberative council.[30]

He also presented material on the history of the Ming Bureau of Military Affairs because it resembled the Border Defense Command in Korea. He traced its origin to palace officials called Nei-shu-mi-shih, created in the 760s in the T'ang period for the purpose of transmitting documents to the emperor and staffed by eunuchs. By the end of the ninth century, one of these officials usurped the authority of the councilors of state (Tsai-hsiang). In the Five Dynasties period (907–60) the eunuchs were removed from this agency, now called the Eunuch's Palace Council (Shu-mi-yüan). In the Sung it was given charge of frontier defense and placed on a par with the Secretariat (Chung-shu sheng) that handled civil affairs.

During the Yüan-feng era of Sung under Emperor Shen-tsung (1078–86), some wanted to abolish the bureau and return all authority over military affairs to the Board of War, but Shen-tsung resisted the recommendation because he preferred a kind of check-and-balance among competing agencies. Thus the agency was carried over through the Yüan dynasty until its abolition in Ming times.[31] Obviously, the history of this institution was enough to convince Yu that Korea was living with the same unfortunate transference of authority that had evolved from an original military crisis, and power had to be restored to legitimate civil agencies.

Next he drew up a table for the reorganization of the existing Six Ministries

(Yukcho), which were to be subordinated to the State Council. This had been an important issue at the beginning of the dynasty because assertive kings found that the State Council posed an obstacle to their will. King T'aejŏng strengthened the Six Ministries in 1405, and in 1414 he limited the jurisdiction of the State Council to conferences on important matters of state and permitted the individual ministries to by-pass the State Council and submit memorials directly to the throne. It was only twenty-two years later that King Sejong restored the primacy of the State Council in 1436 by requiring that the ministers report to and obtain concurrence (*sŏsa*) from the council for their proposals.

The young King Tanjŏng further strengthened its powers, but the usurper King Sejo restored T'aejŏng's practice of allowing direct memorials from the ministries in the 1450s and 1460s. Since these shifts of policy reflected the ebb and flow between royal and bureaucratic authority, Yu's position was clearly supportive of the State Council and the paramountcy of the bureaucracy.[32]

Yu was again inspired by the commentaries of Chung Chang-t'ung, Fan Yeh, and others on this question. Chung had written that when the founder of the Later Han, Emperor Kuang-wu, came to the throne (in A.D. 25), he attempted to reverse the usurpation of imperial authority by officials at the end of the Former Han and assume direct responsibility himself for the supervision of the ministries, but "In seeking to right what had gone wrong, he overcorrected and did not entrust government affairs to subordinates."[33]

Fan Yeh in the *History of the Later Han* also pointed to the problems that arose when the ruler chose to rule directly, without a prime minister:

> In later ages there were many times when [the ruler] was suspicious of people and the responsibilities of the prime minister were divided up and not left unified. The ruler regarded authority as residing in himself and the officials regarded [the seat of] government as residing in the ruler. There was no place where responsibility could be entrusted so that the state could put down rebellion and the people enjoy peace and quiet. For that reason worthy men were not able to put into practice what they had learned, and worthless men were able to gain haphazard acceptance in the midst [of the worthy officials], only because official [organization] was not correct and responsibility was not delegated exclusively [to a single prime minister]. If you want to investigate the ancient [system] in order to establish official posts, you must have a single prime minister to control the empire, for only then can you say that it will be well governed.[34]

Commentators on T'ang organization pointed out another variant of the same problem, the transfer of authority from the apex of the regular bureaucracy to personal secretaries of the emperor. This phenomenon began in the 660s when Emperor Kao-tsung recruited the so-called Scholars of the Northern Gate (Pei-men hsüeh shih) to draft documents. Emperor Hsüan-tsung of the mid-eighth century then created the Han-lin Academy to honor scholars, an event that should have pleased all Confucian statecraft writers, but the measure drew their ire because Emperor Hsüan-tsung was indiscriminate in his recruitment of these supposed scholars, and allowed Buddhist monks, Taoist adepts, experts in painting and chess, lute players, and diviners into their ranks. Then he began to use them as imperial secretaries, and as such they were referred to as his Inner Prime Ministers (Nei-hsiang), or as the emperor's private men (*T'ien-tzu ssu-jen*). All were appointed to the Han-lin Academy, and after a year's stint in that office were given the task of drafting edicts for him. Despite their relative youth, at state banquets they were seated above the first rank officials, second only to the chief ministers of state. The exegete, Hu An-kuo, criticized these practices severely because a true king of virtue was not supposed to operate on the basis of private consideration or consult with his own "private people." Only the prime minister was qualified to perform this function for the ruler.[35]

Yu's sources on the Sung dynasty revealed that there were several councilors of state (Tsai-hsiang) instead of a single prime minister, and they were not chosen exclusively from the heads of the Three Departments (San-sheng), but presumably included a number of other officials as well who may have been less qualified or experienced.[36]

Major deliberation and decision-making was not the exclusive preserve of the so-called outer court or regular bureaucracy where it belonged. Even though the supreme bureaucratic agencies of the T'ang dynasty outer court, like the Department of State Affairs (Shang-shu sheng) and Chancellery (Men-hsia sheng) were retained in the Sung administration, the Secretariat (Chung-shu sheng), which functioned as a deliberative body in the T'ang outer court, had been relegated to paper-shuffling clerical duties, and the Chancellery was also put in charge of rather minor matters as well, such as palanquins, imperial treasures, rank tablets, review of official performance, and other duties.

The most important policy decisions had been usurped by officials in the inner court near the emperor, such as the secretaries (Chung-shu) and members of the Bureau of Military Affairs (Shu-mi-yüan) who met in the inner court in the Hall of State Affairs (Cheng-shih-t'ang) in the emperor's Forbidden Quarters. Financial affairs were run by the Finance Commission (San-ssu) rather than the Ministry of Taxation.[37] The implication of this analysis was that the humiliation of China during the Sung by the Khitan, Jurchen, and Mongol barbarians was undoubtedly the product, in part, of this misallocation of authority.

Ma Tuan-lin argued that in Chou times all officials were chosen because of their superior ability and assembled in the palace to provide advice or rectify mistakes, but after the fall of the Chou dynasty the distinction between "inner" and "outer" officials began in the mid-Former Han dynasty when only eunuchs or imperial favorites were allowed this kind of close access while the "silk-clad" scholar-officials were given posts as clerks in the regular or "outer" bureaucracy.[38]

Finally, in the Ming dynasty when the post of prime minister (Ch'eng-hsiang) was abolished under the reforms of Hu Wei-yung, giving the emperor direct access to the Six Boards, the check on the arbitrary exercise of power by the emperor was eliminated.[39] Ch'iu Chün also pointed out that the abandonment of the supreme governing boards of the T'ang and Sung dynasty, such as the Department of State Affairs (Shang-shu sheng), Secretariat (Chung-shu sheng), and Bureau of Military Affairs (Shu-mi-yüan), had also been designed to increase the growing despotism of Chinese rulers.[40]

Although Yu Hyŏngwŏn did not believe in a literal restoration of Chou institutions, he showed great respect for those Chinese scholars and officials who had stressed the necessity of a supreme prime minister and a civilian State Council, primarily as a means of limiting the arbitrary authority of the king and asserting the primacy of civilian control over the military – despite his view that all civil officials should have an adequate education in traditional military skills and knowledge.

Royal Marriages: Background Checks of Consorts

Yu was especially critical of current practice in the selection of queens and spouses for members of royalty, in particular the summoning of prospective candidates to the palace for an inspection of their faces and physical appearance. He thought that this practice had never been used in Korea until King T'aejong in the early fifteenth century confiscated the property of one man who refused to allow his son to be chosen for T'aejong's son-in-law and then summoned the sons of the officials to the palace for a review of candidates.

Yulgok had criticized this practice in the late sixteenth century and praised the kings of former dynasties who always sought the descendants of "former sages," or virtuous and outstanding men. Yu also counseled against choosing marriage partners on the basis of facial appearance, the magnificence of their clothing, or the advice of fortunetellers. He preferred that queens or spouses for princes and princesses should be chosen by investigating the parents of prospective spouses to see if their families were well run, and the candidates themselves to see if their comportment was in order. Finally, the surname and clan of the candidate had to be checked, and the approval of the top ministers (*taesin*) obtained. He did not specify the purpose of this check of family pedigree, but one might draw some deductions from his discussion of the problem.

Yu advised that marriage partners for royalty be chosen by thorough consultation with officials rather than by the arbitrary act of a king "locked up deep inside the inner recesses of the palace." It was not necessary to reproduce the rites of antiquity in all respects, just to have an official study the ritual classics to devise a workable compromise. Yu felt that the best system for the selection of spouses for royalty in the "later age" since the fall of classical Chou occurred in the Sung dynasty, and he copied out the memorial of Fan Tsu-yü submitted to the grandmother of Emperor Che-tsung (during the *yüan-yu* period, 1086–94) for the purpose of advising her on the method of selection.

Fan had boiled down the essence of correct procedure to four elements. The clan and surname of the candidate had to be reviewed because in ancient China the emperors and kings had to choose their spouses from the descendants in the male line of the feudal lords of large states, sage kings, or illustrious individuals. If there were no suitable candidates from those categories, they might select someone from the female line of descent from those individuals. "They did not take [a spouse] from a low and base family and elevate her to the most respected position [of empress], and it was for that reason that there was much good fortune and they (the rulers) had many illustrious male descendants." The longevity of the Hsia, Shang, and Chou dynasties themselves was attributable to the wise choice of empresses.

Candidates for empresses or queens also had to be women of virtue in the three dynasties of antiquity, and the veracity of that policy was proved by the examples portrayed in *The Book of Poetry* and *The Book of History* of dynasties that fell because their queens were all depraved women. The empress had to serve as a model for all the feudal states, but since it was difficult to judge the potential of young girls for this role, the families and paternal ancestors of the candidate had to be investigated instead. Fan felt that since the Chou there had only been a few examples of empresses of illustrious virtue; the rest were examples of how the wrong empress could lead to failure and confusion. His own Sung dynasty, by contrast, had succeeded in choosing virtuous empresses, and he hoped that this tradition be continued by constant consultation of the ancient texts.

The bridegroom, whether king or prince, had to personally meet his bride and accord her the utmost respect, as Confucius had advised, to symbolize the exalted nature of the relationship and elevate the stature of his empress or princess to a level equivalent to his own, a relationship that Fan compared to that between Heaven and Earth, sun and moon, yin and yang. Fan introduced this proposition into his proposal for procedure in the selection of the imperial consort not because it was justified in any ancient ritual text, but because in the absence of texts for imperial marriages emperors had been following the procedures used by the scholar class (*shih*), which did not accord the bride respect on a level equivalent to the bridegroom. Fan believed that it was uncivil to omit demonstrations of respect for the bride, and that the lower or more vulgar customs of the street or those of the barbarians should not be allowed to infiltrate the norms of the forbidden palace. Current practice, therefore, had to be abolished and revised according to his recommendation.

Finally, the choice had to be made with the full consultation of officials because in antiquity the Son of Heaven consulted his high officials before making a choice, his highest dukes accompanied him in proceeding to greet his betrothed, and the feudal lords managed the wedding ceremony. Even in the Sung dynasty, the Emperor Jen-tsung changed his mind in the selection of a spouse because of the objections of some of the people at court. Fan argued that even though some might believe that the selection of an empress was a family matter to be decided by the emperor himself without outside participation,

> since ancient times many mistakes [in the selection of] rulers resulted from this

> point of view. All matters inside and out are the family affairs of the Emperor and there is no principle which says that the great officials can not participate [in these decisions]. Furthermore, when the Emperor makes even a single appointment to high office or advances even a single official to be close to him, he must consult the views of the world. How much more so when he is selecting an empress to be the mother of the empire?

Yu was obviously enamored of Fan Tsü-yu's plan to bring the selection of imperial consorts within the purview of the scholar-official class by requiring their consultation and limiting empresses and other consorts to the children of that class alone. His requirement that the lineages and clans of each candidate be checked by a committee of officials from the same class would have preserved their exercise of influence through the empress and her male relatives. It was already the practice in Korea that queens were selected from the daughters of the prestigious yangban, and the Sung practice appeared to reinforce what was already accepted social practice. Yangban influence, if not necessarily direct control, over the marriage partners of royalty was an important weapon in the preservation of the social and political status quo in Korea. Yu's ideal society, however, would have replaced the yangban with a class of scholar-officials recruited on the basis of moral behavior, so that his endorsement of Fan's recommendations could be perceived as strengthening the elite of his new society rather than the hereditary yangban of the old. Nonetheless, what he did not want to allow was the king to exercise his own choice to select women outside the class of bureaucrats and scholars. The bureaucrats were to govern the procedure, whether they represented the present yangban or Yu's idealized *sadaebu*.

In addition, Yu also called for abolishing the current practice of early marriage in Korea for all classes of society. He thought that the age of marriage had been reduced over the years from the classical norm of thirty years of age for men and twenty for women to the current norm of sixteen-thirty for men to fourteen-twenty for women primarily because early marriage had first been adopted in the royal house and then adopted by the elite. He also proposed the adoption of Confucius's recommendation to require that all bridegrooms receive the bride as part of the formal marriage rite instead of visiting the bride's house and moving in for a few days – a vestige of matrilocal marriage practice that was preserved in the Chosŏn dynasty. He thought that this practice reversed the proper dominance of the yang or male principle over the yin or female, but what he meant was that the treatment of women should conform to proper Neo-Confucian standards of patriarchy and patrilocal marriage, not to the earlier, more native practice of matrilocal marriage. Finally, he demanded frugality in expenditure at weddings and the reduction of all rituals, clothing, and ceremonial statements to a bare minimum, another example of the power of restraint by Confucian norms against the arbitrary power and propensity for ostentatious display by rulers.[41]

Court Audiences: Accessibility

It is obvious from Yu's advocacy for the restoration of the State Council as the supreme deliberative council of state that he hoped that consultation by the king with the officials of this institution would prevent the tyranny and despotism associated with absolutism in a monarchical system. He did not feel, however, that the mere existence of institutions like the State Council and agencies of remonstrance by themselves would be sufficient to check tyranny. It was also important to win the king's adherence to and application of an ethos of balanced government enshrined by the conduct of rites. The purpose of the council was to open the king's mind to the information and criticism necessary for enlightened rule.

Yu realized that the existence of a bureaucratic structure did not guarantee automatically that the king would make himself accessible to the flow of information and opinion from both these officials and the public at large. He recorded Hŏ Chŏk's plaint about King Injo (r. 1623–49) that he had not opened his court to his own officials. "[Your Majesty] keeps himself deeply ensconced within the nine-layered walls [of his palace] and rarely ever sees the faces of his officials. Every day all the affairs of state are handled only in writing. Decisions that could be made in one word take up ten pages of text, while actions that could be taken in fifteen minutes are delayed for days."

Hŏ believed that Injo's failure to open access to his person by his ministers had created a precedent for inattention that destroyed the efficiency of government operations as a whole.

> It is because the king above is remiss in his attention to government affairs that those below are also lax in attending to their duties. None of the bureau [officials] take their seats in their respective offices, and when they do take their seats there, they pass the whole day floating around. All government business is left to the clerks and petty officials. Rules and regulations are neglected and mistakes are made, and all regulations and provisions are in utter confusion.

He also lamented Injo's abolition of the round-table discussion (*yundae*) that had previously required officials in an audience at court to voice their opinions on governmental affairs. Even though Hŏ realized that Injo had dispensed with the system because he found that the responses had been routine, he argued that there had to be at least one or two ideas worth adopting from a discussion by a large number of officials over several days. Abolishing this "beautiful method" just because of the superficial quality of the discussion would be equivalent to some one "giving up eating just because he happened to choke on the food."

Hŏ's solution to these difficulties was to return to the precedents for the standard audience (*sangch'am*) and court audience (*choch'am*) conducted early in the dynasty and codified in *The Ceremonies of the Five Rites* (*Oryeŭi*), a text that King Sejong ordered compiled and was completed later in 1474. The standard audience was held daily at the Hall of Convenience (Pyŏnjŏn) for his ministers, and the court audience was held every other day at the Hall of Rectitude (Chŏngjŏn) for his officials. These conferences began with reports of any alerts from the network of signal fires strung throughout the hilltops of the country to warn of foreign invasions, and then proceeded to consideration of criminal cases and military affairs. The next order of business was to discuss memorials from officials, impeachments submitted by the censorate, and personnel appointments by the state council and the six ministries. All discussion was held in the presence of the king.

Hŏ noted that this procedure had been abandoned by the "wild and lascivious" King Yŏnsan'gun, but King Chungjong failed to restore them after Yŏnsan'-gun was deposed. In checking the court records for 1537, Hŏ found that the court scribes were dutifully writing down "the regular audience is suspended" every day even though the audience had not been held for thirty years, a symbol of their ardent wish that the procedure might sometime be restored. Unfortunately, when he found that in last year's records (no date) that the court recorders had abandoned their practice of even noting the suspension, tears came to his eyes because he knew it meant that the methods of the founders of the dynasty had been destroyed.

He asked Injo to study *The Ceremonies of the Five Rites*, reinstitute the daily court audiences, and summon officials who had submitted written memorials advance to the throne so that he could ask them specifically what their individual responsibilities were, how much work they had done, how many decisions they had made, and how much they had spent, and then reward them for their accomplishments or dismiss them from office depending on what they had done. Furthermore, all officials in capital bureaus should attend their offices every day and report what they had done the previous day. If this regimen were followed strictly, it would become impossible for the clerks and petty irregular officials to take over the duties of the regular ones.[42]

Another important factor in Yu's consideration of this problem was the memorial that Cho Hŏn submitted on Ming procedure at imperial audiences after he returned from China in 1574. Cho had been impressed at the extent of personal contact between the emperor and his officials. Whenever the Six Boards had business with the emperor, the officials would "face the throne in reporting the matter," and if the remonstrance officials "had something they wanted to talk about, they would hold their written memorial in their hands and personally present it to the Emperor." Furthermore, if any of the governors or prefectural magistrates had a report to make to him,

> he would take along their clerks and runners and lead them into the court where they would kneel down right by the stairs close by the Emperor, . . . announce the name of his bureau, his office rank, what state [*kuo*, i.e., province] it was, and what rank official he was in that state. . . . Even the lowest officials wearing the smallest hats and the shabbiest clothes were all able to look up to view the

> Heavenly Light [the Emperor's countenance], and then bow down, prostrate themselves, and knock their heads on the ground. Even barbarians with braided hair and clothes fastened on the left side [in barbarian style] were all given an audience with *li* [courtesy] whenever the Emperor was on an imperial progress, and he would personally order that they be given food to eat.

Cho was impressed not only by the accessibility of the Ming emperor to all his people, but his openness with foreigners, and he was sure that all his subjects must have felt gratitude and loyalty toward him. By the same token, he was just as sure that the Korean style of monarchical rule was lacking in these august qualities. Even though the attendance of officials of the Six Ministries was required at court audiences, there was no schedule of regular audiences for capital officials to report on affairs of state. Provincial governors might have had some access, but petty officials and clerks had no chance at all to meet the king like their counterparts did in Ming China.

> Your majesty attends court numerous times, but the high ministers of state and advisers in the king's entourage rarely get a chance to see the royal garb. Even when provincial governors and magistrates go [to their assignments], I have never heard that they receive sage [royal] instruction face-to-face. The only thing that happens is that the orders from the royal Secretariat [are issued] which say: "In accordance with the previous royal command, send them off," and that is all. Alas! How can these four words . . . be sufficient to move the minds of the people? If the court conducts its affairs in this way, there is no need to ask why it is that the officials in the outer district towns neglect the people's business.

On the other hand, Cho argued, royal behavior in Korea had not always been that way because in the early fifteenth century King Sejong had diligently attended daily court audiences to discuss current affairs of state and to meet with magistrates about to leave the capital for their posts. In each case he would inform them about natural disasters, famines, or problems that they would have to face when they arrived. He also held daily meetings with the State Council to review all reports from lower echelons of the bureaucracy, and his government was able to manage all affairs without excessive bother to anyone. What Cho Hŏn recommended, therefore, was that King Sŏnjo model himself after the example of the current Wan-li Emperor of the Ming dynasty and King Sejong.[43]

Yu's reason for citing this material was to demonstrate that for at least a hundred years Korean kings had locked themselves inside the palace, failed either to communicate their intentions adequately or to listen to the reports and opinions of the regular bureaucracy, lost contact with the officials on a personal basis, and discontinued routine sessions for the conduct of daily business. What Yu meant by rites in this instance was conformity to procedures of governance by model kings of the past that had obviated the development of current flaws, all of which had been the product of the self-consuming and self-centered concerns of arbitrary or lazy monarchs.

Yu was also dissatisfied with certain types of audiences in Korea because they were held only to receive flattering congratulatory messages from sycophantic officials and not to conduct serious state business. He was particularly discomfited by the major court audiences held to honor the new year, the winter solstice, and the king's birthday because audiences of these types had never been held in the Chou dynasty, and the four seasonal major audiences reported in *The Rites of Chou* and the annual and triennial *ping* audiences for feudal representatives recorded in the *Wang-chih* section of the *Li-chi* were devoted to receiving reports of problems, discussing solutions, or giving admonition. It was only in the "later age" that emperors began to hold audiences to receive congratulations and accept praise, a manifestation of their own human desire (*inyok*) for gratification rather than the Heavenly principle (*ch'ŏlli*) that governed the modus operandi of the ancient sages.

The first occurrence of a congratulatory audience in honor of the new year occurred in the reign of Emperor Kao of the Han dynasty in the tenth month of B.C. 200, following the Ch'in celebration of the new year in that month. Then in the Later Han dynasty, the new year was shifted to the first lunar month. The celebration of the winter solstice began in the Wei and Chin dynasties in the third century A.D., and envoys from local districts and dukedoms were sent to offer congratulations to the emperor. One scholar had justified this kind of celebration because the winter solstice marked the day that the positive, male force of yang began to rise during the year, but it was nonetheless a violation of the practice of antiquity. Finally, Emperor Hsüan-tsung of the T'ang (r. 713–56) began the practice of holding a party on his birthday, and the custom later became an annual tradition followed later in the Sung and Ming dynasties.

Yu quoted the words of two post-T'ang critics who pointed out that Emperor T'ai-tsung of the early T'ang had refused to celebrate his own birthday because it only reminded him of his parents' (i.e., mother's) "ordeal" when he was born. Hsüan-tsung, however, was more than happy to celebrate his birth because he had become arrogant and his officials were all sycophants, but birthday celebrations were not the way for a ruler to honor his parents or for his subjects to honor him.

Yu thought that there might be some justification for celebrating New Year's day even though they were never conducted in ancient China, but it was wrong for the ruler to receive congratulations and presents. The winter solstice was important because the force of yang first emerged in nature, but in earlier times the rulers would honor the occasion by closing the palace gates, not by conducting business. The imperial birthday celebration, however, was totally lacking in moral justification. Emperor T'ai-tsu of the Ming, one of the great promoters of Confucian culture, did in fact refuse to hold such congratulatory audiences either on the winter solstice or his own birthday. T'ai-tsu's piety should have served for a model for later emperors after the late fourteenth century, but unfortunately, his noble intent was undermined by a succession of fawning officials.[44]

Yu concluded that it would be best if the king adopted the ideal court audiences of antiquity devoted to the conduct of government business. He should summon the crown prince and all officials at court on the first day of every month for an audience, and on that day provincial officials would also assemble and carry out a rite at which they would face toward the royal court (the *manggwŏllye*). On five other days during the lunar month all court officials of the first-through-sixth ranks would be summoned to the court audience (*choch'am*) before the king. Every day one official of upper *tangsangwan* rank each from the State Council, the Six Ministries, the National Academy, Office of the Inspector-General, and the Seoul Magistracy, two from the Office of Special Counselors, and every duty official for the day of the State Council and Six Ministries would attend the daily standard audience (*sangch'am*) on a rotating basis. To assure full participation, officials with business to present would take turns mounting the steps to the throne platform to report it directly to the king, and both civil and military officials of all ranks would respond to inquiries by the king every other day in a regular order for the capital offices. All officials appointed to provincial posts would have to report to the king before leaving or after returning to inform the king of their experience "as was done in ancient times."

Yu then described the types of court audiences in the Chou period and Ch'iu Chün's (of the Ming dynasty) commentary that noted that the emperor met his officials every morning to conduct goverment affairs, listened to the officials, who took turns in presenting memorials and answering the ruler's questions, withdrew to his boudoir to ruminate and decide whether he would give his approval to requests, and then reappeared in court for further discussion and deliberation, and listened to advice from his top ministers. Ch'iu argued that this system of thorough discussion and review convinced all officials that final decisions were correct and appropriate, and the procedure inspired them to proceed to their posts in the provinces and carry out the imperial decisions.

Yu also presented some examples from dynasties after the Chou. In the T'ang dynasty all civil and military officials of the first through ninth ranks were summoned to court audiences on the first and fifteenth days of the month; civil officials of the first through fifth ranks attended the regular audience every day; military officials of the first through fifth ranks attended the court conferences on the fifth, eleventh, twenty-first, and twenty-fifth days of the month; those of the first through third ranks and those on duty in their respective bureaus and the top officials attended audiences according to the duties currently under their charge. The Son of Heaven held regular audience every day but convened an audience in the Hall of Convenience in his Purple Boudoir on the first and fifteenth days of the month. Unfortunately, Ch'iu remarked that the Purple Boudoir audiences were handled rather cursorily. In short, Yu's recommended procedure derived from Chou institutions in spirit, but more specifically from the details of T'ang procedure.[45]

His main point was that the formal "rites" or procedures for the conduct of audiences was extremely important as a guide for restoring the proper mode for the king to conduct serious government business. Since kings of the past century at least had failed to maintain proper order in state affairs, the wisdom of the rites could be used as a source of authority outside of and superior to the king's arbitrary power of decision to lead him back to the path of rectitude.

Royal Lectures: Less Intimidation

Yu naturally believed that the royal lectures, an institution created for the education of the king in the classics throughout his life, was an important institution, but he complained that the true spirit of the royal lectures had been lost because the power and majesty of the kings had so overwhelmed and overawed the officials that they were afraid to express their opinions openly and honestly. He felt that true education could not be achieved unless the intimidating atmosphere of the royal lecture sessions were reduced as much as possible. He quoted Cho Kwangjo's remarks that although the royal lecturers had been assured that they might sit at ease in court during such sessions, in fact they were afraid to speak their minds because they were not sure they could take the king at his word.

Cho attributed this atmosphere of intimidation to Queen Chŏnghŭi (the Chŏnghŭi wanghu), who was born in 1418 to a royal relative of the P'ap'yŏng Yun clan, became the queen of King Sejo in 1455, and gave birth to King Yejong and two other children. She became regent for the young Yejong in 1468–69, continued her regency during the minority of King Sŏngjong until 1475, and died in 1483. Cho remarked that the precedent she established continued through Yŏnsan'gun, who once executed one official, Sim Sunmun, for having raised his head to look at the king during a royal lecture session. "So extreme had the majesty of the throne become that the officials trembled with fear. That we still lie prostrate [before the king] is also a custom bequeathed to us from the reign of the deposed king [Yŏnsan'gun]."[46]

Yu also cited Cho Hŏn's disapproval of requiring officials to prostrate themselves on the ground at lecture sessions because it was not a true gesture of respect. At the beginning of the dynasty, kings granted the lecturers the right to sit at ease, and King Sejong in particular would "quietly look around and ask questions, just like a father [did with his] son in a family." As a result, officials were never reluctant to report any source of suffering for the people or difficulty for the country. Queen Chŏnghŭi was the one who forced officials to prostrate themselves before her and the king, but at least King Myŏngjong in the mid-sixteenth century again permitted the lecturers to sit in a relaxed posture.

Cho argued that the denigration and humiliation of officials in the royal presence interfered with the atmosphere necessary for full communication.

> The ruler must empty his mind and look forward to the minister's expression of view, and the minister below should gaze up into the Heavenly countenance to see whether He accepts [his point of view] or not. Only then can there truly be a confluence of wills, a supplementing of what is lacking, a rectification of error, and achievement of a flourishing age of great peace. Since ancient times there was never a case when good government was achieved when the ruler flaunted his power in arrogant fashion and his subjects trembled in fear at his majestic authority.[47]

Yu, in other words, followed closely Cho Kwangjo's and Cho Hŏn's classic defense of open expression of views in an atmosphere of congeniality during royal lecture sessions as a fundamental defense against the evils of tyrannical and despotic governance by an absolute monarch. But the only way that mood could be achieved was by the king's own choice – not by an appeal to any law higher than the command of the king, or to any fundamental right of free expression.

The Personal Bond between Official and King

Yu's attitude toward the king, however, was by no means entirely negative or cautious. The king was still the supreme ruler of the state and the supreme authority over all members of the bureaucracy, but even though Yu accepted the legitimacy of bureaucratic organization, he still believed that the personal bond of loyalty created in feudal times between Chinese lords and vassals was preferable to the impersonal rules and regulations of the bureaucratic system.

To introduce some flavor of the personal bond of feudal times, Yu suggested that the Chou feudal practice of summoning officials to audiences with the ruler at court was indispensable to give both ruler and official alike a feeling of human contact. "If it had not been like this, they would not have had any way to make clear what the proper rules of social behavior [*li*, *ye* in Korean] between ruler and minister were, or to penetrate the feelings of those above and below." At the least, an official would be required to attend an audience at least once in a six-year term of office to make contact with his ruler. Infrequent as it might be, personal petitions to the ruler would be still be preferable to indirect control through superior officials.[48]

Conclusion

Yu's discussion of the ways by which these goals should be carried out were not that simple and straightforward, however, for instead of simply issuing a set of homilies exhorting the kings to change their ways, he attempted to make accommodations with certain accepted practices. The first instance was his attempt to limit the rising costs that had resulted from the proliferation of royal relatives over the generations. He obviously felt he could not simply call for the conversion of royal relatives to commoner status because of the existing rules that preserved privileged royal status to the fifth generation of descent, but he did think that he could introduce a stricter system of ranks with a reduction of expenditures depending on the rank of the noble relative.

Another device he used was to divide princes into eldest and other sons, and sons of the main wife versus the nothoi, or sons of concubines. His purpose was apparently to reduce the emoluments paid to members of lesser categories, but to make these distinctions, he had to accept the traditional Chosŏn bias against nothoi. Since he did, however, urge that the bias against the inherited slave status of some royal concubines be abandoned, he was holding fast to his ultimate objective of reducing inherited slavery as a major feature of Korean life. In total, however, he could not question the utility of the monarchy or the necessity to maintain privileges for four generations of royal blood; the best he could hope for was a reduction of the costs involved.

In some ways he handled the problems of merit subjects in a similar fashion. Even though they represented the practice of showering favors and rewards on people who performed meritorious service for king and country, they were viewed traditionally by Confucian purists as royal favorites at best, political hacks at worst, whose support drained resources from the the national treasury at the expense of the taxpayer. Once again, he dared only call for the abolition of the minor merit subject lists, preserved the major merit subjects, but sought to limit rather than abolish them by establishing a system of ranks and reduced emoluments, shortening their tenure, and hurrying the exit of their descendants into commoner status.

State funerals and banquets were two more categories that involved large expenditures of state funds, but Yu refused to dispense with either of them because he felt they were sacraments that were essential to the civilized state. He was even willing to expand the number of officials and public servants, like frontier soldiers, who might qualify for publicly supported funerals, and he argued for a few more banquets at state expense for officials as well. Instead, he hoped to limit expenditures by setting strict sumptuary regulations and eliminate noncompensated labor service by converting it to hired labor paid for by the state. But at no point did he challenge the legitimacy of rites and sacraments as a necessary state expense.

Even when he made his most direct attack on an institution – his demand that the Royal Treasury be abolished – he was not urging anything like the conversion of the king into a figurehead monarch; only the assertion of bureaucratic control over the royal exchequer to ensure observation of frugality in meeting the king's needs. That this goal could not be achieved until the Kabo cabinet, which was dominated by the Japanese military presence during the Sino-Japanese War of 1894–95, might indicate that the prerogatives of the Korean king were too powerful to be permanently restricted by the assertion of yangban or bureaucratic influence. The yangban, however, were not that concerned about curtailing the king's spending authority – they were happy to grant it to him in exchange for protecting their property rights in land and slaves.

A second theme in Yu's treatment of the king was his use of ritual to achieve certain moral and behavioral objectives among the population. This theme was illustrated by his emphasis on ritual cultivation of the king's plot and royal ceremonies to honor the aged because both were used to illustrate the traditional Confucian arguments about the primacy of agriculture in the economy and the necessity to respect elders. By having the king act out his respect for these two principles by the conduct of ceremonies in public, Yu hoped to rectify lapses from the observance of these two principles over time, that is, the tendency of peasants to neglect cultivation or abandon it altogether for more profitable pursuits, and the weakness or recalcitrance among the peasantry in meeting the needs of elders in society, despite the state's aim to indoctrinate every one in society in Confucian norms.

The third and final theme in Yu's treatment of the king was his attempt to subject royal authority and power to the restraining influence of the bureaucracy, a tendency that was quite conventional in Confucian lore. He sought to create a strong premiership that would act as chief executive in charge of the entire bureaucracy, an obvious attempt to keep the king at some distance from the decision-making process and turn him into a rubber stamp for Confucian, bureaucratic wisdom.

A corollary to his goal of asserting bureaucratic control over the king was reestablishing the supremacy of the State Council over the Border Defense Command, a sixteenth-century ad hoc national security council that had taken over supreme deliberative functions. This was one of the few objectives that was eventually achieved. The leading critic of the Border Defense Command in the early seventeenth century was the statesman Ch'oe Myŏnggil (d. 1647), who compared it to the Shu-mi-yüan or Bureau of Military Affairs of the Sung. He wanted to replace it, however, with a system based on T'ang and Sung institutions adopted in Koryŏ times and some borrowing from the Ming system, not the early Chosŏn State Council.[49]

The problem did not generate a great debate, but in 1864 the minor King Kojong, acting under instructions from the dowager-regent, carried out the essence of Yu's proposal to replace the Border Defense Command with the old State Council.[50] Since the policy was undoubtedly decided by the king's father, the Taewongun, it is possible but unproved that he may have been influenced by Yu's ideas. Even though the reform was not carried out in conjunction with many of Yu's other reforms for bureaucratic reorganization, such as reassigning tasks to the bureaus of the Six Ministries, abolishing the Office of Censor-General, strengthening the governor, reorganizing the boundaries of prefectures and districts, and professionalizing the clerks and runners in the central and local government, one cannot help but suspect the underlying and lingering influence of Yu's thought.

This restoration of the State Council could not have taken place, however, had the dynasty not been shaken to its roots by a serious peasant rebellion in 1862 and the increasing threat of foreign invasion. At the time the Taewongun obviously felt that a restoration of dynastic fortunes had to be dependent on the structure of the bureaucracy itself, as if formal structure could work a transforming effect on the honesty and efficiency of all officials. The Taewongun's reforms may have bought a decade of time in a period of crisis, but too many problems were left unresolved. For example, Yu's recommendation to abolish the Royal Treasury (Naesusa) and to shift control of the king's finances to the regular bureaucracy was essential for the effective use of resources for defense, but it was only achieved under the Japanese-sponsored Kabo reforms of 1894. The failure to reform local government in the seventeenth century meant the accumulation of superfluous officials, duplicated costs, and the increased power of local clerks to exploit the peasantry for gain, all of which contributed to the 1862 rebellion itself.

Yu also sought to surround the king with moral examplars as had been done in the ancient Chou dynasty, the prime minister and two high councilors of state. He wanted to curtail the king's freedom to choose his queens and concubines not only by insisting on the supervision of the choice of consorts by a bureaucratic committee, but by defining the criteria of eligibility according to the norms of the Confucianized ruling class – not that distant from the yangban of his own time. While his comments were somewhat oblique on this question, it was obvious that Yu was not comfortable with the prospect of the king, on a whim, selecting his queen from the lowest and most unrefined classes despite his sympathy for the downtrodden in other areas of life.

Finally, with respect to the king's conduct of daily government business, Yu chose to counter the tendency of monarchs to retreat to the cozy confines of their inner palace quarters with their favorites because it would remove their contact with the problems of the populace. He emphasized the necessity of maintaining accessibility to officials, reestablishing personal contact with them to inculcate the ancient, feudal touch of personal loyalty, and reducing the aura of inviolate superiority and arrogance that had developed in the royal lectures since the late fifteenth century. That arrogance inhibited the lecturers from expressing their views and fulfilling their function of guiding the king to righteousness.

In almost all these problems, Yu Hyŏngwŏn was inspired by classical Confucian norms in which the ruler functions as a symbol of standards, performs rites to illustrate moral standards, reinforces the Physiocratic philosophy of the economy, and subjects himself to bureaucratic regulation and restriction in his expenditure of money, conduct of funerals and banquets, and management of daily affairs of state.

CHAPTER 16
Reforming the Central Bureaucracy

The purpose of Yu's treatment of bureaucratic organization was summarized in a brief paragraph at the end of his essay on the subject that the task of the middle-dynastic period was to reduce the trend toward the increase of officials by the proclivity of emperors to exercise their power to create posts. Emperor T'ai-tsung at the beginning of the T'ang dynasty had proclaimed that he could rule the empire and "sufficiently accommodate the outstanding and talented men of the empire" with a staff of only 730 men, but by the end of the T'ang, the problem of superfluous officials had thrown the system into confusion. Emperor T'ai-tsu of the Ming also began his dynasty by cutting down on posts and making the creation of new ones a crime, but the Ming suffered the same problem that had plagued earlier dynasties.[1]

Proliferation and Complexity in Post-Han China

The Chou Model

Yu derived the fundamental principles of bureaucratic organization from his treatment of classical texts, subsequent commentaries, and post-classical Chinese bureaucratic history. The first of these could be described as the principle of economy, by which organization was to be kept simple and the number of offices reduced to a minimum necessary for the achievement of necessary tasks. This concept was closely tied to a second principle, the rational division of labor in government affairs to eliminate all duplication or overlap, a procedure often referred to by the phrase "establishing offices and dividing up responsibilities" (*sŏlgwan-bunjik*). Yu applied this principle to his own time and called for elimination of all superfluous positions.

Yu believed that the founders of the Chou dynasty had adhered to the principle of simplicity established by the sage emperors of remote antiquity, Yao and Shun, who were able to govern their empires with but one hundred officials. Even when matters became more complex in the Hsia and Shang dynasties (late third and second millennia, B.C.) when more officials had to be created, they still were able to make do with a mere two hundred.[2]

As mentioned in the previous chapter, both the *Book of History* and *Rites of Chou* described six ministers who divided responsibility for administration even though their descriptions did not match.[3]

Proliferation of Officials and Complexity

Yu traced the history of bureaucratic organization from the Han through the Ming, delineating in great detail the structure of central government offices for each dynasty. He interrupted the descriptive detail on occasion to sound the theme that perfection of Chou organization had been lost with the increasing number and complexity of bureaucratic posts. Although the Han government suffered from laxity and inefficiency because it did not continue the Six Ministries and created new agencies that were not appropriate, at least it retained the classical principle of avoiding the creation of idle or superfluous officials, and it was still better than all subsequent dynasties.[4] He cited Tu Yu, compiler of the *T'ung-tien* (ca. 766–801), who remarked that even though the Ch'in and Han did not organize their governments exactly like the six ministers of the Chou, "nevertheless institutions were still not overly complex."[5]

Yu's sources indicated that the superior features of Han administration were gradually lost in the governments of the third century A.D. Wei and Chin dynasties, which began to create more bureaucratic positions and numerous rank titles. It was only in the short-lived Later Chou dynasty (557–81) that the Yü-wen family attempted a literal restoration of the system described in the *Rites of Chou*, an effort that later received the adulation of Chu Hsi.[6]

Unfortunately, this brief period of reform was reversed by the Sui dynasty in the late sixth century when the number of regular officials was expanded and a new category of irregular officials (San-kuan) created.[7] Tu Yu had commented that despite the Later Chou attempt to return to the six ministers of Chou, the Sui emperors decided to return to the organization of the Wei and Chin dynasties because the people had become so used to previous modes of organization that it was difficult for them to adjust to the institutions of antiquity. The Sui emperors called the ministers of the Six Ministries the Masters of Documents (Shang-shu) after the Han imperial secretaries, created additional and separate courts and directorates (Ssu and Chien), and ordered their heads to share responsibility with the six masters of documents. This action destroyed the unity of command that had been exercised exclusively by the six ministers of ancient time. Tu Yu also complained about the overlap of responsibility among the many subordinate bureaus and agencies, let alone the highest ministries in the Sui dynasty, and stressed the necessity of maintaining simplicity and economy in government organization.[8]

As if to punctuate the point, Yu Hyŏngwŏn laid out the complete organization of the T'ang, including the officials of the Six Departments (Sheng), nine courts, five directorates, and a number of other special agencies, including offices serving the emperor and the princes, and the host of their subordinate and attached officials – a task that consumed almost six full pages of text.[9] It was not necessary for Yu to insert his own interpretation of this situation since previous Chinese commentators had written on this situation at length. Tu Yu in the *T'ung-tien* recorded a number of reorganizations (in 662, 670, 691, 705) that apparently did little but change the table of names and responsibilities. Then in 706 over 2,000 supernumerary officials (Yüan-wai-kuan) were created, including some that were sinecures, and after that emperors created new positions by imperial command without regard to the table of organization on the law books. The T'ang government periodically sought to stem the tide by ordering reductions when in 632 Emperor T'ai-tsung cut the number of capital officials to 643, and other emperors ordered reductions in 737 and 740.[10] Later on Chu Hsi paused to remark as well that the problem of superfluous officials in the T'ang was caused by the fatal error of retaining many of the offices of previous dynasties.[11]

The need to eliminate superfluous officials and reduce the size of the bureaucracy had, in fact, been recognized since the beginning of the Later Han dynasty. Emperor Kuang-wu eliminated 400 districts by abolition or combination and reduced the bureaucracy by 10 percent. During Emperor Wu's campaign of retrenchment in the Western Chin dynasty (265–90), Hsün Hsü remarked that not only should regular as well as petty officials be reduced, but the volume of government work had to be diminished as well. He stressed the need to simplify written documents and files and eliminate petty tasks, and he praised Emperor Ming of the Wei dynasty (227–40) for dispatching envoys throughout the empire to recommend staff reductions.[12]

Han Yüan of the early eighth century had also articulated a principle for determining the need for officials. The first task was to calculate the amount and type of work that had to be done, appoint officials to do the work, and hold them responsible for doing it. There was no reason at all to tolerate positions with no work to be done because it would reduce the population engaged in productive tasks – agriculture, sericulture, industry, and commerce.[13]

Tu Yu repeated this theme in the late eighth century. After recounting the history of reductions of administrative staff in the T'ang, he praised the Chou government for appointing only the number of officials they would need and refusing to establish any empty or superfluous positions. Unfortunately, the size of the bureaucracy had not only grown to a figure higher than ten thousand to serve a population of nine million, but approximately one-third the registered population had been lost because of the increase of migrancy after the An Lu-shan rebellion (755–63). The serious changes in population and residence had severely damaged the organization of local districts. "One prefecture would not have as many as three or four thousand households, but there would be fifty or sixty officials [to administer it], like having nine shepherds for ten sheep. They afflict the clerks and burden the people with all kinds of bothersome tasks." Nonetheless, even though a staff reduction would benefit the people by removing the most corrupt and tyrannical officials, it was opposed by officials, who feared the loss of their livelihood.[14]

Li Chi-fu in the early ninth century repeated the same theme, that only 30 percent of the population was left to work the land in arduous labor because so many men were enlisted in the army or functioning as merchants, Buddhist monks, and Taoist adepts. They had to support the 10,000 officials of the capital with their taxes, and the size of districts had shrunk to support the plethora of magistrates. Li, therefore, requested a reduction in the number of officials by combining prefectures and districts, and reducing costs by limiting emoluments, and Emperor Hsien-tsung followed his suggestion by eliminating 808 regular and 1,700 irregular officials.[15]

Attempts to lower the number of officials and the complexity of administration failed in the Sung dynasty because there were no fixed quotas of officials for a number of offices, there was considerable overlap of duties and functions because separate commissions were established to carry out tasks supposedly the responsibility of established offices, and officials were given concurrencies in more than one office. Capital officials, for example, were given additional duties as magistrates of local districts but they often neglected them. Even the reforms of Wang An-shih in the late eleventh century failed to correct the problems of confused organization and superfluous officials.[16]

While administrative rationality and economy had suffered severely in the Sung dynasty, at least an attempt was made in the Ming dynasty to emulate the model of the Six Ministries. Yu was apparently willing to accept the rather forced argument of his favorite Ming writer, Ch'iu Chün, that the Six Boards of the Ming were equivalent to the six ministers of the Chou even though their responsibilities were somewhat different. For example, the Ming Board of Personnel was equivalent to the Chou prime minister, the Board of Taxation was equivalent to the Chou minister of education, and the Board of Public Works was equivalent to the Chou minister of the economy.[17] Nonetheless, he realized that the principles of simplicity and rational assignment of specific tasks to one of six ministers had fallen by the wayside with the destruction of the Chou state by the First Emperor of the Ch'in.[18]

What Yu learned from Chinese experience was that the classical mode of government had to be organized under a prime minister and Six Ministries even though they did not have to be exactly the same as those described in the *Rites of Chou*. All the accretions of later dynasties, in particular additional ministries, courts, directorates, overlapping commissions, and the like had either to be eliminated or their functions combined into or subordinated under one of the six ministries. The creation of sinecures, irregular appointments, and superfluous positions were all to be eliminated.

BUREAUCRATIC REORGANIZATION IN KOREA

Reduction of Agencies and Staff

In turning his attention to contemporary Korea Yu repeated the axiomatic principles of economy and simplicity and called for the reduction of unnecessary officials, duplication, and overlapping areas of responsibility, citing in this instance Yulgok's exaggerated remark to King Sŏnjo in the late sixteenth century that the excessive number of district magistrates had to be cut because there were more posts in the Chosŏn central government than in Ming China. Reduction of capital agencies and district magistracies alike could be achieved by combining duties and territorial jurisdictions of several units.[19]

Yu called for the abolition of the Office of Royal Decrees (Yemun'gwan), an agency divided from the Spring and Autumn Office (Ch'unch'u'gwan) in 1411, because the tasks of this office had already been overlapped by officials in the Office of Special Counselors (Hongmun'gwan) and the historians of the Spring and Autumn Office. In addition Yu wanted to eliminate the Royal Lectures (Kyŏngyŏn) because its posts were held as concurrencies by other officials – including many high-ranking examination passers who used their position to restrict the king's authority.[20] King Sejong had had a similar experience when he created a special agency to honor young scholars called the Book Reading Hall (Toksŏdang), but as time passed these posts declined in prestige. Yu felt that instead of devoting their time to studies, these young officials spent time in impractical activities, engaged in factionalism, and destroyed moral standards.[21] Since the office of Royal Lectures had replicated this sorry experience, it needed to be discarded.

Yu also wanted to eliminate redundant and unnecessary units and agencies in the military establishment as well. Part 2 of his essay covered his decision to reorganize capital and royal defense under the Five Guard system of the early Chosŏn period, to eliminate the Supreme Headquarters (Toch'ŏngbu) because it duplicated the work of the Ministry of War. He recommended also to eliminate four of the Five Military Divisions created since the Imjin War save for the Military Training Agency, and the royal messengers (Sŏnjŏn'gwan) established in the Late Koryŏ period (called Sŏngjŏn sosik at that time). In the last case these tasks could be performed by officials close to the throne or taken over by members of the Inner Forbidden Guards (Naegŭmwi).[22]

A number of other superfluous agencies also merited elimination. The "miscellaneous posts" (Chapchik) had been created in great number without assigning specific tasks and they were often referred to only as recipients of salaries of the lowest rank post (9B). In the districts, the keeper of horse (Kammokkwan) in charge of horse grazing fields in the countryside could be replaced by the district magistrate, and a surplus of recruiters (Kwŏn'gwan) established primarily during Hideyoshi's invasions with underlings like special commanders (Pyŏlchang) and Recruiting Officers (Pyŏlmojang) would be eliminated once

Yu's plan was adopted to combine and reduce the number of military garrisons and small-scale watchtowers. Finally, the number of garrison commanders (Yŏngjang) that had been expanded since the Imjin War and Manchu invasions would also be reduced to tolerable size.[23]

Elimination of Irregular Posts and Concurrencies

In the Chosŏn period kings had made increasing use of commissioners (Chejo) to take charge of special agencies, and most of these posts were held by high ranking ministers as concurrencies. This situation reminded Yu of Sung practice, and he instructed that all commissioners be abolished and all responsibility turned over to the minister (P'ansŏ) or next highest Tangsang (rank 1a–3a) official assigned to the ministry.

Yu was not even willing to make an exception for certain offices, such as the Bureau of Medicine (Ŭisa), the Court of Music (Chang'agwŏn), the Directorate of Astronomy (Kwansanggam), and the Court of Interpreters (Sayŏgwŏn), since commissioners with special expertise in each of those specialties might be usefully employed in addition to the generalist officials appointed as formal heads of those units. He refused to compromise with the principle of unified reponsibility and command, and insisted that it was more important to appoint "the right men" to office rather than to find the most skilled. If skill were needed, instructors (Kyosu) could be employed as underlings in those agencies for that purpose. To use specialist commissioners would only demoralize and weaken the authority of the chief official, causing him to neglect his work, and if the commissioners turned out to be less skilled than expected, no advantage would be gained at all. Yu, in other words, was still strongly committed to the priority of the generalist over the specialist.[24]

He also wanted to abolish concurrencies because 60 to 70 percent of the posts listed in the dynastic law code were concurrencies, and many of them had begun to neglect their duties. Each official, no matter how high or low his position, had to be given exclusive charge of his responsibilities, just as had been done in ancient times. To his knowledge there had never been any concurrent posts in the two Han dynasties, nor even in the slack and shoddy bureaucracies of the Wei and Chin states. Concurrencies had begun in the T'ang and flourished in the Sung, and the Chosŏn government had reproduced that sorry situation. Furthermore, concurrent officials paraded their titles in ostentatious display and their namecards bore titles several lines long because of it.

In addition, the Directorates of Medicine and Astronomy and the Court of Interpreters had irregular sinecures called Ch'ea that Yu defined as officials without regular salaries tested four times a year and assigned salaries on the basis of their test scores. Since these irregular officials occupied the seats of regular officials of those agencies, Yu considered that it deprived them of respect and dignity, resulted in haphazard recruitment of men of no talent, and robbed the unit they worked in of proper organization and chain of command. He insisted that every agency of the government should have regular grades and fixed salaries for its officials, and biannual tests of skill to maintain high standards for officials. Raising and lowering salaries on the basis of on-the-job performance should only be allowed for the lowest level functionaries, like copyists, artists, and musicians.[25]

The establishment of special commissions called General Directorates (Togam) to handle affairs on an ad hoc basis was another practice that had to be eliminated. Yu claimed that establishing such commissions with a full staff of personnel, runners, and slaves was a common occurrence, used even for what would otherwise be considered routine matters. The practice had originated as a symptom of administrative decline in the late Koryŏ dynasty, and had unfortunately been carried over into the Chosŏn era.[26]

Rationalize the Administration of the Capital

Yu sought to abolish superfluous agencies responsible for the control of population and punishment of wrongdoers in the capital. He sought to transfer the responsibilities of officials in charge of the Five Wards (Obu), the separate officials for surveillance and arresting outlaws such as the watch guards handled by the Capital Patrol (Kŭm'owi) since Koryŏ times, and the Agency for the Arrest of Thieves (P'odoch'ŏng), to the Ministry of Punishments, and ultimately the Agency of Punishments (Chŏn'oksŏ). This last agency had been carried over from the Koryŏ dynasty and was used as the repository of suspects charged with a variety of crimes who were transferred to the Ministry of Punishments, the Seoul Magistracy, and the Office of Inspector-General for adjudication and then sent back to the Agency of Punishments. It could be abolished by establishing jails in the Ministry of Punishments, the Seoul Magistracy (Hansŏngbu), and even the Office of Inspector-General.[27] Finally, the useless Agency for the Elderly (Kiroso) for men over seventy years of age and rank 2A was deemed totally worthless because the king would also award the elderly by providing them with rice and meat. The leniency of the king created more expenses than benefits because various grants of fields, parks, fish weirs, and salt flats expanded these funds run by the Agency for the Elderly.[28]

Remonstrance

Yu pared down posts involved in advising the king, criticizing malfeasance in office, and facilitating the transmission of documents. He retained the Office of Special Counselors (Hongmun'gwan), an agency of five officials and fifty-nine assistants charged with speaking their minds in "assisting the virtue and righteousness of the king," it had become one of the de facto agencies of the censorate.[29] He also preserved the Office of Inspector-General (Sahŏnbu) with six officials and sixty-six assistants to criticize shortcomings, rectify mores, and prevent excesses and falsifications, but he discarded the Office of Censor-General

(Saganwŏn) – the third censorate agency – because it was superfluous. Yu was even reluctant to retain the Office of Inspector-General because although special remonstrators had first been appointed in the Han dynasty as a means of "widening the pathways of speech," creating a separate and distinct office for this purpose had actually reduced the opportunity for freedom of speech. Prior to that time every subordinate in each administrative unit had been allowed to voice his criticism of affairs under his jurisdiction, but in later ages only official "remonstrators" were allowed the freedom to criticize, and most of them used their political position not to protest but to protect themselves against their own removal by rulers and reformers.

Yu also cited two cases from China to demonstrate that the professional remonstrators had actually corrupted the politics of the era. Hu Chih-t'ang criticized Empress Wu of the T'ang dynasty for having allowed censors to give heed to false and unjust accusations against officials for wrongdoing, and Ch'iu Chün of the Ming dynasty condemned the continuation of these habits into Sung times and called for a return to factual reporting and prohibition of calumnious charges.[30] In other words, in traditional China and Korea the debate over the issue of the breadth and license for public criticism, as opposed to the defense against libel and false accusation, was carried out in the context of accepted institutions for official surveillance and remonstrance. Yu was trying to strike a proper balance between the two.

Documents and Historical Records

Yu was willing to continue the handling and transmission of government documents by the six Royal Secretaries (rank 3A) and eighty-nine clerks and runners of the Royal Secretariat (Sŭngjŏngwŏn), but the recording of documents for historical references was to be entrusted to officials in the Spring and Autumn Office (Ch'unch'ugwan). One of the aberrant procedures in the keeping of historical archives was the supervising of national history by the prime minister in China. Fan Tsu-yü, a follower of Ssu-ma Kuang in Sung times, criticized the prime minister's access to historical documents, and Liu Chih-chi of the T'ang complained that there were far more official historians than were needed, and most recorders were reluctant to express their opinions. In the Han period, recorders were not keeping pace with the emperor's daily events, and historians were running the risk of jeopardizing enemies and antagonizing members of the nobility by using their posts as vantage points for criticism.

Ou-yang Hsiu of Sung times admonished the historians to keep accurate records of good and bad deeds of officials, and criticized historians who preferred only to restrict themselves to keeping mundane records of those who were appointed or dismissed from office. The records of the *Daily Record of Events* (*Shih-cheng-chi*) and the *Records of Daily Comings and Goings* (*Chi-chü-chu*) were supposed to provide detailed accounts of affairs, but officials acutely sensed the danger involved in such accounts and reduced these documents to simple chronologies. Ou-yang Hsiu advised historians to describe specific crimes of active officials to "encourage the good and chastise the bad" for future generations, and to clarify errors of the ruler to warn against repetition of those mistakes in the future.[31] Obviously, Yu wanted to maintain the integrity of the record-keeping process and immunize it from political interference by high officials.

New Agencies

Bureaus of the Six Ministries

Yu provided each of the Six Ministries with a complement of three specialized bureaus (Sa), designed to establish full and specific jurisdiction over all matters pertinent to the business of each ministry.[32] The organization of these bureaus was close to but not identical with the bureaus of the Six Ministries of either the T'ang or Chosŏn dynasties.[33] They reflected different social circumstances in Korea and some of Yu's special core organizational ideas. By this means he hoped to eliminate a number of independent agencies and commissions created in the manner of the Sung commissions, and incorporate their activities into the appropriate ministry.

Bureau of Forbidden Affairs (State Tribunal)

For example, he proposed the creation of a Bureau of Forbidden Affairs (Changgŭmsa) in the Ministry of Punishments to replace the existing independent Office for the Deliberation of Forbidden Affairs (or State Tribunal, Ŭigŭmbu). The latter was a special tribunal created on an ad hoc basis by kings to try high officials and eminent scholars for malfeasance in office or moral turpitude, since their status was too great to be judged by any but their peers, and the judges were usually high ministers appointed as concurrencies. Yu opposed its continuation because there was no prototype for such a special tribunal in ancient China. Since the Ssu-k'ou in the Chou period and the Ting-wei in the Han were equivalent to the Ministry of Punishments and had assumed responsibility for criminal cases, this task was logically to be entrusted to that ministry.

Yu, however, did not by this measure intend to demean the yangban and throw them into the criminal courts alongside commoners and slaves because he provided that yangban defendants should still be separated from commoners and placed in separate jails. In this instance, at least, he placed more importance on the propriety of institutional format than the rectification of unfair inherited privileges by the yangban.[34]

A Subordinate Slave Bureau in the Ministry of Punishments

Yu also insisted that the independent Slave Bureau (Changyesa) be subordinated to the Ministry of Punishments, but he did not do so because of any dogmatic insistence on adherence to Chinese precedent. The bureau had been established separately in the Chosŏn period to adjudicate disputes over the ownership and status of slaves, a particularly egregious problem for a society that qualified as a slave society by most standards of measurement. A separate Slave Agency (Changyewŏn) had already been established by King Sejo in the mid-fifteenth century, and contrary to the maxim for eliminating duplicate agencies Yu agreed in this instance to retain it along with his proposed Slave Bureau because the great increase in the slave population had increased the volume of lawsuits over ownership. The solution seems strange because the volume of business could easily have been handled simply by expanding the personnel of his Slave Bureau, but he was obviously reluctant to abolish the creation of King Sejo.[35]

Yu acknowledged that there was no precedent in his Chinese sources for a separate slave agency, and like slavery itself, he also argued that it should be abolished, but it could not be dispensed with until slavery disappeared and lawsuits over slave ownership along with it. Not only did he retain the Slave Agency to adjudicate disputes, he also planned to continue using state or official slaves as runners and servants for central government bureaus and agencies. The State Council, for example, was to be staffed by ninety slave runners (*chorye*) in addition to twenty-four clerks.[36]

Administration of Hired Labor in Ministry of Works

Yu did intend to replace labor service with hired wage labor, but he provided that it be administered by the Ministry of (Public) Works rather than the Ministry of Taxation. He provided for flexible expansion in the staff of the Bureau of Construction (Yŏngjosa) to oversee hired artisans and construction workers, and to review their performance on a monthly basis to encourage better quality and efficiency. Quality control was not to depend exclusively on the carrot-and-stick of wage increases and reductions, but with punishment, so many strokes over the legs with a bamboo staff to penalize neglect and dismissal for the incompetent. Nonetheless, he insisted that all labor on state construction projects be done by hired workers paid by wages (*kŭpka koin*). In short, he sought the liberation of workers in state projects from either slavery or corvée labor to wage work, but not the defense of worker rights and dignity from the corporal punishment of state employers.

Administration of Cadastral Survey in Ministry of Works

He also decided to locate responsibility for cadastral surveys of land to accompany his land reform program in the Ministry of Works as well, even though the Ministry of Taxation normally handled this kind of task. In making this choice he felt he had to justify it by taking advantage of ambiguity in the *Book of History* and the *Rites of Chou* relating to responsibilities for supervising production and industry. In the former text, the Ssu-kung was the minister in charge of supervising the land of the country, settling the four classes of people (scholars, peasants, merchants, and artisans) into their residences and proper occupations, and regulating according to the season the profits or production of the land.[37] The *Rites of Chou*, however, stated that the officer of winter (Tung-kuan), was in charge of industry or works. Even though most of the chapter was lost, later commentators assumed it was the model for a Ministry of Works.[38]

Yu pointed out that the Ssu-kung of the *Book of History* had been responsible for land survey, and also that the current Chosŏn Ministry of Taxation was overburdened with work while the Ministry of Works had little to do but supervise construction. Since this was a mistaken limitation of its responsibilities in antiquity, he selected it to carry out the enormous work that would have been required for a national cadastral survey. "Only after [the Ministry of Works carries out a land survey] will we be able to carry out thoroughly the intention [of the sages] to determine land boundaries and make the people secure in their residences in order to ensure the livelihood and care [of the people]."[39]

Ritual and Entertainment Services

Yu wanted to cut the costs of government by eradicating duplication, but it was still necessary to provide services to the state. To meet requirements for ritual performance and the entertainment of guests in a Confucian state the Court of Music (Chang'agwŏn) remained an essential agency, but Yu prescribed a massive reduction of the current 970 musicians to a total of 100 musicians of slave status (*akkong*) by ruthlessly eliminating some musicians and combining others that had been divided between classical and popular musicians (*aak, sog'ak*). He also announced the desirability of restoring the ancient practice of using blind music teachers, even though it had been abandoned when musicians were required to follow Manchurian practice of marching in formal attire.[40]

Yu also provided for specialized agencies to perform entertainment services. The Comprehensive Rites Agency (T'ongnyewŏn) was modeled after the Ming agency for rites and ceremonies (Hung-lu-shih), which also combined entertainment of foreign guests. This latter function was handled separately in Korea by the Korean Ritual Guest Agency (Yebinsi). Yu hoped to cope with the inordinate demands for expenses by paying wages to workers and also by temporarily recruiting idle state slaves in the employ of other government offices. Payment for the entertainment of the king and regally sponsored banquets would be managed by the Royal Cuisine Office (Saongwŏn), and the cost of goods would be shifted from tribute payments to market purchases financed by allotments of funds from central government tax income. Yu took great care to organize a special set of specialized workmen (*ch'abi*) assigned to the king's, queen's, and crown prince's palaces to produce food utensils and bedding, to function as cooks, wine and tea makers, and as tenders of lights and fuel. They were also assisted by the Royal Clothing Office (Sang'ŭiwŏn) and the Royal Stable Court (Saboksi).[41]

Astronomy, Medicine, Foreign Languages

Yu had to provide for agencies to handle technological aspects of government, but to find men with requisite skill he needed to expand opportunity for recruitment more widely. He provided that approximately two dozen duty officials be employed in the Directorate of Astronomy (Kwansanggam), the Agency of Supreme Physicians (T'aeŭiwŏn) – a title shift from the contemporary Directorate of Medicine (Chŏn'ŭigam) – and the Court of Interpreters (Sayŏgwŏn). Any expert that could be found with skills in astronomy, geography, rain gauges, medicine, and language talent would be given a special concurrent position as instructor (Kyosu) or adviser (Hundo), provided with special land grants, tested, and raised in rank and salary.

The Directorate of Medicine would combine medical doctors and pharmacists who would provide service for commoners as well as the king. As opposed to the Ming system, which was covered by a single medical organization, the Korean system was currently subdivided into the Three Medical Bureaus (Samŭisa) such as the Palace Physicians' Court (Naeŭiwŏn), the Directorate of Medicine (Chŏn'ŭigam), and the Office of Benefiting the People (Hyeminsŏ). In addition, Yu planned to combine a Palace Pharmacy (Naeyakkuk) and a School of Medicine (Ŭihak) with an enrollment of forty students. The students would be tested quarterly and the best ones promoted, and while in good standing they would receive a grant of one *kyŏng* of land per student.

Despite Yu's desire to combine all agencies into a single one, he was willing to tolerate the separate existence of the Palace Physicians' Court. His concern, however, was to obtain the best possible students for medical studies, rather than shifting the most talented physicians to the Palace Physicians' Court at the height of their career to care for the king at the expense of the medical needs of the common people. He preferred a single Physicians' Office to assign duties to all physicians and have them serve both kings and commoners alike by sending royal physicians on tours of duty outside the palace to attend commoner patients.[42]

The Interpreter's Court (Sayŏgwŏn) would continue instruction for thirty students in Chinese, twenty in Jurchen (Manchu), fifteen in Japanese, and five in Mongolian reimbursed by monthly rations and a land grant. He preferred to put the language students on a firm financial footing, rather than demean their status by granting them salaries by sinecure (*ch'ea*) appointments. Because interpreters were irregular officials and were not able to deal directly with foreign officials as their equals, Yu wanted to make the head of the Interpreter's Court an official of rank 5A and elevate interpreters to lower but regular official status. This was important especially because in Ming China scholars who had academic careers and *chü-jen* provincial degree-holders could be appointed to office on the basis of foreign languages and might even earn a degree on the basis of merit.[43]

Consolidate Control of Market Regulation

Yu also called for reducing the quota of officials in control of market activities to a minimum and abolishing the Bureau of Market Weights and Measures (P'yŏngsisŏ), an office created in 1392 and given this title in 1466. The Market Bureau regulated shops, weights, measures, the type of goods for sale, and market prices, but Yu was not sure whether he should retain the bureau or distribute its tasks to other agencies. The Ming dynasty (as opposed to specific capital market bureaus from Chou through T'ang) did not have a single market bureau in charge of the nation's business. Yu expressed his own preference for subsuming the capital's market bureau as a subagency of the Seoul Magistracy (Hansŏngbu). The Ministry of Taxation would then control regulation of tax collection and commodity prices, the Ministry of Works weights and measures, the Ministry of Punishments violations of the law and disputes over agreements, and the Seoul Magistracy city shops and marketplaces. His attitude toward both cash and market sales did not indicate much awareness that a growing market and increased demand for currency would require an administrative response to handle new responsibilities. Anyone aware of the massive transforming effects on society that the expansion of production and trade could accomplish would have at least advocated the creation of a Ministry of Trade and Industry rather than divide responsibilities according to the classical division of responsibility into the Six Ministries.[44]

Currency and Warehousing

Another category of government organization included offices related to market and commercial activities. Even though Yu expected to transform labor service to cash payments or wages for workers, he still had not become progressive enough to assume that an expanding economy would require the manufacture of sufficient currency to meet the demand for cash. In fact he suspected that the kings would maintain current prohibitions against minting currency and printing paper money, and he presumed that it would not be necessary to retain the Court for Providing Aid (Sasŏmsi), the office in charge of manufacturing paper money and collecting slave tribute payments. Its reserves could be transferred instead to the Ministry of Taxation.[45]

Warehouses and granaries in the capital were to be divided into three agencies. Yu proposed fusing the Ever-Normal Directorate (Sangp'yŏnggam) with the Military Stores Warehouse (Kunjach'ang) to take charge of stabilization of market prices by buying and selling commodities accumulated in this warehouse. The other two warehouses had specialized purposes: the Surplus Storage Warehouse (P'ungjŏch'ang) or Left Warehouse (Chwach'ang) would store all rice and cash paid into the capital, and the Prosperity Expansion Warehouse (Kwanghŭngch'ang) or Right Warehouse (Uch'ang) would house all rice and cash needed for paying the salaries of regular officials. Yu noted distinctly that the funds kept in the Left and Right Warehouses were to be used for all legitimate costs of government including payments for all salaries and expenses for clerks, government slaves, and soldiers, not just the salaries of the royal family and regular officials. The essence of Yu's whole system of finance was contained in this notice, the centralization of finance, the regularization of all costs to be paid out by government funds rather than by fees, bribes, or gratuities, and the setting of fees for services.

To ensure that the transmission of goods was accompanied by accurate records to eliminate stealing, Yu proposed that the granary and transport officials would at all times be required to sign documents accompanying the transfer of funds. The warehouse manager (Yŏnggwan) would take responsibility for making all payments from warehouse funds, and superior responsibility for warehouse payments would devolve on the high-level officials (Tangsanggwan) of the Ministry of Taxation. In other words, Yu expected that the usual protocol of signed documents and superior levels of jurisdiction would eliminate the loss of government funds, even though that in the past it had not succeeded in doing so.[46]

Miscellaneous Tasks

It is not necessary to describe every last capital agency that Yu wanted to retain, but he did feel it was important to keep bureaus for map keeping, rescuing and saving the sick and indigent, guarding royal tombs, the Four Schools of the capital, and the Military Training Agency (possibly changed to the Capital Soldier Office or Kyŏngbyŏngbu). He stipulated raising the salaries of the twenty tile workers in the Tile Works (Wasŏ) so that the state would guarantee their livelihoods.[47] He lifted the current annual quota on membership in the Hall for Advanced Scholars (Chinsawŏn) of thirty of the best scholars and students from the National Academy to open more opportunity for them. He reduced the quota of eunuchs in the Royal Concubine Office (Aechŏngsŏ) from fifty to thirty but authorized an additional sixty men to be assigned to the king's, queen's, and crown prince's palace as well, and he required that they study fundamental Confucian texts like the *Four Books* and *Small Learning* to obtain an increase in salaries. Yu also declaimed against the current practice of eunuchs living with wives and concubines and recommended that any that did so be punished and dismissed.[48]

Yu did his best to organize most tasks of government within the framework of the traditional Six Ministries, shifting responsibilities from one ministry to another with only marginal justification, assigning new responsibilities for adjudicating criminal cases of high officials and administering control over slaves, and transforming labor service to wage labor.

REGULATING OFFICIALS AND CLERKS

Reducing the Number of Officials and Clerks

Yu's purpose in reorganizing the capital bureaucracy was to economize on the number of officials and assistants and permit the state to finance the total cost of the government, contrary to the reliance on fees and bribes by unsalaried workers of the government. He sought to restrict the total number of capital officials to 540 men, accompanied by 4,480 assistants defined as 45 chief clerks (Noksa), 480 clerks (Sŏri), 2,955 runners (*chorye*) consisting of commoners and slaves, and 1,000 petty clerks, not including a maximum of two-to-three hundred assistants to staff members of the royal family, in-laws, merit subjects, and enfoeffed lords. Ch'ŏn Kwan'u has estimated that Yu's proposals would have reduced one-third the number of total officials from the capital establishment, 60 percent of regular officials, and 565 high-level officials from the Six Ministries and other agencies.

Even though a number of independent agencies would have been reduced, and most of those remaining would have been assigned to one of the Six Ministries for control and supervision, the total number varied from four assigned to the Ministry of Taxation to sixteen under the Ministry of Rites, or a total of thirty-nine. In addition there were thirteen independent agencies still left to handle specialized tasks like remonstrance, royal relatives, the National Academy and other responsibilities. Yu's reforms would have amended and reduced the size of the bureaucracy and reformed the agency of control by strengthening the prime minister and Six Ministries, but it would not have radically changed its overall structure.[49]

Salaries for Support Staff in Capital Bureaus

The usurpation of power and authority from regular officials by clerks had been a prevalent theme among critics and reformers since the beginning of the dynasty. To illustrate this point, Yu cited Hŏ Chŏk's remarks to King Injo early in the seventeenth century that said that because regular officials had no idea of what they were supposed to do on the job, clerks and petty officials had taken over the responsibilities of regular officials. Hŏ referred to the statement of Cho Sik, chief state councilor under King Kwanghaegun (r. 1608–23), that "Things just disappear into the hands of the clerks."[50] What made this situation particularly deleterious was that the clerks were virtually driven to corruption as their only means of support because the central government had eliminated their salaries.

Yu felt that the whole system of support staff for capital bureaus needed to be reorganized and the clerks provided with salaries by the government to ensure their honesty and probity. Yu wanted to approximate the ideal four types of service personnel in the Chou dynasty described in ancient texts: the storehouse manager (Fu), document clerk (Shih), procedural clerk (Hsü), and runner (Tu).

Since the nomenclature and tasks of service personnel in Chou times could not easily be adopted without some modification, Yu substituted his own terms and definitions for Chou terminology: the chief clerks (Noksa), clerks (Sŏri), runners (*chorye*), and boy servants (Sosa). A fifth official called attendant (Chong'in) was assigned in restricted numbers to accompany officials to lead horses for those authorized to ride carriages.[51]

Yu criticized the present Korean system because support staff for capital officials was recruited from the general population as part of their unpaid labor service obligation to the state. Uncompensated service was unrealistic because clerks and runners needed income for support. Not paying salaries to them removed human dignity from their occupations by forcing them to earn income by fees, gratuities, and bribes. As the prestige of their posts declined, there was a decrease in the work performed and the efficiency of their government offices.

Ch'iu Chün of the Ming period commented that the clerks and runners of Chou times supposedly were limited in number and paid salaries to compensate for income lost by giving up farming, and the Han system continued this practice to grant the clerks some dignity and a sense of self-worth. They had become so numerous in later dynasties. however, that the government lost its ability to control and support them.[52]

To ensure the efficiency of government operations Yu sought to put the bureaucratic service personnel on a regular basis, require regular work assignments at specific hours of the day, and guarantee a full staff on duty in every office of the government. He believed this would correct the inadequacies of public offices because in many instances they were conducted more like a private than public operation. Officials as well as service personnel either had no public office, or if they did have one, might choose not to attend it on a regular basis when there were no tasks to perform. "Generally, officials stay at home and very infrequently conduct business. The lower clerks also stay at home and do not go to work to receive orders on a daily basis."[53]

The system lacked both rotating service and permanent duty for civilian staff primarily because there were no specific duties for clerks and runners and no duty hours at specific offices. Yu wanted an official building established for each office, the assignment of a head official to serve on duty in the building, and a schedule of duty for clerks and runners in each government office, even when there was no business to conduct. Capital bureaus, in other words, would have to function like provincial officials and clerks, and the latter would be given time off on rotation. Finally, service officials would all be put on salary and subject to periodic testing of qualifications to permit promotion or demotion.

The highest irregular officials would be the chief clerks (Noksa), who worked in the State Council and Six Ministries to take charge of the handling of official documents. They were currently assigned as assistants to regular officials, but Yu wanted to attach them to an office, presumably to separate them from the control of individual officials and create a more professional system of government clerks. Since they were to be the most talented of all clerks, he intended to reduce their numbers and improve their quality only by recruiting the most qualified men.

Ordinary clerks (Sŏri) would be subdivided into two grades, attendants (Sujŏng) for specific regular officials and those assigned to the post (Chikch'ŏng). These clerks would then provide the only pool for the selection of the best men for promotion to the chief clerk positions. Procedure for the selection would combine a minimum of nine years' of experience followed by an examination held at the Ministry of Personnel. The clerks would be examined on the *Classic of Filiality* (*Hsiao-hsüeh*) and the *Four Books* in addition to the laws and the *Dynastic Code* (*Taejŏn*), writing in the square or exact style, and mathematical calculations. His superior assistant officials would also have to guarantee in writing that the candidate was without fault or had committed no criminal action.

The process of selection of superior clerks and chief clerks owed more to the procedure of examinations than what Yu would have retained for recruiting regular officials. After six years of duty as a chief clerk the Ministry of Personnel would hold triennial examinations to test them on their knowledge of the Six Classics and the *Family Rites* (*Chia-li*) in addition to the other texts. Those who passed the test would receive an increase in salary and an additional grant of land, similar to the recommendation of Chŏng Tojŏn at the beginning of the dynasty to test high-level clerks to raise the quality of their work.[54]

Current practice called for the downward transfer of clerks (Sŏri) who had completed a tour of duty to the post of a post-station clerk (Yŏksŭng). By installing a system for examining and recommending ordinary clerks (Sŏri) for promotion to the post of chief clerk (Noksa), he was seeking to restore the support and prestige for clerks that had declined in the early fifteenth century when the position of clerks was reduced to enhance the status and power of regular officials.

On the other hand, Yu was not willing to allow clerks the right to promotion to the regular bureaucracy after completion of their tour of duty, a practice that had existed in the early Chosŏn period. In early Koryŏ times chief clerks had high status because many of them were recruited from families of officials or the local gentry, called *hyangni*, and they were eligible for promotion to regular official positions after seven years and six months of service, nine years in the late fourteenth century. Until the mid-fifteenth century the approximately 400 to 500 chief clerks could still obtain a promotion to a regular post, but it became more difficult because they first had to serve a minimum of eight to thirty-one years of service as a clerk – or twenty-two years on the average – depending on the office they had worked for. Nonetheless, by the late fifteenth century there were more promoted clerks than passers of the civil service examination who were appointed to regular posts, and 2.2 percent of the passers of the civil service examination (*munkwa*) had also been active chief clerks. To clear the glut of expectant clerks awaiting transfer to regular office, the *Kyŏngguk taejŏn* (law code of 1469) reduced the required term of service for clerks who had reached rank 6B as an irregular official to about eight years, after which a chief clerk could be appointed to district magistrate or a military sinecure (*ch'eajik*) like the armored soldiers (Kapsa), but they could not advance to rank 6A as a regular official. King Sejo had already prohibited promoting clerks to civil posts in the capital, and it became even more difficult for clerks to obtain military sinecures, let alone magistrate's posts. They were only left with completely honorary "shadow posts" (*yŏngjik*).

In the fifteenth century sons of yangban with the special protection privilege (*ŭm*) from their yangban fathers were allowed to become chief clerks, a practice that Sŏ Kŏjŏng once praised in 1473 because the Chou dynasty staff clerks (Fu, Shih, Hsü, Tu) "were also in the stream of scholars," even though sons of common peasants (or men of "good" status) were relegated to less privileged clerk positions. But by 1466, the right to salaries for sinecured military posts was eliminated, and the opportunities for subsequent assignments was restricted to the posts of district magistrate, post-station, and ferry clerks. The growing number of examination passers (of the *munkwa* examination) began to replace ex-clerks in magistrate's posts, and the recruitment of chief clerks by examination was replaced by the increasing appointment of the "protected" (*ŭm*) sons and relatives of high officials (even though they had to pass an examination prior to appointment).[55]

Since salaries had been provided to all officials in Koryŏ times except at the end of the dynasty, including irregular posts like clerks or government artisans, Yu's plan was more a restoration of Koryŏ practice than simply a progressive step forward to compensated labor. In early Chosŏn times, however, uncompensated irregular officials like clerks were not automatically provided with salaries but had to be given the equivalent of a sinecured "salary post" (*nokkwan*, later called *ch'eajik*) just to provide them with income, and they rotated on and off "salary" for brief periods to cut government operating costs. The number of chief clerks with compensated "salary posts" was reduced to about 19 percent in 1414 and 10 percent in 1462, and even this was abolished altogether in 1466, leaving them without any official salaries at all.[56]

Yu wrote that by his time the opportunity for chief clerks to retire to the post of post-station official (let alone district magistrate) had been completely eliminated because only those with influential connections with the aristocracy (*munbŏl*) (sons of high officials with the protection privilege) had the slightest chance for this kind of position. He pointed out that in Chou China commoners were given the chance to serve as one of the four clerk or service positions, but none was allowed to advance to the rank of regular officials. In the period of the unification of China under the Ch'in dynasty, the anti-Confucian rulers "cast off the Confucians and exalted the clerks," and subsequently the Han dynasty began the practice of allowing clerks to become regular officials. This practice was still in effect in Korea to the middle of the fifteenth century, but it had been brought to a complete end by the mid-seventeenth century.

The status of clerks in Korea, even including the chief clerks, had declined so much by the mid-eighteenth century that they became part of the *chung'in* or middle men, and the lowest rank of that pejorative category even below the technical officials. Yu's reforms would have professionalized the service of clerks by requiring examination for office instead of recruiting protected sons of high officials and by permitting promotion of ordinary clerks to chief clerks by examination. Furthermore, uncompensated labor service would be converted to regular salaries, the status of professional clerks and runners would be improved by teaching them moral principles and clearing their ranks of violators of the law. On the other hand, if chief clerks, clerks, or runners took a bribe or commited fraud, they would be dismissed from office and enrolled for military service.

The third-level category of runners (*chorye*) included runners, servants, granary attendants, and guards to be hired from the general population. The number of runners attached to individual government officials would be limited to a maximum of seven for first rank officials and one for seventh rank. The rest would go on duty at their office of assignment. Yu admired the contemporary Chinese system because every government office (yamen) had a staff of runners and each official was provided with individual runners or servants, all of whom were recruited from the general population.[57] In Korea, however, many of the runners were government slaves employed in bureaus so that each office had two separate rosters of men of "good" and "base" (slave) status. Yu commented that because slaves comprised such a large percentage of the population, even private slaves as well as government slaves had to be recruited as runners and servants for government agencies and officials. He conceded that in present circumstances it would be impossible to outlaw slaves from such duties, but if the slave population declined partially by his own proposal for liberating the offspring of commoner mothers in mixed marriages, the government would have to recruit regular soldiers on tours of duty to assume positions as runners and servants for civilian bureaus.

Yu reiterated his belief that any true king was obliged to abolish hereditary slavery, but if he failed to do so, he would at least be obliged to raise the salaries received by slaves to the level of commoners. Even by his own time the duties of slaves and commoners functioning as government runners were the same. In the future commoners and slaves could both be hired as runners, guards, or attendants based only on the qualifications of each individual. Although the government had never provided salaries, specific titles, or duties to commoner and slave runners, it could easily choose to do so. Since private slaves who worked as clerks along with commoners of good status (*yang'in*) had never experienced conflict on the basis of rank, it was feasible for the government to apply a policy of equal treatment for runners as well.[58]

The lowest category of servants and helpers, specific mainly to Korea, were the boy servants (Sosa) distributed to individual officials. Yu described them as young boys who volunteered for the work, and no calculation was conducted to determine whether they were sons of clerks or private slaves. Their social status varied in different provincial regions, particularly in the Hamgyŏng area of the northeast, where the nothoi of officials and slave concubines monopolized the jobs there. Yu remarked that the hiring of young boys was never practiced in classical times and ought to be discontinued in the future. He wanted to allow young men from the age of sixteen or older to enter service without respect to the status of their parents. After they were capped, the best would then be chosen to fill vacancies in the ranks of clerks, and the lesser qualified men could become runners or return home to the village to engage in agriculture. The jurisdiction of these service personnel was handled by the prime minister (*T'ien-kuan*) in Chou times, but in contemporary times the chief official of every office would have responsibility for appointing and recording the names of all employees. The names would be sent to the Ministry of Personnel, which would then send them to the Ministry of Taxation to pay their salaries.

The lowest level of service official would be the attendants (Chong'in), two of which would be assigned to every Tangsang official and one for each Tangha official as his personal servant. Counting the private slaves as well as government attendants, the law would limit the total number to twelve for officials of rank 1A down and three for rank of seven or below, to restrict excessive expenses for these servants.

Yu devised other regulations to limit expenses for carriages, sedan chairs, and horses with accompanying attendants. Only rank one and two capital officials would be allowed to ride a sedan chair, a habit that had been begun by the first emperor of the Ch'in dynasty. Even though the Chosŏn system allowed only high officials the privilege, by the seventeenth century all officials were doing it. Despite Yu's proclivity for raising the status and treatment of slaves and clerks, however, Yu wanted to limit this privilege only to princes and the prime minister and extend the right to ride carriages to others only if carriage-riding in the future became a popular custom among the general population. In other words, men of lesser status should not be granted privileges reserved for the truly superior.

In addition, he wanted to abolish the use of guides for horses except for government horses loaned by post-stations to officials on duty. Yu's method was to provide strict guidelines for the use of servants and assistants according to the rank of the official to curb ostentatious display of good fortune and power, and to reduce total government expenditures.[59]

Official Ranks

Yu then turned his attention to rectifying some of the fundamental errors in the system of official ranks.[60] One of the leading problems was prejudicial treatment of military officials. Not only were civil and military ranks strictly separated by two distinct sets of terms, but the highest rank military official was lowered to the third rank. Inspired by Ma Tuan-lin, who had written that only in later times (after the fall of the Chou dynasty) were civilian and military officials divided in two so that civil officials had no knowledge other than their literary skills and military officials were no longer expected to be literate, Yu wanted to bring military officials to the same level as civil officials with separate but equivalent titles for each of the eighteen grades (superior and minor grades for nine ranks).[61] In Yu's view, rank titles did not begin until the Sui dynasty in sixth-century China, and the Sui government only provided ranks for lesser irregular posts (*san'gwan*) without discriminating against military officers. The full system of ranks was extended in the T'ang dynasty by dividing civil and military officials and increasing the number of ranks by several dozen – what Yu called one of the worst mistakes in later Chinese history.[62]

Irregularities in developing the grading system in Korea had produced a number of minor anomalies as well. Koreans created separate rank nomenclature for the eighteen senior and junior categories of each of nine grades, and the highest third of officials was separated from the rest of regular officials under the title of "officials of the upper end of the hall" (Tangsanggwan), some of whom extended into part but not all officials of the third junior (3B) rank. A firm line was thus drawn between them and their inferiors, including some of those in the third junior rank and below. Instead of advocating that the Tangsanggwan category be abandoned, however, Yu merely suggested confining the title of Tangsanggwan only to officials with senior third rank (3A) or higher. The net result would simply have been to kick the holders of rank 3B out of the most prestigious echelon of officials. The only possible purpose would be to prevent any cheapening of the highest level of bureaucrats by allowing a few lower ranking officials to join their ranks.

Yu also suggested that the Korean custom of treating all officials of ranks 7 to 9 as belonging to one, rather than two ranks (i.e., 7A and 7B), might be retained, but only if the whole system were converted in that fashion. In other words, only if the prevalent distinction between Senior and Junior grades (A and B) were eliminated from every rank could the number of ranks be reduced from eighteen to nine, but if not, then officials in ranks 7–9 should have their rank titles separated into Senior and Junior levels as well.[63]

Hardly any of these revisions of the official rank titles would have led to a revision of the existing system, except for the equalizing of prestige titles for military as well as civil officials. Yu had previously stressed retraining officials to incorporate the liberal arts of the Chou period so that the generalist official should have some knowledge of military skills and music as well as the Confucian canon and Chinese history. Upgrading the military would not be designed to reduce the civil officials to the domination of the military, but to change officials from rote memorizers of formulas for passing the civil service examination to the well-rounded generalists of ancient times.

Yu was trying to adopt eighteen rank titles based, fundamentally but not literally, on the nine mandated ranks (*chiu-ming*) of early Chinese history. He wanted to eliminate nationalistic or idiomatic titles for officials rather than return to any distinctive nomenclature associated primarily with the pre-Koryŏ system of Silla and the earlier Three Kingdoms, mainly because he preferred to find the best possible compromise with ancient Chinese models.

Rectifying Laxity and Dissipation

Desultory Performance on the Job

Yu had quoted Hŏ Chŏk's remarks of the mid-seventeenth century about the confusion that governed public finance. The district magistrates remitted thousands of cash to the Ministry of Works supposedly in payments for their work, but they received nothing in return. The poor peasants were beleaguered with demands for transporting goods for the infantry under the Ministry of War, but the Ministry did not have enough funds to pay them. Officials and clerks were almost completely lacking in information about collecting cash and grain, making official payments, judging criminal cases and civil suits, performing sacrifices at rituals, or conducting important rites.[64]

Hŏ Chŏk ascribed part of the reason for this situation to the failure of regular officials to show up for work in their offices, leaving the clerks in their office to handle affairs in their place. Yu suspected that laxity in attendance was a product of the absence of a formal spirit of dignity and respect that had to be maintained in every yamen. The model for this spirit had been provided by Cho Hŏn's description in 1574 of the manner in which the Ming Board of Rites began each working day by formal procedures similar to a ritual ceremony. Before the chief officials (T'ang-shang) arrived, their subordinates would line up to the left and right of the stairs to the platform in the main hall, bow to each other, and wait for the T'ang-shang to enter from the rear gate, enter the hall, and take their seats. Then all subordinate officials would bow in unison to the T'ang-shang, receive a return bow from them, bow to each other, and then leave the hall. This procedure was followed by the clerks. The duty personnel would then proceed to their own offices and begin the conduct of daily business.

If an official arrived from the provinces with some business, he would follow correct procedure and courtesy, advance to the platform in the main courtyard, genuflect, and hand his petition or report to the chief duty official (Lang-chung), who would then place it on the T'ang-shang's desk. The provincial official would bow and withdraw, and the duty officials would discuss the document and present their recommendations for a decision, and in no case did it take more than one or two days for a decision to be rendered. If a petition once made was submitted a second time, or if a popular petition was presented by the people, the decision would be made the same day. "Thus the procedures at the Chinese court are regular and strict and there are no delays in the conduct of government business, as I have described it."

Cho obviously believed that rites and ritual procedure were obviously of great importance because they induced a proper mood of seriousness and dedication to the responsibilities of office, and he condemned daily procedure in Korean government offices for laxity, wasted time, and desultory performance. The problem was not, however, the lack of formal respect between subordinate officials (Chwarang) and the bureau duty official (Chŏngnang) because they never even dared lift their heads to address him and dutifully turned over all official business to the chief officials of the ministries. It was the delay in the conduct of business that appeared monstrous to him:

> It takes weeks and months before action is taken on public business that has been requested by memorial, and no one ever bothers to submit a second memorial about a decision that has been made [presumably because it would take too long to obtain a decision]. As for suits and petitions from the soldiers and common people, there is no chance for them to get a decision unless they pay a bribe to a clerk. What I fear is that if these evils are not eliminated, there will never be a day when state business is done well.[65]

Yu had also observed himself that officials who worked in the capital bureaus stayed at home during regular office hours instead of going to the office, and in the provinces officials spent their time entertaining private guests or conducting their own private affairs instead of attending to official business. The Tosa, second in command to the provincial governor, who usually assumed the function of chief magistrate of the provincial capital, did not sit with the governor in his yamen to advise him on decisions about provincial affairs; he only inquired after his health once a day. Provincial governors and military commanders were supposed to make periodic rounds of inspection (*sunhaeng*) of all districts in their provinces to see if the officials were doing their jobs and the people were free of suffering, a task that should have required a certain amount of time to accomplish. Governors, however, rushed through the process, spending only a day to cover the affairs of a single district without bothering even to interview the district magistrates.

Yu concluded that if the chief officials were forced to live with their families in the bureau office buildings in the capital and were required to appear in their offices during working hours, "order could be maintained in all government offices, affairs would be handled uniformly, and we could thereby stop people from making requests [for favors from officials simply to get them to do their normal work]." He proposed a general regulation that required all government officials to attend their posts on a daily basis unless they had a reasonable excuse.

In the provinces, not only the Tosa, but the assistants to the provincial army and navy commanders as well, would be required to attend all business meetings at the yamen of their superiors. Governors would be required to select an adequate staff of runners to accompany them on leisurely tours throughout all districts, stay a minimum of three days in a small district and six days in a large one, conduct a thorough investigation, interview all magistrates, and ensure that they participated in the conduct of all government business. All costs for the trip would be paid for from district revenues, and no arbitrary demands would be levied on the peasantry. In addition, the governor and the provincial military commanders as well would be obliged to visit all schools, participate in the rites to Confucius, and conduct lectures for moral education. They were to ask questions of the people to find out what was going on in the locality and inspect all weights and measures to prevent cheating during tax collection by clerks and officials. On the basis of this investigation the governor would have some basis for determining whether to reward the district magistrate or punish him.

To ensure strict daily attendance on the job, a "Keep Order" sign would be pasted up at the office door to indicate an official's presence in his office, but only when he showed up for work. At the end of the day, subordinate officials and clerks would not be allowed to leave for home until a sign was posted stating that the chief official had left. Yu did allow, however, that when there was no business to be conducted in the office, officials would be allowed to do what they wanted, either entertain guests, study books, play the flute, or practice archery – not necessarily because Yu himself believed in liberality as a matter of principle, but because "I hear said that this is the way they do things in China." In short, the main inspiration for Yu's proposed regulations to correct the laxity of Korean bureaucratic practice was Cho Hŏn's memorial of 1574 and his adulation of late Ming bureaucratic behavior.[66]

Since it is well known that the Ming was nearing the end of its days at this time and the signs of decrepitude were already manifest, one might conclude either that Cho Hŏn was really one of the those modern "instant experts" who spend a week or two in a foreign country and then publish a raft of articles on that country, or that Korean bureaucratic practice was so undisciplined at that time that even the Ming bureaucracy in its decline looked like a wonder of displine and rectitude.

Yu Hyŏngwŏn's motives, however, had to have been different since he was undoubtedly writing this section of his book after the two Manchu invasions of Korea, the fall of the Ming dynasty in 1644, and the establishment of Ch'ing suzerainty over Chosŏn. Since the perception of the Manchus as the barbarian destroyers of the greatness of Ming culture was dominant in Korea, and probably in Yu's mind as well, Cho Hŏn's exaggerated view of late sixteenth-century Chinese reality must have been even more convincing to Koreans than when he made his recommendation in late Ming times.

Limits on Parties and Drunkenness

Yu's concern about the evils of profligate spending extended beyond royal banquets to every phase of goverment. He cited Cho Kwangjo's complaint to King Chungjong that in the reign of Yŏnsan'gun the officials had abandoned themselves to partying and pleasure and the mores of the people in general had declined because they tired of hearing the constant and "mournful" admonitions for frugality when they saw before their very eyes examples of the splendor of luxurious parties as if they were living in an age of prosperity.

Yu also cited Cho Hŏn's criticism of the profligate indulgence in partying and drinking that flourished in Korea. Cho reported to King Sŏnjo (in 1574) that the Chinese he observed were always frugal in providing food to guests and limited the number of utensils, the size of the cups, and the number of rounds of drinks served. Chinese officials never dared to expropriate anything from the people to suit their fancies or entertain their guests, not even a single chicken or fish. In his usual hyperbolic praise of Ming culture, he claimed that the Chinese were neither drinkers nor alcoholics, and drunkenness never caused disruption in their administration of government.

Cho believed, however, that Koreans always provided lavish amounts of food and drink on any occasion without ever thinking that they might spend all their property in the process. Officials of the Royal Treasury (Naesusa), who were supposed to eat at home to save costs, were guilty of extravagant expenditures of food and goods, and the poor scholars in the countryside were guilty of the same fault, albeit on a smaller scale, because they always feared criticism for stinginess.

District magistrates in the provinces never adhered to the legal limitations on food and utensils in the entertainment of visitors because they felt that officials who visited them on their way through the provinces only judged their worth on the basis of how lavish they were in offering them food and gifts, and the magistrates lacked the courage to abstain from what they thought was expected of them. Although the king himself had to think twice before butchering an ox to provide meat for himself or his guests, the clerks of magistrates did not hesitate to do so to provide for the magistrate's guests.

The situation was even worse when envoys to or from China arrived at a large district town. Then a nine-course banquet was set out with music and drinking until the wee hours of the night. Not only were oxen slaughtered and huge amounts of rice consumed for making wine, but the people were subjected to demands from the magistrate for goods, the yamen runners were worn out providing oil for lamps, pillows and blankets, and the slaves were run ragged bringing fruit and vegetables from the gardens they tended. So badly were the slaves harassed that some even ran away rather than endure the bad treatment.

Possibly the worst evil of all in Cho's view was the endemic addiction to liquor among the Korean people. Among the worst were the military commanders along the frontier and in remote areas "who in many cases out of their love for spirits abandon their garrisons and cross the border carousing and reveling in drink for several days on end. Not only is this a matter of concern because of the harm done to the poor soldiers, but also because the enemy bandits could take advantage of the abandoned [garrisons], and if they did so, who then would be able to fight them off?"

Koreans simply loved to drink and many had "died young" because of it. Cho warned the king that he had no choice but to take measures to prevent this, and urged that he promulgate Ming T'ai-tsu's prohibition against liquor. He sent him a gift of cups to be sent to the provinces as models for the manufacture of wine cups of small capacity to be used in local wine-drinking and archery rites and in important rites for guests and sacrifices. He also urged Sŏnjo to follow Chinese rites by restricting the number of wine cups offered in any formal situation, and to punish anyone who permitted anything more than three toasts at a banquet.

Cho's recommendations had a great effect on Yu Hyŏngwŏn, who proposed three items of legislation for any monarch to adopt. All officials were to be required to supply their own food at home. Food supplied and utensils used for envoys and guests arriving at district towns were to be limited by his specific regulations, based on the rank of the visitor. Only envoys and officials passing through on official business with orders from the throne, or on their return from an embassy abroad would be entertained at formal banquets, not just a wild and carousing party, and on no other occasion would a banquet be held for them.[67]

CHINESE CLOTHING AND LANGUAGE

Abolish the Horsehair Hat

One of the most significant of Yu's proposals for reform involved what might otherwise appear to have been a matter of little importance – his plan to adopt the Chinese system for clothing and hats "in all respects." But Yu also warned his readers that if there were any "error" in contemporary Chinese clothing, that is, if current Chinese garb was not faithful to ancient norms, then the government should conduct an investigation of the ancient clothing system to rectify the mistake. As a corollary Yu also called for the abolition of the traditional Korean horsehair hat, the adoption of the classical undergarment called the *sim'ŭi* described in the *Li-chi*, the substitution of Chinese-style hats for women, and the provision that officials in the provinces would wear the same garb as those in the capital.

The inspiration for these ideas also came directly from Cho Hŏn's memorial to King Sŏnjo. Cho's admiration of Ming clothing styles reminds one almost of the kind of indiscriminate cultural borrowing advocated by the radical Westernizers of Meiji Japan. Three-quarters of a century later after both the Ming and Korea had been subjugated by Manchu power, Cho Hŏn's Sinophilism must have been overwhelmingly attractive, and Yu chose to quote Cho's lengthy description of the various types of Chinese clothing verbatim.[68]

Cho had done research on the types and dimensions of garments in the Hung-wu period of the Ming (1368–99), and he praised the superiority, utility, simplicity, and economy of those garments compared to the clothing and hats worn by contemporary Koreans. He deplored the poor and rustic attire of Korean clerks except for a few places like Pyongyang and Ŭiju, and proposed that all of them be required to wear formal attire. He advised that Ming hairstyles be adopted for men, straight hair instead of braids for boys under the age of fifteen, and topknots with hats for those older (twenty for the sons of high officials, scholars, and commoners). Women were to adopt the Chinese-style chignon with a long hairpin, and abandon the expensive and extravagant Korean custom of using too much fur in their hats.

For that matter, he admired the variety of hats that the Chinese men wore, particularly the brimmed hats of the Confucian scholars, the fur hats of the military officials, and the other hats worn by clerks and commoners. He noted that the horsehair hat was also worn in China, but by no means exclusively. In Korea, however, every one wore the horsehair hat, "whether noble or base," a habit that he believed imposed too great a cost on the people as a whole. Furthermore, he preferred to have men of different statuses wearing different hats, possibly because the Korean custom was too uniform for his predilection for status discrimination.

Cho commented that he had already heard that the families of some Korean officials and scholars wanted to have their own children copy Chinese hair styles but were afraid to allow them for fear that the king would disapprove. Cho wanted King Sŏnjo to adopt all these Ming styles and he hoped that allowing the families of scholars and officials to do so would set a model for the common people to follow. He hoped that some time in the future the Chinese might say of Korea that it was a country of caps and belts, that is, a civilized country whose people wore the civilized clothing styles of a cultured nation.[69]

Cho not only expressed admiration for the superiority of Chinese clothing, he attacked possibly the most identifiable item of clothing associated with the Korean male – the horsehair hat. Lest his distaste for native custom and his admiration for Chinese superiority be missed, he left no room for doubt when he wrote that he was envious of the Chinese capacity to convert people not only of diverse cultures, but even of barbarian lifestyles, into the unity of the greater Ming Empire as a whole. The provinces of Yün-nan and Kuei-chou in the south and southwest of China, which were 10,000 *li* (3,000 miles) from the capital, were until recent years dominated by non-Chinese or barbarian culture and modes of dress, but now they were all wearing Chinese-style clothing.

"How much more should this be the case [i.e., should it be possible for us] since our land of Kija is only separated from the [Ming] capital by not as much as 4,000 *li* and we are no different from the feudal lords of the five territories of the Chou [in our relationship to the Ming Emperor]. Yet with regard to our clothing and hats, we have much to be ashamed of!"

He concluded by submitting his drawings of all the types of Chinese clothing he had described to be copied and distributed to the provinces as the means for transforming all Korean garb to the Chinese style.[70]

Cho Hŏn's admiration for the superiority of Chinese and Ming culture, and his sense of inferiority about Korean customs might have been a degree more extreme than most educated Koreans at the time, but it should not have appeared outlandish or reprehensible to them. On the contrary, in the twentieth century Cho's statement was a total embarrassment, so much so to the intensely nationalistic North Korean translators of Yu's *Pan'gye surok* that they omitted the above-quoted sentence from the text of their edition of the work.

That Yu Hyŏngwŏn quoted Cho Hŏn's memorial at length, and in fact used it as the model for his own recommendation for the adoption of the Ming version of Chinese clothing is powerful proof of his own admiration for Chinese ways and the corresponding absence of the modern version of nationalistic sentiment that has been so often ascribed to Yu and other members of the supposed Sirhak school of practical learning. Yu's attitude, as well as that of Cho Hŏn, was characteristic of the mentality of the learned Korean scholars of the time who felt that they were participants in a magnificent culture and civilization of universal validity, and that their role was to bring their own people up to that level of culture. Yu was not simply enamored of Ming culture alone, but of ancient and classical standards, because he added that if Ming clothing should in any respects not represent an accurate reproduction of the styles described in the classics, Korean scholars should find the differences and correct the style to conform to the ancient original.

To that end he also quoted Han Paekkyŏm, who wrote a lengthy description of the *sim'ŭi* undergarment prior to his death in 1613. Han based his essay on a thorough analysis of the *Li-chi* in the course of which he disputed some of the interpretations of the design of this garment by two of Chu Hsi's disciples. He concentrated on the original text and attempted by deduction and contemplation to grasp the meaning of the original, a method that antedated the spirit of the school of empirical research (*k'ao-cheng*) of the eighteenth-century Ch'ing dynasty.[71]

Chinese Pronunciation and Colloquial Chinese

Thus far we have seen sufficient evidence of Yu Hyŏngwŏn's devotion to classical Chinese texts, but he never mentioned anything about colloquial Chinese because it was not particularly relevant to the given topic under discussion. But now that he was stressing the adoption of Ming clothing styles, it was obvious that he believed that much was to be learned from the contemporary Chinese, even under Manchu rule. Unfortunately, Yu found that despite the facility of educated Koreans in reading classical Chinese texts, there were absolutely no civil officials who understood the spoken Chinese language.

King Sejong in the early fifteenth century had faced this problem directly by ordering the publication of pronunciation dictionaries for Chinese characters, first Sin Sukchu's annotation of *The Correct Tones of the Hung-wu Era* (i.e., the *Hongmu chŏng'ŭn yŏkhun*), and when that proved too bulky, a shorter version called *A Comprehensive Study of the Four Tones* (*Sasŏng t'onggo*). Yu mentioned that Sejong had founded the Office of Diplomatic Correspondence (Sŭngmunwŏn) and required that all beginning civil officials (in that office?) begin the study of both spoken Chinese and the Korean clerk's script (*idu*). He used the *Sasŏng t'onggo* to educate these officials in Chinese pronunciation, and he required that all officials of the Office of Diplomatic Correspondence use only Chinese pronunciation for all Chinese characters as part of their language-learning process. Unfortunately, because this practice was abandoned, Korean officials and clerks had been using Korean-style pronunciation for Chinese terms ever since. Whenever important matters of state were discussed with China, everything had to be left to the interpreters to handle, a considerable obstacle to proper understanding.[72]

Yu felt that King Sejong's program for Chinese language instruction had to be rehabilitated to facilitate proper communication with the Chinese, but he put it in terms that could only send shivers up the spine of any full-blooded nationalist:

> If you want to follow the intention of our former king [Sejong] and convert [us] barbarians to Chinese culture [*pyŏn i wi ha*], then though it may be difficult to change the speech of the common people totally, [you could still have] people pronounce all characters in the Chinese manner. When the sons of scholars study the classics [in classical Chinese] and Han'gŭl explanations [in the text], you could have them use *The Correct Tones of the Hung-wu Era, Translated and Explained,* [to learn the tones] for reciting the texts.[73]

Yu also wanted all students in his revitalized schools to read the classics in Chinese pronunciation of the characters, even though classical Chinese was not spoken in China. He thought that this method would produce men able to speak Chinese, and as a further incentive he recommended examining all officials in spoken Chinese and either promoting or demoting them depending on their performance. He further devised a law that would require that all civil officials in the capital be assembled at the Office of Diplomatic Correspondence to recite two texts, one in Chinese and the other in *idu*. They would either be promoted or demoted depending whether they were correct in more or less than half their pronunciations. In addition, quota students in the National Academy and Four Schools in the capital and the district schools in the provinces would be tested every three months in reciting from standard Chinese language texts.[74]

Yu's attitude about encouraging, if not forcing, the study of colloquial Chinese to facilitate diplomatic communication with the Chinese government and general understanding of Chinese conditions by a wide range of civil officials was not exclusively a product of a supine attitude toward superior Chinese civilization nor a total denigration of the native language because he did not criticize the use of *idu* among Korean clerks or Han'gŭl orthography for explanations and transcriptions of Chinese sounds. Any nationalist would have acknowledged that knowledge of spoken Chinese would have been far more useful than the traditional "written conversations" that most educated Koreans had to conduct with Chinese on their trips to China. On the other hand, his remark about learning Chinese pronunciation as the means for "converting [us] barbarians to Chinese culture" could only have been uttered in an era when respect for the universal and cosmopolitan standards of Chinese, particularly classical Chinese, culture overrode the particular and hence deficient standards of native Korean culture in the mind of the educated Korean elite.

Conclusion

Yu Hyŏngwŏn was never committed to any fundamentalist or literal recreation of ancient sage institutions, but he did believe that the bureaucracy as a whole required a prime minister and two assistants who might also perform the functions of moral and spiritual guides to the king, and that government business should be divided into Six Ministries. Not only would the Six Ministries conduct its own affairs through its subordinate bureaus, but all independent agencies that had been created since the birth of bureaucratic government would be subordinated to one of the Six Ministries. All duplication, sinecures, overlapping responsibilities, and artificial distinctions between imperial confidantes and regular bureaucrats, and civil and military officials, had to be eliminated.

Yu's plan for eliminating superfluous agencies would have introduced important new principles of organization, not simply attempted a fundamentalist return to the Chou model. He would have reduced the staff of professional remonstrators because they had proved more harmful than beneficial to the goal of healthy politics. He would have cut government costs not only by personnel reductions, but also by converting required services to fully funded and financed activities. He would have consolidated authority over shops and marketplaces in a specific ministry and abolished overlapping responsibility, reduced the superfluity of police agents in the capital, and streamlined the military establishment. He would have abolished the Office of Censor-General and the Office of Royal Documents.

But he would also have created a bureau for slaves along with the previous Slave Agency to handle the case load of ownership disputes, even against his dislike for slavery as an institution. He would have freed the office of historians from the domination of the prime minister, upgraded the skills and grades of doctors, pharmacists, and interpreters, raised the educational levels of eunuchs, and tightened the administration of granaries and warehouses by requiring accurate records and countersigning of receipts and disbursements. A discussion that began with praise for the hallowed institutions of ancient Chou had ended up as an excuse for a significant rationalization in government procedures and costs.

Yu concentrated attention on the weaknesses and anomalies in the service of irregular clerks and runners in capital bureaus. Probably his most significant proposal was to provide regular salaries for all clerks to eliminate one of the major drives toward corruption that was built into the Chosŏn bureaucratic system. Unfortunately, it was never adopted.

He also hoped to transform the organization of clerks completely by dividing them into two levels and permitting promotion of ordinary clerks to chief clerks by the introduction of an examination system. Paradoxically, there was freer access to official posts by clerks in the more aristocratic age of the Koryŏ dynasty than in the supposedly bureaucratic age of Chosŏn, and even by the early sixteenth century, chief clerks (not low-ranking clerks) were regarded as equals in status with sons of high officials and lower degree holders and could take the examinations or transfer to a regular appointment after their clerk service to the sixth rank. He was not willing to restore the early Chosŏn system when clerks had more prestige because he claimed that it was unprecedented for clerks to be regarded as equals of officials in Chou times. It was more likely, however, that he believed, with some others of his time, that a distinction had to be made according to the training and level of education of functionaries. He preferred to accept a fundamental division between regular and irregular officials (contrary to the criticism of that practice by Ma Tuan-lin) but rectify it by improving the professional qualifications of the clerks and establishing their own hierarchy of merit.[75]

Once men had chosen to make a career as a clerk, they were to be recruited by different methods than those used to recruit regular officials (examination versus recommendation) and confined to the system of service personnel. His attitude toward clerks betrayed his favor for the generalists of liberal arts and his prejudice against technical and clerical specialists. Han Yŏng'u has attributed this attitude to the bias of the mid-dynastic Neo-Confucians, rather than the atmosphere of the early fifteenth century, but these biases that Han has mentioned did not necessarily coincide with all of Yu Hyŏngwŏn's attitudes. In fact, some Neo-Confucians of the late fifteenth century were opposed to some of Yu's favorite ideas: greater power for the throne and greater centralization of the bureaucracy, equality of treatment toward military as well as civil officials, and wider opportunity for officeholding among men of all types. Yu opposed the privileges of the yangban class and hoped to raise the qualifications and status of clerks by professionalizing their jobs, but he still intended to keep them separate from the superior class of regular officials who would have undergone half a lifetime of study and training in the "liberal arts" and generalized education in the school system.[76]

Yu hoped to eliminate the use of slaves for government service as runners or clerks by his gradual methods of reform, but until slavery disappeared or was abolished outright he hoped to bring raise the status, pay, and treatment of slaves to the level of commoners. No matter what their status, runners would be provided with regular salaries by the state to eliminate the main reason for corruption and inefficiency. He would also have abolished the use of uncompensated child labor for the boy servants that waited on the officials and converted that position to a regular post as well. There is little doubt that his proposals would have achieved a significant and major reform of the lower bureaucracy.

Yu's comprehensive plans for government reorganization was marked by a spirit of rational reform and planning, but he never asserted the primacy and superiority of the individual intellect as a higher standard than history and mores. His rational powers were always limited by respect for tradition in education, marriage practices, male dominance, and the monolithic bureaucratic structure, but he would have carved away waste, sloth, inefficiency, corruption, and undue discrimination against slaves, women, and illegitimate sons. His idea of replacing required service by wages represented a flexible adaptation to the times, a response to changes that had already been taking place, but he had as yet not been able to sense the potential dynamism of a more modern economy. He professed he owed inspiration to classical principles and institutions and the wisdom of centuries of Chinese commentators, but his analysis of many contemporary Korean problems could not be solved exclusively by relying on these sources alone. It required not only adaptation to changing times but a sharp, rational faculty for dissecting the weaknesses of current administration.

Yu saw absenteeism and laxity in the conduct of daily business as a curse on bureaucratic efficiency, but he felt that the way to rectify these problems was by requiring all officials to greet their superiors in a formal way, garbed in suitable attire, clothing that would reflect a high level of civilization. For this purpose he supported Cho Hŏn's suggestion to replace the Korean horsehair hat and other native garb by Ming-style clothing. Since Chinese models of governance as well as clothing were so important for the continuing process of Korea's civilization, it was also necessary to introduce instruction in the pronunciation of Chinese characters and knowledge of colloquial Chinese. Yu was affected by Cho Hŏn's fascination with many aspects of Ming culture, but he was not influenced by the sixteenth-century Ming alone, for throughout his book he placed more emphasis on the classical norms and models of ancient China than the Ming dynasty.

Nonetheless, Yu's stress on borrowing, whether from classical Chou China or from the Ming or any other dynasty, indicates that the main inspiration for Yu's ideas came from the Chinese tradition, not from a unique respect for material and technological progress, nor confidence in the power of unadulterated reason, nor nationalistic bias in favor of native institutions and customs. His emphasis on rites and ritual for the conduct of government was an ancient, classical idea, and he was convinced that the state of Chosŏn had strayed too far from its rules. He also believed not only that rites or formal rules of behavior had to be performed overtly, but that they had to be followed with the proper spirit to achieve the moral conversion of the participants, even the enlightenment of backward Koreans in his own time.

Appendix to Chapter 16

Table of Agencies Attached to the Six Ministries

- -Ministry of Personnel
    - -Crown Prince Tutorial (Sejigangwŏn)
    - -Royal Cuisine Office (Saongwŏn)
    - -Royal Clothing Office (Sangŭiwŏn)
    - -Grand Physician Hall (T'aeŭiwŏn)
    - -Palace Pharmacy Hall (Naeyakkuk)
    - -Royal Concubine Office (Aekchŏngsŏ)
- -Ministry of Taxation
    - -Office of Cash (Sasŏmsi)
    - -Ever-Normal Granary (Sangp'yŏnggam)
    - -Surplus Storage Warehouse (P'ungjŏch'ang)
    - -Expansive Emergent Warehouse (Kwanghŭngch'ang)
- -Ministry of Rites
    - -Office of Ancestral Sacrifice (Pongsangsi)
    - -Office of Diplomatic Documents (Sŏngmunwŏn)
    - -Office of Honorary Guests (Yebinsi)
    - -Office of Comprehensive Rituals (T'ongnyewŏn)
    - -Spring and Autumn Historians Office (Ch'unch'ugwan)
    - -Office of Printers (Kyosŏgwan)
    - -Office of Music (Chang'agwŏn)
    - -Office of Astronomy (Kwansanggam)
    - -Interpreter's Office (Sayŏgwŏn)
    - -Royal Ancestral Shrines (Chongmyosŏ)
    - -Altars of Land and Soil (Sajiksŏ)
    - -Ice House (Pinggo)
    - -Office of Sacrificial Animals (Sach'uksŏ)
    - -Geographical Documents (Tohwasŏ)
    - -Saving the Destitute Agency (Hwarinsŏ)
    - -Tomb Guardians (within the capital) (Cherŭng)

-Ministry of War
  -Five Guards (Owi)
  -Capital Patrol (Kŭmowi)
  -Inner Forbidden Guards (Naegŭmwi)
  -Righteous-Obedient Guards (Ŭisunwi)
  -Royal Stables (Saboksi)
  -Royal Armory (Kun'gisi)
  -Crown Prince Guards (Seja Igwisa)
  -Gate Guards (Kammunsa)
  -Wall Guards (Sŏngmunsa)
-Ministry of Punishments
  -Slave Agency (Changyewŏn)
-Ministry of Works
  -Directorate of Works (Sasŏn'gonggam)
  -Office of Gardens (Changwŏnsŏ)
  -Bureau of Tiles (Wasŏ)

See also the outline described in Ch'ŏn Kwan'u, *Kŭnse Chosŏnsa yŏn'gu*, pp. 309–10, which includes in addition to the above:
-Royal agencies of the Royal Relatives (Chongch'inbu), Royal In-laws Agency (Ŭibinbu), and Merit Subjects (Kongsin)
-the Teachers with Right to Speak (Sabu), left vacant when no one is qualified
-State Council (Ŭijŏngbu)
-Royal Clan Agency (Chongjŏngbu)
-National Academy (Sŏnggyun'gwan)
-Office of Special Counselors (Hongmun'gwan)
-Office of Inspector-General (Sahŏnbu)
-Office of Royal Secretariat (Sŭngjŏngwŏn)
-Hall of Chinsa Degree-holders (Chinsawŏn)
-the temporary Military Training Agency (Hullyŏn-dogam)

CHAPTER 17

Personnel Policy

Even a devotee of institutional solutions for the ills of government like Yu Hyŏngwŏn could not ignore the fundamental Confucian premise that good government depended on men, not laws. He had paid close attention to this problem in outlining his method for improving the education of men to ensure the cultivation of a superior ruling class (chaps. 4 and 5), but he had also to turn his attention to the problem of ensuring that the best men in the country be retained in office, given the chance to acquire experience in the exercise of bureaucratic authority, and reviewed periodically to weed out the incompetent.

Since the Chosŏn bureaucracy, including both regular officials and clerks, had been the source of corruption, incompetence, favoritism, and obstruction of well-intentioned decrees from the throne, it was obvious to him that he had to work out solutions to eliminate these problems. He pointed out that officials working in the Ministry of Personnel had no knowledge of the personnel records of officials nor of how much time they had spent in office, and the Ministry of War lacked the information to judge the difficulty of service or the length of service that individuals had performed.[1]

The method Yu chose to work out a reform plan, as usual, was to examine the superior norms and examples of classical China, record the deterioriation of those norms and the development of questionable methods in the evaluation of officials in the long history of the bureaucratic age in China and Korea, and attempt to adapt those lessons to his own time. What informed his treatment of this question throughout, however, was not simply the necessity to exhort his readers to moral rectification, but to pick and choose from the institutional arrangements and reform attempts that had been proposed by a host of rulers, officials, and scholars over the ages.

PERSONNEL PROCEDURES IN CHINA

Chou Feudalism: Periodic Review of Performance

Yu's study of the history of personnel procedures in China convinced him that the Chou period, as described in the *Rites of Chou*, had naturally approached a model of near-perfection because the performance of all officials had to be reviewed every three years, and every nine years a grand review was conducted to mete out reward and punishment. The better officials were rewarded by promotion in rank and salary while the incompetents were dismissed from office. The personnel officer (Ssu-shih), a subordinate of the officer of summer (Hsia-kuan), was responsible for recording the feudal ranks of all officials and merits and demerits accumulated every year. He would report the best officials to the king who would appoint them to office for long terms and select those who deserved raises and promotions.

There were six criteria of evaluation defined as follows: *goodness* or doing affairs well; *ability* or carrying out government orders; *seriousness* or not abandoning one's post; *rectitude* or acting without partiality; *law* or maintaining the laws without error; and *discrimination* or not being confused in making decisions. The *Wang-chih* chapter of the *Book of Rites* (*Li-chi*) mentioned also that official appointments required lengthy discussion of top officials for selection of the most advanced scholars (*chinsa*). After the Chou system was discontinued by the Ch'in dynasty all the responsibilities of the Ssu-shih were transferred eventually to the Ministry of Personnel (Li-pu) in the age of bureaucratic organization.[2]

Han Bureaucracy: Long-term Appointments and Recommendations

The Han dynasty was able to preserve certain basic personnel techniques of the Chou because officials were reputed to have been kept on long-term appointments, sometimes for as long as a decade, before earning a promotion, and the emperor personally interviewed every candidate for the post of district magistrate before choosing them. Tung Chung-shu of Emperor Wu's reign proposed that officials be judged for meeting their responsibilities rather than the length of time they spent in office, contrary to current practice. Emperor Hsüan (r. B.C. 73–48) remarked that men recruited for officials of "2,000 picul rank" (*i-ch'ien-shih*), who were eligible for appointment as district magistrates, had to be judged with utmost care since they would be holding office for long terms and could not be transferred frequently lest the peasants lose trust in them. Those who performed their magisterial tasks adequately would then be chosen for higher posts of capital rank. Commanderies (*chün*) and kingdoms (*kuo*) or principates were required to recommend suitable candidates for high ministerial posts and censors (Yü-shih).

When Emperor Ch'eng (r. 32–6 B.C.) established five Masters of Documents (Shang-shu), he assigned two of them to handle personnel matters, one to run the Ts'ang-shih Ts'ao (Office of Constant Attendance) in charge of matters concerning the high ministers of state, and another to control the I-ch'ien-shih Ts'ao (Office of 2,000 Picul Rank Officials). In the Later Han dynasty, Emperor Kuang-wu (r. A.D. 25–58) established an Office of Personnel (Li-pu-ts'ao) to recommend men for magisterial posts. Emperor Ling (r. 168–89) appointed a high official to the post of master of documents in charge of selection of officials (Hsüan-pu Shang-shu), and in the Wei dynasty in the third century, this office was changed to the Ministry of Personnel (Li-pu) headed by a master of documents, a term that became the title for its minister.[3]

Yu was concerned primarily with advertising the merits of the Han personnel system to provide a model for emulation rather than providing a detailed account of its history, and he therefore omitted discussion of any problems of bureaucratic administration until the end of the Former Han, when Tso Hsiung in the reign of Emperor Hsün (r. 126–145) of the Later Han reported that Former Han district magistrates had been transferred too frequently and urged that the best ones be kept in their posts virtually permanently. Yu singled this complaint out for notice because he identified short terms of office as one of the primary problems of seventeenth-century Chosŏn bureaucratic practice.

Major Post-Han Problems in Personnel Administration

After the fall of the Later Han dynasty, personnel administration declined from the heights achieved in the Chou and Han dynasties, and Yu combed the Chinese literature to illustrate the most egregious failures. The problems of short terms of office was one of these, and in addition he dwelled on the influence of pedigree and inherited status on the appointment of officials, the replacement of face-to-face observation in the recruitment of officials by impersonal and remote bureaucratic practices that accompanied the expansion of the empire and the growth of the bureaucracy. His disdain for examinations and the examination system has previously been discussed in chapters 4 and 5, but in this section he explored the routinization of procedure, particularly the emphasis on time-in-grade rather than proper review and evaluation of performance.

He also included a discussion of some of the reform measures that had been adopted in China, particularly the use of recommendation – which he discussed in his program for the establishment of state schools for education (see chap. 5) – and the appointment of subordinates by district magistrates and higher officials in the central bureaucracy. Even though he did not necessarily cite the material he quoted in his proposals for personnel reforms in Korea, he undoubtedly expected his readers to digest this material and apply it to the contemporary Korean situation.

Frequent Transfers versus Long Terms of Office. Yu cited the opinion of Li Chung of the third-century Chin dynasty who deplored the more frequent transfers of officials than in Han times. He hoped to restore the use of triennial reviews of official performance described in the *The Rites of Chou* and prolong the terms of office of local officials.[4] Tu Yu of the eighth-century T'ang dynasty also disliked the reduction of terms of office in the post-Han period from the nine-year tenure system of district officials in antiquity to the six-year term of the Wei and Chin, and the four- and later three-year terms of the Sui and T'ang, even though each official was subject to an annual performance review.[5]

Liu Hsiang-tao, one of Emperor Kao-tsung's officials in the T'ang dynasty, directed his ire against the same question. Since all officials were reviewed once a year for a four-year term of office and then transferred to another post, he blamed the declining prestige of the district magistrate on short terms and frequent transfers. At the beginning of the eighth century, Lu Hui-shen insisted that longer terms in office were essential to eliminating the competition for advancement because in Chou times officials were appointed for life and their posts were passed on to sons and grandsons, and those who proved most meritorious in their work were not immediately promoted or transferred to other posts but received an increase in salary or rank or a letter of congratulations. T'ang officials, however, were kept in office one or two years at the longest, and as briefly as three to five months. For that reason officials had no sense of honesty or shame, spent no time in educating themselves in fundamental moral principles, and ignored the task of providing relief to the destitute.[6]

An undersecretary (Yüan-wai-lang) in the Ministry of Personnel, Shen Chi-ch'i, in 779 sought to extend the term of office beyond the standard four years of Sui and the three years of early T'ang. Although he praised Yao and Shun's supposed use of the nine-year term, he toned down his demand to five years. He also allowed for double promotions to give some leeway for the more rapid promotion of men of exceptional talent. Otherwise all officials would have to complete their terms of office before they could be transferred.[7]

Appointment by Pedigree. Bias in favor of men of aristocratic status was, of course, one of the major problems of Chosŏn Korea, but Yu had devoted much space to this question in discussing education, recruitment, land distribution, and military service. It was, therefore, not surprising that he should devote some attention to the emergence of this question in personnel appointments in Chinese history.

Yu particularly admired Lu Yü's attempts to rectify some of the evils that had crept into the review and appointment process in the Ministry of Personnel after the fall of the Han dynasty. Since personnel administrators were not sure of the quality of candidates for office, they made recommendations on the basis of official rank or showed favor to sons of prominent families or powerful men. Lu wanted to eliminate favoritism and cutthroat competition by using recommendation without consideration for rank and grade as the right method for recruitment because it had proved effective in Han times.[8]

Hsi Shen, an advocate of recommendation in the Chin dynasty (265–90), criticized the use of favoritism and the influence of parents, relatives, and personal connections in personnel matters, and he blamed competition for office for producing factions that distorted the truth. In ancient times feudal lords were not only required to recommend others for office but could have their fief confiscated for a bad recommendation, but in Chin times each official acted on his own and was solely responsible for his own actions, eroding the standards of the Chou recommendation system that held all recommendors liable for the criminal acts of the recommendees.[9]

By the fifth century bureaucratic personnel practice presumably reached the nadir of devolution because of the routinization of procedure and the growth of aristocratic and hereditary status. Neither emperors nor officials of the Ministry of Personnel in the state of Ch'i (479–502) in south China bothered to conduct any investigation of candidates for office because they depended primarily on written records and genealogies of maternal as well as paternal relatives of officials. Sons of the highest ranking families were appointed to office as soon as they reached the age of twenty, and those from lower ranking families were restricted to clerk's posts and given an examination to test their skills when they reached thirty years of age. The Liang dynasty (502–57) established the nine-rank system (*chiu-p'in*) which was not inherently dangerous itself, but in practice it favored hereditary familial and status criteria. The Ch'i methods of recruitment were also carried over into the Ch'en dynasty (557–87) until the reunification of China under the Sui.

In the Southern Dynasties, evaluation of candidates and officials was ignored and vacancies were filled by transferring incumbent officials or appointing their relatives because it was easier than a thorough program of investigation. All appointments were handled by the Personnel Ministry (Hsüan-ts'ao) which merely checked the status of the candidates to judge whether they were "noble or base," and submitted the list of names to the eight highest officials of the regime (the "eight seats" or Pa-tso) for approval. The emperor conducted no interviews of any candidates in advance to determine their capacities but met them for the first time after their appointment. Even though no system was established for reviewing the performance of officials in office, and rank changes were made in an irregular and arbitrary way through the Ch'i dynasty, there were occasional spokesmen like Wang Chien who recommended that local magistrates be chosen on the basis of their past record of governance and support from local residents rather than by selection by officials in the capital.[10]

In Wei and Chin times (third century A.D.), a special recruitment officer, called the Chung-cheng, relied on a man's pedigree instead of a true examination of merit for determining which one of nine grades of rank (*chiu-p'in*) should be assigned to a candidate. Magistrates and city officials were appointed by the Ministry of Personnel (Li-pu), but they were still allowed to hire their own subordinates on the basis of village recommendation.[11] Tu Yu then criticized the Northern Ch'i (r. 570–76) for selling posts, appointing sycophants, and allowing the central government to take over the magistrates' right to appoint subordinates. On the other hand, allowing magistrates to appoint their subordinates could just as easily have been subverted by favoritism for men who had inherited high status.

Wei Hsüan-t'ung in the seventh century remarked that in contemporary practice men had been recruited for office based on their connections with noble families and aristocrats (*munbŏl*) and their ability to pass the civil service examinations that merely tested their skill in writing and comprehension.[12]

Yu recorded the desire of some T'ang dynasty officials for partial restoration of Chou feudal practices after the An Lu-shan rebellion (755–63). Prefect Liu Chih, for example, extolled the Chou custom that men inherited their occupations because it permitted the transmission of important skills from father to son. Even though the inheritance of office had been discontinued at the end of Chou times, retention of inherited occupations was needed in T'ang times because it would guarantee the transmission of technical skills and contribute to ranking men by the quality of their work. It did not mean retaining only the best and casting others out of their jobs, but appointing men of lesser skill and quality to minor occupations.[13]

On the other hand, Shen Chi-ch'i of the late eighth century complained that inherited status had played too important a role in appointing officials. Shen argued that in classical times and even in the Former Han dynasty, no one was deemed noble by birth and all men, including even the son of the Son of Heaven (Chou ruler) was required to engage in study. Not even the sons of a prime minister were allowed an exemption from their household taxes. But by T'ang times none of the sons of men of the nine ranks of officials (*chiu-p'in*) were required to pay taxes and the relatives of the powerful and exalted officials were also granted the protection privilege (*yin*) to encourage the appointment of their descendants to office without further qualifications.

The ancients restricted the number of scholars to guarantee a sufficient supply of workers in productive industries. Although scholars were more exalted, they were not that much better off than the farmers, artisans, merchants, and others. In later times, however, the scholars and officials (*shih*) became a powerful class of superiors who used the whip on peasants and artisans and took over their production for their own livelihood. "Obtaining an official post was like ascending [to the position] of a god, while those who did not have office were like those submerged in a stream. The difference between the pleasure of the former and the difficulties of the latter were as distant from one another as heaven and earth." In other words, the egalitarian spirit of classical times was undermined by class and status differences.

Shen contrasted the perfection of Han bureaucratic law with the mid-T'ang period and condemned the adoption of rank as the basis for promotion in the Sui dynasty because it transformed officials into grasping and avaricious seekers of profit who sought a free ride to a lifetime of wealth and ease. The ultimate message was to reduce the number of officials, the size of their salaries, and their prestige, and increase their responsibilities and accountability to lighten the load on the general population.[14]

Routinization of the Centralized Bureaucracy. Another problem in personnel administration was the growth of impersonal and routine procedure in the evaluation of officials. One manifestation of this problem occurred in north China during the Northern Wei dynasty (424–535) when Minister of Personnel Ts'ai Liang dispensed with evaluations of talent and quality altogether and chose to shift the major criterion for promotion to time in office (*nien-k'o*). Any official had to produce a document of "release" from his past official responsibilities (*chieh*; *hae* in Korean) to obtain qualification for his next appointment. Pi Shu, however, criticized selecting district magistrates just on the basis of the years of experience in office because it would destroy the purpose of official review. Instead of a Ministry of Personnel, "it would be enough just to have one clerk who would control the registers and call out the names." Hu Ch'ih-t'ang also objected vigorously to the emphasis on time in office rather than talent as a criterion for promotion, and he predicted that the failure to ferret out incompetent and corrupt officials would eventually allow them to take over 90 percent of all posts.[15]

In Emperor Hsiao-ming's reign (516–28) Ts'ai Hung confirmed Hu's prediction by stating that since the early sixth century the ratings of performance had been carried out in a thoroughly routine way to handle the review of as many as ten thousand men in the triennial review. Since personnel officials never bothered to investigate merit, the superior or satisfactory rating was given as a matter of course, and the incompetent were included with the able in virtually automatic promotions.[16]

The emperors of the Sui dynasty carried the centralization of authority further in the late sixth century by vesting responsibility for appointments for all "single appointment" posts to the Ministry of Personnel, including the appointment of clerks and assistants.[17] Yu's account showed that the Ministry of Personnel was now overloaded with reams of paperwork in handling appointments, and many critics complained that the record clerks dominated the process because of their special access to the files. After the An Lu-shan rebellion of the mid-eighth century, an attempt was made to restore three annual reviews of performance and to dismiss any official who failed to obtain a promotion before the fourth review.[18]

Classical procedure was retained in T'ang times by requiring that the high ministers of state discuss all candidates for office, and that all officials of the first through fifth rank appointed to office attend an imperial audience to receive their office warrants. Officials below rank six were handled directly by the Ministry of Personnel, and the Ministries of Personnel and War divided the task of examining candidates in their physical appearance, speech, writing skills, and comprehension. All candidates deemed equivalent were then ranked by virtue, talent, and industriousness.[19]

Unfortunately, when full responsibility for recruiting magistrates was turned over to the Ministry of Personnel, the quality and prestige of the magistrate fell because too many military men or war heroes had been appointed to this post. Even when officials from the capital were appointed to magisterial posts, most were inferior in quality.[20]

In T'ang times the whole administration of personnel had fallen into the hands of the clerks and finding suitable officials depended more on rummaging through the record books to ascertain the ranks of officials or judging the writing skills of men than discovering human beings capable of service. Men hoping for office or promotion dispensed with the task of self-cultivation and preferred to establish connections, flatter men of influence, and form factions to obtain a post.[21]

When Emperor Hsüan-tsung tried to extend responsibility for judging candidates beyond the Ministry of Personnel in 725 by establishing a new committee of ten men headed by the Minister of Rites and a Censor to meet inside the Imperial Palace without any participation by the Minister and Vice-Minister of Personnel, Wu Ching objected to any unwarranted imperial interference with duties of his officials, and the emperor acceded and rescinded his edict the next year.[22]

Tu Yu of the eighth-century T'ang dynasty complained that since the Wei dynasty in the third century, personnel officials had neglected direct contact with all incumbents and relied on paperwork as the main means of evaluation. He preferred a system of annual assessment that would rank officials by their performance for a period of six years, after which those who had received inferior ratings would be dismissed, and only those with highest ratings would be promoted. Any officials found guilty of using his own personal feelings in ranking other officials would be impeached.[23]

The trend toward institutionalized routinization continued when in 730 Minister of Personnel P'ei Kuang-ting sought to break the backlog of expectant officials and increase the speed of promotion by eliminating the requirement for subjective judgment of the quality and personality of candidates. All officials were listed on a hierarchical scale based on their office grade and a time limit was set for staying in the same grade. All officials not guilty of criminal acts were then promoted without any review of performance, and no skipping of rank or double promotions were allowed. As a result P'ei Kuang-ting earned the sorry reputation as the father of routinized personnel procedure, dubbed "appointment by seniority."[24]

Yu Hyŏngwŏn then reminded his readers of the remarks of Tung Chung-shu of the Han to demonstrate that P'ei had overturned the wisdom of Han personnel policy: "The ancients established grades of merit based on an official's ability to meet his responsibilities. They never talked about accumulating days of service or long periods of time [in grade]. While the Han did talk about years of service and effort, they never adopted it as the method for appointing people to office."

It was not until Ts'ai Liang of the Northern Wei and P'ei Kuang-ting of the T'ang created the system of promotion based on time-in-grade that the original purpose for reviewing performance of officials was destroyed. In Yu's opinion, locking officials into rank meant that men of talent and moral worth were buried at the bottom of the ranks and were unable to make their way up.[25]

By the late eighth century, personnel administration had deteriorated because of an increase in the number of applicants for a reduced number of posts, the granting of honorific titles and improper promotions, appointments to office to reward soldiers, ministerial and eunuch interference with personnel matters, sale of office, and the takeover of certain provinces by military governors and their direct appointment of their own officials. In 779 Shen Chi-ch'i castigated the procedure of his own department for substituting numerical results of tests on "comprehension and writing" skills for an investigation of "virtue, talent, and hard work" as the basis for recommendations for office because they were overwhelmed with the numbers of applicants for positions.

Shen traced the origin of routinization in personnel administration to the Ch'i and Sui dynasties, which stripped the prefectural and district magistrates of the right to appoint their own subordinates. Although he preferred to return to this practice, he proposed a compromise proposal to allow the Ministries of Personnel and War to participate in discussing the promotion of officials of the fifth through first ranks and bureau chiefs and their assistants to the position of state councilor (Tsai-ch'en). District magistrates would also be given the right to appoint their executive assistants of the sixth rank and below with final approval by the the two ministries. Shen assumed that a strict method of review would lead to a virtual purge of as many as 80 to 90 percent of all officials on the grounds of corruption or incompetence.[26] Yu took this proposal so seriously that he copied the text of Shen's recommendation for amendment of personnel procedures from the *T'ung-tien*.[27]

Excessive Urbanization. Yu also cited other opinions about personnel problems presented in the *T'ung-tien* that attributed the decline in the classical practice of recruiting local people for magisterial posts to the growth in the size and luxury of the capital in the Han period and the abandonment of this practice in Sui times. The prosperity of the capital and large cities and the number of their shops and markets attracted villagers from the countryside because of their desire to achieve a better life. In the Sui dynasty, the institution of the new civil service examination system in the capital to recruit officials attracted swarms of candidates for examinations who clogged the roads and hostels. Men abjured hard work in the villages and sought to achieve their fortunes in the capital, selling off their family property to finance the trip. The result of this change had risked the prosperity of a thousand villages to produce one exalted city. The only solution to the problem was to lock the gates of the capital against itinerant scholars seeking the fortunes of the city and reduce the number of officials.[28]

Although the capital city in Korea was the major urban center of the country, it was not nearly as populated and complex as the major cities of China. Yet the attraction of the capital to scholars still remained strong in the Chosŏn dynasty.

Reform Proposals

Recommendation. Since Yu Hyŏngwŏn had adopted recommendation as one of his major procedures in his plan to reconstitute an official school system to replace the civil service examinations, he was naturally interested in Chinese proposals to use recommendation as a means of evaluating officials. He cited the views of Lu Yü of the third century Wei dynasty, who aspired to restore the classical spirit of yielding to the talents of others to permit selection of the most able and moral men for office. Lu noted that in the classical age officials appointed to office were required to submit letters of thanks and name others who were worthier than they to replace them, but in contemporary times officials wrote perfunctory letters of thanks without bothering to recommend others. Lu wanted to dismiss any official who failed to do so and to require that all such letters of thanks be forwarded to the king for his future reference. Candidates with the most recommendations would be deemed suitable for the next vacancy, and each set of officials would have recommended their own replacements instead of leaving it to the Ministry of Personnel.

Lu naïvely assumed that current officials would then create a mass stampede to exit their posts in favor of those worthier than themselves. The many scholars who had withdrawn from active life to pursue self-cultivation and study would be attracted back into the national search for talent because the horde of inferior men would recommend them to the throne.[29]

In the mid-seventh century Wei Hsüan-t'ung blamed the decline in the quality of T'ang magistrates on the monopoly of personnel review and recommendation by "the hands of only a few men" employed by the Ministries of Personnel and War. Not only were they isolated in the capital from the realities of local affairs in a vast empire, but they were also open to private influence and opportunities for profit. Wei sought to reinstate a division of function modeled after the Chou practice in which the prime minister and court officials made recommendations for rank, salaries, promotions, and dismissals, while the Ssu-t'u and Ssu-ma recommended worthy men for their first appointments. He also wanted to restore the right of officials to appoint their own subordinates.

Wei insisted that officials required a thorough education in school of the so-called six ritual matters: capping, marriage, funerals, ancestral worship, local ceremonies for the honoring of guests, and formalities governing meetings between colleagues, along with the ethical norms governing fundamental social relationships. He felt such training was necessary to break the domination of the aristocracy over the bureaucracy. Wei sought to eliminate these habits by reducing the responsibilities of the Ministry of Personnel and requiring all officials from the third to the ninth rank to recommend candidates for office.[30]

Emperor Kao-tsung (r. 649–83) did in fact ask his officials to recommend others for office, but his prime minister, Li An-chi, complained that each official who did so was immediately charged by his opponents for favoring his own faction of followers (*p'eng-tang*), and many had chosen to remain silent rather than run the risk of criticism.[31] While Yu Hyŏngwŏn was honest enough to include this remark in his book, however, it did not convince him that there was any weakness in recommendation as a system for evaluation.

Yu's last reference to the T'ang period was Lu Chih's criticism during the reign of Te-tsung in the early 790s, a crucially important opinion to Yu since it exerted such influence on his own plans for reform. Lu argued that if you recruited officials according to what they said, there was no way to guarantee that their actions would match their words; if you judged them by behavior alone, many talented individuals would be left out of the search. The only certain method to predict a man's reliability was to depend on village recommendation and recommendations by senior officials for their subordinates and district magistrates. All superficial marks of character, such as "clever words, an insinuating appearance, and sycophancy" had to be discounted, and recommenders had to be held responsible for their word. Empress Wu had been successful in obtaining good men for office because she had not shown favor only to men with official rank. Emperor Hsüan-tsung had also used recommendation, but shortly thereafter charged that recommendations had been based on favoritism and ordered Lu to take full responsibility for recommendations himself.[32]

Appointment of Subordinates by Local Magistrates. Tu Yu, the author of the *T'ung-tien* in 801 and admirer of ancient models, emphasized the division of responsibility between the king of Chou and the rulers of feudal states for appointment of their subordinate officials. Of the three highest ministers (Ching) of rulers of large feudal states, two were appointed by the Son of Heaven (the king of Chou) and the other one by the ruler of the state. In smaller states, the Son of Heaven appointed one of the three ministers, and the ruler of the state appointed the other two. In the second rank of high officials (Ta-fu), three of the top five ranks of feudal lords received a so-called double appointment (one from the Son of Heaven and the other from the ruler of the state), and the lowest two received only a single appointment from his ruler. Only the lowest rank of officials (Shih) received a single appointment from the ruler of their state alone.

This tradition was carried over partly into the Han period when only two of the high officials of a kingdom (Wang-kuo) or marquisate (Hou-kuo) – which were kept separate from the centralized bureaucratic control of most of the empire – were appointed by the emperor; all other officials appointed to these feudal enclaves were appointed by feudal lords themselves. Then with the suppression of the feudal territories in the reign of Emperor Ching (156–140 B.C.), these feudal rulers were stripped of their authority to appoint their officials, and the central government took responsibility for appointing all 2,000-picul rank officials to magisterial posts.[33]

Nonetheless, even though the remnants of feudalism were eliminated, the right of the magistrate to appoint his own subordinates (*tsu-pi*; *chabyŏk* in Korean) from men in the villages (*hsiang-tang*) after a test of their effectiveness was preserved without change to the end of the Han.[34]

Several centuries later Emperor Hsiao-wen of the Northern Wei (r. 470–500) ordered that all officials evaluate their subordinates and assign one of nine grades divided into three general categories (superior, satisfactory, inferior). The minister of personnel (Shang-shu) would take charge of all officials of rank six through nine, and the emperor and his high ministers would discuss officials from ranks one through five. Only those who received an "upper-upper" rating (the highest of nine grades of performance) would be promoted, while those who received the "lower-lower" rating would be dismissed. The others would retain their posts without promotion.[35]

In 779, Shen Chi-ch'i, an undersecretary in the Ministry of Personnel in the T'ang dynasty, proposed allowing provincial officials, including governors, prefects, and district magistrates to appoint their own subordinates with confirmation by the Ministries of Personnel and War. Strict control was to be exerted over provincial officials and magistrates whose recommendations or appointments of subordinate clerks and assistants proved faulty by meting out punishments according to the degree of transgression.[36]

Shen Chi-ch'i believed that the local magistrates would have greater knowledge of the merits of their subordinates than staff officials in the Ministry of Personnel. He thought that since 70 percent of assistants appointed by provincial officials in charge of tax collection, training of soldiers, and border defense were quite good despite the danger of favoritism, the system ought to be extended down to the prefectures, districts, and natural villages as well. Restoring the right to appoint subordinates would raise the morale of many ordinary men who would have the prospect of performing some service.[37]

Unfortunately, the practice of allowing magistrates and other officials to appoint their subordinates was corrupted by the late eighth-century military governors, who ran certain provinces in the northeast without much interference from the central government and used direct hiring (*pi-chao*) as a means of reinforcing their autonomous power against imperial control.[38] In addition, the "Miscellaneous Discussion of Selection and Appointment" (Hsüan-chü tsa-i) in the *T'ung-tien*, which Yu cited in his own study, also claimed that the probity of local government could not be guaranteed by a sudden restoration of direct hiring of clerks and subordinates by district magistrates because local people might well choose to recommend their friends and powerful men.[39]

A number of officials in Korea had been wary of this problem, but Yu felt that it could be checked by a thorough review of performance of all officials, and he appeared to be sympathetic with the idea of using local people to aid in local government.

Failure of Late-T'ang Personnel Reforms. Yu did not conduct a thorough study of some of the problems of T'ang personnel policy, such as the activities of Li Lin-fu, chief minister and minister of personnel between 736 and 752.[40] He ignored Emperor Hsien-tsung's emphasis on increased review of officials and their records, his reduction of official posts after 807, and his success in regaining direct control over some provinces by 817 by forbidding provincial governors from appointing their own subordinates – what Yu had evidently regarded as a superior policy – but in the forty years after his death his achievements were undermined by factional conflict and eunuch interference. Emperor Wen-tsung did attempt to reform examination and recruitment procedures in 827, but in 835 the eunuch Ch'iu Shih-liang blocked his attempt to purge eunuchs from power and forced him to abandon the struggle for reform. The swan song of personnel reform came with the promulgation of regulations for recommendation and review of the performance in 852; thereafter the empire dissolved in corruption and rebellion.[41]

Wang An-shih's Critique of Personnel Procedure

Yu avoided a chronological account of the Sung recruitment and evaluation system and turned immediately to a lengthy memorial of Wang An-shih in the mid-twelfth century.[42] Although Wang's essay introduced no argument that had not been discussed in the literature from the Han to the T'ang, he provided a pithy summary of views that Yu obviously admired. Wang respected the classical system on choosing candidates for office from the local villages and schools by a detailed investigation of their behavior by neighbors, teachers, and acquaintances, a system he much preferred to written examinations or the judgment of a few officials in the Ministry of Personnel in the capital.[43] He preferred employing people in posts according to specialized and technical knowledge in agriculture or industry, appointing the best men to the top posts and men of lesser talent to minor positions, and keeping competent officials in their posts for long terms, even for their whole lives. Instead of rewarding a good official by transferring him to another post, the ancient rulers rewarded excellent performance by increasing his rank and salary.[44]

By contrast Wang deplored the inferior personnel practices of T'ang times: basing promotion on time-in-grade, emphasizing general education over specific knowledge of the administrative problems, and transferring generalists from one post to another. He found that officials in ritual and criminal affairs, for example, were totally lacking in training and experience because they were transferred too frequently to allow them to gain expertise in their specialties. He was unhappy that the fathers and elder brothers of officials were not required to guarantee the probity of their relatives in office, that officials received no instruction in ethics and the arts and were not examined by their own agencies.

Wang believed that in ancient times no advantage was granted to those with rank because officials were chosen on the basis of merit and worth, but the introduction of rank criteria kept men of talent outside the regular bureaucracy and virtually forced men to flatter the powerful to gain posts. In short, except for possibly more emphasis on expertise and practical experience than other T'ang commentators, Wang essentially endorsed the reform proposals of that period.[45]

Ch'eng Hao: The Hall for Inviting the Brave

Yu finally concluded his discussion by citing the recommendation of Ch'eng Hao in Shen-tsung's reign (in the period of 1068 to 1086), who emphasized moral education over writing skills. Ch'eng argued for the creation of a special institute for the recruiting and training of the governing class, called the Hall for Inviting the Brave (Yen-ying-yüan). Suitable candidates from remote places in the countryside would be invited there to study, conduct frequent discussions with the highest officials, draw up detailed regulations, or make recommendations to officials. Lengthy residence in the hall would allow for minute observation of their talents and allow some basis for evaluating their qualifications for office.

Yu concluded that Ch'eng Hao's hall was the institution that would cap off his total system of recruitment, from village recommendation, promotion through a restored system of state schools, appointment to office, and promotion by sponsorship or recommendation. He undoubtedly ended his essay on the Chinese experience on this note, as if virtually nothing new had to be learned for use in Korea from the Sung, Yüan, and Ming periods.[46]

Had Yu been as much of an empiricist as some modern scholars claim, he would have conducted a far more detailed study of post-Sung bureaucratic practices. His confidence in the efficacy of recommendation or sponsorship might well have been undermined had he recognized evidence of the flaws of that system in Sung times. Aspiring officials found it difficult to obtain the required number of recommendations, and it was hard to overcome one bad recommendation from a superior. The system did not guarantee that obscure men of talent would necessarily be discovered, and mandatory sponsorship produced as much sycophancy as in earlier periods.[47]

The Chinese literature on personnel procedures confirmed Yu's belief that face-to-face evaluation of aspirants to office and incumbent officials was absolutely essential for maintaining the integrity of the bureaucracy as a whole. Throughout the long history of bureaucratic practice in China, that integrity had been undermined by laxity in a number of ways. Objective evaluation had been obstructed by routine practices such as promotion based on time-in-grade, the inherited rank of individuals, personal connections, and favoritism. The growth and development of the Chinese empire also brought with it a huge increase in the number of officials, urbanization, and the concentration of ambition on the capital and the other major cities, the development of impersonal procedures in the examination system and the routine of bureaucratic control in the remote Ministries of Personnel and War.

Yu concluded that only a reversal of these trends was bound to confer success, returning from the impersonal to the personal, from big to small, from centrality to locality, and from greed, ambition, and corruption to moral education, training, and rectitude. Part of the reason for this was an attitude that he shared with many Confucians, the feudal ideal of a perfect government that operated in ancient China. He lived in a bureaucratic age but did not admire it much; he had no choice but to compromise with it and seek to rectify its errors because he knew there was no way to return to feudalism.

Reform of Korean Personnel Administration

To ensure that officials who remained in office would meet the highest standards of competence, Yu Hyŏngwŏn also sought to recruit the most talented men in the country, give them ample time to gain experience on the job, evaluate their performance, and allow for promotion of the meritorious and dismissal of the incompetent. Unfortunately, a number of bureaucratic practices had undermined high standards for officials. Short terms of office prevented officials from becoming familiar with their jobs and promoted frequent transfers. As the supervisory capacity of the highest officials declined, responsibility for the conduct of business in capital bureaus was shifted down to lower officials of staff rank (Nanggwan), then eventually to the irregular staff personnel and clerks in the capital bureaus. This was not the enviable shift of responsibility from center to locality that the astute Chinese commentators had mentioned; it was the transfer of responsibility from competent regular officials to poorly trained, irregular officials and clerks.

Review Procedures

Laxity in Review Procedures. Since Yu was convinced that regular review procedures of all bureaucrats would guarantee the purity of officials, he prescribed that on the fifteenth day of the twelfth lunar month the records of all officials be reviewed and final decisions recommended by the State Council, the heads of the ministries (Personnel and War?), and the Office of Inspector-General for promotion or dismissal. It would appear that by expanding participation in the review process Yu was removing exclusive responsibility for final recommendations from the Ministries of Personnel and War alone, let alone the subordinate officials and clerks of those two ministries who might otherwise be guilty of favoritism. This suggestion seems to reflect a tradition of Chinese criticism of those ministries for excessive routinization of procedure and domination by clerks.

Yu also suggested that the process could be streamlined by reducing the number of recommended candidates for each office presented to the king from three to two in conformity with Chinese practice, and if too many vacancies happened to occur, they could be filled by supplementary monthly reviews. The king should interview prospective appointees rather than allow personnel matters to be handled exclusively by the Ministry of Personnel.

Yu presented the views of a number of scholars and officials on the problems of personnel administration. Yi Sugwang, the early seventeenth-century scholar, confirmed that the standard and regular system of appointment was conducted in Koryŏ times twice a year until government was taken over by the military usurper Ch'oe Ch'unghŏn in 1196. Ch'oe then transferred responsibility over appointments from the king and his Ministry of Personnel to a separate agency under his own Personnel Office (*Chŏngbang*) which then proceeded to fill vacancies as soon as they occurred. The rapid process of selection meant abandonment of reviewing past records prior to appointment, still a far cry from the monthly appointment system used by the Ministry of Personnel in China.

What Yi Sugwang's criticism signified was that, contrary to the Chinese experience, the problem of review was not the routinization of the Ministry of Personnel, but the usurpation of the regular personnel ministry by the leaders of the successful military coup against civil authority in 1170. Evidently, laxity in reviewing the performance of incumbent officials may have persisted as a result of that traumatic experience.

Cho Hŏn: Desultory Review Procedure and Labor Costs. Cho Hŏn (pen name, Chungbong), who was killed in fighting against the Japanese in 1592, also praised Chinese caution in reviewing candidates for office primarily because its purpose was to keep criminals or unworthy men out of the bureaucracy. In China, the emperor would evaluate officials every third year and promote only those who completed the full nine-year term of office, but in Korea the quality of men for office was inferior and lacked a good understanding of moral and social principles, and the Ministry of Personnel skipped the elongated review process and made perfunctory recommendations to the king on the very day of appointment.

> Almost all appointments are filled in desultory fashion. They select people from the East and use them to fill up vacancies in the West. They appoint people to office in the morning and transfer them in the evening. The officials in the capital and provinces do not understand what their jobs are all about, and perhaps even before their seats have a chance to get warm they distort the records, steal property, and succumb to the schemes of the wily clerks. When new officials are greeted or when old officials are sent off, men and horses are commissioned to run around for a distance of a thousand *i* [transporting transferred officials to their new posts] thereby destroying the production of the poor people. This is also an evil which does not exist in China!

Cho Hŏn extolled the Chinese system because it was designed to spare the peasants the burden of paying for the traveling costs of all appointed officials by requiring officials to take out private loans to pay their expenses, pay interest rates on the loan, or sell their land and slaves to raise the cost. He also wanted the king to order the Ministry of Personnel to discuss all candidates thoroughly, and permit no recommendation of favorites based on "private and intimate" knowledge. The ministry should select primary candidates for the king, appoint them for long terms of office, and require that they demonstrate some accomplishment in office before gaining eligibility for promotion. Otherwise there would be no guarantee of the diligence of officials in pursuing their tasks.[48]

The Nanggwan in the Ministries of Personnel and War. Yu's methods of correcting the process of personnel appointments differed significantly from the historical development of the sixteenth century. In the fifteenth century the top officials of the Ministry of Personnel and War were responsible for recommending candidates while the censors had the task of rejecting unqualified ones. Nevertheless, because high-level officials proved susceptible to demands from friends for favors, kings decided to delegate responsibility for recommending appointments to the staff-level officials (Nanggwan) in the Ministries of Personnel and War. During the opposition to Yŏnsan'gun and after his deposition by King Chungjong in 1506, the Nanggwan frequently associated with members of the censorate and the Hongmun'gwan (Office of Special Counselors) – particularly the followers of Cho Kwangjo – in criticizing and opposing the high officials. Even after the purge of Cho's adherents in 1519, the Nanggwan continued to act against the overweening authority of the ministerial chiefs. They were transformed from administrative assistants to more important duty officials when they were granted the privilege of recommending candidates for office along with the high officials of the Ministry of Personnel, and their choices were often chosen by the king. Eventually the Nanggwan were allowed to make recommendations independently of the minister and high officials, who in turn were left only with the right to make minor and low-level appointments, as Yulgok had observed in the late sixteenth century.

Yu, however, took note of Yulgok's disapproval of this practice of vesting main responsibility in the hands of subordinate Nanggwan because it overturned the chain of command associated with rank and destroyed the respect of officials for their superiors. Yulgok complained that the higher officials in the Ministry of Personnel neglected their responsibility to conduct a thorough investigation of merit, check diligence and laxity, and recommend promotion or demotion. The function of review had become desultory and the original intentions of the dynastic founders had been abandoned.[49] Yulgok's view of the problems involved in review were obviously more convincing than Yi Sugwang's claim that they stemmed from the military coup of the twelfth century.

Terms of Office

Long Terms of Office. Since Yu convinced by his study of China that long periods of service for officials would put an end to the disruption caused by rapid and frequent tranfers, he was quite sympathetic to Yulgok's protest to King Sŏnjo in the late sixteenth century that officials did not have a chance to warm their seats of office before they were transferred to another post. Even men like the Dukes of Chou and Shao (in early Chou times) would not have had sufficient time in office to achieve anything of merit if they lived in contemporary Korea.[50]

Yu was willing to tolerate the current practice in Korea of transferring competent officials to other posts when needed elsewhere, but only after they completed their current terms.[51] Although he hoped to slow down transfers by having the restored State Council and the Office of Inspector-General retain the right to inspect transfers and impeach incompetent officials, this process had unfortunately never proved successful achieving this goal in the past.

Illness as an Excuse for Transfer. Yu thought that one of the factors that contributed to frequent transfers was the leniency shown to officials who asked for them, particularly as a means of finding a different, temporary post while waiting for a better position to fall vacant, a practice not available to officials in ancient China. He found it still more distressing that officials who had been impeached for their behavior immediately requested a transfer to a different position on the grounds of illness.

In the late sixteenth century Yulgok had insisted that the king prohibit this practice. He wanted at least a minimum of ten days of incapacitation to qualify for release from duty and a letter of support from the chief of the petitioner's agency.

In no case was an official to be allowed a transfer to evade impeachment except when the censorate found that he was unqualified for his post. Even if accused of wrongdoing by the censorate, he would not be allowed to leave his duties unless the Office of Inspector-General formally demanded his interrogation.

Overzealous and Cowardly Censors. Yulgok argued that this phenomenon was not altogether the fault of the ordinary officials because it was brought on by overzealous demands of the censors who demanded that ordinary officials maintain the high moral standards of the sages of remote antiquity in personal as well as official matters. If officials erred in the slightest detail, censors would flood the king with accusations of malfeasance, forcing many officials to request leaves of absence or other pretexts as the only available means of defense.

For that matter some censors found that the constant expectation that they would impeach any and all transgressors induced them to request a transfer on the grounds of illness to save themselves from offending their colleagues or superiors. Thanks to the prestige of their office, they were routinely granted their request, and they were never held liable for shirking their duty. Once the crisis had passed, they were readily reappointed to another censorate position.

Yulgok had criticized the Korean censorate by contrasting their display of cowardice in the face of duty with famous censors in T'ang times like Yang Ch'eng, who held his censorate post for ten years without interruption, and Han Yü, who was impeached for submitting an essay against factional officials but never once used an excuse to escape his office. Even greater was the efficacy of remonstrance officials in ancient China when each felt free to speak his mind. But in Korea the proper function of censors to act as a watchdog over the moral standards of officials was lost because of the careerist desires of censors to avoid criticism and antagonism. Censors even sent messengers to show copies of proposed criticism to any target of attack or impeachment before presenting it as a formal memorial to the king, and they only submitted it formally if they received approval in advance from the presumed violator!

Censors were not only afraid to speak out as individuals, they also collectively opposed any misfit who wanted to express his own views contrary to the wishes of the others. The majority of the Office of Special Counselors (Hongmun'gwan), an extremely prestigious office which had functioned in practice as a de facto agency of remonstrance and surveillance for years, pressured all recalcitrant individuals to conform to their views by signing a joint memorial of protest, obviously to protect themselves against troublemakers who insisted on speaking their own minds. In some instances, a special counselor who disagreed with the majority was allowed to excuse himself from signing the joint memorial but only if he agreed not to utter a contrary view! Yulgok sought to end this practice by refusing to transfer censors, prohibiting the use of illness as an excuse, and permitting each censor to express his own views against pressure for unanimity.[52]

Yu Hyŏngwŏn also observed that censorate behavior had taken a turn for the worse during the reign of King Chungjŏng (r. 1506–44). As the monarch who assumed the throne in 1506 after deposing the paranoid, archtyrant King

Yŏnsan'gun, Chungjong had initially given the censorate liberal rights to impeach regular officials. When their criticism became a political threat to the king and his own officials, however, he checked their power by frequently changing the censorate staff and finally purging the leading spokesman of censorate rights, Cho Kwangjo, in 1519.[53]

Yu softened Yulgok's original request by suggesting that censors be allowed leave or temporary transfer without docking their salaries if their request were plausible, but he joined with Yulgok in opposing transferring them to a noncensorate position and demanded that they be forced to resume their duties as censors. If they qualified for a transfer, they would not be allowed a second transfer unless they stayed on duty for a considerable period of time and compiled a record of superior performance. Yu wanted to restrict transfers for illness by requiring a minimum time interval of three months after the last illness. All officials requesting illness permits of absence would be compiled every ten-day week and dismissed if they did not recover in three months, and any official discovered feigning illness for obtaining leave or transfer would be investigated and impeached.[54]

The Nine-Year Term of Office. Although the average tour of duty for officials was less than the legal standard, Yu was still alarmed that the standard tour was only three years, renewable for another three years. He advocated the classical nine-year term to counteract the clerks and runners whose long-term presence gave them too much power. He pointed out that young officials hoping for successful careers cared nothing about accumulating expertise in their job and preferred frequent transfers and the use of connections, influence, or even luck to gain rapid access to the highest rank. They feared nothing more than being mired in the lowest ranks because of long terms of service, but Yu hoped that the review of past performance and special recommendation for competent officials was the best method to open opportunities for high rank.

Yu wanted to return the basis for promoting officials to education and performance on duty, rather than blind careerism bred by the degeneration of hundreds of years of routinized administration. Although careerism was supposedly not a problem in classical times, after the creation of bureaucratic government in Ch'in and Han times, officials were appointed without any consideration of their intelligence, posts were "changed with annoying frequency, and the minds of the people throughout the world were day-by-day directed toward the busy race for office." After over a millennia of experience in China, "customs and mores became shallow and thin, order was lost and law was abandoned, and nothing could be done right in conducting all the affairs of government." In other words, the standards and values of regular bureaucrats had been lowered not simply by neglecting to promote the small number of good officials, but by routinizing personnel practices in general. The only solution was to restore the moral basis of government service.[55]

Nine-year terms of service would be particularly useful in rectifying the problems of provincial rule, but the government was afraid that provincial governors and army and navy commanders might accumulate military power and rebel against the dynasty, like the An Lu-shan rebellion in T'ang China. Yu was convinced, rather naïvely, however, that selecting the right men for provincial posts would eliminate the possibility that immoral and ambitious power-seekers might build their own power at the expense of the throne: "The positions of provincial governor and military commander were held in ancient times by the Dukes of Chou and Chao. How could they have been anything like the people we have today who are appointed on a haphazard basis? If you truly select the right people, you ought to be concerned that they might not stay long enough in their posts, not that they would be in them too long."

Not only did frequent transfers lead to confusion rather than stability, but the ancient, feudal model of appointment to governors of states or fiefs under the ruler in Chou China was conceived of as a grant to a loyal and devoted servant entrusted with responsibility to run his jurisdiction for life. Even Chou rulers, however, still felt it necessary to oversee governors (Fang-po; Pangbaek in Korean) by appointing three Ta-fu with supervisory control from the capital to prevent disloyalty and rebellion.

When feudalism was abolished by the Ch'in dynasty, life or long-term tenure was replaced by limited tours of duty as an expected feature of bureaucratic government. Nevertheless, a compromise with the classical ideal of unlimited tenure was achieved by establishing a six-year limit to allow the governors time to achieve some results in office. Yu accepted the compromise but warned that fixed terms should not be upheld mechanically but adapted to the qualifications of officials and the need for people in important posts. A competent man needed in a different post should be transferred despite the six-year requirement on his present position, or if his skill in the handling of his job was excellent, he should be kept on despite the legal limits on the term of service. The standard way to reward a competent official was to raise the official's rank and wait for a vacancy to occur to promote him to a post suitable to his talents, not to transfer him – as Wang An-shih had remarked.[56]

*Prohibition Against Family Pedigree (*Munji*)*

While Yu was disturbed about the mechanical and impersonal criteria of personnel administration in a bureaucratic age, he also sought to prevent the obstruction of opportunity for appointment and promotion caused by special favor for children of prominent and illustrious families; he sought to forbid any consideration of family pedigree in personnel matters and require that any discussion of qualifications be confined to "worth and talent." He also sought to abolish the censorate's right to review candidates recommended for office (*sŏgyŏng*) because the candidates were required to present a list of their "four relatives" (father, grandfather, great grandfather, and mother's grandfather), and the four relatives of their wives as well. Censors used this information to check the office, scholarship, and status of former generations, rather than the qualifications of the individual recommendee. "It only promotes the evil of family pedigree [*munji*] and is profoundly contrary to the correct principle by which worthy men should be selected and appointed to office."[57]

Yu was merely reiterating an argument made by famous scholars and officials in the previous century. When Cho Hŏn reported back from his trip to China in 1574, he remarked that in China family pedigree was never brought up in appointment decisions, sons of high officials held minor posts, and even provincial degree-holders (*chü-jen*) and low-level degree-holders called tribute students (*kung-shih*), were appointed to office and even attained high-ranking censorial positions. Korean "families of the great and wealthy" (i.e., yangban), on the other hand, engaged in arrogant and lewd behavior and could not be compared to the abstemious and hard-working Chinese scholars and students who were commoners and nothoi (not aristocrats like Korean yangban)!

The selection of officials in Korea had been narrowed so greatly that most rural peasants were discouraged from risking their family income by incurring the cost of educating their sons. The nothoi of a prestigious father might get as far as registration in a school but few could advance higher, while sons of base or slave status had no hope at all for office, no matter how talented. Cho believed that the Ming government at that time owed its success to its policy of refusing favoritism for the sons of the elite, and he hoped to use his perception of Ming egalitarianism to stir Korean society to reform. Unfortunately, his optimistic view of Ming strength stands in stark contrast to recent studies of the decline of Ming fortune.[58]

Cho's perception of the past glories of Korean history were also flawed because he thought that there had been opportunities for advancement for talented men back in the period of the Korean Three Kingdoms, an age when restrictions based on birth were quite severe under Silla's bone-rank status system and presumably only slightly less so in Paekche and Koguryŏ. Only in the era of the Samhan confederations prior to the fourth century in south Korea could one make a case for more egalitarian opportunity and social institutions, but that was presumably because social stratification was undeveloped in an age of small political communities. Nevertheless, Cho believed that there had not been any discrimination against the use of talented men for office, until the military officers in the late twelfth century seized power by a coup d'état because they feared that "wise scholars might arise from their thatched houses and act as an obstruction to their private interests, so they planned to abolish the examinations for nothoi, and the route [for the advancement of] worthy men gradually became narrowed. Up to the time of our dynasty [1392], the important officials who made policy for the state only thought of benefiting their own sons and grandsons and did not give any consideration to the loss of good men for office for [the future] ten thousand generations."[59] It was interesting that Cho identified the origin of discrimination against nothoi with the military regime of mid-Koryŏ after 1170, contrary to most twentieth century scholars who attribute the practice to the beginning of the Chosŏn dynasty.

In any case, Cho attacked discrimination against the nothoi of yangban and others by prohibiting them from taking examinations (*kŭmgo*). He personally knew cases of nothoi of great learning and scholarship, like Yi Chungho and Kim Kŭn'gong, who ended their days in starvation. Had the Chinese ever observed this rule they would have lost the services of the great Sung scholar, Fan Chung-yen. Any Korean king desirous of transforming Korean society ought to begin by abolishing the restrictions against the nothoi.[60]

Yu also cited the writing of Yu Sŏngnyŏng, who was also a vigorous exponent of expanding opportunities to men of talent. He argued that sages like the Duke of Chou recruited scholars living in ramshackle huts, Kuan-chung of the state of Ch'i chose two robbers to be officials, and Yen Ying appointed his chariot driver to be a high minister (Ta-fu) just because he had made one astute remark. The search for men of talent in the Former Han dynasty yielded so many good men that even the posts of clerks for district magistrates were filled with men of worth. In post-Han times the preference for education as the basis for recruitment in China was undermined by consideration of pedigree (*munji*), which kept the meritorious out of high office to languish in the lowest posts. Cho advised that "One should not speak of whether a man is of high pedigree or from the class of base persons but should only seek for men of worth and talent, and that is all." Furthermore, regional discrimination against men from the northwest was to be offset by purposely appointing men from that region.[61]

In short, the last weakness in personnel administration that Yu chose to mention was the severe social status discrimination of seventeenth-century Korea, a problem that had not been experienced in comparable degree since the Northern and Southern dynasties (ca. 200–600). Yu's predecessors, like Cho Hŏn and Yu Sŏngnyŏng and many others, had objected mightily to this narrowing of opportunity in the Korean bureaucracy, and they all perceived it as a tremendous obstacle to recruitment of the most qualified men for office.

Personnel Reform: Periodic Recommendation Procedures

In devising his own program for reform of personnel administration, Yu Hyŏngwŏn followed Yulgok's criticism against the transfer of responsibility for review and recommendation to the Nanggwan and the censorate. Yu wanted to reduce the censorate from its current staff of three offices (Sahŏnbu, Saganwŏn, and Hongmun'gwan) to the Office of Inspector-General (Sahŏnbu) alone and to abolish the right of review (*sŏgyong*) of proposed appointments by the Office of Inspector-General because it frequently had shown preference for yangban of pedigreed families. Instead he preferred to return to the earlier system of personnel review by the restored State Council, the Ministries (of Personnel and War), and the Office of Inspector-General, and achieve reform by extending tours of duty and conducting periodic review of their performance every three years to eliminate favoritism from personnel procedure.[62]

In addition to the annual review procedures conducted through the Ministry of Personnel, Yu sought also to introduce a periodic recommendation procedure (*ch'ŏn'gŏ*) every nine years to require that all incumbent officials of ranks one through three and officials of fourth rank serving in the Office of Inspector-General, the Office of Special Counselors, and the National Academy would each recommend two able candidates free of any history of criminal action, with supporting letters from officials of ranks five through nine and ordinary commoners. It would appear that this proposal did have an effect on Chosŏn policy, but not until 1870, when the Taewongun ordered high officials to recommend candidates for office.[63]

Yu also called for the establishment of a new office called the Hall for Inviting the Brave (Yŏnyŏngwŏn), named and patterned after the proposal made by Ch'eng Hao of the Sung dynasty, to care for the recommended men by granting them salaries and honoring their rank and scholarly ability. Instead of appointing them immediately to office, they would be assigned as expectant candidates ("awaiting instruction") (*ŭnggyo*) living and studying together in a community. If some problem of government occurred that fit their talents, they could be assigned the duty as a temporary task. Otherwise they might be consulted concerning problems involving the state code or the conduct of rites, or be summoned to royal audiences in consultation with the State Council and Ministry of Personnel. Only after a year in residence in the Hall for Inviting the Brave would they then become eligible for a regular appointment. The whole procedure was defined intentionally to avoid any kind of examination by the State Council, Ministry of Personnel, and Office of Inspector-General because Yu regarded recruitment by single tests as contrary to the methods of the ancients.[64]

Nonetheless, reprimand and punishment for errors in recommendation were still to be preserved to insure the integrity of the recommenders, who would be dismissed from office for any criminal action by recommendees. Even if there were extenuating circumstances, recommenders would still be subjected to a 50 percent cut of their annual salary. If the recommended official were guilty of embezzlement or corruption, the recommender would suffer additional punishment. If the recommender had supported two or more officials who had violated the law, they could themselves be stripped of their office warrants and reduced to the status of commoner. In the recommendation process itself if the recommender acted in response to someone's request for an office, accepted a bribe, acted on the basis of any private consideration or in the knowledge that the candidate was unqualified, he would be held guilty of deception or fraud.

To be sure, recommenders would be entitled to special honors, appointments, and titles if the men they recommended performed well in office, but only after they had accumulated a record of superior performance over a long period. If a recommended official committed malfeasance, his recommender would not be excused even if he had already died; he would be posthumously stripped of his post and all honors and titles taken away, and his son would lose the *ŭm* or protection privilege for appointment to office. To prevent incumbent officials from shirking the duty to recommend candidates to escape the panoply of severe punishments for faulty recommendation, Yu also provided that any evasiveness to recommend qualified men would be punished by immediate dismissal from office.[65]

Another device to insure the steady flow of talented men by use of the recommendation system was adoption of a measure proposed by Lu Yü in the T'ang dynasty that regular court councilors (Ch'ang-ts'an-kuan) of fifth rank or higher recommend the name of a substitute to replace him within three days of his own appointment (*chadae*). In the Sung period the measure was extended to include lower officials such as district magistrates down to the seventh rank and required men with the longest list of recommendations to be appointed to assume the post. Yu was more cautious by restricting recommendation to the top three ranks only for recommendations of censors, historians, district magistrates, and educational officials.

The proposal was also supported by Yu's favorite Ming statecraft expert, Ch'iu Chün, who praised the T'ang and Sung systems because only men with proven talent were recommended and the procedure encouraged the spirit of altruistic willingness to yield their positions to others. Ch'iu recommended that the Ministries of Personnel and War set up a roster of substitutes for every man in office by requiring recommendations by incumbent officials rather than relying exclusively on the impersonal method employed by regular personnel agencies.[66]

CONCLUSION

In his discussion for reform of the means of evaluating the performance of active officials, Yu Hyŏngwŏn sought to recapture the spirit of classical, feudal times and wed it to the bureaucratic system. When he praised the classical ideals of recruiting the most talented men and defining talent as worth and ability, he never meant to divorce moral knowledge and behavior from competency on the job to create a value-free system for evaluating candidates for office. In the search for talent, moral criteria remained primary, and efficiency and competency secondary.

Yu did not believe that it was possible to escape the legacy of centralized bureaucratic organization to return to the alleged purity of feudal norms, but he did believe that the adoption of classical norms and principles would solve the problems that had developed in the age of bureaucracy. His reading of Chinese history revealed that routinization of personnel matters in the hands of a specialized and mechanical Ministry of Personnel and neglect of thorough investigation and evaluation of incumbent officials was responsible for the decline of efficiency and probity in bureaucratic performance.

Maintaining the quality of bureaucratic personnel required constant care and attention to the search for talent by enrolling all officials to recommend those whom they deemed qualified. Promotion also required constant observation of incumbents to recommend promotion, or at least to determine who deserved to keep their jobs. This spirit of dedicated observation of human behavior had been lost because it was replaced by the perfunctory handling of personnel files by clerks.

When the admirable Han dynasty fell in the early third century, the development of an aristocracy and respect for status further impeded the impartial search for talent. Checking genealogies to verify status and family membership usurped the role played by an objective review of performance and obviated any attempt to create a system of equal opportunity for all individuals. An aggressive and intolerant competition for office introduced new structural divisions and a mood of rancor and bitterness within the bureaucracy as officials castigated their opponents and formed cliques to protect themselves against the internecine combat of office-seeking.

When the civil service examination system was introduced in 589 in the Sui dynasty, it was favored because it promised to replace pedigree, status, and connections with an impartial and impersonal testing of individual knowledge as the means for recruitment. Critics soon noted, however, that the stress on rote memorization of texts and literary skills in the composition of poems and essays had not succeeded in producing the elite of moral talent that supposedly ruled over society in ancient times.

Furthermore, the negative consequences of the growth in the size of society and the bureaucracy required to govern it became apparent throughout the T'ang period. As the capital and major cities became the cynosure of interest and attention, flocks of examination candidates assembled at the capital to prepare for examinations, and central government posts superseded the provinces in the growing hierarchy of status and ambition. The older ideal of maintaining good officials in local posts for long periods of time was abandoned by the introduction of short tenure and rapid transfer. Officials in capital bureaus were unable to gain expertise by long experience in a particular post, and magistrates in local districts lost familiarity with the people because they were transferred so frequently. As a result they shifted their attention from the fulfillment of their duties as magistrates to rapid ascent to capital office.

The number of officials and, more important, the number of examination passers and degree-holders and the volume of people in the category of eligible candidates for office and promotion, demanded some kind of rationalization of method to allow the personnel administration to deal with such vast numbers. The solution was to reduce human beings to statistics even before the invention of the computer, by converting them to assigned numbers of rank and introducing the stepladder system of routine promotion based on time-in-grade. This system of appointment by seniority eliminated the need for the enormous expenditure of time and effort needed to carry out a thorough review of all officials and candidates, but it also weakened the central government's knowledge of its pool of officials and its control over the integrity of its functions.

The T'ang dynasty may have suffered from these defects, but its officials were not obtuse to the methods of rectification. Some proposed measures to force the best capital officials to take posts as district magistrates, extend terms of office for all functionaries to gain experience in their posts, and require all officials who aspired to ministerial rank to pass a tour of duty as district magistrate. They requested expanding the system of reviewing officials beyond the Ministry of Personnel by including more officials in evaluating candidates for high office and requiring all officials to recommend others for office under penalty for non-compliance.

Yu accepted the common criticisms of Chinese bureaucratic practice, including short terms of office, frequent transfers of officials, and neglect of provincial posts, because they were all a major part of the Korean scene, but he also addressed some specifically Korean forms of malpractice in the sixteenth and seventeenth centuries. He agreed with the objection to excessive concentration of the recommendation process in the Ministries of War and Personnel, but he was also alarmed by the unique transfer of responsibility from the ministers down to the staff officials (Nanggwan). Not only did this disrupt the chain of command, but by increasing the important prerogatives of the Nanggwan in recommending officials, the focus of struggle between members of rival factions in 1575 for subordinate staff posts in the Ministry of Personnel had actually spawned the emergence of formal, hereditary factionalism. Contrary to the thrust of Chinese criticism, which was to expand responsibility for recommending candidates to all officials rather than just the Ministries of Personnel and War, Yulgok and Yu himself believed that restoring the chain of command in the personnel ministries would achieve more effective evaluation of talent. By the mid-seventeenth century, however, hereditary factions had become so institutionalized that restoring Yulgok's sixteenth-century advice to make cabinet ministers responsible for their duties was hardly likely to eliminate factionalism, the main obstacle to the fair and objective evaluation of talent in Korea. In general, Yu's omission of serious discussion of factionalism has to be counted as one of the major deficiencies of his analysis.

Yu also objected to the excuse of illness because it increased the frequency of transfer among all officials and interfered with maintaining the purity of the censorate. The role of the censorate in government affairs had also become a major scene of struggle in Korean politics during the reigns of Yŏnsan'gun and Chungjong at the turn of the sixteenth century. Censors were originally and theoretically supposed to be neutral observers of political action to exert a moral influence over the behavior of all, and they did become opponents of King Yŏnsan'gun's tyrannical autocracy, and then of entrenched high officials and merit subjects in King Chungjong's reign in the early sixteenth century. They professed they were motivated by a desire to achieve moral purity, but in fact they had become directly engaged in political action of their own, so that King Chungjong decided to purge them and reduce their power in 1519. Censorate power was reduced but not eliminated because censors were still available to perform tasks of surveillance and impeachment, but when hereditary factionalism emerged after 1575, they could not be counted on to act as neutral watchdogs over competing factions and ambitious politicians. They had their own careers to consider, and antagonizing a high official over a minor (let alone major) transgression was sure to jeopardize their own careers.

Yulgok and others had noticed this in the late sixteenth century and sought to cure it by holding censors to their responsibility of honest surveillance of proposed candidates for office. The pressures on them had become so great, however, that they preferred to seek transfers rather than do their duty and ruin their own prospects, and the censorate developed institutionalized procedures for coercing conformity to majority opinion and silencing the remaining men of conscience. This situation was also related to the growth of hereditary factional politics, which made it even more difficult for individual officials to act contrary to the interests of their own faction.

Yu Hyŏngwŏn's solution to the censorate's role was even more drastic because he wanted to reduce the two censorate offices to the single Office of Inspector-General and then abolish its right to sign off on all candidates recommended for office because it had violated its mandate for objective evaluation by favoring the yangban of pedigreed families, not to mention the members of factions. He preferred to confine responsibility to the Ministries of Personnel and War for review and promotion even though that formula had been subjected to attack in China for overly routine evaluation of candidates in impersonal, if not inhuman, terms. He believed that nine-year terms of office and periodic triennial reviews would suffice to eliminate bias from the evaluation of performance.

Yu learned from Chinese experience and the advice of recent Korean scholar-officials that moral education and behavior not only had to become the basis for recruitment, but that it had to be tested and observed constantly in the actions of officials themselves. Since the written examination had provided no guarantee of the individual's adherence to moral norms, the whole process of selection and promotion had to be shifted to techniques of observation and recommendation. Yu sought to achieve this by grafting the characteristics of small community life (i.e., the basis of classical Chou feudalism), where everyone knew everyone else and could vouch for someone's reliability, onto the apparently impersonal and mechanistic universe of bureaucratic practice. In practical terms, he accepted the advice of the Sung period to expand the system of recommendation to all officials and to enforce the system by severe penalties for any failure to recommend candidates. Recommendation would supplement the work of the Ministries of Personnel and War, if not really replace them. And the capstone of the system was to be Ch'eng Hao's Hall for Inviting the Brave, a kind of think-tank of prospective candidates to give advice and be observed in the capital. But how could sponsorship and recommendation in the promotion process have been that successful for seventeenth-century Korea when it had not helped to maintain the purity of Sung officialdom nor staved off the encroachments of foreign aggressors in the twelfth century? It may have been nonetheless tremendously appealing as a method for recruiting men of talent from all classes and regions because in contemporary Korea the road to advancement had been so narrowly circumscribed by criteria of inherited social status.

CHAPTER 18
Provincial and Local Administration

"Let the people and gentry of the village manage the granary publicly but only allow the official yamen to give aid and encouragement."[1]

Four major problems related to Yu Hyŏngwŏn's reform plans for provincial and local administration will be discussed in this and the following two chapters. The first two are related to the method of organizing bureaucracy at the provincial and local levels. The third is the problem of corruption within the bureaucracy, particularly among the clerks, and the fourth was the very difficult question of defining the limits of centralized bureaucratic control. On this last point, many scholars have noted that the Sinitic system of pre-modern bureaucracy contained an endemic weakness at the lowest level – the distance between the district magistrate and the local population, which weakened the ability of the magistrate to control the villages. The proposition will be asserted here, however, that this situation was not caused by laxity and inattention, but an endemic preference for local autonomy that derived from Confucian statecraft thought.

Yu's study of bureaucratic history in China convinced him that the appearance of anomalies in local administration developed as a consequence of growing complexity in the age of bureaucracy after the Ch'in and Han dynasties. Complexity introduced anomalies in administration, particularly variations in the size of local districts, that introduced imbalances into the distribution of tax and labor service burdens. It also created the equivalent of rotten boroughs – small districts with magistrates and their staff of clerks for areas too small to support them. These problems also existed in Korea as well, not because Korea had conquered large territories, created a vast empire, or expanded the numbers of bureaucrats beyond all reason, but because centralized bureaucratic districts had a history of over a thousand years and during that time numerous changes in the size and status of those districts and the territory they controlled destroyed the chance of uniformity and introduced anomalies into the system of organization.

A second problem in local government was the role of the provincial authorities, both the civil governors and the military provincial military commanders and their subordinates. The post of civil governor as a permanent position firmly stationed in a provincial capital with full control over provincial affairs was a late phenomenon in Korean history, established only at the beginning of the Chosŏn dynasty. This meant that the supervisory function of the governor as a watchdog over the district magistrates was relatively weak. Furthermore, the unhappy experience of Hideyoshi's invasions showed that provincial military authorities lacked sufficient autonomy and power to control troops in their districts and provinces. Any desire to strengthen the governor's or provincial military commanders' positions, however, ran up against the traditional statecraft view inherited from the fear of tyrannical regional military commissioners of the T'ang dynasty in China, that too much gubernatorial power would lead to regional rebellion and destruction of the dynasty itself.

A third problem of local administration was, of course, the perennial problem of corruption, but that problem was exacerbated institutionally in Korea by the policy of the early Chosŏn dynasty to eliminate all salaries for clerks. Since fees and gratuities were sanctioned by law, the clerks were virtually given carte blanche to fleece the peasantry and the public.

Finally, the ultimate issue in establishing programs to solve administrative problems in a bureaucratic regime was deciding the level of confidence and trust one could repose in the bureaucracy itself. This was especially difficult for a reformer like Yu Hyŏngwŏn, who believed that the epitome of good government had been achieved in a feudal age in which local autonomy was regarded as a positive advantage, not a sign of the incompleteness and inefficiency of a proper bureaucratic system. For that matter, since this perception was not confined to reformers like Yu, but shared by almost every Confucian of the bureaucratic age (at least intellectually), the bias against excessive centralization of bureaucratic authority and for relative local autonomy was built into the Chinese system of local bureaucracy.

This tug-of-war between central and local interest meant that district magistrates usually controlled relatively large territories and could operate at the village level only by dispatching runners and clerks to natural villages where they had to deal with village chiefs and elders and compromise with local interests. Many of these Korean village leaders were members of larger yangban lineages or members of the central bureaucracy.

When the central government, therefore, hoped to implement the administration of some program, whether taxation or relief, it had to decide generally between two methods: direct control by the representatives of central, bureaucratic power – the district magistrates and their clerks at the local level – or indirect control, in which power and authority for administration was vested in local leaders. In this chapter, the administration of price stabilization, relief, and loan operations will be considered in this context, and in later chapters the question of vesting authority in local associations like the Hyangch'ŏng dominated usually by local yangban, or creating local community compacts (*hyangyak*) as agencies of mutual surveillance, control, moral instruction, and ideological indoctrination will be explored.

PROVINCIAL ADMINISTRATION

Reorganization of Local Districts

In the feudal age of Chou times local administration was divided between the realm of the king or ruler and the autonomous fieflike districts of the feudal lords. Local districts in the king's realm were governed by royal officials, but the fiefs of the feudal lords were governed by the lord's officials. After feudal lords were replaced with local magistrates in the Ch'in dynasty, fiefdoms were replaced by a two-tiered structure of local administration run by bureaucrats, and districts (*hsien*) were organized in larger commanderies (*chün*). Some feudal enclaves retained in the Han dynasty were run by magisterial officials under feudal lords until they were eliminated during the Revolt of the Seven Kingdoms in 154 B.C.[2]

Local administration became more complex in later periods. The Chin regime in the third century A.D. could not maintain an orderly hierarchy of local administrative units because certain commandery prefects and district magistrates independently attacked their neighbors to expand their own territory. Warlords on the frontier also established commanderies on their own authority, granting themselves high-ranking titles even though the population was too small to fit the rank. To establish some kind of regularity among the districts of variable size, the Northern Ch'i government in the late fifth century subdivided commanderies into nine grades according to their size with similar subdivisions for districts as well. Since Minister of War Yang Shang-hsi was particularly alarmed because many districts were too small in area and population and yet had heavy quotas of taxation, he recommended a reorganization of local districts to bring all of them up to a minimum size.

In Sui and T'ang times the commandery was replaced by the Chou (prefecture), the Fu was used for a Chou located in a capital, and the grand protectorate (Tu-hu-fu) was put in charge of several Chou. Sung dynasty local administration became even more complex because of an increase in the types of districts and the habit of appointing many capital officials to magistracies as concurrencies. The hierarchy of prestige among local magistrates derived from the rank of the capital post held by a concurrent official rather than the magistrate's rank.[3]

In the Ming dynasty large-sized Chou were changed to Fu, which either controlled prefectures with their own subordinate districts or ran districts directly. Ch'iu Chün charged that because district boundaries had not been redrawn to keep up with changes in population, some large prefectures (Fu) might control several dozen prefectures and districts while others had barely two or three. Since the disparity in the population of individual districts was just as diverse, he recommended that the Fu, Chou, and Hsien each be divided into three grades according to population. Units that were too small could be joined with others or dropped in rank, and larger ones could be raised in rank. Productivity could also be used to reorganize the ranks of districts to improve the fairness and equality of district quotas of taxes and labor service.[4]

Yu's plan for reforming provincial administration would have required a significant reorganization of prefectural and district boundaries to eliminate major discrepancies between tax and labor service quotas levied on individual districts. Relying on the criticism of Yang Shang-hsi and Ch'iu Chün, Yu complained about the confusion in local administration in Korea because at least seven titles for prefectures and districts were still in use, some reproducing Chinese titles, others preserving terms established in the Three Kingdoms and Koryŏ periods. There was little consistency or order for the use of different titles and a complex system of ranks and grades. The Tohobu in Korean terminology, for example, had nothing in common with the size and responsibility of grand protectorate (Tu-hu-fu) in China. Yu suggested, therefore, that the names used for districts should be adapted to the size and population of each, eliminating the undersized districts and prefectures or combining them into larger units. In addition, the principle of rectification of names – creating a clear and distinct relationship between terms used and the reality they were supposed to describe – had to be applied in this process. Thus, any district with its seat located in a provincial capital should be called Taebu; any district located in a large administrative town should be called Tohobu; any district without jurisdiction over military garrisons should only be called Pu; any medium-sized unit should be called Kun (prefecture), and the smallest unit, the Hyŏn (district). Any fractional districts would then be combined into larger ones. By eliminating the anomalies in the local administration Yu could have reduced the system of local administration to a single file card for the whole country.[5]

Yu also defined each unit by territorial dimension. The Taebu or Tohobu would have 40,000 *kyŏng* (6.7 million acres, 40 *i* or about 13 miles square), the prefecture (Kun) 30,000 *kyŏng*, and the district (Hyŏn) 10,000 *kyŏng*, and each unit would have an administrative town. The Tohobu would also function as a garrison with jurisdiction over a number of lesser administrative towns. The method of calculation would rule out nonarable and nonproductive land, such as mountains, rivers, swamps, and forests. Finally, Yu adopted the advice of Su Ch'o that every district have a magistrate and assistant official, because magistrates might use any pretext to take over the district of a neighboring magistrate as a concurrency, and assistants could watch their actions to prevent them from doing so.[6]

This reorganized scheme of local administration, however, did not represent a serious attempt to build a strict hierarchy of jurisdiction as well as rank. In most Chinese systems several lower level districts were placed under the jurisdiction of the next higher unit, but only the Tohobu or grand protectorate in Yu's plan would have command over a number of subordinate local unit, presumably either prefectures or districts. Otherwise, every prefecture or district would operate independently and report directly to the provincial governor or various capital ministries as they had done in the past. Instead of establishing a number of grades of districts or prefectures as had been done in China, the name "district" or "prefecture" would itself reflect the differences in the area or population of the unit. Furthermore, the rank of the magistrate would vary with the size of the unit, so that the higher ranking – presumably the best – officials would have to be chosen for the more important magistracies. On the other hand, larger units might have presumably less control over their populations than small ones since there would be no regular chain of command over smaller districts and subordinate magistrates.

Yu also wanted to allow district magistrates to appoint their lower ranking officials and staff – one of the most prevalent recommendations in the Chinese literature. This practice had been used throughout the Han dynasty, but because local staff posts were being sold indiscriminately, Emperor Hou-chu of the Later Ch'en in the late sixth century took this power away from the district magistrates and transferred it to the Ministry of Personnel in the capital, a practice continued after the Sui dynasty. Yu was convinced, nonetheless, that the Han system was superior. He wanted to call the irregular district staff assistants in Korea the local officials (Hyanggwan) and have a rectifier (Chŏn'jŏng) and investigator (Chŏn'gŏm) take the place of the head of the seat (Chwasu) and special director (Pyŏlgam), the chiefs of the local yangban or gentry associations (Hyangch'ŏng), who until the late Chosŏn supposedly had supervisory control over the clerks (*sŏri*) of the district magistrate's office. In addition, each jurisdiction would have a specified but varying supply of clerks and boy servants serving in the magistrate's office and the local school (to be discussed later). Not only did he seek to professionalize the ranks of irregular officials by giving them pay, status, and regular posts rather than abandon central government responsibility for their conditions of work, he also wanted to incorporate the officials of the local yangban associations into the local districts and put them directly under the magistrate's jurisdiction.[7]

Provincial Level Officials

In Chinese history the development of the province and its governor as an intermediary unit of local administration developed gradually over several dynasties. Prefects of commanderies were similar to governors since they controlled a number of districts. Even in the Sui and T'ang dynasties, the regional inspector (Tz'u-shih) who headed the prefecture (now called Chou) still controlled districts, but because of the expansion of military activities military units (Fu) and larger military units called superior area commands (Ta-tsung-kuan-fu) were created under the command of regional governor (Tsung-kuan) to oversee as many as several dozen prefectures. Though soon abolished, it revealed the need for a larger unit to assist in the control of regions.[8] In the eighth century, the threat of foreign invasion required the establishment of military commissioners (Chieh-tu-shih) over certain frontier regions with civil as well as military responsibilities. At first civil officials, the posts were then taken over by military men, the most famous of which was An Lu-shan, who rebelled against the dynasty in 755.[9]

In the Ming dynasty, provincial governors above the level of prefects were not appointed until 1430, three-quarters of a century after the dynasty was founded, but they were meant to be circuit inspectors rather than permanent governors. Although they submitted memorials to the emperor, they did not assume full responsibility for tax collection, and provincial commissioners communicated directly with the ministries. As provincial control weakened, circuit intendants assumed control of the administrative and surveillance commissioners. Eventually, grand coordinators (Hsün-fu) dispatched to maintain surveillance over areas were turned into provincial governors by 1550, and they were placed under a supreme commander for military affairs (Tsung-tu chün-wu). In other words, the creation of the permanent governorship to transcend all prefectural and district officials only appeared in full-fledged form a century before Yu Hyŏngwŏn's lifetime.[10]

By the seventeenth century, the Koreans had long since adopted the province and surveillance commissioner as provincial governor (Kwanch'alsa, named after the T'ang term for civil governor, Kuan-ch'a-shih), but provincial administration was still not fully developed and the governor himself still functioned like a temporary circuit inspector. Not only did Yu want to make the governor a permanent official, he also wanted to restructure the governor's staff subordinates to aid him in provincial administration. Yu had found that since the Chou dynasty, kings and emperors were primarily concerned with controlling the powers of the chief local officials without interfering too much with their responsibilities. The Son of Heaven or ruler of the Chou empire sent officials called Ta-fu to oversee (*chien*) the leader of the feudal lords, called the Fang-po, the only lord who had the authority to lead a punitive expedition against a transgressor.

In the Ch'in dynasty, an imperial scribe (later censor) (Yü-shih) was sent to the commanderies as an inspector (Chien) who reported to the emperor, but in the early Han period the post of inspector was abolished. A censor was established to investigate the metropolitan area (San-fu) in the early second century B.C., and investigating censors (Chien-ch'a yü-shih) at the prefectural (Chou) level. Because their surveillance was lax, Emperor Wen (r. 180–157 B.C.) ordered the prime minister to dispatch clerks to investigate the prefectures, but they were not always appointed. In 106 B.C. Emperor Wu then created the post of regional inspector (Tz'u-shih) to oversee one of the thirteen regions and all their commanderies and kingdoms, but Grand Minister of Works (Ta Ssu-k'ung) Ho Wu, in the mid-first century (ca. 32 B.C.) criticized this system because the regional inspector was too low in rank to take charge of criticizing his superiors, and he was replaced by a higher ranking official.[11]

In the T'ang dynasty, civil governors (called variously An Ch'a-shih and Kuan-ch'a-shih) were appointed to the ten (later fifteen) circuits (*tao*) of the empire, and they and the regional military commissioners (Chieh-tu-shih) had about four subordinates, including special commissioners for taxation (Tsu-yung-shih), transport (Chüan-yün-shih), and salt and iron production (Yen-t'ieh-shih) who were not always appointed. The Sung government replaced the circuit with the eighteen (later twenty-three) routes (Lu), each of which was run by a governor

(An-ch'a-shih). The governors had a larger and more complex staff than their T'ang counterparts, but not all posts were filled on a regular basis. The main problem of the Sung, however, was bringing the military commissioners under control to prevent repetition of the An Lu-shan rebellion.[12]

The Ming regime inherited the Yüan dynasty term for province (Sheng), and the governors had four bureaus to handle edicts from the emperor, military affairs, general supervision, and inspection. While Ming provincial administration appeared to be more specialized and efficient, Yu observed that the various posts and officials had divided authority to create checks and balances to prevent the monopoly of power by a single individual. Although he felt that the central government was well organized, provincial government was too complex and hampered by overlapping assignments.[13]

In the late fifteenth century in Korea, the governor had only been assisted by an inspector (Tosa), and several assistants (P'an'gwan) in charge of certain important magistracies.[14] According to the law code of 1469, the *Kyŏngguk taejŏn*, each province had educational officials, interpreters, inspectors of medicine, legal experts, post-station chiefs, and ferry-station officials, but after the revisions of the law codes in 1744 and 1788, all but the single legal expert was eliminated.[15]

Writing in the mid-seventeenth century, Yu Hyŏngwŏn decided to avoid the complexity of the Ming system and reduce the governor's assistants to a minimum of necessary officials, but he would not have eliminated all provincial subordinates. He would have retained three assistants to the governor: the inspector (Tosa) whose title would be changed to consultant (Ch'amni), the inspector of medicine (Simyak), and the legal expert (Kŏmnyul). The governor's yamen was to be staffed by 30 clerks, 140 runners (slaves included), and 28 boy servants.

Since Yu planned to replace the civil service examinations with schools as the means for recruiting officials, the governor would also have jurisdiction over the new Governor's School (Yŏnghak) and its staff to provide for the students' needs. The governor would also continue the tradition of occupying two important concurrent posts, the provincial army commander (Pyŏngma chŏltosa, or Pyŏngsa) and provincial navy commander (Sugun chŏltosa, Susa), each with a staff of about 180 clerks, runners, and boy servants. Since the provincial governor had jurisdiction over military affairs and did not need separate provincial military and naval commanders unless necessary, some provinces had none while others had as many as two each.[16]

Yu suggested the addition of a single official in charge of supervising ocean-going transport for the southern three provinces and the receipt and disbursement of materials in the capital warehouses, to be called the maritime transport commissioner (Haeunsa). Yu was revising the existing system of maritime grain transport officers (Chosol), who lacked a supreme supervisor. He ordered that the officer for maritime transport would be a Tangsanggwan (official of ranks 1A through 3A) without a permanent residence or duty station but make the rounds of inspection. The lower officials would be recruited from residents of the capital, granted salaries from the capital, and divided into two shifts of duty.[17]

Yu also noticed that in the late sixth century in the Sui dynasty special mayors were created to manage the capitals because of the emperor's frequent travels. He suggested following Sui practice by granting the governor a concurrency as mayor of an important city with the special title of special mayor (Yusu), with a high rank of 2B to qualify him as a direct subordinate to the king rather than to any intermediary provincial official. These special cities and each prefectural or district level also had command of a school for training recruits for the central bureaucracy.[18]

The essence of Yu's program was to station the governor in the provincial capital with his family, raise his status by conferring concurrencies on him as a mayor of a special city, maintain the assistants already called for in the original law code of 1469, and expand provincial control over maritime transport. Yulgok had complained bitterly about the offhand treatment of provincial governors in the sixteenth century because, contrary to any six-year limit for gubernatorial service, governors served only one year, had virtually no knowledge of the sentiments of their residents and subordinate officials, and were unable to handle emergency situations. Since the frequent transfer of provincial officials back and forth to the capital merely served to clog the post-stations hostels, Yulgok wanted not only longer terms for governors and provincial military commanders but an order that they take their families with them, choose a suitable town for their seat of office, and assume concurrent duties as magistrate of the town, as only the governors of the two northern frontier provinces were currently permitted to do. He ascribed the military weakness of the border region to frequent transfers of provincial governors, who were virtually unknown to the provincial population. Keeping governors on duty for as long as twelve years would, by contrast, give the population a feeling of stability and confidence and allow governors to take vigorous action against any bandits or invaders of Korean territory.[19]

In the worst possible situation, if incompetent men were chosen to fill provincial posts, the governors would take graft to accumulate wealth and neglect the problems of the peasantry, and the provincial commanders would fleece the soldiers of their property and ignore defensive military preparations. No matter how wise the ruler, the beneficence of his government at the top would never reach the bottom of society to help transform major social problems. Constant review of provincial officials was required to select the best men and weed out the incompetent. Court officials would have to recommend the best candidates for provincial posts and hold them responsible for reform.

Military Command

Since military organization of garrisons had varied requirements that would differ by province, Yu did not expect to create a uniform organization for all provinces, but at least he wanted uniformity of terminology. The highest level provincial garrison would be graded into large and small garrisons, referred to by current titles – the large Ch'ŏmsajin or garrison commanded by the the rank

4B Ch'ŏmjŏl chesa (currently called Chinmu) and the lesser garrison, the Manhojin, comanded by the rank 5B Manho. The objective here was to eliminate all small and useless garrisons and combine their forces into larger ones. Yu summarized the country's local garrison structure as consisting of ninety-two: thirty army garrisons and sixty-two naval garrisons. The army garrisons were commanded by twelve Ch'ŏmsa (i.e., Ch'ŏmjŏl chesa) and eighteen Manho; the navy garrisons were commanded by fourteen Ch'ŏmsa and forty-eight Manho. Yu insisted that the total of ninety-two garrisons had to be reduced by one-third and the troops redistributed.

Yu raised a problem that might be crucial in determining the authority of garrison commanders since some of the Ch'ŏmsa and Manho currently held 3B and 4B rank, each one grade higher than Yu's plan. Since the current rank was equivalent to civilian magistrates, dropping them in rank would subordinate them to their civilian colleagues. Yu claimed that because of the decline in the quality of garrison commanders the government had in recent years sought to attract qualified men for these posts by raising their rank beyond their qualifications and recruiting men from relatives of yangban without jobs (*hallyang*) or from irregular officials. After completing their tour of duty, they would then be transferred to the Ch'amha (ranks six through nine) grades of the civil bureaucracy.

Yu believed that by appointing only qualified military men to be provincial garrison commanders with real government salary payments would he be justified in lowering their rank. Improving the quality of the provincial garrison command and its forces was more important than filling empty quotas by manipulating ranks and other terms of service. Once able men were in command of garrisons, Yu did not expect that civil magistrates would be capitalizing on their rank to outmaneuver their military colleagues in the field. Care also had to be taken to maintain post commanders who had become familiar with the area and not transfer them from one end of the country to the other, a principle that should apply as well to post-station commanders, educational officials, and district magistrates. Yu believed this was consistent with the Han dynasty practice of allowing magistrates to appoint all their subordinate officials, garrison commanders, ferry and post-station officials because it promoted long-term tenure and relations of ease and familiarity between officials and the people.[20]

Kang Hang's Account of Provinces in Japan

Yu turned to Kang Hang's account of his experience in Japan as a prisoner of war during Hideyoshi's invasion to contrast the difference between provincial administration in the two countries. Kang was viewing political institutions that approximated the feudal organization of Chou China, and he praised the Japanese for choosing the most meritorious subjects for office, granting them lifetime tenure in their posts, allowing their heirs to inherit their positions, and giving them the authority to mobilize their own armies – all of which guaranteed them the certitude of military victory. In Korea, however, provincial officials did not always have troops under their command because half the men in a district were assigned to the governor and the other half to the provincial military commander. Men could be under the governor in the morning and then find themselves shifted to the command of the supreme field commander (Towŏnsu) sent out from the capital later in the day. The overlapping jurisdiction of different offices prevented unified control of the province by the governor while each of the military commanders were left without enough troops. There was no connection between one chain of command and another.

Kang recounted the experience of Yi Pongnam who was magistrate of Namwŏn (the Namwŏn-busa) in Chŏlla Province when the war broke out in 1592, but then was transferred to be the magistrate of Naju (Naju-moksa), and shifted to the post of defense commander (Pang'ŏsa). Because his appointment to that post was opposed, he was finally made provincial military commander (Chŏltosa). The governor of Chŏlla, Pak Hongno, was held responsible for defeats against Japanese forces and was replaced by Hwang Sin, but Hwang found the governor's office in ruins and could not find any of the fifty-three provincial magistrates who had been able to mobilize any troops. Kang had been in charge of the district of Tamyang when Namwŏn was surrounded by Japanese forces, but the officials assigned by the capital to take charge of defense only showed up after the military situation was already untenable. When the commanders and a few aides finally arrived, there were no troops available even for ambush attacks against the Japanese.

Kang's advice to the throne was to choose the best men for border commanders on the basis of bravery, courage, talent, ability, and military merit without respect to their rank, their careers as civil or military officials, or their pedigrees. These men should then be appointed as border commanders of garrisons established every 100 *i* (33 miles) near the past invasion points of the Japanese and keep them in command for a period of twelve to fifteen years as the Sung emperors had done. They should not be transferred to another post but only raised in rank, and even if the petition box be filled with complaints against them, they would not be dismissed or transferred until found guilty of a major crime.[21]

The gist of this discussion about governors and provincial officials was that feudal and Japanese traditions could be adapted to the bureaucratic system by long-term service to strengthen command and defense of frontier provinces, and that the political threat to central power could be avoided by careful choice of the best men for office. But this attitude had been disproved by the historical experience of disloyalty, especially in China and Japan. Yu's attitude that education, proper recommendation, and review of official performance would end the autonomous concentration of power by provincial governors and military commanders was a naïve, textbook exercise in purification of the ranks of officialdom.

Upgrading the Status of District Magistrates

In the Chou dynasty every one of the six ministers of state was required to govern a magistracy to prove his qualification for a high position, but in Korea, provincial posts were held in low esteem and assignment to them was only reserved for men whose reputation had been damaged – a complaint made by Chang Chiuling in 714 about provincial posts in T'ang times.[22]

Officials with good reputations were purposely kept out of the provinces, and provincial officials became so demoralized that they neglected the people under their charge. "The best of them just serve their time in office, while the worst of them do harm to the people and fatten themselves." No matter how high the rank, even Tangsang officials of the second rank who were qualified for the post of provincial governor would feel they were being exiled from the center of attention and spend their time "wandering around the various local towns doing nothing more than [associating with] *kisaeng* and wasting their time in drinking." Yulgok's solution would be to require officials from the censorate and the king's palace to rotate in provincial posts, returning to a capital post only after reexamination of their achievement – the standard classical prescription for circulating men of competence between the center and periphery.

Yu paraphrased Yulgok's stress on the importance of district magistrates and provincial officials because they acted in the place of the king in dealing with the ordinary people. Treating magistrates so lightly by reducing their positions to the equivalent of exile would be tantamount to holding the whole population in contempt and threatening the destruction of the state.[23] Yu therefore supported Yulgok's recommendation for governors and provincial military commanders to take their families with them and become concurrent magistrates over the provincial capital. Although he had also hoped to provide the provincial army commander with a regular salary as well, he was willing to continue the current funding of their salaries and garrison expenses from the taxes collected from the peasants who paid military service support.[24]

Staff Officials in Local Government

The solution to the organization of local staff personnel, particularly with respect to clerks, runners, and boy servants, was to double the staff for all employed in governors' and magistrates' yamen, schools, garrisons, and post-stations, but divide them into two shifts where each shift would work fifteen days of the month and be given time off for the other two weeks. They would be compensated by a half-month salary and an extra grant of 50 *myo* of land per person, while clerks and runners employed by administrative towns with daily responsibilities would get a full salary but no land grant. Yu was thinking of the staff personnel employed in the six major magistrate's bureaus (Yukpang) divided into the same categories of the six ministries at the capital. They had to be allowed half a month to rest, otherwise they would be swamped with work, and those off duty would serve by entertaining guests and visitors, or engaging in military affairs. Otherwise, ordinary titles, methods of recruitment, and standards of treatment for these staffs would be kept consistent with the staff personnel in the capital. Given the existing situation, official slaves living near the towns that functioned as the sites for district magistrates would be recruited as runners (*chorye*).[25]

For the staff of a prefectural magistrate (at the Kun) Yu prescribed a quota of fourteen clerks, fifty-eight runners, and eight boy servants with specific jobs for each one. The fourteen clerks were to be divided among six clerks (of the Yukpang) with separate responsibilities for each. In the present system the household chief (Hojang) was a position carried over from the early Chosŏn period but was waning in authority, and the emerging de facto main clerk of the mid-dynastic period, the personnel clerk (Ibang) was taking over his responsibilities, but they performed the same duties concurrently instead of taking turns. The other clerks would be in charge of the Taedong Granary (Taedongch'ang) of grain taxes to purchase tribute items, the Ever-Normal Granary (Sangp'yŏngch'ang) for price-stabilization and relief, the Military Weapons Storehouse (Kun'gigo), assistants for the magistrate and his assistant (Sŭngbal), and other yamen secretaries and scribes for the yamen clerks. The runners were assigned to each of the granaries, special runners for the jailhouse, specialists to care for tea and liquor, house servants as personal servants for the magistrate and his assistant, the assembly of clerks, and other odd officials. The tasks of the boy servants were less specific.

The quota of staff personnel for the governor's yamen (Yŏng) consisted of fifteen (one more than the fourteen for prefectural magistrates), seventy runners, and fourteen boy servants. The governor had the same staff of clerks in addition to a scribe to write official reports to the throne, and a staff of seventeen runners for his own personal needs and six more for his assistant. The rest of the runners were in charge of guarding granaries, serving guests, caring for the horses in the stable, cooking for the whole office, and waiting on the staff of staff officials. The structure of the governor's office varied only by more personal servants than the staff of the prefectural magistrate.

Yu took time to articulate his philosophy of providing liberal staff for the needs of local officials to alleviate the labor service requirement on ordinary citizens for the performance of service personnel in local government offices. He gave consideration to one proposal to save costs simply by cutting the number of runners (Saryŏng, in colloquial language), recruiting residents from communities near the governors' or magistrates' headquarters to perform service, compensating them with a grant of one *kyŏng* of land and a salary of six *mal* of rice per month, and dividing them into six shifts of two months of duty per year. He rejected this idea, however, because he believed that nonspecific general functions required of the labor service system had to be replaced by specialized clerks and runners with specific tasks.

Under the present system, scholars, farmers, artisans, merchants, and even soldiers did not have enough spare time to meet their service responsibilities. Another problem was the conflict between the need for soldiers and personnel for runners and service personnel. Yu pointed out that the service system consumed all available men for work at the magistrate's yamen within a distance of a dozen *i* (four miles) from the yamen, leaving no one to serve as local guard soldiers. The needs of local officials required a specific number of runners depending on necessary duties, and it was unwise to reduce the quota of service personnel. These service personnel also had to be specified for local military commands as well. The equivalent of runners in the military system were Kulloe, who enrolled in ranks distinct from soldiers. Yu wanted a number to be assigned to each military garrison and during wartime they could serve the needs of duty soldiers.[26]

Yu's plan also called for service personnel to serve in the revamped school system that would replace the examination system as the means of recruitment of officials. He singled out the staff for the large prefectural school (Puhak) that would have a single secretary (Sŏgi) and twenty-two runners including cooks, vegetable gardeners, granary guards, room cleaners, and servants to wait on tables. Yu instructed the runners to keep the dormitories warm, serve the students at the dining room table, set up their washing and drinking facilities, establish latrines, and handle collection of night soil for fertilizer. Yu proclaimed his objective was to establish government schools after the manner of Buddhist monasteries in contemporary times, citing the words of Ch'eng I of the Sung, that the monasteries in fact reproduced the dignified life style of antiquity because of simplicity of their communities. In similar fashion Yu outlined the staff requirements as well for the large military Ch'ŏmsa garrison with a staff of five clerks, nineteen runners, and two boy servants (less for a garrison run by the Manho), and a post-station (Yŏk) served by three clerks, fourteen runners, and two boy servants.[27]

Yu's plans to provide for local clerks and eliminate the main cause for corruption was never adopted, but by the next century existing evidence appears to indicate that the clerks, now referred to as middle men (*chung'in* or *ajŏn*), began to rise in prestige and technical qualifications partially as a result of the reduction of their numbers after Hideyoshi's invasions. Membership in their ranks was no longer confined hereditarily to the sons of local clerks alone because magistrates had to appoint temporary clerks to fill vacancies in their ranks. Despite the pejorative label of *chung'in*, they actually asserted themselves by gaining greater control of the six branches of local administration (Yukpang) that had replaced the chief clerk (Hojang) of the early Chosŏn period. They began to overcome their domination by the local yangban associations and assert more independence, partly because more regular funds for their support increased by the growing amount of land surtaxes imposed on peasant taxpayers. As much as one-third of tax revenues may have been devoted to the costs of local clerks by the nineteenth century. As the clerks became more important, it has been suggested that they were no longer so submissive and capitalized on their superior knowledge of local conditions to act as coconspirators with the magistrates in fleecing the peasantry. Although it cannot be proved that local clerks were any more capable of conspiring with corrupt magistrates in the late rather than early dynastic period, there is no doubt that local clerks played a major role in fomenting peasant rebellion by the mid-nineteenth century.[28]

Because the status and work of the local clerks changed in many ways, Yu's formula for providing regular salaries through tax revenues was achieved in practice. It was not done, however, by rational planning of total revenues, but by the ad hoc imposition of surtaxes at local initiative. Whether the growing power, weak status, or corrupt behavior of the local clerks was the main cause, the clerks became a primary catalyst for social disruption in the uprising of 1862.

Women Slave Service Personnel

A significant innovation in reducing the demand on males for service in government offices would have been the use of women slaves in service positions, and Yu was induced to retain the use of women for service jobs but in lesser numbers than men. Those that did perform service for the state would be compensated for their work by grants of salary and land on a scale equivalent to men. On the other hand, Yu was not overjoyed by the retention of female slaves for government service for two reasons: female slaves were being unjustly treated as slaves because they had inherited their social status by birth, and they were subjected to sexual demands by male officials. He also pointed out that neither in ancient nor contemporary times were women required to perform labor service in government offices, and even the Korean law code had no provision for assigning female slaves to work assignments in capital bureaus. Given current circumstances there was no reason why it was necessary to have female slaves perform service duties in both capital and provincial offices.

Yu explained the reasons for excluding female slaves from service jobs altogether. In ancient China men and women guilty of crimes were in fact made slaves and required to perform service for state agencies. The labor service required of slaves in ancient China were imposed as a penalty for criminal behavior, but there was no law providing for the inheritance of slave status from one's parents because hereditary slavery was regarded as a law contrary to the action of a just and virtuous king. Labor service for the state was thus regarded as an entirely legitimate duty of males, but women were only required to accompany their husbands as part of their moral obligation to their spouses. Therefore, the assignment of labor service to women for officials was regarded as a gross miscarriage of justice, especially since they were not guilty of any criminal behavior themselves.

The situation was exacerbated by the behavior of Korean officials who treated women who served them as if they were *kisaeng* (female entertainers) and forced them to have sexual relations. The government did nothing to prevent the exploitative employment of women as service personnel, but instead prohibited female entertainers from marrying lest they damage the institution of marriage and contribute to the destruction of moral standards. Yu insisted that the prejudice against female service obligations had in fact been created by current standards of behavior, and he preferred that women slaves be removed from service altogether as long as inherited slavery could not abolished. Even though some felt that service by female slaves was essential for service, at least as cooks in palaces and offices, others regarded men as superior to women in every job and pointed out that male servants performed all the work in the king's Royal Cuisine Office (Saongwŏn). It would be better that female slaves in service to government agencies be sent home and required to pay tribute to the Court for Providing Aid (in charge of currency) (Sasŏmsi), which also controlled responsibility for collection of tribute from slaves. In addition, until the present hereditary slave law was abolished, children of slaves would be registered on the slave records according to current regulations. Yu's response to government service for female slaves was consistent with his hope to alleviate some of the evils associated with hereditary slavery, a unique protest against the dominant male chauvinism of contemporary mores.[29]

POST-STATIONS AND GRAIN-TRANSPORT GRANARIES

In the mid-seventeenth century there were forty-one chiefs of post-stations (Ch'albang), double the twenty-two that existed in Koryŏ times. Yu intended to reduce the size and expense of this system. He pointed out that in ancient times specific military garrisons did not have to be created because district magistrates were held responsible for the first line of defense against foreign invasion. The number of post-stations could be reduced as well by transferring responsibility for the transmission of documents to district magistrates. Only naval garrisons served by rotating duty soldiers could not be so easily eliminated. Management of the horses and equipment associated with post-station and communication service did require a separate management staff, but economy could be achieved by placing a single chief (Ch'albang) in charge of a number of post-stations, an easy way to allocate resources economically because of Korea's small size.[30]

The Maritime Transport Granaries (Choch'ang), however, were distinct from other provincial agencies. In the Koryŏ period there were twelve transport granaries established along rivers in the southern provinces for internal transport, and ten along the coast for maritime transport of tax grain to the capital.[31] Possibly the number of granaries had fallen into disuse during the period of disorder of King Yejong's reign and the period of military rule in the late twelfth century. In the fourteenth century, most tax grain for the capital had to be sent inland because of the frequent plunder of the seacoast by the Wakō pirates, and at the beginning of the Chosŏn dynasty there were only four granaries along the coast and five on rivers. During Hideyoshi's invasions in 1597 districts along the coast stopped submitting taxes to the grain transport granaries for transshipment to the capital and hired private vessels to ship the grain directly themselves. The cost of the ships for both river and maritime transport was born by the granary workers and sailors who were given tax exemptions as compensation, but it was insufficient to defray the severity of the burden.

There were no regular officials for the river transport granaries and the provincial governors would appoint commissioners (Ch'asawŏn) to proceed to the granary and supervise tax collections with the tax collectors (Kamsugwan) and transport officials (Yŏng'un'gwan). The transport workers and sailors were subjected to demands for fees and bribes from commissioners, other granary officials, and the agents of the Ministry of Taxation at the capital. At times the officials of the capital granary prevented the boats from docking for some time to increase the pressure for payment of fees and bribes, and the agents of princes and princesses in the capital would show up at the docks in Seoul and claim that the sailors were their own runaway slaves. An individual sailor might have to pay a dozen *sŏm* of rice per trip to pay the bribes and fees, and would be forced to borrow grain or money at interest. Some had to flee because they had no way to repay the debt. The creditors might then demand repayment from the residents of the Han River, who would then impose fees on the next group of sailors to arrive. The commissioner of maritime transport in the capital (Haeun p'an'gwan) and all his underlings reaped huge profits from the whole operation.

Yu wanted to eliminate this system by restoring the grain-transport system to its early Koryŏ form. Since there were currently only two maritime granaries on the coast, he wanted to retain those two, restore one that had been abolished, and create five new ones.[32] He also proposed creating five new granaries along rivers for the internal transport of grain to the capital. Since irregular clerks were currently administering the grain-transport system, he sought to appoint an administrator (P'an'gwan of rank 8A) to supervise each granary according to early Koryŏ practice, and a national maritime transport commissioner (Haeunsa, of rank 3A, to replace the current Haeun p'an'gwan), who would make recommendations of men for the post of administrator of the individual granaries.

The maritime transport workers (*chosol*) and river transport workers (*subu*) were to be selected from areas near the granary, provided one *kyŏng* of land and two support taxpayers, and granted a daily rice ration of five *mal* including waiting time en route. The number of transport workers would be restricted by the quota for ships set by the government according to his own calculation of the ratio of thirty-six men per maritime vessel and eighteen for riverine vessels. The state would assume all expenses for building, repairing, and replacing ships from its regular revenues. All private fees for boat loading and the use of horses were to be eliminated and the cost borne by the granary, and any official caught demanding any unauthorized fees from the transport workers and sailors would be indicted for embezzlement. Yu also provided exact measurements for the dimension of each type of vessel and the weight of its grain cargo, and specified that transportation by river should occur three or four times a year, and only two by sea.

For the most part, he preferred to alleviate the responsibilities of the workers and sailors for the sinking of ships, but his idea of alleviation was rather Draconian by modern standards. If a transport sailor were responsible for the loss of a ship, he would received 100 strokes. Otherwise, the ship's captain would receive 100 strokes the first time he lost a ship, but be transported with his family to the frontier as an ordinary soldier if it happened again. The administrator would lose half his salary if his granary lost five ships, and he would be stripped of his office warrant if he lost ten ships in a six-month period. If a sailor was injured, he had to be replaced by one of his support taxpayers, and any unauthorized private substitution was forbidden. He believed that these arrangements would alleviate the current burden imposed on the maritime workers and sailors because they had also been subjected to demands for miscellaneous expenses and outright bribes by officials of the granaries.

Yu set up strict deadlines for the payment of tax grain to the granaries and the departure date for all vessels, and in upland regions, taxes could be paid in cloth, ramie, or silk instead of grain at fixed rates of conversion. The northern two provinces would be exempted from the system because they would keep tax grain on reserve for military expenses. Garrison commanders along the coast were responsible for stationing boats to guide and aid the transport vessels and keep a record of the time of arrival of those vessels to prevent any captain from embezzling the cargo as if the ship had sunk. Contact or trading with private merchants along the way was also to be forbidden, and violators would suffer confiscation of the merchandise. Any captain who transported private goods would suffer confiscation of the goods and assignment to the border as a frontier soldier. All grain that arrived at the capital had to be calculated and recorded by an official of the Ministry of Taxation and a royal secretary along with the granary administrator (P'an'gwan) if he happened to be on board the ship. If the cargo was short, the sailors would have to make up the loss, but the captain would have to pay twice as much as a sailor.[33]

PRICE STABILIZATION AND GOVERNMENT LOANS

The Chosŏn state used two methods inherited from China to provide loans and relief to tide peasants over the planting season or to save them from starvation in time of famine. There were state loans in grain for the spring season or for famine relief, and ever-normal purchase and sale of grain stocks to stabilize the price of rice by balancing short-term fluctuations in the supply of grain. Righteous Granaries (Ŭich'ang) stationed in each prefecture or district, run by the district magistrate and his clerks, provided for state interest-free grain loans to peasants. They were carried over from the Koryŏ dynasty in 1392, and grain reserves in Military Provisions Granaries were also loaned for the same purpose. In 1423, the Righteous Granaries were refunded and a 2 percent interest charge was added to help replenish the stocks, but when the income was not sufficient to maintain the reserve, interest rates were raised later in the century.

Between 1451 and 1470, Chu Hsi's village granary (*sach'ang*) system was introduced in ten districts on an experimental basis. A 20 percent interest rate was charged on loans from the village granaries because Chu Hsi had adopted an interest charge of 2 *tou*/*shih* (20 percent) to pay back the district magistrate for the original capitalization and accumulate an independent reserve fund for future loans. After the reserve was accumulated, regular interest charges were abandoned and only a wastage surcharge of 3 *sheng/shih* (3 percent) was collected. In Korea, the law called for a similar elimination of interest and a reduction to a wastage surchage of 6.7 percent after the original capitalization was repaid. The most important aspect of Chu Hsi's *sach'ang* system, however, was that control over it was supposed to be vested in the hands of local leaders, not the district magistrate, on the presumption that local leaders were more trustworthy and less likely to exploit the indigent peasants. In fifteenth-century Chosŏn, however, the district magistrate was given responsibility to manage the *sach'ang* system.[34]

Since poor peasants had difficulty repaying the principle, let alone the interest, the relief aspect of the system was mitigated and the fiscal demise of the village granaries was assured. Even though 20 percent was less than half the standard 50 percent rate on private loans during the growing season, many people opposed the permanent collection of interest because it contradicted Chu Hsi's original objective to provide relief to the poor. By the end of the fifteenth century, the formal interest rate was abandoned and replaced by a so-called wastage surcharge (*mogok*) that soon grew to 10 percent. Chu Hsi's village granary system had been subverted in two ways: the 10 percent interest charge had become permanent, and the granaries and loans were controlled by the district magistrate rather than the local community. By the mid-sixteenth century, district magistrates began to take an increasing portion of this wastage surcharge for their own expenses as a recording fee (*hoerok*), and in 1650 the Ever-Normal Agency in the capital took it over for its own purposes, leaving 1 percent to the Ministry of Taxation, and only 6 percent for the magistrate's expenses.

Korea also conducted ever-normal price stabilization activities through Ever-Normal Granaries stationed in a few market towns, but in a famine or other crisis, the officials often used Ever-Normal Granary reserves for relief and loans. Furthermore, all state granaries practiced loaning grain in the winter and collecting it again after the fall harvest to prevent rotting. In the seventeenth century, the practice of granting loans to peasants from individual government and military agencies spread throughout the country as a direct means of raising revenues in the face of the fiscal crisis of the central government. By the mid-seventeenth century the ever-normal granaries ceased to have much effect on market prices, and the system of state grain loans had been turned into an agency of repression rather than aid and relief.[35]

State institutions for loans and relief had been obstructed by the administration of the system, the revenue shortage of the state, and the need for income. Interest charges were imposed on relief loans at first to maintain the basic grain fund, and then to raise revenues, and the stock of the ever-normal granary system was depleted by transfers for relief and ordinary revenue requirements.

Yu Hyŏngwŏn was faced with this situation in the mid-seventeenth century, and he sought a solution by examining the Chinese response to these problems in earlier periods. He found that Chinese experience showed that proponents of reform were divided into two camps: those who favored the restitution of the ever-normal price stabilization system, and those who preferred refurbishing the system of state loans to the peasants through district righteous granaries or village granaries.

Lending Institutions: Chou through T'ang

Yu began his essay on the Chinese experience with the views of Li K'uei, prime minister under Marquis Wen of the state of Wei in the late fifth century B.C., not only because he represented the wisdom of antiquity, but because he was an early spokesman for price stabilization. Li K'uei had pointed out that when the price of grain was too high, the "people," that is the nonagricultural, urban consumers, were hurt and were forced to take flight to regions where prices were lower. But if prices were too low, then the farmers were hurt and the country as a whole ended up in poverty. In other words, extremes of grain prices were equally damaging even though the victims may have been different, and the virtuous ruler was bound to maintain fair prices for farm products. He prescribed that the state always had the responsibility of buying up a certain portion of the crop, but the percentage varied according to the size of the crop itself. In a bumper crop year, the government should buy three-fourths of the crop at a price sufficiently high to guarantee a livable income for the farmers. If the crop were moderate, it would only have to buy half the crop; or if it were poor and the price of grain was high, it would only buy one-fourth of the crop. In famine conditions, the state would then distribute the grain reserves it had built up by buying grain during bumper crop years and selling off a sufficient amount to bring the high price of grain down to normal levels. The object of this ever-normal operation was to ensure that farmers were guaranteed moderate incomes and the nonfarming population was able to buy food at reasonable prices.

The *History of the Han Dynasty* also worked out the microeconomic statistics for an average peasant family on the basis of production, tax payments, per capita consumption, and the conversion of the surplus to cash for the purchase of clothing and rituals. It also pointed out that because most peasant families did not save in anticipation of the costs of sickness, death, and funerals, they usually were left short at the end of the year, or failed to apply themselves diligently so that the grain supply never matched demand, and the price of grain rose. It was therefore left to the government to estimate the potential food supply and either buy up a portion of the crop or pay out part of its reserves to ensure a stable price for grain. Under Li K'uei's leadership the state of Wei did this and became rich and powerful.[36]

Yu Hyŏngwŏn then traced the subsequent history of ever-normal and local relief granaries in China. He showed how in the reign of Emperor Hsüan of the Han dynasty (B.C. 73–48) Keng Shou-ch'ang obtained the emperor's approval for establishing Ever-Normal Granaries (Ch'ang-p'ing ts'ang) in districts along the frontier to buy up part of the crop and bid up the price of grain that had slumped during a series of bumper crops. Later in the Sui dynasty in 585 the minister of taxation, Chang Sun-p'ing, established special relief granaries in rural villages called Righteous Granaries (*i-ts'ang*) or Village Granaries (*she-ts'ang*) located at the village shrine to the spirit of the earth (*she*) and financed by contributions of one picul (*shih*) per family, under the supervision of the village chief to store grain for relief in time of famine. These village granaries performed their function for a while, but they declined when the managers of the granary carelessly spent the reserves, used them all up for famine relief, or turned them over to the prefectural magistrate – an example that should have made later statecraft thinkers wary of the benefits of local elite control over district magistrates.

In any case, the village granaries were reestablished in the reign of T'ai-tsung in the T'ang dynasty in the early seventh century, but the same process of decline occurred when the government was forced to take over the Righteous Granary reserves to meet expenses during national fiscal crises in the reigns of Empress Wu (r. 690–705) and Emperor Chung-tsung (r. 705–710).[37]

Yu cited the commentary of Hu (Hung?) of the Sung who said that although the Righteous Granaries of the Sui were not that well stocked, they were effective because they were located in the rural villages and the starving peasants had close access to them. By contrast, after the Sui dynasty the Righteous Granaries were situated in the district towns, at some distance from the villages, and the dispensation of grain was controlled by the yamen clerks who obstructed relief grants by their bureaucratic paperwork or embezzled as much as they could get for themselves. The only beneficiaries of these urban Righteous Granaries were those who lived nearby.

Hu lauded the act of Emperor Shih-tsung of the Chou dynasty for granting relief to the starving population in 959, but he also remarked that relief loans, as opposed to direct grants, presented problems to the peasants. While the peasants were saved from starvation, they did not have the economic capacity to repay the loans. Furthermore, the government's wastage or interest charges gave officials a reason to dun the peasants for interest payments even though they were unable to repay the principle. Some clerks pocketed all repayments without recording them, or collected too much from the peasants during bumper crop years, but in times of famine they were stingy in granting relief and failed to grant tax exemptions in compensation for natural disasters like flood and drought.[38]

Yu also cited Ch'iu Chün's (Ming dynasty) praise of Hu's criticism of the evils attendant on grain loans and his comment that in the Ming period maladministration of Righteous Granaries was just as bad as what Hu had described. Granary clerks were indiscriminate in collecting or buying grain for storage and often sold it in normal times to prevent spoilage from rotting. When they granted loans during a famine, they did not always give it to the needy. In collecting repayment, they were too strict in adhering to deadlines, added wastage or interest charges, demanded repayment in cash for grain loans to profit from the rate of exchange, or drew up false papers indicating that a loan had been made as a pretext for extorting payments from ordinary peasants. In summary, Ch'iu concluded that

> this covers the various types of evils in the Righteous Granaries today. What is said to be righteous is in fact to do things that are not righteous. What was originally meant to benefit the people, on the contrary has come to harm them. The only thing I see is that the business has become bothersome [for the people] and the clerks only act in corrupt fashion, and there is truly no benefit as far as relief is concerned.[39]

In short, Yu ended his treatment of grain loan administration with remarks condemning the Righteous Granaries, that is, the method of magistrate control over loans to the peasantry. This meant that he had brushed aside the equally damaging history of the village granaries of the Sui dynasty.

Ever-Normal and Village Granary Systems

Yu interrupted his historical survey of Chinese relief and loan institutions at this point to comment that the village granary system was obviously superior to the righteous granaries because they were located in the villages, managed by the villages themselves, and designed to encourage frugality and savings by the villagers to accumulate a reserve against the possibility of famine. The village granary reserves were never to be moved to the district or prefectural towns lest these advantages be lost, but in contemporary seventeenth-century Korea the grain reserves for the Korean grain loan system (*hwanja*) were in fact stored in the district town and run by the magistrate's office. Righteous granaries were also established in the district towns to administer annual loans to ordinary peasants, but all the forms of corruption described by Hu Hung (?) and Ch'iu Ch'ün for the Chou and Ming dynasties had been replicated in Korea: rigid adherence to repayment deadlines, harassment for repayment, skimping on lending and overcounting on repayment, forced loans in normal years to collect interest, peasant flight to escape repayment, unauthorized collection of repayments from relatives and neighbors of absconded debtors, and arbitrary collections on the basis of false loan papers. "This kind of system is nothing but a net to ensnare the people; it does not accord with the basic intention [of the system] to save the people from suffering."

Yu criticized the Korean system for lacking the equivalent of village granaries run by the villagers themselves. The Korean administrative structure for loans and relief, therefore, did not replicate the best features of the Chinese system, but rather of the universally condemned green-shoots system (*ch'ing-miao fa*) of Wang An-shih, adopted in 1069 in the Sung dynasty. The ever-normal system was far better than both Wang's green-shoots and the Korean *hwanja* systems because it harmed neither the peasants nor the state and provided benefits to both. It aided the farmer by maintaining a good price for his crops even in the face of a glut of production, and keeping prices down during famine conditions. In early Koryŏ times ever-normal granaries had been established in the capital and in the twelve *mok* or districts headed by magistrates sent by the capital in the tenth century, and that system had been carried over and extended to more provincial districts in the Chosŏn dynasty in the fifteenth century, but by Yu's time in the mid-seventeenth century not one local district retained its ever-normal granary.

The best way, therefore, to solve current Korean problems was to establish ever-normal granaries to stabilize prices through their purchase-and-sale operations, and encourage the elders of every village to establish village granaries and run them themselves, thereby ensuring the fair and just distribution of loans and relief. "Let the people and gentry of the village manage the granary publicly but only allow the official yamen to give aid and encouragement; it will not be able to supervise or excise jurisdiction [over the granary]."

Yu rejected any arguments that corruption could occur in the village granaries after they were established because of the greed of local administrators, or that they might be abandoned by the villagers. He was certain that once established, the villagers would be won over by the obvious advantages of the system, and once the village granaries were accepted, they would become a standard institution. If in the worst instance, village granaries could either not be established or fell into disuse after they were created, no harm would be done and things would still be better off than under the current *hwanja* system of government grain loans because the peasants themselves would have to take responsibility for accumulating their own famine reserve, and the ever-normal granaries could provide relief grants in an emergency.[40]

Chu Hsi's Village Granary System

In addition to the ever-normal granary system, Yu was also a great admirer of the village granary system that Chu Hsi first instituted as district magistrate in 1168 during a great famine. Yu described how Chu Hsi borrowed 600 *shih* (piculs) from the prefectural magistrate, charged 20 percent interest on the loans but with provision for interest rate reduction or no interest at all if the crop yield was too small. By 1176 he repaid the initial capitalization and accumulated an additional reserve of 3,000 *shih*, and then ceased all interest except for the 3 percent wastage surcharge. The head of the village shrine (*she-shou*) and the chief of the *pao* mutual aid unit (*pao-chang*), were to keep the loan records and divide the village population in *pao* units, but the decisions about the initial funding would be calculated by the both permanent and temporary residents of the village, and the disbursement and collection of loans would be conducted by the village elders. Loans would not be forced on anyone who did not want them, and the prefectural and district magistrates would be forbidden from interfering with the management of the loans.

Later Chu Hsi was summoned to court and asked by Emperor Hsiao-tsung to extend the system to a broader area, and to order that the ever-normal granaries in the prefectures and districts and also private wealthy individuals provide a capital rice fund for the establishment of the village granaries (*she-ts'ang*). Not only should the loans be voluntary, but the creation of the village granaries themselves should be voluntary, and the emperor should forbid magistrates from forcing their establishment.

Yu also quoted Chu Hsi's reasons for preferring the village granaries to Wang An-shih's green-shoots system. Chu Hsi objected to the operation of the green-shoots system because loans were made in cash instead of grain, the granaries were located in the district town rather than in the village, the granaries were managed by officials rather than by the elders or men of virtue in the village itself, and the officials were totally lacking in any compassion for the problems of the borrowers.

Chu Hsi was also cognizant of the difficulty of reproducing the perfection of the sage institutions of antiquity, but he believed that the village granaries were a close approximation. The classical principle of accumulating enough savings from every three years of agricultural production to support the village for one year, or saving enough from thirty years of production for a reserve that would last for nine years of famine was the ideal. The ever-normal granary system of the Han was second best and had remained a good system, but in Sung times it only existed on the books. The village granary system was unquestionably superior to anything that existed because it would eliminate the control of corrupt magistrates and end the necessity for punishment, exile, and transportation as means of enforcing repayment of loans. Nonetheless, Chu Hsi warned that men of rectitude had to be recruited to run the village granaries lest deceit and corruption destroy the attempt. He also emphasized the greater need for creating an atmosphere of harmony and instituting irrigation projects to increase crop production and increase savings so that the government would not have to wait until the next famine occurred before taking remedial action.[41]

Workfare Programs

Chu Hsi's village granaries were not extended throughout the Sung empire, and the attempt to introduce them into in the mid-fifteenth century did not last, but these facts did not deter Yu's faith in the superiority and efficacy of the method. Nonetheless, he did not limit his choices only to the village granaries. He felt that they should be used in conjunction with the ever-normal granaries as well, and he was also responsive to the suggestion by Chao Pien, a provincial governor in Sung times, to mobilize the population for the construction of irrigation dikes and induce wealthy families to contribute grain to finance those projects to overcome the effects of drought. Yu expressed admiration in general for the practice of Sung governors in mobilizing people for wall, road, and dike construction, and tree planting as well during periods of famine, a Chinese version of the New Deal Public Works Administration and the South Korean New Village movement (*saemaŭl undong*).

Discounting the brief experiment with Chu Hsi's village granaries, these projects were combined with state grants and loans in the Sung dynasty to provide relief, but the free grants were insufficient to provide more than "a few handfuls" of rice, and the principal and interest charges on loans were so great that the peasants were again left destitute even after the fall harvest. Furthermore, the officials dunned the debtors endlessly or demanded that their relatives and neighbors pay their debts for them, whipping and beating them when they delayed payment, and in the end these brutal methods failed and the reserve system was depleted. Only people with personal connections with relief clerks or village headmen had a chance to obtain a loan, another of the problems that would have been solved by the village granary system.

Nonetheless, the Sung methods of finding all the indigent deserving of free relief grants – the old, the weak, the sick, and unsupported women – and recruiting the starving for dike and irrigation construction at wages paid by the government authorities would solve the problem of relief support by paying wages and reducing the need for grants or loans. And if irrigation projects were not needed, the government could put people to work on other kinds of projects.

> Since the people will be recruited for work and go themselves [to the job], there will be no feelings of resentment. If the wages we pay them for their work are sufficient, they will have enough to provide for the elderly and the young. Thus many people will come to work and the benefits will be extended over a wide area. Irrigation facilities will be promoted everywhere so that there will never again be any harm from famine. The people will not be lacking food to eat, the state will not be short of tax revenues, and we will be able to rely on this for thousands and tens of thousands of years. This system would be as far from the present system [of state loans at interest] as heaven is from earth.

To rephrase this program in twentieth-century terms, workfare was preferable not only to loans at interest, but to welfare as well because it would maintain the morale of the people, increase income and tax revenues, and receive the material benefit of the work done.[42]

Policy for Korea

Replacement of Hwanja with Ever-Normal Granaries. Yu called for the adoption of a policy identical to the program of the conservative opponents of Wang An-shih's green-shoots loan system: abolition of the present *hwanja* grain loan operations, the establishment of ever-normal granaries (Sangp'yŏngch'ang) in every prefecture and district in the country, and the transfer of current *hwanja* funds currently located in the yamen of the district magistrates to the ever-normal granaries. The ever-normal granaries would use rice, grain, cloth, cash, and silver as items for the purchase or sale of goods to stabilize market prices. Prices would be stabilized either by selling or buying goods at a price one-third higher or lower than the market price. Forced loans would be prohibited and violators punished. Every decision for purchasing or selling by the ever-normal granaries would have to be approved by the Ministry of Taxation or state councilors in the capital and submitted for royal approval. In the provinces, district magistrates would have to obtain permission from the provincial governor, and the provincial governors would be required to submit annual reports of their decisions to the Ministry of Taxation. Ever-normal granaries would also be established by governors, provincial army and navy commanders.[43]

Unlike Ssu-ma Kuang of the Sung, who attacked official loans because they were a means of repressing the rich (by forcing loans on them) in the name of welfare for the poor, Yu did not talk about the plight of the rich and focused completely on the plight of the poor under the government-administered *hwanja* grain loans. He acknowledged that some believed that *hwanja* loans were essential to "save the people from poverty" and that some method was necessary to provide this function, but he argued that the ever-normal system would perform that function without the adverse side-effects of loans. Echoing the conservative critics of Wang An-shih, he claimed that loans and the requirement of repayment only converted civil debts into criminal action, and failure to repay loans on time led not only to persistent dunning for repayment by clerks and runners, but to the arrest, beating, and imprisonment of debtors. Sensing the chance for greater profits, officials in the districts would force loans on the people, and if the reluctant debtors chose to flee the district rather than repay, the officials would simply declare their neighbors and relatives liable for the debt (a practice that had already become endemic in the collection of unpaid military cloth support taxes). The existence of loans would, in short, trigger a number of mechanisms for corruption: collusion between clerks and citizens, bribes and payoffs, and arbitrary exploitation by government functionaries:

> So many evils will arise that you will not be able to describe them all, so much so that the prisoners will fill the jails, and whippings and beatings will take place everywhere. It will only lure people into the net [of criminal action] without doing anything to restore the original purpose of benefiting the people. . . . How could this be a good method? How could this have been the intention of the father-and-mother of the people [the king]?[44]

Yu's exposition of the evils of the *hwanja* system was certainly not innovative because it echoed the standard complaints of the conservative opponents of Wang An-shih in eleventh-century China. While some of Wang's conservative critics like Ssu-ma Kuang explicitly defended the interests of the landlords and the rich and attacked the purpose of the expansive, reformist state for intervening in private affairs in the name of welfare for the poor, there was also a general doubt among idealistic reformers as well as conservatives about the capacity of the bureaucratic state for honesty, probity, and justice in the administration of the law.

The capacity of the bureaucratic state for good or evil need not be regarded as fixed and static because it worked well in some periods and badly in others, and the pattern of behavior generally corresponded to the phase of the dynastic cycle. After the establishment of a dynasty when morale was high, the orders of the king were respected, the bureaucracy was staffed with a new complement of officials, and corruption was not a major issue, but in a period of decline officials were demoralized and prone to further their own fortunes at public expense. Yu Hyŏngwŏn was obviously living in an age when the morality of the officials and clerks could not be trusted, and unfortunately, that mood persisted and became progressively worse in the nineteenth century.

Yu believed that loans to the poor became a tool of oppression in the hands of the district officials because of the nature and spirit of the bureaucracy, certainly in his own time, and that the ever-normal granary system could not be used by officials to punish innocent peasants because it was only involved in the purchase and sale of goods to stabilize market prices. The ever-normal system did not jeopardize ordinary people by making them liable for criminal action as the failure to repay a government loan obviously did.

> If you [adopt] the ever-normal system, then in bumper crop years no harm is done to agriculture [the peasant producers who will benefit from an artificial increase in the price of grain], and when there is famine, no injury is done to the people [the consumers who will benefit from an artificial reduction of the price of grain]. Those above and below are benefited, and there are no evil effects to private or public [interests]. What is good about this law is nothing more than this.
>
> Since the grain that is received year after year [by the officials] in the *hwanja* loan system is basically grain that the families of the people should be saving [on their own], [that grain] no longer represents a surplus to be used to provide a supplement for food during a crop failure. I only see that the system harasses the people, eats into their property, and provides opportunities to the clerks for corruption. It truly provides no benefit either to public or private [interests]. Its disadvantages are clear, but if people still have doubts about whether it should be abolished, it is only because they have become used to what is now an established custom and cannot see what is right before their eyes.[45]

Not only were *hwanja* state loans corrupt, but there was no precedent for their existence in Chinese antiquity and there was no record, to his knowledge, of their use in the Liao-tung area of Manchuria, "and yet the people all had enough, enjoyed prosperous times, and were saved from starvation [during famine]." For that matter, the *hwanja* loans had never been used in Seoul and should be kept out at all costs because it would only add extra work for the capital bureaus and draw the capital population into the snares of criminal violations.[46]

Yu indicated that some people raised objections to his appeal to abolish the *hwanja* loans altogether because it would strip the local districts of funds that had to be used for military costs and official expenses. Yu retorted that since the funds for the *hwanja* system came from the portion of national taxes kept on reserve in the magistrate's yamen (the *yuse*), they were already derived from the people to begin with, and there was no necessity to segregate a portion of that reserve under the title of *hwanja* loans. The magistrates should be able to use those reserves for military expenses without being limited by the *hwanja* allocation. In fact, in current practice magistrates even loaned out grain that was supposed to be stored for military provisions anyway, leaving them without resources to pay military costs. The reserve funds of the magistrates should be used to pay for all official expenses, civil as well as military.[47]

Yu conceded, however, that if a famine occurred, officials might be forced to grant loans to peasants even after the *hwanja* system was abolished, but at least it would only be a temporary measure, and it would not continue on a regular, annual basis as an "unlimited evil." Furthermore, magistrates might adopt a version of the workfare system either to take funds from the ever-normal system and use it to hire workers without calling it charity, or to rent land to people.

Village Granary System. Yu did not intend that the *hwanja* system be replaced by the ever-normal system alone but by the adoption of Chu Hsi's village granary system as well.[48] The village granary system would take loans out of the hands of officials and put them under the control of the village elders, and eventually interest charges would be ended after initial capitalization was repaid and a loan fund for the future was accumulated.

The background material that Yu provided prior to expounding his own plan for a village granary was derived exclusively from Chinese sources. Even though he did use Korean materials with regard to other institutions, he neglected to mention Yulgok's regulations for a village granary drawn up in 1577 for the town of Haeju in Hwanghae province, even though Yu later cited Yulgok's statements about the organization and rules for community compacts (*hyangyak*). This was rather a blatant omission since Yulgok's Haeju village granary was tied together with the Haeju community compact and also incorporated many of the norms of the compact in its own regulations.

Yulgok's rules also called for relief loans to poor peasants at a 20 percent rate of interest (2 *toe* per *mal* of grain loaned), or 30 percent if the granary was short of grain, but forbade loans to any persons not members of the village granary association. Since membership in that association required conformity to the extensive list of rules of etiquette and behavior, Yulgok wanted to enforce the adoption of Confucian behavior by eliminating recalcitrants from the local relief system. He did allow loans to be granted to a close relative of a member or a slave (*nobok*) who had not yet joined the granary association, but if they failed to repay, the members would have to repay the loan in his place.

Loans were dispensed three times a month beginning on the first day of the first month, and repayments would begin on the eleventh day of the ninth month through the twenty-first day of the first month of the next year. Every ten families would choose a ten-family head (T'ongju) to supervise repayments. Any borrower who failed to repay the loan after the eleventh month would suffer first-degree punishment (see section on Yulgok's village granary regulations in chapter 19), and the ten-family head would receive third-degree punishment. If the borrower failed to repay by the twelfth month, he would be expelled from the granary association, and the head's punishment would be raised to the first degree. Failure to repay the full amount of the loan would also be punished according to the degree of the shortage. If the granary was short of funds, the members had to contribute 10 *mal* of grain (5 *mal* for lowborn people).[49]

Yu provided that the government should order the establishment of "village" granaries (*sach'ang*) but not in the natural village; rather in each *hyang* (the current *myŏn*), the informal subdistrict (or county) of several administrative villages (each consisting in turn of a number of natural villages) that had no staff of regular officials. The establishment of these village granaries was to be done entirely on a voluntary basis with government help. Volunteers would have to petition the district magistrate, who would then lend rice from his ever-normal granary to them as the initial capital and allow twelve years for repayment after the granary had accumulated the amount from its interest charges. Wealthy benefactors would also be allowed to finance the village granary with their own resources, and the granary administrators would then repay him from the interest received.

All other regulations for the operation of the village granary would simply follow those of Chu Hsi's *she-ts'ang* program except for minor variations to fit local circumstances. The magistrate would grant 1 *kyŏng* of land (under Yu's land distribution system) to the granary as a site, and provide labor service if a new granary has to be built. The granary would have an administration building that would also serve the *hyang* as a lecture hall. The magistrate would exempt the officials chosen by the local communities to run the granary from taxes and military service and three peasants to serve as granary guards from military support taxes, but he would not force any community to establish a village granary against its will, nor would he interfere in any of its operations. The regulations for the village granary system would be incorporated with rules for the conduct of the community compact (*hyangyak*) system since both activities were to be conducted at the *hyang* (county or *myŏn*) level.

Some people objected to Yu that many areas might not be willing to establish village granaries, or if they were, they might run them carelessly or abandon them, but Yu was certain that if the court ordered the magistrates to give full assistance to them, there would be no difficulty in getting people to respond. If the granary then were neglected or abandoned because of the incompetence of its administrators, "it would be because of the evils of the times, not the fault of the law." Or if the granary were not kept in good repair, the ordinary people would still not suffer the beatings and punishments that accompanied the loans of the *hwanja* system. People would remain free from harm and left alone to till the fields, and they would always be able to accumulate emergency reserves by their own savings. Yu confirmed that he had derived his policy of establishing ever-normal and righteous granaries as the perfect antidote for the *hwanja* system from the wisdom of the classic tradition. "It was the ancients who said that they knew that this was the best method; it only depends on our taking this up and putting it into practice."[50]

Workfare and Other Methods of Relief. Yu did not confine his discussion of the methods of providing relief solely to the ever-normal and village granary systems because classical wisdom had provided a number of standard methods to be used in any famine or food crisis. The *Rites of Chou* listed twelve measures to take in a famine that included distribution of existing reserves, reduction of taxes, labor service, and expenditures for mourning rites, ceremonies, funerals, and marriages, relaxation of penalties for criminal acts committed under distress, and prohibitions against using the resources of certain forests, rivers, and waterways. The commentary on the *Spring and Autumn Annals* by Hu An-kuo of the early twelfth-century Northern Sung dynasty (the *Hu-shih Ch'un-ch'iu chüan*) also suggested transferring grain to areas of famine, moving the population, selling off surpluses, and initiating public works projects for the unemployed.[51]

Yu believed that workfare would be preferable to loans to provide relief because the indigent peasants would not have the burden of repayment to make in difficult times. Magistrates might take funds from the ever-normal system and use it to hire workers without calling it charity, or central agencies of the government might hire the starving to work in public works projects. Some parties objected to Yu's workfare program because it lacked the kind of ancient precedent that existed for other remedies like exemptions from taxation and labor service during a famine, but Yu responded that the method had in fact been used by previous kings (as Hu An-kuo's commentary above revealed), and would kill two birds with one stone by obtaining some concrete benefit from providing relief.[52]

Ultimately, however, Yu felt that the solution to relief from famine derived from the general spirit among the population. If a ruler had been able to govern well, he would create a spirit of harmony among the people that would overcome the perversity of some individuals and create a general willingness to obey the ruler's laws and directions and purify their habits and customs. The people would diligently engage in their agricultural tasks, be frugal in their expenditures, and save funds for the future. The government would also be frugal and save as well, and when famine occurred and relief was needed, "everyone would put their minds to relief and be able to save the population [from starvation]." The methods delineated by the *Rites of Chou* and Hu An-kuo's commentary on *The Spring and Autumn Annals* were all useful, but "one has to be sincere in extending them to the times, for only then can you really extend benefits to the people."[53]

The methods Yu advocated to provide relief in times of famine were not the product of original or creative inspiration or the application of superior reason to a complex problem because they were all based on the ever-normal loans devised first by Li K'uei in the Chou dynasty and the village granaries of Chu Hsi in the Sung dynasty. Furthermore, the methods used for relief, like any other problem in government, was less important than the general aura of governance, which could only be established by inculcation of fundamental and eternal Confucian moral principles.

Relief and Loans to the Reform of 1867

Since the history of the *hwanja* loan system has been covered elsewhere, only the crucial features of that story need be summarized here. Far from a successful reform of the *hwanja* system, the problems associated with it increased over the years. The interest charged on loans were largely expropriated by the government for expenditures and not used to refund the reserve for loans, and centralized control over the system was abandoned altogether as individual capital agencies, district magistrates, and provincial military garrison commanders lent out their reserves at will to finance their needs through interest charges. The total volume of loans increased astronomically by the end of the eighteenth century, but the peasants were unable to repay their loans and interest. The unrepaid loans accumulated on the books as the agencies of government continued to collect interest on old loans, converting the whole system into an extra, permanent tax on the poorest segment of the population. Eventually, the oppression of the *hwanja* official loans became one of the main causes of the Imsul rebellion of 1862, let alone the Hong Kyŏngnae rebellion of 1812.

The rebellion delivered a major shock to the government and provided impetus for reform. In 1862 Hŏ Pu proposed the plan Yu Hyŏngwŏn had advocated in the mid-seventeenth century: the replacement of official loans at interest by the ever-normal and village granary systems. Although he never cited the source for his plan, it is quite likely that it was based on Yu's work. Hŏ's proposal, however, was opposed by officials who felt that some portion of official loans at interest had to be retained to provide revenues.

In the fall of 1862 the Reform Bureau proposed a plan that would have adopted several features of Yu's plan. Bad debts were to be written off the books, and those debts that could be repaid would be collected to refinance official relief loans at a more modest level. Interest on loans would no longer be used for ordinary government expenditures, and revenues lost by this measure would be supplemented by surtax on the land tax and a government takeover of land previously under the control of palace estates owned by princes and princesses. The Reform Bureau rejected the adoption of Chu Hsi's village granaries, which were supposed to be organized in conjunction with village *pao-chia* mutual-guarantee organizations and the community compact (*hsiang-yüeh*; *hyangyak* in Korean) systems, because it was not deemed possible to create or recreate these institutions under present conditions. After others opposed any drastic reduction of government loans because the interest was essential for government finance, King Ch'ŏlchong decided not to adopt the Reform Bureau's plan and simply wrote off all bad debts and set limits for loans, but he hoped that the repayment of good loans could still provide some revenue.

By 1866 this last hope proved impossible and the government finally had to recognize that the records of most outstanding loans were worthless, and since it had not abolished the system of loans at interest, it realized it had to refund the system with new capital taken from tax revenues. When tax revenues were not sufficient to bear this burden, in 1867 the government ordered that cash funds from the first minting of multiple-denomination cash in the dynasty's history, the 100-cash, be used to refund the grain loan accounts. Simultaneously, the Ministry of Taxation, undoubtedly at the urging of the Taewongun, King Kojong's father, adopted the village granary system, but simply as a means of eliminating corruption by magistrates and clerks and guaranteeing honesty in the collection of interest for the central government, not to maintain the sanctity of the loan fund itself. And the debts of any borrowers who absconded to avoid repayment would then be reallocated among neighbors of the debtor, one of the chief evils of the *hwanja* system that reformers had long been trying to eliminate. Otherwise, many of the regulations of Chu's Hsi's village granary system that Yu Hyŏngwŏn had advocated were adopted in law.[54]

Yu's ideas about reform of the *hwanja* official loan system were neglected for two centuries, but when reform was finally attempted after the shock sustained by the Imsul rebellion, those ideas became the cornerstone of the most radical proposals made between 1862 and 1867. Since these proposals were based on the hoary traditions of Li K'uei's ever-normal system of the Chou and Chu Hsi's village granary system of the Sung, one could hardly argue that they represented the fruition of modern thought on the problems of relief and credit. But even in the midst of a tide of reform sponsored primarily by the Taewongun, the government was not ready or willing to abandon the *hwanja* loans. They were regarded as indispensable to government finance because of a regressive, unfair, and inadequate agrarian tax base without any major revenues from modern business and industry. When the Taewongun oversaw the adoption of Chu Hsi's village granary system, he distorted its original purpose by converting it to a means for a more efficient method of tax collection rather than for stabilizing relief for the peasantry.

Conclusion

Of the four problems of local administration mentioned in the introduction to this chapter, Yu sought to eliminate discrepancies in the size and tax distribution of individual districts by restructuring the hierarchy of local districts and military garrisons to make local districts at each stage of the hierarchy of administration more uniform in size and population. He wanted to create a stronger provincial administration by advocating that the provincial governor be settled with his family in the provincial seat for relatively long terms of office so that he could become familiar with provincial affairs and gain control over them. At the same time he hoped to control costs by trimming down the staff of assistants of both governors and provincial military commanders. To eliminate the endemic corruption of unsalaried clerks and runners, he would have provided them with standard salaries paid by the state, and to alleviate the burdens on women slaves employed as state workers, he would have exempted them from local service altogether to save them from male domination as well as official exploitation.

The most complex issue, however, was the distribution of power between the central bureaucracy and its agents – the magistrates and their clerks – and the local community. This issue had been discussed in the Chinese literature for two millennia, but no matter which solution was tried, problems continued nonetheless. Since Yu was living in a period when district magistrates controlled the administration of relief, credit, loans, and price stabilization as well as tax collection and labor service, he concluded that the fault derived from excessive reliance on the magistrate. He preferred Chinese institutions that shifted the locus of power from the magistrate to the local community, dominated, of course, by local leaders. He, therefore, insisted on that kind of solution for the conduct of agencies for price stabilization, credit, and relief to the peasantry.

Nonetheless, his solution was not motivated by a commitment to the defense of local – let alone individual – freedoms or rights against the intrusive and oppressive power of bureaucracy, but rather a distrust of distant and corruptible bureaucrats who could not be trusted to protect local people against the distorted application of central power. In working out the rules for local agencies, whether relief or lending institutions, for example, he provided for stiff penalties for violation of his regulations. In other words, the state would be brought in to administer punishment against those violations, whether perpetrated by officials and clerks on one side, or members of the public and the peasantry on the other. As we will see in the next chapter, his concept for local government was also informed by a commitment to tightly knit associations for mutual surveillance as well as mutual aid. Yu did not reject bureaucracy in principle, but he mistrusted it; he favored local control, but not wanton liberalism or freedom from authority. His local autonomy would remain collective and benign, but nonetheless coercive.

CHAPTER 19

The Community Compact System (Hyangyak)

The Reform Bureau of 1862 had objected to adopting Chu Hsi's village granary system because it was too closely connected with the kind of local organization associated with the community compact system, and since that system did not exist in Korea at that time, it would be too difficult to create it in conjunction with the village granaries. The Reform Bureau's description of the relationship between the two institutions was correct. Yu did favor administration of village granaries by local communities because he felt that local control would eliminate bureaucratic corruption and guarantee honest administration, but honest administration was not his only reason for admiring community compacts.

The attempt to create an additional level of organization beneath the local administrator or district magistrate goes all the way back to the early Chou dynasty in Yu's account. Since the ruler of the state in the capital could not always be sure that the district magistrate was faithfully carrying out his orders, maintaining law and order, and assessing taxes equitably, he sought to enlist men in the villages, usually the prominent members of the villages, to act as spies or agents to watch the magistrate and keep him in check. If, however, the local elite was too powerful, the magistrate would find it impossible to carry out the ruler's will, let alone his own desires, and the ruler might find it necessary to reverse the balance of power.

Institutions of local self-government were also established as agencies of mutual surveillance to mobilize the local population to take the place of what otherwise would be an excessively massive and costly apparatus of control. But since villagers might not be overjoyed with spying on their neighbors and reporting malfeasants to the authorities, the state might have to step in and superimpose a mutual surveillance system by fiat on the natural village. The social harmony of village life would have been rapidly ruptured whenever a villager's report of a putative aberrant act was followed up by the bastinado of the magistrate's lictors. To be sure, such mutual surveillance societies were also to be devoted to mutual aid and the mutual inculcation of moral norms and values, but the line between instruction and indoctrination was paper thin in the Confucian tradition.

Were village compacts an attempt to affirm the communal spirit of the local village and protect it against the oppressive power of the magistrate, or was it only a poorly disguised system for penetrating the village to reduce it to total obedience to the state? Was the community compact to be run by the moral elite of the community, which in Korea meant the local yangban, larger landlords, or slaveholders? Was the purpose of moral exhortation designed to affirm the norms of the village, or to replace them with foreign Neo-Confucian values superimposed from the top?

LOCAL SELF-GOVERNMENT IN CHINA

Yu took his model for local control from a Chinese institution described first in the *Rites of Chou* and carried on intermittently through the Sung dynasty. The term he used for local control, *hyangdang*, referred to two of the six hierarchical units of local organization described in the *Rites of Chou*, supposedly for the early Chou period at the beginning of the first millennium B.C. The system of local control was not uniform for the whole country, as described in the *Rites of Chou*, since Chou territory was supposedly laid out in very regular fashion according to the distance of the territory from the capital or royal domain. The organizational units mentioned above were specific to an area referred to as the six *hsiang*, which were located just outside the capital and its suburbs to a point 100 *li* from the capital. These *hsiang* were organized on the basis of a basic, five-family unit called the *pi*, and each succeeding unit increased by multiples of five, so that the *hsiang*, or *hyang* in Korean, was the highest and largest, consisting of 12,500 families, and the *tang* (the *dang* of *hyangdang* in Korean) consisted of 500 families. Each one of the five units was headed by a man of rank and status. The capital and urban areas, and rural areas outside the six *hsiang*, were organized in similar fashion but with different titles.

The task of this local organization was to supervise the triennial census of population and property (the *ta-pi*), and the head official of each unit was to administer all government instructions and edicts handed down from superior units.[1] Note also that the hierarchy of units were based on man-made mathematical proportions, not on the far less tidy pattern of natural villages, topographical features, or market systems. It represented a bureaucratic imposition of a regular, ideal pattern over the irregular and actual pattern of human clusters.

Yu traced the history of this system of local control in later periods as well. Kuan-chung (d. 645 B.C.), the important minister of Duke Huan of the state of Ch'i, was a statesman devoted to the development of economic wealth and military strength. He was the strategist who helped the duke achieved hegemony over an alliance of feudatories in central China against the southern league led by the state of Ch'u, and was also interested in the formation of groups of five families within the suburbs of the capital and a different organization of five-family units in the countryside to increase central control over the population and maximize the strength of Ch'i in its competition with other feudal states. He was primarily concerned about peasants running away from their villages to escape taxes and service, and he believed that a tight, organizational network throughout the country would leave no place for these tax-and service-evaders to escape. The official of each unit also had to supervise military as well as population registration and taxation.[2]

Since this mode of local control was not maintained everywhere in China in the late Chou, Shang Yang (Lord Shang) of the state of Ch'in also revived this system of local control to strengthen Ch'in, preparing it for its eventual conquest of China in the late third century B.C. Although known for his adherence to the principles of Legalist philosophy, Shang Yang extracted this model from earlier Chinese history, and the tradition was later picked up in the post-Ch'in age of bureaucracy by Confucian statecraft thinkers to remedy the decline in local government that had arisen because of general disorder and uncontrolled taxation of peasants.

The Han dynasty regime carried over from the Ch'in state not only the *chün-hsien* (larger commanderies and smaller districts) system of centralized organization of local areas, but also the organization of subdistrict units called *ting* or watchtowers every ten *li* in distance, and a higher unit, called *hsiang*, which in this instance consisted of ten *ting*. The *hsiang* had three officials (the *san-lao* or Three Elders) who administered education, lawsuits and tax collection, and police duties, respectively. The *san-lao* were selected from men in the area who were at least fifty years of age and had a reputation for good behavior. They worked closely with the regular officials and were granted exemption from labor and military service.[3]

In other words, the tightly organized hierarchy of units for local control traced its origins back to the early Chou (or at least what was described in the *Rites of Chou*), the state of Ch'i in the seventh century B.C., and the state of Ch'in in the late Chou, and it was then transferred by the Han dynasty into the age of centralized bureaucratic rule. Although this system was supposedly born in an age of decentralized feudalism, it was obviously designed as a means of increasing the control of the center over the periphery and was found useful in the development of the centralized state. The control of areas beneath the lowest district magistrate, however, was never brought fully into the regular bureaucracy, and after the tight organization described above weakened, local control was left in the hands of local men of influence.

After the Later Han dynasty fell at the beginning of the third century A.D. and north China was taken over by non-Chinese people from the north, local aristocrats played a more dominant role in both local and central government. The movement to recreate greater central control was given impetus by reforms of the Northern Wei state in the late fifth century.

Since census registration and tax collection had grown lax because too many families were "hiding" their existence by registering as members of supposedly large families, in 486 Li Chung proposed a new system of organization called the Three Chiefs (*San-chang*), the head officials of three hierarchical units at the subdistrict level, based on the basic five-family unit. The highest unit was to be the *hsiang*, consisting of 125 families, and headed by a *hsiang-cheng* (*hyangjŏng* in Korean). The chief of each of the three units were chosen from eminent members of the community and exempted from labor service, given a three-year trial period of office and promoted if they did well.

Since some officials opposed the measure because it would be too radical a reform, Li Chung argued that reform was always difficult because the people never understood its purpose even though the plan would benefit them. But if it were implemented when a census was being taken or when taxes were collected after the harvest, the government could win popular support for the measure because the peasants would see that the tighter organization would result in the registration of all families who had hidden their status from the tax collector, more equitable distribution of taxation, and reduction of tax rates to individual families. Yu Hyŏngwŏn commented on Li's plan that even though the rich and powerful were discomfited by the *san-chang* system, "yet after a short time taxes were made more equitable and were reduced, and those above and below were put at ease."[4] Yu, in other words, agreed that a mutual surveillance organization superimposed on the village by the central bureaucracy was justifiable if it resulted in greater equity in the distribution of taxes, even if the short-sighted village inhabitants could not appreciate its benefits.

In the late sixth century Emperor Wen of the Sui dynasty again restored a mutual-surveillance system based on earlier modes of organization based on Su Wei's proposal for a 500-family *hsiang*. Emperor Wen adopted the plan, but a decade later he abolished it when he received reports that the *hsiang-cheng* were taking bribes and the people disliked the institution. In short, mutual surveillance organizations were unpopular with the villagers because they were oppressive.

The T'ang dynasty regime of the seventh century adopted a version of the mutual-responsibility network similar to the Sui, and Yu Hyŏngwŏn used it as the basis for his model for the Chosŏn dynasty in the seventeenth century. The basic unit consisted of the basic four-family *lin*, the sixteen-family *pao* (four *lin*), the hundred-family *li*, and the five-hundred-family *hsiang*. The chief of the *li*, the Li-cheng, was in charge of taking the census, encouraging agriculture and sericulture, investigating criminal acts, and "pressing the people to pay their taxes and perform labor service." The cities were divided into wards (*pang*), each headed by a ward chief (Pang-cheng) who kept the keys to the ward gates and was in charge of police duties and public morals. Villages (*ts'un*) in the countryside were placed under the jurisdiction of the village chief (Ts'un-cheng). The Li-cheng and other officials of this mutual-surveillance network were selected by the district magistrate from commoners and unemployed officials lower than the fifth rank.[5]

Yu cut off his treatment of the history of mutual-surveillance institutions in

China at this point, leaving out any consideration of the *pao-chia* system established by Emperor Shen-tsung in the Sung dynasty in 1070.[6]

Nonetheless, the key element in Yu's plan for the construction of a system of local control was to be his version of the community compact (*hyangyak*), based primarily on two of Chu Hsi's works. The first was Chu's emendation in the twelfth century of a text presumably written by Lü Ta-chün in 1076 called the *Lü-Family Community Compact*, which he designed to be used for the self-cultivation of individuals. The second was his prescription of local government regulations for the district of Chang-chou.[7]

COMMUNITY COMPACTS IN KOREA

The Yuhyangso of the Early Chosŏn Dynasty

Yu did not discuss the institutional history of community compacts in Korea, only references to the institution in the writings of T'oegye, Yulgok, and Cho Hŏn. Tabana Tameo in his recent study of Korean community compacts pursued the same strategy even though he did mention on occasion that in certain cases Korean founders of community compacts modeled them more on existing rules and regulations of existing local self-government organizations than on the *Lü-Family Community Compact* of Sung China.

Tagawa Kōzō, however, has shown that local self-government bodies called Yuhyangso were organized primarily by the local elite (sometimes referred to as *p'umgwan*, or men holding office rank, even though Song June-ho would not classify them as members of the elite) listed in the local yangban register (*hyang'an*) in the countryside. The district was also represented in the capital by Kyŏngjaeso, or the capital headquarters, headed by a government official who came from the district. He found that many of the regulations of the Yuhyangso, called the *hyanggyu*, contained the same moral aspirations and penalties for misconduct as the community compact (*hyangyak*) regulations, Chosŏn dynasty codes, and the Ming code adopted for criminal matters in the Chosŏn period.[8]

At the beginning of the Chosŏn dynasty the Yuhyangso were carried over from the Koryŏ dynasty, associations formed spontaneously by local leaders, men with official rank or local scholars (*yuhyang p'umgwan, hyangjungji saryu*), who were either members of the local elite called *hyangni* or retired officials (*chŏnham*). The *hyangni* were families who provided district clerks to local government, some of whom had also received official sinecures (*ch'ŏmsŏlchik*). They were also appointed to district magistrate's posts, but in the Chosŏn period King T'aejo tried to weaken this local gentry in 1397 by assigning them to duty in the capital guards, but he was afraid to take their sinecures away from them and many of them continued to stay in their home villages where they interfered with the magistrate's control of the population. King T'aejong decided to abolish the Yuhyangso in 1406 to curtail their local influence.

Because some magistrates began to abuse their power, in 1417 the government authorized the creation of a local expert (Sinmyŏngsaek) for each magistrate, supposedly to provide him with advice on local policy, but in reality to prevent magisterial abuse. T'aejong, however, rescinded this order within the year because the Sinmyŏngsaek was exercising too much restraint on magistrates, and in 1420 King Sejong strengthened the magistrates' authority even more by prohibiting any local retired official or *hyangni* from impeaching a magistrate or provincial governor for any act of malfeasance except endangering state security or murder.

When the balance of power appeared to have shifted too greatly to the magistrates, Sejong reinstituted the Yuhyangso in 1428, but he did so by converting it into an agency of central rather than local power by requiring it to supervise local clerks and constrain any criticism of the magistrates by the local elite (*p'umgwan*). In the next few years, any unauthorized criticism of the magistrate or governor was punished by reducing the rank of the district, and officials of the central government in the capital were made heads of the Kyŏngjaeso in the capital to control appointments of the leaders of the Yuhyangso in the villages.

In 1431 Sejong reversed the ban on private suits against magistrates by local people, and King Sejo reconfirmed this policy after 1455. In addition, he dispatched secret censors (Ŏhaeng yusa) to investigate and impeach corrupt magistrates, and in 1467 he abolished the Yuhyangso for the second time, not because they limited the magistrate's power, but because one of them had tried to block a petition against a magistrate's malfeasance by a private individual! Sejo also believed that some of the Yuhyangso had cooperated with the rebellion of Yi Siae that year. As soon as he died, however, his work was undone in 1469 when the ban against private suits against magistrates was reinstituted.[9]

In short, the Yuhyangso as the locus of local self-government was subverted to represent the interests of the local elite against the magistrate or vice versa; it was certainly no bona fide guarantor of official honesty or defender of peasant welfare.

Local Non-Confucian Beliefs and Rituals

At the beginning of the dynasty communal groups also had their roots in native spiritual and ritual beliefs. Incense associations (*hyangdo*) associated with Buddhism were carried over from the previous Silla and Koryŏ periods, but in the late fourteenth and early fifteenth centuries their connection with Buddhism was lost because they were engaged primarily in worship of local deities and animistic spirits in mountains and trees, what the Neo-Confucians condemned as "lewd sacrifices" (*ŭmsa*). They also held meetings to conduct funerals, but because they did so in a festive and joyous spirit and offered wine in prayer to local spirits on behalf of the deceased, the Neo-Confucians were outraged. They regarded such behavior as an immoral desecration of a properly mournful and pious rite. The early fifteenth-century Neo-Confucians felt that a moral crusade was needed to settle people down and create a moral basis for social relations and spiritual values.[10]

Confucian Archery and Wine-Drinking Rites

Yi T'aejin has argued that the movement to revive the Yuhyangso in the late fifteenth century was led by the idealistic wing of the Neo-Confucians known as "the scholars of the forest" (*sarimp'a* or *sarim*) as part of their effort to cleanse the mores and morals of local communities by adopting Chinese institutions, including defining the village according to a set number of households, establishing village granaries, conducting the local wine-drinking and archery rituals, and replicating the Lü-Family community compact that Chu Hsi had advocated in the twelfth century. Yi has also argued throughout his work that the *sarimp'a* and the reform movement of Neo-Confucians was led by small and medium landowners, a popular thesis among other South Korean scholars as well, but it has not been demonstrated by solid empirical research and has been effectively refuted by John Duncan in his recent dissertation on the Koryŏ/Chosŏn transition.[11]

Chu Hsi's village granary (*sach'ang*), designed to take loans out of the control of magistrates and put them in the hands of the elite in the villages, was first advocated in 1440, tried out in thirteen villages in Taegu in Kyŏngsang Province in 1448, and expanded in 1450. The policy was supported by a number of officials and ex-officials committed to Neo-Confucian ideas, but they were either driven out of office or retired after King Sejo usurped King Tanjong's throne in 1455.[12]

In the late fifteenth century some local yangban led a movement to adopt the archery (*hyangsarye*) and wine-drinking rites (*hyang'ŭmjurye*) of the Chinese Chou dynasty. As described in the *Rites of Chou*, the local elite (*hsiang ta-fu*) would listen to a lecture from the Ssu-t'u (minister of education) about the laws of the state, transmit its contents to the head of the local area and select dates for the conduct of the local archery and wine-drinking rites. The archery rite was conducted as a means for rectifying the will, not simply as a contest of military skill, and the wine-drinking rite was conducted to demonstrate respect and deference to people because of their age, virtue, and moral talents. Chŏng Tojŏn supported the conduct of both these rites in the 1390s, and King Sejong included them in his *Five Ritual Ceremonies*.

Kim Chŏngjik, the renowned leader of the *sarimp'a* scholars and officials according to some current scholars, conducted these two rites during his stint as district magistrate of Sŏnsan in Kyŏngsang Province, and his followers praised the rites in King Sŏngjong's court. In a protracted debate that lasted from 1483 to 1488 Kim and his men also supported the restoration of the Yuhyangso because they thought it reproduced the essence of Chou principles of local self-government and was needed to purify the standards of district magistrates and restore harmony to family relations that had been disrupted by intrafamily strife over the inheritance of land and slaves, but they did not perceive it to be an agency for controlling local clerks, as King Sejong had. Eventually King Sŏngjong was persuaded in 1588 to restore the Yuhyangso to rectify the immoral standards of Chŏlla Province that had recently been plagued by a rash of thievery and piracy.[13]

In the early sixteenth century, a number of scholars in Chŏlla Province consistently advocated a reform program that included the performance of the archery and wine-drinking rites, the establishment of Lü-Family community compacts, and greater stress on moral education. The majority of Chŏlla students, however, refused to attend their schools and ridiculed them openly, and some conservative landlords and officials opposed the scholars and even supported the toleration of animistic worship. Was this only a vestige of late Koryŏ cultural barbarism that still infected the minds of the backward villagers of the southwest, or was it a legitimate defense of native beliefs and traditions opposed to the imposition of a new ideology by a narrow intellectual elite?[14]

The Yuhyangso then conducted the archery and wine-drinking rites in a building called Local Archery Hall (Hyangsadang), many of which were built in Kyŏngsang Province, but only two in Chŏlla. Those who attended the rites were seated by age and pledged allegiance to the four principles contained in the Lü-Family compact, and any member who violated rules of moral behavior, criticized the central government, or demeaned the district magistrate was expelled from the Yuhyangso.

The Conflict between Confucian Moralists and Realists

According to Yi T'aejin's analysis, a rivalry developed between the established bureaucrats, merit subjects, and consort relatives of queens (the so-called *hun'gup'a*) and the *sarimp'a* or rural, Neo-Confucian, idealistic scholars for control of the Yuhyangso. By 1492 the criticism by the moralistic reformers of the established bureaucrats reached new heights of vituperation, but what Yi T'aejin has decribed as a confrontation between the *sarimp'a* and the *hung'up'a* Edward Wagner has reinterpreted as a contest between the king and young officials in the Censorate over the limits of legitimate remonstrance and the locus of political authority in the Korean political system.[15]

Nevertheless, Yi T'aejin performed the valuable service of showing how the idea of moral education through self-governing communities, village granaries, and local archery and wine-drinking rites had been thoroughly incorporated into the thought of Kim Chongjik and his disciples in the late fifteenth century, and was not simply the discovery of Chu Hsi's emendation of the *Lü-Family Community Compact* at the beginning of the sixteenth century.

Cho Kwangjo: The Reaction against Community Compacts

During the reign of King Chungjong at the beginning of the sixteenth century, several officials laid the ground for community compacts by their general concern over a number of natural disturbances and murders, which they interpreted as Heaven's revenge for the immoral standards of the times. The king responded in 1511 by publishing a text for moral education, the *Samgang haengsil* (*Exemplars of the Three Moral Relationships*), and discussed resuming the local wine-drinking ritual as a means of promoting rural harmony.

In 1516 he also supported the proposal of the governor of Kyŏngsang Province, Kim An'guk, to publish the *Sohak* (*The Small Learning*) a moral text favored by Chu Hsi and later Kwŏn Kŭn of the early Chosŏn dynasty, and rediscovered in the 1470s by some literati who formed *Sŏhak* clubs (*kye*). It was designed for children from ages of eight to fifteen, but it also contained the text of the *Lü-Family Community Compact*. In 1517 Kim Inbŏm, a rural scholar from Hamyang in South Kyŏngsang Province and a student of another great admirer of the *Sohak*, Kim Koengp'il, recommended publication of the *Lü-Family Community Compact* for the first time in Chosŏn history, and in 1518 Kim An'guk persuaded King Chungjong to publish his edition of the text with his own annotation in Han'gul for the edification of commoners.

King Chungjong ignored the complaints of some officials that since the functions of the community compacts duplicated those of the Yuhyangso, the latter should be abolished. The community compacts spread from Kyŏngsang to Chŏlla Province, and even to districts in Ch'ungch'ŏng to the north, but magistrates were not that zealous in spreading their adoption, and villagers were only half-hearted in carrying out their regulations.

Cho Kwangjo became one of the leading spokesmen for community compacts and the *Sohak*, but he was not a blind advocate, and in 1519 he criticized the ones that had been established because they had not been organized voluntarily but forced on villages by provincial governors. King Chungjong was also annoyed because some compact associations had interfered with the judicial tasks of the Ministry of Punishments and the Seoul magistracy by punishing lawbreakers on their own. Chief State Councilor Chŏng Kwangp'il also argued that since the ancients only intended that community compacts be created in the countryside, the ones in the capital should be banned and the activities of the rest restricted only to funerals, but Chungjong did not approve.[16]

About a month later, the situation changed entirely when Chungjong carried out a purge (the *kimyo sahywa* of 1519) of Cho Kwangjo and his friends, including Kim An'guk, on charges of cliquism. Further executions took place when in 1521 An Tang's sons and friends were executed for allegedly plotting to assassinate the king and replace him with his half-brother.

In 1520 Sŏ Hu of the Inspector-General's office charged that the members of the local community compacts were disloyal to the throne, had been forced to join in the first place, and were recorded in the registers of good and bad deeds only because of favoritism or personal animosity. Since the Lü-Family compact had only been adopted by one village in Sung China, there was no reason to force everyone in the kingdom to join them. He blamed Cho Kwangjo, Kim Sik, and their friends for advertising themselves as true scholars of the Confucian

Way (*tohak*) when, in reality, they spent their time in slander and unwarranted criticism of officials of the court.

Cho Chin of the Censor-General's office demanded that community compacts be abolished because the compact rule for ranking people according to age overturned traditional status distinctions, especially by placing slaves in places of honor. In any case, King Chungjong, who had now lost his enthusiasm for the community compacts, noted that he had already banned the compacts from meeting and interfering in the administration of punishments, and had confined their activities to funerals and mutual aid in time of disaster.[17]

The assistant director of the National Academy, Yi Hang, also charged that a crowd of protestors, including many officials of compact associations, had physically obstructed the lictor responsible for beating Cho Kwangjo. In remarks redolent of Chinese Communist party regulars after the death of Mao Tse-tung about the damage and disgrace they had suffered at the hands of the Red Guard zealots during the Chinese Cultural Revolution, Yi Hang charged that Cho Kwangjo's reforms had stimulated an influx of young men into the bureaucracy, forced the removal of many older officials, and disrupted family relations and social order by opening the door to a rash of criticism by sons, younger brothers, and nephews against their fathers, elder brothers, and uncles. In other words, moralist zealots had done more to destroy moral standards than the most depraved members of society. Chief State Councilor Chŏng Kwangp'il also accused compact officials with harboring fugitives from the purge, Kim Sik and Ki Chun, on the grounds that they were only performing their moral duty to succor neighbors in trouble.

Chungjong agreed that they were only doing their moral duty, but Nam Kon and Yun Kwan accused them of treason, attacked the leaders of the community compacts, and recommended that only scholars (*saryu*) be appointed heads of community compacts in the future. Although King Chungjong did not ban the community compacts, they disappeared nonetheless, and in 1537 Chungjong admitted that the compacts had failed.[18]

Community Compacts and Economic Development

Yi T'aejin has also claimed that since Cho Kwangjo, Kim Chongjik and their colleagues and disciples (the *sarimp'a*) represented the interests of the medium and small landowners in the countryside, they were at once progressive supporters of economic development as well as conservative opponents of the departure of peasants from agriculture for the greater profits of commerce. Where Edward Wagner brought the idealistic, heroic, and virtuous image of the Cho Kwangjo clique down to earth by a sharp and judicious look at its politics, Yi T'aejin built upon the traditional assessment of Cho and his friends as moralistic and idealistic martyrs by adding a modern touch of class analysis and economic progress.[19] He thought that they advocated community compacts to expand irrigation but was not able to find direct evidence to prove it.[20]

Yi's economic argument, however, suffered from a serious contradiction because he admitted that the community compacts had never been designed to act as agents of economic progress. His very argument that they had to be viewed as a moral and stabilizing brake on the disruptive effects of economic progress to save the peasantry from the exploitation of the capital bureaucrats and the Yuhyangso was a clear admission that they favored Confucian moral standards far more than they did the expansion of wealth and the growth of the economy.

Revival of Moral Zeal after 1550

After King Myŏngjong came to the throne in 1545, concern about a general decline in moral standards and moral education revived, but there was not much support for a campaign to establish community compacts. In 1546 Chu Sebung said that community compacts had not been established in rural villages during Chungjong's reign, and Chief State Councilor Yun In'gyŏng opposed their restoration as a national policy because not enough men of high moral standards could be found to lead them. He suggested, however, that local communities be left to organize them spontaneously, and the Dowager Queen concurred.

After King Myŏngjong took over personal rule from the regency of the Grand Dowager in 1553, more scholars and officials than before were sympathetic to the moralistic reformism of Kim Chongjik and Cho Kwangjo. The scholar Sŏ Ŏm praised Cho and called for the adoption of both the *Sohak* and community compacts. In response to complaints in 1554 about recent acts of cannibalism and murder by family members during a recent famine, some officials called for rebuilding schools and emphasizing moral education in Neo-Confucian principles to counter popular fascination with such heterodox religious beliefs as Buddhism, geomancy, yin and yang cosmology, and shamanism.

In 1558 Yun Kae criticized students for abandoning the study of moral principles in favor of preparation for the civil service examinations, and he requested that the curriculum be changed to introduce the *Sohak* before the study of *The Great Learning*, or *The Doctrine of the Mean*, but Myŏngjong refused. In 1559 the scholar Pae Ikkyŏm praised Cho Kwangjo, cited his dedication to the *Sohak* and the *Lü-Family Community Compact*, and urged that the *Sohak* and *Karye* (Chu Hsi's *Family Rites*) be studied every day. In 1560 King Myŏngjong conceded that despite a few errors in office Cho was truly loyal to his king and country and not guilty of treason, and in 1564 T'oegye mourned Cho's death and regretted the neglect of the *Sohak* and the community compact system.

This upsurge of concern for moral education and community compacts reached its zenith when Myŏngjong granted permission for use of the *Sohak* in an education campaign, but Chief State Councilor Yun Wŏnhyŏng, who owed his supreme political position to his blood relationship to his sister, the dowager queen, opposed the request. Although he was forced out of office after the dowager died in 1565, the king took no action to restore the text for the rest of his reign.[21]

T'oegye's Community Compacts

Through the end of Myŏngjong's reign there was thus no progress made in pushing the central government to institute a policy of community compacts for the whole country, but certain individuals were able to do so in their own communities. While recuperating from illness in his home town in Yean district in Kyŏngsang Province in 1556, T'oegye wrote the preface to the articles of a community compact (the *hyangnip yakcho*) based on information supplied by Yi Hyŏnbo and his other friends in the community, and most of the articles in this compact were to be found either in Ming or Korean statute law, or in the provisions of earlier local community organizations. Thus, while community compacts begun in the early sixteenth century were based on the *Lü-Family Community Compact* and Chu Hsi's emendation of it, the principles of local self-government organization and moral rectitude were not confined to one specific institution created in the Sung dynasty, but to the broader traditions and long history of politics and morality in the Chinese experience.

T'oegye's introduction to these articles became an important source for reformers and was quoted extensively by Yu Hyŏngwŏn. Contrary to the argument of Yi T'aejin, however, that T'oegye represented the finest product of the *sarimp'a* movement and presumably should have opposed the Yuhyangso because they were all controlled by capital bureaucrats and relatives of queens, T'oegye asserted that the Yuhyangso performed the same function that the *hsiang ta-fu* did in Chou times, of promoting moral standards and maintaining surveillance over immoral and illegal acts to benefit the nation as a whole. He claimed that the Yuhyangso would succeed in preventing fighting, defending the weak against the strong, and obtaining respect for moral standards if the right men could be found to run them. T'oegye was willing to use the existing structure of local self-government as the locus for moral education without insisting that new institutions called community compacts had to be created independently.

His draft articles called for obedience and respect for the head of the local association as well as punishment for any violations by them of law or moral standards. He and his colleagues in Yean were probably seeking to correct what had happened in Chŏnju in Chŏlla Province in 1546 when a gang of local magnates and official rankholders invaded the assistant governor's (P'an'gwan, who doubled as magistrate of the town) office and wrecked the place, and the local Yuhyangso failed to take any punitive action. In other words, T'oegye sought to make the Yuhyangso a more reliable upholder of law and moral order than it currently was.

Although T'oegye criticized the Lü-Family compact because it emphasized punishment for misdeeds rather than encouragement for the cultivation of virtue, his own set of penalties for violations of moral standards read more like a penal code than a text for moral instruction. The compact prescribed that compact association members might correct other members of the community secretly if their misdeeds were minor, but they had to admonish them publicly at the compact meeting for major transgressions. If the violator failed to correct his ways, the compact secretary (Chigwŏl) would report it to the head of the compact (Yakchŏng), who would then instruct them. If the violators expressed a willingness to reform, their names would be recorded in the book, but if they refused to submit to criticism, they would be expelled from the compact. Anyone who failed to conform to rules for observance of rites and customs, refused to grant a loan to someone in need, missed a repayment deadline, or damaged an object he had borrowed would be recorded for a misdemeanor on the register. Although T'oegye left out the Lü-Family compact provision for recording misdemeanors in a separate register, he provided a system of nine levels of punishment without specifying exactly what these punishments should be, even though presumably he intended that bastinado with a bamboo stick would be included.

Although the Lü-Family compact described a wide variety of violations of the community compact, T'oegye mainly emphasized punishment for failure to encourage others to cultivate their virtue. His draft regulations duplicated, perhaps inadvertently, only twelve of the Lü-Family compact's thirty-one violations: six violations of the moral code, such as perverse confusion of family order, disrespect for parents and elder brothers, unfriendliness to relatives, failure to help those in need, and causing disrespect for the legitimate wife in the family; and six violations of general conduct and public obligations, such as fighting and scolding, using one's strength to lord it over the weak, committing acts of aggression, falsifying or exaggerating facts to accuse others or to set them up for a criminal investigation, and tardiness at compact meetings. The rest of the articles were similar to previous laws or regulations in local organizations like the Yuhyangso.

T'oegye's compact was not original and was never put into practice, but it was respected for the rest of the dynasty as a standard for future advocates of the community compact system. Toward the end of his life he did not display any special zeal for the promotion of the system, and after the succession of King Sŏnjo in 1567, he only praised the *Sohak* as a text for moral education but made no recommendation about the community compact.

T'oegye was even critical of the emphasis in the *Lü-Family Community Compact* on ranking participants according to age because it denigrated the social distinction between the "noble and base," the same kind of criticism leveled by the opponents of Cho Kwangjo! T'oegye's statecraft, in other words, belongs more in the tradition of muscular Confucianism that backed up the rhetoric of persuasion by the threat of force and supported the status quo in discriminatory social relations.[22]

King Sŏnjo and Yulgok, 1571–74

In the 1570s, during the reign of King Sŏnjo, however, a tide of support developed for community compacts among the highest officials. In 1571 a Confucian scholar, Hwang Ŏk, proposed adoption of the *Lü-Family Community*

Compact, but the Ministry of Rites opposed the idea because under current famine conditions any attempt to force peasants to spend time in compact meetings would only lead to disruption. Later that year Yulgok, who was then magistrate of Ch'ŏngju in Ch'ungch'ŏng Province, established the Sŏwŏn Community Compact with the approval of the elders of the district.[23]

In 1572 when Censor-General Hŏ Hyŏp again proposed that the king adopt community compacts for the whole country, King Sŏnjo declined because of the continuing famine and condemned it as a plan that would confuse local customs. In 1573 Yi Kyŏngmyŏng referred to Chu Hsi's remark that the Lü-Family Compact should only be adopted by villages on a voluntary basis, but later that year the Office of Censor-General argued that compacts were essential for reforming the perverse mores and recommended that it be adopted at least in the capital, even though it was presumably designed for villages in the countryside.

The movement to institute community compacts nationwide culminated in a major court discussion of the issue in 1573, when Chief State Councilor Kwŏn Ch'ŏl, Second State Councilor Pak Sun, Third State Councilor No Susin, and Chief of the Military Affairs Commission Hong Sŏm all praised community compacts and mentioned that Korean versions of them called *kye* or *to* had already been tried before a number of times in certain villages. Only Assistant Chief of the Military Affairs Commission Yi T'ak opposed adopting compacts by royal decree and recommended instead that Chu Hsi's corrected edition of the *Lü-Family Community Compact* be printed and distributed nationwide to schools and local communities as a moral text. Sŏnjo decided to print and distribute the text, but he left adoption of community compacts up to individual villages to decide.[24]

The next month Yulgok and Kim Uong of the Office of Special Counselors urged Sŏnjo to support community compacts as the means of national moral regeneration.[25] The king began to waver, and the Ministry of Rites presented a draft set of regulations to bring the community compact model into conformity with Korean circumstances by reducing the number of meetings and the cost of food and wine, and dropping the requirement for a register of demerits.

One of the recommendations, however, was vastly more significant because it transformed the essential nature of the community compact from an agency of self-government into a deputized organization of the district magistrate. The ministry argued that since there were too few local people of superior moral quality to run the compact organization, the district magistrate should act as either the head (Yakchŏng) or secretary (Chigwŏl) of the compact concurrently. Sŏnjo agreed to adopt this form of the community compact for the entire nation, the first official community compact in the dynasty's history, but by the second lunar month of 1574 he stopped the program because of famine and declared that the state was obliged first to provide for the economic support of the people (*yangmin*) before undertaking to educate them in moral standards (*kyomin*).[26]

Sŏnjo apparently still intended to follow through with his initial order after the famine was over, but Yulgok apparently changed his mind about the feasibility of introducing the community compact during a famine. Echoing Mencius, he argued that moral principles could not be successfully inculcated if the people were destitute.[27]

Cho Hŏn and the Ming Model, 1574

After his return from an embassy to Ming China in 1574, Cho Hŏn, who had been a student of T'oegye and Sŏn Hun, submitted a report extolling the community compacts in China. He reported that he had seen them in every village west of Shan-hai-kuan, and that in the Fu-ling area of Manchuria the three leading officials of the community compact were given an audience with the district magistrate twice a month where they each "prostrated themselves once, knocked their heads on the ground three times," and listened to the magistrate read the Ming Emperor T'ai-tsu's Six Edicts issued in 1397. Then they returned to their village and repeated the lecture to the compact members.

> The Instructions were all about filial piety and obedience to parents, respect for elders, harmony and friendship for neighbors in the village, moral instruction for sons and grandsons, diligent effort in agriculture and sericulture, and avoiding unrighteous acts – instructions that Emperor T'ai-tsu of the Ming had determined [at the beginning of the Ming dynasty]. Even though the details did not include the *Lü-Family Community Contract*, the outline was simple and easy for the common people to understand, so that all of them believed it and many in the villages would write moral slogans on the walls or recite them to one another for practice. That is why even though there were many disputes and fights among fathers and sons, elder and younger brothers, they could not bear to divide their families over them.[28]

Cho noted that because of the community compact's role in moral instruction women avoided promiscuity, and on New Year's day, the winter solstice, and [Imperial?] birthdays even the poorest villagers living in small huts honored their family heads by prostrating themselves four times before them. Even slaves bowed to one another when meeting on the road. During weddings the principles all greeted their relatives personally, and both men and women of all ages wore white at funerals and remained in that garb for a month. Even four-year old children knew how to kowtow and knock their heads on the ground, and not even the runners dared to let their hair grow long in unkempt fashion. When standing they all stood erect with their hands clasped and feet lined up neatly. This kind of behavior was typical of all southern Manchuria, demonstrating that despite the legacy of barbarian customs that had prevailed there for over a thousand years, the region had become enlightened under the Great Ming court.

Even though Korea was known as "the land of rites and righteousness," in recent years moral standards had declined, fathers neglected instructing their sons, sons had lost respect for their fathers or elder brothers, husbands could not control their wives, wives showed no obedience to their husbands, and villagers and close relatives engaged in constant disputes. If someone from the village happened to reach high office, he only engaged in corruption, neglected his official duties, and used orders from the king as an excuse for cruel exploitation of the common people. The whole basis of morality – filial respect for parents and and loyal obedience to the ruler – was lost.

Cho recounted an incident illustrating the effectiveness of the community compact as a model for moral instruction. In 1519 a poor man living in Yŏngbyŏn in the north had to abandon his father in a ditch because he did not have enough food to feed him, but when he heard that King Chungjong had just promulgated the text of the community compact to the nation, he turned on his heel, returned to rescue his father, and continued to support him through the rest of his life.

Unfortunately, even though the text of the community compact had been published and distributed throughout the country just last year, it was only gathering dust on book shelves. Since there seemed to be no one with the capacity to seek goodness without waiting for the king's instruction, he advised the king to emulate Ming T'ai-tsu's example by ordering all district magistrates to inform the elders of their districts about the community compacts, and have the village headmen (*li-cheng*) advertise its advantages to the people.

Although Cho agreed that the economic needs of the people (*yangmin*) had to be met before adopting the community compact system, he also pointed out that at the present time the economy was not in bad condition and moral education could not neglected. A son had to be taught that during a famine it was wrong for him to strip the clothes off his father to protect himself from the cold, and a younger brother needed to learn not to steal his elder brother's food to assuage his own hunger. If people were not instructed about these things in advance, they might commit these criminal acts and suffer punishment at the hands of the authorities. Punishing the guilty without providing the people with moral instruction in advance was tantamount to entrapment, a policy that no person with the humane instincts of the enlightened Confucian could tolerate.

Cho insisted, contrary to the earlier proposal of the Ministry of Rites, that there were enough decent officials at court and men of good character in the countryside to run community compacts. If the king could wait until an abundant crop was harvested to guarantee economic security to the people, it would then be possible to achieve the successful adoption of the community compact system.[29]

Cho was tremendously impressed by what was left of the methods of local control and moral indoctrination created by Ming T'ai-tsu in the fourteenth century. Emperor T'ai-tsu came from the peasantry, identified with the troubles and interests of the downtrodden, and attributed the cause of peasant misery to the officials, clerks, and landlords of the late Yüan period. He cracked down on corrupt magistrates, often hauling them in groups to the capital for severe punishment, and he instituted a bold system of local government based on the *li-chia*, units of 110 households under the leadership of the ten wealthiest (not most virtuous!) families. These families controlled ten households each and took responsibility for the equitable distribution and collection of taxes and assignment of labor service, bypassing the regular magistrates altogether!

He also created a parallel system of neighborhood elders (*li-lao*) who assumed many of the responsibilities included in the community compacts under discussion here: adjudication of lawsuits, cases of physical assault, robbery, murder, and sexual offenses, surveillance over vagrants, and reporting of malfeasance by magistrates and clerks to the central government. The elders were also responsible for moral exhortation, particularly the bi-weekly recitations of T'ai-tsu's Six Edicts and the conduct of ceremonies to award local exemplars of morality. The elders were protected from arbitrary arrest by the district magistrates, tax collection was taken out of the hands of the magistrates, and villages were allowed to run their own affairs.

Despite the reputation of the early Ming for the creation of despotic rule, John Watt has showed that T'ai-tsu was "a champion of the rural underdog" who sought "to diminish the power of officialdom over rural society," and in so doing he "displayed a confidence in village society unequaled before the present day." His design was not, therefore, simply to maximize central control, but to hem in local officials "between pressures and controls issuing from all levels," and "to involve rural society itself in the attainment of its [the emperor's] goals.[30]

The early Ming *li-chia* system of local participation and control was never adopted in Korea, and the closest the Koreans ever came to it was the Taewongun's adoption of the village granaries in the 1860s. Cho Hŏn was reporting the situation in Korea in the late sixteenth century after the *li-chia* system had broken down. It proved unstable because emperors after T'ai-tsu lacked his commitment to the perspective of the common peasant, and the growth of population and new markets created discrepancies between wealth and tax assessments, fixed tax quotas and increasing government demands for revenues, and distortions in the structure of wealth in the villages.[31]

What Cho Hŏn observed was the effect of a movement in the early sixteenth century to restore some of the virtues of T'ai-tsu's system, but he failed to record the contributions to community compacts made by the famous statesman-philosophers, Wang Yang-ming, Lo Ju-fang, and Lü K'un, throughout that century.[32] Cho's memorial made no impression on King Sŏnjo himself, but it was very important to Yu Hyŏngwŏn, who copied out over half the text in his *Pan'gye surok*.[33]

Yulgok's Two Community Compacts

Sŏwŏn Community Compact of 1571. In 1571, as magistrate of Ch'ŏngju in Ch'ungch'ŏng Province, Yulgok simplified and modified the *Lü-Family Community Compact* to fit existing Korean *kye* associations and wrote regulations for his Sŏwŏn Community Compact. He insisted that the compact would not work as an agency of moral rectification unless the district magistrate and the head of the *kye* association (*kyejang*) were upright and diligent in encouraging the members of the community and allowing the people to correct their own mistakes before meting out punishment.

Yulgok designed the regulations for this compact to be applied to the twenty-five *kye* of the district of Ch'ŏngju that were organized at the subdistrict or county (*myŏn*) level rather than the natural village. Four General Kye Chiefs (Togyejang) supervised the twenty-five *kye*, and each *kye* compact was headed by a Kyejang and staffed by one instructor for children (Tongmong hunhoe), one chargé (Saekchang) chosen without distinction between commoners and slaves, and one special monitor (Pyŏlgŏm) for each administrative village (*i*).

Yulgok's regulations were similar to Chu Hsi's version of the Lü-Family compact, but the *Sŏwŏn* compact differed from both earlier Chinese models by incorporating distinctions for the treatment of all status groups in Korean society. At the quatriannual sessions for the reading and explanation of the articles of the compact, the compact members would line up along the western wall by age, commoners (*sŏin*) at the eastern end of the south wall with "men of knowledge" (i.e., scholars or yangban) in front of them, and uneducated commoners and slaves at the western end of the south wall – all in order of age. The nothoi (*sŏŏl*) of the scholar class (*sajok*) would form a separate line. Officials of *tangsang* rank, elders among the commoners, and *hyangni* (local clerks) belonging to the compact would be given special places. The list of prohibitions included a ban against acting beyond one's place, especially if one were of base or slave status, and belief in or practice of heterodox doctrines, "lewd [shamanistic] rites," or geomancy (*p'ungsu*) in determining grave sites.

Compact members were required to provide aid in conducting funerals, lend labor to cultivate the land of anyone who was too sick to work, and instruct men under the age of thirty who had not been educated in civil and military matters in the *Sohak*, *Hyogyŏng* (*Book of Filial Piety*), and the *Training Manual for Children* (*Tongjasŭp*). If they failed to read these texts, they would be punished.

The preeminent position of local yangban was illustrated in Yulgok's version of the resolution of disputes. If the Kyejang and the Yusa failed to resolve lawsuits among the people, the case would be turned over to a group of scholars (*saryu*, presumably yangban) within the compact to resolve. If any disputant refused to accept a decision, he would be charged with a misdemeanor, recorded in a demerit register, or even punished if the case were serious.

Any case that could not be solved would be turned over to the district magistrate. The Kyejang or the Yusa had the authority to punish any person on the spot for a misdemeanor that called for less than forty strokes, while more serious punishments were to be discussed at the next compact meeting or turned over to the magistrate.

Yulgok also tried to make the community compact a control agency for the discovery of crime and corruption among local officials. It was to report all demands for bribes and favors by clerks and *kisaeng* of the district magistrate, extortion by the supervisor of agriculture (Kwŏnnong) or chargé (Saekchang), and any unauthorized butchering of oxen to the magistrate. On the other hand the compact was required to petition collectively to obtain a pardon for any person who was about to be executed on false charges.[34]

Haeju Community Compact, ca. 1576. Three years after he had told King Sŏnjo that it would be premature to adopt the community compact system in the midst of a famine, Yulgok composed and instituted his *Haeju Community Compact* (*Haeju hyangyak*) in 1576 while in retirement in Haeju in Hwanghae Province. The Haeju compact was much more detailed and formal than the Sŏwŏn compact and contained an addendum that included a pledge for the members of the compact and articles for a village granary (*sach'ang*).

The Haeju compact was led by a general compact head (Toyakchŏng) and two assistants (Puyakchŏng), one secretary (Chigwŏl) and one treasurer (Sahwa), and the latter two positions rotated between meetings and once a year, respectively. The first meeting of the compact association was to be held in the local private academy (*sŏwŏn*), and the members would bow and burn incense before the paper representations of former sages and teachers, and then genuflect before the general compact head.[35]

Although Yulgok was an outspoken advocate of the voluntary nature of the community compact, he also designed his Haeju regulations to create a closed association of ideological and moral purists by restricting membership to those who could pass strict qualifying tests.[36] Those who wanted to join the compact association first had to write out a formal application explaining their reasons for joining, and the compact members had to accept the application, a process that would take several months. Anyone who was not intelligent or well-behaved would have to show he understood the articles of the compact and could abide by its moral precepts for a probation period of one or two years. Attendance was required at regular bimonthly meetings (up from four times a year in the Sŏwŏn compact). Absence from a meeting required a written excuse in advance, and any member who committed an egregious violation of the rules or failed to rectify any error in behavior after three reprimands would be expelled from the compact association.

The members had to pay dues in cloth and rice, and those dues would be used to pay for the community's funeral expenses. A major ceremony had to be conducted to congratulate any member who underwent his capping ceremony, passed the *munkwa* government examination or obtained the lesser literary or classics licentiate degrees (*chinsa*, *saengwŏn*), received an appointment to office, or was promoted in official rank. Contributions had to be made for food for the slaves who worked at funerals. If any rice were left over at the end of the year, the treasurer could make loans at 20 percent to the members according to the regulations set up for the village granary (*sach'ang*), sell it to buy more cloth, or cease further collections of dues from the members. Cloth would not be loaned but could be used to pay expenses. If a house burned down the community members had to furnish the victim with wood and thatch, furnish one slave, and pay for three days' worth of food while he worked on the house.[37]

Yulgok also provided a separate text for the pledges of the Haeju Community

Compact (*Haeju ilhyang yaksok*) that contained a far longer list of misdemeanors and punishments than the Sŏwŏn compact. This text was significant, however, because it showed that Yulgok shared T'oegye's view that community compact regulations could be used to reform the existing Yuhyangso or *kye* rather than replace them with a new organization. In fact, the pledge regulations specified that the Yuhyangso had the right to nominate candidates for the chief clerk positions in the magistrate's yamen. Membership was not restricted to local yangban or magnates only, but the existence of wealth and status was recognized by allowing any member unable to attend a meeting to send his slave to report it to the association.[38]

Pledges for the Village Granary Kye. Yulgok also included the text of the pledges for the village granary *kye* (*sach'anggye yaksok*), which were quite similar to the community compact in organization and spirit. The community belonging to the granary were organized in groups of five families (*o*) with a five-family head (Ojang), who rotated annually. Members had to pay a small rice fee to the annual fund for relief, and they were required to attend the regular meetings of the granary association. The five-family head was in charge not only of issuing and collecting loans and providing relief, but of recording all good and bad deeds by the members, and the village granary association had the task of admonishing those who violated moral norms, turning recalcitrants over to the magistrate for punishment, or expelling them from the granary association. A local scholar was selected to be instructor (Kyohun) to educate the illiterate, even including slaves.

Pledges for the Village Granary Kye: Mourning and mutual aid. The village granary *kye* pledges stressed proper observation of funerals but forbade drinking wine at such occasions and enjoined frugality in the entertainment provided guests. The bereaved family was not allowed to provide food to them except for fruit or cakes. The regulations also required slaves to perform three-years mourning for the death of a parent, but they were excused from making a grain gift to the bereaved after a death. Slaves were not to be treated on the same basis as commoners since members of the granary association were not required to pay a condolence call on the family of a deceased slave as they had to for all other status groups.

Mutual-aid regulations required a contribution of five *mal* and one able-bodied adult with food to help in reconstruction from all members to anyone whose house and property had been destroyed by fire, with half that contribution and labor service from slaves. If only the house had been burned down, the contribution in grain was eliminated. For lesser fire damage, the members would be required to rush to the site to give aid. If a member was robbed of his property by a thief, all members were required to join in chasing down the thief or making a contribution to recompense the victim. If a person were sick, the members of the association had to find medicine for him or provide labor while he was unable to cultivate his land. If a member were unjustly accused and found guilty of a crime, the members of the association were obliged to come to his defense, and jointly sign a petition requesting his release from jail. The members also had to provide funds for a dowry for poor unmarried women, and for food to the impoverished or starving.[39]

Pledges for the Village Granary Kye: Respect for Age. In addition to a conventional emphasis on pious filial devotion, Yulgok's regulations adhered to the norms of etiquette required between individuals of different age and status groups, with some modifications. For example, a younger person was required to prostrate himself before a respected elder but only bow before an elder if he met him on the road, but Yulgok moved the age difference for prostration down to fifteen years instead of the twenty-year difference for respected elders in earlier texts. Anyone who had a reputation for virtue was to be treated as a respected elder.

Pledges for the Village Granary Kye: Discriminatory Punishment for Slaves. Yulgok's respect for age, however, by no means transcended the conventions of status discrimination in the sixteenth century. His regulations also demanded strict obedience by inferior men (*hain*), that is, slaves, to their masters (*sangjŏn*) and admonished them "to serve their masters with sincerity and not dare to deceive them or hide anything from them in the slightest. If they send you on an errand, run quickly to do the task, never shirking what may be arduous or difficult. Any object you happen to get you must respectfully offer to them. . . . Any act of disrespect by an inferior man to his master was to be punished."

Yulgok also built strict discrimination according to both traditional social status and age into his detailed prescriptions for five grades of punishment for violators of compact rules. One illustration of this principle can be demonstrated in the penalties for assault and battery. The penalty had to depend on the relative ages of the disputants and whether there was justifiable cause for the attack. If an elder (*changja*) struck a younger disputant on just grounds but without causing injury, he would be given the fifth or lowest degree of punishment; more severe fourth-degree punishment if the assault was without just cause but did not cause injury; third-degree punishment if the cause was just but the assault resulted in an injury, and first-degree punishment if the assault was without just cause and resulted in injury. On the other hand, if a younger person (*soja*) assaulted an elder and caused his injury, he would be reported to the magistrate for punishment whether his cause was just or not, and he would suffer first-degree punishment even if had not injured the elder. Nowhere, however, was there any discussion of what kinds of acts were to be interpreted as justifiable reasons for committing assault and battery because Yulgok, in traditional fashion, was content to leave that judgment to the adjudicators rather than attempt to restrict its definition to a written code. He was more concerned that requirements of age and status be accorded their due than that the accused be protected against unjust punishments by arbitrary judges.

In general, Yulgok's rules stipulated lighter punishment for men of higher status who violated rules, norms, or statutory law. The language he used to designate the three statuses involved were ostensibly free of any connotations of inherited status because the elite was described as *sain* (scholars) and the lowest rung of the social ladder as *hain* or inferior persons. The term for commoner (*sŏ*) was not mentioned specifically, but it was obviously assumed that individuals who were neither scholars or lower persons were commoners subject to the penal regulations. Even if Yulgok did not say specifically that his scholars were yangban or their sons who had earned their status hereditarily rather than by scholarship, in the Korea of his time the vast majority of students and degree-holders did come from yangban families. Judging from other parts of Yulgok's text, *hain* referred primarily to slaves (see below).

Thus, if an elder scholar (*sain*, probably yangban) beat a younger person (probably a scholar of his own class), he would only suffer the third-degree of punishment, which in his privileged status only meant a public reprimand at the granary association meeting and half the fines or penalties assessed for ordinary commoners. If a respected elder (*chonja*) committed a violation, one of his sons or younger brothers, or if he had none, a slave, would take the punishment in his place. If a scholar beat a slave on his own authority (i.e., without permission from the authorities), he would be subject to third-degree punishment; if he injured the slave, he would be reported to the magistrate. Beating another yangban who was less than ten years in age difference from the perpetrator would merit a second-degree punishment. These detailed regulations combining age, status, and degree of justification for an assault were redolent of the T'ang code, which was also compiled in an age of status distinctions. These regulations were entirely foreign to the principle of equality under the law that is so important in modern, Western jurisprudence.

The stiffest punishments were naturally reserved for low persons or slaves (*hain*). It is not clear why Yulgok used the term *low people* instead of base persons (*ch'ŏn'in*), the more common term for the lowest rung of social status including slaves, but it is obvious that he was thinking primarily of slaves because he often used it in apposition to the term for "master" (*sangjŏn*). If a low person received the first degree of punishment, he would have to suffer forty strokes, as opposed to an elder (*changja*) (presumably of good or commoner status) who would only be reprimanded to his face before the full granary association meeting, while a scholar (*saryu*) would only have to stand in the courtyard and listen to a discussion of the misdemeanor, or sit at the lowest place at the table during a banquet. Low persons had to suffer at least ten strokes for the fourth category of punishment, and only in the fifth or least onerous, could they get away with a public reprimand. If they were old or sick, they were allowed to substitute a cup of wine penalty for each ten strokes of punishment. A slave would get forty strokes for speaking disrespectfully to a master or scolding him outside the house; thirty strokes for disobedience to a master's order, failure to carry out an order as commanded, or using deception to make a personal profit; twenty strokes for remaining seated on an ox or horse in sight of the master or speaking disrespectfully to a yangban (*sajok*); ten strokes for failure to prostrate himself before a yangban or remaining seated on an ox or horse in his presence, or kneeling instead of prostrating himself before him.

A low person was not allowed even to keep his grievances to himself, for if he failed to report anything bothering him to the Yusa of the granary association, he would receive third-degree punishment. Inducing a low person (and none but a slave would fit this item) to run away from his master was subject to a second-degree punishment.

Pledges for the Village Granary Kye: Landlord Rights and Private Property. One must also call attention to one of the punishments listed separately in the *Pledges for the Commmunity of Haeju* (*Haeju ilhyang yaksok*) that called for the expulsion of a perpetrator from the community compact guilty of "conspiring to do injury to a landlord," a solid indication that Yulgok saw the community compact as a means of enforcing the rights of landlords (and private property) as well as slaveowners against their tenants and slaves. He also prescribed punishments for stealing property from another person, even a Buddhist monk in a mountain monastery, stealing another man's water from his irrigation dike, or taking over another man's land for cultivation. Tardiness in paying taxes, bribery, short-changing borrowers from the village granary, and even laziness or lack of attention to one's work were all criminal actions warranting degrees of punishment specified in the text.[40]

One might pause to ask why Yu Hyŏngwŏn would include Yulgok's defense of landlord rights in his own manuscript since the core of land reform policy was a supposed blending of national and limited private ownership of land. He probably did not want to edit the work of a man he admired greatly, but Yu's condemnation of private property in land indicates a far more radical position than Yulgok's.

Pledges for the Village Granary Kye: Sex Discrimination. There was sex discrimination in his regulations as well: if a woman beat her husband, she would receive forty strokes; if she injured him during the beating, she would be turned over to the district magistrate for more serious punishment. On the other hand, "If a male slave beat his wife who was innocent [of any misdemeanor], he would only receive twenty strokes. If he hurt her, he would receive forty strokes, but would not be reported to the magistrate."

Rape of another man's wife or a single woman would be reported to the magistrate for punishment, but if the perpetrator expressed repentance and willingness to suffer punishment, and "renewed himself," his penalty would be reduced to the first and highest degree punishment by the granary association (the actual penalty, of course, would depend on the status and age of the perpetrator). Obviously, the excessively lenient treatment for male sex abusers was typical of a society that denigrated women's rights.

Pledges for the Village Granary Kye: Penalty for Litigiousness and Profiteering. Litigiousness was also proscribed by the granary association articles. If someone continued to sue in a case that had already been decided, he would suffer third-degree punishment, or first degree if his argument had no justification. Malfeasance in office, such as committing "evil" acts on the pretext of official business, or demanding more than was due in repayment of loans and interest from official granaries were also included. What would be regarded as legitimate (albeit unethical) business practice in the twentieth century, such as pursuing one's own private interest to make excessive profit without showing compassion for the interests of others, merited third-degree punishment.

Pledges for the Village Granary Kye: Restrictions on Speech. The right of speech, if one can even assume that such a concept existed, was extremely limited. Members of the granary association were not free to make pronouncements on what kind of behavior was right or wrong or to satirize others lest they "upset the minds of the people at large." They would suffer first-degree punishment if they did so, and only the head of the association (Yakchang) or the granary clerk (Yusu) had the right to make such statements. Yulgok took special care in differentiating the penalties for false statements: first-or second-degree punishment for destructive slanders, third-degree punishment for false statements or unfair and unjust statements in the context of granary association discussion; fourth- or fifth-degree punishment for ordinary slander. Roisterous behavior, shouting and arguing, laughing and playing pranks, swearing, or criticizing others could be punished by third-or fifth-degree penalties. Finally, belief in heterodox ideas and practice of "lewd [shamanistic] rites" earned second-degree punishment, and the parents and the female shamans involved would receive first-degree punishment as well.

On the other hand, if anyone failed to report a misdemeanor and kept it secret to blackmail or intimidate the perpetrator, he would receive first-degree punishment. Any member who failed to follow the orders of the Yakchang or Yusu would suffer punishment at increasing degrees each time he did so, and after the fourth failure, he would be reported to the magistrate and expelled from the association.

Major Elements of Yulgok's Regulations. Tanaba Tameo believed that late in his life Yulgok placed more emphasis on loyalty to the ruler and the state than Chu Hsi because he added this obligation to his list of obligations in the text of the *Haeju Community Compact* and the *Pledges for the Village Granary Kye* (*Sach'anggye yaksok*), whereas he had not included it the earlier Sŏwŏn Community Compact or in the *Pledges for the Community of Haeju* (*Haeju ilhyang yaksok*) written prior to the *Haeju Community Compact*. He also felt that loyalty to the state was connected with the loyalty owed by a slave to a master that he illustrated in the *Pledges for the Village Granary Kye*. Sakai Tadao felt that both T'oegye and Yulgok were committed to maintaining class distinction and "a social order governed by the *yangban* class," but that Yulgok was more progressive and pragmatic than T'oegye.[41]

Yulgok was definitely a defender of the status quo in social relations, particularly discrimination in favor of yangban, slaveholders, and landlords and against slaves, particularly in his detailed prescriptions for penalties for transgressions of the law and the rules of the compact based on age and status. It is, therefore, hardly justified to praise him for progressivism or pragmatism, for he was much less so than Yu Hyŏngwŏn, who was committed to invading the private property rights of the landlords and slaveholders and reducing (if not abolishing) both the inherited privileges of the yangban and inherited burdens of the slaves.

Sakai has stressed Yulgok's openness and his commitment to the study of all ideas in China, but this interpretation is belied by Yulgok's insertion into Chu Hsi's list of misdemeanors of new bans against heterodox ideas and the conduct of "lewd rites" (by the *sulka* or practitioners of shamanism, acupuncture, and geomancy), specifically those that caused frequent delays in the interment of the dead, suspension of burials because of disease, and reburials of the dead because of interpretations of geomantic forces.

Yulgok's almost obsessive reliance on punishment as the means for coercing conformity to moral norms in his Haeju regulations represented a shift in sentiment from the greater emphasis on moral cultivation in Chu Hsi's community compact and in compacts proposed during Chungjong's reign in the early sixteenth century. His requirement that repeated misdemeanors or gross violations of standards deserved expulsion from either the community compact, the village granary *kye*, or the village itself, was far more severe than Chu Hsi's provision to permit such recalcitrants simply to leave the compact. While Tabana conceded that Yulgok deserved credit for introducing specificity into penal law, he deplored Yulgok's morbid fascination with exposing all possible examples of human immorality and corruption.[42] Furthermore, the essence of that specificity in his penal rules was the gradation of punishment by the social status of both perpetrator and victim – a practice quite typical of the T'ang penal code and Korean slave society.

Finally, Sakai's view that Yulgok's progressive social outlook and his realistic appreciation of the lower classes was to be explained by his belief in the importance of material force (*ki*) in the construction of human nature and the universe, and his objective appreciation of Wang Yang-ming appears totally unjustified.[43] Yulgok's handling of people of lower status and slaves indicates primarily a paternalistic and aristocratic approach to the education of the ignorant, not an inclination to liberate the oppressed from the domination of the yangban and slaveowners.

It was T'oegye, the advocate of the preeminence of principle over psycho-physical energy, who believed that considerations of social status should not intrude on the organization of schools or local government associations! Even if Yulgok had been more sympathetic to the lower classes, there is no reason to believe it would have been the product of his preference for psycho-physical energy as the foundation for objects of the real world and the nature of the human mind.

Injo's Reign, 1623–49

The history of community compacts and the larger concern with moral education in general displayed a pattern of ebb and flow according to shifting national moods. King Injo's interest in moral education and the community compact system was sporadic and weak. In 1629 he approved publication of the *Sohak* and other moral texts, but some officials complained in the early 1630s that young students hardly ever read it because they were too busy studying for the government examinations. Injo mentioned community compacts in a set of regulations to promote schools in 1634, but he did nothing to implement them.[44]

Hwang Chonghae, a retired scholar, did establish a small local association in Mokch'ŏn in 1641 called the Golden Orchid *Kye* (Kŭmnan'gye), based on Chu Hsi's emendation of the Lü-Family compact. The ground rules (*tonggyu*) provided that two yangban would be chosen to act as heads of the association (Yusa) and two low persons (*hain*) to act as secretaries or functionaries. Qualifications for membership were more liberal than the rules for Yulgok's Haeju compact since everyone in the village or township of whatever class ("whether high or low") who were married and had their own residence was permitted to join, and new arrivals to the village were to be allowed to join after having lived and cultivated the land for a few years. Those who refused to join initially would not be eligible for labor sharing in agriculture, assistance in case of flood or drought, or any natural disaster, and if they continued to refuse, they could be beaten and ultimately expelled from the district (*tong*). The compact was to be restricted to the village community alone, and not to any other village or administrative district.

The regulations provided some recognition but no liberation from status by allowing the announcement of awards to lower persons (*hain*) who had done good deeds or had observed three years of mourning for their deceased parents, or to slaves (*nobi*) who had demonstrated strict loyalty to their yangban masters. Strict distinctions were maintained between sons of legitimate wives and the nothoi of concubines (*chŏksŏ*), pointing out that they all shared the same obligations (to their parents), but that nothoi were forbidden from insulting legitimate sons and liable to punishment for such acts in the state law code. On the other hand, if the nothoi of yangban (*sŏŏl*) were found guilty of fighting, they were only to be penalized according to the rules for yangban, not commoners or lower persons.

Hwang maintained Yulgok's schedule for differentiating penalties according to the social status of individuals. He referred to the local elite as yangban rather than *sajok* or *saryu* (scholars or literati) as Yulgok had done in the previous century, and he stated that even though men of all classes were liable for punishment for their misdemeanors, the distinction between yangban and lower persons (*hain*), legitimate son and nothoi, and elder and younger persons had to be kept clear. Unfortunately, because in recent years the lower persons had become used to "lording it over" the yangban and even attacking them physically, these violations had to be punished by beatings, and in severe cases reported to the magistrate.

Yangban as well as low persons had to aid their neighbors in time of disaster and obey the rules for mourning, but a yangban was allowed to send one of his slaves to participate in a funeral as a substitute. If a yangban failed to participate in a funeral, however, he only had to pay a penalty of one *mal* of rice, but the lower person was to be beaten. If a yangban had no slave of his own and not enough money to hire a substitute to perform duties required at a funeral, every one in the community would have to contribute three *mal* of rice to be paid to the bereaved family.

Hwang praised the clannishness of Korean social behavior, particularly the sense of solidarity felt by all descendants of the single head of a clan or lineage group, no matter how distant they were in the degree of blood relationship in the current generation. He expanded the obligations of individuals beyond the family to the clan and provided that failure to treat another lineage relative with the respect due to a close family member would constitute a criminal act. Fighting and altercation was condemned for all classes, whether it included disputes over the pedigree (*munji*) of others among yangban or physical fights among them and the lower persons (*hain*).

Hwang also bent traditional rules to provide mutual aid for the funeral of at least the mother of a wife, a modification of Confucian rules that took into account vestiges of matrilineality in past Korean social life. He justified it because in recent years mutual aid had in fact been provided for the funeral of the parents of a wife even if they lived in another village, if the husband involved had no parents of his own. Nonetheless, since the compact community would not have the economic capacity to pay for this if such events occurred too frequently, it permitted such aid for a funeral only if the deceased mother of a wife lived in the same village, even though it was not called for in the compact's regulations.

Sons would still be obliged to provide aid for the parents even if they lived in another district, and if it were too difficult for one's father in the other district to perform military service himself, members of the community compact would contribute to a military service payment for a substitute or for destitute members of the community who suffered a loss of a parent. If a widow had no children, her brothers or nephews would be allowed to offer assistance to her. Nonetheless, such exceptional acts of aid and assistance were not regarded as the obligation of the community as a whole, but only to blood relatives.[45]

Hwang appears to have been following in Yulgok's tradition of adhering to Korean forms of social status discrimination in the rules of punishment for misconduct. His rules did not reflect any weakening in the desire for physical punishment, but they did show more concern with Korean social customs, including discrimination against nothoi and lower persons or slaves, and greater lingering consideration for the female line of descent.

In 1632 Kim Seryŏng established the P'osan Community Compact when he was magistrate of Hyŏnp'ung, and another one in Hamhŭng when he was governor of Hamgyŏng Province between 1642 and 1644. The Hamhŭng compact was the first Korean compact that incorporated the Six Edicts of Emperor T'aitsu of the Ming dynasty, mentioned by Cho Hŏn after his trip to China in 1574. It also stressed use of the *pao-chia* (*pogap* in Korean), the Ming and Ch'ing version of mutual surveillance among families.[46]

Mid-Seventeenth Century

The community compact movement had not been much of a success in the Chosŏn dynasty, and a brief flurry of interest in the mid-seventeenth century did not indicate that its fortunes had improved. No one disagreed with the notion that moral education and transformation was more of a necessity than ever, but few magistrates had the zeal to establish community compacts in their own districts.

In 1650 King Hyojŏng (r. 1649–59) was alarmed by a rash of murders and the occurrence of natural disasters, and ordered all officials to promote moral education to carry out the spirit of the community compact regulations. He did not, however, order the adoption of compacts in village communities, and most officials paid no attention to his command. In 1657 Yi Kyŏngsŏk deplored the failure of local educational officials and magistrates to carry out the order, but Inspector-General Kim Chwamyŏng argued that since community compacts could not be adopted anyway, the king had no choice but to carry out moral regeneration by the use of punishment against all persons guilty of unfilial and disrespectful behavior, slaves who rebelled against their masters' decisions, and social inferiors who violated standards of social status.[47]

In the first year of King Hyŏnjong's reign (1660), however, Yi Ut'ae, a confidante of the king who had close ties with Song Siyŏl and Song Chun'gil, argued that community compacts, mutual aid and surveillance units (*ogat'ong*) of five, twenty-five, one hundred, and two hundred families, and the village granary system (*sach'ang*) were the best institutional means for the rectification of mores. He suggested that the king print the text either of Chu Hsi's or Yulgok's version of a community compact for educational purposes, but Chief State Councilor Chŏng T'aehwa retorted that community compacts were impractical because Yulgok himself had balked at their adoption, and Yi Ut'ae had insisted that a population census and a land survey had to be conducted before compacts were established. He and others felt that a *hop'ae* or household tally system was not possible and a land survey could only be achieved on a gradual basis. Third State Councilor Wŏn Tup'yo also objected to a five-family system because in the past many families had been left out of registration, and community compacts could not work at all if there were any omissions. In any case, the state of mores in the country was so low that community compacts would not work anyway. Second State Councilor Sim Chiwŏn echoed Yulgok's argument that peasants had been suffering too much from famine over the past years and needed some rest from government demands.[48]

The retired Yi Kyŏngsŏk noted that King Hyojong's nationwide compaign against immoral behavior had failed because bureaucrats were not zealous in carrying it out. In 1664 King Hyŏnjong told Chŏng T'aehwa that he was willing to try the five-family mutual responsibility system (*ogat'ong*), but the times were not ripe for the community compact system and he refused to entertain any more proposals for it for the rest of his reign.[49]

In 1670 the famous Song Siyŏl was asked by friends who had decided to form a Mutual Meeting Association (Sanggwanhoe) modeled after the community compact to embellish their draft of the rules of the compact. Song praised the contributions of Chu Hsi, Cho Kwangjo, T'oegye, and Yulgok, but he only wrote the introduction to the compact and nothing more.[50] Song, like many others, paid lip service to the institution, but did nothing about it.

CONCLUSION

The idea of using local organs of self-government for mutual aid and surveillance derived from the description of local government in *The Rites of Chou* and concrete examples of those practices in Chinese history. Although Yu Hyŏngwŏn began his discussion of community compacts with the *Lü-Family Community Compact* and Chu Hsi's emendation of it, those texts were not introduced seriously until the early sixteenth century.

On the other hand, the principles of mutual aid and surveillance and the emphasis on moral education were present in Korea from the beginning of the Chosŏn dynasty. At that time a movement for moral rearmament was led by a new batch of officials who were ardent students of Neo-Confucian philosophy and attempted to introduce moral texts into the required educational curriculum and moral components into existing institutions of local self-government. Famous scholar-officials like T'oegye and Yulgok wrote compact regulations, but the spirit of their work reflected a strict application of punishment to enforce conformity, and in Yulgok's case, a reaffirmation of the existing Korean code of status relations, many of which had disappeared from Chinese life. Cho Hŏn also advertised the Six Edicts of Ming T'ai-tsu and the importance of community compacts in Chinese local life in the late sixteenth century. The culmination of this movement at the national level, however, yielded only an ephemeral flash of brilliance when in 1573 King Sŏnjo agreed to adopt a program to adopt community compacts throughout the country for moral education, aid, admonition, and punishment. Less than a year later, however, he rescinded the order with the approval of Yulgok himself because of the devastating effects of a famine and peasant economic hardship.

That decision left only private initiative at the local level as the means for adopting community compacts. The few extant examples of the seventeenth century indicated the greater influence of Korean traditions, such as in the provisions of Hwang Chonghae's Golden Orchid Kye of 1641 that referred to Korean aristocrats as yangban instead of scholars, and slaves instead of lower persons, and paid homage to older traditions of respect for members of the matrilineal descent group. Seventeenth-century kings, however, were not active supporters of community compacts.

There was hardly any influence on Korean thinking about these problems from the institutions of the Ch'ing dynasty. Since the Manchu rulers were particularly concerned about gaining the support of Chinese scholars for their regime, the Shun-chih emperor promulgated his own Six Edicts in 1652 and established regulations for community compacts in 1659. The K'ang-hsi emperor expanded the number of imperial exhortations to morality from six to sixteen by his own Sacred Edict in 1670, and the Yung-cheng emperor expanded them still further in 1724, increased the personnel of the community compacts, and required semimonthly lecture sessions in 1729. Imperial edicts were issued periodically thereafter to extend compact organizations throughout the empire, but the purpose of the compacts shifted more to local control than mutual admonition and moral instruction, especially after 1724. A number of Chinese scholars promoted both the Sacred Edict and the community compacts, but most officials could not be bothered with them, scholars of character could not be found to function as lecturers, and the lecture sessions had become a routine and lugubrious burden for both scholars and commoners alike. In any case the Ch'ing community compacts never received much publicity in Korea.

Kung-ch'üan Hsiao listed reasons why the compacts did not succeed in China in the Ch'ing dynasty, and most of them seem to fit the Korean situation as well. The general insufficiency of production was not high enough to sustain any altruistic concern for others, the appeals of the non-Confucian popular religious movements and bandit bands to the illiterate peasants were far greater than Confucian propaganda, the heads of the community compacts used their positions to wield power, and the nature of the compacts themselves were transformed when they took over the tasks of the *pao-chia* and *t'uan-lien* and became the equivalent of a local gendarmerie and militia.[51]

In Korea implementation was obstructed ostensibly because of the sufferings of the population from famine, but what was probably far more important was the popular mistrust of any excessively rigorous mechanism of control and regulation that would have extended the arm of punishment from the magistrate directly into the village, particularly in defense of a hierarchical social structure that was the ideal of the Confucian-educated elite.

Some opponents of the community compacts did point out that they might become more oppressive than the magistrates and clerks if they were taken over by unrighteous individuals, local landlords, or central government officials, and in fact the regulations devised by T'oegye and Yulgok, in particular, could not have convinced too many peasants that they could obtain justice through the community compact when forced to bow and kowtow to the mighty. Contrary to the declamations of the moralists, slaves and nothoi of yangban wanted to escape the debilities of their status, and commoners preferred to run away from their military service taxes or buy themselves official titles to gain some respect from society.

The advocates of community compacts thought of themselves as spokesman for social harmony and justice, but they hoped to ensure it by adopting a strict and regimented system of social organization that would have eliminated almost any opportunity for the untrammeled conduct of private life.

CHAPTER 20

Yu Hyŏngwŏn's Community Compact Regulations

"The custom in this country is that we only pay respect to pedigree [*munji*]. Among those people who engage in the activity of scholars, we also have [a category] that we call yangban, that is, the sons and grandsons and lineage relations [*choktang*] of the higher and lower officials [*taebusa*]. In general, the system of our country is that only the lineage relations of the *taebusa* can obtain regular official posts as civil and military officials."[1]

Yu Hyŏngwŏn probably wrote his draft of a community compact sometime in the 1650s, and he insisted that he had to modify the regulations in Chu Hsi's emendation of the *The Lü Family Community Compact* for two reasons: it was primarily an agreement among members of the scholar class alone and represented their didactic approach to the education of the rest of the population, and it did not include the common people in the community and lacked the cooperative attitude toward the population that Yu felt was necessary. Yu claimed that his own emendations of Chu Hsi's text was based on two sections of *The Rites of Chou* and the compact regulations drawn up by T'oegye and Yulgok, and he also cited about half of the full text of Cho Hŏn's recommendation for community compacts to King Sŏnjo in 1574.[2]

Yu cited statements by T'oegye and Yulgok that praised the emphasis on moral leadership in local communities in Chou times. T'oegye lauded the local men of official rank (*hsiang ta-fu*) in the Chou period who established models of filial piety, brotherly respect, loyalty, and trust for the local communities (*hyangdang*). He and Yulgok both stressed that in the age of decline after the destruction of the Chou dynasty it would not be possible to recreate the laws and institutions of the Chou age, but the moral principles of those times remained intact and the organization of local government as a means of moral training could be reconstituted. Nonetheless, Yu's attribution to T'oegye and Yulgok for the idea that community compacts had to be representative of all class and status groups in the community was partially misplaced, because although both called for participation by commoners and lower people as well as yangban, Yulgok was particularly severe in his discriminatory regulations against the lower classes.[3]

YU'S PLAN FOR KOREAN LOCAL-GOVERNMENT ORGANIZATION

In laying out his proposed regulations for the organization of a mutual-responsibility system for rural villages, Yu adapted the types illustrated in his history of that institution in China. He proposed the establishment of a system based on five families, to be called a *t'ong*, headed by a *t'ong* chief (T'ongjang). Ten *t'ong* or fifty families would make one *i* headed by an Ijang, or the head of a fifty-family unit. Each natural village, what Yu called a neighborhood village (*pugun ch'ŏlli*) and defined as consisting of two fifty-family units, would be called a *kye*, known in common parlance as a village *kye* (*tonggye*). The village *kye* would be divided in two parts, corresponding to the two fifty-family units, and its chief officials would be called the upper and lower *kye* chief (*Sanggyejang*, *Hagyejang*). Their main function was to participate in funeral and mourning rites, while other forms of mutual aid were to be left to the subdistrict village compact association.

Yu called the subdistrict the *hyang*, equivalent to the Korean *myŏn* or county, and specified that it would be created at intervals of 10 *i* (about 3.3 miles), headed by a subdistrict chief (Hyangjŏng) and four assisants and two agricultural officials called Saekpu. The *hyang* was tied into Yu's system of land distribution and was to correspond to 500 *kyŏng* of territory, or 700 *kyŏng* if some of the land was uncultivated. Calculations had to be made about the density of population so that the size of a *hyang* could be adjusted to the population density, rather than the other way around, with a suggested maximum of 600 *kyŏng* of territory. The *hyang* would also have one Yakchŏng or chief official of the subdistrict community compact (*hyangyak*), similar to the situation in contemporary China.

The cities would also be divided into territorial wards (*pang*) consisting of approximately 500 families in the T'ang manner and headed by ward chiefs (Pangjŏng). Municipalities would also have a ward association chief to assume subdistrict compact functions for his ward, similar to the duties of the *yakchŏng* in the rural areas. The government would pay salaries to all functionaries in the mutual responsibility system.

In the countryside, officials of the system were to be selected and appointed from "commoners advanced in years who are diligent and straightforward." In the urban wards, however, appointment was to be restricted to a more elite group: either quota or nonquota students in official schools, or sons of high officials with the protection privilege (*yuŭm*), or relatives of royalty provided they were "pure, fair, and straight." The rural agricultural officials (Saekpu) were responsible for transmitting government orders, collecting taxes, and "pressing [the people] to pay them by the deadlines." The T'ongjang, Ijang, and Pangjŏng were also charged with reporting any peasants who left their villages without permission or the arrival of newcomers from other areas, and they were subjected to a fine if they failed to do so.[4]

It is obvious from the description of duties that Yu was concerned with mobilizing the population to ensure sufficient tax collection as well as the promotion of agricultural production. Furthermore, in conformity with Chinese mutual aid and surveillance organizations, he wanted to keep everyone under control, tied to their villages and urban wards, and registered for taxes and labor service. By binding every individual to a team of families and requiring immediate reports of all movement into and out of villages and towns, there would be no opportunity for individuals to escape from the state's tax and labor service obligations. Despite his encouragement of greater commercial activity in his essay on cash, he by no means could have approved any free migration to the cities to participate in commerce or to supply an increased demand for industrial labor.

At the end of this essay, he also commented on some of the fundamental features of the system. He observed that even if the country were governed by a sage king, it would not be possible to succeed in "nurturing livelihood, carrying out [royal] instructions and orders, unifying customs and mores," and establishing a "government of moral transformation" unless a *hyangdang* system of local control were in place.

In this section he finally referred to the *pao-chia* system of the Sung, not that of the Northern Sung introduced under the sponsorship of Emperor Shen-tsung and Wang An-shih, but the five-family *pao* units proposed by Chu Hsi in his proposed Village Granary Regulations for mutual protection and reliance. Nevertheless, Chu Hsi's lessons were by no means a departure from either the traditional purposes of mutual surveillance or the *pao-chia* system of the Northern Sung during Wang An-shih's era. He pointed out that the *pao* organization would guarantee full tax payments even if some members ran away and would reassign duties annually. It would be able to discover any embezzlement, tax delinquency, evasion of military duty, criminal activity, failure to obey government prohibitions, and malfeasance by the *pao*'s officials themselves. It would then report all such acts to the district authorities, who would then arrest those guilty of wrongdoing, point them out to the community, and administer severe punishment.

Yu commented that even though these remarks of Chu Hsi were connected with his village granary system, he was really talking about the necessity for "organizing households" (*p'yŏnho*), the most important aspects of which were mutual protection for people when they made promises or compacts, rewarding merit, and punishing crime. He added that the creation of mutual aid and surveillance organizations for local control would be far preferable to the laxity and disorder on the current Korean scene.[5]

Regulations for Yu's Community Compact

Principles of Organization

Yu then proposed his own set of regulations in which he evidently copied Yulgok's precedent of establishing community compacts at the subdistrict or county (*myŏn*), which he referred to as *hyang*, not the natural villages. The people of a *hyang* were to nominate men of virtuous reputation who had earned the trust of the people to be general head of all community compact associations at the subdistrict level (Toyakchŏng) for the administrative district (*ŭp*) and his two assistants. The people of every subdistrict would in turn nominate the head of the subdistrict compact association (Yakchŏng) and its secretary (Chigwŏl), a post that would rotate among the ordinary members of the association. Beneath the subdistrict families would be organized not into natural villages but into administrative villages based on Chinese-style units of fifty-family groups (*i*), which would also select "the oldest man in the village who is firm and diligent" to be the head of the fifty-family group (Ijŏng) and his clerk (Saekchang). The Ijŏng would be responsible for admonishing, instructing, and investigating the people of the natural villages.

Yu introduced an interesting twist on the relationship between the community compact and the Yuhyangso by requiring that the head of the subdistrict Compact (Yakchŏng) concurrently take over the leadership of the current Yuhyangso. Such a move would have ensured that the Yuhyangso could no longer function as the agent either of the district magistrate, or of any capital official or nobleman that controlled the district's Kyŏngjaeso.

His regulations governing the positions of lesser compact functionaries were standard. The monthly rotating secretaries (Chigwŏl) and clerks (Saekchang) held their posts only for a year, but none of the regular functionaries of the system were to be transferred from their posts unless their parents had died or were sick, had been forced to leave the village, or had damaged their reputations by some action. Then, the members of the compact association and the village elders would personally ask the man to leave his post or petition the magistrate for his removal. Once the head of the compact was chosen, he was not responsible to the compact members for his position, but the secretary and clerk had to rotate automatically every month and could be removed for malfeasance upon petition, but the final authority in that case belonged with the magistrate.

Wada Sei once remarked that the Chinese institutions of local self-government had been mistakenly advertised by some as demonstrations of Western democracy when they were only extensions of centralized despotic and absolute government. Yu's plan contained elements of popular participation, but the head of the compact was not responsible to the members after he was chosen.[6]

Education and Moral Instruction

In emulation of Yulgok's text of pledges, Yu also included a set of pledges by members of local communities to the subdistrict compact association designed to produce not only compliance with the tax and legal requirements of the state, but to create a moral community for the improvement of individual behavior, interpersonal relations, civic obligation, and social harmony. Yu remarked that in classical times, government affairs (*chŏngnyŏng*) and moral transformation through education (*kyohwa*) were never divided in two. In the Chou dynasty, the local posts of Tsu-shih and Tang-cheng were responsible for education and moral instruction as well as collecting taxes and commanding troops.

Since it was no longer possible to reestablish that kind of unity in local administrations because local officials were no longer autonomous officials (*chajuch'ijigwan*) but were all under the jurisdiction of the district magistrate (*suryŏng*), and individual tasks were divided and distributed among the magistrate's subordinates, there was no choice in current times but to organize a separate community compact. He explained that although an attempt had been made in the Sui dynasty to concentrate both administration and education in the hands of one official like a Tang-cheng, it had not worked well. In Ming times, the head of a one-hundred family group called the Li-cheng was given responsibility to judge minor lawsuits, but he could not control bribery and murder that arose from those disputes.

It did not work not only because the times were bad, but also because the situation had changed from the age of feudalism (*ponggŏnsi*). In the feudal Chou period, the Tsu-shih (the teacher) and Tang-cheng (local administrator) were selected on the basis of their moral worth and were given the official position of *taebu* commensurate with those qualities. Ho Hsiu of Han times, author of a subcommentary on the Kung-yang Commentary on *The Spring and Autumn Annals*, mentioned that people of a eighty-family unit called the *li* established a school and selected a man from among the honored and virtuous elders of the community to run it. He was given the respected title of Father-Elder (*fu-lao*) and a double land allotment, and was granted permission to ride a horse. Local officials as a whole (*hsiang ta-fu*) were treated as if they were capital ministers, and they were given audiences with the ruler of the state at court to discuss official business and given responsibility for education in the provinces. The respect the ancients had for learning was not confined exclusively to formal or legal institutions alone.

After the destruction of feudalism and the institution of the bureaucratic system in the Ch'in dynasty, the local magistrates (*hyanggwan*) were no longer exalted, and it became difficult to find worthy men to be magistrates, let alone headmasters of local schools. They were dropped down to the lowest bureaucratic ranks and afforded few marks of respect. Nevertheless, it was still possible to approximate the Chou situation by the division of labor, a principle that had been followed in ancient times as well. The moral rectification of the population as well as good government could be achieved by cooperation among officials, worthy scholars, and other officials, implying that establishment of the community compact would provide the missing component of moral education in local areas.

Yu argued that in contemporary Korea, as well, it was most important to find worthy men to staff the posts of his Subdistrict Compact Association because not many incumbent district magistrates were worthy or respected. The heads of the compact (Yakchŏng) were obliged to rectify their own behavior to set a moral standard for the community at large, and the members of the compact as a whole had to keep free of any connections or influence lest they use them to gain an advantage over their neighbors in business or any other activity. As Yulgok had proposed, the Subdistrict Compact Association would also be combined with the village granary (*sach'ang*) and run according to ancient precedents. On the other hand, he did not agree with Yulgok that it was possible for the Yuhyangso to be converted into an agency for moral enlightenment, possibly because it had long since became an organization for the yangban alone rather than for the community as a whole. He would have left the Yuhyangso intact but put the head of the community compact in charge of it.[7]

His compact regulations contained the usual four subdivisions for mutual aid and surveillance, and the usual methods of promoting moral perfection through persuasion, education, and social pressure against recalcitrant individuals. Yu commented that currently the Korean people were capable of showing the proper respect to their parents, but they could not show respect for elders and had not been trained how to bow and prostrate themselves. In addition to mutual encouragement of filial piety, respect, and aid to the distressed, each individual was to encourage others to manage one's slaves (*tongbok*) well, stand in awe of the laws, pay taxes on time, and assist the magistrate in carrying out his duties. Despite Yu's frequent protestations against the evils of slavery, his community compact was thus designed to promote peace in master/slave relations by moral appeal and maintain the power and legitimacy of the central government in its control of the countryside.[8]

Mutual Aid

Members of the compact were obliged to provide mutual aid and commiseration in time of disaster, including damage from flood or fire, robbery, sickness, death, support of widows and orphans, damage from slander, and poverty. Yu had nothing significant to add to similar clauses in earlier compacts, but he did not stint in describing the types of catastrophe that required cooperative aid. As in other compacts he enjoined all members to organize a team to collect wood and other materials to help rebuild any house that had burned down, and supply food to the distressed family until it could recover. If a robbery occurred, the members would have to attempt to capture the criminal, and provide compensation and support to the victims if they were poor. If someone suffered a serious illness, the neighbors were to find a doctor and help the family with expenses. In case of death, the association members had to provide material goods and loans to help the survivors. They had to set up trustees to take care of the support of widows and orphans and help them manage their affairs, find a teacher for the instruction of orphans or spouses for those of marriageable age, provide a labor pool to assist in their income, defend them in court against unscrupulous exploiters or take their side in disputes involving the magistrates, oversee the training of young orphans to keep them from bad company, and grant loans to help them in economic distress.

The head and secretary of the community compact association were responsible for overseeing these obligations of the association's members to provide aid to the afflicted by loaning goods, tools, carts, horses, and servants – if they possessed those resources. They would have the duty to punish recalcitrant members who failed to meet these obligations, or recipients of aid who failed to make repayment, and record the names of those who met their responsibilities as a permanent endorsement of their magnanimity and responsibility.[9]

Surveillance Functions

Under the second category of "keeping watch on one another's mistakes," Yu copied many of the provisions that had come down from the Lü-Family compact. He omitted unfilial behavior since it was already penalized in the law code, but he did specify punishment within the compact for failure to look after one parents, raising one's voice or getting angry at them, reproaching them, or squatting disrespectfully in front of them. Other punishable offenses in the conduct of funeral arrangements or ancestral rites included tardiness at burials of family members, so-called straw funerals (*ch'osang*) where straw was laid over the corpse instead of proper burial, drunkenness, neglect of proper rites, failure to conduct ancestral sacrifice on the anniversary of the death of one's parents, or visiting Buddhist temples in the mountains and feeding the monks as an act of piety.

Civil Suits and Slander

Yu adopted the usual admonitions against interpersonal disputes by condemning lawsuits, false accusation to entrap others in the law, mendacity, fabrication, and exaggeration. Civil disputes or lawsuits were to be judged by the head of the compact who would also order the party in the wrong to cease any further action to gain redress. If he failed to do so, the association as a whole would either punish him or report his recalcitrance to the district magistrate, in the old compact tradition.

Moral Checks on Business

Yu's rules governing business and commercial activity were particularly important, especially since scholars like Yi T'aejin have suggested that the *sarimp'a* of the late fifteenth and sixteenth centuries favored the promotion of commercial development. Yu's rules, however, enjoined members not to "go to extremes" in making profits in business transactions, and not to injure others in the conduct of trade. They were not simply to devote themselves solely to making a profit without any consideration of whether their actions were right or wrong, or to demand something in negotiation without a proper reason for doing so, or to deceive someone who made some kind of request from you. For that matter, one was not to spend more than one's means or resources on clothing and adornments or on marriages and funerals, or even to feel discontented if one happened to be poor. If a member of the community happened to be an official, he was to be reprimanded for utilizing his public position to engage in wrongdoing, to make a personal profit, or to oppress others.

These provisions were consistent with the traditional Confucian attitude that business was acceptable but had to be kept within the bounds of moral standards. As will be seen in the chapters on metallic cash, Confucians were not opposed to commerce per se, but to an exaggerated pursuit of profit, an excessive pattern of expenditures, or any depletion in the peasant population by the enticements of huge profits in commerce.

Everyone was subject to chastisement for breaking the law, evading official service obligations or taxes, or associating with criminals. Contrary to conventional practice, men were to be warned against using deception to seduce women, and any man who used force against a woman or committed rape was to be reported to the authorities for punishment. Everyone was enjoined against participating in Buddhist or shamanistic rituals or offering prayers, particularly when a compact association meeting was being held. If that occurred, the general head of all the subdistrict compact associations would transfer the guilty Yakchŏng and have his family servants beaten. Finally, improper behavior at association meetings, such as tardiness, causing a commotion, and leaving the meeting before it came to an end were all misdemeanors subject to punishment.

Punishment for Legal and Moral Violations

Yu's rules for punishment of violations of the regulations and norms of the compact included the regular provisions for admonition, reprimand in the compact meeting, instruction, public apology, and probation, but if the transgressor refused to accept criticism or rectify his mistakes, he would then be indicted for criminal action even though that action might not have been a violation of statutory law but of the rules of the compact association. Even in the case where the perpetrator refused admonition and instruction, the decision for punishment was not to be taken by the Yakchŏng himself, but only with unanimous approval of all members of the compact association. The clerks (Saekchang) of the compact association then had full authority to administer beatings of thirty or less strokes of the bamboo stick while cases requiring more serious punishment had to be reported to the district magistrate. If a clerk refused to carry out the beating, he too would be punished. Finally, in the Sung tradition Yu specified that the community compacts would keep registers of both good and bad deeds and the head of the compact (Yakchŏng) would then determine rewards and punishments if there was no dissent from the congregation.

Penalties for violation of the moral principles of behavior depended on the severity of the deed. Minor transgressions were to be punished by dropping the individual down in the seating order in compact association meetings to a place lower in prestige than their normal position (see later). A perpetrator might regain his original place only after the group granted permission. More serious errors were punished by removal of the perpetrator's name from the compact register, and prohibition against participation in public meetings or village affairs. Any violator who claimed he had rehabilitated himself would be readmitted to the association only after a probationary period of several years and a final face-to-face admonition session that required him to stand in the open courtyard and make a public apology. He would then be allowed to take his seat only if the association members approved.

Yu's list of punishments was not as detailed as Yulgok's five degrees of punishment with a limit of forty strokes, and he reduced the degrees of punishment and the number of strokes to ten, twenty, or thirty, and eliminated some of the light penalties for men of high status. Echoing his desire for the abolition of slavery, one of his regulations declared that "There will be no consideration of nobility or baseness [*kwich'ŏn*] of status [in the determination of] penalties" – a striking reversal of Yulgok's regulations.

Yu did not, however, believe in total equality in the treatment of perpetrators, because punishment had to vary according to the relative ages of the perpetrator and victim. If two brothers happened to fight with one another, the younger brother would be punished more severely than the older. If a transgressor happened to be old or sick and could not endure the full number of strokes prescribed by regulations, he would be required only to remove his hat and lay prostrate on the ground, but his son would take the whipping in his place.[10]

Even though Yu's more general provisions reflected his revulsion against slavery and inherited status, he was hardly more liberal than Yulgok in his commitment to group pressure and physical punishment as the ultimate means for forcing conformity to social norms. Like most other architects of community compacts, he wanted to constrain individuals in the village to vague definitions of requisite interpersonal behavior and make them subject to corporal punishment without requiring that all potentially illegal acts be codified in written form in state laws.[11]

Age versus Inherited Status

In the late sixteenth century, Yulgok had introduced a significant modification into the rules of local self-government organizations by inserting considerations of social status into regulations for punishment in his *Pledges for the Village Granary Kye*. Even though the village granary *kye* was not the same as the community compact, the distinction between the two institutions was not that clear in Yulgok's mind because he carried over many of the moral standards and norms of behavior from the community compact tradition into the granary regulations. Although his list of punishments provided lighter punishments for "scholars" and heavier ones for "lower persons," he had to be referring to the yangban and slaves of Korean society.

Hwang Chonghae, who wrote the regulations for his community compact in 1641 and presumably borrowed Yulgok's concept of differentiated punishments, referred directly to yangban and slaves rather than scholars and lower persons. He was possibly reflecting a more intense perception of inherited privilege in the mid-seventeenth than the mid-sixteenth century, as Yu Suwŏn had argued in the early eighteenth century. Yulgok had thus reversed the emphasis on age as the only legitimate basis for the treatment of individuals in the context of the community compact's functions, and reflected the power of hereditary status in Korean social life.

In his compact regulations on ritual events, however, Yu Hyŏngwŏn sought to affirm the emphasis on age over status in the compact tradition of the Sung dynasty, and he set the standards of behavior required of individuals towards others in prescribed situations according to the five categories of age relationship between ego and alter described in the *Lü-Family Community Compact*. For example, when a "youth" was paying a courtesy call on a "respected one," he had to be wearing a silk gauze hat and formal outer wear, dismount his horse, inquire whether the host was eating, entertaining other guests, or engaged in his own affairs before requesting entry, and present one's name card at the gate. The host would have to reciprocate by sending out a servant to receive the card, descend the stone steps outside his house, or not, depending on the status of his caller. During more formal visits, the number of bows and the attitude of the host was prescribed according to the relative obligations of host and guest.

Congratulatory visits and condolence calls, including funerals and mourning visits, required the head of every household that belonged to the village compact association to call on the affected party, or to present gifts of food, cash, or other goods on felicitous occasions. Even conduct at informal parties had to be governed by strict regulations on the positioning and location of wine cups, the pouring of the wine, the presentation of the wine to guests, the direction toward which host and guest will bow, and the mutual exchange of toasts. The secretary (the Chigwŏl) was obliged to report any violators to the head of the association (Yakchŏng).

Additional degrees of respect were prescribed for visitors or members who might happen to be royal relatives or members of the central bureaucracy with official rank, but otherwise the seating order of individuals at meetings or convocations had to be arranged strictly according to age. In no instance did considerations of social status play a role in these regulations.[12]

There is evidence, however, of the influence of social pressures for the observance of status in the seating arrangements of compact members during the public recitation of the regulations of the compact either at the local school (*hyanggyo*) or at the Local Archery Hall (*Hyangsadang*). Yu's regulations specified that the seating positions of members were to be determined by the age of ego relative to the Yakchŏng under the five categories of the Lü-Family compact, but official and private slaves (*kongch'ŏn* and *sach'ŏn*) would be seated in a separate group apart from people of good status (*yangmin*). Yu's willingness to accept the reality of social life was also reflected in another regulation that permitted a yangban to send a slave or servant to take his place.

On the other hand, if any men who were regular officials of the government bureaucracy or functionaries of the community compact were in attendance at the reading session of the compact regulations, they would be ranked only in accordance with the degree of their position, and not at all according to their good (commoner) or base (slave) status. Though a small concession to the human dignity of slaves, the separation of slaves from "good" men was reminiscent of Yulgok's regulations and reflected Yu's own realistic assessment that slavery was not about to disappear from Korean society despite his ardent wish that it be abolished.

Even though the spirit of the community compact was supposed to be inclusive, there was one practical restriction on full participation. Since the formal requirements of the community compact meeting required that all villagers be dressed in formal attire, if any of the villagers could not afford the required clothing, they might watch the session from outside the courtyard but could not participate in the meeting until the formal ceremonies were over.[13]

Despite his provision to seat slaves away from the rest of the compact association in the formal recitation meeting, Yu was still convinced that the principle of ordering people by age instead of by pedigree or inherited status was sanctioned by classical precedent and essential to a reworking of the social norms of contemporary Korean society. He derived inspiration for this point of view from T'oegye's response to a question by Cho Chin in the sixteenth century as to whether seating arrangements according to age currently in practice in local government (*hyangdang*) meetings did not cause "difficult problems." T'oegye replied that seating order had to be determined on the basis of age in local government meetings. "The difference between nobility and baseness determines the order of rank; what does it have to do with order by age?" He cited the Wang-chih section of the *Book of Rites* (*Li-chi*), which recorded that the various ranks of prestige in Chou times, from the crown prince, secondary princes, court ministers, higher and lower officials, scholars and talented literati, were all admitted to school and thereafter ranked according to their age, not according to the degree of their "nobility or baseness [*kwich'ŏn*]."

T'oegye also referred to description in the *Rites of Chou* of the annual ceremony to local spirits celebrated by the head of one of the local government units (Tang-cheng) where food and drink were offered to people in the community who were ranked according to their age. Ranking by age meant that the oldest people were assigned seats or positions of respect or given the best food, and the purpose was to inculcate norms of filial piety and respect for elders. This principle was the purpose behind the village archery contests, village wine-drinking ritual (*hsiang yin-chou chih li*), and all local laws and rites devised by the sages of Chou times as the means of guaranteeing the very security of the state itself. "How could anyone change an institution that has been carried on since ancient times and abandon the normal seats where fathers, sons, and members of the lineage are aligned, and create a new modus operandi that would destroy the ceremonies of the rural villages and obliterate the teachings of the sages just because some people might feel ashamed to be placed below someone else of low or base status?" T'oegye reminded Cho that "The world only respects three things: virtue, rank, and age. Because virtue and righteousness were most important in school [during Chou times], the princes of the Son of Heaven and the sons of the feudal lords were selected and ranked by age along with the outstanding [youth] of the common people. So much more should respect be based on age in the local villages [*hyangdang*]."[14]

T'oegye himself noted that he had been forced to compromise with current reality because even though there were no official or private slaves in ancient times (or so he thought), presently in Korea they existed and were not allowed to attend schools or to participate in village affairs (in a formal way?), but with respect to any other matter those of low or base status still had to be ranked according to age because there was no other principle to follow. T'oegye thus drew a subtle distinction of the conflict between the hierarchical standards of respect and rank and the egalitarian standards of virtue and merit. Respect for age had to take priority over respect for office and title, but it could only be followed in certain situations where formal boundaries prevented the intrusion of contemporary social norms, such as in schools or in community compact organizations. Yu Hyŏngwŏn probably believed in such a sentiment in general terms, but he was forced to make certain compromises with Korean observance of inherited social status. For that reason, he prescribed that slaves could not sit together with commoners in formal compact meetings.[15]

The Evil of Pedigree

Yu provided that the village *kye* registers (comprising two villages per *kye* in his scheme) would record names of all members of the community whether they were scholars or commoners, but their names would be recorded separately, and slaves were not mentioned at all in this regulation.[16] The regulation reflected his desire to replace the yangban with a meritorious elite of men of virtue who would be trained through continuous observation by their seniors in the village and teachers in his new official schools.

He prescribed that the compact association would require the keeping of a register for the entire district of all officials and scholars (*sabu*), but he probably was using the term to mean the elite of his new society rather than the yangban elite of his own time. Nevertheless, the men to be included in this list did include some elements of hereditary status in contemporary Korean society just as some of his other essays did. Royal relatives and sons of high officials who possessed the protection privilege were included in the *sabu* along with incumbent regular civil and military officials, dormitory students in official schools, *musŏn* (men who passed the select military examinations), and those who had undergone the capping ceremony. In addition each subdistrict or county (*hyang*) would keep a register recording such scions of hereditary privilege as members of high-status royal guards like the Loyal and Righteous Guards and Loyal and Obedient Guards, royal relatives, and those with the protection privilege. as well as extra-quota students in official schools. Naturally, "It would not be necessary to keep a [separate] register for the common people."[17]

Obviously, Yu would not have insisted on a special register for men of higher status and prestige without feeling that they merited more respect than the commoners, but he also insisted that rank or status not affect popular judgment of the behavior of men, and that good deeds be rewarded or bad deeds punished without regard to whether the individual was a scholar or commoner. Distinctions among men of the district were not to be based on the status distinction between scholars (*sa*) and the ordinary people (*min*), or on the prestige of a lineage, but on whether the behavior and actions of people were worthy or ignorant. In explaining this, Yu set out an explanation of the basis of the current status system in Korea:

> The custom in this country is that we only pay respect to pedigree [*munji*]. Among those people who engage in the activity of scholars, we also have [a category] that we call yangban, that is, the sons and grandsons and lineage relations [*choktang*] of the higher and lower officials [*taebusa*]. In general, the system of our country is that only the lineage relations of the *taebusa* can obtain regular official posts as civil and military officials [*tongban* and *sŏban*, or officials of the Eastern and Western files], and for that reason the custom is to call [these people] yangban [men of the two files].

Yu also explained that in addition to yangban, the Korean elite consisted of men of commoner lineages (*sŏjok*) who had either enrolled in official schools or had official posts, and they were referred to as "the middle people" (*chung'in*), the "idlers" (*hansan*), or "irregulars" (*pang'oe*). The lowest category were the nothoi (*sŏŏl*) of the high and low officials (*taebusa*) by their concubines. Yu argued that contemporary local associations did not provide for mixing men belonging to these three different categories in the same ranks or recording them in the same registers because they only recorded the names of the yangban, a statement confirmed by the recent research of Fujiya Kawashima.[18] Therefore, even men of learning, talent, and virtue, including those who had passed the government examinations and held a number of official posts, could not have their names entered into the local registers. Yu condemned this practice as a violation of the intent of former kings who sought to regulate the mores of the people. "All persons who are scholars [*saryu*], should be entered into the [local] register without regard to pedigree, and all should be allowed to sit in order of age at the [compact association] meetings."[19]

Scholarly status did not confer immunity from punishment for any violation of the strict Confucian moral code. Scholars who abhored being forced to participate in the compact association meetings and refused to attend, were to be reported to the magistrate and expelled from the community. Scholars who insulted others and treated them with contempt were especially to be punished for insolence. Nevertheless, their station permitted them certain perquisites like wearing silk hats and garments and riding horses that were forbidden to commoners.[20]

Never before had a compiler of a community compact included such a blistering attack on the system of hereditary restriction of status and officeholding, not even T'oegye or Yulgok. Although Yu felt forced to submerge his distaste for slavery to contemporary social convention in these regulations, he felt less, at least partially, inhibited in challenging the yangban.

Nothoi

Yu also maintained the tradition introduced by Yulgok and continued by Hwang Chonghae in 1641 to punish failure to maintain distinctions between legitimate sons and nothoi (*chŏksŏ*), a distinctly Korean variation not included in Chinese compact texts, but he was more liberal than they by refusing to acknowledge any justification for excluding nothoi from holding a post either as a government bureaucrat or as a functionary of the subdistrict community compact association because the only criterion for officeholding had to be a man's worth, and not family pedigree (*munji*). He, thus, reflected the mood of protest against the discrimination shown the nothoi (*sŏŏl*) that had grown since the early fifteenth century.[21]

Yu, nonetheless, conceded that the registers of the community compact associations still had to distinguish between them and legitimate sons. He explained that while equal opportunity for office should be opened to sons of concubines, within the family proper status distinctions (*myŏngbun*) had to be strictly upheld. Not only did the young have to serve their elders, but those of base (*ch'ŏn*) status were required to serve the noble (*kwi*). This meant that nothoi had to serve the needs of the sons of the legitimate wife (*chŏk*) and show them respect, but at least in one small area no discrimination was to be shown between the sons of concubines of commoner or slave status:

> In all matters they [the nothoi] must not presume to be on equal status with them. They should [sit] in a corner and not dare to sit next to them [legitimate sons]. When seated, they will sit below the elder and younger legitimate brothers, and when standing in a line, they will line up slightly behind [the legitimate sons]. But [within the category of nothoi], all the sons of concubines will be ranked in order of age, and no attention will be paid to whether the status of the concubine [i.e., mother of the nothos] is good or base [*yang* or *ch'ŏn*, i.e., commoner or slave].

Behavior in ordinary situations had to conform to this principle as well. A nothos was not to be allowed to remain seated on a horse if a man of legitimate birth passed by unless the latter was gracious enough to allow him to remain seated there. Nothoi would have to show the same respect for men of legitimate birth that younger commoners had to show to elders, another example of Yu's violation of the predominance of age in respect relations because of this Korean practice that had developed only in the early fifteenth century after the founding of the Chosŏn dynasty.

A nothos might not address a legitimate male younger than he was by the familiar vocative of address, "you," and he had to show respect even though his own family was more prestigious than that of the legitimate man. If he insulted a man of legitimate birth, the local community association had the duty to impeach and punish him. Yu believed that this behavior was justified not only because it was accepted Korean practice, but also because it was practiced in China as well and was therefore a universal standard of behavior. He felt this way because he had heard a story about a Korean visitor to China who was amazed to see an official riding in a carriage on the central part of the road set aside for officials dismount his carriage to greet a scholar passing by on a side road. When he asked the reason, a passerby told him that the official did so because he was the son of a concubine while the scholar was the son of a legitimate wife.

Even though he was convinced that inferior status for nothoi prevailed throughout the world, in Korea they were unjustly prohibited from holding regular office because Koreans were obsessed with family pedigree (*munji*) and thought that allowing nothoi to hold office would disrupt one's moral obligation (*myŏngbun*, i.e., to maintain proper social status distinctions). Unfortunately, in Korea the main criterion for selecting men for office was the artificial ability to compose poems or essays rather than demonstrating virtue and moral worth. If these priorities were reversed, then no men of superior talent in society, including nothoi, would be abandoned in the search for officials, and nothoi would never be inclined to violate the rules of propriety by insulting men of legitimate birth.[22]

Yu's treatment of nothoi was similar to his treatment of slaves. Although he argued for the liberation of both slaves and nothoi from discrimination in the spheres of public life, he could not bring himself to demand the immediate abolition of slavery or discrimination against nothoi in all instances. Instead he sought to achieve workable compromises that would grant more dignity to the discriminated without abolishing the basis for that discrimination totally or too quickly. Yu's reformist impulses in social relations were not radical enough to be disruptive or violent, and he was not a total egalitarian in any case, but his social attitudes differed markedly from Yulgok's because he at least challenged the hereditary privileges of the yangban and the unjust discrimination against nothoi of yangban and their concubines (whether commoner or slave). Yulgok thought only of enforcing existing status discrimination through his detailed list of differentiated punishments. T'oegye was willing to put aside the privileges of rank and subordinate it to age, but only in the context of the school or the compact or *kye* association.

No Freedom of Discussion

Finally, Yu showed no sign of even nascent interest in free and open discussion. In keeping with Yulgok's views, he condemned any discussion of "spirits, false doctrines, or rebellious ideas, or private discussion of court affairs, political matters in the local districts, or exposure of the wrongdoing of others" in the lectures held during the meetings. Since Yu provided that any violators would immediately be charged by the secretary (Chigwŏl) with a misdemeanor, he had no intention of promoting open discussion and criticism of local governance by the members of the compact association.[23]

Maybe it is a function of Western bias to highlight free speech since it is so essential an element of democratic politics, but it does help one to assess the limits of Yu's liberalism. The point has been made in these pages that Yu's opposition to inherited status did not signify his opposition to status and hierarchy altogether. He wanted to transform the criteria of respect from inherited status to virtue and moral action. Since the source of inherited status was not the Confucian tradition, but the subversion of the Confucian ideal by aberrant Korean social practices, those practices could be combatted not by an appeal to a new set of ideals, but by confirmation of classical Confucian ideals. Freedom of speech would only lead to an attack on Confucianism itself, a result more pernicious than perpetuation of the current anomalies in Korean society.

YU'S CONTRIBUTION TO THE COMMUNITY COMPACTS LITERATURE

The idea and inspiration for the institution of community compacts was by no means an innovation, for serious discussion about moral leadership in local self-government organizations had begun in the early fifteenth century, and many of the proposals already included elements of the *Lü-Family Community Compact* and Chu Hsi's emendation of it from the Sung dynasty. Tabana Tameo has correctly pointed out that Yu provided no development of the theory or philosophy of moral education, only another example of an armchair system designed for practical application. While enlightened in spirit, he thought it contained none of the zeal for enlightenment that marked Tasan's work.[24]

Even though Yi T'aejin has attempted to connect the second wave of enthusiasm for community compacts in the late fifteenth century with a progressive movement for the increase of production and commerce, the essence of community compacts was a strong emphasis on moral education to rectify social difficulties or provide aid for economic distress in the countryside. The inspiration for the communal model for mutual aid and surveillance derived primarily from the classical description of Chou institutions of local self-government in the *Rites of Chou.*

The moral overtones of the community compact regulations were amplified in the Sung dynasty because of the renewed emphasis on moral education through fundamental texts like the *Sohak*, which concentrated on reducing moral teaching to the simple and mechanical instruction of untutored children and youth in acts of filial piety and respect for elders. The advocates of the community compacts or other agencies that incorporated similar values did not believe that increasing economic production, or even distributing wealth more widely, was sufficient to create a secure and happy society because ultimately the tranquillity of social life depended on creating a moral atmosphere throughout the local villages. For that reason any attempt by twentieth-century scholars to reduce Neo-Confucian moralism to economic materialism and class interest would simply distort an understanding of the nature of social thought in the Confucian era.

Yu Hyŏngwŏn, however, did represent something new in the history of community compact writing, because he rejected the tendency represented by Yulgok to defend, almost unself-consciously, social status discrimination in the administration of punishment and in the seating order in the compact regulations. Instead, he sought to provide better treatment for slaves and nothoi, but his instincts for reform were limited by the strength of Korean social prejudice. Nothoi would be given more opportunities for advancement in public life, but in the family they would continue to acts as inferiors. Slaves would be judged for their misdemeanors just as commoners within the community compact association, but they would have to sit separately from the rest of the members. Yu's instincts were much closer to the sentiments of T'oegye than Yulgok because T'oegye had written that at least in schools and local self-government organizations men deserved to be treated on the basis of academic accomplishment, capacity for moral behavior, and age. Nevertheless, he had never insisted that those standards be applied in all social institutions or that slaves be liberated from bondage.

It would be difficult to attribute Yu's more active opposition to social discrimination than Yulgok's to T'oegye's philosophical preference for principle over psycho-physical energy in the constitution of the cosmos and the human mind. Nevertheless, it might be possible to speculate that Yu, like T'oegye, may have had greater respect for the principles of governance contained in classical literature rather than the force of contemporary social custom, and he may for that reason have been more willing to challenge social convention. The weakness of this argument, however, was that T'oegye himself was not stirred to socially revolutionary propositions, and that despite Yulgok's support for social status arrangements, he was far more audacious in his concern about practical reform. Yu was fairly free to adopt arguments from many quarters and did so from both T'oegye and Yulgok alike, but he was far from a freethinker; he was as strongly prejudiced against "heterodoxy," or shamanism, geomancy, and Buddhism as Yulgok and other intense Neo-Confucians.

DEVELOPMENTS AFTER YU HYŎNGWŎN

Community Compacts in King Sukchong's Reign

To be sure Yu Hyŏngwŏn's thought did not exert much influence on actual policy over any matter until the middle of the eighteenth century, and the same was true in the area of community compact writing and organization. In general, concern for moral education and enlightenment at the local level continued only sporadically after the mid-seventeenth century. The reign of King Sukchong (r. 1674–1720) was not noted for much concern about moral education, let alone adoption of community compacts at any level.

Community compacts were only mentioned three times between 1682 and 1684. The director of the National Academy, Kim Malli, complained that students in the academy were being treated far too leniently and he asked that they be disciplined according to community compact regulations, but only in the school and not in the outside world, and students guilty of misdemeanors would still be allowed to proceed to the national examinations. Second State Councilor Min Chŏngjung complained about fights that had broken out in the so-called Incense *Kye* (*hwado*) in the capital formed to defray funeral expenses, and he convinced Sukchong to abolish them and order the formation of mutual aid organizations in the capital modeled on community compacts to serve this function. Finally, Second State Councilor Pak Sech'ae criticized the absence of penalties for violations of moral standards in the dynastic law code, and he asked that the important moral regulations contained in community compacts be ordered into penal law. Since there was no record of any implementing edict, the recommendation was probably never carried out.[25]

Despite King Yŏngjo's (r. 1724–76) concern for the *Sohak* and other moral texts in the first part of his reign, there were very few concrete proposals for the adoption of community compacts or measures for moral education. In 1734 and 1745 Yŏngjo approved the requests of the rural scholar from Chŏlla, Wi Sep'ung, and Second State Councilor Song Inmyŏng to institute community compacts, but nothing was ever done. Yulgok's compact was mentioned only briefly at court in 1746 and in 1754, but Yŏngjo never took any action.[26]

Ch'oe Hŭngwŏn's Puindong-dongyak *of 1739–45*

Despite the absence of leadership from the central government, there were a few instances of spontaneous organization. From 1739 to 1745 Ch'oe Hŭngwŏn established a community compact (the *Puindong-dongyak*) and a village granary in conjunction with one another, and he later built a lecture hall for the recitation of the regulations, which were compiled and published later in 1774. Even though Yulgok had established a precedent for combining these two institutions and Kim Seryŏng in the early seventeenth century had called for the establishment of village schools, village granaries, the *pogap* (*pao-chia*) system of mutual aid and surveillance, and community compacts in progression, Ch'oe was apparently not directly influenced by those precedents. He also read and praised Yu Hŏngwŏn's *Pan'gye surok*, but he did so a decade after he established his own compact and granary. He apparently borrowed some of the wording of Ming T'ai-tsu's Six Edicts but was not dependent exclusively on any single model, including Chu Hsi's.[27]

His more explicit delineation of punishments went beyond Yulgok by providing for corporal punishment for scholars (*saryu*) who refused to change their ways, far more severe than Chu Hsi's lenient penalty of "allowing the person to leave the compact." He was more willing than previous scholars and officials to turn violators over to the magistrate than deal with them in the compact organization, and preferred talking about crimes (*choe*) rather than the usual transgressions (*kwasil*) in most community compact regulations. On the other hand, Ch'oe wanted to reward members who performed good deeds and dispensed with the traditional regulation for keeping a separate register of misdemeanors. He also provided that the rules of the compact be read to the members in Han'gul for the edification of all classes. Tabana has commented on Ch'oe's vindictive stress on punishment rather than persuasion as the means for establishing social order, and although this tendency was not true for all writers on the subject, there may well have been a trend since Yulgok (and T'oegye) to convert the compact from an agency of moral teaching to one of coercive enforcement.[28]

Kim Hongdŭk's Community Compact in Poŭn, 1747

Kim Hongdŭk was magistrate of Poŭn in Ch'ungch'ŏng Province when in 1747 he adopted his own version of a community compact to raise the morals of his district. Kim borrowed heavily from Yulgok's delineation of punishments in his Haeju Community Compact and his Village Granary *Kye* Pledges, but as opposed to Yulgok and Ch'oe Hŭngwŏn, he reduced the penalties for the scholars (*saryu*, i.e., yangban) prescribed in Yulgok's regulations because he thought that punishing scholars was unacceptable. Even a scholar who refused to promise that he would reform his errors would only have his name recorded and not be asked to endure a reprimand by the compact's officials.

Kim had some compassion for lower persons (*hain*) or slaves as well, but hardly enough to make a significant difference because he still retained the maximum penalty of forty strokes of the stick for them, but he assured his readers that forty strokes would not be enough to kill anyone, and the head of the *Kye* in any case could be counted on to stop the beating if he thought it might kill the accused. Even though Yu Hyŏngwŏn may have been part of a trend to treat scholars and yangban with less respect, that attitude was not shared by every scholar-official in the kingdom.[29]

An Chŏngbok's Community Compacts

Two Compacts in Kyŏng'an County, 1756. The well-known late-eighteenth century scholar-official, An Chŏngbok, became interested in community compacts from reading the *Sohak* and later the *Hsing-li ta-ch'üan* compendium of Neo-Confucian lore. In his first publication written in 1740, the *Hahak chinam* (*Primer for Lower-Level Learning*), he twice mentioned community compacts as important for moral education and the rectification of social mores, and in 1756 he established a community compact for two villages in Kyŏng'an County (*Kyŏng'an-myŏn iridongyak*), located in Kwangju-bu (in Chŏlla Province). The individual items of his compact were influenced most heavily by the work of Yulgok and Hwang Chonghae, and even though he wrote a chronological biography of Yu Hyŏngwŏn and may have been influenced by his ideas on compacts, he never cited him in his compact regulations.

An's compact regulations are most interesting for his vigorous defense of traditional social status distinctions rather than for any innovations in organization and principles. He insisted that respect for social status (*myŏngbun*) in general and for yangban in particular had to be clear, but yangban also had to be punished for their errors because they had the knowledge to know right from wrong and were obliged to set standards of behavior for commoners (*sang'in*). They were neither to exult in their own pedigrees nor continue their proclivity for factional dispute.

Although some had thought that factionalism had been caused by the inherent nature of scholars and their propensity for argument, he could not believe that such behavior was endemic because they should have been totally preoccupied with study and self-rectification, and should not have thought that correct opinions were the exclusive property only of their own faction. Instead of prescribing punishment for factional behavior, however, he merely urged them to follow King Yŏngjo's declared policy of equal opportunity for all (*t'angp'yŏng*) and strive within the community compact to eliminate the factional tendency.

He deplored the recent habit among students of treating teachers as equals and added a rule that students demonstrate respect for their teachers even though they might be younger. He required commoners (tenants?) and slaves to pay courtesy calls on yangban within three days of the New Year and to prostrate themselves at least once before them, habits that he claimed only the scholars of Kyŏngsang Province were practicing at the time. He provided public rewards for slaves (*nobi*) for displays of loyalty to their masters, but also required them to suffer corporal punishment for moral errors or any sign of disrespect for their masters. He declared that nothoi of yangban were, of course, human, but that the distinction between them and legitimate sons had to be maintained strictly, and any examples of disrespect by them had to be punished, as it was prescribed in the national law code.[30]

He divided his compact organization itself into two *kye* according to the status of the members: the first called Upper *Kye* (*sanggye*) with yangban members, and the second the Middle and Lower *Kye* (*chunghagye*) with commoners and slave members. The Middle and Lower *Kye* had to stand when listening to the recitation of the compact regulations in the colloquial language, but the yangban in the Upper *Kye* could remain seated when listening instead to a recitation of the Lü-Family compact.[31] For a scholar reputed to have been an intellectual follower of Yu, An looks more like a defender of the status quo rather than a social radical.

Village Granary Regulations, 1757. An's regulations for the village granary (*sach'ang*), drafted in 1757, was intimately tied to the community compact. The head of the compact was simultaneously director of the village granary, and other officials of the compact performed duties in the granary. In his preface to the granary's regulations, he discussed the history of ever-normal price stabilization policies in China since the Han dynasty, righteous granaries for relief in villages in the Sui dynasty, and Chu Hsi's village granaries for emergency loans in the Sung dynasty. He acknowledged that the village granary system had developed problems over time, but he blamed it on the people who ran them, not the system itself. He mentioned that while the Korean *hwanja* grain-loan system appeared similar to the village granaries, in fact it was much closer in spirit to Wang Anshih's green-shoots system of loans. He also regretted the failure of the ever-normal system to function effectively even though it was included in the *Kyŏngguk taejŏn* law code of the fifteenth century. He did not bother to include the leading advocates of community compacts in his recitation of their history, but his regulations were quite similar (and often identical) to those made by Yulgok, who combined the community compact and village granary in his regulations, and to Yu Hyŏngwŏn's program to abolish the *hwanja* loans and adopt the ever-normal, village granary, and community compact systems at the local level.

Nevertheless, An did not advocate that these village granaries be adopted at the national level, at least not until a sage ruler appeared who would have the capacity to do it. Tabana has concluded that An originally did not design the village granary to operate in conjunction with the community compact and only added it the next year. Like Yulgok and Yu Hyŏngwŏn, An Chŏngbok designed the granary to operate at the subdistrict or county level and probably did not succeed in carrying it out.[32]

Yu Hyŏngwŏn did not influence An's thought as much as Chu Hsi, Yulgok, Hwang Chonghae, and even Ming T'ai-tsu whose Six Edicts he included in the text. Although usually counted as a prestigious member of the Sirhak scholars, An's conservative defense of social status seems to have hardly been different from the mainstream of social thought throughout the dynasty. Although he was willing to punish yangban for violations of propriety, he had no desire to level the privileges of status nor alleviate discrimination against slaves or nothoi of yangban.

Village Kye for Moral Education in 1776. When An was appointed magistrate of Mokch'ŏn-hyŏn in Ch'ungch'ŏng Province in 1776 he was shocked by the unrestrained behavior of the local residents, and sent out a directive to each of the eight counties (*myŏn*) in the district to provide moral education (*kyohwa*) for the defense of social status (*myŏngbun*). He mentioned that since village *kye* (*tonggye*) already existed in the district, he would use them for the adoption of community compact regulations under the leadership of the educated elite of each community (instead of the county). He cited Ming T'ai-tsu's policy of ordering instruction in his Six Edicts, its effectiveness in transforming local mores, and the traditional respect the Koreans had held for the Ming dynasty in the Chosŏn period. He called for his six admonitions (instead of the four in the Lü-Family compact) against immoral behavior to be recited at monthly meetings in the village.

An emphasized the Chou tradition that moral reform had to begin in the small community, and he hoped that the basic unit would consist of a minimum of one hundred households, the same definition of the administrative village used in the Sui, T'ang, and Ming dynasties. If villages in his district were smaller than that, they would have to combine to form a *tong* (administrative village). The families of the "upper households and officials" (*sangho-daebu*), that is, the yangban, would take charge of guiding "the ignorant people" and organizing them into *kye* (or village *kye tonggye*) for reading the compact regulations and implementing them gradually – a much more hierarchical provision than Yu's predilection from equal social participation. An did not mention a word about the voluntary nature of the community compact stressed by so many other scholars in previous times.[33]

An drew up regulations governing contributions in cash by *kye* households for relief, revenue shortages in the district, and the feeding or replacement of horses in the post-station system. He established collection centers (called Pangyŏkso) for these contributions in the villages and counties to strengthen local self-government because the people should manage what they were responsible for paying for. He also instructed all clerks to refrain from interference.

Unfortunately, his program had just begun when his son died, and he lost his enthusiasm for government service. It was unlikely that his compact system was too successful, especially since it was not even mentioned in the district gazetteer.[34]

King Chŏngjo's Policy toward Compacts

King Chŏngjo ascended the throne in 1776 and approved the adoption of community compacts in 1780, but he did nothing to ensure its implementation and did not respond to further requests for a decade. When Censor-General Sin Ki attacked moral decline and the lack of mutual aid and support for funerals or famines, Chŏngjo developed an interest in community compacts, possibly because of the new tide of fear among conservatives about the developing interest in Christianity and Western learning in Korea. Chŏngjo generally followed the lead of Ch'ae Chegong to respond with more moral education rather than the persecution of Catholics, and in 1795 he ordered the compilation and distribution of the *Combined Edition of the Community Compact and Local (Wine-Drinking) Rite* (*Hyangnye happ'yŏn*) and the recitation of compact regulations when the wine-drinking rite was conducted. Since he believed that community compacts had to be voluntary organizations, however, he opposed forcing them on the population and agreed that they were not necessary in the capital, as Song Siyŏl had once advised. Thus, they were only in certain areas and were viewed more as a means for moral education than as the format for local self-government.[35]

Tasan's Community Compact of 1821

When Chŏngjo died, he was succeeded by his ten-year old son, King Sunjo. The grand dowager of King Yŏngjo, who was sympathetic to the *pyŏkp'a* faction and hostile to the Christians, became regent. The court was consumed with ferocious attacks against Christianity, and the furor was exacerbated when the Christian Hwang Sayong was arrested. His famous silk letter, which outlined a program for military aid from the emperor of France to protect Christianity in Korea and an invitation to the Ch'ing emperor to appoint a Manchu prince to govern Korea was discovered, and the dowager decided to execute a number of Christians and burn their books. Several officials recommended reinforcing moral teaching to strengthen Confucian orthodoxy against Christian subversion, and in 1801 a member of the Inspector-General's Office proposed adopting community compacts and wine-drinking rites as the best means to do this, but the recommendation did not elicit much reaction at court, and the dowager had already decided that strengthening the five-family system (*ogat'ong*) of mutual surveillance to ferret out all Christians would be sufficient.[36]

Further interest in community compacts disappeared, but Tasan (Chŏng Yagyong), one of the scholars arrested for propagating Christianity in 1801 and sent into exile until 1818, wrote the text of a community compact and included it in his famous reform treatise, *A Book from the Heart on Governing the People* (*Mongmin simsŏ*), probably in 1821. Chastened, no doubt, by his close escape from execution, Tasan composed a text that contained nothing new and conformed fully with traditional Confucian standards of behavior.

Nevertheless, Tasan warned his readers that the community compact could easily become a force for evil if a well-intentioned but untalented magistrate appointed members of the elite to be the head and other officials of the organization because they would use their authority to dominate the community, intimidate the people, demand grain and drink, expose secrets, prejudice the adjudication of lawsuits, and use the people to till their own fields. The local elite would possibly split into two factions and wreck community harmony: one faction that controlled the school and another that ran the community compact. Furthermore, since almost everyone could be counted on to steal or act selfishly in a time of famine, the people could only be controlled and steered back to goodness by the intervention of a wise magistrate.

In short, despite the social and economic radicalism of his plan for reform of the land system and elimination of the privileges of the yangban, these elements were not reflected in his community compact draft. In it he did not condemn social status distinction or slavery and, in fact, he appeared to distrust the autonomy of the community compact by calling for its domination by a wise magistrate.[37]

The Hwangyŏ Community Compact of 1823

Tabana also found another text of a Hwangyŏ community compact that he presumes was dated in 1823 because it was based on the five-family system (*ogat'ong*) that the dowager-regent during the beginning of King Sunjo's reign had favored and also contained a condemnation of Christian books. The penalties for violations in this compact were quite similar to the model established by Yulgok because they contained a very detailed differention of five punishments according to the status of the perpetrator.

For example, in the first degree, respected elders had to stand in the courtyard without hats, elders had to endure a reprimand to their faces before all members of the compact, commoners (*chŭngdŭng*, that is, *chung'in* and others) had to strip to the waist and squat on the ground, and lower persons (slaves?) had to suffer thirty strokes of the stick. These penalties were reduced for each stratum for each of the other degrees of punishment. Elders and respected elders could have their sons or nephews accept punishment in their place, or if they had no such relatives, they could have one of their slaves beaten. Slaves that were elderly or sick were allowed to pay a penalty as a substitute for corporal punishment. Otherwise, despite some discrepancies of form and certain ceremonies that appeared more suited for a school or religious meeting, the content of this compact conformed to previous examples in other compacts, particularly with respect to social discrimination.[38]

The Hoeryŏng-gun Compact of 1819

At the end of the dynasty a number of officials wrote community compacts. A magistrate, Sŏ Chŭngbo, wrote one in 1866 modeled after Yu Hyŏngwŏn's version; Han Changsŏk did one in 1890 based on the work of Yu, T'oegye, Yulgok, and Cho Hŏn; Song Chaegyŏng composed one in Hwayang in 1904; Cho Pyŏngsik reputedly did one in the capital in 1904. King Kojong ordered the compilation of a text called *Community Regulations* (*Hyanghŏn*) in 1902 that contained the wine-drinking and archery rituals and a community compact based on Chu Hsi's version.

Finally, a fragment of a community compact from Hoeryŏng-gun in Hamgyŏng Province was published in Japanese sometime after the Japanese annexation in 1910, probably by a district magistrate of the colonial regime, and it appeared to have been based primarily on the compacts designed by Yulgok and Yu Hyŏngwŏn. It was designed to function in support of the magistrate since one of his clerks was to hold the position of head of the subdistrict (county) community compact simultaneously, and possibly other clerks may have held local positions like village elder even though the compact regulations called for popular choice of local elders or scholars (i.e., *hyangban*).

The anonymous Japanese author commented that even though commoners and slaves were admitted into the compact as members, it was still run by the yangban-scholars because the names of the functionaries were all members of the *sarim* (yangban-scholar class). The membership list consisted of just those types of social categories prescribed by Yu Hyŏngwŏn, not only men with civil and military official rank and office, but also students in official schools, *musŏn*, royal relatives and sons of officials with the protection privilege (including nothoi), and members of elite capital guards. Only in the two registers for merits and demerits were men of all social strata to be listed. In short, the author described the compact as "a private compact by the *sarim*" set up to raise local morals and mores, and he portrayed it as a spontaneous, private organization of local self-government that performed some official functions like punishment of misdemeanors and resolution of lawsuits, and was approved and supported by the government's magistrate. It was possible for a hybrid institution that combined private activities and public (or official) duties to exist because modern legal concepts (i.e., especially the necessity for a firm line between public authority and private activity that presumably distinguished the nature of Japanese colonial rule from the late Chosŏn political system) were not strong at the time.

Only the local elite was allowed to attend the quadriannual sessions for the reading of the compact regulations, except for commoners who also happened to be minor functionaries in the compact organization. The rules also contained the usual discriminatory penalties: beatings were reserved for lower persons (*hain*), while scholars (*saryu*) and elders were required only to endure a public reprimand or move to a lower seat during compact meetings. There was, however, no repetition of Yulgok's rule to allow sons, younger brothers, or slaves to suffer a beating in place of an exalted elder.[39] While it would be difficult to assert that an isolated document such as this one reflected the norms of society as a whole, it nonetheless indicates that the forms of distinction and social discrimination of the sixteenth century were still holding fast in the late nineteenth century. While Yu's work on this subject was probably widely known, the thrust of his reforms had still not taken hold.

Yu's Contribution to Community Compacts

The literature on community compacts or, more broadly, on local associations, established for the moral encouragement, mutual aid, and surveillance, began at least at the beginning of the dynasty. The inspiration for the movement came first from the *Rites of Chou*, and was restimulated by a moralistic reform movement in the late fifteenth century under Kim Chongjik. Although that trend came to a sudden end with the purge of Cho Kwangjo in 1519, another upsurge of concern for moral rectification occurred after the mid-sixteenth century with support from T'oegye, Yulgok, and Cho Hŏn, and King Sŏnjo even ordered community compacts adopted on a nationwide basis in 1573, but he suspended the order almost immediately because of a severe famine. Even though these advocates of community compacts were renowned for their concern for moral education, their models placed a greater stress on punishment than persuasion and introduced existing categories of social status discrimination into the compact regulations.

After Hideyoshi's invasions, Korean kings provided little interest or support for the adoption of compacts as a national policy. Yu Hyŏngwŏn's version of a community compact constituted a revival of interest after a lapse of almost a century, but his regulations did not transform their nature and purpose. They did, however, reflect a difficult and agonizing conflict between his ideals of a society based on morality and equality of opportunity and the reality of discrimination against slaves, nothoi, and women, and special favor for the ruling class. He attempted to solve those contradictions by compromise rather than radical revision.

He insisted that marks of inherited social status should not interfere with the admittance of all members of a community to the community compact, that nothoi of concubines (including concubines of slave status) be permitted to hold posts in the compact organization as well as positions in the bureaucracy. He held that status considerations should not be considered in lessening the punishments due prestigious members of the community who violated the law or compact regulations (as Yulgok had provided in his compact regulations), and that age should consistently take precedence over social status in the conduct of ceremonies. However, he still took care to seat slaves separately from commoners and nothoi separately from legitimate sons in formal compact meetings and to provide special status for bona fide scholars and officials and their sons and the elite of his new community of moral worthies.

After Yu's death advocacy of the community compact was either mentioned at court or tried privately in individual districts, but as a whole the movement had lost its drive. In the late eighteenth century, An Chŏngbok's community compact was a model of social conservatism, not radical reform, and Tasan's compact contained nothing of the radicalism of some of his other writings. Although Yu Hyŏngwŏn's work on the subject was either mentioned or copied by some individual compacts from the mid-eighteenth century right through the end of the nineteenth, it had no discernible effect in producing the creation of any distinctly egalitarian compacts even though the number of slaves decreased sharply, at least on the household registers.

Some might relegate the whole literature on community compacts to the category of irrelevant trivia because it did not result in many examples of concrete policy, but it was crucial to understanding some of the fundamental concepts of governance and social discrimination in the Chosŏn period. Contrary to the arguments of some scholars, there is virtually no solid evidence in the compact literature that its authors were motivated by any attempt to reorganize society in a way that would promote the expansion of production and commerce, let alone capitalism, because the method and the content of these compacts and their early Chosŏn predecessors were quintessentially devoted to the realization of Confucian norms of respect and social behavior.

Every advocate of community compacts, including Yu, believed that the community compact association had the duty to oversee and investigate every detail of personal behavior in daily life and mobilize the entire community to enforce conformity to Confucian norms. This was to be implemented first by education and persuasion, but if that did not succeed, then by ostracism and punishment, methods that were antithetical to the Western notion of the right of individuals to protection from the state. As liberal as Yu Hyŏngwŏn may have been on the question of freedom from social discrimination based on inherited status, he was an unshakeable conservative on the question of free inquiry and expression because his aim was to achieve realization of Confucian ideals in full, not the abandonment or destruction of those ideals.

The community compacts were designed to rectify the obvious and periodic decline in popular mores that had occurred over the years, such as an increase of banditry and thievery, overt signs of disrespect for parents, elders, landlords, masters, and husbands, and arguments, fights, and even murder of close relatives. Most of the proponents of the compacts believed that moral education, persuasion, and group pressure were essential to create the mood necessary to restore harmony to society because the apparatus of state power was ineffective or easily subverted by the private and corrupt motives of many officials and most clerks. Yu Hyŏngwŏn shared the sentiment of the moralists of the sixteenth century that a more inclusive network of community organization and control was needed to enforce moral standards.

In the end the community compact movement was a total failure. Only the Taewongun's adoption of the village granary system in the mid-nineteenth century could be regarded as a successful fruition of the long history of ideas about the virtues of local self-government, and even that experiment was mitigated by the charging of interest for central government finance. Instead, the loss of interest in community compacts by kings and active government officials reflected the long-term decline in morale that generally accompanied a political and social regime that doggedly preferred to preserve the position of the elite rather than break the bonds that tied men down.

PART V

Reform of Government Organization: Conclusion

Rationalization and Cost-Cutting

Yu's discussion of bureaucratic reorganization and reform covered all aspects of the bureaucracy, from the king and the central government to local self-government associations. Much of his thought on this subject was based on the concept of rationalization of an inefficient and redundant bureaucracy for cutting wasteful expenditures and taxes. He proposed bringing the king's personal finances under bureaucratic control, cutting the cost of maintaining royal relatives through four generations, reducing the size of the bureaucracy and reorganizing it according to a more rational division of responsibility, and eliminating the equivalent of "rotten boroughs" by incorporating small districts into larger ones.

Bureaucratic Control of the King

Yu thought that the excessive and arbitrary power of the king could be brought under bureaucratic control by establishing the prime minister as chief executive over the six ministries, shifting the selection of royal consorts to the bureaucracy, expanding accessibility by officials to royal audiences, reducing the atmosphere of awe and intimidation that governed the Royal Lectures, and replacing the distance between king and his officials by recreating the feeling of intimacy and reciprocal obligation that accompanied the personal bond between lord and vassal of Chou feudalism. The main problem of Chosŏn government was not royal despotism, however, but the domination of policy by the yangban at court and their defense of their economic interests: private property in land and slaves, tenancy, tax benefits through underregistration of land, and exemption from military and labor service.

Of course, Yu provided for the rectification of these problems by proposing the confiscation of all privately owned land, imposing military service requirements on almost everyone but officials, and abolishing inherited slavery, but in the absence of those reforms his plans for bureaucratic organization were unlikely to achieve their purpose because expanding the control of the existing yangban bureaucrats over the king would only exacerbate the problems of the current age. Thus, when the only serious attempt at bureaucratic reform was carried out in the late Chosŏn dynasty under the Taewongun in the 1860s, the Taewongun expanded the power of the throne at the expense of both bureaucrats and yangban.

Rectification of Personnel Procedures

Yu also presumed that if he abolished the examination system and replaced it with a system of official schools to recruit an elite of morally superior men for government service, the yangban bureaucrats would be replaced by men devoted to the public good rather than their own private interest. He reinforced this plan by providing for reform of the process of reviewing the performance of officials in which his first priority was to eliminate consideration of the pedigree (*munji*) of all candidates for office from consideration and open opportunity to men of talent. His second was to insist upon the use of recommendation as a means of by-passing the deficiencies of current review procedures, and his third was to institute a new training institute for new candidates for office in the capital.

Although all these procedures were based on the recruitment of men grounded in Confucian standards of morality rather than competency or efficiency in administration, they would have undoubtedly improved the quality of officials over the current crop. Unfortunately, the yangban in control of the bureaucracy would have had to sign their own political death warrants to carry it out, and there was as yet no crisis crucial enough to induce them to do it.

Central Bureaucratic Control versus Local Autonomy

Yu's advocacy of the superiority of bureaucratic over royal authority in the conduct of government suggested that he was thoroughly committed to thoroughly centralized bureaucracy as the key to good government. In fact, he deplored the inadequacy of provincial administration because of the temporary aspects of provincial governors and the short terms of service of both governors and magistrates, but his discussion of local government reveals that his strong commitment to local autonomy illustrated his skepticism about the probity and reliability of central bureaucrats.

As always he drew on traditional lore about the importance of local autonomy and self-government as a means of checking the tyranny of the central bureaucrat. He could see that bureaucratic maladministration had converted agencies for ordinary credit and relief into institutions of debtor oppression, so he proposed that the current official grain loan system be replaced by an ever-normal price stabilization system that removed magistrates from functioning as creditors and foreclosers of mortgages, and he transferred authority for relief and loans to subdistrict agencies run by prominent local leaders rather than magistrates or clerks.

Recognizing that the Sinitic style of bureaucratic organization left a big gap between the district magistrate and the village peasants, he echoed the appeals of many in the Chinese and Korean traditions for the creation of local community compacts run by the people themselves, in which the community compact would take over the enforcement of tax payments, the adjudication of low-level criminal and civil cases, the implementation of relief, and the enforcement of Confucian moral standards through group pressure, ostracism, and coercion.

Ironically, the point of local autonomy was not to defend local interest against the center, especially when the local interests of the yangban landlords and slaveholders interfered with state interest and the public good. Local autonomy, he believed, would use the mobilization of the people at the village level and mutual aid and surveillance as a technique to rectify the weaknesses of the existing system of local administration and enforce conformity with central objectives and Confucian norms.

Yu, however, perceived that the interest of the center should be the public good, in which the state acted as defender of the downtrodden peasant and slave against the exploitation of corrupt magistrates and clerks, landlords, and slaveowners, but in the real world the state competed with the landlords and slaveowners for the exploitation of the peasants and slaves. That the community compact never had a ghost's chance of success in the real world only reflected the perception by the local yangban that community compacts would harm their interests.

Elite versus Mass Interests

Yu's bias against pedigree and inherited privilege did not mean that he rejected hierarchy as a standard for social organization. He simply opposed the inheritance of defects and blemishes by the innocent or special privileges by the undeserving. He was relentless in his attack on yangban privilege, but he was willing to make compromises because he fully appreciated the difficulty of a sudden transformation of social norms.

As a result, in working out rules for government reorganization he acknowledged the status that attached to members of the royal family, to officials and their sons, and to scholars and insisted on the respect owed them in public rites and ceremonies. He hoped to open reasonable opportunity to nothoi, slaves, and women to perform functions for state and community, and yet at the same time not undermine powerful conventions. Nothoi would be allowed to hold office and posts in the community compacts but this would not permit them to demand equal status with legitimate sons. Slaves and women in the employ of the state as clerks would be provided with salaries for the first time, but slaves still had to show respect for their masters and line up separately from commoners in local rituals, and women still owed obedience to their fathers and husbands and could not qualify for appointment to regular office. Despite these compromises his attitude toward social discrimination was still far more liberal than that of his contemporaries, but his ultimate goal was to escape contemporary Korean social discrimination for what he regarded as the more benign condition of the late Ming, as described by Cho Hŏn.

Freedom versus Control

Finally, lest the reader construe that Yu's liberality connoted freedom from constraint in all forms, both from social and ideological restriction, keep in mind his list of injunctions and penalties in his community compact regulations that forbade not only discussion of heterodox ideas but of popular criticism of government action. For that reason his community compacts did not represent liberation but conformity to ideas and ideals along with Confucian values and norms. Since the regular bureaucracy and their untutored clerks had not been able to indoctrinate the public to the superiority of Confucian values, he hoped that a tightly organized and voluntary organization of local people would provide the institutional apparatus for the final, successful conversion of all the people to moral norms.

Bureaucratic Reform after Yu Hyŏngwŏn

There appears to have been little influence exerted by Yu's ideas for bureaucratic reform until the decade of the Taewongun after 1863, but reality did not conform in all cases to his description of the situation. The kings of the seventeenth and eighteenth centuries may not have been complete despots, but Kings Sukchong, Yŏngjo, and Chŏngjo definitely maintained their power even though they were not willing or able to challenge the economic interests of the yangban in any serious way. But in the nineteenth century, the power of the king was reduced because of a succession of under-age monarchs dominated by dowager-regents and the male relatives of queens. Since these relatives were all members of yangban clans, the reduction of royal power did not mean the elevation of honest bureaucratic administration, but rather the narrowing of opportunity as consort families monopolized the best posts in the central bureaucracy. Thus, there was no attempt to separate the royal exchequer from the king's nominal control and place it in the hands of the Ministry of Taxation, or to remove control of the palace estates of royal princes and princesses set aside for their benefit. While this represented the continuation of royal excess, it did not also signify the apotheosis of royal power – just the opposite.

Yu had called for the creation of a strong prime minister and the replacement of the irregular Border Defense Command by a reconstituted State Council, but this situation was not changed. The chief state councilor was hardly more important than the councilors of the left and right, and the officials of the Border Defense Command usually held concurrencies in the State Council, so that the domination of the government by the yangban civilian officials over the military was continued without change. But there was no attempt to expand the education and training of civilian officials to broaden their outlook and increase their appreciation of military affairs.

Little was done to lengthen the terms of service for officials. In fact, the trend seems to have been in the opposite direction because officials were shifted so frequently that there was little expectation that they could gain control over their staff officials and clerks. The clerks were never granted salaries by the state, and their corruption continued to be one of the major sources of popular discontent. Community compacts were never established and no institution was created to replace the local clerk between the people and the magistrate. The failure to solve this problem made the magistrates and their clerks the cause of oppression both in the collection of taxes and service and the administration of credit and relief that led to massive peasant rebellions in 1812 and 1862.

Although nothoi were eventually allowed to take the examinations, the social stigma against them still remained strong. After 1800 slaves apparently were able to escape registration as slaves and presumably all the deficiencies concurrent therewith, but what should have been a monumental improvement in social condition did not prevent a devolution toward serious rural discontent and popular rebellion.

When the Taewongun, the father of the minor King Kojong, seized power from 1864 to 1873, however, he made some attempts to institute reforms suggested by Yu and others. In other words, only when the dynasty was facing imminent collapse from the threat of foreign invasion and internal subversion did a leader appear with enough motivation and conviction to attempt some of the reforms that were required. The most important structural reforms, however, included an assertion of royal power, not its subordination to the prime minister or state council. The Taewongun did replace the Border Defense Command with the State Council, but the action did not signify the exercise of bureaucratic responsibility against royal authority.

The Taewongun did adopt the idea of special recommendation of officials for bureaucratic appointments to supplement the work of the Ministry of Personnel, but the result of this effort was to appoint men with connections to high officials, who already represented dominant bureaucratic factions and some of the consort relatives, like the Andong Kim and P'ungyang Cho – not the moral elite of society that Yu Hyŏngwŏn had in mind. He never attempted to eliminate the examination system and replace it with a system of official schools throughout the entire country as the major means of education and recruitment, but the Taewongun's did abolish most of the private academies because they had come to serve only their own private political and economic interests rather than the public good. In personnel policy his main goal was to overcome the domination of the bureaucracy by consort relatives and the members of the Patriarch's and Disciples' Factions, a problem that Yu had virtually ignored in his work. The net result was the creation of a group of officials who were willing to follow the Taewongun's lead in the implementation of policy.

In the realm of local government, however, the Taewongun came close to achieving some of the ideas that Yu put forward in his work. While he did not attempt to put local clerks on government salary or upgrade their status as Yu had suggested, he did establish village granaries to administer grain loans and relief to the peasantry instead of the district magistrate. While the results of this reform were mixed, the measure at least reduced the level of corruption by bypassing the magistrates and their clerks.

While Yu was obviously far ahead of his time, his ideas were not irrelevant to Korean history. In the sphere of bureaucratic reorganization, in particular, they had significant influence on the Taewongun, who succeeded in preventing total collapse for another generation.

PART VI

Financial Reform and the Economy: Introduction

The middle of the seventeenth century witnessed the beginnings of important changes in the Korean economy. The most visible manifestations of those changes – the conversion of the tribute tax in kind into a grain surtax on land to finance market purchases of goods and the minting of copper cash – had begun at the beginning of the century, but they also represented deeper changes in the economy that had begun in the late fifteenth century. They signified that Korea was about to emerge from the near-barter economy of the first quarter of the sixteenth century into the beginnings of a more vigorous market accompanied by the expansion of commerce and a more active role by private merchants outside the restricted system of licensed merchants.

Yu Hyŏngwŏn was not the first scholar to notice the changes that were taking place in his lifetime, but he was far more thorough in his analysis of those changes than anyone before him. He provided one of the fullest treatments of commercial development from the perspective of someone trained thoroughly in the conventional Neo-Confucian curriculum of his era. Did his commitment to the primacy of agricultural production mean that it would be impossible for him, or for any Confucian of his day, to overcome the Confucian bias against commerce and the profit motive? Or would his almost iconoclastic predilection for challenging honored Korean social traditions steer him to a new appreciation of a freer and more expansive commercial and industrial economy?

While Yu was in many ways an original thinker, he in no way played the role of an Adam Smith by clarifying and defining the nature of commercial activity and championing its nature as the key to releasing Korea from economic backwardness. He was, however, an observer of the economic changes that were occurring in his own time. That role as observer operated as a constraint on his vision because he was responding to changes already wrought by a number of Korean officials of his century. Those men were not trying to work out an original philosophy of economic activity but were responding to the injustices of a rigid tribute tax and the impediment against the flow of goods created by the absence of a light and convenient form of currency.

What Yu Hyŏngwŏn contributed to this process was the detached opinion of a scholar removed from direct concern with daily affairs who could derive larger implications about the reforms that had been adopted and recommend extensions and refinements of those reforms. As we will see, from reform of the tribute tax he derived a theory of the rationalization of government finance, and from the introduction of currency he proposed a theory for guaranteeing stability in the use of that currency and the stabilization of prices.

Did his ideas on the reform of tribute and currency then provide a basis for continuous progress and development in the economic realm in subsequent centuries? Many scholars would like to think so, especially those who have been emphasizing the expansion of both agricultural and nonagricultural production and the volume of trade and commerce in the next two centuries. The answer to this question requires a description of the debates over the use of currency and its relationship to industrial and commercial activity in the eighteenth century as a means of determining the flexibility of Confucian statecraft thought in the face of the economic changes underway.

CHAPTER 21

Tribute and the Taedong *Reform*

Yu Hyŏngwŏn's plan for a significant restructuring of state finances was heavily influenced by the major change in the operation of the tribute tax that had been under way since the last half of the fifteenth century. The tribute contracting system carried on sub rosa operated to expand commercial transactions despite the legal bans against it a long time before the first adoption of the *taedong* system in 1594.

The *taedong* law was primarily a recognition of de facto marketing arrangements, a legalization of practices of long standing. At the same time, by removing all legal barriers to government purchases of goods from merchants, the reform also served to remove the costs imposed on the peasant villagers to disguise illegal tribute contracting, such as extra fees, bribes, and high prices for tribute goods purchased. It also stimulated more trade than before and weakened the attempt of the Chosŏn government to control all trade through monopolistic licensing arrangements.

Critiques of the Tribute System

Yu Hyŏngwŏn's treatment of the history of the *taedong* reform was rather brief and cursory, carrying the story only up to 1658, but it was sufficient to indicate the depth of his admiration for the reform and the men who played leading roles in urging it. Even though he was not explicit or effusive in articulating his admiration, one can easily deduce the intensity of his feelings from his use of the *taedong* model for a restructuring of the whole of the Chosŏn fisc (see chap. 22). He also revealed his feelings by incorporating into his own work the key statements on the evils of the tribute system by three sixteenth-century advocates of reform, Cho Kwangjo, Yulgok (Yi I), and Cho Hŏn.

Cho Kwangjo

Yu began his own history of the reform of the tribute system by citing Cho

Kwangjo's (d. 1519) general remarks to King Chungjong about the king's duty to enforce law and punishment to put an end to private requests for favors.[1] He might better have cited Cho's charge in 1518 that local tribute assessments were not uniform throughout the country, *pangnap* contracting had inflated rice and cloth charges to taxpayers at three-to-ten times the real market value of tribute goods, and tribute taxes had become extremely onerous for the peasants compared to the low land-tax rate of one-thirtieth of the crop. Cho told King Chungjong that if he could find a way to reduce the tribute tax, he could begin to restore the original laws and spirit of the dynasty, convert the mores of the people to uprightness, set the minds of the people at ease, and achieve a full dynastic restoration (*yusin*). Cho himself, however, did not provide a plan for reform.[2]

Although Yu failed to cite Cho's concrete proposal, he was aware of the illicit tribute contracting business and the practices of the *pangnap* system. He remarked that while tribute taxes were increasing, the revenues collected by the central government from the land tax were decreasing because of corruption. He had learned from Yulgok's protest to King Sŏnjo in 1574 about King Yŏnsan'gun's extravagant increase in the demands for royal tribute (*chinsang*), the increased quotas listed in the Tribute Ledger (*Kong'an*) of 1501, and retention of those annual levies of royal tribute all the way to 1575.[3]

Yulgok

Yu was also indebted to Yulgok for the view that reform of the tribute system was less important than adoption of the general principle that the government was obliged to pay for goods and services by regular funds (*kyŏngbi*) rather than ad hoc levies or tribute. He quoted Yulgok's remark that in ancient times magistrates were given regular salaries sufficient to feed their families and relatives as well as themselves. Yulgok also said that although Po I, the minister of rites under the sage Emperor Shun, never used state funds for his own private purposes, officials in sixteenth-century Korea had been forced to appropriate public funds and clerks had extorted goods from the people because they were not given salaries. Payment for office expenses and goods, transporting goods by horse and human labor, and entertaining envoys and guests – which were all paid for under the tribute system – should have come from "tax funds kept on hand" (*yuse*) or regular funds (*kyŏngbi*). To limit extortion, the quotas of entertainment funds would be regulated by the size of the hostels and post-stations, and the weights to be transported would be restricted to specific limits. Yulgok's insistence on the necessity of state funding of official salaries and expenses instead of using in-kind tribute and uncompensated compulsory labor was of the utmost importance for Yu's own plans for reform. What Yu did in his own work (see chap. 20) was to provide a thorough study of the system of state finance and provide a complete budget that incorporated all official costs including salaries for all functionaries and the goods, equipment, transport, and labor services required by the state in the performance of official duties.

Yu was, of course, attentive to Yulgok's criticism of the oppressive aspects of tribute demands, in particular the surtax levied on peasant households to pay the cost of obtaining tiger skins (*homaemi*). Originally intended to stimulate the capture of tigers to reduce the threat to the population, the quota of two or three tigers a year had become a source of extortion when the capital bureaus rejected skins for being too small and demanded additional funds in cash and grain. Yulgok wanted to abolish the levy altogether and merely encourage villages to set traps outside the village without levying a quota on them. If a government office wanted tiger skins, they could simply buy them from trappers or merchants.[4]

Yu mentioned that in 1567 Chief State Councilor Yi Chun'gyŏng proposed a reform of the tribute system right after King Sŏnjo came to the throne, possibly a reference to Yi's recommendation to establish a Directorate for Rectification of Tribute (Chŏnggon-dogam) that was accepted by King Sŏnjo in 1570. Yu also cited the plan Yulgok presented in 1569 for abolishing *pangnap* contracting that Sŏnjo never adopted.[5] What Yu referred to but did not cite was Yulgok's sharp critique of the tribute system in his "Questions and Answers at the Eastern Lake" (*Tongho mundap*). In this essay Yulgok was especially critical of the extravagant demands by Korean kings for their own special royal tribute (*chinsang*), in violation of the classical, moral injunction for frugality by a king of true virtue. Yulgok charged that in his own time the smallest and pettiest items of consumption and the vast resources of the sea were thoroughly inspected for selection as tribute for the king's cuisine, "leaving hardly anything left over" for the people's consumption. "The sage kings of ancient times believed that one man should govern the empire, not that the empire should make offerings for the support of one man."

Yulgok argued that even if royal tribute were retained, the king was obliged to reduce quotas to demonstrate his love for the people. He deprecated the popular view that royal tribute was a necessary and sincere fulfillment of the subject's loyalty to his monarch because the real way to show love and respect for the ruler was to govern the state well and ensure the wealth and prosperity of the common people's income. He recalled that in the court of the sage emperor Shun, his esteemed ministers had demonstrated their loyalty by criticizing Shun's use of lacquerware at his own court rather than simply offering more gifts to him.

Yulgok mentioned that the tribute system had not been oppressive in the early Chosŏn dynasty because the people were required to pay tribute items directly to the magistrate, who then remitted them to the bureaus in the capital. There was no opportunity for clerks and runners to deceive the officials or interfere with tribute payments, but as time passed clerks and runners obstructed direct payment of tribute to the king (*pangnap*) and demanded payment in rice and cloth at elevated prices. Since respect for law had fallen into decline by that time, no methods were devised to solve the problem other than prohibiting substitute payments and ordering peasants to pay tribute in kind, but the peasants were forced to rely on contracting because they had long since ceased producing quota goods. The substitution of rice and cloth payments in tribute contracting arrangements had become even more prevalent (after it was prohibited by King Yejong in 1468).

Yulgok observed that in his time the magistrate of Haeju in Hwanghae Province had discovered a solution to the problem of tribute. He had decided on his own authority to levy one *toe* (.1 *mal*) of rice on each *kyŏl* of land to provide funds for purchasing tribute items, collected the tax himself, and paid it to the capital. Since the peasants then only had to pay grain and not search or pay for tribute items, exploitation of the peasantry under the *pangnap* system was eliminated. Yulgok recommended that this method be extended to the whole country, and that a thoroughgoing investigation of population, products, and land area be conducted to establish equitable tax rates and reduce unnecessary tribute requirements.

This plan was not original because in 1468 King Sejo had proposed replacing tribute with a surtax on land. Yulgok did not mention Sejo's idea, nor did he think of it himself; he was merely astute enough to appreciate what the magistrate of Haeju had attempted on his own authority. By advertising the use of a land tax to replace tribute, however, Yulgok provided the basis for the adoption of the plan in 1594.[6]

When Yulgok criticized the expansion of royal tribute quotas in 1501 under Yŏnsan'gun's reign, he pointed out that many districts were no longer producing items for which they had originally been assessed and had to buy them elsewhere. He therefore recommended that the quotas set in the Tribute Ledger (*Kong'an*) be revised downward from Yŏnsan'gun's levels, that all of his additional levies abolished, and that downward revision of quotas be adjusted to the land area of the district and the size of the population to ensure an equal and fair distribution of taxes.

When King Sŏnjo accepted Yi Chun'gyŏng's recommendation to establish a Directorate for Rectification of Tribute (Chŏnggon-dogam), the directorate recommended that tribute levies be assessed according to district population and cultivated land. "Some districts once affluent are now impoverished, some are no longer producing the same goods, some that used to have large populations are now small, some had lands under cultivation which are now laying waste . . ," so that large districts were only paying a tenth of what they should, while small districts were paying the same quota as a large district. Even when magistrates had redistributed tribute taxes by shifting them to a land tax, there were still no standard schedules of payment, and they were levied on tenants as landowners. Despite the urgent need for reform, the attempt was abrogated because of opposition to it from officials.[7]

Then in 1574, when Yulgok was governor of Hwanghae, his observations of conditions in the province reinforced his dislike for the tribute system. The peasants had been forced to go hunting in the hills and fishing in the rivers to obtain tribute for the king, neglecting their fields and leaving their homes in disrepair. If they did not produce the product required, they had to spend an inordinate amount of time and resources to buy it elsewhere. If they were able to catch deer,

deer tongues, and horns that were the special pleasure of the king, they might be rejected if they were not the right species, if the flavor was not up to standard or lost during the several days needed to transport them to the capital, if they spoiled during the heat of summer or were kept too long in the ice house in the capital. And if the items could not be captured or produced, they would have to buy them on the capital market at high prices because they were in demand among the capital aristocrats. He urged the king to reduce the quotas of live deer and salt pork, even if only by a half dozen head, and to demand only "live deer" rather than any particular type of deer. Deer tongues and tails might as well be abolished altogether because they never tasted right, and it would absolve the peasants of one of their most difficult burdens. The least the king could do would be to limit the quotas for live animals or perishable goods to the winter season between the tenth and second lunar months, to eliminate the losses from spoilage.[8] Later in 1576, Yulgok also attempted to set a schedule of values or prices of tribute items for the whole province to prevent magistrates and clerks from overcharging peasants for substitute payments, but only two districts adopted his rates.[9]

Cho Hŏn

Yu Hyŏngwŏn was also heavily indebted to the proposals of Cho Hŏn, a close friend of Yulgok and an advocate of reform of the tribute system when he was assistant to the governor of Chŏlla Province in 1581.[10] After his return from an embassy to China three years earlier, Cho reported that the imperial cuisine agency in Ming China used tax payments in silver to purchase food from the market, a result of the transformation of the two major modes of taxation, the land tax and labor service, into silver payments, a process that became dominant after the middle of the sixteenth century.[11] Not only was China blessed with a large population and many horses, but they also had an extensive system of water transport. Some of the sage rulers of antiquity had concluded that it would be far cheaper to transport perishables by water rather than by land over thousands of miles, and that if they paid for it in silver, it would only take one horse to bring the silver instead of 600 horses to transport the goods in kind. Once this system was adopted, the population was no longer burdened with paying several multiples of the original tax or with heavy hauling of goods at every post-station. Since the markets were always filled with goods and any item could be purchased for silver at market prices, the emperor never lacked any of the delicacies he desired for his table.

Cho contrasted the Chinese situation with the rigors and burdens of royal tribute in Korea. The Chinese population had grown more prosperous and enjoyed the wonders of a solid period of great peace. All along the route between the Yalu River and the Ming capital, even though some areas were obviously barren, the human and animal populations were plentiful and the people was content and prosperous primarily because the imperial court was concerned about popular welfare. The emperor guaranteed salaries to district magistrates in silver and cash for them to purchase their needs on the marketplace, and he had forbidden them from collecting even one foot of cloth or a single chicken on their own authority. The only tax burden the people had to bear was the regular land tax and miscellaneous labor service. "Even the greedy magistrates do not transgress the law to exploit the people; the population increases and the land is productive."

Despite Cho's glowing report of late Ming prosperity, the Ming government was suffering too many of the same difficulties that plagued contemporary Chosŏn: faulty and infrequent cadastral surveys, frequent extra charges and bribes to make up for fixed low taxes and insufficient revenues, and disparities of wealth between rich landlords and impoverished tenants. Nonetheless, the Ming tax system had experienced a major reform in the adoption of the single-whip system of taxation by replacing wheat and cloth taxes and labor service by silver payments, and Cho and other observers were quick to observe the advantages of that system.[12]

Cho was convinced of idyllic circumstances in southern Manchuria and northeastern China, possibly because of the stark conditions he described in the two northern provinces in Korea where the fields were overgrown with weeds and the population had been decimated. Only 10 or 20 percent of the families could afford an ox, and family size was small. The people had suffered from years of unauthorized and arbitrary levies on the people; they had to pay three *p'il* of cotton cloth for every eight *kyŏl* of land and an additional five *p'il* of cloth as their annual military or labor service support obligation (*pongjok*). The agricultural promotion agents (Kwŏnnongsa) organized the peasant households into large and small mutual aid groups (*t'ong*) and called them out to the fields six times a month, and punished anyone who failed to appear for duty by levying a cloth penalty. The peasants also had to perform service as a magistrate's runner or assistant almost every day and had to pay a penalty if they missed their duty. Families had to provide service personnel or substitutes no matter how far they lived from the place of duty or how distant their family relationship, so that the looms of a whole clan could be tied up in weaving cloth to pay the cost for three or four absentees. They had no time or resources left to clothe their own children and protect them against the cold, they were burdened by private debts, and their official taxes were increased at every step in the tax process. If they owed one *mal* of tax, they had to pay four *mal* to the magistrate's granary, an extra eight *mal* to mill the grain, and four times the tax rate to cover transportation of taxes to the capital. They also owed an additional five *mal* a year to purchase the tribute quota in pheasants and deer. By the end of the year the people had to sell their oxen and calves because they had nothing left.

While royal tribute for Hamgyŏng only amounted to 100 *p'il* of cloth per year, the population was also held responsible for levies of fine cloth, a tax on salt flats, provision of minor food costs for officials, and a paper tax, all of which had become standard practice over the generations. Another element of royal tribute, sable pelts, had been preserved even though the animals themselves had disappeared, and the cost of purchasing them in the capital had doubled. The Korean people throughout the country were constantly plagued with demands for royal tribute items no longer produced in their districts, food for the king, fees and bribes to local and capital bureau clerks, and horses or oxen to the post-stations.

Cho appealed to the more modest tribute requirements of Chou China as described in the *Book of History*. In those times the tribute of Yü only required tribute in fish as the only live or perishable item for use in sacrificial offerings, primarily because "the enlightened kings of ancient times did not impoverish the people of the empire to fill their own stomachs." In Korea, however, perishable royal tribute had become a major burden. Tribute in live fish and pheasants had not been required for Kyŏnggi Province in early Chosŏn, but it had become a major ordeal for the people by the sixteenth century.

King Sejong, he argued, had only required that 300 households living along the coast would provide tribute fish in a rotation system three times (a year?), but the cost was so high that revenues were often insufficient. At the end of King Sŏngjong's reign in the 1490s, Son Sunhyo, the governor of Kyŏnggi, became so concerned that fish for the entertainment of a visiting Ming envoy might run out that he collected a double levy on the population, and that double tax quota was later incorporated into the province's tribute quota as a standard levy.

By the end of the sixteenth century, the province had begun to collect a land tax of two *mal* of rice for a parcel of four *kyŏl* of land in each district to provide the cost of purchasing a single fish, and if the revenue was insufficient, it could double the number of *kyŏl* taxed per district. Cho did not know how much fish was currently presented from Kyŏngsang Province, but he did know that they had to supply four palaces. Although it might seem like a small amount, the thirty-two *mal* collected in taxes from sixteen *kyŏl* would produce enough grain to feed a family of eight or nine for a month. In the short spring season when the peasants could neither raise nor borrow the grain to pay for their tribute tax, the magistrate's clerks dunned them for payment, or bound them up and put them in jail if they failed to make payment on time. In effect, royal tribute in fresh fish was depriving a dozen families of half a year's livelihood when the king should have been showing compassion for their suffering. Cho asked that Sŏnjo return to Sejong's more modest fish levy and abolish the double taxes introduced by Son Sunhyo in Kyŏnggi Province.

To lend force to his argument, Cho pointed out that Emperor Hsiao-tsung (the Hung-chih emperor) of the Ming who ascended the throne in 1487 had announced that he was reducing his own daily consumption to one goat and one chicken a day because he was afraid that ostentatious consumption on his part would leave the old and sick without enough to eat, a good example of how a son could change the laws enacted by his father without doing violence to the principle of filial piety.

In Korea, however, royal tribute had started because of fawning and obsequious ministers, and it was exacerbated by the extravagant consumption of King

Yŏnsan'gun at the turn of the sixteenth century. Although Yulgok's reform recommendation of the previous spring (1576?), had not been accepted, King Sŏnjo at least had to prohibit magistrates from excessive tribute collections and order a return to original tribute quotas because the king's previous exhortations to reduce taxes and consumption had not provided any benefit to the people.[13]

Later in 1590, Chŏng Ch'ŏl (a leader of the Westerner faction) complained bitterly that the obstruction of tribute payments and illicit tribute contracting by clerks and runners of the capital bureaus and the district tribute clerks who conspired with them had led to overcharging peasants by ten or a hundred times the value of the original tribute. Although the magistrates could have put a stop to this subterfuge, most were driven by graft to tolerate contracting, and poor peasants who lacked the power and money to prosecute a case against dishonest officials had no choice but to sell their property and flee their homes. Chŏng urged that the government set the values of tribute items and collect a grain tax at the low rate of a few *toe* (.1 *mal*) of rice per *kyŏl*, and if there were any surplus, it would be used to pay the expenses of the district tribute clerks. He claimed that King Chungjong had established a precedent for substituting a land tax for tribute when he ordered the substitution of a grain tax for oil, honey, and other tribute goods in 1515, but unfortunately the measure was regarded only as a temporary means to capitalize on a bumper crop and a surplus of grain, or to alleviate the tax burden in a time of famine or disease; in no case was it deemed appropriate to eliminate tribute levies permanently.[14]

THE TAEDONG REFORM

The Origin of Taedong Reform in 1594

Although the criticism of the Korean tribute system and proposals for replacing it by a grain tax on land had been voiced by Yulgok in 1569 and 1574, Cho Hŏn in 1577, and Chŏng Ch'ŏl in 1590, there was still not enough political support to move King Sŏnjo to action. After Hideyoshi's invasion in 1592, however, the situation changed drastically. The throne cut back tribute demands to 20 to 30 percent of normal years and authorized payment of rice in place of tribute as well as military and labor service. Relief from tribute and tax reductions were offset by the destruction of land, the severe famine that swept across the south in 1594, and the imposition of cruel levies by district magistrates, many of whom were recently appointed military officials, war heroes, or rich yangban who purchased office. The government had been using the 1581 revision of the 1502 *kong'an* tribute registers, but most of its volumes were destroyed or lost during the invasion, and the government was probably relying on the 1473 version. In short, wartime destruction proved an indispensable catalyst to reform.[15]

Yu Hyŏngwŏn stated that the essence of Yulgok's ideas were adopted by Chief State Councilor Yu Sŏngnyŏng (a member of the Southerners, a splinter group of the Easterner faction), who noted in 1594 that the substitution of rice or cloth payments for tribute and the conversion of tribute levies to a land tax were already being practiced, but that no attempt had been made to create a uniform and regular system of taxation based on a survey of land in each district. As a result these land taxes for tribute varied anywhere from one to ten *mal/kyŏl* of rice, and corrupt clerks in the capital bureaus were charging extra for transportation costs. Even though peasants paid one hundred times more than the legal tribute requirements, the state itself only received about 10 to 20 percent of this amount and the difference went into the pockets of the tribute contractors, district tribute clerks, and capital bureau clerks and runners. Furthermore, royal tribute (*chinsang*) was even more corrupt than ordinary tribute.

Yu Sŏngnyŏng then echoed Yulgok's earlier recommendation that the tribute required from one province be calculated and adjusted to the amount of land in the province to ensure a uniform rate of tribute taxes for every district, payable in cloth, rice, or beans. He estimated that not only would a uniform tax of one to two *mal/kyŏl* pay for capital tribute, but that additional levies of tribute for special occasions (*pangmul*) could also be eliminated by an additional land tax of a few *toe* or less, payable in rice, cloth, or beans. The costs for royal tribute might also be abolished by the same method.

Yu proposed that specific granaries in each province be designated as repositories for the land surtax for tribute and that the government set a schedule of fair and uniform prices in cotton for goods that would be purchased on the market. He assumed that emergency requirements for military expenses or state needs could be met by reducing demands and diverting funds stored in rice and beans in tribute warehouses to those purposes.

He also mentioned that in Ming China there was no requirement to collect tribute to pay any foreign emperor, nor did they have any equivalent for special royal tribute (*chinsang*) like Korea. Instead all thirteen provinces paid silver to the Kuang-lu-ssu that was used to purchase goods to be presented at court; if there were any emergency needs, the emperor would simply finance them from silver reserves by ordering a reduction of his own consumption. The Chinese thus did not have to transport tribute or mobilize artisans to make items to be shipped to the capital. Yu Sŏngnyŏng's inspiration, therefore, did not derive solely from the ideas of Yulgok and Chŏng Ch'ŏl, but from the replacement of silver taxes for grain and service already in use in Ming China (cf. Cho Hŏn). His program incorporated three major elements previously proposed: substitution of land taxes for tribute items, replacement of labor service in transport and other activities by a land surtax to pay for hired labor, and state regulation of rice and cloth equivalency rates for substitution payments to prevent overcharging.[16]

Under the pressure of war King Sŏnjo approved the recommendation to allow rice payments in lieu of ordinary tribute (but not royal tribute) as well as for support payments for rotating capital soldiers and personal tribute (*sin'gong*) to support rotating official slaves sent to the capital (*sŏnsang nobi*). After a good crop was harvested in 1594, he approved reducing the land tax substitute for tribute sent to the capital from an average of seven to eight *mal/kyŏl* to a uniform two *mal/kyŏl*, which was supposed to yield an annual revenue of 70,000 *sŏm*, greater than the 60,000 *sŏm* collected from the land tax. When the actual receipts proved to be only 50,000 *sŏm*, it became clear that the new tribute surtax had not been applied thoroughly and peasants were not able to pay full taxes. Since land under cultivation was not resurveyed until 1604, it could not be expected that a land surtax would yield its full potential.

Critics of the system claimed that two *mal/kyŏl* was still too heavy a tax in wartime, especially when transportation costs, personal fees (or bribes), and a half-dozen other types of land levies were also being charged by magistrates. Capital merchants were hard pressed to find the goods demanded by capital bureau clerks, especially at the low prices offered by them, while the government had difficulty paying the costs for Chinese envoys and the rations for Chinese troops stationed in Korea. The revenues from the low land surtax were too low to replace the profits made by clerks, runners, and slaves, and the administrative costs of local as well as capital officials. The beneficiaries of corruption and illegal tribute contracting joined forces in opposing the new law, and King Sŏnjo abolished Yu Sŏngnyŏng's reform, probably in 1599.[17]

The Taedong System for Kyŏnggi Province, 1608

Yu Hyŏngwŏn reported that in 1608, Han Paekkyŏm charged that tribute collected from the people had grown so large and oppressive that the viability of the dynasty was threatened. He also commented that Han explained that Yu Sŏngnyŏng's reform in 1594 had not been rescinded in 1599 because the law itself was flawed, but because of anomalies in the application of the law. While a land surtax rate of two *mal/kyŏl* to finance the replacement of tribute in Kyŏnggi Province had been extremely light for coastal districts that shipped their tax payments to the capital by boat, the taxpayers in the more remote and mountainous (upland) regions were burdened by the cost of transporting the tax to the capital and other government offices. Transportation cost more than three times the tax itself. Merchants and shopkeepers in the capital resented the demands of capital bureau clerks to lower the prices of goods the government purchased from them in place of tribute items.

Furthermore, because the reform was first adopted soon after the king and his court returned to the capital when there was a shortage of goods available in the shops, the government reintroduced special tribute levies in kind on the peasants, who regarded this measure as a form of double taxation. What had been advertised as a means of lowering tax rates and creating a uniform and equitable rate then appeared to have become only a subterfuge for heavier taxes. Finally, local officials opposed the system because the government did not abide by its new method and had lost the trust of the people in the reliability of the laws, and the clerks and runners naturally resented the reform because they had lost their opportunities for illicit profits under the previous *pangnap* system. Han charged that because the government failed to follow up enactment of reform by careful surveillance over the laws and continued to rely on the clerks who used the *pangnap* method to collect special levies of tribute items, the clerks were as corrupt as ever, and the rice surtax had proved more troublesome than the tribute system.

Han believed that tribute reform failed in the 1590s because the government was too concerned about raising as much tax revenue as possible and neglected the problem of establishing a fair and uniform tax rate on the taxpayers. While the standard surtax rate of two *mal/kyŏl* might be retained, he felt it should be lowered by grades for districts located farther than two days transportation from the coastal transshipment port. The discontent of the capital merchants could be alleviated by guaranteeing a generous price for market purchases, anywhere from two to five times better than the market price, neither raising (tax rates and prices) in a bumper crop year or reducing them during a bad crop. Guaranteed good prices would allow all those people participating in illicit *pangnap* contracts to function like honest brokers engaged simply in the transfer of goods from areas of surplus to areas of need with proper and legitimate opportunities for profit. If goods unavailable in the capital shops were needed for ritual celebrations or for the king's use, officials would be allowed to make special demands for tribute in kind from a given locality, but to prevent double taxation they would have to deduct the value of the goods in rice and cloth from the new surtax revenues.

The essence of Han's proposal was recommended by Second State Councilor Yi Wŏn'ik in 1608. King Kwanghaegun adopted the new proposal, called the *taedongbŏp* or *taedong* system, but to test the plan he restricted its application to Kyŏnggi Province only. He established the Taedong Agency (Taedongch'ŏng, later changed to the Office for the Dispensation of Benevolence, Sŏnhyech'ŏng, in 1614) to handle the surtax revenues, and set the annual tax rate at sixteen *mal/kyŏl* of rice, collected half in the spring and half in the fall, without any variation in the rate according to the quality of the annual crop – eight times higher than Han Paekkyŏm's proposal (or Yu Sŏngnyŏng's tax rate in 1594). The tax rate was not only calculated to raise sufficient revenue to pay for purchasing tribute goods (*kongmul*) and special royal tribute (*chinsang*), but two of the sixteen *mal* were used to pay for items and salaries required by district magistrates' offices and the cost of horse transportation in the capital (*kyŏngswaema*). The new law was supported by a half dozen high officials at court, praised in a petition of 263 Kyŏnggi residents, and backed by young censors and lower ranking gentry and commoners. Kwanghaegun, however, rejected a proposal to extend the *taedong* system to Kangwŏn Province in 1610, probably because he was dissuaded by its opponents.[18]

In reviewing the history of the *taedong* reform to 1608, Yu began his account with Yulgok's astute observation of the injustices of the tribute question and the intriguing institution of a land-tax substitute for tribute finance by the magistrate of Haeju. Yu also cited Yulgok's criticism of royal tribute in Korea because it was subject to expansion by kings who were profligate spenders and consumers of luxuries.

Yu recorded the admiration that Cho Hŏn and Yu Sŏngnyŏng had shown for the beneficial effects of the single-whip tax reform and the conversion of land and labor service taxes to silver in Ming China in the sixteenth century and repeated their recommendation that some parallel to the Ming tax system be adopted. Even though metallic currency, let alone silver, was still not a major medium of exchange in Korea, it was obvious to them that a tax in grain or cloth would be preferable to tribute in kind.

Nevertheless, this growing awareness needed a stimulus to create reform, and it was provided by the devastation wrought by Hideyoshi's invasion after 1592. Yu Sŏngnyong became the prime mover in the adoption of the *taedong* method of replacing tribute with a land tax in 1594, but the reform could not be sustained beyond 1599. The rescission of tribute reform did not, however, depress Yu because Han Paekkyŏm had explained that there were some understandable reasons for the failure of the reform, notably the inadequacy of the land surtax to replace tribute costs and the excessive concern of officials with raising funds in the wake of wartime destruction.

Although the *taedong* system was not adopted permanently until 1608 by King Kwanghaegun, it had been proposed by two more officials that Yu admired, Han Paekkyŏm and Yi Wŏn'ik. Although Kwanghaegun was dissuaded from extending the reform beyond Kyŏnggi Province by some who profited from tribute contracting and corruption, and others who feared the disruption that might attend any major change in a system of taxation, the groundwork had been laid for reform by the general awareness of the corruption of the tribute system, the superiority of a simpler and fairer land tax, and the positive example of the single-whip tax reform in Ming China.

Kangwŏn Province, 1623

The *taedong* system was extended to Kangwŏn Province in 1623, but Yu Hyŏngwŏn did not refer to it and omitted any reference to the struggle to expand the reform until King Hyojong came to the throne in 1649.[19] Nonetheless, a brief discussion of the extension of the *taedong* system to Kangwŏn will help us to evaluate the quality and nature of the reform effort.

Shortly after the coup d'état against Kwanghaegun by the Westerner faction and the enthronement of King Injo in 1623, the new minister of taxation, Yi Sŏ, suggested a *taedong* tax for two or three provinces at a rate of ten *mal/kyŏl* to provide some relief for the peasants. A few months later the Ministry of Taxation recommended extension of the *taedong* system to the whole country. Anxious to avoid underfinancing the cost of tribute items, it suggested levying a higher land surtax of twenty *mal/kyŏl* of rice in two or three additional provinces, half to be collected in spring and fall to reduce the burden of paying the tax at one time. It expected to collect a gross amount of 600,000 *sŏm* (1 *sŏm* was equivalent to 15 *mal*) nationally, deduct 200,000 *sŏm* to pay for military expenses in the southwest and north and the cost of the Japanese hostel (Waegwan) in Tongnae in Kyŏngsang Province, and use the remaining 400,000 *sŏm* to pay for the purchase of tribute items. One official, however, pointed out that it would better to confine its application to Kangwŏn Province, where the amount of arable land was small rather than any of the southern provinces where landlord opposition would be strong.[20]

This objection was of crucial importance for understanding one of the reasons why extension of the *taedong* system was so protracted: the fear of the landowners and landlords – the wealthiest class in the country – that the reform would increase their tax burdens. Limiting application of the law to a province of marginal fertility and poor peasants would enable the king and court to avoid a major political challenge.

The leading supporter of extension was Cho Sik, a section chief (Chŏngnang) in the Ministry of Personnel, who argued that in ancient times funds for the salaries of officials and rulers of feudal states came from a single source, a tithe levied on grain, while the feudal lords (*chu-hou*) were also authorized to collect tribute. Unfortunately, in the Chosŏn dynasty tribute taxes in kind had become too onerous, especially since the influential, wealthy, and unscrupulous men were able to evade taxes, but as the current land tax was so low, raising taxes on land was the best way to eliminate tribute and other miscellaneous taxes. If annual production from (one *kyŏl*?) of land was 20 to 30 *sŏm* (i.e., 300 to 450 *mal*), it would be possible to raise taxes to 22 to 23 *mal* (per *kyŏl*) and still not reach the classical tithe (which would have been 30 to 45 *mal/kyŏl*). Rich landlords had so much land and labor power under their command that their complaints about the new tax could not be taken seriously, and the profiteers who engaged in illegal tribute contracting (*pangnap*) were criminals who deserved no consideration at all.

Although some also complained that shipments of surtax grain to the capital would be shipwrecked, Cho responded that very few grain ships had been lost at sea. Whenever they had, it was because of overloading or sailing during the dangerous winds and waves of the fall season, which could be overcome by limiting maritime transport to the spring. Other complaints about the possibilities of fire in granaries were also invalid because each granary could be built at some distance from private homes and protected by constructing fire walls. In any case, in the past two hundred years there had not been a fire in the two major granaries of the capital.[21]

King Injo finally decided in the fall of 1623 to adopt the *taedong* system for Kangwŏn, Ch'ungch'ŏng, and Chŏlla provinces, but he also disliked variations in the *taedong* surtax rate among the provinces and regretted that the cost of human labor and goods needed by the district yamen were not calculated in devising the tax rate. At his request the Taedong Agency for the Three Provinces then advised the king to adopt a rate of fifteen *mal/kyŏl* for Ch'ungch'ŏng and Chŏlla, and sixteen *mal/kyŏl* for Kangwŏn. Of this amount, ten *mal* would be paid to the Taedong Agency (Taedongch'ŏng) to defray the cost for purchasing tribute items needed by capital bureaus, remuneration for the costs of specific service (*kiin*), clerks, and runners, and paper for the Ministry of Rites and the Directorate of Astronomy (Kwansanggam). The remainder of the *taedong* (five or six *mal/kyŏl*) revenues would be retained in the province to pay for royal tribute, ordinary tribute items levied in kind, medicine for the Palace Physicians' Court (Naeŭiwŏn), goods consumed by the magistrates, and horse transport costs. In short, this proposal represented a major step in simplifying and rationalizing the state's system of finance by replacing the poorly regulated levies of tribute, official expenses, and labor service with a simple land surtax.

Early in 1624, the secret censor (Amhaeng ŏsa) for Chŏlla Province, Chang Yu, cautioned the king against the possible loss of transport vessels at sea and theft by the transport sailors, and warned that local districts might have to be taxed a second time to replenish the losses. Since the *taedong* land surtax was too low, revenues would be insufficient to allow local districts to buy what they needed. Furthermore, the costs of horse transport and personal fees were not included in the revenue calculations.[22]

Before King Injo could decide on the merits of these complaints, however, Yi Kwal's rebellion broke out and wrecked the operation of the *taedong* system. To alleviate the financial difficulties of the peasants after the rebellion, the government then cut the *taedong* tax rate to four *mal/kyŏl*, but at the cost of adequate funding to replace tribute and uncompensated labor service. Except for *taedong* taxes collected already, the rest of the provinces involved in the reform were allowed to revert to tribute payments in kind, a system cynically dubbed "the half-*taedong*" system. Peasants naturally resented this immediate reversal of government policy even though it was designed to benefit them, but Chief State Councilor Yi Wŏn'ik, who had recommended the *taedong* system for Kyŏnggi Province in 1608, explained that famine conditions had rendered the system inoperable. The devastating effects of the rebellion on the *taedong* reform is important because it meant that the delay in extending the *taedong* system to the rest of the country was caused by an extraneous circumstance unrelated to the capacity of the Chosŏn government's capacity for institutional reform.

In 1624, Ch'oe Myŏnggil, one of the leaders of the Injo Restoration coup in 1623, made a blistering attack in the Royal Lectures on the bookish and inept work of Yi Wŏn'ik and Cho Ik, who had drawn up the *taedong* regulations. He asked that the system be abolished, and proposed that additional revenue be raised instead by adopting the household tally system (*hop'ae*) and requiring cloth tax payments from the sons and younger brothers of yangban.

Ch'oe Myŏnggil argued that since the majority of the people in the capital and major towns were opposed to the *taedong* system, tribute should be restored but prices of tribute goods in contracting arrangements revised downward to prevent profiteering from substitutions of tribute goods. In other words, he wanted to recognize tribute contracting as a legal operation but legislate prices charged by the tribute middlemen, a proposal that would have been almost impossible to enforce. The tribute middlemen did their business with individual peasants or whole districts in which official involvement was far less than the *taedong* system when purchasing agents employed by government agencies bought goods from the merchants.

So Sŏng also supported abolition because the tribute system of the early Chosŏn dynasty was only a copy of the ancient system of tribute, the people resented the replacement of tribute by a land surtax, and the clerks and runners were just as corrupt as they had been before. Second State Councilor Yun Pang also remarked that when the *taedong* system was first adopted, only the powerful people and residents of large (or important) districts opposed it, but now everyone but the king hated it.[23]

At the end of the year the Taedong Agency for the Three Provinces proposed reducing the tax rate for Ch'ungch'ŏng Province from fifteen to fourteen *mal/kyŏl*, five *mal* of which would pay for all the operational costs of each district and the governor's office, local tribute (*pangmul*) and royal tribute (*chinsang*) as well. Not only would this leave a surplus of 10,000 *sŏm* of revenue, but the remaining nine *mal* (per *kyŏl*) of the surtax could be remitted to the capital for the cost of ordinary tribute goods (used by the capital bureaucracy). Yun Pang, however, demanded total abolition of the *taedong* surtax, or at least adjustment of the tax rate according to the needs of each magistrate, and he reminded King Injo that he had only approved that the law be tested until the end of the year. Undoubtedly aware that Chief State Councilor Yi Wŏn'ik had turned against the *taedong* law, he also urged Injo to ask his opinion.

Third State Councilor Sin Hŭm also reported recent complaints that a single surtax payment was too hard to pay and tax burdens were heavier in remote provinces than Kyŏnggi. Although he had also "heard" that the ordinary people favored the *taedong* system, wealthy landlords complained that the more land they owned, the higher the taxes on them, an average of one *sŏm* (fifteen *mal*) per *kyŏl*. Sympathizing with the plight of the rich, he predicted that their bitter resentment might signal the onset of an "age of decline" (*soese*). While he admitted that he had heard that the residents of Chŏlla favored the *taedong* law, those in Ch'ungch'ŏng at least wanted a reduction of the tax rate to fourteen *mal/kyŏl*. Since the court could not be sure whether reports of popular feelings were true or simply representations by the provincial governors, he also suggested that King Injo ask Yi Wŏn'ik's opinion. Yi Wŏn'ik finally abandoned his support of the *taedong* system because of popular discontent and recommended canceling the law immediately or at the end of the month.[24]

King Injo's response as recorded in the *Veritable Record* (*Sillok*) was rather cryptic since he decreed that matters be carried out in accordance with regulations in other provinces, and that no "additional" land tax of five *mal/kyŏl* (for paying provincial and other costs) be adopted. On the second point, the Taedong Office had not requested an "additional" tax of five *mal*, but had recommended that it only be deducted from the overall taedong rate of fourteen *mal/kyŏl* for Ch'ungch'ŏng Province. Injo may have mistakenly believed that the *taedong* rate had been reduced from fourteen to nine *mal/kyŏl*, and that the other five *mal* was a request for an additional tax to cover provincial costs.

At the beginning of the next year the Taedong Agency explained that it had suggested that the revenues from the five *mal/kyŏl* portion of the *taedong* tax be retained in the province to pay for provincial expenses, transport, and royal and local tribute because the people of the province had mistakenly thought that the *taedong* proposal was intended to be a "half-*taedong*" system that would only replace ordinary tribute sent to the capital bureaus while the district magistrates would be left to harass the peasants by collecting their own tribute levies without any uniform standards.

The Taedong Agency, however, was determined to limit taxes to anticipated expenditures (*yangch'ul wiip*), contrary to established convention. They sent out staff officials (Nangch'ŏng) to Ch'ungch'ŏng and Chŏlla to examine provincial taxes, the expenses of each district, local tribute and service paid to the provincial governor and provincial army and navy commanders, the costs of royal and local tribute and horse transportation, and the taxes collected on each *kyŏl* of land cultivated by the people, and they compared their statistics with the ledgers forwarded by the provincial governor to the capital. On the basis of this detailed survey they concluded that the *taedong* levy need not exceed fourteen *mal/kyŏl*, of which five *mal* would pay provincial obligations. They intended only to use this in Ch'ungch'ŏng, and then wait until a similar investigation were done for Chŏlla before the *taedong* rate was set for that province. They also explained that they had submitted this memorial to correct the king's misconception about their original plan, and they were submitting the Ch'ungch'ŏng governor's ledgers to aid him in reconsidering his decision. Injo, however, refused to concede that he had misconstrued the plan; he merely explained that he had prohibited the adoption of the five *mal/kyŏl* "additional" tax because the governor had not been thorough in his investigations to implement the reform and it was not timely to impose this tax at the time.[25]

There was no clear edict, however, to rescind his previous order to extend the *taedong* system to the three provinces because he only ordered that regulations in other provinces be adopted. It was obvious, however, that he was ready to cancel the *taedong* system for all provinces except Kyŏnggi because he later rejected Royal Secretary Cho Ik's strong demand that the system not be abandoned. Cho argued that abolition would only benefit corrupt officials at the expense of the people, and that Chu Hsi would have supported the *taedong* reform because he had always been concerned about reducing discriminatory inequality between the rich and poor. Injo merely said that he had already made up his mind on the issue, that is, that he was about to cancel it.[26]

Nonetheless, he did change his mind early in 1625 when a number of students and scholars from Kangwŏn Province petitioned that the *taedong* system be retained because the people of that province liked it. He then adopted Yi Wŏn'ik's recommendation to keep the *taedong* law for Kangwŏn Province alone (possibly because landlord resistance was not as strong there), and he set the tax rate at sixteen *mal/kyŏl* to provide sufficient revenues not only for tribute items, but also for yamen expenses and salaries for district yamen, human and horse transport costs, and medicine for the king. After he made his decision, he urged the governor of Kangwŏn to canvass the population again, and the governor reported that the public was in favor of the law.[27]

In the provinces, especially Ch'ungch'ŏng and Chŏlla, the large landlords were apparently the leading opponents of the *taedong* land tax, but poor peasants may have resented it as well because they must have suffered loss of income from Yi Kwal's rebellion and a bad crop in 1623. Even though Injo called a brief halt to the *taedong* substitute tax and reverted to assessments of tribute goods to alleviate the impact of a new land surtax in the wake of the rebellion, the peasants may still have taken a jaundiced view of government fickleness over reform and perceived the surtax as an additional tax, not a replacement for tribute. It may thus be mistaken simply to blame rich landlords alone for opposition in Ch'ungch'ŏng and Chŏlla to the *taedong* system at that time because many peasants may not have perceived that the reform was in their best interest.

Furthermore, King Injo was persuaded by opponents of the reform after a campaign of a couple of years that the peasantry did not like the *taedong* system. He did his best to order his officials to conduct surveys, but he had to operate on a poor system of communication and incomplete information. Even though he did decide to eliminate the *taedong* system for Ch'ungch'ŏng and Chŏlla provinces, he attempted to preserve it for Kangwŏn (as well as Kyŏnggi) when he was told that the population favored it. In short, the effects of the Yi Kwal rebellion, the retreat to a half-*taedong* system to accommodate peasant hardship, the apparent vacillation by the government in its determination to abolish tribute altogether, and the imperfect means of assessing public opinion helps to explain King Injo's partial abandonment of the reform by 1625.

Ch'ungch'ŏng, 1652; P'yŏng'an and Hwanghae, 1646

The period after the Yi Kwal rebellion was hardly more conducive to the adoption of a major tax reform because of the two Manchu invasions of 1627 and 1637. In 1633, when the government was in desperate need of revenue and soldiers, King Injo was intrigued by a report from the Office of the Censor-General that the late ex-governor of Ch'ungch'ŏng Province, Kwŏn Pun, had investigated tribute taxes and devised a reform system almost as good as the *taedong* system, but he was not moved to adopt it.[28] After the second Manchu invasion in 1637, Censor-General Yi Sik proposed an extension of the *taedong* system to raise funds for military expenses and to eliminate corruption of the tribute system by clerks.[29]

In 1638 Kim Yuk, the governor of Ch'ungch'ŏng Province, argued that the *taedong* system would be suitable for his province because of the large amount of arable land there. In an act of hyperbole motivated by his enthusiasm for reform Kim estimated that even with a very low tax rate, the revenues from a *taedong* land surtax would pay not only for royal and regular tribute, but also for warships, horse transportation, and magistrates' yamen expenses – and still yield an extra twenty or thirty thousand *sŏm* surplus. He regretted that Kwŏn Pun's plan had not been adopted when he was governor even though the district magistrates all favored the idea, and he asserted that the *taedong* system would free the peasants from hard labor and the excessive demands of officials. The Border Defense Command agreed with Kim's arguments but refused to support it because, contrary to Kim's claims, the tax rate would be too low to pay all the costs involved.

Kim initially proposed a rate divided into cloth and grain portions: one *p'il* of cloth and two *mal* of rice per *kyŏl* of land. Since he calculated the value of one *p'il* of cloth at five *mal* of rice, the tax rate calculated in grain would have been equivalent to seven *mal/kyŏl*. The close advisers of the king, however, had asked that the tax be based on a formula of two *p'il/kyŏl*, which at the current rate of exchange at five *mal/p'il* would have been equivalent to ten *mal* of rice.

Kim pointed out, however, that since the relative values of rice and cloth varied according to the size of the crop, any year in which a bumper rice crop flooded the market with rice the cost in rice of purchasing cotton cloth for paying the tax would automatically rise and impose a hardship on the peasantry. He argued that he had purposely intended that combining rice and cloth in the tax rate would take care of variations of supply and price by creating an "equal" or uniform tax rate that would still guarantee sufficient revenue for the state. He held that his current evaluation of the value of one *p'il* of cloth at five *mal* of rice was nothing more than a reflection of current prices, but he was willing to countenance adoption of the higher tax rate (two *p'il* of cloth costing ten *mal* of rice on the market, rather than his seven *mal* equivalent) proposed by the Royal Lectures temporarily (presumably to ensure sufficient revenue) and wait until the next good harvest to adopt his method to prevent a bumper crop and a cheap rice price from alienating the taxpayers.

The Border Defense Command then responded by saying that it had reviewed the equivalent value (*chŏlka*) of (tribute?) taxes sent from Ch'ungch'ŏng with the expenditures of the Ministry of Taxation and found that the equivalent value of receipts from the *taedong* reform would have been quite close to expenditures at Kim's suggested rate, but it would not have covered the miscellaneous taxes or costs (*chabyŏk*) as well as the cost of tribute. The ministry, therefore, implied that since Kim Yuk's estimates of revenue from a *taedong* reform would fall short of revenues, the government would have to impose a (higher) rate that taxpayers would not support.

Furthermore, the ministry did not approve of switching back and forth from the higher rate advocated by the Royal Lectures to Kim's rate, presumably because the public might think that the government was switching rates to manipulate market prices for its own advantage. In any case, it would be important to revise the tribute ledgers (*kong'an*) first, and then discuss the possibilities of the *taedong* system later on. King Injo decided not to adopt Kim Yuk's proposal for

Ch'ungch'ŏng Province, but he did remark that it would be possible to adopt the *taedong* reform some time in the future without first revising the tribute ledgers.[30]

The conservative tide of opinion began to shift slightly in favor of the *taedong* reform when in 1646 Second Minister of Taxation Yi Sibang, who had previously opposed the *taedong* system in 1623, now decided to support it because the tribute burden in Ch'ungch'ŏng was twice as high as Chŏlla even though it had less land. Although he won over two other ministry officials to his position, Ch'oe Myŏnggil, however, the leading opponent of the plan in 1624, blocked any chance of a change in policy by insisting that the *taedong* system was only a revenue-raising measure and would not provide relief to the peasants.[31]

It is clear that Kim Yuk's attempt to spread the *taedong* reform to Ch'ungch'ŏng Province was blocked by the fear that a new surtax on land would either constitute a new and additional tax or be perceived as such by the taxpayers. By exaggerating the amount of revenue that the new surtax would generate, he opened himself to the charge that he was simply trying to sweeten the pill of a new tax. Even though he was obviously guilty of either a miscalculation of expected revenues or a purposeful deception, he also believed that those problems were minor compared to the continuation of a thoroughly corrupted and unbalanced tax system like the current combination of tribute in-kind and uncompensated labor service in transporting the tribute items. Any reform of major magnitude required a willingness to take certain risks, but in this instance King Injo adopted the conservative advice of his Ministry of Taxation.

Following the conservative mood of the times in 1646, King Injo also decided to cancel a special land tax for Hwanghae and P'yŏng'an provinces called the Western provision tax (*sŏryangmi*) or the Mao or Chinese provision tax (*moryangmi, tangnyangmi*), a rice surtax of 1.5 *mal/kyŏl* established in 1611 on Kado (Ka Island) just off the Hwanghae coast to provide rations for the troops of Ming general Mao Wen-lung. Even after Mao's garrison was withdrawn, the surtax had been kept on in the name of a special rice tax (*pyŏlsumi*). In compensation for this extra burden on these two provinces after 1611, their tribute quotas were shifted to Ch'ungch'ŏng and Chŏlla provinces, but in 1646 when the Western provision tax was canceled, the original tribute quotas were returned to Hwanghae and P'yŏng'an provinces, providing some relief in tribute demands for Ch'ungch'ŏng and Chŏlla. As things turned out, a special rice tax was retained in Hwanghae Province, but the rate was dropped from seven to five *mal/kyŏl* and the revenue was used to buy tribute to present to the Ministry of Taxation, in effect converting it into a *taedong*-type of land surtax.

In P'yŏng'an Province, as well, a partial implementation of *taedong* principles was adopted when thirteen districts along the direct route of travel to China were required to pay a grain tax at a rate of five *mal/kyŏl*, and twenty-nine other upland districts paid a rate of six *mal/kyŏl*. Of this amount, three *mal* (60 percent of the revenue from the lowlands and 50 percent from the uplands) was used to buy tribute for the Ministry of Taxation, and the other three *mal* was kept in the province for military expenses and hiring horses.

Thus, despite the conservative reaction to the *taedong* system, it had begun to penetrate P'yŏng'an and Hwanghae provinces, and Kim Okkŭn has gone further and argued that in these two provinces, and in the case of royal tribute (*chinsang*) in Hwanghae Province, tribute had already been changed to a land tax in practice, an arrangement called the private *taedong* system (*sadaedong*). Kim did not specify the date when this transformation occurred, but as proof he referred to the statement in 1697 of the minister of personnel, who in response to a formal proposal to adopt the *taedong* system in Hwanghae Province in 1694, pointed out that the gist of the *taedong* system was already in practice. Formal and legal acceptance, however, did not occur until fifteen years later, in 1708.[32]

After Injo died and King Hyojong ascended the throne in 1649, the situation for reform became more favorable. When Prince Yŏnch'ŏn (Yŏnch'ŏn'gun), Yi Kyŏng'ŏm, recommended adoption of the *taedong* system for the three southern provinces, many of the high officials, including Councilor of the Left Yi Kyŏngsŏk, Councilor of the Right Chŏng T'aehwa, and Director of the Office of the Royal Clan (Tollyŏngbu Yŏngsa) Kim Sanghŏn, favored it, but discussion was delayed for three months by mourning requirements for the deceased king, Injo.

After Kim Yuk was appointed councilor of the right, he again proposed adopting the *taedong* reform for Ch'ungch'ŏng and Chŏlla provinces, but he revised his earlier tax rate proposal upward from the equivalent of seven *mal/kyŏl* to the equivalent of ten *mal/kyŏl*, the rate suggested in 1638 by officials of the Royal Lectures. He did so in order to meet objections against revenue shortage, but he still insisted that the tax be divided into cloth and rice: one *p'il* of cotton defined as worth five *mal* of rice in current prices, and two *mal* of rice in the spring, and an additional three *mal* in the fall. The tax equivalent of ten *mal* (or two *p'il*) would still have been much lower than the sixteen *mal/kyŏl* (eight *mal* each in the spring and fall) in Kyŏnggi and Kangwŏn provinces.

Since the total amount of land in Ch'ungch'ŏng and Chŏlla was 270,000 *kyŏl*, Kim estimated tax revenue from the surtax at 5,400 *tong* (270,000 *p'il*) of cloth, equivalent to 1,350,000 *mal* of rice, and 85,000 *sŏm* (1,275 million *mal*) of rice, which would pay for royal tribute, miscellaneous labor service, and expenses of magistrates' yamen in addition to ordinary tribute. The Border Defense Command responded to Kim's written memorial by proposing that the system be tried only in Ch'ungch'ŏng Province first.

When Kim Yuk was summoned to court to testify about his plan, he mentioned that he expected opposition from wealthy landlords in the south but felt it was more important to legislate on behalf of the ordinary people. He was supported by Cho Ik and Yi Sibaek, and opposed by two or three officials. When King Hyojong then asked whether he had more to fear from peasant or landlord resentment on this issue, all officials agreed that peasant chagrin would be greater if the king failed to pass the law.[33]

The conflict over the issue became so bitter that the court was split apart. In 1650, the minister of taxation, Kim Chip, was so offended by Kim Yuk's remarks at court during the debate that he left court altogether and retired to his home in the country, and his disciple, Song Siyŏl, then a second inspector (Chib'ŭi) in the Office of the Inspector-General, resigned as well. Kim Yuk, in turn, felt that Kim Chip's withdrawal from court impugned his own integrity, and he defended his honor by submitting his own resignation. Hyojong accepted Kim's resignation and reappointed him to a sinecure in the ceremonial Military Affairs Commission (Chungch'ubu). After that, discussion over the *taedong* reform was suspended for half a year.[34]

In 1650 the tide of official opinion turned in favor of the *taedong* reform. The Office of Censor-General and the Border Defense Command both recommended that the time had come to try out the *taedong* system in the coastal areas of Ch'ungch'ŏng because tribute taxes there were particularly egregious. Chief State Councilor Yi Kyŏngyŏ, Third State Councilor Cho Ik, Ministers of Punishments and War Yi Sibang and Yi Sibaek, and Censor-General Min Ŭnghyŏng supported the adoption of the *taedong* reform for lowland Ch'ungch'ŏng, but King Hyojong put off a decision because other high officials were still firmly opposed to it, and he shifted his attention to the problem of Manchu objections to Korean military preparations.

After this issue had been settled, in 1651 Hyojong appointed Kim Yuk to the post of chief state councilor and a number of other reformers to high office, and in July he supported Min Ŭnghyŏng's recommendation for a low three *mal/kyŏl* land surtax in Ch'ungch'ŏng and Chŏlla provinces just to replace tribute alone. Hyojong liked the idea of a tax less than a fifth of the rate in Kyŏnggi Province because the people should have welcomed it, but Wŏn Tup'yo and Hŏ Chŏk scotched his hopes by objecting that the people would regard it simply as an additional tax. Hŏ argued that since tribute taxes were heavier in Ch'ungch'ŏng than Chŏlla, the logical way to create an equitable distribution of provincial tax burdens would be to reduce taxes in Ch'ungch'ŏng and raise them in Chŏlla. Unfortunately, the desirable but light three *mal/kyŏl* surtax in Ch'ungch'ŏng would not be sufficient to replace tribute in kind, and the people of Chŏlla Province would resist any attempt to raise their rate.

Hyojong must have taken Hŏ Chŏk's advice to heart because he later abandoned any intention of adopting a *taedong* plan for all three southern provinces at once and decided to focus on Ch'ungch'ŏng Province alone. He still favored a three *mal* tax for Ch'ungch'ŏng, but only if its revenue would cover the cost of tribute and he could promise not to raise the rate further. Wŏn Tup'yo, who wanted to block any *taedong* replacement for tribute altogether, immediately reminded him that it certainly would not be sufficient to cover the costs of yamen expenses and the *kiin* service costs, and it might lead to greater loss of grain ships at sea. Later that month the Border Defense Command confirmed Wŏn's argument that the tax rate would be too low, but it still suggested that the *taedong* tax be adopted for Ch'ungch'ŏng alone.[35]

Hyojong by now had decided to favor some kind of reform. When in August Second State Councilor Han Hŭng'il proposed adoption of the *taedong* reform for all three provinces in the south, the king indicated he still favored the three *mal/kyŏl* rate, but only for Ch'ungch'ŏng Province. A few days later Kim Yuk agreed even though it was not as good as a higher tax rate, and Yi Sibang also argued that tax revenues would be insufficient. Hyojong said it would be worth testing the three *mal/kyŏl* surtax in Ch'ungch'ŏng first to decide whether the peasants or the private merchants (*sajuin*) would end up paying the greater part of the tax, but Yi insisted that the *taedong* system should be adopted immediately because it had worked well in Kangwŏn Province. Hŏ Chŏk reaffirmed his previous advice that the reform be confined to Ch'ungch'ŏng Province because its tribute burden was almost double that of Chŏlla even though it had only 140,000 *kyŏl* of land to Chŏlla's 190,000 *kyŏl*, but he supported Kim Yuk's and Yi Sibang's preference for the higher *taedong* rate because it would cover all administrative and transportation costs as well as tribute.

When the conference apparently ended with Hyojong's decision to adopt a three-*mal* surtax for Ch'ungch'ŏng alone, Kim Yuk obtained Hyojong's approval to put Yi Sibang and Hŏ Chŏk in charge of implementing the order. In the next few days, however, Hyojong changed his mind and decided in favor of the higher *taedong* rate and signified his willingness to adopt the views of Kim Yuk, Yi Sibang, and Hŏ Chŏk for a more ambitious policy of eliminating all miscellaneous charges for goods and services as well as tribute payments.[36]

When King Hyojong finally promulgated an edict decreeing adoption of the *taedong* system in Ch'ungch'ŏng Province in the fall of 1651, he recounted how the tribute system had only provided an opportunity for the capital tribute middlemen (*kyŏngjuin*) to reap twenty to thirty times the value of tribute items by their market transactions in the *pangnap* scheme and double the tax burden on the local districts. He noted how officials had been split between those who preferred keeping but reforming the tribute regulations and those who wanted substitute rice or cloth for tribute in kind, and he gave full credit to Kim Yuk for his forceful and persuasive advocacy of the *taedong* system.[37]

Ching Young Choe has asserted in his study of this case that extension of the *taedong* throughout the country was prolonged, among other reasons, by "the characteristic . . . weakness of the authority of the king and the absence of any other co-ordinating and directing center of government operations." He also argued that bold decisions required a king of "exceptionally strong character and of constructive and realistic imagination," and that the *taedong* system had been advanced by "a few reformers" who responded to a "grave national crisis."[38] Choe's conclusions were generally valid, but in this instance the advocates of reform were well placed in the highest ranks of the central government, and the king himself had been favorably disposed to it from the beginning of his reign. He had been constrained against bolder moves not only by the opposition of wealthy landlords and conservative bureaucrats, but by the fear that people of moderate wealth and poorer peasants might not trust government promises to solve their problems by imposing a new tax. Hyojong initially favored the three-*mal* rate because the people were more likely to accept a low surtax, but he changed his mind and decided in favor of a rate that was more than three times larger because he wanted to make sure he could cover all costs and not have to raise the rate again.

Of course, he was urged on not only by Kim Yuk, but Cho Ik, Min Ŭnghyŏng, Yi Sibang, Hŏ Chŏk, and some of the censors, but he also had to defy the opposition of Ch'oe Myŏnggil, Wŏn Tup'yo, Cho Sŏgyun, Kim Chip, and last but not least, the strong supporter of his anti-Manchu policy, Song Siyŏl.[39] By no means was Hyojong willing or able to impose his decision on a court whose opinion was split on the issue, but it would be a disservice to describe him as a weak king because his support was ultimately crucial in reversing policy. The decision represented a noble victory for the reform wing of bureaucrats in the government.

Implementation of the decision would not prove to be that easy because the official Hyojong appointed to administer the *taedong* tax resigned in opposition. When Hyojong chose Minister of Taxation Wŏn Tup'yo to take over that responsibility, it could have been interpreted as a sly method of ensuring the failure of the *taedong* system because Wŏn had previously been opposed to it. Kim Yuk was incensed by this choice and accused Wŏn of being so determined to win his way that he would never carry out any policy he disliked. Kim had little respect for Wŏn's talents and accused him of violating the chain of command by never once meeting with him to discuss methods of implementation. King Hyojong defended his appointment of Wŏn, and even after he dismissed him, he appointed him to an important post in the Taedong office, presumably because he must have expected that top officials would abandon their own personal views to carry out his commands.[40]

Nonetheless, there were many critics of the law. Yi Sibang said it might work for the coastal region, but not for the hilly or upland area. Although Kim Yuk argued that the cloth tax was only equivalent to two *p'il* per *kyŏl*, he had to concede that if the peasants did not weave cloth, they would have to buy cloth with rice to meet their *taedong* cloth taxes at a price of more than twelve *mal* per *p'il* of cloth (instead of the current exchange rate of five mal per *p'il* set in the Taedong regulations) after a bumper crop and a drop in rice prices. But Kim also concluded that this problem could be eliminated by requiring a cash payment instead of rice (for upland peasants who did not weave cloth). Kim, of course, had been the leading advocate of introducing copper cash into the economy as a major medium of exchange, but this idea was a generation in advance of his time and the use of cash instead of cloth was not adopted until King Sukchong's reign in the late seventeenth century.[41]

Chŏlla Coastal Districts, 1658

King Hyojong's adoption of the *taedong* system for Ch'ungch'ŏng, however, did not cow its opponents into silence. In 1652, the fourth censor (Chŏng'ŏn) of the Office of Censor-General, Yi Man'ŭng, attacked two of Kim Yuk's favorite measures – adoption of copper cash as a medium of exchange and the *taedong* system. Yi Man'ŭng's opposition to cash as well as the *taedong* reform indicates that the conservative agenda was broader than preservation of the tribute system and included a reaction to the perceived dangers that expanded commerce and a cash economy would bring to the older economic order in Korea.

Yi was convinced that the people of Ch'ungch'ŏng Province were strongly opposed to the *taedong* system. If it had been as good as advertised, how come the king had not decided to adopt it for the whole country? He blamed the governor, Kim Hong'uk, for failing to have conducted a thorough investigation of the "feelings of the people" (*minjŏng*) right after he was first appointed to office. For this reason negative popular opinion was never reported to the throne, and the virtuous intentions of the court was never transmitted to the people.[42]

Yi Man'ŭng also held the *taedong* surtax should not have been levied at a time when peasants were in dire need of relief, especially since the *taedong* surtax on land had increased the taxes of poor peasants as well as wealthy families. He charged Inspector-General Hŏ Chŏk of failing to inform King Hyojong of problems in the system in Ch'ungch'ŏng Province. He claimed that he had heard that the councilor of the right was bombarded with written petitions when he visited the province but failed to report them to the throne, and that Chief State Councilor Chŏng T'aehwa, who had never agreed with the *taedong* law, showed no interest in its success. These officials should have emulated the behavior of Yi Wŏn'ik, who after advocating the *taedong* system for Kangwŏn, Ch'ungch'ŏng, and Chŏlla provinces, later changed his mind when he was out of office and wrote a letter to the high ministers opposing the system.[43]

There were, in fact, several reports about the *taedong* system in Ch'ungch'ŏng Province that corroborated some of Yi Man'ŭng's criticisms. Contrary to the intent of the law, soldiers on duty in the provincial army and navy garrisons were still required to pay fees for service, food, fish, pillows, ramie, straw, and a number of other items that were worth double the cost of cloth taxes for the support of soldiers. Some peasants did perceive the *taedong* surtax only as an addition to their own tax burden, and in 1657 the Office of Censor-General confirmed that extra levies on soldiers had become oppressive. Agents sent out from the Ch'ungch'ŏng provincial army commander's headquarters were making the rounds of coastal villages to buy six times the normal allotment of fish products, and after they had paid the villagers for them, they immediately took the payments back as a fee to pay for transportation of the goods to the camp. The coastal residents had also been bankrupted and were forced to leave their villages to evade further depredations. Contrary to the legal limit of 10 *mal/kyŏl* on the *taedong* grain surtax, a report was received in 1653 that in Hongju an extra 1.3 *mal*, colloquially dubbed "private *taedong* taxes" (*sadaedong*) was collected on the pretext that it was needed to repay grain borrowed from the granary by the previous magistrate. Cloth taxes were demanded according to standards of measure longer than the legal dimensions, and good cloth was switched for short and mediocre cloth to use for payments to merchants or remittance to the capital.[44]

Provincial officials were ignoring the *taedong* provisions to compensate peasants for labor service, and were spending surplus *taedong* rice revenues for themselves. Song Siyŏl claimed in 1657 that officials spent funds as soon as they received them and then attempted to replenish what they had spent by levying extra taxes, a perversion of the formula for setting tax quotas on the basis of anticipated expenditures (*yangch'ul wiip*). In any case, he preferred the time-honored procedure of limiting their expenditures to revenues actually received (*yang'ip wich'ul*).

If there did happen to be a surplus of revenues, officials and clerks loaned them out at interest for their own profit rather than keeping them as a reserve, and tribute agents and underlings of capital bureaus were also buying inferior merchandise on the market at prices lower than authorized by the government to earn profits for themselves. He therefore asked that the *taedong* tax be cut to provide relief to the peasants.[45]

King Hyojong did not respond to Yi Man'ŭng's proposal, but he did not believe that there was sufficient evidence of success in Ch'ungch'ŏng Province to justify Kim Yuk's proposal in 1654 to extend the *taedong* system to Chŏlla. In 1656, Kim Yuk complained that in Chŏlla the required labor service assessed for the repair of thirteen warships that had been lost at sea, or the substitute cloth taxes to pay for this service (*yŏkp'o*), was costing peasant families about fifty to sixty *p'il*. "The people of Chŏlla were in great sorrow and wondered why [the king] only loved Ch'ungch'ŏng and took no pity on us?" If the Ch'ungch'ŏng *taedong* surtax of ten *mal/kyŏl* were adopted, not only the repair of warships but also the costs of royal tribute could be financed as well.[46]

In 1657, Kim Yuk claimed that the several million people of Chŏlla had been clamoring for the adoption of the law in their province, but their desires had been frustrated by the opposition of fifty-odd magistrates. Since peasants were already paying over sixty *mal* of rice per *kyŏl* to meet their tribute obligations under the tribute contract system, the adoption of the *taedong* surtax would reduce their taxes to less than one-fifth their current burden and meet all revenue requirements for the province as well. Contrary to Yi Man'ŭng's earlier assertion, Kim argued that despite the opposition of the Ch'ungch'ŏng magistrates to the *taedong* system, the peasants were overjoyed with it, and the province had become the envy of its neighbors.[47]

Hyojong ordered his high officials to discuss Kim's proposal in September, but they had become cautious after censor Yi Man'ŭng's insistence that no further extension of the *taedong* law be enacted until a full study be conducted of its effect in Ch'ungch'ŏng. Minister of Taxation Hong Myŏngha and Minister of the Right Yi Huwŏn warned that even though coastal residents favored the law, there was no maritime transport system established in Chŏlla to send tribute products to the capital so that they could be purchased on the open market, and in any case the population of the upland region was opposed to the *taedong* system altogether. Two months later, the next Minister of Taxation, Chŏng Yusŏng, objected to open market purchases of goods by the government because experience in Ch'ungch'ŏng had shown that medicines formerly sent to the capital as tribute had now been replaced by inferior products available on the market. After the abolition of required labor service by the professional gatherers of medicinal herbs, the work had been taken over by men with no specialized knowledge.

Despite these objections Chief State Councilor Chŏng T'aehwa ordered Ho Chŏk to take responsibility for consulting with Minister of Taxation Chŏng Yusŏng to work out draft regulations for the *taedong* system for Chŏlla and to request the governor of Chŏlla to canvass the views of the magistrates. Even though his report was not included in the *Veritable Records*, Kim Yuk, now director of the Office of the Royal Clan, quoted the governor's report, which he assumed included false statements. Nonetheless, since it stated that of the fifty-three magistrates in Chŏlla, thirty-four favored the *taedong* system, sixteen were opposed, and six were neutral, Kim used it to refute an earlier report that all the district magistrates were opposed to the *taedong* reform. Han Yŏngguk found in his research that opposition to the reform from Left Chŏlla Province came almost totally from the upland region since twenty of the twenty-seven districts in Left Chŏlla were upland while only six of the twenty-three districts of Right Chŏlla were upland and three of these were later reclassified as coastal.

Kim Yuk reported that the residents of the uplands did not want the *taedong* system because they estimated their current taxes at the excessively low rate of ten *mal/kyŏl* that reflected the discriminatory shift of taxes to the right province or coastal region by the government in the past. He insisted that Hyojong take immediate action on his own authority to lower the tax burden in Left Chŏlla and equalize the taxes for the whole province by establishing a uniform *taedong* tax rate of ten *mal/kyŏng* for the whole province. He urged that five *mal* be collected before the end of the year and the next portion in the spring, but that after the fall payment the tax rate could be adjusted, possibly to conform to the rate in Ch'ungch'ŏng. Hyojong, however, refused to act without prior discussion with his ministers.[48]

Chances for the extension of the *taedong* system to Chŏlla were given an added boost when Song Siyŏl, one of King Hyojong's closest confidants, returned from a trip to Chŏlla in 1658, reported that the people favored the *taedong* reform, and declared himself that he thought it was "a good law."[49] Kim Yuk then recommended that the *taedong* system only be adopted in the twenty-seven coastal districts of Chŏlla, and in his last memorial to the king before his death on October 23, he asked Hyojong to appoint his protégé, Sŏ P'ilwŏn, to the governorship of Chŏlla Province to ensure that implementation of reform not be stymied after his death.

In his laudatory obituary of Kim Yuk, King Hyojong said that in his youth during King Kwanghaegun's regime Kim had been blocked from office because he was the descendant of a colleague of Cho Kwangjo, one Kim Sik, who was dismissed and banished in 1519, escaped from exile, and later committed suicide when his whereabouts were revealed. Kim Yuk was first appointed to office after the Injo Restoration in 1623, began an illustrious career, and was the prime advocate for the *taedong* system in Ch'ungch'ŏng and Chŏlla provinces. Unfortunately, his vituperative attacks on Kim Chip left him open to the charge of overweaning self-confidence that plagued him until the day he died. Yet Hyojong indicated that he was inclined to carry out Kim's deathbed desire by declaring that he could not have found a firmer person to take charge of government affairs than Kim Yuk.[50]

King Hyojong then appointed Kim's protégé, Sŏ P'ilwŏn, governor of Chŏlla, but because an estimate had revealed that a ten *mal/kyŏl* surtax would leave the budget short by over 5,000 *sŏm*, he decided to raise the rate for that province to thirteen *mal/kyŏl* to preclude any need to raise the rate in the future. Minister of Taxation Chŏng Yusŏng also proposed to solve the transportation problem by having tribute merchants from the capital go to Chŏlla, receive payments from the authorities for the purchase of any goods needed in the capital, and then pay for the costs of transportation themselves from their own profits, but the other court officials opposed the idea. In the fall of 1658 Hyojong finally decided to apply the *taedong* system to the coastal districts of Chŏlla at a rate of thirteen *mal/kyŏl*, mostly in accordance with regulations currently in use in Ch'ungch'ŏng, and he rejected Chŏng's proposal for private transportation of taxes by merchants.[51]

Hyojong himself passed away in 1659 before making a decision on the upland districts of Chŏlla. He was willing to do so because he displayed a serious sensitivity to popular grievance and he was not content to accept the governor's reports about unanimous opposition to reform by the district magistrates. His request for a further report from the governor provided Kim Yuk with the indirect testimony of district magistrates that at least the lowland districts favored a transfer of tribute taxes to a land tax. Since everyone agreed that the tribute burden on coastal Chŏlla was excessively onerous, Hyojong's own sensitivity to popular suffering as well as Kim's zealous advocacy and general support for reform among many active ministers, persuaded him that the time had come for a change.

Yu Hyŏngwŏn ended his coverage of the *taedong* reform with the events of 1658, but it is obvious that on balance the history of the reform indicates one of the most successful examples of institutional reform in the dynasty. It had to overcome the opposition of a large percentage of the landlord class, the upland residents of some of the provinces in the south, those peasants who feared that it would only lead to an additional tax, and officials who feared that the system would not produce sufficient revenues. Kim Yuk, the leader of the reform, was one of the most impressive reformers of the dynasty, but he had support from other officials as well, including members of the Southerner faction like Hŏ Chŏk, and even the Westerner Song Siyŏl, who originally opposed the reform and later changed his mind when he interviewed the peasants of the south. King Hyojong, who provided ultimate authority for the reform, naturally played the key role, capping what should be regarded as a significant and remarkable reform effort. Contrary to other areas of administration, the *taedong* reform provided an example of success for others interested in reform.

Upland Districts in Chŏlla, 1662

Prior to his death, King Hyojong left instructions with Song Siyŏl to postpone further discussion of the upland districts in Chŏlla until the fall. After King Hyŏnjong ascended the throne, Chief State Councilor Chŏng T'aehwa reported that since five of the upland districts actually favored the *taedong* system, it would be wiser to adopt it for the whole province rather than those five districts alone.

Debate continued into 1660, however, over the complex question of the grain/cloth commutation or conversion rate as well as the surtax rate on land. The government had to determine a tax rate that would guarantee sufficient revenue to replace the tribute goods without imposing too heavy a tax burden on the population, and it had to set a commutation rate setting the price of cloth in grain that would not discriminate against upland residents who had to pay their taxes in grain equivalents of cloth. Thus, the tax rate was set in cloth at two *p'il* of cloth per *kyŏl*, but only those districts designated to pay their tax in cloth would pay the tax at this rate. Other districts would pay in grain according to the commutation rate. That commutation rate, by the way, was not necessarily the same commutation rate used for the land tax, or for other provinces.

Furthermore, even though the *taedong* surtax was assessed in either rice or cloth, officials frequently discussed total tax revenues not by listing *both* rice and cloth revenues separately but rather by combining them into a single figure, most usually in terms of rice measured in *mal*. In other words, the *mal* would then become a unit of account rather than units of rice itself, and the cloth tax revenues would be converted to *mal* according to the government's rice/cloth commutation rate.

In Ch'ungch'ŏng Province, the tax rate was two *p'il/kyŏl* and the rice tax was thus ten *mal/kyŏl* (i.e., a five *mal/p'il* grain/cloth commutation rate). The commutation rate was supposed to ensure exact equivalency whether the tax was paid in cloth or grain, but if peasants living in districts in which the *taedong* tax had to be paid in cloth did not weave the cloth themselves, they had to buy it on the market. If the market price of cloth was higher than the five *mal/p'il* commutation rate fixed by the government, it cost them more than the legal grain tax equivalent of ten *mal/kyŏl* to pay their *taedong* tax; if the market price were lower, the peasant taxpayer would have benefited by a smaller payment.[52] Since the price of rice was cheaper in Chŏlla Province than in Ch'ungch'ŏng because production was higher there, the government decided that the *taedong* tax rate of ten *mal/kyŏl* that was used for Kyŏnggi and Ch'ungch'ŏng provinces was too low for Chŏlla Province and had to be raised to thirteen *mal/kyŏl* to ensure sufficient revenue. This action then required raising the rice/cloth commutation rate for the upland region of Chŏlla to six and one-half *mal/p'il* rather than the five *mal/p'il* commutation rate for the coastal district and the other two provinces.

In the middle of 1660, King Hyŏnjong decided he would apply the *taedong* system for the upland districts of Chŏlla after the fall harvest. Minister of Taxation Hong Myŏngha mentioned that during King Hyojong's reign, when officials were discussing regulations for the *taedong* system in the upland region (*san'gun*) of Chŏlla, the consensus had been that the tax would be levied at two *p'il/kyŏl*, but the rice/cloth commutation rate would be set at seven *mal/p'il*. This meant that residents of the upland region who had to buy cloth had to pay fourteen *mal* to purchase the two *p'il* required for each *kyŏl* of land, one *mal/kyŏl* higher (or 7.7 percent) than the tax rate for the lowland or coastal region of the province. When Yi Sibang had recommended that the commutation rate be lowered to six *mal/p'il*, it would have reduced their taxes to twelve *mal/p'il* but cut revenues as well.[53]

Chief State Councilor Chŏng T'aehwa argued, however, that if the purpose of the *taedong* tax was to benefit the people, they would be better off with a seven *mal/p'il* commutation rate, but Minister of Taxation Hŏ Chŏk supported Yi Sibang's six *mal/p'il* commutation rate because he thought it was closer to the real price of cotton cloth in rice. He pointed out that even in Ch'ungch'ŏng Province, where the commutation price of rice was set at five *mal/p'il*, the peasants found it difficult to buy cloth at that price on the market, and in the coastal districts (where cloth was more expensive than upland), they had to pay six to seven *mal* for one *p'il* of cloth.[54]

When King Hyŏnjong suggested that it might be best to compromise by setting the tax rate at thirteen *mal/kyŏl* in grain and two *p'il/kyŏl* in cloth (a six and one-half *mal/p'il* commutation rate), Chŏng agreed because it would split the difference between the two proposals. Splitting the difference between the two proposals was certainly a reasonable solution, but if this commutation rate were not an accurate assessment of the real market prices of rice and cloth at the time, it would have imposed a penalty on taxpayers who had to buy cloth or reduce the government's revenues. Unfortunately, the information available to the court consisted of hearsay reports, and the king did not order the conduct of a thorough study of prices throughout the province to determine what the price of cloth really was.[55]

King Hyŏnjong ordered that the *taedong* tax be adopted for the upland region of Chŏlla in 1660, but when Minister of Taxation Hŏ Chŏk and Third State Councilor Wŏn Tup'yo (a long-time opponent of the tax) complained that crop conditions were bad in the province, Hyŏnjong postponed the decision until the spring of 1661 and ordered that all *taedong* surtaxes collected already in the coastal area of Chŏlla be retained in the districts for use as relief funds (rather than returning them to the taxpayer). Further discussion ceased until 1662, when Kim Yuk's son, Kim Chwamyŏng, then minister of rites, reminded King Hyŏnjong of his promise. The king then agreed to adopt the *taedong* system for the upland region of Chŏlla in the fall and put Kim in charge of its implementation.[56]

The taedong *System in Ch'ungch'ŏng and Chŏlla*

The *taedong* surtax was levied in rice or grain in coastal districts, and in cloth in upland districts except that grain payments at the commutation rate fixed by the government was also allowed. All land was subject to the tax except for special tax-exempt land (*kŭppokchŏn*) set aside for expenses for the king, exemplary filial sons, and other recipients of state honors. Otherwise, the commutation rates and the grain tax rates differed by province, from sixteen *mal/kyŏl* set for Kyŏnggi Province in 1608, to ten *mal/kyŏl* for Ch'ungch'ŏng in 1651, to thirteen *mal/kyŏl* for coastal Chŏlla in 1658 and upland Chŏlla in 1662. Since the rates varied by province, the system lacked uniformity and fairness as well, since the fixed commutation rate may not have reflected market prices.

The *taedong* surtax was to be paid twice a year in spring and fall, and the government defined the dimensions of the *p'il* of cloth for tax payment in the upland region as thirty-five "feet" long by seven "inches" wide in Korean measure, with a thread count of five *sŭng*. Since the quality of the cloth was only one-fourth the value of the superior cloth (*sangmok*) used as a standard by the Ministry of Taxation, the purpose was obviously designed to lower the tax burden on the upland peasants.[57]

Taedong tax revenues not only paid for the purchase of goods previously paid in kind as tribute, but also for expenses for rites, paper, textiles, wages for hiring labor previously performed as corvée labor service, the cost of ocean and land transport of rice and cloth taxes to the capital, and expenses for provincial gubernatorial offices and magisterial districts. These expenses included tax income collected directly by magistrates from land previously set aside for provision of district salaries (*arokchŏn*) and official expenses (*kongsujŏn*) and exempted from tax collection by the central government (*kakcha susejŏn*).

That portion of the *taedong* taxes remitted to the capital was used to pay for what was previously required as tribute, and it was divided into three types: tribute payments to the Ch'ing court (*chinhŏn*), also called annual tribute (*sep'ye*); royal tribute for the Korean king, estates of royal relatives, and celebration of three national holidays (*chinsang*); and general tribute (*wŏn'gong* or *kongmul*) to bureaucratic agencies. *Taedong* funds for the purchase of items for government bureaus, however, increased over time. For example, one district paid for sixty items of former tribute paid to sixteen bureaucratic agencies in the capital in the 1660s, but by 1751, it was paying for the purchase of two hundred items for twenty-three government bureaus.[58]

The provincial Taedong Agencies (Taedongch'ŏng) for Kyŏnggi, Kangwŏn, Ch'ŭngch'ŏng, and Chŏlla were placed under a single Office for Dispensing Benevolence (Sŏnhyech'ŏng) governed by a system of commissioners. The three supreme commissioners (*Tojejo*) were the top three state councilors (of which Kim Yuk was chief state councilor in 1651). One of the commissioners (*Chejo*) was the minister of taxation, and two others took responsibility for the provincial offices and the Ever-Normal Bureau (Sangp'yŏngch'ŏng). The staff officers (*Nangch'ŏng*) were placed in direct charge of running these agencies.[59]

Of the 131,490 *kyŏl* of cultivated land taxed in Ch'ungch'ŏng Province in 1652, 6,673 *kyŏl* of tax exempt land (*kŭppokchŏn* or *pokho*) used to pay funds for the king's palace expenses, honored exemplars of morality, post-stations, ferries, and the like, was deducted from the *taedong* tax rolls, leaving 124,746 *kyŏl* of taxable land (thereafter an annual average of 124,000 *kyŏl*). This exemption from the law was an important modification of the principle of fair and equal distribution, but the amount was not large at the outset. The total *taedong* revenue for the province that year was 83,164 *sŏm* (or 1,247,460 *mal*), of which 58 percent (48,280 *sŏm*) was remitted to the capital for the purchase of former tribute items, 36.8 percent (30,922 *sŏm*) was kept in the provinces to meet yamen expenses, salaries, and other costs, and 4.7 percent (3,962 *sŏm*) was set aside to defray maritime and overland transport costs. To alleviate the burden on small districts that could not meet their tax quotas for capital tribute purchases, surpluses were collected from large districts to make up the difference.[60]

In Chŏlla Province the *taedong* surtax was levied on about 200,000 *kyŏl* a year of taxable land (*silkyŏl*) in 1662, yielding revenues of 147,134 *sŏm*, of which 61,218 *sŏm* (41.6 percent) was remitted to the capital, and 61,218 *sŏm* (58.4 percent) was retained in the province – a proportion almost the reverse of the pattern in Ch'ungch'ŏng. In Chŏlla Province, the first half of the tax payment (6 *mal/kyŏl*) was due in the spring and was sent to the capital to pay for tribute purchases and other capital expenses, but any shortages of revenues needed in the capital was supplemented from large districts that had a surplus. The second tax payment (seven *mal/kyŏl*) was retained in the province. Evidently for the calculation of the total value of *taedong* revenues, cloth payments were converted to units of account in rice (*mal*).[61]

Han Yŏngguk has called attention to interprovincial discrimination in the *taedong* tax. Under the tribute system Ch'ungch'ŏng Province paid 83.3 percent of the amount of tribute that Chŏlla paid (exclusive of special tribute and personal labor service costs) even though Ch'ungch'ŏng had only 55.5 percent of the population and 71.4 percent of the land in Chŏlla. Han estimated that Ch'ungch'ŏng should only have paid 62.5 percent of Chŏlla's tribute (1/1.6, the average between the population and land ratios for the two provinces).[62]

The cost of purchasing tribute items for shipment to China was, of course, quite onerous after the second Manchu invasion of 1637. Initially Korea had to send 100 *yang* of gold, 10,000 *yang* of silver and 20 other articles. The amount and type of tribute to the Ch'ing court was reduced in 1647, 1654, and 1711, and in the last year gold and silver was eliminated, but even in the eighteenth century more than thirty kinds of goods were sent.

Of the 56,889 *sŏm* of grain sent to the capital from Chŏlla Province in 1662, 1,661 *sŏm* was spent to purchase quality paper, 9,333 *sŏm* (actually half in cloth and half in rice) for large and small quality cotton cloth for tribute to the Ch'ing imperial court, and 1,388 *sŏm* for over 26,000 rolls of quality paper for the Ch'ing emperor and his family – a total of 12,382 *sŏm* or 21.8 percent of *taedong* remittances to the capital. Of these amounts, half the cotton tribute was reduced in 1711. Other provinces had to pay a proportionate share of these amounts as well.[63]

Provincial District Capital Agent Replaced. The *taedong* system also brought in its wake a transformation in the supply of tribute items to the capital. Since the mid-Koryŏ period each provincial district sent a commoner to the capital under the system of compulsory labor service to serve as the district's capital agent (Kyŏngjŏri or Kyŏngjuin). He was responsible for supervising the flow of written communications between the district and the central government, and orders from the throne were distributed through him to his district. The capital agent only ceased acting as the conduit of edicts to districts in 1730, when King Yŏngjo required that all royal orders and ministerial directives be funneled through provincial governors. The district's capital agent also guaranteed the attendance of rotating duty soldiers in the capital and rotating *kiin* clerks responsible for wood and fuel supplies to capital bureaus, and had to pay the cost for replacing any *kiin* or serviceman absent without leave. They provided room and board for officials and clerks from their districts in their own homes or those of their friends (reimbursed with interest by the district magistrate). Since they also had to make advance payments of tribute items to the central government when necessary, they were given the opportunity to reap large and illicit profits as middlemen between the peasants or districts and the central government by selling quality tribute goods and purchasing cheaper items for presentation to the government under the *pangnap* method of profiteering.

Under the *taedong* system, however, the work of the district's capital agent was no longer performed by a local clerk (*hyangni*) or commoner from the district on rotating labor service, but by a resident of the capital hired as agent for each district and paid a "service fee" (*yŏkka*) or salary. The province's Taedong Agency in the capital used revenues received from the *taedong* tax to pay their annual service fee of twenty *sŏm* in rice (for Chŏlla, fifteen *sŏm* for Ch'ungch'ŏng) and to grant them funds for purchasing goods on the market to present to the king or central bureaus in lieu of tribute payments. At times the capital agents complained that the funds given them were too low for a reasonable profit despite exhortations issued by high officials and government laws to provide liberal prices and guarantee incentives for the private supply of commodities to the capital without the system of forced supply.

On the other hand, the district's capital agent learned to utilize his position to make large profits, primarily by making loans to commoners and clerks who owed cloth or service payments or to magistrates who needed funds in advance to meet government deadlines for tax payments or to pay for their food and lodging expenses. They profited by lending funds at rates as high as 10 percent per month, and as their profits increased, the level of their "service fees" or salaries rose by the eighteenth century to 100 *sŏm* for agents of ordinary districts, 240 *sŏm* for the agent (*chuin*) of the provincial governor, 30 *sŏm* for the provincial army commander, 4 *sŏm* for the provincial navy commander, and 170 *sŏm* for petty clerks working in official warehouses (*konggo chabyŏk*). Since the position of district capital agent guaranteed the prospect of wealth, officials and yangban began to purchase the positions themselves for 5,000 *yang* of cash for agents in the capital, and 10,000 *yang* for those in the provincial capitals.[64]

Kiin Costs Paid for by Taedong. Taedong revenues were also used to pay for costs previously supplied by the *kiin. Kiin*, who also had been liable for making paper for the Ministry of Works, were also paid a fee for their service by the provincial Taedong Agency, a hybrid arrangement by which *taedong* funds were used to pay for the cost of paper products made by the *kiin* rather than purchasing them on the open market. A similar system was also adopted for paying tribute agents (Kongjuin) who previously worked for the Ministry of Taxation and were paid wages from land tax (*chŏnse*) revenues. Their wages were now shifted to *taedong* revenues, and they engaged in obtaining items formerly required as tribute. Furthermore, *taedong* regulations were revised in 1653 to pay for special tribute items for the entertainment of guests, and in other cases the *taedong* system was further extended to replace tribute horses presented to the Royal Stable Court (Saboksi).[65]

Costs Paid by the Taedong. The *taedong* revenues retained in the provinces were used to replace all previous levies on provincial districts to pay the office expenses of district magistrates, the provincial governor, and provincial military and naval commanders. To determine district expenses all districts were divided into four categories on the basis of the amount of land they contained, and *taedong* provincial funds paid for office expenses for pen and ink, paper, medicine, oil, official guests, soldiers in annual bivouac training, holding the first stage of the triennial civil service examinations, and assistance to chartered private academies. Since the cost of making muskets, gunpowder, and bullets had previously been paid for by extra land levies, these expenses were also included in the *taedong* revenues.

Costs associated with the transportation of *taedong* taxes to the capital such as boat construction and repair and maintenance of horses were budgeted in the *taedong* account as well, eliminating previous charges collected from the peasants. Remuneration was provided for inspectors on board ship to ensure that taxes reached the capital. Others feared that the existing fleet of grain transports for the land tax was too small for the increased grain and cloth revenues without special expense funds. In addition, *taedong* funds also paid for horses used in remitting royal tribute, official travel, and overnight costs for local officials in the capital, but with strict provisions to prevent wasteful expenditures. The *taedong* fund also paid for support of sailors, oarsmen, and horse grooms.

Full Accounting. Magistrates had to provide a full accounting of their expenditures and ferret out "hidden" or unreported cultivated land, collect *taedong* taxes from it, and enter it on the registers. To reduce the cost for the support of official guests, each magistrate had to post a schedule of payments on the walls of government offices on major thoroughfares. Any surplus revenues generated by the *taedong* tax would be stored as insurance against any future crop disasters, or loaned out at interest to maintain a fresh fund to pay for costs, and records would be kept to prevent any waste. Funds from the Ever-Normal Bureau (Sangp'yŏngch'ŏng) would be also used as a reserve in case of shortages. To ensure fair tax distribution, the smallest of the four categories of districts paid only one-twelfth the amount required of the largest ones.

Taxes Replaced by Taedong Tax. In Chŏlla Province some taxes collected for royal tribute were retained in the province for the governor to purchase special types of food and other items for presentation to the national Royal Ancestral Shrine (Chongmyo). Magistrates were authorized to obtain local tribute products for the entertainment of foreign visitors, furs and pelts for royal tribute, clerical costs for the triennial household (census) registers, fees for the manufacture of nitrates and explosives, expenses in transfer ceremonies for magistrates transferred prior to the expiration of their full term of office, provincial examinations for civil and military candidates, and musicians. A serious omission from the *taedong* financial system, however, was the continuation of arbitrary levies on the people for payments of pheasants, chickens, ice, and firewood used by the district magistrate.[66]

Benefits and Weaknesses. Han Yŏngguk felt that although the half-dozen types of tribute or labor service that were not eliminated did preserve the legality of arbitrary tribute or service levies, the *taedong* system was rational and modern because on balance it eliminated most of the unplanned, arbitrary, and excessive collections of the tribute system. It improved the distribution of taxes by replacing communal taxpaying by administrative district with a more equitable system of individual taxation. It simplified the multifold and various types of tribute payments to rice and cloth taxes, reduced transport costs by allowing upland areas to pay cloth instead of rice, prohibited all irregular levies beyond those specified by law, and reduced government costs by setting prices to be paid for the purchase of tribute goods and dividing provincial districts into four categories to determine the level of their tax expenditures. It also provided special measures for supplementary funds if tax revenues fell short, and replaced compulsory labor service with wage payments.

As a compromise with existing conditions, however, the *taedong* regulations excluded currently tax-exempt land owned primarily by members of the privileged elite from the *taedong* surtax, permitted tribute levies of common items of consumption, and allowed governors to demand special and rare products from areas in their jurisdictions for the consumption of prestigious visitors. Han argued that these compromises were produced by the constraints of what he called the "feudal state system."[67]

Extension to Chŏlla. Kim Yuk had believed that extension of the *taedong* system to Chŏlla was particularly urgent because of the importance of the province to agricultural production and the need to alleviate the tax burden on the provincial population. In 1587, Chŏlla had 442,189 *kyŏl* of the national total of 1,510,194 *kyŏl* of land in the country (29.3 percent), paid 353,744 *sŏm* of 1,087,477 *sŏm* of national grain taxes (32.5 percent), including 230,789 *sŏm* of 492,222 *sŏm* of national rice taxes (46.9 percent). Chŏlla suffered severe loss and destruction after Hideyoshi's invasion, but still accounted for similar proportions of land and grain taxes. In 1646, it only had 200,437 *kyŏl* of registered land, less than half the previous amount, but still paid 75,720 *sŏm* of the 272,912 *sŏm* of national grain taxes (27.7 percent), including 38,281 *sŏm* of the 95,422 *sŏm* of national rice taxes (40 percent).[68]

Transformation of Tax Structure. The *taedong* reform transformed the tax structure of the dynasty. In 1717, the governor of Ch'ungch'ŏng, Yun Hŏnju, reported that the total of all legal and regular taxes levied on land was twenty-five *mal/kyŏl* in rice, of which twelve *mal* (the rate had been dropped from thirteen *mal*) (50 percent) represented the *taedong* surtax, six *mal* (25 percent) the land tax (*semi*) and rice surtax for the three types of troops (*samsumi*), and six *mal* (25 percent) the miscellaneous expenses, district levies for pheasants and chickens, and wood and coal for fuel.[69] What this meant was that the old tribute tax that consisted of something in the range of half of the national tax receipts was converted to a system that required the open circulation of goods and stimulated the market and merchant transactions as the main means of supplying goods where needed. To a large extent these activities were already practiced under the *pangnap* system of illicit tribute contracting, but the *taedong* reform removed all legal barriers to trade in goods with government tax revenues.

Abolition of taedong *for Upland Chŏlla, 1667–68*

Opponents of the *taedong* system, however, did not give up the fight against it just because King Hyŏnjong had extended it to Chŏlla. In 1664 Pae Ki and other scholars from Chŏlla Province demanded abolition of the system in the upland region of the province because taxes had been assessed more severely on the uplands than on the lowlands since the turn of the century. In the first cadastral survey made after the Imjin War in 1603 the government had lowered the grade of classification for the fertility of land in the coastal or lowland regions because it had been devastated and peasants had fled to the hills, where they first began to reclaim land in the uplands. Consequently in subsequent years the quality of land in the uplands was assessed at a higher rate, and taxation of the upland region became several times heavier than the coast by 1663.

Pae and the others also charged that the commutation rate for the cost of cloth in rice or grain for tax payments had been set at 6.5 *mal* for each 35 "foot" length of 1 *p'il* of cloth, but the quality of cloth had improved from the standard 5 *sŭng* (180 threads) to 6 or 7 *sŭng*, and the length had increased from 35 to 39 "feet," so that the price of a bolt of cloth had gradually risen by 6 or 7 *toe* (*sŭng*, i.e., .6 or .7 *mal*) per bolt. This was equivalent to a 9.2–10.7 percent price increase (in grain) for 1 *p'il* of cloth, which was equivalent to a tax increase for those peasants who paid the *taedong* tax in grain.

When the merchants demanded better quality cloth in payment for the purchase of items that had previously been rendered to the government as tribute, the government found it could not reject merchant demands and passed the cost on to the taxpayers. Taken at face value, this rise in the cost of the *taedong* tax may have occurred because it was difficult to maintain parity between the government-established commutation rate and the real market price of cloth, a price that fluctuated with the value of cloth as well as the value of grain, which was commonly subject to annual variations in the size of the crop. The price of cloth could have risen because of an improvement in the quality of manufacture, or an increase in demand, or shortage of supply. Whatever the cause in the rising price of cotton cloth, it was bound to increase taxes on those upland residents who did not weave the cloth themselves but had to pay grain to buy cloth to pay their *taedong* tax in cloth.

Pae and his colleagues also charged that the *taedong* tax failed to achieve an equal and just distribution of taxes throughout the country according to the method used in the ancient "tribute of Yü" (*Yü Kung*), by which tribute levies varied according to the type of grain and the distance of the area from the capital. By contrast, in contemporary Korea residents of Chŏlla Province were paying thirteen *mal/kyŏl* while those living in Ch'ungch'ŏng only paid a lower ten *mal/kyŏl* rate. Since Ch'ungch'ŏng was closer to the capital than Chŏlla, its districts were allowed to accumulate large surpluses of revenue in their granaries.

Cloth taxpayers in the uplands of Chŏlla were also subject to arbitrary rejections of their cloth taxes on the grounds of poor quality, something that rice taxpayers presumably did not have to suffer, and transportation costs by land were still being collected in violation of *taedong* regulations, increasing the real tax rate to the equivalent of twenty-five to twenty-six *mal/kyŏl*, compared to the thirteen *mal/kyŏl* paid by the lowland farmers. Instead of charging a constant rate in all districts in upland Chŏlla, magistrates were allegedly charging rates that varied considerably. This complaint, however, seems to have been directed against favorable treatment for large landlords in particular because the magistrates were accused of levying the same tax on large landlords who had seven to eight *kyŏl* as well as smallholders who had only one or two *kyŏl* of land, in obvious violation of the law.

Naturally, these Chŏlla scholars preferred the old tribute system because no matter how burdensome it had been, the government could obtain any item it wanted directly without needing a reserve fund of rice and cloth. The *taedong* system also drove up the price of some items in the capital that were relatively cheap where they were produced locally. Market purchases had multiplied the cost to the government many times over and increased taxes on the landowners.

Prior to the introduction of the *taedong* reform, taxes in the upland districts in the south were collected twice a year, the first half was the land tax (*chŏnse*), and the second half the miscellaneous taxes (*chabyŏk*). Pae Ki and his comrades complained, however, that the six *mal/kyŏl* land tax and commuted *taedong* cloth tax (on the uplands) were collected in the spring and summer, and the *taedong* rice tax (thirteen *mal/kyŏl*) on the lowlands was collected in the fall and winter – a far too burdensome tax schedule.[70] Since there were not enough revenues to cover the miscellaneous taxes (*chabyŏk*) and the rice taxes on land were too large to raise further, the magistrates instituted new levies on individual households (*inho*). Pae Ki and his friends concluded by asking that the *taedong* tax for upland Chŏlla be abrogated so that at least a couple of dozen districts would be given some tax relief.

Nevertheless, two governors of Chŏlla later reported to King Hyŏnjong that even though popular opinion had always been divided on the merits of the *taedong* system, evils developed in any law as time passed, Pae Ki's criticisms were not sufficient justification for abolition, and some of the problems were not the product of the *taedong* system. Even though it was unjust that large households with several dozen adult males as well as fractional families of widows, orphans, and single sons were all counted as single households, the population still approved of the *taedong* system.[71]

In 1663, Chief State Councilor Chŏng T'aehwa then reported that all but three of the upland districts in Chŏlla were opposed to the *taedong* law, and only one of the five districts that had favored the idea in 1659 still felt that way. Third State Councilor Hong Myŏngha also concluded that although the coastal region favored it, the uplands were opposed. A battle broke out between Second State Councilor Wŏn Tup'yo, who demanded its abolition as always, and acting mayor of Seoul Hŏ Chŏk, who wanted to preserve it. Nevertheless, since both Chŏng and Hong approved of the law in principle and opposed abolishing it in half a province, they advised King Hyŏnjong to retain the *taedong* system in Chŏlla.

Chŏng T'aehwa, however, pointed out that the commutation rate was no longer realistic because cotton cloth had become more expensive and rice cheaper, and he recommended raising the rice price of cloth in the commutation rate used in the uplands from six and one-half to seven and one-half *mal/p'il*, a recommendation that Hyŏnjong accepted in 1664. The increase in the commutation price of cloth probably benefited peasants who were growing cotton and weaving cotton cloth and selling it on the market to meet the demand for tax payments, if not consumption, but raised the taxes paid by peasants who had to pay the *taedong* tax in grain or buy cloth. When Hyŏnjong raised the commutation rate again in 1665 to eight *mal/p'il*, upland residents of Chŏlla continued their opposition while upland cloth weavers resident in Ch'ungch'ŏng Province now complained that their cloth was now egregiously undervalued at only five *mal/p'il*. (On the other hand, peasants who paid the *taedong* tax in rice or bought cloth to pay the tax in Ch'ungch'ŏng enjoyed a lower tax than the residents of Chŏlla).[72]

Kim Okkŭn has argued that a small increase in the *taedong* tax caused by a change in the commutation rate would not be that onerous to small landowners and cultivators, a dangerous underestimate of the sensitivy of the poor to tax rates. In any case, the increase in the price of cloth also antagonized the rich and large landowners who had to pay more grain to pay the *taedong* cloth tax. A rise in the commutation rate from six and one-half to eight *mal/p'il* raised the tax by 23 percent from thirteen to sixteen *mal/kyŏl*, which also meant that upland residents of Chŏlla were paying 23 percent more in taxes than the coastal residents who were still paying thirteen *mal*. Even though the real tax may well have been as high as twenty-five *mal/kyŏl* as Pae Ki and the other scholars of Chŏlla had charged, an increase in the commutation rate still would have added to the heavier tax burden for the upland districts. The upland residents, therefore, had a legitimate reason for their discontent with the *taedong* tax system.

If the government were still committed to maintaining an equal and uniform tax for all persons in the province, it would have raised the tax rate on the lowlands to sixteen *mal/kyŏng* or allowed residents of the uplands to pay rice instead of cloth at the thirteen *mal/kyŏng* rate. As long as it insisted that upland districts pay their taxes in cloth, changes in the market price or commutation rate were bound to create discrimination.

In January 1666, governor of Chŏlla Min Yujung then recommended that the *taedong* law be rescinded in the upland districts on the basis of his survey of public opinion. King Hyŏnjong accepted the recommendation, ordered a return to the old tribute system for upland Chŏlla, and reduced the rice tax rate for the lowlands from thirteen to twelve *mal/kyŏl*. One censor then reminded the king that a survey of land and official needs had to be undertaken to redistribute tribute quotas, but before this task could be completed Hyŏnjong suddenly changed his mind after receiving a more detailed report from the secret censor (Amhaeng ŏsa) for Chŏlla, Sin Myŏnggyu. Sin reported that he visited each district individually and found that it was only the large households living in the larger and more important districts that opposed the *taedong* system, while the poorer and smaller households living in smaller districts all wanted the law restored. Chŏng T'aehwa and Hong Myŏngha (now councilor of the left) both agreed that public opposition to *taedong* had been misrepresented.[73]

Ex-governor Min Yujung then admitted that he recommended abolition of the *taedong* tax in upland Chŏlla because while making his tour of inspection in the province he had heard people complaining that the rise in the commutation rate had increased the grain paid to buy cloth for the tax. He expressed regret, however, that after the *taedong* tax had been rescinded in favor of a return to tribute taxes in kind taxpayers were once again subjected to demands for gratuity payments and arbitrary rejection of tribute goods on the grounds of poor quality. Not only did common people prefer the *taedong* system, but even agents of the capital bureaus (*kyŏng kaksajuin*) felt that funding for obtaining tribute had never been as good as when the *taedong* tax was in effect.

King Hyonjong then accepted Min's recommendations to restore the *taedong* tax for upland Chŏlla in the next year (1668), cut the tax rate from thirteen to twelve *mal/kyŏl* and retained the commutation rate of 8 *mal/p'il*. As Kim Okkŭn put it, Hyŏnjong's original decision to abolish the *taedong* system in upland Chŏlla was based on the misrepresentation of the views of the wealthy and landowning class as if it were the majority opinion of the whole population. Hyŏnjong provided some relief to the lowland rice-paying districts by cutting the rate by one *mal*, but by restoring the eight *mal/p'il* commutation rate he created a tax rate of sixteen *mal/kyŏl* for the upland region, 33 percent higher than the twelve *mal/kyŏl* rate in the lowland districts. He may have intended to punish the large landlords of upland Chŏlla for defying his will, but the same rate fell on the small cultivators as well.[74]

In any case, the difficulty in establishing a fair tax rate for the *taedong* tax because of the variation between the market prices of cloth and grain and the government's commutation rate and the variation in the tax rates between one province and another explains why resistance to the law itself continued even after the extension of the law to four provinces and parts of two others as well. These difficulties, however, did not impinge too severely on the favor by which the reform was generally held by most commoner peasants.

Extension to Hamgyŏng, 1666

During the time that the court was debating the extension of the *taedong* system to upland Chŏlla, in 1666 the governor of Hamgyŏng Province, Min Chŏngjung, complained that taxes on the peasants had increased because there had been no regulation of tax rates. He received approval from King Hyŏnjong to carry out tax reform in the name of the Detailed Tax Regulation Law (*sangjŏngbŏp*) which was a close approximation to the *taedong* system elsewhere. Taxes in rice, cloth, or other goods assessed on land were to be used to pay for regular and royal tribute assessed on each district, and the remainder left after these tribute items were purchased was kept in the province to pay for administrative costs. The Ever-Normal Bureau (Sangp'yŏngch'ŏng) received all *sangjŏng* taxes from the districts and took charge of payment to capital bureaus in place of the magistrates of each individual district.[75]

Thus, by 1666 the *taedong* system or its equivalent had been extended to all provinces but Kyŏngsang in the southeast, P'yŏng'an, and Hwanghae, but in the latter two provinces some aspects of the *taedong* substitution of land taxes for in-kind tribute payments had been adopted as well.

THE TAEDONG SYSTEM AFTER 1666

The handling of the *taedong* tax in Chŏlla in the decade after 1658 demonstrated concern by King Hyŏnjong and some of his officials for public opinion in general and sympathy for the plight of the small landowning and poorer peasants. The reason why Hyŏnjong apparently vacillated over the suitability of the law was the inexactitude of his information about public sentiment. In that period, since no one was aware of any possibility of conducting large scale surveys of opinion, the king and court had to rely on reports submitted by the provincial governor, who could accept, reject, or color reports from his district magistrates. Hyŏnjong's lack of faith in this regular channel of information, however, was demonstrated by the alacrity of his response to the secret censor's more detailed account of public opinion and his immediate restoration of the *taedong* system for upland Chŏlla. Even Min Yujung and Chŏng T'aehwa, who were influenced by negative reports from Chŏlla to recommend abolition of the *taedong* tax for upland Chŏlla, reversed their opinions and readily admitted that they must have been operating on the basis of partial and incomplete information.

Ching Young Choe's criticism of the weakness of the king's authority and the necessity of having a strong and constructive leader like Kim Yuk at court to achieve extension of the *taedong* system was exaggerated.[76] Although Kim's role was very important, in the decade after his death the kings and high court officials generally favored the reform but were unwilling to force it on the population against its will. Choe may have been right in criticizing the eulogizing of these attitudes as proto-democratic, but the behavior of the government in this period demonstrated a serious concern for the popular will even though its transmission was obstructed by premodern methods of observation, investigation, and communication. When Hyŏnjong decided to reinstate the *taedong* system for the upland districts of Chŏlla, he knew that wealthy landlords were opposed to the law, but he ordered its adoption almost as a direct challenge to their interests.

There was still opposition in Chŏlla to the idea of collecting the full year's *taedong* taxes as well as the land tax on newly cultivated land during the spring season when the peasants were running out of their food reserves, contrary to Ch'ungch'ŏng when tax collections had been divided in half between spring and fall. To remedy this Hyŏnjong accepted Min Yujung's proposal to extend the Ch'ungch'ŏng practice to Chŏlla.[77]

Nonetheless, not all problems in the administration of the *taedong* system in Chŏlla Province were solved in this period. After 1662, some magistrates failed to supervise tax collections themselves, and either turned the responsibility over to their petty officials or conspired with them to collect heavier taxes. Fishermen along the coast were dunned for tribute levies on various pretexts without receiving payment from the authorities. When high quality paper products sent to China as tribute could no longer be found readily in the capital markets, the government reverted to a temporary allocation of tribute paper. Clerks working in the Royal Cuisine Office had been demanding high amounts of cloth to buy bamboo shoots (*chuksun*) and accepting illicit gratuities; even though the authorities punished them for the practice, they continued the same practices because they were were allowed to keep their posts.

In 1671, an official of the Weapons Bureau (Kun'gisi) was arrested for profiteering by holding *taedong* revenues back until the price of rice shot up and then selling off the grain. The Military Training Agency was profiteering by demanding more tax funds than were necessary for the purchase of muskets. Government officials ignored the *taedong* prohibition against forced labor service from peasant households by requiring Buddhist monks to work on construction projects without pay, and if the monks ran away, they conscripted ordinary peasants to replace them.

Since capital bureaus often demanded extra goods from the tribute agents (*kongjuin*) beyond the limits of the *taedong* law and left them no margin of profit, in 1666 Minister of Taxation Kim Suhŭng requested that rice reserves from the land tax in P'yŏng'an Province be taken over for a year and transferred to the Office for Dispensing Benevolence. Shortages in the supply of meat required by the king for the royal table occurred because the introduction of firearms into the countryside had increased the efficiency of hunting, depleted the number of animals, and raised their cost on the market. Higher prices could not solve the problem of demand, and officials had to recruit peasants forcibly to go on hunts to trap animals for tribute. King Hyŏnjong tried to solve the problem by reducing the meat required for the palaces of two queens in 1670 to reduce the pressure on the villages. In 1668, the government reduced the number of guards, attendants, and tomb construction workers for the funerals of queens, princesses, and high officials.[78]

Despite all these difficulties with the implementation of the *taedong* tax in the upland area of Chŏlla, Han Yŏngguk, the leading scholar of the *taedong* reform, still believed that the population must have welcomed the reform. Although the evidence for this assertion was sparse, Han discovered some important indications. In 1673 court officials, disturbed by the shortage of *taedong* revenues in Ch'ungch'ŏng Province, argued that the *taedong* system in that province should be abolished because it was no longer possible to raise the tax rate. A classics licentiate (*saengwŏn*) from Ch'ungch'ŏng, Kim Mindo, however, wrote to the court that the *taedong* system had reduced the taxes on the peasants in Ch'ungch'ŏng from eighty to ninety *mal/kyŏl* before 1658 to ten *mal/kyŏl*. If the tax rate were increased to the twelve *mal/kyŏl* rate currently used in Chŏlla and Kyŏnggi, the peasants would have no grounds for protest.[79]

A few days later Third State Councilor Kim Suhŭng remarked that Kim Mindo's request for a two *mal/p'il* raise in the *taedong* rate was based on popular opinion in Ch'ungch'ŏng and the Office for Dispensing Benevolence's need for more revenue, and King Hyŏnjong mentioned that the new governor was also in favor of some act of reform. Minister of Taxation Min Yujung reminded them that the stubborn and violent people of Ch'ŏngju were opposed to abolishing the *taedong* system because it would mean that the district magistrate would then make demands on them for his daily requirements. A minor official in the Office of Special Counselors, Yi Inhwan, however, opposed a raise in the tax rate because it would would hardly be different from abolishing the *taedong* system altogether. When Kim Suhŭng disparaged Yi's objection because it was only a personal defense of his hometown of Ch'ŏngju, King Hyŏnjong accepted Kim's advice to raise the *taedong* tax by two *mal*.

The *Sillok* historian (writing in King Sukchong's reign, 1674–1720) chose to insert his opinion into the record that it was not the *taedong* system itself but the profligate spending of the government that necessitated the unfortunate raise in the tax rate:

> Even though the *taedong* system might not have been consistent with the in-kind tribute system adopted at the beginning of the dynasty, there was no better system for guaranteeing sufficient revenues to the state without afflicting the population. If only the government could have economized on its expenses and issued funds consistent with revenues, there would never have been any need to worry about financial shortages. At the present time we have not been able to do this, and [officials] want to raise taxes on the poor and starving peasants, or if not, abolish a good law that has already been operating [effectively]. It would be a mistake in policy to double the hardships of the people instead of offering them relief. In general the problem is that there are standard limits on tax revenues, but no limits on expenditures. If you fail to economize, you could raise taxes every year and still not raise enough revenues. Yi Inhwan was only saying that the local population did not want [a tax increase], but he could not understand that the real way to spare the people [excessive taxes] was to economize on expenditures.[80]

Finally, Han Yŏngguk found additional evidence about the popularity of the *taedong* policy by citing the remarks of Royal Secretary Yi Wŏnjŏng in 1677 that the people of Kyŏngsang Province were earnestly hoping for the adoption of the *taedong* system to provide relief from tribute levies that were twice as bad as any other province.[81] Han concluded that the the *taedong* tax had proved successful in Chŏlla, a province that was a crucial part of the financial base of the dynasty. Later on, when the effects of the *taedong* system became worse and the peasants came to think of it primarily as a new land tax and an extra burden, it was not the fault of the system itself but the general decline of order and the disruption of the economic system.[82] Han also believed that the extension of the *taedong* surtax over thirty years of debate was significant because the policy had been adopted when the government sought to place priority on the wishes of the people over the rich landlords, magistrates, and conservative officials at court.[83]

CONCLUSION

Although the *taedong* system provided the basis for Yu Hyŏngwŏn's plan for a thorough reform of the whole system of government salaries and expenses, his account of the history of the *taedong* movement was fairly abbreviated. After mentioning Yi Wŏn'ik and the adoption of the *taedong* system in Kyŏnggi Province in 1608, Yu only referred next to Kim Yuk's important role in extending the system to Ch'ungch'ŏng Province during King Hyojong's reign in 1651 without quoting any of Kim's now famous memorials to the throne, although he may not have had access to them at the time. Yu did say that when the people of Ch'ungch'ŏng demonstrated that they approved the reform, Kim then tried to persuade the king to adopt it for Chŏlla Province as well, but because of opposition among court officials, Hyojong only applied it to the coastal region of Chŏlla.

He also explained that the *taedong* land tax rates in the last two provinces were not the same and a uniform rate or system could not be devised for the whole country primarily because *taedong* taxes had been adopted to replace tribute quotas for each province that had never been assessed at a uniform rate. The fairness of the *taedong* tax depended on the quality of cadastral surveys used for the land tax, but these records were flawed by imperfect registration or corrupt concealment or "hiding" of cultivated land – an astute observation of one of the institutional flaws of the system. It was for this reason that the *taedong* tax rate for Kyŏnggi had been set at a rate higher than other provinces.

Yu's account of the *taedong* reform came to an end in 1658 and did not include the debate over its extension to upland Chŏlla in the 1660s even though Yu had moved to Puan in that province in 1653 and did not die until 1673. He also wrote that the only material he had to work with at the time was just one volume of the *Taedong Regulations* (*Taedong chŏrmok*) devised by Kim Yuk for Ch'ungch'ŏng Province.[84]

Although Yu Hyŏngwŏn was not privy to the full debates over the *taedong* system at court, and ended his account prior to the extension of the system or some modification of it to upland Chŏlla, Hamgyŏng, and Kyŏngsang, there is no question but that he was swept up in the strong tide of reform that had reached its height in the 1660s. Certain key statesmen like Yulgok, Cho Hŏn, Yu Sŏngnyŏng, Han Paekkyŏm, Yi Wŏn'ik, Kwŏn Pun, Kim Yuk, and Hŏ Chŏk played crucial roles in this process, but in addition the Imjin Wars provided a major catalyst. There was a solid core of reformers at court, and the disposition of kings like Kwanghaegun and Injo as well as the more aggressive Hyojong and Hyŏnjong illustrate that historical forces of long duration were the most important spur to Yu's adoption of the *taedong* model for his own plan for rationalizing and reforming state finance.

The history of the adoption of the *taedong* system throughout Korea shows that a reform effort directed at the alleviation of the arbitrary exactions of individual officials and clerks had to be waged against the determined opposition of conservative officials who sought to protect the source of their graft and landlords who rebelled against the idea of a surtax on their landed property. The *taedong* reform reduced not only the cost of purchasing tribute items on the market under the previous illegal tribute-contracting system, it eliminated a host of other other costs for rituals, certain central and local government expenses, incidental expenditures, and the panoply of uncompensated labor service requirements associated with the delivery of goods to the king and government offices. For that reason the *taedong* system marked a rational advance over the unplanned, arbitrary, and excessive exactions of the tribute system. It improved the distribution of taxes by simplifying the multifold and various types of tribute payments to cloth and rice taxes, prohibited all irregular levies beyond those specified by law, reduced government costs by setting prices to be paid for the purchase of tribute goods, divided provincial districts into four categories to determine the level of their tax expenditures, provided special measures for supplementary funds if tax revenues fell short, and replaced compulsory labor service with wage payments funded by *taedong* revenues. Finally, it acted as a stimulus to trade and commerce by opening up the process of allocation to greater market transactions than existed before.

The major deficiency of the system was that it was not carried out to completion. The government still permitted officials to levy tribute for common items of consumption and governors to demand special and rare products from areas in their jurisdictions for the consumption of prestigious visitors. It also failed to establish a uniform system of taxation to eliminate differential provincial tax rates and create a workable formula for establishing a fair commutation rate between cloth and grain. The most serious weakness, however, was that despite transferring the basis of the tax to land, the government failed to maintain an accurate and periodic survey of arable land to ensure a just distribution of the tax burden on landowners. By the nineteenth century, the problem of the tribute tax had been converted into a problem of the land tax, which became one of the major causes of peasant rebellion, but that was a matter of the deterioration and corruption of the *taedong* system after it had been established.

CHAPTER 22

The Taedong *Model for Official Salaries and Expenses*

> "If anyone should speak out and say that [royal tribute] has plagued the country and caused the loss of virtue, others only point to them and say that they have no respect for their king. This is the reason why it would never end until every district in the country was destroyed."[1]

> "After the commercial shops have flourished and all kind of goods are circulating, then even though you may have some urgent need [for them], you need not worry."[2]

Despite his sketchy history of the *taedong* system, Yu endorsed it as a major improvement over the traditional tax structure that was based on a fundamentally light tax that produced insufficient revenues and therefore required the government to approve ad hoc levies on the population without any limit on the amount and frequency. The *taedong* system, by contrast, made clear just what the peasants were supposed to pay in taxes every year by establishing a public tax rate. It provided for a "calculation of financial needs, the collection of tax rice to meet those needs, and control exercised by the government at court over expenditures." Despite these advantages, however, Yu pointed out that many officials were opposed to adopting the system nationwide because they opposed shifting tribute to the land tax.

Yu argued that the current land tax had been in a state of confusion because low-level clerks (*sŏwŏn*) had been allowed to control land registration, let alone steal and expropriate land from peasants, while the district magistrates purposely kept land "hidden" from the registers themselves. Presumably, since district quotas for the land tax were determined by government figures of registered land in all districts, those districts with the highest amount of unregistered cultivated land benefited the most from laxity in cadastral surveys. The only chance ordinary peasants had for relief was to negotiate privately with holders of hidden land about the division of tax quotas within the district.

If a district had been assessed for only one-tenth the amount of cultivated land it actually contained, it would produce a revenue shortage that would force the state to demand special levies to make up the difference. If the government needed an additional 100 *p'il* of taxes, it would spread it out among all the provinces simply on the basis of the amount of registered land, without providing any regular or uniform standards. The provincial governor would set quotas for each administrative district, each district would divide the quota among the number of household heads (in the household registers), and the household heads would then allocate taxes among the peasants. In every step of this process officials, clerks, and runners raked in profits from the transaction or demanded payoffs and bribes, increasing the burden on taxpayers beyond the legal limit. In traditional tribute particularly, the people did not know what the quotas were, and officials and clerks took advantage of them to set arbitrary rates and to make profits every time tax items were shipped and transferred. Even if the clerks were honest, they had to collect more than was legally due to provide a surplus for wastage.[3]

Furthermore, if tribute products were no longer produced where the tribute was assessed, the peasants were forced to purchase them through contractors. More likely, neither officials nor peasants even bothered to ask whether the tribute items were local products or not because tribute taxes had come to be assessed only on the basis of the amount of registered cultivated land and the number of able-bodied males in the district, and the district's faulty quota had become a permanent basis for the tax. Eventually, the clerks were given full leeway in filling their pockets at the expense of both the state and the people.[4]

The whole process of mobilizing the country to raise this extra tax would "disrupt the population of all eight provinces, make the heads of households run back and forth, force the magistrates and clerks to circulate communications, increase the circulation of paperwork in dunning people for taxes, and expand the opportunities for bribery."[5] The net result of this kind of supplementary, ad hoc taxation would end up costing the people no less than 200,000–300,000 *p'il*, for a net return to the central government of only 100 *p'il* of taxes. The result of almost daily repetitions of this process would be to destroy people's peace of mind, and since the regular salaries of the officials were too low to begin with, and the clerks and runners had no regular salaries at all, they had to use public funds, corruption, and bribery to support themselves. The truly honest clerks and runners ended up in destitution; those who were reasonably honest were forced into corruption just to exist; the most avaricious and corrupt of their colleagues simply became wealthy.

Yu concluded that since "our customs have become like this, and the legal system caused it to be this way," it was not clear that the *taedong* system would be sufficient to eliminate the arbitrary and unregulated additional taxes on the population. Since the current version of the *taedong* system (up to 1658, the last point Yu discussed in his work) involved an estimation of the amount of funds the state needed and a calculation of the tax rate on land in rice or cloth to raise those funds, it was a rational method to eliminate the need for additional ad hoc levies. Nevertheless, since this method of producing revenues to finance what the government felt it was necessary to spend (*yangch'ul wiip*) was contrary to the classical principal of limiting state expenditures to available revenues received (*yang'ip wich'ul*), true economy could only be achieved if the state itself reduced current levels of expenditure.

Yu remarked that all court officials had rejected the *taedong* system because it would require a cadastral survey for it to be effective. Although Yu did not list the reasons why they objected to a cadastral survey, one might speculate not only that the cost of a national survey would have been too great, but that the taxes of the rich landlords would have increased significantly by more accurate registration. As Yu did say, there were only two ways to explain their attitude: "If all they wanted (by their opposition) was (to perpetuate) unregulated tax quotas, it was either a case of delusion or ignorance, or an extreme case of injustice and national betrayal."[6] Since Yu wanted to expand the *taedong* system beyond replacing the cost of purchasing the old tribute items to cover almost all government revenues, including some of the costs of military defense, he had to demand an accurate, nationwide survey of all cultivated land to guarantee a fair and equal distribution of taxes on the landowning and tenant population. Of course, in his chapter on land he went much further by proposing the abolition of landownership and tenancy and the redistribution of basic plots of land to all peasant families.

Yu believed that obstruction to the *taedong* reform was the product of a virtual conspiracy among provincial governors and magistrates. While attending a public discussion of the problem he once heard a governor and a magistrate thanking each other for the role they had each played in keeping the *taedong* system out of the province because if the reform were enacted, the magistrates would have "no handhold or foothold" to rely on for their support. The conversation appeared bizarre to him because they should have been talking about the need for a public-spirited desire to serve the national and popular interest; the only foothold worth considering was a national system of regular taxes and standard salaries for officials. Instead, what they had in mind was the satisfaction of their own private interests and desires, behavior intolerable in a government run under the laws of a virtuous king (*wangbŏp*).[7]

Yu was convinced that rational budget allocations for paying the costs of government goods and services and human and horse transport for the shipment of those goods to the capital would replace all forms of tribute for the central government and the king. Miscellaneous forms of compulsory labor service (*chabyŏk*) that varied greatly from one district to another would be made equal and uniform by calculating its cost, levying sufficient taxes, and paying those costs from regular tax revenues. The honesty and probity of government officials and the efficiency of government operations could only be secured if the government assumed full responsibility for paying adequate salaries for all functionaries of the state, providing all costs required by government offices and agencies, and prohibiting magistrates from levying arbitrary surtaxes to pay the salaries of all their clerks and officials. Government finance would be based on funds raised legally and openly by authorized state taxes (*kyŏngse*), and all expenditures would be made from funds (*kyŏngbi*) raised by those taxes. He meant that such funds would be based on tax rates set by the state in quantities determined in advance by the state, and no opportunity would be allowed for magistrates or individual officials and their army of clerks and runners to impose arbitrary and excessive extra taxes.

He stated that his intent was to copy the *taedong* system without using the word itself because he hoped to avoid the stigma that had been attached to it over the decades of debate. He preferred to talk only about "regular expenditures" (*kyŏngyong*) to be paid out of regular tax receipts (*kyŏngse*) to clarify what the real issues would be. He criticized the current *taedong* system because it involved establishing tax rates on the basis of a calculation of expenditures (*yangch'ul wiip*) – the equivalent of a modern budget – because he preferred the classical formula of limiting expenditures only to revenues received (*yang'ip wich'ul*) since it would put an end to the more serious evil of current government finance – the unlimited use of extra, arbitrary, or miscellaneous taxation.[8]

Even though Yu was committed to a radical and progressive rationalization of government finance, his radicalism was restricted by a quite conservative aversion to the risks involved in commiting expenditures in advance. Despite what he said, however, he appears to have been talking about a balanced budget. Since he refused to countenance any possibility of a national debt, or borrowing from private parties to finance government deficits, to prevent the possibility of a budget deficit he calculated expenditures in advance, reduced them to match expected revenues, and made no allowance for annual shortages produced by emergencies, unforeseen developments, or miscalculations. But without the possibility of a national debt, the only way to prevent a financial deficit based on undercalculation of expected revenue was to allow additional taxes on the spot, a practice that Yu was trying to overcome.

TRIBUTE REFORM

*Royal Tribute (*Chinsang*)*

One of the significant features of the Korean tributary system had been the important and oppressive role played by tribute set aside for the king alone and administered by his own palace bureaucracy. Echoing the views of Cho Kwangjo and Yulgok against the excesses of royal tribute (*chinsang*), Yu proposed that it be abolished and the king's expenses be paid for and managed by one agency of the regular bureaucracy, a plan that was not carried out until adoption of the *Kabo* reform program of 1894.[9] Yu provided that this bureaucratic agency would calculate the equivalent of the king's living expense in accordance with the ancient Chinese principle used in feudal times, that the ruler of a state was only entitled to an income ten times greater than the salary of his chief minister. The new agency would pay that sum to the Royal Cuisine Office (Saŏngwŏn) or Royal Clothing Office (Sang'ŭiwŏn) from tax revenues shipped to the capital by maritime transport. Since there would no longer be any need for the Royal Treasury (Naesusa), it too could be abolished along with the current requirement that the capital bureaus provide daily offerings to the king. Instead, the Royal Cuisine Office would simply follow the practice used at the Chinese court by paying a price in rice or cash that would be at least twice the amount of current market prices to designated purchasing masters or agents (*chuin*). For special items like bean sauce, vinegar, wine, and salt, the office would make and store the items for use. The only possibility of a tribute levy might occur during ritual ceremonies that occurred once or twice a year when fruit like oranges or pomelos that only happened to ripen at certain times of the year would be needed. Otherwise, all goods consumed by the king and even construction projects for the king would be funded by regular taxes without any special levies.

All expenses of the king and queen, including clothing, upkeep of palaces, and salaries for eunuchs and palace lady attendants would be paid from regular tax revenues, especially since the ancients had quotas for these palace functionaries. The crown prince would receive one-fifth the king's income for his upkeep, and the other princes and princesses would be granted support from regular state revenues when they left the palace for their own separate quarters. Yu argued that an income of this size was especially generous since in Chou China the crown prince was only entitled to a fief equal in size to those held by the feudal lords. The queen's palace would also receive one-sixth the king's income for her own expenses and her ladies-in-waiting, and concubines of former kings (the Rear Palace or Hugung) would also be given funds for food and clothing and support for their male and female slaves. Yu justified these government grants according to the classical principle that from the Son of Heaven down to the common people, each person was entitled to a share of support in descending order of rank. Although the highest ministers had to support their parents from their own salaries, the ruler was entitled to separate funding for his mother and the queen.

Yu also proposed to abolish monthly royal tribute offerings from provinces and allow the presentation of tribute to the king as a matter of moral obligation only on New Year's day. Even then, the offerings would be purchased on the market from regular tax revenues by using a purchasing master. If governors of provinces were involved in these offerings, they too would use purchasing agents and pay for them from tax funds kept in reserve in the province, or hire artisans for any construction that might be necessary. In no case would the governors be allowed to reallocate tribute or tax levies to meet these needs of the king to the districts, and the provincial army and navy commanders would be absolved from royal tribute obligations.

Yu justified this proposal because he held that even in Chou times the kings really did not demand tribute. Although he conceded that the feudal lords did present particular goods produced in their own states to the Son of Heaven (King of Chou) as a matter of ritual etiquette (*ye*), he always refused them. In contemporary Korea it would be all right to purchase items on the market once a year as a tribute offering to the king as a matter of ritual obligation (*ye*). If the items were found wanting in quality, however, then in accordance with classical feudal practice, only the "lord of the province" (*toju*), as if he were a lord of an ancient fief, should be reprimanded for an act of discourtesy, but the items should not be rejected or demanded again as clerks in the capital had been doing in the past.

Yu was serious about the ritual required in presenting letters of felicitation (*chŏnmun*) and gifts of tribute on New Year's day and suggested that procedure in use in either the T'ang or Yüan dynasties in China might be adopted. During the Yüan dynasty, the Ministry of Rites presented commissioners from each province to step forward before the king, read their letters of felicitation, present gifts as tribute from the provinces, and receive a statement of "instruction" (*kyo*) from the emperor. Yu suggested that this procedure could be used for any ritual performance, the entertainment of guests, and provisions for the king's support. The goods received would then be sent to the particular bureaucratic ministry responsible for its disposition, such as the Ministry of Taxation. In short, the responsibility for managing and paying for all ritual acts performed by the king in addition to the costs of his upkeep would be taken over entirely by the regular bureaucracy as a means of checking the unrestrained greed of a despotic king. The model for the ideal form of limited monarchy was to be found in the feudal arrangements of the Chou when ritual behavior conferred a religious sanction to restraints on monarchical excess.[10]

Yu also cited Yulgok's words back in the late sixteenth century that tribute for the king should not require more than a small supply of goods, and that the sage kings of antiquity never believed that it was proper to mobilize the whole nation merely to support the consumption of the ruler. Yu expanded on Yulgok's comment by emphasizing the moral basis for tribute offerings: "The people offer tribute on the basis of their righteous obligation [to demonstrate their loyalty to the king] [*ŭi*], and the ruler receives them as an act of ritual propriety [*ye*]." Over the years, however, the royal tribute presented from the provinces had come to include an endless variety of tasty food items offered as frequently as two or three times a month, a custom that began in the middle of the dynasty and was never the custom at the beginning. All these levies were in addition to regular tribute, and because the provincial governors were otherwise occupied, they turned responsibility over to the district magistrates.

In Kyŏnggi Province, the magistrates then shifted the responsibility to the chiefs of the major post-stations (Ch'albang) and redistributed taxes among the people allowing brokers (*kaek*) and clerks to reap profits from bribes, gratuities, or tribute contracting. As Yu put it, "the royal tribute runs through you like a roasting skewer, and the gratuities are piled on you like a horse load." The actual operation of the system had nothing to do with the righteousness and ritual propriety that inspired tribute at the outset. The amount and variety of goods demanded in all sorts of weather without consideration for spoilage or difficulty in transport had destroyed the production of a thousand families and caused harm to tens of thousands only for supplying things "that the ruler of men has no interest in and have never passed before his eyes."

> Truly if the ruler of men gave one look at how the people had been dunned for payment, kicked and beaten in the back alleys of the towns, made to suffer from the cold and heat along the roads, and left with no one to whom to utter their grievous sighs of distress, then even though the king might desire such goods, he would not be able to bear [listening to] the sobs of the people. How much less [would he have tolerated] some of these rank-smelling goods which people easily abhor, which are no good to mouth or stomach, and which cause injury to thousands of people.
>
> This is not hard to understand, but the ruler only sits on his fine rug in the inner recesses of the palace and thinks that since he is the ruler, there is no way that he would purposely have planned for these evils to exist. But the obsequious and fawning ministers think that this is the natural way to express love for their ruler and do nothing about it. If anyone should speak out and say that [royal tribute] has plagued the country and caused the loss of virtue, others only point to them and say that they have no respect for their king. This is the reason why it would never end until every district in the country was destroyed.[11]

Yu then damned the Korean institution of royal tribute by an invidious comparison with the situation in China. Not only was there no record of any equivalent to the royal tribute of Korea in the three dynasties of Chinese antiquity (*san-tai*), but since Han and T'ang times the Chinese had a separate agency, that is a bureaucratic office that purchased all tribute items from regular tax revenues. "Never have I heard of tribute presented to the throne from the outer provinces [*oebang chinsang*]." Nor for that matter was there any Chinese term equivalent to the *chinsang* (royal tribute) used in Korea. Even Emperor Te-tsung of the T'ang dynasty, a ruler thoroughly castigated by historians for his excessive collections of gifts, never received anything more than silk, certainly not the monthly offerings of fish presented to Korean kings. In the Ming dynasty, imperial gifts became more complicated, but still tax revenues in silver and cash were paid to the Court of Imperial Entertainments (Kuang-lu-ssu), which then purchased all items presented to the emperor on the market. This system furnished abundant supplies to meet the emperor's needs without ever having an equivalent of Korean royal tribute (*chinsang*) levied on peasants as a separate tax.

In Korea, royal necessities were never funded by regular taxes and there was never an agency in the regular bureaucracy to handle royal tribute, because all royal tribute items were paid directly to royal agencies that handled cuisine, bedding, clothing, and other functions. Two-thirds of royal tribute was presented by the capital bureaus to the king, and districts in the provinces had to make royal tribute payments monthly or daily. So many men were involved in the transportation and handling of tribute in the capital that it appeared that 80 or 90 percent of the population was occupied in transporting royal tribute offerings through the post-stations to the capital.[12]

Yu attributed the inability of Korean kings to achieve good government to the adoption of improper laws and institutions almost at the outset of Korea's recorded history. In ancient times Korean institutions suffered by comparison with Chinese models because Koreans were isolated and inferior culturally. Yu traced the origin of royal tribute to a statement in the *T'ung-tien*, which had noted that when the state of Koguryŏ conquered the petty state of Okchŏ along the northeastern coast of the peninsula in the third century A.D., it had made Okchŏ responsible for transporting fish, salt, and maritime products over a distance of a thousand *i* (333 miles) to the Koguryŏ court. China, by contrast, had at least passed through an era of rule by sage kings in antiquity before it had declined to a period of "dirt and filth" – the post-Chou era of centralized bureaucracy – but at least it had something to admire in its past. "As for our country, we only had the customs of barbarians, so that even in the clean-washed and new [atmosphere] of this dynasty we still have not completely changed the vulgar [customs] of the past."[13]

Now the time had come to restructure Korean institutions in conformity with those of the ancient Chinese sages so that kings would be guaranteed adequate provisions and all evils associated with royal tribute could be eliminated. If the king's private Royal Treasury (Naesusa) and his concept of treating the product of his kingdom as his own private property (*sajae*) could be eliminated, "we could reduce the plague on the mass of the people, be in accord with the minds of all under Heaven, make the country wealthy and the military strong, achieve education and moral transformation, and bring about the Great Peace."[14]

In Korea the king's private and selfish interests and the satiation of the physical needs of his palate and stomach had taken precedence over concern for the sickness of the state or fatigue of the people. Yet despite his inordinate desire for the fanciest foods and the best materials, tribute goods were still poor in quality. The superiority of the Chinese system was obvious because it placed priority on the livelihoods, occupations, or strength of the people. Thus, Yu urged adoption of the Chinese system of establishing a bureaucratic agency and purchasing goods for the king from ordinary tax revenues. The vestige of feudal ritual tribute could be maintained at a ceremony conducted on New Year's day, "and if the court also accepts [the tribute] with ritual propriety, we will perhaps come close to the rites of the ancients."[15]

Although Yu had been influenced in his criticism of royal tribute by the views of sixteenth-century statesmen like Yulgok and Cho Hŏn, he was also indebted even more to his belief that royal tribute in Korea was inferior to Chinese methods because it originated in the barbaric and immoral institutions of the Koguryŏ dynasty. Yu obviously hinted that warlike Koguryŏ was most likely to have subordinated reciprocal obligation and ritual respect to the avaricious desires of the ruler, and he appealed for an adoption of the Chinese system because he believed it preserved the essence of classical norms defined by the ancient Chinese sages. Although his respect for those norms was probably motivated by his admiration for the wisdom of the sages dissociated from their Chinese ethnicity, his derogation of the barbaric nature of Korea's early history and the preservation of barbaric norms into the seventeenth century could in no way be construed as an exercise in incipient – let alone fully developed – nationalism, contrary to the recent interpretations of some writers on the Sirhak movement in the twentieth century.

*Tribute for Capital Bureaus (*Kaksa*)*

As opposed to royal tribute Yu found that there had in fact been precedent for ordinary tribute in ancient China when feudal lords levied tribute according to the special products of different areas, but the gift and receipt of tribute was connected with the moral principle of ritual etiquette (*ye*) between the king and his feudal vassals. If the feudal lord presented goods of inferior quality, it was not the peasant who was blamed, but the feudal lord himself. The feudal system, therefore, did not allow clerks in capital bureaus the right to reject tribute goods on the grounds of inferiority (*chŏmt'oe*), let alone transfer extra burdens to the peasants. Under the bureaucratic system in Chosŏn, however, ordinary people had to present goods all at once and were vulnerable to the clerks' power of rejection. Every time rejected tribute had to be replaced, the peasants became vulnerable to graft and corruption at every link in the administrative hierarchy.[16]

Furthermore, in classical feudalism under the rules for the tribute of Yü, the government of a virtuous king only taxed 10 percent of the crop or 10 percent of the income of merchants in the market towns, and supposedly prohibited all other irregular taxes, but in contemporary Korea tribute was levied in addition to other taxes, contrary to the ancient method. In ancient times rice and millet was paid in taxes in the ruler's bailiwick around the capital (*kinae*), but no tribute was required. In the fiefs or feudal states ruled by the lords outside the king's domain (*kioe*), goods offered as tribute were obtained by a 10 percent tax and the proceeds used to purchase the goods. Therefore, the only obligation imposed on the peasants was the land tax. In contemporary Korea, however, every district had to offer a variety of local products as an additional tax, so that modern tribute corresponded only nominally to ancient Chinese practice.[17]

Purchasing and Marketing Arrangements

Purchasing Masters to Replace Tribute Middlemen

Yu prescribed that present tribute items be listed for all goods spent by the capital bureaus. After eliminating unnecessary expenditures, quotas would be determined and each bureau would record the inventories of each item on hand. A separate quota would be maintained for items used in rituals and in the Royal Ancestral Shrine (Chongmyo). In accordance with the *taedong* system, tribute offered in kind either by local districts or the older tribute masters or middlemen (*kongmul chuin*) would be replaced by the purchase of goods on the market by purchasing masters (*mubijuin*). The government would grant these purchasing masters liberal funds from tax revenues to buy goods at prices several times higher than market prices for items needed by the bureaus, and these government allocations would remain standard even through bad harvests and famine years. Yu also provided that such funds for purchases would also be kept in reserve, half in cash and half in rice.

Yu expected that the purchasing masters would function as semiprivate merchants rather than government officials, financed by government tax funds. All purchases would take place in the capital for every item of consumption, down to the smallest mustard seed. The provincial governors would likewise purchase what they needed in the provincial capitals and would refrain from demanding any tribute goods from the districts. Yu also warned against permitting forms of corruption that had grown up in the tribute system, such as capital bureau clerks illicitly rejecting tribute goods on the grounds of poor quality (*chŏmt'oe*), or demanding fine goods for cheap prices on the market.

Yu warned that even under the *taedong* system that was currently operating in several provinces, extra allocations of tribute items in emergencies had in fact allowed magistrates to impose extra levies on the people and opened the door for bribes and obstruction of the flow of goods to the capital because there were no ironclad regulations for determining purchasing agents and setting prices in all circumstances. Permanent and binding regulations were necessary to eliminate all the evils that accompanied the tributary system. Provincial governors would not be allowed to redistribute royal tribute that had been specifically assigned to them (rather than to the districts) by demanding that the districts pay for it. If emergencies demanded a reallocation to districts to obtain necessary items, the governor would also have to hire purchasing agents to buy the goods on the market or directly from the producer.[18]

Liberal Prices as Stimulus for Market Development

Yu remarked that some people had expressed the reservation that because goods did not circulate in the market as they did in China, even providing liberal prices for those goods would not be sufficient to attract them to the capital, and the bureaus would always be short of the goods that they needed. Yu conceded that goods had not been purchased in the capital markets for some time, but he believed that the goods had not been attracted to the capital because tribute was not being purchased for a price. He was certain that within two or three years after the institution of market purchases, these fears would disappear. Despite the hazardous character of Korean roads, the opportunity for profit would overcome difficulties in transportation. "Once you set a price that is better [than the market price], the people will definitely go to the place where profits are to be obtained, and even if you wanted to prohibit them from doing so, you would not be able to do it." Since tribute in kind had long since been replaced by substitute purchases or tribute contracting called *pangnap*, people were already used to collecting funds to buy tribute items and pay bribes.

In the case of some items that were difficult to buy in the capital, the price of the goods in the capital would be calculated and deducted from the taxes sent by a given district, and the district magistrate would retain these tax revenues to hire a purchasing agent. He would provide the agent with funds and send him out as his commissioner, a person colloquially called "the tribute elder" (*kongmul puro*), to purchase those goods where they were produced, similar to the system used in the capital. The government would also pay horse and transportation costs and arrange for any emergency allocation of goods to be bought in this way on the market rather than by continuing the practice under the tribute system of making extra, ad hoc allocations of tribute goods on individual districts.[19]

The Government-Regulated Market: Subsidized Prices

Yu's perception of the operation of market purchases did not include any theoretical proposition about the necessity for prices to be determined only by private negotiation between sellers and purchasing agents. On the contrary, he did argue that the government should determine liberal prices to be paid to merchants over current market prices – an argument that followed Han Paekkyŏm's proposal in 1608 to remedy the practice of officials to demand lower prices for goods from merchants after the adoption of Yu Sŏngnyŏng's *taedong* reform of 1594. Yu thus implied that to preclude merchant opposition to the *taedong* system the government was obliged to guarantee the private merchants a profit for their sales to the government and an incentive for a constant flow of goods to the capital. He wanted the state not only to subsidize the replenishment of merchant stocks, the continuous reproduction of goods, and the profits of the merchants, but also to guarantee the health and viability of the market system itself. The state would have the power to accomplish these objectives because it would be the major purchaser of goods previously remitted to the king and government as tribute.

Even though the *taedong* system undoubtedly provided a major stimulus to the development of the market, Yu did not develop an economic theory to justify the beneficial effects of a theoretically free market in disciplining producers to cut costs and prices through competition or to eliminate inefficient producers. On the contrary, his plan for a government subsidy for prices would reduce thrift and efficiency by guaranteeing profits for higher cost producers. He felt that since the state would be the primary consumer of many products, it was obliged to defer the opportunity to use its monopsony on consumption to obtain better prices from merchants because it would inhibit the operation of the market to maintain a continuous flow of goods to the national capital and provincial districts.

Since Yu's economic reasoning was based on moral criteria rather than value-free analysis of the effects of impersonal economic forces, it was natural – but also naïve – for him to have assumed that government functionaries would have subordinated their own interests to protect and guarantee the profits of the merchants and producers. The opponents of the *taedong* reform were on solid ground when they held that officials and clerks were more likely to underpay merchants or force them to sell at low prices. Despite his belief, however, that the superior moral standards of a class of well-educated and morally trained and selected bureaucrats would be able to overcome human greed to ensure a plentiful supply of goods without oppressive taxation of the common peasants, in this instance he called upon the coercive power of the state to enforce government payments above market prices to prevent official exploitation of the merchants under a *taedong* system.

OFFICE, TRAVEL AND OTHER EXPENSES

Market Purchases for Office Expenses

Yu specified that the Ministry of Taxation be made responsible for establishing quotas for office expenses of capital bureaus and provincial and district government units and setting "designated prices" (*chŏngga*) for the purchase of goods by the purchasing agents from rice funds set aside for the purchase of goods (*kami*). Yu remarked that since clerks in the governors' yamen had been responsible for supplying the pens and ink used in their offices, and they had used this requirement as an excuse for squeezing the funds from the peasants to pay for them, henceforth every magistrate, military garrison, post-station, and official school would pay for these costs from their own official funds.[20]

Even though in his own time labor service taxes and in-kind tribute had been replaced by cloth taxes or grain and cloth substitute payments in tribute contracting arrangements, Yu noted that officials still had authority to demand additional goods and services to meet emergency expenses, and they frequently crossed the line separating official and private needs. Because government salaries were quite low, high officials in the capital felt justified in demanding gifts from officials in the provinces. District magistrates had to send gifts to their friends at court as well as high officials and noblemen, especially when they first obtained their posts, and they had become so bound by the obligations of courtesy and gift-giving to superiors (*insa*) that they had transformed what originated as a private act into a public duty. Yu criticized Chief State Councilor Hwang Hŭi in the mid-fifteenth century because he had indicted one official for failing to present a gift to a higher court official: "Nowadays everyone regards this kind of action as beautiful and thinks that the purpose behind it is for the provinces to show respect for the court. In addition, everyone says that anybody who becomes a magistrate is obliged to help his friends, for a magistrate is not the same as other officials. This is also one of the current opinions around."[21]

Yu, however, reminded his readers of the aphorism that bribes – including gifts of tea, medicine, paper, and ink – should not be brought "to the gates of a high officials [*taebu*]" because all such gifts were ultimately "taken from the people." Even though the highest capital officials were expected to behave with the utmost integrity, when they first started their careers as district magistrates, they were expected to exploit the people to aid their own friends. The common practice of gift-giving could be eliminated by providing adequate salaries for the whole bureaucracy. "If those who make the laws are affected by even one iota of private thoughts, mistakes will be made in the correct handling of all affairs." Drawing a firm line between public and private (*kongsa*) interests was indispensable to distinguishing between moral and immoral behavior, between Heaven's principles (*Ch'ŏlli*) and human desires (*inyok*). "When you are managing a state's affairs and establishing institutions, you cannot permit the slightest degree of private interest [to be involved]."[22]

Currently government offices were stocked with a variety of private as well as public materials and there was no system of rigid accounting to prevent the mixture and confusion of the two, especially when envoys and guests arrived to be entertained. Yu wanted a system of budgeted costs to provide for a basic quota of rice that could be stored in advance. Instead of listing the cost of each item like honey, oil, pheasants, and chickens, magistrates could allocate available funds as they saw fit. Then "there will no longer be the evil situation whereby official and private expenditures in an official yamen are mixed together."[23] Furthermore, Yu anticipated that the future development of the market would ensure a sufficient supply of all anticipated necessities: "Moreover, after the commercial shops have flourished and all kind of goods are circulating [in the market], then even though you may have some urgent need [for them], you need not worry [about finding them in the marketplace]."[24] Not only the standard items of yamen costs, but even more ordinary purchases of consumption items like fish and salt could be bought directly by the magistrate's yamen on the market.

Nonetheless, even though the needs of a magistrate's yamen was more varied than the costs of a capital bureau, Yu emphasized that reliance on the market could not mean that officials be allowed to use their power to force merchants to sell their goods at cheap and unprofitable prices. Although the private households of high officials in the capital were in the habit of making daily purchases from merchants in the marketplace without attempting to use their influence and prestige in an oppressive way,

> in the district towns [the officials] have the lives of people completely under their grasp. Even in the case of a low-ranking district [*hyŏn*], the situation there is in fact run like a small state. If [the officials] were to trade directly with people in the market, it goes without saying that it would lead officials and clerks to pursue their own private interests, and in every case it would produce an evil situation for the people.[25]

This had to be avoided by determining what goods needed to be purchased and what their prices should be, a procedure that was already in practice in the capital since the capital bureaus negotiated prices of various goods with merchants. Once a series of commodity prices were established, it would always be possible to revise them in the future as conditions changed. Once prices in rice were determined, funds for the purchase of all commodities consumed by officials (oil, honey, pheasants, and chickens) could be added to the salaries for officials and magistrates, governors, provincial army and navy commanders, their assistants, and the local petty officials (Hyanggwan) of magistrates.[26]

In advocating the purchase of pheasants and chickens, in particular, Yu proposed a more radical measure than the *taedong* law itself, which provided that a pheasant and chicken had to be provided by one peasant from every eight *kyŏl* of land. Yu insisted, however, that no in-kind levies of this nature would be required and all costs in rice equivalents would be included in the official's budget because clerks had used the pheasant and chicken levy as an excuse for corrupt extortion of further profits. The officials had to calculate a fair price, conduct purchases according to fixed regulations, and "let [the merchants] keep the surplus for their profit. . . . Only after things are done like this will both public and private interests both be put at ease."

The purchase of oil and honey would also be conducted by the same procedure. Officials should set a generous price for these commodities and ensure that neither private nor public interests be harmed.

"If it happened that payment was made at a cheap price and purchase was forced, the clerks and runners will extort payments and the harm will affect the people. Anything like this ought to be profoundly punished."[27]

Yu also objected to the argument that the desire for bribes by corrupt and avaricious clerks could not be solved simply by converting a tribute item or in-kind levy to funded purchases on the market. If items were purchased on the spot just when the need arose, it might be difficult to prohibit corruption in the purchase transaction, but if the costs could be budgeted and funds provided to designated purchasing agents in advance to guarantee them a sufficient surplus over their cost for a fair profit, "they would either use the funds to take care of their families, buy the goods from the market, seek out salesmen who gather round, go and buy goods where the prices are cheap, or engage [in a futures market] by paying rice before the deadline and receiving chickens [from merchants] when the deadline arrives." This method would be far preferable to the current system of tribute payments that permitted clerks to demand bribes when each peasant showed up with goods to offer.[28]

Envoys and Travel Expenses

Yu also planned that official expenses for sending envoys to China and entertaining Chinese envoys and other guests in Korea had to be budgeted and paid for by the state. Currently the government did not provide travel and expense funds for envoys to China while they were traveling through Korean territory but allowed them to make their own demands from provincial governors, military commanders, and magistrates en route. Because there were no fixed quotas limiting these expenditures, "they all [make demands for] hard labor and irregular taxes that cut deeply into the fat of the people. . . ." Since one stint as an envoy to China "in most cases will make a wealthy man of you," Yu wanted to prohibit Korean envoys from demanding bribes as well as travel expenses from the population and from selling goods in China that they had received in their arbitrary collections from the provinces. The central government would provide travel expenses, including bribes to Manchu officials if they were unavoidable. Bad as this might seem, it was still better than granting carte blanche to envoys to squeeze what they needed from the peasants living along the travel route.[29]

Yu regarded the custom of granting Korean envoys the right to collect what they wanted from the population one of the ultimate causes of moral decline and dynastic failure because it was similar to the domestic tribute system that lacked anything more detailed than a large quota for each province and then allowed provincial officials and clerks to work out the details of tax collection down to the individual peasant. Just as the central government had lost control of the administrative process below the level of the province, so too did the central government abjure responsibility for controlling demands by Korean embassies en route. Even back in the feudal age of Chou China any time the ruler of a state demanded "something he liked," everyone in the social ladder emulated that behavior by making their own demands on their subordinates. "If the king makes demands, those below will see this and be influenced [by his behavior]. The high officials [*taebu*] will definitely make demands in order to benefit their families. The lower officials [*sa*] and common people will definitely make demands in order to benefit themselves, and they will not shirk even from seizing [the property of others] and killing the king and usurping the throne."

Yu argued that the *Spring and Autumn Annals* (*Ch'un-ch'iu*) had shown that this mode of behavior had been stimulated by immoral urges on the part of officials, their greed for extravagant expenditure, the loss of a sense of honesty and shame, and the growth of favoritism and bribery. Not until the decline and fall of the Chou dynasty itself were these practices finally brought to an end. The only way to combat this tendency was to exercise frugality, set quotas for expenditure in accordance with an official's place in rank, and eliminate arbitrary demands.[30]

In addition to Korean envoys traveling abroad, the upkeep of imperial envoys from Ch'ing China was a serious financial problem because a number of individual districts had been given quotas to provide for costs and labor service even though some of them were located at considerable distance from the main route of transportation. A district remote from the hostel where an imperial embassy was staying might only have to provide two or three men, but they would have to gather the materials allocated and travel anywhere from two to six days to deliver them.

> The magistrates drop their business [to show them hospitality] and there is confusion and trouble along the boundaries between districts. Ten thousand people are burdened with labor and expenses so that even the chickens and dogs have no rest. The harm from this evil is so great that it cannot be described. One man's responsibilities at the hostel still cannot be met by a hundred men put to work in the remote districts, and one *sŏm*'s worth of expenses at the hostel can-

> not be met even though it takes a hundred *sŏm* of expenses in the remote districts. Isn't it a thousand times worse when corrupt officials and clerks take advantage of the situation to work their corruption?[31]

Yu urged that all allocations of tax quotas among districts (*punbae*) and all construction of temporary hostels or thatched huts to house imperial envoys in the districts be abolished. If financial responsibility were placed only on the districts where government hostels (*ch'am'ŭp*) were located, total expenditures of labor and revenues for envoys could be reduced to one-tenth of current levels. Further savings could be achieved by building some permanent, tile-roofed hostels for envoys and travelers. Any local district was not to have more than one hostel, and any hostels located other than where the district seat was situated would be assigned to a nearby district for its financing. All costs of these hostels were to be estimated in advance and paid for from regular tax revenues. If there were not enough regular runners (*sahwan*) available, then members of "idle households," or those without other responsibilities, would be required to do the work and be compensated by a fair deduction from their tax obligations. In an extreme labor shortage, the hostel could then hire workers at wages of .5 *mal*/day (15 *mal*/month) and the magistrate could deduct the cost from taxes that were to be transmitted to the capital, or recruit men on military service for the work and reduce the time of their military duties by an equivalent number of days.

Yu stipulated that a shortage of labor or funds could not be used as an excuse for issuing arbitrary orders to other districts, and in extreme emergencies the central government could ultimately allow all district magistrates to keep their tax revenues in the district or supplement their funds with some revenue allocations from adjacent districts. Although some objected to abolishing the traditional distribution of such costs among all provincial districts because a single district town could not afford to pay for the costs of a hostel, Yu countered with the argument that all revenue should be considered as national revenue, not just the revenue of one district, and any costs could be deducted from the national account.

Despite the objection that fish, meat, fruit, and vegetables needed to feed traveling imperial envoys could not be predicted and budgeted in advance but would require ad hoc levies, Yu responded that if officials paid for the purchase of food and drink, there would be no reason for any ad hoc levies of goods in-kind. For that matter, if the people were suffering from famine and destitution, even the king would not be justified in mobilizing peasants for a royal hunt for food, let alone paying the expenses for traveling imperial envoys.

Nor could labor shortages be used as a legitimate argument to defeat Yu's reform, since wage labor could be hired by funds saved by tax quota reductions on the hostels, and by exemptions from other forms of labor service by towns with hostels in them. In addition to using all the town's tax revenues and taking some from neighboring towns, the quotas of runners, slaves, and workers for hostels and post-stations could be increased, so that there would be sufficient funds and personnel in each hostel to provide room and board for an imperial delegation of about forty to fifty people. Under the *taedong* law operating in some provinces the Office for Dispensing Benevolence (Sŏnhyech'ŏng) had provided the cost for buying some of the items involved in entertaining envoys, but Yu argued that since it had not funded the construction of permanent hostels everywhere, it would be better simply to abolish the current system altogether.[32]

Yu justified these proposals by appealing not simply to abstract reason or economic logic, but to the superiority of classical precedents established in late Chou China. The states of the late Chou period appointed officials to receive visitors and envoys, including those from enemy states, and paid the cost of their upkeep. In contemporary Korea, however, there was neither an office nor a system to take sole responsibility for hostels for foreign envoys and guests. Not only did the district magistrates, local clerks, slaves, and the rural population in general have to abandon their work to provide for the entertainment of visitors, but the highest officials in the capital also had to devote their time to this task as well. "This is a situation where the state can be driven to ruin without waiting for a war to occur." In addition to establishing permanent hostels in the districts, officials in the capital could be selected to administer these tasks, even as a concurrent appointment.[33]

Finally, Yu complained about the exorbitant costs required to pay for the ceremonies that accompanied the departure of magistrates, garrison commanders, educational officials, and post-station chiefs who had finished their term of office and the welcoming of their replacements. Requisitions of men and horses, food, utensils, and banquets were so onerous that the practice had become one of the major evils in local administration and had been responsible for "destroying the livelihood of the people." Some peasants had been recruited as bearers and were sometimes required to stay in the capital for long periods; others had to pay several *p'il* of cloth taxes to provide support. In the case of Hŭngdŏk (Hŭngdŏk-hyŏn), a district of only 1,000 households, the magistrate had been changed ten times in nine years and the total levy on the population to pay the expenses of the ceremonies and transportation came to 700 *tong* (35,000 *p'il*, or 3.88 *p'il* per household per year).

He also cited the words of Cho Hŏn in the late sixteenth century that the Korean system was especially egregious because transfers of officials occurred too frequently. No sooner had they arrived at their posts than they spent the entire accumulated resources of the district before being transferred elsewhere, and every time a change was made the people had to pay for the transfer ceremony and travel costs for an average trip of about three hundred miles. The Chinese did not have this problem because they required all officials to pay their own moving costs even for distances of over three thousand miles.

Yu proposed to reduce costs and limit the number of authorized attendants for provincial officials in transit. The provincial governor and his assistant (Tosa) and the provincial army and navy commanders and their aides (Uhu) could only be accompanied by three or four clerks and slaves if they were traveling to the capital. Possibly the ceremony for the departure of local officials from the capital might be eliminated, or they might be welcomed at their home towns and sent off ceremonially to their next posts. While the government would pay the costs of an official proceeding to his post from the capital or reimburse him for out-of-pocket costs from his home town to his post, the official himself would take responsibility for hiring bearers and horses for transporting his family between posts. When he left his post, his own district would pay his cost and his petty officials would escort him to the border of the next district.

Yu also prescribed a list of travel costs for officials by rank ranging from a low of 15 *mal* for a low-ranking magistrate to a high of 30 *mal* for a magistrate of an important district (Puyun, Tohobusa) for every 100 *i* (33 miles) of distance over 100 *i*. For long distance trips, he could be given a customs-station pass to enable the station to pay the bills and deduct the cost from their own funds. Provincial governors, army and navy commanders, educational officials (Kyogwan), and post-station chiefs (Ch'albang) would be required to take their families with them so that they would settle in their districts and get to know the population better, and the government would provide travel costs matching the above schedule for long tours of duty.

Yu pointed out that the Chinese had more reasonable regulations because an official assuming a post in the provinces had to use his own draft horses and his private attendants to transport his family belongings, and the people in his assigned district were only obliged to meet him at the district boundary. He was even opposed to allowing districts to provide riding and draft horses for transporting officials and their families to reduce the burden on the post-station system because he feared that the peasants would ultimately bear the costs whether the districts or post-stations had responsibility.

Yu also felt that currently government offices were stocked with a variety of private as well as public materials and there was no system of rigid accounting to prevent the mixture and confusion of the two, especially when envoys and guests arrived to be entertained. A system of budgeted costs should provide for a basic quota of rice that could be stored in advance and paid out to meet costs. Since the cost in rice would be allocated to officials, they would not have to list the cost of each item like honey, oil, pheasants, and chickens, but could allocate available funds as they saw fit. Then "there will no longer be the evil situation whereby official and private expenditures in an official yamen are mixed together."[34]

Local Government Costs

Yu capped his discussion of government finance by drawing up a budget of salaries and administrative costs for every unit of government, one example of which should illustrate his mode of thought. His scheme of local organization provided for four grades of prefectures and districts: the Tohobu, Pu, Kun, and Hyŏn. Converting Yu's *kok* (10 *mal*) to the *mal* and *sŏm* (15 *mal*) for easier comparison with contemporary units, the budget for the Tohobu would be 11,190 *mal* or 745 contemporary *sŏm*, and that for the Hyŏn would be 6,595 *mal*. The Hyŏn budget was broken down as shown in table 8.[35]

TABLE 8
YU'S SAMPLE DISTRICT BUDGET

Category	Amount per mo.	per year
District magistrate	95 *mal*	1140 *mal*
Asst. magistrate	50 "	600 "
Official expenses		2500 "
Honey	25 *mal*	500 "
Pure oil	30 *mal*	300 "
Perilla oil	15 *mal*	150 "
Pheasants and chickens		450 "
Paper, equipment, etc.		1000 "
TOTAL:		6595 "
		or (439 *sŏm* 10 *mal*)

NOTE: Yu's *kok* was equal to 10 *mal* (or *tu* in Sino-Korean pronunciation). A *sŏm* (*sŏk* in Sino-Korean pronunciation), the contemporary unit of grain, was equal to 15 *mal*.
SOURCE: PGSR 19:13a-b.

Yu drew up this budget with careful consideration for variations in expenses in different areas and by the size of the district. His estimate of rice costs for guests and envoys varied from 1,500 *mal* for a district located on a major thoroughfare to 150 *mal* for districts in remote places, like the island of Chindo along the coast. He also allocated supplemental grants of 500 *mal* for busy towns like Pyongyang, Kaesŏng, and Chŏnju, and towns located at major crossroads, and lesser amounts for districts that had put up fewer envoys. He calculated the value of rice provided for governors and provincial army commanders who toured the province on their rounds of inspection and added the cost to the budgets of each individual district. He noted that under the present terms of the *taedong* tribute system, provincial governors had been allowed 75 *mal* of expense rice per trip, but he regarded this as inadequate and raised the budget to 100 *mal* each for the governor and provincial army commander for each visit to a district, or 200 *mal* each for two trips per year. Any additional business trips had to be paid for from funds set aside for for envoys and guests. Since their budgets were based on the principle of compensation for work performed, they were not entitled to any payment from the state's accounts if they made no official trips. Yu thought it was entirely unreasonable that the governor of Ch'ungch'ŏng Province should be allowed to collect expense rice when he in fact had not been making rounds of inspection. Expenses for the travel of Chinese and Korean envoys and equipment expenses of post-stations also had to be budgeted separately.[36]

Expenses for the purchase of oil, honey, chickens and pheasants used for private as well as official purchases would be paid monthly to the magistrate and his assistant, 60 percent to the former and 40 percent to the latter. Quotas for the expenses of the local petty officials (*hyanggwan*) and the gate guards (*kun'g-wan*) would also be budgeted in this manner. Once all official expenses had been allocated in this fashion, it would then become possible to abolish all the official colony lands (*kwandunjŏn*) used currently to defray yamen costs. Vegetable lands currently used to supply districts, public schools, military garrisons, and post-stations would be maintained, but in carefully regulated amounts. Salaries and expense costs were also to be budgeted for local yangban associations that performed semiofficial duties in supervising local clerks (the Hyangsoch'ŏng). The chief (Pyŏlsu) of this association would receive 180 *mal*/year, and his assistants (Pyŏlgam) 120 *mal*/year, and their office would receive support for food and fuel as well. Other allocations were included for officials and expenses of school and educational officials, constables (*changgwan*), military districts, post-station and grain-transport officials.[37]

Labor Service on Fishing Weirs and Salt Flats

Yu provided that fishing weirs (*ŏjang*) and salt flats that had been set aside for the income of estates of princes and princesses (*kungbang*) and used for official expenses should also be abolished and turned back to the common people, a policy that was not adopted in earnest until the Taewongun's regime in the 1860s. The peasants would be given legal permission to raise fish and produce salt for their own benefit and simply be taxed on their income, instead of requiring that they work in the weirs as part of their labor service under the supervision of officials. The same principle would be followed in abolishing required labor service for raising of horses, nurturing beehives, and fishing in rivers. In short, all forms of required labor service would be thoroughly eliminated by Yu's broad reform of the system of government finance.[38]

Crop Damage Assessment Costs

This system of budgeted expenses also required provisions for relief and investigation and supervision of degrees of crop damage and tax reduction that had been left out of the tribute system but had been part of the land tax in the first two centuries of the dynasty. If crop conditions qualified for famine relief, official salaries and expenses, and funds for entertaining envoys and guests would all qualify for a 20 percent reduction. A famine would be defined as a loss of up to 60 percent of tax revenues and the condition would be declared for all villages in a district. The governor might do so for a province, and the king might declare it for the whole country. If the loss in tax revenues was greater than 60 percent, the budget could be reduced even more.[39]

Assessing crop damage also required investigation of exactly how much land had suffered from flood or drought, but the cost of the investigation would be deducted from the regular budget, not by demanding payment from the peasants. Since Yu realized that the annual damage assessments of all land (*taphŏm*) had been a serious problem for peasants because too many clerks had been used for this job, he allowed only one or two to perform this task. By establishing the correct procedure, simplifying the process, and putting it under the officials, he hoped to restrict interference by clerks by confining their responsibilities only to receiving written documents. Yu specified that the amount of paperwork required be reduced to about three days by discarding the current requirement that the complete land registers (*chŏn'an*) be copied out in triplicate every year; instead he simply permitted records of damaged land to be inserted into the file. Finally, he allowed that the district magistrate would petition the governor for the cost for repairing walls, moats, and official buildings, and the throne for special budgeting for any large projects.[40]

Procedure for Disbursement of Official Funds

Yu declared that his system would require a calculation of the price of all the above-mentioned goods and services and extra considerations for wear-and-tear or replacement costs in terms of their rice value (*chŏrmi*) and payment by the government's treasuries to each bureau each month. The Ministry of Taxation, in other words, would "make disbursements" (*chiha*) from "government funds" (*kyŏngbi*) obtained by regular revenues. The Ministry of Taxation would then summon the designated purchasing masters or agents (*chŏng juin* or simply *chuin*) to take charge of the purchase of paper, firewood, and other goods as the "tribute middlemen" (*kongmul chuin*) had done under the *taedong* system. The current practice of demanding bedding, paper or its value in cloth for stationery used in lawsuits, and firewood, torches, and candles used in capital bureaus by levies on the people would be abolished. Furthermore, all office expenses traditionally paid for by income from office expense land (*konghaejŏn*) would be eliminated and provided by ordinary tax revenues from government funds.[41]

Yu also charged that yamen or government offices unjustly levied surtaxes of rice and cloth on peasants in addition to ordinary tribute. Runners working as constables in legal or criminal cases demanded fees for their own support, military garrisons had the clerks squeeze the soldiers for their expenses, and clerks in magistrates' yamen extorted wood and fuel from soldiers on duty. The Royal Secretariat in the capital demanded that any magistrate who left his position had to pay them a "pen debt" (*p'ilch'ae*), which they collected by levying another cloth surtax. Yu remarked that all these practices had in fact become accepted practice, and officials did not seem to realize that the situation was deplorable.[42]

Full Salaries for All Officials

Ancient Principles

One of Yu's contributions to the literature on financial reform was his idea that the creation of a fund raised by revenues from the land tax – a key feature of the *taedong* reform as a means of eliminating tribute levies – could also be used to finance almost the entire cost of administration, create a sufficient surplus to convert unpaid clerks into compensated functionaries of the state, and replace compulsory labor service with wage payments for transportation and other work performed for the state. His main goal was not simply financial reorganization, but removing the economic causes of corruption and immorality in the bureaucracy and excessive labor service demands on the ordinary peasantry.

While this mode of thought suggests that Yu derived his inspiration for this measure exclusively from the *taedong* reform of the seventeenth century, he also sought justification in the Chinese classics and histories. Yu held that the principle of open and legal financing of government service had been articulated by the ancients and remained valid for all modes of government, whether feudal or bureaucratic. All government began with the proposition that officials were entitled to support by the people: "Those who are ruled by others feed them; those who rule others are fed by them, a principle that exists throughout the world." Nevertheless, this obligation had to be regulated to prevent exploitation of the people. The people were not to be taxed at a rate higher than 10 percent of their income "lest it cause harm to the cultivator," nor should the tax rate be any less than 10 percent in order that state finances be guaranteed. The lowest ranking government official was entitled to a salary at least equivalent to the income he would have received had he been left to cultivate his own fields, and the highest officials were entitled to larger salaries to allow them to "treat their close relatives with humaneness. Only after ensuring [that their salaries are sufficient] will you be able to encourage a sense of shame (i.e., moral standards) and achieve [good] rites and customs."[43]

These supposedly ancient and universal principles also required open and legal responsibility and accountability, not the nonlegal, irresponsible, and arbitrary methods of funding official income and costs that had developed over the years. The expansion of the number of officials, particularly superfluous ones, had strained government finance and led to a overall reduction of the level of salaries. Not only were the highest officials left without adequate income, but the lowest ranking officials had devised "lax and careless practices" to raise their incomes and serve "their private interests."

Yu attempted to demonstrate in a separate study of the history of bureaucratic salaries in China and Korea that not only in ancient times, but also in the bureaucratic period after the Ch'in and Han dynasties in China, full schedules for sufficient salaries for ranked officials had been drawn up to ensure fairness. According to the *Rites of Chou*, in Chou times the prime minister and two other chief ministers first allocated ranks of nobility (*chüeh*) based on their virtue, and then assigned salaries on the basis of merit or accomplishments. The size of their salaries varied according to the length of time they served on duty. Ch'iu Chün of Ming times commented that titles of rank determined degrees of honor and were prerequisite to an imperial salary grant, and both rank and salary were the means by which the Son of Heaven could control officials, "respect virtue, compensate meritorious performance, and cause [officials] to give all of their mind and effort." He also stressed that these rewards of rank and salary had to be recommended to and issued by the ruler, not by ministerial officers alone.

Mencius had already commented that in Chou times there were two separate systems of rank and grade, the five ranks of noble titles (duke, marquis, earl, viscount, and baron) and the six grades of office – the Chün or ruler (the feudal lord of a state or fief), the Ching or chief minister, and the lesser ranks of Ta-fu and Upper, Middle, and Lower Shih (i.e., Shang-shih, Chung-shih, and Hsia-shih). The five grades of nobility corresponded to the size of their fiefs. The Son of Heaven (the king of Chou) had his own royal estate of 1,000 *li* on each side, the dukes and marquises had fiefs of 100 *li* square, the earls had 70 *li*, the viscounts and barons 50 *li*, and feudal lords (Chu-hou) with less than this amount were assigned as dependencies (*fu-yung*) to higher feudal lords. The Chou king could confer these feudal titles on anyone within the empire while the six grades of officials were confined to the officials who ran the royal domain and the fiefs of the feudal lords.

The salaries were ranked in two separate grades defined as multiples of each lower level official's salary. In the largest fief (a *ta-kuo*) the ruler (Chün) or enfoeffed duke or marquis received ten times the salary of a Ching, the Ching received a salary four times greater than a Ta-fu, the Ta-fu and each salary down through the Hsia-shih was each twice as high as his subordinate. In short, the salary of a ruler was 320 times greater than the salary of a lowly Hsia-shih, but in smaller fiefs the salary ratio was smaller, 240/1 in fiefs of 70 *li* on each side, and 160/1 in those of 50 *li* on each side. The lowest salary of regular officials was defined as "the same salary as that of commoners serving as officials, a salary sufficient to replace [the income that would have been earned if the man had engaged in] cultivation." A commentator noted that commoners serving as government officials referred to the four grades of clerks and runners (Fu, Shih, Hsü and Tu) discussed previously.

The income of a peasant was also differentiated by establishing five different degrees of production based on the effort and zeal of different peasants. A superior farmer (Shang neng-fu) was defined as one who could support nine people from the production of a standard-sized plot of 100 *mou* (*myo* in Korean pronunciation, 16.7 acres) assuming the application of manure. The less efficient peasants were presumed to have supported eight, seven, six, or a minimum of five persons from the same plot. Thus, commoners who served as officials were likewise divided into five grades corresponding to the productivity of the five standards of peasant productivity, and their salaries were ranked according to the importance of their work.

Chu Hsi of the Sung dynasty summarized the significance of this system by emphasizing that the salaries of the rulers or feudal lords of states and their subordinate officials were paid for by the system of Aid (the *chu-fa*) or labor service on public fields (*kung-t'ien*, or *kongjŏn* in Korean), or taxes or rent (*tsu*) on the land they cultivated, while the officials (*shih*) and commoners who served in office "only received salaries from the government, which was like the income from the land." In other words, the only legitimate basis for the income or salaries of officials had to be a scheme of payment beginning from the lowest rank defined as an equivalent of a single peasant family's production to the highest rank of 320 multiples of that income, funded by an optimum tithing of agricultural production.[44]

Yu also believed that the theoretical justification for a sufficient and adequate salary scale for all officials was provided in the Great Plan (Hung-fan) in the *Book of History* (*Shu-ching*): "Only if you provide ample salaries to those people who are in office will they do their work well. If you do not do so, and you cause people who have the zeal and will to perform affairs for the state not to do well, then these people will end up in crime."[45]

Yu cited several famous Chinese philosophers, statesmen, and emperors who supported this idea. For example, in Han times when two officials, Chang Ch'ang and Su Wang-chih, complained that low-ranking officials were perpetually concerned about the welfare of their families because their salaries had been too low, Emperor Hsüan (r. 73–48 B.C.) authorized a 50 percent increase in their salaries.[46] Emperor Kuang-wu of the Later Han also raised salaries as well, and Ch'iu Chün of the Ming praised both emperors for their understanding of the ancient dictum that a generous salary was essential to ensuring an honest performance of duty. Emperor T'ai-tsu of the Sung dynasty also insisted on the importance of controlling petty officials by reducing their numbers and increasing their salaries.[47]

Salary Schedules in Various Dynasties

Yu then provided lists of the salary scales of the major dynasties from the Han through Ming. The standard was set in the Han schedule by which the San-kung or three advisers to the king received 350 *hu* (*kok* in Korean) per month or 4,200 *hu* per year. The body of regular officials, however, contained fourteen salary grades from the medium two-thousand picul to the hundred picul rank. The highest rank received 180 *hu*/per month (2,160 *hu*/year) to the lowest of 16 *hu*/month (192 *hu*/year). The ratio between the highest and lowest salaries was 21.9/1 if the San-kung is included, or 11.25/1 if the San-kung are excluded. Although the disparity between highest and lowest salaries appeared more modest than the 360/1 ratio of Chou times, since the commentator Yen Shih-ku claimed that salaries of petty clerks in Han times were 10 and 8 *tou* (since the *hu* was equivalent to 10 *tou*, or *mal* in Korean, these were equal to 1 and .8 *hu* per month), the salary ratio could be calculated at 437.5/1.[48]

Yu was evidently satisfied that exact uniformity between Chou and Han standards was not necessary to capture the essence of Chou principles, and despite variations over subsequent dynasties, salary schedules had not departed that much from Han standards. The salary of the highest Ming rank was nominally only half that of Han times, but the grain measures were twice as large.[49] He also assumed whatever the disparity of salaries between the highest and lowest functionaries all such legal and open systems had been fair because they were consistent with the available economic resources of the country and based on an equitable tax rate. Even the high salaries of top officials in the Han dynasty were not irresponsible manifestations of excessive imperial largesse because they were consistent with the positions of the officials involved and also provided for the salaries of their assistants, clerks, and runners as well. For that matter, the salaries (or feudal allotments) of seventeenth-century Japanese daimyo were sufficient to pay for the living costs of hundreds or thousands of troops under their command.[50]

Yu ended his survey of salary schedules by treating the Koryŏ and Chosŏn dynasties in Korea. He only included the salary schedule in the reign of King Munjong (r. 1047–83) of the Koryŏ dynasty because it represented the culmination of various changes that had taken place since the beginning of that dynasty in the early tenth century, and presumably remained valid until the military coup d'état of 1170. He noted, presumably with great favor, that the annual income of 139,700 *sŏm* of revenue in rice, millet, and wheat were stored in the Left Warehouse (Chwach'ang) and distributed to all officials according to their grade, based on the principle that "anyone who had a post received a salary." The salary range was from a high of 400 to a low of 10 *sŏm* per year per person, or a modest ratio of 40/1, and all provincial officials as well as clerks were also entitled to full salaries.[51]

The salary schedule of the early Chosŏn dynasty was more complex because salaries were paid in grain, silk, cotton cloth, and paper money. A rank 1A official received 98 *sŏm* of grain, 6 *p'il* of silk, 15 *p'il* of cotton cloth, and 10 *chang* of paper money, while a rank 9A official received only 12 *sŏm* of grain, no silk, 2 *p'il* of cotton cloth, and 1 *chang* of paper money. The salary ratio was apparently consistent with rates in other dynasties, but financial difficulty sustained from Hideyoshi's invasions in 1592–98 had a disastrous effect on official salaries. Yu estimated the annual grain salary of rank 1 officials in his own time as barely more than 60 *sŏm*, and no grants of silk, cotton, or paper money at all, while a rank 9 official received barely 12 *sŏm*. The latter could only support themselves by receiving "offerings" of food from the provinces called (*chinbong*), and they also divided up funds that were left over from bureau expenses (*pun'a*) for their own use. There was no fixed salary schedule for provincial officials, and their incomes varied considerably and derived from different sources, primarily from irregular levies and additional taxes. Since the military officers in the provinces, from provincial army and navy commanders to the commanders of garrisons, were not provided with regular salaries either, they raised income by releasing their troops from duty and collecting cloth support payments instead.

While some clerks received no salaries at all, others might receive a ration equivalent to 6 *mal* of grain, but even capital clerks were deprived of salaries if they were under punishment for some misfeasance or were on duty at a granary or yamen. None of the clerks and runners serving district magistrates and none of the male and female slaves in the capital as well as the provinces was granted grain rations or salaries, and had no choice but to steal and embezzle goods to support themselves.[52]

Yu concluded therefore that every functionary of the state, no matter was his rank or status, was entitled to a government salary: "From the highest minister of state [Kyŏngdaebu, i.e., Ching and Ta-fu] down to commoners [*sŏin*], men of noble status [*kwija*] will have enough to provide for ancestral rituals for all their relatives, while people of base status [*ch'ŏnja*] will have enough to support their parents and take care of their wives and children."[53]

Yu's Salary Proposal

Yu was determined to put the Korean system back on the track established by the Han dynasty salary schedule by converting all salaries to a rice equivalent, set in *kok*, the equivalent of the *hu* used in Han times and valued at 10 *mal* or pecks of grain. Since the Korean *sŏm* was then worth 15 *mal*, not 10, Yu preferred using the *kok* as the main unit of account and redefining the *sŏm* as 10 *mal*. The highest ranking 1A official would receive 600 *kok* (6,000 *mal*, or 400 contemporary *sŏm*) a year, and the lowest regular official of rank 9B would receive 60 *kok*, or a ratio of $^{10}/_{1}$. The ratio of salaries between the highest and lowest functionaries, from chief state councilor to boy clerk in the provinces who would be paid 144 *mal*/year (14.4 *kok*, see next section), was $^{41.7}/_{1}$, a relatively modest differential compared to other dynasties. Actual payment of salaries would be divided: one-third in cash, one-third in white rice, one-sixth in hulled millet, and one-sixth in yellow beans.[54] Since Yu mentioned elsewhere that partial cash payments could take place after "cash was put into circulation" (*haengjŏn*), we might presume that he hoped to encourage the use of copper currency to facilitate trade.[55]

Yu believed that he could adapt ancient Chinese principles to the realities of contemporary Korea. Although Korean tax revenues were only a fraction of those in China, it would be simple to coordinate actual revenues with the smaller number of Korean officials to provide compensation to officials and their families. Since he had already proposed land grants to officials, the income from them would be calculated together with salaries for office to determine their total income. Salaries would be paid monthly rather than the current quarterly payments to provide adequate compensation during intercalary months, and a high official of Tangsanggwan rank would be granted retirement benefits such as a half-salary and an exemption of part of his state land grant after the age of seventy. To tide the nation over the financial burden of providing salaries for all officials, he suggested that initially the government might provide only one-half or two-thirds of his salary schedule, and then increase them to the full amount later.[56]

Superfluous costs to the government would be reduced by abolishing military sinecures called *ch'ea* attached to the Military Affairs Commission (Chungch'ubu), an agency that had lost its significance and was used for appointments of elderly, prestigious officials to serve as ministers-without-portfolio. Censors and royal attendants (Sijonggwan) who could not be dismissed from office but were under investigation for malfeasance in office would have their salaries reduced by half.

Current opportunities for state grants or salaries to be passed on hereditarily (i.e., hereditary salaries or *serok*) by so-called Loyal Subjects (Ch'ungsin) and Pure Officials (Ch'ŏngbaengni) were to be limited only to the eldest or designated heir of the patrimonial line down to the great-grandson. By no means should they be entitled to these honorary salaries if their fathers were still alive or if they also held posts on their own merits. In case of famine the salaries of all such officials would be reduced by 20 percent or more except for soldiers serving on duty.[57]

Salaries for Clerks, Slaves, and Women

One of Yu's most radical proposals was to put all functionaries on state salary including clerks, runners, artisans in government employ, and men and women slaves who functioned as runners or servants. He found that the law code of 1469, the *Kyŏngguk taejŏn*, listed over 5,000 runners (Chorye, Najang, and Chewŏn) who served this duty as part of their labor service obligation. Since these duties had driven almost all of them into bankruptcy after a few years' service, the government sought to alleviate their burden by expanding the number of shifts from three to twelve a year of one month's duration, which extended the interval of free time between tours of duty from three months to a year. Yu reported that this system of rotating service had long since disappeared since officials usually exempted common peasants in return for a cloth fee of two *p'il* and used the funds to hire substitutes, who supposedly received the cloth fee as their monthly salary and six *mal*/month of rations – an unfortunate practice that had occurred in the operation of the military service system as well.[58]

Yu sought to replace this irregular system with a schedule of published, legal provisions for compensation to clerks and runners. The chief clerk (Noksa) would be given a salary in white rice, millet, and cash equivalent to 40 *mal*/month (480 *mal*/year), and in addition receive a land grant of 2 *kyŏng* (200 *myo*). This land would be exempted from the military service requirement and be held for the life of the recipient, and for three years after his death by the widow. Thereafter she would retain half the land until her own death.

Ordinary clerks (*sŏri*) and runners (*chorye*), however, would not be entitled to a land grant. The clerks would receive thirty-five *mal* and the runners twenty-five *mal* per month, and official male slaves (*sano*) and female servants (*yŏbok*) would be entitled to the same wage as well. Boy servants, many of whom were recruited from the sons of official slaves, were also to be entitled to a monthly salary of fifteen *mal* (one *sŏm* in contemporary measure) as well. The salaries for local clerks and runners were less: two *kok* or twenty *mal* for clerks (*sŏri*) and twelve *mal* for runners and official slaves.[59]

Yu also prescribed that soldiers in the capital guard (*kyŏngbyŏng*) would be paid a salary of fifteen *mal*/month in addition to eight *p'il* of cotton cloth by their support taxpayers, and their commanders and cavalrymen would be given higher salaries. Yu kept their salaries lower than the runners because their duties were far lighter and they were also eligible for cloth support payments. Artisans in state employ (*chang'in*) were also to be granted twenty-five *mal*/month, but they would be subject to severe investigation of the quality of their work, and if found wanting, they could suffer beatings, reduction of salary, and dismissal. Craftsmen who made bows, arrows, armor, knives, woven cloth, and jade objects would be eligible for a salary raise to the equivalent of a 9B regular official.[60]

Clerks and runners in the provinces were also to be granted fifty *myo* of land in addition to their salaries. Their land grants would be exempted from firewood and brush levies, and they would be exempted from labor service required of ordinary land-grant peasants. Yu specifically listed the costs of salaries for all clerks and runners in all district magistracies, military headquarters, schools, and post-stations as part of each office's expenses. To reduce the work loads of clerks and runners he divided them into two shifts and excused those off duty from running personal errands for officials. They were only to be used for entertaining guests, assisting at ritual sacrifices, and performing military duties. They would retain their salaries even when transferred and be protected against any illegal attempts by magistrates to deprive them of their salaries. Any magistrate who arbitrarily reduced the number of shifts and took over the salaries owed to clerks and runners for his own use would be subject to the charge of embezzlement.[61]

Yu rejected the idea that clerks and runners might simply be paid daily rations or wages for the days that they served on tours of duty because they were entitled to regular salaries equivalent to what the head of a peasant household would earn and should be held fully responsible for completion of their tasks. In contemporary Korea the local clerks and runners had gained so much power and wealth through corruption that they frequently controlled almost all the land in the vicinity of the magistrate's or military commander's district. Without government provision for full salaries for them, there would be no way to eliminate their domination of local real estate.

Yu opposed the suggestion that government funds could be saved by granting local clerks and runners only a half-salary and half a land grant because they deserved the same full salaries and grants that their counterparts in the capital were to receive. He reminded his readers that previous Confucian scholars had praised the Chou system because it provided clerks and runners with land grants in addition to salaries to provide for the support of their families and guarantee honest behavior. Since these petty officials were in charge of administering the land and population of magistracies, they had to be on daily duty for a host of responsibilities, unlike the clerks and runners of the capital who were only assigned specialized tasks and had much free time. Two shifts were required because they had to provide service for entertaining guests and military affairs in addition to their ordinary duties.[62]

The classics had declared that clerks and runners were commoners who served in office and were entitled to salaries in the range of 25–35 *mal* (per month?), equivalent to the average income or production of a peasant. Yu estimated that average annual production from a superior farmer working 100 *myo* (1 *kyŏng*) of land – the minimal land grant to a peasant family under his program of redistribution – was from 130 to 140 *kok* (1,300–1,400 *mal* or *mal*) of unhulled grain, and 60–70 *kok* (600–700 *mal*) per *kyŏng* for an average farmer.[63] The monthly equivalent of those figures was from 50–117 *mal* per month per family. Yu asserted that since the farmer would be assisted by his wife and sons and a few more adult men for occasional assistance, he was justified in estimating the monthly income of a single adult male at 25–35 *mal*. He also felt that his proposed salary for clerks and runners would in fact be more generous than a peasant's income because they would not have to pay the land tax, military support tax, and the costs of an ox and seed.[64]

How realistic was Yu's estimate of peasant production as the basis for determining the minimum salary for a clerk or runner? To begin with, he did not attempt to calculate the annual production of an average peasant under contemporary conditions of ownership and tenancy. Kim Yongsŏp has shown that in the districts he studied in the late Chosŏn period very few owners or tenants owned or cultivated more than 1 *kyŏl* of land, and most possessed between .35 to .68 *kyŏl*. If this were grade 4 land, they would have possessed between 1.6 to 3.2 acres. Since current productivity averaged approximately 6.48 *sŏm* or 97.2 *mal* per acre, such peasants would have produced between 156 *mal* and 311 *mal* per year, or 13 to 26 *mal* per month.

Yu's estimation of 100 *myo* or 16.7 acres would have meant a vast improvement over per capita land occupation and peasant income at the time. Since the peasants would have possessed or cultivated five to ten times more land than they did, his estimate of production by a single peasant family on 16.7 acres of 600 to 1,400 *mal* per year was four to five times greater than the 156 or 311 *mal* that might be estimated from an average peasant holding at the time, or eight to ten times greater than the income of tenants who had to share half (or more) of their crop with the landlord.[65]

Yu's exaggerated estimate of peasant productivity as the basis for granting minimal salaries to clerks and runners show that he did not intend that the plan could be carried out under present circumstances. The whole plan for full compensation must have been part of Yu's attempt to justify a full cadastral survey against the opponents of the *taedong* reform who had resisted a resurvey of cultivated land. Yu realized that if a national cadastral survey were carried out justly and honestly in conjunction with his program for nationalization and distribution of land, it would produce sufficient revenue for the government to pay full salaries for all officials and all office expenses, and still leave an adequate income for the livelihood of the peasants.

According to Kim Yongsŏp's figures, which may underestimate the amount of land in his sample villages, since large landowners seemed to be absent from his examples, 10 to 15 percent of registered cultivators might have owned 40 to 70 percent of the land in a village. Therefore, it might not have been so far fetched for Yu to have assumed that his plan for nationalization and redistribution would have uncovered a sufficient amount of unregistered or "hidden" land to enable a grant of 100 *myo* (16.7 acres) of land to each peasant family. On the other hand, since the adoption of the *taedong* land surtax alone took the whole seventeenth century to implement, the total nationalization and redistribution of land would have been impossible without a revolutionary struggle. That kind of radical reform had not become part of the accepted language of discourse among active officials in the previous century.

In addition to commoners of good status, many official slaves occupied posts as clerks and runners in the seventeenth century. Yu would have preferred to abolish slavery altogether, except for those under criminal punishment, but he conceded that the times were not ripe for this kind of reform. Nonetheless, he hoped to provide salaries for official slaves because they were equivalent to the salaried clerks and runners of ancient China. Contrary to the popular opinion that the ancient Chinese used slaves to serve as runners, Yu pointed out that these runners (Tu) were enslaved specifically as punishment for crimes they had committed, or were barbarian prisoners-of-war who had violated norms of proper behavior. Even if they did perform service for the state, they were also provided with clothing and food all the way through the T'ang dynasty. Ancient laws also provided three steps of "exemption" from slave status to eventual manumission, and even if a criminal remained a slave for life, there had never been any decree ordering the hereditary transmission of slave status to descendants. By contrast Korean law required state service from hereditary slaves and even included them in the quotas of clerks and runners for government offices.

"How are these responsibilities not those of people who are slaves in name but runners in fact? Since their responsibilities are like this, we have no choice but to grant them salaries given the runners in ancient times."[66]

Furthermore, by keeping slaves on service as runners, he would alleviate the pressure on magistrates to carry out forcible conscription of peasants or assessment of labor service from the neighbors and relatives of peasants who had run away. Those men who had been enslaved as punishment for their crimes might be penalized by reducing their salaries lower than the standard for official slaves who inherited their status.[67]

The treatment of female slaves in government service offered similar difficulties. Yu noted that even though it was improper to require women to perform government service, since the government had already been doing so, their salaries ought to be the same as men – an astounding proposal for equal pay for equal work even though confined only to women of servile status working in government jobs. He conceded that it might be justified to reduce salaries for female slaves because their strength or labor power was lower than men, but they deserved additional consideration because they had been required to perform the kind of oppressive labor that had never been required of women in China. As if to add insult to injury, the state also took their offspring from them by forcing them into inherited slave status. Yu argued that the current quotas of male and female slave service for each government office only caused confusion in the requirements of service and in the support budgets, which could be eliminated by providing a uniform grant of fifty *myo* of land in addition to equal salaries. On the other hand, by no means did Yu advocate that women be allowed into his new school system and made eligible for positions of regular office.[68]

In short, the essence of Yu's plan for the support and compensation of officials was to extend government responsibility not only to clerks and runners in the lowest unit of local administration, but also to include male and female slaves and those of base status as functionaries deserving of remuneration for the work expended. If the abolition of slavery became impossible or protracted, the government was obliged to refrain from compounding an unjust inheritance of slave status by failing to provide them with adequate salaries. One cannot help but be impressed by Yu's humane concern for the welfare of the men and women of the lowest rank in government service, and his rational proposals, had they been met, would have served to alleviate much distress in the operation of the current system of remuneration.

Estimate of Annual Expenditures

Finally, Yu drew up an estimate of annual national expenditures based on reports of current expenses adjusted for reductions that could be made in his plan for cutting down the size of the bureaucracy. These expenditures included the cost of salaries for all employees of the state including military officials, clerks, official slaves, and women servants – not just regular civil officials – the expenses of government offices, and miscellaneous costs involving transportation of goods, entertainment of foreign guests, rituals, and even tribute to China. Presumably the budget would be funded according to his calculations of revenues under his reform plan for land redistribution and taxation. Table 9 shows Yu's budget, converted to contemporary *sŏm* (15 *mal*).

This proposed budget of expenditures for the whole government was based on the model provided by the *taedong* reform, which had already replaced ordinary tribute and a large percentage of royal tribute, transportation costs, and office expenses by provision of funds from tax revenues on land. Yu expected that this wholesale rationalization of government finance could have been made feasible by the elimination of superfluous posts and the reduction of expenditures.

TABLE 9

ESTIMATED NATIONAL ANNUAL EXPENDITURES (IN *sŏm*)

Capital expenditures	
Palaces	6,667
Goods for capital bureaus	66,667[1]
Salaries:	
1. Official salaries	54,027[2]
2. Salaries for royal relations, merit subjects, transferred, officials on half-salary, *chinsa* degree-holders, guards, students	26,667[3]
Expenses of capital bureaus	6,700
Salaries of clerks and runners	
1. Of capital bureaus	86,653[4]
2. Of above category 2 royal relations, etc.	14,667
Salaries of 2,000 capital soldiers	33,333
Tribute to China and entertainment of envoys from China	6,667
Miscellaneous expenses	20,000
TOTAL	322,048[5]
Provincial expenditures[6]	
Governor's yamen (8 officials at 3,524 *sŏm* each)	28,192
Prov. Army commanders' yamen (8 at 3,172 *sŏm*)	20,576
Prov. Navy commander's yamen (8 at 2,896 *sŏm*)	17,376
Civil districts (145):	
Taebu and Tohobu (33 at 4,380 *sŏm*)	144,562
Pu (22 at 3,80 *sŏm*)	83,835
Kun (60 at 3,229 *sŏm*)	193,760
Hyŏn (30 at 2,682 *sŏm*)	80,480
Garrison districts (65):	
Ch'ŏmsa(jin) (20, at 740 *sŏm*)	14,813
Manhojin (45 at 592 *sŏm*)	26,640
Post-stations (40):	
Ch'albang routes (20 at 475 *sŏm*)	9,506
Ch'amha Ch'albang routes (20 at 414 *sŏm*)	8,293
Granaries (Ch'ang) (12, at 62 *sŏm*)	752[7]
Hyangjŏng (7,000 men at 6.7 *sŏm* per man)	46,667
TOTAL	675,452[8]
Miscellaneous provincial expenditures	
Provisions for soldiers in district towns, 620,000 men paid 5 *toe* (.1 *mal*)/day, twice/year, not including men on regular military service shifts	41,333

Expenditures by all districts for upkeep of envoys and guests, governors and provincial military commanders making the rounds:	15,333
Men and horses for transport:	16,667
Ritual objects and silk for ties at shrines for Earth and Grain and Confucius	6,667
Repair of weapons, banners, etc.	33,333
Upkeep for guests at post-stations	4,000
Cavalry and larger garrisons with more than standard quotas	13,333
Repair of warships and grain transport ships	6,667
Royal tribute paid by provincial governors, and transport costs	3,333
Costs for Chinese imperial envoys and Korean envoys en route to China, plus men and horses for transport	16,667
Additional soldier rations for NW frontier	26,667
Miscellaneous costs	66,667
TOTAL	250,667[9]
GRAND TOTAL	1,248,267

[1] Yu attributed the basis of his calculation to the table drawn up by Chief State Councilor Kim Yuk and the assistant section chief (Chwarang, rank 6A, presumably of the Ministry of Taxation) for substitution of *taedong* taxes for tribute for Ch'ungch'ŏng Province. Their calculation was 92,000 *sŏm* or 138,000 *kok*. Since this figure included provision for food and clothing for the king, worth 9,000 *kok*, Yu deducted it, to yield a total of 129,000 *kok*, or 86,000 contemporary *sŏm*, but since he felt that this sum was unjustifiably large, he urged that purchases be reduced and a quota be set at 100,000 *kok* (i.e., 66,667 *sŏm*).

[2] This sum for salaries would have paid for the salaries of 565 civil and military officials from ranks 1–9 according to Yu's revised and reduced list of officials (see chaps. 14 and 16).

[3] Yu noted that in average times the cost of salaries and support for the people listed here would have been more than 80,000 *sŏm*. His reduction of two-thirds of this cost was achieved by eliminating superfluous bureaus and officials including the *ch'ea* sinecures that were four or five times more numerous than regular officials (*chŏngjik*). He argued that a complete weeding out of these posts could make his plan to increase salaries by four or five times the current level fiscally feasible.

[4] These salaries for capital clerks and runners would pay for 45 chief clerks, 475 clerks, 3,005 runners including slaves, and 985 boy servants.

[5] Yu's grand total was slightly inaccurate, 318,667 *sŏm*. He noted that, although his calculations were in rice, it included the cost of cash, cloth, and yellow bean expenditures.

[6] These figures include expenditures for military aides, local yangban associations, constables and guards, bannermen, weapons directors, ritual officials, runners and slaves, educational officials, and regular dormitory and irregular students in schools. The cost of the school in the provincial capital seat was not included.

[7] Yu noted that the salaries of clerks and runners and maritime grain transport workers at granaries could not be estimated because they were only given rations and did not work all the time.

[8] Yu's calculated the total at 1,020,300 *kok* or 680,200 *sŏm*. Yu also noted that his budget of expenditures was designed to be a temporary calculation that could be changed after reform was carried out.

[9] Yu estimated the total at 380,000 *kok* or 253,333 *sŏm*.

SOURCE: PGSR 19:31b-34b.

CONCLUSION

The inspiration for Yu's financial reforms came from the *taedong* reform in the first half of the seventeenth century, but he carried it much further than the current law by expanding it to cover almost all costs of government except regular military service. The tribute system had already been converted to taxes levied in grain and cloth through tribute contracting arrangements even prior to the adoption of the *taedong* system. That system, therefore, was less important for changing the real tax situation than for legitimizing current, illegal practice and restricting it to a public system of tax quotas and rates based exclusively on the amount of land under cultivation. Since Yu realized that the *taedong* system had converted the national tax system by making the land tax its most important component, he believed not only was it essential to carry out a complete and accurate survey of all cultivated land to ensure a fair and equitable distribution of taxes, but also that the time had come for a more equitable system of land distribution to provide stability for peasant livelihood as well as national tax revenues. Unfortunately, Yu's expectation that a strong king would have been willing and able to confiscate land from the powerful landlord class in Korea to redistribute it to smallholders and tenants proved to be an Utopian and anachronistic fantasy. Nonetheless, he was convinced that the *taedong* formula would provide the key for a more rational system of budgeting, accounting, and finance.

The rational aspect of Yu's thought was certainly not a manifestation of Western concepts of progress or modernity because there is no evidence that such influence reached him at the time. He derived the notion of rational planning and cost-cutting efficiency from the superior methods of classical Chinese government and late Ming dynasty finance. Although he agreed that the world was always subject to change, neither he nor his intellectual predecessors had developed any theory of upward progress from primitive to more developed economic systems, probably because they felt that contemporary times had never and probably could never reach the heights of the ancients.

He objected to royal tribute as a separate category of tribute not only because it was an obvious excuse for unlimited demands on the peasantry, but also because there was no precedent for it in feudal Chou China, let alone the post-Han bureaucratic age. He believed that the Chinese had always paid for the ruler's needs by using national tax revenues, and had put an agency of the regular bureaucracy in charge of the ruler's finances (a measure not adopted in Korea until the 1894 Kabo reform).

He blamed the Korean custom of royal tribute on the absence of an age of sage rule in Korean antiquity and a barbaric tradition established by the Koguryŏ court over its hapless tributary, Okchŏ. Since this sign of barbarism had never been routed out over the past millennium of Korean history, the time had arrived for reconstructing the care and feeding of the king according to the model of moral and limited monarchical prerogative established in classical Chou times. The excessive demands of Korean kings was an epiphenomenon of despotic acquisitiveness that had never been restrained by the proper spirit of rites and etiquette or by the control of well-trained bureaucrats. Because of Yu's respect for classical Chinese models and the superiority of more recent Chinese institutions, and his embarrassment at some of the inferior practices of the Korean past, those scholars who have identified Yu Hyŏngwŏn as one of the first nationalists in Korean thought have misconstrued the fundamental basis of his thinking. His goal was to improve government and finance by the best methods he could find, but he in no way glorified the special features of the indigenous tradition.

In addition to royal tribute, Koreans in the Chosŏn period had also allowed officials on tributary missions to China to make demands on local districts along the route of travel for expense support, and magistrates had made a habit of presenting gifts to the king and their superiors as a matter of courtesy or ritual respect. Yu also found that neither of these habits were justified in classical practice.

Although ordinary tribute had been used in classical times, Yu also noticed that they had never demanded tribute items in kind as Korean governments had done until the seventeenth century. Instead, all items used for tribute were purchased with regular tax revenues, and the tax burden on the peasants supposedly was limited to the tithe. Since the history of the tribute system in Korea had not demonstrated that the tolerance of tribute contracting by King Sejo between 1559 and 1568, or the introduction of the *taedong* method of shifting tribute to the land tax in the 1590s and 1608 had been motivated by an appeal to classical institutions but rather by an attempt to overcome practical administrative problems, Yu could be accused of merely gilding the lily by citing classical precedent to justify his more practical considerations. One could only adopt that point of view, however, if one refuses to believe the testimony of his writings that the remote past rather than a Utopian future provided the inspiration and models for his vision.

In his discussion of the mechanism by which market purchases of all goods consumed by king and bureaucracy should operate, his hearty advocacy of the advantages of the market appeared to have adumbrated the arguments of Adam Smith. He, however, justified it as a classical means for obtaining items of consumption by the ruler and government, not by any developed or sophisticated statement of the theoretical economic advantages of a free market in solving problems of scarcity and promoting the supply of goods through the law of supply and demand. He did understand the role of the market in circulating goods, but he felt that since the government would function as chief if not monopsonistic purchaser of commodities, it would have to play the crucial role of stimulating commercial activity and guaranteeing the flow of goods to the capital by subsidizing the prices of commodities and guaranteeing profits for producers and purchasing agents designated by the government. He insisted that the government officials would have to pay higher than market prices to guarantee the viability of the tribute agents or merchants lest those officials be tempted by the virtual monopsony of the market to force producers and merchants to sell below cost. This mode of thought was an almost bizarre adumbration of Park Chung-hee's nurturing care of the *chaebŏl* after 1965, by which in the current Republic of Korea the state controlled capital, savings, investment, income, and food prices to guarantee the development of capitalism. Yet, this adumbration does not mean that Yu had anticipated modernity, but that South Korean capitalism in the twentieth century trod a path congenial to the traditional bureaucratic mentality toward the market.

Yu did not believe that the classical tradition simply meant bureaucratic control, monopoly, or obstruction of merchant or market activity, but he still felt that bureaucratic subsidies to purchasing agents and producers and state regulation of prices was necessary for the healthy practice of the *taedong* tax system. He never argued that the market should be allowed to operate autonomously and automatically without the need for any positive, government intervention to achieve good ends. Nor did he believe that either commerce or industry should grow so large and profitable that it would attract peasants into those occupations, reduce the number of cultivators, and decrease the volume of agricultural production in the country.

Instead of concluding that the key to the *taedong* system was the shift from a controlled economy to a free market and the development of the private accumulation of capital for investment in nonagricultural production as the means to the creation of greater personal and national wealth, Yu preferred to use the *taedong* model as a scheme for funding all costs of government to reduce the cost of government, the tax burden on the peasantry, and the root causes of bureaucratic corruption. Since Yu believed that the corruption of unsalaried clerks, runners, and government slaves was caused by inadequate compensation by the state, he prescribed that the government take responsibility for paying salaries for all state functionaries down to clerks and runners, including official slaves and women.

Although his plan for financing both government purchases and the salaries of government officials through the *taedong* system consisted of an eminently rational method of solving the deficiencies of government finance, he did not argue that that human rationality freed from the encumbrance of inherited wisdom was the essence of his method. Instead, he took the theoretical basis for his policy from the *Book of History* and the hierarchical model of salaries from the feudal era of Chou China. He also admired the salary scheme that had been worked out after the Han dynasty in China's bureaucratic age, and especially in early Koryŏ in the late tenth century. By contrast he severely criticized the irrationalities of the system of compensation in the Chosŏn dynasty and compared it invidiously to the more moral and rational methods of classical China.

Although an advocate of the total abolition of slavery, he felt he had to accept it for the time being because slavery had become too ingrained in the psyche of the Korean yangban to permit sudden abolition by a single decree. Nonetheless, although slavery could be reduced gradually by stricter laws governing inheritance of status, in the interim daily discrimination against official slaves had to be corrected by guaranteeing salaries for them as well as those of good or commoner status.

While flexible in his toleration of slavery for the moment, he was adamant about the necessity for abolishing private property in land and replacing it with land grants for the peasants. Given current conditions in which the majority of cultivators were either poor or marginal landowners or tenants, he assumed that the state would receive sufficient revenue to assume all costs for salaries and expenses only if the redistribution of land were carried out and a land tax limited to 10 percent of production, and he based his financial calculations on the assumption that each peasant household would be cultivating his proposed standard plot of 100 *myo* or 16.7 acres, instead of the minuscule holdings of the average cultivator in the mid-seventeenth century.

Yu concluded his study of the *taedong* system shortly after 1658, just before expansion of the *taedong* tax to the upland districts of Chŏlla Province. Between 1653 to 1659 a major cadastral survey was then carried out undoubtedly as a means of felicitating expansion of state revenues now that the land tax was fast becoming the most important component of national revenue. Yu may well have been living at one of the most opportune times for the adoption of a land redistribution program, because after his death major surveys were conducted only in 1718–20, 1820, and 1898–1904, intervals of 50 to 100 years.[69]

As Han Woo-keun pointed out in his survey of socioeconomic conditions in this period, the land tax (*chŏnse*) had been graded in a range of tax rates from 4 to 20 *mal/kyŏl* according to fertility and climatic conditions by King Sejong in 1441, but the assessments on land had been reduced gradually over the years so that by the beginning of Sukchong's reign in 1674, almost all land was graded at the lowest category (lower-lower) and taxed at the rate of 4 *mal/kyŏ*, with some land in the southern provinces at 6 *mal/kyŏl*. After 1708, the lower six provinces had replaced tribute with the *taedong* land tax, and the rate of all land taxes in 1717 was 24 *mal/kyŏl*, of which 12 *mal* was the *taedong* tax, 4 *mal* was the old land tax, 2 *mal* was the *samsumi* for support of the three types of soldiers (including the new musketeers) in the army, 2 *mal* was for miscellaneous expenses, 3 *mal* was for pheasants and chickens consumed by the district magistrate, and 1 *mal* was for four types of firewood, straw, and coal for fuel. Since Han found an estimate in 1737 that average production in husked rice was 300–375 *mal/kyŏl* or an average of 350 *mal/kyŏl* for low-quality land, the combined land tax rate was still low, only 24⁄350 *mal* or 7 percent of production.[70]

Despite this reasonable tax rate, in the eighteenth century the central government was plagued by a chronic shortage of revenues. The Ministry of Taxation was responsible for collection of the land tax and the Office for Dispensing Benevolence for the *taedong* tax. Han Woo-keun found that in 1717 annual revenues for the Ministry of Taxation was no more than 130,000 *sŏm*, but because of a major crop disaster in 1716, tax receipts had been reduced to only 58,000 *sŏm*. In 1726, the Ministry of Taxation stated that its annual revenues were around 100,000 *sŏm* of rice, 70–80,000 *p'il* of cloth, and 160–170,000 *yang* of cash, which was sufficient to balance its budget, but that year revenues were down to 60,000 *sŏm* of rice, 20–30,000 *p'il* of cloth, and 40–50,000 *yang* of cash (from the upland regions of Hwanghae and five other districts that paid their taxes in cash). The shortage had to be supplemented by taking rice taxes from Kanghwa Island and using cloth and cash from P'yŏng'an Province. Again, in 1738 the Minister of Taxation reported that his annual (rice?) expenditures were around 110,000 *sŏm* but revenues were only 68,000 *sŏm*.[71]

In 1738 King Yŏngjo was informed by Third State Councilor Song Inmyŏng that expenditures by the Office for Dispensing Benevolence had annual expenditures of 140,000 *sŏm*, or 240–250,000 *sŏm* if cotton cloth expenditures were added (i.e., about 100,000 *sŏm* in grain equivalents). When Yŏngjo proposed cutting the *taedong* tax in half in 1740, Song replied that if he cut the *taedong* tax (in half), he would be left with 240,000 *sŏm*, and if he cut the land tax (*chŏnse*), he would have 170,000 *sŏm* (combined total for rice, cloth, and cash?). Han Woo-keun therefore deduced that total revenues from the *taedong* tax must have been twice 240,000 *sŏm*, or 480,000 *sŏm*. He also estimated that of this total revenue, approximately half was used to pay tribute agents to purchase what had been tribute items for the capital, and the other half was retained in the provinces for use by provincial governors, military commanders, district magistrates, and military garrisons. Since any surplus left over from the *taedong* tax was probably being used to supplement shortages in the Ministry of Taxation's budget caused by reduction in land tax revenue, the Office for Dispensing Benevolence's *taedong* tax resources had also diminished.

Han estimated the combined revenues of both the Ministry of Taxation and the Office for Dispensing Benevolence at 350,000 *sŏm* per year (why not 410,000 *sŏm* based on funds available to the capital?), which had been sufficient for paying the salaries of regular officials and rations for duty soldiers (exclusive of support taxes for soldiers) in normal years, but at the end of King Sukchong's and the beginning of King Yŏngjo's reigns (ca. 1715–40) a series of crop disasters and famines had created chronic fiscal shortages. Although Han lacked detailed statistical information, he found a report in 1718 that reductions of tax revenue from poor crop conditions had meant that the government had not been able to meet salaries for regular officials and rations for troops, and another report in 1760 that the combined revenues of the Ministry of Taxation and the Office for Dispensing Benevolence was short by 20–30,000 *sŏm* on an annual basis.[72]

Kim Okkŭn's far more detailed study of the *taedong* system has shown that in the last part of the Chosŏn dynasty about 1,450,000 *kyŏl* of land was registered for the whole country, but the amount of "true land" (*silkyŏl*) or taxable land that was left after deducting tax-exempt land, damaged land, or land exempted because of temporary climatic conditions or natural disaster amounted to 800,000 *kyŏl*. An additional 50–60,000 *kyŏl* was also deducted as special tax exempt land (*kŭppokchŏn*), leaving about 750,000 *kyŏl*. Total national revenues from this taxable land yielded a total of 600,000 *sŏm* of rice, which was about three times the revenues of 180,000 *sŏm* from the land tax (120,000 *sŏm* for paddy land and 60,000 *sŏm* from dry land). Kim found that the total *taedong* revenue for 1769 was 565,225 *sŏm*, of which 315,853 *sŏm* (56 percent) was remitted to the capital (*sangnap*) for the purchase of items that had previously been remitted as tribute in kind. Han had mentioned a figure of 480,000 *sŏm* total revenue for 1740, of which 240,000 *sŏm* (50 percent) was remitted to the capital. Kim's estimate that 56 percent of national *taedong* taxes (or its equivalent) was sent to the capital was a more accurate figure than Han's 50 percent since he took into account wide-ranging provincial variety in the division of revenue between the capital and the province. For example, P'yŏng'an Province retained 75 percent of their *taedong* revenues in the province, while Kyŏngsang Province only kept 34 percent. Kim noticed that the fiscal crisis in the provinces increased toward the end of the dynasty as the overall proportion of *taedong* revenues kept in the provinces declined.[73]

Flaws that were detrimental to the operation of the land tax naturally became problems of the *taedong* tax as well. Kim pointed out that the system of grading the productivity of land for tax purposes in 1441 by measuring fertility and weather conditions had virtually been abandoned since almost all land was graded at the lowest or next-to-lowest category of fertility. This development meant that the progressive feature of the land tax had been lost, and the only method for easing taxes was a special royal order of exemption following investigation of local conditions (*taphŏm*). Kim found that for Kyŏnggi Province, for example, between 1657 and 1760, a period of 111 years, Korean kings granted 38 reductions, or an average of 1 reduction for every 4 years. Only in 3 cases were all taxes exempted, and most reductions varied from 1 to 3 *mal/kyŏl*.[74]

Han Woo-keun found several examples of inefficient, useless, or corrupt investigations of crop damage in the early eighteenth century, such that peasants who merited relief did not get it, and large landlords who did not deserve it received them. In 1746, King Yŏngjo even forbade provincial governors from granting damage exemptions on their own authority. Swidden fields were often registered erroneously as land under constant cultivation and subjected to annual taxes. In addition, land registration itself was hampered by corruption, so that much cultivated land was left out of the records, contributing to low taxes for the wealthy and oppressive and confiscatory taxes for the poor and unprotected small peasants. Surcharges for fees or bribes increased real tax rates, and some powerful landlords who took over the lands of smallholders had registered themselves as the sole owner of the combined holdings, and collected taxes as virtual rent from the real petty smallholders.

The concentration of land in the hands of the wealthy and the corruption of officials and clerks in the administration of the land tax exacerbated the position of poor peasants and tenants. As Kim Okkŭn put it, the *taedong* reform did provide some benefits to peasants who had been oppressed by the corruption of the tribute system, but by shifting tribute to land, it had become a kind of feudal land rent imposed on the peasantry. The percentage of tenants among peasants expanded and rental rates increased to as high as 70 to 90 percent of the crop. Ultimately, corruption and injustice in land distribution and taxation became one of the three major sources for peasant rebellion, especially in the *imsul* rebellion of 1862 in the south.[75]

Although Yu's writings on the *taedong* system was celebrated in the late eighteenth century revision of the *Munhŏnbigo* by Yi Man'un, there is no evidence to indicate that Yu's attempt to expand *taedong* principles to finance all government costs including the salaries of clerks, runners, official slaves, local irregular officials, and chiefs of yangban associations was ever adopted.[76] Although he showed great foresight in many of his recommendations, he was still a creature of the mid-seventeenth century because he derived inspiration from the tide of reform that accompanied the gradual adoption of the *taedong* system. Had his program been adopted, and had all salaries of all functionaries and all administrative costs of government yamen been funded by government tax revenues, it might have improved the probity of government officials and reduced the volume of corruption. Unfortunately, his program would have depended on an efficient and dutiful registration of land, let alone nationalization and redistribution – a chimerical wish considering the preference of officials and clerks to maintain the status quo. The subsequent decline of the land and *taedong* tax systems after 1700 indicates that private competition for land and insatiable greed by officials and clerks required something better than government salaries or the self-policing mechanisms of the centralized bureaucracy.

CHAPTER 23

Copper Cash and the Monetary System

Kim Yuk, the leading protagonist of the extension of the *taedong* system, was also the leading advocate of the adoption of copper currency in the mid-seventeenth century, and Yu Hyŏngwŏn was sufficiently influenced by his ideas to propose collecting part of national taxes in cash under his own plan for restructuring national finance on the basis of the *taedong* system. Since copper currency became an important medium of exchange in the Korean economy in the late seventeenth and eighteenth centuries, and the development of metallic cash has been seen as one of the signs of a growing market economy and the beginning of Korea's modern development, Yu has been perceived as one of the intellectual pioneers of modernism.

Since copper cash disappeared from the market in the middle of the sixteenth century, its reemergence in the mid-seventeenth century should be considered both consequence and cause of commercial development in the economy. The mechanics of the process of commercial development, however, are quite difficult to verify by quantitative measures. There is a marked lack of evidence despite a host of scholars who have been asserting the growth of surplus production in the agricultural economy from the late fifteenth century.

By the late fifteenth century Korean peasants had begun to switch from broadcast seeding of dry fields and the use of the fallow system to wet-field rice agriculture, and the application of fertilizer to permit yearly cultivation, methods associated with the Chiang-nan or southern region of China during the Sung period. Attempts by the government to copy Chinese and Japanese versions of the water wheel for irrigation failed by 1431, but by the late fifteenth century irrigation was expanded from small-scale damming of upland streams to more costly redirection of water from downstream rivers through barriers and gateways into lowland sluices. Yi T'aejin argued that as production of land expanded, the established capital officials, royalty, and consort relatives used the local Yuhyangso to mobilize peasant labor for the construction not only of irrigation facilities but for the reclamation of land along the coastal regions to increase their own private estates. The spread of irrigation also brought with it the benefits of transplantation in the cultivation of rice with improved crop yields.[1] Undoubtedly total agricultural production was expanded as a result of these innovations, but it is not clear whether greater production exceeded the growth of population to produce a marketable surplus or simply kept pace with rising population.

Commercial activity did appear to be growing. There was the increase in cotton production, the transformation of military service from actual duty to cloth taxes, and the replacement of tribute taxes by merchant purchases by tribute middlemen under the *pangnap* system. The volume of trade was reinforced by the development of private trading with the Chinese in the sixteenth century, particularly the imports of silk and the mining of silver to pay for those imports.

Yet concerted attempts to introduce copper cash into the economy as a more efficient exchange medium were constantly thwarted by the reluctance of both officials and peasants to accept it in place of bolts of cloth and bags of grain that had constituted the only exchange medium for most of the countryside since the mid-sixteenth century. The eventual victory of this effort was a combination of two factors: enlightened leadership by the proponents of copper cash from the top, and a growth in the market and demand for a better medium of exchange from the bottom.

What was also significant about the protracted process for the reintroduction of copper cash in the seventeenth century – one that was marred by setbacks as well as successes – was the debate over policies associated with the nature of currency, its purposes, and the role of the state in the regulation of the money supply, exchange rates between various media of exchange, and commodity prices. These debates were complex but they can be crudely summarized as a division between a loose-money policy designed to ease the state's financial problems and to stimulate the commercial economy, and a conservative money policy of control to prevent the ravages of inflation. It may seem strange that within the first few decades after the reintroduction of copper cash, when the volume of that cash was small and did not circulate in all markets throughout the country, that more sophisticated problems of money supply, exchange rates, and prices could have been so significant. But they were, and the attitudes and policies toward those questions had an important effect on the Korean economy in the eighteenth century.

By the same token, Yu Hyŏngwŏn's analysis of the role and function of money and the state's role in its management provides an interesting model for comparison with the policies adopted at the time and in the first half of the eighteenth century. It was only in the mid-eighteenth century that his ideas became more widely known, a century after he wrote his work on money, and a period when a hundred years of experience with copper cash had changed perspectives from the time when cash was being introduced.

COPPER CASH IN THE SEVENTEENTH CENTURY

Reviving the Use of Cash, 1551–1627

Interest in currency resumed briefly in 1551 when the government considered minting copper cash as the fastest way to raise funds to provide revenues and relief in the midst of a famine.[2] Later in that century Yulgok complained about the absence of metallic or paper money and recommended copper cash over paper bills and suggested that it be enforced by stiff penalties. Yi Hangbok agreed that metallic cash was the most convenient form of currency, but he was more cautious because it had been used a few times in the past without success, copper was in short supply in Korea, and official permission for mining would not be sufficient to attract poor peasants into mining. He urged that thorough consideration of methods to gain its circulation had to be attempted before it should be adopted permanently.[3]

The next suggestion for metallic currency came in 1598 from Yang Hao, a Ming general stationed in Korea during the Imjin War against Japanese invaders. Since Ming China already had a cash economy, he thought the Korean government would be able to provide some financial support for their own government as well as funds for purchasing supplies for Ming soldiers by minting copper cash. Korean court officials opposed the idea and King Sŏnjo politely declined the suggestion because copper and other metals were in short supply and economic conditions were currently so bad that any attempt to mint cash might cause popular unrest. When Yang returned home later that year, Chinese pressure for currency was relaxed.[4]

After the war was over, a group of fourteen officials led by Chief State Councilor Yi Tŏkhyŏng in 1603 urgently proposed minting copper cash, but opposition led by the ministers of the left and right blocked the plan because copper and other metals were not plentiful in Korea. Furthermore, bad relations with Japan blocked Korea's main source of copper imports. Then, in 1625 the late Ming general, Mao Wen-lung, who had established an island base at Kado (Ka Island) near Manchuria had suggested that Korea import Ming cash. Injo did not accede to this request, but he did accept the recommendation of Minister of Taxation Kim Sin'guk that the Korean government mint its own copper cash to provide government revenue. Injo minted two coins at this time, the Eastern Country Circulating Treasure (*Tongguk t'ongbo*) and the multiple denomination Ten-cash Circulating Treasure (*Sipchŏn t'ongbo*). Injo suspended operations only a few months later but resumed minting again in 1626. However, only 600 strings (or 6,000 *yang* at 100 *yang*/string, in which the *yang* (tael, or 1.3 ounces), originally a measure of weight, functioned as a unit of account) of cash were minted until the Manchu invasion of 1627 brought operations to a halt.

King Injo's Ever-Normal Bureau and Chosŏn T'ongbo, *1631*

In 1633, King Injo established the Ever-Normal Bureau (Sangp'yŏngch'ŏng) in charge of price stabilization activities and ordered it to mint a coin called the Chosŏn Circulating Treasure (*Chosŏn t'ongbo*), and he forbade minting by other agencies of government or private individuals. The coin was modeled after the Wan-li Circulating Treasure (*Wan-li t'ung-pao*) that was larger and weighed twice as much as the Chosŏn Circulating Treasure coins minted in the previous decade. The original regulations established the exchange rate for the coin at 1 *toe* (.1 *mal*) of rice per *mun* of cash (100 *mun* per *yang*), but because of objections that the coin would be overvalued, the Ministry of Taxation proposed reducing its value in half to .5 *toe/mun* but setting the value of coins cast in pewter at 1 *toe/mun*. The ministry also proposed allowing one-third or one-fourth of all taxes and tribute owed the state in cloth or grain to be paid in cash. This would include the land tax or grain rations for musketeers, bowmen, and pikemen (*samsubyŏng*) of the Military Training Agency, but the ministry anticipated that residents in remote districts would have difficulty in obtaining enough cash to make payments. In the capital, redemption payments in lieu of punishment, office expenses for the capital bureaus, royal grants, and compensation for labor service could all be paid in cash. Injo accepted these suggestions but rejected the ministry's idea of allowing interpreters in embassies to China to bring back Chinese cash to circulate along with the *Chosŏn t'ongbo*.[5]

In 1634 Injo adopted the Ever-Normal Bureau's recommendation to remedy obstructions in the flow of currency. It had already permitted the *samsu* soldiers to receive one-tenth of their rations in cash, but it had not recommended imposing any cash taxes on the people. The *samsu* soldiers were authorized to present their cash to the Ever-Normal Bureau's granary to buy food, but because there was not enough grain on reserve to supply their needs, people were already beginning to lose confidence in the cash. Then, when the government allowed peasants who had not yet paid their taxes to do so in cash, many living near the capital took advantage of it, and its circulation and availability increased there.

Not enough cash had been minted for distribution in the countryside, so profiteers took cash to the provinces and demanded higher exchange rates than authorized by the government. To counteract this problem, the agency asked that 30,000 *kŭn* of the year's Japanese "tribute" copper be allocated to regional centers for minting in major towns in the south – Andong (later shifted to Taegu), Chŏnju, and Kongju to insure uniformity of distribution in the countryside. The value of coins minted in these districts would be slightly greater than those in the capital and a part of their taxes could be paid in cash so that the use of cash would not constitute a de facto increase in the tax rate. These tactics were designed not only to spread the circulation of cash throughout the countryside, but to eliminate the tricks of the clerks and runners by rejecting tax payments because the quality of the cloth or grain they presented for taxes was not up to standard.

The agency rejected the idea currently popular in some quarters that the introduction of currency was creating a differential in prices between the capital and the countryside by arguing that the free exchange of goods in an open market would balance prices throughout the country. Residents of the capital would take their cash to the countryside to buy up grain, while peasants and other holders of rice in the provinces would come to the capital to sell it for cash. "Thus rice could accumulate in the capital and cash could be sent back to the villages." Cash would circulate without hindrance by the use of cash in the tax system because peasants would be able to pay grain to the magistrates, and the magistrates would use cash to pay the people. In other words, if King Injo wanted cash to circulate, he had to allow its use in the tax system, otherwise it would be "like expecting a river to flow downstream even though its source had been blocked off."

When Injo called for further discussion about the possibility that the minting of cash had created different values for the coin between capital and countryside, the agency officials replied that the king ought to declare that the value of the coin would remain constant throughout the country. Furthermore, the attitude of the public at large could be assessed by the residents of Andong, who had requested the establishment of a mint, and by the people of Kaesŏng, who had been using copper cash for some time and deserved a mint in their city as well. Injo finally ratified the proposal, choosing to select those towns that either had flourishing commercial activities or were close to Japan or sources of copper ore.[6]

In 1635 the Ever-Normal Bureau argued that Korea had been unable to achieve the circulation of cash in over two hundred years since the dynasty was founded even though metallic currency had been in use throughout the world since remote antiquity. The problem was that the people had no trust in the country's laws because too many policies, like the *taedong* system and the *hop'ae* household tally system had been dropped not long after they were first adopted. Even though the people understood the advantages of cash, they had doubts that it would become a permanently acceptable means of exchange. Something had to be done to instill public confidence in cash, like the Koryŏ practice of announcing a new edict to the royal family's ancestral shrine. The government had to demonstrate its resolution to carry out the law and put an end to idle gossip and confusion about the laws.

The agency's program permitted shopkeepers and merchants to establish cash markets or set up shops at will in the capital and provincial districts and along the major thoroughfares in the countryside to accept cash payments. It ordered capital bureaus and district magistrates' yamen to collect fines and pay for expenses in cash, required markets in the capital to accept cash for ordinary purchases of fuel and vegetables and require cash for the purchase of large items like oxen and horses with fines for failure to adhere to the law.[7] Injo also established a special cash tax in Kyŏnggi Province and granted permission for private minting of cash in Haeju and Suwŏn, a violation of the original terms of the law in 1633. Yi Sŏ had even suggested this in 1623 when Injo came to the throne, but this was the first time it was allowed.[8]

Although minting was suspended at the beginning of 1637[9] because of the second Manchu invasion, cash continued to circulate in Kaesŏng and Hwanghae Province, stimulated by the active production and trade of brassware and private minting. An ex-magistrate of Kaesŏng had reported in 1634 that most of the residents there had approved the use of cash, but it had been opposed by the yangban.[10]

Kim Yuk's Promotion of Cash, 1637–50

In 1644 Kim Yuk returned from an official embassy to the Ming capital full of progressive ideas he had picked up from China. He wanted the king to adopt the Chinese system of carts for transporting goods, and he wanted every magistrate along the route traversed by envoys to China to establish shops to stimulate the circulation of copper cash. In that event, envoys and their retinue of doctors, interpreters, and guards would be able to pay cash for food and lodging instead of having to drag their food and horse fodder with them. Local peasants would supply rice, cloth, firewood to the magistrate, travelers could purchase it for cash, and the local peasants would benefit from the demonstration effect of cash transactions by learning how to buy things at stores for cash themselves.

Kim believed that Korea had never succeeded in promoting the circulation of cash throughout the country because cash was used only in the capital, and the rural population had no idea of its utility. He believed that it should be possible to circulate cash in Hwanghae and P'yŏng'an because the roads were busy with traffic there, and he suggested that cash held by the Ministry of Taxation be sent to those provinces. Furthermore, government silver should be used to purchase cash in Beijing to obtain a supply of tens of millions of strings for Hwanghae and P'yŏng'an provinces. He also noted that cash was as popular in Kaesŏng then as it was in China, and it could provide a model for Hwanghae and P'yŏng'an. Official travelers would be overjoyed at not having to carry excess baggage, shopowners would be happy to receive so much cash from travelers, and the local peasants would be relieved because they would no longer be forced to pay rice to travelers as part of their local tax obligation.

He also testified that many officials in the north had indicated their agreement with the use of cash there, including the governor of P'yŏng'an and a few magistrates. He proposed a change in government strategy for promoting the circulation of cash by purchasing Chinese cash with Korean silver to increase the supply of currency. The Border Defense Command then recommended that the governors and magistrates of the two provinces be canvassed about their views on cash and the other reforms, especially since Kim Yuk had already discussed the issues with them on his trip, but Injo took no action.[11]

When Kim Yuk was magistrate of Kaesŏng in 1648 he expressed chagrin in a memorial to the king that his past petitions requesting the use of cash had not been permitted. Now that he had been on duty for a year in Kaesŏng, he had already noticed that cash had been used in Kaesŏng since 1643 and had spread to neighboring districts like Kanghwa, Kyodong, P'ungdan, and Yŏnbaek. "Large items like land, houses, and slaves, and small items like firewood, brush, vegetables, and fruit were all purchased for cash. . . . I am happy to say that I know that cash can be adopted because even the young boys you meet in the marketplace would never be deceived [by the use of cash]."

Even if the king were not willing to adopt cash for the whole country, he could authorize it for P'yŏng'an and Hwanghae provinces. The people there would at least benefit from not having to carry rice around with them whenever they traveled.

He proposed that the governors of these two provinces first establish mints in provincial districts, and allow people to use cash to pay fines, redemption payments, or taxes, so that its circulation could take place without the need for any coercive orders by the state. Kim urged the king not only to follow the successful circulation of currency in Kaesŏng, but to copy precedents for metallic currency established in ancient China:

> In the past during the Sung dynasty, Chang Tsai wanted to buy a piece of land in order to try to establish the well-field system. Even though the well fields had been abolished since the age of antiquity, he still wanted to carry it out. How is that the system of cash that has been in use from ancient times to the present [in China] could be so difficult to carry out only in our country? The use of cash in my district has in fact been [equivalent to Chang Tsai's] trial of the well field system.[12]

In 1650, Kim Yuk returned from an official embassy to China with 150,000 *mun* (or 1,500 *yang*) of cash that he purchased with funds saved from his travel expenses, and with King Hyojong's approval he distributed the cash to tax collection centers (*tohoe*) in Pyongyang and Anju to see whether it would stay in circulation. Hyojong agreed that if it did, he would then order minting of cash to take place in the upland regions to promote the circulation of more cash.

King Hyojong's Adoption of Cash, 1651

Since King Hyojong resented his treatment by the Manchus while under detention in Manchuria and was determined to seek revenge against them for their two invasions of Korea, he was only to happy to find some means of financing the strengthening of Korean military power. The king was contemplating using cash for this purpose, but in 1651 the Border Defense Command reported that the supply of cash for P'yŏng'an and Hwanghae provinces was insufficient even though the population was used to using it in the market. Hyojong was intrigued by Minister of Taxation Wŏn Tup'yo's suggestion that it would be cheaper to buy cash from China than mint it in Korea. Chinese merchants in Manchuria had flocked to Liao-tung to sell cash to Korea when they heard of the possibility that Korea was preparing to circulate cash in the economy, and they worked out an agreement with the Korean interpreters to sell 80 *ch'ing* of cash for 1,600 *yang* of silver (850 *mun* of cash per *yang* of silver).[13] The current envoy to China could take silver to pay for it and bring the cash back on his return. The Border Defense Command proposed that the Ministry of Taxation pay two-thirds the cost and the Ever-Normal Bureau the rest.

Hyojong was overjoyed with this prospect, but since Korea was currently suffering under a famine and the Minister of Taxation reported that his treasury was empty, he thought it would be almost impossible to find the silver needed. The minister proposed sending 800 *yang*, but Hyojong settled for ordering district magistrates on the frontier to buy cash with rice to obtain currency for circulation. He had decided to wait to see whether the cash circulated successfully before authorizing any more purchases.[14]

Hyojong then ordered the Military Training Agency to mint cash, presumably to use the profits to pay for their expenses from the profits of seigniorage. He also permitted the private minting of cash for only the second time since 1635 and forbade the use of rough cloth (*ch'up'o*) as currency to promote the circulation of metallic cash. The Border Defense Command then charged that officials in charge of enforcing the ban against the circulation of cloth had failed because they could not discipline their own underlings. Nevertheless, the situation in P'yŏng'an and Hwanghae provinces looked promising because cash was actually circulating there, and the residents of Seoul favored the use of cash, but there was not enough available.

To meet the short supply, the Border Defense Command requested that copper and other metals from Tongnae (imported from Japan) be sent to Seoul and that the Military Training Agency cease its current manufacture of weapons to smelt copper into coins. Hyojong agreed and ordered that cash be banned temporarily in the capital until this was done.[15] The next month Kim Yuk told Hyojong that the need for cash was too urgent to wait for the current Korean ambassador to Beijing to return from China to bring more cash.[16] A few months later Hyojong revealed that he had decided to grant a request from a sinecured official in the Military Affairs Commision, Yi Kyŏngyŏ, Third State Councilor Han Hŭng'il, and Second State Councilor Yi Sibaek to permit private minting.[17]

The Ever-Normal Bureau's Stimulation Plan, 1651

At the end of 1651 the Ever-Normal Bureau obtained approval from Hyojong for a more ambitious cash circulation policy. It noted that the use of cash had been permitted in the capital, but warned that fluctuations in its value ought to be avoided by setting its exchange value at ⅓ *toe* of rice, the prevailing value in Hwanghae and P'yŏng'an provinces. This appears to have been the first attempt by the government, at least in the seventeenth century, to fix the value of cash, or set an exchange rate between cash and rice – a policy fraught with serious policy implications. In the absence of specific testimony, one might speculate that the officials of the Ever-Normal Bureau had little ideological commitment to free market principles and preferred to ensure a stable value of the currency by fiat to build confidence in the minds of a suspicious public in the worth of the new medium of exchange. Decreeing the value of cash in grain at the prevailing market rate may have seemed like a safe-and-sane policy, but any variation in the supply of or demand for grain would throw havoc into the system of legal values.

The Ever-Normal Bureau also suggested permitting payment of cash to obtain royal permission to take the examinations, to gain release from base status to become commoners, to purchase blank office warrants, or to gain exemption from corporal punishment for criminal action. Cash would be permitted for the purchase of all commodities on the market including rice, and the bureau would also act as a clearinghouse for people who wanted to obtain cash for the payment of rice taxes or vice versa. By these devices, "currency would circulate without rest and commodity prices would shoot up, and a correct, harmonious and standard balance [between commodities and currency would be achieved]." Evidently these measures were adopted, but they did not prove effective.[18]

At the beginning of 1652 a dispute broke out between Yun Sunji, a supporter of Hyojong's cash policy, and Hŏ Chŏk, who claimed that there had been some "obstructions" in the system. Hyojong conceded that cash could not be forced on the people and agreed to conduct an investigation of popular feelings about cash. A few days later a royal lecturer, Hong Myŏngha, who was lecturing on the Great Plan (Hung-fan) of the Chou dynasty, mentioned that the text had stressed the necessity that all laws of the state had to be drawn up in accordance with the feelings of the people. By contrast, however, King Hyojong's intention to provide benefit for the people by adopting copper cash had been frustrated because officials were actually forcing people to use cash by beating anyone who refused to do so. Merchants and shopkeepers were refusing to use it, and everyone was complaining about the situation.

Hyojong replied that the policy required patience and that cash had circulated without trouble in the northwest. He had planned to begin its circulation in the capital as well and was not willing to rescind his order because the sages of ancient times taught that it took a long time to obtain successful implementation of a law. His currency edicts would continue and cash would be stimulated by requiring all penal redemptions to be paid in cash. Kim Yuk, now councilor of the left, was overjoyed to hear this and promised to discuss it with Hŏ Chŏk and convince him that slow and methodical planning was needed to solve the problem.[19]

Yi Man'ŭng's Criticism of Cash, 1652

In 1652, the fourth censor of the Office of Censor-General, Yi Man'ŭng, attacked

Kim Yuk's support of copper cash as a medium of exchange at the same time that he had criticized his advocacy of the *taedong* system for Ch'ungch'ŏng Province. Yi could not understand why King Hyojong had adopted cash since it obviously had no value and could not be eaten or worn like rice and cloth. He felt that cotton already functioned as a satisfactory medium of exchange in Korea, the supply of copper cash was too small to provide a national metallic currency, and even King Injo had tried and abandoned it. He claimed that the people would never be happy with copper cash even though Kim Yuk had claimed that it would benefit the people as a whole rather than a few with commercial interests. King Hyojong, however, was not moved by Yi's arguments to change his policy.

By contrast, Kim Yuk reported in 1653 that people in the capital were able to pay taxes and fines in cash as well as rice, and that travelers were able to purchase goods for cash while traveling through the country. He obtained Hyojong's permission to establish mints in Chŏlla and Kyŏngsang provinces as well to continue the spread of cash throughout the country.[20]

Negative comments about cash policy continued to appear, however. Later that year the Office of Special Counselors (Oktang or Hongmun'gwan) memorialized that the virtuous rule of Hyojong had declined since he first came to the throne because some of his policies had not succeeded, and the top state councilors were sharply divided over the issues. Although cash policy had been designed to enhance the flow of currency and promote the exchange of goods, the country was lacking in copper and had to rely on imports from abroad, making the minting of copper coins difficult. Before cash could be brought into circulation, enough of it had to be minted, and the people had to be educated gradually to the benefits so that they would realize they would not be harmed by its use. Forcing the people to use cash before they had learned to trust it would cause them suffering rather than contribute to their wealth.[21]

In the spring of 1654, a middle rank official in the Office of Special Counselors, Kim Suhang, reported that in a recent trip through the villages of Hwanghae and P'yŏng'an provinces he found that every person was carrying cash with him, but he was surprised when they informed him that they had been forced to do so by a new order from the Ever-Normal Bureau that required all persons to carry 50 *mun* of cash personally, and that any violators would be punished by a corps of special officers (Pyŏlchang). Kim commented that the law made no sense in requiring that people have a certain amount of cash on their persons because the point of ordering the use of currency was to spend it and keep it in constant circulation, not to retain a fixed amount.

When Kim Yuk questioned the veracity of his report, Kim Suhang denied that he was spreading false information. He remarked that he had been told prior to his trip by friends in the capital that cash circulated throughout the two northwest provinces, and when he went there, he saw for himself that everyone was carrying cash around in their belts. He had assumed it was a natural development until he heard directly from the people and magistrates he met that the special officers roamed around the villages rounding up people up to check them for cash and meted out beatings or demanded redemption payments for those who had none on them. Their behavior was so tyrannical that the villagers ran off as soon as they heard they were coming.

Kim Yuk was set back by this statement, and the next day he obtained Hyojong's permission to put the assistant governors (Tosa) of the provinces in charge of circulating cash. Since the way to do it was merely to have magistrates collect cash for taxes and use it for expenditures, he also won approval for P'yŏng'an to follow the practice in Hwanghae by collecting 1 *mal* of rice for the (land?) tax (probably 16–25 percent of the tax).[22]

Yi Kyŏngyŏ's Objections to Cash Policy, 1654

After a severe flood in the summer of 1654, the sinecured Yi Kyŏngyŏ submitted a lengthy moral lesson to Hyojong in which he chastised the king for faulty planning, and failure to adopt the ancient precedent of choosing some material other than food and clothing to use as currency to offset shortages of goods in some areas and to create an equal distribution of products throughout a country. Yi was himself criticial of copper cash, but he was even more critical of Hyojong's vacillation in determining a policy of action and following it through with conviction. He believed that for the four or five thousand years of Korea's history since Tan'gun, all Korean kings had been aware that cash was beneficial to both the country and its people alike, but that no king who had adopted cash for currency had ever changed his mind and abolished it after he had done so. This was a flawed premise because not all kings since Tan'gun were advocates of metallic cash, and a number of kings in the fifteenth and early sixteenth centuries had tried with considerable effort both cash and paper money and abandoned it only after it failed to circulate properly.

Unfortunately, Yi continued, Korea was then faced with insurmountable obstacles to the successful adoption of metallic currency. Since copper and other metals used for cash were not produced in much quantity in the country, Korea had to depend on foreign imports of metallic raw materials. What was more important, however, was that economic conditions did not justify the use of cash because the population as a whole was too poor, and few had any surplus wealth. Most people lived on a hand-to-mouth basis,

> cultivating the land for food and weaving cloth for clothes. Although there were artisans and merchants, the artisans worked mostly in construction, leatherwear, and linen, and cloth and rice were used for the circulation of these goods. The people were barely able to provide enough for themselves, and people had to run away from their homes and become vagrants because they were starving and freezing from the cold. There just was not enough surplus property saved up to allow people to purchase a stock of cash to be lent out at 10 percent interest.[23]

The people did not consider that cash would ever be of any utility to them for conducting the business of everyday life. "The peasants in the fields, the residents of the towns, and the patrons of the *makkŏlli* [grog] shops only thought of finding a few grains of rice to get through the vicissitudes of the next day, and when because of their empty bellies their parents, wives, and children sought the breast of sustenance, they never thought that having a few coins of cash on them to take home would ever be of any aid in surviving."[24]

While the circulation of cash throughout the economy was deemed to be beneficial, it should have occurred as a matter of course, and not been coercive. Coercion had created obstacles against currency and caused problems in both public and private life. Officials were making private profits in the name of public duty, and residents of the northwest were suffering hardship from the policy. High ministers and loyal officials in the capital failed to study the policy adequately and used force to implement the use of cash in the name of benefiting both the nation and the people without taking cognizance of its ill effects.

In fact, the whole apparatus of the state was bound to a policy of deceit because officials believed false stories and refused to believe accurate accounts; governors, magistrates, and scholars selected for court appointments did not know the basic intention of the court's policy, nor were they or any court officials willing to speak clearly on the deficiencies of the program; they only confirmed that it was possible to put cash into circulation, and they were encouraged in this by disreputable profiteers. The only solution was for Hyojong to summon all important capital officials to submit their honest views on the situation and carry out changes that would take into account the needs of the people themselves.[25]

Yi Kyŏngyŏ did not object to the use of metallic currency itself since it was fully justified by both classical and historical precedent in China, but he did claim that economic conditions and popular attitudes were not appropriate for it, and forcing the use of currency by punishment had only created a tyrannical regime without any prospects for success. His conservatism, in other words, was ostensibly not based on any Confucian or ideological commitment to the priority of agriculture over commerce, but on the impropriety of a forced-draft transformation of a backward economy. Nevertheless, his complaints, like those of Kim Suhang the previous year, resembled the standard resistance to change in almost any age by people unwilling to pay the costs associated with creating a presumably more beneficial system.

The Use of Cash for taedong *Tax Payments, 1654*

Kim Yuk was undaunted by this kind of conservative opposition. In late 1654, he tried to spread the use of cash by requiring it for *taedong* tax payments for the upland districts of Ch'ungch'ŏng Province. Although many residents of the area complained about the tax, Kim noted that the tax should not have caused them too much suffering because the *taedong* tax was only two *p'il* of cloth per *kyŏl* of land when the peasants wove the cloth themselves. On the other hand, those who could not weave cloth had to buy cloth on the market, and during a bumper crop year when the price of rice declined because of oversupply, it could cost them over twelve *mal* of rice just for one *p'il* of cloth. This situation indeed caused them hardship, but it could be remedied if cash were used to pay the tax.

Kim proposed that the magistrates of the twenty-odd upland districts of Ch'ungch'ŏng should collect copper scrap from the people or save on office expenditures to buy copper and other metals to engage in minting of cash. Even if not enough cash were minted to replace cotton cloth for the payment of all the *taedong* tax, it might be possible for them to pay anywhere from one-third to one-half of the tax and reduce the cost of transporting cloth bolts. Anticipating that a royal command to order all magistrates to mint cash would undoubtedly elicit protest, he suggested that only those magistrates who agreed with the policy would be asked to mint cash; no force would be used to pressure magistrates to do so against their will.

Kim was aware that appreciation in the price of cloth or depreciation in the value of grain could lead to an increase in the tax burden on taxpayers who did not weave cloth themselves, but he naïvely assumed that metallic cash would provide a stable medium for the payment of taxes on the assumption that it would not vary in value like cloth and grain did. As we will see, he believed that the government could set the exchange rates or relative prices between silver, cash, grain, and cloth without fear that market forces might undermine the fixed rates. Unfortunately, fluctuation in the value of coins because of a number of factors including supply, demand, and debasement was one of the major problems in the history of metallic currency in China. Kim was so anxious to introduce copper cash into the economy that he did not anticipate the problems that might arise from a flood of cash on the market from unrestricted minting, not to mention the possibility of counterfeiting and adulteration by private parties. These were not problems that Kim had to face in 1654, but they did appear by the end of the century.

Kim also said that he had been encouraged by success in the use of cash in the capital. Already 10 to 20 percent of tribute payments to capital bureaus were being paid in cash, and he anticipated that before long the amount would rise to 50 percent. Although minting had been ordered for Kyŏngsang Province and then suspended, he had also heard that the current governor was minting cash again, thanks to Kim's own encouragement. Since the king had already permitted private minting, there should be no obstacle to his encouraging magistrates to engage in minting as well. He suggested that cash be used along major thoroughfares in Chŏlla and Kyŏngsang provinces and that capital bureaus use cash to make purchases of their needs in cash as well. Once again, Kim's enthusiasm for the success of his plan to monetize the Korean economy led him to approve minting by private parties and local officials, another measure that was roundly criticized in the Chinese literature because it stimulated an excessive increase in the money supply in addition to the loss of control over the manufacture of standardized coins that could win public confidence.

Kim had already discussed the issue with Minister of Taxation Yi Sibang, who agreed with the idea of having the Ever-Normal Bureau buy scrap copper with its silver and cloth reserves, hire men to cut wood for fuel, and pay wages to vagrants to go to work minting cash. By this means it would be possible to supply raw materials and labor without burdening government finances for minting twenty or thirty thousand strings of cash, and it would obviate the need for importing cash from Liao-tung or Shen-yang.

In other words, sensitive to the criticism of Yi Kyŏngyŏ and others that cash should not be forced on either officials or the people, Kim believed that restricting the policy only to willing magistrates, allowing the taxpayer to pay taxes in cash of stable value rather than depreciated rice, and restricting the portion of tax payment to a gradually increasing fraction of their tax quotas, would be better methods to achieve successful circulation of cash. Kim, however, was either unaware of the inflationary potential for an unchecked minting policy that would render cash less stable than grain unless carefully managed by monetary authorities, or he put it out of his mind because of his determination to introduce cash into the economy at any cost. Kim's proposal was obviously motivated by an attempt to respond to Yi Kyŏngyŏ's diatribe against a coercive policy to preserve the king's policy to introduce cash as a favored medium of exchange.[26]

Kim Yuk's Revised Regulations of 1655

Sensing that he was coming to the end of his career as well as his life, Kim tried to initiate more action to guarantee the success of the cash policy before he died. In mid-1655 Kim, now chief state councilor, obtained King Hyojong's permission to discuss revisions in cash policy with Minister of War Wŏn Tup'yo and Minister of Taxation Hŏ Chŏk.[27] Kim was then elevated to a sinecured post as director of the Agency for Royal Relatives (Tollyŏngbu Yŏngsa), and at the end of the year declared in court that he was much concerned over the failure of cash to circulate in any great quantity in the marketplace. Since Kim was not in good health, he proposed that another man who currently held no post but had been recommended to him for his capacities, Pak Susin, be given a military post of sufficient rank, appointed to the post of staff official (Nangch'ŏng) of the Ever-Normal Bureau, and put in charge of the circulation of cash as well as the activity of the markets.

Although Kim was still not entirely optimistic that revised regulations under Pak Susin's supervision would be successful because Hyojong's cash policy had been in effect for five years already without favorable results, he had discussed cash policy at length with Minister of Taxation Hŏ Chŏk and the two had submitted a revision of the regulations, but Hyojong had decided to move slowly on the proposal and eventually brought the changes to a halt. Lingering precariously on the edge between life and death, and faced with a ten-year limit that Hyojong himself had imposed on the policy, Kim's only prospect for success would come if Hyojong adopted his and Hŏ Chŏk's revised regulations, hold both of them responsible, let Pak Susin take charge of implementation, and dismiss him if he failed. Hyojong accepted Kim's advice, appointed Pak to the post of temporary tomb guardian (Ch'ambong), and passed the order to the Ever-Normal Bureau.[28]

The revised regulations provided that one *mal* of the eight *mal/kyŏl taedong* rice tax in years of normal production, or two *mal* when rice was short and too expensive would be replaced by payment in cash, an obvious benefit to the taxpayers and a real inducement to use cash. These figures do not jibe with our knowledge of the *taedong* tax rate, which varied from province to province, but in 1655 the tax rate was two *p'il* in cloth or sixteen *mal* in rice in Kyŏnggi and Kangwŏn provinces, but not in Ch'ungch'ŏng. Hence eight *mal* appears to have been the commuted rice payment for one-half of a two-*p'il* tax. Allowing one *mal* of eight *mal* to be paid in cash might indicate one-sixteenth of the overall *taedong* tax (one-fourth if two *mal* were payable in cash), a modest decrease from Hyojong's previous ruling to allow one-tenth the tax to be paid in cash.

In addition, shops would be established in Kyŏnggi as well as Hwanghae and P'yŏng'an to promote the use of cash. Half of the cloth redemption payments for punishment would be allowed by the Ministries of Taxation and Punishments, the Seoul Magistracy (Hansŏngbu), and the Slave Agency (Changyewŏn). One-fifth of the old tribute products owed to capital bureaus and one-third of the rice and cloth rations paid by the Ministries of Taxation and War for hired or service labor for the capital bureaus would also be paid in cash. Because the value of currency had been subject to fluctuations, he proposed that the government set the value of cash and rice against silver, 600 *mun* of cash equivalent to 1 *sŏm* (15 *mal*) of rice or 1 *yang* of silver. Thus, 1 *mun* of cash would be worth ¼ *toe* (or 1/40 *mal*) of rice. Finally, the government would maintain its strict prohibition against melting or converting cash to other uses.

Nonetheless, the historian who wrote the *Sillok* account inserted his own negative assessment of the reform because he noted that despite the prohibition against the melting and conversion of cash to pots, pans, and other utensils, secret smelters had already been in operation in the hills, reducing the supply of copper still further. He estimated that since the cash reserves of the Ever-Normal Bureau were all disbursed to the provinces, they amounted to less than two or three hundred thousand strings of cash, which he estimated was barely equivalent to the household property of ten *chung'in* (hereditary technical clerks) employed and living in the capital. Thus, despite Kim's claim that the currency law was not being enforced and that more detailed and harsher revisions were necessary, the *Sillok* historian inferred that the real reason for the failure of cash to circulate widely was the shortage of cash itself.

> Every time [the law] was revised, the people immediately suffered a loss in profit, and all those knowledgeable about it believed it was wrong. The king also disliked it but Kim Yuk still stubbornly defended it. Pak Susin was a rather common and inferior resident of the capital who once managed a "house" [*ŏk*, business?] by employing a number of woodcutters. Because somebody said he was

> talented and he himself claimed that if he were appointed, he could see to it that the circulation of cash would be achieved, Kim Yuk heard of it and recommended him to the court. Unfortunately, Pak got sick and died.[29]

The *Sillok* historian obviously resented Kim Yuk's choice of Pak Susin for the management of cash policy because he was a commoner who lacked an official position, and this attitude may have betrayed his own personal bias as the main reason for his opposition to the policy. The contemporary historian, Wŏn Yuhan, accepted the *Sillok* account as a completely trustworthy explanation of the reason for the failure of the cash policy and the weaknesses of Kim Yuk's character, and he also concluded that people lost confidence in cash because there was too little of it in circulation. Wŏn also found additional testimony about Kim Yuk's intractable disposition from Hyojong himself, who remarked in 1656 that Kim was "stubborn and uncompromising in nature, would never stop until completing what he wanted, and would pay no attention even though the world said he was wrong. People praised him for his strength, but those who did not share his views rejected him, and that is why most thought he was wrong."[30]

On the other hand, Wŏn omitted considering the extenuating circumstances in this case. Kim had just submitted his resignation from office because when he had been in charge of the Ever-Normal Bureau and the Office for Dispensing Benevolence, the two agencies in charge of cash and the *taedong* taxes, he had given 70 strings of cash and 2,000 *yang* of silver alloy (*paekkŭm*) to two of his clerks with dispensation to trade them for goods at a profit for the purpose of promoting the circulation of cash in Hwanghae and P'yŏng'an provinces, but the governor of Kyŏnggi Province later charged them with illegal activity and charged that they be arrested and punished. Kim offered his resignation because he took the blame for the actions of these two clerks and claimed that he was only thinking of the nation's good without a thought of the consequences. He said that his neglect was even more serious because Hyojong's decision to use cash had only then occurred and was under considerable attack, so that his mistake had threatened the success of the policy. Hyojong may well have criticized Kim's character because he felt piqued by Kim's involvement with the two clerks, but he refused either to accept Kim's resignation or order the punishment of the clerks.[31]

Furthermore, Yi Man'un, who wrote the first revision of the *Munhŏnbigo* after 1782, simply described the cash policy at this time without any negative comments about Kim Yuk or Pak Susin. He prefaced his summary of this revised legislation with a brief synopsis of the important role that Kim played in the attempt to introduce cash into Korea after his second mission to Ming China in 1650.[32]

King Hyojong's Abandonment of Copper Currency, 1656

King Hyojong himself finally decided to bring down the curtain on his attempt to circulate cash in 1656 because he thought that the economic burden imposed on the Ever-Normal Bureau to provide the initial capital for financing the minting of cash was causing the bankruptcy of that agency. Since the government would have recouped its initial expenditures by using the cash that it minted by paying bills, the basic problem may have been the shortage of capital in government hands. Yi Sibang told Hyojong that the Ever-Normal Bureau had been loaning out a stock of 20,000 *sŏm* of grain at 10 percent interest to collect 2,000 *sŏm* (per year) income, but it was not even enough to pay for the expenses for one Ch'ing ambassador's stay in Korea. Despite the shortage in the bureau's funds, it had also granted a thousand *sŏm* of grain to the merchants and people of the city but had still not received repayment (in cash).

Hyojong replied that it was his cash policy that had led to a gradual loss of state finances, and that unless he could think of some way to solve the problem, the only alternative left was for him to order an end to the use of cash immediately. Yi Sibang told him that Kim Yuk himself really was not aware of how difficult it was to keep cash in circulation, particularly since last year's revision to collect part of the *taedong* tax in Kyŏnggi Province had been suspended, and there were no (cash?) funds to pay the tribute masters (*kongmul chuin*). Hyojong remarked that it was already too late to remedy the situation and asked how many years his cash policy had been in effect.

The chief royal secretary (Tosŭngji), Chŏng Ch'ihwa, replied that it had been in operation for six years. Even though the original purpose of the law was to increase state revenues and provide benefits to the people, most people were opposed to it, and it was hard to maintain cash in circulation. Hyojong then concluded that since the six years of his cash policy had been worthless and state finances had been drained, presumably by honoring cash payments for taxes and penalties, the time had come to abolish cash.

The Border Defense Command claimed that it had opposed the use of cash ever since the policy was first adopted because it would be too hard to achieve successful circulation, but for the first three years of the policy everyone's objections had been overridden by the defense of the "great minister" (*taesin*), obviously Kim Yuk. After the third year, they were able to obtain Hyojong's promise to limit the experiment to a decade, but they kept silent from that time on even though they were convinced that the public was opposed to it. Now that Yi Sibang had reported what was happening, they were convinced that the "great official in charge" (*chugwan-daesin*) must have realized that cash was never going to circulate. Hyojong now felt he had full support for his decision to abolish the use of cash. Simultaneously he ordered that all rice that had been paid or loaned out for cash recently be repaid in rice instead of cash.[33]

Yi Man'ŭn's Evaluation of Kim Yuk's Cash Policy

Yi Man'ŭn chose to embellish his treatment of Hyojong's final decision to end his experiment with copper currency in his account in the revised edition of the

Munhŏnbigo in the 1780s by quoting the remarks of Kim Yuk, who recounted his lifetime experience in spearheading the movement to introduce copper cash into Korea beginning with his first trip to China as an envoy in 1636. He remarked that Kim was overwhelmed by the level of Chinese civilization at the time and had tried to recommend the adoption of both cash and wagons. On his way back from a second mission to China, Kim sent in another memorial from Shen-yang in Manchuria again requesting the adoption of cash, but without success. Later, while magistrate in Kaesŏng, he was inspired by the active circulation of cash in the area but failed to gain adoption of his recommendation to spread its use throughout Hwanghae and P'yŏng'an provinces. In 1650, on the way to China again, he sent another request from Pyongyang, and when he arrived in Beijing used his travel funds to buy 150,000 *mun* of cash. On the way back he heard in Ŭiju that the court had accepted his recommendation, and he distributed the cash to the districts along the coastal route, but the measure did not succeed in stimulating widespread circulation.

In the spring of 1651, when he first became a member of the highest councilors of state, the whole population was still using the cheap rough cloth (*ch'up'o*) for currency, and even though Hyojong prohibited its use, it continued. Because he thought that if cash were legally introduced, the use of cloth would stop on its own, he requested that cash be minted and that old, cheap *Wan-li* coins be purchased from the Liao-tung area of Manchuria. This coin was lower in value than the *T'ien-ch'i* and *Ch'ung-chen* coins, but when they were brought into Korea they were mixed with newer Korean minted coins and circulated with them. Within a year, this cash had begun to circulate in Hwanghae and P'yŏng'an provinces until opposition to it arose at court in 1652 before circulation had had a chance to spread widely. Finally Hyojong decided to adopt Yi Sibang's recommendation to abolish it in the ninth month of 1657.[34]

The simplicity of Yi's laconic description of these events was by no means a neutral recitation of the facts. His main point was that Hyojong had finally understood what Kim had been advocating for fifteen years, that copper currency would prove enormously beneficial to the economy and help Korea catch up to the level achieved by Ming China. Converting the Korean population to appreciation of cash would take some time, but signs of success had been achieved within a year after Hyojong's adoption of the policy in 1651. What stopped the signs of initial success was the protest of court officials.[35]

Wŏn Yuhan's Explanation for the Failure of Cash Policy

The contemporary scholar Wŏn Yuhan, however, has chosen to assign a modicum of responsibility to Kim Yuk and Hyojong for the failure to achieve success in the circulation of cash. Kim Yuk had advocated methods too rash and radical, and King Hyojong had supported the use of cash only because he wanted to raise funds for a military campaign of revenge against the Manchus. Kim was inspired by the use of cash in Ming China and thought that its circulation in

Kaesŏng proved that it not only could but had to happen in Korea as well, but because of his strong convictions and stubborn personality, he refused to listen to any objection to his methods. Hyojong was also at fault for attempting to force cash on the population when the economy was not ready for it because he believed it would increase government revenues. In fact, Wŏn argued that the failure of this radical approach to cash, the abolition of copper currency as legal tender, and the reversion to cheap cloth as a medium of exchange after 1657 even "dulled or repressed" the circulation of currency where it had already progressed, in Kaesŏng, Anju, and Pyongyang.

Nonetheless, Wŏn did not think that Kim's rashness and stubborness was the main reason for the demise of Hyojong's cash policy in 1657. Commerce and industry had been repressed by traditional respect for agriculture and disdain for less productive or nonproductive occupations like commerce or nonagricultural industries. The yangban ruling class based its wealth on land and agriculture and objected to both commerce and currency because the emergence of a wealthy commercial or industrial class would pose a threat to the security of their own political and social dominance. They feared that economic changes through commerce might destroy the social order and forced them to drop to the level of the despised commoners.

Wŏn may have been right in concluding that the use of cash did not derive from any natural or direct demand arising from economic development in the Korean economy. Despite the arguments of several economic historians that increases in agricultural production had led to a surplus over the consumption of a growing population, the economy remained primarily agricultural and surplus production was subjected to the constraints of periodic drought and flood as well as population pressure. Industry remained confined to handicrafts without any advance to factory production, and commercial activity had not developed sufficiently to require metallic cash as a medium of exchange. There was not sufficient demand to stimulate the mining of copper and other metals. Even the mining of gold and silver had been repressed after the government obtained an exemption from Ming demands for tribute in those precious metals because they were in such short supply. To retain the exemption, the government probably repressed active mining operations. When the government did attempt to mine more copper and other metals, it was hampered by backward technology, irrational methods of management, scattered locations of mining sites, and poor transportation.

Wŏn also argued that the primary reason for the failure of cash policy by 1656 and further constraints on expanding the supply of cash after it was again legalized in 1678 was the shortage of copper in Korea. Imports of copper from Japan did increase the supply but the government was reluctant to increase her dependency on Japan by expanding those imports. The only alternatives left were to break up metal utensils to extract the copper, import cheap cash from China, and permit private minting of coins, measures of only temporary effectiveness. The amount of cheap cash that could be imported from China was limited in quantity because it had to be done in nominal violation of Chinese law against its export to foreign countries. Decentralizing authority over minting by permitting local officials and private persons to mint cash was a policy error. The central government should have retained control over minting as it had done in the past, probably because debasement or counterfeiting would have destroyed the attempt to build confidence in the cash. The ordinary people never conceived of copper cash as having any value greater than its intrinsic metallic value, and brassware craftsmen melted cash down to get the raw material for making their products because they would be more valuable.

Wŏn also argued that the lack of development of the market and the lack of demand for metallic currency was also produced by damage to the basic production of agriculture and other commodities by the Japanese invasions of 1592–98 and the two Manchu invasions of 1627 and 1637. The government's policy to adopt copper cash in 1625 and again in 1633 was brought to a halt by the latter two of those invasions. The vacillation of the government in promoting the use of cash, as well as in adopting the *taedong* reform or the *hop'ae* household registration system, must have created doubts in the mind of the public about its commitment to the use of cash as legal tender. Wŏn also blamed the high ministers of state for their contentious opposition to the government's cash policy, but despite the failure of that policy by 1657, Wŏn was willing to concede that the experience gained in attempting to circulate cash into the economy brought Korea to a higher stage of economic development and laid the foundation for a more successful effort after 1678.[36]

Wŏn's interpretation that the efforts of Kim Yuk, Hyojong, and other officials to introduce copper cash into the Korean economy failed because the king finally decided to withdraw cash from circulation in 1657 was excessively negative. The evidence that appeared after the reinstitution of cash in 1678 indicates that the circulation of cash continued in the private economy even after the government stopped accepting cash for tax payments and suspended minting by government agencies. It is difficult to fault the advocates of copper cash and paper money in the Chosŏn period because they used the best methods they could devise in the hope of introducing cash and other modes of currency into the economy. A number of kings and officials attempted repeatedly to introduce currency throughout the fifteenth and early sixteenth centuries. Kings Injo and Hyojong as well as Kim Yuk and others were thoroughly convinced of the importance of bringing the Chosŏn economy at least to the level achieved in Ming China. While it may be true that the policy proved extremely difficult because the level of commercial activity had dropped below what had been achieved in the late Silla and Koryŏ dynasties, it would be difficult to argue that there was a total lack of progressive leadership in the seventeenth century, let alone the fifteenth. It would therefore be mistaken to believe that progressive support for the adoption of cash could only have originated in the writings of a few nascent scholars of Practical Learning in this period because, as we will see, inspiration for this policy came from active officials like Kim Yuk and kings like Hyojong, and the scholars derived inspiration from the arguments of these men.

CONCLUSION

In Korea higher levels of trade and the use of supposedly more advanced forms of currency than bolts of cloth or bags of grain had been achieved earlier in the Silla and Koryŏ periods. After copper cash had largely disappeared from Korean markets by the mid-sixteenth century, a number of officials were inspired to reintroduce it because of the example of the more advanced and prosperous late Ming economy and because of the government's need for revenue. The policy was supported by Kings Injo and Hyojong and a number of officials in addition to Kim Yuk, but it was not easily sustained because of the public's mistrust of cash and of government officials, who often used illogical and coercive means to enforce its use. At times the policy was reversed because of the disruption caused by the Manchu invasions, which caused the population to question the seriousness of the government's commitment to the permanent use of cash, and its penalizing of those who had begun to use it. Since the supply of copper was such a crucial drawback to the policy's success, the failure of the government to ensure a sufficient supply of cash, or copper to mint cash, to meet the needs for the payment of taxes, loans, and fines also weakened the willingness of the public to accept its use.

The record does not seem to indicate that the anti-commercial bias of Confucian thought was the main obstacle to the adoption of copper cash in the first half of the seventeenth century, despite Wŏn Yuhan's arguments to the contrary. Although many officials did argue that the peasantry was not ready to accept cash primarily because they were happy with a subsistence level of consumption, had nothing but simple needs, and did not need or want copper cash, in my view they did so because of what they perceived to be the state of mind among the peasantry. It is certainly not clear that the interests of the landlords, whether yangban or commoner, would have been adversely affected by the introduction of copper coinage into the economy, because as moneylenders and creditors they could easily have profited as much from loans of cash as loans of grain.

When King Hyojong abandoned the attempt to introduce cash into Korea in 1657, it did not mean the failure of the effort, merely its postponement. After minting was resumed in 1681, cash became a permanent feature of the economy, and part of the reason was that the use of cash in some parts of the economy continued even after minting had been suspended in 1657. One must assume that there had been a sufficient increase in the volume of internal trade to sustain the use of cash and the demand for more of it in the leading commercial areas to ensure its acceptance after 1681.

Yu Hyŏngwŏn, who was probably working assiduously on his masterwork in the period after King Hyojong's decision to cease more minting of cash, was greatly influenced by Kim Yuk's heroic efforts to introduce copper cash into the Korean economy, and he became intimately involved in what had become a national debate over the issue. When he presented his views on currency in his masterwork, he did so in the hope that they might have some influence on the consequences by recommending measures that would ensure the success of Kim Yuk's goals. Even though his ideas did not penetrate the higher levels of the government and society until the middle of the eighteenth century, he did his best to apply the lessons of history to a program geared toward the use of copper cash, and by anticipating some of the problems that might occur once cash became a part of the Korean economy, he provided an alternative plan to the policies that were adopted after 1681.

CHAPTER 24

Yu Hyŏngwŏn's Analysis of Currency

"Why currency does not circulate is not because it cannot do so; it is only because the people do not use it."[1]

In his usual fashion, Yu Hyŏngwŏn sought to ground his policy recommendations for money on a thorough study of the history of currency since early Chou times, but it would be naïve to assume that Yu was conducting an inductive study to discover whether currency was truly beneficial or harmful to the Korean economy. We cannot be certain exactly when Yu wrote his essay, but it is safe to assume that he was aware of the general outlines of Kim Yuk's campaign to introduce currency into Korea against great odds. In my view, he must have been aware that King Hyojong had supported Kim in this effort from 1651 to 1656. Since the king had made no effort to resume the policy of monetizing the Korean economy after 1656, the main issue after that date was whether Kim Yuk's policy was right or wrong. As we will soon see, Yu Hyŏngwŏn had obviously decided for himself that Kim Yuk was on the right track. He may have reached that decision based on his study of the classics and the Chinese historical experience, but I suspect that he mined those resources to reinforce the conclusion he had drawn from observing the Korean experience with cash in his own time.

Yu found that the Chinese had a long history of metallic currency, but the record by no means demonstrated unmitigated success in the utility of metallic cash in all periods. It was, of course, of crucial importance to Yu to find whether the sages of antiquity cast their favor on currency or not, but it was also important to determine whether currency had proved to be an unmitigated blessing after the decline from perfection that accompanied the fall of the Chou dynasty. During the Han dynasty, metallic cash grew tremendously along with the expansion of the empire, and that growth carried with it more complex problems in the use and regulation of cash than had existed in classical times. But after the fall of the Han, and particularly the "barbarian" incursions into north China in the fourth century, the use of cash declined and even disappeared from the market in many areas in a fashion that was similar to the situation in medieval Europe after the fall of the Roman Empire.

The disappearance of cash and the reversion to a more primitive economy based on either barter or the use of grain and cloth (silk or ramie) as media of exchange provided historical material for a comparison between cash and noncash economies in Chinese history. Not surprisingly, there were two points of view on this question: that the Chinese cash experience had been either disadvantageous or downright evil, or that the use of grain and cloth as media of exchange presented even more problems than the use of metallic cash, proving that with all its drawbacks it was far better than grain and cloth as a medium of exchange and indispensable to the free circulation of goods if not the growth of production and wealth.

As things turned out, the reunification of China under the Sui and T'ang dynasties after the late sixth century was accompanied by an economic resurgence and the remonetization of the Chinese economy as a whole. In the subsequent period covered by Yu from the Sui to the late Ming, the problems that emerged in a Chinese economy that was far more developed than seventeenth-century Korea provided a textbook account of methods of money management. Many of the problems associated with currency in the later Chinese dynasties were only repetitions of those that had occurred in the Han.

The effort to reintroduce cash into Korea in the seventeenth century after a hiatus of a half-century or more resembled most closely that period in Chinese history when metallic cash disappeared from Chinese markets particularly in the north, during the Northern and Southern dynasties from the early fourth through the late sixth centuries. What this meant was that the problems associated with the Chinese economy during the periods of its greatest advancement and monetization, like the T'ang, Sung, and Ming, was less relevant to Korean needs than the situation of north China in the late fifth century. What Yu wanted to find out primarily was whether a country was better off with or without metallic cash. What would happen after cash was fully incorporated into the economy was still interesting from an intellectual standpoint, but it was a problem that was not that relevant to the situation in Yu's own time.

Kim Yuk's attitudes toward cash discussed in the last chapter provide a useful illustration to this question. Since Kim was the leading agent of the movement to introduce cash in the face of inertia and opposition, he ignored what could have been the serious consequences of unrestrained minting, debasement, counterfeiting, fluctuations in the value of rice and cloth as well as money itself, and the oversupply of money in the economy. Yu Hyŏngwŏn also had to face the question of whether Korea would be better off with metallic cash, but he was also a scholar who had the advantage of detachment and perspective that Kim lacked. He could therefore work out a policy to deal not only with the introduction of cash, but the creation of stable prices and equitable taxes once that cash had become a medium of exchange, albeit not the only medium of exchange.

CURRENCY IN CHINA

The Sages Sanction Currency

Yu must have been overjoyed to discover that the Great Plan (*hung-fan*) in the *Book of History* proposed to King Wu by the venerable Kija (Ch'i-tzu in Chinese), a Korean culture hero as well as a Chinese sage, had proclaimed that the terms *shih* and *hua* (*sik* and *hwa* in Korean), usually translated into English as food and money, were fundamental to the economy of a sage ruler. *Hua* was defined as means of exchange, "things like gold, knives, cash, and cowry shells that were used to distribute profit and circulate goods, both of which were the basis for providing livelihood to the people." According to the "Treatise on Food and Money" of the *History of the Han Dynasty* (*Han-shu*), cowry shells were purportedly the main form of currency until the Grand Duke (T'ai-kung) Lü Shang, an acquaintance of King Wen, the father of the founder of the Chou empire (B.C. 1122), minted the first form of metallic currency called the *huan-fa* to replace cowry shells, and established an agency (Chou-fu) to handle the administration of cash.[2] Only one type of currency was presumably used until King Ching (r. B.C. 544–520) presumably minted a coin called large cash (*ta-ch'uan*), probably a larger coin to circulate along with the earlier, smaller cash.[3]

The *Rites of Chou* also claimed that the Chou state had set up several agencies for regulating markets and currency. The Wai-fu or Outer Agency acted as the treasury for currency outside the capital, handled the receipt of taxes and expenditure of funds in currency, and paid for the expenses of the officials, rites, entertainment of foreign guests or envoys, funerals, field training for the army, and imperial progresses. The Ch'uan-fu (Currency Agency) took charge of collecting market taxes in cash and buying unsold goods that had been accumulating on the market, functioning presumably to stabilize prizes by intervening in purchase and supply operations. Yu provided additional reinforcement from post-classical times by citing his favorite Ming scholar, Ch'iu Chün, who praised cash because it was easier to move around than large and heavy items and stimulated the circulation of goods, and also because small coins allowed the determination of minute differences in prices.

The Ssu-shih (Market Agency) of the Chou era also regulated the boundaries and shop sites for the permanent market, decided which shops would market which goods, set fair prices for goods, prohibited the circulation of luxury items, and ensured the circulation of both goods and money. It also intervened in the market to mitigate the effects of economic disasters. During a poor harvest or famine it would aid the merchants and the consumers by suspending market taxes on shops and counteracting the high prices of food and goods by minting more cash.[4]

The thrust of Yu's message here was that metallic cash had been invented at the beginning of the first millennium B.C. in China and was successfully supported by the state's use of cash to collect taxes and pay salaries and other expenses. The rulers also took responsibility for regulating the organization of markets by licensing specific merchants to sell certain goods, setting fair prices, and buffering prices by actively intervening with state reserves of cash and commodities in market transactions. Not only was Yu pointing out that Korea was almost three millennia behind the ancient example of the successful use of cash in the economy, but that the fundamental methods for introducing cash into the Korean economy were already delineated in ancient Chinese texts.

Yu commented that regulations for cash dovetailed with the well-field system of Chou, which meant that cash did not interfere with the primacy of agricultural production. Not only were peasants granted the means to earn a living but shopkeepers and merchants were given an area to conduct business so that "the people of the four occupations [officials, farmers, artisans and merchants] would each obtain a place [*samin kaktŭk kiso*]." Cash was used as a means of measuring the value of goods, and the merchants performed the task of circulating money. The merchants were indispensable to general economic welfare because they had to prosper before sufficient goods could be exchanged to guarantee the flow of currency, and the flow of currency was necessary for supplying food to the people in a period of famine and shortage.

Yu indicated that cash had been more useful than grain or cloth as a medium of exchange because the state could choose to mint more cash in an emergency simply by an expenditure of labor; the supply of cash did not fluctuate like grain supplies, which depended on weather conditions. He also found another late Chou source, the *Kuan-tzu*, that illustrated another advantage of currency – providing relief to the starving. It stated that the founders of the Hsia and Shang dynasties of the late third and mid-second millennia B.C., Yu and T'ang, had mined gold and minted gold currency to save the common people from starvation during famines caused by drought and flood, not because currency represented an article of consumption that could feed or clothe people, but because its supply could determine the prices of things and the government could lower prices by putting more currency into circulation. It was for that reason that the ancients commonly referred to money as "the scale" (*heng*) because it could raise or lower prices.[5]

Currency Problems after the Fall of the Chou

Debasement, Private Minting, and Counterfeiting. Unfortunately, as Wang Ch'eng explained in the early sixth century, the centralized regulation of currency described in the *Rites of Chou* and the uniform cash standard of that period had been lost by the Ch'in unification. There were so many types of coins that trading across provincial boundaries was sometimes stopped because districts refused to accept strange coins.[6]

The ability of money to raise or lower prices depended as much on the money supply as the quantity of goods for sale in the marketplace, for an imbalance in that relationship could result in either inflation or deflation. In addition, the ability of money to act as a stabilizing influence over prices depended on public confidence in the value of the coins in circulation. In a period when paper money and bills of exchange had yet to make their appearance in market transactions, the public was usually suspicious of any coins whose intrinsic value was markedly less than the value of the metal used to make them plus the cost of production. On the other hand, problems in public confidence might occur if the minters of coins debased their intrinsic value by using cheaper metals in the alloys or cut the weight of the coin.

During the Ch'in dynasty (255–206 B.C.) the government minted the *pan-liang* or "half-*liang*" cash, but in the Han dynasty (after 206 B.C.) the government abandoned the Ch'in coin and minted lightweight cash that rapidly lost value and caused inflation, driving the price of a picul (*shih, sŏk*) of rice up to ten thousand pieces of cash. The problem of inflation was solved in 175 B.C. when another "half-*liang*" coin was minted that actually weighed 4 *shu* (1/6 *liang*). Even though the actual weight of the coin (2/12 *liang*) was less than the face value (6/12 *liang*), it was probably close enough to restore some confidence in the ability of the coin to retain its value. In other words, minting debased cash or too much cash could be just as disastrous as not having enough of it.[7]

Chia I: State Control over Minting. Counterfeiting was another factor that resulted in the debasement of currency and an unwanted increase in the money supply. It had been prohibited in Han times, but because ordinary persons were allowed to mint cash privately, the control over the content of cash was less than perfect. Chia I of Emperor Wen's reign (180–157 B.C.) in the Former Han dynasty held that counterfeiting and debasement of the coinage could not be stopped as long as private minting was allowed. He explained that the government allowed private minters to alloy copper with tin, but prescribed a punishment of branding on the face for the use of any alloys with lead, zinc, or iron. The punishment, however, could not deter the crime because the potential for profit was too great. The state did not have the capacity to monitor what had been granted as a legal occupation to everyone, and punishment for such an easy violation was tantamount to entrapment of ordinary persons.

He also pointed out that because the state had not been able to guarantee a uniform weight and quality of all cash in circulation in every region, people refused to accept cash that was not common to their own area. The plethora of different coins merely created confusion in the markets while the profits from private minting or counterfeiting only increased the number of copper miners, reduced the number of productive peasants, and damaged the standard of honesty among the general population.

Chia I's warning was quite relevant to Korea in the 1650s because King Hyojong had permitted private minting and Kim Yuk had even urged more of it to ensure a sufficient cash supply for the cash-short Korean economy. Had cash been accepted by the Korean population, Korea might have been forced to confront either a debasement of the currency or an oversupply of money and price inflation almost immediately, but she was spared this difficulty because the king decided to withdraw cash from circulation.

Despite the problems of private minting and debasement, however, Chia I did not call for the *permanent* withdrawal of cash from the marketplace. On the contrary, he argued that prohibiting the private minting of cash was also fraught with difficulty because it would reduce the supply of cash and increase the value of coins remaining in circulation, enticing more counterfeiters to risk even greater profits. The state could increase its laws and prohibitions and decapitate counterfeiters by the dozen without bringing an end to the practice. In the end, the only solution to counterfeiting and private minting was not only for the state to prohibit minting of coins, but also to collect all available coins in circulation, and return all the private minters to agriculture. The circulation of adulterated coins would cease, and trust and confidence could be restored to the people once the state gained exclusive control over the minting process.

Rather than assume that metallic currency might be replaced by another medium of exchange or barter, he apparently supposed that after the government had collected all outstanding coins, it could recirculate them and use them to regulate grain and commodity prices by buying and selling goods on the market. The only one who could become rich from this system was the government, while the "persons engaged in the lesser occupations" – not only merchants and artisans but presumably counterfeiters and profiteers as well – would have a hard time making a living. In effect, cash would remain legal tender but its volume would be restricted to the amount possessed or disbursed by the government, as if greedy men and ex-counterfeiters would have permanently abandoned the opportunity for profiteering by minting debased coins.

Chia I then argued that the surplus cash generated by monetary retrenchment could then be given as gifts to the hated Hsiung-nu, the nomads who constantly raided the Chinese frontier, to destroy their society by enticing their own people to engage in the nonproductive and contemptible struggle for profits that was then plaguing Han society. Chia I's lesson for policy planners was not an optimistic view that cash or unrestrained free market activities were beneficial, but a livid fear of the capacity of money to induce illegal and immoral behavior, and of private minting and adulterated coinage to wreak inflationary havoc. Cash might have been a necessity, but its misuse had to be checked by state control over the money supply and commodity prices.[8]

Yu also cited another Former Han statesman, Chia Shan, who shared a pessimistic view about the deleterious effects of private minting and private control of cash, but from a slightly different perspective. Chia Shan told Emperor Wen that although cash had no utility in itself, it could be transformed into "wealth and nobility," which situation posed a danger to the ruler of a state because private parties would have the power to enrich and ennoble themselves irrespective of the ruler's wishes. Since control over wealth and nobility was the means by which the ruler of the state held power, he should not allow any private parties the ability to create their own independent wealth.

Emperor Wen ignored the advice, and his neglect only exacerbated the problem. The plutocrat Wu Wang-bi not only earned enough money by minting cash to match the emperor's own treasury, but he rebelled against the throne. Teng T'ung spent forty years accumulating a greater fortune by mining and minting more cash than what Emperor Wu (r. 140–87 B.C.) possessed when he came to the throne. Although Teng did not rebel, he set a bad example for district magistrates who sought to increase their depleted funds by establishing mints in the mountains themselves. Since other private persons also engaged in counterfeiting, the net increase in the money supply reduced the value of the coinage and created commodity price inflation.[9]

Han Wu-ti and Uncontrolled Minting. The expansion of the money supply by uncontrolled minting and counterfeiting reached a crisis point in the reign of Emperor Wu, and in 118 B.C. he adopted measures that appeared similar to Chia I's proposal except that they were accompanied by the mailed fist of the state. He minted the new five-*shu* coin that was more difficult to counterfeit because it was heavier in weight than the current coin and had a rim around the edge and a design on the face. As the conqueror of vast territories, however, he was unwilling to leave the fate of the money supply to chance, so he prohibited private minting, executed as many as twenty or thirty thousand counterfeiters unmercifully, and terrorized hordes of small counterfeiters into confessing their crimes in advance to obtain pardons. He created three officials under the office of the Imperial Forest Park (Shang-lin-yüan) who controlled all the cash of the empire and gave them the exclusive right to mint cash, and he ordered that all previous coins be melted down. The cost of minting the new coin was so high relative to the nominal value of the coin that none but a few skilled craftsmen could profit from counterfeiting. As we will see, the elements of Emperor Wu's policy made a lasting impression on Yu Hyŏngwŏn: the application of technological skill to create well-made coins difficult to copy, severe punishment for counterfeiters and private minters, and the minting of a coin that allowed no profit for counterfeiters.[10] What Yu learned from the literature on the Han dynasty was, therefore, not that cash was an abomination that had better be abolished or that its use created insoluble problems, but that the assertion of control by the ruler backed by coercion could bring all anomalies under control.

Copper Cash over Cloth and Grain

Ch'iu Chün and Kung Yu's Obscurantism. On the other hand, despite Emperor Wu's Draconian solution to the problems of monetary debasement, excessive money supply and inflation continued past his death, and a new group of moralists emerged who demanded the abolition of cash because it was the source of immorality. To illustrate this view Yu cited the opinion of Kung Yu in the reign of Emperor Yüan of the Han dynasty (r. 48–32 B.C.), who believed that cash itself had stimulated peasants to abandon agriculture for the prospect of filling their own private treasuries to the brim with their cash profits from commerce. He proposed that the emperor outlaw cash as legal tender, abolish Emperor Wu's agencies in charge of minting cash, and decree that cloth and grain would henceforth replace metallic cash as the main media of exchange. The emperor ignored the proposal when Kung Yu's opponents argued that trade currently depended on the circulation of cash, and that cloth could not be readily subdivided into smaller units for small transactions.[11]

Yu Hyŏngwŏn was only too happy to introduce into his essay a rebuttal of Kung Yu's bias against cash written by one of his favorite Ming dynasty authorities, Ch'iu Chün, who pointed out that cloth and grain were simply no match for the convenience of metallic coins as a medium of exchange. He also quoted K'ung Lin of the Chin dynasty (late third century A.D.) who praised the sages of antiquity for having chosen materials that were of no value as articles of consumption to function as media of exchange for goods that had some utility. Not only were they able to avoid wasting useful goods for the function of transaction exchange, but by using items that were smaller and lighter in weight than bolts of cloth and bags of grain they also economized on transportation costs. In addition, dividing up bolts of cloth or bags of grain into small parts to cover small transactions was just too difficult and burdensome to be practical. In any case, if the people had attempted to substitute cloth and grain for cash, the officials at the time would not have allowed it.[12]

Ch'iu Chün, of course, was living in the midst of the cash economy of the Ming dynasty when arguments in favor of the preferability of grain and cloth over cash (let alone silver in the bimetallic currency system of China in the sixteenth century) as media of exchange must have appeared like an exercise in obscurantism. Yu Hyŏngwŏn used Ch'iu to counter the obscurantists in Korean society who wanted to prevent progress to the level of the Han or Sui dynasties, let alone the sixteenth-century Ming dynasty.

Ts'ao P'i's Reversion to Grain and Cloth. Kung Yu, of course, launched his attack on cash in the middle of the Han dynasty when the amount of cash in circulation had reached unprecedented heights, but after the Han dynasty fell the commercial situation deteriorated markedly with deleterious effects on the role of metallic cash in the economy. Yu recounted how Ts'ao P'i, who established the Wei dynasty in northeast China in 220, abolished the five-*shu* cash and allowed only grain and cloth to be used as media of exchange. This policy failed not simply because using grain and cloth meant that items of consumption had to be withdrawn from the market to function as currency, but because bags of grain could be debased by sprinkling water over them to increase their weight, or bolts of silk cloth by reducing the number of warp threads in the weave. For these reasons grain and cloth were abandoned, and at the suggestion of Ssu-ma Chih the five-*shu* coin was minted again and continued into the Chin dynasty (Western Chin, 265–317; Eastern Chin, 317–420).

The debate over the advantages of cash versus grain and cloth was continued in the Chin dynasty when Hsüan Hsüan (during the period from 397 to 419) proposed to abolish cash. Yu cited the rebuttal of K'ung Lin that money had been no less important than food in the Great Plan of antiquity because of its necessary function as a medium of exchange. He was willing to concede that if the peasants were, in fact, devoting all their time to the production of coins, it would be justified to abolish its use, but he argued that in fact the peasants were keeping to agriculture, and the artisans were engaged in making utensils even with cash in the economy. The rulers maintained control over currency to maintain the exchange of goods, and the use of coins reduced transportation costs in exchange transactions and allowed more grain and cloth to be consumed. "This was why cash carried on the tradition established by the use of tortoise and cowry shells [in ancient times] and has never been abolished since."

Yu also quoted Chung Yu, who had also argued that grain and cloth were by no means superior to cash as media of exchange because both those materials could be debased as easily as metallic cash. He asserted that the adulteration of grain and cloth was so pronounced in the Wei dynasty that severe punishments were useless in controlling it, and cash areas seemed to prosper over regions that used grain and cloth for money. Because of the adverse affects of the replacement of cash with grain and cloth in Emperor Ming's era (227–40) almost everyone at court favored the restoration of cash, and the emperor approved it.[13]

Further corroboration to this point of view was provided by Chuang Kuei, a regional official on the western frontier of the Western Chin dynasty, who established a base where Kansu Province is today from 306 to his death in 314. Governing an area where the barbarian invasions had set the economy back to a more primitive level, Chuang was able to achieve prosperity by fostering trade with non-Chinese peoples beyond the frontier, and he adopted the suggestion of his chief of staff, So Fu, to restore the use of the five-*shu* coin of the Han era to facilitate this goal.[14] Yu must have admired this account because it corroborated the view expressed in previous centuries that the minting of cash was bound to create prosperity by increasing the circulation of goods in the market.

The Spread of Copper Cash to the Barbarians. Yu also believed that an important but humiliating lesson for the Koreans of his own time was that non-Chinese peoples, usually regarded as the barbarians of the world by enlightened Confucians, had understood and mastered the use of cash as a medium of exchange, leaving the Koreans even farther behind on the scale of world development. He found references to the use of cash in the period of division after the fall of the Later Han and in several states in the so-called Western Region to the west of the Han boundary. The state of Shu (present day Szechwan) minted iron cash, and several states in the Western Region used silver cash with designs and likenesses of rulers on the face.

Yu was impressed by the widespread use of cash even beyond the confines of China, but he was not ready to admit that any and all media of exchange beyond grain and cloth were acceptable. He pointed out that iron cash had been abandoned because it was too heavy, and the paper money (*chiao-tzu*) of the Sung dynasty in the 1041–49 period was simply "evil," but he praised copper and tin for being the most suitable materials for minting cash. He lauded the Khitan, who established the Liao dynasty (tenth through early twelfth centuries) in Manchuria and northeast China, because they had "enriched their country and benefited their people" by regulating the circulation of cash.

Yu also mentioned that he had personally met some Westerners who had recently been shipwrecked in Korea and confirmed that their country, located in the western ocean generally to the south of the Western Region in proximity with the southern barbarians, was using silver and copper cash as media of exchange. Despite the garbled geographic description of the location of Holland, it appears likely that these men must have been members of the shipwrecked Dutch vessel *Sparrowhawk*, compatriots of Hendrik Hamel, who were detained as prisoners from 1653 to 1668.[15] What Yu gained from this conversation and his other research was that Korea was virtually alone in the world in its forms of currency because "throughout the world, there is no country that can not use cash."[16]

Reversion to Silk and Cloth in North China. Metallic cash disappeared from circulation in north China during the Northern Wei dynasty (424–534) until Emperor Hsiao-wen (r. 471–500) minted the *T'ai-hua* five-*shu* coin. Although minting of this coin continued in the early sixth century, cash was not used in some districts, and merchants often refused to accept it. Yu found corroboration for his view about the inferiority of grain and cloth from Wang Ch'eng in the reign of Emperor Hsiao-ming (r. 516–28), who stated that since silk and other types of cloth posed serious problems as media of exchange because bolts of cloth had to be ripped apart for small purchases, a task not easily performed and a waste of the arduous weaving women had done to make the cloth in the first place. Grain was also inconvenient because it required measures and scales to test its volume and weight. Furthermore, silk and cloth were not as useful as cash in providing relief against the vicissitudes of hunger and cold.

The situation was partially remedied when Emperor Hsiao-wen (r. 471–500) minted the *T'ai-hua* coin and another five-*shu* coin to circulate with it and prohibited all other previous forms of nonstandard, depreciated coins like the "goose-eye cash" to restore confidence in copper cash. Unfortunately, because the five-*shu* coin of the *T'ai-hua* period in the late fifth century was not backed by the kinds of regulations that would guarantee its permanence (like the five-*shu* coin of the Han dynasty), it circulated only in the capital. Wang recommended that in this situation the emperor should reinstate all existing coins except the underweight "goose eye" (*ngo-yen*) or "ring chisel" (*huan-tso*) cash as legal tender, and establish stiff penalties to stop counterfeiting and eliminate chicanery by shopkeepers in the markets.[17] In other words, even bad cash was preferable to grain and cloth as a medium of exchange, an argument that warmed Yu's heart.

Other Aberrations, Northern and Southern Dynasties

Deflation and Copper Shortage. In south China during the period of the Northern and Southern dynasties currency did not disappear, but there was a serious shortage of coins. This situation was just the opposite of the problem prevalent in the early Han dynasty, the flooding of the market with cash through private minting and the debasement of coinage – problems that Chia I had sought to remedy. Chia I, himself, had mentioned that any attempt to reduce the money supply by curtailing coinage might create a shortage of cash that would create a deflationary situation.

In the Liu-Sung dynasty in south China during the *yüan-chia* year period (424–54) officials were faced with a shortage of the recently minted four-*shu* cash in state coffers. One proposal was made to prohibit the private minting of copper cash to allow the state to monopolize the copper reserves so that it could mint the heavier five-*shu* cash, while others argued that the shortage of copper cash could be solved by melting copper utensils down for more cash. Fan T'ai objected because converting copper utensils to cash could create shortages in the goods regarded as necessities.

What Fan probably did not understand was that the shortage of copper had driven up the price of the metal beyond the face value of the coins in circulation, so that there was an economic incentive to melt cash down to copper. He reasoned that the the capacity of currency to sustain trade might not depend on the amount of cash (in circulation?) because the government could avoid a shortage of cash by maintaining what he called an "equal" circulation of it throughout the economy. He probably meant that since cash gravitated to a few urban areas or transportation routes, it left the rest of the country with a cash shortage. If that cash could be distributed more equitably throughout the country, it would enable meeting the demand for coins and stabilize prices by creating a balance between the volume of cash and the amount of goods in circulation for maintaining stable prices. It is unlikely that by "equal" circulation he meant high velocity or rapid turnover in market transactions, a concept too advanced for the time.

Fan T'ai did observe that the state would have been better off solving the copper cash shortage by using tortoise or cowry shells, as it had in ancient times, and preserve copper for the manufacture of useful products, but this was only a frivolous suggestion because no one was willing to accept cowry shells for money any longer. Despite Yu copying out Wang's point of view in his account, he did not abandon his view about the priority of copper cash.[18] As we will see later, Yu believed that increasing the supply of copper was the only means of providing the material for the minting of an adequate supply of cash that would allow the circulation of goods at stable prices.

Multiple-Denomination Coins and Avarice. Another problem that plagued theoreticians of money in the era after the fall of the Han dynasty was the appearance of the first multiple denomination coins in which the face value was far greater than the metallic value of the coin. Sun Ch'üan of the Wu dynasty in the third century A.D. minted two such coins, the 500-cash coin called the *Ta-ch'üan wu-pai*, and another 1,000-cash coin called the *tang ch'ien-ch'ien*, but the the coins failed to gain acceptance possibly because they were too valuable for most transactions, and the people had no confidence that others would honor them. Sun was forced eventually to admit failure, melt all the cash down, and reimburse all holders of the coins still in circulation.

Yu Hyŏngwŏn, however, did not accept Sun's excuse that he had simply made an error in judging popular trust in the coin. Instead he accused him of an avaricious desire to reap huge profits, violating the basic purpose of money, which was only to permit the free exchange of goods. Goods and cash were to be exchanged for amounts of "equivalent" value, and it was improper for there to be any major discrepancy between the value of a product and its price. Minting a multiple denomination coin was simply an immoral act of deception for profit with adverse consequences for his kingdom as a whole.[19]

Even though Yu had learned that sage rulers of ancient China had used objects of no value such as cowry shells as a medium of exchange, or that the use of metallic coins was preferable to rice and cloth for money because they had less utility as objects of consumption, he could not appreciate that money could function as a symbol rather than simply as a good with a value content and price. Yu could not countenance using a coin, let alone a piece of paper, to represent large units of wealth even if their symbolic use would have conferred enormous benefits by eliminating the high cost of transporting carts of cash to purchase large items. He therefore believed that multiple denomination coins (and paper money) constituted an immoral scheme to maximize profits.

Reemergence of Counterfeiting and Excess Cash. Fan T'ai of the southern Liu-Sung dynasty was also concerned about destabilizing fluctuations in the value of coins, which he attributed to the desire by counterfeiters to gain from the profits of seigniorage. Instead of reducing those profits to a minimum so that the face value of a coin would approximate its intrinsic value, the counterfeiters had adulterated their coins to increase their profits, thereby destroying public trust and confidence in the coins. He praised the policy in the Later Han dynasty during the *yüan-chia* year period (151–53) to drive counterfeiters out of business by eliminating the profits of seigniorage. They did this by minting a new four-*shu* copper coin, shaped like the older five-*shu* coin and with a raised rim, that had a face value very close to its metallic value.

Unfortunately, when another four-*shu* coin was minted in the *hsiao-chien* year period in the Liu Sung dynasty (454–56), the results were disastrous because the coin was small and light and the outer rim was poorly made. Counterfeiters had no trouble in reproducing it and compounded their transgressions by adulterating the coins with lead. Stiff penalties and even executions of corrupt officials failed to stem the practice, and commodity prices skyrocketed. Then the government responded by increasing the quality of the coin and forbidding the circulation of coins that were too small or lacked raised rims.[20]

Later during the Liu-Sung dynasty the better coins were driven off the market by cheaper ones, and the less valuable two-*shu* coin was minted. Counterfeiters had difficulty matching its weight and size, but the market was flooded by a variety of irregular coins. The oversupply of cheap cash was exacerbated around 465 when Ch'en Ching-chih obtained permission to allow private minting of cash. The private minters cut the weight and thickness of the coins so severely that some wags coined some memorable phrases in honor of the situation: that coins were so light that they floated on top of water, that you might crush them if you grabbed them too tightly, or that a string of a thousand coins took no more than three inches of space. The price of a *t'ou* of rice (*mal* in Korean) rose to 10,000 pieces of cash, and retail sales were brought to a halt because consumers did not have enough cash to make purchases.[21]

K'ung I of the Southern Ch'i dynasty (ca. 479–83) provided his explanation for the deterioration of copper currency after the mid-fifth century in the Liu Sung era. By contrast with the previous five hundred years when the five-*shu* coin of the Han had remained constant in shape, size, and weight, the government after that period was too stingy in its use of copper in casting cash and too sparing of the technology used to mint coins, primarily because they aimed to maximize the supply of coins from the available metal raw materials by making each coin smaller and lighter. Unfortunately, the government by its own minting policies only succeeded in debasing the currency and destroying its value as a medium of exchange. K'ung thought that the only solution was to return to the greater weight and higher standards of the five-*shu* coin of the Han dynasty.[22]

In short, the lessons Yu learned from the monetary experience of the Northern and Southern Dynasties period was that neither the reduction or disappearance of cash from the market (north China), nor the debasement of coins and the flooding of the market with cheap cash (south China) were desirable developments. A better way had to be found to find a stable currency.

Ch'iu Chün: Penny Cash. Yu felt that Ch'iu Chün of the Ming dynasty had found the answer to this problem. Ch'iu wrote that no one had discovered the fundamentals of creating an unchanging and permanent method for minting cash until K'ung I had warned the government against being stingy in the use of copper or sparing in the technology of manufacture (*pulsoktong pur'aegong*). Ch'iu explained that K'ung meant that the coin had to be thick and pure, the metal evenly distributed, and the outer rim round and made correctly. It should cost one piece of cash (*ch'ien*) to make one coin so that the profits for counterfeiters would be reduced to zero. In other words, the only guarantee against counterfeiting was no-profit minting, which obviously ruled out any possibility of a multiple denomination coin.

Ch'iu commented that in the history of cash in China to the mid-Ming dynasty there had been numerous small, poorly made, or underweight coins in addition to multiple denomination coins, but only the five-*shu* coin of the Han, or later the *K'ai-yüan t'ung-pao* coin of the T'ang, "hit the mark for perfection." Later multiple denomination coins like the "three-cash" or "ten-cash" soon were driven from the marketplace and only those coins minted in the fashion of the the *Ka'i-yüan* coin continued in circulation to the mid-Ming.[23] In other words, history had taught the world that there were only a few coins that had retained public confidence and prevented debasement and inflation because the face values were close to the intrinsic values and the technology of coinage was too difficult for the counterfeiters to reproduce cheaply.

Cash in the Reunified Empire

When the unified empire was restored by the Sui and T'ang dynasties in the late sixth century, the reestablishment of a single central government laid the basis for creating coinage of standard size. Yu described how Emperor Kao-tsu of the T'ang dynasty abolished the five-*shu* coin and minted the *K'ai-yüan t'ung-pao* that weighed about seven *shu* each, the coin that Ch'iu Chün had praised as having attained the standards of the five-*shu* coin of the Han dynasty.

Nonetheless, the history of cash in the T'ang was by no means free of problems. Emperor Kao-tsung was determined to prevent the reappearance of private minting that been so troublesome in the Han dynasty, and in 682 he ordered the execution by strangling of any private party who minted coins. These ruthless penalties failed to solve the problem, however, and Emperor Hsüan-tsung in 734 solicited opinions from officials about the wisdom of legalizing private minting.

Liu Chih: Price Regulation by Ever-Normal Operations. Yu reproduced only one of the opinions, that of Liu Chih, who introduced a sophisticated analysis of the effect of supply and demand on prices, and of the money supply on the value of money. He argued that if the price of agricultural products were too low, it had a damaging effect on agriculture, presumably because peasant income might be reduced below the cost of production. And if cash were too "light" (probably in weight, but also low in value), it would have hurt the income of merchants, presumably because they would have to pay higher prices for agricultural goods or commodities.

His answer to the problem of dampening the fluctuations in prices was not the untrammeled free market, but the reponsibility of the state to monitor the prices of goods and the value of currency and take steps to remedy any disequilibrium that might occur in the market. His explanation was similar to the operation of the ever-normal granary to stabilize grain prices because he reasoned that if the prices of goods rose and the value of cash declined, the cause could be attributed to a surplus of cash in the market. The government then had to devise means to collect or extract cash from the marketplace, reduce its quantity, and drive its value up. If, on the other hand, cash became too valuable, the government had to put more cash into circulation to drive its value down to some acceptable norm. These ever-normal price stabilization operations, however, would be frustrated if private persons were allowed to mint cash on their own and increase the money supply.

Liu Chih: Debasement and Private Minting. The second problem in controlling the dependability of currency was preventing the debasement of coins. Echoing the views of Chia I of the Han dynasty, Liu called for a ban on private minting as well as counterfeiting. His concern was not, however, restricted to debasement of coinage, but to the reduction of agricultural production and resulting famine and deprivation because the lure of profit from private minting would induce peasants to abandon their fields in favor of a more lucrative profession. Private minting would also exacerbate existing disparities of wealth, especially because the wealthy were the only ones who had sufficient capital to undertake private minting.

Liu Chih: Copper Restriction and Copper Price. Liu also felt that the supply of copper cash was too small and the price of raw copper too high, but he did not attribute the cause to a deficiency in copper mining, but the excessive use of copper for the manufacture of utensils, weapons, and other products. He also complained that even though more cash was being minted than ever before, the value of individual coins was too high because they weighed too much, and the raw copper cost more than the heavy copper coins were worth. Counterfeiters had been melting the heavy coins down to mint lighter ones even though this was prohibited, and enforcement was too lax to obstruct it.

Since iron was better than copper for making weapons, and lacquerware better for making utensils, he advised the emperor to prohibit the use of copper for those purposes to liberate more copper for use as cash, and drive the price of copper down. Once the price of copper was reduced, it would become unprofitable for counterfeiters to melt down heavy coins to make lighter ones, and the coinage could be stabilized once again. Liu Chih recognized fully the relationship between the supply of copper, whether in ore or copper utensils, and the value of copper cash, but it did not occur to him to economize on the cost of money either by minting multiple denomination coins or printing paper money. In any case, his ideas were opposed by all the chief officials of the T'ang court, and the emperor decided only to order the district magistrates to eliminate all debased cash.[24]

Tu Yu's Summary of Wisdom on Currency. Yu also cited Tu Yu's essay on cash in the *T'ung-tien* that surveyed developments through 756 A.D. Tu broke no theoretical ground on monetary policy, but he reinforced many of the ideas that Yu had covered in his survey of Chinese monetary history. He reinforced Liu Chih's lessons about the valuable function of money to regulate the value and distribution of goods, and the duty of the enlightened ruler to intervene in the marketplace to stabilize prices. He confirmed the beliefs of earlier statesmen and commentators that the establishment of currency or money was "profound and far-reaching" in its effects because it allowed the calculation of the value of the products of the world in terms of "number." Since gold and silver were used for utensils or jewelry and grain and cloth were too difficult to transport or subdivide, cash was the only suitable medium of exchange "because it flows and does not reside [in one place] just like a stream of water." It can be moved from one place to another, divided in parts and used for subdivisions of weight and length.

Coinage was invented by a sage, the Grand Duke (T'ai-kung) of the Chou dynasty. It was later withdrawn from circulation but reinstated in the feudal state of Ch'i. Kuan-chung praised currency because it neither added nor detracted from the supply of food and clothing, and former rulers used it to store wealth, govern the people, and pacify the world. While the wealth and prosperity, or the poverty and destitution of nations and people depended on the production of food and silk, the problems of a surplus or shortage of goods, and the inflation or deflation of prices could be controlled through ever-normal price stabilization operations – the inspiration no doubt for Liu Chih's recommendations a millennium later. As Kuan-chung had put it, cash was used to achieve a balance between extremes in prices, and Tu Yu confirmed this judgment.

Tu Yu also criticized some of the methods of rulers and statesmen in more recent times who tried to increase the supply of copper cash by economizing on the amount of copper or simplifying the technology of minting, or minting multiple denomination cash to make greater profits from seigniorage. He deplored counterfeiting and the private minting of cash, the failure of severe punishments to bring it to an end, and the loss of agricultural productivity because peasants gave up farming in the hope of making huge profits by doing it. It was necessary to adhere to the rule set down by one ancient sage that the people should not be allowed ready access to copper, and the authority to mint coins should be controlled by the ruler.[25]

Tu Yu summarized and represented a relatively conservative body of opinion on currency. He approved of cash because it was extolled by sages and worthies of the Chou period, not because it represented the tide of modern development. He feared the potential for inflation that accompanied any form of currency that inflated or misrepresented the intrinsic content of the symbol used for that currency. And he disliked the dangers implicit in free activity in the choice of occupation, particularly the presumed loss of agricultural production and loss of control over the money supply. While he deplored the use of violence as a means of coercion, he still insisted on state regulation of cash in the economy.

Government Restraint on Cash Possession: Immorality and Private Accumulation. At the end of the T'ang dynasty in the early ninth century another period of deflation in commodity prices occurred. What was interesting to Yu about this case was not so much the phenomenon of deflation, but Emperor Hsien-tsung's response to it. In 817 the emperor and his government decided that deflation had not been caused either by a drop in the supply of copper or an increase in the demand for cash that might have been a consequence of an increase in commerce, but by the hoarding of cash by wealthy individuals. Hsien-tsung assumed a self-righteous moral tone and denounced some of the regional commanders for accumulating vast fortunes in cash of a half million strings each and driving up real estate prices by their purchases of land and house sites. He was angered because wealthy merchants were justifying their own immense holdings by claiming that they had full support from the military officials, and district magistrates were unable to exercise any restraint on their control of wealth.

Hsien-tsung sought to solve the problems of cash shortage and high real estate prices at once by decreeing that no single individual from civil and military officials to commoners, merchants, innkeepers, and monks would be allowed to keep more than 5,000 strings of cash. Any commoner who had accumulated a surplus in cash was encouraged to buy goods on the market as a means of reducing their total liquid holdings, but if they violated the 5,000-string limit after the deadline, they would be executed. Officials guilty of the same crime would be exempted from execution, but they would suffer a demotion in rank.[26]

In the capitalist world of the 1980s piling up a vast fortune was seen by many as one of the happy consequences of free enterprise, and the rise of real estate values in New York, Los Angeles, Tokyo, and Seoul as an understandable though regrettable consequence of too much money chasing after limited resources. To my knowledge no one was executed for accumulating a high bank account or bidding too much for a piece of property, but in the moralistic world of the late T'ang, wealth was still a sign of the ill-gotten gains of the manipulator, the speculator, and the cheat. It was not surprising that Hsien-tsung preferred coercion and the death penalty to rectify a cash shortage rather than simply minting more cash or ordering government treasuries and bureaus to spend more cash in the market to drive prices down, especially since Tu Yu and others had already argued that intervention in ever-normal manipulation of goods and cash was one of the major duties of a responsible ruler.

Emperor Hsien-tsung was simply incapable of either separating market actions from moral implications or tinkering with the market mechanism – as Kuan-chung and Liu Chih had suggested – to remedy any imbalance by varying the supply of either metallic copper or cash. But why did Yu Hyŏngwŏn choose to include this tale in his coverage of the history of currency in China? Probably because Yu admired a display of moral fortitude by the ruler of an empire in the face of what he, too, must have agreed was an illustration of the capacity of avarice to destroy proper balance in the distribution of wealth and commercial activities.

Government Restraint on Cash Possession: Ma Tuan-lin and Limits on Cash. Emperor Hsien-tsung's attempt to force imperfect human beings into compliance with rational and moderate economic behavior, particularly by setting an upper limit on the private possession of cash, called into question the role of ruler and state as economic guide and overseer. Ma Tuan-lin, compiler of the *Wen-hsien t'ung-k'ao* in the early thirteenth century in the Southern Sung dynasty, had a more reasonable solution to the problem of avaricious private accumulation.

Ma's approach differed from Emperor Hsien-tsung because he brought a sense of historical perspective to the problem. He was aware that the ruler felt a responsibility to control and regulate the economy, but the historical situation determined the kinds of methods he should use. He believed that after the end of the Chou dynasty and the loss of the well-field system, the emperors of subsequent dynasties lost the power to control economic production and maintain equal distribution of wealth among the people. The only means they had left to achieve this was by restraining the accumulation of vast estates by limiting the maximum amount of land that any individual or family might own or possess (*hanmin myŏngjŏn*).

Ma did not comment on the rather obvious failure of this tactic in the Han dynasty because it was not that important for his argument. He wanted to make the point that the imposition by the state on the rights of ownership over real estate had been deemed an acceptable tactic, but no one had ever thought of achieving the same objective by limiting the amount of cash that anyone could accumulate. The reason for this was that most understood that the "purpose" of accumulating cash was not to aggrandize wealth, but to create "liquidity and circulation" in the flow of goods (*yut'ong*). Therefore, there was no need for the ruler to establish laws to instruct people in trade or the exchange of goods.

He understood that Hsien-tsung's restriction on the amount of cash that could be accumulated had been instituted because the shortage of cash in the marketplace had driven up its value and deflated the price of goods, and he did not question Hsien-tsung's judgment that the cause was the greed of hoarders and profiteers. But he opposed limiting their cash possessions because he felt that the avaricious could be more easily controlled by allowing people to impeach them for their behavior without disrupting the flow of currency throughout the market. He also pointed out that in practice the method just did not work: a similar limit on the volume of cash savings in the *shao-hsing* period (1131–63) of the Southern Sung period had failed miserably.[27]

Yu Hyŏngwŏn did not comment on the contrasting methods of Emperor Hsien-tsung and Ma Tuan-lin, but it is obvious that he shared Ma's point of view without denigrating Hsien-tsung's attitude and purpose. Yu, after all, was a moralist who must have shared Hsien-tsung's distaste for the more egregious forms of avarice, but he was also convinced of the classical dictum about the immense utility of cash as the penultimate lubricant for the circulation of goods. The circulation of goods was a positive good, but not because it permitted all individuals the opportunity to become rich; rather it ensured a flow of necessities to the population at large once an economy had passed beyond the stage of rural self-sufficiency for all products. Thus, Yu must have agreed with Ma when he concluded that avarice could not go unpunished, even though the possession of vast amounts of wealth would be regarded as a mark of high accomplishment in a capitalist world, let alone a sign of the Devil's work. But that punishment had to be done without disrupting the flow of cash or stable prices that would occur if every one were forced to divest themselves of surplus cash and flood the market with it. Cash was, after all, a function of the market that operated according to rules that the sages had already discovered, and those rules should not be violated even if the purpose was to punish immorality.

Lü Tsu-ch'ien: The Solid Penny Cash. Ma Tuan-lin opposed artificial limits on the possession of cash because he felt cash was necessary for the exchange of goods, but he still was uneasy about the stimulus to profit through the manipulation of money because profiteering, itself, was immoral. He was not, of course, the only scholar who viewed cash with a certain ambivalence. Lü Tsu-ch'ien (1137–81) of the Southern Sung also felt that cash was necessary to the operation of market activities but was not an object of use in itself. Yu cited Lü's argument that "currency was nothing more than something used for balancing the prices of commodities" while grain and cloth were the only real forms of wealth. For that reason the ancients always spoke of the necessity to accumulate a nine-years' reserve of food for every thirty years of normal production as a defense against famine, never of accumulating "a reserve of twenty or thirty thousand strings of cash," which would have been of no use in feeding the starving. Lü, evidently, was unwilling to acknowledge that a starving man might be able to buy some food to feed himself.

Lü pointed out that in classical times taxes and tribute were collected for the most part in grain and local products and only a small amount in cash, and that salaries for officials were in land grants rather than the cash used currently in Sung times. Because most of the people in ancient times were in fact agriculturalists settled on the land, there was little reason for many of them to be engaged in the peripheral occupation of commerce. Even in the Han dynasty the ranks of officials were defined by the number of piculs of grain they received in salary until Emperor Wu departed from this norm by emphasizing the importance of cash and requiring that all persons had to report their cash savings to the government. From this time on people began to accumulate cash by the thousands of strings, and cash, which had functioned only as a balance or scale (*kwŏn*) to enable the achievement of balanced prices, then became more important than useful items like grain and cloth. In other words, Lü believed that cash was useful as long as it was not treated as something that possessed value; only when its possession became the end of economic activity did it possess a potential for evil.

Nonetheless, Lü had no special admiration for Kung Yu of the Han who wanted to abolish cash altogether and return to an economy of grain and cloth because it was unrealistic to hope for a return to the past of antiquity. He agreed with several others that when cash dropped out of use during the reign of Emperor Wen of the Wei dynasty (220–26) the absence of cash did not eliminate cheating on commercial transactions.

Cash had become indispensable, but to perform its function as a medium of exchange it had to be standard in weight and quality of manufacture lest debasement and counterfeiting ruin its proper function. Unfortunately, only the five-*shu* coin of the Han and the *K'ai-yüan* coin of the T'ang dynasties had met the standard, and in the Sung dynasty during the reign of Emperor T'ai-tsung (r. 976–98) Chang Ch'i-hsien had wrecked the currency by issuing new coins that were too light in weight and poor in quality, primarily because he was interested mainly in the profits of seigniorage. Lü preferred the solution of K'ung I of the Southern Ch'i that the profit of seigniorage be reduced to zero to drive the counterfeiters out of the minting business and leave the government in exclusive control of issuing cash and regulating prices by ever-normal market purchases.

Since the economy should depend primarily on the production of food and textiles, cash should be kept small in quantity and high in value to function as a medium of exchange; it should function as a lubricant for trade, but never thought of an object of real wealth.[28] The ambivalence of Lü's attitude toward cash was that it had become an indispensable medium for the Chinese economy, but that the medium could not become the message lest the desire for money undermine production of basic necessities. To achieve this end, K'ung I's prescription for minting a solid penny cash close to the intrinsic value of the metal was the only guarantee of success.

Yeh Meng-te: Cash as an Object of Value. Despite Lü Tsu-ch'ien's admonition against treating money as an object of wealth, it was apparent that many Chinese had been doing that since the Han dynasty. Yu felt it was worth quoting the views of Yeh Meng-te of the Sung dynasty (ca. 1090s) on this point. Yeh complained that in his dynasty the accumulation of cash fortunes had become so commonplace that the apparently astronomical personal fortunes of the Han dynasty in the first century B.C., which reached as much as ten million pieces of cash for some noblemen in particular, was now attainable by even middle or lower-class households. Yeh's reaction to this situation, however, was not one of pride in the accomplishment of his age in spreading the wealth of kings to the common man. Instead, he reached the same conclusion that Emperor Hsien-tsung of the T'ang dynasty had reached: that the concentration of cash in private hands had left the Sung government desperately short of funds for its own expenses.

The government, unfortunately, decided that the only way out of that problem was to mint multiple denomination coins manufactured with a tin alloy of copper and a face value of ten cash to make up the deficit. Unfortunately the tactic had proved futile because the public lost confidence in the coin. In an age when the public valued cash as an object of wealth, the accumulation of money in private hands forced the state to abandon a sound coinage policy.

Like Lü Tsu-ch'ien, Yeh much preferred the subsistence economy of the well-field system of the ancient Chou dynasty where cash was used only in small amounts. He quoted Li K'uei of the Wei dynasty, who provided statistics to prove that very point. According to Li each peasant family under the well-field system consisted of five individuals who shared in the cultivation of its plot of 100 *myo*, producing 1.5 piculs (*sŏk*) per *myo* or a total of 150 piculs. The 10 percent tax cost 15 piculs, the five family members ate 90 piculs/year, leaving a surplus of 45 piculs, worth 30 pieces of cash per picul, or a surplus of 1,350 pieces of cash. Annual costs for shrine and ritual expenses cost 200 cash/year, leaving 1,150 pieces of cash or enough to buy clothes for the entire family. In that situation of perfect agrarian equality there had never been problem because of the insufficiency of cash in circulation.[29]

Now Yeh Ming-te, a subject of perhaps the most prosperous commercial age in Chinese history, was advising his readers to look back to the frugal model of well-field subsistence when cash, to be sure, was used, but never too much to divert attention away from the production of food and clothing. In this instance, I would suspect that Yu Hyŏngwŏn had decided to cite Yeh's work because he admired the thrust of his argument, not because he regarded it as absurd.

Fluctuations in Sung Dynasty Money Supply. According to Yu's account, after the fall of the T'ang dynasty, cash went out of use briefly until Emperor Shih-tsung (r. 944–60) of the Later Chou dynasty confiscated copper utensils and Buddhist statuary and resumed minting different types of coins after 960. For the Sung dynasty, founded that very year, however, the cash glut became the source of problems as Yeh had pointed out. Yu cited Ch'iu Chün's criticism of the Sung emperors' habit of minting new coins every time they changed the year period within a reign. Emperor Jen-tsung changed year periods nine times in the forty years of his reign with a coin for each, and the costs involved in minting new cash, such as finding copper ore, smelting the ore or melting down scrap copper, employing artisans and workers, and paying for supervisors and officials placed an enormous burden on the population.[30]

From the time of Wang An-shih's administration at court after 1068, the supply of copper available for cash and state finances had been depleted. Yu attributed the phenomenon to the abandonment of the prohibition against private ownership of copper and the failure of the government to prevent the export of copper or cash from the country by ship.

By subscribing to the first of these two explanations, Yu indicated that he might have been won over to the views of Emperor Hsien-tsung and Yeh Ming-te except that he also saw fit to quote the argument of Hu Hung (?) (1100–55), who explained that the main reason for the cash shortage was that people were melting copper cash and selling raw copper because it was then worth ten times more than the face value of the copper cash. Hu argued that the emperor could counteract this trend by imposing a prohibition against melting cash down, a more economical way of maintaining the supply of cash than by minting more of it. Failure to maintain the ban against the export of copper utensils only exacerbated the problem because it meant that copper would end up in the hands of the "barbarians," bona fide cash would shrink in quantity, counterfeit cash would rise, and the possibility of finding enough copper to meet the need for cash would be lost.[31]

What was important about Hu's critique was that it demonstrated that the supply of copper was the crucial factor in explaning a cash shortage, and that the price of copper ore relative to the value of cash and foreign trade in copper were instrumental in explaining both why a shortage might exist, or how it could be solved.

Paper Money: In Sung, Chin, and Yüan Dynasties. Yu ended his discussion of currency with a special section on paper money, first introduced in Sung China. During the reign of Emperor Chen-tsung (r. 997–1022), Chang Yung, the local military commander in the Szechwan area who was dissatisfied with iron cash because it was too heavy, began to circulate paper scrip (*chih-chi*) called *chiao-tzu* in which each piece of paper money was designated as equivalent to one string of cash, theoretically a thousand coins. One might well speculate that the main stimulus to the use of paper money was the expansion of trade and commerce that rendered the penny cash too cumbersome a vehicle to maintain a growing market.

Because a number of unspecified difficulties occurred, there was a debate over whether the paper money should be withdrawn from circulation. Emperor Jen-tsung (r. 1023–63) decided to adopt the suggestion of a transportation commissioner, Hsieh T'ien, to prohibit private printing of paper money, and to establish an agency to print the money and oversee its use. Paper money was continued after the Sung was forced into south China by the Jurchen Chin forces in the twelfth century, and the name of the paper money was changed to *hui-tzu* and administered by the Board of Taxation. At first paper money was backed up by full convertibility to metallic cash, but convertibility was later dropped.

In the Chin dynasty in north China and Manchuria, the government adopted its own paper money, called *chiao-ch'ao*, and in the Yüan period the Mongols printed its own paper note in the Chung-t'ung era (1260–64) called the *Chung-t'ung yüan-pao-ch'ao*. All paper money from the Sung period on was stamped with a seal denoting its value, but by the end of the Yüan convertibility to cash been suspended. The value of the paper money itself plummeted in value as commodity prices inflated steeply, but Yu did not make clear whether he thought that the lack of convertibility was the cause of the depreciation of paper money or not.

Paper Money: Ch'iu Chün on Paper Money. Yu then appended Ch'iu Chün's view that paper money was a preposterous invention, far inferior to copper cash. During the T'ang dynasty, a man named Wang Yü had once used paper to simulate copper cash to burn for sacrifices to the spirits, but no one at the time had had the remotest inkling that it would ever be used for real money. Ch'iu stigmatized Chang Yung, the originator of paper money, as the equivalent of the man who first used wooden models for human beings in Shang sacrifices, one of the favorite epithets of Confucius for the man whose ingenuity later led to human sacrifice itself. And he condemned Hsieh T'ien for preserving the system at a time when others had called it into question.

Ch'iu argued that Heaven in its graciousness had conferred on Earth the birth and procreation of living and growing products to supply the needs of man, and had granted to the rulers of states the ability to use money to achieve a balance among the values of products, but the purpose of these gifts was to benefit the people of an empire as a whole, not to create profit just for the benefit of the ruler alone. For a ruler to fail to balance the relative supply of goods and money was tantamount to a violation of Heaven's trust. It was an even greater betrayal of his responsibility to use trickery and deceit by converting something that had no intrinsic value into something that was given value or utility just to gain profit for himself.

Ch'iu was not arguing that all money was bad, but that the nominal value of money had to bear some relation to its material content and the amount of skill and labor that went into its production. A single bill of the paper money (*ch'ao*) of the Sung and Yüan dynasties, by contrast, only cost three to five pieces of cash to print, and yet it could be used to purchase goods worth a thousand coins! Ch'iu's reason for why paper was so cheap and so unsuitable as a representative of value appeared similar to the older critique against multiple-denomination cash, but he also developed a new monetary theory that bore a remote resemblance to the concept of a labor theory of value, inspired by Adam Smith, embellished by Ricardo, and inherited by Marx among others.[32] Even though Ch'iu's theory had no relationship to any subsitution of commodity exchange values as a source of wealth, the division of labor as the key to increased production, labor's conflict with capital, and class struggle between the proletariat and bourgeoisie – none of which existed at the time – Ch'iu did believe that labor and human effort was indispensable to the creation of value; not only use-value but exchange-value as well:

> Even though the things of the world may be produced in the natural world [in the realm of Heaven and Earth], everything must be assisted by human labor [*illyŏk*, Korean pronunciation] before it can achieve its utility [*yong*]. In substance [*ch'e*] it may be large or small, or skillfully or poorly [made], and the skill used in labor [*kongnyŏk*] may be shallow or deep, [according to which] its price may be high or low. If [the price of an object] is as high [in value] as 1,000 pieces of cash, in substance it may not be large in size, but it has to be made with the kind of skill that would certainly take more than one day. Would it in any way be possible that one would be able to buy this with a piece of paper money about a foot square in size that only cost three to five pieces of cash [to print]? If the common people can think of exploiting others by this means without the ruler being able to prohibit it, the ruler would have lost his function as ruler – let alone if the ruler thought of doing it for himself![33]

Despite Ch'iu reaching a point close to modern economics, he did not quite attain a concept of exchange value, let alone a view of the commodity aspect of currency that fluctuated in price according to its supply and the demand for it. He could only see the value of paper money in terms of the price of the paper used to make it, but given his classical education he should not have taken umbrage at this since the vaunted and hallowed cowry shell of ancient times was hardly more valuable. In any case, in an age when nickels, dimes, and quarters (i.e., multiple-denomination cash) were regarded as a fraud perpetrated by charlatans, it was not likely that a hundred or thousand dollar bill could have earned much respect from Ch'iu Chün.

Paper Money: Paper Money and Drafts. It is obvious from Yu's own proposals for currency policy that Ch'iu Chün's prejudice against paper money influenced him greatly. Possibly his excessive empirical and historical approach to the lessons of past behavior had limited his conception about the possible functions of money and prejudiced him against the adoption of written instruments of exchange, bills, drafts, or more modern banking arrangements. Curiously, even though his own country had experimented with paper money unsuccessfully for the better part of the fifteenth century, and kings like T'aejong and Sejong had led the way in the effort to introduce it, he neither studied nor analyzed the reasons for that failure, but merely assumed that the failure of paper money to last into the Ming era must have proved that it was flawed as a medium of exchange. In that respect, one suspects that his attitude toward money was perhaps more conservative than those aforementioned kings of the early Chosŏn dynasty!

THE WISDOM OF CHINESE MONETARY EXPERIENCE

Yu concluded his essay on the history of money in China with Ch'iu Chün's biting critique of paper money in the Sung and Yüan because he was convinced that Chiu's analysis was correct and should be kept in mind in planning a currency policy for Korea in the mid-seventeenth century. Whereas previous writers had distinguished between products of utility like grain and cloth because they could be consumed with some benefit to the consumer, Ch'iu shifted the focus of value to the role of labor and skill in the act of production. Presumably he meant that only metallic cash, which required both effort and skill in the minting process, could constitute something of value that could then function as a medium of exchange.

Was there, however, any justification for Ch'iu Chün's bias against both multiple denomination metallic cash and paper money specifically on the grounds that issuing money at a far greater nominal value than the cost of the raw materials, labor, and skill required to make the money itself constituted a profiteering and exploitative deception of an unwitting general population? Ch'iu believed that money had a proper function as a medium of exchange to lubricate the flow of goods, but that it should never be used by either private citizens or rulers to make profits. He thought that past experience had demonstrated that the public lost confidence in both multiple denomination cash and paper money, and as a result the value of the money deteriorated along with rampant inflation in prices.

Some traditional experts on money like Liu Chih of T'ang times had realized that there was or might have been some connection between the volume of money in circulation and the amount of commodities for sale in the market, and some had in fact asked whether changes in the value of money or fluctuation in commodity prices were caused by demand or supply. It had become common knowledge that no matter what the media of exchange, prices of agricultural goods shifted markedly between periods of glut and scarcity caused by changing weather conditions. Some observers had noted that from the T'ang period on there were periods when the value of cash increased not only as a result of a surplus of agricultural production, but also because of a shortage of the supply of cash itself, and merchants and other private individuals had no difficulty in basing their business on calculations of current market conditions rather than on some classical moral precepts about the use of money.

On the other side, it had become fairly common knowledge that the value of money could be reduced by an oversupply of the currency either by purposeful debasement of its content (whether cash, grain, or cloth), private minting, counterfeiting, and excessive issuance by the government. Although many may have regarded government minting of multiple denomination coins as just too transparent a means of government profiteering, private minting and counterfeiting were both deemed bad, not just because the private minters and counterfeiters always debased coins, but because there was no control over volume. In fact, some policy makers even proposed reducing the money supply and asserting central control over minting or issuing money to restore its value and public trust in it.

When paper money began to be issued in the Sung period and continued throughout the Yüan, it reflected a progressive development in the Chinese economy and an attitude toward money that was closer to twentieth-century conceptions of money as symbols of value that did not necessarily have to be converted to bona fide objects of value on demand. When one considers that Chinese scholars had been saying for centuries that money itself represented an exercise in sage wisdom because the rulers of antiquity had purposely used objects of "no value" to function as media of exchange, mainly to preserve items of use for consumption, Ch'iu Chün was not necessarily obliged to argue that using paper for money was ipso facto immoral.

Why did Ch'iu Chün, a Ming scholar, however, take such a conservative view of multiple denomination copper cash and paper money in the Sung and Yüan dynasties, especially when he appeared otherwise to have been a progressive statecraft writer? Judging individual opinion simply on the basis of trends in historical developments and modes of thought is often a dangerous business, but it has become conventional to think of the Ming regime as a period of conservative and nationalistic reaction to the more open and cosmopolitan economies and policies of the Sung and Yüan eras.

Nevertheless, even in the Yüan dynasty the Mongol rulers restricted legal foreign trade to the government in 1284, and then stopped foreign trade in the early fourteenth century. After Emperor T'ai-tsu of the Ming dynasty restricted trade to tributary missions, further restrictions were imposed in the late fourteenth century, and the large-scale foreign trade missions to South Asia and East Africa that began in 1405 under the eunuch-admiral Cheng Ho, were brought to an end in 1433.

Trade was probably hindered as well by the raids of the so-called Japanese pirates (Wakō), who raided the China coast from the Yangtze delta south between 1549 and 1561. The ban on trade was lifted for Southeast Asia, Taiwan, and the Philippines after 1567, but reimposed again toward the end of the Ming and carried over into the Ch'ing period (1644), with the exception trading for copper from Japan.

Mark Elvin has argued that conservative economic policies restricted the volume of cash in the economy and caused a recession in the fourteenth century that lasted until the resurgence of prosperity after 1570. These policies also had effects on currency. The inconvertible paper money of the Yüan period led to a depreciation of paper money and the flight of silver from China to Western Asia. After 1400 the Ming regime tried to ban the use of silver currency and enforce paper money, but it weakened its value by inflationary expenditures for military campaigns. The government then supported a shift to the use of silver currency in 1436 by allowing its use for tax payments, a practice that spread widely by the end of the century, and in the sixteenth century silver imports from Japan were increased by Spanish and Portuguese silver.[34]

In short, even though the major monetary outcome of these conservative and isolationist policies was the shift from paper to silver, these trends may well have produced Ch'iu Chün's conservative views on paper money and copper cash. Since Yu was influenced by Ch'iu's ideas, one might also deduce that he himself was by no means a proponent of either the free market, expanded foreign trade, or a more flexible monetary system to support a trade system of greater volume.

MONEY IN KOREAN HISTORY

Koryŏ Dynasty and Resistance to Change

Even though Yu concluded his survey of money in China on a negative note, when he turned his attention to Korea he argued positively for the need for money in the Korean economy even though the first attempt to adopt metallic coins in the Koryŏ dynasty had not been marked by success. He wrote that King Sŏngjong of the Koryŏ dynasty first ordered the use of iron cash in 996, and that the prime minister, Han On'gong, in 1002 recommended the adoption of cash and the abolition of rough cloth (*ch'up'o*) as a means of exchange, "but because this was startling to local custom and gave rise to resentment, [the use of cash] was abolished."[35]

The first successful attempt occurred in 1102 when King Sukchong established an official Directorate of the Mint (the *Chujŏn-dogam*), minted 15,000 strings of a coin called "The Circulating Treasure of the [Country] East of the [Yellow] Sea" (*Haedong t'ongbo*), and accompanied the coin with the statement that Korean customs had been too simple and that putting cash into circulation was the best means available for promoting "the wealth of the people and profit of the nation." The mint then declared that because the people all thought that cash was a good idea they were requesting the king to legitimize the decision to mint cash by announcing it to the royal ancestral shrine. The cash was distributed to all civil officials and soldiers and shops were established in the capital at Kaegyŏng to accept payment in cash.

Yu noted, however, that the government had to establish more wine and food shops to accept cash in 1104, presumably because the new cash had not been welcomed by the population. As soon as Sukchong died, King Yejong was immediately hounded by the opponents of cash. Yejong responded with a spirited defense of Sukchong's cash policy, reminding the critics that the sage kings of ancient China had in fact begun the use of currency for the same purpose of enriching the country and benefiting the people, not because they wanted to make profits for themselves. Since even the Liao dynasty's emperor had recently adopted cash as well, it was even more incumbent on Koryŏ to do the same. The problem with Korea, however, was that whenever "a law is established, crowds of people arise to criticize it incessantly" to block its legislation. Particularly annoying was the argument of the critics that cash could not be adopted because King T'aejo (Wang Kŏn, the founder of the dynasty) had admonished his successors in his famous testament (*yuhun*) to prohibit the use of T'ang and Khitan customs. Yejong argued that T'aejo was only warning against the adoption of the habit of extravagant and wasteful expenditure, not culture and institutions in general, because "if you abandon Chinese [culture and institutions] what do you have left [to copy]?" In any case, no matter how inspired his arguments, Yejong eventually succumbed to the critics.[36]

Yu Hyŏngwŏn then interrupted his description of mid-Koryŏ cash policy by endorsing the views of the Koryŏ progressives. He criticized the Korean people at the time for being too "crude and simple" in their customs and for expressing amazement and resentment over the abolition of rough cloth and the adoption of copper cash back in 1002. He praised Sukchong for his astuteness in adopting cash but condemned the critics of cash after 1105 because of their general negativism. As an illustration of the difficulty the Koryŏ regime had in adopting Chinese institutions, he pointed out that So T'aebo (1034–1104) and other chief ministers of state had opposed the idea that the state should pay for the room and board of students at the National Academy (*Kukhak*) as in China because it would cause too much harm to the people, presumably by raising their taxes. Since this kind of opposition only showed that even men in high position had no understanding of what was right, King Yejong was powerless to resist the negative views of his officials. Even though Yejong was an admirer of culture and refinement, he was surrounded with men whose tastes were given to "luxury and ostentation, and who spent their time mumbling lines of poetry and had no far-reaching understanding of what it took to govern a state."

Yu also blamed resistance to the adoption of cash on a pervasive resistance toward change among Koreans in general. "The feelings of ordinary people are that if you are happy with something, you continue doing it, but if you dislike it, you change things, [an attitude that] is even more valid in our country." Furthermore, the inability of Koreans to maintain a law or system for any length of time was aptly summed up in an old aphorism about Koryŏ times, that "in Korea if some public policy lasted for three days, why wouldn't you trust [that it would continue permanently]?" In short, Yu was not only an admirer of more advanced Chinese institutions and methods, he believed that the Korean people in general preferred the status quo to reform and lacked the patience to test new programs for enough time to allow some chance of success. High officials, particularly in the Koryŏ era, simply lacked understanding and foresight.[37]

Superiority of Cash to Paper

Yu ended his account of currency in the Koryŏ period by citing two proposals on currency made in 1391. Judging from the way he edited these two proposals and the content of his own commentary endorsing the use of metallic cash, it is clear that he had adopted Ch'iu Chün's view about the worthlessness of paper money. Yu copied out in his own text a copy of a proposal made by Pang Saryang in the third lunar month of 1391, but he amended the text by disingenuously omitting one key phrase in Pang's memorial to make him appear to have been an advocate of the superiority of metallic cash to any other medium of exchange.

Pang argued that even though the world was divided into regions each of which had its own differences and special customs, society as a whole was divided into four occupational groups, scholars (or scholar-officials), farmers, artisans, and merchants, each of which earned its living by its own calling. Cash performed the necessary function of allowing people to exchange what they had for what they lacked and maintain a constant circulation of goods. Metallic currency been in circulation in the world since the Grand Duke of Chou (T'ai-kung) initiated its use, primarily because of its physical virtues: it was light and easy to transport, firm and indestructible, unlike grain that could be eaten by rats in storage or cloth that could be cut into pieces. In Korea, coarse cloth had been used as the prime medium of exchange primarily because it had originated in the Eastern Capital (Kyŏngju) and other surrounding districts, no doubt a tradition borrowed from the Silla dynasty. When stored in warehouses it could rot from dampness, burn up in fires, or be eaten by rats. According to Yu's version of Pang's memorial, Pang then proposed that metallic cash be minted and that the use of coarse cloth for currency be prohibited, but he omitted the key phrase that paper money be printed along with copper cash and that *both* be used as currency![38]

The power of Yu's conviction about the superiority of copper cash had led him to a serious violation of the high standards of honesty and truth in historical reporting that was part of the Korean, as well as the Chinese, tradition. Perhaps because of a certain uneasiness over this misrepresentation of Pang's true words he did include another proposal by the Supreme Council of State (Top'yŏng'ŭisasa) in the seventh lunar month of 1391 advocating the use of paper money *instead of cash*, but to indicate his disdain for the recommendation he relegated it to a footnote written in half the size of the main portion of his text.

The Supreme Council carried the history of currency further back to the use of gold coins by the sage Emperors Yü of the Hsia (B.C. 2205) and T'ang of the Shang (B.C. 1766), and praised the utility of cash and its long history in China and Korea as well, citing the examples of purely Korean coins since the Three

Kingdoms period.[39] It also noted that so-called silver jar money (*ŭnbyŏng*) had also circulated with copper cash and bolts of cloth as well, but because of problems in the law both silver and copper cash had been dropped. It had been replaced by the five-*sae* (*sŭng* in Sino-Korean pronunciation) cloth[40] but this cloth had been devalued in thread count to two-or three-*sae* cloth. It was still inconvenient as a currency because it required labor to manufacture it, was too heavy to carry around, and was eaten by rats when in storage. It provided a poor reserve for the state when it needed relief against famine or expenses for the army.

The council's conclusion, however, was that despite the advantages of copper coins, it would be too difficult to attempt to revive them at the time and far simpler to print paper money designed like the *hui-tzu* of the Sung or the *pao-ch'ao* of the Yüan dynasties. They recommended that it be stamped with the slogan "Koryŏ Circulating Paper Money" (*Koryŏ t'onghaeng chŏhwa*) at a value of one bolt of five-*sae* cloth, that all the "rough" cloth of lower than standard thread count and quality be abolished, and that both five-*sae* cloth and paper money be accepted as legal tender.[41]

Even without his own commentary on the history of currency in the Koryŏ period, it should have been obvious from his treatment of the last two notices that he had already decided in favor of copper cash. In his own commentary, he made it explicit that cash was the necessary medium of exchange because it would help to fill the state's financial needs and promote people's standard of living, but he wondered how it was possible that of all the countries of the world, only Korea could have failed to put cash into circulation permanently. He rejected the common argument that the main cause for failure was that the land was infertile and the population poor, that is, that Korea had insufficient production of surplus wealth to justify an active commercial market, because the quality of the land in the country (hence average productivity) was not uniformly bad but varied in quality and in that respect hardly differed from any other country. The tastes of the Korean people, the distribution of the population in the universal four categories of occupations, the means by which they earned their living, and the exchange of goods to satisfy demands or trade surpluses were as much features of Korean life as in any other country. In other words, both economically and sociologically there was no special reason why Koreans could not have had a cash economy.

Wŏn Yuhan has argued that Yu's position here was unrealistic because of his excessive admiration for the Chinese experience. Wŏn felt that the situation in Korea was vastly different from contemporary China and that Yu exaggerated Korea's capacity to adopt currency because there had been no long tradition of metallic currency, the Korean government was facing a fiscal crisis, and the population was still suffering the effects of three invasions in the mid-seventeenth century.[42]

Yu also felt that the argument that Korea lacked copper and tin for minting cash was also misguided because those metals could easily be imported from abroad, especially since the raw metals were not that expensive. It was obvious to him that a large amount of copper had been used by the Korean people to make bowls, basins, and other implements, and the dozen or so Buddhist monasteries and temples located in almost every district of the country must have had a large number of bronze bells. He did not suggest that these utensils and bells would necessarily have to be melted down to mint cash, but he did argue that if the nation's entire resources could be mobilized, it should not be difficult to raise funds to pay for copper and tin imports. Furthermore, since domestic copper ore was in short supply, the state would not have to worry too much about illegal private or mining or counterfeit minting of cash that might depreciate the value of the coins. Again, Wŏn Yuhan accused Yu of being unrealistic and impractical because Korea did not have the financial resources to import large quantities of copper from Japan.[43]

Lack of Leadership at the Top

Yu did believe that the real responsibility for the failure of cash policy had to be ascribed to the lack of leadership by the man at the top (*wisangjiin*) of government, although he could have been referring to "men at the top," including the king's highest ministers and advisers as well, since his classical Chinese (*hanmun*) text did not distinguish between singular and plural. He pointed out that King Sukchong of Koryŏ wisely ordered the adoption of cash but failed to provide guidance for ensuring that it would be put into permanent circulation, something that cash itself could not have achieved on its own, or by any natural process. The main means for providing guidance was for the government simply to collect taxes in cash and use that cash to pay for official purchases and expenses. Sukchong had failed to do this because he was content merely to issue cash to high officials and soldiers on a one-time basis and set up wine shops in the wards of the capital to accept cash for payment for a limited service rather than convert all or part of the tax system to cash.

To indicate his flexibility in the face of resistance to conversion of the tax and salary system to cash, Yu was willing to accept a more moderate conversion to cash of just half official taxes and salaries as the minimum requirement for achieving a permanent adoption of cash as the main medium of exchange. He made this concession because he thought a certain minimum amount of cash in circulation and a minimum volume of cash and frequency of transactions had only to be reached to break through the logjam of obstructionism. To illustrate his point he used the metaphor of the gates of irrigation dikes in controlling the flow of water into the fields. Cash was like water but could not flow easily if the dikes were closed. Only if the manager of the dikes tripped open the gates would the water then cascade freely into the fields. Without the guidance of the ruler in providing stimulus for the flow of cash, even China would not have succeeded in promoting the use of cash.

Yu's Formula and Early Chosŏn Experience

Yu did not discuss the specific attempts to promote the circulation of metallic cash, let alone paper money, in the fifteenth and early seventeenth centuries, a serious omission since the validity of his argument might have easily been tested against past experience. But he did say that in recent times whenever the government had tried to adopt cash, in every instance the policy was reversed, mainly because the government had not provided guidance or stimulation by collecting the land tax in cash. Bolts of rough cloth persisted in the market even though the government had prohibited its use. Using cash for currency, by contrast, would be tantamount to taking material of no utility and converting it into something useful. If poorly woven cloth could retain its tenacious hold on the marketplace for such a long time, there was no reason why cash could not do likewise if only "the man above" demonstrated some constancy of purpose and ceased "rescinding orders at dusk that had been issued at dawn."[44]

Yu's statement about the capacity of the Korean people to adopt copper currency and the need for better leadership on the part of Korean kings and high officials was immortalized by Yi Man'un, who included the gist of this memorial in the revision to the *Munhŏnbigo* compiled after 1782. He placed it just after his evaluation of Kim Yuk's role in the adoption of cash immediately after King Hyojong had rescinded the use of cash in 1656. Yu's opinions had obviously become well known sometime before this date, at least by the mid-eighteenth century, although I have yet to discover evidence that they influenced cash policy at that time. In any case, by that time the Korean experience and knowledge of cash and its problems had advanced beyond the stage of Yu's wisdom.[45]

One could easily charge Yu with dereliction of his scholarly reponsibility when he chose to omit the monetary history of the Chosŏn dynasty, in particular the experiment with paper money in the fifteenth century, because he should have tested the validity of his arguments against the facts. Even though Yu had no use for paper money, there is no need for us denizens of the twentieth-century world in which paper money is being replaced by even less substantial electronic recordings on plastic disks to accept the validity of Yu's anti-paper prejudice. Our only obligation is to compare Yu's views with the state of knowledge at the time.

The monetary history of the Chosŏn dynasty also requires examination of the possible reasons why both metallic cash and paper money failed to gain acceptance. Were those media of exchange universally perceived as inherently worthless and hence prone to rapid devaluation? Did the kings and their advisers fail to provide sufficient guidance and support by requiring at least one-half the taxes, official salaries, and official purchases to be transacted in cash (or paper money as well)? Did they err by not ensuring a sufficient supply of copper by foreign imports, or by not paying enough attention to controlling the value of money and the prices of commodities in the market?

In introducing paper money in 1402, King T'aejong did not meet Yu's criterion for converting half of all taxes and expenditures to paper because he relied mainly on punishment to coerce the use of paper bills. However, from 1410 to 1415 he required payment in paper money for all prebendal rents paid to designated officials and government offices (probably constituting most if not all the land in Kyŏnggi Province), tribute taxes on slaves and base persons, repayment of government grain loans to peasants, one-third the salaries paid to officials, and a number of minor taxes on merchants and artisans. Technically speaking, he may have missed Yu's criteria by a few percentage points in each case, but it would appear unreasonable to charge him with lack of effort in providing support and guidance. The unwillingness of the population to accept paper money at face value could easily have derived from their belief that the money had no value of its own, but a modern economist might conclude that their suspicions were the products of traditional psychological prejudice that could only have been broken down by the kind of aggressive support for the use and acceptance of cash that Yu favored.

After 1425 when King Sejong minted cash, he also required cash payments for slave tribute, and taxes on merchants, shamans, and home sites, but he did not require it for payment of the land tax, replacement of tribute levies, or the military support tax (instead of cloth). He also relied heavily on coercion and punishment to enforce the use of cash but did not take sufficiently aggressive action to import sufficient copper to guarantee enough cash for the economy. As a result, he soon found that the restriction to cash as the only legal tender for transactions in the marketplace had simply brought market activities to a standstill. He did not anticipate that because of the copper shortage, copper itself or items made from copper would become more valuable than the cash, and that people would melt down copper and smuggle it out of the country to make greater profits than by using cash – a lesson that Yu had learned from the experience of the Liu-Sung dynasty in the fifth century and Liu Chih of the T'ang dynasty in the eighth century. These developments, however, could have been prevented by adoption of another of Yu's admonitions, to import enough copper from abroad to ensure a sufficient supply of cash, but Sejong failed to live up to this responsibility.

After 1469 King Sŏngjong tried to introduce paper money again, but he did not require larger payments of ordinary taxes in paper money than had been attempted before, and in 1470 he retreated by permitting official slaves to pay their tribute in grain or cloth. Throughout the decline of paper money and cash into the early sixteenth century, there was no evidence that any king made a serious attempt to convert the majority of tax payments into cash or paper money. The one criticism about the weakness of the central government's effort might have been the lack of sufficient pressure from the king and capital to force lesser officials and district magistrates to accept paper money and pay for purchases with either cash or paper money. Although it would appear unreasonable to place blame on the king and his court for the inertia of the lower bureaucracy since it was such a common feature of centralized bureaucratic regimes, there may be no other scapegoat to find if one insists on searching for human error rather than natural forces. In other words, the wisdom of Yu's emphasis on the need for guidance and leadership from the top cannot be discredited by examining the concrete performance of currency policy in the fifteenth and early sixteenth centuries that Yu ignored. His criticism about the lack of sufficient government guidance and support rather than a public perception of the worthlessness of paper might well have been true about the failure of cash and paper money to circulate successfully in the fifteenth and sixteenth centuries.

Some of the same problems of insufficient government support for cash recurred after the late sixteenth century. King Sŏnjo rejected the suggestion of Yang Hao, the Ming general, to adopt cash, and King Injo's cash policy in 1625 was frustrated by the shortage of copper, but in 1633 he went further than any previous king by requiring that one-fourth to one-third of all tribute, one-tenth of the tax to support the new *samsu* special troops, and expenses for bureaus and hired labor in the capital be paid for in cash. Nonetheless, not enough cash was minted to meet the demand and circulation was interrupted by the Manchu invasions early in 1637. Since the government noticed that most cash was circulating only in the capital, it pressed the Ever-Normal Bureau throughout the 1630s to spread the use of cash to the provinces and allow the use of cash throughout the tax system.

When Kim Yuk first entered the picture in 1644, he introduced a number of recommendations, but his main interest was to spread the use of cash to ease travel expenses throughout the main transportation route between Seoul and China, and he sought to solve the shortage of copper by importing cash directly from China. After his proposal was ignored, he then hoped to persuade King Hyojong simply to adopt cash for a few provinces, preferably in the northwest. In 1650 he brought in a supply of cash from China and urged Hyojong to purchase more with silver, but Hyojong was faced with an immediate fiscal shortage and could not afford the cost. In 1654 Hyojong decided to collect in cash either 12.5 or 20 percent of *taedong* taxes, 20 percent of tribute offered to capital bureaus, and 33.3 percent of the tribute paid by official slaves in addition to other items. By 1654 Hyojong was coming closer to meeting Yu's criterion for serious government support of a cash policy but was still some distance from meeting Yu's requirement that half of all taxes and government payments be paid for in cash, and that the government finance all copper and cash needed by imports from other countries.[46]

Currency Proposals for Korea

Upgrading Mint Technology

After finishing his account of cash in the Koryŏ period, Yu then plunged immediately into his concrete proposals for a cash policy in his own time, presumably written after 1656. He again rejected the popular contention that Koreans could not accommodate themselves to cash because their customs were so different from the Chinese. He declared that the reason "why currency does not circulate is not because it *cannot* do so; it is only because the people *do* not use it" (emphasis added). It was the task of "the man [or men] at the top" to recognize the advantages of cash and resolutely undertake methods to guarantee its circulation, but it did not mean that he should "force people to do so or disrupt [their lives]." If the proper measures were adopted, it would only take a few years for cash to circulate naturally, "just as if the sluices [in the irrigation dikes] had been opened for the water to flow." Once it did, "the country would be enriched and the people would prosper, and our country would be changed from a [collection] of decrepit, isolated, and indolent villages to a land of glorious and resplendent civilization, the benefits of which would last forever."[47]

To prevent confusion and loss of confidence in the currency that might occur if there were a variety of coins of different weight and quality, Yu wanted to restrict minting to a single type of coin. He prescribed that a brass (*tusŏk*) coin modeled in size, shape, and weight after the Circulating Treasure of the K'ai-yüan year period (713–41) of Emperor Hsüan-tsung's reign (the *K'ai-yüan t'ung-pao*) in the T'ang dynasty be struck, and that it have the title "Circulating Treasure of the Eastern Country [*Tongguk t'ongbo*]" on its face. Yu reported that the *K'ai-yüan t'ung-pao* was reported in the *History of the T'ang Dynasty* and Tu Yu's *T'ung-tien* to have weighed .1 tael (.1 *liang* or 1 *ch'ien*). Even though the scales used in China (probably northeast China) in Yu's own time yielded weights three times greater than the T'ang era, since Korean scales were equivalent to T'ang, not contemporary Chinese, scales, the weight of the *Tongguk t'ongbo* should weigh 1 *chŏn* or .1 *yang* according to Korean scales.[48]

Yu also insisted that the quality of the coin be maintained at a high standard by careful selection of craftsmen and high salaries for them. He complained that in the seventeenth century Korean coins had been very poor in quality, but this did not mean that Koreans had never done better, for coins minted in King Sejong's reign in the fifteenth century were all extremely fine and even surpassed some Chinese coins.

The quality of minting could be improved by a search for a talented man to take charge of the mint and manage the work of first-class artisans, who would be allowed to select their own assistants, given ample provisions, and permanently employed at their specialty, contrary to the current lax standards. The work of the craftsmen was to be investigated by officials, the best rewarded and promoted and the worst punished, according to the standards of performance he recommended for the regular system of education.

Penny Cash versus Multiple-Denomination Cash

In accordance with Ch'iu Chün's views, he prohibited either "large" or multiple denomination cash or "small" cash weighing some fraction of the main coin, and insisted that there should only be a single, standard coin. "The face value of the coin should not be too far from the cost of the copper [used to make it] and the cost of labor, which might otherwise open the door to counterfeiting or the destruction [melting down] of cash." Since Yu stipulated that each coin would weigh 1 *chŏn* or .1 *yang* and that 200 *mun* or individual coins of the new cash would be equivalent to 1 *yang* of silver, then one coin would be worth .005 *yang* of silver. He also remarked that the market price of brass from which he recommended that the coins be minted could be calculated from the present price of 1 *yang* of silver for 25 or 26 *yang* of brass. Since a coin would weigh 1 *chŏn* or .1 *yang*, the cost of brass in one coin would be on the average 1/25.5 *yang* or 1/255 *chŏn*, or .0039 *yang* of silver. In other words, the face value of Yu's new coin (equivalent to .005 *yang* of silver) would be about 25 percent higher than the cost of the brass. Because he made no specific calculation about the overhead and labor costs for minting the coin, it is not possible to estimate what the profits of seigniorage would have been without further study of minting operating costs in general. In light of his cash philosophy, however, he probably planned to reduce the profits of seigniorage as much as possible to reduce the incentive for counterfeiting.[49]

Yu's calculations present a complex problem, however. If the metallic cost of making a coin was .0039 *yang* of silver, then even if we did not consider the labor and production costs, then 256 coins or *mun* is the maximum amount that could be minted from 1 *yang* of silver's worth of brass. Any exchange rate lower than that would have meant that the coins would have circulated at a value less than the metal's intrinsic worth, if the cost of the brass remained constant. As we will see, the price or exchange rate for copper coins after they began to be minted again in 1678 was set at 400 *mun* per *yang* of silver, doubled in value temporarily in 1679, and then immediately dropped to the original rate because it was the real market rate at the time. Since this policy could not have succeeded if the cost of minting had produced a net loss, one must assume that an increased supply of copper and other metals like tin and zinc for an alloy with copper must have bid down the cost of the intrinsic metallic value of the coin to allow even for a minimum of zero profit. It cannot be determined just when he wrote his essay on cash and made his calculations because he could have done so any time between 1656 and 1670, but he must have based them on market prices for brass at the time.

Yu opposed the use of multiple denomination cash because it would overvalue the intrinsic metallic value of coins and stimulate counterfeiting by guaranteeing sure profits over the cost of minting, and he also opposed undervaluing coins to the point where they would be worth less than their metallic value because people would then melt their coins down to obtain more value for the metal, reduce the supply of money in the market, increase the value of cash, and depreciate commodity prices.[50]

Providing an Optimum Money Supply

Yu stipulated that a certain amount of cash would be necessary to ensure its successful circulation throughout the country, and he estimated the optimum volume of cash according to the total annual revenues from total or annual taxes, which he concluded was approximately four or five million *kok* (40–50 million *mal* because his *kok* consisted of 10 *mal*, or 2.7–3.3 million contemporary *sŏm* of grain). Unfortunately, he did not explain the basis for his estimate of total standard tax revenue, but in his chapter on government expenditures for the support of the government after he had cut several costs from the current budget, he estimated a total expenditure of 1,248,267 *sŏm*, or 18,724,005 *mal* (at 15 *mal* per *sŏm*).[51] This amount also had to represent the total tax revenue in his reformed system of government, but the estimate of 40–50 million *mal* (2.7–3.3 million contemporary *sŏm*) in this chapter was over twice his estimate for total national expenditures.

A rough estimate of contemporary national revenues might yield a figure closer to his estimate of regular national tax income. If a liberal 300,000 *sŏm* per annum were estimated for the land tax, and another five times that amount for the *taedong* tribute tax and all illict surcharges, it would total 1.8 million *sŏm*. If the equivalent of the cloth support tax for military service was estimated at 1 million *p'il* of cloth (presumably 2 *p'il* on the average for 500,000 taxpayers), at Yu's proposed exchange rate of 6 *mal/p'il*, the amount would come to 3,000,000 *mal* or 200,000 *sŏm*, bringing the national total to 2.1 million *sŏm*, still 28 to 33 percent less than his estimate.

In any case, he believed that 100,000 to 200,000 strings of cash (100 to 200 million coins at 1,000 coins per string) would supply enough cash for the economy, and if 7 to 8 million strings (7 to 8 billion coins) could be minted, there would never ever be any further need to mint more cash.[52] If his estimate of 40 to 50 million *mal* for national tax revenues was correct, it would require 800 million to 1 billion coins (at a conversion rate of 20 *mun/mal*). He only hoped, however, to convert one-third tax revenues to cash, and at the beginning of the campaign he would have settled for 10 or 20 percent. In other words, he would have settled for either 80 to 100 million or 160 to 200 million coins at the initial stage, and 267 million coins eventually, to convert one-third tax revenues to cash payments. Therefore, his call for 100 to 200 million coins would in fact have matched his goal for converting 10 to 20 percent of his estimated national tax revenues to cash, but his figure of 7 to 8 billion coins for total conversion of all taxes to cash was exaggerated by a factor of three decimal points, possibly a typographical error in the text.[53]

If he had also estimated the velocity of cash transactions, he might have been able to reduce the money supply necessary for the successful introduction of cash into the economy to some fraction of 800 million to 1 billion coins. In fact, his estimate of replacing one-third national tax revenues, or 267 million coins by his figures, might in fact have represented an optimum amount.

Kwŏn Yŏng'ik has justifiably concluded that Yu's estimate of 7 to 8 million strings for the money supply was astronomical by comparison with the money supply/GNP ratio he found in South Korea in 1974. Both he and Wŏn Yuhan believed that Yu was totally unrealistic to expect that Korea had the financial capacity to import this much cash from Japan, but if his estimates were revised downward to a more realistic estimate of the money supply necessary to replace grain (and cloth) in taxes, his proposal would not have appeared so outlandish.[54]

As we will see later, he was aware that despite a national cash shortage it was also quite possible to experience a cash surplus and commodity price inflation, but he assumed that local variations could be managed by ever-normal price stabilization methods. Stability in prices at the national level had to be guaranteed by minting enough cash for the nation as a whole.

No Private Minting, No Cash to Copper

Yu believed that care had to be taken to inform the entire population at the beginning of the year that cash would be circulated later to Tax Collection Centers (Tohoegwan) in each province to allow taxpayers to pay their taxes in cash. To guarantee the quality and amount of the cash minted by the government, the private minting of cash would be forbidden. To prevent any reduction in the amount of cash in circulation, the government would also forbid private persons from melting cash down to make utensils. Although both the Han and T'ang dynasty governments in China had punished private minting by execution, he recommended less brutal punishments: one hundred strokes for the perpetrator and sixty strokes, increased labor service, or exile for the master of the shop or residence involved; one year's transportation for neighbors of the perpetrator in the mutual security group, and sixty strokes to urban ward or village chiefs. As was common, informants were to be rewarded with the guilty party's property, and confession in advance of discovery would exempt one from punishment.

Cash and Taxes and Salaries

To succeed in guaranteeing the permanent adoption of cash throughout the economy, the government had to order the use of cash in the payment of taxes and official salaries, but he did not hold to his previous minimum requirement of 50 percent of all taxes and salaries. He was willing to settle for only one-third of the land tax, whether it was due to be paid in rice or cloth, and one-third of all government expenditures, from the king's own expenses to the salaries of clerks, slaves, and soldiers. He also allowed that the proportion of cash payments might be reduced to 20 or 10 percent in remote places in the countryside until cash circulation penetrated those districts. The district magistrates would be responsible for collecting cash taxes, not the tribute middlemen still engaged in tribute contracting (*pangnap*) in provinces where the *taedong* replacement for tribute in kind had not been adopted. By reducing his minimal requirement for taxes and salaries from one-half to one-third the total, Yu's proposal really appeared less radical than what the government had attempted in the reigns of Kings Injo and Hyojong. On the other hand, his demand for the minting of millions of coins presumably backed by imports of copper from abroad, would in fact have meant a far greater investment of funds by the government to ensure a sufficient supply of money.

Not only did Yu insist on providing a new brass coin of high standard of manufacture and a sufficient supply of it to spread its use throughout the market, he also agreed with many previous advocates of currency (and paper money) that the rough bolts of cloth (*ch'up'o*) that had been used for currency had to be abolished altogether. He also noted that paper money had already disappeared from the Korean economy by his own time.

Unravel Monetary Bolts of Cloth

He remarked that currently fine cloth of six-*sae* thread count was being used in both official and private transactions in which a thirty-"foot" length was defined as one *p'il* and a fifteen-"foot" length as one-half *p'il*, but that the bolts of cloth used as currency had been devalued by reduction of the thread count to two to three *sae*, creating commodity price inflation. He charged that government and private savings stored in warehouses had virtually been rendered worthless, the skill and labor of the women weavers wasted, and many ordinary people bankrupted and driven to thievery to support themselves. The king should order the unraveling of all bolts of rough cloth currently possessed, prohibit any weaving of it in the future, search the marketplaces for bolts of this cloth, and administer beatings to the violators! His willingness to impose punishment reflected his determination to eliminate any expectation that the government might soon reverse its policy, as it had done so many times in the past. Only after the rough cloth disappeared from sight and was replaced by cash as the medium of exchange could the government allow cloth to be traded on the market again.[55]

Establish Shops to Circulate Cash

Yu also prescribed that the government use the familiar device of establishing shops in the wards of the capital, district and garrison towns, post-stations, and hostels to accept cash for transactions, but according to a set quota of shops for each site. In the capital city officials would capitalize these shops so that they might loan rice, grain, and other articles on favorable terms, and allow them liberal limits for repayment of the loans in cash, and in the provinces private parties would be allowed to establish their own shops and be granted exemption from the ordinary shop tax. Government aid for the establishment of shops in tiles, kitchen utensils, plates, tables, and the like would be established by government loans from *taedong* tax reserves to shopkeepers.

In the provinces those merchants allowed to establish new shops under the numerical limits he proposed would be given land grants according to his land distribution scheme, but in the villages individuals who wanted to establish shops in villages would be allowed to do so without a grant of land from the state. The district magistrate would provide them some support by exempting them permanently from the shop tax and granting them loans in grain to get started.

Yu's policy was to keep the number of shops within limits set by the government but allow capitalization and benefits to private shopkeepers outside the licensed monopolies, even those who would not have qualified for land grants under his land distribution system.[56] Nevertheless, this proposal was by no means a radical proposition for the liberalization of commerce to create a free market; on the contrary, it remained within the constraints of the current system under which licensed monopoly shops coexisted with a growing private shop and market sector, a pattern that persisted to the middle of the nineteenth century, even though the number and economic power of the private merchants increased.

Promotion and Regulation of Cash Transactions

Yu insisted that any transactions in cash would be held to the strictest standards of honesty. Any yangban (civil or military official in this case) or clerk who dared to charge as much as one *mun* of cash over a fair price for any transaction would be subject to severe punishment, and an admonition against price gouging would be engraved on a board and hung over the doorways of shops. Yu therefore assumed that the government would have to regulate prices and monitor sales to prevent tradesmen and other persons from using unfamiliarity with cash and prices to hoodwink the gullible.[57]

The government would also promote the use of cash for room, board, and service in the hostels (*ch'am*) established on the main thoroughfares by paying daily travel costs of one *mun* per person and another *mun* for every horse for any person on government business. It would provide costs for hiring torch-bearing guides for night travelers in the vicinity of the hostel town. He insisted that this policy be followed even though the government had not been paying travel expenses to civil and military officials (yangban in the narrow sense of the term). This policy would also eliminate the depredations of court officials and yangban on funeral processions who sent their retainers in the villages to demand people to serve as porters and torchbearers. Perpetrators of this behavior would henceforth be subject to punishment, and if the local official felt powerless to take action against them, he would be obliged to report it to the provincial governor. Government provisions for travel expenses would put an end to the actions of eunuchs from the capital, commanders of garrisons in frontier towns, and military aides and officers (*kun'gwan*) who demanded far more for their upkeep as they passed through hostels and towns on their travels. The magistrates of each district would also provide fodder for the horses of these last three categories of officials.

The state also had the obligation to provide for the upkeep of the hostels, and it could do this by eliminating their obligation to pay support taxes in cloth for military service (*pop'o*), leaving them with only the household (*hose*) and shop taxes (*p'ose*). Hostels would only pay a tax of 40 *mun*/year, and shops established by officials in the capital would pay 120 *mun*/year. Shops granted land by the state under Yu's scheme of land distribution would pay a heavier tax, 240 *mun*/year, and no taxes would be imposed on private shops in the residential areas of local villages, defined as shops that received no grants of land from the state. Prior to the adoption of his land grants system, shopkeepers would not be subjected to personal labor service, but after its adoption, they would be liable for it.[58]

Cash Payments and Respect Relations

Yu realized, of course, that his plan for government-funded travel expenses for anyone on official business conflicted with accepted sensibilities about the privileges of rank. The government previously had not provided travel expenses to yangban not because they had sufficient wealth, but because their exalted status allowed them the privilege of making demands on the local population for services. Yu noted that it was proper to make a distinction between noble and base (*kwich'ŏn*) people and require that commoners treat yangban with respect: "To treat as noble those who are noble and to respect the worthy is really an appropriate principle, and if commoners do not treat yangban with respect but insult them and encroach upon them, they would really deserve to be punished."

Nevertheless, the principle of respect had nothing to do with government compensation for travel expenses. The problem with respect for status, however, was that

> in our country whenever we mention the two words, nobility and baseness, we only do it [to justify] oppressing and coercing people, and when someone is called a yangban it causes trouble everywhere. The people who live by the side of the road hate the yangban and regard them as the source of suffering, and for that reason they try to keep their homes small and simple. How could the yangban help but feel ashamed over this? The reason why the products made by artisans are so shoddy is because the officials force them to do it, and why merchants and shopkeepers do not go to the market is because the officials force them to sell [at low prices]. We must change our customs with respect to these matters, for only then could all these things be done the right way and could it be possible for [common] people to meet their obligation to treat men of true nobility with respect.[59]

Yu's explication for his reason for government funding of all travel expenses irrespective of the status of the individual was designed to put to rest any fear that his advocacy of cash in the market would destroy the nexus of interpersonal relations based on respect that was so fundamental to Korean society at that time. The traditional elite must have feared that cash was the symbol of a society oriented toward profit, and that the exaltation of currency might well destroy the best aspect of traditional Korean society. Yu, however, insisted that cash would not interfere with proper moral standards, only with the abusive use of social distinction to enslave the commoner population to the uncompensated service of the yangban, a class of people who owed more to the inheritance of their status from their forebears than their own inner virtue. His reasoning on this issue, to provide government compensation for travel to eliminate unjust labor demands by traveling yangban without thereby destroying the necessity of respect by social inferiors for their superiors, was very similar to his argument to replace slavery with wage labor because he had assumed that wage laborers would continue to show respect for their employers instead of claiming equal status with them.

Government Regulation of the Exchange Rates

Of course, in this chapter, Yu's primary interest was the circulation of currency itself more than rectification of social evils, and he insisted that the value of coins could be established by the government in relation to rice, cloth, and silver. In other words, once cash were minted and the government controlled the quality and quantity of the money, it could set prices of those three basic goods permanently in cash. He worked out a schedule of exchange rates himself after reviewing standards set for taxes and salaries since ancient times and set the primary standard exchange rate of his new coin at 200 coins (*mun*) per tael or ounce (*yang*) of silver, or 20 *mun* of cash for each tenth of a tael (*chŏn*) of silver (.005 tael of silver for each coin or *mun*). Twenty copper coins would be equivalent to 1 *mal* of rice or a five-"foot" length of cotton cloth (*myŏnp'o*). He determined the ratios of the standard units – husked rice (*paengmi*), a bolt of cotton cloth (*myŏnp'o*), cash (*chŏn*), and silver (*ŭn*) – as shown in table 10.[60]

TABLE 10
YU'S PROPOSED EXCHANGE RATES

Substance	Cotton Cloth	Cash	Silver	Rice
Cotton, 1 *p'il*	—	120 *mun*	.6 *yang*	6 *mal*
Cash, 20 *mun*	5 feet	—	.1 *yang*	1 *mal*
Silver, 1 *yang*	1 *p'il*, 20 ft.	200 *mun*	—	10 *mal*
Rice, 1 *mal*	5 feet	20 *mun*	.1 *yang*	—

NOTE: 1 *p'il* or 1 bolt of cotton cloth defined as 30 "ft." by 8 "inches," of 6 *sŭng* thread count (480 warp threads).

He claimed that although Chinese authorities allowed cash to circulate (freely?), they also set prices to avoid fluctuations. Someone had pointed out to him that despite Yu's admiration for government price-fixing in China, this policy had not succeeded in establishing constant prices in contemporary times because the price of a *mal* of rice cost no less than several hundred coins, and that private families who had accumulated savings of twenty or thirty thousand cash were not regarded as wealthy.

To defend his belief in the vaunted superiority of fixed cash prices and exchange rates against this embarrassing empirical evidence, he claimed that the current price inflation in China only represented the unfortunate result of an age of decline produced by a government policy of unrestrained minting of cash, and an undersupply of grain, silk, and goods in general. The best comparison ought to have been made with earlier times, as in the Han dynasty when the price of one *hu* (either five or ten *mal* or pecks) was twenty to thirty coins, or the Warring States period when Li K'uei once said that one *hu* was worth thirty coins. In ancient China, cash was valuable (i.e., worth something rather than nothing) and could be exchanged for grain and silk, and there was no "stagnation" in the market, or no interruption in the free flow of goods. Even though the money supply was small at the time, it was more than enough to meet demand. A perfect balance had been achieved between the supply of goods and the supply of money, so that "the families of the people kept stores of rice and millet, and there was mutual aid between the root and branch [agricultural production and money and market activities]." In other words, Yu was an advocate of a hard money policy and stable currency, an opponent of easy money and inflation.

In examining recent reports of prices in Manchuria and China in Ming times (up to 1644) he also found that they were not as inflated as they had been in Sung and Yüan times. He had heard that in Liao-tung Province in Manchuria 1 *chŏn* (.1 *liang*) of silver was exchanged for 60 copper coins in the past (late Ming dynasty?), or 600 coins (*mun* in Korea) per *yang* of silver, a rate only one-third the value of the 200 *mun* per *yang* of silver Yu wanted to establish for a new Korean coin. The new Ch'ing rulers (after 1644) had increased the value of copper coins by one-third to 400 coins per *liang* of silver, only 50 percent cheaper than Yu's proposed rate.

When King Sukchong began to mint copper cash in 1678, five years after Yu's death, he set the exchange rate of copper cash against silver at 400 coins (*mun*) per *yang* of silver, raised its value to 200 *mun* in 1679, and lowered its value again to 600 *mun* per *yang* of silver in 1680 to adjust the legal rate of exchange to the real market rate. Although the supply, demand, and prices of copper, silver, and commodities may have differed from the Manchurian situation at time, it appeared that the value of cash against silver in Korea was moving toward the value in Manchuria probably because of an increase in the supply of cash in circulation relative to the amount of goods for sale in the market. Yu's proposed rate of 200 *mun* per *yang* of silver overestimated the eventual value of cash in the market probably because he assumed that the government would be able to constrain the money supply and keep cash at a relatively high value.

There is some ambiguity in Yu's own text about whether he intended to establish a fixed and unchanging exchange rate for copper cash in relation to silver, or believed in a flexible adaptation of that rate according to economic conditions. When some of his friends told him that he should have decided on an exchange rate of 400 *mun*/*yang*, he replied that "If the value of cash declined, there would be no reason why the exchange rate could not be adjusted to the situation at the time. The only thing [that is important] is that at the time the rate is set you do your best to fit the rate to conditions. Even though you may set the rate in this manner, once the rate is set, it should last permanently and never be changed." Yu's flexibility on the cash/silver exchange rate was apparently limited to the period prior to the final determination of the exchange rate; thereafter it was to remain constant.[61]

Yu also set the exchange rate of cash in rice at twenty *mun* of cash for one *mal* of rice, but he did concede that in the short term the price of millet and rice could fluctuate widely, that the price of rice might rise to sixty *mun* of cash (300 percent) after a poor crop. In other words, the cash/silver exchange rate was to be fixed and fundamental, but the exchange value of cash with grain, cloth, and other commodities could fluctuate.[62]

Yu explained that since the *t'ou* (peck) in Liao-tung was twice the volume of the Korean *mal*, cash prices for grain were not as high as Koreans thought, and in any case the price of grain was determined by what price the government chose to set. Even though Manchurian coins might appear to be only half the value that Yu proposed for the new Korean coin since 400 Manchurian coins were needed to purchase 1 *yang* of silver, because of the difference in grain measures, Korean cash could buy twice as much rice in Korea than in Manchuria, and his proposed rate of exchange for Korean cash would be equivalent to the Manchurian rate.

He contrasted the contemporary situation in China with recent monetary history in Korea. He pointed out that cash had not been circulating in Korea except for the area around Kaesŏng, and then when cash was first adopted, the value of cash was set at 30 *mun* of cash for 1 *chŏn* of silver (or 300 *mun* per *yang* of silver). Later, however, the value of cash dropped severely to 500, 700, and then 1,000 *mun* per *yang* of silver. Yu provided an intriguing hypothesis to explain this phenomenon by arguing that the inflation in the value of silver was produced because cash was really not used anywhere but in the Kaesŏng area and all the cash minted in the country found its way to Kaesŏng, glutting that district with cash. Cash was attracted to the Kaesŏng area because the government did not do enough to spread the supply of it throughout the kingdom nor stimulate its use by requiring that cash be used for taxes or expenditures, leaving only private persons to conduct trade in cash on their own. Yu's explanation of the reasons for this depreciation in the value of cash might seem entirely conjectural except that the experience with cash after King Sukchong reinstated the minting of copper currency in 1678, to be described later, displayed similar symptoms: surplus cash concentrated in the capital and very little of it reached the countryside.

When the government finally introduced cash in 1635 and later in 1650, it set its value at one *mun* of cash made of brass (*tusŏk*) per *toe* (one-tenth *mal*) of rice (ten *mun* per *mal*) and two *mun* of cash made of red copper (twenty *mun* per *mal*), but later on only one type of cash (which?) circulated at a cheaper rate of three *mun* per *toe* of rice, that is, thirty *mun* per *mal* of rice. Because the coin failed to circulate, presumably because it was still overvalued, the price of one *mal* was raised to fifty and later seventy *mun* of cash. Even though the government used cash for salaries, it only used cash to pay for extra grants instead of the basic salaries of officials. The hope that the people would adopt cash for use in private transactions was doomed to failure, and when the circulation of the cash ceased, the government had no choice but to abolish it as legal tender.[63]

Yu presupposed that an ideal cash economy would consist only of a single coin similar to a U.S. penny, and that its value could be set at 200 *mun* or coins per *yang* of silver and 20 *mun* per *mal* of rice. Although large transactions would require transporting cartloads of strings of a thousand coins each, he assumed that a cash economy would not be subjected to disruptive volatility in price fluctuations because the king would maintain control over the money supply, set the face value of the single coin based on an equivalent to the cost of the metallic content and labor, and fix prices of other commodities in cash. These prices would be maintained in perpetuity by state regulation of the money supply, not only in preventing commodity price inflation by checking excessive minting of cash, but also by stopping commodity price deflation and an increase in the value of cash by guaranteeing a sufficient supply of copper to meet the increased demand for cash as its circulation spread throughout the country by importing foreign copper. As we will see, after 1678 Korean money managers had to deal with both problems, and Yu's overall proposal for the creation of stable prices in a money economy appeared to be more logical than the remedies adopted by Sukchong and subsequent kings.

Progressive Conservatism

Yu's advocacy of cash when Korea was advancing beyond the stage of cloth and grain as media of exchange appears to have been progressive, but his fundamental attitudes toward cash were rooted not only in classical thought, but also in the classical model of ancient society and economy by which the market served only to move goods from areas of surplus and concentration to those of shortage and deprivation, and money only played the role of lubricating the flow of goods.[64] Despite his willingness to import as much copper as needed to expand the supply of currency throughout the nation, he had no concept of stimulating production and expanding market activities to escape the constraints of a fundamentally agrarian economy, or using cash as a means of accumulating capital for large-scale commercial, let alone industrial, projects.[65] Had he believed in the virtues of large-scale capital formation to fuel commercial or industrial expansion, he would have been aware of the bottleneck created by having no medium of exchange other than pennies.

He also provided another excellent indication of the conservative nature of his vision for the economy in his appendum to his essay on cash, a short treatise advocating that the state abolish what he called "empty markets" (*kongjang*) or "empty markets in outer [i.e., suburban] areas" (*oech'ŏ kongjang*). Judging from his own description of these places, they appear to have been the equivalent of flea markets held in open fields rather than either constructed shops built in market areas designated by the state, or even periodic five-day markets held in market towns. He was willing to approve the periodic markets since they allowed local villagers to exchange goods among themselves, and he even advised the government to cease the current market taxes (*changse*) that district magistrates and their clerks and runners were levying on trade among ordinary peasants in periodic markets. In his view, market taxes were warranted only if levied on professional merchants who had their designated shops in market areas.

He did not believe that the choice of occupation was to be left to the free will of all individuals lest the basic population of cultivators be reduced by unrestrained pursuit of commerce. The "empty" or flea markets were undesirable because they attracted flocks of troublemakers and starving peasants who had no legitimate occupations of their own, got drunk, and started fights with others. "They don't hesitate to butcher oxen, they drink together without any restraint, they do damage to mores and destroy customs, and they brew trouble and commit robbery." The very existence of these markets provided a "den of evil for vagrants escaping famine in their home towns." Only if such markets were held farther than thirty *li* (seven and one-quarter miles) from any town or post-station, could they be tolerated. In short, the commercial economy, let alone industrial production, was to be kept under control and restraint, and left to perform a subsidiary role in an agricultural economy.[66]

Conclusion

Yu Hyŏngwŏn's advocacy of copper cash certainly appeared enlightened and progressive in his own time because the lack of an adequate currency had made the Korean economy appear backward by comparison with trade and commerce in Ch'ing China and Tokugawa Japan. Yu was obviously caught up in the movement for cash that had started at the beginning of the century, but he derived most of his ideas about the proper mode of currency, the regulation of its value in the market, and measures to stimulate and ensure its successful adoption from the Chinese experience and major commentaries on the problems of cash by Chinese statesmen and writers over two millennia, not just the recent history of the late Ming (he refrained from commenting on the early Ch'ing) and the information he obtained from Hendrik Hamel's compatriots about currency in the Western world. He was acutely aware of Korea's inability to develop a permanent cash economy on its own except for a few brief experiments, and he blamed it on the backward and barbaric legacy of the Korean Three Kingdoms. While it is possible that a sense of nationalistic pride motivated Yu to advocate policies that would bring Korea abreast of China and sought to borrow methods and models previously worked out by the Chinese, it appears more likely that the classical model of ancient China provided his own standard of perfection, and experiments in post-Ch'in China informed him about some of the problems involved in administering the use of currency and cash. Instead of bragging about the superiority of native institutions, as most modern chauvinists are prone to do, Yu measured Korea against cosmopolitan standards of perfection that transcended national identity within the world of East Asian cultural awareness.[67]

He learned from classical Chinese texts that currency was important as a medium of exchange rather than as a source of wealth or as a means of increasing nonagricultural production. He learned that a money economy might threaten instability by over-or undersupply of either money itself, or the commodities for sale on the market, and he advised that the government had the responsibility to provide for cash, either through minting or importing, and to stabilize the value of money by regulating its supply. It also had to prevent any actions that would decrease the value of money or weaken public confidence in it as legal tender, whether by private minting, counterfeiting, debasement, or excessive minting, or conversely increasing money's value by melting it down or exporting it abroad.

This type of conservative approach to the money supply by no means indicated *by itself* any hostility to commerce, since advocates of sound or hard money who preferred silver coins or specie payments instead of paper money or bank notes unbacked by things of value was also part of the program of Andrew Jackson and the radical Democrats in the United States in the 1830s. They did battle with the American system of Alexander Hamilton and the Federalists, who were devoted to high-tariff protectionism, the monopoly of the state-supported private U.S. Bank and its issuance of bank notes and paper money, and state support for the economy.[68] It shares the approach of twentieth-century hard money advocates of the gold standard for currency or maintenance of the stability of the currency against the potential effects of inflation and the desire of governments to print money and expand the money supply to meet budget deficits.

The circumstances in mid-seventeenth century Korea, however, were somewhat different. Gold and silver did not circulate, and silver was only used as a standard for setting the value of grain, cloth, and copper cash. The absence of an adequate currency meant that the circulation of goods was obstructed, and now that the *taedong* taxation system had been adopted, a more rapid circulation of goods was necessary for the market purchases of necessities by the state to work efficiently.

Yu's predilection for his concept of hard money – penny cash close to the intrinsic value of the copper in it – was coupled with his belief in the positive role of the state. With reformist officials of his generation he believed that the state had a necessary role to play in stimulating the spread of cash throughout the economy, instead of leaving the fate of cash to any free-market philosophy untrammeled by government interference. He presumed that the main means of providing for the flow of cash was converting taxes and government payments to cash, rather than by stimulating expanding production, liberating merchants from government constraint, or encouraging peasants to go into commercial or industrial activity or foreign trade, even though he advocated establishing shops to accept cash from consumers. He believed that with proper planning and regulation, the government could calculate just how much cash was needed to enable the conversion of most taxes and government payments to cash, and set a face value on the coin that could be maintained indefinitely.

In one of his suggestions he displayed a kind of courage that some other advocates of cash could not bring themselves to advocate, that the endemic shortage of copper be overcome by importing whatever was needed from Japan to achieve a full conversion of taxes to cash. Had he also proposed expanded exports to Japan to pay for the copper, he might have taken another step toward more advanced economic thinking. Unfortunately, he did not develop the idea that trade could produce wealth, or even the mercantilist notion that a favorable balance of trade with foreign countries would produce wealth through a constant import of specie to pay for those exports.

His idea of a fixed value of cash to be maintained by government flexibility in controlling the money supply appears to have been reasonable and cautious, but it was not likely to stimulate the benefits of trade by providing more liquid capital to merchants and producers. It certainly did not allow any adjustment that might benefit the poor, debt-ridden, and taxpaying peasants, who might have been well served by a looser monetary policy that would allow moderate inflation in difficult times. His more conservative monetary policy would have prevented the damaging effects of inflation, but it would also have guaranteed a steady return to the creditor class of landlords, state grain-loan officials, and merchant moneylenders by preserving the value of loans at the expense of debtors and the poor.

His calculation of the total money supply that would be needed to monetize taxes presupposed a fixed volume of currency because it had not occurred either to his Chinese sources or Korean contemporaries that it might be possible for the economy to expand by nonagricultural production and foreign trade, and that the demand for cash might increase indefinitely in the long term without necessarily causing inflation. Certainly, if he had hoped for an ever-expanding economy, or had been interested in expanded commercial (let alone industrial) production, he could never have rested content with a cash economy based on the penny alone. Had his Chinese sources provided some clue about the convenience of bills of exchange and drafts for long-distance trade, he might have been awakened to the economic benefits of nonagricultural activity, but he was unable to appreciate the use of paper money in Sung and Yüan times in China. He only thought that paper money had been tried in Koryŏ and fifteenth-century Chosŏn and had failed because it was too susceptible to adulteration and inflation, and he believed the same fate was destined for any multiple-denomination coin. In short, Yu was more progressive than the majority of Koreans in the sixteenth century but was still too firmly attached intellectually to the wisdom of economic thought in classical times, which to him appeared far more advanced than contemporary Korea.

CHAPTER 25

A Cycle of Inflation and Deflation

By stimulating the exchange of goods the *taedong* reform created a need for a better medium of exchange to regulate calculations of value if only to maintain an equitable assessment of taxes. The *taedong* system itself involved the use of a kind of dual currency system based on grain and cloth, but the manipulation of the grain/cloth exchange rate and the use of the *chŏmt'oe* or "check-off" system by which clerks had rejected cloth payments on the grounds of poor quality had caused discontent and created more pressure for the use of metallic currency as a more reliable and less easily manipulated medium of exchange.

In other words, the expansion of market transactions had stimulated the demand for copper cash, and the state took responsibility for supplying cash to the market. But once that decision was made in 1678 by King Sukchong, the problem of controlling the money supply emerged. Sukchong decided it was preferable to limit the minting of coins to a single source, preferably in the capital, but since the cost of transporting the cash to the provinces was too high, he had to allow local officials to mint cash on their own, which weakened central controls over the money supply. Local officials were prone to mint as much cash as possible to pay for their own expenses, and to mint inferior coins to increase the profits of seigniorage. This debasement of coins only destroyed public confidence in the money and drove its value down. Instead of cash replacing cloth as a medium of exchange, the reverse began to take place.

Another stumbling block that appeared was slow circulation. The central government's agencies were dependent on the remission of cash tax collections in the countryside to make purchases of goods in the capital market, but provincial cash receipts were slow to arrive. King Sukchong then authorized additional minting by various capital agencies to provide them with the cash for purchase of goods, and this additional minting raised the money supply and caused price inflation. In addition, the king was under pressure to mint cash to provide relief in case of crop failures and famine conditions, and this function also led to the increase of the money supply by the late 1680s. Thus, by 1689, the surplus cash had returned to the capital, inflating the prices of goods, but it had either disappeared or was replaced by bolts of cotton cloth in the countryside. The problems associated with initiating the proper circulation of cash had been quite formidable.

King Sukchong wanted to spread cash use and had to increase the supply of cash in the economy to do so, but inflation and debasement had forced him to curtail the money supply and stop the minting of cash – a serious contradiction in policy. The minting of cash in the seventeenth century did not solve all the economic problems caused by the lack of an adequate money supply because the management of money was also a problem for which the Koreans lacked adequate experience. Maintaining a stable value of currency was complex because copper cash was not used in many areas of the country, and there were delays in its flow from the countryside to the major market and urban areas. Because mints were not concentrated under a single source of authority, controlling the money supply was difficult. And the desire for restraint to dampen the potential for inflation was often countered by the need for cash to finance government operations or relief in times of famine and distress. By the end of the seventeenth century conservative spokesmen against inflation had emerged to do battle against the more liberal advocates of greater market activity.

THE FIRST CYCLE: INFLATION IN A PRIMITIVE CASH ECONOMY

Resumption of Minting, 1681–89

King Sukchong authorized the minting of cash in 1678, five years after Yu Hyŏngwŏn's death, but only two years later the country suffered from inflation caused by the excessive minting of cash, followed by contraction of the money supply and deflation. When King Sukchong began to mint copper cash in 1678, he set the exchange rate of copper cash against silver at 400 coins (*mun*) per *yang* of silver, raised its value to 200 *mun* in 1679, and lowered its value again to 600 *mun* per *yang* of silver in 1680 to match the real market value of cash in an inflationary situation. Since a severe famine had occurred in 1680, Sukchong had probably minted too much cash to provide relief to the peasants, lowering its value on the market.

The pattern was now about to be repeated, but now over a protracted period, and this experience fostered changes in attitudes toward cash and its merits. Sukchong's suspension of minting in the provinces continued until the beginning of 1681, when he adopted Second State Councilor Min Chŏngjung's request to resume minting both in the capital and the provinces, but under the direction of the Ministry of Taxation in the capital and the provincial governors in the provinces. Min made his proposal not simply to expand the volume of cash in circulation, but to eliminate the corrupt manipulation of the rules for commuting grain taxes to cloth by officials and clerks. He was inspired by the semiretired Song Siyŏl, who complained that peasants required to pay a cloth commutation of the *taedong* rice tax were being charged too much by the district magistrates. In 1623

King Injo had prohibited this kind of illegal manipulation of the standards of quality for rice and cloth tax payments and defined the bolt of cloth at 35 "feet" of length and 5 *sae* (400 threads) in width, but by 1681 the peasants were asked to pay finer cloth of 6 *sae* (480 threads). This phenomenon was part of a general trend toward demands by tax collectors for better quality cloth than the rough cloth (*ch'up'o*) that had been used primarily as the main medium of exchange in the market.[1] Min claimed that tax collectors were not only demanding 6 *sae* cloth from the taxpayers, they were also cheating the central government as well by remitting only 5 *sae* cloth to the capital (a practice dubbed *hwanmok* or "switching the cotton"), or collecting whiter or more polished rice from the taxpayers and remitting an inferior grade to the capital. He suggested that district magistrates supervise tax collections and ban illegal switching of tax payments.

Once Sukchong agreed, Min pressed for even greater reform. Even though the government tightened procedures for collecting taxes in cloth, the Ministry of War alone would still be entitled to collect 7 *sae* (560 thread) cloth under the present rules. The only way to eliminate all corruption in cloth taxes would be to accept Minister of Taxation Cho Sasŏk's advice to convert cloth taxes to cash at commutation rates established in exact tables. He also warned that this policy could only succeed if the government resumed the minting of more cash to ensure the circulation of cash throughout the country, and King Sukchong granted his approval. Even though Wŏn Yuhan has observed that the primary factor in the decision was a desire to eliminate the cost of transporting cash minted in the capital to the provinces, Min's main motive was to eliminate corruption in the collection of taxes paid in cloth or rice.[2]

Flaws developed in the new program almost immediately. Provincial governors could not be trusted to restrict the minting of cash in the provinces to a proper level because in 1682 Yi Samyŏng, the governor of Chŏlla Province, was charged with blatant profiteering and excessive minting.[3] Furthermore, early in 1683 the Ministry of Taxation reported it had run out of rice and cloth funds and had no cash at all because tax receipts were so low, and Minister of Taxation Yun Kye complained that the coins minted by other capital agencies and the provincial governors were so bad that the public lost confidence in them and the value of cash had plummeted. He then obtained Sukchong's approval to make the Ministry of Taxation the only agency with authority to mint cash, eliminate corruption, and convince the public that the officials were not simply trying to profit by minting coins.

The chief of the Office of Royal Relatives, Min Yujung, also complained to Sukchong about difficulties in the distribution of cash minted in the capital to the provinces. When the Ever-Normal Bureau and the Office of Benefiting the People previously sent cash to south Chŏlla and Kyŏngsang provinces, the commissioners (*ch'ain*) entrusted with distributing cash throughout the villages were ordered to make purchases of goods in the provincial markets for cash. Unfortunately, these commissioners made personal profits by paying prices much lower than those in the capital market. Peasant taxpayers who had to sell their bolts of cotton to obtain cash to pay the commuted support taxes for soldiers, artisans, or labor service workers, or official slaves who wanted to pay their slave cloth tribute in cash, now had to pay a premium for this transaction.

Min pointed out that the corruption of the commissioners over the past several years had not only wrecked the plan to spread the use of cash, it had stopped the circulation of cash and commercial activity in the southern provinces, and the commissioners themselves became liquor merchants or local tavern owners. Since many people had come to believe that the royal court had, in fact, abolished its circulation of cash purposely, it would now be even more difficult to reinstitute its use in the market. Min then won Sukchong's approval to turn responsibility for transporting newly minted cash to the market towns and villages over to the provincial governors and district magistrates, and set prices or exchange rates for goods according to prices in the capital market to eliminate price differentials between the capital and the countryside.[4]

Unfortunately the policy to centralize minting in the capital under the Ministry of Taxation was frustrated when meager cash tax revenues for government offices throughout the country left them without enough cash to pay bills or make purchases. In 1683 Sukchong was forced to grant permission to mint cash for a limited period of time on an ad hoc basis to capital ministries suffering critical shortages of funds or local districts in dire need of relief funds to combat famine. Wŏn Yuhan interpreted this decision as a significant change in the purpose of minting cash from promotion of the circulation of cash in the economy to raising additional revenues from the profits of seigniorage, but that view is neither fair nor accurate. Sukchong had been forced to modify his plan for central control of minting and the money supply to meet emergency demands for funds for relief as well as ordinary expenses, not simply to increase revenue by minting as much cash as possible. Had he really been devoted to maximizing the profits of seigniorage, he might have favored multiple-denomination cash or paper money instead of the less profitable "penny" cash in current use.

1689–91, Contracting the Money Supply

Once he opened the door to ad hoc minting by local agencies, however, more cash flowed into the market and the value of cash declined. Then, early in 1689 Minister of Taxation Kwŏn Taejae won Sukchong's approval to contract the money supply by suspending his ministry's minting operations.[5] Later that month Chief State Councilor Kwŏn Taeun told Sukchong that reports of a surplus of cash were misleading because it was only true of the capital and little was circulating in the countryside. Not only was cloth still the main medium for the payment of taxes by the rural people, it had even replaced cash in the revenues of the capital bureaus. He then suggested that the capital bureaus be required to collect at least one-third their revenues in cash to restore confidence among the taxpayers in the value of cash and help expand its use in the provincial economies. He also argued that using cash instead of cloth for tax payments would prevent the familiar "check-off" (*chŏmt'oe*) tactic that tax clerks used to reject cloth on the grounds of alleged inferiority. Third State Councilor Kim Tŏgwŏn also reported that public confidence in cash had declined because officials in the capital had been refusing to accept cash for tax payments. Sukchong adopted Kwŏn's suggestions, but he maintained his decision to suspend further minting to curtail the increase of cash in the capital market. Had Sukchong merely wanted to increase revenues, he would not have suspended minting.[6]

Sukchong had minted cash without restraint between 1683 and 1689, but then authorized a "temporary" ban on minting. He continued the ban to 1691 because he was afraid of the possibility of reproducing the deleterious effects of an excessive money supply. In the seventh month of 1691, he allowed Kaesŏng to mint cash to provide funds for military expenses and entertaining Ch'ing envoys, but he remained cautious about restraining the money supply to prevent inflation and preserve the value of the currency, especially since Kaesŏng was the heart of the cash economy outside the capital. He restricted coinage in Kaesŏng to twenty smelters for a period of five months, and required that the Ministry of Taxation inspect the quality of the coins. In 1692, he also allowed the Military Training Agency to mint cash briefly under controlled regulations to provide for defense costs for Kanghwa Island, and granted similar permission to the Anti-Manchu Division (Ch'ongyungch'ŏng). Even though Sukchong allowed the resumption of minting after 1691, he did not do so primarily to raise revenues because he favored a conservative and restrictive control of the volume of cash.[7]

Probably for this reason government offices were still short of sufficient cash revenue. In 1693 Minister of Rites Yu Myŏnghyŏn asked for additional funds for famine relief – the Office of Benefiting the People had exhausted all its reserves to counteract the drought that had been suffered in several provinces that year. The Border Defense Command won Sukchong's approval for minting more cash at the beginning of the fourth lunar month, but the supplies of copper had been exhausted. Copper imports from Japan in official trade had only averaged between 26,000 to 29,000 *kŭn* (catties) prior to 1678, and had increased to 300,000 *kŭn* a year by 1693, but the Border Defense Command reported that the three agencies that were minting cash (presumably the Ministry of Taxation, Military Training Agency, and Central Division?) required more than 4,000 *ch'ing* (400,000 *kŭn*) to produce their quota of cash. The Office of Benefiting the People had also been authorized to mint cash to meet its expenses, but there was no copper available. Yu suggested that since the two military agencies had only been given a twelve-month limitation on minting, on the first day of the first lunar month in 1694 the Office of Benefiting the People should take over minting from the Military Training Agency and the Anti-Manchu Division. In other words, the amount of cash available was used for relief and military expenses, and imported copper was not sufficient to allow further minting.

Chief State Councilor Kwŏn Taeun objected to the diffusion of minting among several agencies because it had depleted the supply of copper, driven its price sky high, and stimulated counterfeiting and the debasement of coins. Yu

Myŏnghŏn added that allowing so many separate agencies to mint cash had obstructed spread of cash in the economy because it increased the cost of materials and resources and contributed to the deterioriation in coin quality. Now that a national shortage of copper had occurred, minters had begun to use lead as alloys and some coins were so poorly made that they crumbled when handled, destroying public confidence in their quality, and reducing the general value of all coins in the market – a problem that Yu Hyŏngwŏn had warned against in his writings. Kwŏn urged Sukchong again to economize on the use of copper by concentrating all minting operations in a single office, but Sukchong followed Yu Myŏnghŏn's suggestion to wait until the beginning of the next year.

Paradoxically, the shortage of cash had reduced, rather than increased, its value because it promoted cash adulteration in compensation. Yu Myŏnghŏn felt that by concentrating minting in the Ministry of Taxation and the Office of Benefiting the People, the government would economize on production cost and maximize seigniorage profits for the state, provide standard coins for use in the market, and eventually succeed in extending the use of cash throughout the country. Sukchong agreed to abolish minting by all but the Ministry of Taxation and one other capital agency, but he chose the Ever-Normal Bureau instead of the Office of Benefiting the People to join with the Ministry of Taxation as the sole agents for minting and supervising cash.[8]

A little over a year later in 1694, however, Sukchong reneged and granted the Royal Division (Ŏyŏngch'ŏng) the right to mint cash to provide enough revenues for the completion of wall construction work. After debating whether the Royal Division should be permitted to mint more cash for a six- or twelve-month period, Sukchong compromised by agreeing to ten months.

The battle between liberality and restraint in the minting of cash was exacerbated by a horrendous famine in 1695, reputedly more severe than the one in 1680. Sukchong initially granted permission to the governor of Kangwŏn Province to mint cash for relief funds but rescinded the order when two ministers objected that his compassion would destroy the government's control over the money supply by setting a precedent for other governors to make similar requests. They asked instead that he have the Ever-Normal Bureau mint extra cash and send it out to Kangwŏn Province. Sukchong overrode their objection and permitted more minting by the governors of Hwanghae, Ch'ungch'ŏng, and Kangwŏn provinces to fulfill his responsibility to care for the welfare of the people. He only agreed to impose a limit of 10,000 *yang* (1 million coins) of cash to be minted in the capital and sent to those three provinces, but he assigned responsibility for this to the Office of Benefiting the People instead of the Ever-Normal Bureau. Even though Sukchong chose to violate his own law to limit the minting of cash to two agencies in the capital, he was forced to do so primarily by a moral compunction to provide relief, not by a desire to maximize government revenue for ordinary expenditures. All authorizations for additional minting between 1691 and 1695 were necessitated by emergencies and limited by cautious fears about the effects of inflation.[9]

Rising Interest Rates and Inflation

It was at this point that a crucial turning point in general attitudes toward cash occurred when more people began to blame cash itself for some of the evils in the economy. Third State Councilor Ch'oe Sŏkchŏng attacked the role of cash for exacerbating the interest rate and the debt burdens imposed on poor peasants. He said that prior to the introduction of cash, peasants in the villages borrowed rice or cloth from others in the difficult spring planting period, and repaid the debt in rice after the fall harvest. For every ten *mal* of rice borrowed in the spring planting season, fifteen *mal* for the principal and interest combined had to be repaid after the fall harvest, 50 percent interest for the time borrowed (referred to as *changni*).

Ch'oe accepted this 50 percent interest rate (closer to 60 percent per annum since the term of loan was probably around ten months) with astonishing sangfroid because it was sanctified by tradition, but he was really angered because the use of cash for loans had provided an opportunity for creditors to raise real interest rates still higher. If someone borrowed 1 *yang* of cash in the springtime when rice was in short supply and its price was high, the borrower could only purchase 2 *mal* of it on the market. After the harvest in the fall the borrower would have to repay 1 *yang* 50 *mun* (1.5 *yang*), but since the temporary surfeit of grain on the market would have driven the price of grain down to 5 *mal* per *yang* of cash, it would cost the borrower 7 *mal* 5 *toe* (7.5 *mal*) to obtain the 1.5 *yang* of cash to repay the lender's principal and interest, 3.75 times the grain value of the original loan in cash borrowed in the spring, or 375 percent for the growing season.[10]

Furthermore, during the growing season interest was calculated at the rate of 10 *mun* per month on a 1 *yang* loan, but if the borrower had to delay repayment for sixteen or seventeen months, he would have to pay as much as 1.6–17 *yang* in interest alone. If cash was short and moneylenders were reluctant to grant cash loans and peasants were desperate for funds, peasants would have to offer as much as 100 percent interest for a cash loan during the growing season and repay 2 *yang* for every *yang* borrowed. In that situation, if the fall price of grain dropped to 5 *mal* per *yang*, the borrower would have to sell as much as 15–16 *mal* of rice in the fall to obtain enough cash to repay capital and interest on the loan, an interest rate in grain at 800 percent for the growing season. Poor peasants would have to spend the income earned by a year's arduous labor just to pay off their taxes and private debts.

Since the standard interest rate on loans of silver and cash had been 20 percent for the growing season ever since ancient times, even though the universal interest rate for rice or grain loans repaid in grain in the fall had been 50 percent for the season, Ch'oe believed that the rate for all loans in cash ought to be set at 20 percent, or 20 *mun* (.2 *yang*) of cash for each *yang* borrowed. Since cash had been put into circulation,

> the rich were getting richer and the poor poorer. It has been less than twenty years since cash has circulated, but the problem [of loan interest] has become so great that all the people in the provinces hoped that it would be abolished. But because cash had circulated for both official and private transactions for such a long period of time, it had become difficult to abolish it immediately. We should establish a law changing the discriminatory interest rate on cash loans, so that the poor and lowly people would perhaps be granted the benefit of some relief.

Ch'oe argued that interest rate reduction was the least the government could do since the peasants also had to deal with the avarice of the district magistrates, the demands for bribes from the district clerks, and the predations of bandits.[11]

Ch'oe's account of the multiplying effect of cash loans on interest rates may not have taken account of the benefits conferred on borrowers by the depreciation of the currency because if the value of cash dropped by 50 percent in the space of a year, the cost of a loan even with a usurious interest rate might be reduced by half. Unfortunately, cutting a seasonal interest of 800 percent in half might not have succeeded in saving the impoverished debtor from financial ruin. Ch'oe's castigation of the adverse affect of cash on interest rates marked the development of a negative reaction to cash that was born of direct experience rather than the hackneyed moralism of traditional anti-cash prejudice.

The historian responsible for compiling this section of the *Veritable Record for King Sukchŏng* (*Sukchong sillok*), probably in the late 1720s when anti-cash bias was at its height, inserted a statement in the text right after the above notice describing three of the ill effects of cash that may also been perceived in 1695 as well. He charged that cash made people prone to spend their savings more freely than other media of exchange, stimulated them to pursue commerce at the expense of agriculture (because it was less arduous and provided the prospect of easy money), and put debtors at the mercy of wealthy usurers who gained as much as five or six times the amount of the original loan when they converted cash payments into grain.[12]

Sukchong's Ban on Minting, 1697

At the end of 1695, Sukchong again authorized the Royal Division to mint cash for a ten-month limit, and his authorization of military as well as civilian agencies to mint cash to provide funds for relief produced inflationary consequences and a drop in the value of copper cash. The compiler of the *Sillok* section that reviewed this period expressed his own admiration for the pioneers of cash in the seventeenth century, Yi Wŏn'ik, Kim Yuk, and Kim's grandson, Kim Sŏkchu, but he charged King Sukchong with irresponsibility by authorizing the excessive minting of cash to make up for financial shortages caused by periods of famine.[13]

King Sukchong did, however, become wary of the negative consequences of an excessive cash supply and specified that he was authorizing this additional short-term minting only to provide humanitarian relief in the face of desperate famine conditions. Nevertheless, the cash supply in the capital and other urban areas had grown too large and cash had become so cheap that people melted it down either to obtain raw copper or make utensils because it was more valuable that way. Even though specific figures for copper imports from Japan are not available for these years, total Japanese copper exports increased from approximately 430,000 *kŭn* a year in 1691 and 1692, to close to 700,000 *kŭn* in 1693 and 1694, dropped to 327,252 *kŭn* in 1695, rose to 628,348 *kŭn* in 1696, and peaked to 1.4 million *kŭn* in 1697. What percentage of that total was shipped to Korea is not known, but the sum presumably exceeded the 300,000 *kŭn* mark mentioned in 1693. For that reason, in the eighth month of 1696 Sukchong accepted the proposal of the Fourth Inspector of the Office of the Inspector-General, Song Ching'ŭn, to end all special permission for short-term minting operations by government agencies when the current limits on such loans expired in the third lunar month of 1697. This decision brought all government-authorized and legal minting of cash to an end for over twenty years.[14]

THE SECOND CYCLE: DEFLATION, 1697–1731

Ban on Minting and Deflation, 1697–1724

Sukchong's suspension of all government minting aided tremendously in reversing the tide of cash surplus and price inflation in the markets, especially since the use of cash and the production and sale of nonagricultural goods in markets continued to spread geographically, and created more demand for cash. In the ensuing twenty years the cash supply could not keep up with the rising demand for its use, and the value of cash was driven so high that it became almost as valuable as silver.

Licensed vs. Unlicensed Merchants. The demand for cash increased with the expansion of commercial activity, and the growth of unlicensed merchants (*nanjŏn*). At the beginning of the dynasty the commercial activities of the licensed capital shopkeepers (*sijŏn*) were restricted to supplying the palace and central government with their material needs and marketing whatever surpluses were left in the state treasuries, but by the end of the fifteenth century the population of the capital was increased by the migration of peasants whose land had been taken over by landlords. Many of them became merchants and set up shops around the city, and King Chungjong in the early sixteenth century tolerated their presence to enable them to support themselves.

As these unlicensed merchants (*nanjŏn*) became more prosperous by the end of the century, the licensed capital merchants began to demand government permission to ban competitors and grants of monopoly privileges for a wider range of commercial activities than they previously enjoyed, especially since taxes on licensed merchants had increased considerably after Hideyoshi's invasions. The government was now constrained to comply with their request since it faced a fiscal crisis after the invasion, did not have the funds to pay the licensed capital shopkeepers for the goods they had presented, and had to rely on them to obtain their own supplies and goods for entertaining Chinese envoys and holding state funerals. Government grants of monopoly privileges to licensed capital merchants marked the beginning of the so-called *yug'ŭijŏn*, or six categories of shops, each dealing in a different category of goods, which were authorized to establish warehouses (*toga*) for storing their category of goods, and to collect taxes from other, nonlicensed merchants.

The unlicensed operators consisted not only of professional merchants, but of guard soldiers seeking to supplement their limited salaries, slaves of the powerful yangban families, and artisans in handicraft manufacture who sold their products directly to the public. A more serious challenge to the licensed monopolies was posed by the development of large-scale commercial ventures not only by wealthy merchants, but also by yangban and clerk-representatives of local districts in capital agencies (*chŏri*). They also established warehouses to engage in wholesaling, and contracted with producers to buy products in large quantities and to sell at prices cheaper than the licensed merchants.[15] Kang Man'gil traced the origin of wholesaling to the government's decision in 1681 to build warehouses to provide paper and cushions to the government and to store goods for subsequent use. This measure was taken because the *kong'in* tribute agents were unable to meet government demands for goods on time. Later on, private merchants began to construct their own warehouses (*toga*) to buy products in quantity or corner the market in a given commodity to restrain supply and drive prices up.[16]

The 1716 Famine and Demand for More Cash. The commercial activities of the unlicensed merchants and private wholesalers contributed to the demand for cash and exacerbated the cash shortage during the moratorium on official minting in the early eighteenth century, but the hardships of deflation were not sufficient to stimulate government interest until another famine in 1716 created crisis conditions. At that time Second State Councilor Yi Hŭimyŏng declared that the time had arrived for the government to purchase copper and mint more cash to provide relief funds for the starving.[17] Yi's request for humanitarian relief failed to generate much support because general attitudes toward cash had become extremely negative. Min Chinwŏn, in particular, complained about the usurious loans associated with cash and the insufficiency of copper. Two other similar proposals in 1717 and 1719 for relief for famine in P'yŏng'an Province and Cheju Island were initially approved by King Sukchong but later rescinded because of opposition to the perceived evils of cash. In 1724, the next king, Kyŏngjong, also agreed to mint cash to meet a fiscal crisis, but Second State Councilor Yi Kwangjwa opposed it from the outset and then, with the support of the Minister of Taxation, persuaded the king to cease further minting because copper was too expensive, the cost of relief would break the goverment's budget, and the use of cash would itself only stimulate corruption and deceit.[18]

A New Basis for Anti-Cash Prejudice. By the second decade of the eighteenth century the attitudes toward cash and its role in the economy had been almost totally reversed from what they had been in the early seventeenth century. From King Injo through the first half of King Sukchong's reign, kings and a growing percentage of high officials had favored a positive policy to introduce cash into the economy and promote its circulation throughout the country. Officials like Kim Yuk and Hŏ Chŏk and scholars like Yu Hyŏngwŏn believed that the absence of cash demonstrated the persistence of backwardness if not barbarism in the level of civilization. Both Sukchong and Kyŏngjong remained faithful to their moral obligation to succor the starving, and they were willing to use cash to do it, but even though the cash shortage and price deflation in the second decade of the eighteenth century provided sufficient economic and rational grounds for a small increase in the money supply, neither king could overcome the anti-cash prejudice of their top officials.

Even though the introduction of cash had always been opposed by a hard core of conservatives who preferred the imagined simplicity of a natural, agrarian economy, the new conservative opposition to cash was now the product of reaction against anomalies in prices, exchange values, and interest rates that was now attributed exclusively to a lack of constraint in restricting the money supply in the 1690s. Conservative critics might easily have focused attention on administrative mismanagement by the government caused by insufficient reporting and monitoring of price conditions, or the lack of sophistication in regulating not only the national volume of cash but its unequal distribution throughout the country. They chose, however, to reduce the problems of monetary management to a simple, moral conception of the capacity of cash itself to create evil. Negativism toward cash that appeared in the first two decades of the eighteenth century was therefore a recent development, a reaction to a "modern" trend rather than simply the obscurantism of the Confucian fundamentalists.

By the latter part of the 1720s, however, the increasing use of cash and the gradual expansion of market activities had so exacerbated the shortage of money and the deflation of commodity prices that officials began to see that since the development of cash in the economy had virtually become irreversible, the government was obliged to meet its responsibility to enlarge the money supply and bring down prices.

King Yŏngjo's Anti-Cash Prejudice: 1727

Unfortunately, the most powerful person in the political system, King Yŏngjo, had become the captive of anti-cash prejudice. Even though he agreed with the request of some officials in 1725, a year after he ascended the throne, to mint cash to provide relief to alleviate the severity of the famine, he did so only with the greatest reluctance and imposed a time limit on minting.

Yŏngjo reminded his officials that even though cash had been used in China at least since the Chou and Han dynasties, Ssu-ma Kuang had warned against its evils in his *Tzu-chih t'ung-chien*, and the history of cash in Korea had reproduced some of the same problems the Chinese had experienced. He expressed his admiration for Kings Sukchong (r. 1674–1720) and Kyŏngjong (r. 1720–23), not because Sukchong had initiated a public program to stimulate the spread of cash, but because both he and Kyŏngjong had displayed sagacious caution by prohibiting any excessive minting. A shortage of cash was not worth worrying about anyway because cash could neither be eaten or worn like food or cloth. It would have been better if cash had never been used in the first place, but now that it had, he had no choice but to mint more of it. Considering his animus against cash, it was not surprising that only a couple of months later he reconsidered his decision and decided to abolish any further minting because of his fear of a repetition of the inflation of 1696.[19]

Hong Ch'ijung: Ban on Cash for Tax Payments. Less then two years later in the third lunar month of 1727, Yŏngjo presided over a major debate among his officials over the best means for meeting the problems created by the extraordinarily high value of cash in the market. Although there were some officials who shared his bias against cash, the majority had recognized that the circulation of cash had spread to more areas of the country, and that no matter what problems had occurred because of its use, it was now an indispensable medium of exchange. They had also learned from the previous generation's experience that the stability of prices had to be maintained by adjusting imbalances between the supply of cash and the supply of commodities for sale in the market. Nevertheless, in view of Yŏngjo's feelings they were forced to be defensive and apologetic in supporting their recommendation for minting more cash.

Second State Councilor Hong Ch'ijung tried to persuade Yŏngjo that in that year of crop failure and famine when the impoverished peasants had spent everything they had produced, they were suffering not from surplus cash and inflation but from cash shortage, the excessively high value of cash, and deflation. By this he intimated that the prices of grain and cloth had been driven so low that it cost the peasants too much to obtain cash to pay taxes or to repay cash loans, and that the government should make cash cheaper by minting more of it, an argument that would have been quite congenial to the cheap silver Populists and Bryan Democrats in the late nineteenth-century United States, who sought to ease the debt burden of poor farmers by a cheap money policy at the expense of the creditors and bankers (that is, moneylenders) of the cities.

Hong said other high officials had agreed with him in private conversation that the time had come to mint more cash, but their hopes had been frustrated by Yŏngjo's stubborn opposition. If the king conceded that he had to tolerate the use of cash in the economy, he had to allow additional minting. If, on the contrary, he opposed more minting, he would have to abolish the use of cash altogether to protect poor peasants against debt and usurious interest in a money economy where cash was short and its value was too high.

Since Hong realized that Yŏngjo could not be persuaded to mint more cash and Hong himself believed it would be disastrous to abolish the use of cash altogether, he proposed a compromise to salvage the retention of cash at least in the private market. To gain Yŏngjo's favor for his plan, he was even willing to propose a policy that would have set the Korean tax and currency system back to the sixteenth century, an idea that would have offended Kim Yuk, Yu Hyŏngwŏn, and other great proponents of a cash economy. Hong suggested that Yŏngjo abolish the requirement that part of the *taedong* land tax, the military cloth tax (*kunp'o*), and the cloth tribute owed by official slaves be paid in cash. The peasants would pay these taxes in cloth alone, the government would cease paying any of its bills in cash, and cash would be allowed only for petty purchases on the market in the capital (and probably other commercial and market towns as well). Hong believed that by removing government demands for cash commutation of taxes, available cash would then be funneled into the market, reducing the value of cash and commodity prices, and providing some relief to provincial peasants who had to buy cash with grain at a prohibitive rate of exchange to pay all or part of their taxes.

Yŏngo was intrigued but not overwhelmed by the proposal because he still thought that there was more to be feared from the evils associated with minting more cash than there was from an excessively high value of cash in the market. He declared that his own preference really was not simply to prohibit more minting, but to do away with cash altogether, to cleanse the human mind of the devious tricks of monetary manipulation. Even though cash was now in short supply, the population of the capital had no reason to fear any loss in the food supply unless grain transport ships were lost at sea in their voyages from the south.

Since King Yŏngjo realized that only rich creditors benefited in a cash economy when the money supply was short, he reasoned that peasant debtors would have everything to gain from outright abolition of cash. He knew from experience what the problems of a cash surplus (and inflation) were, but since he could not predict what would happen if he abolished the use of cash altogether, he was willing to accept Hong's compromise by abolishing the use of cash for everything but small transactions in the "private" market and monitor its effects for a year or two. He then asked the assembled officials to voice their own views as if he were willing to be dissuaded by skilled and effective argument to the contrary.

Two officials supported Yŏngjo's basic inclination to abolish cash altogether instead of Hong's compromise. Minister of Personnel Sim T'aekhyŏn agreed but not because he thought cash had the capacity to create evil inclinations in the human mind. On the contrary, he agreed with Hong's view that the increase in the value of cash had imposed such heavy costs on taxpayers that the government had no choice but to mint more of it, but because Yŏngjo was so firmly opposed to it, he had not dared express his views until this conference. Now he believed that the best policy was simply to abolish the use of cash altogether, because if the government were permitted to spend its cash reserves in private markets under Hong's plan, it would create other kinds of problems that he did not specify.

Chang Pung'ik, a fifth rank military officer, agreed with Yŏngjo's belief that cash was responsible for stimulating man's capacity for sharp practices and deception, and he preferred Sim's recommendation to abolish cash outright. When stationed in Pukchŏk (in North P'yŏng'an Province) he observed how the circulation of cash had spread from the area around Kilchu to the districts south of Hoeryŏng in the space of only two years – an observation that would have thrilled men like Kim Yuk and Yu Hyŏngwŏn because it proved that supposedly "backward" Koreans had the capacity to learn the utility of cash as well as any other people. Sim, however, was convinced that the spread of cash into communities where it had never been used before was an evil to society because it had created a cash shortage and made it rare and valuable, a phenomenon that he believed would occur for any commodity if its circulation (or sale) expanded in official and private transactions throughout the country.

Chang had accurately observed that the spread of the money economy had increased demand for cash, which required more minting to maintain balance in commodity prices, but instead he agreed with Yŏngjo that abolishing cash as legal tender would benefit the lower class at the expense of the interests of the wealthy (moneylenders). He urged Yŏngjo to confiscate all cash stored by government offices and private individuals and convert it into brassware. To prohibit the use of cash by the government but permit it to ordinary people for their private transactions under Hong's compromise would only "delude the people [*mangmin*]," presumably by incorporating a moral contradiction into the law.

On the other hand Yi Pyŏngsang, an official in the Office of Royal Relatives, defended Hong's compromise solution because eliminating cash taxes and cash transactions by the government would reduce the burdens on the debt-laden and taxpaying peasantry. When he had been stationed in the south he had noticed that the wealthy were saving cash in anticipation of a further increase in its value, while the poor had to sell almost their entire harvest to obtain enough cash to pay their taxes because of the high value of copper money. The deflation of grain prices caused by the increased value of cash meant that even after a moderately successful harvest, it took a *sŏm* (15 *mal*) of rice to obtain 1 *yang* of cash (100 coins, as opposed to only 5 *mal* under Yu Hyŏngwŏn's exchange rates around 1670, a 67 percent drop in the cash price of rice or a 300 percent rise in the value of copper money in the last half-century). Since the peasants had come to regard a successful harvest as a disaster, Hong's suggestion to collect all *taedong* and military support taxes in cloth was fully justified.

Yi Pyŏngsang and Brevet Fifth Rank Military Officer Yi Pongsang defended the compromise and the legal use of cash in private markets because government offices would at least be able to spend their current cash reserves and by so doing lower the value of cash on the marketplace. Minister of Rites Sin Sachŏl also wondered what the Ministry of Taxation, the Office for Dispensing Benevolence (that collected *taedong* taxes), and the Military Divisions and garrisons would do with all their cash reserves if cash were abolished altogether. Yŏngjo, however, scoffed at the idea that they would not be able to find a way to spend their cash reserves. "Just let them spend what they have already collected, and they would use it up overnight."

Yŏngjo felt that disposing of government cash reserves was only a minor issue, but Left Royal Secretary Han Ijo said that despite the assertions of the Ministry of Taxation, the military agencies and divisions in the capital, and the governors' and military commander's offices in the provinces that they had spent all their funds, he believed that they still had large reserves of cash, more than what private families had. Since cash had been circulating for such a long time, it was almost impossible to find any other substance that could take its place as a medium of exchange despite its current inflated value, and it would be mistaken to declare all that potential revenue illegal.

Yŏngjo weakened slightly by finally expressing concern about how the government could dispose of its cash reserves. Hong could have seized on this sign of weakness in Yŏngjo's resolve to abandon his own compromise plan and even argue for expansion of the money supply, but he must have concluded already that his own compromise solution was the best he could hope for. He told Yŏngjo that it was in fact because the problem of cash reserves was indeed insurmountable that he had devised his compromise solution by which cash would remain as legal tender in the marketplace. While it was true that neither the Ministry of Taxation nor the Office for Dispensing Benevolence were currently holding any cash reserves, the king could not abolish cash outright because various military divisions or agencies and wealthy private individuals still must have had huge cash reserves. Or even if he prohibited the use of cash as legal tender, it would never be carried out because too many individuals and government agencies would be unwilling to witness the obliteration of their savings at one stroke of the regal pen. If the government simply ceased using cash for taxes and disbursements, it would free more cash for use in private markets, drive down the market value of cash, and eliminate the need to mint more of it. Besides, cash had been used in the marketplace since the Han dynasty in China, presumably with no untoward effects.

Sim T'aekhyŏn, who had earlier proposed abolishing cash altogether from the private market as well as from government finances, did make a concession to Hong's argument about the importance of government cash reserves by pointing out that Yŏngjo could only prohibit the government from using cash for its finances if state treasuries showed a surplus. Unfortunately, at the current time the reserves were almost fully depleted and government agencies had no other choice but to use their cash reserves to meet their obligations. This argument, however, only confirmed Yŏngjo's belief that the government's expenditure of cash could be continued until all government agencies spent all the cash they had, but not beyond that time.

While Yŏngjo approved Hong's compromise primarily to relieve the tax and debt burdens of the common people and eliminate usurious loans, some officials took issue with his assumption that cash was responsible for these problems. Third Inspector Kim Uch'ŏl of the Office of Inspector-General conceded that it might be better to abolish cash altogether, but he felt it would be far better to reduce the value of cash simply by minting more of it. He also refuted Yŏngjo's declaration that the use of bolts of cotton prior to the introduction of cash had been trouble-free because local clerks had always been guilty of rejecting cloth tax payments on the false grounds of poor quality (*chŏmt'oe*) to demand bribes or gratuities. Cash at least eliminated the perennial struggles over the quality of the cloth. Yŏngjo conceded Kim's point but insisted that gratuities were less of a problem than than those caused by cash itself.

Censor-General Sin Ch'ŏsu opposed abolishing the use of cash because it was bound to create a revenue shortage. He also warned Yŏngjo that converting taxes to cloth would not eliminate shortages in the money supply because failure of the cotton crop would cause the price of cotton to rise and peasants would have to pay high prices in rice or grain to obtain bolts of cotton to pay their taxes. Yŏngjo dismissed this objection by the feeble argument that prior to the adoption of cash in the first place (1631?) the country had been collecting taxes in cloth for centuries even at times when the cotton (or ramie) crop was poor, presumably without any difficulty. Yŏngjo's assertion, however, was not backed by any detailed knowledge or investigation of the history of cloth taxes, and he was soon to be embarrassed when Sin's forecast came true.

Hong Ch'ijung granted the feasibility of Sin's point and conceded that cloth might well appreciate in value just as cash had, but he argued that if any district suffered a poor cotton crop and bolts of cloth became too expensive, the government could grant temporary permission for taxpayers of such districts to pay their taxes in cash, especially since his plan would preserve cash as legal tender in the marketplace. Nonetheless, it was still necessary to convert taxes from cash to cloth because even after the catastrophic crop failure in Chŏlla Province in 1726, the price of rice remained so low that peasants were still forced to sell their entire crop to collect enough cash to pay their creditors and the tax collectors. Furthermore, eliminating the demand for cash for tax payments would also reduce the real interest rate on loans by increasing the money supply.

Yŏngjo was now ready to admit that it was possible that collecting the *taedong* tax in cloth instead of cash might cause hardship for taxpayers, but Hong was by now so fully committed to his compromise solution that he sought to calm Yŏngjo's fears. He admitted that when crops were good, the value of cash went up, and when crops were bad, the price of rice went up. Because the same rule also operated for cloth and cash as well, the people of the capital were happy to pay taxes in cash if the price of cloth happened to be high, but not if it were cheap. Yŏngjo need not worry about shifting tax payments from cash to cloth if a shortage in cloth caused a rise in its price because the government could prevent that simply by fixing the cloth/cash exchange rate at 1 *p'il* for every *yang* of cash (that is, 100 *mun* or coins per *p'il* of cloth, a 16.7 percent increase in the value of cotton than the 120 *mun/p'il* exchange rate that Yu Hyŏngwŏn prescribed around 1670). What he failed to see was that if the market price of cotton rose higher than the government price of cloth, the producers of cotton and cotton cloth would either have to sacrifice profit, take a loss on sales, or suspend the manufacture of cloth. Fixing the cloth/cash exchange rate might not work, and if the legal exchange rate were ignored, urban taxpayers would eventually have to pay more cash to obtain cloth for tax payments. Even Sim T'aekhyŏn, who preferred that cash be abolished altogether once Yŏngjo had decided to prevent government offices from using it, still believed that converting all taxes to cloth would create new problems, and he advised Yŏngjo to test the system for two or three years before adopting cloth taxes permanently.

Yŏngjo said that since opinion was divided, he needed to study the problem for a few more months, and he wondered why Korea had faced such difficulties in the circulation of cash when the Chinese had never had such trouble since the five-*shu* coin was adopted in the Han dynasty – an erroneous assumption. Although conceding that the Korean government was obliged to solve whatever problems arose after cash was introduced, he was still amazed how cash had succeeded in circulating at all in Korea because rice and grain were products that were indispensable to life and always seemed to circulate without any major problems – another erroneous assumption. It was easy for him to prohibit its use, but he would then have to decide what substance could best replace it as a medium of exchange.

If he adopted Hong Ch'ijung's compromise and prohibited the official use of cash but permitted its use in the private market, he agreed it would produce other kinds of problems. If he ordered people in the southern three provinces to pay taxes in cloth but allowed them the right to make substitute payments in cash under certain circumstances as Hong suggested, it would only be justified as a temporary adjustment whenever a poor cotton crop cause an abnormal rise in the price of cloth. He could allow provincial taxes to be paid in cloth but have capital bureaus use cash in the capital to purchase tribute items from the market. After one or two years of this, he would expect that the price of cloth would rise and the value of cash would decline as Hong had predicted.

Yŏngjo announced his decision to modify Hong's original proposal by prohibiting the use of cash only in the payment of *taedong* taxes for the southern three provinces of Ch'ungch'ŏng, Chŏlla, and Kyŏngsang, but Hong quickly urged Yŏngjo to extend the scope of cloth payment to the military support taxes for cavalrymen (*kibo*) and infantrymen (*kunp'o*), and other taxes where the law allowed 50 percent payments to be made in cash in addition to cloth. Yŏngjo relented and also added on tribute taxes owed by official slaves of which 50 percent had been previously paid in cash. He also mentioned that he would reserve the option to reverse the policy after a couple of years no matter how much embarrassment he might suffer.

Yi Pyŏngsang then said that the state always had the power to reduce an excessively high value of cash by minting more of it, but if Hong's compromise policy succeeded, the king might be able to change the policy later on, presumably by reinstating the use of cash for taxes and official disbursements. Yŏngjo concluded the session by praising Hong's compromise as providing a means of solving current problems without having to mint more cash, and he predicted that the reduction in the government's use of cash would naturally drive the value of cash down.[20]

In 1726 Hong Ch'ijung succeeded in preserving the use of cash in the market by blocking Yŏngjo's original inclination to abolish its use altogether. Yŏngjo's moralistic condemnation of the evil effects of cash was far less "progressive" than the sentiments of any king since Injo in the early seventeenth century and most of the kings of the fifteenth century as well, who struggled to introduce either cash or paper money into the Korean economy. Yŏngjo yearned for his idyllic perception of a more natural and primitive, cash-free economy in which the population never had to suffer the contrary risks of inflation and deflation. He deplored the recent rise in real tax and interest rates caused by the cash shortage, but he attributed the phenomenon to the propensities of cash itself, primarily the ease by which moneylenders could manipulate seasonal shortages and surpluses to maximize their interest and the automatic multiplier effect the payment of taxes in cash had on taxpayers.

Of the eight officials who expressed their views at this meeting, however, only one agreed with Yŏngjo's moral condemnation of the evils of cash itself. The other seven, whether positively or reluctantly, believed that minting more cash was the most logical and reasonable solution to the current extremely high value of cash in the market. By contrast with Yŏngjo, they were either the intellectual heirs of the pro-cash advocates of the seventeenth century, or by their practical experience and observation of market conditions, had realized that the use and circulation of cash had progressed too far throughout the economy to abandon it.

Failure of Hong's Plan, Search for other Media. Six months after Yŏngjo decided to adopt this major policy change, however, he was forced to retreat for reasons predicted in the preceding debate. The governor of Hwanghae complained that restricting provincial taxes to cloth was working a hardship on the people, and current Second State Councilor Cho T'aeŏk reported that when he had visited Wŏnju (in Kangwŏn Province) many people were upset because the failure of the cotton crop had driven both the cost of cotton and their tax payments too high. Minister of Taxation Yi T'aejwa also pointed out that since the government could no longer receive taxes or pay bills in cash (except for disposing of current cash reserves), the flow of goods between the capital and the provinces had been obstructed. Cho requested that the taxpayers again be allowed to commute taxes into cash if they desired, and Yi requested reinstatement of the previous rule that half the taxes be paid in cash. Yŏngjo conceded that the situation in Kangwŏn probably represented other provinces as well, and he agreed to cancel his order restricting tax payments to cloth alone.[21]

Since Yŏngjo did not, however, abandon his desire to abolish cash, he asked his councilors what medium would be most suitable to replace it. Yi T'aejwa and Cho T'aeŏk proposed paper money, and Cho remarked that it could be used to pay for fodder or for official salaries except that the bills would not last long and had to be replaced. As for other possible alternatives to cash, Yi suggested three types that he had personally witnessed. In his youth he had noticed a kind of ordinary bolt of cotton cloth used in the market that was fairly wide and short in dimension called the *choryangmok*, then another type of cotton called the *hamsanp'o* that usually was of poor weave and turned black but was only used by private families in making purchases at early morning or evening markets, and lastly, a small coin (*soch'ŏn*) that was one fourth the weight of a "large coin" (*taejŏn*). Yŏngjo said he had seen neither paper money nor the *choryangmok* cotton bolts, but he was still opposed to cash because since its introduction "the minds of the people and the mores of the time have gradually become more contrary and mistaken." He could not abolish cash, however, until he found a suitable replacement, and he directed his court officials to continue discussing alternatives.[22]

Two months later Yŏngjo convened another court audience to discuss a suitable replacement for cash and reform of the military support tax system (*yangyŏk*) simultaneously. The conference must have been a deep disappointment to him because only three officials were willing to accept any medium of exchange other than cash; the thirteen others who expressed their views either denigrated alternate choices or argued that cash was indispensable to the economy. Nonetheless, the testimony of the officials revealed an interesting variety of opinions about the relationship between principles of taxation, interest rates, prices, and the medium of exchange.

Minister of Punishments Sŏ Myŏnggyun and Magistrate of Seoul Kim Tongp'il supported reinstatement of Hong Ch'ijung's compromise plan and urged Yŏngjo to continue collecting the military support tax in cloth and forbid the military divisions and units from accumulating cash reserves, but not primarily because cotton cloth was necessarily superior to cash as a medium. Kim Tongp'il, for that matter, was really in favor of minting more cash but he also retreated to Hong Ch'ijung's compromise. Instead of trying to defend the superiority of cotton or any other medium to cash, however, he forthrightly admitted that not only bolts of common cloth but even paper money were worse than copper cash as the failure of the fifteenth-century experiment with paper money had demonstrated.

Censor-General Song Chinmyŏng argued that if the king chose to abandon cash for either of these alternatives, he would be forced to reinstate it soon after and so damage the prestige of his reign that the people would take it as a sign that the dynasty was declining rapidly toward its own demise. Cash savings in the private and public sector were so extensive that the king had no alternative but to mint more. Kim Tongp'il also pointed out that since every country in the world had been using cash since ancient times, the main problem was not the physical nature of the medium but finding the right way to manage it.

Kim also told Yŏngjo that if he abolished cash as legal tender, it would wipe out the monetary value of both government and private cash savings, anger poor debtors by obliterating the cash they already possessed and needed to pay their current debts, and increase the dependence of the poor on the rich for loans, an argument echoed later by Yi Ikhan, Third Deputy Director of the Office of Royal Relatives. Usurious interest rates, which several believed had been exacerbated by the circulation of cash itself, would reappear under any other medium of exchange as well. Obviously more cash had to be minted, but the king had been blocked from doing so because opinion among his officials was divided – a rather transparent distortion since everyone knew that Yŏngjo was the leading opponent of cash.

Kim admitted that if more cash were minted, the price of copper and the cost of minting cash would rise, reducing the profits of seigniorage to nothing. Contrary to the argument of Censor-General Song Chinmyŏng that cash was irreplaceable and had to be minted even without a profit because it was the king's obligation to do so in a crisis, Kim believed that some profit from seigniorage was necessary to provide an economic incentive for minting.

Kim explained that what he meant by the government's obligation to manage cash in the right way referred to controlling the money supply: "If it is expensive, make it cheaper, and if it is cheap, then make it more valuable. It only depends on managing it in the right way [*sŏnyong*]."

After making this spirited argument for additional coinage, one might have expected him to have supported the idea of importing more copper from Japan, as Yu Hyŏngwŏn had proposed, but instead he retreated to a reinstatement of Hong Ch'ijung's compromise plan because it would eventually succeed in raising the money supply in the market simply by removing it from tax payments.

Kim introduced several significant ways of interpreting the role of cash in the economy. Like Kim Yuk and Yu Hyŏngwŏn in the previous century, he treated cash or money in an instrumentalist rather than moralist fashion by stressing the government's obligation to manage or regulate the money supply. He believed that the increases in interest rates through moneylending had not been caused by some innate attribute of cash itself, but by the shortage of cash and its subsequent rise in value, a problem that could occur no matter what the medium of exchange happened to be.

This same instrumentalist attitude toward interest was also taken up by Cho Wŏnmyŏng, the third minister of the Ministry of Works, who criticized the conventional view that loans *in cash* had driven up interest rates and immiserated the poor. It was true that rich moneylenders insisted on loaning only cash to the peasants in the spring and multiplied the value of the nominal 50 percent interest rate in the fall to as much as 500 percent because a cash loan of 1 *yang* worth no more than 2 *mal* in the spring yielded 10 *mal* when the principle and interest in cash (1.5 *yang*) was converted to rice and repaid in the fall. Cash itself, however, was not to blame for this, for if there were no cash, the lenders would continue to refuse to loan rice or grain directly in the spring but use whatever medium of exchange had replaced cash. The real problem had been the contraction of the money supply because of the government ban on minting, which could be solved if Yŏngjo agreed to establish mints in Tongnae, Kyŏngju, Taegu, and other towns in Kyŏngsang Province as well as in the Ministry of Taxation and the military divisions and agencies in the capital.

Brevet Minister of War Yi T'aejwa, who had previously suggested printing paper money, now proclaimed that no other medium besides cash could be found and rejected Kim Tongp'il's endorsement of Hong's compromise plan. He told Yŏngjo that he had forewarned Hong that his plan would fail because a prohibition against government use of cash would only create a roadblock in the flow of trade and obstruct the purchase of former tribute items on the market by the capital bureaus, a prediction that had recently proved valid. He advocated minting more cash to correct the shortage and ease tax burdens caused by the government's ban on minting for the past thirty years. Furthermore, since the high value of cash had also attracted more counterfeiters, he recommended that they be decapitated and their heads displayed on the district border as a warning to others.[23]

Cho Wŏnmyŏng, the third minister of the Ministry of Works, opposed replacing cash with cotton cloth because it, too, could rise in value because of shortages. Diverting cotton cloth to use as a medium of exchange would also reduce the supply of cotton available for clothing, and the weavers of the south would never be able to produce enough cloth to meet the needs of the people of Kangwŏn and Hamgyŏng provinces during the winter. Weavers would begin weaving cloth of lesser value to serve as currency, which would then lose its value in a few years.

Sixth Royal Secretary Yi Chŏngp'il favored retention of cash because he thought it was essential for a successful reform of the military support tax system. He thought the fiscal shortage in the military system was the product of Korea's incomplete adoption of the tripartite tax system of the T'ang dynasty. Of the three taxes of the T'ang dynasty, the Chosŏn government had only adopted the land (*tsu*) and labor service (*yung*) taxes, but had never had an equivalent to the *tiao* or household tax, which in T'ang times was a cash tax. In other words, Yi was advocating a graded version of a household cash tax as the best means of expanding the tax base beyond the the personal cloth tax that had been limited to a shrinking pool of adult male *yangmin*. The household tax would be divided into three grades (according to the number of either adult males or family members), four to five *yang* of cash for a large household, three for a medium-sized household, and two for a small one. Cash was essential to permit emulation of the T'ang *tiao*, especially since paper money and bolts of cloth would produce the same kinds of problems that plagued cash if the government failed to manage their use properly. The king also had to mint more cash to prevent the price of rice from falling and damaging the income of the people engaged in agriculture.

Yi Chŏngp'il's justification for cash was directly related to his conviction that the expansion of the tax base for the military support tax could best be achieved by shifting the object of the tax from the adult male of a restricted population of *yangmin* to the majority of households in the country. Possibly because the household cash tax had at least been used successfully during the early T'ang, he must have assumed that this precedent would carry weight with Yŏngjo. Of course, since no version of the household tax, whether in cloth or cash, was adopted until the Taewongun's regime in 1870, primarily because it was opposed not only by yangban, but by all those who had gained exemption from the military support tax over the years, Yi's argument by itself was not likely to gain much support for the retention of cash.[24]

Second Minister of Rites Yŏ P'iryong agreed that most people thought cash should be abolished, but he and Yun Pin, third inspector of the Office of Inspector-General, felt that if cash were abolished now in the midst of a succession of crop failures, there would be no resources left for providing relief. Yŏngjo revealed at this juncture that despite the prolonged debate over the utility of cash and the history of its use since the seventeenth century, he still did not understand its function in the economy. He told Yun that he just could not understand how anything besides food could be used to provide relief to starving peasants since neither gold nor pearls, let alone cash, could be eaten or worn. Yun then had to instruct him that wealthy people with grain reserves would be willing to ship their grain to the areas of shortage and sell it for cash if the state provided cash to the peasants for that purpose.

Not everyone at the conference, however, was unwilling to discuss other alternative media of exchange, particularly paper money. Cho Chinhŭi, the junior sixth counselor in the Office of Special Counselors, did not recommend paper money as a suitable alternative for cash, but at least he blamed its failure in China on timing rather than any intrinsic weakness in paper money itself. Since the Han dynasty various dynastic governments in China had in fact made changes in the type of currency used from time to time, but unfortunately no matter what the type, it exacerbated the disparity of wealth between the rich and poor. The Chinese government (probably in Sung times) had attempted to remedy this by abolishing copper cash and replacing it with paper money, but unfortunately it did so too late, after the (Sung) dynasty had already entered into irreversible decline. Since Yŏngjo's recent attempt to stop using cash for taxes and government expenditures had failed, he concluded that there was no other alternative to cash, but he had refrained from making a strong argument for increasing the money supply earlier out of respect for Yŏngjo's feelings.

Pak T'aehang, by contrast, agreed that a suitable substitute had to be found for cash, and he, Third Royal Secretary Cho Chibin, and Chief State Councilor Yi Kwangjwa, supported the adoption of paper money. Pak justified paper money by arguing that the primary problem was not the type of currency but the relative exchange value between currency and commodities. Cash worked best if it were "light," or less in value than the price of commodities on the market, but because at the present time cash was "heavy" or more expensive than commodities, wealthy lenders were loaning cash to the peasants and demanding repayment in grain, collecting twenty or thirty times their capital in the transaction. The famous Han Yü of the T'ang dynasty had in fact been able to discern that the reason for the "heaviness" or high value of cash at the time was the prohibition against the use or minting of cash and its distribution (or dispersion) beyond the "five passes." Han had prescribed that the value of cash could be reduced below the prices of commodities by prohibiting the use of copper for casting Buddhist statues and bells, thereby increasing the copper supply for minting cash.

Pak might also have mentioned King Sukchong's ban against melting down cash to make brassware to reverse a trend toward the depletion of the cash supply, but he was either unaware of it or preferred to hinge his case on the word of an acknowledged Chinese Confucian master of the ninth century. Pak, therefore, took a tolerant attitude toward paper money, but by observing that the money supply would always remain a problem that required proper regulation and management by the government, he weakened whatever influence he might have had on Yŏngjo who, at this time, was looking for some means of exchange that would work better than cash in precluding high interest rates, exploitative moneylending, superfluous consumption, and general immorality.

Third Secretary Cho Chibin also proposed printing paper money, but to be used in addition to cash, not to replace it entirely. He wanted to preserve cash as legal tender lest creditors suffer a loss of debts owed them, and he felt that paper money would be needed to make up for the recent shortage of cotton cloth caused by the decline in its production and the diversion of it for use as currency. As Cho Wŏnmyŏng argued, there was not enough cloth left for clothing, the burden of cloth taxes under the *taedong* and military support tax (*kunp'o*) had increased, and the quality of the cloth and its length had been reduced.

Pak argued that the cost of printing paper bills was much less and the profits of seigniorage were much greater than minting cash. Depending on the quality of the paper used, it would be possible to print bills worth 324 *yang* at a cost of only 60 to 70 *yang* of copper cash. The government could adopt paper money as a medium of exchange to circulate with cash and silver and use it to pay for the tribute items purchased by the capital bureaus and to provide relief to people in the capital. Not only was paper money cheaper and quicker to make than cash, it would reduce Korean dependency on the Japanese trade center (Waegwan) at Tongnae for imported copper. Since he had heard a few years ago that the Office for Dispensing Benevolence bought copper from the Waegwan for silver but did not receive the full quota of the order, paper money would free Korea from this kind of loss at the hands of undependable Japanese traders.

Only four of the officials at the conference spoke out in favor of abolishing cash: Yi Hae, Second Minister of Personnel Yun Sun, Third Royal Secretary Chŏng Uju, and Prince Yŏhŭng (Yŏhŭnggun). Yun attempted to refute the argument that cash had been circulating for so long that it was impossible to abolish it as legal tender. The public was generally not aware that in the beginning of the dynasty, Chosŏn kings had tried using silver currency and paper money together and later switched to cotton cloth. All three were unsatisfactory until 1674 [*sic*, 1678], except for Kim Yuk's abortive attempt to introduce cash (in the 1650s). Nevertheless, by 1727 the people had become so used to cash that they erroneously believed it was the only material suitable for currency and had been in use for the entire three hundred years of the dynasty. In short, Yun dismissed the experience of the seventeenth century in the spread of cash to make it appear less important than it was.

Prince Yŏhŭng and Yun Sun agreed on moral grounds that cash had to be abolished because it caused evil. Prince Yŏhŭng claimed that cash was responsible for turning the human mind toward deception, dishonesty, thievery, and banditry. Yun wanted to abolish it because it was so light in weight and represented so much value that its very existence made it an irresistible object for thievery, embezzlement, and bribery. Cash attracted peasants into commerce and away from agriculture to satisfy their hopes for easy profits, stimulated trickery and deception in commerce, and increased the indebtedness of the poor peasants to the wealthy moneylenders. He also believed that cash loans to peasants had even multiplied interest rates from the nominal 50 percent per season to an actual 750 percent, even higher than Cho Wŏnmyŏng's estimate.

Yun pointed out that as more people gained exemption from registration or payment of the military support tax by fair means or foul, the tax base had been narrowed to the so-called *yangmin*, an ever-narrowing group of men who were still retained on the military support tax rosters. The burden of this tax had been increased by the usurious loans that the taxpayer had to incur to finance payment of the tax. A small family might have to borrow four *yang* of cash (worth eight *mal* of rice on the market?) to obtain enough cloth to pay the military support tax (*panp'o*) in the spring, and they would have to repay eight *yang* (not six *yang*?) in the fall, which could then be converted to five to six *sŏm* (75–90 *mal*). The peasants were stripped clean by this burden, and were understandably overjoyed when Yŏngjo decreed that taxes be collected in cloth, not cash.

Yun thought that because it was cash itself that permitted moneylenders to force cash loans on peasants in the spring and recoup more than ten times the principle in the fall, the regressive military support tax was only an exacerbating factor rather than a prime cause of peasant destitution. He was unconvinced by the argument already put forward by a number of officials that inequities caused by the shortage of cash could be redeemed by increasing the money supply, for he asserted that if Yongjo now decided to mint one million *yang* of cash to ease the shortage, it would only end up in the hands of the rich and make the poor peasants even more dependent on the wealthy for loans and credit. Since the country was able to get along quite well prior to the use of cash in 1676 [*sic*], there was no reason to think that it would be impossible to abolish its use. He did not even broach the question of whether an increase in the money supply, or a "cheap money" policy, would have cut debt burdens on peasants who had contracted loans in cash.

Royal Secretary Chŏng Uju, who also agreed that cash should be abolished because of the problems it had caused, disagreed with Yun Sun's analysis of the priority of evils associated with the military support tax and the burden of peasant taxation and debt. From his experience as magistrate in nine districts throughout the country he had learned that the regressive structure of the military support tax was more important than cash or interest rates. The burden of that tax fell most heavily on the *yangmin* or commoner peasants because of the tax exemption granted to yangban, scholars, and students (*yugyosaeng*), and that the *yangmin* peasants had to increase their burden of debt to the wealthy to pay taxes. The families of the scholars, officials, and students paid no tax at all, while the commoner families paid at the rate of two *p'il* per adult male, or six to twelve *p'il* per household if they had three to six adult males. He therefore advocated that Yŏngjo begin by cutting the military cloth support tax rate by one *p'il*, and then move toward a major reform by establishing a uniform rate of one *p'il* per adult male for all forms of service for all families from the highest minister of state to the ordinary commoners (*sŏmin*). The expansion of the tax base would lower the family tax and increase revenue simultaneously.

Even though Chŏng Uju thought that the regressive military support tax was more important than cash and interest in explaining the economic burden on the peasants, he still felt that cash was not necessary for stabilizing peasant welfare and the general economy. It deserved to be abolished and replaced by another medium of exchange, but not until the Ministry of Taxation and all military divisions and units that held cash reserves spent it to pay for their expenses. Of course, this policy would have made the merchants and private persons who accepted cash from the government the ultimate losers by then declaring that the cash they would have just received would no longer be legal tender!

Yun Sun, by contrast, dismissed the objection that abolition of cash would cause tremendous losses of both government reserves and private wealth because the cash could readily be converted to brass utensils that were in popular demand in Korea. The metal might then be exported to Japan, but even if the export outlet for brass at the Japanese enclave (Waegwan) at Tongnae were closed, the exchange value of the copper in cash could be calculated in cotton or rice and gradually sold off for the manufacture of weapons or utensils, saving the wealthy from the disaster of a complete loss of their cash reserves. He estimated that it would take about a decade for the country to use up the national cash supply for these purposes. Since the poor peasants would be overjoyed at the order, Yun urged the king to make a decision on their behalf.

Yun had to have been thinking of the welfare of the common peasant at the expense of the government's finances and the wealth of private families with large cash reserves because it is hard to imagine why any person of property would savor the prospect of salvaging some of their cash savings by converting it to metal tools or utensils as long as cash remained more valuable than those items. Certainly many practical officials had already complained over the potential loss of their cash reserves that would result from the king's decision to abolish cash, and they were undoubtedly too embarrassed to express their fears over a personal financial loss.

Yun urged that Yŏngjo summon the mental determination to follow in the active tradition established by the first two kings of the dynasty, T'aejo and T'aejong, by making a bold decision to abolish cash and return to the monetary system of the early Chosŏn kings. Even the laudable *taedong* reform of the seventeenth century, which provided immediate benefits at the time and was still regarded favorably by the people, had been established only through the resolute orders of seventeenth-century kings.

In arguing for the abolition of cash, Prince Yŏhŭng and Yun Sun, just as Yŏngjo himself had done previously, were asserting that moral combat against evil was more important than the instrumental manipulation of the money supply to redress imbalances among the prices, values, and interest rates. Third Magistrate of Seoul Yi Chŏngje agreed that moral issues could not be divorced from the economic problems associated with the use of cash, but contrary to the other moralists he held that it was not cash itself but the human mind (*insim*) that was the true source of evil. Since Chou and Han times in China, every Chinese dynasty used cash, but if the spirit of virtue was able to work its way gradually into the human mind, and the mores and standards of society remained firm even to a limited degree, people would be able to rectify their own problems without the need to abolish the use of cash. On the other hand, if mores and standards had not been established, then even if cash were abolished and another medium of exchange found, it would not improve the situation. Those who thought that the minds of men were already corrupt and minting more cash would make them even more corrupt would never be persuaded that additional minting could alleviate the cash shortage or solve the fundamental problems associated with cash. As a good moral philosopher he disagreed with the association of cash with immorality, but as an unsteady economist he could not appreciate the argument that minting more cash would solve imbalances in prices and interest rates. Nevertheless, he may have at least weakened the bond in Yŏngjo's mind between cash and immorality.

Possibly the most significant recommendation of the day was made by Second Royal Secretary Yi Chunggwan, who was strongly opposed to abolishing cash because cash was essential to the economy and its abolition would eliminate the best means for providing relief to the poor. He favored expanding the volume of cash in circulation and solving the problem of usurious interest rates by imposing a legal maximum on interest rates at 20 percent per season, but he never discussed whether the existing bureaucracy would really be capable of enforcing the interest limit in every village.

He also proposed that the king cut the value of cash to silver so that 1 *yang* of silver would be equal to 2 *yang* of cash, that is, 100 coins. If Yi's assessment of the current value of cash were accurate, the value of cash would have increased 800 percent over the cash/silver exchange rate of 800 coins/*yang* of silver that King Sukchong set in 1680.[25]

Yi opposed a cut of one *p'il* per adult male in the military cloth tax rate, but he favored a reduction of one *yang* of cash per adult male on the presumption that half the military support tax be paid in cash and half in cloth. He predicted this would have an immediate effect, and after a few years, state finances would have recovered enough so that an additional tax cut of one *yang* of cash and two *p'il* could be made.[26] By this means he hoped that the problems in the military support tax system (*yangyŏk*) could be solved without the need for further remedial action such as a major revision of the tax system.

In other words, Yi Chŏngje worked out a plan to solve the problems of both military support taxes and cash simultaneously. He favored retaining the cash portion of the military cloth tax and the use of cash in the economy, but he also hoped to provide relief to peasant taxpayers by reducing the military support tax by one *yang*/adult male and imposing a 20 percent limit on interest rates on cash loans. Although interest rate limitation would at least theoretically rein in the moneylenders, Yi's package appears to have been a conservative attempt to reform the military cloth tax system without eliminating current exemptions and expanding the tax base. He opposed adopting either a household or per capita tax that would have placed a uniform levy on all households of all social status groups, two of the favorite proposals of the egalitarian reformers.

Yŏngjo then complained to his state councilors that although he had summoned officials to come to court to present their views, only about a dozen or so had actually made their appearance, too few upon which to make decisions on these important matters. This was a rather flimsy excuse for inaction since the debate over this issue had been one of the most complex and comprehensive discussions of currency in the history of the dynasty. He realized that the cash reserves in government treasuries was a serious problem especially if it had to be spent after a new medium of exchange was chosen, but he had already made up his mind to get rid of cash to put an end to chicanery and permit human beings to purge their minds of evil inclinations – a solid endorsement of his original views and those of Prince Yŏhŭng and Yun Sun. In the past he had agreed to the demand of his high officials to mint more cash, and the Office for Dispensing Benevolence had as a result imported more copper from the Japanese at the Waegwan, but he felt that it was fundamentally wrong. He knew that it would be improper and insincere for him to permit more cash to be minted, but he was so troubled over the possibility that he might be persuaded to do so against his will that he had not been able to sleep through the night. Nonetheless, he postponed a decision to abolish cash because he was also worried about losing the government's current cash reserves.[27]

A few days later the discussion resumed, but some of the participants were more forceful in their arguments. The practical Second Minister of War Cho Munmyŏng derided the bookish scholars who advocated the abolition of cash without ever having learned the real facts. Had they done so, they would have realized that, "Since ancient times there has never been a country that did not have cash, and once you have it, you have to mint it because it would be contrary to reason to stop minting it after you have decided to use it." When cash was first introduced into Korea, it was minted annually by capital and provincial offices, and each coin had a single character on the reverse side of the coin identifying the mint. The last big minting occurred in 1696 when the governor of Chŏlla, Kim Man'gil, obtained permission from King Sukchong to mint about 120,000 *yang* (1.2 million *mun* or coins or 1,200 strings) to provide relief funds for the province during a severe famine, and Sukchong had to overcome the same kind of opposition to cash recently expressed in Yŏngjo's court. It saved the people of the province from starvation at that time and should have been done for the whole country. Only when the censorate began to complain about counterfeiting did minting become taboo and the idea of abolishing cash so popular, but he thought the only choice left was to mint more currency.

Third State Councilor Sim Suhyŏn, however, preferred that cash be abolished because it gave rise to immoral behavior and thievery, and was also too costly for Korea to afford because the copper would have to be imported from Japan. Chief State Councilor Yi Kwangjwa, however, pointed out that because no cash had been minted for thirty years and much of it had been lost or worn out, the value of cash had increased so much that the price of grain was still cheap even after a poor harvest. Formerly, one could buy three *mal* of rice for one *yang* of cash, but at present one could buy as much as four to five *mal* for that amount of cash even during the spring when rice prices were high.[28] Moneylending had become immensely profitable for the rich, who tripled their cash loans over the planting season, or quadrupled them if they took advantage of occasional gluts or shortages of the grain crop.

Nonetheless, Yi argued that usury was not the fault of cash. When he had been passing through Kongju, people along the road asked him to abolish cash and set market prices, but they did not realize that even if the wealthy had accumulated grain or cloth instead of cash, they still would have been caught in the same trap. Furthermore, if cash were abolished, about 120–130,000 *yang* (1.2–1.3 million coins) of government cash reserves as well as private savings would lose its value entirely.

Yŏngjo, however, rejected the idea that paper money like cash would create similar problems if it were more or less expensive than commodities ("heavier" or "lighter"). He was still convinced that human beings did not hold any special honor for paper money while cash had exacerbated tendencies toward trickery and deception because it was light in weight and easy to carry. Nonetheless, Yŏngjo was finally forced to compromise his basic position when he made his final decision. He issued a decree stating that because every country had used cash since ancient times, he could not now abolish it in Korea until he could find a substitute, but he would not mint more of it, and would eliminate some of the worst problems that had been created because of its use.[29] In short, King Yŏngjo joined with the most conservative officials in his court who were incapable of seeing the advantages of metallic currency and associated cash with evil human inclinations. Forced by the majority of his officials to concede that cash had become indispensable, he was not moved to increase the money supply and solve the severe deflationary situation that had been created by previous policy.

Limits on Interest

One of the worst problems created by the use of cash, at least in Yŏngjo's mind, was high interest rates for loans, but he was incapable of drawing a connection between the shortage of cash, high value of money, and high interest rates. Had the money supply been increased by more minting, interest rates should have declined, but some officials at court preferred to reduce those rates by government command. Yi Kwangjwa recommended that Yŏngjo limit *interest payments* by forbidding the total amount of interest payments ever to rise above the amount of the initial loan (100 percent of the principal). Yi did not articulate this principle in terms of the *interest rate*, but since loans were normally granted throughout the growing season for a maximum of ten months, he probably conceived of an upper limit of 10 percent per month simple interest (for a term of ten months).

This figure was only Yi's theoretical upper limit, for he really intended to reduce interest rates far more severely. He pointed out that the current interest rate for a cash loan of one *yang* was 2 percent (two *p'un*, *pun* in Sino-Korean pronunciation) per month (for ten months), but borrowers never had sufficient resources during the growing season to repay their loans, and almost always did so after the fall harvest. Since the usual period of the loan was ten months, interest was calculated at 20 percent for a ten-month loan (2 percent times 10). He now proposed that no additional interest be charged after the ten-month period even if took the debtor ten years to repay the loan, fixing the interest limit at a 20 percent maximum by limiting the time when interest could be charged. If the lender then broke the law by demanding more interest, he would be subject to physical punishment, cancellation of interest, and repayment of the principal alone. Yi believed that his formula would prohibit not only the current usurious loans (*changni*), but the practice of refinancing unpaid loans by adding the unpaid interest to the principle (i.e., compound interest) as well.

Yi also hoped to end the practice of loaning grain in the spring and demanding repayment in cash. Even though a loan in the spring might be calculated in cash according to the spring price of grain, the borrower would only be obliged to repay the loan *in grain*, at a simple interest rate of 5 percent per month, or 5 *toe* (.5 *mal*) per 10 *mal*, or a total of 50 percent (5 *mal* for a 10 *mal* loan) for ten-month limit, with no additional interest thereafter.

Thus, though a theoretical limit on *total interest payments* for any type of loan, not the interest rate, would be a sum equal to the size of the original loan, in practice interest could only be charged for ten months, and *total interest payments* could not exceed 20 percent for cash loans and 50 percent for grain loans for the ten-month period. The per annum simple interest rate would have been 24 percent and 60 percent, respectively, but these figures would have been meaningless because the key feature of the proposal was to limit the time for interest to be charged to ten months. The interest rate for official debts would be still less, 10 percent interest for a ten-month time limit for either cash or grain loans.

Any officials who violated these limits to charge higher interest for their own, "private" profit would be subject to criminal charges and exile. Yŏngjo climaxed his decree on the issue with a stern moral warning against the rich moneylenders who profited at the peasants' expense: "Though cash cannot be worn in the cold nor eaten in hunger, still the rich get richer and the poor poorer because of it. The rich accumulate cash and manipulate it at will while the poor are faced with immediate crises without giving a thought to the profit from interest."

There were two aspects of Yi Kwangjwa's plan that might have eventually brought moneylending to an end and closed off access to credit by the ordinary peasants. If the interest *rate* were set too low, creditors might choose to redirect their savings elsewhere to obtain a higher rate of return. Furthermore, the time limit on interest charges not only limited total interest payments, but also deprived the creditor either of a year's interest charges or a significant proportion of his capital itself. If the theoretical limit of interest *payments* were restricted to the initial size of the loan, and the borrower failed to make any further payments, the creditor would have received his capital back but not any interest on the loan. Since private cash loans and grain loans, and official loans (either cash or grain) were set at the 20 percent, 50 percent, and 10 percent rates cited above, far lower than the 100 percent limit suggested by Yi Kwangjwa, if the borrower refused or failed to make any further payments after ten months, the creditors would only have received back those percentages of their initial capital investment and would in fact have lost all interest payments for the ten-month period. Even if the peasants chose to repay their debts some time in the future, the creditor would have no access to that capital and would be deprived of interest income from loans to others. In short, Yi's measure would have benefited peasant debtors at the expense of the rich moneylenders, but Yŏngjo did not approve the idea.[30] We do not know the reasons, but we might speculate that Yŏngjo was not as moved to take direct action against moneylenders and creditors since he was convinced that abolishing the use of cash would solve the problem anyway.

Yi Ik [Sŏngho]

Between 1726 and 1727 a struggle was waged over Yŏngjo's desire to abolish cash, his adoption of Hong's compromise plan, and the failure of that plan. While Yŏngjo's hopes were frustrated by the strength and vigor of the opposition to his conservative thinking on the role and nature of cash in the economy, he also had some unwitting support from one of the leading examples of statecraft scholarship in the early eighteenth century, and a reputed admirer and follower of Yu Hyŏngwŏn. Yi Ik (pen name, Sŏngho), passed the highest level civil service examination in 1705 and probably did the bulk of his writing on practical affairs in the decade of the 1720s, but he was far more the product of his times rather than the propagator of Yu's ideas. As we have seen, however, the 1720s permitted a fairly wide and open debate on the pros and cons of cash, and by no means was it necessary that a serious thinker would be forced to conform with the majority point of view. But because Yi Ik lived in an age when many officials had begun to react against some of the negative consequences of a mismanaged cash economy at the end of King Sukchong's reign, like King Yŏngjo he adopted an extremely negative attitude toward cash and preferred that it be abolished altogether.

Yi argued that the circulation of cash contributed to the decline of agricultural production, the loss of national income, the desertion of peasants for the attractions of moneymaking and profiteering in the markets and cities, the rise of usurious moneylending, the stimulation of ostentatious consumption, the growth of banditry, and the decline of public mores. The peasants abandoned frugality and saving to squander their money to satisfy their tastes in food, drink, and clothing, leaving themselves poor and destitute. The rich saved their cash and lent it at usurious rates of interest, increasing their profit still further by taking advantage of the difference in the price of rice between spring and fall. The moneylenders made profits far greater than the return on investment for agriculture and commerce, while the poor were unable to repay their loans and had to sell their land and homes to satisfy their creditors. The whole process simply made the rich richer and the poor poorer, destroyed the putative equality and balance of the natural village, and reduced state revenues in the process. Only "the tax gougers, profiteers, conspicuous consumers, and thieves wanted cash; it was not of much aid to those who worked hard to feed themselves and were content with a life of poverty."

Yi reasoned that if cash were abolished, people would lose the means for satisfying their desires for luxury products and would be forced to adopt the ways of frugality, simplicity, and self-sufficient production in the only items necessary for sustenance – food and clothing. Prior to the introduction of cash for tax payments, the people had only to pay part of the grain they had grown as taxes without suffering any harm to their subsistence, but after the adoption of cash taxes, they had to exchange more and more grain to buy the cash as the value of cash increased (because of the cash shortage). While the advocates of cash praised it for its ability to produce wealth for the common people, the common people were poor to begin with and needed nothing besides salt, iron, tools, and medicine. Anything else was a waste of money.

Cash was unnecessary for facilitating the exchange of goods because land transportation could be avoided simply by taking advantage of Korea's peninsularity by shipping all goods by sea. The abolition of cash would eliminate usurious loans, reduce profligate expenditures, drunkenness, and thievery, return the peasants to agricultural production and simpler and purer lives, and eliminate inequality in the distribution of income.

> Cash has been circulating now for about forty years. Was there any harm done before we had it, or any advantages after we circulated it? Production

> among the people has declined, the mores of the people have become worse, state finances have been depleted. The harm done has been plain to see except that some think that it is beneficial because it makes it easier to collect taxes. But if the people have suffered harm, how could it be possible that the state might benefit?

He conceded that if cash were replaced with cloth and grain for taxes, the cloth might be woven too thinly and the grain might rot in storage, but faced with a choice of evils, these problems were far less damaging than the evils wrought by cash.[31]

Nevertheless, Yi recognized that cash had become so widespread by the 1720s that it would be impossible to outlaw its use overnight, primarily because both officials and private wealthy individuals would resist any attempt to rob them of their wealth. Instead he thought the government should first issue a decree that it would abolish cash entirely ten years hence, and that in the interim it should ban tax payments in cash. He assumed that this measure would drive the value of cash down to the level of copper and tin so that final abolition of cash would not cause any serious loss of wealth either to the rich or the government agencies.[32]

Curiously this was the same tactic that was proposed by several officials who sought to solve the cash shortage and reduce the high value of cash by freeing more cash for the market given Yŏngjo's reluctance to spend more resources to import either cash or copper from abroad. In fact, the measure to ban cash from tax collections and replace them with grain and cloth was adopted in 1726 but discontinued six months later. Yi Ik's plan to force the depreciation of cash by this means might well have taken a decade at the least.

After the ban on cash for tax payments was dropped in 1727, Yi proposed minting a large, multiple-denomination coin weighing .5 *yang*, equivalent in value to fifty coins, but marked on the face with a value of sixty coins, to yield a surplus of ten coins for each new large coin over the cost of the metal. This surplus would then be used to cover the cost of the metalworkers engaged in minting the cash so that the face value of the new large coin would be exactly equivalent to the cost of production, an idea proposed earlier by Yu Hyŏngwŏn, not for the purpose of destroying the value of coins, but to maintain the constancy of their value and enable them to function as a perpetual medium of exchange. Assuming that Yi had read Yu's work, Yi turned Yu's idea on its head because he wanted to mint a coin with a face value exactly equivalent to its production value, not to ensure the stability of cash in the market, but rather to cause its demise. He calculated that if the government confined its expenditures exclusively to the new large fifty-cash coin while absorbing all the small coins in the possession of the people through tax collections, the small coins would eventually disappear from the market first. Then, as the large coins proved too unwieldy and yielded no profit from minting, people would abandon their use of multiple-denomination coins as well, leaving only grain and cloth as the media of exchange. The process would take place so gradually that neither official agencies nor the public would feel any pain.

Wŏn Yuhan has pointed out that Yi Ik's proposal was unique for the 1720s but was repeated later by Chŏng Sanggi (1678–1752), who wanted to remove cash from the economy because the extremely high value of cash had caused deflation in commodity prices and economic hardship to people engaged in commerce as well as agriculture. He proposed a progressive program of minting multiple-denomination cash beginning with a 15-cash coin and advancing over a period of forty years to a 100-cash coin. When that stage was reached, the weight and value of the coin would become so great that the people would realize that bolts of cloth and bags of rice would be far more convenient than cash and abandon the use of copper coins altogether. Wŏn had dubbed this idea one of the best examples he has found of erroneous, unrealistic, impractical, conservative, and retrogressive thought in the annals of the writings of the so-called practical learners (*sirhakcha*).

Wŏn was indubitably correct because most opponents of multiple-denomination cash believed that the public would never have confidence in the face value of the coins in the first place, and the value of the new cash would fall precipitously. One might expect the same thing that happened in 1867 after the 100-cash was minted, that the suspect multiple-denomination cash would drive the trustworthy penny cash off the market – not because the latter was worthless, but on the contrary because it retained its value and its possessors would seek to save it rather than spend it according to Gresham's law. Yi Ik and Chŏng Sanggi, both opponents of cash in whatever form, thought that the public would trust multiple-denomination cash immediately, that it would drive "penny" coins off the market by some process of absorption, and that the public would realize that multiple-denomination cash was too heavy, too high in value, and too unwieldy.

All other positive advocates of multiple-denomination cash sought to preserve cash and maximize the profits of seigniorage and solve the national shortage of copper, while other conservatives resisted its use because they thought it would cause inflation. Chŏng Sanggi and Yi Ik sought to promote its use to destroy cash entirely. No matter how bizarre their tactics, they shared the sentiments of other conservatives who sought to return the Korean social order to an ideal of simplicity and purity sustained by a predominantly agricultural economy.[33]

Yi Ik was determined to turn back the tide of economic change to the conditions of the sixteenth century. If a reversion to rice and cloth produced problems of their own, they could be remedied by using money woven of silk temporarily. Silk would be preferable to paper because paper money soiled quickly and could be easily counterfeited and had already failed its major practical test in the fifteenth century. Furthermore, Yi reasoned that because silk would be too valuable to use for small transactions, it would never catch on with the public as a convenient medium of exchange, and as it gradually disappeared from the market, it would be replaced by grain and cloth once again.

Wŏn Yuhan has charitably called this idea "unique" because no one else ever thought of it, but it only involved a rather perverted mode of rationality by which more advanced means of exchange could be used to destroy themselves instead of relying on the king's command to abolish any form of currency other than cloth and grain. Wŏn Yuhan also astutely observed that although the positive support for cash by Yu Hyŏngwŏn and the negative reaction to it by Yi Ik were diametrically opposed, both of them lacked the foresight to predict what consequences would be produced in society by the introduction of currency, or to formulate policy responses to these changes.[34]

YŎNGJO RESUMES MINTING OF CASH, 1731

The Disastrous Harvest of 1731

King Yŏngjo adhered to his decision neither to abolish cash nor mint more of it until the harvest of 1731 proved disastrous and the funds of the Office of Benefiting the People (relief agency) had been depleted. Minister of War Kim Chaero asked Yŏngjo to mint more cash in the capital and use it for government expenses, permitting taxes due to be remitted to the capital from the southern provinces to be retained at home for relief. Minister of Taxation Kim Tongp'il confirmed this account and reported that his ministry only received 70,000 *sŏm* of grain in tax revenue that year, hardly more than half the previous year's revenue of 130,000 *sŏm*, and hence was not equipped to provide relief to the provinces. He was supposed to purchase what had formerly been tribute items with cash revenues on the market, but he was so short of funds that he had been forced to dip into the so-called "sealed and immovable" (*pongbudong*) reserves set aside for emergencies. The only resources left were land taxes from Hwanghae Province and about 20,000 *yang* of cash, which would be used up shortly. Since the metallic copper stored in the ministry had no value as currency, he also proposed that it be used to mint cash to purchase items presented as tribute prior to the *taedong* reform instead of rice.

Kim Chaero contributed the news that a grain transport ship had sunk en route to the capital in the summer causing a loss of 48,000 *sŏm* owed to the Office for Dispensing Benevolence and 10,000 *sŏm* for the Ministry of Taxation. Kim Tongp'il added that the Office for Dispensing Benevolence usually could count on 300,000 *sŏm* of annual revenue and the Ministry of Taxation about 120,000 *sŏm*, indicating that their losses had amounted to about 16 percent and 8.3 percent of their annual income. Kim Tongp'il's account of the Ministry of Taxation's revenue of 70,000 *sŏm* was only 58.3 percent of that estimate, and probably represented revenues available to the Office for Dispensing Benevolence as well, that is, a 42.7 percent reduction in grain revenues for the capital for that year.

Minister of Personnel Song Inmyŏng pointed out that rice had become so expensive that 1 *yang* only purchased 2 *mal* of rice (vs. 5 *mal* according to the rate cited in 1626), while grain loan funds had been depleted despite the rule that half the granary funds were supposed to be kept on reserve, and rice reserves in military granaries had not been kept intact either. The Office of Benefiting the People in the capital was then left with no more than 40 to 50,000 *sŏm* for use throughout the year, but he estimated that its reserve should be totally depleted after two or three sales were made by next spring. He also recommended using cash and cloth to save using government rice and grain, even though he realized that Yŏngjo strongly objected to it.

Yŏngjo noted that if he decided to mint more cash, he could at least be certain that because cash still retained a high value on the market, it would be easy to get soldiers and merchants who provided tribute goods to accept government cash payments in lieu of grain. Kim Chaero warned him, however, that there would be problems after minting was carried out and the value of cash was driven down. Ordinarily 1 *sŏm* (15 *mal*) of rice could be bought for only 3 *yang* of cash (5 *mal/yang*), but now it took 5 *yang* (3 *mal/yang*, a somewhat better price than Song Inmyŏng's report) to buy the same amount. It took this kind of crisis to move Yŏngjo to abandon his previous policy and agree to authorize minting additional cash for the first time since 1696, but he took the action reluctantly as a temporary measure to provide emergency relief.[35]

Song Chinmyŏng and Multiple-Denomination Coins

Nonetheless, the shortage of copper must have inspired some officials concerned by the high value of cash to think of better ways to economize on the cost of increasing the money supply. The two most economical alternatives in that age were paper money and multiple-denomination cash (i.e., nickels, dimes, and quarters rather than pennies), but paper money had many detractors, and people like Yu Hyŏngwŏn believed that ordinary people would never believe that multiple-denomination cash would be honored at its face value.

After mints were reestablished in 1731, however, Second Minister of Taxation Song Chinmyŏng attempted to overcome the traditional prejudice against multiple-denomination cash by defending its utility in rational and logical terms. In tracing the history of currency in Korea, he noted that paper and cloth had been used for brief periods of time and then abandoned when certain problems developed in their use, but that experience did not invalidate their utility because in China metallic currency had been used without interruption for over two millennia because any difficulties that had emerged were solved by reforms or changes in the system. In Korea, however, when any problem associated with the use of cash appeared, people were ready to abolish it immediately, "like someone who stopped eating just because he got something stuck in his throat" – a rather daring and dangerous parody on the attitude of King Yŏngjo himself.

Song then moved on to his justification for multiple-denomination coins by pointing out that King Ching of the Chou dynasty (r. 544–520 B.C.) and Liu Pa had used a 100-cash coin, as did Chu-ko Liang of the Wei state (third century A.D.). The only difference between "large" and "small" cash was that one was worth more than the other, a principle no different than the use of precious metals like gold and silver along with silk and copper cash. A large coin could be made larger and thicker along the edge with a different design on its face than the ordinary coin and given a value equivalent to five or ten common coins. There was no reason to fear that the common people would refuse to use the new coins, or that small coins would disappear from the market and bring the sale of small and cheap goods to a halt. Minting a large coin would not require that the older, cheaper coins be withdrawn from circulation (i.e., that nickels, dimes, and quarters could easily circulate with pennies). In fact, the smaller coins could be used for items of low cost while the larger ones for more expensive items like land and houses, or the state could use the larger coins and leave the small coins for use among the people in the marketplace. And if any change took place in conditions and a coin went out of use, the government could always make changes in the denominations of coins.

For that matter, there had never been any fixed rule about the weight of a coin because it had always varied according to the times. Contrary to what some people thought, there was no reason why gold had to be dearer than silver, or silver dearer than cash, or why it would be improper for a 10-cash coin (dime) to be worth more than a silver one. Every item was worth more or less than another, and there was no fixed rule as to the order of precedence. Silk was supposed to be worth more than cotton, but some varieties of finely woven cotton could in fact be worth more than silk. There was no reason that any new coin would be free from some sort of difficulty, but in planning the currency system of a country, one should simply choose the best alternative among many and then change whatever problems emerged after it was adopted, rather than expect perfection before one adopted a plan,

It was obvious, however, from the subsequent discussion at court, that only a few officials shared Song Chinmyŏng's views about the utility of multiple-denomination cash, let alone paper money. Second State Councilor Song Inmyŏng and Third Minister of Personnel Yi Chongsŏng both mentioned that Yi Kwangdo had previously proposed printing paper money, but even though it had been used in Sung and Yüan times, contemporary Koreans were too easily confused or deluded and would not place any trust in it.

Yŏngjo also expressed his skepticism about the utility of multiple-denomination cash because the common people were too devoted to small coins to appreciate large ones. If large or multiple-denomination coins were introduced, he was certain that the smaller coins would disappear and the larger ones would all end up in the hands of the rich. Like Yi Ik, Yŏngjo did not understand Gresham's law that the smaller coins would be drawn off the market by rich and poor alike because they would retain their value while the depreciated large coins would be left alone in the market.

Sixth Royal Secretary Yi Ilche confirmed Yŏngjo's fears when he said that even though King Ching of the Chou dynasty approved the use of multiple-denomination cash "to benefit the people," Duke Mu (Mu-kung) did not approve it. The people living in a lesser age of decline, that is, any dynasty after the fall of the Chou, in Korea as well as China, would certainly be suspicious of it. Yŏngjo then said that a lot more study of the problem was needed before he could reach a decision because he had learned that it would be unwise to leap at the first suggestion for any change without insisting that every official be allowed to express his views and commoners be given the opportunity to oppose any policy initiative.

Yi Chongsŏng added that multiple-denomination cash might increase the profit from seigniorage, but those profits would prove so attractive to counterfeiters that the government would be helpless to prevent them from flooding the market with coins. Yi Ilche expected that the rich would be attracted to the multiple-denomination coins and accumulate huge savings in them, increasing their own wealth and their own power over the market to a degree that would surpass the state's. He did not realize that the rich would be no less cautious than ordinary people about the value of these coins and would hardly dare to tie up their savings in rapidly depreciating currency. He compared the evil consequences of multiple-denomination cash to the overthrow of the great well-field system of the late Chou dynasty because after it had been destroyed by the state of Ch'in, private property in land was created. Once the landlords had become land rich, they were able to accumulate savings in cash as well, and it was impossible for the state to stop them from doing so. In other words, introducing multiple-denomination coins would be an epochal reform that would transform the Korean economy from stable and conservative agricultural production to a more volatile and instable cash economy that would allow the amassing of great wealth by counterfeiting and monetary manipulation. In those circumstances the Korean state would find it as difficult to prohibit counterfeiting as to prevent the monopolization of land by rich landlords after the fall of the Chou dynasty.

Yi Ilche was convinced that minting multiple-denomination cash would be of some utility, but only for about a decade because it would drive small coins out of the market, leave the common peasants without a medium of exchange for small transactions, and allow the rich to control all multiple-denomination cash. Second Minister of War Cho Wŏnmyŏng remarked that multiple-denomination cash had been adopted in Chinese history mainly as a means for enriching the state, but the policy did not last long, and soon after it had to be replaced by cash of small denomination, a process that also resulted in a large financial loss for the state as well. In other words, conservatives like Yi Ilche and Cho Wŏnmyŏng confirmed Yu Hyŏngwŏn's fears about the dangers of multiple-denomination cash.

Song Inmyŏng, by contrast, expressed some limited approval for multiple-denomination cash. He did not care that much for cash in the first place, but he was willing to approve its adoption on an experimental basis because the king had the option to abolish its use if it did not work out. For that matter, since small coins were not that useful either, the king would be better off abolishing them as well. When Yŏngjo asked him what would be used to replace cash, he replied that rice could be used for small transactions, and cotton or silk for large transactions, and after about twenty or thirty years, he might be able to reintroduce small cash again. Yŏngjo made no reply, but after struggling vainly for years to obtain acquiescence to a total abolition of cash from ministers who had a far more astute understanding of the operation and function of cash in the economy than Song, he must have regarded him as either an obscurantist or an ignoramus out of touch with the recent debates of 1726–27.

Yi Chongsŏng, who had opposed the use of large cash because it would stimulate counterfeiting, also showed some flexibility. Counterfeiters would be attracted by the prospect of large profits of seigniorage, but the government's purpose should not be to increase its profit, but to solve some of the problems that existed in the cash market at the time. The king had the option to choose between small or large denomination cash. If he chose small denomination cash and problems developed, he could change the currency and introduce multiple-denomination cash, or vice versa. When Yŏngjo asked him if he really believed that the people would not suffer no matter which type he used, Yi replied that in fact in Chinese history, a large variety of coins had been used, evidently without any ill effect. Some were so light that "they floated on water" or so fragile that they could be "crushed in the hand." Paper bills were used in the reign of Hsüan-tsung in the T'ang, and in the Southern Sung, and these examples proved that there was never any single or fixed monetary system, but that Chinese emperors might convert small cash to multiple-denomination coins or vice versa, as the situation demanded.

Yŏngjo said that people were now suggesting that he convert small cash to multiple-denomination coins, but how could he be sure that if he did, there would not be even worse problems if he were forced to convert multiple-denomination coins back to small denomination coins in the future, a justifiable question since "floating" or "crushable" cash had long since become cliches for the kind of debasement that automatically produced commodity price inflation.[36] Yŏngjo did not reach a final decision on the question of multiple-denomination cash at this time, but a few months later in 1736 when Yi Kwangjwa told him that in his view it would be wiser not to do so, the idea was abandoned.[37] Nonetheless, not only Song Chinmyŏng, but even Yŏngjo and a few of his officials were willing to discuss multiple-denomination cash as if it were a possible, if not entirely feasible, alternative. The level of discussion on monetary policy had ostensibly become more liberal than the ideas of Yu Hyŏngwŏn a half-century before because Yu believed that the face value of coins always had to be virtually equal to the cost of minting, but the result of the debate in 1731 was adoption of Yu Hyŏngwŏn's preference for penny cash based on an aversion to either paper money or multiple-denomination coins, without any knowledge at court of Yu's position. Once King Yŏngjo had been forced to realize that cash had become indispensable to the Chosŏn economy, he preferred to opt for the most conservative policy available.

CONCLUSION

The leading advocates of cash in the seventeenth century wanted to promote the extension of its circulation throughout the country by an aggressive policy of converting tax payments to cash. That policy had proved successful in stimulating the spread of cash throughout the country, but positive support for the minting of cash was ruined by unregulated and uncontrolled minting and the concentration of the volume of money in the capital and other special marketing areas long before sufficient cash had circulated throughout the rural provinces to justify the conversion of all taxes to cash payments. When cash dropped in value and created commodity price inflation in the 1690s, King Sukchong sought first to limit, and then to prohibit the minting of more cash after 1697, a policy that remained intact when King Yŏngjo came to the throne twenty-seven years later.

The success of the campaign to introduce cash into the Korean economy in the seventeenth century led to a gradually increasing demand for more cash to meet the needs of the market, but the government was not able to understand that the growing market justified a renewal of minting to balance the supply of coins with the demand for them. Instead the reaction against the inflation of 1696 was inherited by King Yŏngjo after 1724, and he persisted in maintaining a harmful deflationary policy.

King Yŏngjo did not perceive of himself as a money manager with the responsibility to regulate the money supply to ensure stable values and prices, nor did he inherit the seventeenth-century spirit to bring Korea up to the economic level of China by promoting the circulation of cash. If he had had his way, he would have abolished cash altogether and returned to the era of cloth and grain of the late sixteenth century because he naïvely believed that those two media of exchange had the magical property of insulating the ignorant peasant against sharpsters and manipulators. The battle to defend metallic cash had to be fought all over again because of the ill consequences of an earlier inflation and the artifically induced problems of price deflation and high interest rates caused by regal mismanagement and blindness.

Because a large number of influential officials understood the basic mechanics of regulation, they persuaded Yŏngjo that his own prejudices were unworkable. Hong Ch'ijung's compromise solution of 1726 was the natural product of a stalemate between the king and his officials. Yŏngjo was persuaded that the use of cash in private markets had to be retained if only to permit the expenditure of government cash reserves, and that bolts of cloth might just as readily produce the same difficulties as cash since any medium of exchange would be subjected to the same rules of supply, demand, and price. Hong was also able to persuade Yŏngjo to accept cash commutations in tax payments in emergencies, and convince him that eliminating cash from government finance while preserving it in the marketplace would reduce the demand for cash, decrease the value of currency, and eventually restore some equilibrium or stability to the market itself. Yŏngjo, in fact, endorsed this argument even though it would mean that restored stability would ensure the continuation of cash rather than its elimination. These were significant concessions from a king who began his reign as a reactionary opponent not only of cash, but also of progress in the commercial or nonagricultural industrial sectors of the economy.

Yŏngjo's conservatism was not simply the product of the uneducated mind, because the most renowned statecraft scholar after Yu Hyŏngwŏn, Yi Ik, also shared his moral bias against cash. There could be no better example to disprove the notion that the nonofficial statecraft scholars necessarily represented a thoroughly progressive and developmental class of thinkers just because they spent more time studying the issues than most officials did.

When Yŏngjo finally capitulated and agreed to mint more cash in 1731, he was forced to do so by another of the frequent famines and crises in state finances that plagued the last half of the dynasty, not simply by his acquiescence to the virtues of superior argument. Furthermore, throughout the debate that began in 1726, a number of officials made serious arguments for multiple-denomination cash, paper money, and interest-rate limitation that took the level of debate far above the simple, "penny-cash" mentality of Yu Hyŏngwŏn, but because Yŏngjo was not positively disposed to seek new and progressive solutions to monetary problems, he refused to adopt any of them. Had he possessed even a modicum of the more adventurous spirit of Kings Injo, Hyojong, and Sukchong, he might have given any or all of these ideas a try.

For that matter, there was no further development to the use of paper money, bills of credit, or banking. Even multiple-denomination metallic cash was not attempted until 1867, and because it depreciated quickly and caused inflation in commodity prices, it was quickly abandoned – not because it was intrinsically susceptible to such a development, but because the Taewongun was primarily concerned with raising revenue and ignorant of the need for restraining the money supply. Even though the volume of copper cash in circulation increased appreciably after it was first introduced in the mid-seventeenth century, by the nineteenth century its condition and quality had deteriorated. Adulteration by counterfeiters and lack of sufficient uniformity and dependability made it unusable for financing foreign trade with Japanese and other foreigners after 1876.[38]

CHAPTER 26

Cash and Economic Change after 1731

King Yŏngjo's decision to mint more cash in 1731 appeared to mark the end of an era of government conservatism and guarantee the permanence of the role of cash in the Korean economy. In actuality, cash had already won its place by the gradual expansion of commercial activity since the seventeenth century; it was only a matter of time before Korean kings acknowledged its necessity. Did the grudging acceptance of cash as a permanent part of the Korean economy mean that a significant advance over the seventeenth century was underway in general attitudes toward the economy, and did Yu's prescription on the role of cash and commerce in the economy appear irrelevant and outdated just when his ideas were beginning to spread among scholars and officials?

Yu Suwŏn

The Development of Merchant Capital

While many scholars and officials were still opposed to problems that they attributed to cash itself, some of their more enlightened fellows began to face some of the implications raised by the emerging role of commerce in the economy. In some ways, the most enlightened of these men was Yu Suwŏn, an official affiliated with the Disciple's Faction (*Soron*) purged in a factional dispute with the Patriarch's Faction (*Noron*). He was one of the first writers to challenge traditional Confucian restrictions on the function of commerce in the economy.[1]

Between 1729 and 1737 Yu wrote a book called *Usŏ*, which advocated greater respect for the "despised" occupations of commerce and industry, and he began his discussion of this topic by directing his sympathies toward the growing class of yangban literati who had failed the civil service examinations and were unable to obtain an official appointment. Since Korean law prohibited anyone from standing for the official examinations or holding high civil office if any of their ancestors had ever engaged in commerce or handicrafts, yangban families were prevented from engaging in those occupations no matter how poor and desperate they might become for fear they might lay an eternal curse on their male progeny. Yu's goal was to liberate the yangban class from its hereditary restriction to a life of scholarship and idleness.

The problem of unemployed yangban had been growing by the eighteenth century because an increasing number of people had been able to escape the confines of hereditary slavery and *yangmin* or commoner status, and some had obtained qualifications for official posts by purchase or contribution, but the number of bureaucratic positions remained constant, increasing the supply of unemployed and frustrated aspirants for office. Because they were unable to earn a living by commercial activity, they were either reduced to penury, had to seek a patron of influence, or engage in moneylending or bribery to survive.

Yu Suwŏn believed that if unemployed scholars were given the chance to earn a living in commerce, not only would they be able to support themselves, but they would participate in the formation of a new merchant class of better educated men. He was inspired by contemporary Ch'ing practice where commercial activity did not disbar any man or his descendants from taking the national examinations.

Critics of Yu's ideas objected to opening commerce to yangban because they believed that commercial activity would have a deleterious effect on morals by stimulating the search for profit, not only for individual yangban, but for their sons and descendants as well. Yu retorted, however, that commerce and industry were not base or ignoble occupations, and in fact merchants maintained a higher standard of ethics than many of the fallen yangban or corrupt officials who in a desperate struggle for survival entered into contractual arrangements (*pangnap*) with peasants to pay their taxes in advance, lent money at usurious rates, or conspired to seize slaves and land from others in trumped-up lawsuits.

He pointed out that by the late 1720s only government-licensed shops had been authorized in certain major cities and towns like Seoul, Pyongyang, Kaesŏng, Chŏnju, Suwŏn, and a few others, and he wanted to spread licensed shops not only to every major administrative town, but to commercial market towns as well. He was not, however, an advocate of free market commercial activity because he wanted to retain the system of government licensing and opposed the growth of unlicensed or unauthorized shops (*nanjŏn*), small-scale itinerant merchants or subcontractors, itinerant peddlers, periodic markets (held usually once every five days), or the ad hoc markets or fairs held in "open fields" that Yu Hyŏngwŏn had objected to.

Anyone tied to the Western notion that capitalism can only develop by the destruction of the feudal bonds of corporate guild relations to permit individuals to create their own enterprises and participate in a free market system might well believe that Yu Suwŏn's plan was misguided or illogical if he expected to promote greater commercial activities by forcing all merchants to accept state control. To be sure, he wanted to expand commerce but to do it by strengthening government licensing of shops to repress the competition of the rising number of unauthorized small-scale merchants and peddlers. He anticipated that the licensed merchants would become bigger and stronger because their profits would be guaranteed and the opportunities for accumulating capital increased. Government would benefit as well because it would be easier to collect taxes from them than from small merchant subcontractors and itinerant peddlers. It did not occur to him that expansion of gross national product might be his primary objective.

He was aware, however, that if the government restricted the sale of each category of goods to specific licensed shops, those shops might readily withhold goods from sale to drive up prices and profits. To counteract this possibility he advised the government to grant licenses to a number of shops in many areas of the capital and in district and market towns and allow them to sell the same product. Under his system of government-sponsored oligopoly, purchasers would presumably be able to take their business to another shop if the store refused to sell at a reasonable price.[2]

Kang Man'gil has argued that Yu Suwŏn ultimately felt that unrestrained competition from small-scale merchants and peddlers would threaten the viability of the larger, licensed merchants by taking away sales and profits, and that only an oligopolistic system could guarantee sufficient profits for capital accumulation. Yu, however, did not want to drive the small merchants into destitution, but to organize them into larger and more viable units. He envisioned three different types of combination: (1) amalgamation of small merchants into large conglomerates; (2) agreements between yangban businessmen who would invest capital in a licensed main store and subcontracting merchants who would act as sales agents, or partners and managers of branch shops in provincial towns under the control of the yangban owner or partner in the capital; and (3) commercial capitalist enterprises run by wealthy merchants who would cut costs and increase production and profits by hiring wage labor and rationalizing work procedures and record-keeping similar to large-scale food processing shops in contemporary Ch'ing China. Kang pointed out that Yu's three alternatives were not random suggestions, but reflections of the historical evolution of evolving capitalism itself. Yu was ahead of his own time because he was prescribing remedies for the current reluctance of Korean merchants to invest too much money in wage labor.[3]

Yu Suwŏn also envisioned a growth of commercial cities and towns dominated by the wealthy merchants, but not solely in economic affairs. Even though these merchants would be guaranteed their profits and wealth by a system of state licensing, he perceived that they would be capable of running civic affairs as well, particularly building and supervising walls and moats for local defense, bridges, schools, charitable estates, and roads. He envisioned this system of local self-government under merchant-yangban leadership as providing local initiative by cooperation and capital investment in place of the more communal cooperation portrayed in the ideal image of the ancient well-field system. The wealthy merchants would also be expected to establish charitable funds for the starving and found schools to educate the youth in Confucian learning. He did not realize, however, that since the new merchant-yangban class would have to take the lead in promoting an ethical system that in Korea denigrated merchant activity, they might have to the modify the hallowed Confucian canon to bring it in line with contemporary Ch'ing practice.

As Kang Man'gil pointed out, Yu's preference for maintenance of government licensing of merchants was not a negative reaction to commercial development, but a positive method for promoting not only the development of wealthy merchants, capital accumulation, and urbanization, but also "bourgeois" leadership in politics and government as well. Yu's "bourgeoisie," however, was not to be based on maximum freedom and individual liberty to pursue gain and profit without restriction; it was to be a class under government control that would cooperate with the government by paying commercial taxes and providing leadership for local civic tasks based on communal norms.[4] In any case, his view for the role of merchants in society represented a significant advance over the ideas of the seventeenth century.

Cash Policy

Yu Suwŏn also considered methods of solving the recurrent cash shortages that had occurred since the government stopped minting cash in 1697. He agreed with the critique of some officials that the cash shortage had been caused by the retention of cash reserves of capital and local civil and military agencies, but he criticized their proposed remedy that the government be prohibited from storing any cash reserves at all because the agencies would still have to store their savings or surpluses in some form. Unfortunately, cash was the only suitable medium for storage because both grain and cloth would spoil, rot, or be eaten by vermin over any period of time.

The best possible solution was to prohibit any "private" accumulation of reserves in government offices because he believed that traditionally the government had been obliged to keep its tax resources in constant circulation. Even though nine-years' savings from crop surpluses was the ideal reserve against famine or crop disaster in ancient times, government granaries never kept their reserves immobile but rotated them every year by using cash to buy grain on the market for military rations and official salaries and then replenishing them from the next year's tax receipts. Unfortunately, because the civil and military agencies of the government were at present rigidly defending the benighted principle of maintaining "immovable" (*pongbudong*) reserves, cash had been withdrawn from circulation and its value had been driven up.

Yu also believed that cash had not been put into circulation and tended to gravitate into the treasuries of wealthy families because commercial activity had not been fully developed, but the solution of many observers to ban rich merchants from accumulating cash savings was also "laughable." "Even the awe and majesty of the First Emperor of the Ch'in Dynasty would not have been able to stop them from saving their money, because it was the decision of the rich merchants themselves that determined whether they saved their cash or spent it."

Yu blamed the problem on the Korean tendency to honor appearances over reality. Because scholarship was honored and commercial and industrial activity despised, even the profiteers in Korea made a show of disdaining commerce and avoided engaging in any profitable activity in public view while piling up their cash savings and secretly lending it at high interest or advancing it to others for tax payments in advance at a premium (*pangnap*). In other words, public embarrassment over profiteering and commercial activity had restricted the propensity to spend cash for consumption, and small merchants and peddlers could not earn enough cash from their sales of handicraft manufacture to accumulate capital to expand their commercial activity. Because the number of petty merchants was too small, there were not enough of them to bring them together in cities, and because the rich merchants also had no incentive to exchange their cash for goods, it was inevitable that currency would stagnate.

The only solution to the problem, therefore, was not to tinker with cash policy, but to eliminate the sense of shame that people had toward commerce and industry, and to spend as much money as it would take to lure merchants to undertake the large-scale joint ventures in establishing commercial shops. If that were done, the country would have a hundred times more commerce than it presently did, cash would end up circulating everywhere, even in the most remote rural villages, and it would no longer be locked up in private treasuries.

A third key to ensuring the permanent adoption of cash was for the government to adopt a quota for the annual minting of cash, designate official smelters, purchase copper and tin, and prohibit the manufacture or circulation of debased coins. If the government set the annual cash quota so that the volume of cash in circulation would always be equivalent to the value of commodities for sale on the market, long-term circulation of cash would be guaranteed.

Unfortunately, the problem with current cash policy was that "we only know how to mint cash, but we don't know anything about the right way [to mint and use] cash." Because no one knew about the right metals for minting, or the right weights or dimensions for producing cash of high quality, the types of cash that circulated throughout the country varied widely in size, weight, and quality. "How would any one be surprised that cash stagnated and did not circulate, or that it varied in weight and was not equal and uniform, or that it would be minted one day and abolished another, be either too expensive or too cheap, and cause great problems for commerce and industry as well as agriculture, for private parties as well as the government?" Cash of varying sizes and weights had to be abolished or withdrawn from circulation and replaced by new cash according to standard and uniform measures, and private minting or counterfeiting had to be prohibited. Replacing the money supply with new coins required that the government not stint on expenditures for copper, coal or labor costs – an idea in tune with Yu Hyŏngwŏn's views – and commerce and industry had to be opened to the population. These were the methods for securing the successful circulation of cash and attaining "wealth and power" for the country.[5]

Yu Suwŏn's proposals were radical departures from conventional thought in a number of important ways. Instead of the traditional admiration for agriculture and frugality, he promoted commerce and spending as the means for promoting national and popular welfare. The stimulation of spending would ensure a more thorough circulation of cash and induce merchants into capitalizing more ambitious ventures once they could look forward to profits from larger sales of goods. The number of shops and commercial towns would expand, and the demand for cash would increase, requiring the government to replace the current money supply of coins of mixed sizes and standards with a uniform coin, and it would have to purchase whatever raw materials were needed to achieve this task. To ensure the viability of commercial enterprises, the state would reorganize commerce by licensing all shops and combining small merchants into larger, licensed ones, creating an oligopolistic system to allow sufficient competition to eliminate market cornering by individual merchants and sufficient profits to capitalize each enterprise. The yangban would be encouraged to engage in commercial activity, creating a new class of educated merchants who would then be urged to perform civic duties in welfare and local governance. In short, Yu proposed a system of commercial, oligopolistic capitalism with a civic culture of duty and participation by a new commercial yangban class, managed and restricted by the state to ensure profits and prevent irresponsible speculation and price manipulation.

Yu Suwŏn's ideas would not have been possible in the seventeenth century, but in the 1730s when the Korean economy was already functioning with copper currency despite the shortage of money and the reduction of commercial profits by increased competition from private merchants, his solutions were a logical, albeit unusual, response to current problems. At the same time, the untaxed yangban, augmented by tax evaders seeking to escape the military cloth support tax, would be converted into productive citizens by opening the doors to profitable commercial enterprise to them. It is not clear whether his writings had much influence on his contemporaries or subsequent generations, but at the least he anticipated Pak Chega's promotion of commercial activity by a half century.

COMBATING ANOTHER CASH SHORTAGE, 1742

Even though the money supply expanded after 1731, King Yŏngjo was not as fully committed as Yu Suwŏn to the expansion of commerce and the steady expansion of cash in circulation by an annual minting quota. It may not be possible to estimate the national money supply for Korea after 1731, but it probably bore some correlation to the increase in the central government's cash receipts and disbursements. As table 11 shows, the central government's annual cash revenues advanced steadily from about 82,000 *yang* in 1700 to about 120,000 *yang* in 1727, and jumped suddenly to near 200,000 *yang* in 1731. It apparently declined somewhat in 1749, rose above previous levels in 1785 and approached 300,000 *yang* per annum at the end of the eighteenth century (i.e., from 8.2 million to 30 million coins, or from 8,200 to 30,000 strings).

TABLE 11
NATIONAL REVENUES AND DISBURSEMENTS, 1700–1807

Year	Revenues	Disbursements (in *yang*)
1700	84,260	81,850
1723	115,026	106,675
1727	118,300	127,000
1731	N.A	198,790
1749	169,790	N.A.
1785	219,830	N.A.
1792	N.A	274,890
1807	306,986	323,338

SOURCE: Wŏn Yuhan, "Chosŏn hugi hwap'ye yut'ong e taehan ilgoch'al" [A study of currency circulation in late Chosŏn], *Han'guksa yŏn'gu* 7 (March 1972):134, based on the *Man'gi yoram: Chaeyongp'yŏn* [Handbook of government affairs] (Keijō: Chōsen sōtokufu chūsūin, 1938), Hojo illyŏn kyŏngbi [Annual accounts of the Ministry of Taxation].

The increase in the cash revenues undoubtedly reflected an increase in the money supply, but it did not mean that the money supply necessarily kept pace with the demand for cash because apparently the circulation of cash was spreading to different areas of the country and the supply of commodities for sale increasing. Further study would be necessary to estimate the money supply at the time, but according to a statement made by one official in 1742, Yŏngjo apparently did not approve continuous minting of cash on an annual basis and only approved minting 300,000 *yang* of cash (three million coins or 3,000 strings) in 1731, a sum that was apparently not reflected in table 11 of government revenues and expenditures until 1785. Thus, in 1742, a decade after Yŏngjo had authorized this amount, Pak Munsu complained that the value of cash had risen again, but this time he suggested that the cash shortage be overcome by importing Chinese cash from Ch'ing China and ordering that brassware be melted down for minting.[6]

Pak Munsu: Import Cash from Ch'ing China

The cyclical pattern in the rise and fall in the quantity and value of money had created another crisis, but few officials favored importing Chinese currency. Two months later, Chief State Councilor Kim Chaero objected to it because it would be tantamount to legalizing smuggling, presumably because the government had established a noncash buffer zone along the Yalu River to prevent the import of Chinese cash.[7] Even if it could be done, it would lead to trouble because the ignorant common people would not be able to distinguish between Korean and Chinese cash. On the other hand, if Korean cash were abolished or withdrawn from circulation and only Chinese cash were allowed in the marketplace, Korea would be passing control of its own currency over to Ch'ing China. Kim had not been able to find a single official who agreed with Pak Munsu's recommendation, and Yŏngjo agreed almost immediately that it would be a major mistake to have two different types of cash circulating concurrently.[8]

Pak Munsu responded that other officials back in King Sukchong's reign had recommended importing cash from China, but Yŏngjo was unimpressed by this point. Pak then told Yŏngjo that he had one of three choices: to abolish cash altogether, mint more of it, or import some from abroad. More cash was needed because the cash shortage had made it impossible for families to support themselves. If Ch'ing cash could not be imported, then at least brassware could be replaced by porcelain and the metal used to mint more cash. Later in the day, Sixth State Councilor Yun Yangnae also proposed minting iron cash to increase the money supply, but the idea was dropped after Kim Chaero pointed out that since iron was the favorite metal of the counterfeiters for debasing coins, government approval of the use of iron in coinage would only legalize all the debased cash the counterfeiters had minted.

Song Inmyŏng: Replacing Old Cash with New

Councilor of the Left Song Inmyŏng also agreed that there was no alternative to minting more cash, but the government had to maintain control over the money supply and not allow private individuals to mint or counterfeit cash. Faced with the opposition either to import Ch'ing cash or adopt iron currency, Song suggested that the government at least prevent any further contraction. Since the rising value of cash had acted as an incentive for cash savings over consumption, speculators were saving as much cash as possible in anticipation of an even greater rise in the value of their money. To counteract this tendency he proposed that new cash be minted right away and put into circulation with the old cash for a period of three years, presumably to reduce the value of cash in the market and deplete the expected profits of the rich speculators. Thereafter, the government would place a ban on the old coins and prohibit the rich from saving them, allowing only the new coins to circulate. Melting down all the old coins after three years and converting them to new coins would force the rich speculators to spend all their savings before it lost its value as legal tender, thereby pumping more cash into the market and curtailing the need for imported cash or copper.

Yŏngjo again declared his willingness to mint more cash even though he still would have preferred to abolish it altogether, and he also agreed to Song's plan to replace all current coins three years hence. Neither Yŏngjo nor any of his officials, however, proposed an expansion of copper mining or increased imports of copper from Japan, as Yu Hyŏngwŏn had in the previous century, but in this period it may not have been possible anyway because the Japanese had cut back on their copper exports.

Song added that changing the entire money supply by reminting was a tactic that could be repeated but no more often than once every fifty years, a rather conservative estimate since the cash shortage had reached a crisis situation thirty years after minting was banned in 1697, and only twelve years after Yŏngjo agreed to more minting in 1731. Pak Munsu feared that once the old cash was banned as legal tender, there would be a sharp reduction in the money supply until the old coins were reminted as new cash, presumably causing a sharp deflation in prices. Whether the new cash was minted by official agencies or private parties, the artisans might illicitly debase the coins with lead or steal copper for their own use. Coins debased with lead would be darker in color and readily detected by the people, and the government would ultimately lose as much as 30 or 40 percent (of the copper) in the process of reminting the cash. Yŏngjo agreed that the point was well taken, but the officials in charge should be able to prevent it.

Kim Yangno: Multiple-denomination Cash

Because changing the currency to force savings onto the market must have seemed barely adequate to solve the cash shortage, Second Minister of Rites Kim Yangno again raised the suggestion of minting multiple-denomination coins like the 10-cash or 100-cash, to be used in conjunction with the old small coins. Two other officials supported Kim's idea, and even Yŏngjo appeared to soften his earlier stance by remarking that it might be all right to do so, but Fourth Royal Secretary Yun Hwijŏng objected because circulating multiple-denomination cash along with small denomination coins would only make it easier for the counterfeiters. Yun's objection was apparently sufficient to dissuade Yŏngjo.

Thus far four plans had been discussed to increase the money supply: importing Ch'ing cash, minting iron cash, introducing multiple-denomination cash, and replacing the entire money supply to force the expenditure of savings, and only the last, the most cautious plan, had been approved. The discussion then moved away from these practical remedies to more fundamental consideration of the possible moral causes of the cash problem. Fifth Counselor of the Office of Special Counselors Yun Kwang'ŭi thought that the problem was not the volume of currency in circulation, but whether the king could practice frugality and show special concern for popular welfare, but Yŏngjo, as much a moralist as any man, was put off by Yun's self-righteousness and told him he was talking like a scholar who had no knowledge of the real world.

Yŏngjo must have felt constrained to demonstrate his ethical concerns by asserting that despite the advice of scholars and officials to the contrary, he had always thought cash should be abolished because the amount of cash in circulation had nothing to do with whether "rites and music" flourished after a century of rule (i.e., whether a king had succeeded in producing a record of virtuous leadership), but everything to do with the moral transformation produced by education (*kyohwa*). Yŏngjo defended his reign by transferring blame to the population at large; it was because the minds of the people had gradually changed for the worse that it had become impossible for him to abolish cash, leaving him no alternative but to mint more of it.

Even though he had been forced to mint more cash contrary to his moral principles in 1731, he was still skeptical of the advantages of increasing the money supply. Previously Yun Chihwan had said that the more cash minted, the better things would be, but Yun was badly mistaken. Many thought that minting more cash would benefit the state rather than private individuals, but "private minting" or counterfeiting of large amounts of cash for private profit had taken place as well. Yŏngjo also had doubts about the utility of melting down brassware to create more copper for minting cash. Pak Munsu had formerly said that it was wrong to melt down brassware because it was a daily necessity, not a luxury item, and melting it down would cause hardship and distress to the general population. That was why Yŏngjo originally had intended to use cloth in place of cash because he thought it would suit the simple and pure tastes of the common people.

King Yŏngjo Canvasses "Public Opinion"

Despite these ruminations about the material and moral advantages and disadvantages of solutions to the cash shortage, Yŏngjo decided to canvass the opinions of people beyond the small body of government officials, a method that he was later to use more frequently. He ordered the magistrate of Seoul and the Office for Dispensing Benevolence to solicit the views of the people of the capital and provinces on minting more cash or introducing multiple-denomination coins. Kim Yangno, however, advised him to restrict his search to the people of the capital, not the whole country, and Song Inmyŏng urged him to dispense with public opinion altogether and just make up his own mind. Pak Munsu also suggested he simply order provincial governors and district magistrates to select talented people to take responsibility for minting operations.[9]

A couple of weeks later the debate moved toward a final conclusion as all alternatives brought up for solving the cash shortage were presented for discussion. Cho Sanggyŏng, the magistrate of Seoul, reported that a few "knowledgeable" gentlemen and the "masses" of the population of Seoul were impregnably opposed to both multiple-denomination and Ch'ing cash, but they did agree that more of the current small coins should be minted. Minister of Punishments Min Ŭngsu also said he had heard the same views from the court officials and commoners he had talked with.

Cho also reported that some respondents believed that the high value of cash had been exacerbated because government agencies in both the capital and provinces, not just the rich speculators, had been storing cash away and treating it as an "immovable reserve," just as Yu Suwŏn had observed in his analysis of the cash shortage. If these agencies were to store silver instead and spend their cash savings, it would drive down the value of cash. They also thought that the copper cash reserve could be expanded still further and the value of copper cash reduced from its high value if the government either melted silver into smaller pieces, minted more small cash of the value of one or two single coins, or circulated silver coins instead of using cash.[10] But Cho himself was not sure which of the two views was correct.

Min Ŭngsu: Silver Coins or More Copper Cash

As commissioner (Tangsang) of the Office for Dispensing Benevolence, Min Ŭngsu supported the idea of allowing the government to mint silver coins and use them to pay its bills while granting the common people full freedom to use copper cash in their market transactions because it would free more copper cash for the market and reduce the high value of cash. There was enough silver in Korea to make the plan feasible, but he predicted the tribute middlemen (*kong'in*) would dislike it, and tax payments made by distant villages in cash would have to be sent back (and replaced with silver currency payments).

Kim Chaero, however, was more afraid of the profits counterfeiters might make from silver coins than of the problems of the cash shortage. He predicted that the government would have as much trouble in stamping out counterfeiters as it had had in prohibiting the smuggling of ginseng by merchants, and he asserted that most people simply preferred to retain only the old coins without experimenting either with multiple-denomination coins or silver cash. Yŏngjo agreed that the inability to enforce prohibitions was the reason why the people had no respect for the law and the country lacked a spirit of law and order.

Min Ŭngsu also raised serious questions about the efficacy of Song Inmyŏng's plan to force rich hoarders of cash to spend their savings within the next three years before the old cash was declared illegal, because the people would doubt whether any law could be maintained consistently for any length of time in the future. Instead of forcing them to spend their cash, they would on the contrary hold onto it even more tightly. He preferred forcing government agencies to release their stagnating cash reserves on the market by ordering them to use their cash to buy rice or silver for their reserve fund – a device similar to the usual ever-normal commodity price stabilization system used for grain. Yŏngjo took seriously Min Ŭngsu's warning that a total conversion of the currency in three years might shatter public confidence in the validity and longevity of all government laws. He agreed that the only way the laws could be made to work was first by establishing respect for law itself (*ipkang*), and that the only way to solve the currency problem was by minting more cash.[11]

Pak Munsu: Silver Cash

Pak Munsu also proposed minting of silver coin of (a weight of?) 1-*yang* (8–9 *sŏng* or "stars") with a (face?) value of 2 *yang* (equivalent to 200 copper coins) of cash (an increase of 400 percent in the value of cash since 1680). Yŏngjo asked him why anyone would want to continue using copper cash if they could have silver, and Pak assured him that even if that were true, there was enough silver in the country to replace copper cash entirely with silver coins. Practically, however, it would not be necessary to mint all the silver into coins right away, just 200,000 *yang* of silver coins each year (equivalent to 20 million copper coins – an apparent underestimate of the money supply) until silver replaced copper cash.

Yŏngjo told Pak he was talking nonsense, presumably because he thought that it was absurd to think that Korea could either mine or import enough silver to replace copper cash. Song Inmyŏng, however, took Pak's suggestion more seriously. He recalled that when he had traveled to China during an official embassy, the embassy was accompanied by a few Ŭiju merchants with the right to trade in ginseng (*p'alp'o*), and they had about 80,000–90,000 *yang* (of silver by weight, not silver coins) with them. Of this amount 80,000 *yang* was high-grade silver (*ch'ŏn'ŭn*) and 10,000 *yang* was pure silver (*chŏng'ŭn*). Nonetheless, he did not know where such large quantities of silver were to be found.

Yŏngjo mentioned that Chŏng Sŏksam had once told him about silver mining operations in China, and Song noted that even though there was not enough silver in Korea, it might be possible to mine about 200–300,000 *yang*. What he knew of the situation in Beijing, however, was that the use of silver was confined to the top (the government, or the highest levels of society?), while copper cash was used in the side streets, but that the Chinese, by contrast, had more than enough copper cash. He said that Pak must have been talking about the silver in the silver shops attached to the Ministry of Taxation. He suggested that the military divisions and agencies should dispatch officers to investigate how much silver could be mined to estimate whether enough could be found to pay for the daily food and clothing needs of the soldiers.

Yŏngjo said that Pak's recommendation was somewhat different from the chief state councilor's recommendation that silver be used alongside copper cash. Yŏngjo was afraid that the government might end up violating the canonical Confucian prohibition against competing with merchants for profit by seeking control over silver, a strange attitude since he had not raised the same reservation about government minting of copper cash. In any case, Pak assured him that it was not his intention to do so, and he guaranteed that silver coinage would not cause any loss of profit for the merchants. He would not have proposed any plan by which the court would be responsible for causing trouble for the merchants by competing with them for profits.

A number of court officials provided strong support for silver coins. Kim Sanggyŏng said he had canvassed the views of many ordinary people and found that they opposed any abolition of cash and favored the idea of using silver currency as well. Ku Sŏnggyo, an official in the Military Training Agency, thought that it was a shame that silver was not being used as currency in Korea since it was the most plentiful precious metal in the country, and Song Inmyŏng said that although he did not know what the size of the immovable cash reserves were, it would be a good idea to have the Ministry of Taxation exchange its cash reserves for silver as a means of recirculating idle copper cash in the market.

Yŏngjo asked the officials to provide concrete ideas about what form silver currency would take before he would approve the idea. Kim Chaero asked if ten-*sŏng* silver would be best? Pak Munsu also favored the use of ten-*sŏng* silver for currency, but Song Inmyŏng said that (even?) seven- or eight-*sŏng* silver could not be put into circulation in Korea. Pak Munsu thought that Korean silver was similar to Japanese silver, and Kim Sanggyŏng said Korea had been importing even more silver from Japan in recent years, suggesting that any shortage of silver could be satisfied by imports. Kim Yangno agreed with using silver, but thought that Japanese silver was different from Korean. Kim Sangsŏng thought it would be all right to use (both Japanese as well as Korean silver), but that the policy would only be acceptable as long as the government did not end up competing with merchants for profit.

Others raised the question of the domestic supply. Min Ŭngsu thought that there was a lot of high-grade silver (*ch'ŏn'ŭn*) in Korea but not much in the silver shops. When he had been traveling along the Western Route (between Seoul and Ŭiju in the northwest), he had collected 50,000 *yang*, and also heard that the provincial military commanders and district magistrates must have collected more than 120,000 *yang* or so. The supply of silver in the silver shops varied from time to time, but he believed that the people would not be opposed to the idea of having silver circulate with copper cash. Chief State Councilor Kim Chaero mentioned that since silver miners were currently not producing much silver and the taxes they paid to the Ministry of Taxation had not been that large, he did not anticipate that much silver would be obtained by mining. Yŏngjo finally asked whether further minting of cash would be necessary if silver currency were adopted, and Pak Munsu said that it could not be dispensed with. He thought that silver should just be used to pay for military expenses.

Silver Imports from Japan

The participants in this debate had only limited knowledge of the extent of the Korean silver trade with Japan. Trade with Japan was renewed in 1609 but declined after 1637 when private Korean traders dealt directly with the Japanese in the smuggling of sulphur, gunpowder, muskets, and swords. They also began to engage in a triangular smuggling trade with China and Japan, selling ginseng for silver through Tongnae to Japan, and using the silver to import Chinese goods.

Although figures from the Japanese side for the export of silver to Korea are not exact, Tashiro Kazui had estimated that silver exports averaged about 17,000 pounds per year from 1684 to 1695 and then dropped to about half that amount because Korean traders were reluctant to accept a series of new coins issued by the Tokugawa Bakufu after that date with appreciably less silver content than earlier ones. The Bakufu responded to a complaint from Tsushima, the intermediary in trade with Korea, that Korean merchants were reluctant to accept depreciated silver coins for high-quality ginseng, and decided to mint a special high-quality coin for the Korea trade in 1710. Trade with Japan then revived and Japanese silver exports rose to an average of 8,700 pounds per year in the 1714–32 period, about 7 to 8 percent of the silver coins minted in that period in Japan.

Expansion of that trade was limited by the Bakufu which restricted the amount of silver that could be exported to Korea annually, 9,418 pounds per year in 1686, raised to 15,696 pounds in 1700. In 1714 Arai Hakuseki urged that the limit of silver exports to trading partners like Korea, the Ryukyus, and China be reduced still further to five or six thousand pounds a year, but it could not be enforced in the Korea trade because the Sō family of Tsushima complained that the trade was essential to maintain the welfare of the island and the prestige of Japan against a foreign state. Because of the silver shortage, in 1736 the Bakufu was again forced to reduce the silver content of coins to almost half of what they had been in the mid-seventeenth century, and the policy of minting special, high silver-content coins for the Korea trade proved too burdensome. In 1737, the Bakufu then simply cut down the amount of silver it supplied to Tsushima han, and in the 1740s silver exports to Korea declined sharply and came to an end in 1752. Thereafter, Tsushima financed the Korea trade with exports of copper.[12]

In short, conditions inside Japan made it unlikely that Japan would have been able to supply Korea's silver needs if King Yŏngjo had decided to replace all copper cash with silver coins, but there was no reason why he could not have minted silver coins and circulated them with copper as a reasonable means of increasing the money supply.

Yŏngjo and Alternatives to Penny Cash

In the end, after one of the most sophisticated discussions of alternative policies to solve the problem of currency shortage in the history of the dynasty, Yŏngjo declined to adopt any of the new policies and decided only to approve the minting of more copper cash by various offices in the capital and provinces.[13] This meant that Yŏngjo had been influenced not only by the negative views of some of his high officials against the counterfeiting of silver coins, but by reports of the opposition of "public opinion" to the use of multiple-denomination cash. He also abandoned the idea of forcing the hoarded cash savings of rich speculators onto the market by a total conversion of existing coins. It may well have been "public opinion" that persuaded Yŏngjo to reject multiple-denomination cash, but one must assume that "public opinion" represented the richer denizens of the capital who would have resisted any kind of "cheap money" policy to reduce the value of their savings and loans.

The rejection of multiple-denomination cash and silver coins left the minting of more "pennies" as the only solution to the cash shortage – strangely enough, the conclusion that Yu Hyŏngwŏn had reached as part of his argument for a progressive reform to liberate seventeenth-century Korean society from the primitivism of a cashless economy. King Yŏngjo, by contrast, arrived at the same conclusion independently, but from the opposite direction. Desirous of returning to the less complex realm of the cashless economy, he was forced to admit that it was no longer possible to do so, and he settled for penny cash as the least of evils.

Yu, however, had seen fit to lay out a scheme for maintaining price stability in a cash economy, and one of its most important measures was to ensure a sufficient money supply by liberal importation of copper. A few days after Yŏngjo made his decision, Kim Chaero and Pak Munsu agreed that it had to be done. Pak warned, however, that the country was lacking a sufficient supply of metal to provide an adequate money supply for the nation. Copper could be obtained from the Japanese in Tongnae but not in great quantity – an accurate assessment of the current situation. On the other hand, despite Yŏngo's aversion to melting down brassware to obtain its copper, brassware was in fact plentiful because everyone owned some, from the royal palace and highest officials to the lowest commoners. If it were used to provide the material for minting more coins, the cash crisis could be solved.

As a result, Yŏngjo authorized the minting of 500,000 *yang* of cash (50 million coins or 50,000 strings) by capital agencies, the governors of P'yŏng'an, Kyŏngsang, and Chŏlla provinces, the magistrate of Kaesŏng, and the Naval Command for the southern provinces (T'ongnyong). Whatever the total money supply was at the time, in 1731 and 1742 Yŏngjo had authorized the minting of 800,000 *yang* or 80 million coins, two-thirds of what Yu Hyŏngwŏn had estimated as a minimal money supply to assure the successful adoption of copper cash in the economy. Yŏngjo reluctantly agreed to this policy, postponing these decisions at first for seven years, and then an additional eleven years, a far cry from the more aggressive support for cash and commerce that Yu Suwŏn recommended in the 1730s.[14]

The *Sillok* account of the decision was a poor summary of the complex discussion that had been raised over a number of important issues. It only stated that most officials opposed Pak Munsu's proposal to mint silver currency, and that Yŏngjo dismissed it as nonsense but did concede that silver cash might be used to pay military expenses.[15] A fuller discussion of the debate would have revealed that Yŏngjo rejected the importation of cash from China because it would violate the Korean ban on the use of cash along the Yalu River border and yield Korean control over its currency to the Chinese. He abandoned the idea of multiple-denomination cash because of the opposition of a number of officials and "public opinion," undoubtedly dominated by rich, conservative residents of the capital who were afraid of inflation and wanted to preserve the high value of cash and the profits of moneylending for as long as possible. Because of their opposition he declined to employ the intriguing idea of replacing the entire money supply to force the speculators to turn their cash back to the marketplace.

Despite his own initial disdain for the proposal to supplement copper cash with silver currency, he seriously entertained discussion of the idea because quite a few officials thought the supply of silver was sufficient to justify a bimetallic currency system – a view that was quite feasible despite the cessation of Japanese silver exports to Korea after 1752. The Chinese experience with silver was cited as a useful precedent for bimetallism, but it was dismissed rather cursorily because China had a plentiful supply of copper cash to begin with, and only the wealthy elite used silver for their transactions. Importing silver from Japan and the production of Korean silver mines were discussed as well, but no action was taken to pursue these alternatives.

Yŏngjo was ostensibly open to a variety of opinion about policy alternatives, and he did not actively attempt to restrict the growth of commerce or the role played by merchants in the economy because he believed that the government had a moral responsibility to stay out of any profit-making venture in competition with merchants. He was forced to concede that he did have a public duty as a benevolent ruler to intervene in the circulation of cash to eliminate any imbalance or destabilization of prices, interest rates, and taxes, but his powerful prejudice against cash yielded only slowly to arguments for a more positive role in expanding the money supply. He was skittish about the prospects of using any form of cheap money, whether paper money or multiple-denomination cash, because he was fearful that it would cause inflation, and even after he reluctantly agreed to mint more cash in 1731, he placed a severe brake on the development of the cash or nonagricultural economy by holding down the money supply. This conservative fear of inflation was also characteristic of Yu Hyŏngwŏn's ideas as well.

Unfortunately, Yŏngjo's policy deflated commodity prices by maintaining a high value of cash and dampened opportunities for investment in nonagricultural industries by keeping interest rates high as well. He never believed that it was his duty to promote industrial or nonagricultural production for the benefit of the people or the national economy as a whole, and he was by no means a mercantilist monarch who sought to increase national wealth against other national rivals. On the contrary, he was fearful that foreign trade might lead to foreign domination, particularly if Korea became dependent on Ch'ing China for imports of cash, or Tokugawa Japan for imports of copper ore.

Since the peasants were desperate for loans to tide them over the spring planting season or the vicissitudes of flood or famine, Yŏngjo's tight money policy must have increased the burdens on the peasantry by adding high interest costs and heavier cash taxes to an increasingly regressive tax system, remedied only partially by a 50 percent cut in the military service tax under the equal service tax reform (*kyunyŏkpŏp*) in 1750. After a brief conversion of some cash taxes to cotton prior to 1731, optional payment of military support taxes in cash was reintroduced. In 1750 just after the equal service reform had been adopted, a number of officials recommended the adoption of multiple-denomination cash to meet the demand for more currency for tax payments. Even though Yŏngjo agreed that the equal service tax reform did require more cash for tax payments, he decided only to mint more of the ordinary "penny" cash.[16]

More small cash was minted periodically to keep up with the demand for cash generated by the spread of commercial activity throughout the country, and in 1750 a request was made by the Border Defense Command to concentrate all minting in one agency to economize on the use of copper because its price had been increasing, but this idea was not implemented until 1785 when King Chŏngjo agreed to give that task exclusively to the Ministry of Taxation.[17]

King Yŏngjo fought fiercely to rid the Korean economy of cash, but circumstances forced him to acknowledge its indispensability to the Korean economy at the time. When he did so, he was constrained not only by his own conservative inclinations but the declining exports of copper from Japan. While agreeing to mint more cash to reduce the disadvantages of extreme deflation, he still maintained a conservative policy designed to keep the money supply at a minimum. The net effect of that policy was to restrain the potential for economic growth and development by elevating commodity prices and raising interest rates.

THE EXPANSION OF PRIVATE MERCHANT ACTIVITY

The Challenge to Licensed Monopoly, 1741–1813

King Yŏngjo was forced into his reluctant capitulation to the growing demand for more currency by the expanding scope of the commercial economy and the increased importance of private, unlicensed merchants. Just as Yu Suwŏn had written in the 1730s, in 1741 the magistrate of Seoul complained that the supremacy of the licensed merchants had already been threatened by hordes of small merchants and traders who set up shop in the capital. At times the government enforced the rules against competition. They closed down unlicensed lumber dealers who set up their own warehouses along the banks of the Han River in 1753 and petty officials of the National Academy who took over the bankrupt capital salt shops and established salt warehouses in 1769. They took punitive action against private rice merchants who hoarded rice in their warehouses and drove up the price in 1782.

At other times, however, the government was gradually forced to abandon its resistance to the activities of unlicensed merchants and private wholesaling activities. In 1742 and 1747 government agencies finally ceased opposing the activities of previously unlicensed merchants in tobacco and soybean paste, but they chose to grant monopoly rights to them rather than tolerate unlicensed competition as a matter of principle. When the second magistrate of Seoul, Yi Pohyŏk, asked in 1742 that all new shops founded in the capital in the previous sixteen years be banned, the Border Defense Command modified the proposal by agreeing only to ban private shops competing in the sale of necessities.

Once the power of the licensed shops in the capital to ban competition had been cracked, they too began to compete with private merchants in the provincial capitals by establishing warehouses and wholesale operations, and they too sought to manipulate prices by gaining control over supply, often with the collusion of officials and clerks of government offices.[18]

The establishment of unlicensed monopolies had serious repercussions when the merchants of the capital and the so-called Five Rivers cornered the rice market and drove the price "ten times" higher than normal in 1779. The government banned the practice but without success. A similar crisis occurred in the rice market in 1786, and unlicensed merchants continued to make inroads into the profits of the monopoly shops by cornering the supply of fish, tobacco, ramie, and other products. Wealthy businessmen from P'aju and wholesalers from Seoul took over part of the tobacco crop, and yangban commercial entrepreneurs in the capital contracted directly with peasant ramie growers in seven districts in South Ch'ungch'ŏng Province to buy their crops and market the product. Private merchants set up shop in markets outside the downtown Chongno licensed market area, in places like Yangju, P'och'ŏn in the northeast, and Nuwŏnjŏm in the northern outskirts, and Songp'a and Samjŏn in the Kwangju area, to intercept products flowing into the capital and sell them in competition with the licensed merchants.

The licensed merchants in Seoul complained in 1754 that the Songp'a market was supposed to be held only six times a month but in fact merchants there stockpiled goods and sold them on a daily basis. In 1789 licensed fish merchants pointed out that whereas they had previously bought the whole catch from commercial ships that arrived in Seoul, now ships only sold one-tenth their cargo and kept the rest to sell themselves, and in 1807 they complained that officials had failed to stop private merchants in P'aju, Songp'a, and Samjŏndo from cornering the fish market. By the nineteenth century the private wholesalers were able to develop nationwide networks, including not only major cities but also areas of production, crucial junctions along transportation routes, new market towns, and export market towns like Ŭiju and Tongnae, and even centers of production, whereas the licensed merchants' wholesale activities were confined mainly to the consumption markets of the major cities.[19] There was also growing resentment against the wholesalers who interfered with the earnings of small merchants. In 1781, the third inspector of the Office of Inspector-General, Ku Suŏn, remarked that

> I have heard recently that the system of wholesale monopolies [*togo*] has just appeared whereby one merchant gains control over others and does not permit them to make their own private [and independent] purchases. Wealthy people form their own *kye* organizations [*kyebang*] and buy up products at cheap prices

> and then sell them to people outside their own *kye* at double the price. Thus the profit ends up in the hands of one man, while the harm extends to tens of thousands.[20]

Despite the complaints of the licensed merchants the government was unable to enforce the ban against illegal competition, and it lost its resolve to maintain the very system of licensed monopolies as well. For that reason Yu Suwŏn's program for the expansion of licensed shops and the creation of oligopolies under state control was becoming less feasible. In 1781 when the hat monopoly demanded the arrest of capital guardsmen for selling woolen hats illegally, King Chŏngjo decided to allow the agency in charge of capital markets to adjudicate each complaint individually lest total enforcement of the law bankrupt the soldiers involved in unlicensed production of the hats and arouse their animosity. As partial compensation to the licensed merchants the government tried to reduce some of their tax burdens by collecting part of them from the weavers directly, but the Ministry of Taxation refused to go along and demanded more taxes from the licensed merchants and drove them to the edge of insolvency.

The ministry sought to achieve a reconciliation of conflicting interests by granting the wool monopolists a ten-year 5,000-*yang* loan to buy silver from China, putting them in charge of collecting commercial taxes from the soldier hat-sellers, but the wool monopolists feared that eventually the unlicensed operators would drive them out of business. In 1782 the iron monopoly, and in 1784 the lacquer ware and wood products monopolies, demanded government action to ban unlicensed sales by merchants and producers, but the government admitted that it was powerless to block unlicensed sales in the countryside.

In 1787 the government again tried to bring competition from unlicensed manufacturers and merchants under a modicum of control by attempting a compromise solution. It instructed the knife monopoly that it could not simply ban all unlicensed sale of knives and would have to permit unlicensed vendors to operate alongside the licensed merchants, a policy referred to as joint sales (*t'ong-gong parmae*). It permitted independent ironmakers to buy scrap iron from the monopoly iron shops to make small tools and sell them on the market on their own, but it also attempted to assuage the licensed merchants in Seoul by granting them, tribute middlemen (*kong'in*), and capital guardsmen 157,000 *yang* of interest-free loans to help tide them over their financial difficulties. The ambivalence of government policy continued in 1788 when the government enforced the ban against unlicensed sale of candles but refused to ban unlicensed sales of honey. In 1791 licensed fish merchants complained that private owners of ships were selling their catch directly to the public, while the private entrepreneurs claimed that selling small quantities of fish directly to consumers was accepted convention.[21]

Pak Chega's Advocacy of Greater Commerce

Pak Chega, a nothos of an official, was able to establish a reputation for scholarship and gain a post as librarian of the Kyujanggak archives in 1779. He returned from four visits to China that began in 1776 as an exponent of the superiority of late Ch'ing civilization and wrote essays on Chinese carts, boats, walls, tile, roads, bridges, markets, medicines, and weapons. While also interested in the technological aspects of farming and animal husbandry, he was also a strong advocate of commerce and foreign trade, and like Yu Suwŏn forty years before, he believed that the idle and parasitic yangban could be turned into productive individuals by encouraging them to engage in commerce, an idea he proposed to King Chŏngjo in 1786. His open praise for the accomplishments of the Manchu Ch'ing dynasty, however, earned him criticism from those who continued to view the Manchus as a barbarians who had destroyed the beloved Ming dynasty and twice violated the peace and security of Korea. Forced out of his capital post to a provincial position, Pak was able to survive until he was arrested, tortured, and exiled during the anti-Christian persecution of 1801.[22]

In his "Treatise on Learning from the North [i.e., Ch'ing China]" (*Pukhag'ŭi*), Pak described the thriving markets he witnessed in Yenching and other towns in China, but he rued the incapacity of fellow Koreans to appreciate the Chinese love of commerce because they regarded it as an inferior pursuit of profit. Even though over a century of experience with copper cash and commercial development had taken place, Pak claimed that Koreans were still unable to perceive that commerce was indispensable to society. When they visited China and witnessed the magnificence and prosperity of Chinese palaces, vehicles, decoration, and textiles, they condemned them all as examples of the wasteful and ostentatious consumption that had been responsible for the fall of the Ming dynasty.

Virtually echoing the sentiments of Yu Hyŏngwŏn, Pak insisted that while merchants did not produce things of value, they were engaged in the useful occupation of circulating goods. The ancient sages had perceived the essential utility of the circulation of goods and had invented the use of precious stones and shells as media of exchange, and carts and boats as means for transporting goods past topographical barriers.

By contrast with Ch'ing China, Pak felt that Korea was in danger of declining not from conspicuous consumption, but from its love of frugality. Unfortunately, Koreans interpreted frugality to mean that you never spent your savings to buy anything, but the consequence of that proclivity resulted only in reducing popular demand and eliminating the stimulus for the production of goods otherwise available in China. Koreans had no concept of the utility of those goods, and

> If you don't know what the utility [of the goods are], you don't know any reason to produce them. If you don't have any reason to produce them, then more and

> more people are driven to destitution every day. I would compare these goods to a well. If you draw water from it, it will [continue] to refill, but if you stop, then it goes dry. So if you don't wear brocade, then the country won't have any weavers and the skills of the women will decline. If you have no distaste for cracked cups or don't care for fine workmanship, there won't be any mechanics and potters in the country, and the skills and arts [of technology] will disappear. Even agriculture will go to ruin and its methods will be lost, and commerce will be weakened and the occupation will be lost. The people in all the four basic occupations [scholarship-and-government service, agriculture, commerce, and manufacture] will end up in difficult circumstances, and they will be unable to render assistance to each other. The treasures that exist in our country will not be accepted within its territories, so when you visit a foreign country, you will find their people waxing wealthy while ours descend into poverty.[23]

Because of his instrumental approach to the mechanics of economic behavior, Pak Chega had been able to derive the relationship between demand and production, and his logic had led him to see the economic danger involved in the constant moral emphasis on frugality. Kim Yongdŏk has written that Pak's belief in the benefit of consumption over saving as the means to stimulate greater and more varied production was unique to Korean thought, even including the scholars devoted to practical affairs, and was characteristic of modern economic thought.[24] Unfortunately, it is not clear today that an emphasis on consumption over savings is necessarily a characteristic of "modern" thought, since many economists in the late 1980s and early 1990s have explained the decline of the U.S. economy in part as a result of consumerism coupled with a low rate of saving. Others have praised the high rate of saving in countries like South Korea and Japan as a means of capital formation for productive investment. The real problem was the misuse of savings in a precapitalist economy, the failure to use those savings to expand investment in industrial production, infrastructure, trade, and marketing.

Pak Chega also claimed that there were two fundamental differences between the Chinese and Korean economies: the widespread network of shops and markets in China and their superior circulation and distribution of goods, and greater toleration of commercial activity and the merchant class. Since there was no stigma attached to commerce in China, anyone could go into business without damaging his dignity or reputation. Even the highest ministers of state personally went shopping for antiques in the market district of the capital, and they had been doing so since the Sung and Ming dynasties. But in Korea, the *sadaebu* (the yangban elite) avoided those mundane activities because they were overwhelmingly attached to the superiority of literary talent, what Pak deprecatingly referred to as their "empty" scribblings. Those who lacked a post and had no money had no experience in working the fields and no knowledge of agriculture. Since commerce was taboo, they were left without any means of making their own living and had no choice but to wander the country penniless with their ink and inkstones, sponging off the largess of others, making demands for favors, or looking for some stroke of good fortune. It was obvious to him that the merchants of China were far better than the scholars of Korea.

Pak also felt that an increase in foreign trade was essential to the well-being of the Korean nation. He pointed out that Korea had been paying for its imports of Chinese silks and medicines for years by the export of Korean silver because it had no goods or products it could sell to them, and the depletion of silver had caused its price to go up.[25]

Pak gained a greater appreciation for commerce and cash from his travels in China, and he became an advocate of greater consumption as the means of promoting greater production of goods. It was not by chance, however, that it required the stimulus of the more advanced Ch'ing economy to provide the inspiration for these views, because no matter how much economic change had occurred in Korea since the seventeenth century, not enough had occurred to produce greater awareness of the advantages of commerce and production among government officials. Nonetheless, one might conclude that despite the conservative aspect of Yu Hyŏngwŏn's love for penny cash, his openness to the benefits of commerce laid the groundwork for Pak's more advanced views.

Ch'ae Chegong's Joint-Sales Decree of 1791

The result of the conflict between private merchants (and private artisans engaged in the selling of their own wares) with the licensed merchants in the 1780s represented a significant advance for free market principles, but not a total victory for unrestricted competition. King Chŏngjo opted to institutionalize the compromise solution of 1787 by promulgating the "1791 joint-sales" decree (*sinhaek t'onggong*). The idea was fathered by Councilor of the Right Ch'ae Chegong, an acquaintance of Pak Chega and other progressive proponents of commercial activity in the 1780s, who indicted the licensed monopolies for raising commodity prices artificially by three- to fivefold since his youth because of their control over the supply of goods. But instead of recommending an end to all monopoly privileges, he obtained King Chŏngjo's approval to restrict monopoly privileges only to the "six shops" (Yug'ŭijŏn or Yukchubijŏn) over the products they traditionally sold and to allow unlicensed merchants to sell any products not covered by the six shops. The six shops were the highest level shops in the capital with the largest obligations to meet state demands for royal and government products, and they had been established either in 1637 or the early seventeenth century after the Imjin War (1592–98).

Ch'ae sought to take vengeance on the licensed monopolies by allowing more opportunity for the private merchants, but he could not call for the abolition of all monopolies probably because the throne had to depend on the "six shops" for supplying certain goods on demand. Nonetheless, he had less respect for monopoly or oligopoly than Yu Suwŏn in the 1730s, who planned to reorganize all merchants into licensed oligopolies on the theory that the creation of a number of shops in different neighborhoods and towns would prevent any one of them from cornering the market. He presumed that his new "educated yangban-merchants" would behave honestly and altruistically, and he did not imagine that they might enter into any kind of conspiracy to control the market and raise prices. Ch'ae Chegong had seen what monopolists could do and sought to counter them by opening the market still more.

The licensed merchants were incensed at Ch'ae's measure, and after he was transferred to the post of magistrate of Suwŏn, they followed him there to demonstrate against him. Contrary to the expectation that the private merchants would have jumped for joy at the news of Ch'ae's policy for greater liberalization, some of the owners of independent shops condemned it because they, too, had never believed in the concept of free market competition and were hoping themselves to attain a grant of monopoly privileges from the government. Now they had lost that chance.

The fish and ramie cloth shops, for example, both applied for admission into the privileged community of licensed monopolies, but in 1794 the government refused to grant permission and reiterated the policy of joint or open sales (*t'ong-gong parmae*), which meant that monopoly sales would only be permitted for the so-called six shops. Kang Man'gil has argued that the motive for this decision was initially financial: since the government could no longer protect the monopolies against competition, it chose to profit by imposing commercial taxes on all unlicensed merchants. On the other hand, Ch'ae Chegong clearly designed his open sales policy to weaken the strength of the monopolies and permit the growth of independent merchants.[26]

The effects on some of the shops no longer covered by monopoly privileges was adverse. By 1803, sixteen unlicensed shops had suffered bankruptcy, and they demanded relief from the government either by granting new or restoring old monopoly and wholesaling rights or by reduction of their tax and service obligations to the state. The government was only willing to grant them the right to collect taxes from other merchants, not the right to reestablish warehouses and wholesale selling operations, because it would only lead to artificial commodity price inflation at the expense of the poorer capital residents.[27]

Private wholesaling, however, continued despite the ban against it, and in 1813 licensed fish shops complained that they were losing business to private wholesalers. In addition, small-scale independent merchants were also outmatched by the wealthier and rich merchants who used their capital to corner supplies and elevate prices. To alleviate their plight the government occasionally granted permission to the small private merchants to sell their goods to the government.[28]

Commercial developments in the eighteenth century had outrun the perspective of both Yu Hyŏngwŏn and Yu Suwŏn. The former might not have been comfortable with the independence of private merchants because he had always believed that the role of commerce was secondary to agriculture, and the latter would have been discomfited by the toleration of private merchant business because he wanted to organize all small merchants into larger units and create oligopolies in major products.

The government's solution after Ch'ae Chegong's joint or open sales policy of 1791 and 1794 was to cut back the scope of licensed monopolies and create more opportunity for free trade, but the prospect of bankrupty in an atmosphere of freer (if not totally free) trade stimulated a reactionary demand for state protection. There was no total solution to the problem, neither an advance to totally free market conditions nor reversion to licensed monopoly sales for the capital and major towns. As a result, commercial competition by both licensed and unlicensed shops, some large wholesalers and some petty merchants, continued to the end of the nineteenth century.

THE EXPANSION OF CASH AFTER 1785

The decline of licensed monopolies and the growth of private merchant activities in the late eighteenth century indubitably fueled greater demand for cash. King Yŏngjo had always been reluctant to mint more cash, but his death in 1776 removed an obstacle to expansion of the cash supply. In 1785 King Chŏngjo decided to mint cash on a more regular basis (five times between 1785 and 1798), and he authorized an annual import of 50–60,000 *yang* of copper from Japan to provide the raw material for the cash.

One is bound to wonder whether Yu Hyŏngwŏn's advocacy of reliance on Japanese imports for copper ore had some effect on Chŏngjo's thinking because Yu's *Pan'gye surok* was first published with an introduction by the governor of Kyŏngsang Province in 1770, and in the early 1780s Yi Man'un was working under the king's order on the revision of the *Munhŏnbigo* encyclopedia of Korean institutions. In his revised text Yi quoted Yu's arguments on the advantages of cash in the *Pan'gye surok*.

The gist of Yu's argument was as follows: that it was absolutely necessary for any country to use cash because it would provide more resources for state expenditures and improve the living standards of the people. Korea was the only country in the world that had not been using cash (when Yu lived), but there was no reason why this should be so since Koreans were no different from the people of other countries: they all cultivated land, had the same tastes, and supported themselves by trading what they produced for things they did not produce themselves. Since Korea had the capacity to adopt the use of cash, the only reason why it had failed to do so was the inability of Korean kings to provide leadership and guidance for its circulation. While King Sukchong of the Koryŏ dynasty sought to promote the circulation of cash by paying cash out to officials and soldiers, and establishing wine shops to accept cash payments, he and others who wanted to stimulate the exchange of cash in Korea failed to understand the means needed to do so. They erroneously thought that if they could collect half the taxes and pay out half the salaries of officials in cash, that cash would circulate naturally without requiring much discussion.

In the Chosŏn period, kings had decided to circulate cash a number of times, but each attempt was curtailed shortly thereafter, not only because there was much opposition to it, but because the government had not sought to collect the land tax in cash. The mere fact that cheap cloth was functioning as a medium of exchange in the market already simply proved without a doubt that copper cash had to circulate if given a chance. The reason why government prohibitions against the use of cheap cloth had not succeeded in stopping its use as a medium of exchange was because cash was not yet circulating throughout the market.

The argument that cash could not circulate because copper and tin were not produced in sufficient supply in Korea was simply wrong because those metals could be purchased abroad at reasonable prices. Even the poorest peasants living in thatched huts in remote villages deep in the mountains or valleys used copper to make their eating and drinking utensils. It was certainly possible to salvage copper from bronze statues, bells, chimes, and implements in the dozen or so Buddhist temples found in almost every district of the country and mobilize the entire country to find enough cash that would be needed, especially since ordinary people were already counterfeiting coins on their own even though there were no copper mines in the country. There was, Yu concluded, no reason why cash could not circulate.[29]

In 1785, Yu's advice was outdated since cash had been in continuous use for a century, but the problem of securing a sufficient supply of copper was still a major problem. King Chŏngjo, however, was so confident that importing copper from China and Japan would be easy that he also decided to ban the mining of copper and silver ore in Korea to conserve Korea's national resources. Unfortunately, statistical evidence indicates that the Tokugawa Bakufu limited copper exports to Korea to 100,000 *kŭn*/year (133,000 lbs?) from 1713 to 1736, and that available figures for the mid-1760s apparently stayed near that amount.[30]

By the late eighteenth century Japan was faced with a copper shortage and the Sō clan on Tsushima Island could not find sufficient copper to pay for maintenance, let alone expansion of trade. Therefore, despite King Chŏngjo's policy of liberal imports, the annual import total decreased to 28,000 *yang* in 1816. As the source of supply fell, the price of copper rose and the profit of seigniorage on minting cash fell, as shown in table 12.

Minister of Taxation Kim Iyang complained that reliance on China and Japan for these metals increased their price because of the cost of transportation and reduced the profits of seigniorage, but the major reason had to have been the copper shortage in Japan and Bakufu restriction on copper exports. King Sunjo was then forced to suspend minting and rescind the ban Chŏngjo had imposed on copper mining in 1787.

TABLE 12
SEIGNIORAGE ON COPPER CASH, 1706–1814

Amount of Copper for 1 *yang* of Silver		Profit on Minting	
Year	Copper (in *kŭn*)	Year	Profit(%)
1706	8.3	1731	50
ca. 1723	1.5	1775	30
ca. 1780	1.2	1798	20
ca. 1810	1.0	1814	10

Not until 1828 did King Sunjo turn to copper mining as the solution to the problem of supply by establishing the Kapsan copper mine in Hamgyŏng Province and developing it into a major source of copper. In 1836, it was reported that domestic supplies had replaced Japanese imports and reduced the price of copper on the market, and by the 1840s there were twenty-seven active copper mines in the country.[31]

Prior to the expansion of copper supplies by Japanese imports and domestic mining, the shortage of copper forced the government in the late eighteenth century to consider more economic alternatives to "penny" coins, like imported cash, multiple-denomination cash, silver currency, paper money, or paper notes. Seven requests for multiple-denomination cash were made in the reign of King Chŏngjo and two more at the beginning of Sunjo's reign, but none of these proposals was accepted and no more requests were made after 1816 until the Taewongun adopted a 100-cash coin in 1866. The only adaptation to proposals for increasing the face value of coins was a gradual decrease in the weight of the coin, from .25 *yang* of copper (in 1678?), to .20 *yang* in 1724, to .17 *yang* in 1752, and .12 *yang* in 1757. In other words, the weight of the standard coin dropped to half its original weight by 1757.[32]

Despite the evidence of increased liberalization of trade, the introduction of mining, and government willingness to mint more copper cash, these developments did not lead to the indigenous creation of more advanced media of exchange, such as multiple-denomination cash, silver coins, paper money, bills of exchange, or banks.

Conflicting Views of Practical Scholars on Cash

Pak Chega and U Chŏnggyu. In light of the economic developments of the eighteenth century, it was not unusual that some of the practical scholars of the late eighteenth and early nineteenth centuries approached the problems of cash and commerce from a different perspective than either Yu Hyŏngwŏn or Yi Ik. The most significant development in that period was an increase in the number of late eighteenth-century scholars who were awestruck by the advanced technology, commerce, and culture of late Ch'ing culture during the reign of Emperor Ch'ien-lung, and they usually argued in favor of emulation of Ch'ing commercial practice, including either the minting or importation of more cash.

Pak Chega, whose ideas on commerce we have explored above, complained about the poor quality and lack of uniformity of Korean cash in comparison with Ch'ing coins of the K'ang-hsi and Ch'ien-lung eras, and he suggested the possibility of importing superior Ch'ing coins into Korea, an idea that had been mentioned before in Korea but not attempted until the late 1860s. Pak favored the import of Ch'ing cash as the means of alleviating the perennial cash shortage and price deflation that usually plagued the Korean economy.[33]

U Chŏnggyu was another scholar-official of the late eighteenth century who had relatively liberal economic views for the time. In 1788 he had sent a memorial to the throne urging the adoption of silver currency, and in his *Rustic Views on the Management of the Country* (*Kyŏngje yaon*) he wrote that gold (or metal, i.e., metallic currency) was as valuable to the country as grain and was therefore the secret to national wealth and the prosperity. The use of silver had been proven useful as a medium of exchange in China because it was both lightweight and valuable, and for that reason Korean interpreters and merchants who accompanied tribute missions had taken large quantities of silver with them to purchase goods in Yenching and promote trade with China.

Because the export of silver had led to the exhaustion of Korean silver reserves, the government should have been stimulated to increase silver mining, but to the contrary officials had condemned the silver shops in Korea, and the government had banned them, allowing only copper and copper shops to exist. But if the silver shops had been so bad, how could the copper shops have been guilt-free? On the contrary, U Chŏnggye continued, both silver and copper shops, and by extension the use of silver and copper currency, were beneficial. Local officials should be allowed to recruit people to engage in the minting of silver cash. It would only become a problem if that activity took the peasants away from agriculture, but in fact it would create more opportunities for employment for peasants without land or for those who were not engaged in agriculture by stimulating wealthy merchants to invest their capital in hiring laborers to do the mining of silver and minting of cash, and they would pay taxes to the state as well. The condemnation of silver shops and silver currency was obviously erroneous because the merchants would earn a return on their investment, and the landless workers would earn enough to support themselves, "benefiting both private and public interests alike."[34]

He also intended that silver coins circulate along with copper cash because copper cash had been in use as the most important medium of exchange since the Chou dynasty in China. Imbalances in commodity prices had always been regulated by either increasing or decreasing the money supply. Like Yu Hyŏngwŏn, he commented that Korea had in its past experimented with silver jar money and paper money, but they had not worked out because they were too light or irregular. Cash had now been in circulation for over a hundred years, but the difficulties involved in using it (shortage of supply?) had led some to advocate its abolition. This was obviously mistaken because similar proposals made in the Han and Chin dynasties in China had been rejected.

U was convinced that the current high value of cash had been created because too much cash, probably two to three hundred thousand strings (two to three million coins), had been collected from the people in taxes and was being held in reserve by the treasuries of state officials and agencies. No more than 10 or 20 percent of those tax receipts had been spent and recirculated into the market, and in recent years the percentage of retained cash savings had grown even greater as military units and divisions had been buying and storing copper and iron.

The solution to the problem was simple: just order all government agencies to buy grain with their cash reserves or loan it to the people to recirculate it. In addition all copper and other metals in reserve should be used to mint more cash not only in "penny" cash, but in multiple denominations of ten, a hundred, or a thousand. These remedies would solve the problem of cash shortage, the excessively high value of currency, and the stagnation of circulation of both cash and commodities, because then cash would be performing its "ever-normal" function of creating a balance between goods and currency and stabilizing prices.[35]

Pak Chiwŏn. Pak Chiwŏn was another of the famous travelers to China who wrote a well-known travelogue after his first visit in 1779 called *Diary of My Trip to Jehol* (*Yŏha ilgi*). When King Chŏngjo ascended the throne in 1776, Pak decided to go into self-imposed exile because one of Chŏngjo's closest officials, Hong Kugyŏng, intensely disliked Pak's patron, Hong Naksŏng, who was a member of the *pyŏkp'a* faction that had supported King Yŏngjo when he committed filicide against Chŏngjo's father, the Sado crown prince in 1762. Like Pak Chega, Hong Taeyong, and many other travelers to China in this period, Pak Chiwŏn was greatly impressed by the splendor of late Ch'ing civilization, the architecture, the boats, and carts, the tiles, and standards of measure as well as agriculture, sericulture, and animal husbandry. He entered a career as an official in the late 1780s, and in the late 1790s submitted a land-limitation scheme to restrict the private estates of the landlords.

Because of the content of one of his popular novels, *The Biography of Master Ho* (*Hosaengjŏn*), he has earned a reputation as a progressive thinker on the matter of commerce and trade because the protagonist of the novel borrowed money from a wealthy man, led a band of robbers to an island off the coast, and accumulated a fortune by trading with the Japanese. He then returned to the peninsula and distributed his wealth in humanitarian, Robin-Hood fashion, to the impoverished peasants. During his conversations with friends Master Ho extolled trade with China and praised it as the means for enriching Korea, and denigrated the awkward and impractical traditional long-sleeved, white-cotton clothing of the Korean elite.[36]

A number of scholars have praised Pak for his progressive views, but there was also a strong conservative tendency in his thought that affected his ideas about commerce and currency. He, traditionally, believed that agriculture was the primary source of wealth, that commerce could only play an auxiliary role in the economy, and that cash was only a means for circulating goods, not a source of tangible products or real wealth. This point of view was shared by reformers and progressives like Yu Hyŏngwŏn as well as conservative opponents of metallic cash. His sources for these concepts were not restricted to the Confucian giants of antiquity, but to the practical statesmen of the Chou era, Kuan-chung of the Ch'i state and Shang Yang of the Ch'in state. Kuan-chung had said that "the fields and the market areas of a country were engaged in competition [to attract] the people [to them], and gold and grain competed to be held in greater esteem," but the secret to production was commitment by the people to cultivation of the fields (not gold or money) because it was the only route to greater production and the wealth and prosperity of the country. Shang Yang also remarked that gold and grain were related adversely to one another: "If gold [or metal] were produced, then grain died; if grain grew, then gold died. . . . If you liked to produce gold in your country, then both gold and grain would die, the treasuries of the state would be empty, and the state weakened. If you like to grow grain in your country, then both gold and grain would grow, the treasuries would be filled to overflowing, and the state would be strong."

In other words, Kuan-chung, the spokesmen for the hegemons of ancient Chou, and Shang Yang, the architect of Legalist materialism, shared with Mencius and other Confucians the devotion to the supremacy of agricultural production. "Gold [or metal]," that is cash or money, could only be produced as an adjunct to the production of things of real value like food, while abandonment of agriculture for commercial profits would end by reducing labor power and production. Unfortunately, most people only thought of cash as a useful means of providing food and clothing against the evils of famine and cold and stored as much cash as they could in normal times as a hedge against flood, drought, and war, but they did not realize that money alone was not enough.[37] This point of view, by the way, was not too far from that of Yu Hyŏngwŏn.

Despite his apparent agreement with Yu Hyŏngwŏn on the secondary relationship of currency to agriculture, Pak was more progressive than Yu in his prescriptions for coinage reform. In a letter Pak wrote to the Councilor of the Left Kim Iso in 1792, he expounded his views on the problems of adjusting the money supply according to the volume of commodities in circulation by raising or lowering the value of money to create stability in commodity prices. Facing the current shortage in the supply of copper as well as copper cash, he advocated the minting not only of multiple-denomination cash in addition to "penny" coins, but silver currency as well, with a guaranteed profit of seigniorage of 10 percent in the process. Silver was bound to gain public confidence because the metal itself was precious; Koreans were simply unused to using it as coins.

He also noted how silver ingots had been used primarily by Korean interpreters and merchants to finance the China trade, but contrary to U Chŏnggyu, he viewed that trade as damaging to the economic interests of Korea because an annual average of 100,000 *yang* of silver had been exported to China to pay for luxuries and perishable items like felt hats. Once Korea began to mint silver coins, it would reduce the silver supply available for export, so that the government should take action to prevent the flight of silver from Korea by closing off the China trade. The government should reduce the number of people authorized to travel to Yenching on tribute missions and ban the export of silver to China as well as forbid the import from China of any products other than medicines. Even though Pak believed in the utility of currency and was more "advanced" in his ideas on the money supply than Yu Hyŏngwŏn had been a century before, the large outflow of silver frightened him because he perceived it as an exchange of real wealth for production of goods of no utility to meet the frivolous demands of Korean consumers. Wŏn Yuhan has praised these ideas for manifesting a nationalistic spirit, but if so, it was the nationalism of the modern mercantilist or protectionist rather than the free trader. Like Pak Chega, he favored the development of roads and transport vehicles to expand the distribution of articles of local production throughout Korea, but he was afraid of the consequences of foreign trade because he really could not envision any potential for the development of an export market, no matter what his hero, Master Ho, had to say in the *Hosaengjŏn*.[38]

Pak also wrote elsewhere that the Korean government should prohibit private minting, maintain exclusive government control over the minting of cash, and reject the idea of importing Ch'ing cash. He suspected that the last idea reflected the hopes of the official Korean interpreters who expected to turn at least a 600 percent profit on the purchase of cheaper Chinese cash, and he objected to it because Korean currency was already too irregular and confused. The coins first minted in 1678 weighed .12 *yang* each, but in 1679 the weight was doubled to .25 *yang* and treated as equivalent to two of the original coins, and this 2-cash coin, or "old cash" (*kujŏn*), was the best of all coins minted after that. A second type called the cash of the three military divisions (*samyŏngjŏn*) were minted around the middle of the century and had much less copper and were smaller in size, the worst type of coins put into circulation. The copper content of coins minted in this period were .20 *yang*, in 1742, .17 *yang* in 1752, .12 *yang* in 1753, and .12 *yang* around 1810. Finally, the coins minted in King Chŏngjo's era after 1776, called "new cash" (*sinjŏn*), were better in quality, but eventually all three types of coin circulated at the same face value. Pak insisted that the highest quality "old cash" be taken as the standard for the "penny," that the value of "new cash" be cut to half the value of "old cash," and that the use of the "three military division cash" and all other coins of poor quality be prohibited. By this means the government could restore public confidence in the currency.[39]

Both Wŏn Yuhan and Kwŏn Yŏng'ik have claimed that Pak Chiwŏn's ideas on currency were a product of his own nationalistic self-consciousness. Kwŏn explained that the key concept of his monetary wisdom was that only goods or products had real utility because they satisfied the desire for existence, whereas cash only had relative economic value because it functioned as a means of weighing and balancing the value of products. Although he regarded agriculture as fundamental to the economy, he did not ignore or degrade cash and commerce.

Hence, Pak's theory of money was unprejudiced, objective, and practical. The only aspect of modernity lacking from his theory were perhaps the absence of any theory of purchasing power or quantitative analysis.

Kwŏn also remarked that Pak believed in putting the power to mint and manage cash completely in the hands of the state and removing all outside influence from the Korean monetary system. To create national self-sufficiency he proposed prohibiting foreign trade and the export of raw metals for minting coins, like silver. Even though this was to be a national currency system for a unified state, it was not a philosophy of national essence (presumably like the chauvinists and ultranationalists of the Japanese in the 1930s), nor did it have any aspects of the ambition for national power that characterized the Western mercantilists who sought to maximize the national possession of precious metals.[40]

Kwŏn's analysis, however, is unsatisfying because Pak's emphasis on the primacy of agriculture and the secondary role of currency was an eminently classical statement of the relationship of cash to agricultural production, one that Yu Hyŏngwŏn adopted as well, back in the mid-seventeenth century. There was nothing "objective" (let alone modern) about it at all. His proposal to create a currency system that, if not totally uniform, would at least consist of quality coins of easily discernible value was hardly a departure from what Yu had also advocated, another standard goal of the better monetary theorists in the Chinese tradition, but his advocacy of multiple-denomination cash and silver coins represented a more enlightened attitude toward money than Yu's penny cash. Kwŏn's assertion that Pak's fear of foreign trade and the exhaustion of the silver supply was not mercantilist is not so clearly demonstrated. The mercantilist at least believes that trade can be an engine for the expansion of national economic power as long as a favorable balance of trade and the resulting inflow of specie from abroad can be maintained. Pak's opposition to trade with China because of the current adverse balance of trade had mercantilistic implications, from the losing rather than the winning side of the equation, but his conservative protectionism was not conducive to any expansion of trade as a means of promoting Korean economic growth.

Tasan. Even though the great statecraft scholar of the late eighteenth and early nineteenth centuries, Chŏng Yagyong (Tasan), generally had a conservative attitude toward commerce, he was also a well-known advocate of multiple-denomination cash. Like Yŏngjo, Yi Ik, Pak Chiwŏn, and other conservatives before him, he insisted on the primacy of agriculture over commerce and opposed ostentatious expenditures on luxury items. Like Pak Chiwŏn he also deplored the export of gold and silver to China for the import of fancy silks, and he favored a ban on the import of silks and the private mining of gold. He explained that the circulation of cash had not developed in Korea until late in its history because easy maritime transportation around the coast lessened the need for cash. He conceded that cash was easier to transport than other media of exchange and promoted the volume of trade. However, when cash finally arrived in Korea, instead of creating prosperity, it undermined morals by stimulating deceit and deception in the search for profit, ostentation and profligate expenditure, bribery and corruption among government clerks, the abandonment of agriculture, and the decline of production and the daily income of the peasantry.

Nevertheless, after his nineteen-year exile for his involvement in the Christian movement ended in 1818, he took a more positive attitude toward cash. Because Korean cash had been poor, light, and fragile, he suggested that some of it be recast into multiple-denomination 10- and 100-cash coins that would circulate together with the ordinary "penny" cash. The larger coins would be useful for large commercial transactions conducted over great distances while the smaller coins could remain in use for local market transactions.

He proposed Pak's method of minting gold and silver coins to circulate at a value of fifty copper coins each to inhibit the export or smuggling of precious metals out of the country, and banning the consumption of imported fancy Chinese silks for all but the most respected rituals or celebrations. The ban on silk consumption alone would reduce the export of gold and silver by 90 percent of current totals and help to keep enough wealth in the country to buy off any potential foreign aggressors in the future.[41]

Tasan also believed that cash was the best medium for tax payments because it eliminated the kinds of cheating that existed in the measurement of grain and cloth, and again like Pak Chiwŏn, he thought it was essential to concentrate all minting activities in one government mint to maintain high standards and uniformity in the production of coins. The same agency would also become the sole agency for the production of weapons and musical instruments as well. If these measures were undertaken, cash (and commerce in general) would fulfill its proper role, as a medium for the exchange of goods and the proper and equal distribution of those goods throughout the country.

Furthermore, since the national tax structure was excessively dependent on the land tax and merchants were hardly taxed at all, the imbalance in taxation had to be redressed by raising taxes on merchants. On the other hand, they were not to be fleeced by double taxation or demands for bribes by officials who collected transit taxes at the ferries or customs stations. The purpose of these changes, however, was not to promote expansion of commerce and industry or shift the work force from agriculture to these occupations but, on the contrary, to preserve the primacy of the agricultural peasant by eliminating the advantages that merchants had accrued over the years and to ensure the equitable distribution of income among all occupations. Kim Yongdŏk has commented that Tasan was not as progressive as Pak Chega or Yu Suwŏn in his economic thinking because he did not push for the expansion of commerce and industry, but he was more progressive than Yi Ik because he reserved second place for commerce after agriculture.[42] Kim's analysis of Tasan, however, was hardly more convincing than Kwŏn Yong'ik's treatment of Pak Chiwŏn, because Tasan's reduction of cash and commerce to a secondary role was not only not progressive, it was the essence of classical wisdom as advertised by Yu Hyŏngwŏn in the late seventeenth century.

Tasan's views on cash (like Pak Chiwŏn's) may have been more advanced than

Yu Hyŏngwŏn's because he advocated multiple-denomination copper, gold, and silver cash, but these ideas were by no means innovative at the time. Furthermore, he showed no inclination for an aggressive expansion of copper, gold, and silver mining that was eventually only partially remedied by the establishment of the Kapsan copper mine in 1828.

Wŏn Yuhan has explained the failure to mint multiple-denomination cash until 1866 to conservative resistance to change, domestic tranquillity and the absence of any military threat, and popular distrust of coins if their face value was greater than the intrinsic value of the metal. There was also a fear of inflation in commodity prices, and the expectation that multiple-denomination cash would only increase savings and profits by usurers, weaken the central government control of the money supply, stimulate thievery by increasing the value of cash, and sully the mores of the population in general. Wŏn argued that these factors also explained the limitations on the capacity for change and adaptation as a whole.[43]

The problem with Wŏn's analysis is that his list of obstacles is too inclusive and general, and he failed to search for fundamental problems. A number of officials had proposed means of increasing the money supply and using more convenient forms of money, but the kings of the dynasty were not willing to try these alternatives and back them by adequate policies. Furthermore, even the scholars who advocated multiple-denomination cash were not really radical supporters of commercial and industrial development and growth.

Tasan's conservatism may not have been identical to the conservativism of the seventeenth century and earlier where men opposed the transition from grain and cloth to copper cash. It was closer to the limited reformism of Yu Hyŏngwŏn, who believed that Korea was destined to catch up to the economic principles of early Chou, if not late-sixteenth century Ming China (or in Tasan's case, early nineteenth-century Ch'ing China) and develop commerce to the point where it could play a useful function in easing the transmission of goods from areas of surplus to areas of shortage. The primacy of agriculture remained the dominant economic principle of the Chosŏn dynasty and the practical learning scholars as well, with the possible exceptions of Yu Suwŏn and Pak Chega.

Cash in the Nineteenth Century

Although all cash remained in the form of the "penny," once the supply of copper was increased by domestic mining after 1828, the volume of minted cash increased appreciably, by 5,001,100 *yang* or 500 million coins between 1807 and 1857, more if the amount minted by the new mint established at the Hamgyŏng Provincial Governor's headquarters in Hamhŭng in 1862 could be calculated. In addition, the profits of seigniorage were only 10 to 12 percent in 1807, 1814, and 1825, but after the founding of the Kapsan copper mine in 1828, they increased to 20 to 27 percent in 1830, 1832, 1855, and 1857 (see table 13).

The expansion of minting had also been accompanied by a breakdown of the government's policy to concentrate all minting in the Ministry of Taxation, a trend that Tasan had hoped to redress. After 1806 the Office for Dispensing Benevolence and other capital agencies were authorized to mint cash as well because the Ministry of Taxation had failed to keep pace with the increased demand for cash since 1798 and the value of cash had risen once again. Centralization of minting had lasted only for about twenty years, and in the early nineteenth century both central and local government agencies began to shift responsibility for minting to private parties to cut production costs. These private parties were wealthy individuals who requested permission from officials and received a permit to assume all costs for privately minting a specified amount of cash and paid a tax for the privilege. Even though the central government refused to grant formal permission for requests by private parties to mint cash, the practice continued, and the volume of cash probably increased during King Ch'ŏlchong's reign, from 1850 to 1864, and in 1874 Pak Kyusu attributed the increasing amount of poorly made cash in the money supply to private minting. Because the margin of profit left to the private minters was so small, the only way they could make a profit was to work their employees overtime and mint more cash than was authorized in the agreement they signed with the officials.

TABLE 13
QUANTITY OF COPPER COINS MINTED, 1807–57

Year	Quantity Minted (*yang*)
1807	300,000
1814	326,400
1825	367,500
1830	733,600
1832	784,300
1855	1,572,500
1857	916,800
TOTAL:	5,001,100

SOURCE: Wŏn Yuhan, "Chosŏn hugi hwap'ye chŏngch'aek e kwanhan ilkoch'al: Koaekchŏn ŭi chuyong non'ŭirŭl chungsimŭro" [A study of late Chosŏn currency policy: Proposals to mint multiple-denomination cash], *Han'guksa yŏn'gu* 6 (September 1971), pp. 89–93, 95–97.

Wŏn Yuhan regarded these figures as displaying an escape from the confines of traditional custom and ideology in favor of a pursuit of profit, and a change in the mode of management of minting from public to private enterprise. He also believed that the main reason why the requests by officials to mint multiple-denomination coins disappeared after 1816 was because the surplus in the supply of copper and adequate profits of seigniorage rendered them unnecessary – although why nickels, dimes, and quarters should not have been a boon to a nation of consumers lugging carts of penny cash around is hard to understand. He also believed that this situation opened the prospect for the healthy development of a cash economy, and by 1862 officials were even discussing the possibility of converting taxes and official grain loans to cash.[44]

On the other hand, not all statistical evidence reinforces Wŏn Yuhan's optimistic view about the steady development of a money economy. It is true that the percentage of cash in government revenues grew and eventually exceeded Yu Hyŏngwŏn's goal of one-third of tax receipts by 1820 when 52.8 percent of government taxes were collected in cash, compared to 29.2 percent for rice and 14.1 percent for cotton and cotton cloth. Nonetheless, this may have been a peak figure for the role of cash in tax revenues, for the available figures on year-end balances in agencies of the central government show a peak of 48.7 percent of all taxes in cash from 1827 to 1836, and a decline to 36.4 percent from 1868 to 1876. Although the year-end balance does not measure the total amount of cash revenue collected or spent during the year, An Pyŏngt'ae concluded that the decline in the year-end reserves must have represented not only a decline in the central government's cash tax income, but a decline in the percentage of commodity products relative to total production as well. It may be possible that commodity production and sales declined as a product of the general political and social troubles that culminated in the 1862 rebellion in the south.[45]

Finally, the history of the use of cash in the Korean economy took an ironic twist right after King Kojong ascended the throne in 1864. Presumably under the direction of the Taewongun, King Kojong ordered the governor of Hamgyŏng to cease minting cash in Hamhŭng and close down the Kapsan copper mine in that province because mining activities had been causing the local residents hardship. By so doing, the government was now deprived of its domestic copper supplies when the demand for government funds rose sharply to finance national defense in the face of foreign threat, the resuscitation of the population in the wake of the 1862 rebellion, and the construction of the Kyŏngbok Palace to increase the prestige of the royal house.

The new administration reversed previous cash policy by shutting down mining and minting in the north and instituting the 100-cash coin, the first multiple-denomination coin in the dynasty, a decision that was not imposed solely by the Taewongun but agreed to collectively by the top government leaders. Since one source estimated that the minting of this coin in 1867 produced sixteen million *yang* of cash (equivalent in face value to 1.6 billion of the "penny" coins), it was not surprising that rapid inflation and the fall in the value of the new coins drove the old "penny" coins out of the marketplace, and the government was forced to suspend further minting of the 100-cash in June, 1867. The inflationary situation had disastrous political consequences for the Taewongun because it appeared to fulfill the warnings of centuries of monetary conservatives against the consequences of multiple-denomination cash. From a twentieth-century perspective, however, this experience only proved the necessity of a careful and effective management of the money supply, not the disutility of multiple-denomination cash.[46]

PART VI

Financial Reform and the Economy: Conclusion

Consideration of the history of cash and the development of commerce and industry in the period after 1600 indicates clearly that most statecraft writers did not play a major role in stimulating institutional changes because they often followed the initiatives of reform-minded officials who preceded them or more progressive foreign examples, primarily from China. In fact, one of Yu Hyŏngwŏn's key concepts was that the economy of the ancient Chou had already surpassed contemporary, seventeenth-century Korea, and he hoped that Korea would be able to catch up to Chou levels by instituting the safe and dependable penny cash to convert at least one-third of the nation's revenues to cash receipts.

Still a believer in the primacy of agriculture, he thought that the state would have to grant merchants and artisans some minimal allotment of land because he neither foresaw nor desired the development of independent merchant activity. He did realize that the government would have the important task of regulating the money supply to ensure stable prices, but it never occurred to him that the economy could, or should, grow in size because he did not believe that new wealth could be created indefinitely, especially by nonagricultural production. Thus, his estimate of the optimum money supply was erroneously based on the assumption of a static economy.

He did not foresee the problems in prices and interest rates that would be created by regional as well as national shortages of currency. Although he planned to guarantee a sufficient supply of copper from Japanese imports, he did not anticipate the Japanese copper shortage and the reduction of copper export quotas in Japan that began under Arai Hakuseki in the early eighteenth century and continued into the late eighteenth and early nineteenth centuries. He did not realize that regulation of the money supply, prices, and interest rates would be a difficult and complex affair that would require constant attention.

The times surpassed Yu's monetary vision, but his successors did not always build upon some of his more progressive attitudes. The progressive, pro-cash climate of the seventeenth century was followed by the emergence of animosity toward cash in the early eighteenth century, and this mood swept up statecraft writers like Yi Ik. The majority of statesmen and practical scholars, however, did remain committed to the extension of cash in the economy. After further minting was reinstituted in 1731, King Yŏngjo restrained further monetary progress by declining to experiment with the recommendations in 1742 of more progressive officials like Pak Munsu, Kim Yaro, and Min Ŭngsu for multiple-denomination copper, silver cash, or imported Chinese cash, let alone paper money.

Copper cash was accepted fully by the eighteenth century, but only in the form of pennies. For that matter, the government came increasingly to accept the development of private merchant activity and wage labor as well, and even participated in the weakening of the state-authorized licensed monopolies, but in the end the expansion of private enterprise was not able to overcome the limits of licensed commerce or agrarian physiocracy.

Those few statecraft scholars in the eighteenth century who did begin to challenge the supremacy or primacy of agriculture were still limited by certain aspects of tradition. Yu Suwŏn wanted to promote the circulation of cash and commercial activities, but he saw it as a means of converting idle yangban who had been unable to obtain official posts into useful and productive citizens who would at least be able to support themselves by commerce rather than continue their parasitic reliance on the support of others. Pak Chega and Pak Chiwŏn also advocated similar ideas, that commerce be opened to yangban as well as commoners to reduce the number of yangban who depended on gratuities, bribes, or general support by the whole population, and convert them to more useful lives.[1]

They took their model of development from contemporary Ch'ing China, which meant that they hoped to eliminate the prejudice against both manual labor and commerce that had become so deeply ingrained in the yangban psyche and create an economy and a social elite like that of the late Ch'ing. Their economic vision was limited because their model of progress was not an appeal to commerce and industry as the lifeblood of the economy. They lacked the capacity to see the need for infrastructural improvements, the expansion of overseas trade, and the development of more efficient institutions for mobilizing savings and stimulating investment. Some scholars and officials did recognize the benefits of silver coins and multiple-denomination copper coins – let alone commercial paper and banks – but they could not win enough support among the bureaucracy and persuade kings to take bold initiatives. Some also criticized the evils that flowed from status restrictions and argued for permission for yangban to engage in business, but too many felt that the open pursuit of profit was a demeaning affair. Private merchants succeeded in putting a dent in the armor of the licensed monopolies, but the result was only a compromise between the two. Once they had broken through the barriers, too many private merchants sought to become monopolists themselves rather than destroy the licensed monopoly system completely. Yu Suwŏn could see the advantages of state-led economic development, but hardly anyone sought total liberation from government restraint as a means of creating opportunity for individual entrepreneurship, and the government never did adopt his plan for state-controlled oligopoly. By the end of the eighteenth century the state was content to act as referee between licensed monopolies and private merchants without stepping forward to lead the way toward rapid economic development.

One doubts that traditional attitudes toward agriculture and commerce would have blocked all economic progress by itself because interesting changes had already occurred. Nevertheless, despite the achievement of private merchants, wholesalers, and artisans in breaking loose from the narrow framework of licensed production and commerce of the early Chosŏn period, the capitalist class was extremely limited in size, and the industrial proletariat hardly existed at all, since most manufacture was limited to small-scale handicraft production.

The government seemed incapable of taking a leadership role in expanding the economy. While it agreed to mint more cash, it limited it to penny cash alone, restricted mining activities, took no steps to improve domestic transportation, maintained certain monopolies primarily to ensure a flow of former tribute goods, and kept foreign trade within the narrow confines of tribute relations with China and extremely limited restrictions with Japan. In fact, when foreign traders and missionaries showed up at Korean gates in the nineteenth century after the Opium War, they were regarded by Korean officials as the harbingers of national destruction.

EPILOGUE

The Complexities of Korean Confucian Statecraft

This book has been devoted to a study of Confucian statecraft in the last half of the Chosŏn dynasty with respect not only to its ideas, but to its relevance to government policy and action. The material presented in the text reveals that it is very difficult, if not impossible, to define Confucian statecraft in action in simple terms for a number of reasons. The ideas that constituted the Confucian statecraft tradition were not always internally consistent. The conflict between historical contingency and ideal Confucian objectives inhibited or obstructed the achievement of those objectives; antinomies within Confucian thought and practice guaranteed conflict over the definition of goals and priorities; and the impossibility of recovering the ideal norms of classical antiquity because of the irreversibility of the transition from the Chou feudalism to Ch'in centralized bureaucracy meant that difference of opinion was unavoidable over the crucial question of compromise between the ideal and the real. For these reasons, the statecraft thought of Yu Hyŏngwŏn, which has constituted the focus of this study, cannot be taken as the only, the best, or the most representative example of Korean Confucian statecraft thought in Korea. Some of his ideas were truly unusual and some were acceptable to most Confucians, but others were rejected as unworkable, even by those who regarded themselves as his intellectual disciples. The reason why I chose him as the focus for this study was because he was the first Korean scholar of the Chosŏn dynasty to write a thorough and comprehensive analysis of the deficiencies of his society in the seventeenth century, providing us with an excellent entrée into statecraft writing and the nature and complexity of a Korean Confucian society under stress. His scheme for the rectification of institutions provides a template for us to compare the ideas and policies of both scholars and officials involved in the contemplation of policy to the end of the dynasty.

The Incompleteness of the Confucian Transformation

At the beginning of the Chosŏn dynasty, there were very few people in Korean society who would be regarded as thoroughgoing Confucians because despite the presence of Confucian ideas for two millennia, Buddhism functioned as the dominant religion at the upper levels of society, and folk religion, which included animistic spirit worship and shamanism, was pervasive among the rural peasantry. The new dynasty was ushered in by a small coterie of converts to the Neo-Confucian doctrines of Sung dynasty China, particularly as digested and recapitulated by Chu Hsi in the twelfth century. These men set out on an effort to convert all of Korea to belief in Neo-Confucian principles and the practice of Confucian norms.

They and their successors at the top of government and society went a long way to achieving their aims, but they never fully completed their task. Even though the peasants were eventually converted to Confucian ancestor worship and patrilineal family organization and the like, they never fully discarded their fear of the spirits in general. Total conversion of Korean society to Confucian belief was also hindered because its educational enterprise was underfunded. The early Chosŏn state's official school system proved a failure even before the end of the fifteenth century, and even the private academies after the mid-sixteenth century were not created to educate all benighted peasants. Their Confucian overlords needed them more in the fields than in the schoolroom.

The inadequacy of mass education was not the only reason for the violation of Confucian norms and standards in real life. Many of the officials who had been schooled and indoctrinated in Confucian moral standards placed private interest over the public good, took bribes to enrich themselves and their own families, exploited peasants and slaves to increase their wealth, and foreclosed on mortgages to expand their landed properties instead of fulfilling their role as moral examplars for society at large. Even though Neo-Confucian bureaucrats were supposed to run Korean affairs as they would a moral order, many of them were incapable of living up to the high standards of the moral code.

In this sense the history of the Chosŏn dynasty could be viewed as a morality play in which a solid core of true believers did battle with the reality of human weakness and foible. Neo-Confucians understood the persistence of human imperfection because they had been taught that inner goodness in the mind was obscured or obstructed by psychophysical force. Historical experience had also demonstrated that dynasties were not static or perpetual; they had a life of their own that led to decline marked by the breakdown of social order and rebellion in which the forces of evil seemed to win the day.

Confucianism, however, was not discredited despite its failure to halt moral and dynastic decline because of the view that chaos and disorder was the fault of leadership, education, or institutions, not the moral philosophy itself. Confucian standards could outlive one dynasty and be resuscitated by the next. Confucian thought was thus preserved as the dominant system of belief and the source of statecraft wisdom from the Sung through Ch'ing dynasties in China despite the overthrow of individual dynasties. Korea had only one dynasty dominated by the Confucian vision, the Chosŏn dynasty. It should have come to an end in

1592 when Hideyoshi invaded Korea because by that time the Chosŏn state had been weakened by maladministration, internecine bureaucratic factionalism, unfair taxation, the concentration of wealth, the evasion of responsibility, and the deterioration of national defense. If Confucian statecraft were to be judged by consideration of the results of a government run by Confucians, Confucian statecraft should have been deemed a failure in 1592. But when the war was over in 1598 both the Chosŏn state and the Confucian philosophy that guided it remained intact.

Confucianism in the Midst of Contingent Circumstance

When Neo-Confucianism was adopted as the leading belief and ideology at the beginning of the Chosŏn dynasty, society and social institutions were already well developed. The state was organized as a monarchical bureaucracy, and society was structured hierarchically on the basis of hereditary or semihereditary principles, including strict discrimination between status categories. This situation alone meant that the early Chosŏn Neo-Confucians had inherited institutions that were less than ideal.

Monarchy and Centralized Bureaucracy. The existence of a ruler or monarch had been recognized by Confucians as a necessity for civilized government since Confucius himself, but absolute monarchy and a centralized government organization had always been major problems for Confucian statecraft thinkers. Rulers could be a danger and threat to the Confucian moral and social order because they were usually more concerned with the retention of their political power than conformity to moral norms. Confucians had an ambiguous if not contradictory attitude toward rulers, particularly the bad ones. Mencius had taught that since an immoral ruler lost his Heavenly Mandate to rule, the population had the right to overthrow him and replace him with another. Confucians might justifiably withdraw their loyalty from such an immoral ruler, but they might also feel that it was their duty to stick with him to lead him from immorality to morality.

Because Confucian thought emphasized loyalty to the ruler, some have believed that Confucian thought was conducive to the creation of monarchical despotism, especially in the Ming and Ch'ing dynasties in China. The Korean situation was somewhat different because most Confucian officials were drawn from yangban families with a long history of honor, wealth, prestige, and status that outshone the royal clan. It is true that at the beginning of the dynasty they supported an army general in his usurpation of the throne because they felt that greater royal authority was essential for transforming society from Buddhism and animism to Confucian belief. But once the new dynasty was in place, the Confucian officials began what became a protracted battle against most kings to preserve their own families' hold on power, wealth, and position, and to induce them to accept Confucian standards of statecraft.

When the Chosŏn dynasty appeared, Korea had long been organized as a centralized bureaucracy, but centralization had been incomplete, at least by the standards of most Chinese dynasties. The Neo-Confucian supporters of the new dynasty successfully overcame that deficiency by extending central control to all the districts of the kingdom, but they were never enamored of centralized bureaucracy as the best form of government organization because it represented the political system of the Ch'in dynasty that had destroyed the beloved feudal political configuration of the Chou dynasty in the late third century B.C.

The Ch'in bureaucratic system was based on Legalist thought that seemed diametrically opposed to Confucian moral philosophy. The Legalists took a negative view of human nature, eschewed moral education and persuasion as useless methods for the establishment of order, and insisted on the necessity of reward and punishment as the only means for keeping human beings under control. All Confucian officials who served bureaucratic dynasties after the Ch'in had to use punishment as the means for enforcing conformity. Some sought to temper it with Confucian compassion, but others became such adept users of coercion that punishment became as much a feature of the bureaucratic Confucian state as moral suasion. Even the most moralistic Neo-Confucians resorted to punishment as the ultimate recourse for forcing the ignorant and recalcitrant to conform to Confucian moral ideals, revealed only so clearly in Yu Hyŏngwŏn's regulations for the conduct of his proposed schools. Yet most Confucians believed that the unmitigated use of punishment was symptomatic of the moral failure of the ruler and the state.

Unfortunately centralized bureaucracy had proved to be permanent, and Confucians had to adjust to these unfortunate circumstances as the only way for their philosophy to survive. The conflict between the two ideals – moral suasion versus coercion – was never solved, and the dividing line between the two was left to arbitrary judgment or circumstance.

The Social Legacy: Heredity, Property, and Slavery. The ruling class of the early Chosŏn dynasty consisted of yangban families that constituted a semiaristocratic bureaucratic elite that owed much of their prominence to the inheritance of status, and they ruled over a slave society sustained by the system of inherited slave status. Neo-Confucians in the first two centuries of the dynasty barely raised the question of the moral conflict between Confucian principles and semihereditary bureaucracy and hereditary slavery. It was not until the immense pressure exerted on the Chosŏn state by a series of catastrophic invasions after 1592 that the Confucian bureaucrats began to think of requiring idle yangban and slaves to perform military service.

The inheritance of social status, whether yangban or slave, was not only responsible for revenue shortages and inadequate defense because of tax-exemption privileges, it also contributed significantly to obstructing the achievement of the Confucian ideal of expanded opportunity for education and officeholding. The preservation of class interest by yangban landlords and slaveowners was the main obstacle to converting society to a moral basis for the distribution of prestige, office, and wealth, but reform was made doubly difficult by the antinomies within the Confucian moral system. Confucians were morally obliged to preserve the patrimony of their families, including slaves as well as real estate, and to show the utmost respect for one's elders and superiors in the social order, a moral obligation used by landlords and slaveowners to legitimize private property and slavery.

Even though the idealistic Confucians agreed that the virtuous ruler was obliged to guarantee subsistence to the common peasant, ideally through the grant of a minimal plot of arable land according to the well-field model of the Chou dynasty, they were faced with the reality of private property that had determined land tenure in Korea for over a millennium. Since the early Chosŏn kings ignored appeals for nationalization and egalitarian redistribution, they confirmed the private property of the landlords and opened the door to the recreation of the same conditions in the maldistribution of wealth that had prevailed in the late fourteenth century. As a result most Confucians paid only lip service to the notion of national ownership and egalitarian redistribution.

Even less attention was paid to hereditary slavery that had been in practice since the tenth or eleventh centuries, possibly because slavery itself had never been condemned as immoral. At least the question of hereditary enslavement of the innocent should have been raised by committed Confucians, but few did so. In any case, the class interests of the landlords and slaveowners in a slave society constituted an insuperable obstacle to idealistic Confucian purists.

Agriculture over Commerce and Industry

These class interests were abetted by the overpowering and enduring belief by Confucian scholars and officials alike that agricultural production was the only legitimate way to produce wealth. Food and clothing were necessary to subsistence, but all else was superfluous and contributed to unnecessary, ostentatious, and immoral consumption. Industry and commerce were acknowledged as necessary activities, but only in a limited way. Artisans had a role to play in providing the population with necessary nonagricultural goods, but any expansion in the production of luxury items would corrupt the morals of the people. Likewise commerce was necessary for the circulation of goods, but any excessive profiteering would reduce the production of necessities by inducing peasants to abandon their primary agricultural tasks in pursuit of commercial profit.

These ideal principles were compromised in real life because the nobility, yangban, landlords, and the rich were allowed to enjoy the luxuries of life, the skilled artisans were employed, often by the state, in producing the brocades, silks, fine pottery, and other "unnecessary" items of conspicuous consumption, and merchants were subsidized, often with monopoly licenses, to provide those items to the king and upper class. Only the peasants were left to fulfill the Confucian moral norms of frugality, but more by deprivation and the lack of wealth than by adherence to abstract moral norms. These violations of Confucian norms of simplicity, frugality, and modesty existed in every dynasty because those with the wealth to buy luxury goods refused to dispense with them. Confucians had either to engage in constant scolding of the recalcitrant or resign themselves to tacit or hypocritical acceptance of human weakness. The Physiocratic emphasis on agricultural production and the concomitant denigration of industrial and commercial activity in Korean Confucian thought supported the preeminent economic and political position of the landlords by hindering the accumulation of wealth by artisans and merchants, and by forbidding their participation in the competition for bureaucratic office.

International trade did not provide a major stimulus to commerce in general because of the restrictions of the tributary system with China, the suspicion and lack of trust between Koreans and their Chinese or Manchu suzerains, the predatory aggressions of the Wakō pirates from Japan in the fifteenth century, the involvement of the Japanese with their own internal wars in the sixteenth century, and the reimposition of severe limits on foreign trade activity after the Shimabara Rebellion of 1636. In fact, these real limits on international trade probably accounted as much as Confucian doctrine for the restrictions on the development of the economy.

Bureaucratic Routinization and Crisis

Chinese had experienced the rise and fall of dynasties so frequently in their long history that they became convinced that dynasties had a life of their own governed as much by bureaucratic routinization and laxity as the loss of moral fiber. Korean dynasties lasted for much longer periods than the Chinese for a number of complex reasons, but the Chosŏn dynasty began to exhibit characteristics of bureaucratic deterioriation by the end of the fifteenth century.

Laxity and corruption in administration that increased over time meant that registration of the taxpaying population was not maintained, taxes and services were levied more heavily on the poorest peasants, and military service was eroded by evasion.

Bureaucratic laxity and corruption was exacerbated by the elimination of salaries for all clerks at the beginning of the dynasty. The policy was undertaken by the regular officials to elevate themselves over the influential local *hyangni* or local clerk class of the late Koryŏ and prevent them from rising to the regular bureaucracy, but it forced all clerks into a life of corruption by demanding fees and gratuities to make a living.

By the end of the sixteenth century the capacity of the bureaucracy to rectify the problems of maladministration was weakened by the emergence of internecine factional strife within the bureaucracy after 1575. The unfortunate consequence of this sad state of affairs was the devastation wrought by Hideyoshi's invasions in the 1590s. Someone looking at Korea in 1598 after the last of the Japanese returned home, might well have concluded that both the Chosŏn dynasty and the experiment in Confucian statecraft had been a failure.

THE SEVENTEETH-CENTURY GOVERNMENT REFORM PROGRAM

Even before the Japanese invasions a number of Confucian bureaucrats had sounded the clarion call of reform. Yulgok (Yi I), by his analysis of the failure of domestic institutions and the weakness of the military, and Cho Hŏn, by his comparison of Chosŏn deficiencies with Ming advantages in administration, commerce, and other areas, led the appeal for institutional rectification, but their appeals were largely ignored.

Ironically the devastation of the Imjin Wars solved some of the major problems of the dynasty and gave Confucian statecraft a second chance. While the destruction of land and property reduced both individual wealth as well as state revenue, it alleviated population pressure on the land, induced a period of tax remission, and allowed peasants a period to revive agricultural production. Even though the government had a lower tax base, it was able to begin land and population registration again as a basis for future revenues and service. The irregularity of the local product tribute tax and the injustice of its operation in practice led to conversion of the system. Intimate contact with Ming officials made Korean officials more aware of the far greater development of commerce and economic activity in China than Korea, and stimulated the emulation of some Ming commercial practices. In short, national catastrophe laid the basis for a reform effort in the seventeenth century that was by no means totally successful, but resulted in important institutional reforms.

Defeat in battle awakened the regime to the problem of tax and service evasion and stimulated measures to broaden requirements by bringing idle yangban, tax evaders, and slaves into the military service system. It stimulated the establishment of new divisions and the adoption of Western firearms. The leading role in this reform effort was played by active officials rather than armchair scholars.

Of course, the record of accomplishment in this century was mixed. The most obvious failure in the reform effort was the attempt to reconstitute a viable military force. The formation of new divisions was influenced more by political considerations than by the logic of national defense, and the Yi Kwal rebellion of 1624 shifted priorities from national defense to the prevention of rebellion.

A second factor was the inability of the regime to recruit and retrain a sufficient force of foot soldiers, and to recognize the importance of firearms and training in their use. The government must have relaxed its efforts after conclusion of a treaty with the Japanese in 1609 and underestimated the military strength of the Manchus.

Probably the most important reason for the disasters of the two Manchu invasions of 1627 and 1637, however, was the change in foreign policy from Kwanghaegun's regime, a change that has to be attributed to Confucian influence. It was, after all, the Westerner faction that seized power in a coup d'état in 1623 and insisted on outright support for the Ming dynasty because of its moral obligation to the Ming Wan-li emperor for his (belated) dispatch of reinforcements to Korea in 1592. The Westerners were intellectually and morally incapable of continuing Kwanghaegun's more pragmatic policy of adaptation and delay. What was worse, after the Manchu imposition of sovereignty over Korea, it became impossible for Korean kings to rebuild Korean military forces in the face of Manchu surveillance.

Under the protection of the Manchu Ch'ing dynasty, however, the threat of foreign invasion was removed and a strong military defense became unnecessary. The armed forces were kept in place mainly to ensure domestic tranquillity, but because its cost was far too large for that purpose, it functioned more and more as an oppressive mode of taxation. Since military service was deemed demeaning to begin with, the tendency to evade it grew, and a smaller and smaller group of commoner peasants were left to carry the whole fiscal burden. The most serious weakness of the Ch'ing peace, however, was the desuetude with which officials considered military defense because when the Ch'ing state lost its power in the nineteenth century to defend itself, let alone its Korean tributary, Korea found itself helpless and isolated.

The need for more adult males for the payment of the military support tax, if not actual duty as soldiers, continued to stimulate plans for drawing more slaves into the military service system or liberating them from inherited slavery. During the Imjin Wars slaves were incorporated in considerable numbers into the *sog'o* units and manumitted in return for military merit or purchase, but after the war the price of purchase was too high to allow much reduction of the slave population. The need for adult males subject to military service, however, kept slaves as military support taxpayers. The same motive also explains the origin in official circles of the long debate over the matrilineal rule for the manumission of offspring of the sons of commoner mothers in mixed slave/commoner marriages, first instituted in 1669. This marked an important step in the state's interference with the slaveowner's control over his slaves.

The idea for reforming the local products tribute system began in the late fifteenth century, but the stimulus needed to accomplish the task also occurred as a result of the Imjin Wars. The illicit system of tribute contracting underway since the late fifteenth century demonstrated the advantages of market purchases of goods over in-kind tax payments, and state officials simply applied to the whole country what had already been tried by some officials – financing the cost by an extra tax. The *taedong* reform carried out in the seventeenth century contributed to even greater commercial activity than before.

Almost the same officials who championed the adoption of the *taedong* reform also pioneered the introduction of metallic currency. From their observation of the Ming economy they realized that metallic currency was needed to overcome the cumbersome use of grain and cloth as media of exchange to lubricate market transactions.

The reform of the military system, the matrilineal rule in mixed marriages, the *taedong* law, and the currency reform of the seventeenth century represented a series of positive responses to serious problems by active Confucian officials, and their policies provided both inspiration and working models for the new statecraft scholars.

Yu Hyŏngwŏn's Reform Plans

The response to crisis is certainly one of the main reasons why Korean scholars in the seventeenth century began to shift their attention from Confucian moral metaphysics to the problems of statecraft. The same thing happened in the late Ming dynasty and spawned the statecraft writings of Ku Yen-wu and Huang Tsung-hsi, but Yu Hyŏngwŏn, unaware of their existence, derived no inspiration from them.

In China the reaction against Sung learning in the sixteenth-century Ming period took the form of Wang Yang-ming's emphasis on the inner, meditational approach to self-rectification rather than the apparently external and superficial approach to book learning and scripture by Chu Hsi and Sung Learning. Since Wang Yang-ming had been condemned as a heretic by T'oegye (Yi Hwang) in Korea in the mid-sixteenth century, very few Koreans became followers of his thought. Born into the Northerner faction, Yu must have abided by T'oegye's condemnation to adhere to the teachings of Chu Hsi and the Sung school, but he insisted that the study of institutions as well as book learning was critical to the rectification of self and society.

Using better institutions to find moral men to assume office was only part of his plan. He also believed that there was only one model for perfect institutions – the systems used by the sages in ancient China, but because he agreed that a literal recreation of ancient institutions was unworkable, he did his best to extract principles that would work in quite different circumstances under the mode of centralized bureaucracy.

The degree to which he departed from ancient institutions and compromised with current reality varied from one institution to another. In some cases, he appeared tainted by blind fundamentalism, despite his demurral to the contrary, when he insisted that the carving out of embossed squares in the landscape would remedy the administrative problems caused by population growth, geographical mobility, and laxity in registration. In others, he modified ancient institutions by compromising with post-Chou reality whether of the Chinese or Korean variety.

For example, he was most adamant in demanding a program of nationalization and redistribution of land to eliminate the evil of private property, and yet he rejected the idea that he was simply copying the well-field system of ancient Chou China. Since he felt that it was as necessary to create a hierarchy of wealth that would match the moral capacity of his new officials rather than the inherited prestige of the yangban or their talent in literary composition, he prescribed extra allotments to those officials – a plan that he compared to the limited-field system of the Han dynasty. In short, he claimed he was fusing Chou and Han models as the optimum accommodation to post-Chou circumstance. Furthermore, he supported his argument for the 100 *myo* basic land allotment by a practical proof, rather than just a blind appeal to the classics, by demonstrating that there was sufficient land area in Korea to provide for the the Korean population.

Although Yu argued that he selected crucial elements of ancient patterns on reasonable and empirical grounds, many of his choices were really arbitrary and idiosyncratic. Other Confucians could and did ignore his insistence on the embossed square and the superiority of the 100-*myo* unit, for example, let alone the need for confiscation and nationalization of private property.

In his rejection of hereditary slavery, he argued that slavery was unjustified because all human beings were essentially the same and none deserved to be treated as chattel, but by no means did he really signify an absolute commitment to equality or a justification on rational grounds alone. To the contrary, he sought ultimate authority in classical precedent, which prescribed slavery as an appropriate punishment for certain serious crimes, but never as a status to be inherited by innocent children. True to this principle he never called for the total manumission of all slaves, just an end to inherited slavery. On the other hand, he clearly communicated his willingness to compromise with Korean tradition by tolerating the continuation of slavery for a period far longer than one generation. He provided for them to continue to work for their masters, receive a land grant from the state, continue their participation as soldiers and support taxpayers, serve as clerks and runners in official agencies, and assume inferior roles in his regulations for his community compacts. His support for adoption of the matrilineal rule also reflected his acknowledgment that the reduction of slaves in society would take several generations.

He extolled the virtues of the Chou system of militia service, but his plan for the reform of military service was only indirectly related to the militia ideal. Instead, he urged a return to the early Chosŏn system of discrete rotating duty soldiers supported by a separate body of support taxpayers, but he justified its relation to the militia system by arguing that it was a self-sufficient method of finance that did not drain revenues from the state exchequer. Assigning support taxpayers to duty soldiers was far better than loading a heavy tax burden on the population for financing the burdensome professional soldiers created by expansionist dynasties in the post-Chou era. Here again, he demonstrated flexibility in one dimension countered by dogmatic rigidity in another. After all, a professional military corps might have been just what Korea needed in view of the sorry performance of regular Chosŏn troops against the Japanese and Manchus.

His respect for early Chosŏn military organization was not matched, however, by his rejection of the tribute system, which he condemned in practice even though it had been created by the venerated founders of the Chosŏn dynasty. He was convinced of the logical and empirical superiority of an increased land tax as a method for financing both material purchases and other administrative costs of both the king and the state, but he was not content to rely on logic alone.

He defended his position on the grounds that tribute, particularly royal tribute, was an immoral and unrestrained exercise in monarchical acquisitiveness that deserved to be brought under control by a more reasonable system of taxation.

His admiration for hired or wage labor as a means of replacing slave cultivators on the estates of the large landlords or uncompensated labor service by commoners certainly appeared as a rational and innovative response to changing circumstances rather than a dogmatic mimicking of classical precedent. He argued that wage or hired labor was preferable to slave labor on moral grounds because it would eliminate the cruel and coercive treatment of slaves, and on apparently liberal grounds because hired laborers entered into employment by free choice and willing agreement.

These arguments undeniably had aspects of humaneness and liberalism to them, but his thinking was by no means free of the constraints relevant to his times. He did not argue that wage labor had proved its superiority by his own observation of contemporary facts, but rather by hearsay information about wage labor in China. Wage labor was not a new phenomenon; it had been around since long before the beginning of the dynasty without doing damage to Korean social custom. In fact, he argued that hired labor would not promote the freedom of the individual laborer at all. To the contrary, he guaranteed that the Chinese experience demonstrated that hired laborers were as respectful and subordinate to their employers as Confucian standards required. Choosing one's employer was neither to produce freedom of choice in society at large, or to transform laborers into commodities and wage slaves in a capitalist system.

One of Yu's overarching themes was the establishment of a truly moral society ruled by moral officials. He denigrated the examination system for its failure to producing honest and dedicated officials, but he saw the answer in adapting ancient institutions, particularly resuscitating the moribund official school system and initiating the face-to-face evaluation of candidates for office. Yu's ideal society was to be as hierarchical as contemporary Korean society, but on an almost completely different basis – demonstrated superiority in Confucian ethical behavior.

Yu was a defender of popular or peasant welfare, but his sympathies for the common peasants, slaves, lowly clerks, and women were often balanced or offset by his commitment to the necessity of hierarchical relations. He sought to level the playing ground by having the state confiscate the landed property and reduce the slaves of the yangban and landlords, but he often made certain concessions to social reality by accommodating aspects of inherited status that favored members of the noble family, merit subjects and their relatives, and the sons of officials without office of their own, and to denigrate nothoi, clerks, slaves, and women. He was willing to prolong the period of slavery because he felt that the yangban were emotionally and physically as yet incapable of dispensing with their slave labor. At one point, he even assured the yangban families that his reforms would not destroy them because their wealth and traditional respect for education would guarantee the success of their sons in his new system of schools. He could make such concessions to existing privilege because of his commitment to the propriety of hierarchical respect relations, and his sympathy for the members of his own class.

His plan to refurbish the schools would only have provided for the body of regular officials. He also had to cure the endemic corruption of the petty clerks without elevating them to the same level as the regular officials. His solution was to provide them with salaries through an improved system of taxation. Whether guaranteed salaries for clerks would have eliminated corruption as Yu hoped is something that one can never know because it was never tried, but it would certainly have been an improvement over the existing situation.

Finally, at the lowest end of the bureaucracy, the local district, where the magistrate and his irregular local clerks, village headman, and village officials came into direct contact with the people, he hoped to overcome the damage done by corrupt local officials by replacing them with semiautonomous institutions like community compacts and village granaries, copied from models created in the Sung dynasty, staffed by prominent men of virtue. They were to take charge of teaching villagers and common peasants to practice Confucian moral standards, provide mutual aid, relief, and loans, and implement mutual surveillance against criminals and wrongdoers.

Unfortunately, Yu's plan for the moral reformation of all levels of the bureaucracy was the least effective of all his ideas. The examination system was never replaced by a refurbished school system and a serious and sustained method of recommendation. A salary system for petty clerks was never instituted to the end of the dynasty, and the community compacts were attempted only in a few instances. Only the adoption of village autonomy for the administration of loans was attempted under the Taewongun in the 1860s. Otherwise, local nonofficial organizations were dominated almost exclusively by local yangban in protection of their own interests and local clerks were left unchecked to profit from bribery.

Yu's recommendations for improvements in the economy, particularly the use of metallic cash, did have some influence on the next century. When Yu began to write his masterwork around 1650, active officials were already attempting to introduce metallic currency to lubricate market transactions. Yu responded to their initiative and sought to add some wisdom to it by consulting the Chinese classics and histories.

Consulting the classics did not necessarily mean that he was conservatively tied to backward economic ideas because what he found in those sources was often more developed than contemporary practice in Korea. In fact, Chou China appeared to have had a larger commercial sector than Korea, certainly a more advanced use of money. He found that industry and commerce were not evil, as some ideologues believed, but necessary for the production and circulation of items of utility among the population. It was just that they were secondary to agricultural production and had to be limited lest the attractiveness of profit lured too many peasants from the primary occupation of agricultural production.

Yu agreed with the most progressive Korean officials of his time that market development should be encouraged, certainly as a means of reforming the corrupted tribute system. He admired Cho Hŏn's reports of the more advanced Ming economy, but he did not intend to move as far as the Chinese had by allowing sons of merchants to take the examinations. Since he included land allotments for merchants in his ideal land distribution scheme, it is obvious that he expected commercial activity only to supplement basic income from farming, not replace it. His economic vision was quite a bit behind late Ming economic developments, not to mention earlier dynasties.

Nonetheless, it was his fear of the adverse consequences of inflation because of mistakes in the management of currency in past Chinese dynasties that makes him look quite conservative. To be sure, many economists in favor of sound money and stability in the twentieth century fear the adverse consequences of inflationary policies, but this concern for stability does not interfere with their progressive perspective on the capacity of a healthy capitalist economy to expand steadily. Yu, however, was witnessing the beginnings of a cash economy when the mistrust of the value of that cash was powerful. The slightest symptom of inflation was liable to destroy confidence in the cash and destroy the whole experiment. For that reason he felt that the only secure way to use cash was to limit its type to the penny cash, where the face value was only slightly more than the intrinsic worth of the metal.

A money system based exclusively on copper pennies was by itself a brake on the potential for expanding the economy. He favored it because his economic concepts were tied closely to moral rather than utilitarian objectives. Nickles, dimes, and quarters, let alone dollar bills, were not only sure guarantees of inflation, they were also evil seeds that would burgeon into moral decay by stimulating greed and avarice, destroying frugality, and leading the peasants to abandon their fields in search of easy profit.

In short, Yu's economic thought was progressive by comparison with the relatively backward situation of Korea in the sixteenth century, but quite limited with respect to developments in Ming China or Tokugawa Japan, let alone the West.

EIGHTEENTH-CENTURY DEVELOPMENTS

Institutional Changes

There were four major institutional changes in the eighteenth century about which Yu Hyŏngwŏn had something to say: slavery, military service, land, and the economy. The reform of the slave system was probably the most significant of any reform in the dynasty. The matrilineal succession rule was adopted permanently in 1730, official slaves were abolished in 1801, and the percentage of private slaves in the population dropped below 10 percent after 1780, but the abolition of hereditary slavery and of slavery altogether did not occur until the end of the nineteenth century. Scholars like Kim Yongsŏp would like to attribute this phenomenon to the emergence of an entrepreneurial spirit among the peasantry that allowed slave cultivators to accumulate surpluses and buy their way out of slavery, but the concrete evidence for this thesis is weak. Even though the high opportunity cost involved in recapturing runaway slaves and the easy economical alternative of replacing slaves with tenants and hired laborers were more likely causes, it is difficult to discount the effect of Yu's direct challenge to slavery on Confucian moral grounds, particularly because his views became widely known among the educated class in the late eighteenth century. His contribution to the decline of slavery and Korea as a slave society may be his most outstanding contribution to the improvement of Korean life.

Yu had much less direct influence on the debate over the equal service reform (*kyunyŏkpŏp*) of 1750, a misnomer if there ever was one. Yu's idea had been to reconstitute and rebuild the military establishment by which the military cloth tax paid by a discrete group of support taxpayers would finance rotating duty soldiers. He had also argued for the reïntroduction of military affairs into the education and training of officials, the adoption of Western firearms, and the reorganization of a defense system.

By the eighteenth century, however, the Chosŏn military system lost its raison d'être and the military cloth tax became a bane on the existence of the commoner peasant. Because of the widespread evasion of registration and service, the shrinking number of commoner peasants had to bear the full weight of the military cloth tax. Yu did not anticipate this outcome, but his concern for the maldistribution of tax burdens was carried on by many other active officials, who promoted some method of lightening the tax load on commoner peasants by shifting slaves to commoner status and including the service-exempt yangban and the legions of tax-evading scholars and putative students in the ranks of the support taxpayers. Slaves did escape servitude primarily by running away, but they escaped the net of the military service registrars by fair means or foul. The result of three quarters of a century of discussion to extend the military cloth tax to yangban was disappointing, however, because King Yŏngjo finally capitulated to their interests and only reduced the tax on commoners. The tax reduction had but temporary and limited effects, for by the middle of the nineteenth century it became one of the major causes of peasant rebellion.

Another issue was the land tax, an issue where Yu's ideas were far beyond the capacity of his age. He had recognized that the maldistribution of land, not just the land tax, was the primary cause of peasant poverty in an agrarian society. His appeal for national confiscation and redistribution did not elicit much of a response in the seventeenth century because the land tax was still quite light. The adoption of the *taedongmi* rice surtax on land to provide funds to replace local tribute, however, increased the severity of the land tax in the structure of taxation.

Even then the nominal land tax rate still remained relatively low, but the trend toward the concentration of land in the hands of large landlords, the loss of land by smallholders, and their decline to landless sharecroppers and laborers exacerbated their economic hardship. By the end of the eighteenth century, the time had become ripe for some kind of remedial action. The armchair statecraft scholars in the eighteenth and nineteenth centuries, often referred to as the Sirhak school, were by no means unified on the solution. Some like Tasan (Chŏng Yagyong) backed the radical nationalization and redistribution plan, but others like Sŏngho (Yi Ik) opted for a more conservative land limitation system than Yu Hyŏngwŏn's. Most serious officials dismissed redistribution as unrealistic because the defense of landed property had become impregnable. The turning point was reached in the 1790s when King Chŏnjo put out a call for advice on the land question but he failed to take any serious action to alleviate the problems of land distribution and taxation. The land problem carried over into the nineteenth century with disastrous consequences, because it was identified as one of the three major causes of the Imsul rebellion of 1862.

The third of the major causes of that rebellion was the maladministration of credit, loans, and relief handled mainly by district magistrates and their clerks. As more peasant smallholders were reduced to the margin of subsistence by the loss of land to landlords and then driven over the edge to starvation by natural disaster, they were reduced to dependency on relief payments and loans. Unable to repay the loans because of their marginal economic position, the loans were turned over and the interest payments became a permanent tax. When rebellion broke out in 1862 the peasants directed their ire against the district magistrates and their clerks, the ones responsible for the administration of the land and military service taxes and the collection of interest payments on loans.

In the recovery plan of the Taewongun in the 1860s, a few of Yu Hyŏngwŏn's recommendations for action played a small role. His plan for nationalization and redistribution was simply ignored, only a half-hearted effort was made to carry out a cadastral survey to register cultivated land for fairer collection of the land tax, and his suggestion for the adoption of recommendation in the selection of officials was tried as a supplement to the examination system. The Taewongun was the first to mint multiple denomination cash, as the more advanced eighteenth century experts on currency had advocated, but that policy was contrary to Yu's advice to limit metallic currency to penny cash. His prediction that it would produce inflation came true.

On the other hand, his idea of extending military service to all male adults but officials, modified in the course of the debate in the eighteenth century to an extension of the military service tax to yangban households, was finally adopted. And his recommendation for the transfer of relief and loan administration from the district magistrates to the leadership of prominent gentry was adopted.

It was not to be expected that Yu's seventeenth-century perspective would have remained relevant to nineteenth-century circumstance, but Yu did inspire a number of well-known reformers in the eighteenth century, and the germ of several of his reform ideas was preserved in the frost of two centuries of administrative deterioriation, recalled to life by the Taewongun to save the dynasty from collapse.

Commerce and Industry

Yu Hyŏngwŏn learned much from the debate over the emergence of a more active commercial economy in the seventeenth century, and he was one of the spokesmen for progress in the context of that time. He expected commerce to play a more active role in the economy than in the past century, and he welcomed the introduction of copper cash to promote a more fluid exchange system, but his ideas were only known to a few until the turn of the eighteenth century. When they did, some of his ideas that were progressive for the seventeenth century had become conservative in the eighteenth.

The reason was that King Sukchong was unable to manage the currency to prevent inflation in those arteries of trade that used cash, and he shut down the mints in frustration. The fear of inflation was inherited by King Yŏngjo in the 1720s, who believed that a return to a noncash agrarian economy would be better for the Korean population. The policies of these two kings did not reflect the dominant opinion at court. In fact the kings were far less enlightened or progressive than a number of officials, contrary to Kings T'aejong, Sejong, and Sejo who unsuccessfully sought to introduce metallic and paper money into Korea in the fifteenth century. Only reluctantly was King Yŏngjo persuaded that cash had become a permanent aspect of Korean commerce, and that minting cash was the best way to solve the economic bottlenecks created by long-term deflation.

Even though a number of active officials had become more open and progressive in their attitude toward currency and suggested the minting of multiple-denomination and silver cash and paper money, Yŏngjo refused to go beyond penny cash, a policy left intact until the Taewongun's regime in the 1860s. This was essentially the same attitude of Yu Hyŏngwŏn in the mid-1600s, but after currency became indispensable to the economy, the fear of inflation and penny cash led to deflation and a serious brake on economic growth.

The development of commerce had also led to the rise of private, unlicensed merchants and artisans – even members of the official establishment who engaged in both private as well as official production of goods – who challenged the licensed monopolies and took over an increasing share of the market without government permission. This phenomenon represented a departure from the licensed monopoly system of the early Chosŏn dynasty, but government officials tolerated it nonetheless. They did not ban it as an unacceptable violation of Confucian principle. In fact, Confucian officials often warned against direct government involvement in business activity because it was too demeaning, too close to the selfish pursuit of profit.

Yu Hyŏngwŏn had no idea that this development would take place, but his armchair statecraft successors as well as government officials devised policy recommendations to deal with the problem. The debate, however, was not conducted in twentieth-century terms between free trade versus a state-managed economy. On the contrary, the eighteenth-century Korean economy looked more like the kind of goulash economic system currently underway in China in the early 1990s, except that industrial factory production had no place in Korea at that time. In addition to the licensed monopoly shops of the capital and slave and commoner artisans of the government, there were private artisans and merchants. Wholesale merchants cornered the market in goods like rice and fish, or put out raw materials to peasant cotton spinners and weavers, official artisans supplemented their income by using their spare time to produce goods for the private market, and rotating duty soldiers in the capital entered into the hat and glove trade to compete with licensed shops. The competitors with licensed monopolies did not always challenge the system of monopoly in favor of a completely free market; many demanded membership in the ranks of the privileged monopolists themselves.

Yu Suwŏn in the 1720s did argue for more organization by the government of the small-scale merchants to form oligopolies that would reduce the evils of the untrammeled pursuit of profit while maintaining competition to engender efficiency and cheaper prices. His Confucian perspective did not prevent him from considering positive aspects of commercial organization beyond the framework of licensed monopoly. Pak Chega and Pak Chiwŏn also urged increased international trade because they admired its greater development in China, where it was not deemed un-Confucian. Nonetheless, almost all agreed that commerce and industry would still remain subordinate to agriculture.

In any case, the armchair scholars were not the architects of government policy on the economy. Instead, the government mediated the dispute by a compromise between the licensed and unlicensed merchants and artisans that divided the market between them. This solution apparently was acceptable to most, and the economy neither reverted to restricted monopoly nor advanced much toward industrial capitalism until sometime after the introduction of foreign trade in the 1880s. Korean Confucian thought could easily have tolerated greater commercial activity than what existed in Korea, but the stimuli to greater production and trade were lacking in the economy.

Commercial agriculture did not receive a big boost until the export of grain to Japan in the 1880s, and a serious start to industrial capitalism did not occur until the cessation of the ban on private business by the Japanese colonial regime after 1919. Contrary to much scholarly opinion, by the end of the dynasty the commercial and industrial economy did not really transform the agrarian, agricultural economy.

Statecraft Scholarship and the Late Chosŏn Dynasty

Recent scholarship on the late Chosŏn period has distorted an understanding of some of the fundamental aspects of that society because of its search for proof to demonstrate the capacity of the Korean people to achieve change and progress on their own initiative. That body of scholarship has been successful in demonstrating some of the major changes that did take place, such as the growth of the nonagricultural commercial sector, the decline of slavery, and the shifts in the tax system. But the desire to demonstrate progress has shifted attention away from the domination of agriculture, the maintenance of yangban power, and the influence of Confucian statecraft concepts on the thinking of the educated class.

Confucian statecraft ideas were by no means translated directly into policy choices, as this book should make clear, but the emphasis on the moral basis for government never lost force even while the state was losing ground to human weakness, corruption, and immorality. The ultimate goal of producing a moral order according to Confucian standards was maintained. The primacy of agriculture and the fear of the immoral consequences of commerce and the profit motive were still deemed important, but not enough to blind the vision of Confucian officials and scholars to some advantages of economic activity. Despite the growth of the commercial economy, merchants and artisans were still few in number and too weak to challenge the predominance of the yangban families who monopolized education, dominated the upper bureaucracy, and controlled the chief source of wealth, land and agricultural production.

Finally, the locus of statecraft ideals remained the institutions of Chinese antiquity described in the Chinese classics; the chief source of wisdom in the conduct of practical statecraft was the immense literature on Chinese history and institutions; the main prop of Korea's security was still the protection afforded by the suzerain state, the Manchu Ch'ing dynasty, until the Sino-Japanese War of 1894. These elements may be lugubrious reminders of subjugation to foreign culture for modern Korean nationalists, but they also are symbols of the membership and participation of the Korean Confucians in a world much broader than the confines of the Korean peninsula, governed by levels of complexity and civilization far higher than most in world history.

Notes

Introduction

1. Ch'ŏn Kwan'u, "Pan'gye Yu Hyŏngwŏn yŏn'gu: Sirhak parsaeng esŏ pon Yijo sahoe ŭi iltanmyŏn" [A study of Yu Hyŏngwŏn: One aspect of Yi dynasty society as seen from the birth of practical learning], part 1, *Yŏksa hakpo* 2 (October 1952):35–36; part 2, ibid. 3 (January 1953):123–25; idem, "Chosŏn hugi sirhak ŭi kaenyŏm chaeron" [Reconsideration of the concept of *sirhak* in the late Chosŏn period], in idem, *Han'guksa ŭi chaebalgyŏn* [The rediscovery of Korean history] (Seoul: Ilchogak, 1974), pp. 107–85.

2. Ch'ŏn Kwan'u, "Pan'gye Yu Hyŏngwŏn yŏn'gu ŭibo [A corrigenda to my study of Yu Hyŏngwŏn], in idem, *Kŭnse Chosŏnsa yŏn'gu* [Studies in the history of Chosŏn in recent times) (Seoul: Ilchogak, 1979), pp. 338–43 n. 11; "Pan'gye Yu Hyŏngwŏn yŏn'gu: Sirhak parsaeng esŏ pon Yijo sahoe ŭi iltanmyŏn" [A partial view of Yi dynasty society as seen through the emergence of *sirhak*], in ibid., pp. 229–32; Chŏng Kubok, "Pan'gye Yu Hyŏngwŏn ŭi sahoe kaehyŏk sasang" [Yu Hyŏngwŏn's ideas for the reform of society], *Yŏksa hakpo* 15 (March 1970):1–3; Kim Chunsŏk, "Yu Hyŏngwŏn ŭi pyŏnbŏpkwan kwa silliron" [Yu Hyŏngwŏn's view of legal reform and his thesis of true principle], *Tongbanghak chi* 75 (June 1992):71–73 n.3, et passim. Kim noted that as a youth Yu studied with Yi Wŏnjin, his maternal uncle, and Kim Seryŏm, the husband of his paternal aunt, when he was a child. Yi was the man who was the magistrate on Cheju when Hendrik Hamel and his friends were shipwrecked off the Korean coast in 1653.

3. Ch'ŏn Kwan'u, "Pan'gye Yu Hyŏngwŏn yŏn'gu" [A study of Pan'gye Yu Hyŏngwŏn], in *Chosŏn kŭnsesa yŏn'gu* [Studies in the recent history of Chosŏn] (Seoul: Ilchogak, 1979), pp. 233–34.

4. For information on the history of the *Pan'gye surok*, see the Han'gukhak kibon ch'ongsŏ ed., no. 10, *Chŭngbo pan'gye surok* (Seoul: Kyŏng'in munhwasa, 1974), pp. 620–23.

5. For the history of the *Munhŏnbigo*, see *Kuksa-daesajŏn* 2, 1475; MHBG *pŏmnye* (rules of compilation):1a-b;*su*, *ŏje* (royal notices):5a-b.

6. "Yu Hyŏngwŏn ŭi pyŏnbŏpkwan kwa silliron" [Yu Hyŏngwŏn's view of legal reform and his theory of real principle], *Tongbanghak chi* 75 (June 1992):83–89.

7. Peter Bol has preferred "pattern" over "principle" as a translation of *i* (*li* in Chinese). Peter K. Bol, *"This Culture of Ours": Intellectual Transitions in T'ang and Sung China* (Stanford, Calif.: Stanford University Press, 1992).

8. I have chosen "psycho-physical energy" instead of Carsun Ch'ang's "matter" or Wing-tsit Chan's "material force" as a translation for *ki* (*ch'i* in Chinese). See Carsun Chang, *The Development of Neo-Confucian Thought*, 2 vols. (New York: Bookman Associates, 1957, 1962); Hoyt Cleveland Tillman, *Utilitarian Confucianism: Ch'en Liang's Challenge to Chu Hsi* (Cambridge: Council on East Asian Studies, Harvard University, 1982); Wing-tsit Chan, *A Sourcebook in Chinese Philosophy* (Princeton, N.J.: Princeton University Press, 1963).

9. *Pan'gye sŏnsaeng yŏnbo* (Seoul: Tongguk munhwasa, 1961), pp. 6–7.

10. *Pan'gye chapko* (Seoul: Yŏgang ch'ulp'ansa, 1990).

11. Yi Usŏng, "Ch'ogi Sirhak kwa sŏngnihak kwa ŭi kwan'gye: Pan'gye Yu Hyŏngwŏn ŭi kyŏng'u" [The relationship between early practical learning and the learning of nature and principle], *Tongbanghak chi* 58 (June 1989):15–22.

12. Kim Chunsŏk, "Yu Hyŏngwŏn ŭi pyŏnbŏpkwan kwa silliron," p. 72.

13. Ibid., pp. 94–104.

14. Ibid., pp. 104–9.

15. Leszek Kolakowski, "Mind and Body: Ideology and Economy in the Collapse of Communism," in Kazimierz A. Poznanski, ed., *Constructing Capitalism: The Reemergence of Civil Society and Liberal Economy in the Post-Communist World* (Boulder, Colo.: Westview Press, 1992), pp. 10–13.

CHAPTER 1. Confucian Statecraft in the Founding of Chosŏn

1. Min Hyŏn'gu, "Sin Ton ŭi chipkwŏn kwa kŭ chŏngch'ijŏk sŏnkyŏk" [Sin Ton's administration and its political nature], *Yŏksa hakpo* 38 (August 1968):49. John Duncan has provided a very useful discussion of the power and functions of the late Koryŏ monarchs and the domination of the great official families of the capital in late Koryŏ, the families that I prefer to label yangban. See his manuscript, "The Koryŏ Origins of the Chosŏn Dynasty," submitted to the University of Washington Press, 1993.

2. Martina Deuchler, *The Confucian Transformation of Korea: A Study of Society and Ideology* (Cambridge, Mass: Harvard University Press, 1992).

3. Chŏng Tojŏn, *Sambongjip* (Seoul: Kuksa p'yŏnch'an wiwŏnhoe, 1961); James B. Palais, review of Han Yŏng'u, *Chŏng Tojŏn sasang ŭi yŏn'gu* [A study of the thought of Chŏng Tojŏn] (Seoul: Han'guk munhwa yŏn'guso, 1973), *Journal of Korean Studies* 2 (1980):199–244.

4. The sources for this section are too numerous to list, but for an English account, see Ki-baik Lee [Yi Kibaek], *A New History of Korea*, trans. by Edward W. Wagner (Cambridge: Harvard University Press, 1984).

5. Chŏng Tojŏn, "Chosŏn kyŏnggukchŏn, ha" [Institutes for the management of the state, pt. 2], *Sambongjip* (Seoul: Kuksa p'yŏnch'an wiwŏnhoe, 1961), p. 218.

6. Kang Man'gil, "Sugong'ŏp" [Handicrafts], *Han'guksa* 10, *Chosŏn: Yangban kwallyo kukka ŭi sahoe kujo* [History of Korea, 10, Chosŏn: The social structure of the yang-

ban-bureaucratic state] (Seoul: Taehan min'guk Mungyobu, Kuksa p'yŏnch'an wiwŏnhoe, 1974):369–75, 382–85.

7. Ibid., pp. 386–89.

8. Sung Jae Koh, "Myŏn'ŏp" [Cotton textiles] in Kuksa p'yŏnch'an wiwŏnhoe, ed., *Han'guksa* 10:320–25.

9. Sin Chihyŏn, "Yŏm'ŏp" [The salt industry] in Kuksa p'yŏnch'an wiwŏnhoe, ed., *Han'guksa* 10:389–95.

10. Yu Sŭngju, "Kwang'ŏp," *Han'guksa* 10:335–43.

11. Ibid., pp. 348–55.

12. Yi Sangbaek, *Han'guksa: Kŭnse chŏn'gip'yŏn* [The history of Korea: Early modern period] (Seoul: Ŭryu Munhwasa), pp. 476–82; Yu Wŏndong, "Sang'ŏp" [Commerce] in Kuksa p'yŏnch'an wiwŏnhoe, ed., *Han'guksa* 10:295.

13. It is unlikely, however, that they took deposits, issued and accepted bills, and functioned like banks in issuing bills at a discount to purchasers on the basis of collateral in real estate as they did by the end of the nineteenth century. It is not clear just when some of these more advanced banking practices began. See Yu Wŏndong, "Sang'ŏp" [Commerce] in Kuksa p'yŏnch'an wiwŏnhoe, ed., *Han'guksa* 10:305–8.

14. Yu Wŏndong, "Sang'ŏp," *Han'guksa*, 10:278–87.

15. John K. Fairbank, "A Preliminary Framework," in John K. Fairbank, ed., *The Chinese World Order* (Cambridge: Harvard University Press, 1968), pp. 1–9; Chun Haejong, "Sino-Korean Tributary Relations in the Ch'ing Period," in idem, pp. 90–111.

16. Yu Wŏndong, "Sang'ŏp," *Han'guksa* 10:313–19.

17. For the role of the *kongsin*, see Edward Willett Wagner, *The Literati Purges: Political Conflict in Early Yi Korea* (Cambridge: East Asian Research Center and Harvard University Press, 1974); for the *san'gwan*, see Yi Sŏngmu, *Chosŏn ch'ogi yangban yŏn'gu* [A study of the yangban in the early Chosŏn period] (Seoul: Ilchogak, 1980), pp. 116–74.

18. For the *chung'in*, see Yi Sŏngmu, *Chosŏn ch'ogi yangban yŏn'gu* [A Study of the yangban in the early Chosŏn dynasty] (Seoul: Ilchogak, 1980), p. 31, n.114, and for the *hyangni*, and clerks, see ibid., pp. 31–38, and idem, "Chosŏn ch'ogi ŭi hyangni" [The *hyangni* of the early Chosŏn period] *Han'guksa yŏn'gu* 5 (1970):65–96.

19. For the *nothoi*, see Yi Sŏngmu, *Chosŏn ch'ogi yangban yŏn'gu*, pp. 38–39; Song June-ho [Song Chunho], "Chosŏn sidae ŭi kwagŏ wa yangban mit yang'in" [The civil service examinations of the Chosŏn period and the yangban and commoners] *Yŏksa hakpo* 69 (March 1976):101–35. See also James B. Palais, book reviews of these two works in *Journal of Korean Studies* 3 (1981):191–212.

20. Ping-ti Ho, *The Ladder of Success in Imperial China: Aspects of Social Mobility, 1368–1911* (New York: Columbia University Press, 1962), pp. 41–52, 68–72.

21. John Breckenridge Duncan, "The Koryŏ Origins of the Chosŏn Dynasty," 1988. Rev. ed. submitted for publication 1993, pp. 102–3.

22. John Breckenridge Duncan, "The Koryŏ Origins of the Chosŏn Dynasty: Kings, Aristocrats, and Confucianism" (Ph.D. diss., Seattle: University of Washington, 1988); idem, "The Social Background to the Founding of the Chosŏn Dynasty: Change or Continuity?" *Journal of Korean Studies* 6 (1988–89):39–80.

23. Yi Sŏngmu, "Yangban," in Kuksa p'yŏnch'an wiwŏnhoe, ed., *Han'guksa*, 10:549–55; Yi Sŏngmu, *Chosŏn ch'ogi yangban yŏn'gu*, pp. 4–17.

24. Yi Sŏngmu, "Yangban," *Han'guksa* 10:552.

25. Song June-ho, "Chosŏn yangban'go" [A study of the Chosŏn yangban], in idem, *Chosŏn sahoesa yŏn'gu* [Studies in the social history of Chosŏn] (Seoul: Ilchogak, 1987), pp. 165–71; Yi Sŏngmu, *Chosŏn ch'ogi yangban yŏn'gu*, pp. 2–4, 366–67; Han Yŏng'u, "Chosŏn ch'ogi sahoe kyech'ŭng yŏn'gu e taehan chaeron" [A reconsideration of studies on social strata in early Chosŏn], *Han'guk saron* 12 (February 1985):334; Yu Sŭngwŏn, *Chosŏn ch'ogi sinbunje yŏn'gu* (Seoul: Ŭryu munhwasa, 1987), pp. 6–174; Yongho Choe, *The Civil Examinations and the Social Structure in Early Yi Dynasty Korea: 1392–1600* (Seoul: The Korean Research Center, 1987), passim and esp. pp. 161–66.

26. Yu Suwŏn, *Usŏ* (Seoul: Sŏul Taehakkyo kojŏn kanhaenghoe, 1971), pp. 131, 165; Han Yŏng'u, "Yu Suwŏn ŭi sinbun kaehyŏk sasang" [Yu Suwŏn's ideas about the reform of social status], *Han'guksa yŏn'gu* 8 (September 1972):40–41, 47; Paolo Santangelo, *La Vita e l'opera di Yu Suwŏn Pensatore Coreano del XVIII Secolo* (Naples: Istituto Universitario Orientale, Seminario di Studi Asiatici, 1981), pp. 78–79.

27. Yu Sŭngwŏn, *Chosŏn ch'ogi sinbunje yŏn'gu*, passim, esp. pp. 6–174. Song argued that the term *yang* was only used in apposition to *ch'ŏn* (lowborn, slave). See Song June-ho, "Chosŏn yangban-go," pp. 172–74, 210, 217–18, 242. But Han Yŏng'u pointed out that when the term yangban was used in apposition to other terms for commoners besides *yang'in*, such as *paeksŏng*, it meant "those who possessed office" (yangban) vs. "those who did not possess office" (*paeksŏng*); in other words, a yangban was simply someone who was a person of good status (*yang'in*) who held an official post, not someone who possessed superior social status. See Han Yŏng'u, "Chosŏn ch'ogi sahoe kyech'ŭng yŏn'gu e taehan chaeron" [A reconsideration of studies on social strata in early Chosŏn] *Han'guk saron* 12 (February 1985):321–22.

28. A number of Song's arguments that have been refuted or proved irrelevant to the problem by Han Yŏng'u and Yu Sŭngwŏn will be eliminated from discussion. Song, however, made an appeal to logic by arguing that no society with a significant slave population could be divided so simply into two classes of free men (*yang'in*) and slaves (*ch'ŏnmin*) because all of them had, and would have to have, a ruling class superior to the ordinary class of commoners. Yu Sŭngwŏn and Han Yŏng'u have argued that neither of them denied the existence of the yangban as a ruling stratum; they only denied that it was based on inherited status.

Song also argued that the existence of a yangban elite status group was demonstrated by numerous statements about the aristocrats (*kwijok*), aristocratic families (*kwiga*), great families (*taejok*), hereditary families (*sejok*), hereditary officials (*sesin*), officials of hereditary salaries (*serok chi sin*), *sadaebu*, aristocrats (*munbŏl*), or hereditary factions (*sebŏl*). Han, however, argued that the existence of such terms was only a matter of names or nomenclature, and did not prove the existence of hereditary status.

Song also argued that he was never able to find a concrete instance when the term *yang'in* was ever used to represent the yangban or *sajok*. The difference between yangban and commoners was almost exclusively expressed by the terms *sajok* (i.e., yangban) and *sŏin* (commoners) used in apposition. But both Han and Yu have responded to the charge and found a number of instances when the terms *yang'in* or *yang* were apparently used in a broad sense to include yangban. Yu Sŭngwŏn, *Chosŏn ch'ogi sinbunje yŏn'gu*, pp. 50–53.

29. Yu Sŭngwŏn stated explicitly that in his view the hereditary aristocracy of the Koryŏ period was obliterated and replaced by a new *sadaebu* elite that arose from the class of small-to-medium landowners. Ibid., 50–51.

30. Song June-ho, "Chosŏn yangban-go," pp. 175–80, 200–201, 222–23. Han Yŏng'u specifically rejected the citation of Yang Sŏngji's statement to prove that the great families or yangban were a status elite because Yang was mainly concerned with preserving their ownership of slaves and was advocating a new policy to grant them privileges that they did not already possess. He also pointed out that since Yang proposed that men from all social status groups, including the highest, be subjected to military service, he was not a supporter of status. But this argument could be turned against Han by using the same kind of argument used regarding yangban slave ownership. That is, if Yang was advocating military service for high status groups, it must have been because they were currently not subjected to it – an implicit recognition of the existence of a privileged status elite! See Han Yŏng'u, "Chosŏn ch'ogi sahoe kyech'ŭng yŏn'gu e taehan chaeron," pp. 331–32.

31. Yu and Han rejected the idea, but John Duncan is apparently at work on this subject at present. See the section entitled "Marriage Relations of the Great Families" in chapter 3 of John Duncan, *The Koryŏ Origins of the Chosŏn Dynasty,* University of Washington Press, forthcoming. See Song June-ho, "Namwŏn chibang'ŭl yero hayŏbon Chosŏn sidae hyangch'on sahoe ŭ kujo wa sŏnkyŏk" [The structure and nature of village society in the Chosŏn period as seen in the Namwŏn area), in idem, *Chosŏn sahoesa yŏn'gu* (Seoul: Ilchogak, 1987), pp. 277–306; idem, "Namwŏn e tŭrŏonŭn Ch'angp'yŏng ŭ Wŏlkusil Yu-ssi, Yangban segye e issŏ hon'in i ŭimi hayŏttŏn'gŏt [The Wŏlkusil Yu clan of Ch'angp'yŏng that moved into Namwŏn, the meaning of marriage in the yangban world], in *Chosŏn sahoesa yŏn'gu* (Seoul: Ilchogak, 1987), pp. 307–25.

32. Song June-ho, "Chosŏn yangban-go," p. 243.

33. On the nothoi and the Poch'unggun, see ibid., pp. 249–59 et passim. In seeking to refute Song's view that a prominent ancestor was necessary for the maintenance of a family's yangban status, Yi Sŏngmu claimed that if this condition were important, it would have been mentioned in the late fifteenth-century law code, the *Kyŏngguk taejŏn*. Song's discovery of just such a provision in the sources effectively refuted Han's objection.

34. Ibid.

35. Yi Sŏngmu stated that the importance of a prominent ancestor disappeared by the sixteenth century, *Chosŏn ch'ogi yangban yŏn'gu*, p. 218. Song's study of the seventeenth and eighteenth century yangban does not necessarily refute this and Han Yŏng'u's opinions because both argued that by the seventeenth century the yangban had become a status group, particularly in local communities. But Song's discovery of explicit provisions for granting privileges to those with a prominent ancestor in the "four ancestors" (*sajo*) in both husband and wife's families does refute this view.

36. Song June-ho, "Chosŏn yangban-go," p. 248.

37. Ping-ti Ho, *Ladder of Success in Imperial China*, pp. 165–67 et passim.

38. Hilary J. Beattie, *Land and Lineage in China: A Study of T'ung-Ch'eng County, Anhwei, in the Ming and Ch'ing dynasties* (Cambridge: Cambridge University Press, 1979).

39. Edward W. Wagner, "The Ladder of Success in Yi Dynasty Korea," *Occasional Papers on Korea*, no. 1 (April 1974), p. 4.

40. Yi Sŏngmu, *Chosŏn ch'ogi yangban yŏn'gu*, pp. 59–65.

41. James B. Palais, "The Aristocratic/Bureaucratic Balance in Korea," *Harvard Journal of Asiatic Studies* 44, no. 2 (December 1984):427–68.

42. See the discussion of the origin of choronyms in Chinese history in David G. Johnson, *The Medieval Chinese Oligarchy* (Boulder, Colorado: Westview Press, 1977).

43. Song June-ho, "Chosŏn yangban-go," pp. 282–87, 320.

44. For a description of *sajŏn* in the early Koryŏ period see James B. Palais, "Land Tenure in Korea: Tenth to Twelfth Centuries," *Journal of Korean Studies* 4 (1982–83): 73–206. In the sixth lunar month of 1388 King U said that "the land laws had been destroyed" because the rich and powerful had accumulated too much land. The Supreme Council (Top'yŏng'ŭisasa) noted that there was not supposed to be any prebendal land (*sajŏn*) in the northwest and northeastern provinces, and if an investigation revealed that any existed illicitly, it was to be confiscated by the government. In the ninth lunar month of 1390 King Kongyang ordered the burning of all registers for both *kongjŏn* and *sajŏn* in the streets of the capital. *Koryŏsa* [History of the Koryŏ dynasty] 2 (Seoul: Yŏnhŭi taehakkyo ch'ulp'anbu, 1955):78:24b; 714:38a. Hereafter referred to as KRS.

45. See the discussion on *kongjŏn* and *minjŏn* during the early Koryŏ dynasty in Palais, "Land Tenure in Korea," p. 120. On occasion *minjŏn* was also referred to colloquially as *sajŏn* in the sense of "privately [owned] land" rather than in its normal sense as "prebend," an unfortunate habit for later historians who have had difficulty in determining when and whether that term referred to prebendal allotments or private property.

46. KRS 78:38a, 5th lunar month, third year of King Kongyang's reign (1391).

47. Ibid. 78:20b–28a, especially the proposals listed from 78:26a on, proposing the adoption of a new prebendal system. For the remarks of the censor, Yi Haeng, and the Minister of Justice, Cho In'ok, see ibid. 78:29a, 32b.

48. A chaste widow without children received only half her husband's prebend after his death, ibid. 78:40a, 5th lunar month, 1391. For discussion of grants to widows (*kubunjŏn* or *susinjŏn*) and orphans (*hyuryangjŏn*) see Yi Kyŏngsik, *Chosŏn chŏn'gi t'oji chedo yŏn'gu*, pp. 87, 152–53.

49. KRS 78:26a–b. Cho was not averse to state takeovers of land, but he only called for a temporary confiscation of land in the northern two frontier provinces for a period of three years prior to a major program for a cadastral resurvey to provide emergency provisions for the troops there and salaries for incumbent officials, ibid. 78:25a–26a, 78:38b, 5th month, 1391.

50. Ibid. 78:34b.

51. See in particular the memorial of Hŏ Ŭng, ibid. 78:34a.

52. Ibid. 78:36a–b, King Kongyang, accession year (1389), 12th month. For final adoption of this provision in 5th month, 1391, ibid. 78:40a–b.

53. Yi Kyŏngsik, *Chosŏn chŏn'gi t'oji chedo yŏn'gu*, pp. 101, 284. Yi's explanation of the purpose of the *kwajŏn* prebends is much preferable to that of Ch'ŏn Kwan'u, who thought that the objective was only to provide for salaries of officials, but Ch'ŏn was right when he said that the reform was more of a fiscal or revenue reform than a land reform. Ch'ŏn Kwan'u, "Han'guk t'oji chedosa, ha" (part 2) [The Korean land system, part 2], in *Han'guk munhwasa-daegye* [A grand outline of Korean cultural history] (Seoul: Koryŏ taehakkyo minjok munhwa yŏn'guso, 1965), p. 1397.

54. KRS 78:36b.

55. Ibid. 78:36b–37a.

56. Ibid. 78:39b. Yi Kyŏngsik, *Chosŏn chŏn'gi t'oji chedo yŏn'gu*, pp. 103–4; Ch'ŏn Kwan'u, "Han'guk t'oji chedosa, ha" (part 2), p. 1438.

57. KRS 78:40b.

58. Yi Kyŏngsik, *Chosŏn chŏn'gi t'oji chedo yŏn'gu*, pp. 277, 293; Han Yŏng'u, "Taejong, Sejongjo ŭi taesajŏn sich'aek: sajŏn ŭi hasamdo igŭp munje rŭl chungsim ŭro" [Policy toward *sajŏn* in T'aejong's and Sejong's reigns: Particularly the problem of transferring grants of *sajŏn* to the southern three provinces], *Han'guksa yŏn'gu* 3 (March 1969):47, and Ch'ŏn Kwan'u, "Han'guk t'oji chedosa, ha" (part 2), p. 1439, give different figures: 149,300 *kyŏl*, of which 84,100 *kyŏl* for *kwajŏn*, 21,240 *kyŏl* for *kongsinjŏn* (merit subject land), and 4,460 *kyŏl* for *sasa* (temples and shrines). In addition 39,280 *kyŏl* quasi-*sajŏn* prebendal grants to granaries, palaces (of princes and princesses), yamen for expenses, and land for salaries to incumbent officials. Ch'ŏn estimated that three-quarters of the land of the province was devoted to prebends or "semi-prebends."

59. Chŏng Tojŏn, "Chosŏn kyŏngguk, sang" [The management of Chosŏn, part 1], *Sambongjip* (Seoul: Kuksa p'yŏnch'an wiwŏnhoe, 1961), pp. 214–15.

60. See Duncan, "Koryŏ Origins of the Chosŏn Dynasty."

61. Yi Kyŏngsik, *Chosŏn chŏn'gi t'oji chedo yŏn'gu*, pp. 192–98. Yi discussed here the situation under the *kwajŏn* system in the early fifteenth century, but his description also holds for the Koryŏ period as well.

62. Ibid., pp. 135–37. Two notices in 1394 and 1397 indicated that there was a ban against tenancy, and the latter explicitly forbade sharecropping except for plots smaller than 3–4 *kyŏl* and only in the case of widows and orphans without slaves who were unable to cultivate the land themselves. See Yi Kyŏngsik, "Simnyuk segi chijuch'ŭng ŭi tonghyang" [Trends in the landlord stratum in the sixteenth century], *Yŏksa kyoyuk* 19 (April 1976):163–64.

63. Fukaya Toshitetsu had defined land tenure in the Koryŏ period in terms of multiple rights to the same parcel of land according to which total and absolute ownership was limited by other rights, but his views were the product of his assumption that land was ultimately owned by the state. Since that notion has been rejected by most scholars, his theory has been weakened, but it still retains a germ of truth. See Palais, "Land Tenure in Korea, pp. 135–36, 144–50.

64. Chŏng Tojŏn, "Chosŏn kyŏnggukchŏn, ha" [Institutes for the management of the state, part 2], *Sambongjip* (Seoul: Kuksa p'yŏnch'an wiwŏnhoe, 1961), pp. 233–34, 237–38.

65. For more detail see part 4, Military Reform, below.

66. Ch'ŏn Kwan'u, "Han'guk t'oji chedosa, ha" (part 2), p. 1402.

67. Yi Kyŏngsik, *Chosŏn chŏn'gi t'oji chedo yŏn'gu*, pp. 277, 293.

68. Ch'ŏn Kwan'u, "Han'guk t'oji chedosa, ha" (part 2), p. 1430.

69. Ibid., pp. 1426, 1430; Han Yŏng'u, "Taejong, Sejongjo ŭi taesajŏn sich'aek: sajŏn ŭi hasamdo igŭp munje rŭl chungsim ŭro," p. 45.

70. The tribute system was evidently not applied to every province since it was not extended to Cheju Island until 1408, and P'yŏng'an and Hamgyŏng provinces until 1413. Tagawa Kōzō, *Richō kōnōsei no kenkyū*, pp. 3–4, 6, 21.

71. Ibid., pp. 49–56, 59 n 15, 74–79. Tagawa describes a number of hereditary occupations assigned as designated service for men of commoner or slave status to gather firewood, produce salt, raise and train falcons, or raise different types of birds, p. 234 et passim.

72. Ibid., pp. 275–94.

73. Ibid., pp. 27–29, 91–97.

74. The equivalent of *pangnap* methods are mentioned in 1321 and 1352 in the Koryŏ period when merchants paid tribute to the capital bureaus first and then recouped them from local residents at a profit, or when capital bureaus demanded advance payments from capital residents of people from local districts and then allowed them to collect repayment from the district. Ibid., pp. 253–57, 335–37.

75. Yi Sangbaek, *Han'guksa: Kŭnse chŏn'gip'yŏn*, p. 484; Ch'oe Hojin, *Han'guk hwap'ye sosa* [Short history of currency in Korea] (Seoul: Sŏmundang, 1974), pp. 11–36.

76. Ch'oe Hojin, *Han'guk hwap'ye sosa*, pp. 11–36; KRS 79:10a–16a. The dimension of the bolt of cloth measured 35 "feet" (*ch'ŏk*) by 2 "feet" two "inches" (*ch'on*), Korean measure. For this information and the thread count of the *sae*, see Sudō Yoshiyuki, "Kōrai makki yori Chōsen shoki ni itaru orimonogyō no hattatsu" [The Development of the textile industry in late Koryŏ and early Chosŏn], *Shakai keizaishigaku* 12, no. 3 (1942):16–18. See also Yi Sangbaek, *Han'guksa: Kŭnse chŏn'gip'yŏn*, pp. 484–85.

77. For discussion of T'aejong's adoption of paper money in 1402 and 1410, see Ch'oe Hojin, *Han'guk hwap'ye sosa*, pp. 55–58; Miyahara Tōichi, "Chōsen shoki no choka ni tsuite" [Paper money in early Chosŏn], (Tōyōshigaku kenkyūshitsu, Tokyo Kyōiku Daigaku, *Tōyōshigaku ronshū*, 1954), no. 3, pp. 369–82; see p. 380 for Miyahara's cited opinion; Yi Chongyŏng, "Chosŏnch'o hwap'yeje ŭi pyŏnch'ŏn" [Changes in the currency system of early Chosŏn], *Inmun kwahak* 7 (1962):295–308.

78. Between 1406 and 1422 the value of paper bills dropped from 10 to 30 *chang* or bills per string of cash (presumably cash imported from China). Its value dropped to 1/12.5 its initial value by 1425 since the redemption fee to avoid ten strokes of punishment had gone up from six to seventy-five bills of paper money. Cash minted by Sejong in 1423 was supposed to be worth one *toe* (.10 *mal*) of rice and 1/200 *p'il* of cotton cloth, but by 1425 it had fallen to .33 *toe* and 1/300 or 1/400 *p'il* of cotton cloth. It was worth less against cloth of a higher 6–7 *sae* thread count (vs. the standard 5 *sae*), 1/600 or 1/700 *p'il*. By 1427, one *mun* of cash had fallen to 1/7 or 1/8 *toe* of rice, and by 1429 it had fallen to 1/12 or 1/13 *toe*. Miyahara Tōichi, "Chōsen shoki no dōsen ni tsuite" [Copper cash in Chosŏn] *Chōsen gakuhō* 2 (October 1951):88–90; Yi Chongyŏng, "Hwap'yeje," pp. 314–15; Ch'oe Hojin, *Han'guk hwap'ye sosa*, p. 72.

For discussion of T'aejong's adoption of paper money in 1402 and 1410, see Ch'oe Hojin, *Han'guk hwap'ye sosa*, pp. 55–58; Miyahara Tōichi, "Chōsen shoki no choka ni tsuite," pp. 369–82; Yi Chongyŏng, "Chosŏnch'o hwap'yeje ŭi pyŏnch'ŏn," pp. 295–308.

79. Yu Sŭngju, "Kwang'ŏp," *Han'guksa* 10:350–55.

80. Ch'oe Hojin, *Han'guk hwap'yesa*, pp. 61–76; Miyahara, "Dōsen ni tsuite," pp. 75–88.

81. See n. 79.

82. Yi Chongyŏng, "Hwap'yeje," pp. 316–24; Miyahara, "Dōsen," pp. 90–98. Ch'oe Hojin says that some nickel alloy cash was minted, *Han'guk hwap'ye sosa*, pp. 66–67, see also pp. 71–76.

83. Miyahara, "Dōsen," p. 97; pp. 90–98 for previous material.

84. Yi Chongyŏng, "Hwap'yeje," pp. 324–29.

85. Ibid.

86. Mun Ikchŏm was reputed to have been the first to bring back cotton seeds from China in 1363, and he was recommended for a national commendation by King T'aejo of Chosŏn in 1401 for having introduced the material that supposedly was providing cotton cloth for everyone's clothing at the time. Although Sudō Yoshiyuki disputed the accepted story about Mun Ikchŏm's personal introduction of the cotton plant to Korea and suggested that cotton may have been brought to Korea by sea from the Chiang-nan region of China a decade or two earlier than that, Sudō did discover that the late Koryŏ scholar Yi Saek had mentioned receiving a gift of cotton seed from a relative in 1375. Nonetheless, cotton and cotton cloth did not become widespread until 1430. Ch'oe Hojin, *Han'guk hwap'yesa sosa*, pp. 43–47; Sudō Yoshiyuki, "Kōrai makki yori Chōsen shoki ni itaru orimonogyō no hattatsu" [The development of the textile industry in the late Koryŏ and early Chosŏn period), *Shakai keizaishigaku* 12, no. 2 (February 1942):1–10; Yi Chongyŏng, "Hwap'yeje," pp. 329–31; Wŏn Yuhan, *Chosŏn hugi hwap'yesa yŏn'gu* [A study of the history of currency in the late Chosŏn period] (Seoul: Han'guk yŏn'guwŏn, 1975), pp. 10–12; Miyahara, "Dōsen," pp. 98–99.

87. Yi Chongyŏng, "Hwap'yeje," pp. 334–35, and n.28. Contrary to Miyahara Tōichi's finding that paper money simply decreased in value in a straightforward pattern after Sejong reintroduced it in 1445, Yi Chongyŏng discovered that Sŏngjong's policy had worked by bidding up the value of paper bills.

88. Ibid., pp. 335–38.

89. Wŏn Yuhan, *Chosŏn hugi hwap'yesa yŏn'gu*, pp. 10–12; Miyahara, "Dōsen," pp. 98–99; Yi Chongyŏng, "Hwap'yeje," p. 338; Ch'oe Hojin, *Han'guk hwap'ye sosa*, pp. 45–55.

CHAPTER 2. The Disintegration of the Early Chosŏn System to 1592

1. See the biographies of Yun Wŏllo, Yun Wŏnhyŏng, and Yun Im, in KSDSJ 2:1068–71.

2. See Ou-yang Hsiu's memorial of 1045 "On Parties," in Wm. Theodore de Bary, Wing-tsit Chan, and Burton Watson, comps., *Sources of Chinese Tradition* 1 (New York: Columbia University Press, 1964 ed.):391–92.

3. Han Yŏng'u, building on a suggestion proposed by Sudō Yoshiyuki, was the first scholar to propose that contrary to the view of Fukaya Toshitetsu that *sajŏn* was transferred south to increase the supply of land for more *kwajŏn* prebendal grants, the real reason was to alleviate the suffering of the peasants in Kyŏnggi Province, reduce the losses from wrecked grain transport ships bringing tax grains to the capital, and divert land in Kyŏnggi Province to military expenses. Han Yong'u, "Taejong, Sejongjo ŭi taesajŏn sich'aek: Sajŏn ŭi hasamdo igŭp munje rŭl chungsim ŭro" [The policy of Kings T'aejong and Sejong toward *sajŏn*: The problem of the transfer of *sajŏn* to the lower three provinces], *Hanguksa yŏn'gu* 3 (March 1969): 39–88, esp. pp. 66–70; Yi Kyŏngsik, *Chosŏn chŏn'gi t'oji chedo yŏn'gu: T'oji pungŭpche wa nongmin chibae* [A study of the land system in the early Chosŏn dynasty: Land distribution and the control of the peasantry] (Seoul: Ilchogak, 1986), pp. 192–211. See also Ch'ŏn Kwan'u, "Han'guk t'oji chedosa, ha" [The Korean land system, part 2], in *Han'guk munhwasa taegye*" [A grand outline of Korean cultural history] (Seoul: Koryŏ taehakkyo minjok munhwa yŏn'guso, 1965), p. 1449; Sudō Yoshiyuki, "Kōraichō yori Chōsen shoki ni itaru densei no kaikaku" [Land Reform between the Koryŏ and Chosŏn dynasties], *Tōagaku* 3 (1940):115–91.

4. Yi Kyŏngsik, *Chosŏn chŏn'gi t'oji chedo yŏn'gu*, pp. 211–15. In Han Yŏng'u's view, the transfer of *sajŏn* prebends south from 1417 to 1431 was more revolutionary than the burning of the *sajŏn* registers in 1390. Han Yŏng'u, "Taejong, Sejongjo ŭi taesajŏn sich'aek," pp. 50, 53, 86.

5. Yi Kyŏngsik, *Chosŏn chŏn'gi t'oji chedo yŏn'gu*, pp. 212–40; Han Yŏng'u, "Taejong, Sejongjo ŭi taesajŏn sich'aek," pp. 77–79, 83–84.

6. Yi Kyŏngsik, *Chosŏn chŏn'gi t'oji chedo yŏn'gu*, p. 232.

7. Even in King Sejong's reign prior to the adoption of the *kongbŏp* in 1444, only 0.1–0.2 percent of the land was upper grade, and only 1–2 percent was middle grade; all the rest was low grade. Ch'ŏn Kwan'u, "Han'guk t'oji chedosa, ha" (part 2), in *Han'guk munhwasa daegye*," pp. 1491–93, 1511–13; Han Yŏng'u, "Taejong, Sejongjo ŭi taesajŏn sich'aek," pp. 80, n.126, 84.

8. Yi Kyŏngsik, *Chosŏn chŏn'gi t'oji chedo yŏn'gu*, pp. 241–43.

9. Ibid., pp. 248–50.

10. Ibid., pp. 260–62, 265.

11. Ibid., pp. 265–76.

12. Ibid.

13. Ibid., pp. 272–79.

14. For the early Koryŏ dynasty, see James B. Palais, "Land Tenure in Korea: Tenth to Twelfth Centuries," *Journal of Korean Studies* 4 (1982–83): 73–206. For the Chosŏn dynasty, see Pak Pyŏngho, *Han'guk pŏpchesa t'ŭksu yŏn'gu: Yijo sidae ŭi pudongsan maemae kŭp tambobŏp* [Special studies on the history of the Korean legal system: Sale and guarantee of immovable property] (Seoul, 1960); idem, "Han'guk kŭnse ŭi toji soyukwŏn e kwan han yŏn'gu" [A study of landownership rights in recent Korean history], *Seoul taehakkyo pŏphak* 8, no. 1 (1966):63–93; 8, no. 2 (1966):78–104; 9, no. 1 (1967):157–85.

15. Yi Kyŏngsik, "Simnyuk segi chijuch'ŭng ŭi tonghyang [Trends in the landlord stratum in the sixteenth century], *Yŏksa kyoyuk* 19 (April, 1976):148–50.

16. Ibid., pp. 143–46.

17. Ibid., p. 142.

18. Ibid., pp. 154–62.

19. Ibid., pp. 163–68. See also chap. 6, below, on slavery.

20. Yi Kyŏngsik, "Simnyuk segi chijuch'ŭng Yi tonghyang," pp. 169–75; Pak Sŏngsu, "Kogong yŏn'gu" [A study of hired labor], *Sahak yŏn'gu* 18 (1964):527–54; Miyahara Toichi, "Jūgo-roku seiki Chōsen no kokō ni tsuite" [Hired labor in fifteenth and sixteenth century Chosŏn], *Chōsen gakuhō* 11 (1957):93–116.

21. Yi Kyŏngsik, "Simnyuk segi chijuch'ŭng ŭi tonghyang," pp. 177–81.

22. *Chungjong sillok* 32:10b, Chungjong 13 (1518).2.*kyŏng'in*, cited in Yi Kyŏngsik, "Simnyuk segi chijuch'ŭng ŭi tonghyang," p. 146.

23. Ibid., p. 141, n. 7. See Sin Yonggae in 1515, *Chungjong sillok* 21:52b–53a, Chungjong 10.2.*kyŏngja*, who remarked that the big landlords had holdings of over 100 *kyŏl* while the poor peasants were left with little or none. See the remarks of the Royal Lecturer Ki Chun on the beauties of the well-field system, *Chungjong sillok* 36:34b–35a, Chungjong 14 (1519).7.*kyesa*.

24. *Chungjong sillok* 51:54b–55a, Chungjong 19 (1524).9.imsin. See also the remarks of Chŏng Yugil to King Myŏngjong in 1548 that land limitation was the best possible idea since the well-field system was not possible in present times. He pointed out that even though the Chinese Han dynasty and the Koryŏ dynasty had tried it [*sic*], it had never been carried to completion in those dynasties. Nonetheless, he thought it was the only remedy for the concentration of land by large landowners and the loss of land by ordinary peasants that characterized the current situation in Korea. *Myŏngjong sillok* 7:48b, Myongjong 3 (1548).3.*kyesa*. These sources are cited in Yi Kyŏngsik, "Simnyuk segi chijuch'ŭng ŭi tonghyang," p. 141, n.7.

25. Tagawa, *Richō kōnōsei no kenkyū*, pp. 338–45.

26. Ibid., pp. 27–36, nn. 10, 11, 38 n.15, 39, n. 17; 231–32, 751–53; Kim Okkŭn, *Chosŏn hugi kyŏngjesa yŏn'gu*, (Seoul: Sŏmundang, 1977), pp. 15–16.

27. Tagawa, *Richō kōnōsei no kenkyū*, pp. 386–408, 428–37.

28. Ibid., pp. 440–45.

29. Ibid., pp. 282–334.

30. Ibid., pp. 446–70, 486–96, 751–53; Kim Okkŭn, *Chosŏn hugi*, pp. 15–16. For Yulgok's proposal, see later in this chapter.

31. The law also included exclusion from future official appointments for any yangban or official who engaged in contracting. The law was later incorporated in the 1485 revision of the *Kyŏngguk taejŏn*. Tagawa, *Richō kōnōsei no kenkyū*, pp. 497–509.

32. Tagawa has insisted that these slave-clerks of the capital bureaus must have developed after 1510 into a completely professionalized guild (*kumiai dantai*) rather than just a simple group of individual operators, and were to evolve into the tribute masters (*kongmul chuin*) engaged in the tribute contracting business after the adoption of the *taedong* reform in 1594. Tagawa claimed that they engaged in capital accumulation by squeezing huge illicit profits and developed in one of the overlooked interstices of a bureaucratic aristocracy (*kanryō kizoku*). The evidence Tagawa presented on this point, however, was not sufficient to prove beyond a doubt that the capital bureau clerks and slaves had

really developed a guild-like structure of the *za* in feudal Japan, nor that tribute masters of the seventeenth century were exclusively limited to them, rather than to private merchants, or déclassé yangban. Tagawa, p. 635, and n.33, below.

33. Ibid., pp. 528–37, 539, 543–45, 588–96, 610–35; p. 627 for the quotation. Tagawa has argued that master or private master was used in two ways: private tribute contractors who began as hostel-keepers and warehousemen along the banks of the Han River in Seoul, or as clerks and slaves of the capital bureaus. He believed that when the term was used in this memorial, the Office for Dispensing Benevolence was referring only to the clerks and slaves, but I believe that he could not be so positive that it did not extend to private masters as well.

34. Wakita Osamu, "The Social and Economic Consequences of Unification," in John Whitney Hall, ed., *The Cambridge History of Japan* 4 (Cambridge: Cambridge University Press, 1991):99–110.

35. Yi Hyŏngsŏk, *Imjin chŏllansa* [History of the Imjin War] 1 (Seoul: Sinhyŏnsilsa, 1974):37–43.

36, Ibid. 3:1253.

37. Yi Hyŏngsŏk remarked that Yulgok's military advice, supposedly given in 1582 at the time of a Jurchen attack in the north, was held in such low esteem that it was not even recorded in the *Sillok*. Ibid. 1:125–27; 3:1262–63, 1356–57; Yi I, *Yulgok chŏnsŏ* (Seoul: Sŏnggyun'gwan taehakkyo, Taedong munhwa yŏn'guwŏn, 1958), pp. 9–10.

38. Yi Hyŏngsŏk, *Imjin chŏllansa* 3:1256–59.

39. Ibid. 1:88–91.

40. Ibid. 3:1244–52.

41. For the Korean-Japanese negotiations leading to the war from 1587–92, see ibid. 1:88–110. During the court discussion over Hideyoshi's intentions, one Easterner, Kim Sŏng'il, also insisted on the imminence of an invasion. He also refrained from promoting Yi Sunsin from magistrate to naval commander of Chŏlla Province. Ibid. 3:1369.

42. Ray Huang, "The Lung-ch'ing and Wan-li reigns, 1576–1620," in F. W. Mote and Denis Twitchett, eds., *Cambridge History of China* 2, part 1 (Cambridge: University of Cambridge Press, 1988): 566–67.

43. Ibid., pp. 511–63; Jonathan Spence, *The Search for Modern China* (New York: W. W. Norton, 1990), pp. 15–21.

44. Yi Hyŏngsŏk, *Imjin chŏllansa* 1:37–43, 83.

45. Ibid. 1:116–21. For Yi's survey of Japanese opinion on the invasion, see 3: 1380–83. Jurgis Elisonas, "The Inseparable Trinity: Japan's Relations with China and Korea," in John Whitney Hall, ed., *The Cambridge History of Japan* 4 (Cambridge: Cambridge University Press, 1991):268, 270; Asao Naohiro, "The Sixteenth-Century Unification," in ibid., pp. 70–71, 76–68.

46. For the Korean-Japanese negotiations leading to the war from 1587–92, see Yi Hyŏngsŏk, *Imjin chŏllansa* 1:88–110. Yi Hyŏngsŏk made two different estimates of the troop strength of the Japanese invaders. The figures in the text are based on the material shown on pp. 134–35, which jibes with the figures presented by Elisonas (see below). On p. 201, Yi wrote that the total mobilized force in Japan was about 330,000 men, while the invading force constituted 200,000 men. About 100,000 men were stationed at Nagoya,

and 30,000 men stationed at Kyōto to guard the capital. See also Asao Naohiro, "Sixteenth-century Unification," p. 71; Elisonas, "Inseparable Trinity," p. 271.

47. Yi Hyŏngsŏk, *Imjin chŏllansa* 1:32, 36–37; Asao Naohiro, "Sixteenth-century Unification," pp. 53–57, 72; Elisonas, "Inseparable Trinity," p. 272. For descriptions of Japanese weapons used in the war, see Yi Hyŏngsŏk, *Imjin chŏllansa* 3:1311–15.

48. Yi Hyŏngsŏk, *Imjin chŏllansa* 1:31–36. Yu Songnyŏng's essay on Japanese tactics comes from his *Sŏae sŏnsaeng munjip, chapchŏ* [Miscellany], *Waeji yongbyŏng* [Japanese method of using troops] 16:34a-b, in idem, Taedong munhwa yŏn'guwŏn, ed., *Sŏaejip* [Collected works of Yu Sŏngnyŏng] (Seoul: Tongguk munhwasa, 1958):288, which cited the testimony of Yi Sigyŏng, a Ch'albang (chief of a post-station), who followed his father, Yi Yangwŏn, to the Yangju and P'och'ŏn areas during the invasion and studied the Japanese order of battle.

49. Elisonas, "Inseparable Trinity," pp. 273–76.

50. For an account of the capture of the two princes, see Yi Hyŏngsŏk, *Imjin chŏllansa* 2:807, 824–26.

51. Elisonas, "Inseparable Trinity," pp. 276–78; Yi Hyŏngsŏk, *Imjin chŏllansa* 2:650–65, 674–83, 843–58.

52. Yi Hyŏngsŏk, *Imjin chŏllansa* 1:258–64 for the events surrounding Yi Il. Yi reported that Yi Il was only able to muster a force of about 800 men, but the *Sillok* reported he had a force of about 6,000. According to the *Sŏnjo sujŏng sillok* 26:3b, Sŏnjo 25.4 (1592) (Kuksa p'yŏnch'an wiwŏnhoe ed., *Chosŏn wangjo sillok* [1957] 25:612). See also the brief summary in *Sŏnjo sillok* 26:1a, and Yu Sŏngnyŏng, *Chingbirok* 1:14a, Sŏnggyun'gwan, Tong'a munhwa yon'guso ed., *Sŏaejip, pu Chingbirok* (Seoul: 1959):498. Yu Hyŏngwŏn's account is not exactly the same as the *Sillok*. His version either paraphrases, garbles, or leaves out a number of statements recorded in the *Sillok*. It is likely that he did not have access to the *Sillok* and obtained his information from another source. See Yu Hyŏngwŏn, PGSR 21:17a-b. For Cho Kiryong, see Yi Hyŏngsŏk, *Imjin chŏllansa* 1:280. See pp. 248–89 for description of fighting in 1592, sixth lunar month.

53. Yi Hyŏngsŏk, *Imjin chŏllansa* 1:258–64 for the events surrounding Yi Il. For Cho Kiryong, see p. 280. See pp. 248–89 for description of fighting in 1592, 6th lunar month.

54. *Han'guk kunjesa: Kŭnse Chosŏn chŏn'gip'yŏn* [The military history of Korea, early modern period: Early Chosŏn dynasty] (Seoul: Yukkun ponbu, 1968) 1:321–24.

55. Ibid., pp. 300–301.

56. This information comes from a statement presumably written by a *Sillok* historian, sometime between 1641 and 1657, the dates when the revised *Sŏnjo sillok* was first begun and completed. It is possible that he was one generation removed from the Hideyoshi invasions, three from the 1555 incident. *Sŏnjo sujŏng sillok* 25:19b–20a, Sŏnjo 25.10.kyesa (1591); also cited in *Han'guk kunjesa* 1: 301 n.214. On the dates of the compilation of the original *Sŏnjo sillok* and revised *Sŏnjo sujŏng sillok* see Kuksa p'yŏnch'an wiwŏnhoe ed., *Chosŏn wangjo sillok*, 48 vols. and index (Seoul: 1957), vol. 25, *pŏmnye* [explanatory notes] by the general editor, Sin Sŏkho, pp. 1–2, dated 1957.

57. Yi Hyŏngsŏk, *Imjin chŏllansa* 3:1391.

58. Ibid. 1:443–44 (on tactics), 465–78, 497; 2:692, 707–12; 3:1389–95, 1398–99.

59. See ibid. 3:1287–91, for a discussion of men who ran away from battle.

60. For heroes, see the description of Chŏng Pal's exploits at the battle of Pusan in ibid., pp. 235–41, and those of the Tongnae magistrate (Pusa), Song Sanghyŏn, at the battle of Tongnae (4.15 lunar) against a Japanese force of 20,000, in ibid., pp. 240–49. For the failure of Sin Rip, the general circuit defense commander (Tosunbyŏnsa), to defend Bird Pass (Saejae) at the battle of Ch'ungju on May 17–19, 1592, see ibid., pp. 254, 266–77. Yi Hyŏngsŏk rebutted the charges against Sin, that he erred in failing to defend Bird Pass, and said that he was just overwhelmed by superior and better trained troops. For the battle at Mugye, see ibid., pp. 324–26, for Wŏn Ho at Kumip'o, see pp. 334–36, for the battle at Un'am, see ibid., pp. 362–64. Korean forces suffered disastrous defeat soon after at the battle of Yong'in just south of Seoul (July 7–14, 1592) and opened the path to Seoul despite an enormous numerical advantage (50,000 to only 2,000 Japanese troops) because of poor tactics and organization. See ibid. 1:327–34. For the failure to defend the route to Seoul, see ibid. 1:198–204; 3:1280–85.

61. Ibid. 1:143–47, 152–53, 287–91, 314–24.

62. Elisonas, "Inseparable Trinity," pp. 276–78; Yi Hyŏngsŏk, *Imjin chŏllansa* 2:864–70.

63. Hideyoshi's seven conditions that were not revealed to the Ming emperor were: (1) investiture of a Ming princess as the queen of Japan; (2) conclusion of a treaty of trade and friendship between Japan and Ming China; (3) an exchange of oaths and pledges between officials of the two countries; (4) cession of four Korean provinces to Japan; (5) conveyance of a Korean prince and a couple of high officials to Japan as hostages; (6) return of the two captured Korean princes; and (7) a pledge signed by Korean officials and presented to Japan to abide by the treaty. Yi Hyŏngsŏk, *Imjin chŏllansa* 2:876.

64. Ibid. 2:889, 914–23. Yi Hyŏngsŏk believed that the peace negotiations were maintained mainly by the efforts of Konishi Yukinaga and Shen Wei-ching, including their willingness to take the risk of forging the letter of submission from Hideyoshi to the Ming emperor. They sent Konishi Joan with the seven conditions imposed by Hideyoshi to China to ask for *ponggong* (investiture and tribute), dispatched two Chinese officials to Japan to conduct peace talks with Hideyoshi, and created two phony officials on their own authority to further the negotiations, a Chinjusa (envoy to present a memorial to the emperor) and a Ming imperial envoy (from the Ming emperor to Hideyoshi). Ibid. 2:863.

65. Ibid. 2:922–29. Shih Hsing, the Ming minister of war, who was the leading official at the Ming court responsible for the negotiations, and Shen Wei-ching, the leading negotiator, were both cashiered after the negotiations fell apart. Shih died in jail, and Shen was executed. Ibid. 2:931–39; Ray Huang, "Lung-ch'ing and Wan-li Reigns, 1576–1620," p. 571.

66. Yi Hyŏngsŏk said that Third State Councilor Yi Wŏn'ik was the only Westerner who refused to take sides. Yi Hyŏngsŏk, *Imjin chŏllansa* 2:992–98. Yi Wŏn'ik's biography in KSDSJ 2:1191–92 does not give his factional affiliation, but notes that early in his life he was something of a loner who had few friends, but Yu Sŏngnyŏng (Southerner) recognized his capacity and recommended him for office. Later he served under Yulgok (esteemed by the Westerners after his death) in Hwanghae Province, was appointed chief state councilor under King Kwanghaegun (who was supported by the

Great Northern splinter faction of the Easterners), but was exiled for opposing the plan to depose the grand dowager. He was finally recalled to office by the Westerners after they deposed Kwanghaegun.

67. Yi Hyŏngsŏk, *Imjin chŏllansa* 2:761, 767, 791–94, 835–36, 945–48, 990, 1032–39; 3:1400; Elisonas, "Inseparable Trinity," pp. 278–87.

68. Elisonas, "Inseparable Trinity," pp. 288–90; Asao Naohiro, "The Sixteenth-Century Unification," pp. 72–73; Yi Hyŏngsŏk, *Imjin chŏllansa* 2:949.

69. Yi Hyŏngsŏk, *Imjin chŏllansa* 3:1254.

70. Ibid.

71. Ibid. 3:1255, 1318–21.

72. Ibid. 1:47; 3:1264, 1304.

73. Ibid. 1:453–62; 3:1305. On the introduction of muskets, see 1:122, 3:1305–06. Korean defenses suffered a major blow at the beginning of the war when some residents of Seoul burned down the weapons bureau (Kun'gisi), destroying its cache of weapons. This was part of a number of spontaneous risings against the regime by the population, such as the destruction of the Ministry of Punishments with its slave records, and uprisings at the Imjin River, Kaesŏng, and Pyongyang. Ibid. 1:464.

74. PGSR 21:42a–44b, 14a-b; Yi Hyŏngsŏk, *Imjin chŏllansa* 3:1357. For a discussion of Ch'i's methods in fighting pirates in Che-chiang during the Chia-ch'ing era (1522–66), a list of the contents of the *Chi-hsiao hsin-shu*, and Yu Sŏngnyŏng's recommendations, see *Han'guk kunjesa: Kŭnse Chosŏn hugip'yŏn* 2:3–10.

75. For descriptions of the various types of cannon used, see Yi Hyŏngsŏk, *Imjin chŏllansa* 3:1306.

76. Ibid. 2:700, 766.

77. Ibid. 2:1163.

78. Ibid. 1:183, 186; 2:745, 765. For Yi Sugwang's support for the Military Training Agency and the deficiencies of military training see ibid., pp. 1260–61.

79. Kyŏnggi Province was excluded after the Manchu invasion of 1636–37. KSDSJ 1:676. For studies of the founding of the Military Training Agency, see Ch'a Munsŏp, "Sŏnjojo ŭi Hullyŏn-dogam [The military training agency of King Sŏnjo's reign], in idem, *Chosŏn sidae kunje yŏn'gu* [Studies of the military system of the Chosŏn period] (Seoul: Tan'guk taehakkyo ch'ulp'anbu, 1973), pp. 158–78, and *Han'guk kunjesa* 2:13–19, written by Yi Kyŏmju. On the founding of the agency, see also *Man'gi yoram*, kunjŏngp'yŏn, pp. 215–17, 227; Yi Hyŏngsŏk, *Imjin chŏllansa* 2:745.

80. Yi Hyŏngsŏk, *Imjin chŏllansa* 3:1265. The source, unavailable to me, was Cho Kyŏngnam's *Nanjung chamnok* [Miscellany on the Imjin War], *kwŏn* 2 (Seoul: Minjok munhwa ch'ujinhoe, 1977).

81. The terms *chujin* (main garrison) and Chŏlchesa (main garrison commander), that Yu Sŏngnyŏng used, were different titles for the same kind of provincial garrison organization adopted in 1466. *Han'guk kunjesa* 1:114–17. For the late Koryŏ period see ibid. 1:103–10; for figures on types of troops in Sejong's reign, see 1:123 for Kyŏngsang Province, 1:129–134 for the whole country, and the table on type of soldier and troop strength on 1:118; for discussion of the Three-Wing reform of Sejo, see 1:157–59; for

chin'gwan system, see 1:159–162. The map facing 1:168 gives a good picture of the disposition of the various levels of garrisons throughout the country.

82. PGSR 21:17a–18a; Yi Hyŏngsŏk, *Imjin chŏllansa* 2:769.

83. PGSR 21:17a-b; *Sŏnjo sillok* 49:24b (1594); Yu Sŏngnyŏng's *Chingbirok* 1:14a, Sŏnggyun'gwan, Tong'a munhwa yon'guso ed., *Sŏaejip, pu Chingbirok* (Seoul: 1959), p. 498. The account in *Han'guk kunjesa* 1:296–98, discusses Yu Sŏngnyŏng's role in criticizing the *chesŭng pangnyak* system at the time and gives the dates for the period during which Yu's proposal was adopted by King Sŏnjo. The second volume of this study, *Han'guk kunjesa: Kŭnse Chosŏn hugip'yŏn* (Seoul: Yukkun ponbu, 1977), pp. 3–10, gives a brief synopsis of the Imjin War, 1592–98; 2:23–26, reviews Yu Sŏngnyŏng's discussion of the *chesŭng pangnyak* system and his proposal for restoration of the *chin'gwan* system. This source is hereinafter referred to as *Han'guk kunjesa*, vol. 2.

84. PGSR 21:19a–20b. For another discussion of Sung dynasty border defense tactics see Yi Hyŏngsŏk, *Imjin chŏllansa* 3:1253–54.

85. *Han'guk kunjesa* 2:26–37; Ch'a Munsŏp, "Sog'ogun yŏn'gu," pp. 179–228. See *Sŏnjo sujŏng sillok* 28:15a-b, Sŏngjo 27.10.ŭlsa (1594). Yu said that he learned about the *Chi-hsiao hsin-shu* from the Korean official Yi Tŏkhyŏng who was informed about the text by the Chinese general, Ch'i Chin, the son of Ch'i Chi-kuang. Yu had it copied by scribes and recommended it to the king on 1593.4.kyesa. See *Chingbirok* 3:10b–11a, Sŏnggyun'gwan ed. (1959), pp. 539–40, and *chüan* 1 of Ch'i Chi-kuang, *Chi-hsiao hsin-shu*, *Wan-yu wen-k'o* series, ed. Wang Yün-wu (Shanghai: Commercial Press, Chung-hua min-kuo 27th year, 1939), pp. 21–29.

86. On March 28, 1593 (2.26 lunar) an order allowed official and private slaves who joined the army to be entered into the registers for *yang'in* (commoners). On July 12 (6.14 lunar) tests for skill were instituted for slaves in accordance with the regulations for the Sam'ŭisa (Bureau of Doctors) *chapkwa* examination, and those who passed were immediately treated as *yang'in* and attached to the Ingnimwi (Winged Forest Guard). Slaves were also manumitted for presenting decapitated heads of Japanese or making grain contributions. Yi Hyŏngsŏk, *Imjin chŏllansa* 3:1297, 1353.

87. Ibid. 1:799; 2:1238.

88. Ibid. 2:1159, 1163, 1665, 1668.

89. The new *sog'o* troops were organized into 11-man squads (*tae*) headed by a squad leader (Taech'ong). A banner or platoon (*ki*) was made up of 3 squads, 33 men under a platoon leader (Kich'ong); 3 banners a company (*ch'o*) of 99 men under a company commander (Ch'ogwan); 5 companies a battalion (*sa*) of 495 men under a battalion commander (P'ach'ong). Yu Sŏngnyŏng, "Regulations for the Organization of Troop Units" (P'yŏn'o samok) 15:18a-b, attached to a directive to the Sunch'alsa of Kyŏnggi Province, dated 1595.12.8, in *Sŏae munjip*, p. 696; cited in Ch'a Munsŏp, "Sog'ogun yŏn'gu" [A study of the Sog'o soldiers], pp. 13, 17. This was the model for organization at the battalion level and below, but the quotas were not strictly observed. Yu Sŏngnyŏng, in discussing the advantages of the *sog'o* system, said that battalions consisted of 360 men, divided into 5 companies with 3 banner-platoons (*ki*) each, 3 squads (*tae*) of 8 men per platoon, and 2 files (*o*) per platoon of 4 men each. The source is *Sŏae munjip* 14:6a

(Seoul: Taedong munhwa yŏn'guwŏn, 1958):240, cited in Ch'a Munsŏp, "Sog'ogun yŏn'gu," p. 184.

90. The detailed description of *sog'o* organization up to and including battalions is for the Haeju area in 1595, see *Sŏnjo sillok* 65:18a, Sŏnjo 28.7.kyŏngjin, cited in *Han'guk kunjesa* 2:29, 33 n. 59. The figures for Kyŏnggi Province are from ibid. 2:32, which is based on Yu Sŏngnyŏng, "Kunmun tŭngnok" (Record of the military establishment) in *Chingbirok* 15:1a–3b; "I Kyŏnggi Sunch'alsa mun" [Message sent to the mobile inspector of Kyŏnggi Province, a post held concurrently by the provincial governor] in ibid. 15:3b–4b; "Pyŏn'o samok" [Regulations for military organization] in ibid. 15:18a–20b. See Sŏnggyun'gwan ed. (1958):688–90, 696–97. See also the section on *sog'o*, *Sŏae munjip* 14:5b–6b, p. 240.

The number of regiments per province evidently varied. According to the *Soktaejŏn* [Dynastic code, continued] of 1746, Kangwŏn Province had only three, while four provinces had six, and Pyŏng'an had nine. *Han'guk kunjesa* 2:33, n.60. For an extensive discussion of the composition of the Kyŏnggi and other provincial regiments, see Ch'a Munsŏp, "Sog'ogun yŏn'gu," pp. 191–95.

91. The information for this battalion was part of a report dated the fifth month of 1596 for the regiment (*yŏng*) headquartered at the Anju *chin'gwan*. See *Han'guk kunjesa*, 2:33–35, esp. the table on p. 34. The information derives from the *Chin'gwan kwanbyŏng p'yŏn'o chankwŏn* [A fragment of the organization of government troops in a *chin'-gwan*]. See also Ch'a Munsŏp's discussion of the organization in P'yong'an and Anju in "Sog'ogun yŏn'gu," pp. 191–92.

92. *Han'guk kunjesa* 2:33.

93. *Pibyŏn chamnok* [Miscellaneous notes on national defense], in Yu Sŏngnyŏng, *Kugyŏk Sŏaejip* 2 (Seoul: Minjok munhwa ch'ujinhoe, 1977):46–47 of the original *Hanmun* (classical Chinese) portion of the text. I am indebted to Yi Kyŏmju, the author of the section of *Han'guk kunjesa* 2:35–36, for discovering these ideas in Yu Sŏngnyŏng's works.

94. Directive to the Sunch'alsa and Pyŏngsa of P'yŏng'an Province, "Kunmun tŭngnok," in the *Chingbirok*, 16:13b–14b, Sŏnggyun'gwan ed. (1959):714; "Pibyŏn chamnok," in *Kugyŏk sŏaejip* 2:46–47; *Han'guk kunjesa* 2:36.

95. *Han'guk Kunjesa* 2:37.

96. *Sŏnjo sillok* 111:2b–3a, Sŏnjo 32.4.chŏngsa, cited in Ch'a Munsŏp, "Sog'ogun yŏn'gu, p. 195.

97. For citations, see the discussion in ibid., pp. 96–97.

98. Yi Hyŏngsŏk, *Imjin chŏllansa* 3:1278–79. Yi put the blame on King Sŏnjo for laxity in attending to rebuilding of the army.

99. Ibid. 3:1322–23.

100. Ibid. 2:972.

CHAPTER 3. Post-Imjin Developments in Military Defense and the Economy

1. The names of some of the factions have nothing to do with regional loyalties.

2. Yi Sangbaek, *Han'guksa: Kŭnse hugip'yŏn* [History of Korea: Late recent times]

(Seoul: published by Ŭryu Munhwasa for the Chindan hakhoe, 1965), pp. 82–87; Franz Michael, *The Origin of Manchu Rule in China* (Baltimore: Johns Hopkins Press, 1942), pp. 39–47; Frederic Wakeman, Jr., *The Great Enterprise: The Manchu Reconstruction of Imperial Order in Seventeenth-Century China* (Berkeley and Los Angeles: University of California Press, 1985), 1:49–82.

3. Yi Pyŏngdo, "Kwanghaegun ŭi tae Hugŭm chŏngch'aek" [Kwanghaegun's policy toward the Later Chin], *Kuksasang ŭi chemunje* 1 (March 1959): 135–73; Wakeman, *Great Enterprise* 1:62–63; Inaba Iwakichi, *Kōkaikun jidai no mansei kankei* [Manchurian-Korean relations in the age of Kwanghaegun] (Keijō: ōsakaya goshoten, 1933), esp. chap. 5.

4. Yi T'aejin, "Chung'ang Ogunyŏngje ŭi sŏngnip kwajŏng" [The process of the establishment of the central five division system], *Han'guk kunjesa* (1977), pp. 88–89; Chŏn Haejŏng, "Kado ŭi myŏngch'in e kwanhan sogo" [A short study on the name, Ka Island], *Seoul taehakkyo nonmunjip*, inmun sahoe kwahak, no. 9 (1959), included in idem, *Han-Jung Kwan'gyesa yŏn'gu* [Studies in the history of Korean-Chinese relations] (Seoul: Ilchogak, 1970), pp. 156–64; Wakeman, *The Great Enterprise* 1:127.

5. Kim Yongdŏk has argued that in foreign policy the realism of Kwanghaegun was replaced by the almost mindless commitment of the Westerner Chu Hsi Neo-Confucianists to principles of moral obligation, duty, and honor. "Sohyŏn seja yŏn'gu" [A study of Crown Prince Sohyŏn], *Sahak yŏn'gu* 18 (Sept. 1964):436–37.

6. Even though the king authorized a force of only 500 men for the Howich'ŏng, the unit's commanders continued to recruit men on their own until it had grown to 1,000 men by 1624. Yi T'aejin, "Chung'ang Ogunyŏngje ŭi sŏngnip kwajŏng," chap. 2 in *Han'guk kunjesa* (1977), pp. 74–75; idem, *Chosŏn hugi ŭi chŏngch'i wa kunyŏngje pyŏnchŏn* [Politics and changes in the army division system in the late Chosŏn period] (Seoul: Han'guk yŏn'guwŏn, 1985), pp. 81–93, 98–102.

7. Yi T'aejin, *Han'guk kunjesa* (1977), p. 73; idem, *Chosŏn hugi*, p. 84.

8. Yi T'aejin, *Han'guk kunjesa* (1977), pp. 76–80; idem, *Chosŏn hugi*, pp. 90–96.

9. The king's 6,000 men consisted of a couple of thousand troops in the Military Training Agency, 1,000 at Changdan, 2,000 at Suwŏn, a mere 200 in the new Royal Division, and 500 under the four generals of the Howich'ŏng (Royal Retinue Office). Yi T'aejin, *Han'guk kunjesa* (1977), pp. 79–80; idem, *Chosŏn hugi*, pp. 94–96.

10. Its men were also exempted from service on the northern frontier, in contrast to the Military Training Agency troops, whose musketeers in particular were often transferred to the north for duty. Yi T'aejin, *Han'guk kunjesa* (1977), pp. 80–82; idem, *Chosŏn hugi*, pp. 96–98.

11. Yi T'aejin, *Han'guk kunjesa* (1977), pp. 83, 85–87; idem, *Chosŏn hugi*, pp. 98–106.

12. Only after the invasion did the government authorize the mobilization of 30,000 more troops from the southern provinces. Yi T'aejin, *Han'guk kunjesa* (1977), pp. 90–91; idem, *Chosŏn hugi*, pp. 109–13.

13. The Nosŏ were also referred to as the Kongsŏ (or merit-subject Westerners). One of their leaders was Kim Yu, who favored the appointment of a member of the Small Northerner faction, Nam Igong, to the post of censor-general in 1625. Kim was trying to build up a base of political followers and King Injo wanted to limit the dominance of

the Westerner merit subjects. They were opposed by Yi Kwi and a younger group of Westerners, known as the Young Westerners (Sosŏ), connected with the later Ch'ŏngsŏ or Pure Westerner faction. According to O Such'ang, however, Yi Kwi and Kim Chajŏm were not on the best terms with Yi Sŏ and Kim Yu, the original conspirators against Kwanghaegun, because they did not join the plot until 1622. In other words, the members of the supreme commander's forces and the rear capital guard were also divided among themselves. O Such'ang, "Injodae chŏngch'i seryŏk ŭi tonghyang" [Trends in political forces in King Injo's reign], *Han'guk saron* 13 (August 1985):84–92; *Kuksadaesajŏn* 1:354; Yi T'aejin, *Chosŏn hugi*, pp. 113–14.

14. Yi T'aejin, *Han'guk kunjesa* (1977), pp. 90–94; idem, *Chosŏn hugi*, pp. 114–16; O Such'ang, "Injodae chŏngch'i seryŏk" (1985), p. 94. The agreement was signed on 1627.3.3 lunar, only two months after the invasion. The king agreed to cease using the Ming year-period and to send a hostage to the Later Chin court. By the fifth lunar month Manchu forces withdrew from the peninsula.

15. He remained tsar even after he resigned command of the Anti-Manchu Division in 1634.

16. Kim Yu refused the request of Yi Sibaek, then head of the Defense Command (Suŏsa), to replace troops assigned to his unit from the distant Kyŏngsang and Kangwŏn provinces with men living in Kyŏnggi Province, a decision that later returned to haunt him. Yi Kŭng'ik recounted the story that when Injo asked Yi Sibaek why his command was in such bad condition, Yi replied that it was because the supreme commander, Kim Yu, had refused his requests for troop reassignments. Kim Yu was so angered by the remark that he had Yi Sibaek arrested on some other charge and beaten bloody, shocking everyone around. Yi Kŭng'ik, *Yŏllyŏsil kisul*, 27 Pyŏngja horan chŏngch'uk Namhan ch'ulsŏng (Keijō: Chōsen kosho kankōkai, 1913) 5:120–21, cited in Yi T'aejin, *Chosŏn hugi*, p. 121 n.37.

17. Yi T'aejin, *Han'guk kunjesa* (1977), pp. 94–101; idem, *Chosŏn hugi*, pp. 117–27.

18. Yi Kŭng'ik, *Yŏllyŏsil kisul*, 27, 5:120–21, cited in Yi T'aejin, *Chosŏn hugi*, p. 133 n.86.

19. Yi Kŭng'ik, *Yŏllyŏsil kisul*, 27, 5:121–22.

20. For the account of these events, see ibid., pp. 121–59; Yi T'aejin, *Han'guk kunjesa* (1977), pp. 102–8; idem, *Chosŏn hugi*, pp. 127–36; for domestic politics at the time of the invasion, see O Such'ang, "Injodae chŏngch'i seryŏk" (1985), pp. 97ff.

21. Yi Kŭng'ik, *Yŏllyŏsil kisul*, 27, 5: 120.

22. Kim Yongdŏk, "Sohyŏn seja," pp. 442–44, 448; Yi T'aejin, *Han'guk kunjesa* (1977), pp. 108–11; idem, *Chosŏn hugi*, pp. 136–43.

23. Yi T'aejin, *Chosŏn hugi*, pp. 143–45.

24. The governor of Hwanghae Province, Kim Hong'uk, in a courageous memorial delivered to King Hyojong in 1654, charged that Kim Chajŏm had conspired with Lady Cho, Injo's favorite, to falsify the charges against Princess Kang, and that he had also been responsible for the deaths of Prince Sohyŏn's two sons. Kim Yongdŏk "Sohyŏn seja yŏn'gu," pp. 433–90, pp. 482–83 for the last item; Yi T'aejin, *Han'guk kunjesa* (1977), p. 114; idem, *Chosŏn hugi*, pp. 146–47; O Such'ang, "Injodae chŏngch'i seryŏk," pp. 97–98; Yi Kung'ik, *Yŏllyŏsil kisul*, 29, 5:266–81.

25. Yi T'aejin, *Han'guk kunjesa* (1977), pp. 111–15; idem, *Chosŏn hugi*, pp. 147–50; O Such'ang, "Injodae chŏngch'i seryŏk," pp. 111–12.

26. Ch'ŏn Kwan'u, "Han'guk t'oji chedosa, ha" (part 2), in *Han'guk munhwasa taegye* [A grand outline of Korean cultural history] (Seoul: Koryŏ taehakkyo minjok munhwa yŏn'guso, 1965), p. 1430.

27. Ibid., pp. 1505–7, table, p. 1507.

28. Ibid., p. 1506.

29. By 1807, 37,926 *kyŏl* of land, or 2.6 percent of the total registered land in the nation belonged to this category. Ibid., p. 1508–10.

30. These figures for average acreage corresponded more or less to the least two fertile categories of *kyŏl* since the areas of the six grades of one *kyŏl* in the early Chosŏn dynasty were 2.25, 2.65, 3.21, 3.786, 5.63, and 9.01 acres. The survey conducted by the Japanese in 1901 reported that the average size of a *kyŏl* varied by province, reflecting the greater fertility of land in the south where double-cropping of wet rice agriculture was more productive than the greater dry-field farming of the north. Ibid., pp. 1492, 1495.

31. Kim Yongsŏp, *Chosŏn hugi nong'ŏpsa yŏn'gu: nongch'on kyŏngje, sahoe pyŏndong* [Studies in the agricultural history of late Chosŏn: The village economy and social change] (Seoul: Ilchogak, 1970), pp. 160–61.

32. Ibid., pp. 136–37, 149–53.

33. Ibid., p. 155.

34. Ibid., pp. 164–65.

35. Ibid., p. 162, table 61.

36. Shikata Hiroshi, "Richō jinkō ni kansuru ichi kenkyū" [A study on Yi dynasty population], in *Chōsen shakai hōseishi kenkyū* [Studies in the social and legal history of Korea] (Tokyo: Iwanami shoten, 1937), pp. 257–388; idem, "Richō jinkō ni kansuru mibun kaikyūbetsuteki kansatsu" [An investigation of Yi dynasty population in terms of status and class], in Chōsen teikoku daigaku hōgakkai, ed. *Chōsen keizai no kenkyū* [Studies in the economy of Korea] (Tokyo: Iwanami shoten, 1938) 3:363–482, appendix, pp. 1–33 and attached charts; Kim Yongsŏp, *Chosŏn hugi nong'ŏpsa yŏn'gu: Nongch'on kyŏngje, sahoe pyŏndong* (1970), pp. 158–59; p. 158, table 59.

37. Kim Yongsŏp, *Chosŏn hugi nong'ŏpsa yŏn'gu: Nongch'on kyŏngje, sahoe pyŏndong* (1970), pp. 149–54, 157, tables 38–56.

38. Kim Yongsŏp, "Chosŏn hugi ŭi sudojak kisul: Iyangbŏp ŭi pogŭp e taehayŏ" [The technology of rice culture in late Chosŏn: The spread of transplantation], in *Chosŏn hugi nong'ŏpsa yŏn'gu: Nong'ŏp pyŏndong, nonghak sajo*, [Studies in the agricultural history of late Chosŏn: Changes in agriculture and trends in agricultural studies] (Seoul: Ilchogak, 1971), pp. 2–18, originally published in *Asea yŏn'gu*, vol. 13 (March 1964). For a discussion of the necessity of water supplies, especially during the crucial transplanting of seedlings from the seed bed to the main fields, see idem, "Chosŏn hugi ŭ sudojak kisul: Iyang kwa suri munje" [The technology of wet rice agriculture in late Chosŏn: The problems of transplantation and irrigation], in *Chosŏn hugi nong'ŏpsa yŏn'gu: Nong'ŏp pyŏndong, nonghak sajo* pp. 72–76. See also Tony Michell, "Fact and Hypothesis in Yi Dynasty Economic History: The Demographic Dimension," *Korean Studies Forum*, no. 6 (Winter-Spring 1979/1980), pp. 83–84.

39. Kim Yongsŏp, "Chosŏn hugi ŭi sudojak kisul: Iyangbŏp ŭi pogŭp e taehayŏ," pp. 18–37. See idem, "Chosŏn hugi ŭ sudojak kisul: Iyang kwa suri munje," (1971), pp. 78–79, for evidence that magistrates were required to report damage to crops for assessment of tax reductions even though transplanting was used.

40. Kim Yongsŏp, "Chosŏn hugi ŭi sudojak kisul: Iyangbŏp ŭi pogŭp e taehayŏ," p. 35, n.82.

41. Kim Yongsŏp, "Chosŏn hugi ŭi sudojak kisul: To, maek imojak ŭi pogŭp e taehayŏ" [The technology of wet rice agriculture in late Chosŏn: The spread of rice/barley double cropping], in *Chosŏn hugi nong'ŏpsa yŏn'gu: Nongch'on kyŏngje, sahoe pyŏndong*, (1970), pp. 40–71.

42. Yi Sangbaek, *Han'guksa: Kŭnse chŏn'gip'yŏn*, pp. 476–78.

43. I reach this conclusion despite the recent argument by Ch'oe Yun'o in his "Sipp'alshipku segi nong'ŏp koyong nodong ŭi chŏn'gae wa paltal" [The expansion and development of agricultural hired labor in the eighteenth and nineteenth centuries] *Han'guksa yŏn'gu* 77 (June 1992):57–88, who asserts the creation of a full-scale wage system and commodification of labor in this period. Even though his focus is on agricultural rather than industrial labor, his evidence is mostly qualitative and insufficient to prove the percentage of work performed by wage labor and the degree of increase over the fifteenth century.

44. Kang Man'gil, "Sugong'ŏp" [Handicrafts], in Kuksa p'yŏnch'an wiwŏnhoe, ed., *Han'guksa*, vol. 10, *Chosŏn: Yangban kwallyo kukka ŭi sahoe kujo* [Chosŏn: The social structure of the yangban-bureaucratic state] (Seoul: Taehan min'guk Mungyobu, Kuksa p'yŏnch'an wiwŏnhoe, 1974), pp. 375–82.

45. Sung Jae Koh [Ko Sŭngje], "Myŏn'ŏp" [Cotton textiles]), in Kuksa p'yŏnch'an wiwŏnhoe, ed., *Han'guksa*, 10:325–35.

46. Yi Sangbaek, *Han'guksa: Kŭnse chŏn'gip'yŏn* [History of Korea: Early Modern Period] (Seoul: Ŭryu munhwasa, 1962), pp. 476–78.

47. Yu Wŏndong, "Sang'ŏp," in Kuksa p'yŏnch'an wiwŏnhoe, ed., *Han'guksa* 10:287–305; Yi Sangbaek, *Han'guksa: Kŭnse chŏn'gip'yŏn*, pp. 482–83.

48. Yu Wŏndong, "Sang'ŏp," in Kuksa p'yŏnch'an wiwŏnhoe, ed., *Han'guksa* 10:294–95.

PART II. Introduction

1. See James B. Palais, "Confucianism and the Aristocratic/Bureaucratic Balance in Korea," *Harvard Journal of Asiatic Studies* 44, no. 2 (December 1984):427–68; Robert P. Hymes, *Statesmen and Gentlemen, The Elite of Fu-chou, Chiang-hsi in Northern and Southern Sung* (Cambridge, Cambridge University Press, 1986); Peter K. Bol, *"This Culture of Ours": Intellectual Transitions in T'ang and Sung China* (Stanford, Calif.: Stanford University Press, 1992).

2. This statement conflicts with much contemporary research in South Korea, which posits the disruption of the social structure and the weakening of the yangban in the eighteenth and nineteenth centuries. This question will be raised later.

CHAPTER 4. Remolding the Ruling Class through Education and Schools

1. Yu Hyŏngwŏn, *Pan'gye surok*, with *Purok p'oyu* [Supplement], ed. by Kojŏn kanhaenghoe [The Classic Publication Society] (Seoul: Tongguk munhwasa, 1958) 12:49a. This edition of Yu Hyŏngwŏn's *Pan'gye surok* will be used throughout this book and referred to as PGSR with numbers referring first to the *kwŏn* and then to the folio pagination. See also the *Chŭngbo Pan'gye surok*, Han'gukhak kibon ch'ongsŏ, no. 10 (Seoul: Kyŏng'in munhwasa, 1974). I also used the Korean translation and annotation by Han Changgyŏng, *Kugyŏk chuhae Pan'gye surok*, 6 vols. (Seoul: Ch'ungnam taehakkyo, 1962) (for vol. l). There is another translation by the Chosŏn minjujuŭi inmin konghwaguk kwahagwŏn, *P'an'gye surok* (Pyongyang: Kwahagwŏn ch'ulp'ansa, 1963) (for vol. 4), but vol. l covering the land system was not available to me.

2. PGSR 12:48a.

3. See Hoyt Tillman's discussion of the views of Chang Tsai and the Ch'eng brothers in the Northern Sung dynasty over the possibility of restoring ancient institutions. Hoyt Cleveland Tillman, *Utilitarian Confucianism: Ch'en Liang's Challenge to Chu Hsi* (Cambridge: Harvard University, Council on East Asian Studies, 1982), pp. 42–43.

4. PGSR 12:48b.

5. Ibid. 10:30b

6. Ibid. 12:49a.

7. Ibid. 12:48a.

8. Ibid. 12:48a.

9. See Tillman, *Utilitarian Confucianism*, for a discussion of the utilitarian thought in the Sung dynasty, particularly that of Ch'en Liang.

10. PGSR 10:30b

11. Ibid. 11:1a-b.

12. For the Ssu-t'u, Yu cites the *Book of History* (*Shu-ching*) and *Rites of Chou*, ibid. 11:1b, 2b. For description of other officials, like the *shih-shih*, *pao-shih*, *ta ssu-lo*, and *lo-cheng*, and the school hierarchy, see ibid. 11:4a, 6b–7b, 9a–b, 10b–12a, 14a, 15a.

13. Ibid. 11:9b, 3a, 7b.

14. Ibid. 11:12a. See Wm. Theodore de Bary's discussion of Chu Hsi's ideas for establishing a graded scheme of education from childhood in "Chu Hsi's Aims as an Educator," in Wm. Theodore de Bary and John Chaffee, eds. *Neo-Confucian Education: The Formative Stage* (Berkeley and Los Angeles: University of California Press, 1989), pp. 186–218.

15. PGSR 11:3a; see also the Wang-chih section of the *Book of Rites*, ibid. 11:9b.

16. Peter Bol, *This Culture of Ours: Intellectual Transitions in T'ang and Sung China* (Stanford, Calif.: Stanford University Press, 1992).

17. PGSR 11:9b.

18. Commentary on the *Rites of Chou*, ibid. 11:4a.

19. PGSR 11:2a, 9a-b; see also the Lu-shih commentary.

20. Ibid. 11:3a.

21. Ibid. 11:4a-b.

22. Ibid. 11:5a-b; see also the Wang-chih section of the *Book of Rites*, ibid. 11:9b, and the Hsüeh-chi section of the *Book of Rites*, 11:6b.

23. Ibid. 11:9b–11a.

24. Ibid. 11:14b. John Chaffee discusses the problem of regional quotas in the Sung dynasty in *The Thorny Gates of Learning in Sung China: A Social History of Examinations* (Cambridge: Cambridge University Press, 1985).

25. PGSR 11:13a.

26. Ibid. 11, 2b, 4a, 10a, 14b.

27. See Yu's quote of Chu Hsi about the correspondence between clothing and rank in ancient times, ibid. 11:13b, and exemption from miscellaneous labor service (*yoyŏk*) for the "accomplished scholars" (*chosa*), ibid. 11:10b.

28. Ibid. 11:6b–7a; 10b; commentary of Mr. Fang; 11a; 11b.

29. Ibid. 11:11b, 11a.

30. For the *Book of Etiquette and Ceremonial* (*I-li*) portion, see ibid. 11:41–55a; for the *Book of Rites*, see 11:53a–55a.

31. Yu also appended to this section reference to the use of the wine-drinking rite in the T'ang dynasty in association with the presentation of degree-holders or examination passers at the *chou* or prefectural level. Here men of worth were honored as guests and the degree-holding expectant officials took part in the ceremony along with the district magistrate (Tz'u-shih) who functioned as host. In the winter other wine rituals were held for honoring the elderly. The T'ang-chih section of the *T'ang-shu*, for the *chen-kuan* period, 627–50, cited in ibid. 11:55a–60b.

32. Ibid. 12:25a-b. In 178 B.C., Emperor Wen of the Han dynasty ordered the recommendation of scholars for positions, and in 165 B.C. he also ordered feudal lords, princes, and high officials to recommend worthy and good men. Ibid. 14:2b. Another case of recommendation was mentioned for high officials in the reigns of Emperors Wen (r. 180–157), Ching (156–140), and Yüan (r. 48–32). Ibid. 14:2b–3b.

33. Ibid. 12:1b–12a, 3a–b.

34. Ibid. 12:3b–4b.

35. Ibid. 12:28a-b.

36. Ibid. 12:29a.

37. Ibid. 14:4a–5a, 30a-b, *T'ung-tien*, ch. 18, p. 103. See Ch'ing-lien Huang, "The Recruitment and Assessment of Civil Officials under the T'ang" (Ph.D. diss., Princeton University, 1986), p. 106.

38. Miyazaki Ichisada, *Ajia rekishi jiten* [Dictionary of Asian history] (Tokyo: Heibonsha, 1962) 2:391–92; Miyazaki, *Kyūhin kanjinhō no kenkyū* (Kyōto: Tōyōshi kenkyū, 1956).

39. PGSR 12:6a-b. At first the Chung-cheng was assigned to the Chün or commandery. Later in the Chin dynasty (265–90) the system was expanded and a hierarchy of officials were established to perform these tasks at other administrative levels.

40. Ibid. 14:8b–9b.

41. Ibid. 12:7a–8a for the views of Liu I; 8b–9a for the views of Wei Chüan.

42. Ibid. 12:26b–27b.

43. Ibid. 12:10a–b.

44. See ibid. 12:28a for examples.

45. Ch'en quoted Liu I's famous statement that "Among the lower *p'in* grades no important households were to be found, and among the high *p'in* grades no mean families were to be found." Ibid. 12:28b.

46. Ibid. 12:28b.

47. Ibid. 12:27b.

48. Ibid. 12:27b–28a. The emperor, by the way, did not adopt Fu's recommendation.

49. Ibid. 12:29a.

50. Ibid. 12:10b, 29a.

51. Ibid. 12:10b.

52. Ibid. 14:11a-b.

53. Ibid. 12:29b. See also Tu Yu's complaint in the *T'ung-tien* that the Chung-cheng graded people only according to aristocratic status (*men-fa, munbŏl* in Korean). Ibid. 12:6a.

54. Ibid. 10:5a.

55. Ibid. 10:5b.

56. Ibid. 12:4b–6a.

57. Ibid. 12:4b–5a, 26b–27a; also the memorial of Wei Piao of the early first century A.D., 12:26a. For coverage of complaints about the examination system in China, see Chaffee, *Thorny Gates of Learning in Sung China*; Peter K. Bol, "Chu Hsi's Redefinition of Literati Learning," in de Bary and Chaffee, eds., *Neo-Confucian Education*, pp. 151–85; de Bary, "Chu Hsi's Aims as an Educator," in de Bary and Chaffee, eds., *Neo-Confucian Education*, pp. 186–218.

58. PGSR 12:6a, 12a–14a.

59. Arthur F. Wright and Denis Twitchett, eds., *Perspectives on the T'ang* (New Haven, Conn.: Yale University Press, 1973), pp. 4–7, 26–27, 47–49, 52–58, 63–68, 78–82. In Twitchett's opinion, although the examinations still produced only a small fraction of the total posts in the T'ang bureaucracy, the real breakthrough came as a result of more opportunities for employment in provincial administration. Ibid., p. 79.

60. PGSR 12:30a-b, by Li E.

61. Ibid. 12:37a, cf. similar remarks of Tu Yu in ibid. 12:41a. For other statements, see ibid. 12:30a-b, 37a, 33b–34a. The Ministry of Personnel located only in the capital would never be able to gain sufficient information to discipline the magistrates because it judged merit exclusively on literary talent and rank, let alone the deceptions of candidates who illicitly hired skillful writers to take tests for them or paid bribes to clerks. PGSR 12:35b, 39a. See the remarks of Lu Chih during the reign of Te-tsung in the early 790s, ibid. 14:33b–35b.

62. Ibid. 12:35b, 39a.

63. Ibid. 12:14a.

64. Ibid. 12:39a-b.

65. Ibid. 12:37a-b.

66. Ibid. 12:39b, 37a-b.

67. Ibid. 12:32b. He calculated that this figure would adequately fill the roughly 14,000 posts of the early T'ang bureaucracy since that the average official career was about thirty years.

68. Ibid. 12:39b–40a.

69. Ibid. 14:14b. Ch'ing-lien Huang cited Ma Chou's views in "The Recruitment and Assessment of Civil Officials under the T'ang Dynasty," pp. 73–74, and summarized briefly with extensive material in footnotes all criticism of recruitment and assessment in the T'ang, pp. 281–91.

70. PGSR 14:15b–16a; Huang, "Recruitment and Assessment of Civil Officials," p. 283, n. 605, item 2.

71. PGSR 14:15b–16a; Huang, "Recruitment and Assessment of Civil Officials," p. 283, n. 605, item 2.

72. PGSR 14:16a-b.

73. Ibid. 14:33b–35b. Huang discussed two of Lü Chih's memorials between 792 and 794. He also criticized short terms of office and frequent transfer of officials. Emperor Te-tsung, however, did not adopt his ideas. "Recruitment and Assessment of Civil Officials," pp. 183–87; Denis Twitchett, "Lu Chih (754–805): Imperial Adviser and Court Official," in Arthur F. Wright and Denis Twitchett, ed., *Confucian Personalities* (Stanford, Calif.: Stanford University Press, 1962), p. 105.

74. PGSR 12:15b.

75. Ibid. 12:15b–17a.

76. Ibid. 12:42a, 43a.

77. Ibid. 12:41b.

78. Ibid. 12:20a.

79. Thomas H. C. Lee, *Government Education and Examinations in Sung China* (Hong Kong: Chinese University Press, 1985), pp. 241–43.

80. PGSR 12:20b–21a.

81. Ibid. 12:20b.

82. Ibid. 12:46a, 45b.

83. Chaffee, *Thorny Gates of Learning*, pp. 67–68.

84. Ibid., pp. 47–48.

85. For his description of the Ming system, see PGSR 12:21a-b.

86. Ibid. 12:21b–22a.

87. Ibid. 12:22b.

88. Ibid.

89. Ibid.

90. See Hugh Kang, "Institutional Borrowing: The Case of the Chinese Civil Service Examination in Early Koryŏ, *Journal of Asian Studies* 24, no. 1 (November 1974):109–26.

91. PGSR 12:22b–23a.

92. Ibid.

93. For his coverage of Chosŏn, see ibid. 12:23b–24b.

94. Ibid. 12:12b.

95. Ibid. 12:24b.

96. Yi Sŏngmu, "Sŏnch'o ŭi Sŏnggyun'gwan yŏn'gu" [A study of the National Academy in the early Chosŏn dynasty], *Yŏksa hakpo* 35–36 (December 1967):219–68.

97. PGSR 9:40b. For a description of Sung academies, see Chaffee, *Thorny Gates of Learning*, pp. 89–91.

98. PGSR 9:40b.

99. James B. Palais, *Politics and Policy in Traditional Korea* (Cambridge: Harvard University Press, 1975), pp. 110–31.

100. The Taewongun abolished all but forty academies, transferred the Taebodan shrine of the Mandongmyo to the capital, and made no provisions for local shrines. Palais, *Politics and Policy*, chap. 6.

101. See James B. Palais, "Confucianism and the Aristocratic/Bureaucratic Balance in Korea," *Harvard Journal of Asiatic Studies* 44, no. 2 (December 1984):427–68.

102. See Peter Bol's analysis of Chu Hsi's definition of true learning, in "Chu Hsi's Redefinition of Literati Learning," in de Bary and Chaffee, eds., *Neo-Confucian Education*, pp. 156–67.

103. PGSR 10:29a-b.

104. See Peter Bol's description of Chu Hsi's balanced treatment of Wang An-shih and his acceptance of some of Wang's premises, despite his claim that Wang lacked a true understanding of the Confucian Way. "Chu Hsi's Redefinition of Literati Learning," pp. 167–71.

105. PGSR 12:42b.

106. Ibid. 12:43a–44a, 19b.

107. Ibid. 12:44a-b.

108. Ibid. 12:44b–45a.

109. Tillman, *Utilitarian Confucianism*, pp. 145–52.

110. PGSR 12:47a.

111. Ibid. 12:47b.

112. Ibid. 11:18a, 20a-b.

113. Ibid. 11:21a-b.

114. Ibid. 11:22a.

115. Ibid. 11:19a–20a.

116. Ibid. 12:45a.

117. Ibid. 14:40a–41b. For Ch'eng Hao's plan in the Sung dynasty, see Lee, *Government Education and Examinations in Sung China*, p. 241

118. PGSR 11:15b–17b

119. Ibib. 11:17a-b. For Wu Heng's views on the beauties of the ancient schools, see ibid. 11:22a–23a; for Chang Shih's views see 11:23a-b; de Bary, "Chu Hsi's Aims as an Educator," pp. 194, 201.

120. PGSR 11:27a–28b.

121. Ibid. 11:29a–31b.

122. Ibid. 11:31b–41a.

123. Ibid. 11:35a-b.

124. Ibid. 11:36a-b.

125. Ibid. 12:22a-b.

126. Ibid. 10:30a.

127. Ibid. 10:29a–30b.

128. Ibid. 10:10a.

129. Ibid. 10:27b–28a.

130. Ibid. 10:18b–19a. See similar remarks by Yulgok [Yi I] in ibid. 10:32b.

131. This test was similar to the *hsiao-lien-k'ua* of the T'ang. Edward Willett Wagner, *The Literati Purges: Political Conflict in Early Yi Korea* (Cambridge: East Asian Research Center and Havard University Press. 1974), pp. 92–103.

132. PGSR 10:27a.

133. Wagner, *Literati Purges*, p. 98.

134. PGSR 10:32b–33b.

135. Ibid. 10:28a-b.

136. Ibid. 10:26a.

137. Ibid. 10:30b.

138. Ibid. 10:2b, see also 10:31a–32a.

139. For the views of Yü Chi, see ibid. 10:2b–3a; for those of Ch'iu Chün, see 10:3a–4a; for Ma Tuan-lin's (*Wen-hsien t'ung-k'ao*) praise of the careful selection of education officials during the yüan-feng era of the Sung (1078–86), see ibid. 10:2b.

140. Ibid. 10:1a. Yu noted that the idea of separate quarters was copied from Ch'eng-tzu's [Ch'eng Hao's] proposal for a Yen-ying-yüan.

141. Ibid. 10:1b. For a previous, similar proposal by Yulgok, see ibid. 10:33a.

142. Ibid. 10:1b–2a. After review by the Ministry of Personnel in the capital, the candidate would be appointed to the post. If there were a major discrepancy between the man's current rank and that of the *kyogwan*, he would be given a brevet appointment.

143. Ibid. 10:9a, 12b, 15b.

144. Ibid. 9:37a-b.

145. Ibid. 9:38a.

146. Ibid. 10:27b.

147. Ibid. 10:16b–17a.

148. Ibid. 9:31a-b.

149. An exception to this scheme would be Kyŏnggi Province where the capital was located. Here the Middle School would take the place of the Governor's School.

150. Ibid. 9:32a-b.

151. Ibid. 10:35a-b.

152. Ibid. 9:32b–33a. For specific ranks for these officials, see ibid. 9:32b. See also the note where Yu says that the new posts of Kyodo (Teacher) and Kyosu (Instructor) of ranks 4B and 6, respectively, would be created to function exclusively as teachers, as opposed to the current situation where teachers of the Four Schools were concurrent posts held by incumbent officials.

153. Ibid. 9:33a.

154. Ibid. 9:35a–36a.

155. Ibid. 9:39a.

156. Ibid. 9:40b.

157. Watanabe Manabu, *Kinsei Chŏsen kyōikushi kenkyū* [A study of the history of education in the recent Chosŏn period] (Tokyo: Yūsankaku, 1969), p. 406.

158. PGSR 9:39a. Watanabe pointed out that Yu's *hyang* or subdistrict was also defined as a unit of 500 households, hence equivalent to the *tang* referred to by K'ung An-kuo. Watanabe, *Kinsei Chōsen kyōikushi kenkyū*, p. 406.

159. PGSR 9:39a–40a.

160. Ibid. 9:39b.

161. Ibid. 9:39b–40a.

162. Lee, *Government Education and Examinations in Sung China*, pp. 245–49.

CHAPTER 5. New Schools: Conservative Restraints on Radicalism

1. PGSR 9:27a-b.

2. Ibid. 9:25b, 10:4b.

3. Ibid. 10:7b.

4. Ibid. 9:34a

5. Ibid. 9:33a.

6. Ibid. 9:34a-b.

7. Ibid. 9:34b.

8. Ibid.

9. Ibid. 10:22a.

10. Ibid. 10:25b.

11. Ibid. 10:24a.

12. Ibid. 10:25a.

13. Ibid. 10:25a, 22b–23b.

14. Ibid. 10:22b–23b. See these pages for specific quotas for the current examinations at all levels.

15. Ibid. 9:3b.

16. Ibid. 10:24b–25a.

17. Ibid. 10:24a.

18. Ibid. 10:13b.

19. Ibid. 10:14a-b.

20. Ibid. 10:13a.

21. Ibid. 10:14b–16b.

22. Ibid. 10:19b.

23. Ibid. 10:11a.

24. Ibid. 10:19a-b.

25. For an explanation of the San-shu in the Later Han dynasty, see Charles O. Hucker, *A Dictionary of Official Titles in Imperial China* (Stanford, Calif.: Stanford University Press, 1985), p. 401.

26. PGSR 10:17b. Yu also recommended consulting the ancient rites for establishing procedure.

27. Ibid. 10:18a.

28. Ibid. 10:29b.

29. Ibid. 10:20a.

30. Ibid. 10:20b–21a.

31. Ibid. 10:21b.

32. Ibid. 10:21a.

33. Ibid. 10:5a, 9a-b.

34. Ibid. 10:10b.

35. Ibid. 10:13a. See similar regulations for failure of promoted students to pass initial examinations upon entering higher schools, ibid. 10:14b–15a.

36. Ibid. 10:15a, see also regulations for dismissal of students who failed initial examinations at the T'aehak or National Academy, 10:16a.

37. Ibid. 9:25b, 36a.

38. Ibid. 9:25b.

39. Ibid. 9:26a. What would this man have thought of rock and roll?

40. Ibid. 9:26a. For references to quiet sitting, consult the index to Wm. Theodore de Bary and the Conference on Seventeenth-Century Chinese Thought, *The Unfolding of Neo-Confucianism* (New York: Columbia University Press, 1975).

41. PGSR 9:26b–31a.

42. Ibid. 9:30b–31a.

43. Ibid. 10:26b.

44. Ibid. 10:27a.

45. Ibid. 9:27a-b.

46. Ibid. 9:25b, 10:4b.

47. Ibid. 10:10b.

48. Ibid. 9:36b.

49. Ibid. 10:4b.

50. Ibid. 10:10a, 11a.

51. Ibid. 10:8b, 11b. He also called for archery ranges to be established next to every school, 9:36b.

52. Ibid. 10:12a.

53. Ibid. 10:13a.

54. Ibid. 10:47b–48a.

55. For regulations pertaining to other schools, see ibid. 10:44a–53b. The main reforms included an entrance examination for prospective candidates, the provision of salaries and extra land grants for students, triennial selection examinations and quarterly review examinations (*kogang*) of students and elimination of the failures.

56. Ibid. 10:48a-b, 53a.

57. Ibid. 10:45a–57a.

58. Ibid. 10:47a-b.

59. Ibid. 10:53a-b.

60. Ibid. 10:48b. For medicine, see 10:49a; for astronomy, 49a-b; for geography, 49b; for languages, 49b–50a; for law, 50b; for mathematics, 50b; for calligraphy, 51a; for art and painting, 51b; for music, 51b–52b.

61. Ibid. 10:51b–52b.

62. Ibid. 10:7b.

63. Ibid. 10:7b.

64. Ibid. 10:7b–8a.

65. Ibid. 10:4b. For a fuller discussion of age, particularly the 40-year age minimum for appointing scholars, except in the case of talented men, see 10:20b.

66. Ibid. 10:5a.

67. Ibid. 10:5b.

68. Ibid. 10:4b.

69. Ibid. 10:4a.

70. Ibid.

71. Ibid. 10:13a, 14b–15b.

72. Ibid. 10:33b.

73. Ibid.

74. Ibid. 10:15a.

75. Ibid. 9:36b.

76. Ibid. 9:35b, 38b.

77. Ibid. 9:35a–36a.

78. Ibid. 9:38b.

79. Ibid. 9:36a.

80. Ibid. 9:38a.

81. Ibid. 10:51b.

82. Ibid. 10:22a, 46a.

83. Ibid. 10:5b.

84. Ibid. 10:21b.

85. Ibid. 10:26a.

86. Ibid. 10:5a.

87. Ibid. 10:8b.

88. Ibid. 10:35a.

89. Ibid. 10:36a.

90. Ibid.

91. Ibid. 10:5a.

92. Ibid. 10:5b–6a.

93. Ibid. 10:6a-b.

94. Ibid. 10:6b.

95. Ibid. 10:6b–7a.

96. Ibid. 10:7a.

97. Ibid. 10:7a-b.

98. The term *sŏ* could refer to the division between eldest legitimate son and other sons – Song Siyŏl's position in the mourning debate – but in this context the distinction was clearly between legitimate sons of the yangban's wife and the sons by concubines, commoner, or slave.

99. Ibid. 10:7a.

100. Ibid. 10:8a.

101. Ibid.

102. Ibid.

103. Thomas A. Metzger, *Escape from Predicament: Neo-Confucianism and China's*

Evolving Political Culture (New York: Columbia University Press, 1977), pp. 60–61 et passim.

104. PGSR 10:8a.

105. Ibid.

106. Ibid. 10:8b.

107. MHBG 187:20b–21b.

108. Ibid. 184:3b–4a.

109. Ibid.

110. Ibid. 186:1b–2a.

111. Ibid. 186:17b–18b, 187:2a.

112. Ibid. 188:15b–18b.

113. James B. Palais, *Policy and Politics in Traditional Korea* (Cambridge: Harvard University Press, 1975), chap. 6.

114. Watanabe Manabu, *Kinsei Chōsen kyōikushi kenkyū* [A study of the history of education in the recent Chosŏn period] (Tokyo: Yūsankaku, 1969), p. 398.

115. Ibid., pp. 54, 128.

CHAPTER 6. Slavery: The Slow Path to Abolition

1. PGSR 26:8b.

2. PGSR 26:5b–6a.

3. William L. Westermann, *The Slave Systems of Greek and Roman Antiquity* (Philadelphia: The American Philosophical Society, 1955); M.I. Finley, *The Ancient Economy* (Berkeley and Los Angeles: University of California Press, 1973), pp. 40, 49, 62–94, 106; idem, *Ancient Slavery and Modérn Ideology* (New York: Viking Press, 1980) pp. 9–92; Ronald B. Levinson, *In Defense of Plato* (Cambridge, Mass.: Harvard University Press, 1953) pp. 139–94, 571; Gregory Vlastos, "Slavery in Plato's Republic," *The Philosophical Review* 50 (1941):289–304, reprinted in M. I. Finley, ed., *Slavery in Classical Antiquity* (Cambridge: W. Heffer and Sons, 1960) pp. 133–49. See other articles by M. I. Finley, A. H. M. Jones, and W. L. Westermann in this volume. Ernest Barker, *Greek Political Theory: Plato and His Predecessors* (1918. London: Methuen and Co., 1951) pp. 29–33, 75, 107, 119–20, 266–67; Ernest Barker, *The Politics of Aristotle* (New York: Oxford University Press, 1958), pp. xiii-xxiv et passim; Allan Bloom, trans., *The Republic of Plato* (New York: Basic Books, 1968); Alvin W. Gouldner, *Enter Plato: Classical Greece and the Origins of Social Theory* (New York: Basic Books, 1965), pp. 24–34, 136, 145, 241–43, 307, 319, 334, 351–59; Roger Chance, *Until Philosophers are Kings: A Study of the Political Theory of Plato and Aristotle in Relation to the Modern State* (New York: Oxford University Press, 1929), pp. 12, 23, 137, 179–80, 219; David Brion Davis, *The Problem of Slavery in Western Culture* (Ithaca, N.Y.: Cornell University Press, 1966), pp. 66–72; Keith Hopkins, *Conquerors and Slaves: Sociological Studies in Roman History*, vol. 1 (Cambridge: Cambridge University Press, 1978).

4. Finley, *Ancient Slavery and Modern Ideology*, pp. 127–28; Davis, *Problem of Slavery*, pp. 17–18, 72–106.

5. Davis, *Problem of Slavery*; Edith F. Hurwitz, *Politics and the Public Conscience: Slave Emancipation and the Abolitionist Movement in Britain* (London: George Allen and Unwin; New York: Barnes and Noble Books, 1973); Orlando Patterson, *Slavery and Social Death: A Comparative Study* (Cambridge: Harvard University Press, 1982), pp. 72–76; Eugene D. Genovese, *Roll, Jordan, Roll: The World the Slaves Made* (New York: Vintage Books, 1976), pp. 161–68.

6. Marc Bloch, *Slavery and Serfdom in the Middle Ages*, trans. William R. Beer (Berkeley and Los Angeles: University of California Press, 1975); Finley, *Ancient Slavery and Modern Ideology*, pp. 124–49.

7. Eugene D. Genovese, *The World the Slaveholders Made* (New York: Pantheon Books, 1969); Genovese, *The Political Economy of Slavery* (New York: Vintage Books, 1967), pp. 157–79; Eric Williams, *Capitalism and Slavery* (Chapel Hill: University of North Carolina Press, 1944); Elizabeth Fox-Genovese and Eugene D. Genovese, *Fruits of Merchant Capital: Slavery and Bourgeois Property in the Rise and Expansion of Capitalism* (New York: Oxford University Press, 1983), pp. 34–60, 272–98.

8. Robert William Fogel and Stanley L. Engerman, *Time on the Cross: The Economics of American Negro Slavery* (Boston and Toronto: Little, Brown and Co., 1974). For a sample of some of the criticism aroused by this book, see Paul A. David, Herbert G. Gutman, Richard Sutch, Peter Temin, Gavin Wright, with an introd. by Kenneth M. Stampp, *Reckoning with Slavery: A Critical Study in the Quantitative History of American Negro Slavery* (New York: Oxford University Press, 1976); Genovese and Genovese, *Fruits of Merchant Capital*, pp. 136–71.

9. Davis, *Problem of Slavery*, pp. 292–389.

10. Chŏn Hyŏngt'aek, *Chosŏn hugi nobi sinbun yŏn'gu* [A study of slave status in late Chosŏn] (Seoul: Ilchogak, 1989), pp. 14–15, 32–39.

11. For a discussion of Korean slaves as chattel, see Kameda Keiji, "Kōrai no nuhi ni tsuite [The slaves of Koryŏ]," part 1, *Seikyū gakusō* 26 (1936):100–124; Hong Sŭnggi, *Koryŏ sidae nobi yŏn'gu* [Slavery in the Koryŏ period] (Seoul: Han'guk yŏn'guwŏn, 1981), pp. 8, 20, 23–35, 41–50, 69–75, 82–85, 189–93, 207–12; Hong Sŭnggi, *Koryŏ kwijok sahoe wa nobi* [The aristocratic society of Koryŏ and slavery] (Seoul: Ilchogak, 1983), pp. 4, 8–10, 33–42, 46–50, 63–80, 214; Ellen Salem, "Slavery in Medieval Korea" (Ph.D. diss., Columbia University,1978), pp. 33–118.

The main differences between Chinese and Roman law were supposed to be that Chinese slaves could own property (including slaves of their own), contract debts, institute suits, legally marry other persons of base or slave status, be adopted, and be held legally responsible for their actions. They were protected by law from unreasonable injury, and in some cases had surnames. On this basis some scholars referred to them as half-human and half-chattel. The laws of Korea, Japan, the ancient Hebrews and Hittites were regarded as similar to those of China. Niida Noboru, *Shina mibumpō shi* [The history of the law on personal status in China] (Tokyo: Tōhō bunka gakuin, 1942), pp. 2, 88–90, 860–61, 900–937, 979–85. Niida, following Harada Keikichi, stated explicitly that in principle slaves were not regarded as human during the Roman Republic but that toward the end of the Republic, aspects of the slave's humanity included family relations and protection from cruel and arbitrary punishment were admitted into law; the Emperor Constantine further liberalized the law by prohibiting conspiracy to murder slaves and division of slave property upon the death of the master (ibid., p. 901). Niida discusses the nature of slavery in Korea in pp. 904–5, largely based on the work of Sudō Yoshiyuki, to be cited later.

See also Niida Noboru, "Chūgokuhō ni okeru dorei no chii to shujinken: doreihō shoshi" [The position of slaves and the rights of masters in Chinese law], in idem, *Chūgoku hō seishi kenkyū: dōrei nōnohō, kazoku sonrakuhō* [Studies in the legal history of China: Slave and serf law, family and village law] (Tokyo: Tokyo daigaku shuppankai, 1962), pp. 5–19. Originally published in *Chūgoku hō seishi* [A history of the Chinese legal system] (Tokyo: Iwanami zensho, 1952). Nishijima raised the question of the half-human/half-chattel thesis, but preferred to stress the importance of social status in the Chinese system of slavery. Nishijima Sadao, "Chūgoku kodai nuhisei no saikōsatsu" [Another investigation of the ancient slave system in China], in *Kodaishi kōza* [A course on ancient history] (Tokyo: Gakuseisha, 1963) 7:162–73; Hamaguchi Shigekuni, *Tōōchō no senjin seido* [The base person system of the T'ang dynasty] (Kyoto: Tōyōshi kenkyūkai, 1966), pp. 18–61. Wilbur simply discusses slaves as chattel, in C. Martin Wilbur, *Slavery in China During the Former Han Dynasty, 206 B.C.–A.D. 25* (New York: Russell and Russell, 1943), pp. 118–26.

Contrary to Niida's description of classical Western slavery, M. I. Finley has written of the "ineradicable double aspect of the slave, that he was both a person and property," asserting that neither of the two theoretical extremes – of the slave as property or the perfectly free man – has ever existed. "A person possesses or lacks rights, privileges, claims and duties in many respects. . . . The combination of these rights, or lack of them, determines a man's place in the spectrum, which is, of course, not to be understood as a mathematical continuum, but as a more metaphorical, discontinuous spectrum, with gaps here, heavier concentrations there." Finley, *Ancient Economy*, pp. 63, 67–68. Patterson has also stated in similar fashion that, "As a legal fact, there has never existed a slaveholding society, ancient or modern, that did not recognize the slave as a person in law." Orlando Patterson, *Slavery and Social Death: A Comparative Study*, (Cambridge: Harvard University Press, 1982), p. 22.

12. Patterson, *Slavery and Social Death.*

13. KRS 85:40b–41a.

14. *Kwanghaegun ilgi* 80:13a, Kwanghaegun 6.7.pyŏng'in (1614). The *Kwanghaegun ilgi* is included in Kuksa p'yŏnch'an wiwŏnhoe [National Historical Compilation Committee] ed., *Chosŏn wangjo sillok* [The veritable records of the kings of the Chosŏn dynasty] (Seoul: Tongguk munhwasa, 1955), vols. 26–32. See also the memorial of the Saganwŏn in ibid. 87:1a, Kwanghaegun 7.2.kimyo (1615); cited in Hiraki Makoto, "Shipch'il segi e issŏsŏ ŭi nobi chongnyang" [The attainment of commoner status by slaves in the seventeenth century], *Han'guksa yŏn'gu* 3 (March 1969):109, 119.

15. *Sukchong sillok*, 21:49b, Sukchong 15.12.ŭrhaek (1689), cited in Yi Sangbaek, "Ch'ŏnja sumogo" [A study of the inheritance of the mother's status by slaves], *Chindan hakpo* 25, no. 7 (December 1964):175.

16. The historian's remarks were a rebuttal of the proposal of the State Councilor, Nam Ung'un, to follow the matrilineal rule and allow the offspring of women of good status to inherit that status to increase the number of able-bodied males available for military service. The historian was particularly incensed at Nam's suggestion that King Myŏngjong should issue an edict without bothering to discuss it with his ministers. *Myŏngjong sillok* 12:25a, Myŏngjong 6.9.kyech'uk (1551), cited in Yi Sangbaek, "Ch'ŏnja sumogo," p. 171.

17. KRS 85:40b–41a.

18. The *Munhŏnbigo* was originally compiled in 1770. A second edition was compiled in 1782 but not published. A third edition was published in 1908 under the title *Chŭngbo munhŏnbigo*. See KSDSJ 2:1475.

19. KRS 85:40b–41a. For the commentary of Yi Ki(?), see MHBG 162:8a. See also Kameda, "Kōrai no nuhi," part 1, p. 95; Salem, "Slavery in Medieval Korea," p. 35.

20. KRS 85:41a-b, 93:21a-b; MHBG 162:10a.

21. KRS 1:12a-b, T'aejo 1.8.sinhaek (918).

22. Modern scholars have been skeptical of T'aejo's motives and have suggested that he was trying either to expand the tax base or weaken the economic base of the old followers of Kungye and other political rivals in a period rife with plots and conspiracy. Hong Sŭnggi, *Koryŏ kwijok sahoe wa nobi*, pp. 60, 142–57; Kameda, "Kōrai no nuhi," part 1, p. 100 ff. See also Kim Ch'ŏlch'un, "Ch'oe Sŭngno ŭi simu isipp'alcho" [The eighteen-point memorial of Ch'oe Sŭngno], in Hyosŏng Cho Myŏnggi paksa hwagap kinyŏm Pulgyo sahak nonch'ong kanhaeng wiwŏnhoe [Publication committee for essays on the history of Buddhism in honor of the sixtieth birthday of Dr. Cho Myŏnggi], ed., *Pulgyo sahak nonch'ong* [Essays on the history of Buddhism] (Seoul: 1965), pp. 227–56.

23. Kameda, "Kōrai no nuhi," part 1, pp. 93–148. *Samguk sagi* [Record of the Three Kingdoms] 50:17a (Keijō: Koden kankōkai, 1931); KRS 2:8b, T'aejo 18.6 (935).

24. He also mentioned low status post-station and ferry workers, KRS 2:16b, T'aejo 26.4.(943).

25. *Koryŏsa chŏryo* (Seoul: Asea munhwasa, 1973), hereafter referred to as KRSCY 11:26a-b, Uijong 12.6 (1158), cited in Hong Sŭnggi, *Koryŏ kwijok sahoe*, pp. 142, 148–51.

26. KRS 85:43b–44a, cited in Hong, *Koryŏ kwijok sahoe*, p. 142; Salem, "Slavery in Medieval Korea," p. 77.

27. KRS 85:1a–2a, KRSCY 2:7b Kwangjong 7 (956); Salem, "Slavery in Medieval Korea," p. 77.

28. KRS 31:31b–33a, 35a–36a, 85:43a–44a; 108:5b–6a; MHBG 162:20a-b.

29. See Kameda, "Kōrai no nuhi," part 1, pp. 96–98, 119–21; part 2, p. 58; Sudō Yoshiyuki, "Sensho ni okeru nuhi no benrei to suisatsu to ni tsuite [On the investigation and adjudication of slaves in the early Chōsen period] *Seikyū gakusō* 22 (November 1935):2, 6–10.

30. Kameda, "Kōrai no nuhi," part 1, pp. 128–30; part 2, p. 61; Sudō Yoshiyuki, "Kōrai makki yori Chōsen shoki in itaru nuhi no kenkyū" [A study of slavery from late Koryŏ to the early Chosŏn period], part 1, *Rekishigaku kenkyū* 9, no. 1 (1939):8.

31. Chŏng Tojŏn, the famous radical reformer and supporter of Yi Sŏnggye and the new Chosŏn dynasty, emphasized the problem associated with commendation in late Koryŏ:

> There was no way to settle the people down in security and some of them probably died of hunger and cold. The population was reduced by the day, and those who were left could not bear the burden of taxes and labor service, so they cut it off [gave up?] and commended themselves to the families of the great and rich and to the people of power and influence. Some engaged in artisanry and commerce, or ran off and wandered about, so that 50 to 60 percent of the people were lost [from the tax rolls?], and this does not even include those who became official and private slaves of the Buddhist temples.

Chŏng Tojŏn, "Chosŏn kyŏnggukchŏn, sang p'anjŏk," [Institutes for the management of the state of Chosŏn, part 1], in idem, *Sambongjip, sang* [Collected works of Chŏng Tojŏn] (Seoul: Kuksa p'yŏnch'an wiwŏnhoe, 1961), p. 214, cited in Hong, *Koryŏ sidae nobi yŏn'gu*, p. 229.

32. Salem, "Slavery in Medieval Korea," pp. 119–39; Hong, *Koryŏ kwijok sahoe wa nobi*, pp. 309–40.

33. Sudō Yoshiyuki, "Kōrai makki yori Chōsen shoki in itaru nuhi no kenkyū," part 3, *Rekishigaku kenkyū* 9, no. 3 (1939):289–91; Hong, *Koryŏ kwijok sahoe wa nobi*, pp. 342–404. This development, an obvious violation of the legacy of T'aejo, antagonized the Confucian bureaucrats who, as educated men trained in morality and statecraft, felt that the use of slaves and eunuchs as ministers to the king made a travesty of government.

34. KRS 132:6b–7a. See also the story of the slave of Chang Hae in KRS 32:7a; Kameda, "Kōrai no nuhi," part 1, pp. 122–23, 129–30; part 2, pp. 58–59.

35. Yi Sugŏn estimated over 100,000 official slaves in the first quarter of the fifteenth century, over 200,000 slaves in the second quarter, and over 350,000 in the last quarter. Idem, *Yŏngnam sarimp'a ŭi hyŏngsŏng* [The formation of the *sarim* group in the Kyŏngsang area] (Taegu?: Yŏngnam taehakkyo minjok munhwa yŏn'guso, 1979), p. 174.

36. Memorial of An Nosaeng, an official in the Ministry of Punishments, dated 1407.5.ŭrhaek, cited in Sudō Yoshiyuki, "Nuhi no benrei," p. 46.

37. This regulation could, however, be superseded by a written will. KRS 85:45a–46a, notices dated 1391–1392. *Ponson* is a synonym for *sason*. Sudō defines the *sason* as the group of relations including nephews, grandnephews, father's elder brothers (uncles), and older male paternal cousins. "Nuhi no benrei," pp. 38, 61, n.15.

38. In 1397 it was decided that sons and grandsons of concubines should have the right to inherit family slaves in the absence of legitimate heirs. In 1405 revised regulations also provided that if there were no heirs of a family either by the legitimate wife or a commoner concubine, then the children of a slave concubine would be entitled to a one-seventh share of the family slaves. If there were no legitimate heirs, but sons of a commoner concubine, then the children of a slave concubine would still be entitled to a one-tenth share of family slaves. If the legitimate wife had daughters and the commoner concubine had sons, the sons would get one-third of the slaves, and the son of a

commoner concubine who was responsible for ancestral sacrifice would get one-half. Sons of concubines were to be given a one-third share of family slaves even when legitimate daughters survived. For adjustments in the 1405 regulations, see Sudō, "Nuhi no benrei," pp. 41–47, 51–53.

39. Ibid., pp. 40–47.

40. KRS 118:12a, discussed in Hong Sŭnggi, *Koryŏ sidae nobi yŏn'gu*, pp. 218–21; Hong, *Koryŏ kwijok sahoe wa nobi*, pp. 259–60.

41. Sudō Yoshiyuki, "Kōrai makki yori Chōsen shoki in itaru nuhi no kenkyū," part 1, pp. 10–11.

42. KRS 85:45a-b.

43. Ibid. 85:46b.

44. Ibid. 85:47a; Hong Sŭnggi remarked that the statement that slaves were not chattel but human beings was unprecedented, but that the Office of Remonstrance did not desire to improve the lot of the slave on the basis of humanitarianism. It was speaking for the Yi Sŏnggye faction, which sought to repress the influence of the powerful families and Buddhist temples whose economic and political position was heightened by the increase in the number of slaves they held through free purchase and gift. Even though it was only a side effect of the Yi Sŏnggye faction's intentions, it nonetheless somewhat improved the social position of slaves. Hong Sŭnggi, *Koryŏ kwijok sahoe*, p. 231.

45. For the 1388 memorial, see KRS 84:35b; for the 1389 memorial see KRS 85:34b–35a. Both are cited in Kameda Keiji, "Kōrai no nuhi," part 1, p. 126.

46. In this case, the term used was "release from service" (*pangyŏk*). Hong Sŭnggi summarized the scholarly debate on the question of whether release from service was equivalent to manumission. At first Hong agreed with Yi Kibaek that service and status were closely correlated and release from slave service for official slaves must have meant a rise in status as well. The Koryŏ system may have been analogous to the T'ang rule that official slaves who retired from service at the age of sixty also rose in status to *kuan-hu*, and then became commoners at the age of seventy. Despite the lack of evidence that such a rule was literally followed in Koryŏ, there were age categories that were similar to those of the T'ang.

Kim Seyun took a critical view of this interpretation, arguing that there was no evidence that commoners released from service duties also enjoyed a rise in status to commoner. In his later work Hong adopted a more cautious attitude and declined to make a positive judgment on the situation in early Koryŏ. For his earliest view, see Hong Sŭnggi, "Koryŏ sidae kongnobi ŭi sŏnkyŏk" [The nature of official slaves in the Koryŏ period], *Yoksa hakpo* 80 (Spring 1978):48–49, in which he concluded that release from service at age 60 meant manumission to commoner (status). See also Yi Kibaek, "Koryŏ sidae sinbun ŭi sesŭp kwa pyŏndong: Han'guk chŏnt'ong sahoe e issŏsŏ ŭi sinbun" [Changes in status inheritance in the Koryŏ period: Status in Korean traditional society], in idem, *Minjok kwa yŏksa* [The nation and history] (Seoul: Ilchogak, 1971), pp. 94–96; Kim Seyun, "Koryŏ hugi ŭi oegŏ nobi" [The outside resident slaves of late Koryŏ], *Han'guk hakpo* 18 (Spring 1980):73 n.16; Hong Sŭnggi, *Koryŏ kwijok sahoe wa nobi*, pp. 71–77.

47. KRS 85:47a-b; Hong Sŭnggi argued that the government was more interested in gaining control over slaves than freeing them from servitude, and that the Kaesŏng and

Hwaryŏngbu slave registers that he has studied shows an expansion of state control over the outside resident slaves in particular. Hong, *Koryŏ sidae nobi yŏn'gu*, p. 221; idem, *Koryŏ kwijok sahoe*, pp. 75, 261.

48. Special slave investigation agencies were established in 1269, 1288, 1301, 1356, 1381, 1388, and 1391 with Yi Sŏnggye in charge but disbanded in 1392. See Sudō, "Nuhi no benrei," pp. 2–6.

49. *Sejo sillok* 46:40b, Sejo 14.6.pyŏng'o (1468), cited in Sudō, "Nuhi no benrei," p. 22.

50. Sudō, "Nuhi no benrei," pp. 47–51.

51. On 1414.6.chŏngsa, Chief State Councilor Yu Chŏnghyŏn told T'aejong that 12,797 cases had been petitioned to the Togam. *T'aejong sillok* 27:44a, cited in Sudō, "Nuhi no benrei," pp. 21–22.

52. *T'aejong sillok* 33:68a, T'aejong 17.6.sinhaek (1417).

53. King Sejong reached the same conclusion. Yi Sugŏn, *Yŏngnam sarimp'a ŭi hyŏngsŏng*, pp. 175–76, 180.

54. Sudō, "Nuhi no benrei," pp. 28–31; Sudō, "Nuhi no kenkyū," part 4, *Rekishigaku kenkyū* 9, no. 4 (1939):422–26.

55. Scholars have recently pointed out that T'ang law prohibited the marriage of male slaves to commoner women, and that even though there was no mention of this in early Koryŏ, it may have been the rule because it seems to have been the law in late Koryŏ. Sudō, "Nuhi no kenkyū," part 3, p. 261; Yi Sangbaek, "Ch'ŏnja sumogo," pp. 160–61.

56. Yi Sangbaek summarized the Yüan regulations pertaining to the status of offspring of mixed marriages as follows. 1. The children of commoner fathers and slave mothers became commoners. 2. The children of a commoner father and a mother who was a daughter of a male slave would be commoners. 3. Children of a slave father and a mother who was a daughter of a commoner who petitioned for marriage would be slaves. 4. Children of a male commoner who illegally married a female slave would become slaves and be returned to the master. 5. Children of a male slave who illegally married a daughter of a commoner would be commoners, but registered differently.

In the first three cases the son adopts the father's status; in the fourth and fifth cases, because the marriage is illicit, the children take the mother's status. Nevertheless, because marriage was relatively free, this system was quite different from T'ang and Sung as well as Koryŏ practice. Yi Sangbaek, "Ch'ŏnja sumogo," pp. 160–61. See also Sudō, "Nuhi no kenkyū," part 3, pp. 262–63.

Niida Noboru cited the Yüan code, which stated that if the daughter of a *liang* (good, *yang* in Korean) family wanted to marry the male slave of someone else, then she would become a slave. If (a male slave) married the daughter of a *liang* family and they were [illegally] sold off as slaves, then they would be converted to good status (*liang*). Both seller and buyer would be deemed guilty of a crime and the sale price confiscated by the authorities. *Yüan-shih* [History of the Yüan dynasty] 103:22b.

Niida pointed out that there was more latitude for commoner/slave marriage during the Yüan period than before. Because more people of good status were being seized, confiscated, or sold off and the number of slaves was increasing, it became impossible to maintain the iron rule against commoner/base (*liang/chien*) marriages. Daughters of *liang* families who married male slaves became slaves, but the daughter of a male slave once permitted to marry a *liang-jen* (good person) would instantly become a *liang-jen* herself. Her children would also adopt their father's status whether *liang* or slave. Niida cited *Yüan-shih*, 104:9b–10a. Niida Noboru, *Shina mibumpōshi*, pp. 927–28.

57. For sources on the above section see KRS 31:31b–33a, 35a–36a, 85:43a–44a; 108:5b–6a. See Kameda, "Kōrai no nuhi," part 1, pp. 96–98, 119–21; part 2, p. 58; Sudō, "Nuhi no benrei," pp. 1–61; Yi Sangbaek, "Ch'ŏnja sumogo," p. 158 ff; Hong Sŭnggi, *Koryŏ sidae nobi yŏn'gu*, pp. 20–23.

58. KRS 85:46a. See the memorial of the nobleman, Kwŏn Chunghwa, who complained about the loss of able-bodied males for military service because male slaves were marrying women of good status and under Korean law their children all became private slaves. He asked that they be prohibited from doing so, and that where such marriages existed, the state would divorce the couple. And if the master of the male slave were found guilty of violating the law, he too would be punished. T'aejong approved the recommendation. *T'aejong sillok* 2:6a-b, T'aejong 1.7 kab'in (1401); ibid. 10:17a, T'aejong 5.9.kab'in (1405); ibid. 26:21b, T'aejong 13.9.chŏngch'uk.

59. Kameda Keiji, "Kōrai no nuhi," part 1, pp. 98–99; part 2, pp. 47–48; Yi Sangbaek, "Ch'ŏnja sumogo," pp. 158–62; Hong Sŭnggi, *Koryŏ sidae nobi yŏn'gu*, p. 221; idem, *Koryŏ kwijok sahoe wa nobi*, p. 261.

60. *T'aejo sillok* 12:2b. T'aejo 6.7.kapsul.

61. *T'aejong sillok* 27:48b, T'aejong 14.6.mujin. Sources in nn. 74–76 are cited in Sudō, "Nuhi no kenkyū," part 3, p. 267.

62. *T'aejong sillok* 27:48b, 1414.6.mujin, cited in Sudō, "Nuhi no kenkyū," part 3, pp. 267–68, and Yi Sangbaek, "Ch'ŏnja sumogo," p. 163.

63. *Sejong sillok* 45:9a, 1429.7.kisa.

64. Ibid. 55:22a, 1432.3.kapsul.

65. Ibid. 55:26b–27a, 1432.3.kapsin. This and the notices in n. 81 and n. 82 cited in Yi Sangbaek, "Chŏnja sumogo," pp. 162–65. See also Sudō, "Nuhi no kenkyū," part 3, pp. 268–69.

66. *Sejong sillok* 55:27a. If Yi Chaeryong's description of the onerous service and tribute burdens of early Chosŏn official slaves is to be believed, it is hard to imagine why a private slave would necessarily prefer official slavery, but it is possible that the prospects for manumission were better as an official slave. Yi pointed out that after the state abolished most Buddhist monastic slaves in 1406 and converted them to government or official slaves, it raised the rate of tribute hitherto levied on official tribute-paying slaves (*napkong nobi*) to the same levels as that paid by the former monastic (private) slaves. I have deduced, therefore, that unless Sejong's officials were mistaken about the motives of slaves, the prospects of manumission or escape must been brighter for official than private slaves. Yi Chaeryong, "Chosŏn chŏn'gi ŭi nobi yŏn'gu" [A study of the slaves of the early Chosŏn period], *Sŭngjŏn taehakkyo nonmunjip* 3 (1971):169–88.

67. Children born of such marriages between 1414 and 1432 were also exempted from the law. *Sejong sillok* 55:26b–28a, Sejong 14.3.ŭryu, pyŏngsul.

68. *Sejo sillok* 46:32b, 1468.6.im'in, cited in Yi Sangbaek, "Ch'ŏnja sumogo," pp. 166–67. See Sudō, "Nuhi no kenkyū," part 3, pp. 272–73. See the *Kyŏngguk taejŏn* of

1471 (Chōsen sōtokufu, Chūsūin ed., 1934), p. 490, which states the matrilineal rule of succession for offspring of base persons except that offspring of male slaves and female commoners would inherit base or slave status. P. 486 includes among the exceptions to the matrilineal rule the provision that the offspring of officials (*taeso wŏn'in*) as well as royal relatives by their slave wives or concubines would be regarded as commoners (*yang*).

69. Yi Sugŏn, *Yŏngnam sarimp'a ŭi hyŏngsŏng*, p. 175, n.47. Han Yŏngguk's study of the same 1609 Ulsan registers indicated that the percentage distribution by status among the household heads was 10 percent for yangban, 62 percent for commoners and 28 percent for slaves, but because private slaves living in the families of yangban and commoners were not counted among the household heads and children tended to be underreported, he amended these figures to his own estimation 3 percent yangban, 57 percent commoners, and 40 percent slaves. Han also pointed out that 10 percent of the *solgŏ nobi* (family male and female slaves) and 45 percent of the *oegŏ nobi* (outside-resident male and female slaves) had taken commoner women as wives, and all children of such mixed slave/commoner marriages were claimed by slaveowners (official as well as private), in most cases the owner of the female slave. Han believed that the masters must have been forcing their male slaves to marry commoner women. Han Yŏngguk, "Chosŏn chungyŏp ŭi nobi kyŏlhon yangt'ae, sang: 1609 nyŏn ŭi Ulsan hojŏk e nat'anan saryerŭl chungsimŭro" [Marriages of slaves in mid-Chosŏn, part 1: Examples in the Ulsan household register of 1609], *Yŏksa hakpo* 75–76 (Dec. 1977):185–86, 189–91, 197.

70. *Chungjong sillok* 101:7a-b; Min Hyŏn'gu, "Kŭnse Chosŏn chŏn'gi kunsa chedo ŭi sŏngnip," p. 219.

71. *Myŏngjong sillok* 12:24b–25a, Myŏngjong 6.9.kyech'uk (1551), Yi Sangbaek, "Ch'ŏnja sumo-go," p. 171.

72. *Myŏngjong sillok* 12:24b–25a. The *Myŏngjong sillok* compilation was begun in 1568 and completed in 1571. See the preface to the Kuksa p'yŏnch'an wiwŏnhoe [National Historical Compilation Committee] ed., *Chosŏn wangjo sillok* [Veritable record of the Chosŏn dynasty] 19 (Seoul: Tongguk munhwasa, 1955): 6.

73. Yi Sangbaek believed that the historian's opinion was a product of an emphasis on social order, class structure, and rigid formalism in attitudes that accompanied the growing influence of Confucian thought on Korean society. Actual policy, such as the adoption of the patrilineal and matrilineal rules, was determined more by the socioeconomic demands of real life than by theoretical or ideological considerations, which were only used to reinforce real or material interests. There is, however, no need to draw a line between Confucian theory and material interest on the slave question, because the conservative Confucian line against mixing of status groups was consonant with the material desires of the slaveowners for the preservation, if not increase, of their property. Yi Sangbaek, "Ch'ŏnja sumo-go," pp. 171–72.

Yi Chaeryong's views are closer to those of the *Sillok* historian than my own. Yi argued that, as opposed to late Koryŏ or late Chosŏn, in early Chosŏn the opportunities for manumission were almost completely closed off. "Chosŏn ch'ogi ŭi nobi yŏn'gu," pp. 179–80.

74. KRS 85:43a-b, Ch'ungnyŏlwang 24.1 (1298), cited in Hong Sŭnggi, *Koryŏ kwijok sahoe wa nobi*, p. 106.

75. Hong mentioned that Kang Chinch'ŏl's opinion to the contrary, the 1298 decree meant that only the domestic slaves of the yangban were exempted from service while their outside resident slaves were liable for it because in the early Chosŏn period outside resident slaves were responsible for miscellaneous labor service (*yoyŏk*). Hong, however, felt that the latter rule was an early Chosŏn innovation. Hong, *Koryŏ kwijok sahoe wa nobi*, pp. 106, 115–17, 230–31, 251, 254–58; Kang Chinch'ŏl, *Koryŏ t'oji chedo yŏn'gu*, p. 302.

76. Hiraki Makoto, *Chosŏn hugi nobije yŏn'gu*, p. 183.

77. Sudō, "Nuhi no kenkyū," part 4, pp. 413–20; Kameda Keiji, "Kōrai no nuhi," part 2, pp. 29–34; Hong Sŭnggi, *Koryŏ kwijok sahoe wa nobi*, pp. 106, 115–17, 230–31, 251, 254–58; Hiraki Makoto, *Chosŏn hugi nobije yŏn'gu*, p. 183; Arii Tomonori, "Richō hojūgun kō" [A study of the auxiliary soldiers of the Yi dynasty], *Chŏsen gakuhō* 31 (April 1965):21–22; Ch'ŏn Kwan'u, "Chosŏn ch'ogi Owi ŭi pyŏngjong" [Types of soldiers in the early Chosŏn five guards], *Sahak yŏn'gu* 18 (September 1965):59–95; Hiraki Makoto, *Chosŏn hugi nobije yŏn'gu*, pp. 153–54. Yi Chaeryong claims that all opportunities for manumission, presumably by service in the auxiliaries, were closed off after 1481, but he does not cite his source. Yi, "Chosŏn chŏn'gi ŭi nobi yŏn'gu," p. 180.

78. Min Hyŏn'gu, "Kŭnse Chosŏn chŏn'gi kunsa chedo ŭi sŏngnip" [The establishment of the early modern military system in the early Chosŏn period]," in Yukkun saggwan hakkyo Han'guk kunsa yŏn'gusil, ed., *Han'guk kunjesa: kŭnse Chosŏn chŏn'gi-p'yŏn* [The history of the Korean military system: The early modern early Chosŏn period) (N.p.: Yukkun ponbu, 1968), pp. 214–22.

79. Ibid., pp. 153–55.

80. *Sŏnjo sujŏng sillok* 26, Sŏnjo 25.4.kimi (1592). The *Sŏae sŏnsaeng munjip* [The collected works of Teacher Yu Sŏngnyŏl] 16, *Kiran husa* [Record of the aftermath of the invasions], gives the date of imjin (1592) 4.30 for the attack and burning of the slave records, cited by Hiraki Makoto, *Chosŏn hugi nobije yŏn'gu*, p. 153.

81. Hiraki Makoto, *Chosŏn hugi nobije yŏn'gu,* pp. 154–65.

82. Ibid., pp. 185–87; idem, "Sipch'il segi e issŏsŏ ŭi nobi chongnyang" [The attainment of commoner status by slaves in the seventeenth century], *Han'guksa yŏn'gu* 3 (March 1969):100 ff; Ch'a Munsŏp, "Sŏnjojo ŭi Hullyŏn-dogam" [The military training agency of Sŏnjo's reign], *Sahakchi* 4 (November 1970):11–30; Ch'a Munsŏp, "Chosŏnjo hugi ŭi yŏngjang e taehayŏ" [The *yŏngjang* of the late Chosŏn dynasty], *Sach'ong*, 12–13 (September 1968):495–518; Chŏn Hyŏngt'aek, *Chosŏn hugi nobi sinbun yŏn'gu*, pp. 169–70; James B. Palais, *Politics and Policy in Traditional Korea* (Cambridge, Mass: Harvard University Press, 1975); p. 89.

83. Chŏn Hyŏngt'aek found that only 14 percent of the list of 69 official slaves who died without heirs from 1677–1764 owned enough land to generate enough of a surplus to purchase freedom. *Chosŏn hugi nobi sinbun yŏn'gu*, p. 267. For the reference to Im Pok, see Hiraki Makoto, *Chosŏn hugi nobije yŏn'gu*, p. 166.

84. Hiraki Makoto, "Sipch'il segi e issŏsŏ ŭi nobi chongnyang," pp. 100–105. Man-

umission by purchase continued to be practiced, probably to the end of the dynasty. See also Hiraki, *Chosŏn hugi nobije yŏn'gu*, p. 43; Ch'oe Yŏnghŭi, *Imjin waeranjung ŭi sahoe tongt'ae* [Social dynamics during the Imjin Japanese invasions] (Seoul: Han'guk yŏn'guwŏn, 1975); pp. 74, 111–25 (on the *napsok* system). Chŏn Hyŏngt'aek has written that the *napsok* or *songnyang* fee might be as high as 160 *sŏm* of rice, but generally it only cost 50 *sŏm*. He refrained from estimating just how many slaves bought their freedom this way, but in 1669 Kim Chwamyŏng noted that 5,000 *sŏm* had been raised from 100 people as *songnyang* fees. Chŏn pointed out that in 1662 the price for manumission dropped to 50 *sŏm*, and in 1718 50 *sŏm* for men between ages of 15–30, 40 *sŏm* for those 30–40, 30 *sŏm* for those 41–50, 20 *sŏm*, for those 51–55, and 10 *sŏm* for those 56–60. He concluded that a slave had to own at least 1 *kyŏl* or more of land to accumulate 50 *sŏm* of rice, an amount that would classify him as a rich peasant. For 100 *yang* of cash or 50 *p'il* of cloth a slave could pay 25 years' worth of *sin'gong* to buy one's freedom, the legal means to obtain escape from heavy service and slave status, but obviously only the rich slaves could afford it; the poor ones remained slaves. Chŏn Hyŏngt'aek, *Chosŏn hugi nobi sinbun yŏn'gu*, pp. 31, 207–9.

85. MHBG 62:20a-b.

86. Ibid. 62:20b–21a.

87. Ibid. 62:21a.

88. Ibid. 62:19b. The *Chungbo munhŏnbigo* also contains an undated account of Yu Kŭngnyang, whose mother had originally been a female slave of a high official but fled from her master's house in fear of punishment because she had broken a jade bowl. She then met and presumably married a man, no doubt a commoner, and gave birth to Yu. After Yu grew up, he passed the military examinations and rose to a prominent post in the civil administration. Only then did his mother reveal her origins to him. Yu was so upset he sought out his mother's old master and said he wanted to report himself to the court, give up his military examination degree, and become his male slave as was his due. The old master refused and even granted him a warrant of manumission. Yet in the future, whenever his mother's former master summoned him, he responded immediately, even when in the midst of his official duties at court. The point of this story is to illustrate the sense of duty, if not honor, that some people had toward the fulfillment of their proper roles in society. Similarly, manumission did not eliminate the sense of duty of the freed slave. MHBG 162:19b–20a.

89. Chŏn Hyŏngt'aek, *Chosŏn hugi nobi sinbun yŏn'gu*, pp. 121–42.

90. MHBG 62:19b.

91. Ibid. 62:19a-b; Yi I, *Yulgok chŏnsŏ* [The complete works of Yi I] 15:26a (Seoul: Sŏnggyun'gwan taehakkyo, Taedong munhwa yŏn'guwŏn, 1958). Hiraki Makoto has written that Yulgok's prestige was so great at the time that had he been fully committed to reform, he could have persuaded the king to take action. Hiraki, "Jūshichi-hachi seiki ni okeru nuryōsai shosei no kisoku ni tsuite" [On the status of offspring of male slaves and commoner wives in the seventeenth and eighteenth centuries], *Chōsen gakuhō* 61 (October 1971):49.

92. Kim Yŏngmo, "Chosŏn hugi sinbun kujo wa kŭ pyŏndong" [The social status structure and its change in late Chosŏn] *Tongbanghak chi* 26 (1981):123.

93. Cho Ik, *P'ojŏjip*, 13, pyŏnt'ong kunjong ŭi sangch'a, cited in Hiraki, "Jūshichi-hachi seiki nuryōsai," p. 50. This source was not available to me.

94. MHBG 162:23b–24a; *Hyŏnjong sillok* 20:20b–21a, which only refers to Song's recommendation; Song Siyŏl, *Songja taejŏn* [The great works of Master Song] (Taejŏn: Namyun chongsa, 1927) 13:32b–33a. It appears that the first concrete proposal to a king for adoption of the matrilineal rule was made in 1657 by the governor of Ch'ungch'ŏng province, Yi Kyŏng'ŏk, to King Hyojong, but it was not accepted. The account in the *Chŭngbo munhŏnbigo* states that Yi recommended that sons of mixed marriages adopt their father's service or status, and that daughters adopt their mother's; also that the king approved and a set of regulations were drawn up on this basis. But King Hyŏnjong's reference to Yi's proposal in 1669 noted that it was aimed at adoption of the matrilineal rule for sons as well as daughters of official or private male slaves and their commoner wives, the same plan as that of Yulgok, which was blocked by the State Council (Myodang). Shikata noted that neither the law code of 1744, the *Soktaejŏn*, nor subsequent notices in the *Munhŏnbigo* mentioned the adoption of any rule in 1657. Shikata Hiroshi, "Richō jinkō ni kansuru ichi kenkyū" [A study of Yi dynasty population], in idem, *Chōsen shakai hōseishi kenkyū* [Studies in the social and legal history of Korea] (Tokyo: Iwanami shoten, 1937):352–53.

95. The *Soktaejŏn* states that the matrilineal rule was adopted in 1669, rescinded in 1675, readopted in 1681 and rescinded in 1689, but Hiraki has found that readoption was only proposed in 1681 and not promulgated until 1684. *Soktaejŏn* [Dynastic code, continued] (Keijō: Chōsen Sōtokufu Chūsūin, 1935), p. 436; *Sukchŏng sillok*, Sukchong 10.10.ŭrmyo; Hiraki, "Jūshichi-hachi seiki ni okeru nuryōsai," pp. 45–75; see pp. 53–54 for discussion of the 1684 date. On the matter of Hŏ Chŏk's attitude, Yi Sangbaek believed that even though Hŏ Chŏk agreed to Song Siyŏl's proposal for the matrilineal law in 1669, he secretly opposed it. By asking that the matter be turned over to the *taesin* for discussion shows that he was trying to avoid responsibility. Yi Sangbaek, "Ch'ŏnja sumogo," pp. 173–74.

Chŏn Hyŏngt'aek adopted the rather simple line that Song Siyŏl, as a follower of Yulgok, favored adoption of the matrilineal rule as a means of expanding the commoner population because he and the Westerners (and the Westerner splinter Disciple's Faction, the Noron) represented not only the more practical orientation of Yulgok but the interests of large absentee landlords in the Kiho area (Kyŏnggi and Ch'ungch'ŏng) provinces who were satisfied with cultivating their estates with tenants and hired labor (not slaves). He blamed the Southerners like Hŏ Chŏk for opposing the matrilineal law and defending the interests of the slaveowners and the defense of social status (*myŏngbun*) because they supposedly represented the idealist and moralistic wing of Neo-Confucian thought sponsored by T'oegye (Yi Hwang), and because they represented the smallholding yangban of Kyŏngsang Province who relied on their outside resident slaves for cultivation. This formulation, however, is not proved by any demonstration about the nature of the yangban landowners in the three provinces or any differing degree of dependence on slave labor. And he does not mention that Hŏ Chŏk supported the matrilineal law prior to 1672. He also noted that the Sirhak scholars like Yu Hyŏngwŏn, Tasan, and others, while connected to the splinter factions of the Easterners, did favor the matrilineal reform and the reduction of slavery because of a practical idealism fostered by their exclusion from the political system. See Chŏn, *Chosŏn hugi nobi sinbun yŏn'gu*, pp. 212–16, 234, 238–39, 275.

96. Chŏn Hyŏngt'aek, *Chosŏn hugi nobi sinbun yŏn'gu*, p. 177, table 37, shows the quotas by status of troops in the Changyong *oeyŏng* as recorded in 1798. The quotas are subdivided into 6 districts (Suwŏn, Yong'in, Chinwi, Ansan, Sihŭng, and Kwach'ŏn, of which most were assigned to Suwŏn). The number of commoner troops was about 15,500 vs. 6,436 slave soldiers, or 30 percent of the total of 22,022, and the distribution was about equal for all the districts. If all the *sog'o* soldiers and the *abyŏng* were slaves, the percentage may have been over 30 percent.

97. Chŏn Hyŏngt'aek reported that during King Sukchong's reign all the commoners were excluded from service or cloth tax payments in the *sog'ogun*, and by Kyŏngjong's reign (1720s) all their soldiers were slaves. Chŏn, *Chosŏn hugi nobi sinbun yŏn'gu*, p. 170–71.

98. That is, children who had not yet lost their milk teeth. For a discussion of this text, see E. G. Pulleyblank, "The Origins and Nature of Chattel Slavery in China," *Journal of the Economic and Social History of the Orient* 1, pt. 2 (April 1958):199.

99. PGSR 26:9a–10a.

100. In 176 B.C. Emperor Wen freed slaves, but no reason was noted. In 140 B.C. Emperor Wu released from slavery the wives and children of the rebels of the Seven Feudatories because "he took pity on them." In A.D. 39 an imperial decree manumitted all persons in I-chou who had been made slaves since A.D. 34. PGSR 26:10–11a; Ch'ü T'ung-tsu, *Han Social Structure* (Seattle: University of Washington Press, 1972), p. 157.

101. PGSR 26:10a; cited in Wilbur, *Slavery in the Former Han Dynasty*, pp. 197–98, 312–13.

102. The system of pardons is discussed in great detail in Hamaguchi Shigekuni, *Tō ōchō no sennin seido* [A study of the system of base people in the T'ang dynasty] (Kyoto: Tōyōshi kenkyūkai, 1966); Niida Noboru, *Shina mibumpōshi*. For regulations pertaining to slaves in English translation, see *The T'ang Code*, vol. I, transl. Wallace Johnson (Princeton, N. J.: Princeton University Press, 1979).

103. Wilbur, *Slavery in China*, pp. 138–39.

104. There is only brief mention of Yu's discussion of slavery in Ch'ŏn Kwan'u's earliest study of Yu's thought, "Pan'gye Yu Hyŏngwŏn yŏn'gu," part 1, *Yŏksa hakpo* 2 (1952):69–70. The first extensive and scholarly treatment was the very important article by Chŏng Kubok, "Pan'gye Yu Hyŏngwŏn ŭi sahoe kaehyŏk sasang" [Yu Hyŏngwŏn's ideas for the reform of society], *Yŏksa hakpo* 15 (March, 1970):31–38. I wish to acknowledge my debt to the last article in providing a useful introduction to Yu's ideas, but for the sake of brevity I will cite it only on certain points of interpretation.

105. PGSR 26:4a-b.

106. Ibid. 26:4b. See also 21:38b.

107. PGSR 26:4b–5a.

108. Ibid. 26:4b; 26:1b.

109. Ibid. 26:1b, 4b.

110. KSDSJ 1:1439–40.

111. PGSR 26:3a-b.

112. Ibid. 26:3b–4a.

113. Ibid. 26:5a,7a-b.

114. Ibid. 26:7a.

115. Ibid. 26:8b; Chŏng Kubok, "Pan'gye kaehyŏk sasang," p. 33.

116. PGSR 26:8b–9a.

117. Wilbur, *Slavery in China*, pp. 452–53, doc. 122. dated A.D. 9. For an alternate translation see Pan Ku, *History of the Former Han Dynasty*, trans. by Homer H. Dubs (Baltimore: Waverley Press, 1955), p. 285.

118. PGSR 26:1a. See also 21:39a.

119. Ibid. 26:1a.

120. Ibid. 26:1a.

121. MHBG 162:23b–24a; *Hyŏnjong sillok* 20:20b–21a, which only refers to Song's recommendation. The memorial does not seem to be in his collected works in the section on memorials presented in 1669, *Songja taejŏn* 13:10b–27b.

122. See n.88. Chŏn Hyŏngt'aek, *Chosŏn hugi nobi sinbun yŏn'gu*, pp. 238–39, 275.

123. PGSR 26:5a.

124. Ibid. 26:5a-b.

125. Ibid. 26:5a.

126. Ibid. 26:5b–6a.

127. Pak Sŏngsu, "Kogong yŏn'gu," [A study of hired labor], *Sahak yŏn'gu* 18 (September 1964):539, 544, 546, 548–51.

128. PGSR 26:6a.

129. Pak Sŏngsu, "Kogong yŏn'gu," pp. 527–54.

130. Ibid.

131. PGSR 26:6b–7a.

132. Ibid. 26:6b.

133. Ibid.

134. Ibid. 26:6b–7a.

135. Ibid. 26:7a.

136. Ibid.

137. Kim Yongsŏp, *Chosŏn hugi nong'ŏpsa yŏn'gu: Nongch'on kyŏngje, sahoe pyŏndong* [Studies in the agricultural history of late Chosŏn: The village economy and social change] (Seoul: Ilchogak, 1970); idem, *Chosŏn hugi nong'ŏpsa yŏn'gu: nong'ŏp pyŏndong, nonghak sajo* [Studies in the agricultural history of late Chosŏn: Changes in agriculture and trends in agricultural studies] (Seoul: Ilchogak, 1971). See his other articles in the bibliography.

138. Ch'oe Chun'o, "Sipp'al shipku segi nong'ŏp koyong nodong ŭi chŏn'gae wa paltal" [The expansion and development of agricultural hired labor in the eighteenth and nineteenth centuries], *Han'guksa yŏn'gu* 77 (June 1992):57–88.

139. Kang Man'gil, "Chosŏn hugi koripche paltal" [The development of the late Chosŏn hired labor system], *Han'guksa yŏn'gu* 13 (July 1976):73.

140. Han Yŏngguk, "Chosŏn hugi ŭi kogong: 18–19 segi Taegu-bu hojŏk esŏ pon kŭ silt'ae wa sŏnkyŏk" [Hired labor in late Chosŏn: The real situation and character of hired

labor as seen through the household registers of Taegu in the eighteenth and nineteenth centuries], *Yŏksa hakpo* 81 (March 1979):81–124.

141. Ibid., see table 2, p. 86, table 4, p. 87, table 6, p. 89.

142. Ibid., pp. 90–95.

143. Ibid., pp. 106–7.

144. Ibid., pp. 97–102.

145. Ibid., pp. 114–16.

146. Ibid., pp. 116–19. Even though this kind of lifetime indentured servitude was presumably abolished in 1783, it still continued. Ibid., p. 123.

147. Ch'oe Chun'o, "Koyong nodong," pp. 82–83.

148. Fernand Braudel, *Civilization and Capitalism, 15th-18th Century*, vol. 2, *The Wheels of Commerce* (New York: Harper and Row, 1982), pp. 49–54.

149. Georges Duby, *The Early Growth of the European Economy: Warriors and Peasants from the Seventh to the Twelfth Century*, trans. Howard B. Clarke (Ithaca, N.Y.: Cornell University Press, 1974), p. 226.

150. Han Yŏngguk, "Chosŏn hugi ŭi kogong," p. 86.

151. Chŏn Sŏkchong, *Chosŏn hugi sahoe pyŏndong yŏn'gu* [A study of the social changes in the late Chosŏn period] (Seoul: Ilchogak, 1983), pp. 279–87.

152. Han Yŏngguk, "Chosŏn chungyŏp ŭi nobi kyŏlhon yangt'ae" [Marriages of slaves in mid-Chosŏn], *Yŏksa hakpo* 77 (1978):123.

153. Pak Nouk. "Chosŏn sidae komunsŏsang ŭi yong'ŏ kŏmt'o: t'oji nobi mun'girŭl chungsim'ŭro" [An investigation of the use of terms in old documents of the Chosŏn period]. *Tongbanghak chi* 68 (October 1990):112–13, 118. Edward W. Wagner deduced that in the 1663 household register for the northern district of Seoul, the term *pan,* when used for a female slave married to a male slave, indicated that her owner was the same as her husband's, or that the slave listed was the possession of an owner already listed in the document. "Social Stratification in Seventeenth-Century Korea: Some Observations from a 1663 Seoul Census Register," *Occasional Papers on Korea*, no. 1 (April, 1974), pp. 52–53. Pak Nouk, however, amended this interpretation of *panno* to mean "a slave of the same category," that is "a slave who did the same kind of work or service as other slaves," or "a slave of the [same] family" (p. 111), not Wagner's interpretation of "slave of the above-listed owner."

154. *Sukchong sillok* 7:12b–13a, Sukchong 4.4.kisa (1678), cited in Yi Sangbaek, "Ch'ŏnja sumogo," p. 173; Hiraki Makoto, "Jūshichi-hachi seiki ni okeru nuryōsai shosei no kisoku ni tsuite" [On the status of offspring of male slaves and commoner wives in the seventeenth and eighteenth centuries], *Chōsen gakuhō* 61 (October 1971):53–54; Hiraki, *Chosŏn hugi nobije yŏn'gu*, pp. 132–34; Chŏn Hyŏngt'aek, *Chosŏn hugi nobi sinbun yŏn'gu*, pp. 238–39, 275. Hiraki in the second of his works cited above has shown that the chronology in the *Soktaejŏn* of 1744 is wrong. According to this source, the matrilineal rule was supposed to have been rescinded in 1675, but the evidence is lacking from the primary sources save for a reference later in 1730 to Ho Chŏk's supposed opposition to the matrilineal rule in 1675. See ibid., n.13, reference to SJW 716, Yŏngjo 6.12.26, 1730. Susan Shin deduced from her study of the Kŭmhwa household register of 1672 that the matrilineal rule of 1669 was obviously not being enforced. "The Social Struc-

ture of Kŭmhwa County in the Late Seventeenth Century," *Occasional Papers on Korea*, no. 1 (April, 1974), p. 14. Ellen Kim found that the matrilineal rule was not fully observed in her study, "The Enduring Institution: A Case Study of Slavery in Traditional Korea" (B.A. thesis, Harvard College, 1991).

155. *Sukchong sillok* 21:49b, Sukchong 15.12.ŭrhaek (13th day), cited in Hiraki, *Chosŏn hugi nobije yŏn'gu*, p. 136, n. 22.

156. Hiraki Makoto, "Jūshichi-hachi seiki ni okeru nuryōsai shosei," pp. 55–61; Hiraki, *Chosŏn hugi nobije yŏn'gu*, pp. 134–36. For proposals made in 1680 see *Sukchong sillok* 11:11a, Sukchong 7.1.kyŏng'o. On this day, Min Chŏngjung praised the effectiveness of the matrilineal rule for producing more men of good status for the state and the wisdom of Yulgok for proposing the idea. For proposals made in 1684 see *Sukchong sillok* 15,ha:32b–33a, Sukchong 10.10.ŭrmyo (1684); for rescission of the law in 1689 see *Sukchong sillok* 21:49b, Sukchong 15.12.ŭrhaek.

For a discussion of the history of the matrilineal rule from 1669 to 1731, see also Chŏn Hyŏngt'aek, "Sipkusegich'o naesinobi ŭi hyŏkp'a" [Changes in government slaves in the early nineteenth century], *Han'guksaron* 4 (March 1978):204–11. Chŏn emphasized the factional basis for the dispute over the matrilineal law.

157. *Yŏngjo sillok* 27:25a, Yŏngjo 6.9. pyŏngsul, cited in Hiraki Makoto, "Jūshichi-hachi seiki ni okeru nuryōsai shosei," pp. 69–72. See also Yi Sangbaek, "Ch'ŏnja sumogo," p. 176; Chŏn Hyŏngt'aek, "Sipkusegich'o naesinobi ŭi hyŏkp'a," pp. 208–10.

158. Hiraki, "Jūshichi hachi seiki," p. 74.

159. Kim Yongsŏp, "Yang'an ŭi yŏn'gu: Chosŏn hugi ŭi nonka kyŏngje" [A study of the land registers: The peasant households in the late Chosŏn dynasty], in idem, *Chosŏn hugi nong'ŏpsa yŏn'gu* 1 (Seoul: Ilchogak, 1970):164.

160. Chŏn Hyŏngt'aek, "Sipkusegich'o naesinobi ŭi hyŏkp'a," pp. 192–204; Kim Yongsŏp, "Chosŏn hugi sinbunje ŭi tongyo wa nongji soyu" [The shakeup of the status system and the ownership of agricultural land in late Chosŏn], in idem, *Chosŏn hugi nong'ŏpsa yŏn'gu: nongch'on kyŏngje, sahoe pyŏndong* [Studies in the agricultural history of late Chosŏn: The village economy and social change] (Seoul: Ilchogak, 1970), pp. 424–26.

161. Hiraki, *Chosŏn hugi nobije yŏn'gu*, pp. 165–81, discusses different types of manumission by purchase or merit and prices by age category in the seventeenth and eighteenth centuries. Chŏn Hyŏngt'aek, *Chosŏn hugi nobi sinbun yŏn'gu*, chap. 2 and pp. 188–201; Kim Yŏngmo, "Chosŏn hugi ŭi sinbun kujo wa kŭ pyŏndong," pp. 127–33.

162. The official was Yun Tongdo, SJW 1192, p. 686d, Yŏngjo 37.4.17, cited in Chŏn Hyŏngt'aek, "Sipkusegich'o naesinobi ŭi hyŏkp'a," p. 203.

163. For a full discussion of the sources, see Chŏn Hyŏngt'aek, "Sipkusegich'o naesinobi ŭi hyŏkp'a," pp. 211–13. For the reference to Hong Ponghan's statement in 1761, see SJW 1200, p. 192a, Yŏngjo 37.12.1 (1761). The record of Yi Ikp'o's scolding of Hong Ponghan is in Sŏng Taejung's *Ch'ŏngsŏngjip*, cited in Chŏn Hyŏngt'aek, p. 212.

164. Ellen Kim, "Enduring Institution," pp. 87–88.

165. Shikata Hiroshi, "Richō jinkō ni kansuru mibun kaikyūbetsuteki kansatsu" [An investigation of Yi dynasty population in terms of status and class], in Chōsen teikoku

daigaku hōgakkai, ed. *Chōsen keizai no kenkyū* [Studies in the economy of Korea] 3 (Tokyo: Iwanami shoten, 1938): 363–482.

166. Ibid., pp. 388–89. My calculations based on his raw data vary slightly from Shikata's own percentages. These calculations show a drop in slave households from 37.1 percent in 1690, to 26.6 percent in 1729–32, to 8.5 percent in 1783–89, and finally to 1.5 percent in 1858. Ibid., p. 386–87.

167. Ibid., pp. 392, 394.

168. Yi Chun'gu, "Chosŏn hugi yangban sinbun idong e kwanhan yŏn'gu, ha" [A study of the movement of yangban status in late Chosŏn], *Yŏksa hakpo* 97 (March 1983):3, n. 171; Kim Yŏngmo, "Chosŏn hugi ŭi sinbun kujo wa kŭ pyŏndong," pp. 53–153.

169. Pak Nouk, "Chosŏn sidae komunsŏsang ŭi yong'ŏ kŏmt'o," pp. 98–108. The term *solgŏ nobi* used to be interpreted as "domestic slaves," but Pak Nouk has demonstrated that this is a mistranslation because they did not necessarily live in the master's house. They were slaves who were regarded as members of the master's household and whom the master "could lead, command," or "mobilize for personal service according to his needs (pp. 98–99)." Pak thinks that they could be regarded as "service slaves" (*angyŏk nobi*), who owed service to their masters wherever they might have lived (pp. 100–101).

170. Chŏn Sŏkchong, *Chosŏn hugi sahoe pyŏndong yŏn'gu*, pp. 248–49; 279–81.

171. Ellen Kim, "Enduring Institution," pp. 71–73, 107, including table 4, p. 71, and fig. 5, p. 72.

172. Yi Ik, *Sŏngho saesŏl*, Insamun, 16b–17b (Seoul: Kyŏnghŭi ch'ulp'ansa, 1967) 1:414.

173. Yi Ik, *Sŏngho saesŏl yusŏn* (Keijō: Chōsen kosho kankōkai, 1915), pp. 356–57; Chŏn, "Sipkusegich'o naesinobi," p. 150; Hiraki Makoto, *Chŏsen gōki nuhisei kenkyū*, pp. 215–17; Han Woo-keun, *Yijo hugi ŭi sahoe wa sasang*, pp. 287–98.

174. Yu Suwŏn, *Usŏ* 168d (Seoul: Sŏul taehakkyo ch'ulp'anbu, pref. dated 1969), pp. 7–8; Han Yŏng'u, "Yu Suwŏn ŭi sinbun kaehyŏk sasang" [Yu Suwŏn's ideas about the reform of social status], *Han'guksa yŏn'gu* 8 (September 1972):35–39; Paolo Santangelo, *La Vita e l'opera di Yu Suwŏn Pensatore Coreano del XVIII Secolo* (Napoli: Istituto Universitario Orientale, Seminario di Studi Asiatici, 1981), pp. 73–79; Hiraki Makoto, *Chŏsen gōki nuhisei kenkyū*, pp. 218–19.

175. He must be referring to the *chŏnsikwa* system of the tenth to twelfth centuries. See James B. Palais, "Land Tenure in Korea: Tenth to Twelfth Centuries," *Journal of Korean Studies* 4 (1982–83):73–206.

176. Yu Suwŏn, *Usŏ*, pp. 8–9; Han Yŏng'u, "Yu Suwŏn," p. 40.

177. Yu Suwŏn, *Usŏ,* pp. 7c-d.

178. Ibid, p. 8b; Han Yŏng'u, "Yu Suwŏn," p. 41.

179. *Usŏ*, p. 131; Han Yŏng'u, "Yu Suwŏn," p. 41.

180. Yu Suwŏn, *Usŏ*, p. 131, 165; Han Yŏng'u, "Yu Suwŏn," pp. 40–41, 47; Santangelo, *La Vita*, pp. 78–79.

181. Yu Suwŏn, *Usŏ*, pp. 165–67, p. 166 for the above quote; Han Yŏng'u, "Yu Suwŏn," pp. 32–38.

182. Han Yŏng'u, "Yu Suwŏn"; pp. 42–48, 53, 55–58.

183. Yu Suwŏn, *Usŏ*, pp. 160–61; Han Yŏng'u, "Yu Suwŏn," pp. 58–60.

184. Chŏn Hyŏngt'aek, *Chosŏn hugi nobi sinbun yŏn'gu*, pp. 175–76.

185. The material in this section is based on Chŏn Hyŏngt'aek, "Sipkusegich'o naesinobi ŭi hyŏkp'a," pp. 189–260.

186. Chŏn Hyŏngt'aek, *Chosŏn hugi nobi sinbun yŏn'gu*, pp. 121–42.

187. Chŏn Hyŏngt'aek, "Sipkusegich'o naesinobi," p. 218. Table 1 gives a breakdown of central bureau and royal treasury and palace slaves. MHBG 162:18a lists for the year 1484, 261,984 capital and provincial male and female slaves and 90,581 district (and?) post-station male and female slaves, a total of 352,565.

188. The quotas of slaves for each province under the fixed quota system based on the *ŭrhak naesi nobi kamgong kŭptae samok* of 1755 are shown in table III-A and III-B in Chŏn Hyŏngt'aek, "Sipkusegich'o naesinobi," p. 236. There were major differences among the provinces. Most of the capital bureau slaves were in Kyŏngsang, and most of the royal treasury slaves were in the north, in Hamgyŏng, P'yŏng'an, and Hwanghae. Many slaves were needed in Hamgyŏng at the two palaces located in Hamhŭng and Yŏnghŭng for the conduct of ancestral rites, and there was a lot of palace land (*sagung changt'o*) in Hwanghae. There were many *sinobi* or central bureau slaves in Kyŏngsang because of the large numbers of artisans there. Table III-A shows 30,617 capital bureau slaves, with 20,350 in Kyŏngsang (14,101 of which were female slaves) and 5,678 in P'yŏng'an. Table III-B shows 5,574 royal treasury slaves, with 1,200–1,500 in the three northern provinces. See also Chŏn Hyŏngt'aek, *Chosŏn hugi nobi sinbun yŏn'gu*, pp. 43–47 and 231 for complaints about the shortages of substitute revenues after the rate reduction on slave tribute in 1755.

189. The provincial quotas were too high to begin with because the slave population of 1750 was taken as the standard; there were in fact far fewer official slaves in existence when the law was adopted. After the abolition of the slave registrars district magistrates were lax in investigating the slave population and turned over the work to clerks who either took bribes or neglected runaways. Even though the slave population of individual districts changed, magistrates were reluctant to report the results because an increase in the number of reported slaves would naturally mean an increase in the slave tribute due from the district. In general, quotas tended to remain constant even though there were reductions in the actual number of official slaves in some districts due to runaways, deaths, old age exemption from service, epidemics, and famine, and in some areas slave service was three or four times greater than what it was supposed to be. Chŏn Hyŏngt'aek, "Sipkusegich'o naesinobi," pp. 227–41.

190. Ibid.

191. *Yŏngjo sillok* 122:5a-b, 7a, Yŏngjo 50.2.chŏngyu, 50.3.pyŏng'in; SJW 1349, Yŏngjo 50.3.11, 12, 13, vol. 75, pp. 581, 584, 586, 588, 590 of the *Kuksa p'yŏnch'an wiwŏnhoe* ed., cited in Chŏn Hyŏngt'aek, "Sipkusegich'o naesinobi," pp. 225–26.

192. For discussion of the high percentage of runaway official slaves, see Chŏn Hyŏngt'aek, *Chosŏn hugi nobi sinbun yŏn'gu*, pp. 230–31.

193. MHBG 162:10b–11a.

194. "Only by consulting the blood line [of people], are they treated as slaves for a hundred generations. For this reason some ignorant and base person could control the life or death of others, and even if someone of outstanding talent should appear among [the slaves], he too would be confined to being the slave of another. How is this reasonable [lit., By what principle]?" MHBG 162:22b; PGSR 21:38b–39a, 26:4a-b; Chŏn, "Sipkusegich'o naesinobi," p. 250.

195. A revised edition was presented to King Chŏngjo in 1783. Yi Usŏng, annotated commentary, in Chōsen kosho kankōkai ed., apparently photographically reproduced, An Chŏngbok, *Tongsa kangmok*, 3 vols. (Seoul: Kyŏng'in munhwasa, 1970), frontpapers. Yun Namhan gives the dates 1756–59 for completion of the text, annotated introduction to An Chŏngbok, *Kugyŏk Tongsa kangmok* (Seoul: Minjok munhwa ch'ujinhoe, 1977) 1:3–8.

196. An Chŏngbok, *Tongsa kangmok* 2:20–21; 1977, 3:221–22; idem, *Kugyŏk tongsa kangmok* 2:221–22. The *Chŭngbo munhŏnbigo* selection is a slightly contracted version of this quotation. MHBG 162:9a–10a.

197. For references to An's discussion of Kija and instances of slavery in early Korean history to the early Koryŏ period, see the following pages in the Chōsen kosho kankōkai edition of An Chŏngbok, *Tongsa kangmok* 1:105, 118, 233, 2:98, 147–48. For these and other later references, check the index under *nobi* in vol. 10 of the Minjok munhwa ch'ujinhoe 1977 edition. KSDSJ 1:884; *Chōsenshi* [History of Korea] (Keijō: Chōsen sōtokufu, 1937), series 5, 10: 670 states that An became tutor or advisor to the crown prince in 1772, probably until his appointment as district magistrate four years later.

198. An Chŏngbok, *Tongsa kangmok* 3:221–22.

199. Ibid. 2:48, dated 987.7th month; enactment of the *nobi hwanch'ŏnbŏp* (law returning slaves to base status).

200. Ibid. 2:129–30; Minjok munhwa ch'ujinhoe ed. (1977), 4:80, notice about first adoption of the *ch'ŏnja chongmobŏp* (matrilineal succession law) in 1039.

201. Chŏngjo himself commented that since slaves who became commoners gained no particular tax advantage since they still had to pay the 1 *p'il yangyŏk* (commoner cloth tax) – the same rate as commoner support taxpayers – the reason so many of them were anxious to become commoners was because they hated being called slaves. *Chŏngjo sillok* 32:37a-b, Chŏngjo 15.3.kyemyo, (1791). In 1796 the magistrate of Pŏun, Yun Chedong, said that "People preferred being noble to base, just as they preferred life to death . . . and that they evaded tribute because there was nothing baser than the name of slave." MHBG 162:32a-b, dated Chŏngjo 20 (1796). These statements along with examples of people who ran away to evade slave status rather than tax levies are cited in Chŏn Hyŏngt'aek, "Sipkusegich'o naesinobi," pp. 242–47.

In 1795, Yang Chuik proposed fusing commoners and slaves and abolishing slavery. He argued that both slaves and commoners were the children of the king. While commoners were controlled by the state, slaves were under the control of the state and private families and thus carried a double burden. Ibid., p. 250, citation of Yang Chuik, *Agŭkchip* 3, so (memorials). Chŏng Sanggi also wrote that the burden on slaves was worse than commoners because they paid tribute either to their masters or to the capital bureaus and also owed labor service to the local magistrate. Further, the requirement that female slaves pay tribute (*pigong*) only made the slaves poorer. He also advocated joining slaves and commoners together and adjusting personal tribute according to wealth. Ibid., citation of *Nongp'o mundap*, kyunminyŏk (on the equalization of service obligations of the people; full quote on p. 220, n. 103.

202. Ibid., pp. 246–47.

203. *Chŏngjo sillok* 32:37a–39a, Chŏngjo 15.3.kyemyo (1791); Chŏn, "Sipkusegich'o naesinobi," p. 249; Hiraki, *Chosŏn hugi nobije yŏn'gu*, pp. 192–94.

204. See ibid., p. 194, n. 8 for sources.

205. A total of 66,067 male and female official slaves were abolished, including 36,974 *naenobi* of the various palaces, and 29,093 *sinobi* of the various capital bureaus. The order did not include all official slaves, but the *sŏnsang* and *ibyŏk* for the *kaksa nobi* (slaves of the capital bureaus) was abolished and people from the capital were hired to take their place. The liberated *naesi nobi* were enrolled for *yangyŏk* commoner service and some were assigned to the palaces in Hamhŭng and Yŏnghŭng to pay 1 *yang* of cash as *sinyŏk* (personal service tax payments), and they were called *kungsok kasol* (temporary dependents attached to the palaces); the *kasol* were equivalent to *poin* or support taxpayers. Official slaves were still left in other places, especially slaves confiscated from people who had been guilty of criminal offenses as punishment. Chŏn Hyŏngt'aek, *Chosŏn hugi nobi sinbun yŏn'gu*, pp. 241, 244, 247–66.

206. Her title was Chŏngsun wanghu, 1745–1805, of the Kyŏngju Kim clan. The daughter of Han Ku, she became Yŏngjo's second queen in 1759. She had no children of her own and did not get along well with Crown Prince Sado. She and her father calumniated the prince and contributed to his virtual execution. KSDSJ 2:1356–57.

207. The government in 1800 consisted of the leaders of the Noron, Yi Pyŏngmo, Chief State Councilor Sim Hwanji, Councilor of the Left Yi Sisu, Councilor of the Right Sŏ Yongbo, Minister of Taxation Yi Sŏgu, and Sŏnhyech'ŏng tangsang Cho Chin'gwan and Yun Haeng'im. Chŏn Hyŏngt'aek, *Chosŏn hugi nobi sinbun yŏn'gu*, p. 239.

208. ILSN 18, Sunjo sinyu.1.38, sinyu.2.4 (1801) cited in Hiraki Makoto, *Chosŏn hugi nobije yŏn'gu*, pp. 196–99; MHBG 162:34a–36a.

209. Hiraki Makoto, *Chosŏn hugi nobije yŏn'gu*, pp. 197–202; Chŏn Hyŏngt'aek, "Shipkusegich'o naesinobi," pp. 241–60; Chŏn Hyŏngt'aek, *Chosŏn hugi nobi sinbun yŏn'gu*, pp. 243–46.

210. Chŏn Hyŏngt'aek, "Shipkusegich'o naesinobi," pp. 248–50. Chŏn Hyŏngt'aek has concluded that the debate over the abolition of official slaves was divided primarily, but not exclusively, along factional lines. Although some members of all hereditary bureaucratic factions were found on both sides of the fence, most of the advocates of abolition were from the Patriarch's faction descended from Song Siyŏl. They were more concerned with practical problems of state finance than the Southerner and *sip'a* factions, who were the leading proponents of status discrimination. The *sip'a* were those who had defended Chŏngjo's father, Crown Prince Sado (the Sado seja), when he was murdered by his own father, King Yŏngjo, 1762. (They were opposed by the *pyŏkp'a* who defended Yŏngjo's action.) For a discussion of the Sado seja's murder, see JaHyun

Kim Haboush, *A Heritage of Kings: One Man's Monarchy in the Confucian World* (New York: Columbia University Press, 1988). Since the *sip'a* and Southerners supported Chŏngjo's elevation to the throne, they inhibited his natural sympathy for the slaves. If the Southerners and *sip'a* were responsible for obstructing slave reform, one wonders why Yŏngjo himself did not himself abolish official slavery when the bureaucracy had very few Southerners in it. For that matter, even when there were more of them in Chŏngjo's government (1776–1800), there was continuous progress in easing the opportunity for manumission.

211. Hiraki attributed the following statement made in court conference in 1601 to Yun Sŭnghun, but it seems to be included in remarks made by Cho Suik, who was complaining about the shortage of troops. In any case:

> In my humble opinion the law of private slavery exists only in our country. Heaven gives birth to the myriad people and endows them equally. You cannot say at all that at the time they are born on this earth, they [people] are already divided into noble and base. Even though the standards [of elegant living?] of our country are very common and inferior, if our ancestors happened to have a few slaves, they were able to sit at ease and enjoy the pleasures of dukes and marquises. How could there be such a principle?
>
> Earlier Confucian scholars have said about the well-field system that the only time you can implement it is right after a major upheaval [war or rebellion] in the world. At the present time the situation of our country is [as precarious as if it were hanging by] a hair. Even though we have slaves, no one dares talk about it. We must use the law of China and abolish forever the adult males and slaves granted to the families of the chief ministers on down and make them soldiers.
>
> It is said that in the past during the Koryŏ [period] at the time that the Eastern Expeditionary Headquarters was established [by the Mongols], the Chinese officials asked about our law of private slavery because they wanted to abolish it, but at the time our king and high ministers stopped it. These were the views of inferior rulers and ministers. How can they be taken up for discussion? At the present time the fortunes of the country have taken a turn for the better. It is a time when all institutions have been renewed. We cannot stick stubbornly to the mistaken laws of former times. (*Sŏnjo sillok* 142:15a, Sŏnjo 34.10.kich'uk, cited in Hiraki Makoto, *Chŏsen hugi nobije yŏn'gu*, p. 221)

212. Chŏn Hyŏngt'aek pointed out that the tribute tax rate on official slaves had been reduced to half that of commoners because they also had to pay the personal tribute tax to their private masters. *Chosŏn hugi nobi sinbun yŏn'gu*, pp. 173–74.

213. The regulations also specified that once a person had sold himself into slavery, even if for only a day, his status became fixed and irreversible; he could not lightly be exempted from slavery. MHBG, 162:36b–37a.

214. Barry Hindess and Paul Q. Hirst, *Pre-capitalist Modes of Production* (London, Henley and Boston: Routledge and Kegan Paul, 1975), pp. 115–16, et passim, especially pp. 125–77.

CHAPTER 7. Land Reform: Compromises with the Well-Field Model

1. PGSR 1:1a-b.

2. Ibid. 1:2b–3a.

3. Yu Hyŏngwŏn cited a host of classical sources and later commentaries on the nature of the well-field system (*ching-t'ien* in Chinese, *kyŏngjŏn* in Korean). I have decided to use the model described in the *Mencius*, for which see James Legge, *The Chinese Classics*, copyright reissue in 5 vols. (Hong Kong University Press, 1960), pt. 3, bk. 1, sec. 3, 19, and PGSR, 5:15a, 16a-b. For Yu's treatment of Mencius with several commentaries, see pp. 100–103 of the Kojŏn kanhaenghoe edition of the PGSR. For the *Han-shih* account by Pan Ku, which varies in certain respects from the *Mencius*, see ibid. 5:7a. Mencius's account indicates the absence of private ownership since land was distributed to people at the age of fifteen and taken back at the age of sixty. Several poems in the *Shih-ching* (*Book of Poetry*) suggest that the peasants distinguished between their own "private" (*sa*) fields and the "public" (*kong*) fields of their lords. PGSR 5:6a, 11b–12a, and the Shan Man-shan ode of the *Shih-ching*, Legge, pp. 373–74, pt. 2, bk. 6, ode 6, sec. 1; the *Ta-t'ien* ode, Legge, p. 381, pt. 2, bk. 6, ode 8, sec. 3; and the *E ho* ode, Legge, p. 584, pt. 4, bk. 1 (ii), ode 2. Yet "private" fields obviously refers only to a right of cultivation, not ownership in the modern, Western sense.

4. According to the *Shih-chi*, in the third year of Ch'in Hsiao-kung, Duke Hsiao adopted the reforms of Yang of Wei. In the twelfth year the well fields were abolished and the *ch'ien* and *mo* (*ch'ŏn* and *maek* in Korean pronunciation) were "opened up." See *Shih-chi*, Chung-hua shu-chü (Peking 1962) 1:203, for the adoption of Wei Yang's reforms and 7:2230, for a description of the system of mutual surveillance that was established; 7:2232, for the "opening up" of the *ch'ien* and *mo*. The Harvard Index to the *Shih-chi* also refers to the Wu-chou t'ung-wen shu-chu ed., pp. 647a, 1525b, and 685a, the last referring to the Lieh-chüan biography of Lord Shang.

See also *Tzu-chih t'ung-chien*, compiled by Ssu-ma Kuang, Shang-mu yin-shu-kuan ed., 33:6a-b, and the *Tzu-chih t'ung-chien kang-mu*, compiled by Chu Hsi, 7:53a-b, 1701 edition of a commentary by Ch'en Jen-hsi (1581–1636). See also the remarks of Su Hsün in Wm. Theodore de Bary, Wing-tsit Chan and Burton Watson eds., *Sources of Chinese Tradition* (New York: Columbia University Press, 1964) 1:406.

For a discussion of the origins of private ownership and its practice in the Han dynasty, see William Gordon Crowell, "Government Land Policies and Systems in Early Imperial China" (Ph.D. diss., University of Washington, 1979), pp. 42, 92–110.

5. PGSR 5:24a-b.

6. Yu Hyŏngwŏn's discussion of the relationship of private property to the feasibility of the well-field system in Chinese thought begins with Chu Hsi's commentary on Lord Shang's abolition of the well fields and his "opening up of the *ch'ien* and *mo* [*ch'ŏn*, *maek*]." Chu Hsi argued that the *ch'ien* and *mo* referred to the system of waterways already mentioned in the *Chou-li* that was used in areas other than where the well-field system had been adopted. The Ch'in found that the system of dikes and pathways was using too much land that otherwise could be cultivated, and to increase production, destroyed these as well as the well fields. Yu's text states:

> [Lord Shang] opened up [i.e., destroyed] the *ch'ien* and *mo* and completely eliminated all prohibitions and restrictions [on the use and ownership of land] and allowed the people [private persons] to accumulate large holdings and buy and sell [land] in order to fully utilize human labor and open up to cultivation land that had been abandoned. All land was treated as arable land and not an inch's worth was left [uncultivated], so that there would be complete utilization of the profits from the land." Ibid. 5:21b.

In any case, Chu Hsi's commentary clearly shows his preference for the Chou system of boundaries and allotments and his distaste for unrestrained private ownership and economic exploitation for profit.

7. Ibid. 5:21b–22a.

8. Yu also noted that the opinion of Ch'iu Chün of the Ming was similar to his own. Ibid. 5:23a.

9. Ibid. 5:23a-b. Yu also cited the Kung-yang commentary to the *Spring and Autumn Annals* to the effect that too low a tax rate, i.e., below the rate of one-tenth the crop, was not right either. Yu omitted Ho Hsiu's explanation, which was that the barbarians had a light tax because they did not need to provide funds for the conduct of rites, something any civilized state should be doing. See also *Ch'un-ch'iu kung-yang chuan chu-shu* 16:8a, Ssu-pu pei-yao ed. (Shanghai 1936?), v. 157–62; PGSR 5:18a.

10. PGSR 5:23b; *T'ung-tien, chüan* 1, *shih-huo, 1*, Kuo-hsüeh chi-pen ts'ung-shu ed., p. 11.

11. PGSR 5:24a-b; *T'ung-tien*, ch. 1, *shih-huo*, 1, Hsin-hsing shu-chü ed., p. 9b.

12. PGSR 5:36a.

13. Ibid. 6:14a-b.

14. Ibid. 1:1a-b.

15. Ibid. 1:1a.

16. The discussion of the well-field system (*ching-t'ien* in Chinese, *kyŏngjŏn* in Korean) is most complex because of conflicting accounts in the source materials. Yu Hyŏngwŏn cited a host of classical sources and later commentaries on this problem. I have decided to use the model described in the *Mencius*, for which see Legge, *The Chinese Classics*, and PGSR 5:15a, 16a-b. Yu's treatment of Mencius with several commentaries is quite extensive, covering pp. 100–103 of the Kojŏn kanhaenghoe edition of the PGSR. Yu also described the *Han-shih* account by Pan Ku, according to which 8 farmers of farm families received 100 *myo* (*mu* in Chinese), plus 10 *myo* each of *kongjŏn* (*kung-t'ien* in Chinese), a total of 880 *myo*. An additional 20 *myo* was set aside for land for houses. PGSR 5:7a.

For a recent discussion of the well-field system, see Crowell, "Government Land Policies and Systems in Early Imperial China," pp. 42–61. For a valuable survey of the well-field system see Katō Shigeshi, *Shina kodensei no kenkyū* [A study of the ancient land system of China] (Kyōto: Kyōto hōgakkai, 1916).

All technical terms, whether in Chinese or Korean, will be rendered in Korean pronunciation unless otherwise indicated.

17. PGSR 5:18b.

18. Ibid. 1:5a.

19. Ibid. 1:19b; *Kuksa-daesajŏn* [Great dictionary of Korean history], Yi Hongjik ed. 1 (Seoul 1962):247.

20. See n. 3, supra.

21. Consult Katō Shigeshi, *Shina kodensei*, and Hori Toshikazu, *Kindensei no kenkyū*. [A study of the equal-field system] (Tokyo: Iwanami shoten, 1975).

22. PGSR 5:18a. See also *Ch'un-ch'iu Kung-yang chüan-chu-shu*, Ssu-pu pei-yao ed. 16 (Shanghai 1936?):8a.

23. See the article by Miyazaki Uchisada on *shih-ta-fu* (*sadaebu* in Korean) in *Ajia rekishi jiten* 4 (Tokyo: Heibonsha, 1962):174a, and the article by Masubuchi Tatsuo on the Spring and Autumn period in ibid. 4:343a-b.

24. PGSR 1:2a, 6b–7a.

25. Ibid. 1:10a.

26. Ibid. 1:2a.

27. Ibid. 5:21b–22a; *Tzu-chih t'ung-chien*, Shang-mu yin-shu-kuan ts'ang-fan ed. 33:6a-b; de Bary et al., *Sources of Chinese Tradition* 1:216–18; Joseph R. Levenson, "Ill Wind in the Well-field: The Erosion of the Confucian Ground of Controversy," in Arthur F. Wright, ed., *The Confucian Persuasion* (Stanford, Calif.: Stanford University Press, 1960), p. 273.

The phrase *hanmin myŏngjŏn* means "limit the name-land of the people" where "name-land" refers to land registered in someone's name.

28. PGSR 5:22b.

29. Hori Toshikazu, *Kindensei*, pp. 19–27; William G. Crowell, "The Land Limitations of Emperor Ai – A Reexamination," paper presented at the Asian Studies on the Pacific Coast Conference at Eugene, Oregon, June 1977.

30. *Tzu-chih t'ung-chien kang-mu* 7:53a-b.

31. Chu Hsi's paraphrase was close to a verbatim transcript of Ssu-ma Kuang's text in the *Tzu-chih t'ung-chien* 33:6a-b, but since Chu Hsi's *fan-li* (introduction and explanation of the principles used in the text) explicitly remarked that he was emulating the cryptic, didactic style of *The Spring and Autumn Annals* to praise moral deeds and condemn immoral ones, Yu Hyŏngwŏn obviously felt he had the license to interpret Chu Hsi's motivations.

The *fan-li* provides among other things the code language Chu Hsi used to assess praise and blame with regard to legitimate rulers and usurpers. The opening lines of Hsüan-tsung's preface notes that the *Tzu-chih t'ung-chien kang-mu* is based on the format of the *Ch'un-ch'iu* classic and its traditions (*chüan*, commentaries) and that its purpose is to "clarify Heaven's principles, rectify moral relationships, praise good, and blame bad. . . ."

32. PGSR 5:22b; *T'ung-tien*, ch. 1, *shih-huo*, 1.

33. For a thorough survey of the equal-field system and its antecedents, see Hori Toshikazu, *Kindensei*.

34. Yu accepted the statement in the *History of the Koryŏ Dynasty* (*Koryŏsa*) that the early Koryŏ *chŏnsikwa* land system was a replica of the equal-field system, but recent scholarship has demonstrated that this interpretation was incorrect. See James B. Palais,

"Land Tenure in Korea: Tenth to Twelfth Centuries," *Journal of Korean Studies* 4 (1982–83):73–206.

35. PGSR 6:2b.

36. Ibid. 6:1b.

37. Ibid. 6:5b.

38. Ibid. 6:3b.

39. Ibid. 6:4a-b.

40. Ibid. 6:5b.

41. Ibid.

42. Ibid. 6:1b.

43. Ibid.; this refers to the Northern Wei.

44. Ibid. 6:2b, 3a.

45. Ibid. 6:3b–4a.

46. For the Sui dynasty, see ibid. 6:4b; for the T'ang see ibid. 6:5a,6b.

47. Ibid. 6:7a.

48. Ibid. In a footnote, Yu corrected Ma Tuan-lin by stating that it was not until the reign of Emperor Wu of the Chin dynasty, 265–290, that the household tax (*tsu*) was begun, not in the Han dynasty.

49. Ibid. 6:8b.

50. Ibid.

51. Ibid. 6:8b–9b.

52. Ibid. 6:8b.

53. Ibid. 6:9b.

54. Ibid. 6:9a, Yu's commentary in smaller type.

55. See Palais, "Land Tenure in Korea."

56. Ibid.

57. PGSR 6:12a.

58. Ibid. 6:13a-b.

59. Ibid. 6:9a–10a.

60. Ibid. 6:10a.

61. See ibid. 6:10a-b, for a brief account of some of these changes.

62. There are two possible meanings for *sajŏn*: either privately owned land or a prebendal grant from the king that included exemption from taxes as a benefit. The literature on this is too extensive to cite here; for summaries see Palais, "Land Tenure in Korea," and Yi Kyŏngsik, *Chosŏn chŏn'gi t'oji chedo yŏn'gu: t'oji pungŭpche wa nongmin chibae* [A study of the land system in the early Chosŏn dynasty: Land distribution and the control of the peasantry] (Seoul: Ilchogak, 1986).

63. PGSR 6:12a-b.

64. Yi here may have understood the early *kubun* grant as equivalent to the basic *k'ou-fen-t'ien* allotment of the T'ang, or he he may have used the term *kubun* as a synonym for T'aejo's *yŏkpunjŏn*.

65. PGSR 6:13a.

66. Ibid.

67. Ibid. 6:11a.
68. Ibid. 6:13a.
69. Ibid.
70. Ibid. 6:12b.
71. For a survey of Sung thought on the well-field, limited-field, and equal-field systems, see Sudō Yoshiyuki, "Sōdai no tochi seidoron: Seidenron gendenron o chūshin to shite" [Land system proposals of the Sung period: Proposals for the well-field and limited-field systems], in *Tōsō shakai keizaishi kenkyū* [Studies in the social and economic history of the T'ang and Sung] (Tokyo: Tōkyō daigaku shupankai, 1965), pp. 233–320.
72. PGSR 6:13b–14a.
73. Ibid. 6:14a-b.
74. Ibid. 6:14b.
75. Ibid. 6:15a.
76. Ibid. The memorials of Cho Chun and Yi Haeng can be found in "The Treatise on Food and Money [*sikhwaji*]," section on the land system, in the *Koryŏsa*. See *Koryŏsa* 78 (Seoul: Yŏnhŭi taehakkyo, 1955):20b–31a; 36a–42b.
77. See Palais, "Land Tenure in Korea."
78. PGSR 1:2a-b.
79. Ibid. 5:24a.
80. Ibid. 5:24b–25a.
81. Ibid. 5:25a-b.
82. Sudō, "Sōdai no tochi seidoron," pp. 266, 312, 258, 269–70, 238–85.
83. Ibid., pp. 267–79.
84. Ibid., pp. 304–9.
85. PGSR 5:25a, 27a, 29a-b, 34b.
86. Ibid. 5:26b–27a.
87. In addition he hoped to induce the resettlement of peasants who had turned to commerce by prohibiting commercial activity, forcibly lowering the price of land, and selling office titles to those who reclaimed land. Sudō, "Sōdai no tochi seidoron," pp. 254–55.
88. Ibid., pp. 256–62, 269–73, 276–85, 312–14.
89. PGSR 5:25a, 27a, 29a-b. For Fan Tzu-yü's biography, see *Ajia rekishi jiten* 7:459.
90. PGSR 5:34b–35b.
91. Ibid. 5:35a-b. Lin's plan was praised, albeit with some reservations, by Hsüeh Chi-hsüan, Ch'en Liang, and Chu Hsi.
92. Ibid. 5:35b–36a. Ch'en Liang flourished in the late twelfth century.
93. Ibid. 5:36a. Yu neglected to mention Chu Hsi's disparaging remark about Su Hsün's limited-field plan. It is curious that although Yu cited the opinion of Lü Tsu-ch'ien, he did not discuss his writings at all. A brief perusal of Lü's opinions indicates that Yu would have found them congenial. Lü believed that the various land systems adopted in the Han, Chin, Later Wei, Ch'i, and T'ang dynasties were varying approximations of the ancient (well-field?) system. What was important was that people should have knowledge of the ideal ancient systems, otherwise their ignorance would prevent them from achieving proper land reform. Land had to be under the control of officials and not pri-

vate individuals if either the well-field or equal-field systems were to be adopted. A land limitation scheme could not work as long as private property continued to exist.

> Even if you should want to adopt the limited fields and name fields [*ming-t'ien* or *myŏngjŏn* in Korean pronunciation] of the Han dynasty, those who have land will occupy large amounts and will be able to buy up even more without limit while the government will not be able to stop them from doing so. And those who do not have land will not even have enough to stand an awl on. Even if you wanted to set limits [on landholding], there would be no way to do it.

Li-tai chih-tu hsiang-shuo, ch. 9, t'ien-chih, chih-tu, in *Hsü Chin-hua ts'ung-shu*, compiled by Tung-lai hsien-sheng Lü Tsu-ch'ien, Po-kung 9:3b.

He also suggested that the government should look around for areas where there was available land, take control of it, and set up a well-field system in such places as a start toward overall reform. Ibid. 9:4a. Lü flourished in the late twelfth century.

94. Sudō, "Sōdai no tochi seidoron," p. 281. The source for Chu Hsi's evaluation of Lin Hsün is the "Essay on the People" (*Lun-min*) in *Chu-tzu yü-lei*, ch. 111. See also Sudō, "Sōdai no tochi seidoron," pp. 286–91, 315.

95. That is, there is no explicit statement by Chu Hsi in the text cited by Yu in PGSR 5:30b–34a. For the statement about the Later Chou, see ibid. 5:34a for a reference in Yu's commentary to Ou-yang Hsiu's *Wu-tai-shih* [History of the Five Dynasties].

96. PGSR 5:25b.

97. Ibid. 5:25a-b.

98. Ibid. 5:35a-b.

99. Ibid. 5:26a-b.

100. Sudō, "Sōdai no tochi seidoron," pp. 264–65, 273.

101. Ibid., pp. 292–97.

102. Sudō Yoshiyuki, "Hokusō ni okeru hōden kinseihō no shikō katei" [The process of the adoption of the square-field equal-tax system in the Northern Sung], in idem, *Chūgoku tochi seidoshi kenkyū* [Studies in the history of Chinese land systems] (Tokyo: Tokyō daigaku shuppankai, 1954), pp. 434–509.

103. Ibid., p. 447.

104. Sudō, "Sōdai no tochi seidoron," pp. 273, 299–300, 302–4, 316–17; Sudō, "Nansōmatsu no kōdenhō" [The public field system of the Southern Sung], in idem, *Chūgoku tochi seidoshi kenkyū* [Studies in the land systems of China] (Tokyo: Tokyo daigaku shuppankai, 1954).

105. PGSR 1:1a-b.

106. Ibid.

107. For a discussion of *kongjŏn* in the early Koryŏ context, see Palais, "Land Tenure in Korea," *Journal of Korean Studies* 4 (1982–1983):73–205.

108. PGSR 1:2a.

109. Ibid. 1:2a-b.

110. Ibid. 1:1b–2a et passim.

111. Ibid. 1:2b–3a.

CHAPTER 8. Redistributing Wealth through Land Reform

1. PGSR 2:12a-b.

2. Ibid. 2:13a.

3. This dialogue is contained in a special appendix to this section entitled "Miscellaneous Discussion on the Land System, Appendix" (*Chŏnje chabŭi, pu*), PGSR 2:10b–18b.

4. Ibid. 2:11a.

5. Ibid. 2:12a-b.

6. Ibid. 2:12b.

7. Ibid. 2:13a.

8. Ibid.

9. Ibid. 2:13b.

10. Ibid. 2:13b–14a.

11. Ibid. 2:14a-b.

12. Ibid. 2:14a.

13. Ibid. 2:14b.

14. Ibid. 2:10b–11a.

15. Ibid. 2:11a.

16. Ibid.

17. Ibid. 2:14a.

18. Ibid. 2:14b–15a.

19. Ibid. 2:15a.

20. Ibid. 2:12b.

21. Ibid. 2:15a-b.

22. Ibid. 2:15b.

23. Ibid.

24. Ibid.

25. Ibid. 2:11b. See also ibid. 1:35a where Yu permitted someone to exchange his own allotment for his parents after they died, or neighbors to swap allotments. He did not allow exchange of allotments between villages, however.

26. Ibid. 2:11b–12a.

27. Ibid. 2:12a.

28. Ibid.

29. Ibid. 2:12a-b.

30. Ibid. 2:15b.

31. Ibid. 2:16a.

32. Ibid. 2:16a-b.

33. Ibid. 25:45b–49b.

34. Ibid. 1:11a.

35. Ibid. 1:11b, 14a.

36. Kim Yongsŏp has noted that the original six "feet" of the "Chou-foot" were lost during the Imjin War. He then calculated the areas of the six grades of *kyŏl* according to the *kapsul* or 1634 "Chou foot." Kim, "Yang'an ŭi yŏn'gu: Chosŏn hugi ŭi nonka kyŏngje"

[A study of the land registers: The peasant households in the late Chosŏn dynasty], pt. 1, *Sahak yŏn'gu* 7 (May 1960):47.

THE SIX GRADES OF LAND AREA

Grade	*P'yŏng*	Acres (1224 *p'yŏng*/acre)
1	3,117.36	2.55
2	3,655.29	2.97
3	4,446.38	3.63
4	5,660.72	4.62
5	7,793.40	6.37
6	12,469.44	10.19

37. PGSR 1:13b. The material summarized above is taken from ibid. 1:11b–13b.

38. Ibid. 1:13a-b.

39. Ibid. 1:13a.

40. Ibid. 1:16b.

41. Ibid. 1:16b–17a.

42. Ibid. 1:13b.

43. Ibid. 1:14b–15a.

44. Ibid. 1:15a-b.

45. Kim, "Yang'an ŭi yŏn'gu," pt. 1, pp. 34–48, 63, 94–95.

46. PGSR 2:19a.

47. Ibid. 2:16b.

48. Ibid.

49. Ibid.

50. Ibid. 2:17a.

51. Ibid.

52. For discussions of leadership in North Korea, see Bruce Cumings, "Corporatism in North Korea," *Journal of Korean Studies* 4 (1982–83):269–94; Robert A. Scalapino and Chong-sik Lee, *Communism in Korea*, vol. 2, *The Society* (Berkeley and Los Angeles: University of California Press, 1972):752–56; Dae-sook Suh, "Communist Party Leadership, in Suh Dae-sook and Chae-jin Lee, eds., *Political Leadership in Korea* (Seattle: University of Washington Press, 1976):159–61. For Park Chung-hee [Pak Chŏnghŭi] in South Korea, see David C. Cole and Princeton N. Lyman, *Korean Development: The Interplay of Politics and Economics* (Cambridge: Harvard University Press, 1971), pp. 49–50.

53. PGSR 2:17a-b.

54. Ibid. 2:17b–18a.

55. C. A. Peterson, "Court and Province in Mid- and Late T'ang," in Denis Twitchett and John K. Fairbank, eds., *The Cambridge History of China*, vol. 3, *Sui and T'ang China, Part I* (Cambridge: Cambridge University Press, 1979):510–52.

56. PGSR 2:18a.

57. Ibid. 1:3a.

58. Ibid. 1:19b–20b.

59. Ibid. 1:20b, 21a.

60. Ibid. 1:12b–13a.
61. Ibid. 1:19a-b.
62. Ibid. 1:18b–19a.
63. Ibid. 1:58a.
64. Ibid. 1:57a–58a.
65. Ibid. 1:22b.
66. Ibid. 1:22a.
67. Ibid. 1:23b.
68. Kang Chinch'ŏl, "Han'guksa ŭi sidae kubun e taehan ilsiron" [An attempt at the periodization of Korean history], *Chindan hakpo* 29–30 (December 1966):175–98.
69. PGSR 1:3b.
70. Ibid. 1:3b, 24a-b.
71. Ibid. 1:24a.
72. Ibid. 1:3a-b.
73. Ibid. 1:3b.
74. Ibid.
75. *Taebusa* might indicate officials of middle and lower rank, judging from the use of terms *taebu* and *sa* in the table of offices in the *Chou-li*, whereas *sadaebu* usually indicates scholars (*sa*) plus officials (*taebu*), i.e., scholar-officials.
76. PGSR 1:6b–7a.
77. Ibid. 1:7a.
78. Edward Willett Wagner noted that the term *sol* ("caring for") in the 1663 household register for the northern part of Seoul indicated "children or others living in the household." Presumably this did not indicate slaves, which were listed separately. "Social Stratification in Seventeenth Century Korea," *Occasional Papers on Korea*, no. 1 (April 1974), p. 41. The compound *solchong* is not listed either in Morohashi Tetsuji, ed., *Daikanwa jiten* [The great Sino-Japanese Dictionary], 12 vols. (Tokyo: Taishū-kan shoten, 1955–59), or Yi Kawŏn, Kwŏn Odon, and Im Ch'angsun, eds., *Tong'a Hanhandaesajŏn* [The Great East Asia Sino-Korean Dictionary] (Seoul: Tong'a ch'ulp'ansa, 1982).
79. PGSR 1:36b; see also 1:35b.
80. Ibid. 1:7a.
81. Ibid.
82. Ibid. 1:7b.
83. Ibid.
84. Ibid.
85. Ibid.
86. This was a feature of the late Koryŏ-early Chosŏn *kwajŏn* system.
87. PGSR 1:7a-b.
88. Ibid. 1:7b.
89. Ibid.
90. Probably the land taxes were to be paid by the cultivators, who Yu might have thought would be retainers or slaves of the royal family rather than common peasants.
91. PGSR 1:8b.

92. Yu provided equivalents in terms of land area, but since productivity and fertility varied, a 500-*kok* prebend would vary in land area from 50 *kyŏng* of first-grade land to 250 *kyŏng* of ninth-grade land. Ibid.

93. Ibid. 1:8b–9a.

94. Ibid. 1:9a.

95. Ibid. 1:9b.

96. Ibid. 1:10b.

97. Ibid. 1:10a.

98. Ibid.

99. Ibid. 1:10a-b.

100. See the definition of *yüeh-ti* (*yŏlchi*) in Morohashi Tetsuji, ed., *Daikanwa jiten* 10:214.

101. PGSR 1:10b–11a.

102. Ibid. 1:11a.

103. Edward Willett Wagner, *The Literati Purges: Political Conflict in Early Yi Korea* (Cambridge: East Asian Research Center, Harvard University, 1974); see also Chŏng Tuhŭi, "Chosŏn ch'ogi samgongsin yŏn'gu: kŭ sahoejŏk paegyŏnggwa chŏngch'ijŏk yŏkhwarŭl chungsimŭro" [A study of the three merit subject lists of the early Chosŏn period, in particular their social background and political role], *Yŏksa hakpo* 75–76 (December 1977):121–76.

104. PGSR 1:57b–58b, 66a. James B. Palais, *Politics and Policy in Traditional Korea* (Cambridge: Harvard University Press, 1975), pp. 78–82.

105. PGSR 1:21a.

106. See the definition in Yang Chudong, Min T'aesik, and Yi Hongjik, ed., *Hanhan-daesajŏn* (Seoul: Tong'a ch'ulp'ansa, 1963), p. 1139.

107. PGSR 1:53a.

108. Ibid.

109. Ibid. 1:53a.

110. See Bruce Cumings's analysis of the use of organic or corporate models in contemporary North Korea. "Corporatism in North Korea," pp. 269–94.

111. PGSR 1:53a-b.

112. For land grants, see ibid. 1:32b; for membership in the royal guards, see ibid. 1:53b.

113. Ibid. 1:32b.

114. *Sŏ* in this context means nothoi, but as the debate over mourning rites in the mid-seventeenth century brought out, some believed that *sŏ* only meant all sons but the eldest son of a wife, not the sons of a concubine.

115. PGSR 1:33a.

116. Ibid. 1:32b.

CHAPTER 9. Late Chosŏn Land Reform Proposals

1. See B. A. Holderness, *Pre-Industrial England: Economy and Society, 1500–1750* (Totowa, N.J.: J.M. Dent and Sons, 1976), pp. 75–82, for the conversion of seigneurial

lands to freeholds by 1640 and ownership and leasing by 1750, pp. 51–61 for period of enclosure from 1500–1800, pp. 69–75 for the agricultural revolution of 1560 to 1760; pp. 83–94 et passim for the development of commerce and industry between 1660 and 1870; Aldo de Maddalena, "Rural Europe, 1500–1750," in Carlo M. Cipolla, ed., *The Fontana Economic History of Europe: The Sixteenth and Seventeenth Centuries* (Glasgow: William Collins Sons, 1974), pp. 300–304; Fernand Braudel, *The Wheels of Commerce: Civilization and Capitalism, 15th–18th Century*, vol. 2 (New York: Harper and Row, 1982), esp. chap. 3.

2. It even had its day in England from 1620 to 1720 or to the end of the Anglo-French War in 1763. See C. H. Wilson, "Trade, Society and the State," in *The Cambridge Economic History of Europe* 4 (Cambridge: Cambridge University Press, 1967):487–575; Fernand Braudel, *Wheels of Commerce* 2:542–49; Betty Behrens, "Government and Society," in E. E. Rich and C. H. Wilson, *The Cambridge Economic History of Europe*, vol. 5, *The Economic Organization of Early Modern Europe* (Cambridge: Cambridge University Press, 1977):573–88, 595–97, 602.

3. See Nakamura Takafusa, *Economic Growth in Prewar Japan*, trans. Robert A. Feldman (New Haven: Yale University Press, 1971). In particular, see pp. 145, 213–31 for post-WWI trends, but Takafusa blames the boom and bust of the period from World War I through the Great Depression for the creation of monopoly formation and the wage or income differential of the double structure (advanced vs. modern economic sectors) rather than any intent on the part of the government. He also credits the Japanese government for marginal intervention to offset some of the more adverse effects on the urban proletariat in the second two decades of the twentieth century, but its performance on that score was hardly impressive.

4. Barrington Moore, Jr., *Social Origins of Dictatorship and Democracy: Lord and Peasants in the Making of the Modern World* (Boston: Beacon Press, 1967). Theda Skocpol also emphasized the role that entrenched landlords played in obstructing peasant revolutionary potential in France, China, Prussia, and England, in *States and Social Revolutions: A Comparative Analysis of France, Russia, and China* (Cambridge: Cambridge University Press, 1979).

5. Bruce Cumings, *The Origins of the Korean War*, vol. 1, *Liberation and the Emergence of Separate Regimes*; vol. 2, *The Roaring of the Cataract, 1947–1950* (Princeton, N.J.: Princeton University Press, 1981, 1990).

6. C. H. Wilson noted that in the age of mercantilism every Castilian burgher wanted to raise his family to hidalgo rank and purchase exemption from taxation. See C. H. Wilson, "Trade, Society and the State," in *The Cambridge Economic History of Europe* 4 (Cambridge: Cambridge University Press, 1967):494. Fernand Braudel cited cases of successful merchants in the pre-capitalist age who bought fiefs to gain status in a lingering feudal environment, but this was slightly different from a landed gentry who were supposedly on the path to becoming capitalists, as Kim Yongsŏp argues. See Braudel, *Wheels of Commerce* 2:249. Thomas C. Smith showed how the *gōno,* or rich peasants, in late Tokugawa Japan used their wealth to vie for samurai privileges and mimic the samurai life style, in *The Agrarian Origins of Modern Japan* (Stanford: Stanford University Press, 1959), pp. 175–79.

7. For the entrepreneurial activities of Koreans after the 1920s see Carter J. Eckert, *Offspring of Empire: The Koch'ang Kims and the Colonial Origins of Korean Capitalism, 1876–1945* (Seattle: University of Washington Press, 1991).

8. The detailed articles on these topics have been collected and published in Kim Yongsŏp, *Chosŏn hugi nong'ŏpsa yŏn'gu: nongch'on kyŏngje, sahoe pyŏndong* [Studies in the agricultural history of late Chosŏn: The village economy and social change] (Seoul: Ilchogak, 1970); in particular, see the two articles on the *yang'an* or land registers, pp. 78–188, 208–94. One of his examples should suffice to illustrate the problem. In one village of 382 men in the district of Chinju in 1846, about 6 percent owned 44 percent of the land while 63 percent owned only 18 percent. The rich peasant averaged over 1 *kyŏl* per person, while the poorest peasants held less than 1/4 *kyŏl*. Since the opportunities for increasing as well as losing one's property were available to men of all status groups, even though there were differences of fortune depending on the status of the individual, a few slaves were able to become rich peasants, even landlords. An increasing number of yangban were forced to till the earth and were reduced to tenancy as well, even though the household registers appeared to indicate that the yangban population was growing. In the same village in Chinju, most of the landlords and rich peasants were yangban in status, but 8 percent of the men of good status (*yangmin*) or commoners and 3 percent of the slaves also fell into this category. On the other hand, 55 percent of the commoners and 73 percent of the slaves owned the smallest parcels and were poor peasants. Kim Yongsŏp, "Sipp'alku segi ŭi nong'ŏp silchŏnggwa saeroun nong'ŏp kyŏngyŏngnon" [The agricultural situation in the eighteenth and nineteenth centuries and the new managerial agriculture], in idem, *Han'guk kŭndae nong'ŏpsa yŏn'gu* [Studies in the history of modern agriculture in Korea] (Seoul: Ilchogak, 1975), pp. 2–6.

9. Pak Nouk, "Chosŏn sidae komunsŏsang ŭi yong'ŏ kŏmt'o: t'oji nobi mun'girŭl chungsim'ŭro" [An investigation of the use of terms in old documents of the Chosŏn period], *Tongbanghak chi* 68 (October 1990):90, 119.

10. Kim Yongsŏp, "Sipp'alku segi ŭi nong'ŏp silchŏng," pp. 7–15.

11. Braudel, *Wheels of Commerce* 2:281–82; Holderness, *Pre-Industrial England*, pp. 69–75 et passim.

12. See Kim Yongsŏp, "Yang'an ŭi yŏn'gu: Chosŏn hugi ŭi nonka kyŏngje" [A study of the land registers: The peasant households in the late Chosŏn dynasty], pt. 1, *Sahak yŏn'gu* 7 (May 1960):1–95; also published in idem, *Chosŏn hugi nong'ŏpsa yŏn'gu* [Studies in the agricultural history of late Chosŏn] vol. 1 (Seoul: Ilchogak, 1970).

13. Kim Yongsŏp, "Sipp'alku segi ŭi nong'ŏp silchŏnggwa," pp. 15–29.

14. Ibid., pp. 29–72.

15. Kim Yongsŏp, *Chosŏn hugi nong'ŏpsa yŏn'gu: nongch'on kyŏngje, sahoe pyŏndong* (1970), pp. 158–59, table 59.

16. Ibid., pp. 149–54, 157, tables 38–56, pp. 149–54, 157. The specific district was Nanjŏn-myŏn, Wansan-gun in the Chŏnju area. Ibid., p. 80. In only one subdistrict in Wansangun near Chŏnju in Chŏlla Province did yangban totally dominate landholding. Although all yangban in the district, 23.6 percent of the total number of registered *kiju*, owned 45.5 percent of the land, the 97 yangban (8.4 percent of the population) who owned more than 1 *kyŏl* held 35.5 percent of the land. Yet few were very large landowners; only

one yangban held a parcel of 10.11 *kyŏl* and 8 others had average holdings of 7.59 *kyŏl*. One commoner owned 6.33 *kyŏl* and 73 others had an average holding or 1.52 *kyŏl*, but there were no major slave landowners. Ibid., p. 153, tables 54–56, p. 153.

17. Kim Yŏngmo, "Chosŏn hugi sinbun kujo wa kŭ pyŏndong" [The social status structure and its change in late Chosŏn], *Tongbanghak chi* 26 (1981):53–153; Song June-ho, "Chosŏn yangban'go" [A study of the yangban of Chosŏn], in idem, *Chosŏn sahoesa yŏn'gu* [Studies in the social history of Chosŏn] (Seoul: Ilchogak, 1987), pp. 118–259.

18. Edward Willett Wagner, "The Ladder of Success in Yi Dynasty Korea," *Occasional Papers on Korea*, no. l (April 1974), pp. 1–8.

19. My view on this question differs from that of Martina Deuchler, who regards the inheritance pattern in late Chosŏn to have so heavily favored the eldest legitimate son that it was tantamount to primogeniture. If, as Deuchler suggests, Neo-Confucian influence was tending toward primogeniture in property inheritance, one would expect to see a continuation of large landholdings. The problem cannot be resolved without more thorough empirical research of actual wills and agreements for the division of property. See Deuchler, *The Confucian Transformation of Korea: A Study of Society and Ideology* (Cambridge: Harvard University Press, 1992).

20. Chōsen sōtokofu, Chūsūin, ed., *Richō no zaisan sōzokuhō* [The property inheritance laws of the Yi dynasty] (Keijō, 1936).

21. *Sejong sillok* 49:14a–21b, Sejong 12.8.muin, cited in Han Yong'u, "Taejong, Sejongjo ŭi taesajŏn sich'aek: Sajŏn ŭi hasamdo igŭp munje rŭl chungsim ŭro" [The policy of Kings T'aejong and Sejong toward *sajŏn*: The problem of the transfer of *sajŏn* to the lower three provinces], *Han'guksa yŏn'gu* 3 (March 1969):79 and n.125.

22. If one were to guess that the average size of the *kyŏl* on the last two grades of land was 8 acres, slightly better than the worst quality of land, then average productivity would have been 2.5 *sŏm* or 37.5 *mal* per acre. – or if 1 *kyŏl* was equal to either 20 *majigi* on the best and 40 *majigi* on the worst land, and production was 10/1, then production should have been 400 *mal* for 40 *majigi*, the worst land, or 26.7 *sŏm/kyŏl*, but this would be an estimate for the early nineteenth century.

23. Kim Yongsŏp, *Chosŏn hugi nong'ŏpsa yŏn'gu: Nongch'on kyŏngje, sahoe pyŏndong* (1970), p. 167ff. For the late Koryŏ estimate I cited the work of Kim Chaejin, "Chŏn'gyŏlche yŏn'gu" [A study of the system of land measurement], *Kyŏngbuk taehakkyo nonjip* 2 (January 1958):75–113.

24. Kim Yongsŏp, *Chosŏn hugi nong'ŏpsa yŏn'gu: nongch'on kyŏngje, sahoe pyŏndong* (1970), pp. 168–69.

25. Kim calculated 800 *mal* at 40 *sŏm*, or 20 *mal* per *sŏm*. Ordinarily, one *sŏm* should have consisted of 15 *mal* in which case 800 *mal* should have been 53.3 *sŏm*, but I would hesitate to correct Tasan's firsthand testimony, and it is possible the *sŏm* in Chŏlla Province at that time did consist of 20 *mal*. Ibid., p. 169.

26. Ibid.

27. Fernand Braudel, *Civilization and Capitalism, 15th–18th Century* 1, *The Structures of Everyday Life: The Limits of the Possible* (New York: Harper and Row, 1981):120–21. Braudel mentioned that 1.5 hectolitres (about 4.13 bushels of wheat seed at 2.75 bushels/hectolitre) would be planted on each hectare to yield that crop.

28. Hoon K. Lee, *Land Utilization and Rural Economy in Korea* (Shanghai, Hong Kong, Singapore: Kelly and Walsh, Ltd., 1936), p. 56, table 19. For Hishimoto's figures, I made conversions based on the formula of 1 *koku* = 4.96 bushels. See Appendix E, "Tables of Measures,"in James I. Nakamura, *Agricultural Production and the Economic Development of Japan, 1873–1922* (Princeton, N.J.: Princeton University Press, 1966), p. 220. Thus, 7.7 *to* x 1.984 pecks = 15.28 pecks/4 pecks = 3.81 bushels per 0.10 hectare, or 38.1 bushels/ha, or 15.55 bushels/acre. 7.7 *koku* = 39.4 bushels/ha, or 1.16 metric tons/ha. Hishimoto Chōji, *Chōsen-mai no kenkyū* [A study of Korean rice] (Tokyo: Sensō shobo, 1938), p. 7. See table 1, n."a" in Yūjirū Hayami and Saburō Yamada, "Agricultural Productivity at the Beginning of Industrialization," in Kazushi Ohkawa, Bruce F. Johnston, Hiromitsu Kaneda, eds., *Agriculture and Economic Growth: Japan's Experience* (Princeton, N.J.: Princeton University Press, 1970), p. 108, equates 0.15 metric tons with 1 *koku* or 4.96 bushels of brown rice. Thus the weight of brown rice per bushel would be 0.03 metric tons or 60 pounds. R. H. Tawney also equates 1 bushel of rice with 60 pounds, in *Land and Labor in China* (Boston: Beacon Press, 1966), p. 49.

29. 9.88 *koku* x 4.96 bushels/ha = 49.0 bushels of rice per hectare. Hishimoto Chōji, *Chōsen-mai no kenkyū*, p. 7; Hoon K. Lee, *Land Utilization and Rural Economy in Korea*, p. 56, table 19.

30. Nakamura, *Agricultural Production and the Economic Developmnent of Japan*, pp. 90–92, estimates the average yield for around 1880 at 1.6 *koku/tan*, but I will use the 1.64 *koku/tan* presented in table 1 in Yūjirū Hayami and Saburō Yamada, "Agricultural Productivity at the Beginning of Industrialization," p. 108. To convert metric tons to bushels I converted *koku/tan* shown in table 1 to bushels/ha by multiplying by 10 to find *koku*/hectare, and by 5.12 to convert *koku* to bushels.

31. See Yūjirū Hayami and Saburō Yamada, "Agricultural Productivity at the Beginning of Industrialization," p. 108.

32. Nakamura, *Agricultural Production and the Economic Development of Japan*, tables 4–6, p. 103.

33. 1,000 to 7,000 kg/ha, or 7.6–53 bushels/ha.

34. Francesca Bray [Joseph Needham], *Science and Civilisation in China*, vol. 6, *Biology and Biological Technology*, pt. 2: *Agriculture* (Cambridge: Cambridge University Press, 1984):508, table 13.

35. Dwight H. Perkins, *Agricultural Development in China, 1368–1968* (Chicago: Aldine Publishing Co., 1969), p. 17. I converted Perkins's estimates of 139 catties/*shih mou* for 1400, 203 catties/*shih mou*, and 243 catties/*shih mou* to kilograms per acre by multiplying catties by 1.1 (to convert to pounds) and by 6 (to convert *mou* to acres), and then dividing by 60 to convert pounds to bushels.

36. Perkins, *Agricultural Development in China, 1368–1968*, p. 17. For the early twentieth century, Tawney calculated the average rice yield per acre in China at 10.8 bushels for 1916–18. Tawney, *Land and Labor in China*, p. 49. According to John Lossing Buck, Owen L. Dawson, and Yuan-li Wu, *Food and Agriculture in Communist China* (New York: Frederick A. Praeger, 1966), p. 22, the yield was 2,972 kilograms (1,351 pounds) per hectare, which at the rate of 60 pounds per bushel yields 22.51 bushels per hectare, or 9.19 bushels/acre, for the period 1929–33.

According to Yi Yŏnghun, *Chosŏn hugi sahoe kyŏngjesa* [The social and economic history of Late Chosŏn] (Seoul: Han'gilsa, 1988), p. 234, a book consulted after the galleys were finished in this volume, the estimated average production in Kyŏngsang Province around 1910 was 20.79 bushels/acre of hulled rice, about double Chinese yields in the early twentieth century, but production in Kyŏngsang was far higher than the average for all of Korea.

37. Or 49 bushels/ha. See Hishimoto Chōji, *Chōsen-mai no kenkyū*, p. 7.

38. Tony Michell, "Fact and Hypothesis in Yi Dynasty Economic History: The Demographic Dimension," *Korean Studies Forum*, no. 6 (Winter–Spring 1979–80), pp. 77–79, and table of estimated population during the Yi dynasty, pp. 71–72. Michell admitted that his estimates might be inaccurate because of underreporting in the censuses, but he insisted on the validity of the trends shown. He, therefore, ignored population totals and multiplied the number of households recorded by 7.95, a figure consistent with the radical estimates of Kwŏn Tai-hwan in the Population and Development Studies Center, Seoul National University, *The Population of Korea* (Seoul: Seoul National University, 1975), and *Han'guk sahoe, in'gu wa palchŏn* [Korean society, population and development] (Seoul: Seoul National University Press, 1978).

Ishi Yoshikuni supplied a table of adjusted population estimates for 1640–1780 on p. 53, but his estimates for the eighteenth century are about 4 million less than Michell's, and he claimed that population leveled off at 7.28 million people about 1730. I find Michell's discussion more convincing. See Ishi Yoshikuni, *Kankoku no jinkō zōka no bunseki* [An analysis of population growth in Korea] (Tokyo: Keiso, 1972), pp. 46–49, 56.

39. Bray, *Science and Civilisation in China*, vol. 6, pt. 2, *Agriculture*:601.

40. Han Woo-keun, "Sŏngho Yi Ik ŭi sasang yŏn'gu" [A study of the thought of Sŏngho Yi Ik], in *Yijo hugi ŭi sahoe wa sasang* (Seoul: Ŭryu munhwasa, 1961), pp. 141–42, 144–48.

41. Ibid., pp. 203–11, 215, 238–45.

42. Ibid., pp. 246–48. He did not believe that Shang Yang of the Ch'in dynasty destroyed the well-field system by "breaking down" the embankments between the well fields because, following Chu Hsi, he thought that Shang Yang had only leveled those embankments to open the fields up to irrigation.

43. Han, "Sŏngho Yi Ik ŭi Sasang Yŏn'gu," pp. 250–54. Takahashi Toru wrote that Yi was not completely clear about the size of the permanent plot, and he estimated that he must have envisioned a plot in the range of 1–2 *kyŏng*. Ibid., p. 254.

44. *Yŏngjo sillok* 51:8a-b, Yŏngjo 16.2.kapsin (1740), cited in Han, "Sŏngho Yi Ik ŭi sasang yŏn'gu," p. 249.

45. Yi calculated productivity at 60 *mal* for every 1 *mal* planted, except in the southern provinces where broadcast seeding instead of transplanting reduced the yield by 1/3 to 40 *mal* per *mal* planted. Han Woo-keun, however, pointed out that in the eighteenth century, Yi Chunghwan, in his *T'aengniji* described the production from one *mal* of seed as varying from 60 *mal* for the best to 30 *mal* for the worst, a 2/1 ratio for the highest and lowest grades that would have prevented the equality of taxation that Yi hoped for, yet under Yi's scheme the owners of the least fertile land would have been undertaxed

because their production would have been double Yi's estimate, an even less regressive rate than what Yi intended. Ibid., pp, 268–74, 284.

46. He cited Yu Hyŏngwŏn's statement that peasants living in the uplands could earn more than subsistence by planting only 20 *mal* of rice annually, while the peasants in the lowlands or plains were left starving by spring even though they planted more than 30 *mal* of seed. The reason was that the upland peasants were more diligent in their practices and reaped a crop twice as plentiful as the lazier downland peasants. Based on similar calculations, Yi criticized Yu's plan for reimbursement of officials to award the 50 percent rent on 6 *kyŏng* of land to lower officials of rank 7 and below because it would be too low to pay for their upkeep, and the clerks and runners, who would get only half of that amount, would be left in destitution. Ibid., pp. 268–74, 284.

47. Kim Yongsŏp, "Sipp'al segi nongch'on chijig'in ŭi nong'ŏpkwan" [The views on agriculture of rural intellectuals in the eighteenth century], in idem, *Chosŏn hugi nong'ŏpsa yŏn'gu* (1970), pp. 4–25. For the source for Chŏngjo's comment in 1799, see ibid., p. 22, n.40, cited from the *Ilsŏngnok*, Chŏngjo 23.2.11. He must have thought that the *chikchŏn* system consisted of land grants to officials, but in fact *chikchŏn* referred to prebendal grants of tax income rather than the land itself.

48. Ibid., pp. 29–46.

49. Kim Yongsŏp believed that his essay on land (*chŏllon*) had to have been written much later than his essay on the well-field system (*kyŏngjŏllon*) in his *Kyŏngse yup'yo*. See Kim Yongsŏp, "Sipp'alku segi ŭi nong'ŏp silchong," pp. 93–94.

50. Hong Isŏp, *Chŏng Yagyong ŭi chŏngch'i kyŏngje sasang yŏn'gu* [A study of the political and economic thought of Chŏng Yagyong] (Seoul: Han'guk yŏn'gu tosogwan, 1959), pp. 107–8.

51. Ibid., pp. 78–88.

52. Ibid., pp. 93–94.

53. Ibid., pp. 95–99; Pak Chonggŭn, "Taṣan, Tei Jyakuyō no tochi kaikaku shisō no kosatsu: Kōsaku (nōryoku ni ojita) tochi bunpai o chōshin to shite" [A study of Tasan, Chŏng Yagyong's ideas on land reform: Distribution of land in accordance with labor], *Chōsen gakuhō* 28 (July 1963):83–85, 104; Hong Isŏp, *Chŏng Yagyong ŭi chŏngch'i kyŏngje sasang yŏn'gu*, p. 110.

54. Hong Isŏp, *Chŏng Yagyong*, p. 110, n.43; Pak Chonggŭn, "Tasan," pp. 85–86; Chŏng Yagyong [Yun Set'aek, ed.] *Chŏng Tasan chŏnso* [The collected works of Chŏng Tasan] 2 (Seoul: Munhŏn p'yŏnch'an wiwŏnhoe, 1961): 220. He referred to Pak Chiwŏn's version, but he just as easily could have cited Yi Ik's.

55. Kim Yongsŏp, "Sipp'alku segi ŭi nong'ŏp silchong," pp. 101–7.

56. Pak Chonggŭn, "Tasan," pp. 86–98; Hong Isŏp, *Chŏng Yagyong*, pp. 111–12.

57. Pak Chonggŭn, "Tasan," pp. 86–98; Hong Isŏp, *Chŏng Yagyong*, pp. 111–12.

58. Pak Chonggŭn, "Tasan," pp. 79, 104, 109. For direct references to Tasan's works, see the footnotes in Pak's article and in subsequent sources cited.

59. Kim Yongsŏp, "Sipp'alku segi ŭi nong'ŏp silchong," pp. 99–101, 107–10.

60. Ibid., pp. 110–25.

61. Ibid., pp. 125–28, 134–36.

62. Ibid., pp. 129–31, 133; Pak Chonggŭn, "Tasan," pp. 86–98; Hong Isŏp, *Chŏng Yagyong*, pp. 111–12.

63. Kim Yongsŏp, "Sipp'alku segi ŭi nong'ŏp silchong," pp. 131–33.

64. Ibid., pp. 136–41. Pak Chonggŭn also tried to argue that there were progressive elements in Tasan's thought, such as the use of rational means for increasing agricultural production, technological improvement, expansion of mining, minting currency, and the establishment of independent and separate vocations for all people. He was convinced that these ideas must have been inspired by the transition occurring in the Korean economy at the time, the transition from a feudal to a capitalist economy. Nevertheless, his argument was not as thorough and sophisticated as that of Kim Yongsŏp. Pak Chonggŭn, "Tasan," pp. 79, 104, 109.

65. Kim Yongsŏp discussed Sŏ's early writings, in "Sipp'alku segi ŭi nong'ŏp silchong," pp. 141–46.

66. Ibid., pp. 153–54.

67. Ibid., pp. 154–58.

68. Ibid., pp. 164–58.

CHAPTER 10. The Royal Division Model

1. Ch'a Munsŏp, "Chosŏnjo Hyojong ŭi kunbi kwangch'ung, sang [Expansion of military defenses under King Hyojong of the Chosŏn dynasty, pt. 1] *Nonmunjip* (Tan'guk taehakkyo) 1 (1967):28 n. 9.

2. Ibid., pp. 25–28; Yi T'aejin, *Chosŏn hugi ŭi chŏngch'i wa kunyŏngje pyŏnjŏn* [Politics and changes in the army division system in the late Chosŏn period] (Seoul: Han'guk yŏn'guwŏn, 1985), pp. 154–56; Yi Kŭng'ik, *Yŏllyŏsil kisul* 32 (Keijō: Chōsen kosho kankōkai, 1912–13) 5:352–61, "Hyojongjo kosa ponmal, Kim Chajŏm ok" [The complete details of Hyojong's reign, the treason case of Kim Chajŏm].

3. Ch'a Munsŏp, "Hyojong ŭi kunbi kwangch'ŏng," pt. 1, pp. 28–36.

4. Pak's last proposal was simply for repair of bronze cannon on ships stationed off the southern coast.

5. Ch'a Munsŏp, "Hyojong ŭi kunbi kwangch'ung," pt. 1, p. 41; see *Hyojong sillok* 10:20a-b.

6. Ch'a Munsŏp, "Hyojong ŭi kunbi kwangch'ung," pt. 1, pp. 41–42, see n.17, which quotes passages from *Hyojong sillok* 11, Hyojong 4.i7.kimi, and *Pibyŏnsa tŭngnok*, Hyojong 4.i7.28. This note also gives a figure of 204,229 men for the total absent or missing from the military registers in 1648.

7. Ch'a Munsŏp, "Hyojong ŭi kunbi kwangch'ung," pt. 1, pp. 43–44, and KSDSJ 1:319.

8. KSDSJ 2:1494, article on *chinyŏngjang*, another term for *yŏngjang*; Ch'a Munsŏp, "Hyojong ŭi kunbi kwangch'ung," pt. 1, pp. 45–46.

9. Ch'a reports this as the creation of Hyojong, but the KSDSJ 1:365 states that Yi Kwi was responsible for its establishment in Injo's reign, and that it continued in operation until 1882. Until this discrepancy is solved by a search through the sources, I would tend to prefer Ch'a's account. Ch'a, "Hyojong ŭi kunbi kwangch'ung," pt. 1, p. 46.

10. This regulation appears to indicate that slaves owned, rather than simply occupied or possessed, the land on which they paid the land tax, for if the master were the registered owner, one would expect that he also would have been the subject of tax reduction.

11. Ch'a, "Hyojong ŭi kun'gi kwangch'ung," pt. 1, pp. 47–48.

12. PGSR 21:31a–32a, for this and previous quotations. The order of the quoted material has been rearranged slightly. Yu's short commentary to his proposed law to remedy the practice of substitute cloth taxes contains a brief summary of the points made above. Ibid. 21: 30a-b.

13. Ibid. 21:68b; see also 21:31b.

14. Ibid. 21:68a-b.

15. Ibid. 26:68b.

16. Ibid. 21:31b–32a.

17. Ibid. 21:30b–31a.

18. Ibid. 21:31b–32a.

19. Ibid. 21:30b.

20. Ibid. 21:31a.

21. Ibid. 21:30b–31a.

22. Ibid. 21:30b, 32b.

23. Ibid. 21:71a-b; KSDSJ 2:1439–1440.

24. PGSR 21:34a-b, 69b.

25. Ibid. 21:24b, 36a. On 21:69b Yu stipulated that troops on frontier duty could be used as the servants (*saryŏng*) of garrison commanders, but their duties should be limited to carrying firewood. The rest of their time was to be spent in practicing archery and shooting.

26. Yu cited the memorial of Chungbong, Cho Hŏn, and Yi Sugwang's *Chibong yusŏl*, preface dated 1614, but the latter states on 3:28a (Seoul: Kyŏng'in munhwasa ed., 1970, p. 56) that total strength of soldiers and support personnel in Korea (date unspecified) was no less than 500,000 of which 180,000 were soldiers. PGSR 21:64a.

27. *Chibong yusŏl* 3:28b–29a.

28. These figures were exclusive of marines (*sugun*) for which Yu had only sparse information. The total number of registered soldiers is slightly higher than Minister of War Wŏn Tup'yo's report in 1653 that there were only 150,000 men on the national military registers.

29. PGSR 21:64b–68a. There are some minor discrepancies in Yu's arithmetic, hardly worth fussing about. Yu noted elsewhere that the *sog'ogun* were not provided with support personnel like the regular troops of good status, an added deficiency that only they had to suffer. Ibid. 21:30b; Min Hyŏn'gu, "Kŭnse Chosŏn chŏn'gi kunsa chedo ŭi sŏngnip," [The establishment of the early modern military system in the early Chosŏn period], in Yukkun sagwan hakkyo Han'guk kunsa yŏn'gusil, *Han'guk kunjesa: Kŭnse Chosŏn chŏn'gi-p'yŏn* [The history of the Korean military system: The early modern Chosŏn period] (N.p.: Yukkun ponbo, 1968), pp. 43–46.

30. Chŏn Hyŏngt'aek, *Chosŏn hugi nobi sinbun yŏn'gu* [A study of slave status in late Chosŏn] (Seoul: Ilchogak, 1989), pp. 176–77.

31. The Later Han commentator, Cheng Hsüan, in interpreting the Hsiao ssu-tu sec-

tion of *The Rites of Chou* wrote that the basic component of the 12,500-man army was the 5-man squad recruited from 5 families who furnished 1 adult male each, PGSR 23:1a-b. Pan Ku's treatise on the military in his *Han-shu* stated that the well-field had 8 families, but each unit of 64 well-fields furnished 75 soldiers, a little less than 1 soldier for every 7 families on average. The 64 well-field units (*t'ien* in Chinese) also had to provide 1 military chariot and 16 oxen and horses. See ibid. 23:2a-b. For a similar, but slightly different set of figures in Hu An-kuo's commentary on the *Spring and Autumn Annals* (the *Hu-shih chüan*), see ibid. 23:5a.

Yu also cited a commentary by Chu Hsi on the *hyangsu* (*hsiang-su* in Chinese) system. According to this there were two separate systems of organization culminating in units called *hyang* or *su*, each with an identical 12,500 households. The basic cellular unit for both structures was the 5-family group; since each family furnished 1 man each, the 5 men constituted a squad. Companies, battalions and the rest, up to the 12,500-man army were based on multiples of the 5-man squad. Chu Hsi noted that the *hyangsu* system was based on multiples of 10, and the well-field system on multiples of 9. Later on, Confucian scholars tried to combine the 2 into a unified system, but Chu Hsi did not see how that was possible. Ibid. 23:3b.

32. Ibid. 23:1a.

33. Ibid. 23:5a.

34. Ibid. 23:1b,2a.

35. The Han military system is discussed in ibid. 33:6a–7b. One Sung scholar, I Fu, captured the essence of the system in one brief paragraph:

> In the Han dynasty military system nothing was more detailed in its organization than the Southern and Northern Armies of the capital. At that time soldiers and farmers were not yet divided in two, and the Southern and Northern Armies were in fact made up of the common people [as a whole] much like the well-field system of ancient times. The Southern Army's soldiers were recruited from the commanderies [*chün*] and feudalities [*kuo*], while the soldiers of the Northern Army were recruited from the Left, Right, and Capital *fu* [i.e., the *San-fu* or three districts around the capital]. Ibid. 33:6a

Compare a similar statement of a Mr. I, quoted in the *Wen-hsien t'ung-k'ao*, 156, *ping-k'ao* (essay on military affairs), pt. 2, cited in Hamaguchi Shigekuni, "Zenkan no Nambokugun ni tsuite" [The Southern and Northern Armies of the Former Han], idem, *Shinkan zuitōshi no kenkyū* [Studies in the history of the Ch'in, Han, Sui and T'ang] (Tokyo: Tokyo daigaku shuppankai, 1966), p. 254.

Although scholars have debated whether the Northern Army recruits came only from the capital regions or the whole country, there seems to be no major dispute about the basic system of rotating military service for the male population at large. For the dispute on areas of recruitment, see Hamaguchi, "Zenkan no Nambokugun ni tsuite," pp. 253–54. Hamaguchi, by the way, would accept the view of I Fu against present-day Chinese scholarly critics, on the grounds that the administration of troops in the capital environs differed from that of the ordinary commanderies, and the *chung-wei* or commander of the Northern Army (i.e., Capital Guards) had direct control of the village or *hsiang* soldiers in the capital districts.

36. He traced the origin of shifts for frontier duty to the Ch'in method of treating exiled criminals, hence not a proper method for ordinary peasants. PGSR 23:6b–7b.

37. Hamaguchi has a chapter on the division of soldiers and peasants in the end of the Later Han and under the regime of Ts'ao Ts'ao of the Wei (in the third century A.D.) in *Tōkan zuitōshi no kenkyū*, pp. 326–35. See also ibid., p. 33.

38. See PGSR 23:8a–9a for the general outline of the system, and ibid. 8a–12b for commentaries by later Chinese writers of the T'ang and Sung.

39. Hamaguchi Shigekuni has pointed out that the number of *fu* varied from one time to another but usually there were about 600 to 630 of them. There were also three grades of *fu* based on the number of soldiers attached, 1,200, 1,000, or 800. These troops were also assigned to the capital guards (*wei*) or frontier garrisons for rotation duty there. PGSR 23:8a–9b; *Hsin T'ang-shu* 50, *ping-chih* [Treatise on military affairs], 40:1b–3a. See also Hamaguchi Shigekuni's article on the *Che-ch'ung-fu* in the *Ajia rekishi jiten* 5:249, and Charles O. Hucker, *A Dictionary of Official Titles in Imperial China* (Stanford: Stanford University Press, 1985), pp. 119–20. For more detail see Hamaguchi, "Fuhei seido yori shinheisei e" [From the *fu-ping* system to the new-soldier system], in *Shinkan zuitōshi no kenkyū*, pp. 3–83, first published in *Shigaku zasshi* 41 (1930):11–12.

40. PGSR 23:10b–11a; *Hsin T'ang-shu* 50, *ping-chih*, 40:1a.

41. PGSR 23:11b, *Hsin T'ang-shu* 50, *ping-chih* 40:1b–3a.

42. PGSR 23:10a.

43. These long-term soldiers were dubbed *kuang-chi* in 724.

44. Lin Chiung of the Sung also deplored the decline of the *fu-ping* system by the late seventh century, and the conversion of the militia soldiers to permanent or long-term troops in 723. PGSR 23:10a, 11a–12a; *Hsin T'ang-shu* 50, *ping-chih* 40:1a-b, 3a.

45. The first were the palace and capital guards, the second the garrison troops of the various prefectures attached to the walled town of the prefectural seat, and the third were the local troops (*hsiang-chün*) who were selected from the household registers, formed into units where they were recruited for service, and trained as a defensive reserve. PGSR 23:12b.

46. Ibid. 23:12b–14b.

47. Ibid. 23:14b–15a.

48. See his citation of Su Shih's praise of the system in *Shinkan zuitōshi no kenkyū*, p. 35.

49. Hamaguchi, "Fuhei seido yori," pp. 10–11, 32–33. This arrangement had not been typical of the system when first founded in the Western Wei. In his account in the *Ajia rekishi jiten* 5:249, he said that 80 percent of the *Che-ch'ung-fu* were in the capital area and 20 percent on the frontier, somewhat different percentages than one would derive from the statements in his article.

50. Hamaguchi, "Fuhei seido yori," pp. 15–16.

51. A system of matching copper tallies in the form of a fish was used when peasants were called up to ensure that no unauthorized service was imposed on families. And when on duty, soldiers were exempted from labor service and local products tribute pay-

ments. Hamaguchi also cited the view of the famous late Ming anti-Manchu scholar, Wang Fu-chih, in his *Essays on Reading the Comprehensive Mirror*, that the creation of an independent network of *Che-ch'ung-fu* military outposts was not as good as the previous system of having a couple of military officials attached to the district magistrate's yamen assume responsibility for the training, recruitment, and mobilization of soldiers. Ibid. pp. 18–21, 30–32.

52. The troop complement of a *wei* was 5,600 men, subdivided at two levels into five "thousand household units [*so*]," and "hundred household units," of 1,120 and 112 men, respectively. PGSR 23:15b, 16a.

53. James B. Palais, "Land Tenure in Korea: Tenth to Twelfth Centuries," *Journal of Korean Studies* 4 (1982–83):73–206.

54. Ibid.

55. PGSR 23:16a-b.

56. Ibid. 23:17a.

57. Palais, "Land Tenure in Korea," pp. 89–114, esp. p. 105.

58. PGSR 23:16b. See the glossary in Palais, "Land Tenure in Korea," for *yŏn'ip*.

59. PGSR 23:17a-b.

60. See n.49 supra for this and following quotations.

61. PGSR 21:29b–30a.

62. Ibid. 21:37a-b.

62. Ibid. 21:37b–38a.

64. Ibid. 21:30a. While the *sog'o* units consisted of slaves and commoners together when they were first created in the Imjin War, Yu specified that in his system they would be reserved for slaves alone to accommodate the aversion of commoners to mingling with their inferiors.

65. The provisions for slaves or slave soldiers, grain transport workers, sailors, beacon station soldiers, able-oarsmen, reconnaissance soldiers, and other types of troops to be discussed later, were different.

66. PGSR 21:12a-b.

67. See the *Kyŏngguk taejŏn* [Great code for managing the state], preface dated 1469, subsequently revised four times by 1485 (Keijō: Chōsen sōtokufu chūsuin, ed., 1934):406ff. for regulations pertaining to rotating shifts for regular soldiers and others, and pp. 453–54 for provision of support taxpayers to various types of soldiers. For the date of publication, see KSDSJ 1:64.

68. Ch'a Munsŏp, "Hyojong ŭi kunbi kwangch'ung," pt. 1, p. 38; Yi T'aejin, *Chosŏn hugi*, pp. 163–67.

69. The reform of the Royal Division is discussed in detail by Ch'a Munsŏp in "Hyojongjo ŭi kunbi kwangch'ung [The military defense build-up of King Hyojong's reign], in idem, *Chosŏn sidae kunje yŏngu* (Seoul: Tan'guk taehakkyo ch'ulp'anbu, 1973), pp. 254–55. See also Ch'a, "Imnan ihu ŭi yangyŏk kwa kyunyŏkpŏp ŭi sŏngnip" [The commoner service system after the Imjin Wars and the establishment of the equal service system] *Sahak yŏn'gu* 11 (July 1961):117. The primary source for the reform is *Hyojong sillok* 8:84a-b, Hyojong 3.6.kisa. Ch'a estimated the interval between tours of duty at 21 months, but if one thousand men served a 2-month shift and there were 21,000

men in the unit, there must have been 21 shifts with an interval of 42 months between shifts. For additional details on the founding of the Royal Division and its regulations at the beginning of the nineteenth century, when it consisted of 16,300 duty soldiers, 17,475 equipment support taxpayers (*chabo*) and 50,175 ration support taxpayers (*kwanbo*), plus other miscellaneous soldiers and support taxpayers, see *Man'gi yoram*, kunjŏngp'yŏn [Section on military affairs] (Keijō: Chōsen sōtokufu chūsūin, 1938), pp. 327–32.

70. PGSR 21:32a-b.

71. Ibid. 21:29b.

72. Ibid.

73. Ibid. 21:29b, 34a.

74. Ibid. 21:30b. Yu's statement about the Special (Cavalry) Unit, presumably of the Military Training Agency, is hard to understand since its troops were provided support taxpayers, as will be shown in chap. 11. He may have meant that the registration of support taxpayers as called for in the regulations lagged behind the recruitment of duty soldiers.

75. Ibid. 21:30a.

76. Ibid. 21:55a-b.

77. Ibid. 21:32b.

78. Ibid. 21:56a–57a; see *chüan* 1 of the *Wan-yu wen-k'o* series edited by Wang Yün-wu (Shanghai: Commercial Press, Chung-hua min-kuo 27th year, 1939), pp. 21–29.

79. PGSR 21:29b–30b.

80. Ibid. 21:36a, 57a.

81. Ibid. 21:35b.

82. Ibid.

83. Ibid. 21:35a-b. For the arrangements for support taxpayer payments at the time of the reform of the Royal Division in 1651, see *Hyojong sillok* 8:84a-b, Hyojong 3.6.kisa.

84. PGSR 21:36a.

84. Since the Royal Division only had 12,000 men just prior to the 1651 reform, Kim may have been exaggerating, or he may have been talking about the total troop strength of a number of capital divisions in addition to the Royal Division.

86. Ch'a Munsŏp made this point in "Imnan ihu ŭi yangyŏk," pt. 2, p. 117.

87. *Hyojong sillok* 8:84b–85a, Hyojong 3.6.kisa.

88. PGSR 21:57a-b.

89. Or three months if their duty assignment fell within the agricultural work season from the fourth through the seventh lunar months. Ibid. 21:36b. He provided different training regulations for cavalrymen.

90. Ibid. 21:36b–37a.

91. Ibid. 21:32b–33b.

92. Ibid. 21:34a.

93. Ibid.

94. Ibid. 21:34b.

95. At the same time he sought to reduce and simplify some of the categories of sol-

diers created in the wake of the Japanese invasions. These types are listed in a note (in small-sized type) on ibid. 21:29a.

96. Ibid. 21:29b, 21:46a, 21:48a-b, 21:62b.

97. Ibid. 21:11a-b. For Yu's remarks on how low the two *p'il* rate was, see ibid. 21:36b.

98. This form of evasion as practiced in the late seventeenth and eighteenth centuries is discussed in detail in Chŏng Yŏnsik, "Sipch'il-sippal segi yangyŏk kyunilhwa chŏngch'aek ŭi ch'uui" [The trend in policy toward a uniform labor service tax on men of good status in the seventeenth and eighteenth centuries], *Han'guksaron* 13 (August 1985):121–82.

99. PGSR 21:11b–12a. See the memorial of Uch'amch'an (State Councilor) Kwŏn Chŏk in 1750, *Yŏngjo sillok* 71:24b–25a.

100. PGSR 21:14a, 41a-b.

101. Ibid. 21:29b.

102. Ibid. 21:57a.

103. Ibid. 21:29b.

104. Ibid. 21:9a. At the beginning of the dynasty the Forbidden Soldiers (i.e., Soldiers of the Forbidden Quarters) consisted of three units attached to the Dragon Tiger Regiment (Yonghoyŏng): the Naegŭmwi, Kyŏmsabok, and Urimwi. According to one source, when a Forbidden Soldier Agency (Kŭmgunch'ŏng), or Agency of the Three Forbidden Soldier Guards (Kŭmgun samch'ŏng), was created in 1666, there were 200 men each in the Kyŏmsabok and Urimwi, and 300 in the Naegŭmwi, somewhat less than Yu's estimate. KSDSJ 1:226. See also Yi Kŭng'ik, *Yŏllyŏsil kisul*, pyŏlchip Yonghoyŏng (article on the Dragon Tiger Regiment), cited in Ch'a Munsŏp, "Sŏnch'o ŭi Naegŭmwi" [The Inner Forbidden Guards of early Chosŏn], in idem, *Chosŏn sidae kunje yŏn'gu* (1973), p. 54.

105. PGSR 21:6a.

106. Ch'a Munsŏp, "Sŏnch'o ŭi Naegŭmwi," pp. 52–56, 64–82. For the exemption from the military examinations in obtaining an appointment to the Naegŭmwi, see *Kyŏngguk taejŏn* (Keijō: 1934), p. 341.

107. Ch'a Munsŏp made this point about the trends in quotas in the fifteenth and early sixteenth centuries. As one example, he cited the recommendation of Chŏng Inji and Sin Sukchu in 1474 to cut the Naegŭmwi back from 200 to 100 on the grounds there were too many poor soldiers in it. Despite opposition to this, King Sŏngjong, known as a rather meek and mild-mannered king, accepted the proposal. Nonetheless, the law code promulgated in 1485 did have a quota of 190. Yŏnsan'gun increased the quota in 1505. He changed the names of the duty soldier and the reserve guards as well. Ch'a reports that the quota right after the Imjin Wars was 440, almost 200 less than Yu Hyŏngwŏn's estimate for the mid-seventeenth century. "Sŏnch'o ŭi Naegŭmwi," pp. 87–89.

108. The Loyal and Righteous Guards were established in 1417 to provide opportunities for service and posts to the descendants of the three lists of merit subjects who had backed both T'aejo and T'aejong in their political struggles. They were organized independently, divided into four groups and served on guard duty in the palace.

Then in 1445, Sejong created the 600-man Loyal and Obedient Guards to provide opportunities for nephews and sons-in-law as well as direct descendants of the top three ranks.

They were assigned to the Ministry of War, divided into four groups of 150 men each and served on guard duty at the palace, three days on and nine off, not a very demanding schedule. The unit was established after Sejong had come to the throne, but the retired T'aejong was himself still in command of the armed forces. The unit was abolished in 1456 and restored in 1469 but without any quota limit.

After Sejo usurped the throne, he rewarded his own merit subjects by allowing their descendants to enlist in the Loyal and Righteous Guards, and in 1456 he expanded opportunities for special service for descendants of minor merit subjects (*wŏnjong kongsin*) who had been previously excluded from the other elite guards by abolishing the Loyal and Obedient Guards and replacing them with new units – the Loyal Assistant Guards (Ch'ungch'anwi) and the Tiger Wing Guards (Hoigwi). He intended by this means to placate local yangban who might be upset over his usurpation. King Yejong restored the Loyal and Obedient Guards in 1469. The Loyal Assistant Guards were divided into four groups and served rotating nine-day shifts on palace guard.

In 1471, the terms of service of all three guard units were changed by King Sŏngjong. The quota limits were eliminated, the Loyal and Righteous Guards were converted into long-term service while the other two were divided into five groups rotating on and off every four months. The duties of the Loyal and Obedient Guards were later increased by dividing them into seven groups serving every two months, a measure adopted because of financial problems.

For a discussion of these privileged guard units in the early Chosŏn period, see Ch'a Munsŏp, "Sŏnch'o ŭi Ch'ung'ŭi, Chungch'an, Ch'ungsunwi [The Loyal and Righteous Guards, Loyal Assistant Guards, and Loyal and Obedient Guards of the early Chosŏn period], in idem, *Chosŏn sidae kunje yŏn'gu*, pp. 90–135. For discussion of the depletion of students in the National Academy, see ibid., p. 131.

109. PGSR 21:9b–10b.

110. Ibid. 21:10b, 12a-b. See Ch'a Munsŏp, "Chungjongjo ŭi Chŏngnowi [The Jurchen Quelling Guards of Chungjong's reign], in idem, *Chosŏn sidae kunje yŏn'gu*, pp. 136–57.

111. PGSR 21:38b–39b.

112. Ibid. 21:42a, 44a.

113. Ibid. 21:43b.

114. Ibid. 21:44a.

115. Ibid. 21:44b.

116. Ibid. 21:38a-b.

117. Ibid. 21:29b, line 6. For a discussion of the origin of the *sog'ogun*, see Ch'a Munsŏp, "Sog'ogun yŏn'gu [A study of the *sog'o* soldiers], in idem, *Chosŏn sidae kunje yŏn'gu* [Studies in the military system of the Chosŏn period] (Seoul: Tan'guk taehakkyo ch'ulp'anbu, 1973), pp. 179–228.

118. PGSR 21:37a, 38a.

119. Ibid. 21:29b, 32a.

120. Ibid. 21:38a-b.

121. Ibid. 21:39b.

122. Ibid. 21:39a-b, 40b.

123. Ibid. 21:39b–40a, 43b–44a.
124. Ibid. 21:43b, 21:64b–68a.

CHAPTER 11. The Debate over the Military Training Agency, 1651–82

1. PGSR 21:12b–13a.

2. Ibid. 21:12b–13a. For discussion of the commercial activities of Military Training Agency troops, see Yi T'aejin, *Chosŏn hugi ŭi chŏngch'i wa kunyongje ŭi pyŏn'ch'ŏn* [The politics of the late Chosŏn Period and changes in the capital division system] (Seoul: Han'guk yŏn'guwŏn, 1985), pp. 178–89; see p. 189 n.10.

3. PGSR 21:11a-b. For Yu's remarks on how low the two *p'il* rate was, see ibid. 21:36b. See Ch'a Munsŏp, "Imnan ihu ŭi yangyŏk kwa kyunyŏkp'ŏp ŭi sŏngnip [The yangyŏk system from the Imjin Wars on and the establishment of the equal service system] *Sahak yŏn'gu* 10 (April 1961):115–30.

4. Ch'a Munsŏp, "Hyojong ŭi kunbi kwangch'ung" [The military defense build-up of King Hyojong's reign], in idem, *Chosŏn sidae kunje yŏngu* (Seoul: Tan'guk taehakkyo ch'ulp'anbu, 1973), pp. 49–51; Yi T'aejin, "Chung'ang Ogunyŏngje ŭi sŏngnip kwajŏng" [The process of the establishment of the central five division system], in *Han'guk kunjesa, 2 Kŭnse Chosŏn hugip'yŏn* [The military history of Korea, vol. 2. Early modern period: Late Chosŏn dynasty] (Seoul: Yukkun ponbu, 1977), pp. 123–32; Yi T'aejin, *Chosŏn hugi ŭi chŏngch'i wa kunyŏngje pyŏnch'ŏn* [The politics of the late Chosŏn period and changes in the capital division system] (Seoul: Han'guk yŏnguwŏn, 1985), pp. 169–73. See also the brief historical account of the Military Training Agency written by the compiler of *Hyŏnjŏng kaesu sillok* [The revised veritable record of King Hyŏnjong] 10:8b–9a, in Kuksa p'yŏnch'an wiwŏnhoe [National Historical Compilation Committee] ed., *Chosŏn wangjo sillok,* vol. 37 (Seoul: Tongguk munhwasa, 1955).

5. Ch'a Munsŏp, "Hyojong ŭi kunbi kwangch'ung," pp. 49–51; Yi T'aejin, *Han'guk kunjesa* (1977), pp. 123–32; *Chosŏn hugi*, pp. 169–73.

6. *Hyŏnjong kaesu sillok* 7:5b, cited in Yi T'aejin, *Chosŏn hugi*, pp. 176–77. See also chap. 10, above.

7. *Sŭngjŏngwŏn ilgi* [Records of the Royal Secretariat] 11:411–21 (Seoul: Kuksan p'yŏncha'n wiwŏnhoe, 1962). This text is hereinafter referred to as SJW. For a briefer summary, see *Hyŏnjong sillok*, 16:10a, same date.

8. *Hyŏnjong kaesu sillok* 20:22b–23a. A draft memorial in Song Siyŏl's collected works, undated but inserted after another document dated the ninth lunar month of 1670, clearly indicates that he intended to phase out the agency completely. Song Siyŏl, *Songja taejŏn* 6 (N.p.:Kigukchŏng, 1926): 10b–12b. This draft memorial is located between one dated *kyŏngsul* (1670).9.19 and another dated *sinhaek* (1671).1.17.

9. SJW 11:400. I am indebted to Ch'a Munsŏp's discussion of this matter for the above source. See Ch'a Munsŏp, "Kŭmwiyŏng ŭi yŏn'gu" [A study of the Royal Guard Division), in idem, *Chosŏn sidae kunje yŏn'gu*, p. 345. Unfortunately, the quote in Ch'a's book on this page is not from the SJW, which he cites in n.12 on p. 345, but from the *Hyŏnjong kaesu sillok* 20:22b–23a.

10. Ch'a Munsŏp, "Kŭmwiyŏng yŏn'gu," pp. 342–45.

11. SJW 11:411–21, Kanghŭi 8 (Hyŏnjong 10).1.23 chŏngsa. For a briefer summary, see *Hyŏnjong sillok*, 16:10a, same date. According to the *Man'gi yoram* (MGYR), Kunjŏngp'yŏn (volume on military administration) (Keijō: Chōsen sōtokufu chūsūin, 1938), p. 218, Yi Wan, who was commander of the agency, was appointed minister of war concurrently in *pyŏn'go* year or 1666, but he balked at assuming the burden of two posts.

12. See n.14, below, for the material above and following.

13. See n.14.

14. SJW 11:411–13. Ch'a Munsŏp, "Kŭmwiyŏng yŏn'gu," p. 346, relies primarily on the *Hyŏnjong kaesu sillok*, 20:25a-b, Hyŏnjong 10.1.chŏngsa (23rd day) for the account of this day's discussion. This source is much more abbreviated and less illuminating than the SJW, which takes up eight full folio pages as opposed to a few lines in the *Sillok*. For a brief summary, see also *Hyŏnjong sillok*, 16:10a same date, and *Chōsenshi*, series 5, 4 (Keijō: Chōsen insatsu KK, 1934):378.

15. This would account for 6,656 men, leaving 9 extras.

16. This would yield a total of 508 men overall, 4 less than the 512 called for.

17. Ch'a Munsŏp attributed this idea to Song Siyŏl's recommendation that the Military Training Agency be reduced by attrition, but since Hyŏnjong was preserving the agency and recruiting new soldiers prior to considering letting old ones go, the scheme seems closer to Hŏ Chŏk's suggestion.

18. *Pibyŏnsa tŭngnok* [Record of the Border Defense Command] 3 (Seoul: Kuksa p'yŏnch'an wiwŏnhoe, 1949):14, Hyŏnjong 10.2.20 (1669); *Hyŏnjong sillok* 16:14b–15a.

19. *Hyŏnjong sillok*, 21:29b–30a; Ch'a Munsŏp, "Kŭmwiyŏng ŭi yŏn'gu," p. 346.

20. *Hyŏnjong sillok*, 17:48b–49a (1669), cited in Yi T'aejin, *Chosŏn hugi*, p. 183 n.21.

21. The phrase was literally, "In general, [it was because] the king kept military affairs in his mind." *Hyŏnjong sillok* 16:15a.

22. Yi T'aejin discovered this historical account by the historian of the *Veritable Record* after a notice in 1663, six years prior to the creation of the special unit. The account contains one slight error: the historian notes that Yu Hyŏgyŏn was appointed commander of the Military Training Agency in *sinhaek* year (1671), when it was actually 1669. This slip probably does not mean that the figures of soldiers and support taxpayers are erroneous. *Hyŏnjong kaesu sillok* 10:9a (1663), cited in Yi T'aejin, *Chosŏn hugi*, p. 183 n.22.

23. *Songja taejŏn* 13:30a-b.

24. It may be that Song's account is garbled. He gave the date, *chŏngmyo*.4.12 (1627), but I cannot find a record of the incident he describes. Kim Yejŏng was in fact a musketeer of the Military Training Agency who in 1629 reported a conspiracy led by the former Hundo (interpreter?), Im Kyŏngsa, in league with five company commanders of the agency. Im planned to put out the word that the spiritual forces of the capital at Hansŏng were on the wane, call for the establishment of a new capital at Yŏnsan, proceed to Naep'o on the coast and seize a few districts nearby to interdict sea traffic, and then call on their coconspirators in the agency in the capital to kill the agency commander, set fire to the royal ancestral temple and capital gates and call for the restoration of the deposed Kwanghaegun. Thanks to Kim's report, Im was executed and Kim was awarded by being promoted to *tangsang* rank (1A to 3A) and granted all the confiscated family property of Im Kyŏngsa. *Injo sillok*, 20:25b; *Chōsenshi*, series 6, 2:219, Hyŏnjong 7.i4.19; Yi Hongjik,

ed. *Kuksadaesajŏn* [Great dictionary of national history] 1 (Seoul: Chimun'gak, 1963):285 (hereafter KSDSJ). There does not appear to be any report in the court records of a plot reported by Kim Yejŏng in 1629.

25. *Songja taejŏn* 13:30b–32a.

26. Ibid. 13:32a. Song's complaints were echoed by a *Sillok* historian, so much so that one wonders if he were not, in fact, a disciple of Song's. "The fact that as before vacancies in the ranks of the Military Training Agency's soldiers caused by deaths or desertions continued to be filled was a major violation of the recommendation that Song Siyŏl made to the King. And everyone said that when the recruitments were carried out there was tremendous resentment and criticism, but throughout Hŏ Chŏk and Yu Hyŏgyŏn assisted in its accomplishment. They could do so because the king's main concern was with military affairs." *Hyŏnjong sillok* 16:15a. The editor of this volume of the Kuksa p'yŏnch'an wiwŏnhoe ed., Sin Sŏkho, commented that the compilation of the *Hyŏnjong Sillok* began in 1675, the year after Sukchong came to the throne, when the court was dominated by members of the Southerner (Namin) faction, the opponents of Song Siyŏl, leader of the Westerners at the time. Because of delays the first draft was not completed until the fifth month of 1677. It would appear, however, that the historian in charge of this section was sympathetic to Song and hostile to the Southerner, Hŏ Chŏk. *Chosŏn wangjo sillok* 36 (Seoul: Kuksa p'yŏnch'an wiwŏnhoe, 1957):1–2.

27. *Songja taejŏn* 13:32b.

28. *Hyŏnjong kaesu sillok* 24:7b–8a (1671); *Hyŏnjong sillok* 19:21b; Ch'a Munsŏp, "Kŭmwiyŏng ŭi yŏn'gu," p. 347.

29. *Hyŏnjong kaesu sillok* 24:20a (1671). Ch'a Munsŏp, "Kŭmwiyŏng ŭi yŏn'gu," p. 347.

30. *Pibyŏnsa tŭngnok* 3:106–07 (1671); Ch'a Munsŏp, "Kŭmwiyŏng ŭi yŏn'gu," pp. 347–48.

31. *Hyŏnjong kaesu sillok* 24:27b–28b (1671); Ch'a Munsŏp, "Kŭmwiyŏng ŭi yŏn'gu," p. 347.

32. For a thorough discussion in English of the issues involved, see JaHyun Kim Haboush, "A Heritage of Kings: One Man's Monarchy in the Confucian World" (Ph.D. diss., Columbia University, 1978), pp. 47–55. Haboush points out that Song Siyŏl's position was too challenging to Hyojong's legitimacy to present to the throne, so a different argument was made to justify a lesser degree of mourning: that Korean law, as opposed to the *I-li*, required only one (instead of three) years' mourning of a wife for all her husband's sons.

The only objection I would raise in Haboush's account is her statement that it was extraordinary that there should have been any debate over Hyojong's credentials at all. She ignored the probable poisoning of Crown Prince Sohyŏn and the setting aside of his heirs because of King Injo's suspicion that he was collaborating with the Manchus to gain the throne for himself. In addition, he wreaked horrible vengeance on Lady Chang and her family, and he may have set aside Sohyŏn's sons because of his hatred for the Changs as well as his suspicions of Sohyŏn's loyalty. Haboush states that Injo only banished the three sons of Sohyŏn to eliminate any question of the legitimacy of the newly designated heir, later King Hyojong, and she suggests that the debate over Hyojong's legitimacy was only a legal technicality. But if Injo had in fact murdered or ordered the murder of Crown

Prince Sohyŏn and bypassed his sons who would normally have succeeded their father, the legitimacy of Hyojong was by no means merely a legal or technical question. And if Sohyŏn had died a natural death, there would have been no reason to set aside his heirs. Ibid., pp. 49–50. See also idem, *A Heritage of Kings: One Man's Monarchy in the Confucian World* (New York: Columbia University Press, 1988), pp. 23–25.

33. Yi T'aejin, *Han'guk kunjesa* (1977), pp. 136–39; *Chosŏn hugi*, pp. 177–78, 181–84; see also chap. 10, above. The point of view that Southerners Hŏ Chŏk and Yu Hyŏgyŏn supported the creation of the special unit only to control it and continued to fill vacancies in the Military Training Agency instead of allowing it to shrink by attrition as Song had requested, is that of the historian and compiler of this section of the *Sillok*. Although the statement appears prejudicial to the interest of the Southerner faction, the compilation of the *Hyŏnjong sillok* was begun in 1675 and completed in 1677, in a period when Southerners were in a dominant position at court. The director of the *Sillok* compilation (Ch'ongjaegwan) was Hŏ Chŏk, and one of the members of the second section (Ibang tangsang) was Mok Naesŏn, a man later instrumental in the purge of Westerners in 1689. *Hyŏnjong sillok* 16:14b–15a cited by Yi T'aejin, *Chosŏn hugi*, p. 178 n.8. For information on compilation, see Sin Sŏkho, ed., *Chosŏn wangjo sillok* 36 (Seoul: Kuksa p'yŏnch'an wiwŏnhoe, 1957):1–3.

34. Haboush, "A Heritage of Kings," pp. 55–61.

35. These two men also had important relatives and family connections. Kim Man'gi was the father-in-law of King Sukchong, Kim Sŏkchu was the nephew of the father-in-law of King Hyŏnjong, son of a minister of war, and grandson of Kim Yuk, of the Ch'ŏngp'ung Kim clan. Yi T'aejin, *Han'guk kunjesa* (1977), p. 143 n.36, and *Chosŏn hugi*, pp. 189–90.

36. Yi T'aejin, *Chosŏn hugi*, pp. 184–87; idem, *Han'guk kunjesa* (1977), pp. 139–41. For the figure of 6,250 Crack Select Soldiers see p. 142 n.33.

37. Yi T'aejin, *Han'guk kunjesa* (1977), p. 146 n.51, explains that the animosity of Kim Sŏkchu for Song Siyŏl and many Westerner literati began because of Kim Chip's opposition to the plan of his grandfather, Kim Yuk, for the *taedong* system, and impeachment of his father's conduct of the funeral for Kim Yuk. See also Yi T'aejin, *Chosŏn hugi*, pp. 186–89.

38. Yi T'aejin, *Han'guk kunjesa* (1977), pp. 143–45. Yun Hyu's motives derive from the remarks of the *Sillok* historian, see n.42, and *Sukchong sillok* 4:46b; Yi T'aejin, *Chosŏn hugi*, pp. 190–92.

39. Yi T'aejin, *Han'guk kunjesa* (1977), p. 145; idem, *Chosŏn hugi*, p. 191–93; Yu Hongnyŏl, "Mankwa sŏlhaeng ŭi chŏngch'aeksajŏk ch'uui: Chosŏn chunggirŭl chungsim'ŭro" [Trends in policy behind the establishment of the *mankwa* examination in the mid-Chosŏn period] *Sahak yŏn'gu* 18 (September 1964):207–46.

40. Yi T'aejin, *Han'guk kunjesa* (1977), pp. 145–46 n.48, *Chosŏn hugi*, pp. 192–93.

41. Yi T'aejin, *Han'guk kunjesa* (1977), pp. 141–42, 145–47; *Chosŏn hugi*, pp. 193–96.

42. *Han'guk kunjesa* (1977), pp. 142–43 n.57, pp. 147–48; *Sukchong sillok* 9:10b–11a (1680).

43. Yi T'aejin, *Han'guk kunjesa* (1977), pp. 148–49, see esp. p. 148 n.58; idem, *Chosŏn*

hugi, pp. 196–98 n.58. The notes contain references to notices in the *Sukchong sillok*. The name of the incident, *Sambok*, or "three *pok*," derived from the three princes' having the character *pok* (happiness) as part of their princely titles. This incident is also covered in Haboush, "A Heritage of Kings," pp. 62–64, but she claims Yun was executed for his heterodox, anti-Chu Hsi beliefs. There is no citation of a source for p. 64 n.91, however. See also Kang Chujin, *Yijo tangjaengsa yŏn'gu* (Seoul: Seoul Taehakkyo ch'ulp'anbu, 1971), pp. 285–93.

44. *Sukchong sillok* 11:10b–11a, Sukchong 7.1.kyŏng'o, cited in Yi T'aejin, *Chosŏn hugi*, p. 199 n.60; *Han'guk kunjesa* (1977), pp. 149–50.

45. The number of special unit soldiers (along with aides or *p'yohagun*) was listed in the third lunar month of 1682 as 13,949. These 13,949 soldiers are referred to as *Yŏngbu p'yoha pyŏltaegun*, literally "the aides and soldiers of the division-regiments of the special unit of the Military Training Agency." *Yŏngbu* or Division-Regiment is not a usual appellation for the Military Training Agency, to which the special unit was attached, but on the other hand, the agency was part of what became the *Ogunyŏng* (Five Military Divisions) in 1682. See *Sukchong sillok* 13, sang:18a-b.

It was initially proposed that these 13,949 troops be divided into 80 companies (of 134 men each), or a total of 10,748 soldiers. This reorganization yielded a surplus of 3,201 soldiers who were to be transferred to support taxpayer status along with their previous 3,201 "material support persons" (*chaboin*), a total of 6,402 who would be reassigned as support taxpayers in addition to what I would estimate as 32,244 (10,748 times 3 support persons) support taxpayers of the 10,748 soldiers, or a subtotal of 38,646. By converting some duty soldiers to support taxpayers, it alleviated the pressure to find new support taxpayers for the new unit.

To this 80 companies of special unit soldiers were added 3,773 Crack Select Soldiers. They were supposed to be reorganized into one division 25 companies of 134 men each, or a total of 3,350 men. The new Forbidden Guards thus consisted of 10,748 men from the special unit and 3,350 from the Crack Select Soldiers, or a total of 14,098. The reorganization of the Crack Select Soldiers also involved a shift of 423 duty soldiers (3,773–3,350) and their 423 "materiel support persons," or a total of 846 persons, to the status of support taxpayer. These were added to the existing 11,628 existing Crack Select Soldier support taxpayers, increasing the number to 12,474. Of this figure, 6,595 were made "rice taxpayers" and the remaining 5,879 were shifted to the Ministry of Taxation. The reason was not stated, but it may have been to provide funds to the ministry, which did pay some salaries and expenses of the Crack Select Soldiers. Thus, if you add these 6,595 support taxpayers to the 38,646 support taxpayers for the special unit soldiers, you get a total of 45,241.

Yi T'aejin's estimated figure of support taxpayers differs considerably from mine. He estimates 14,098 regular soldiers of the combined Forbidden Guards, and a total of 78,195 support taxpayers consisting of 14,098 materiel support persons (*chabo*) and 64,097 support taxpayers (*poin*). Of the latter category, he claims 57,502 support taxpayers carried over for the special unit soldiers, but this number is not mentioned in the *Sillok* text. It contains within it an estimate of 41,100 original support taxpayers for the special unit soldiers, but since he already has estimated 10,748 materiel taxpayers for the same number of soldiers, there could not have been more than two more support taxpayers (*poin*), or a total of 21,496, in this category.

I also think he double counts 3,350 material support persons for the Crack Select Soldiers because the *Sillok* mentions a total of 12,474 of Crack Select *poin* combined with the 846 downgraded soldiers and their support taxpayers, reduced to 6,595. He should not add on another 3,350, I believe.

On the other hand, in 1704 when almost all military units were reorganized in a major reform effort, the Reform Bureau of that time stated that under "the old system" the Forbidden Guards consisted of 136 companies of 127 men each (i.e., 17,272 soldiers), which, combined with three support taxpayers for every man, capital and provincial Standard Bearers (P'yoha), Special Cavalry (Pyŏlyowi), and Cannoneers (Pyŏlp'ajin), et al., came to a total of 91,696 men. If you subtract the 17,272 rotating duty soldiers from this, it leaves 74,424 for support taxpayers and miscellaneous types of soldiers. This is not far from the figure of 78,195 that Yi T'aejin gives for support taxpayers in 1682. Even though there were a few thousand more duty soldiers in 1704, I would accept Yi's estimate even though its derivation is not clear. Possibly this figure should include miscellaneous soldiers as well as support taxpayers. See *Sukchong sillok* 13, sang:18a-b; *Hyŏnjong sillok* 21:29b–30a; Ch'a Munsŏp, "Kŭmwiyŏng ŭi yŏn'gu," pp. 346, 348–54; Yi T'aejin, *Chosŏn hugi*, pp. 200–201, especially the table on p. 201. See p. 226 n.7. See also *Sukchong sillok* 40:55b.

46. In 1704, when the size of the force was cut back, there were 136 companies of 127 men each with 3 support taxpayers per man, exclusive of miscellaneous soldiers. At this time, the 136 companies were divided into 13 rather than 10 shifts of two months each, which meant that the interval between duty was extended from 20 to 36 months. These figures would yield a total of 69,088 duty soldiers and support taxpayers combined, but in fact the actual figure was 91,696, almost 32 percent higher than one would expect. Hence, in 1682, if my calculations are increased by a factor of 32 percent, the estimated total of soldiers and support taxpayers combined should have been around 60,000 men. Ch'a Munsŏp, "Kŭmwiyŏng ŭi yŏn'gu," p. 353.

47. *Sukchong sillok* 13, sang:25a-b; Ch'a Munsŏp, "Kŭmwiyŏng ŭi yŏn'gu," pp. 349–50.

48. *Sukchong sillok* 11:10b–11a, Sukchong 7.1.kyŏng'o, cited in Yi T'aejin, *Chosŏn hugi*, p. 199 n.60; *Han'guk kunjesa* (1977), pp. 149–50.

49. Ch'a Munsŏp, study of the Kŭmwiyŏng in *Taegu sahak* 7:8 (1973), included in his *Chosŏn sidae ŭi kunje*; *Han'guk kunjesa* (1977), pp. 150–53; Yi T'aejin, *Chosŏn hugi*, pp. 202–3, esp. nn. 70–72.

50. See Haboush, "A Heritage of Kings," pp. 66–69 for explanation of the issues surrounding the Patriarch/Disciple split.

51. Yi T'aejin, *Han'guk kunjesa* (1977), p. 153, notes that in fact the dispute between consort relatives that began around 1680 changed the mode of factional politics that had prevailed up to this time.

52. Yi T'aejin, *Chosŏn hugi*, p. 206.

53. Yi T'aejin, *Han'guk kunjesa* (1977), pp. 153–58; idem, *Chosŏn hugi*, pp. 205–8, 210–13.

54. Yi T'aejin, *Han'guk kunjesa* (1977), pp. 159–62; idem, *Chosŏn hugi*, pp. 215–18. The post of commander remained until King Yŏngjo restored the Yusu system in the eighteenth century.

CHAPTER 12. The Search for Alternative Modes of Military Finance

1. For the above discussion, see Ch'a Munsŏp, "Imnan ihu ŭi yangyŏk kwa kyunyŏkp'ŏp ŭi sŏngnip" [The yangyŏk system from the Imjin wars and the establishment of the equal service system], *Sahak yŏn'gu*, pt. 2, 11 (July 1961):97–102; Chŏng Yŏnsik, "Sipch'il-sippal segi yangyŏk kyunilhwa chŏngch'aek ŭi ch'uui" [The trend in policy toward uniform labor service tax on men of good status in the seventeenth and eighteenth centuries], *Han'guksaron* 13 (August 1985):124. For a discussion of the changes in the meaning of *yuhak* and other terms for students and scholars see Young-ho Ch'oe [Ch'oe Yŏngho], "Yuhak, haksaeng, kyosaeng-go" [A study of *yuhak, haksaeng*, and *kyosaeng*] *Yŏksa hakpo* 101 (March 1984):1–21.

2. An Chŏngbok, "Kun'guk ch'ongnok [Total national statistics], in *Chaptong san'i* [Miscellaneous information] (Seoul: Han'gukhak munhŏn yŏn'guso, ed., Han'gukhak kosajŏn ch'ongsŏ series, 1981), p. 446, cited in Chŏng Yŏnsik, "Yangyŏk kyunilhwa," p. 139. The statistics are undated, but the note to the first entry on p. 446 mentions the *Soktaejŏn* law code published in 1746.

3. An Chongbok, *Chaptong san'i* [Miscellaneous information] Han'gukhak yŏn'guso, ed., Han'gukhak kosajŏn ch'ongsŏ series, 1981), pp. 446–47. The 6,316 soldiers of the Military Training Agency were presumably permanent, salaried soldiers. The figures for soldiers for the other four divisions includes the aides or P'yohagun. The Defense Command and Anti-Manchu Division were evidently not financed by support taxpayers except for 2,468 assigned to the 1,022 aides of the Anti-Manchu Division.

4. These included the following types: support taxpayers of rotating duty soldiers of each (divisional?) headquarters, ivory soldiers (*abyŏng*) who paid taxes instead of serving on rotation, the total of single equipment taxpayers assigned to each rotating duty soldier of the Royal Division and Forbidden Guard Division, ibid., p. 446.

5. Ibid.

6. Ibid., pp. 446–47. There were approximately 110,000 *sog'o* soldiers in 1641 and 200,000 in 1711. Ch'a Munsŏp, "Imnan ihu ŭi yangyŏk," pt. 2, p. 96.

The total of all subcategories in An's statistics comes to 1,412,638, which is vastly larger than his announced grand total of 1,083,784, so either he or I have double-counted somewhere. If we were to assume that *sog'o* slave soldiers and slave post-station workers are not included in his announced total of 1,083,784, this would reduce the total of subcategories to 1,151,502. The discrepancy is now reduced to 68,000, but there are no other categories that could be suspected of double counting.

If the percentage of *sog'o* soldiers plus slave post-station workers is calculated as a percentage of 1.4 million men, it comes to 19 percent; if the lesser total of 1,083,784 is taken, then 24 percent of all servicemen and taxpayers were of base status. This is considerably lower than Yu Hyŏngwŏn's estimate in the seventeenth century, but nonetheless considerable. Yu, however, may have been comparing different quantities.

7. *Yŏngjo sillok* 73:79a.

8. Ibid. 75:7b–8a.

9. For citations, see Ch'a Munsŏp, "Imnan ihu ŭi yangyŏk," pt. 2, *Sahak yŏn'gu* 11:116–17.

10. Chŏng Yŏnsik, "Yangyŏk kyunilhwa," pp. 129–30.

11. Ch'a Munsŏp claimed that there were only 2,000 Howigun (Royal Attendant Guards) in 1636, which may have been equivalent to the later Royal Division soldiers. "Imnan ihu ŭi yangyŏk," pt. 2, p. 120.

12. Chŏng Yŏnsik, "Yangyŏk kyunilhwa," pp. 124, 138. See the proposal of Hŏ Chŏk in 1669 to reduce the district quotas of school students described in chap. 7, and the discussion of reforms in the 1650s in chap. 12.

13. Ch'oe Yŏngho, "Yuhak, haksaeng, kyosaeng-go," pp. 7–14.

14. *Hyojong sillok* 12:2b; Ch'a Munsŏp, "Chosŏnjo Hyojong ŭi kunbi kwangch'ung, sang" pt. 2, p. 43; Chŏng Manjo, "Chosŏn hugi ŭi yangyŏk pyŏnt'ong non'ŭi e taehan kŏmt'o: Kyunyŏkpŏp sŏngnip ŭi paegyŏng" [A study of the debate over reform of the commoner service system in late Chosŏn: Background to the establishment of the equal service system], *Tongdae nonch'ong* 7 (April 1977):11 n.34; James B. Palais, *Politics and Policy in Traditional Korea* (Cambridge: Harvard University Press), pp. 96–97.

15. *Hyojong sillok* 21:8a–9a (1659), cited in Ch'a Munsŏp, "Hyojong ŭi kunbi kwangch'ung," pt. 2, p. 50.

16. Ibid.

17. Ibid. 21:9a-b.

18. Ibid. 10:a-b.

19. Ibid. 14:6a, cited in Ch'a Munsŏp, "Hyojong ŭi kunbi kwangch'ung," pt. 2, pp. 45–46.

20. Ch'a Munsŏp, "Hyojong ŭi kunbi kwangch'ung," pt. 2, pp. 46–47. See the discussion of slave participation in examinations in the early part of the dynasty in Choe Young-ho [Ch'oe Yŏngho], "Commoners in Early Yi Dynasty Civil Examinations: An Aspect of Korean Social Structure, 1392–1600," *Journal of Asian Studies* 33, no. 4 (August 1974):611–31.

21. *Hyŏnjong kaesu sillok*, 28:21b–22a, Hyŏnjong 15.7.ŭrch'uk. Ch'oe Yŏngho argued that after 1626 sons of yangban enrolled in private academies rather than government schools like *hyanggyo* because they could not bear to associate with commoner students, but this statement suggests that by the third quarter of the century private academies were by no means restricted to sons of yangban. Ch'oe, "Yuhak, haksaeng, kyosaeng," p. 15.

22. *Hyŏnjong kaesu sillok* 28:22b–23a, Hyŏnjong 15.7.chŏngmyo.

23. *Hyŏnjong kaesu sillok* 17:30b; 28:26a–27a; *Hyŏnjong sillok* 22:27b–28a, same date. These and previous citations on this case are cited in Chŏng Manjo, "Yangyŏk pyŏnt'ong non'ŭi," 1977, p. 12 nn. 35–40.

24. *Sukchong sillok* 10:66a; Chŏng Manjo, "Yangyŏk pyŏnt'ong non'ŭi," pp. 13–15.

25. Yi Tanha's memorial is in *Sukchong sillok* 11:31b–32a, Sukchong 7.4.pyŏngsul. For an interpretation of Yi Tanha's memorial, see Chŏng Manjo, "Yangyŏk pyŏnt'ong non'ŭi," pp. 16–17.

26. James Legge, *The Chinese Classics*, vol. 2, *The Works of Mencius*, bk. 6, pt. 1, chap. 7 (Shanghai, 1935) pp. 405–6.

27. *Sukchong sillok* 11:31b–32b (1681).

28. The reason why the figures do not add up is because of the nature of the classical Chinese language used. Yi Samyŏng said there were "something over" one million households, "something over" 400,000 and 700,000. As a general rule, I add a factor of two out of the next ten.

29. *Sukchong sillok* 12:60a–61b (1681); Chŏng Manjo, "Yangyŏk pyŏnt'ong non'ŭi," pp. 15–16.

30. Yi Samyŏng's statistics are interesting but not entirely clear. It is not certain that the 800,000 combined total of soldiers and support taxpayers he mentioned also included the 200,000 *sog'o* soldiers. If not, then the total number of men supposedly involved in the entire military service system came to one million, about the same as the figure discovered by An Chŏngbok in the middle of the eighteenth century. Since this is contrary to most other opinions, either his 800,000 was inclusive of the 200,000 *sog'o* soldiers, or his overall estimates are significantly exaggerated. See An Chŏngbok, *Chaptong san'i*, Han'gukhak munhŏn yŏn'guso ed. (Seoul: Asea munhwasa, 1981), pp. 446–47.

31. *Sukchong sillok* 12:60a–61b (1681); Chŏng Manjo, "Yangyŏk pyŏnt'ong non'ŭi," pp. 15–16. The corrigenda to *kwŏn* 12 of the *Sukchong sillok* 12 ha:2a-b, contains a paragraph by the historian who claimed, in what appears a bit of character assassination, that Yi Samyŏng was a skillful advocate who masked his perverse ideas behind purple prose. Because his mother was the sister of Kim Sŏkchu, he participated in the secret conspiracy of Kim Sŏkchu in 1679–80 to obtain the execution of Hŏ Chŏk and other Southerners. He also used his contact with a eunuch, Kim Hyŏn, to gain admittance to the final examinations without taking the preliminary *chŏnsi* examination, and he found out from Kim Sŏkchu, who was in charge of the test, what the examination question was to be. He also was registered as a merit subject for his work in the execution of Hŏ Kyun, Hŏ Chŏk's son. It appears his merit status may have been revoked because he skipped a stage in the examinations and was promoted out of turn, but when Sukchong later held a special examination (*chŏngsi*), he passed in first place. He used his appointment to the Office of Special Counselors (Hongmun'gwan) to get his name put back on the merit subject rolls, and when others opposed it, the king granted him a special promotion and enrollment as a second-grade merit subject. He had now advanced to the highest ministerial ranks.

The historian explained that he proposed the household cloth tax to gain Sukchong's favor. It was not that the purpose of the household cloth tax to eliminate existing evils in military support taxes was a bad idea – it had even been proposed before by many people; his motives were suspect because putting forward a dangerous plan at a time when the common people were suffering from famine and their trust in their ruler's benevolence was shaken could only have been undertaken for the purpose of winning power and influence at court.

Without a more thorough study of the conspiratorial politics of the period and an attempt at verifying the charges, one cannot be completely sure that the historian's remarks were an expression of political or personal bias. Nevertheless, the compilation of the *Sukchong sillok* was begun in 1720, right after the death of Sukchong, and completed in 1728. We know that because of the problems of recording the history of factional disputes, the historians were shifted several times. In the second year of the project, the radical Disciple (Soron) leader, Kim Ilgyŏng, impeached the head of the *Sillok* project, Kim Ch'angjip, and three others of the top Patriarch (Noron) leaders, and after the execution of the four, a Disciple took over as director of the *Sukchong sillok* compilation. He, too, was dismissed in 1723. Then in 1724, King Kyŏngjong died, and King Yŏngjo, supported by the Patriarchs, came to the throne and purged some of the Disciples.

In 1725, the directorship of the *Sillok* project was shifted to the Patriarchs until its completion in 1727, but in that year, too, there was a purge of over 100 Patriarchs, and a return of some Disciples to the government. These Disciples then demanded revision of some portions of the *Sukchong sillok*, which was done by adding corrigenda to the end of each *kwŏn*. Since the historian's remarks cited above were included in one of these corrigenda, we might assume that he was affiliated with the Disciples and probably biased against Kim Sŏkchu, even though Kim was not on good terms with Song Siyŏl, the patron saint of the Patriarch's faction, and, by extension, Yi Samyŏng. The tenor of his criticism makes it appear that he was using an ad hominem argument to discredit the household cloth proposal. For the history of the compilation, see *Chosŏn wangjo sillok* 38:1–3.

32. *Sukchong sillok* 12:61a.

33. Ibid. 12:61b, same date; 12:63b–64a.

34. Ibid. 13 sang:1a.

35. Ibid. 13 sang:1b.

36. Ibid. 13 sang:1b–2a.

37. Ibid. 13, sang:2a, 6a, 6b–7a. For the above discussion, see Sukchong 8.1.kyŏng'o.

38. Ibid. 13, sang:7a–8a.

39. Ibid. 13, sang:8b. Further requests for rescission of orders to transfer the members of the censorate who criticized the governor and provincial military commander of P'yŏng'an were made. Ibid. 13, sang:9b.

40. Chŏng Manjo says that the great majority opposed the plan because of famine conditions. Since some of those people also suggested adopting it when crop conditions improved, it would not be correct to say that the vast majority opposed the plan, at least in principle. I do not believe that the position that implementation had to be delayed until improvement in harvests meant outright opposition. Chŏng Manjo, "Yangyŏk pyŏnt'ong non'ŭi," p. 16.

41. *Sukchong sillok* 13, sang:10b, 11b–13a, Sukchong 8.1.pyŏngja, 8.2.kyŏngjin, 8.2.kapsin (1682). One other attempt to solve the shortage of commoners for military service ought to be mentioned here as well. An elderly sinecure, Yi Kyŏngyŏ, in 1653, pointed out that so many commoner peasants were escaping state control by commending their lands to powerful landlords and becoming slaves that, "it won't be long before there are no *yangmin* left in the country at all." His solution was one that Yu Hyŏngwŏn had also advocated: use of the matrilineal succession rule in mixed commoner/slave marriages, which Yi argued would guarantee a multiplication of the *yangmin* population within

a decade's time. *Hyojong sillok* 11:9a-b, cited and discussed in Ch'a Munsŏp, "Hyojong ŭi kunbi kwangch'ung," pt. 2, p. 42.

42. Chŏng Yŏnsik, "Yangyŏk kyunilhwa," pp. 121–44.

43. Ibid., pp. 139, n.74, pp. 183, 129–30; Chŏng Manjo, "Yangyŏk pyŏnt'ong non'ŭi," p. 10.

CHAPTER 13. Military Reorganization, Weapons, and Walls

1. PGSR 21:29a. See Ch'a Munsŏp, "Kŭmwiyŏng yŏn'gu [A study of the Royal Guard Division]," in idem, *Chosŏn sidae kunje yŏn'gu* (Seoul: Tan'guk taehakkyo ch'ulp'anbu, 1973), pp. 342–431. It is difficult to find information on the other two categories. Ch'a mentioned that the Special Musketeers was one of the minor types of provincial troops that supplemented the main force of provincial soldiers, the *sog'ogun*. Ch'a, "Sog'ogun yŏn'gu [A study of the *sog'o* soldiers], in ibid., p. 204.

2. PGSR 21:29a. The units he excluded were the Kapsa, P'aengbae, Taejol, Pajin'gun, and Pandang.

3. Yi T'aejin, *Chosŏn hugi chŏngch'i wa kunyŏngje pyŏnjŏn* [Politics and changes in the army division system in the late Chosŏn period] (Seoul: Han'guk yŏn'guwŏn, 1985), pp. 160–63.

4. PGSR 21:12a-b.

5. Ibid. 21:35a.

6. In addition to the Military Training Agency and the Royal Division, two other units were, strictly speaking, not capital guards, but they did have responsibility for defense of the capital region. In 1624 the Anti-Manchu Division (Ch'ongyungch'ŏng) was charged with the defense of Kyŏnggi Province, and in 1626 the Defense Command (Suŏch'ŏng) was established to defend the Namhan mountain fort (Namhan sansŏng). KSDSJ 1:906, 788; KSDSJ 2:1546.

7. In 1393, King T'aejo established the Righteousness Flourishing Three Armies (Ŭihŭng samgunbu) in command of ten guard units of Righteousness Flourishing King's Personal Guard (Ŭihŭng ch'in'gunwi). This system was reorganized in 1457 under King Sejo into three armies and Five Guards (Samgun owi). From the beginning of the dynasty in 1392 there was a single command agency, but the title was changed a number of times until the adoption of the Five Guards Directorate (Owi toch'ongbu) in 1466. This agency was kept separate from the Ministry of War. but its top two officials were concurrent appointments. Its responsibilities were taken over by the Border Defense Command (Pibyŏnsa) after 1545, even though the agency itself was not abolished until the military reforms of 1882. See the articles on the Owi and Owi toch'ongbu in KSDSJ 1:952–53.

8. PGSR 21:2a, see also 21:1a–2a, 4b.

9. Ibid. 21:2b.

10. Ibid. 21:3b.

11. Ibid. 21:2b, 13a.

12. Ibid. 21:9a. At the beginning of the dynasty the Forbidden Soldiers (i.e., Soldiers of the Forbidden Quarters) consisted of three units attached to the Dragon Tiger Regiment (Yonghoyŏng): the Naegŭmwi, Kyŏmsabok, and Urimwi. According to one

source, when a Forbidden Soldier Agency (Kŭmgunch'ŏng), or Agency of the Three Forbidden Soldier Guards (Kŭmgun samch'ŏng) was created in 1666, there were 200 men each in the Kyŏmsabok and Urimwi, and 300 in the Naegŭmwi, somewhat less than Yu's estimate. KSDSJ 1:226. See also Yi Kŭng'ik, *Yŏllyŏsil kisul*, pyŏlchip, Yonghoyŏng (article on the Dragon Tiger Regiment), cited in Ch'a Munsŏp, "Sŏnch'o ŭi Naegŭmwi" [The Inner Forbidden Guards of early Chosŏn], in idem, *Chosŏn sidae kunje yŏn'gu* (1973), p. 54.

13. The salary would be 15 *mal* of rice, 6 *mal* of millet, and 9 *mal* of yellow beans per month, rather generous by comparison with his ration schedule for other soldiers. PGSR 21:9a, line 10.

The quota had risen to 180 in 1440, when Sejong decided to reduce to it 60 to maintain the high quality of its troops. He raised it to 100 in 1445. King Sejo later put 100 men on reserve and created 200 new duty troops, thus tripling the number to 300. He also divided the men into three shifts and required that one-third or 68 men serve on duty at any one time. The conservative King Yejong (r. 1468–69) reduced the quotas of all special guard units by 13,040, from 35,240 men to 22,200. The Naegŭmwi quota was cut from 200 to 100. The quota of 200 in the *Kyŏngguk taejŏn* (1469–74) probably represented an increase resulting from recruitment through skill examinations. The breakdown for all royal guards was as follows:

REDUCTION IN ROYAL GUARD QUOTAS, 1468–69

Name	Old quota	New quota	Reduction
Pyŏlsiwi	2,400 [3,400?]	2,500	900
Kapsa	20,000	10,000	10,000
P'ajŏgwi	3,000	2,500	500
Taejol	3,400 [3,440?]	3,000	440
Naegŭmwi	200	100	100
Ŭngyangwi	200	100	100
TOTAL	35,240 [30,240?]	22,200 [18,200?]	13,040 [12,040?]

SOURCE: Ch'a Munsŏp, "Sŏnch'o ŭi Naegŭmwi," p. 86.

14. PGSR 21:7b–8a. The regulations for the examinations are in ibid. 21:5b–7b.

15. As opposed to ordinary infantry, who were divided into eight shifts and served for two months at a time, these night patrol soldiers would be divided into ten shifts of a month's duty. They would be provided with a monthly ration of 9 *mal* of rice. Ibid. 21:2a-b, 4a–5b.

16. Yu mentioned that these police boxes were currently called Kyŏngsuso.

17. Ibid. 21:5a-b.

18. Ibid. 21:2b.

19. Ibid. 21:2b–3b.

20. Ibid. 23:32b–34b.

21. Ibid. 21:15b–17a. Chŏn Noksaeng was born in 1318 and died while on the way to exile in 1375, KSDSJ 2:1323.

22. PGSR 23:34b–35a.

23. Ibid. 23:35a-b.

24. The version of Yu Sŏngnyŏng's proposal quoted in ibid. 21:71a is not dated but

described as having been made after the Imjin invasions (1592). It appears to be an extended version of a proposal Yu first made in 1591, just prior to the invasion. The proposal was not adopted at the time. This second version was made in 1594 when Yu was chief state councilor, *Sŏnjo sillok*, 49:24a-b (1594), cited in Yukkun sagwan hakkyo, Han'guk kunsa yŏn'gusil [R.O.K. Army Military Academy, Research Hall for Korean Military History], *Han'guk kunjesa: Kŭnse Chosŏn chŏn'gip'yŏn* [The military history of Korea: Recent times, the early Chosŏn period] (Seoul: Yukkun ponbu, 1968), p. 298 n.194, for an abbreviated version. This source is hereafter referred to as *Han'guk kunjesa* (1968). For the original proposal, see *Sŏnjo sujŏng sillok* 25:19a-b (1591), cited in *Han'guk kunjesa* (1968), p. 297 n.193.

25. PGSR 21:20b.

26. *Han'guk kunjesa* (1968), pp. 380–81. Hideyoshi issued orders dividing up his invasion units on 3.18 (May 29, 1592). Corps 1–9 had 158,700 men (avg. of 17,633 per corps), with 118,300 men in camp in Japan. The Eighth Corps of 10,000 men was stationed in Tsushima, the Ninth Corps of 11,500 in Ikki Island, so that the actual number of troops embarking on the invasion was 137,200 men. The front line was to consist of the First Corps of 18,700 men and the Second Corps of 22,800 men and the Third Corps of 11,000 men, a total of 52,500 men. By the end of the year, the Japanese had 18,000 men in P'yŏng'an, 22,000 in Hamgyŏng, 11,000 in Hwanghae, 25,000 in Kaesŏng, 20,000 in Hansŏng, 13,000 in Kangwŏn, 15,000 in Ch'ungch'ŏng, and 40,000 in Kyŏngsang, a total of 166,000 men. Yi Hyŏngsŏk, *Imjin chŏllansa* [History of the Imjin War] 1 (Seoul: Sinhyŏnsilsa, 1974), pp. 135, 151.

27. *Han'guk kunjesa* (1968), p. 291.

28. The history and causes of the breakdown of the *chin'gwan* system are discussed in detail in ibid., pp. 275–91.

29. PGSR 21:20b, 60a.

30. Ibid. 21:21b–22a; see ibid. 21:20b ff. for above material.

31. Ibid. 21:22b.

32. Ibid. 21:23b–25b.

33. Ibid. 21:26a-b. These liaison officials were not part of the original *sog'o* system in the 1590s.

34. Ibid. 21:26b–27a.

35. Ibid. 21:57b.

36. Ibid. 21:58a.

37. Ibid. 21:17a.

38. Ibid. 21:71b–72a. For the text of Yu Sŏngnyŏng's discussion of the principle of subdivision that was the essence of *sog'o*, see *Sŏae munjip*, 14:5b–6b, Taedong munhwa yŏn'guwŏn, ed. (1959), p. 240.

39. PGSR 21:69b.

40. Ibid. 21:71a.

41. Ibid. 21:40a-b on testing, ibid. 44b et passim on training, ibid. 21:6a ff. on failure to select officers on the basis of skill or training.

42. Ibid. 21:70b.

43. Ibid. 21:45a-b.

44. Ibid. 21:52b–53b, 56a, 61b.

45. Ibid. 21:52b–53a.

46. Ibid. 21:49a–50a, 51b–52a.

47. Ibid. 21:52b.

48. Ibid. 21:47b–49a, 50a.

49. Yu discussed the poor quality of conventional weapons and armor, ibid. 21:28b; cited Yulgok's famous proposals to reform the system for raising battle horses, ibid. 21:70b–71a; discussed the history of horse-raising in China, ibid. 24:17a–21b, 34a; suggested regulations for wall construction, ibid. 21:61a; discussed the history of wall construction, ibid. 24:1a–5b; carts and war chariots, ibid. 24:6a–16b; the need for shipbuilding and repair, ibid. 21:51a; post-stations, ibid. 24:21b–23a; beacons, ibid. 21:55b–56a.

50. Ibid. 21:42a-b.

51. Ibid. 21:42b–43a.

52. Ibid.

53. Ch'a Munsŏp, "Chosŏnjo Hyojong ŭi kunbi kwangch'ung" [Expansion of military defenses under King Hyojong of the Chosŏn dynasty], pt. 2, *Nonmunjip* (Tan'guk taehakkyo) 2 (1968):17–20.

54. Ibid., pp. 20–21. Ch'a points out that he cannot be certain that this action in 1654 was limited to Ch'ungch'ŏng Province or included the whole country but he thinks the former is likely.

55. Yi T'aejin, *Chosŏn hugi*, p. 162.

56. Ch'a Munsŏp, "Hyojong ŭi kunbi kwangch'ung," pt. 2, p. 2.

57. PGSR 21:42a–44b, 14a-b.

58. Ibid. 21:28a-b.

59. Ch'a, "Hyojong ŭi kunbi kwangch'ung," pt. 2, p. 25, and *Hyojong sillok* 10:21a-b (1653).

60. Yi T'aejin, *Chosŏn hugi*, p. 162.

61. Ch'a Munsŏp, "Hyojong ŭi kunbi kwangch'ung," pt. 2, pp. 25–26.

62. Ibid., p. 26.

63. The above material on weapons and gunpowder is based on ibid., pp. 26–29.

64. Ibid., pp. 34–38.

65. PGSR 24:5b. For the whole discussion of walls and moats in classical antiquity, see ibid. 24:1a–6a.

66. Ibid. 24:5b–6a.

67. Ibid. 22:1b–2a.

68. Ibid. 22:2a, 5a.

69. Ibid. 22:3a-b.

70. Ibid. 22:4b.

71. For discussion of the details of Yu's and other writers' plans, see Yi Hyŏngsŏk, *Imjin chŏllansa* 3:1323–25.

72. PGSR 22:8b for the quote, 5a–10b for the discussion of wall construction.

73. Ibid. 22:8b.

74. Yi Hyŏngsŏk, *Imjin chŏllansa* 3:1412.

75. PGSR 23:17b.
76. Ibid. 21:49a–52b.
77. Ibid. 21:23b.
78. Ibid.
79. Ibid. 21:60b–61a.
80. Ibid. 21:61a-b.
81. For Yulgok's proposal, see *Han'guk kunjesa* (1968), pp. 368–69 and n.28, which quotes the text of Yulgok's Memorial on Contemporary Problems [*Chin sisa so*] in *kwŏn* 7 of the *Yulgok chŏnsŏ*. See PGSR *p'oyu* (supplement), *kunhyŏnje* (on the system of local administration).
82. PGSR 21:61b–62a.
83. Ibid. 21:62a.

CHAPTER 14. The Military Service System, 1682–1870

1. Yi T'aejin, "Chung'ang Ogunyŏngje ŭi sŏngnip kwajŏng" [The process of the establishment of the central five division system], *Han'guk kunjesa* 2 *Kŭnse Chosŏn hugip'yŏn* [The military history of Korea, vol. 2 Early modern period: Late Chosŏn dynasty] (Seoul: Yukkun ponbu, 1977), pp. 165–66; idem, *Chosŏn hugi ŭi chŏngch'i wa kunyŏngje pyŏnjŏn* [Politics and changes in the army division system in the late Chosŏn period] (Seoul: Han'guk yŏn'guwŏn, 1985), pp. 223–25; JaHyun Kim Haboush, "A Heritage of Kings: One Man's Monarchy in the Confucian World" (Ph.D. diss., Columbia University, 1978), pp. 62–71; Kang Chujin, *Yijo tangjaengsa yŏn'gu* [A study of the history of factionalism in the Yi dynasty] (Seoul: Seoul Taehakkyo ch'ulp'anbu, 1971), pp. 285–93.
2. *Sukchong sillok* 38 sang:2a–5a.
3. *Sukchong sillok* 38 sang.
4. For the text of the day's discussion, see *Sukchong sillok* 38 sang:8a–10a. The material is discussed at length in Ch'a Munsŏp, "Imnan ihu ŭi yangyŏk kwa kyunyŏkp'ŏp ŭi sŏngnip" [The yangyŏk system from the Imjin Wars and the establishment of the equal service system), pt. 2, *Sahak yŏn'gu* 11 (July 1961):125–26; idem, "Kŭmwiyŏng yŏn'gu" [A study of the royal guard regiment], in idem, *Chosŏn sidae kunje yŏn'gu* [Studies of the military system of the Chosŏn period] (Seoul: Tan'guk taehakkyo ch'ulp'anbu, 1973), p. 353; Yi T'aejin, *Chosŏn hugi* (1985), pp. 232–33 n.23.
5. See the tables in Ch'a Munsŏp, "Imnan ihu ŭi yangyŏk," pt. 2, p. 126, and Chŏng Yŏnsik, "Sipch'il-sippal segi yangyŏk kyunilhwa chŏngch'aek ŭi ch'uui" [The trend in policy toward uniform labor service tax on men of good status in the seventeenth and eighteenth centuries], *Han'guksaron* 13 (August 1985):155 n.130. These tables are based on the final regulations and figures incorporated in the *Kagyŏng ijŏngch'ŏng tŭngnok, Ogunmun kaegunje pyŏnt'ong chŏrmok*, which are somewhat different from the figures cited in the *Sillok*, cited below. Ch'a Munsŏp, "Kŭmwiyŏng ŭi yŏn'gu" [A study of the royal guard regiment], in idem, *Chosŏn sidae kunje yŏn'gu* (Seoul: Tan'guk taehakkyo ch'ulp'anbu, 1973), pp. 353–54; *Sukchong sillok* 40:54a–59b. According to the remarks of the *Sillok* historian, the reorganization of the Five Military Divisions of the capital region was largely the work of Min Chinhu; the reduction of the cloth tax rate on marines

was proposed by Kim Ku. Yu Chib'il was in charge of drawing up the Reform Regulations, and Yi Yu drafted the regulations for fining school dropouts on his own. *Sukchong sillok* 40:59b.

6. *Sukchong sillok* 40:59b; Ch'a Munsŏp, "Imnan ihu ŭi yangyŏk," pt. 2, p. 127; Chŏng Yŏnsik, "Yangyŏk kyunilhwa" (1985), pp. 155–63.

7. *Sukchong sillok* 40:58b–59b; Ch'a Munsŏp, "Imnan ihu ŭi yangyŏk," pt. 2, p. 127.

8. Cloth tax revenues would also be used to pay for all miscellaneous costs associated with ships including "land goods." *Sukchong sillok*, 40:56b–57b; Ch'a Munsŏp, "Imnan ihu ŭi yangyŏk," pt. 2, p. 127.

9. For details, see Yi T'aejin, *Han'guk kunjesa* (1977), pp. 169–71; idem, *Chosŏn hugi* (1985), pp. 225–28. For the original source for the reforms of 1704 in this and other notes to follow, see *Sukchong sillok* 40:54a–59b, Sukchong 30.12.kabo.

10. Yi T'aejin, *Han'guk kunjesa* (1977), pp. 173–75; idem, *Chosŏn hugi* (1985), pp. 230–32.

11. For Pak's later recommendations, see *Sukchong sillok* 50 ha:36b–37b; for Yi Imyŏng's, see n. 12, following.

12. Pak Kwŏn's version of a capitation tax is to be found in n.11. For the rest of the debate, see *Sukchong sillok* 50 sang:38b; for Yi Imyŏng's proposal, see ibid. 50, ha:3a–5b, although the introductory statement to his memorial indicates that Yi submitted it a few days before.

13. PBSDN 6:306–10, but the discussion appears to have been held earlier, on 10.23. The best source for the regulations is PBSDN 6:320–25. A comprehensive but slightly abridged version is in *Sukchong sillok* 50 ha:34b–36a. The main points are summarized in Ch'a Munsŏp, "Imnan ihu ŭi yangyŏk," pt. 2, pp. 129–30.

14. Chŏng Yŏnsik, "Yangyŏk kyunilhwa" (1985), pp. 129–30, 141, 154–63.

15. *Sukchong sillok* 55:31a–32b. See also Kim Chinbong, Ch'a Yonggŏl, and Yang Kisŏk, "Chosŏn sidae kunyŏk chawŏn ŭi pyŏndong e tae han yŏn'gu: Hosŏ chibang ŭi kyŏng'ŭrŭl chungsimŭro [A study of the changes in the sources of military service taxes in the Chosŏn period: The case of Ch'ungch'ŏng Province] *Hosŏ munhwa yŏn'gu,* no. 3 (1983), p. 75.

16. *Kyŏngjong sillok* 4:11a.

17. *Yŏngjo sillok* 27:25a.

18. Ibid. 28:29b–30a.

19. SJW 42:953, 956–58; *Yŏngjo sillok* 36:34b–37a; idem 37:11a-b.

20. Chŏng, "Yangyŏk ŭi kyunilhwa" (1985), pp. 139–41.

21. *Yŏngjo sillok* 58:10b; ibid. 67:44b; cited in Ch'a Munsŏp, "Imnan ihu ŭi yangyŏk," pt. 2, p. 131.

22. Ch'a, "Imnan ihu ŭi yangyŏk," pt. 2, pp. 131–33.

23. The following comments derive from *Yŏngjo sillok*, 71:18b–34b, and SJW 58:81–144. Because of the press of time, I have only covered the material from pp. 81–144, but intend a more thorough study in the future. The material through the end of the seventh lunar month in the latter source ends on p. 242.

24. See n. 26 below for references to the context of the debate.

25. I owe thanks to Jack Dull for pointing out an anachronism in this quotation. The

pa, or hegemon, was a phenomenon of the Chou period in the eighth century B.C., several centuries after the purported discussion between King Wen and his adviser, T'ai-kung. The citation may be accurate, but the text had to be written some time after the mid-Chou period. It is also his view that *sa* (*shih* in Chinese) ought to be translated as "petty official," an opinion supported by the *sa* being treated as lower in rank than the *taebu* (*ta-fu*) in the *Chou-li.*

26. SJW 58:141a–143a; *Yŏngjo sillok* 71:24b–25a, same date.

27. SJW 58:141a-b.

28. *Yŏngjo sillok* 71:22b–23b.

29. Ibid. 71:24a. For Cho Hyŏnmyŏng's statement in favor of a cloth tax on land (*kyŏlp'o*), see ibid. 71:18b–19a.

30. SJW 58:162–66; Haboush, "Heritage of Kings," p. 262.

31. SJW 58:171:c-d.

32. *Yŏngjo sillok* 71:29a–30b; SJW 58:169–75.

33. SJW 58:164b, 172a.

34. Ibid. 58:173:b–175a.

35. Ibid. 58:189–93; *Yŏngjo sillok* 71:32b–33a, same date.

36. *Yŏngjo sillok* 75:7b–9b; Ch'a Munsŏp , "Imnan ihu ŭi yangyŏk," pt. 2, pp. 136–37; Pak Kwangsŏng, "Kyunyŏkpŏp sihaeng ihu ŭi yangyŏg'e taehayŏ" [Commoner service after the adoption of the equal service system], *Sŏnggok nonch'ong* 3 (1972):135–36.

37. *Yŏngjo sillok* 72:23b–24a, 27a-b; Pak Kwangsŏng, "Kyunyŏkpŏp sihaeng ihu," pp. 136–37.

38. *Yŏngjo sillok* 71:9b–10b.

39. Ch'a Munsŏp estimated this income at 372,045 *yang* minus 80,416 left in the provinces, leaving a balance of 291,629 *yang* for the central government. "Imnan ihu ŭi yangyŏk," pt. 2, p. 140.

40. Pak, "Kyunyŏkpŏp sihaeng ihu," p. 146.

41. Chŏng Yagyŏng, *Mongmin simsŏ* [Essays from the heart on governing the people] 3:13a-b, in idem, *Chŏng Tasan Chŏnsŏ* [The complete works of Chŏng Tasan], *ha* (vol. 3) (Seoul: Munhŏn p'yŏnch'an wiwŏnhoe, 1961), p. 476.

42. For developments in the military service and tax system after the equal service reform of 1750, see Pak Kwangsŏng, "Kyunyŏkpŏp sihaeng ihu," pp. 161–84; Kim Yŏngsŏp, "Chosŏn hugi kyunyŏkche ijŏng ŭi ch'uri wa hop'obŏp [The reasoning behind reform of the military service system in the late Chosŏn period and the household cloth system] *Sŏnggok nonch'ong* 13 (1982):7–46; Kim Yŏngsŏp, "Chosŏn hugi kunyŏkche ŭi tongyo wa kunyŏkchŏn" [The shake-up of the equal service system of late Chosŏn and military-service land] *Tongbanghak chi* 32 (September 1982):97–147; James B. Palais, *Policy and Politics in Traditional Korea* (Cambridge: Harvard University Press, 1975), p. 107. This article deals in particular with the questions of quotas, *kyebang*, and collective payment by villages.

43. Palais, *Policy and Politics*, p. 107.

44. Tax-exempt yangban or the low-level elite comprised 38 percent of the households; 20 percent were slaves, and 17 percent were exempted for special reasons (Buddhist

monks, shamans, willow-basket weavers, single-woman households). See Kim Yŏngsŏp, "Chosŏn hugi kunyŏkche ijŏng ŭi ch'uri wa hop'obŏp."

PART IV. Conclusion

1. Kang Man'gil, "Kunyŏk kaehyŏngnon'ŭl t'onghaebon sirhak ŭi sŏnkyŏk [The nature of Practical Learning as seen through proposals for the reform of military service], *Tongbanghak chi* 22 (June 1979):153–69; Kim Yongsŏp, "Chosŏn hugi kunyŏkche ŭi tongyo wa kunyŏkchŏn" [The reasoning behind reform of the military service system in the late Chŏson period and the household cloth system] *Sŏnggok nonch'ong* 13 (1982): 100.

2. Yi asserted this opinion in his commentary on a story about Chien-tzu, the ruler of the state of Chao in the Warring States period of Chou China, who gave orders to cut household taxes in the territory of Chin-yang. Yi anachronistically interpreted this statement as if the Chao tax system were identical to the T'ang triple tax system of the ninth century A.D. by remarking that a wise ruler who sought to alleviate tax burdens on the people only had the option of reducing the household tax because the land tax was a fair and just tax that simply had to be collected, and personal service was a necessity because men were needed to fight in wartime. Yi Ik, *Sŏngho saesŏl yusŏn*, ed. An Chŏngbok (Seoul: Kyŏngmunsa, 1976, reprint of Keijō: Chōsen kosho kankōkai, 1915), *sang* (vol. 1), p. 351, cited in Han Woo-keun [Han Ugŭn], *Yijo hugi ŭi sahoe wa sasang* [Society and thought in the late Yi dynasty] (Seoul: Ŭryu munhwasa, 1961), p. 287. Yi Kawŏn, Kwŏn Odon, and Im Ch'angsun, eds., *Tong'a Hanhandaesajŏn* [The Great East Asia Sino-Korean Dictionary), (Seoul: Tong'a ch'ulp'ansa, 1982), p. 1199, gives the original source of the story as the the section on the hereditary house of Chao in the *Shih-chi*. I am indebted to my colleague, Jack Dull, a specialist in the Han dynasty, for pointing out to me that Yi Ik's commentary on the Chao tax system as if it were the same as the triple tax system of the T'ang era is a gross anachronism.

3. Yi Ik, *Sŏngho sŏnsaeng chŏnjip* 46:6b–7a (Seoul: Kyŏng'in munhasa, 1974), *ha* (vol. 2), pp. 206–7, cited in Han Woo-keun, *Yijo hugi ŭi sahoe wa sasang* [Society and thought in the late Yi dynasty] (Seoul: Urchi munhwasa, 1961), p. 288.

4. Yi Ik, *Sŏngho saesŏl* 1:356. These issues are discussed and summarized in Han Woo-keun, *Sŏngho Yi Ik yon'gu* [A study of Sŏngho Yi Ik] (Seoul: Sŏul taehakkyo ch'ulp'anbu, 1980), pp. 200–201.

5. Han Woo-keun, *Yijo hugi*, p. 292; original quoted from the *Kwagurok*, "Saengjae" [Production of wealth], section, not available to me. See also ibid., p. 291, and Yi Ik, *Sŏngho sŏnsaeng chŏnjip* [The complete works of master Sŏngho] (Seoul: Kyŏng'in munhwasa, 1974) 46:6a–7b; Han Woo-keun, *Sŏngho Yi Ik yŏn'gu*, pp. 202–4.

6. Yu Suwŏn, *Usŏ* (Seoul: Seoul Taehakkyo Kojŏn kanhaenghoe, 1971), pp. 109, 112–13, 117, 128.

7. An Chŏngbok, *Chaptong san'i* [Miscellaneous information] (Seoul: Han'gukhak munhŏn yŏn'guso, 1981) 2:118–20.

8. Yi Kyugyŏng, *Oju yŏnmun changjŏn san'go, ha* (vol. 2) (Seoul: 1959), pp. 307–8.

9. Chŏng Yagyong, *Mongmin simsŏ* [Essays from the heart on governing the people]

18:12a–14a, in *Chŏng Tasan chŏnsŏ* [The complete works of Chŏng Tasan] *ha* 3 (Seoul: Munhon p'yŏnch'an wiwŏnhoe, 1961): 475–76.

CHAPTER 15. The King and His Court

1. PGSR 25:12a.

2. Ibid. 15:26a–27a.

3. Ibid. 25:27a.

4. Ibid. 15:27b–28a. For that matter, noble ranks were also assigned to princes (Ŭibin) and husbands of princesses (Kongju, Ongju, Kunju, and Hyŏnju).

5. Ibid. 15:27a.

6. Ibid. 15:27b. Yu also traced the history of feudal titles and ranks from the Chou through the Sung, ibid. 18:14b–17a.

7. See Song June-ho [Song Chunho], "Chosŏn sidae ŭi kwagŏ wa yangban mit yang'in" [The civil service examinations of the Chŏson period and yangban and commoners], *Yŏksa hakpo* 69 (March 1976):101–35.

8. Edward Willett Wagner, *The Literati Purges: Political Conflict in Early Yi Korea* (Cambridge: East Asian Research Center and Harvard University Press, 1974), pp. 42–50, 70–73, 95–120.

9. PGSR 15:28a–29b.

10. Ibid. 25:20a–26b.

11. Ibid. 13a–15a.

12. Ibid. 16:14a–15b.

13. Ibid. 16:15b. Other superfluous units such as the Naejasi, Naesŏmsi, and Sadosi were to be abolished because their duties were also performed by the Royal Cuisine Office (Saongwŏn), Pongsangsi, and Yebinsi. Ibid. 16:16a.

14. Ibid. 16:16b–17a. For elimination of a number of other unimportant agencies, see 16:17a–18b. The abolition of guard commanders of the Kyŏmsabok and Ingnimwi was ordered because their units had been eliminated; the Wine Bureau (Saonsŏ) was to be eliminated because of duplication; and special warehouses for oil, honey, and other items, such as the Ŭiinggo and Changhŭnggo were to be abolished. Ibid. 16:20a-b.

15. Ibid. 7:13b–15b; 16a–18a; 26:15a-b.

16. Ibid. 7:18a; 26:15b–17a.

17. Ibid. 7:15b–16a; 26:13a–14a. For a description of the ceremony in Chou times, 16:14a–15a.

18. Ibid. 26:20b–25a.

19. Ibid. 26:17a–20b.

20. Ibid. 17:2b–3a. See 17:1a-b for description of these six officials, and the *Chou-kuan* section of the *Shang-shu*, Ikeda Sueri, ed., *Zenyaku kambun taikei* ed. 11 (Tokyo: Shūeisha, 1976):632–34.

21. Ch'en Pu-liang of the Sung made a similar comment about the possibility that the San-kung and Six Ministers could hold positions concurrently. He also remarked that the statement in the *Book of History* that the ancients did not bother with quotas

of officials, and were only interested in obtaining the right men meant that they would leave positions in the San-kung or San-ku vacant if there were no men of virtue available.

The commentary by Ts'ai Ch'en noted a discrepancy with the *Rites of Chou*, which described the Ssu-kung as the officer of winter (Tung-kuan) in charge of industry, and also the continuation of this tradition by scholars of the Han dynasty. PGSR 17:2a–3b; *Zenyaku* 11:634–5.

22. PGSR 18:21b–22b.

23. The Korean pronunciation of these officers is Ch'ŏn'gwan, Chigwan, Ch'un'gwan, Hagwan, Ch'ugwan, and Tonggwan. For Cheng Ssu-neng's remarks and the codes of law, see ibid. 17:4a; for the 60 subordinates, see 17:5a-b. For detailed description of the responsibilities of the six ministers as copied from the *Rites of Chou*, with commentaries, see ibid. 17:4a–16b. Yu also claimed that in the Chou dynasty there were presumably 3,190 of the king's court and metropolitan area, but he rejected the 2,643 listed in the *T'ung-tien* and the unsupported figure of 61,032 for the bureaucracy of the feudal lords. Ibid., 18:10b.

24. Ibid. 17:29b–32b; 18:13a–14a.

25. Ibid. 15:2b; 16:1b.

26. Ibid. 17:19b.

27. Ibid. 17:20a. Yu's main interest was economy of personnel in the top command structure, because he also pointed out that the total number of officials by the reign of Emperor Ai (6–1 B.C.) had reached 130,285. Elsewhere, when he listed only 7,567 officials in the Later Han, he must have been referring to regular officials alone. Ibid. 18:10b.

28. Li Lin-fu, a member of the imperial family, worked his way to the top of the T'ang administration by 736, purged his political enemies, and wielded dictatorial power until impeached by Yang Kuo-chung. Yang, a relative of the famous consort Yang-kuei-fei, succeeded to power after Li's death in 752. He fell out with his friend, An Lu-shan, one of the factors contributing to An's rebellion. Yüan Tsai became an important official and a favorite of Emperor Tai-tsung later in the eighth century, engaging in ostentatious self-indulgence and tyrannical personal behavior. *Ajia rekishi jiten* 9 (Tokyo: Heibonhsa, 1962):112, 318; 3:150; C. A. Peterson, "Court and Province in Mid- and Late T'ang," in Denis Twitchett and John K. Fairbank, eds., *The Cambridge History of China*, vol. 3, *Sui and T'ang China*, pt. 1 (Cambridge: Cambridge University Press, 1979), pp. 409–53; Edwin G. Pulleyblank, *The Background of the Rebellion of An Lu-shan* (London: Oxford University Press, 1955), pp. 82–104.

29. PGSR 17:28b.

30. Ibid. 16:1b, 5a. After the Border Defense Command was established in 1555, the State Council's authority was severely weakened during the rule of Kwanghaegun (r. 1608–23) and its functions taken over by the Border Defense Command. Yi Sugwang (d. 1629) advocated its abolition and a restoration of the State Council. MHBG 216:12b–14a, 22b–29a.

31. PGSR 17:39a–40a.

32. Yi Sangbaek, *Han'guksa, kŭnse chŏn'gip'yŏn* [The history of Korea: Early modern period] (Seoul: Ŭryu munhwasa, 1962), pp. 159–60.

33. PGSR 17:19b.

34. Ibid. 17:20a. Yu's main interest was economy of personnel in the top command structure, because he also pointed out that the total number of officials by the reign of Emperor Ai (6–1 B.C.) had reached 130,285. Elsewhere, when he listed only 7,567 officials in the Later Han, he must have been referring to regular officials alone. Ibid. 18:10b.

35. Ibid. 17:28b–29b.

36. Ibid. 17:29b–32b; 18:13a–14a. Yu agreed that there were a large number of officials in Sung times but made no attempt to assess the accurate number because of overlapping responsibility, vacant offices, extra or irregular officials, and general irregularity. Ibid. 18:11a.

37. Ibid.

38. Ibid. 18:22b–23b.

39. Ibid. 17:33a, 35b; 18:14b. Yu estimated the total number of officials in the Sung dynasty at 20,400. Ibid. 18:11a.

40. Ibid.

41. Ibid. 25:15b–18b.

42. Ibid. 25:5a–6b.

43. Ibid. 25:3a–5b.

44. Ibid. 25:6b–9b.

45. Ibid. 25:1a–3a.

46. Ibid. 25:12a; KSDSJ 2:1383.

47. PGSR 25:12a–13a.

48. Ibid. 13:4a-b.

49. MHBG 216:24b–25a. For other opinions, see ibid. 24b–27b.

50. MHBG 216:28a–29a.

CHAPTER 16. Reforming the Central Bureaucracy

1. PGSR 15:46b.

2. Yu took the time to draw up a list of total government offices for major dynasties from the 200 (or 120) officials of the Hsia, 200 (or 240) of the Yin (Shang). The number in parentheses was supplied by the Han commentator, Ch'eng Hsüan. Ibid. 18:10a.

3. Ibid. 17:2b–3a. See 17:1a-b for description of these six officials, and the *Chou-kuan* section of the *Shang-shu*, Ikeda Sueri, ed., *Zenyaku kambun taikei* ed. 11 (Tokyo: Shūeisha, 1976):632–34.

4. PGSR 17:19a.

5. For dates of publication, see *Ajia rekishi jiten* 6 (Tokyo: Heibonsha, 1962):384–85.

6. PGSR 17:20a–21a. The reduction of officials in the Later Chou reflects Yu's statistics in the post-Han period: 6,836 for the Chin, 6,172 for the Sung, 7,764 for the Later (Northern) Wei, and 2,989 for the Later (Northern) Chou, in ibid. 18:10b

7. Yu's figure for the Sui dynasty was 12,576 officials, of which 2,581 were capital officials and 9,995 provincial, ibid. 18:10b–11a, 13a.

8. Ibid. 17:21b–22a. My colleague, Jack Dull, has informed me that the Masters of Documents were Han imperial secretaries and that the Nine Courts were modeled after

the Nine Ministers (Chiu-ch'ing) of the Han dynasty, but in the Sui and T'ang they were virtually sinecures. Michael Loewe, "The Former Han Dynasty," in *Cambridge History of China* 1 (Cambridge: Cambridge University Press, 1986):181 et passim. Yu Hyŏngwŏn, in an addendum to this section, also described the six Shang-shu of the Han, PGSR 17:33a. For the T'ang Six Boards (Liu-pu) and their twenty-four bureaus (Ssu), see ibid. 17:34a–35a.

9. PGSR 17:22a–25b. Yu also listed the total number of T'ang officials at 18,805, of which 2,621 were capital officials (Nei-kuan) and 16,185 provincial officials in prefects and districts, ibid. 18:11a.

10. Ibid. 17:26a; see also citations from the *T'ung-tien* in ibid. 18:18b; Denis Twitchett and John K. Fairbank, eds., *The Cambridge History of China* 3 (Cambridge: Cambridge University Press, 1979):203.

11. The citation is to *Chu Hsi Yü-lu* [A record of the sayings of Chu Hsi]. PGSR 17:27a.

12. PGSR 18:17b–18b.

13. Ibid. 18:19a.

14. Ibid. 18:19a–21b.

15. Ibid. 18:21b.

16. Ibid. 17:29b–32b; 18:13a–14a. Yu agreed that there was a large number of officials in Sung times but made no attempt to assess the accurate number because of overlapping responsibility, vacant offices, extra or irregular officials, and general irregularity, ibid. 18:11a.

17. Ibid. 17:3b.

18. Ibid. 17:17b.

19. Ibid. 15:1a-b.

20. Ibid. 16:10b–11b; *Kuksadaesajŏn* [Great dictionary of national history] (hereafter, KSDSJ) 1:941; Ch'ŏn Kwan'u, "Pan'gye Yu Hyŏngwŏn yŏn'gu" [A study of Yu Hyŏngwŏn], in idem, *Kŭnse Chosŏnsa yŏn'gu* (Seoul: Ilchogak, 1979), pp. 308–9.

21. PGSR 16:12a–13a; KSDSJ 1:426.

22. PGSR 15:19a–10a.

23. Ibid. 16:13a–14a, 20b–22a.

24. Ibid. 16:2a–2b.

25. Ibid. 16:3b–4b.

26. Ibid. 16:4a.

27. Ibid. 16:18b–19b; KSDSJ 1:233; 2:1330.

28. PGSR 16:13a–14a.

29. The highest officials were the Taejehak, Chehak, and Pujehak. Ibid. 15:6b.

30. Ibid. 15:6b; 16:9b–10a.

31. Ibid. 15:6b–8b.

32. Ibid. 15:2b–4b.

33. Ibid. 17:35a.

34. Ibid. 16:8a–9a; 15:4a–5a.

35. There was a Slave Bureau (Changyesa) in the *Kyŏngguk taejŏn*, the law code first promulgated in 1469, that was responsible only for maintaining the slave registers, not the adjudication of lawsuits over ownership and status. Han Woo-keun [Han Ugŭn] et

al., eds., *Yŏkchu Kyŏngguk taejŏn* [Translated and annotated Great Code for managing the state] (Sŏngnam, Kyŏnggi Province: Han'guk chŏngsin munhwa yŏn'guwŏn, 1985), p. 20, referred to hereafter as Han Woo-keun, KGTJ. The same description is contained in the 1865 revised code, the *Taejŏn hoet'ong*, *Kyōshu Taiden kaiden* [The emended and annotated edition of the *Taejŏn hoet'ong*] (Keijō: Chōsen sōtokufu Chūsŭin, 1939), p. 78. This text is referred to hereafter as TJHT.

36. PGSR 15:2a, 2b, 4a, 11a; 16:9a–b.

37. Ibid. 17:2a.

38. Ibid. 17:2a, 12b.

39. Ibid. 15:5b.

40. Ibid. 15:12a–13a.

41. Ibid. 15:13a–16a.

42. Ibid. 15:16b–18b.

43. Ibid. 15:19a–20a.

44. Ibid. 16:18b; 15:20b–21a; KSDSJ 2:1620, article on Pyŏngsisŏ. This office was not abolished until the Kabo reform of 1894, a sign of the influence of tradition over Korean life.

45. PGSR 15:16b.

46. Ibid. 15:18b–19a.

47. Ibid. 15:22b, 23b.

48. Ibid. 15:22b–23b.

49. Ibid. 15:24a. The whole central government reorganized by Yu's plan would work out as follows, with separate agencies organized under the control of one of the six ministries. See appendix to chap. 16.

50. Ibid. 25:3a–5b.

51. Ibid. 15:30a. See the description of these clerks in Chou times in ibid. 18:23b–26a.

52. Ibid. 18:24b–25a.

53. Ibid. 15:30a.

54. Ibid. 15:29b–31a; Han Yŏng'u, "Chosŏn ch'ogi ŭi sanggŭp sŏri 'Sŏngjunggwan,'" [On the collective posts of high-level clerks in the early Chosŏn period] *Tong'a munhwa* 10 (September 1971):19.

55. *Songjo sillok* 33, Sŏngjong 4.8.kyehaek, cited in Yi Sŏngmu, *Chosŏn ch'ogi yangban yŏn'gu* [A study of the yangban in the early Chosŏn period] (Seoul: Ilchogak, 1980), pp. 105–7, esp. p. 106 n.278. Han Yŏng'u pointed out that of an estimated 400 to 500 high level clerks in the capital, about twenty a year were promoted to rank six regular positions, "Chosŏn ch'ogi ŭi sanggŭp sŏri 'Sŏngjungwan,'" [On the collective posts of high level clerks in the early Chosŏn period], *Tong'a munhwa* (September 1971), pp. 4–5, 18, 20–41. Han Yong'u's general position on the early Chosŏn period was that the rational, bureaucratic stress on examination replaced the aristocratic, status proclivities of the late Koryŏ dynasty, but that this general spirit was lost by the fifteenth and sixteenth centuries. There are many others, however, who would dispute the sharpness of Han's portrayal of the radical transformation of early Chosŏn society. Ibid., p. 45.

56. A schedule of *nokkwan* posts for 24 of the 128 chief clerks, or 19 percent, was established in 1414. Eight of 18 chief clerks of the Six Ministries received salaries, or

about 44 percent, the highest percentage of all. Later in 1460, only about 10 percent or 46 of the then 430 chief clerk positions were *ch'ea* or salaried posts, mainly because of fiscal shortages. Rotation of shifts occurred more frequently so that chief clerks got only half of their previous income. Han Yong'u, "Chosŏn ch'ogi sanggup sŏri 'Sŏngjunggwan,'" pp. 70–78.

57. Yu appeared to have been following the view of Ch'iu Chün that although criminals were reputedly enslaved and used for penal labor as runners (Tsui-li), it would not have been appropriate for the classical age. PGSR 18:26a.

58. Ibid. 15:31b–33a.

59. Ibid. 15:33a–34a.

60. Yu briefly traced the history of official rank in China in ibid. 18:11a–12b.

61. Ibid. 18:22b–23b.

62. Ibid. 15:25b.

63. Ibid. 15:25a-b.

64. Ibid. 25:3a–5b.

65. Ibid. 25:27b–28b.

66. Ibid. 25:26b–28b.

67. Ibid. 25:31b–33b.

68. Ibid. 25:34a–36a.

69. Ibid. 25:36b.

70. Ibid. 25:36b–37b.

71. Ibid. 25:37b–38a; Han Paekkyŏm, *Kuam yugo* [The leftover writings of Han Paekkyŏm] (Seoul: Yŏrhwadang, 1972), pp. 26–38.

72. PGSR 25:44a–45b.

73. Ibid. 25:45a. The North Korean translation of this section toned down the remark about converting barbarians to Chinese culture to "convert those of backward culture." *Pan'gye surok* 4 (Pyongyang: Kwahagwŏn ch'ulp'ansa, 1963):332.

74. PGSR 25:44a, 45a-b.

75. Han Yong'u also cited Sŏ Kŏjŏng's remark in 1473 that the clerks and runners (i.e., the Fu, Shih, Hsü, and Tu of Chou times) were members of the scholarly stream (*saryu*). Han Yong'u, "Chosŏn ch'ogi sanggup sŏri 'Sŏngjunggwan,'" pp. 78–82.

76. PGSR 15:31b; Han Yong'u dated the beginning of prejudice against technical officials and specialists to 1477, even though Kim Chongjik, the intellectual father of the later opponents of merit subjects and King Yŏnsan'gun, made similar remarks in 1464. "Chosŏn ch'ogi sanggup sŏri 'Sŏngjunggwan,'" pp. 65–67.

CHAPTER 17. Personnel Policy

1. PGSR 25:3a–5b.

2. Ibid. 14:1b–2b, 41a-b. For recommendation in the Chou dynasty, see E. A. Kracke, Jr., *Civil Service in Early Sung China, 960–1067* (Cambridge: Harvard University Press, 1953), pp. 6–7.

3. PGSR 14:3b–4a; 41b–42b.

4. Ibid. 14:9b–10b.

5. Ibid. 14:14a-b. See corroborating remarks in 14:31a–32b. For the T'ang assessment of review system, see Ch'ing-lien Huang, "The Recruitment and Assessment of Civil Officials under the T'ang Dynasty" (Ph.D. diss. Princeton University, 1986), pp. 100–188. For the origins of the annual and triennial assessments of officials, see pp. 103ff.

6. PGSR 14:16b–17a; Tsukiyama Jisaburo, *Tōdai seiji seido no kenkyū* [A study of the T'ang system of government] (Ōsaka: Sōgenshi, 1967), p. 200.

7. PGSR 14:29a–30a; *T'ung-tien* (T'ai-pei: Hsin-hsing shu-chü, 1966), ch. 18, pp. 103–4.

8. In 178 B.C., Emperor Wen of the Han dynasty ordered the recommendation of scholars for positions, and in 165 B.C. he also ordered feudal lords, princes, and high officials to recommend worthy and good men. PGSR 14:2b. Another case of recommendation was mentioned for high officials in the reigns of Emperors Wen (r. 180–157), Ching (156–140), and Yüan (r. 48–32). Ibid. 14:2b–3b, 5a–8b.

9. Ibid. 14:8b–9b.

10. Ibid. 14:11a-b.

11. Ibid. 14:30a-b, *T'ung-tien* ch. 18, 1: 103. See Huang, "Recruitment and Assessment of Civil Officials under the T'ang," p. 106.

12. PGSR 14:15b–16a; Huang, "Recruitment and Assessment of Civil Officials," p. 283, n.605, item 2.

13. PGSR 14:21a–22a.

14. Ibid. 14:23b–24a; *T'ung-tien* ch. 18, 1:101–2; Huang, "Recruitment and Assessment of Civil Officials," p. 240.

15. PGSR 14:11b–12a.

16. Ibid. 14:44b.

17. Ibid. 14:13a-b; Huang, "The Recruitment and Assessment of Civil Officials," p. 107.

18. PGSR 14:14a-b. See corroborating remarks in 14:31a–32b. For the T'ang assessment of review system, see Huang, "Recruitment and Assessment of Civil Officials," pp. 100–188. For the origins of the annual and triennial assessments of officials, see pp. 103ff.

19. PGSR 14:14a-b; Huang describes this process in more detail, "Recruitment and Assessment of Civil Officials," pp. 62–63.

20. PGSR 14:14b. Huang cited Ma Chou's views in "Recruitment and Assessment of Civil Officials," pp. 73–74, and summarized briefly with extensive material in footnotes all criticism of recruitment and assessment in the T'ang, pp. 281–91.

21. PGSR 14:17b–19a. For other references to Chang Chiu-ling's advocacy that candidates for magistrates be reviewed thoroughly for their talent and investigated by the censorate (Yü-shih-tai), see Tsukiyama Jisaburo, *Tōdai seiji seido no kenkyū*, pp. 198, 201; Denis Twitchett, "Hsüan-tsung," *The Cambridge History of China* 3 (Cambridge: Cambridge University Press, 1979):352–53. For an account of the increase in volume of officials appointed and corruption in the sale of offices after Empress Wu's reign in 697 to Emperor Jui-tsung's reforms in 710, see Huang, "Recruitment and Assessment of Civil Officials," pp. 206–11.

22. PGSR 14:20a; Huang, "Recruitment and Assessment of Civil Officials," pp. 216–19; Twitchett, "Hsüan-tsung," p. 389.

23. PGSR 14:43a–44a.

24. Ibid. 14:20a-b. Ch'ing-lien Huang described a 30 percent increase over the number of ranking officials in 657 to 17,686 ranking officials in 733 to 18,085 in 737. The number of lesser central and local government officials also rose from 183,361 in 589–600 to 349,863 in 737. Still the increase in offices was not sufficient to meet the growth of candidates seeking posts, for in 737 there were 160,000 eligible candidates for the ranking posts, nine times more than the 17–18,000 posts. "Recruitment and Assessment of Civil Officials," pp. 95–98, 211–14. For further discussion of P'ei Kuang-ting's reform, see ibid., pp. 219–20. Twitchett noted that the reforms also allowed more opportunity for clerks to be promoted to regular positions, threatening the advantages that examination passers had gained under Empress Wu's regime, and that the seniority system was relaxed in 733. "Hsüan-tsung," pp. 393, 396–97. Huang also mentioned the shift of responsibility for conducting the literary and civil-service examinations from the Ministry of Personnel to the Ministry of Rites in 736, in "Recruitment and Assessment of Civil Officials," pp. 221–22.

25. PGSR 14:20b–21a. For Hu Ch'ih-t'ang's criticism of Ts'ai Liang and P'ei Kuang-ting, see 14:32b–33b. According to Ch'ing-lien Huang, the establishment of a list of officials by rank was established by P'ei Kuang-ting's father, P'ei Hsing-chien in 669. P'ei Kuang-ting reintroduced the same measure and based promotion on seniority in 730. Huang also traced the origin of appointment by seniority to Fu Ch'ang (d. 330) of the Chin dynasty; "Recruitment and Assessment of Civil Officials," pp. 155–58, 220 n.248.

26. PGSR 14:22a–23b; Tsukiyama Saburō, *Tōdai seiji seido no kenkyū*, pp. 201–202. See ibid., p. 222 for the date of Shen's memorial in the *Tzu-chih t'ung-chien* 226, the 14th year of Tai-li in Tai-tsung's reign. For background of the late eighth century, see Ch'ing-lien Huang, "Recruitment and Assessment of Civil Officials," pp. 228–43.

27. PGSR 14:29a–30a; *T'ung-tien* ch. 18, 1:103–04.

28. PGSR 14:24b–25a.

29. Ibid. 14:5a–8b.

30. Ibid. 14:15b–16a; Huang, "Recruitment and Assessment of Civil Officials," p. 283 n.605, item 2.

31. PGSR 14:16a-b.

32. Ibid. 14:33b–35b. Huang discussed two of Lu Chih's memorials between 792 and 794. He also criticized short terms of office and frequent transfer of officials. Emperor Te-tsung, however, did not adopt his ideas. "Recruitment and Assessment of Civil Officials," pp. 183–87; Denis Twitchett, "Lu Chih (754–805): Imperial Adviser and Court Official," in Arthur F. Wright and Denis Twitchett, eds., *Confucian Personalities* (Stanford, Calif.: Stanford University Press, 1962), p. 105.

33. PGSR 14:12b–13a. For Tu Yu's commitment to classical models, see E. G. Pulleyblank, "Neo-Confucianism and Neo-Legalism in T'ang Intellectual Life, 755–805," in Arthur F. Wright, ed., *The Confucian Persuasion* (Stanford, Calif.: Stanford University Press, 1960), p. 100.

34. PGSR 14:13a-b. Similar remarks about the Wei and Chin dynasties and the lat-

ter's takeover by the central government of the appointment of officials and their clerks as well is discussed in a memorial by Wei Hsüan-t'ung of Emperor Kao-tsung's reign (r. 650–684) in the T'ang. Ibid. 14:14b–15a, 30a.

35. Ibid. 14:44a. For Emperor Hsiao-wen's attempt at reform see Huang, "Recruitment and Assessment of Civil Officials," p. 106.

36. PGSR 14:27a–30a; *T'ung-tien* ch. 18, 1:103–4.

37. PGSR 14:24b–26b; *T'ung-tien* ch. 18, 1:103.

38. PGSR 14:23b–24a; Huang, "Recruitment and Assessment of Civil Officials," pp. 237–41.

39. PGSR 14:24b–26b, *T'ung-tien* ch. 18, 1:103.

40. In 744, Li scandalized the court by an act of nepotism in the selection examinations that was later discovered by Emperor Hsüan-tsung, and he waged bloody factional war against his rivals in 746. Others have attributed equal blame for violating standard procedures for examinations and appointments to Yang Kuo-chung, the archenemy of An Lu-shan. Yang was a distant relative of Yang-kuei-fei, the emperor's paramour. Huang, "Recruitment and Assessment of Civil Officials" pp. 224–28; Twitchett, "Hsüan-tsung," pp. 398, 409–47 for Li Lin-fu's regime, and pp. 428–30, 447–53 for Yang Kuo-chung.

41. Huang, "Recruitment and Assessment of Civil Officials," pp. 256–72.

42. For review of the Sung recruitment, promotion, and recommendation or sponsorship systems see Kracke, *Civil Service in Early Sung China*.

43. See also ibid., p. 85, which stresses Wang's preference for selection of men of character rather than adherence to legal regulations.

44. PGSR 14:35b–39a.

45. Ibid. 14:35b–39a. Yu also admired Ssu-ma Kuang's disapproval of jealousy among officials, the cultivation of associates among colleagues and others to obtain promotion, and the use of literary and writing skills rather than administrative competence. He cited Ch'iu Chün of Ming times, who reiterated in succinct form a version of the points raised by Wang and Ssu-ma, admired long-term employment of officials, and criticized the T'ang practice of time-in-grade as the basis for promotion rather than a thorough investigation of performance. Ch'iu deplored the disappearance of thorough review of performance because the number of officials had become too large, and he endorsed Tung Chung-shu's preference for emphasizing merit and ability over time-in-grade. See his comments in Yu's discussion of personnel review procedures, in ibid. 14:39a-b, 42a-b.

46. Ibid. 14:40a–41b.

47. Kracke, *Civil Service in Early Sung China*, pp. 165–68; for general review of sponsorship, pp. 103–85.

48. PGSR 13:8a–9a.

49. Ibid. 13:22b–23a. This problem has been discussed in detail by Ch'oe Idon, "Simnyuk segi Nanggwankwŏn ŭi hyŏngsŏn kwajŏng" [The process of the formation of the rights of nanggwan in the sixteenth century], *Hanguksaron* 14 (February 1986):3–50.

50. PGSR 13:4b–5a.

51. Ibid. 13:1b.

52. Ibid. 13:23a-b.

53. Edward Willett Wagner, *The Literati Purges: Political Conflict in Early Yi Korea* (Cambridge: East Asian Research Center and Harvard University Press, 1974).

54. PGSR 13:2b–3a; for the comments of Yulgok, see 5a-b.

55. Ibid. 13:3a-b.

56. Ibid. 13:3b–4b.

57. Ibid. 13:12a.

58. Ray Huang, *1587, A Year of No Significance: The Ming Dynasty in Decline* (New Haven, Conn: Yale University Press, 1981).

59. PGSR 13:13a.

60. Ibid. 13:12a–13b.

61. Ibid. 13:13b–14a.

62. Ibid. 13:18aff.

63. James B. Palais, *Politics and Policy in Traditional Korea* (Cambridge: Harvard University Press, 1975), p. 54.

64. PGSR 13:9b–10a.

65. Ibid. 13:10a-b. Yu supplied a sample form to be filled out by the recommender on 13:10b–11a.

66. Ibid. 13:11a–11b. The T'ang regulations were adopted in the reign of Emperor Tetsung (r. 780–805) and in Sung times by Emperor Chen-tsung (r. 997–1022).

CHAPTER 18. Provincial and Local Administration

1. PGSR 7:34b–35b, 50a-b.

2. PGSR 18:1a–3a; Michael Loewe, "The Structure and Practice of Government," in Denis Twitchett and Michael Loewe, eds., *Cambridge History of China* 1 (Cambridge: Cambridge University Press, 1986):463–90; Hans Bielenstein, "The Institutions of Later Han," in ibid. 1:472–73, 506–11.

3. PGSR 18:3a–6a.

4. Ibid. 18:7a-b.

5. Ibid. 15:39b–40a.

6. Ibid. 15:35a–36a. Provincial magistrates (T'ai-shou) in the Ch'in dynasty had assistants called Ch'eng, and the Han magistrates had assistants called Wei or Tu-wei, ibid. 18:3a.

7. Ibid. 18:15a; 15:39b–40a. For the local gentry associations (Hyangch'ŏng) or the list of its members (*hyang'an*), see Fujiya Kawashima, "The Local Gentry Association in Mid-Dynasty Korea: A Preliminary Study of the Ch'angnyŏng Hyangan, 1600–1839," *Journal of Korean Studies* 2 (1980):113–38; Kim Yongdŏk, *Hyang'an yŏn'gu* [A study of the local yangban associations] (Seoul: Han'guk yŏn'guwŏn, 1978).

8. Howard J. Wechsler, "The Founding of the T'ang Dynasty: Kao-tsu (Reign 618–26)," in Twitchett and Fairbank, eds. *The Cambridge History of China* 3:174–75.

9. C. A. Peterson, "Court and Province in Mid-and Late-T'ang," ibid. 3:466–68.

10. Ray Huang, *Taxation and Governmental Finance in Sixteenth-Century Ming China* (Cambridge: Cambridge University Press, 1974), pp. 27–29; Frederic Wakeman, Jr.,

The Great Enterprise (Berkeley and Los Angeles: University of California Press, 1985), pp. 37–38.

11. Derk Bodde, "The State and Empire of Ch'in," *Cambridge History of China* 1:54; Michael Lowe, "The Former Han Dynasty," ibid. 3:156–57; PGSR 18:17b–18a.

12. PGSR 18:8a–9a.

13. Ibid. 18:9a–10a.

14. KSDSJ 1:413; 2:1614; Chōsen Sōtokufu Chūsūin, ed., *Kyŏngguk taejŏn* (Keijo, Chōsen Sōtokufu Chūsūin, 1934), pp. 116–33.

15. The Korean terms for these officials are: instructors (Kyosu), adviser (Hundo), inspectors of medicine (Simyak), legal experts (Kŏmnyul), post-station clerk (Yŏksŭng), and ferry-station official (Tosŭng). In 1744 the inspector of medicine had been eliminated, and by 1788 the pharmacist was removed. The post-station clerks were promoted to Ch'albang, and ferry-station officials were replaced by special officers (Pyŏlchang) under the Ministry of War. Chōsen Sōtokufu Chūsūin, ed., *Soktaejŏn* (Keijō: Chōsen Sōtokufu Chūsūin, 1935), pp. 94–99; Chōsen Sōtokufu Chūsūin, ed., *Taejŏn hoet'ong* (Keijō: Chōsen Sōtokufu Chūsūin, 1939), p. 136.

16. PGSR 15:36a–37b. Kyŏnggi had no army commander, Chŏlla had a second navy commander (one for the Left and Right Provinces), Kyŏngsang had second army and navy commanders; P'yŏng'an had no navy commander and an extra army commander for the north and south subprovinces; Hamgyŏng had a second army commander; Kangwŏn and Hwanghae had neither army or navy commanders, until an army commander was established in Hwanghae during Hideyoshi's invasion. Furthermore, a navy commander was given the concurrent post of navy commander for the southern three provinces (T'ongjesa) retained since its creation during Hideyoshi's invasion. Thus, provinces that did not separate army or navy commanders were directed by the provincial governor. Yu had no objection to raise to varying the number of provincial military commanders according to the perceived need for defense.

17. Ibid. 15:36a–38a.

18. Ibid. 15:39b–40a.

19. Ibid. 13:5b–6b.

20. Ibid. 15:40a–41a; 13:14b–15a.

21. Ibid. 13:6b–7b.

22. Yu cited the remarks of Chang Chiu-ling in 714 to Emperor Hsüan-tsung that there were hardly any talented men in the posts of prefects or district magistrates because most of them had obtained office primarily because of their personal connections. Most officials regarded magistrate posts as tantamount to exile from the capital, and the soldiers and irregular officials who were appointed to them used their positions to accumulate time-in-grade. This system was totally contrary to the Chou practice of recruiting magistrates for central government office and sending the best officials in the capital to take over magistrates' positions. Ibid. 14:17b–19a.

23. Ibid. 13:15a–17a.

24. Ibid. 13:5b–6b.

25. Ibid. 15:42a–42b.

26. Ibid. 15:42a–44a.

27. Ibid. 15:44a–45b.

28. Kim P'iltong, "Chosŏn hugi chibang sŏri chiptan ŭi chojik kujo, sang" [The structure of organization of the group of local clerks in the late Chosŏn dynasty, Part 1] *Han'guk hakpo* 28 (Fall 1982):79–116; idem, "Chosŏn hugi chibang sŏri chiptan ŭi chojik kujo, ha" (Part 2) *Han'guk hakpo* 29 (Winter 1982):87–116.

29. PGSR 15:45b–46b.

30. Ibid. 15:41a.

31. The list of the twelve early Koryŏ river granaries is in ibid. 3:10a.

32. The list of his proposed granaries is in ibid. 3:9a-b.

33. Ibid. 3:8b–15b, 15:41b–42a.

34. Hsiao Kung-chuan claimed that Chu Hsi only charged 10 percent on loans, but Yu Hyŏngwŏn recorded Chu Hsi's village granary rate at 2 *tou/shih* or 20 percent. Hsiao Kung-chuan, *Imperial China: Rural Control in the Nineteenth Century* (Seattle: University of Washington Press, 1970), pp. 175–76, 55; PGSR 7:36a.

35. James B. Palais, *Politics and Policy in Traditional Korea* (Cambridge: Harvard University Press, 1975), pp. 132–37.

36. PGSR 7:31a–32a; *Ajia rekishi jiten*. 10 vols. (Tokyo: Heibonsha, 1962) 9:183.

37. PGSR 7:32a–32b.

38. Ibid. 7:33b.

39. Ibid. 7:34a-b.

40. Ibid. 7:34b–35b, 50a-b.

41. Ibid. 7:36b–37a. Yu also cited the remarks of Lü Tsu-ch'ien, Chu Hsi's close friend and associate, who agreed that advance preparations for storing surplus and Li K'uei's ever-normal granaries were the best and second-best systems. The third best method was simply to distribute whatever grain you had to the population and have them migrate to places where some reserves existed. The worst method was making gruel and distributing it to the people on a daily basis. Ibid. 7:37a.

42. Ibid. 7:37a–38b.

43. Ibid. 3:49b–50a.

44. Ibid. 3:53a-b.

45. Ibid. 3:53b–54a.

46. Ibid. 3:54a.

47. Ibid. 3:54a-b.

48. Ibid. 3:54a.

49. Yi I, *Yulgok chŏnsŏ* 16 (Seoul: Sŏnggyun'gwan taehakkyo, Taedong munhwa yŏn'guwŏn, 1958): 45a–46b; Tabana Tameo, *Chōsen kyōyaku kyōkashi no kenkyū* [A study of the history of the community compact and moral education in Korea) (Tokyo,1972), pp. 336–37.

50. PGSR 3:54a, 55b–56b.

51. Ibid. 3:56b–57a.

52. Ibid. 3:54a.

53. Ibid. 3:57b–58a.

54. Palais, *Politics and Policy in Traditional Korea*, pp. 147–57.

CHAPTER 19. The Community Compact System (*Hyangyak*)

1. PGSR 7:1b. The reference is to the "Ta Ssu-t'u" section of the *Chou-li*, and the numbers of households come from Cheng Hsüan's commentary.

2. Ibid. 8:1a; *Ajia rekishi jiten* (Tokyo: Heibonsha, 1962) 2:305–6.

3. PGSR 7:2b–3a; Wada Sei, *Chūgoku chihō jiji hattatsushi* [History of the development of local self-government in China] (Tokyo: Kyūko shoin, 1975), pp. 6–8.

4. PGSR 7:3a-b.

5. Ibid. 7:3b–4b.

6. The issues involved in the Sung *pao-chia* system are too complex to investigate here, but it is likely that Yu refrained from praising any policy supported by Wang unless he was overwhelmed by its obvious utility. See Higashi Ichio, *Ŏ Anseki simpō no kenkyū* [A study of the new laws of Wang An-shih] (Tokyo: Kazama shobo, 1970), pp. 742–811.

7. Yu's version of the text was probably based on Chu Hsi's collected works (*Chu wen-kung wen-chi*), the most reliable text, but with some erroneous emendations included in the *Hsing-li ta-ch'üan*. See "Chu-tzu tseng-sun Lü-shih hsiang-yüeh," PGSR 11:3b–41a; "Chu-tzu Chang-chou pang-yü," ibid. 11:28a–31b; Tabana Tameo, *Chōsen kyōyaku kyōkashi no kenkyū* [A study of the history of the community compact as moral education in Chosŏn] (Tokyo: Chōhōsha, 1972), pp. 1–13; Kung-chuan Hsiao, *Rural China: Imperial Control in the Nineteenth Century* (Seattle: University of Washington Press, 1960; paperback ed., 1967), pp. 201–2.

8. Tagawa Kōzō, "Richō no kyōkyu ni tsuite" [Local regulations in the Yi dynasty], part 1, *Chōsen gakuhō* 76 (July 1975):35–72; part 2, ibid. 78 (January 1976):45–88; part 3, ibid. (October 1976):179–210.

9. Yi T'aejin, "Sarimp'a ŭi Yuhyangso pongnip undong" [The movement by the sarim group to restore the Yuhyangso], in *Han'guk sahoesa yŏn'gu: nong'ŏp kisul paltal kwa sahoe pyŏndong* [Studies in the social history of Korea: The development of agricultural technology and social change] (Seoul: Chisik san'ŏpsa, 1986), pp. 125–30. Published originally in *Han'guk munhwa* 4 (December 1983):1–38. Tagawa, "Richō no kyōkyu," pt. 1, p. 40. Kim Yongdŏk, *Hyangch'ŏng yŏn'gu* [Studies of the local self-government office] (Seoul: Han'guk yŏn'guwŏn, 1978), pp. 16–21.

Yi T'aejin has accepted Yi Kŭkpae's account and rejected the statement made by the royal secretary, Sŏng Chun, in 1482 that Sejo abolished the Yuhyangso at the time of Yi Siae's rebellion in the northeast because he had been told that men of official rank (*p'umgwan*) in the local Yuhyangso had joined in the rebellion. King Sŏngjong expressed doubt about this reason and asked his officials to check the record the *Sejojo ilgi* [Diary of Sejo's reign], a text no longer extant, and then he dropped consideration about restoring the Yuhyangso. Yi could not find any notice in 1467 about any abolition of the Yuhyangso in that year, but given Sŏng Chun's attempts as governor of Hamgil Province after that time to use his authority as a high official to win over as many local gentry as he could, he might have been trying to prevent the resurgence of the gentry by the restoration of the Yuhyangso to preserve his own political control of the Hamgil literati. Yi T'aejin, "Sarimp'a ŭi Yuhyangso," pp. 157, 181–82.

10. Yi T'aejin, "Sarimp'a ŭi Yuhyangso," pp. 136–49. Kim Ch'ŏm, for example, con-

vinced King Chŏngjo in 1400 to adopt the Chinese-style artificial village (*isabŏp*) because it would eliminate the local practice of lewd sacrifices by creating a village shrine for a hundred-family unit dedicated to the altars of earth and grain (*sajiktan*), a system used extensively in Ming China. Because the policy did not succeed in restructuring the villages or eliminating the animistic rituals, however, the idea was dropped.

11. John Duncan, "The Social Background to the Founding of the Chosŏn Dynasty: Change or Continuity?" *Journal of Korean Studies* 6 (1988–89):39–79; idem, "The Koryŏ Origins of the Chosŏn Dynasty: Kings, Aristocrats, and Confucianism" (Ph.D. diss. University of Washington, 1988).

12. Yi T'aejin, "Sarimp'a ŭi Yuhyangso," pp. 148–56.

13. Ibid., pp. 156–62.

14. Chang Chiyŏn, *Chosŏn yugyo yŏnwŏn* [The source of Confucianism in Korea] (Masan, 1922), pp. 133–34, cited in Yi T'aejin, "Sarimp'a ŭi Yuhyangso," p. 165; Kim Yongdŏk, *Hyangch'ŏng yŏn'gu*, pp. 22–25.

15. *Yŏnsan'gun ilgi* (in *Chosŏn wangjo sillok*) 31:a-b, Yŏnsan'gun 4.8.kyeryu; Yi T'aejin, "Sarimp'a ŭi Yuhyangso," pp. 176–81; Kim Yongdŏk, *Hyangch'ŏng yŏn'gu*, pp. 25–26; Edward Willett Wagner, *The Literati Purges: Political Conflict in Early Yi Korea* (Cambridge: East Asia Research Center and Harvard University Press, 1974), pp. 33–50.

16. Tabana Tameo, *Chōsen kyōyaku*, pp. 21–53, 83–87. See p. 53 for the discussion between Chungjong and Chŏng Kwangp'il. Tabana could not tell from the sources whether Kim Inbŏm or Kim An'guk was the first to talk about the community compact, ibid., pp. 103–5. Yi T'aejin, "Sarimp'a ŭi Hyangyak pogŭp undong" [The movement among the *Sarimp'a* to spread community compacts], in idem, *Han'guk sahoesa yŏn'gu*, pp. 253–66, 268–74; Wagner, *Literati Purges*, p. 112.

17. *Chungjong sillok* 38:2a-b; Wagner, *Literati Purges*, pp. 104–12; Tabana Tameo, *Chŏsen kyŏyaku*, pp. 54–55, 108. On p. 52 Tabana noted that the MHBG, *kwŏn* 84, recorded that Chungjong approved the extension of the community compact system to the capital and the whole country, but Tabana could not find any record of royal approval for that order in the *Sillok*. Nam Kon made a number of similar accusations against the community compact and the habits of the scholars in 1521, Tabana Tameo, *Chŏsen kyŏyaku*, p. 57. Wagner wrote that King Chungjong called a halt to the community compact program in 1520, but it was not a total halt. Wagner, *Literati Purges*, p. 112; *Chungjong sillok*, 38:2b. See also Yi T'aejin, "Sarimp'a ŭi hyangyak," pp. 266–68.

18. *Chungjong sillok* 38:2b–3b, 8a–b; Tabana Tameo, *Chōsen kyōyaku*, pp. 55–57.

19. Wagner, *Literati Purges*, pp. 121–23.

20. Yi T'aejin, "Simnyuk segi ch'ŏnbang (po) kwan'gae ŭi paltal: Sarim seryŏk taedu ŭi kyŏngjejŏk paegyŏng iltan" [The development of irrigation dikes in the sixteenth century: Part of the economic background to the emergence of the power of the sarim], in idem, *Han'guk sahoesa yŏn'gu*, pp. 187–219; idem, "Sarimp'a ŭi hyangyak," in ibid., pp. 274–88; idem, "Yŏnhae chiyŏk ŭi yŏnjŏn kaebal: ch'ŏksin chŏngch'i ŭi kyŏngjejŏk paegyŏng iltan" [The development of reclaimed fields along the coast: Part of the economic background of the consort-relative regime], in ibid., pp. 222–52.

21. Tabana Tameo, *Chōsen kyōyaku*, pp. 63, 82–83, 97, 109–10, 126–59.

22. Ibid., pp. 183–97; Tagawa, "Kyōkyu," pp. 37–43, 50; Sakai Tadao, "Yi Yulgok

and the Community Compact," in William Theodore de Bary and JaHyun Kim Haboush, eds., *The Rise of Neo-Confucianism in Korea* (New York: Columbia University Press, 1985), pp. 323–27; PGSR 9:21a.

23. Tabana Tameo, *Chōsen kyōyaku*, pp. 213–20. Tabana doubted whether the elders really agreed with the plan because only two years later Yulgok told the king that community compacts should not be adopted until the poverty of the peasants was taken care of. Ibid., p. 292.

24. Ibid., pp. 213–20, 234–38. See p. 219 for Tabana's phrase. Tabana also pointed out that the MHBG mistakenly recounted that the king had ordered the community compacts to be carried out in all local communities, ibid., p. 220.

25. Ibid., pp. 221–23. The long text of Yulgok's remarks were only carried in the *Sŏnjo sujŏng sillok* [The revised veritable record of King Sŏnjo], and the two versions of the *Sillok* are slightly different.

26. Tabana Tameo, *Chōsen kyōyaku*, pp. 223–26.

27. Ibid., pp. 226–27. Later in the fifth lunar month Sŏnjo approved a list of regulations governing etiquette between men of different ages and statuses according to the recommendation that Yu Hŭich'un had made some months before. Ibid., pp. 230–31, 287–90; *Sŏnjo sujŏng sillok* 19:a-b.

28. For references to this quote and succeeding material on Cho Hŏn, see n.29.

29. *Sŏnjo sujŏng sillok*, 36b–38a; Tabana Tameo, *Chōsen kyōyaku*, pp. 241–43, 247–48.

30. John R. Watt, *The District Magistrate in Late Imperial China* (New York: Columbia University Press, 1972), pp. 105–18, quotes on pp. 113–14, 117.

31. Ibid., pp. 119–38.

32. Ibid., pp. 139–51; Joanna Handlin, *Action in Late Ming Thought* (Berkeley and Los Angeles: University of California Press, 1983), pp. 41–54, 114, 125–29, 143–49, 151, 154, 186–207. Handlin has shed far more light on Lü's humanism than Watt, who thought that Lü simply represented the advocates of coercion.

33. Handlin, pp. 232–34.

34. Yi I, *Yulgok chŏnsŏ* (Seoul: Sŏnggyun'gwan taehakkyo, Taedong munhwa yŏn'guwon, 1958), 16:2a–7a; Tabana Tameo, *Chōsen kyōyaku*, pp. 291–98; Sakai Tadao, "Yi Yulgok and the Community Compact," pp. 327–29. As Tabana Tameo has pointed out, Yulgok's *sŏwŏn* omitted the pledge to support the four categories of obligations and the items for the mutual exchange of rites and ritual (*ye*) included in the *Lü-Family Community Compact*. He retained only five of its articles for aid to the distressed, that is, only aid for funerals, unwed young girls, sick families who could not work, and those unjustly accused of crime. He did borrow Chu Hsi's provision for the reading of the compact regulations at the compact meetings, but he reduced the provisions for food and clothing, introduced a different seating order, and omitted any mention of the etiquette to be followed at the meeting, supposedly to fit Korean custom. He reduced Chu Hsi's list of thirty-seven "virtuous" deeds and duties to eighteen "so-called good" deeds, of which only eleven were identical to Chu Hsi's emendation of the Lü-Family compact. Instead of the "errors" in the Lü-Family compact, Yulgok listed twenty-six "bad" deeds and a number of others in separate articles as well.

35. Sakai Tadao, "Yi Yulgok and the Community Compact," pp. 300, 330–33; Tabana

Tameo, *Chōsen kyŏyaku*, pp. 353–56. Tagawa dated the Haeju compact at 1578 or 1579, "Kyŏkyu," part 1, p. 63.

36. Tabana Tameo, *Chōsen kyōyaku*, pp. 353–56.

37. Tabana Tameo, *Chōsen kyōyaku*, pp. 298–304; Yi I, *Yulgok chŏnso* 16:7a–12a; for the text of the *Lü-Family Community Compact*, see Yi I, 16:12a–26b; for the text of the reading of the compact at a full session of the association, see 16:26b–32a.

38. For the text, see Yi I, *Yulgok chŏnsŏ* 16:48a–60a; Tabana Tameo, *Chōsen kyōyaku*, pp. 318–24; Tagawa, "Kyōkyu," part 1, pp. 54–60.

39. Yi I, *Yulgok chŏnsŏ* 16:34a–45a; Tabana Tameo, *Chōsen kyōyaku*, pp. 327–36.

40. Yi I, *Yulgok chŏnsŏ* 16:51a; Tabana Tameo, *Chōsen kyōyaku*, p. 346. See the next reference for the full citation for the material in the village granary regulations.

41. Tabana Tameo, *Chōsen kyōyaku*, pp. 344–45; Sakai Tadao, "Yi Yulgok and the Community Compact," pp. 334, 337.

42. Tabana Tameo, *Chōsen kyōyaku*, pp. 345–48, 356, 359; Sakai, "Yi Yulgok and the Community Compact," p. 340.

43. Sakai, "Yi Yulgok and the Community Compact," pp. 340–41.

44. Ibid., pp. 365–75.

45. Ibid., pp. 375–84, 388–95.

46. Tabana Tameo, *Chōsen kyōyaku*, pp. 401–5.

47. Ibid., pp. 427–35.

48. Ibid., 450–54, 472–74. Tabana thought that the text of the community compact Yi recommended for adoption was probably Yulgok's, ibid., p. 474.

49. Ibid., pp. 454–58.

50. Introduction to the *Hwangyŏ hyangyak*, cited in Tabana, *Chōsen kyōyaku*, pp. 474–75, 495–502, 520–21.

51. Hsiao, *Rural China*, pp. 184–205.

CHAPTER 20. Yu Hyŏngwŏn's Community Compact Regulations

1. PGSR 9:12a-b.

2. The sections of the *Rites of Chou* were the *Hsiang san-wu* [The three local officials] and *Hsiang pa-hsing* [The eight punishments for local areas], PGSR 9:20b. Tabana wrote that Yu probably wrote this section during Hyŏnjong's reign, but could also have done so in Hyojong's reign (1649–59) as well. Tabana Tameo, *Chŏsen kyōyaku kyōkashi no kenkyu* [A study of the history of the community compact as moral education in Chŏson] (Tokyo: Chōhōsha, 1972), p. 524.

3. PGSR 9:21b–23a. Tabana Tameo has pointed out that Yu's copy of Cho Hŏn's memorial was, however, flawed in a few instances based on his comparison of the *Pan'gye surok* with Cho Hŏn's memorial in the *Sujong Sŏnjo sillok* 8:36b–38a. Yu mistakenly recorded that Cho wrote that Chinese community compacts met only once a month instead of twice a month on the first and fifteenth days of the lunar month. He failed to record that in China the head, assistant, and secretary of the community compacts first called on the district magistrate to listen to his recitation of the Six Edicts of Ming T'ai-tsu, after which they lectured the compact members on its contents. He left out Cho's state-

ment that the Chinese community compacts also met on new year's day, the winter solstice, and (the emperor's?) birthday. Where T'ai-tsu had issued instructions to the people "for each to rest secure in the principle of continuous reproduction" (*kag'an saengni*), Cho recorded this as "be diligent in conducting agriculture and sericulture" (*kŭnjak nongsang*), even though the meaning of the two phrases was essentially the same. Yu cut the text from 1,119 characters to 610 in the regular text, plus another 56 in a footnote. Tabana Tameo, *Chōsen kyōyaku,* pp. 52–53, 243–47.

4. PGSR 3:1a–2a; 9:14b–15a.

5. Ibid. 3:2a-b.

6. Ibid. 9:11a-b; Wada Sei, *Chūgoku chihō jiji hattatsushi* [The history of the development of local self-government in China] (1939. Tokyo: Kyūko shoin, 1975), p. 2.

7. PGSR 9:18a-b; Tabana Tameo, *Chōsen kyōyaku*, pp. 550–53.

8. PGSR 9:1a-b. The content of this category of Yu's text was quite close to Chu Hsi's *Tseng-sun Lü-shih hsiang-yüeh*; Tabana, *Chōsen kyŏyaku*, pp. 7–8.

9. PGSR 9:7b–8a.

10. Ibid. 9:15b, 16a. For further discussion of penalties as related to social status, see following sections, this chapter.

11. Ibid. 9:1a–3a; 15b–19b.

12. Ibid. 9:3a–7a.

13. Ibid. 9:8a–9b, 14b–15a.

14. Ibid. 9:12b–13a.

15. Ibid. 9:13b.

16. Ibid. 9:15a.

17. Ibid. 9:11b–12a. Tabana has raised the question whether Yu meant that no register would be kept for commoners, or that commoners would not be registered at all. He pointed out that Yu's directions for the two registers recording good and bad deeds would record both scholars and commoners, and he assumed that even those not registered would be so recorded. Tabana, *Chōsen kyōyaku*, pp. 552–53. On the other hand, Yu did say that commoners would be listed in the *kye* registers.

18. Fujiya Kawashima, "A Study of the *Hyangan*: Kin Groups and Aristocratic Localism in the Seventeenth and Eighteenth Century Korean Countryside," *Journal of Korean Studies* 5 (1984):3–38.

19. PGSR 9:12a-b.

20. Ibid. 9:15b–17a.

21. Tabana, *Chōsen kyōyaku*, pp. 8, 115–17. The language of Yu's text differed in many other instances as well from Chu Hsi's version. Martina Deuchler, "'Heaven Does Not Discriminate': A Study of Secondary Sons in Chosŏn Korea," *Journal of Korean Studies* 6 (1988):121–63.

22. PGSR 9:19b–20b.

23. Ibid. 9:10a; 13b–14b.

24. Tabana, *Chōsen kyōyaku*, p. 554.

25. Ibid., pp. 562–64.

26. Ibid., pp. 569–89.

27. Ibid., pp. 590–602.

28. Ibid., pp. 602–7, 617, 628. Tabana concluded that Ch'oe Hŭngwŏn worked out his own formula from a thorough digesting of the previous literature but was influenced mostly by the Lü-Family compact, Chu Hsi, and T'oegye, rather than Yulgok. Nevertheless, Ch'oe's emphasis on punishment appears to have derived from Yulgok.

29. Ibid., pp. 607–30.

30. Ibid., pp. 652–58, 671.

31. Ibid., pp. 663–64. Tabana, however, was unwilling to draw a conclusion whether the *kye* referred to a formal organization based on status, or simply to an informal "group" of people.

32. Ibid., pp. 659–72. Tabana also suggested that An's ideas were closely related to Yu's on these points, and that An's concept of the *kye* differed from that of Yulgok, who designed his *kye* to be a specific and separate organization that ran the granary as its function in conjunction with the community granary. An's *kye*, which was possibly more like an informal group divided by the status of the residents, was to function as part of the community compact organization. Although Tabana Tameo has praised An Chŏngbok's Kyŏng'an County Two-Village compact and granary as a unique and creative contribution to that subject, apart from his greater detail and the clearer emphasis on social status differentation than others, there was little to distinguish his thought from the previous literature.

33. Ibid., pp. 711–15. Small villages probably were organized as individual *kye* no matter how small their population, because forty of the village *kye* in An's district of 3,336 households (or 16,267 persons) had only an average of 83.4 families per *kye*.

34. Ibid., pp. 715–24.

35. Ibid., pp. 672–711.

36. Ibid., pp. 712–36.

37. Ibid., pp. 745–49. One of the two texts that Tabana used also contained an addendum quoting Yulgok's remarks that it was premature to initiate community compacts while the people were still suffering from famine and deprivation.

38. Ibid., p. 756

39. Ibid., pp. 770–83.

CHAPTER 21. Tribute and the *Taedong* Reform

1. PGSR 3:29b.

2. Cho Kwangjo, *Kugyŏk Chŏng'am Cho Sŏnsaeng munjip* [The collected works of Cho Kwangjo, transl.] (Seoul: Chŏng'am Cho Sŏnsaeng kinyŏm saŏphoe, 1978), p. 391, or 3:17a–18b of the original text, cited in Han Yŏngguk, "Hosŏ e silsi toen taedongbŏp, sang" [The Taedong system in Ch'ungch'ŏng Province, part 1] *Yŏksa hakpo* 13 (October 1960):77 n.1, and in Ching Young Choe, "Kim Yuk (1580–1658) and the Taedongbŏp Reform," *Journal of Asian Studies* 23, no. 1 (November 1963):23 n.8.

3. PGSR 3:29b–30a. For Yulgok's memorial to Sŏnjo, see ibid. 4:12b, and the "10,000-Word Memorial" (*manŏn pongsa*) in Yi I, *Yulgok chŏnso* (Seoul: Songgyun'gwan taehakkyo, Taedong munhwa yŏn'guwŏn, 1958) 5:31b–32b. Tagawa Kōzō has pointed out

that even though tribute was carried over from the Koryŏ dynasty, Chŏng Yagyong in the early nineteenth century believed that the practice of levying miscellaneous forms of tribute on the population had been the product of Yŏnsan'gun's infamous regime in the early sixteenth century, a tale that originated in the mid-seventeenth century. The story probably originated because Yŏnsan'gun was famous for exorbitant levies of special royal tribute. Hŏ Kyun, however, in his writings in 1611, and Yi Kung'ik in his *Yŏllyŏsil kisul,* written in the late eighteenth century, both said that this was an apocryphal story. See Tagawa Kōzō, *Richō kōnōsei no kenkyū* [A study of the tribute system of the Yi dynasty], pp. 1–2, 119 n.11.

4. PGSR 3:27b–28b.

5. Ibid. 3:30a.

6. Ibid. 4:10b–12b; Yi I, *Yulgok chŏnsŏ* 15:22b–24a, pp. 324–25. He also referred briefly to the *pangnap* problem in his "10,000 Word Memorial" of 1574, in ibid. 5:22a, p. 100; cited in Han Yŏngguk, "Hosŏ, part 1," p. 77 n.2. Han provided the explanation for opposition to Yulgok's proposal. See also Tagawa, *Richō kōnōsei no kenkyū*, pp. 750–51; Ching Young Choe, "Kim Yuk," p. 23.

7. PGSR 4:12b–13b; Kim Okkŭn, *Chosŏn hugi kyŏngjesa yŏn'gu* [A study of the economic history of the late Chosŏn] (Seoul: Sŏmundang, 1977), pp. 1–15.

8. PGSR 4:13b–15a; Yi I, *Yulgok chŏnsŏ* 5:42b–44b.

9. Tagawa discovered this in Yulgok's letter to Sŏng Hon in 1576. Yi I, *Yulgok chŏnsŏ* 11:7a, cited in Tagawa, *Richō kōnōsei no kenkyū*, p. 741; Kim Okkŭn, *Chosŏn hugi*, p.15 n.5.

10. I have reorganized and combined statements in two of Cho Hŏn's memorials that Yu cited under the same topics. The first one is found in PGSR 4:15a–18a, the second, in 4:18a–20a.

11. Liang Fang-chung, *The Single-Whip Method of Taxation in China* (Cambridge: Chinese Economic and Political Studies, Harvard University, 1956).

12. Ray Huang, *1587 A Year of No Significance: The Ming Dynasty in Decline* (New Haven, Conn.: Yale University Press, 1981), p. 62; Liang Fang-chung, *Single-Whip Method of Taxation*.

13. PGSR 4:15a–18a; KSDSJ 2:1439–40.

14. Tagawa, *Richō kōnōsei no kenkyū*, pp. 743, 751–53.

15. Ibid., pp. 754–57; Kim Okkŭn, *Chosŏn hugi*, p. 17.

16. PGSR 3:29b–31a; Yu Sŏngnyŏng, *Sŏae munjip* [Collected works of Yu Sŏngnyŏng] (Taedong munhwa ed., 1958), 16a–17a; *Sŏnjo sujŏng sillok* 28:7a–8a, Sŏngjong 27.4.kiyu. Tagawa Kōzō stated that Yu Sŏngnyŏng did not want to replace the tribute system altogether but just permit tribute contracting and use the land tax as a substitute payment. Nevertheless, even though the essence of the *taedong* reform supposedly eliminated tribute by substituting a land tax, the schedule of taxes was drawn up to pay for the cost of replacing tribute goods that were either paid for in kind or had to be replaced on the market. In other words, the spirit of replacing tribute with substitute payments was retained through the adoption of the *taedong* system. Otherwise, one would have expected that grain or cloth quotas would have been adopted without tying them to indi-

vidual tribute items, and the purchase of tribute could have been controlled exclusively by budgets adopted for each capital agency. Tagawa, *Richō kōnōsei no kenkyū*, pp. 751, 757–59.

17. Ibid., pp. 760–65.

18. PGSR 3:31a–33b. Of the 16 *mal/kyŏng*, 2 *mal* would be paid to the district magistrate for his personal and public expenses. Tagawa also found that the Sŏnhyech'ŏng was also mentioned prior to the adoption of the Kyŏnggi land surtax, back in the fourth lunar month, as part of a proposal to eliminate some problems in the tribute system, and Yi Wŏn'ik was borrowing that precedent to justify the creation of a special office "to confer benevolence on the suffering people." Tagawa, *Richō kōnōsei no kenkyū*, pp. 766–70, esp. p. 769; Kim Okkŭn, *Chosŏn hugi*, pp. 74–75.

19. The *taedong* reform was first studied by Chŏng Hyŏng'u, "Taedongbŏp e taehan ilyŏn'gu" [A study of the *taedong* system] *Sahak yŏn'gu* 2 (Dec. 1958):50–85, but a pathbreaking effort was made by Han Yŏngguk in his six articles on the subject: "Hosŏ e silsi toen taedongbŏp sang" [The Taedong System in Cholla Province, part 1] *Yŏksa hakpo* 13 (October 1960):77–108; Ha (part 2), ibid. 14 (April 1961):77–132; idem, "Honam e silsi toen taedongbŏp, sang," [The *taedong* system in Chŏlla Province, part 1), ibid. 15 (September 1961):31–60; I (part 2), ibid. 20 (April 1963):29–80; Sam (part 3), ibid. 21 (August 1963):67–100; Sa, Wan (part four, completion), ibid. 24 (July 1964):91–118. The study by Kim Okkŭn, *Chosŏn hugi*, was also devoted almost exclusively to the *taedong* reform. In addition to providing some more detailed information about the adoption of the system, he also tracked changes that took place between the seventeenth and nineteenth centuries. See also Ching Young Choe, "Kim Yuk," pp. 21–35.

20. Han Yŏngguk, "Hosŏ," part 1, pp. 80–81. The quote is in *Injo sillok* 2:24b–25a, Injo 1.7.kyŏngja; Kim Okkŭn, *Chosŏn hugi*, p. 103.

21. "Non Sonhyech'ŏng so" [Memorial proposing the establishment of the Office for Dispensing Benevolence], in *P'ojŏ sŏnsaengjip*, *kwŏn* 2, cited in Han Yŏngguk, "Hosŏ," part 1, pp. 82–83, and Kim Okkŭn, *Chosŏn hugi*, p. 104.

22. *Injo sillok* 6:48b–49b, Injo 2.8.sinhaek, cited in Han Yŏngguk, "Hosŏ," part 1, pp. 85–89; Kim Okkŭn, *Chosŏn hugi*, pp. 105–7.

23. *Injo sillok* 7:30a-b, Injo 2.11.kyech'uk; ibid. 7:46b, Injo 2.12.pyŏngsul, cited in Han Yŏngguk, "Hosŏ," part 1, pp. 91–92, and Kim Okkŭn, *Chosŏn hugi*, pp. 107–8.

24. *Injo sillok* 7:48b–49a, Injo 2.12.chŏngyu. This material is covered in Han Yŏngguk, "Hosŏ," part 1, pp. 92–93, except that he omitted Sin Hŭm's key statements about the opposition of the wealthy landlords.

25. *Injo sillok* 8:7a-b, Injo 3.1.imsul; Kim Okkŭn, *Chosŏn hugi*, pp. 108–10, see especially Kim's explanation on p. 110.

26. Han Yŏngguk, "Hosŏ, part 1," pp. 95–96; *Injo sillok* 8:7a, Injo 3.1.sinyu.

27. Han Yŏngguk, "Hosŏ," part 1, pp. 94–95; Kim Okkŭn, *Chosŏn hugi*, pp. 108–11.

28. *Injo sillok* 28:45a, Injo 11.10.kyŏngja.

29. *Ibid.* 33:21a, Injo 14.9.kab'in.

30. *Ibid.* 37:22b–23a, Injo 16.10.pyŏngsul; ibid. 37:32a-b, Injo 16.11.muin; Han Yŏngguk, "Hoso," part 1, pp. 95–96; Kim Okkun, *Chosŏn hugi*, p. 156.

31. Han Yŏngguk, "Hosŏ, part 1," pp. 97–98; Kim Okkŭn, *Chosŏn hugi*, p. 157.

32. Kim Okkun, *Chosŏn hugi*, pp. 264–66.

33. Han Yŏngguk, "Hosŏ, part 1," pp. 98–100; Kim Okkŭn, *Chosŏn hugi*, pp. 156–58; Ching Young Choe, "Kim Yuk," pp. 26–28; *Hyojong sillok* 2:20a–21a, Hyojong accession year (*chŭgwinyŏn*).11.kyŏngsin.

34. *Hyojong sillok* 3:4a–5a, Hyojong 1.1.pyŏngja, cited in Han Yŏngguk, "Hosŏ," part 1, p. 101 n.73; Kim Okkŭn, *Chosŏn hugi*, pp. 159–60; Ching Young Choe, "Kim Yuk," pp. 28–29.

35. *Hyojong sillok* 6:38a-b, Hyojong 2.6.musin; ibid. 6:57b, Hyojong 2.6.ŭrch'uk, cited in Ching Young Choe, "Kim Yuk," p. 30; Kim Okkŭn, *Chosŏn hugi*, pp. 160–61. Min Ŭnghyŏng had complained in 1650 that since Hideyoshi's invasions the government had failed to revise tribute regulations for the three southern provinces, reform would be justified in Ch'ungch'ŏng because her taxes were heavier than Chŏlla's, and Chŏlla's heavier than Kyŏngsang. Kim Okkŭn, *Chosŏn hugi*, pp. 160–61 and PBSDN 14:176–77, Hyojong 1.6.9.

36. *Hyojong sillok* 7.3b, Hyojong 2.7.kapsin; ibid. 7:5b–6a, Hyojong 2.7.ŭrch'uk; ibid. 7:8b–9a, Hyojong 2.7.musul; Ching Young Choe, "Kim Yuk," p. 30.

37. *Hyojong sillok* 7:23b–24b, Hyojong 2.8.kisa; Han Yŏngguk, "Hosŏ," part 1, pp. 104–5; Kim Okkŭn, *Chosŏn hugi*, p. 163.

38. Ching Young Choe, "Kim Yuk," p. 34.

39. Kim Okkŭn, *Chosŏn hugi*, p. 164.

40. Ibid., p. 31; Han Yŏngguk, "Hosŏ," part 1, pp. 103–4; Kim Okkŭn, *Chosŏn hugi*, p. 162; *Hyojong sillok* 7:14a-b, Hyojong 2.8.musin; 7:16a, Hyojong 2.8.kiyu. Hyojong also rejected resignations submitted by Chief State Councilor Kim Yuk, Second State Councilor Yi Sibaek, and Third State Councilor Han Hŭng'il, ibid. 7:17a.

41. MHBG 152:13b, cited in Han Yŏngguk, "Hosŏ," part 2, p. 130. See MHBG 152:11b for the grain/cloth exchange rate in the Taedong Regulations. These regulations divided Ch'ungch'ŏng Province into three categories for determining whether taxes should be paid in rice or cloth. Thirty-five coastal districts were to pay grain, thirteen mountain or hilly districts would pay cloth, and six districts defined as "half coastal and half hilly" paid half in grain and half in cloth. MHBG 152:12b.

42. Kim Hong'uk was appointed governor of Ch'ungch'ŏng in 1652, Hyojong 2.10.3 (chŏngmi), in CSS, series 5, 3:412.

43. *Hyojong sillok* 8:36b–38a, Hyojong 3.4.sinch'uk. For Hŏ Chŏk's appointment to this post, see CSS, series 5, 3:452, Hyojong 3.3.20 (sinmyo), but he was replaced in this office shortly thereafter. Kim Yuk was appointed councilor of the right in 1651, Hyojong 2.12.7, CSS, series 5, 3:417.

44. For discussion and references, see Han Yŏngguk, "Hosŏ," part 2, pp. 125–28.

45. Ibid., pp. 128–29; MHBG 152:13b. See the discussion of *yang'ip wich'ul* by Lien-sheng Yang in "Notes on Dr. Swann's *Food and Money in Ancient China*," in idem, *Studies in Chinese Institutional History* (Cambridge: Harvard University Press, 1961), p. 88.

46. Han Yŏngguk, "Honam," part 1, pp. 31–60, esp. pp. 31–34; Kim Okkŭn, *Chosŏn hugi*, p. 198.

47. *Hyojong sillok* 19:5a–6a, Hyojong 8.7.imja, cited in Han Yŏngguk, "Hosŏ," part 2, p. 129; Han, "Honam," part 1, pp. 34–35; Kim Okkŭn, *Chosŏn hugi*, p. 199. Ching Young Choe called this Kim Yuk's "deathbed memorial," "Kim Yuk," p. 32.

48. *Hyojong sillok* 19:52a-b, Hyojong 8.11.pyŏng'o; Han Yŏngguk, "Honam," part 1, pp. 35–38; Kim Okkŭn, *Chosŏn hugi*, pp. 199–200; Ching Young Choe, "Kim Yuk," p. 33; MHBG 152:13b–14a.

49. Han Yŏngguk, "Hosŏ," part 2, p. 10 n.121; Ching Young Choe, "Kim Yuk," p. 33; *Hyŏjong sillok* 20:31a, Hyojong 9.7.chŏngmi.

50. Edward W. Wagner, *The Literati Purges, Political Conflict in Early Yi Korea* (Cambridge: East Asian Research Center and Harvard University Press, 1974), pp. 104–8; *Hyojong sillok* 20:36a-b, Hyojong 9.9.kihaek; Ching Young Choe, "Kim Yuk," p. 33. For two other memorials by Kim Yuk presented in 1658 that have not been dicussed elsewhere in secondary studies, see MHBG 152:15a–16b. The first objected to the statement of a previous governor of Chŏlla that the people were opposed to the law, especially when the secret censor for the province had interrogated people in the streets and villages and found that they would have welcomed the *taedong* surtax even if had been as high as fifteen to twenty *mal* (per *kyŏl*). He also said it was the governor's obligation to tell the people that the thirteen *mal/kyŏl* rate was not etched in stone and could be reduced.

51. Hyojong suggested the thirteen *mal/kyŏl* rate earlier in the year, in the second lunar month. Han Yŏngguk, "Honam," part 1, pp. 39–40; Kim Okkŭn, *Chosŏn hugi*, pp. 200–201; MHBG 152:14a-b. Three other districts were added to the coastal, rice-paying region later on, or thirty of the fifty-three districts in all. MHBG 152:14a-b.

52. See Minister of Taxation Hŏ Chŏk's remarks about the higher cost of cotton in Ch'ungch'ŏng, in Han Yŏngguk, "Honam," part 1, p. 43.

53. Of the two versions in the *Hyŏnjong sillok* and *Revised Hyŏnjong sillok* the former is obviously garbled and the latter far more reliable, and Han Yŏngguk has relied on it in his article. *Hyŏnjong sillok* 3:6a-b, Hyŏnjong 1.6.kihaek, and *Hyŏnjong kaesu sillok*, 3:49a-b, same date. Han Yŏngguk, "Honam," part 1, p. 42; Kim Okkŭn, *Chosŏn hugi*, pp. 201–3.

54. Han Yŏngguk, "Honam," part 1, p. 42; Kim Okkŭn, *Chosŏn hugi*, p. 203.

55. *Hyŏnjong kaesu sillok* 3:49a, Hyŏnjong 1.6.*kihaek*; Han Yŏngguk, "Honam," part 1, p. 43; Kim Okkŭn, *Chosŏn hugi*, p. 203.

56. The regulations for the *taedong* system for that province were promulgated in 1663. The law was suspended briefly again between 1666 and 1667, but for all practical purposes it had really begun in 1662. Han Yŏngguk, "Honam," part 1, pp. 44–45; Kim Okkŭn, *Chosŏn hugi*, p. 203.

57. For the dimensions of the *p'il*, see Han Yŏngguk, "Hosŏ," part 2, p. 83.

58. For this point see Han Yŏngguk, "Honam," part 2, pp. 55–61, et passim; part 3, passim; part 4, pp. 91–99. In the first of these articles Han studied the operation of the *taedong* system in Ch'ungch'ŏng after 1651 based on the promulgation of the eighty-two articles of the law (*Hosŏ taedong samok*), in "Hosŏ," part 2, pp. 77–132. Implementation of the articles for Chŏlla Province were published in ibid., pp. 67–100. Since

this is the main source for the following information about the details of the Ch'ungch'ŏng *taedong* system, I will only cite specific pages if it might be of some use for consulting primary references. The *taedong* system is discussed in the eighteenth-century MHBG *kwŏn* 152–54; the text of the regulations for Ch'ungch'ŏng (*Taedong chŏrmok*) is in MHBG 152:10b–12b, and tax rates and first year's revenues for Chŏlla are in MHBG 153:18b–19a.

59. MHBG 10b–11a.

60. Han Yŏngguk, "Hosŏ," part 2, p. 90 n.96, pp. 90–96; "Honam," part 2, p. 33.

61. Han Yŏngguk, "Honam," part 2, pp. 33–34.

62. Han found that between 1744 and 1834 Ch'ungch'ŏng's taxable land rose to 76.9 percent (from 71.4 percent), which might have reduced the tax differential between the two provinces, since Ch'ungch'ŏng's basis for taxes increased. Ibid., p. 33 n.67. Han also pointed out that since the average number of persons per household was 3.5, he assumes that the statistics only counted adult males and females and not children.

63. Ibid., part 2, pp. 39–47.

64. In 1653 instructions were issued that liberal prices ought to be paid from *taedong* revenues from Ch'ungch'ŏng Province for food items used by the Royal Cuisine Office (Saongwŏn) to attract a sufficient supply of goods through the open market, and Kim Yuk sought to reduce costs by substituting more plentiful and cheaper pigs or calves for the costlier deer previously required for royal tribute or ritual ceremonies. Han Yŏngguk, "Hosŏ," part 2, p. 90 n.96, pp. 90–96; "Honam," part 2, pp. 38, 57, 76 n.115. For discussion of the district's capital agent, see Yi Kwangnin, "Kyŏngjuin yŏn'gu" [A study of the district's capital agent] *Inmun kwahak* 7 (June 1962):237–67. For his discussion of the rise in the annual wages of the district's capital agents by 1800, see ibid., p. 262.

65. Han Yŏngguk, "Hosŏ," part 2, pp. 90 n.96, 90–96; "Honam," part 2, pp. 73–80. For *kiin*, see Tagawa, *Richō kōnōsei no kenkyū*, pp. 744–46 et passim.

66. Han Yŏngguk, "Hosŏ," part 2, pp. 99–125; "Honam," part 3, pp. 88–99; part 4, pp. 91–121; pp. 83–99; MHBG 152:10b–11b.

67. Han Yŏngguk, "Hosŏ," part 2, pp. 118, 123–24.

68. Han Yŏngguk, "Honam," part 1, p. 46 n.41. The source of these figures was Wada Sei, *Chōsen no tochi seido oyobi chisei seido chōsa hōkoku* [A report of an investigation of the land and land tax systems of Korea] (Keijo: 1920), pp. 703–29.

69. Han Yŏngguk, "Hosŏ," part 2, p. 125, which cites *Sukchong sillok* 60:31b, Sukchong 43.8.sinhaek.

70. Yi Man'ŭn's commentary in the MHBG, written between 1782 and 1791, also reported that the *taedong* tax was divided into a seven *mal/kyŏl* levy in the fall, and six *mal/kyŏl* in the spring, as established by law in 1658 prior to the adoption of a cloth tax for upland Chŏlla in 1662, MHBG 152:18b–19a.

71. *Hyŏnjong kaesu sillok* 9:40a–45a, Hyŏnjong 4.10.im'in (8th day, 1663), Han Yŏngguk, "Honam," part 4, pp. 100–102 n.135; "Honam," part 1, pp. 57–59.

72. Han Yŏngguk, "Honam," part 4, p. 104; for the 8 *mal/p'il* commutation rate in 1665, see MHBG 152:18b; Kim Okkŭn, *Chosŏn hugi*, pp. 204–5.

73. Han Yŏngguk found the comment by the *Sillok* historian who said that Hyŏnjong

had in fact decided to rescind the *taedong* law for upland Chŏlla because court officials believe that everyone opposed the law when it was only true of the wealthy families and large households. For the reference see "Honam," part 4, p. 107. Kim Okkŭn also goes over this story in *Chosŏn hugi*, pp. 205–6. Yi Man'ŭn's commmentary in the MHBG records Chŏng T'aehwa and Min Yujung's remarks in Hyŏnjong's sixth year, but the twelfth lunar month was January 1667; MHBG 152:19a. The secret censor's report and Hyŏnjong's reversal of his decision is in MHBG 152:19a-b. For Hyŏnjong's reduction of the rice tax rate for the lowlands, see MHBG 152:19b.

74. Han Yŏngguk, "Honam," part 4, pp. 104–7; Kim Okkŭn, *Chosŏn hugi*, pp. 206–7; MHBG 152:19a–20a. In the MHBG account Min Yujung also said he thought that the reduction of the rice tax rate in the lowlands to twelve *mal/kyŏl* was not enough, and he advised another reduction to eleven *mal/kyŏl*. Chief State Councilor Chŏng T'aehwa replied that while the people might be pleased by this, the government would suffer a loss in revenue and force it to raise taxes again. It would be better to store the revenue surplus, and if there was enough, they reduce the tax rate in the future, an idea consistent with the adoption of the *taedong* system in Hyojong's reign. MHBG 152:19b–20a.

Han Yŏngguk estimated that *taedong* revenue was decreased by a value equivalent to about 20,000 *sŏm* annually when the rice/cloth commutation rate for upland districts in Chŏlla was changed to eight *mal/p'il* in 1666, and then when the tax rate was reduced from thirteen to twelve *mal/kyŏl* later that same year to raise the value of cloth against rice. The tax reduction from the first change of the commutation rate was 6,068 *sŏm*, and 12,723 *sŏm* for the second. One problem is why the tax revenues should have declined by over 6,000 *sŏm* when the rise in the commutation rate should have yielded more revenue, but Han suggested that it might have been due to a decline in the amount of land under cultivation. Han, "Honam," part 2, p. 30 n.60.

75. Kim Okkŭn, *Chosŏn hugi*, pp. 304–5.

76. Ching Young Choe, "Kim Yuk," p. 34.

77. Min wanted simply to split taxes in half, but Hyŏnjong ordered that taxes from older land be commuted to cloth payments in the fall, and taxes on new land be collected in rice in the spring. The governor, however, objected because since the taxes for 1665 had already been collected prior to transplanting, if half the taxes were collected in the fall under a semiannual basis, the peasants would think that they would be paying an extra half-year's taxes (i.e., at a rate of eighteen rather than twelve *mal/kyŏl*. Hyŏnjong accepted his suggestion to call off the the fall tax collection and collect all taxes for the year on both new and old land in the next spring. The new regulations called for thirty coastal districts to pay their taxes in rice, twenty-one upland districts to pay half in cash and half in cotton cloth, and two district to pay half in cash and half in ramie cloth. Han Yŏngguk, "Honam," part 4, pp. 107–8; MHBG 152:20a.

78. Also because of reductions of revenue caused by famine conditions, in the decade after 1667, the amount of tax-exempt land for filial sons, chaste women, and loyal subjects and the grain and cloth allocations to the Office for Dispensing Benevolence for the purchase of goods was reduced. Han Yŏngguk, "Honam," part 4, pp. 106–16.

79. *Hyŏnjong kaesu sillok* 27:42b, Hyŏnjong 14.11.*sinsa*, cited in Han Yŏngguk,

"Honam," part 4, p. 115 n.180. The MHBG cites King Hyŏnjong's acceptance of another memorial from Kim Minhaeng (Kim Mindo?) in 1674 for an additional two *mal* (per *kyŏl*) raise in the rice tax in his province, and reduction of the cloth commutation rate (from twelve *mal/p'il*?) to six *mal/p'il*, and five *mal/p'il* for Kyŏnggi Province. MHBG 152:21a.

80. *Hyŏnjong kaesu sillok* 27:46b, Hyŏnjong 14.12.kyech'uk, cited in Han Yŏngguk, "Honam," part 4, p. 116.

81. *Sukchong sillok* 6:33b, Sukchong 3.6.chŏngsa, cited in Han Yŏngguk, "Honam," part 4, p. 115 n.182. The first proposal for the *taedong* tax rate in Kyŏngsang was twelve *mal/kyŏl*, the same rate currently in use in Chŏlla, but the Office for Dispensing Benevolence anticipated a serious shortage of revenue and proposed raising the rate to thirteen *mal/kyŏl* of rice, commuted to cloth at the rate of seven *mal/p'il*, slightly more than half the twelve *mal/p'il* commutation rate for Chŏlla. MHBG 152:1a-b; Kim Okkŭn, *Chosŏn hugi*, pp. 237–39.

82. Han Yŏngguk, "Honam," part 4, p. 116.

83. See the reference to King Hyŏnjong's order to Min Yujung, governor of Chŏlla, in 1665 to find out what the feelings of the people really were, since he had previously been reluctant to do so and only relied on the views of the rich that the common people did not like the *taedong* law and recommended that it be abolished. Ibid., "Honam," part 1, p. 47 n.43.

84. PGSR 3:33b; KSDSJ 2:1045.

CHAPTER 22. The *Taedong* Model for Official Salaries and Expenses

1. PGSR 3:23a–24a.

2. Ibid. 19:17a-b.

3. Ibid. 3:34a–35b; 3:19b.

4. Ibid. 3:19a-b.

5. Ibid.

6. Ibid. 3:34a–35b. This memorial was also excerpted in MHBG 152:16b–17a. Similar arguments in favor of the *taedong* system were also made in PGSR 3:19a-b.

7. PGSR 3:35b–36a.

8. Ibid. 3:16b–17a.

9. Yu cited Cho Kwangjo on this point, but not the attack on royal expenditures in Yulgok's *Tongho mundap*. See chap. 21.

10. PGSR 3:21b–22b.

11. Ibid. 3:23a–24a.

12. Ibid. 3:24a–25a.

13. Ibid. 3:25a. For Koguryŏ's subjugation of Okchŏ, see Ki-baik Lee, *A New History of Korea*, trans. Edward W. Wagner (Cambridge: Harvard University Press, 1984), p. 24.

14. PGSR 3:21b.

15. Ibid. 3:25b.

16. Ibid. 3:19a-b.

17. Ibid. 3:20a.

18. Ibid. 3:18b.
19. Ibid. 3:18b.
20. Ibid. 19:11b, 5b.
21. Ibid. 19:16b.
22. Ibid. 19:16b–17a.
23. Ibid. 19:17b.
24. Ibid. 19:17a-b.
25. Ibid. 19:17b.
26. Ibid. 19:17b.
27. Ibid. 19:14b–15a.
28. Ibid. 19:15a.
29. Ibid. 3:36b–38b.
30. Ibid. 3:38b. The quote is taken from the *Hu-shih chüan* [The Tradition of Mr. Hu, Hu An-kuo?].
31. PGSR 3:40a-b. Yu illustrated the costs involved in putting up imperial envoys with the example of Chip'yŏng-hyŏn. The district was required to forward one ox for transport (or two if the magistrate was corrupt), three or four roebucks, several hundred chickens, and sixty to seventy pheasants, pigs, eggs, oil, honey, fish products, vegetables, salt, bean sauce, fruit of all kinds, rice, noodles, utensils, straw mats, dustpans, brooms, pots, cauldrons, gourds, bedding, tents, cushions, painted screens, all of which had to be loaded on carts and drawn by oxen and horses for several hundred *i* (30–100 miles). If the envoy stayed in a hostel at the capital for more than a ten-day week, the district's men and horses had to return home and be ready to go back to the capital for the return journey, with an additional levy of similar goods. Ibid. 3:41a–42a.
32. Ibid. 3:39a, 40a, 42a, 43a-b.
33. Ibid. 3:42b–43b
34. Ibid. 3:43b–46a.
35. Ibid. 19:13a-b, for budgets for the other three districts, see ibid. 19:12a–13b.
36. Ibid. 19:13b–14a.
37. Ibid. 19:15a-b, 18a–22a, 31b.
38. Ibid. 19:15b.
39. Ibid. 19:16a.
40. Ibid. 19:16a-b.
41. Ibid. 19:5b, 3:26a.
42. Ibid. 3:16b.
43. Ibid. 19:2a-b. During the debate over the *taedong* reform in 1623, Cho Sik cited Chou dynasty practice to justify payment of salaries to all officials by the state, but Yu did not refer to Cho in his historical coverage of the *taedong* system (see chap. 21, above).
44. Ibid. 20:1a–3a. Yu also included the discussion in the Wang-chih section of the *Book of Rites* (*Li-chi*) that described the ratio of salaries in the royal domain as if it were analagous to salary grades in feudal states. It also described the basis of salaries for commoners who served as officials on the same basis but included the point that the Hsia-shih or lowest regular official received a salary equal to a superior farmer who could support nine persons from a plot of 100 *mou*. The T'ang dynasty commentator, Ku Kung-

yen, and the Ming commentator Ch'iu Chün also described details of the salaries for the four grades of clerks and runners. Ibid. 20:3a–4b.

45. See as well the commentary on the meaning of terms by Mr. Ts'ai in ibid. 20:4b. He translated the passage as follows: "Only after those people in office are provided with salaries which they can look up [forward?] to, will it be possible to hold them responsible for doing good [or performing well]. If their salaries are not continued, clothes and food not given to them, so that they are not able to live in harmony at home, then these people will in the future fall into crime and perversity." I have adopted the translation in Sahagwŏn, ed., *Pan'gye surok* (1963) 4:42. See also the translation by Han'gukhak kibon ch'ongsŏ, ed., no. 10, *Chŭngbo pan'gye surok* 3 (Seoul: Kyŏng'in munhwasa, 1974):553. The translation by Clae Waltham in *Shu Ching: Book of History*, p. 128, appears vague and ambiguous. Legge's translation appears to have missed the mark: "All right men, having a competency, will go on to be good. If you cannot make men have what they love in their families, they will only proceed to be guilty of crime." *Chinese Classics* 3:330–31, p. 5, b. 4, par. 13.

46. PGSR 20:4b–5a. See the comment on this issue by the Sung official, Hsia Sung, in the mid-eleventh century.

47. Ibid. 20:5b.

48. Ibid. 20:6a-b.

49. Ibid. 19:2b–3a. The salary lists from the Former Han through Ming are discussed in ibid. 20:6b–13b.

50. Ibid. 19:2b.

51. Ibid. 20:14a-b.

52. Ibid. 20:16b–18a; 3:25b.

53. Ibid. 3:26a.

54. Ibid. 19:1a-b, 4b. To convert Yu's *kok* to contemporary *sŏm*, one would have to multiply by 10 *mal* and divide by 15.

55. Ibid. 3:29a.

56. Ibid. 19:3a.

57. Ibid. 18:3b–4a, *Chŭngbo Pan'gye surok* 3:466.

58. PGSR 19:5a.

59. Ibid. 19:4b–5a, 22b. Yu noted that boy servants in the capital, who were called *ch'ŏngjik*, were sons of clerks and official slaves who volunteered for the job. They were referred to in Kyŏnggi Province as *t'ong'in*. In the southern provinces, however, they were called *kongsaeng* (tribute students) and recruited from the sons of officials and clerks. In the north (*yŏngbuk*) they were recruited from sons of official slaves and called *yŏnjik*.

60. Ibid. 19:4b–5a.

61. Ibid. 19:22b–28b.

62. Ibid. 19:29a-b.

63. Since the *kyŏng* was 100 *myo* or 16.7 acres, then Yu's estimated production for a superior farmer was 1,300–1,400 *mal* or 86.7–93.3 in contemporary *sŏm* (i.e., 15 *mal*, not 10 *mal* as in Yu's *sŏm*), or 5.19–5.59 *sŏm* per acre. Production for an average farmer would be 600–700 *mal/kyŏng* or 40–46.7 *sŏm/kyŏng*, or 2.4–2.8 *sŏm*/acre.

64. Ibid. 19:29b. Yu's monthly salary scale for capital clerks was 40 *mal* (4 *kok*) for

chief clerks (*noksa*), 35 *mal* (3 *kok*, 5 *mal*) for clerks (*sŏri*), 25 *mal* for runners (*chorye*) and official slaves (*sano*). The boy servants, however, would only receive 15 *mal*. Ibid. 19:4a-b.

65. The chief source for figures of acreage, average holdings, and production are to be found in Kim Yongsŏp, *Chosŏn hugi nong'ŏpsa yŏn'gu* [Studies in the agricultural history of the late Chosŏn period] (Seoul: Ilchogak, 1970). For an estimate of the size of the land held by the majority of peasants, I used an eyeball estimate of categories D and E in the tables on pp. 240–45, which are almost the same as Kim's remarks on p. 246. For further discussion, see his Appendix on Ownership and Production.

66. PGSR 19:30a-b.

67. Ibid. 19:30b.

68. Ibid.

69. James B. Palais, *Politics and Policy in Traditional Korea* (Cambridge: Harvard University Press, 1975), p. 61.

70. Han Woo-keun [Han Ugŭn], *Yijo hugi ŭi sahoe wa sasang* [Society and thought in the late Yi dynasty] (Seoul: Ŭrchi munhwasa, 1961), pp. 33–35. The production figure for 1737 was 40–50 *sŏm* or 600–750 *mal*, but since Han estimated this at 300–375 *mal*, he must have regarded the figures in the *Sillok* as referring to unhusked rice. Polished rice could be calculated by dividing the figure in half.

71. Han Woo-keun, *Yijo hugi*, pp. 36–37.

72. Ibid., pp. 37–38.

73. Kim Okkŭn, *Chosŏn hugi kyŏngjesa yŏn'gu* [A study of the economic history of late Chosŏn] (Seoul: Sŏmundang, 1977), pp. 406–8.

74. Ibid., pp. 79–80.

75. Ibid., pp. 410–11; Han Woo-keun, *Yijo hugi*, pp. 40–46.

76. PGSR 152:16a–17a; see also ibid. 3:34a–35b.

CHAPTER 23. Copper Cash and the Monetary System

1. Yi T'aejin, "Simnyuk segi ch'ŏnbang (po) kwan'gae ŭi paltal: Sarim seryŏk taedu ŭi kyŏngjejŏk paegyŏng iltan" [The development of irrigation dikes in the sixteenth century: Part of the economic background to the emergence of the power of the *Sarim*], in Yi, *Han'guk sahoesa yŏngu: nong'ŏp kisul paltal kwa sahoe pyŏndong* [Studies in the social history of Korea: The development of agricultural technology and social change] (Seoul: Chisik san'ŏpsa, 1986), pp. 274–88; idem, "Sarimp'a ŭi Yuhyangso pongni undong" in ibid., pp. 125–85, published originally in *Han'guk munhwa* 4 (December 1983):1–39.

2. Wŏn Yuhan, "Chosŏn hugi ŭi kŭmsok hwap'ye yut'ong chŏngch'aek: Sipch'il segi chŏnban ŭi tongjŏn yut'ong sidogirŭl chungsim'ŭro" [Metallic currency policy in late Chosŏn: The attempt to circulate copper cash in the first half of the seventeenth century] *Tongbanghak chi* 13 (December 1972):100.

3. MHBG 159:5a–6a.

4. Ch'oe Hojin, *Han'guk hwap'ye sosa* [Short history of currency in Korea] (Seoul: Sŏnmundang, 1974), pp. 81–83.

5. *Injo sillok* 28:52b–53a, Injo 11.11.imjin.

6. Ibid. 29:6a-b, Injo 12.2.chŏngch'uk.

7. Ibid., 31:44a-b; Injong 13.7.imsul.

8. Additional references for material covered to this point: MHBG 159:6a; Chang Kukchong, "Sipch'il segi kŭmsok hwap'e (tonghwa) ŭi yut'ong e taehayŏ" [Circulation of metallic currency in the seventeenth century], *Yŏksa kwahak* 76 (1961):44–47; Wŏn Yuhan, "Yijo Sukchongjo ŭi chujŏn tonggi" [The motive for minting coins in Sukchong's reign], *Tongguk sahak* 9–10 (1966):37, 40–41; idem, "Yijo hugi ch'ŏngjŏn ŭi suip yut'ong e taehayŏ [Circulation of imported cash in the late Yi dynasty], *Sahak yŏn'gu* 21 (September 1969):145; idem, "Yijo Sukchong sidae ŭi chujŏn e taehayŏ" [Minting of cash in Sukchong's reign], *Sahak yŏn'gu* 18 (1964):627–74; idem, "Kŭmsok hwap'ye (1972)," pp. 100–103, 108, 112–15; idem, "Chosŏn hugi ŭi kŭmsok hwap'ye," *Tongbanghak chi* 13 (December 1972):107; idem, *Chosŏn hugi hwap'yesa yŏn'gu* [Studies in the history of currency in the late Chosŏn period] (Seoul: Han'guk yŏn'guwŏn, 1975), pp. 27, 84–85; Ch'oe Hojin, *Han'guk hwap'ye sosa*, pp. 83–84.

9. The twelfth lunar month of previous year.

10. Chang Kukchong, "Sipch'il segi," p. 47.

11. *Injo sillok* 45:46a–47b, Injo 22.9.pyŏngsul, cited in Wŏn Yuhan, "Chosŏn hugi ŭi kŭmsok hwap'ye," pp. 104, 114–16.

12. MHBG 159:6b–7a; Kim Yuk, "Chamgok sŏnsaeng yugo p'oyu" [Supplement to the bequeathed manuscripts of Kim Yuk], 5b–6b, dated twelfth lunar month of *chŏnghaek* year, probably January, 1648, in *Chamgok chŏnjip* [The complete works of Kim Yuk] (Seoul: Taedong munhwa yŏn'guwŏn, Sŏnggyun'gwan Taehakkyo, 1975), p. 279. Kim Yuk was appointed magistrate of Kaesŏng in the fourth lunar month of 1648, "Chamgok sŏnsaeng yŏnbo" [Chronological history of Kim Yuk], in *Chamgok chŏnjip* [The complete works of Kim Yuk] (Seoul: Taedong munhwa yŏn'guwŏn, Sŏnggyun'gwan Taehakkyo, 1975), p. 477. Chang Kukchong believed that cash had already been circulating even before 1634, not 1643 as Kim Yuk remarked, and that private minters must have been coining cash, "Sipch'il segi," pp. 48–49. See also Wŏn Yuhan, "Chosŏn hugi ŭi kŭmsok hwap'ye," pp. 104, 112–16.

13. One *ch'ing* contained 70 strings or 17,000 *mun* of cash. 80 *ch'ing* meant 5,600 strings or 1,360,000 *mun*.

14. *Hyojong sillok*, Hyojong 2.3.kyŏng'in, 2.3.chŏnghaek, cited in Wŏn Yuhan, "Yijo Sukchong sidae ŭi chujŏn," pp. 634–35; idem, "Chosŏn hugi ŭi kŭmsok hwap'ye," pp. 117–18. Just a few days before this meeting Hyojong had agreed to provide relief to peasants starving from famine by selling military grain reserves in Ŭiju, Anju, Pyongyang, and other places for cash. This action only indicated that the use of cash had become so widespread that it was preferable to convert rice stocks to currency as a means of providing relief rather than transporting rice directly to various points around the provinces. Contrary to what Wŏn Yuhan intimated in the first article cited above, this was not part of a general plan to finance an increase in the supply of cash.

15. MHBG 159:7a; *Hyojong sillok* 6:25b, Hyojong 2.4.kyŏng'o; Wŏn, "Chosŏn hugi ŭi hwap'ye," p. 118.

16. *Hyojong sillok* 6:31b, Hyojong 2.5.kich'uk.

17. Ibid. 7:3b, Hyojong 2.7.kapsin, cited in Wŏn, "Yijo Sukchong sidae ŭi hwap'ye," p. 636.

18. *Hyojong sillok* 7:38b, Hyojong 2.11.kyeryu, cited in Wŏn, "Chosŏn hugi ŭi kŭmsok hwap'ye," p. 118; "Yijo Sukchong sidae ŭi chujŏn," p. 641.

19. *Hyojong sillok* 8:20b, Hyojong 3.2.kiryu; ibid. 8:23a, Hyojong 3.2.kab'in; ibid. 8:24a, Hyojong 3.2.ŭrmyo. Wŏn Yuhan suspects that the opposition between the two men must have had some factional basis since Yun was Westerner and Hŏ was a Southerner, "Yijo Sukchong sidae ŭi chujŏn," p. 641 n. 31; idem, "Chosŏn hugi ŭi kŭmsok hwap'ye," pp. 118–19.

20. *Hyojong sillok* 10:16a, Hyojong 4.1.kapsin.

21. Ibid. 10:37b–38a, Hyojong 4.3.mujin; Wŏn gives the date at 4.3.kyŏng'o, but that date seems to be missing from the text, "Chosŏn hugi ŭi kŭmsok hwap'ye," p. 119 n. 78.

22. *Hyojong sillok* 12:18a, Hyojong 5.3.pyŏngjin; 12:19a-b, Hyojong 5.4.sinyu; 12:29b, Hyojong 5.4.chŏngmyo; Wŏn, "Yijo Sukchong sidae ŭi chujŏn, p. 643.

23. See n.25, below.

24. See n.25, below.

25. *Hyojong sillok* 12::39a–41a, Hyojong 5.6.muin; MHBG 159:7b–8a; Wŏn, "Yijo Sukchong sidae ŭi chujŏn," pp. 646–47 n.42.

26. MHBG 159:7a-b; Kim Yuk, "Chamgok sŏnsaeng yugo," 4:22a–22ba, dated kabo (1654), presumably between the ninth to eleventh lunar month; Wŏn, *Chosŏn hugi hwap'yesa yŏn'gu*, p. 87; idem, "Yijo Sukchong sidae ŭi chujŏn," p. 635. It seems strange that scholars who have worked on this problem have not found the text of Hyojong's edict and Kim's memorial in the *Sillok* or other sources. I have not had the time to conduct a search myself, but judging from Kim's reference to Hyojong's prohibition against the use of rough cloth for currency, the memorial should have been submitted shortly after the edict was issued.

27. *Hyojong sillok* 15:1a, Hyojong 6.7.sinmyo; 15:33b–34a, Hyojong 6.7.sinyu; Wŏn, "Yijo Sukchong sidae ŭi chujŏn," pp. 644–45. Kim was appointed chief state councilor in Hyojong 6.7.kab'in, *Hyojong sillok* 15:2b.

28. *Hyojong sillok* 15:33b–34a, Hyojong 6.12.sinyu, cited in Wŏn, "Yijo Sukchong sidae ŭi chujŏn," p. 645 n.36.

29. *Hyojong sillok* 6.12.kyehaek.

30. Ibid. 16:29a-b, Hyojong 7.4.kyŏngsin; SJW 7:783, cited in Wŏn, "Yijo sukchong sidae ŭi chujŏn," p. 644.

31. Ibid.

32. MHBG 159:9a-b; Wŏn, "Yijo Sukchong sidae ŭi chujŏn," pp. 644–45.

33. The best account is in SJW 7:968–69, Hyojong 7.9.26. The account in the PBS 2:510–11 is abridged, but Yi Man'ŭn appears to have extracted elements from the SJW for his account, in MHBG 159:8b–9a.

Hyojong's demand for repayment of grain loans in grain caused a brief flurry of debate after the low-ranking censor (Chŏng'ŏn) in the Office of the Censor-General, Min Yujung, argued that recalling loans in rice rather than allowing the people to repay them in cash was a betrayal of its promise to the people when it first granted the loans, and it had caused much ill feeling because most people had already accumulated cash to make repayment. SJW 7:979–88, Hyojong 7.10.15 through 7.10.23.

34. MHBG 159:9a-b.

35. MHBG 159:10a-b.

36. Wŏn, "Yijo Sukchong sidae ŭi chujŏn," pp. 642–47; "Chosŏn hugi ŭi kŭmsok hwap'ye," pp. 122–32.

CHAPTER 24. Yu Hyŏngwŏn's Analysis of Currency

1. PGSR 3:3b–4a.

2. Chung-hua shu-chü, ed., *Tz'u-hai* (Shanghai: 1947), p. 309.

3. PGSR 8:1a–2a. The "Treatise on Food and Money" from the *History of the Han Dynasty* (*Han-shu*) described the Chou-fu system of the Duke of Chou, the use of pearls, jade, gold, knives, and cloth as media of exchange in ancient China, and the shape of the ancient gold coin as round with a square hole. Ibid. 8:2b. See also Morohashi Tetsuji, comp., *Daikanwa jiten* [The great Sino-Japanese dictionary] (Tokyo: Taishū-kan shoten, 1955–59) 1:382.

4. PGSR 8:1a–2a.

5. Ibid. 8:2a-b.

6. Ibid. 8:10a–11b.

7. Ibid. 8:3a.

8. Ibid. 8:3a-b.

9. Ibid. 8:4b.

10. Ibid. 8:4b–5a.

11. Ibid. 8:5a-b.

12. Ibid. 8:5b.

13. Ibid. 8:7b–8a.

14. *Ajia rekishi jiten* 6:276, biography of Chang Kuei; PGSR 8:8a-b.

15. Gari Ledyard, *The Dutch Come to Korea* (Seoul: Royal Asiatic Society and Taewon Publishing Company, 1971).

16. PGSR 8:6a.

17. Ibid. 8:10a–11b.

18. Ibid. 8:8b–9a.

19. Ibid. 8:6b–7a.

20. Ibid. 8:8b–9a.

21. Ibid. 8:8b–9a.

22. Ibid. 8:9a–9b.

23. Ibid. 8:9b–10a.

24. Ibid. 8:11b–13a.

25. Ibid. 8:13b–14a.

26. Ibid. 8:14a-b.

27. Ibid. 8:14b–15a.

28. Ibid. 8:15a–17a.

29. Ibid. 8:17a-b, source cited is the *Shih-lin yen-yü* by Yeh Meng-te.

30. PGSR 8:17b–18a.

31. Ibid. 8:18a-b. Tillman described Hu Hung as one of the fundamentalist advocates of the literal restoration of the well-field system, Hoyt Cleveland Tillman, *Utilitarian Confucianism: Ch'en Liang's Challenge to Chu Hsi* (Cambridge: Harvard University Press, 1982), pp. 50–51.

32. David McLellan, *Karl Marx: His Life and Thought* (New York: Harper and Row, 1973, Harper Colophon ed., 1977), p. 162; Tom Bottomore, ed., *A Dictionary of Marxist Thought* (Cambridge: Harvard University Press, 1983), pp. 86, 377.

33. PGSR 8:19a; for the previous material, see 8:18b–19b.

34. Mark Elvin, *The Pattern of the Chinese Past* (Stanford: Stanford University Press, 1973), pp. 215–25; for the Wakō pirates and post-1570 commerce, see John E. Wills, Jr., "Maritime China from Wang Chih to Shih Lang," in Spence and Wills, eds., *From Ming to Ch'ing* (New Haven, Conn.: Yale University Press, 1979), pp. 210–20.

35. PGSR 8:19b–20a.

36. Ibid. 8:20a-b.

37. Ibid. 8:20b–21a.

38. Ibid. 8:21a-b; compare 8:21b, line 4, with KRS 19:4b, lines 2–3.

39. The *Samhan chungbo*, *Tongguk t'ongbo*, *Tongguk chungbo*, *Haedong chungbo*, and *Haedong t'ongbo*, PGSR 8:21b.

40. Referred to here as the five-*chong* cloth, since *chong* was synonymous with *sae* or *sŭng*.

41. Ibid. 8:21b–22a; KRS 19:14b–15b.

42. Wŏn Yuhan, "Pan'gye Yu Hyŏngwŏn ŭi kungjŏngjŏk hwap'yeron" [Yu Hyŏngwŏn's positive views on currency], in *Yu Hongnyŏl paksa hwagap kinyŏm nonch'ong* [Essays in commemoration of the sixtieth birthday of Dr. Yu Hongnyŏl] (Seoul: Hyeam Yu Hongnyŏl paksa Hwagap kinyŏm saŏp wiwŏnhoe, 1971), p. 300.

43. Wŏn Yuhan, "Kŭngjŏngjŏk hwap'yeron," p. 295.

44. PGSR 22a–23b.

45. MHBG 159:10a-b. Kwŏn Yŏng'ik has also stressed Yu's fundamental emphasis on the need for bold and decisive leadership to accomplish reform and overcome the forces of conservatism. Kwŏn Yŏng'ik, "Yu Hyŏngwŏn ŭi hwap'ye sasang e kwanhan yŏn'gu" [A study of Yu Hyŏngwŏn's thought on currency], *Taedong munhwa yŏn'gu* 11 (1977):63–64.

46. See chap. 23, above, for the background for this discussion.

47. PGSR 3:3b–4a.

48. Yu also noted that Tu Yu in the *T'ung-tien* wrote that that 1 *liang* or tael was equivalent to 24 *shu*. One *ch'ien* or .1 tael would then have been 2.4 *shu*, but since the calibration of the scale yielded figures three times greater than in T'ang times, the weight of .1 tael should have been three times greater, or 7.2 *shu*. Yu himself calculated that the present .1 tael (or 1 *chŏn* in Korean pronunciation) would be 7 *shu* by present scales, or 2 *shu* more than the five-*shu* coin. Ibid. 4:1a.

49. Yu also remarked that the price of brass was higher in the capital where it took 3 *yang* of brass to purchase 1 *p'il* of ordinary cloth (*sangmok*) but over 4 *yang* in Tongnae

(near Pusan). He anticipated that when it came time to mint a new coin, the authorities could expect that they would have to pay a high price for brass. Ibid. 4:4b.

50. Ibid. 4:1a-b, 5a.

51. See table 9, pp. 846–47.

52. PGSR 4:1b.

53. Ibid. 4:1a-b.

54. Kwŏn Yŏng'ik, "Yu Hyŏngwŏn ŭi hwap'ye sasang," p. 70 n. 40. Although not crucial to his argument, he appears to have mistaken Yu's estimates of grain and cash. Wŏn Yuhan wrote that Yu estimated annual grain taxes at four to five million *sŏm* (*sŏk*), but Yu used the term *kok*. Although *kok* could have been synonymous for *sŏm* in colloquial parlance at the time, Yu defined the term *kok* as equivalent to 10 *mal*, not 15 *mal* in the contemporary *sŏm*. Wŏn also cited Yu's estimate of 100–200,000 strings of cash as equivalent to 1–2 million *yang*, but I have chosen to estimate the number of coins rather than units of account. Besides, *yang* can only be determined by dividing the number of coins by Yu's proposed exchange rate with silver at 200 coins per *yang* of silver, so that the amount of *yang* for 100–200 million coins would be 500,000 to 1,000,000 *yang* (of silver). The same rule ought to apply as well for Yu's upper estimate of optimum copper imports. Wŏn Yuhan, "Kungjŏngjŏk hwap'yeron," pp. 295–96. Song Ch'ansik has covered the same issue, but he mistakenly reported that Yu estimated national tax revenues at 400–500,000 *kok* of grain, when it should have been 4–5 million *kok*. He also wrote that the cash equivalent of 400–500,000 *kok* of grain was 800,000 to 1 billion strings, but it should have been 4–5 million *kok* or 40–50 million *mal* converted to 800 million to 1 billion *coins!* Song Ch'ansik, "Chosŏn hugi haengjŏnnon" [The circulation of cash in the late Chosŏn period] *Han'guk sasang taegye* 2 (Seoul: Taedong munhwa yŏn'guwŏn, Sŏnggyun'gwan taehakkyo, 1976):793.

55. PGSR 4:5b–6a.

56. Kwŏn Yŏng'ik stressed this last point in "Yu Hyŏngwŏn ŭi hwap'ye sasang," pp. 72–73.

57. PGSR 4:1b–2b.

58. Ibid. 4:3b.

59. Ibid. 4:3a-b.

60. Prices and exchange rates are listed on ibid. 4:1b, 4b.

61. Ibid. 4:5a. Kwŏn Yŏng'ik also stressed this point and cited the writings of several Chinese scholars like Yeh Meng-te, Fan T'ai, and Lü Tsu-chien of the Sung to illustrate their belief that the volume of production was as much if not more responsible for price fluctuations than the money supply. "Yu Hyŏngwŏn ŭi hwap'ye sasang," p. 75, and p. 76 n. 52. See also Song Ch'ansik, "Chosŏn hugi haengjŏnnon," p. 791. Chang Kukchong's discussion of the value of cash relative to silver and rice was extremely useful, in "Sipch'il segi kŭmsok hwap'ye (tonghwa) ŭi yut'ong e taehayŏ" [The circulation of metallic currency in the seventeenth century], *Yŏksa kwahak* 6 (1961):55.

62. PGSR 4:5b, or after a poor crop 1 *chŏn* of silver would only buy 1 *mal* of grain but 3 *mal* after a bumper crop.

63. Ibid. 4:5a-b.

64. I disagree with the interpretation of Wŏn Yuhan that Yu regarded currency as second only in importance to land and agricultural production for the prosperity of the state and the people, because the classical point of view was that currency functioned primarily as a means of exchange that aided the circulation of goods, and not something that produced wealth independently. See Wŏn, "Sirhakcha ŭi hwap'ye kyŏngjeron" [Theories of a cash economy by *sirhak* scholars], *Tongbanghak chi* 26 (March 1981):157, 161; Wŏn Yuhan, "Kŭngjŏngjŏk hwap'yeron," p. 290.

65. While Wŏn Yuhan has contended that Yu wanted to expand "productive activities and productive capacity in society," the most that he may have desired might have been increased production of agricultural products, and possibly cotton cloth, but I have found no evidence that he was willing to expand industrial production as the main way for creating greater wealth. Wŏn Yuhan, "Sirhakcha ŭi hwap'ye kyŏngjeron," p. 163.

66. PGSR 4:6a–7a.

67. As mentioned above, Wŏn Yuhan accused Yu of being unrealistic by applying more advanced Chinese standards to Korea in the seventeenth century, but I agree with Yu's argument that the Koreans did have the capacity to adopt cash successfully at that time for a number of reasons: the commercial economy was already making progress both because of a probable increase in surplus production and greater private commerce outside the bounds of the licensed monopoly merchants in the capital, cash was already circulating in some parts of Korea because of minting undertaken by kings Injo and Hyojong in the 1620s, 1630s, and 1650s, and cash was adopted permanently only five years after Yu's death. See Wŏn Yuhan, "Kungjŏngjŏk hwap'yeron."

68. Arthur Schlesinger, Jr., *The Age of Jackson* (New York: Book Find Club, 1945).

CHAPTER 25. A Cycle of Inflation and Deflation

1. Pang Kijung has traced this trend and also found a statement by Song in 1681 that government officials were demanding cloth for tax payments of 8 *sae* and 45 "feet" in length, versus the legal regulations of 5 *sae* and 35 "feet." Song also said the people were predicting that the officials would increase their demands to 10 *sae* and 50 "feet" before they were through. Pang also cited Yu Hyŏngwŏn's statement (written some time before 1673) that 1 *p'il* of higher quality 6 *sae* "correct cloth" (*chŏngp'o*) was worth 30 *p'il* of rough cloth (*ch'up'o*). "Sipch'il-sipp'al segi chŏnban kŭmnap chose ŭi sŏngnip kwa chŏn'gae" [The establishment and development of money taxes in the seventeenth and first half of the eighteenth centuries], *Tongbanghak chi* 45 (November 1984):147, 154 n. 117. For other material in this section, see n.2 below.

2. SJW 14:966a-b, Kanghŭi 20 (Sukchong 7).1.15 (kisa). Wŏn Yuhan did not discuss the problem of cheating in the collection of rice and cloth taxes under the *taedong* system in "Sukchong sidae ŭi chujŏn e taehyŏ" [Minting of cash in Sukchong's reign] *Sahak yŏn'gu* 18 (1964):657.

3. *Sukchong sillok* 13 ha:31a, Sukchong 8.11.kyeryu; *Sukchong pogwŏl chŏng'o* [Errata] 13 ha:1b, *Chosŏn wangjo sillok* 38:618b, same date; Wŏn, "Sukchong sidae ŭi chujŏn," p. 657.

4. SJW 15:818c, Kanghŭi 22 (Sukchong 9).1.30; reported two weeks later in *Sukchong*

sillok, 14 sang:4a, Sukchong 9.1.ŭrmyo, and PBS 3:604, Sukchong 9.1.15; Wŏn, "Sukchong sidae ŭi chujŏn," p. 657.

5. SJW 17:723a, Sukchong 15.3.3 (kyŏng'o); *Sukchong sillok* 20:21a, Sukchong 15.3.kyŏng'o. For other citations requesting that individual central agencies or provinces be allowed to mint cash after 1685, see Wŏn Yuhan, "Sukchong sidae ŭi chujŏn," p. 657. Pang Kijung also remarked that Sukchong's main goal in minting and circulating cash was to raise more revenue for the government, "Sipch'il-sipp'al chŏnban segi," p. 159.

6. PBSDN, 4:236, Sukchong 15.9.7; SJW 16:921d–922a, Kanghŭi 28.9.7 (kyŏngja); *Sukchong sillok* 21:31a; Wŏn, "Sukchong sidae ŭi chujŏn," p. 658. It is difficult to judge just what cloth taxes were to be commuted to cash at this rate, but the table of cash commutations of the cloth tax in 1679 presented by Pang Kijung shows only that the *taedong* tax payable in cloth for Chŏlla and Kyŏngsang provinces were to be commuted to cash for one-third the taxes due, and only with the agreement of the taxpayer. For other cloth taxes, the percentage of tax to be commuted to cash was either 50 or 100 percent. Possibly Kwŏn intended to require one-third of all such cloth taxes to be commuted to cash. See Pang, "Sipch'il-sipp'al chŏnban segi," p. 159.

7. PBS 4:422, Sukchong 17.10.24; SJW 18:569a-b, Kanghŭi 31.8.23 (kyŏngja); *Sukchong sillok*, 24:21b, Sukchong 18.8.kyŏngja; PBS 4:854, Sukchong 18.10.4.

8. SJW 18:742c-d, Kanghŭi 32.7.3 (ŭrsa); Wŏn, "Sukchong sidae ŭi chujŏn," p. 659; Tashiro Kazui, *Kinsei Nitchō tsūkō boekishi no kenkyū* [A study of the history of Japanese-Korean trade in recent times] (Tokyo: Sōbunsha, 1976), pp. 272–75. The annual import of 300,000 *kŭn* of copper up to 1693 was 44 percent of total Japanese copper exports ($^{300,000}/_{681,387}$ *kŭn*) in 1693. If that import figure were constant, it would have been 68.5 percent and 71 percent in 1691 and 1692 when total Japanese exports were only 437,667 and 421,874 *kŭn*, respectively. Tashiro argues that the expansion of Japanese copper mining was stimulated by increased Korean demand for copper after 1678. Ibid., p. 274, table II-11.

9. SJW 19:266c-d, Kanghŭi 33.9.13 (muin), (1695); PBSDN 4:725–6, Sukchong 21.9.29, 21.10.2; ibid. 4:740, Sukchong 21.11.21; MHBG 159:12b.

10. To compare these prices in 1694 with Yu Hyŏngwŏn's exchange schedule, Kim said that in the spring 1 *mal* of rice was worth .5 *yang* or 50 *mun* of cash, or 50 coins. This price was 2.5 times Yu's fixed value of 20 *mun*/*mal*, but this was exactly the rice/cash exchange rate that Ch'oe said existed after the fall harvest when rice was at its cheapest level. If the average rice price were taken at 3 *mal*/*yang* or 33.3 coins per *mal*, then either Yu's estimate of the cash price of rice was $^{13.3}/_{33.3}$ or 40 percent higher than the "real" market price, or the price of rice had dropped by that amount between 1670 and 1694.

11. MHBG 159:13a-b.

12. *Sukchong sillok* 29:33b, Sukchong 21.12.musul; Wŏn Yuhan, "Sukchong sidae ŭi chujŏn," p. 658.

13. *Sukchong sillok* 29:33b, Sukchong 21.12.musul; Wŏn Yuhan, "Sukchong sidae ŭi chujŏn," p. 658.

14. *Sukchong sillok* 30:44a-b, Sukchong 22.8.pyŏngsul; Wŏn Yuhan, "Sukchong sidae ŭi chujŏn," p. 662; Tashiro Kazui, *Kinsei Nitchō tsūkō boekishi no kenkyū*, p. 274. Japanese copper exports plummeted precipitously from 1.4 million *kŭn* in 1697 to 26,453 *kŭn*

in 1698. While part of this reduction may have been caused by stricter export controls in Japan, a large part had to have been the product of King Sukchong's ban on further minting. Ibid., p. 274.

15. Yu Wŏndong, *Han'guk kŭndae kyŏngjesa yŏn'gu* [Studies in the recent economic history of Korea] (Seoul: Ilchisa, 1977), pp. 214–24. Kang Man'gil mentioned two private slaves steering two ships back from P'yŏng'an Province to the capital with a load of salt in 1710 who were driven by a storm to China. He speculated that they were either merchants themselves or in the employ of private Han River merchants in the capital. Kang Man'gil, *Chosŏn hugi sang'ŏp chabon ŭi paltal* [The development of commercial capital in the late Chosŏn period] (Seoul: Koryŏ taehakkyo ch'ulp'anbu, 1973), p. 70.

16. Kang Man'gil, *Chosŏn hugi sang'ŏp chabon ŭi sŏngjang: Kyŏngsijŏn Songsangdŭng ŭi Toga sang'ŏb'ŭl chungsimŭro* [The growth of commercial capital in late Chosŏn: Wholesaling by the licensed monopolies in the capital and the merchants of Kaesŏng], *Han'guksa yŏn'gu* 1 (September 1968):80–87; Kang, *Chosŏn hugi sang'ŏp chabon ŭi paltal*, pp. 168–75.

17. Wŏn Yuhan, "Sukchong sidae ŭi chujŏn," pp. 662–63; Chang Kukchong, "Sipp'al segi ŭi tonghwa chujo wa chŏnhwang munje" [The minting of copper cash and the problem of the shortage in the money supply in the eighteenth century], *Yŏksa kwahak* 1 (1963):41, 49.

18. Wŏn Yuhan, "Sukchong sidae ŭi chujŏn," pp. 664–65; MHBG 159:14a; SJW 30:622c-d, Yunjŏng 2 (Kyŏngjong 4).2.9 (kyech'uk).

19. The above remarks combine statements Yŏngjo made on two occasions: PBSDN 7:726–7, Yŏngjo 1.8.8; ibid., 7:764–65, Yŏngjo, 1.10.6; MHBG 159:14a-b; Wŏn Yuhan, "Sukchong sidae ŭi chujŏn," p. 55; Han'guk ŭnhaeng, *Chŭngbo Han'guk hwap'yesa* [The revised edition of the history of currency in Korea] (Seoul: Han'guk ŭnhaeng, 1969), pp. 49–50.

20. PBSDN 8:68d–72b, Yŏngjo 3.5.11; Wŏn Yuhan, "Sippal segi e issŏsŏ ŭi hwap'ye chŏngch'aek: tongjŏn ŭi chujo sajŏp chungsi" [Currency policy in the eighteenth century: The minting of copper cash], *Sahak yon'gu* 19 (April 1967):56.

21. PBSDN 8:129d, Yŏngjo 3.9.21; Wŏn Yuhan, "Sippal segi," p. 56.

22. *Yŏngjo sillok* 13:7b, Yŏngjo 3.9.ŭrchuk; Wŏn Yuhan, "Sippal segi," p. 57.

23. Other officials who opposed abolishing cash included the following. Yu Manjung, fourth minister of the Ministry of War, agreed that cash corrupted mores and stimulated thievery, but nothing better could be found to take its place, and the king had no choice but to mint more of it. Sŏ Myŏngyŏn, the third minister of the Ministry of Taxation, merely affirmed the general view that even though Yŏngjo's desire was to abolish cash, another medium of exchange would produce consequences as difficult as the present troubles.

24. James B. Palais, *Politics and Policy in Traditional Korea* (Cambridge: Harvard University Press, 1975), p. 107.

25. Or 400 percent higher than the 200 coins/*yang* of silver rate of 1679 and Yu Hyŏngwŏn's recommended rate of about 1670.

26. This recommendation would have cut 2 *yang* and 2 *p'il* from the tax rate, and would only make sense for those taxpayers who owed 3 *p'il* per person.

27. SJW 35:516a–526c, Yungjŏng 5.11.5 (chŏngsa) (1727); *Yŏngjo sillok* 14:3a-b, Yŏngjo 3.11.chŏngsa. Brief summary in Wŏn Yuhan, "Sippal segi," p. 56.

28. This meant that the price of rice had declined by 33 or 67 percent in the past few years, but it must have risen since the early 1670s because Yu Hyŏngwŏn had prescribed a rice/cash exchange rate of 5 *mal/yang* (100 coins) of cash.

29. See n. 27, above.

30. SJW 35:516a–526c, Yungjŏng 5.11.5 (chŏngsa) (1727); *Yŏngjo sillok* 14:3a-b, Yŏngjo 3.11.chŏngsa. Brief summary in Wŏn Yuhan, "Sippal segi," p. 56.

31. Han Woo-keun, *Yijo hugi ŭi sahoe wa sasang* [Society and thought in the late Yi dynasty] (Seoul: Urchi munhwasa, 1961), pp. 218–23, esp. p. 222 for the quotation. Wŏn Yuhan, "Sŏngho Yi Ik pujŏngjŏk hwap'yeron" [Yi Ik's negative view of cash], *Yŏksa hakpo* 48 (December 1970):53–66.

32. Wŏn, "Sŏngho Yi Ik," pp. 66–67.

33. Ibid., pp. 68, 70–72.

34. Ibid., p. 69. See also Wŏn Yuhan, *Chosŏn hugi hwap'yesa yŏn'gu*, pp. 190–98.

35. SJW 40:469a–70b, Yunjŏng 9 (Yŏngjo 7).9.20 (kyŏngjin); *Yŏngjo sillok*, 30:26b, same date; Wŏn Yuhan, "Sippal segi," pp. 57–58; Han'guk ŭnhaeng, *Chŭngbo Han'guk hwap'yesa*, p. 50.

36. SJW 45:384c–385c, Ongjŏng 13 (Yŏngjo 11).2.10 (ŭrhaek); *Yŏngjo sillok* 40:52b, same date.

37. *Yŏngjo sillok* 41:8a, Yŏngjo 12.2.kyesa; SJW 45:690a-b, Kŏllyung 1.2.29 (kyesa). Another proposal for multiple-denomination cash was rejected again later in 1737, Han'guk ŭnhaeng, *Chŭngbo Han'guk hwap'yesa*, p. 51.

38. Palais, *Politics and Policy in Traditional Korea*, chap. 8, "Monetary Policy."

CHAPTER 26. Cash and Economic Change after 1731

1. Han Yŏngguk, author of the preface to Yu Suwŏn, *Usŏ* (Seoul: Sŏul taehakkyo kojŏn kanhaengsa, 1971), pp. 1–9; Kang Man'gil, "Chosŏn hugi sang'ŏp ŭi munjejŏm: *Usŏ* ŭi sang'op chongch'aek punsŏk" [Problems in commerce in the late Chosŏn period: An analysis of the commercial policies contained in the *Usŏ*], *Han'guksa yŏn'gu* 6 (September 1971):53 n.1.

2. Kang Man'gil, "Chosŏn hugi sang'ŏp ŭi munjejŏm," pp. 54–61, 65–68.

3. Ibid., pp. 61–65.

4. Ibid., pp. 69, 72.

5. Yu Suwŏn, *Usŏ*, pp. 144–45. I have rearranged the order of the arguments made in the original.

6. *Yŏngjo sillok* 55:26a, Yŏngjo 18.4.imja; Han'guk ŭnhaeng [Bank of Korea], *Chŭngbo Han'guk hwap'yesa* [Revised edition of the history of currency in Korea] (Seoul: Han'guk ŭnhaeng, 1969), p. 52.

7. The *Munhŏnbigo* included a memorial submitted in 1737 by Councilor of the Left Song Inmyŏng that mentioned the noncash buffer zone in the northern two provinces, but also reported that the population was ignoring the ban. He opposed punishing all the violators right away because the state had the obligation to "instruct" them before met-

ing out punishment. He recommended that the provincial governors again issue orders promising strict punishment for illegal circulation of cash, after which the government could use all the cash it received to buy grain at market prices to provide relief in advance of an anticipated shortage in the next harvest, or to distribute the cash to districts south of the buffer zone to provide cash loans to the peasants, and then collect the repayments in cash, part of which would be used to buy grain, and part diverted to the income of the magistrate (the *hoerok* or recording fee). MHBG 159:16a-b.

8. James B. Palais, *Politics and Policy in Traditional Korea* (Cambridge: Harvard University Press, 1975), p. 169.

9. *Yŏngjo sillok* 55:30b–31a, Yŏngjo 18.6.sinmyo; SJW 51:674a–675b, Kŏllyung 7.6.4; *Chŭngbu Han'guk hwap'yesa*, p. 52.

10. A small multiple-denomination coin worth 2 pieces of cash (*tang'ijŏn*) was first minted in 1679. It weighed .25 *yang* (8.375 grams). Han'guk ŭnhaeng, *Chŭngbo Han'guk hwap'yesa*, p. 43.

11. SJW 51:691b-d, Kŏllyung 7.6.16 (kyemyo); *Yŏngjo sillok* 55:33a, Yŏngjo 18.6.kyemyo; Han'guk ŭnhaeng, *Chŭngbo Han'guk hwap'yesa*, p. 52.

12. Tashiro Kazui, *Kinsei Nissen tsūkō bōekishi no kenkyū* [A study of the Japan-Korea trade in recent times] (Tokyo: Sōbunsha, 1981), pp. 323–29, 334–39.

13. SJW 51:695d–696c, 697c, Kŏllyung 7.6.19 (p'yŏng'o); *Yŏngjo sillok* 55:33b–34a, Yŏngjo 18.6.p'yŏng'o; PBS 11:270–71. For a brief summary of the debate in 1742, see Wŏn Yuhan, "Chosŏn hugi hwap'ye chŏngch'aek e taehan ilkoch'al: Koaekchŏn ŭi chuyong non'ŭirŭl chungsimŭro" [A study of late Chosŏn currency policy: Proposals to mint multiple-denomination cash], *Han'guksa yŏn'gu* 6 (September 1971):77.

14. Ibid.

15. *Yŏngjo sillok* 55:33b–34a, Yŏngjo 18.6.p'yŏng'o.

16. Ibid. 71:18a, Yŏngjo 26.5.sinhaek; MHBG 159:16b–17a.

17. Wŏn Yuhan, "Chosŏn hugi hwap'ye chŏngch'aek e taehan ilkoch'al," p. 81 n.28; Wŏn Yuhan, "Sipp'al segi e issŏsŏ ŭi hwap'ye chŏngch'aek: Tongjŏn ŭi chujo sajŏp chungsim" [Currency policy in the eighteenth century: The minting of copper cash], *Sahak yŏn'gu* 19 (April 1967):62.

18. Kang Man'gil, *Chosŏn hugi sang'ŏp chabon ŭi sŏngjang: Kyŏngsijŏn songsangdŭng ŭi toga sang'ŏb'ŭl chungsimŭro* [The growth of commercial capital in late Chosŏn: Wholesaling by the licensed monopolies in the capital and the merchants of Kaesŏng] *Han'guksa yŏn'gu* 1 (September 1968):80–87; idem, *Chosŏn hugi sang'ŏp chabon ŭi paltal* [The development of commercial capital in the late Chosŏn period] (Seoul: Koryŏ taehakkyo ch'ulp'anbu, 1973), pp. 168–75, 197.

19. Yu Wŏndong, *Han'guk kŭndae kyŏngjesa* [Studies in the recent economic history of Korea] (Seoul: Ilchisa, 1977), pp. 224–28; Kang Man'gil, *Chosŏn hugi sang'ŏp chabon ŭi paltal*, pp. 73, 175–83. For the origins of the *yug'ŭijŏn*, see Yu Kyosŏng, "Soŭl Yug'ŭijŏn yŏn'gu" [A study of the Seoul six licensed shops], *Yŏksa hakpo* 8 (1955):377–434.

20. *Chŏngjo sillok* 12:55b, Chŏngjo 5.11.kihaek, cited in Kang Man'gil, *Chosŏn hugi sang'ŏp chabon ŭi paltal*, p. 197.

21. Ibid., p. 197.

22. Sin Sŏkho, "Haeje" [Explanatory note], in Pak Chega, *Chŏngyujip: pu Pukhag'ŭi*

[The collected works of Pak Chega, with the essay on learning from the north appended] (Seoul: Kuksa p'yŏnch'an wiwŏhoe, 1971), pp. 1–5 at the end of the volume.

23. Pak Chega, *Chŏngyujip*, p. 408; Kim Yongdŏk, *Chosŏn hugi sasangsa yŏn'gu* [Studies in the history of thought in late Chosŏn] (Seoul: Ŭryu munhwasa, 1977), p. 170.

24. Ibid., pp. 170–71.

25. Pak Chega, *Chŏngyujip*, pp. 408–9; Kim Yongdŏk, *Chosŏn hugi sasangsa yŏn'gu*, p. 170.

26. Yu Wŏndong, *Han'guk kŭndae kyŏngjesa*, pp. 229–37, 248–53, 290–93, 300. Ironically, the ironmakers granted monopoly sales over tools made from scrap iron suffered from this decision as well because the old licensed iron shop recaptured the business. Kang Man'gil, "Chosŏn hugi sang'ŏp chabon ŭi sŏngjang," pp. 88–90; idem, *Chosŏn hugi sang'ŏp chabon ŭi paltal*, pp. 74–75, 188–95; Yu Kyosŏng, "Sŏul Yug'ŭijŏn yŏn'gu," pp. 389–93.

27. For a discussion of the effects of the Ch'ae Chegong's joint-sales policy of 1791, i.e., the limit on monopoly privileges to the six shops, on metalworkers, furriers, hatmakers, and other artisans, see Kang Man'gil, *Chosŏn hugi sang'ŏp chabon ŭi paltal*, pp. 133–50; Song Ch'ansik, *Yijo hugi sugong'ŏp e kwanhan yŏn'gu* [A study of manufacture in the late Yi dynasty] (Seoul: Sŏul taehakkyo ch'ulp'anbu, 1973), pp. 22–42.

28. See n. 27.

29. MHBG 159:10a-b.

30. Tashiro Kazui, *Kinsei Nitchō tsūkyō bōekishi no kenkyū*, pp. 360–62, 367, 371–72. Wŏn Yuhan found less exact statistics in Korean records. He found one report in 1734 that annual imports had come to several hundred thousand *kŭn* of copper, and that 30,000 *kŭn* was imported in 1634, and 45,000 *kŭn* in 1693. Copper imports were also suspended in 1742 because it was costing too much silver to buy. Import of zinc from China was also restricted by both the Korean government to reduce silver exports and by the Chinese government to restrict the outflow of zinc. Wŏn Yuhan, "Sipp'al segi e issŏsŏ ŭi hwap'ye chŏngch'aek," pp. 75–78.

31. Wŏn Yuhan has interpreted the reduction of dependence on Japanese copper imports, and the production of surplus copper from Korean mines as important indicators of economic development, in "Chosŏn hugi hwap'ye chŏngch'aek e taehan ilkoch'al," pp. 93–95. For his discussion of copper mining, see idem, "Sipp'al segi e issŏsŏ ŭi hwap'ye chŏngch'aek," pp. 78–83.

32. The magistrate of Suan, Kang Chunhŭm, also proposed a 2-cash coin in 1813. Wŏn Yuhan, "Chosŏn hugi hwap'ye chŏngch'aek e kwanhan ilkoch'al," pp. 78–87; Palais, *Politics and Policy in Traditional Korea*, p. 169.

33. Pak Chega, *Chŏngyujip*, pp. 408–9; Kim Yongdŏk, *Chosŏn hugi sasangsa yŏn'gu*, p. 170.

34. U Chŏnggyu, *Kyŏngje yaon* [Views from a rustic on the management of the country], Yi Iksŏng, trans. (Seoul: Ŭryu munhwasa, 1973), pp. 295–96.

35. Ibid., pp. 293–95.

36. Chŏng Iksŏp, "Pak Chiwŏn ŭi saeng'ae wa sasang" [The life and thought of Pak Chiwŏn], in Honam munhwa yŏn'guso [Institute of Chŏlla culture], ed., *Yi Ŭrho paksa chŏngnyŏn kinyŏm Sirhak nonch'ong* [Collected essays on practical learning in honor

of the retirement of Dr. Pak Ŭrho] (Kwangju: Chŏnnam taehakkyo ch'ulp'anbu, 1975), pp. 475–83.

37. Kwŏn Yŏng'ik, "Pukhakp'a ŭi hwapye sasang e kwanhan yŏn'gu" [A study of the thought on currency of the northern learning scholars], *Han'guk kyŏngje* 4 (September 1976):24–26.

38. Wŏn Yuhan, "Sirhakcha ŭi hwap'ye sasang palchŏn e taehan koch'al: Kŭm ŭnhwa ŭi t'ongyongnon'ŭl chungsimŭro" [A study of the development of practical learning thought on currency, in particular the idea of circulating gold and silver currency], *Tongbanghak chi* 23–24 (February 1980):152–56; Kwŏn Yŏng'ik, "Pukhakp'a ŭi hwap'ye sasang," pp. 36–38; Kang Man'gil, "Sang'ŏp kyoyŏngnon," in Taedong munhwa yŏn'guwŏn [Taedong Institute of Culture], *Han'guk sasang taegye: sahoe kyŏngje sasang p'yŏn* [Grand outline of Korean thought: Volume on social and economic thought] (Seoul: Sŏnggyun'-gwan taehakkyo, 1976), pp. 543–46.

39. Kwŏn Yong'ik, "Pukhakp'a ŭi hwap'ye sasang," pp. 35–36; Wŏn Yuhan, "Sipp'al segi e issŏssŏ ŭi hwap'ye chŏngch'aek," p. 73.

40. Kwŏn, "Pukhakp'a ŭi hwap'ye sasang," pp. 39–41.

41. Kim Yongdŏk, *Chosŏn hugi sasangsa yŏn'gu*, pp. 192–96; Chŏng Yagyong, *Kyŏngse yup'yo* 2:31a–32a, in *Chŏng Tasan chŏnso* [The collected works of Chŏng Tasan], *ha* (vol. 3), p. 38; idem, *Tasan nonch'ŏng*, Yi Iksŏng, trans. (Seoul: Ŭryu mun'go, 1972), pp. 213–15, 312–13; Wŏn Yuhan, "Sirhakcha ŭi hwap'ye sasang palchŏn e taehan koch'al: Kŭm ŭnhwa ŭi t'ongyongnon'ŭl chungsimŭro" [A study of the development of practical learning thought on currency, in particular the idea of circulating gold and silver currency] *Tongbanghak chi* 23–24 (February 1980):157–61.

42. Kim Yongdŏk, *Chosŏn hugi sasangsa yŏn'gu*, pp. 202–6.

43. Wŏn Yuhan, "Chosŏn hugi hwap'ye chŏngch'aek e kwanhan ilkoch'al," pp. 87–89.

44. Ibid., pp. 89–93, 95–97.

45. An Pyŏngt'ae, *Chōsen kindai keizaishi kenkyū* [A study of modern Korean economic history] (Tokyo: Nihon hyōronsha, 1975), pp. 109–14.

46. Wŏn Yuhan, "Chosŏn hugi hwap'ye chŏngch'aek e taehan ilkoch'al," pp. 97–98; Palais, *Politics and Policy in Traditional Korea*, pp. 170–73.

PART VI. Conclusion

1. Pak Chega, *Chŏngyujip: pu Pukhag'ŭi* [The collected works of Pak Chega, with the essay on learning from the north appended] (Seoul: Kuksa p'yŏnch'an wiwŏnhoe, 1971), p. 409; Song Ch'ansik, "Pak Chiwŏn ŭi *Yŏnhaengjip*" [The travelogues of Pak Chiwŏn's trips to Yen-ching], in Yŏksa hakhoe, ed., *Sirhak yŏn'gu immun* (Seoul: Ilchogak, 1973): 179–81.

Glossary

aak 雅樂 classical musicians
abyŏng 牙兵 officers' personal aides known as the ivory soldiers
aengnaesaeng 額內生 regular quota students
aengnaeyŏk 額內役 regular quota service
aeg'oe kyosaeng 額外役生 extra-quota school students
aeg'oe samosok 額外私募屬 recruitment by official of extra-quota men for low-rate service
aeg'oesaeng 額外生 extra-quota students. See *aeg'oe kyosaeng*
aeg'oeyŏk 額外役 extra-quota service
ajŏn 衙前 yamen attendants
akkong 樂工 slave musicians
aksaeng 樂生 commoner musicians
alsŏng 謁聖 special examinations
Amhaeng ŏsa 暗行御史 Secret Censor
amun tunjŏn 衙門屯田 yamen colonies
An-ch'a-shih (Ch.) 按察使 governor; see Kuan-ch'a-shih.
arokchŏn 衙祿田 land previously set aside for provision of district salaries
ch'abi 差備 specialized workmen
chabo 資保 equipment support persons
chaboin 資保人 material support persons
chabyŏk (*tsu-pi*, Ch.) 自辟 right of the magistrate to appoint his own subordinates
chabyŏk 雜役 miscellaneous forms of compulsory labor service or taxes
ch'adae 自代 having a high official recommend the name of a substitute to replace him within three days of his own appointment
chaebŏl 財閥 cartel
ch'aeji 采地 prebends granted by King Wen (Chou) for hereditary official families
ch'aek 策 (essays) on policy
ch'aek hyŏllyang 策賢良 asking the worthy and good to write answers to policy questions
chaemul 才物 chattel goods
ch'aeŭp 采邑 fiefs of feudal vassals
ch'ain 差人 commissioners
chajuch'ijigwan (Ch.) 自主治之官 local autonomous officials
Ch'albang 察訪 chief of a Post-station
cham 站 hostels
Ch'ambong 參奉 tomb guardian
Ch'amha 參下 officials of ranks 6-9
Ch'amji 參知 assistant vice-minister of

the Ministry of War
Ch'amni 參理 consultant
ch'am'ŭp 站邑 government hostels
chang 長 elder, one 10-20 years older than ego
Ch'ang 倉 granary
Chang-chou (p.n.) 漳州
Chang-ku 掌固 Chou dynasty official in charge of walls and moats
Ch'ang-p'ing ts'ang (Ch.) 常平倉 Ever-Normal Granaries
Ch'ang-ts'an-kuan (Ch.) 常參官 Regular Court Counselors (Sung) of fifth rank or higher
chang-tsung (Ch.; Kor., *changjong*) 長從 long-term, professional soldiers
Chang'agwŏn 掌樂院 Court of Music
Changch'o 壯抄 Robust Select Soldiers
Changdan (p.n.) 長湍
Changgŭmsa 掌禁司 Bureau of Forbidden Affairs
changgwan 將官 constable, guard officer
Changgyo 將校 general or commander in charge of the battalions
Changhŭnggo 長興庫 Long Prosperity Warehouse
chang'in 匠人 artisans in state employ
changja 長者 an elder
changjong (Ch., *chang-tsung*) 長從 long-term, professional soldiers
changmun 場門 local markets
changni 長利 usurious loans
changse 場税 market taxes
Changyesa 掌隸司 Slave Bureau, proposed by Yu Hyŏngwŏn
Changyewŏn 掌隸院 Slave Agency (early Chosŏn dynasty)
Changyongdae 壯勇隊 special military unit est. 1459
Changyongwi 壯勇衛 Robust and Brave Guards
ch'anong 次農 secondary farmers
ch'ao (Ch.) 鈔 single bill of paper money (Sung)
Chapchik 雜職 miscellaneous posts
Chapch'ŏlchŏn 雜鐵廛 metal scrap shops
chapkwa 雜科 technical examinations
chapsaekkun 雜色軍 miscellaneous reserve soldiers
chapse 雜税 miscellaneous taxes
Ch'asawŏn 差使員 (river transport grain) commissioners
Chasŏm chŏhwago 資贍楮貨庫 Paper Money Treasury (late Koryŏ)
chayŏn ji ri 自然之理 principle of nature
ch'e (Ch., *t'i*) 體 substance, essence
ch'ea 遞兒 sinecures
ch'eajik 遞兒職 sinecure
Che-chiang system (Ch.) 浙江 Late Ming military organization of Ch'i Chi-kuang
Che-ch'ung-fu, or *fu* (Ch.) 折衝府, 府 One of 600-odd assault-resisting garrisons in the Sui and T'ang *fu-ping* military system
chegam 諸監 chiefs of directorates
chehu 諸侯 feudal lords
Chejo 提調 commissioner, or assistant commissioner (of the Border Defense Command or other agencies)
Ch'en dynasty (Ch.) 陳 (A.D. 557-87).
Ch'eng (Ch.) 丞 assistant magistrate (Ch'in)
Ch'eng-chün 成均 National Academy
Ch'eng-hsiang (Ch.) 丞相 prime minister
Cheng-shih-t'ang (Ch.) 政事堂 Hall of State Affairs
chesa 祭祀 ancestral rites
chesŏn 諸選 men who passed selection examinations
chesul 制述 written examination
chesŭng pangnyak 制勝方略 "victory strategy" adopted at the time of the Japanese pirate attack of 1555, the

ŭlmyo waebyŏn
ch'et'ong 體統 the legitimate order of society
Chewŏn 諸員 runners
Ch'i dynasty 齊 A.D. 479-502
Ch'i, state of (China)
Chi-chü-chu 起居注 *Records of Daily Comings and Goings*
Chi-hsiao hsin-shu 紀效新書 book by Ch'i Chi-kuang
chi-t'ien (Ch.) 籍田 see *chŏkchŏn*.
Chia-ch'ing era (Ch.) 嘉靖 Ming dynasty, 1522-66
Chia-li (Ch.) 家禮 *Family Rites*
Chiang-nan 江南 region in South China
chiao-ch'ao (Ch.) 交鈔 paper bill in Chin dynasty (12-13th c.)
chiao-tzu (Ch.) 交子 paper scrip issued in early 11th c., Sung dynasty
Chibong yusŏl 芝峰類說 text by Yi Sugwang
Chib'ŭi 執義 second inspector in the Office of the Inspector-General (Sahŏnbu)
chieh (Ch.) 解 document of "release" granted to an official who had been transferred absolving him of financial or other responsibilities for his post
Chieh-tu-shih (Ch.) 節度使 military commissioners
Chien (Ch.) 監 inspector
ch'ien (Ch.) 賤 base
ch'ien (Ch.) 錢 piece of cash
ch'ien-pu fang-t'ien (Ch.) 千步方田 thousand-paced square fields
Chien-ch'a yü-shih (Ch.) 監察御史 investigating censors
Chigwan 地官 officer of earth
Chigwŏl 直月 secretary of a community compact
chigyŏk 職役 service
chih-fen-t'ien (Ch.) 職分田 office land
chiha 支下 to make disbursements
chih-chi (Ch.) 質劑 paper scrip
chik 職 job
chikchŏn 職田 "office land," or prebendal grants to officeholders
chikchŏng 直定 direct recruitment
Chikch'ŏng 直廳 attendants assigned to a post or office
chikpunjŏn 職分田 office land
Ch'ilch'ŏllyang (p.n.) 漆川梁 Kŏje Island
ch'ilchŏng 七情 seven emotions
chin 鎮 garrisons
chin 陳 fallow
ch'in 親 having a royal parent; royal relationship
Chin dynasty (Ch.) 晉 A.D. 265-90
Chin dynasty (Ch.) 金 A.D. 1115-1234
Ch'in dynasty (Ch.) 秦 227-207 B.C.
chin-shih (Ch.) 進士 advanced scholar
Chin-ssu Lu 近思錄 *Record of Things Near at Hand*
chinbo 鎮堡 local garrisons and forts
chinbong 進奉 offerings of food from the provinces to capital officials to supplement short salaries after the Imjin War
ch'inch'ŏk 親戚 close relatives
Chindo (p.n.) 珍島 Chin Island
Ching (Ch.) 卿 chief minister (Chou)
Ch'ing dynasty (Ch.) 清 A.D. 1644-1911
Chingbirok 懲毖錄 "Precautions Against Attack" (by Yu Sŏngnyŏng)
ch'ing-i (Ch.) 清議 pure discussion
Ching-lüeh (Ch.) 經略 military commissioner (Ming)
ch'ing-miao (Ch.) 青苗 green shoots grain loan policy of Wang An-shih (Sung), A.D. 1069
Ching-t'ien lei-shou 井田類收
chin'gwan 鎮管 regional command garrison of central garrison system of 1457

chinhŏn 進獻 tribute payments to the Ch'ing court
chinjang 鎮將 garrison commanders
ch'injin 親盡 limiting inheritance of royal blood to four generations
Chinju (p.n.) 晉州
Chinjusa 陳奏使 envoy to present a memorial to the emperor
Chinmu. See Chŏmjŏl chesa 鎮撫
chinsa 進士 advanced scholar. Literary licentiate degrees
Chinsa 鎮使 garrison commander
chinsang 進上 royal tribute; tribute in local products to the king and royal family
Chinsawŏn 進士院 Hall for Advanced Scholars
chinyŏngjang 鎮營將 another term for *yŏngjang*
Chip'yŏng-hyŏn (p.n.) 砥平縣
chiu-ming 九命 the nine mandated ranks of early China
chiu-p'in 九品 nine ranks
cho 租 tax or rent
cho (Ch., *tiao*) 調 the T'ang capitation tax for tribute
ch'o 哨 company (military organization)
ch'ŏ 妻 wife
Chobangjang 助防將 auxiliary defense officer
choch'am 朝參 court audience
Choch'ang 漕倉 Maritime Transport Granaries
choch'ong 烏銃 fowling piece or musket
ch'odae 召待 royal audience
choe 罪 crimes
Ch'ogwan 哨官 company commander
chŏhwa 楮貨 paper money
Chojisŏ 造紙署 papermaking agency
chojol 漕卒 grain transport workers
chŏk 嫡 legitimate sons
chŏk 族 local community unit (Chou)
chŏkcha 嫡子 legitimate son
chŏkchangja 嫡長子 eldest son of a legitimate wife
chŏkchang-jason 嫡長子孫 eldest sons and grandsons of legitimate wives
Chokch'inwi 族親衛 Royal Relative Guards
chŏkchŏn 籍田 ruler's ceremonious cultivation of his own plot
chŏkchŏng 足丁 full quota land grant to an adult able-bodied male liable for military service (Koryŏ)
chokse 族世 hereditary lineage
chŏksŏ 嫡庶 legitimate sons and nothoi (sons of concubines)
choktang 族黨 sons and grandsons and lineage relations
chŏl 節 nodes of a bamboo stalk
Chŏlchesa 節度使 commissioners of ordering and organizing
chŏlka 折价 the equivalent value or price of one thing in terms of another
Chŏlla Province 全羅
Ch'ŏlli (Ch., *T'ien-li*) 天理 principle of Heaven, heavenly principle
chŏllon 田論 Tasan's essay on land
Chŏllyegwan 典禮官 ritual officials
chŏlsu ib'an 折受立案 royal certificate granting cession of rights to individuals, as in the grant of salt flats and fishing weirs to royal princesses
Chŏltosa 節度使 provincial military (army or navy) commander
Ch'ŏmjŏl chesa 僉節度使 commanders of the seventeen garrisons or *chin* (early Chosŏn).
chŏmjŏn yuhan 占田有限 limited possession of land
Ch'ŏmsa 僉使 see Ch'ŏmjŏl chesa
Ch'ŏmsajin 僉使鎮 prefectural-level naval garrisons
ch'ŏmsŏlchik 添設使 official sinecures
chŏmsu 占受 receive

chŏmt'oe 點退 rejection of tribute goods by a bureau clerk
Ch'ŏn 天 Heaven
chŏn 錢 cash
chŏn 佃 land unit of 4 *kyŏng*
ch'ŏn 賤 base status
chŏn ki-ji 專其地 exclusive control over land
chŏn'an 田案 the complete land registers
chŏnbong 專封 feudal lords given exclusive control over land
Chŏnbŏpsa 典法司 Ministry of Justice
Ch'onch'ong 千總 officer in charge of infantry
chŏng 丁 adult male
chŏng 情 human emotions
chŏng kyŏnggae 正經界 land boundaries
chŏn'gaek 佃客 the "tenant-guest," peasant cultivator of land, presumably an owner, on prebends to men of official rank under the *kwajŏn* system
Ch'ŏngbaengni 清白吏 pure officials; chief officials of top rank of the important state offices
Chŏngbang 政房 Personnel Office (Koryŏ)
chŏngbyŏng 正兵 regular soldiers of commoner status
chongch'in 宗親 male relatives of the royal clan
Chongch'inbu 宗親府 Office of Royal Relatives
Chŏngch'och'ŏng 精抄廳 Crack Select Agency
Chŏngch'ogun 精抄軍 Crack Select Soldiers
Ch'ŏngch'ŏn River 清川江
chŏngga 定價 designated prices for the purchase of goods by the purchasing agents under the *taedong* system
Chŏnggon-dogam 正供都監 Directorate for Rectification of Tribute, agency established by King Sŏnjo in 1567
chŏnggun 正軍 regular duty soldiers
Chonghak 宗學 Yu's Peer's School
Chong'in 從人 attendant
ch'ŏngjik 廳直 boy servants
chŏngjik 正職 regular officials
chŏngjŏn 正田 regular fields
Chŏngjŏn 正殿 Hall of Rectitude
Ch'ŏngju (p.n.) 清州 in Ch'ungch'ŏng Province
chŏngjuin 定主人 designated government purchasing masters or agents
chŏngjwa chonsim 靜坐存心 concentration of the mind
chongmobŏp 從母法 matrilineal succession law
chongmojibŏp 從母之法 matrilineal succession law
Chongmyo 宗廟 the Royal Ancestral Shrine
chŏngmyŏng 正名 rectification of names
Chŏngnang 正郎 a bureau section chief
Chongno (p.n.) 鍾路 Bell street in downtown Seoul
Chŏngnowi 定擄衛 the Jurchen Quelling Guards
chŏngnyŏng 政令 government affairs
ch'ŏn'go 薦擧 recommendation procedure
Chŏn'gŏm 典檢 investigator
Chŏng'ŏn 正言 fourth censor of the Office of Censor-General (Saganwŏn)
chŏngp'o 正布 correct cloth
chŏngsi 庭試 special palace examination
Ch'ŏngsŏ 清西 Pure Westerner faction
Chŏngsun, Queen 貞純王后 King Yŏngjo's second queen, dowager regent for King Sunjo
chŏng'ŭn 精銀 pure silver
ch'ŏn'gunbo 賤軍保 slaves with military service responsibilities

Ch'ŏn'gwan 天官 Officer of Heaven
Ch'ongyungch'ŏng 摠戎廳 the Anti-Manchu Division (the Kyŏnggi Province Division)
ch'ŏnha taech'e 天下大體 essential core of the world
chŏnham 天銜 retired officials
Chŏnhyŏndang 尊賢堂 Yu's Hall for Respected and Worthy Scholars
ch'ŏn'in 賤人 base person, i.e., slaves and others of low status
chonja 尊者 a respected elder
ch'ŏnja 賤者 people of base status (including slaves)
Chŏnje sangjŏngso 田制詳定所 Bureau for the Determination of the Land System
chŏnji 專地 officials given exclusive control over land
chŏnji chohwa 天地造化 transforming power of nature
chŏnjo 田租 land tax
Chŏn'jŏng 典正 rectifier
chŏnju 田主 "landlord," or recipient of a *sajŏn* prebend in Kyŏnggi Province under the *kwajŏn* system
Chŏnju (p.n.) 全州 in Chŏlla Province
chŏnmaek 阡陌 ridges and dikes
ch'ŏnmin 賤民 base people, including slaves
chŏnmun 箋文 letters of felicitation
chŏnnonggwan 典農官 agricultural managers
Chŏn'oksŏ 典獄署 Agency of Punishments; agency that received suspects of crimes prior to remanding them to the Ministry of Punishments, the Seoul Magistracy, and the Office of Inspector-General
chŏnse 田税 land tax
chŏnsi 殿試 palace examination
chŏnsikwa 田柴科 system of prebendal distribution of arable land and hillside land for the gathering of tree branches for fuel (early Koryŏ)
Ch'ŏnsim 天心 mind of Heaven
chŏnsŏn 戰船 warships
Chŏnsu kiŭi 戰守機宜 "Essentials of Military Strategy" (by Yu Sŏngnyŏng)
Chŏn'ŭigam 典醫監 Directorate of Medicine
ch'ŏn'ŭn 天銀 high-grade silver
ch'ŏp 妾 female base person (in the *Rites of Chou*)
chŏri 邸吏 representatives of local districts in capital agencies
chŏrmi 折米 rice value of replacement cost of equipment
choryangmok 助糧木 wide and short cotton bolt, used for currency
Chorye 皂隷 runners, see also Najang
Choryŏng 鳥嶺 Bird's Peak. See Seje
chosa 朝士 court officials
chosa 造士 accomplished scholars
ch'osang 草葬 straw funerals
Chosŏn dynasty 朝鮮
Chosŏn t'ongbo 朝鮮通寶 Chosŏn Circulating Treasure
chou (Ch.) 州 prefecture
Chou dynasty (Ch.) 周
Chou-fu (Ch.) 九府 the monetary agency of the early Chou dynasty
Chou-kuan (Ch.) 周官 *Rites of Chou*; section of the *Shang-shu*
Chou-kung (Ch.) 周公 Duke of Chou
Chou-li (Ch.) 周禮 *Rites of Chou*
chu 州 prefecture
chu (Ch.) 助 aid
Ch'u dynasty 楚
chu-fa (Ch.) 助法 system of aid (Chou dynasty) in well field system by which farmers working on eight private plots contribute their labor to cultivate the ninth plot of the lord
Chu-hou (Ch.) 諸侯 the feudal lords
Chu Hsi Chang-chou pang-yü 朱熹漳州榜諭 Posted Instructions for Chang-chou

Chu Hsi tseng-sun Lü-shih hsiang yüeh 朱熹增損呂氏鄉約 Emendations on the Village Oath System of Mr. Lü
chü-jen (Ch.) 擧人 provincial degree holders (Ming and Ch'ing China)
Ch'uan-fu (Ch.) 泉府 Currency Agency (Chou dynasty) which took charge of collecting market taxes in cash and buying unsold goods that had been accumulating on the market, functioning presumably to stabilize prices
Chüan-yün-shih (Ch.) 轉運使 Regional commissioner for transport
chüeh (Ch.) 爵 ranks of nobility
chugwan-daesin 主管大臣 "the great official in charge," an oblique reference to Kim Yuk
chuho 主戶 main householder
chuin 主人 warehousemen called the masters or private masters (*sajuin*)
chuin 主人 bureau masters in charge of tribute collection; or government purchasing master or agent to buy items from the market; see *chŏngjuin*
chuin 主人 agent of the provincial governor
chujin 主鎭 main garrison in the *chin'gwan* systems
Chujŏn-dogam 鑄錢都監 Directorate of the Mint (Koryŏ, est. 1102)
chuksun 竹筍 bamboo shoots
ch'ulbyŏng 出兵 military service
ch'ulse 出稅 taxes
ch'ulsin 出身 holder of the military examination degree
chün (Ch.) 郡 commandery or prefecture in Chinese dynasties; see *kun*
Chün (Ch.) 君 ruler
Ch'un-ch'iu 春秋 *Spring and Autumn Annals*
chün-hsien (Ch.) 郡縣 commanderies and prefectures, or the generic term for centralized bureaucracy
chün-shui fa (Ch.) 均稅法 equal tax system
chün-tzu (Ch.) 君子 man of superior virtue
Ch'unch'u'gwan 春秋館 Spring and Autumn Office
Ch'ung-chen (Ch.) 崇禎 Chinese coin
Chung-cheng (Ch.) 中正 personnel evaluation official (Wei and Chin)
Chung-shih (Ch.) 中侍 Middle *Shih*, official rank (Chou)
Chung-shu (Ch.) 中書 secretaries (T'ang and Sung)
Chung-shu sheng (Ch.) 中書省 Secretariat (T'ang and Sung)
Ch'ung-tsai (Ch.) 冢宰 Prime minister in *Book of History*
Chung-t'ung era 中統 Yüan dynasty, 1260-64
Chung-t'ung yüan-pao-ch'ao (Ch.) 中統元寶鈔 paper bill issued in 13th c. Yüan dynasty
chung-wei (Ch.) 中衛 commander of the Northern Army (i.e., Capital Guards)
Chŭngbo munhŏnbigo 增補文獻備考
Ch'ungch'anwi 忠贊衛 Loyal Assistant Guards
Ch'ungch'ŏng Province 忠清
Chungch'ubu 中樞府 Military Affairs Commission (or Office of Ministers-without-portfolio) (Chosŏn)
Chungch'ubu Yŏngsa 中樞府領事 Chief of the Military Affairs Commission (Chief Minister-without-Portfolio)
chŭngdŭng 中等 *ch'ung'in* and others
chunggong 衆共 mass participation
Chunggun 中軍 provincial governor's military aide; subordinate to divisional commander (Taejang)
chunggwangsaeng 增廣生 extra quota or irregular students
chunghagye 中下契 Middle and Lower *Kye* reserved for commoners

and slave members in An Chŏngbok's community compact

Chunghak 中學 Middle School

Ch'unghunbu 忠勳府 Office of Merit Subjects

chunghŭng 中興 restoration (of a dynasty)

Chunghwa 中和 district in South P'yŏng'an Province

Ch'ung'igwi 忠翊衛 Loyal Aide Guards

chung'in 中人 "middle men" or "middle people"; (1) defined by Yu Hyŏngwŏn as commoners or men of commoner lineages (*sŏjok*) who held office or were enrolled in official schools, and were also called the "idlers" (*hansan*), or "irregulars" (*pang'oe*); (2) holders of specialist positions through passage of technical examinations in astronomy, mathematics or calculations, writing, medicine, etc.; came to hold posts hereditarily and intermarried with others of the same class; (3) sometimes used for holders of clerk positions, also *ajŏn*

Ch'ungju (p.n.) 忠州

Chungnyŏng 竹嶺 Bamboo Peak

Ch'ungsin 忠臣 Loyal Subjects

Ch'ungsunwi 忠順衛 Loyal and Obedient Guards

Ch'ung'ŭiwi 忠義衛 Loyal and Righteous Guards

Ch'un'gwan 春官 officer of spring

ch'up'o 麤布 cheap rough cloth

chusa 舟師 *sugun*

Ch'uswae-dogam 推刷都監 General Directorate of Slave Registration

Ch'uswaegwan 推刷官 slave registrars

ch'ut'al 追奪 posthumous stripping of office warrants

Chwach'ang 左倉 Left Warehouse, for rice and cash paid into the capital

Chwaŭijŏng 左議政 councilor of the left, or second state councilor

Chwarang 佐郎 assistant section chief in one of the Six Ministries

Chwasu 座首 Head Seat, chief of the local yangban or gentry associations (Hyangch'ŏng)

Chwaŭijong 左議政 councilor of the left or second state councilor

fa (Ch.) 法 laws

fa (Ch.) 閥 status

fan-chen (Ch.) 藩鎮 system of frontier garrisons in the Chinese Eastern Chin dynasty that combined several civil districts in one military district with a large garrison (*ta-chen*) under a single commander

Fang-po (Ch.) 方伯 leader of feudal lords (Chou); see Pangbaek; provincial governor

fang-t'ien (Ch.) 方田 square-field system

fa-yüeh (Ch.) 閥閱 aristocratic family status

fu (Ch.) 府 district; see *Che-ch'ung-fu*

fu (Ch.) 賦 a type of poem

Fu 府 Storehouse manager (Chou)

fu-lao 父老 father-elder, in charge of local school (Chou)

fu-ping (Ch.) 府兵 military service system (T'ang)

fu-yung (Ch.) 附庸 dependencies (ancient China)

hae 解 document of "release" granted to an official who had been transferred absolving him of financial or other responsibilities for his post

Haedong chungbo 海東重寶 a Korean coin

Haedong t'ongbo 海東通寶 a coin (Koryŏ); the Circulating Treasure of the [Country] East of the [Yellow] Sea

Haeju (p.n.) 海州 Hwanghae Province

Haeju hyangyak 海州鄉約 Haeju community compact

Haeju ilhyang yaksok 海州一鄉約束 Pledges of the Haeju Community Compact

haeng 行 behavior

haengjŏn 行錢 putting cash into circulation

Haeun p'an'gwan 海運判官 commissioner of maritime transport in the capital

Haeunsa 海運使 maritime transport commissioner

Hagwan 夏官 Officer of summer

Hagyejang 下契長 lower *kye* chief in Yu Hyŏngwŏn's plan for local government

Hahak chinam 下學指南 *Primer for Lower-Level Learning*, by An Chŏngbok

haho 下戶 households of lower status

hain 下人 inferior or lower men, men of low status

hakchŏn 學田 special school land

Hakkyo samok 學校事目 Yu's "Proposals for Schools"

Hakpin 學賓 Yu's Visiting Scholar

haksaeng 學生 student in school

hallyang 閑良 unemployed sons of civil and military officials

hallyanggwan 閑良官 "idle officials"; see *hallyang*.

Hamgil Province 咸吉 see Hamgyŏng Province

Hamgyŏng Province 咸鏡 Hamgil Province

Hamhŭng (p.n.) 咸興 in Hamgyŏng Province

hamsanp'o 咸山布 cotton bolt used for currency that usually was of poor weave and turned black

Hamyang (p.n.) 咸陽 in South Kyŏngsang Province

Han dynasty 漢

Han-lin Academy (Ch.) 翰林院

Han River 漢江

Han-shu 漢書 *History of the Han Dynasty*

hang'ŏp 恒業 steady occupations

han'in 閑人 idle persons, sons of officials without posts

han'injŏn 閑人田 prebendal grants of tax income to "idle" sons of officials without posts

hanjŏn 限田 limited field

hanjŏnbŏp 限田法 limited field system

hanjŏng 閑丁 unemployed or "idle" relatives of yangban

hanmin musangjik 閑民無常職 Yu Suwŏn's idle people without regular occupations

hanmin myŏngjŏn 限民名田 limiting the amount of land that any individual or family might own or possess

hanmun 漢文 classical Chinese

hansan 閑散 "idlers"

Hansan Island 閑山島

Hansŏng 漢城 Seoul

Hansŏngbu 漢城府 Seoul Magistracy

happo 合保 See *pyŏngbo*

heng (Ch.) 衡 "the scale," referring to money because it could raise or lower prices

Hoenggan 橫看 the Horizontal Ledger, a list compiled from 1456 to 1473 of all expenditures made from tribute collected in kind, including the cost of manufacturing tribute items by artisans

Hoerodang 會老堂 Elder Assembly Halls

hoerok 會錄 "recording fee," actually a portion of the interest on state grain loans

Hoeryŏng (p.n.) 會寧 in Hamgyŏng Province

Hoeryŏng-gun (p.n.) 會寧郡 Hamgyŏng Province

hoesi 會試 regular civil service examination

Hoigwi 虎翼衛 Tiger Wing Guards

Hojang 戶長 Household Chief, main clerk of a district magistrate (Chosŏn)

hojŏk 戶籍 household registers

Holch'i 忽只 the core of Royal Guards, also called the Sŏngjung aema

homaemi 虎贖米 surtax levied on peasant households to pay the cost of obtaining tiger skins

hongbŏm 洪範 Great Plan

Honghwamun 弘化門

Hongmu chŏng'ŭn yŏkhun 洪武正韻譯訓 *Correct Tones of the Hung-wu Era*, by Sin Sŏkchu

Hongmun'gwan (Oktang) 弘文館（玉堂）Office of Special Counselors

hongp'ae 紅牌 special red warrants

Hŏnsa 憲司 Office of Surveillance

hop'ae 號牌 household tally, est. 1458

hop'o 戶布 household cloth tax

hŏryŏk 歇役 low rate service

Hŏsaengjŏn 許生傳 *The Biography of Master Hŏ*. Novel by Pak Chiwŏn

hose 戶稅 household tax

Hosŏ taedong samok 湖西大同事目 Regulations of the *taedong* law for Ch'ungch'ŏng Province.

hosu 戶首 household head

Hou Han-shu (Ch.) 后漢書 *History of the Later Han dynasty*

Hou-kuo (Ch.) 侯國 Marquisate

Howich'ŏng 扈衛廳 Royal Retinue Office

Hsia dynasty (Ch.) 夏

Hsia-kuan (Ch.) 夏官 Office of Summer

hsiang (Ch.) 鄉 unit of 12,500 families in the Chou dynasty, 125 families in the Northern Wei, 500 family unit in the Sui and T'ang dynasties

hsiang-cheng (Ch.) 鄉正 chief of a *hsiang* in the Northern Wei dynasty

hsiang-chün (Ch.) 鄉軍 local troops

Hsiang pa-hsing (Ch.) 鄉八刑 the eight punishments for local areas

Hsiang san-wu (Ch.) 鄉三物 the three local officials

hsiang shih-ta-fu (Ch.) 鄉士大夫 local scholar-officials of ancient China

hsiang ta-fu (Ch.) 鄉大夫 local elite, or local officials (Chou)

hsiang-tang (Ch.) 鄉黨 village communities

hsiang yin-chou chih li (Ch.) 鄉飲酒之禮 village wine-drinking ritual

hsiang-yüeh (Ch.) 鄉約 community compact

hsiao (Ch.) 少 one 10-20 years younger than ego

hsiao-chien (Ch.) 考建 year period in the Liu Sung dynasty (454-56)

hsiao-hsüeh. (Ch.) 小學 grammar school

Hsiao-hsüeh (Ch.) 小學 "The Small Learning" (Instructions for the Young)

hsiao-jen (Ch.) 小人 "small man," of limited moral capacity

hsiao-lien k'ua (Ch.) 孝廉 recommendation of filial and honest men (T'ang)

Hsiao ssu-tu (Ch.) 小司徒 Vice-Minister of Education

Hsia-shih (Ch.) 下士 lower shih, official rank (Chou)

hsien (Ch.) 縣 district in Chinese dynasties; see *hyŏn*.

hsing-li (Ch.) 性理 philosophy of nature and principle

Hsing-li ta-tien (Ch.) 性理大典

Hsü 胥 procedural clerk (Chou)

Hsüan-chü tsa-i (Ch.) 選舉雜記 miscellaneous discussion of selection and appointment

Hsüan-pu Shang-shu (Ch.) 選部尚書

master of documents in charge of selection of officials (Han)

hsüan-shih (Ch.) 選士 selected scholars

Hsüan-ts'ao (Ch.) 選曹 Personnel Ministry

Hsüeh-chi (Ch.) 學記 section of the *Book of Rites*

Hsün-fu (Ch.) 巡撫 grand coordinators

hu (Ch.) 斛 Chinese measure of volume (Kor., *kok*) equivalent to 5 or 10 *tou* or pecks (Sino-Kor. *tu*, Kor., *mal*)

Hu (*Hou*, Ch.) 侯 Marquis

Hu-shih chüan 胡氏傳 *The Tradition of Mr. Hu* (Hu An-kuo?)

Hu-shih Ch'un-ch'iu chüan 胡氏春秋傳 Hu An-kuo's commentary on the *Spring and Autumn Annals*, early twelfth-century (Northern Sung)

Hua (Ch.) 貨 means of exchange, money

Huai River 淮河

huan-fa 圜法 reputedly the first metallic coin (Chou). 1122 B.C.

huan-tso (Ch.) 鐶鑿 ring chisel cash

Hugung 後宮 the Rear Palace, for concubines of former kings

hui-tzu (Ch.) 會子 paper scrip, term first used in Jurchen Chin dynasty (12-13th c.)

Hullyŏn-byŏltae (Pyŏltae) 訓練別隊 Special Cavalry unit of the MTA

Hullyŏn-dogam 訓練都監 Military Training Agency, est. 1593

hu-ma-fa (Ch.) 戶馬法 household horse system of (Sung)

hundo 訓導 local educational official

Hundo 訓導 adviser

Hung-fan (Ch.) 洪範 Great Plan, of the Book of History (*Shu-ching*) (early Chou)

Hung-lu-shih (Ch.) 鴻臚寺 agency for rites and ceremonies (Ming)

Hung-wu (Ch.) 洪武 year period of the Ming dynasty (1368-99)

Hung-wu cheng-yün (Ch.) 洪武正韻

Hŭngdŏk (p.n.) (Hŭngdŏk-hyŏn) 興德

hun'gup'a 勳舊派 established bureaucrats, merit subjects, and consort relatives of queens

Hŭngyang (p.n.) 興陽

huse 後世 the later age(s)

hwabyŏng 火兵 firearms soldier

hwa-i 華夷 civilized versus barbaric

hwach'a 火車 war wagon

Hwanghae Province 黃海

hwangjap'o 黃字砲 *Hwang*-type cannon; the long-barreled cannon

Hwangyŏ 黃驪 community compact

hwanja 還上 state-sponsored grain loans

hwanmok 換木 "switching the cotton" when government officials collected high-quality cloth from taxpayers but remitted only low-quality cloth to government warehouses

Hwat'ong-dogam 火熥都監 Firearms Directorate

Hwayang (p.n.) 華陽

hyang 鄉 local; subdistrict in Yu Hyŏngwŏn's local government plan, 12,500 families; equivalent to the contemporary *myŏn*

hyang-daebu 鄉大夫 local officials

hyang sŏnsaeng 鄉先生 local teachers

hyang'an 鄉案 local yangban register

hyangban 鄉班 local yangban

hyangch'ŏng 鄉廳 local yangban associations

hyangdang (*hsiang-tang*) 鄉黨 subdistrict (*hyang*) and village (*tang*), or local communities in Yu's system of local control

hyangdo 鄉徒 incense associations

hyanggun 鄉軍 provincial soldiers

hyanggwan 鄉官 local (petty) officials

hyanggyo 鄉校 local, provincial schools
hyanggyu 鄉規 regulations of the Yuhyangso
hyanghak 鄉學 subdistrict schools
hyanghoe 鄉會 subdistrict convocations
Hyanghŏn 鄉憲 *Community Regulations*
hyangjŏng (*hsiang-cheng*) 鄉正 official of a subdistrict in charge of 500 families
hyangjungji saryu 鄉中之士類 local scholars; see *yuhyang p'umgwan*
hyangjuŭmnye 鄉酒飲禮 wine drinking rite
hyangni 鄉吏 local elite, lit., "local clerks"; in Koryŏ could be appointed to magistrate's post, but not in Chosŏn
hyangnip yakcho 鄉立約條 articles of a community compact
Hyangnye happ'yŏn 鄉禮合編 *Combined Edition of the Community Compact and Local (Wine-Drinking) Rite.*
hyangp'um 鄉品 local gentry with rank titles
hyangsa 鄉祠 village shrines
Hyangsadang 鄉射堂 Local Archery Hall
hyangsang 鄉庠 Yu's local schools
hyangsarye 鄉射禮 the local archery rite
Hyangso 鄉所 local yangban association
Hyangsoch'ŏng 鄉所廳 local yangban associations that performed semi-official duties in supervising local clerks
hyangsu (*hsiang-su*, Ch.) 鄉遂 local-government system
hyang'ŭmjurye 鄉飲酒禮 local wine-drinking rites
hyangyak 鄉約 community compact or subdistrict community compact association in Yu Hyŏngwŏn's local government plan (otherwise translated as local contract or oath association)
hyehyul 惠恤 benevolent compassion
Hyeminsŏ 惠民署 Office of Benefiting the People (a relief agency)
Hyogyŏng 孝經 *Book of Filial Piety*
Hyŏkp'yech'ŏng 革弊廳 Reform Bureau
Hyŏkp'ye-dogam 革弊都監 General Directorate To Eliminate Evils
hyŏllyang-kwa 賢良科 special recommendation examination urged by Cho Kwangjo in 1518
hyŏllyŏng 縣令 district magistrate
hyŏn 縣 district (Chosŏn)
hyŏn 賢 worth
hyŏn and *nŭng* 賢能 worthy and able
Hyŏnjong Sillok 顯宗實錄 *The Veritable Record of King Hyŏnjong*
hyŏnju 縣主 daughter of a crown prince by a concubine
Hyŏnp'ung (p.n.) 玄風
hyŏnson 玄孫 4th-generation male descendant
hyŏryŏk 歇役 light-rate service
hyuryangjŏn 恤養田 land grant to orphans

i 里 administrative village
i 里 one-quarter of a mile
i 里 10-*t'ong* or 50-family unit in Yu Hyŏngwŏn's plan
i 里 50-family group
i-ch'ien-shih (Ch.) 二千石 officials of so-called "2,000 picul rank"
I-ch'ien-shih Ts'ao (Ch.) 二千石曹 Office of 2,000 Picul Rank Officials
I Ching 易經 *Book of Changes*
I-li (Ch.) 儀禮 *Book of Etiquette and Ceremonial*
i-ts'ang (Ch.) (Kor., *ŭich'ang*) 義倉 Righteous Granaries
ib'an 立案 estate registration

Ibang 吏房 personnel clerk, main clerk of a magistrate's district (later Chosŏn)
ibyŏk nobi 立役奴婢 service slaves
Ich'ŏn 伊川屯 Military Colony
idu 吏讀 Korean clerk's script
igi 理氣 principle (*i*) and psycho-physical energy (*ki*, pronunciation changes to *-gi* after a vowel)
Igun 二軍 Two Armies
Igwi 翊衛 Wing Guards
Ijang 里長 head of a 50-family unit in Yu Hyŏngwŏn's plan
Ijŏng 里正 head of a 50-family group
Ijŏngch'ŏng 釐正廳 Reform Bureau
Ikki Island 壹岐
Iksan (p.n.) 益山 south of Seoul
illo yŏng'il 一勞永逸 perpetual ease after a single effort
illyŏk 人力 human labor
illyu 人類 human beings
Imjin 壬辰
Imjin River 臨津江
imsin 壬申 year of 1728 rebellion
imsul 壬戌 year of 1862 rebellion
Ingnimwi 羽林軍 Winged Forest Guard
inho 煙戶 individual households
Inhogun 煙戶君 Prince Inho
Injo Restoration 仁祖反正
injŏng 人情 feelings of people, human nature
Inmul ch'ubyŏn-dogam 人物推辨都監 Directorate for Inspection of Slaves
inp'um 人品 personal quality
insa 人事 obligations of courtesy and gift-giving to superiors
insim 人心 human mind, imperfect, beclouded by psycho-physical energy within
insun kosik 因循姑息 accommodation and appeasement
inyok 人慾 human desire
Ipchŏn 立廛 Seoul silk shops
ipho ch'ulbyŏng 立戶出兵 military service
ipkang 立綱 establishing respect for law
ippangjigun 入防之軍 frontier duty troops
Irye 吏隸 runners and slaves
isabŏp 里社法 artificial village

jisŏ 支庶 sons and younger brothers of branch lines of the *sadaebu* or yangban
Jurchen 女真

Kabo 甲午 year of 1894 reform
kach'uk 家畜 household servants
Kado (Ka Island) 椵島
Kadŏk Island 加德島
kaek 客 see *kaekchu*
kaekchu 客主 wholesalers, brokers
Kaesŏng (p.n.) 開城
kag'an saengni 各安生理 for each to rest secure in the principle of continuous reproduction
K'ai-yüan t'ung-pao (Ch.) 開元通寶 Chinese coin (T'ang)
kakcha susejŏn 各自收稅田 land exempted from tax collection by the central government
Kaksa 各司 the Capital Bureaus (of the Six Ministries)
kamgwan 監官 steward of coastal properties
kami 價米 rice levy to pay for cost of masts, oars, and sails; rice funds for the purchase of goods under the *taedong* system
Kammokkwan 監牧官 keeper of horse
kammun 監門 palace gate guards
Kamsugwan 監收官 tax collectors
Kanghwa Island 江華島
Kangjin (p.n.) 康津
Kangwŏn Province 江原
Kan'gyŏng-dogam 刊經都監 Direc-

torate of Buddhist publications
kanryō kizoku (J.) 官僚貴族 bureaucratic aristocracy
Kansu Province (Ch.) 甘肅
Kanyangnok 看羊錄
kap'o 價布 substitute cloth payment or fee in lieu of labor service
Kapsa 甲士 Armored Soldiers
Kapsan copper mine 甲山 in Hamgyŏng Province
Karye 家禮 Chu Hsi's *Family Rites*
Khitan 契丹
ki 氣 psycho-physical energy (pronunciation changes to *-gi* after a vowel) (Ch., *ch'i*)
ki 旗 banner or platoon, of 3 squads
ki 起 cultivated
ki chaemul 己財物 private property
kibo 騎保 cavalryman support taxpayer
kibyŏng 騎兵 cavalryman
Kich'ong 旗摠 platoon leader
Kiho 畿湖 region of Kyŏnggi and Ch'ungch'ŏng provinces
kiin 其人 rotating clerks from local districts responsible for wood and fuel supplies to capital bureaus
Kija (Ch., Ch'i-tzu) 箕子 Shang-Chou culture hero portrayed by Koreans as the sage transmitter of culture to Korea
Kijŏn tosŏl 箕田圖説 *The Land System of Kija, with Illustrations and Explanations*
kiju 起主 lit. master of cultivation; the term appears in *yang'an* land registers, and Kim Yongsŏp has interpreted it to mean "landowner," but Pak Nouk convincingly demonstrated that it only meant "cultivator" with no indication whether the cultivator possessed ownership rights or not
Kilchu (p.n.) 吉州
Kimhae (p.n.) 金海
kimyo sahywa 己卯士禍 the purge of Cho Kwangjo, 1519
kinae 畿內 the ruler's bailiwick around the capital
kioe 畿外 the fiefs or feudal states ruled by the lords outside the king's domain
Kip'aegwan 旗牌官 Officer of the Banner and Tally, Bannermen
Kiroso 耆老所 Agency for the Elderly
kisaeng 妓生 female entertainers
kisasu kiriil ya 其事殊，其理一也 the principle is the same despite the variety of things
kisŏn'gun 騎船軍 marines or maritime soldiers
Kobu (region) 古阜
kogang 考講 written classics examination
kogong 雇工 hired labor, or agricultural wage workers, *mŏsŭm*
Koguryŏ dynasty 高句麗
koja 庫子 warehouse clerks
kŏjin 巨鎮 main garrison
kok 斛 10 *mal* in Yu Hyŏngwŏn's units of volume
kolp'um 骨品 bone rank
Kŏmnyul 檢律 Legal Expert
kong 共 sharing in common
kong 公 fair
kong 公 petty feudal rulers
kong'an 貢案 tribute ledgers
kongbŏp 貢法 law of 1444 that graded land tax revenues by land fertility and weather conditions
Kongbu sanjŏng-dogam 貢賦詳定都監 General Directorate for Determining Taxes
kongch'ŏn 公賤 official slaves
konggo chabyŏk 工庫雜役 petty clerks working in official warehouses
konggong-ji-ron 公共之論 open and public opinion
konghaejŏn 公廨田 office expense land

kong'in 貢人 tribute middlemen or merchants
kongjang 空場 "empty markets" or flea markets or "empty markets in outer areas"; see *oech'ŏ kongjang*
kongjang 公匠 official artisans
kongjŏn 公田 public field, or Lord's field; see *kung-t'ien;* public land system
Kongju (p.n.) 公州
Kongju 公主 princess
Kongjuin 貢主人 tribute agents employed by the Ministry of Taxation prior to the *taedong* reform of the sixteenth century
kongmul 貢物 tribute goods paid to various bureaus of government in the capital; see *wŏn'gong*
kongmul chuin 貢物主人 tribute middlemen, or tribute masters
kongmul puro 貢物父老 the tribute elder, commissioner of a district magistrate sent out to purchase goods under the *taedong* system, as a means of replacing tribute
kongni 貢吏 tribute clerk
kongnyŏk 功力 skill used in labor
kongp'ae 空牌 blank warrants
kongsa 公私 public and private
Kongsa 貢士 tribute scholars
kongsaeng 貢生 "tribute students," or boy servants; see *t'ong'in, ch'ŏngjik,* and *yŏnjik*
kongsang 供上 the expenses of the royal house
kongsang 供上 tribute
kongse 公税 public taxes
kongsin 功臣 merit subjects
kongsinjŏn 功臣田 merit subject land or prebends
Kongsŏ 功西 see Nosŏ
kongsujŏn 公須田 land set aside to pay official expenses
kong'ŭm 功蔭 forebears (?)
Koryŏ dynasty 高麗
Koryŏsa 高麗史 *History of the Koryŏ dynasty*
Koryŏ t'onghaeng chŏhwa 高麗通行楮貨 late Koryŏ dynasty paper bill, the "Koryŏ Circulating Paper Money"
kosin 告身 blank office warrants to men who joined the armed forces
k'ou-fen-t'ien (Ch.) 口分田 mouth-share land, i.e., per capita share land
Ku-wen yin-lü 古文韻律
Kuan-ch'a-shih (Ch.) 觀察使 governor; see Kwanch'alsa
kuang-chi (Ch.) 彍騎 long-term soldiers
Kuang-lu-ssu 光祿寺 Court of Imperial Entertainments (Ming)
Kuan-tung feng-su chüan 關東風俗傳
Kuan-tzu 管子
kubun 口分 "mouth share"
kubunjŏn 口分田 "mouth-share land," Korean pronunciation of Chinese *k'ou-fen-t'ien*; widow's support land (Koryŏ and Chosŏn)
kuei (Ch.) 貴 noble
Kuei-chou 貴州 province in China
kuga sejok 舊家世族 old families and hereditary lineages
kuje 舊制 the old system; Yu Hyŏngwŏn's term for military units established from the founding of the Chosŏn dynasty to the Imjin War
kujŏn 口錢 mouth (head or capitation) tax
kujŏn 舊 old cash
kukcha (*kuo-tzu*, Ch.) 國子 sons of the state
Kukhak 國學 National Academy
kukka kyŏngbi 國家經費 state expenses
kukka tanmun 國家袒免 blood relationship of lowest degree of mourning
kullo 軍奴 military police

Kulloe 軍牢 military runners
kŭmgo 禁錮 prohibition against taking examinations
Kŭmgun 禁軍 Forbidden Soldiers
Kŭmgun samch'ŏng 禁軍三廳 Agency of the Three Forbidden Soldier Guards
Kŭmgunch'ŏng 禁軍廳 Forbidden Soldier Agency, or Agency of the Three Forbidden Soldier Guards (Kŭmgun samch'ŏng), est. 1666
kumiai dantai 組合団体 completely professionalized guild
Kumip'o (p.n.) 龜尾浦
Kŭmnan'gye 金蘭契 Golden Orchid Kye
Kŭm'o 金吾 capital night patrol
Kŭm'owi 金吾衛 Capital Patrol
Kŭmsan (p.n.) 錦山
Kŭmwi pyŏltae 禁衛別隊 Forbidden Guard Special Unit
Kŭmwigun 禁衛軍 Forbidden Guard Soldiers
Kŭmwiyŏng 禁衛營 Forbidden Guard Division.
kun 郡 large district (or prefecture) (Chosŏn); see *chün*.
kun 君 royal relatives
kŭn 斤 unit of weight
k'un 閫 military region in China (Sung)
kunbojijŏn 軍保之田 funds or lands in a village for the purpose of paying the village's tax quota; see *yŏkkunjŏn*
kung-shih (Ch.) 貢士 tribute students (Ming and Ch'ing) China
kung-t'ien (Ch.) 公田 public land, or lord's field (Kor., *kongjŏn*)
Kung-yang 公羊 commentary on *The Spring and Autumn Annals*
kungbang (or *kungga*) 宮房（宮家） palace estates of princesses et al.
kungbangjŏn 宮房田 land or estates granted to princes and princesses
kungga 宮家 see *kungbang*
Kun'gigo 軍器庫 Military Weapons Storehouse
Kun'gigam 軍器監 Weapons Directorate
Kun'gi kamgwan 軍器監官 Weapons Director
Kun'gisi 軍器寺 Weapons Bureau
kun'gwan 軍官 military officer, gate guards
kunho 軍戶 military households
Kunhyangch'ŏng 軍餉廳 Military Ration Agency
kun'ik 軍翼 the Army Wings
kunja 君子 man of virtue
Kunjach'ang 軍資倉 Military Stores Warehouse
Kunjagam 軍資監 Quartermaster Bureau
kunjajŏn 軍資田 land available for military expenses and provisions
kŭnjak nongsang 勤作農桑 be diligent in conducting agriculture and sericulture
kunjŏn 軍田 land grants to soldiers
Kunju 郡主 princess
kunp'o 軍布 military cloth tax
kunp'ogye 軍布契 village collective tax associations
kunsa 軍士 soldiers
kuo (Ch.) 國 kingdoms or feudalities
kuo-hsüeh (Ch.) 國學 National Academy; Kor., *kukhak*
kŭpchŏn chŏngbyŏng 給田定兵 granting of land in combination with assigning military service to the grantee
kŭpka koin 給價雇人 hired workers paid by wages
kŭppok 給復 granting land tax exemptions
kŭppokchŏn (*pokho*) 給復田（復戶） special tax-exempt land
kwa 科 rank
kwagŏ 科擧 civil service examinations

kwajŏn 科田 "rank land (system)" 1389, i.e., prebendal grants to men of official rank

kwalli noye 官吏奴隷 slaves in service to officials

kwamok 科目 highest civil service examination

kwanbo 宮保 ration support taxpayers

Kwanch'alsa 觀察使 Surveillance Commissioner, term for provincial governor; see Kuan-ch'a-shih

kwandun 官屯 official colonies

kwandunjŏn 官屯田 civil official colony land

Kwanghŭngch'ang 廣興倉 Prosperity Expansion Warehouse, also called the Right Granary (Uch'ang) to store rice and cash in the capital for payment for official salaries

Kwangju (p.n.) 光州\廣州

Kwangju-bu (p.n.) 光州府\廣州府 magistracy in Chŏlla and Kyŏnggi provinces

Kwansanggam 觀象監 Directorate of Astronomy

Kwansu 官需 official expenses

kwasil 過失 transgressions

kwi 貴 noble

kwich'ŏn 貴賤 noble and base

kwich'ŏn mu pyŏlbun 貴賤無別分 no distinctions between noble and base

kwiga 貴家 aristocratic families

kwija 貴者 men of noble status

kwijok 貴族 families of noble status

kwŏn 卷 chapter of a book

kwŏn 權 scale

Kwŏn'gwan 權官 recruiters

Kwŏnnong 勸農 supervisor of agriculture

Kwŏnnongsa 勸農使 agricultural promotion agents

kye 契 associations organized for purposes such as pooling capital and lending to members in rotation, for the sharing of tax quotas by its members; natural village in Yu Hyŏngwŏn's plan for local government (see *t'onggye*); also used for community compact organizations (*hyangyak*)

kyebang 契房 an association formed to protect members against military taxes; see *kyebangch'on*.

kyebangch'on 契房村 a whole village whose residents would sign up with an official for low-rate service in order to reduce the tax burden collectively

kyejang 契長 head of a kye association

kyejŏn ch'ulbyŏng 計田出兵 "furnishing soldiers by measuring the amount of land"

kyo 教 "instruction" from the Korean king or a Chinese emperor, equivalent to an edict (Chosŏn)

Kyodo 教導 teacher

Kyodong (p.n.) 喬桐 Kyŏnggi Province

kyogwan 教官 educational official; prefectural or district level

Kyohun 教訓 instructor (of a village granary *kye*)

kyohwa 教化 moral transformation through education

kyŏl 結 a constant measure of crop yield produced by an area that varied from 2.2 to 9.0 acres depending on the fertility of the land

kyŏl-bu 結負 system of land measurement using the *kyŏl* and *-bu* (1/100 *kyŏl*)

kyŏlchŏn 結錢 cash surtax on land

kyŏlmi 結米 the 2-*mal* rice surtax on land to supplement military costs, 1751

kyŏlp'o 結布 cloth surtax on land

kyŏm chu ki inmin 兼主其人民 combined overlordship over its people

kyŏmbyŏng 兼倂 accumulation of large amounts of land by landlords (at the expense of small peasants)

kyomin 教民 to educate the people in moral standards

Kyŏmsabok 兼司僕 Concurrent Royal Stables (of the Dragon Tiger Regiment or Yonghoyŏng of the Forbidden Soldiers)

kyŏng 卿 high ranking officials

kyŏng (*ch'ing*, Ch.) 頃 100 *myo*

kyŏng 敬 seriousness; keeping one's mind under strict control at all times, as if one were conducting a rite at an ancestral shrine or having an interview with one's father or ruler

kyŏng kaksajuin 京各司主人 agents of the capital bureaus

kyŏng-myo 頃畝 system of land area measurement

Kyŏng'an County (p.n.) 慶安面 located in Kwangju-bu in Chŏlla Province

kyŏngbi 經費 expenditures made from government funds from regular tax revenues

Kyŏngbok Palace 景福宮

kyŏngbyŏng 京兵 capital soldiers

Kyŏngbyŏngbu 京兵部 Capital Soldier Office, Yu's proposed name to replace the current Hullyŏn-dogam or Military Training Agency

Kyŏngch'agwan 敬差官 special crop assessors

Kyŏngdaebu 卿大夫 the Ching and Ta-fu, officials of the Chou dynasty

Kyŏnggi Province 京畿道

Kyŏngguk taejŏn 經國大典 Great Code of 1469, revised 1474

kyŏnggun 京軍 capital soldiers

kyŏnggye 境界 land boundaries

Kyŏnggyejang 境界狀 Chu Hsi on land boundaries

Kyŏngjaeso 京在所 capital headquarters of a local district

Kyŏngje yaron 經濟野論 *Rustic Views on the Management of the Country*, by U Chŏnggye

kyŏngjŏllon 井田論 Tasan's essay on the well-field system

Kyŏngjong, King (r. 1720-24) 景宗

Kyŏngjŏri (Kyŏngjuin) 京邸吏（京主人） a district's Capital Agent

Kyŏngju (p.n.) 慶州

Kyŏngjuin 京主人 see Kyŏngjŏri

kyŏng'o waeran 庚午倭亂 The Japanese rising of 1510

Kyŏngsang Province 慶尚道

kyŏngse 經税 regular tax receipts, funds raised legally and openly by authorized state taxes

Kyŏngse yup'yo 經世遺表 text by Tasan

Kyŏngsigam 京市監 Directorate of the Capital Markets

Kyŏngsuso 警守所 police boxes

kyŏngswaema 京刷馬 cost of horse transportation in the capital

Kyŏngyŏn 經筵 the Royal Lectures

kyŏngyong 經用 regular expenditures

kyŏngyŏnghyŏng punong 經營型富農 managerial rich peasants

Kyŏnnaeryang (p.n.) 見乃梁

kyosaeng 校生 students in provincial schools

Kyosŏgwan 校書館 Publications Office

Kyosu 教授 instructor

Kyōto (p.n.) 京都

Kyujanggak 奎章閣 archival library of the Chosŏn dynasty

kyujŏn 圭田 land grants by King Wen of Chou to his officials at the end of the second millennium B.C.

kyun 均 equality, equity

kyunjŏn 均田 equal-field system (China)

kyunmin 均民 making the people equal

kyunyŏk 均役 equal service

kyunyŏkpŏp 均役法 the Equal-Service Law of 1750

Kyunyŏk sasil ch'aekcha 均役事實冊子 "The True Facts of Equal Service," by Hong Kyehŭi

Lang-chung (Ch.) 郎中 chief duty official (Ming)
Later Ch'en dynasty 後陳
Later Chin dynasty 後晉
Later Chou dynasty (Ch.) 後周
Later Han dynasty (Ch.) 後漢
li (Ch.) 里 land measurement
li (Ch.) 里 100-family unit (T'ang), 80 family unit (Chou)
li (Ch.) 禮 see *ye*; courtesy, rules of social behavior
Li-cheng (Ch.) 里正 chief of the 100-family *li* (T'ang)
Li-chi 禮記 *Book of Rites*
li-chia (Ch.) 里甲 Ming system of local control and surveillance
li-lao (Ch.) 里老 neighborhood elders (Ming)
li-ming (Ch.) 禮命 courtesy appointment, plan of Ch'eng Hao; *yemyŏng* in Korean
Li pu (Ch.) 吏部 Ministry of Personnel
Li-pu-ts'ao (Ch.) 吏部曹 Office of Personnel (Han)
liang (Ch.) 兩 see *yang*; 1 tael, weight measure
Liang dynasty (Ch.) (502-57) 梁
Liao dynasty (Ch.) 遼
Liao River 遼水
Liao-tung (Ch.) 遼東 peninsula, river in Manchuria
lin (Ch.) 鄰 4-family unit (T'ang)
Liu Sung dynasty 劉宋
Lo-cheng (Ch.) 樂正 official in charge of instruction, National Academy
Lu (Ch.) 路 route, i.e., province
lu-t'ien 露田 open or treeless lowland fields

madae 馬隊 horse platoons
maek 貊 ridges
magun 馬軍 horse soldiers
makkŏri grog
mal Colloquial for *tu*, 1/15 of a *sŏm* (coll. for *sŏk*)
mal 末 branch
malbo 末保 marginal support taxpayers; see *pyŏngbo*, *happo*
manggwŏllye 望闕禮 a rite at which provincial officials would face toward the royal court
mangmin 罔民 deluding the people
Manho 萬戶 lesser garrison commander
Manhojin 萬戶鎮 small garrison
mankwa 萬科 new recruitment examination for soldiers
Meiji period 明治 Japan, year period
men-fa (Ch.) 門閥 aristocratic status; see *munbŏl*
Men-hsia sheng (Ch.) 門下省 Chancellery (T'ang and Sung)
men-hu 門戶 family line
men-ti (Ch.) 門地 family pedigree; see *munji*
min 民 the people, general population
mindun 民屯 civilian colonies
Ming dynasty (Ch.) 明
minjŏn 民田 people's land, or land owned privately by "the people"
minjŏng 民情 feelings of the people
minjung 民衆 the masses
mogok 耗穀 "wastage surcharge" or interest charge on state-sponsored grain loans
mogun 募軍 soldiers conscripted directly by base and unit commanders or civil officials
moipkun 募入軍 recruited soldiers
mok 牧 district headed by magistrates sent from central government (Koryŏ)
Mokch'ŏn (-hyŏn) (p.n.) 木川（縣）in Ch'ungch'ŏng Province
Mongmin simsŏ 牧民心書 *A Book*

From the Heart on Governing the People, by Tasan

moryangmi 毛糧米 the Mao or Chinese provision tax (*tangnyangmi*) of 1611; see *sŏryangmi*

mŏsŭm hired labor, or agricultural wage workers; see *kogong*

mubijuin 貿備之人 purchasing masters, semi-private merchants to take the place of existing tribute masters or *kongmulchuin*

mudang 巫堂 female shamans

Mugye (p.n.) 茂溪 Kyŏngsang Province

muhak 武學 military student archers

mukwa 武科 highest military examinations

mulgo injŏng p'o 物故人丁布 death gratuity in cloth

mulli 物理 the principle of (material) things; see *wu-li*

mun (*wen* in Ch.) 文 culture, the written word, representation

mun'an 文案 official permit

munbŏl 門閥 aristocracy, noble families and lineages

munho 門戶 family line

Munhŏnbigo 文獻備考 see also *Chŭngbo munhŏnbigo*

Munhwa Yu clan 文化柳氏

munji 門地 pedigree

munjok 門族 family lineage

munkwa 文科 highest level civil service examination

munmu yangban 文武兩班 civil and military officials (yangban in the narrow sense of the word)

muryok 物慾 material desire

musŏn 武選 men who passed military selection examinations

myo 畝 the Chinese *mu*, land area unit

myŏn 面 subdistrict (or county)

myŏnbyŏng 免兵 exemption from military service

myŏnch'ŏn 免賤 exemption from base status, slavery, or manumission

myŏngbun 名分 one's moral obligations, but often used to indicate the moral obligation of upholding proper status distinction since social status should accrue to morally superior individuals

myŏngjŏn 名田 possession of land (name-land, or land registered to someone by name)

Myŏngnyang (p.n.) 鳴梁 in Chŏlla Province

myŏnp'o 綿布 five-"foot" length of cotton cloth

myŏnse 免稅 land tax exemption

myŏnyŏk 免役 exemption from military service

Naegŭmwi 內禁衛 Inner (Palace) Forbidden Guards

Naejasi 內資寺 Court of Palace Cuisine

naeno 內奴 male slaves employed in the palace

naenobi 內奴婢 Royal Treasury (Naesusa) and royal relative palace (*kungbang*) slaves

Naep'o (p.n.) 內浦 in Kyŏngsang Province

Naesa 內舍 Inner House

naesasaeng 內舍生 school or regular dormitory student

naesi nobi 內寺奴婢 palace and official bureau slaves

Naesŏmsi 內贍寺 Court of Palace Provisions

Naesusa 內需司 the Royal Treasury

Naet'ang 內帑 King's Treasury

Naeŭiwŏn 內醫院 Palace Physicians' Court

Naeyakkuk 內藥局 Palace Pharmacy

Nagoya (p.n.) 名古屋

Najang 羅將 runners, see also Choye

Naju (p.n.) 羅州
Naju-moksa 羅州牧使 magistrate of Naju
Naktang 落黨 Fallen Party, of Kim Chajŏm
Namhan sansŏng 南漢山城 Namhan mountain fortress
namjŏng 男丁 adult males
Namwŏn (p.n.) 南原 district in Chŏlla Province
Namwŏn-busa 南原府使 magistrate of Namwŏn
Nan-chün 南軍 Southern Army (Han), imperial guards
Nangch'ŏng 郎廳 staff officers in a bureau
Nanggwan 郎官 duty officers in ministries
Nangsa 郎舍 Office of Remonstrance
nanjŏn 亂廛 unlicensed shops
napkong nobi 納貢奴婢 tribute-paying slaves
napse 納稅 land tax
napsok 納粟 grain contribution to purchase manumission from slavery or office titles
Nei-cheng (Ch.) 内政 Internal Administration chapter of the *Kuan-tzu*
Nei-hsiang (Ch.) 内相 Inner Prime Ministers
Nei-shu-mi-shih (Ch.) 内樞密使 officials for transmission of documents (T'ang)
ngo-yen (Ch.) 鵝眼 "goose eye" cash
nien-k'o (Ch.) 年格 time in office or time-in-grade
Nit'anggae 尼湯介 uprising of 1583
nobi 奴婢 slave
Nobi ch'uswae-dogam 奴婢推刷都監 Directorate for Investigation of Slave Status
nobi isejibŏp 奴婢以世之法 the law by which slavery is determined by heredity
nobok 奴僕 slave
nojŏn 露田 open or treeless lowland fields
nokchŏn 祿田 salary land
nokkwan 祿官 sinecured "salary post"
Noksa 錄事 registrar, chief clerk
nong 農 peasants, agriculturalists
nongjang 農場 estates
Noron 老論 Patriarch's Faction
Northern Ch'i dynasty (Ch.) 北齊
Northern Chou dynasty (Ch.) 北周
Northern Sung dynasty (Ch.) 北宋
Northern Wei dynasty (424-535) (Ch.) 北魏
Noryang (p.n.) 露梁 Kyŏngsang Province
Nosŏ 老西 Merit-Subject Westerner faction; also Kongsŏ.
nŭng 能 ability
Nŭngmaach'ŏng 能麼兒廳 Military Academy, est. 1655

o 伍 group of five families
o 伍 file, military, of 4 men
Obu 五部 Five Wards (in the capital)
ŏbyu 業儒 a nothos scholar
oebang chinsang 外方進上 tribute presented to the throne from the outer provinces
oech'ŏ kongjang 外處空場 "empty markets in outer areas," flea markets (*kongjang*)
oegŏ nobi 外居奴婢 outside-resident official slaves
Oesa 外舍 Outer House
ogat'ong 五家統 5-family mutual aid and surveillance unit; see *oga chakt'ong*
oga chakt'ong 五家作統 5-family mutual surveillance units
Ogunyŏng 五軍營 Five Military Divisions (late Chosŏn)
Ŏhaeng yusa 御行有司 secret censors
Ojang 伍長 5-family head

ŏjang 漁箭 fishing weirs
ŏk 屋 "house" or business
Okchŏ (state) 沃沮
Oktang 玉堂 nickname for Hongmun'gwan. Office of Special Counselors
ŏmjŏksŏjibun 嚴嫡庶之分 maintaining strict distinctions between legitimate sons and nothoi
Ongju 翁主 princess
ongsan 甕算 nonsense
ŏp 業 function or occupation
ŏrindo 魚鱗圖 fish-scale registers
Oryeŭi 五禮儀 *The Ceremonies of the Five Rites*
Ŏsa 御史 secret censor
Owi 五衛 Five Guard system (early Chosŏn)
Owi toch'ongbu 五衛都摠府 Five Guards Directorate
Oyŏng 五營 Five Divisional Headquarters of the General Army (Kyŏnggi Province Division)
Ŏyŏngch'ŏng 御營廳 Royal Division
Ŏyŏnggun 御營軍 Royal Division Soldiers

pa (Ch.) 霸 hegemon
Pa-tso (Ch.) 八座 "8 seats" or 8 highest officials
P'ach'ong 把總 battalion commander
Paekche dynasty 百濟
paekchŏng 白丁 (1) Koryŏ dynasty, men of intermediate status between commoners and base persons; (2) Chosŏn dynasty, outcastes including willow basket weavers and butchers
paekkŭm 白金 silver alloy
paeksŏng 百姓 common people (Chosŏn); less than commoner but higher than slave (Koryŏ)
P'aengbae 彭排 military unit
paengmi 白米 husked rice
Pai-lu t'ung shu-yüan chieh shih 白鹿洞書院揭示 Chu Hsi's "Posted Instructions for the White Deer Academy"
Pajin'gun (p.n.) 罷陣軍
P'aju (p.n.) 坡州
p'aksagwan 博士官 erudites or specialists in the classics (Han). See *po-shih kuan*.
p'alp'o 八包 trade in ginseng
P'alwi 八衛 Eight Guards
pan-liang (Ch.) 半兩 the "half-*liang*" coin
pandang 伴倘 personal aides of high officials, see *pan'in*.
pang 坊 ward
Pang-cheng (Ch.) 坊正 ward chief (T'ang)
Pangbaek 方伯 provincial governor
panggun sup'o 放軍牧布 excusing duty soldiers from service and collecting tax payments from them instead
pangjŏn 方田 square-field system
Pangjŏng 坊正 chief of a ward in Yu Hyŏngwŏn's local government plan
pangmul 方物 tribute goods
pangnap 防納 tribute contracting; see *taenap*
pang'oe 方外 "irregulars"
Pang'ŏsa 防御使 Defense Commander
Pang'ŏyŏng 防御營 Defense Regiment
pangp'aesŏn 防牌船 armored ships
pangsang 坊庠 ward schools
P'an'gwan 判官 assistant to a provincial governor; administrator of grain transport
pangyak 方略 defense strategy of Yi Il
Pan'gye surok 磻溪隨錄 Collected works of Yu Hyŏngwŏn.
Pangyŏkso 防役所 collection centers for relief contributions in the villages

pan'in 伴人 estate agents or managers; personal aides of high officials; see *pandang*.
panno 班奴 a slave of the same category or family as other slaves
panp'o 番布 military support tax
P'ansŏ 判書 minister
pao (Ch.) (or *she*) 保（社） 16-family unit (T'ang); household cluster or mutual aid unit (Sung)
pao-chang (Ch.) 保長 chief of the *pao* mutual aid unit (Sung)
pao-ch'ao (Ch.) 寶鈔 Yüan dynasty paper money
pao-cheng (Ch.) 保正 mutual surveillance
pao-chia (Ch.) 保甲 mutual aid and responsibility system (Sung)
pao-ma-fa (Ch.) 保馬法 raising horses by household clusters (Sung)
P'ap'yŏng Yun clan 坡平尹氏
Pei-chün (Ch.) 北軍 Northern Army of the Han dynasty, capital guards
Pei-men hsüeh shih 北門學士 Scholars of the Northern Gate to draft documents (T'ang)
p'eng-tang (Ch.) 朋黨 factions
pi (Ch.) 比 5-family unit (Chou)
pi 鄙 local community
pi-chao (Ch.) 辟召 direct hiring by governors of subordinate officials
Pibyŏnsa 備邊司 Border Defense Command
pich'ongbŏp 比摠法 provincial quota system
Piguk 備局 see Pibyŏnsa
p'il 疋 cloth measurement
p'ilch'ae 筆債 "pen debt" or cloth surtax levied by the Royal Secretariat
p'in (Ch.) 品 grades
ping (Ch.) 聘 annual and triennial audiences for feudal representatives (Chou)
pip'anjŏg'imyŏ silchŭng [chŏn'gŏ] juŭijŏg'in hangmun t'aedo 批判的實證（典據）主義的學問態度 critical verification based on the citation of evidence
po 步 paces
po 保 support unit for duty soldiers
p'o 鋪 police box
p'o 布 cloth tax
pobusang 褓負商 peddlers
pobyŏng 步兵 infantrymen
P'och'ŏn (p.n.) 抱川 suburbs of Seoul
Poch'unggun 補充軍 unit of auxiliary soldiers
P'odoch'ŏng 捕盜廳 Agency for the Arrest of Thieves
pogap (*pao-chia*) 保甲 system of mutual aid and surveillance
pogye 僕隷 school slaves; servants and runners
poin 保人 support persons or taxpayers
pokho 復戶 see *kŭppokchŏn*
pŏl 閥 status
pŏn 本 root
pŏn 番 shift of rotating duty soldiers (Chosŏn)
pongbudong 封不動 "sealed and immovable" emergency reserves
pongch'aek 封冊 noble titles
ponggŏn 封建 granting of fiefs, feudalism; (Ch. *feng-chien*)
ponggong 封貢 investiture and tribute
ponggŏnsi 封建時 the age of feudalism
Pongsangsi 奉常寺 Court of Ancestral Rites
pon'gung nongsa 本宮農舍 agrarian huts of the main palace
pon'gwan 本貫 choronym; place name used to identify lineages
pongjok 奉足 support taxpayer (for duty soldiers)
pono 保奴 support slaves

pŏnsang kyŏngjik 番上京職 duty soldier
pŏnsang-ji-gun 番上之軍 rotating service troops
ponson 本孫 close relatives; those relatives entitled to inherit property when parents die without children; *sason*
pop'o 保布 support taxes in cloth for military service
pŏryŏl 閥閱 aristocratic family status
P'osan Community Compact 苞山鄉約 of Kim Seryŏng
po-shih kuan (Ch.) 博士官 erudites, or specialists in the classics (Han); see *p'aksagwan*
p'ose 鋪稅 shop taxes
p'osu 砲手 musketeers
Poŭn (p.n.) 報恩 in Ch'ungch'ŏng Province
Poŭn community compact 報恩鄉約
pu 負 a hundredth of a *kyŏl*
pu 府 prefecture; second largest unit in Yu Hyŏngwŏn's plan for local government
pu 夫 male farmer, farm family
pu 賦 tax, rent?
pu 部 regiment, of the MTA
pubyŏng 府兵 regular troops, soldiers
pugun ch'ŏlli 附近村里 neighborhood village in Yu Hyŏngwŏn's local government plan
Puhak 府學 Large Prefectural School
Puindong-dongyak 夫仁洞洞約 the community compact established by Ch'oe Hŭngwŏn from 1739 to 1745
Pukhag'ŭi 北學議 "Treatise on Learning from the North" (i.e., Ch'ing China)" by Pak Chega
pukpŏl 北伐 King Hyojong's "attack the North" policy
Pullyanggi (Fou-lang-chi) 佛狼機 Portuguese or simply, Western-style) cannon
pullyu 分類 dividing people into classes
pulsoktong pur'aegong 不惜銅不愛工 excessive laxity in the technology of manufacture
p'um 品 rank
p'umgwan 品官 title listed next to names of men in the household register (*hojok*) or land register (*yang'an*); some interpret this to mean "men of rank and office," but Song June-ho believes it was a title designating a petty local clerk of low status
p'umnyu 品流 class
pun 分 share, role
pun 分 area of measurement
pun'a 分兒 funds left over from bureau expenses
punbae 分配 allocations of tax quotas among districts
P'ungdan (p.n.) 豐湍
p'ungsu 風水 geomancy
P'ungjŏch'ang 豐儲倉 Surplus Storage Warehouse
punjŏng 分定 allocations that provincial governors and provincial army and navy commanders were required to raise any way they could and pay to the central government to offset the loss of revenue from the 1-*p'il* tax cut as a result of the 1750 Equal Service system
punsu 分數 quotas
Punwŏn 分院 Branch Agencies of the Saongwŏn or Pottery Agency
Pusa 府使 district magistrate
Pusan (p.n.) 釜山
Puwŏnsu 副元帥 vice-field commander
Puyakchŏng 副約正 assistants of the Haeju community compact
Puyun 府尹 magistrate of an important district
p'yohagun 標下軍 standard bearers,

aides
Pyŏkchegwan (p.n.) 碧蹄館 place of famous battle in Imjin War
pyŏkp'a 僻派 faction that supported King Yŏngjo when he starved his son, Crown Prince Sado, to death
Pyŏlchang 別將 special commanders; special officers
Pyŏlchoch'ŏng 別造廳 Special Armory
Pyŏlgam 別監 special director, assistant to the chief of a local yangban or gentry association (Hyangch'ŏng or Hyangsoch'ŏng)
Pyŏlgŏm 別檢 special monitor
pyŏlho sano 別戶私奴 see *oegŏ nobi.*
pyŏlkunjik 別軍職 special or auxiliary posts
Pyŏlmadae 別馬隊 Special Horse Unit
Pyŏlmojang 別募將 recruiting officers
Pyŏlmuban 別武班 special military unit during the reign of Sukchong, (1095-1105)
Pyŏlp'ajin 別破陣 Special Destruction Corps (cannoneers)
Pyŏlp'osu 別砲手 special musketeers
pyŏlsajŏn 別賜田 special royal award land
Pyŏlsiwi 別侍衛 Special Attendant Guards
Pyŏlsu 別首 chief of the Hyangsoch'ŏng
pyŏlsumi 別收米 special rice tax, continuation of the *sŏryangmi* of 1611
pyŏltae 別遂 (Hullyŏn-byŏltae) Special Cavalry of the Military Training Agency.
p'yŏn 偏 skewed
p'yŏng 坪 measure of area; 1,227.2 per acre
Pyŏng'an Province 平安道
pyŏngbo (*happo*) 併保 combining support taxpayers; a program to recruit additional support taxpayers by offering a reduced tax rate
Pyŏngja 丙子 year of the second Manchu invasion, 1637
pyŏngjang 邊將 border garrison commanders
pyŏngjŏn 兵田 land for the support of soldiers
pyŏngma 兵馬 cavalryman
Pyŏngma chŏlchesa 兵馬節制使 garrison commander in *chin'gwan* system
Pyŏngma chŏltosa 兵馬節道使 Provincial Army Commander; see Pyŏngsa
P'yŏngnowi 平擄衛 the Jurchen Pacifying Guards
Pyŏngsa 兵使 Provincial Army Commander, short for Pyŏngma chŏltosa
pyŏngsŏn 兵船 troopships
P'yŏngsisŏ 平市署 Bureau of Market Weights and Measures
Pyongyang (P'yŏngyang) (p.n.) 平壤
Pyŏngyŏng 兵營 provincial military commander's headquarters
p'yŏnho 編戶 "organizing households"
Pyŏnjŏn 便殿 see Hall of Convenience
p'yŏn'ogun 編伍軍 soldiers organized into regular military units

sa 士 petty officials; scholar-officials; scholars; retainers or knights
sa 事 work
sa 私 private
sa 司 battalion
Sa 司 bureaus, of the Six Ministries
Saboksi 司僕寺 Royal Stable Court
sabu 射夫 archers
sabu 士夫 officials and scholars; see *sadaebu*
sabyŏng 私兵 private soldiers
sach'ang 社倉 (Chu Hsi's) village granaries
sach'anggye yaksok 社倉契約束 pledges for the Village Granary *Kye*
sach'ŏn 私賤 private slaves

Sach'ŏn (p.n.) 泗川
sadaebu 士大夫 scholar-officials
sadaedong 私大同 the private *taedong* system
sadan 四端 the four basic virtues in the human mind
sadan ch'ilchŏng 四端七情 the Four Origins and Seven Emotions
Sadosi 司導寺
sae （升）(*sŭng* in Sino-Korean pronunciation); a unit defined as 80 warp threads by Cheng Hsüan in his commentary on the funeral rituals of the classic *I-li* (*The Book of Etiquette and Ceremonial*)
Saekchang 色掌 chargè, or clerk
Saejae (Choryŏng) (p.n.) （鳥嶺）Bird's Peak
Saekpu 穡夫 rural agricultural officials
saengwŏn 生員 classics licentiate
Saganwŏn 司諫院 Office of Censor General
sago 四庫 the Four Granaries of the capital to pay for the expenses of the royal house (*kongsang*)
sagun 四郡 the four prefectures in the northwest, est. 1443
Sahak 四學 Four Schools
Sahŏnbu 司憲府 Office of the Inspector-General
sahusŏn 伺候船 patrol boats
Sahwa 司貨 treasurer of the Haeju community compact
sahwan 使喚 regular runners
sain 士人 scholars
saja serok chi miŭi 仕者世祿之美意 a beautiful idea that (represented) the intent of King Wen of the Chou dynasty to provide hereditary salaries for those (officials) who served him
sajae 私財 private property
sajang 私匠 private merchants
Sajaegam 司宰監 office for supplying the costs of guest expenses
sajik 社稷 altars of earth and grain; see *sajiktan*
sajiktan 社稷壇 altars of earth and grain
sajo 四祖 four ancestors
sajok 士族 families or lineages of scholar-officials; often used in Korea for the yangban whether they were scholar-officials or not
sajŏn 私田 "private land": prebends or rights to collect the *cho* or tax granted to certain individuals in place of the state; or privately owned land; prebend
sajŏn 賜田 royal grants of land to private individuals
sajuin 私主人 warehousemen called private masters, private merchants
sajuin 私主人 private masters of the bureaus in charge of tribute collection
salsu 殺手 "killers" or close-combat sword, pike, and spearmen
Sama 司馬 Kor. for Ssu-ma, the chief military official in the capital of the Chinese Chou dynasty
Samaso 司馬所 Centers for Classics and Literary Licentiates; see Yuhyangso
Sambok plot 三復
Samgang haengsil 三綱行實 *Exemplars of the Three Moral Relationships*
samgo 三考 inspection periods
Samgong 三公 three moral advisers to the king
Samgun Toch'ongjebu 三軍都摠制府 Three Armies Command Agency
Samgun'mun 三軍門 Three Armies Office
Samhan 三韓 The three Han states in south Korea, ca. A.D. 1-300: Mahan, Pyŏnhan, Chinhan
Samhan chungbo 三韓重寶 a Korean coin.
samin kaktŭk kiso 四民各得其所

that the four occupations (officials, farmers, artisans, and merchants) would each obtain a place (in the world)

Samjŏn (p.n.) 三田 near Yangju, close to Seoul

Samjŏndo (p.n.) 三田渡 near Seoul

sammyŏn 三免 triple pardons

samosok 私募屬 initiation of low-rate service or *hŏryŏk* by officials on their own authority

samp'o waeran 三浦倭亂 the Three Ports Uprising of Japanese in Korea in 1510

Samsa 三司 Financial Commission (Koryŏ)

samsu 三手 the three skills: musketry, swordsmanship, and archery

samsubyŏng 三手兵 musketeers, bowmen, and pikemen

samsuryang 三手糧 three types of soldiers' rice surtax on land in the southern three provinces

samsumi 三手米 the rice surtax to support the *samsu* (the three types of soldiers), including musketeers, created during the Imjin War

Sam'ŭisa 三醫司 Bureau of Doctors

samyŏngjŏn 三營錢 the cash of the three military divisions

San-chang 三長 Three Chiefs of 486 A.D. (Northern Wei)

San-fu (Ch.) 三府 three districts around the capital

San-ku (Ch.) 三孤 three subordinate advisers to the ruler, below the San-kung

San-kuan (Ch.) 散官 irregular officials

San-kung (Ch.) 三公 three advisers to the ruler in *Book of History*

san-lao (Ch.) 三老 three elders of local (Han) government who administered education, lawsuits, and tax collection police duties

San-sheng (Ch.) 三省 Three Departments (T'ang)

San-shih (Ch.) 三師 Three Teachers (Sung)

San-shu (Ch.) 三署

San-ssu (Ch.) 三司 Finance Commission

san-tai (Ch.) 三代 the three dynasties or ages of Chinese antiquity: Hsia, Shang [Yin], and Chou

sang 庠 a local school in ancient China, below the district level; Yu's new type of school

sangbŏn 上番 on duty, or on a tour of duty (soldiers)

Sangbu 相府 Prime Minister's Office, equivalent to Yu's Ŭijŏngbu

sangch'am 常參 daily Standard Audience

Sandang 山黨 Mountain Faction of Kim Chip, Song Siyŏl, and Song Chun'gil

sanggye 上契 the Upper *Kye* reserved for yangban in An Chŏngbok's community compact

Sanggyejang 上契長 Upper *Kye* Chief in Yu Hyŏngwŏn's local government plan

Sanggwanhoe 相觀會 Mutual Meeting Association

sangho-daebu 上戶大夫 upper households and officials, in An Chŏngbok's village *kye* community compact

sang'in 常人 commoners

sangjik 常職 people in regular occupations

sangjŏn 上典 master of a slave

sangjŏng 詳定 detailed tax regulations

sangjŏngbŏp 詳定法 the Detailed Tax Regulation Law adopted in Hamgyŏng Province in 1666 that closely approximated the *taedong* system

Sangju (p.n.) 尚州

sangmok 上木 superior cloth
sangnap 上納 portion of tax receipts remitted to the capital
Sangp'yŏngch'ang 常平倉 Ever-Normal Granaries
Sangp'yŏngch'ŏng 常平廳 Ever-Normal Bureau, for price stabilization
Sangp'yŏnggam 常平監 Ever-Normal Directorate
Sang'ŭiwŏn 尚衣院 Royal Clothing Office
san'gun 山郡 upland region
san'gwan 散官 sinecures, posts without duties, salaries, or prebendal grants
sano 私奴 private slave
sano 司奴 official slave
sanobi 私奴婢 private slaves
sansŏng 山城 mountain fort
Saongwŏn 司饔院 Royal Cuisine Office
Saonsŏ 司醞署 Wine Bureau
sap'ae 賜牌 prebendal grants under royal warrant
sap'ae nobi 賜牌奴婢 royally granted slaves
sarim 士林 see *sarimp'a*.
sarimp'a 士林派 "the scholars of the forest," supposedly scholars of high moral standards in the countryside who were shut out of office
saryŏng 使令 runner, servant
saryu 士類 the class of scholars
sasa 寺社 temples and shrines
sase 賜税 royal grant of tax revenues to an individual; prebendal grant?
sasejŏn 賜税田 prebend
Sasŏmsi 司贍寺 Court for Providing Aid, in charge of paper money and slave tribute
sason 使孫 see *ponsŏn*
Sasŏng t'onggo 四聲通考 *A Comprehensive Study of the Four Tones*, by Sin Sukchu
sasu 射手 archers
Sayŏgwŏn 司譯院 Court of Interpreters
se (Ch., *sui*) 歲 term used to represent the age of a person in which the individual's age at birth is one year
se 税 taxes
sebol 世閥 hereditary lineage
sech'o 歲抄 annual selection of unregistered men for military service
segong 歲貢 annual tribute recommendees
segyŏng 世卿 hereditary ministers
Sejojo ilgi 世祖朝日記 diary of Sejo's reign
sejok 世族 heirs to the family line; hereditary clans
sejŏn 税田 taxable land
sejŏn kwanha 世傳管下 hereditary hired laborers
semi 税米 land tax
seŏpchŏn 世業田 permanent land grants
sep'ye 歲幣 tribute to the Chinese emperor
serok 世祿 hereditary salaries
serok chi sin 世祿之臣 officials of hereditary families
serokchŏn 世祿田 hereditary salary lands
sesin 世臣 hereditary officials
Shan-hai-kuan (p.n.) 山海關
Shang dynasty 商
Shang-lin-yüan (Ch.) 上林苑 the Imperial Forest Park, given control over cash and the right to mint cash by Emperor Wu (Han)
Shang neng-fu (Ch.) 上農夫 superior farmer (Chou), defined as one who could support nine people from the production of a standard-sized plot of 100 *mou*
Shang-shih (Ch.) 上士 Upper Shih (official rank in Chou dynasty)
Shang-shu (Ch.) 尚書 *The Book of*

History
Shang-shu (Ch.) 尚書 minister, of one of the Six Ministries in China; Master of Documents (Sui)
Shang-shu sheng (Ch.) 尚書省 Department of State Affairs (T'ang and Sung)
Shang-shu ta-chüan (Ch.) 尚書大傳 Commentary on the *Shu-ching*
shao-hsing (Ch.) 紹興 year period (1131-63) of the Southern Sung dynasty
she (*pao*) (Ch.) 社（保）household cluster
she (Ch.) 社 spirit of earth
she-shou (Ch.) 社首 head of the village shrine (Sung)
she-ts'ang (Ch.) 社倉 village granary
Shen-yang (p.n.) 瀋陽 in Manchuria
Sheng (Ch.) 省 province (Yüan-Ch'ing)
Shih (Ch.) 史 document clerk (Chou)
shih (Ch.) 實 true, real, actual substance
shih (Ch.) 石 Chinese unit of grain volume, 1 picul
shih (Ch.) 士 scholar-officials, scholars; low-level official (Chou)
shih (Ch.) 食 food
shih (Ch.) 詩 a type of poem
shih and *hua* (Ch.) 食貨 food and money
Shih-cheng-chi 時政記 *Daily Record of Events*
Shih-chi 史記 Ssu-ma Ch'ien's *Records of the Grand Historian*
Shih-lin yen-yü (Ch.) 石林燕語 Text by Yeh Meng-te
shih-ta-fu (Ch.) 士大夫 scholar-officials
shih-tsu (Ch.) 士族 families or lineages of scholar officials
shih-yung (Ch.) 實用 practical utility
Shōgun. (J.) 將軍 military ruler
shu (Ch.) 術 tactics
shu (Ch.) 庶 commoners
shu (Ch.) 銖 weight, used for coins: as in 2-*shu*, 4-*shu*, or 5-*shu* coins
Shu-ching (Ch.) 書經 *The Book of History*
Shu-Han dynasty 蜀漢
Shu-mi-yüan (Ch.) 樞密院 Bureau of Military Affairs (Sung)
shuai (Ch.) 帥 special military commanders (Sung)
si 仕 on duty
Sibwi 十衛 the Ten Guards
sig'ŭp 食邑 prebend, grant of tax income only to a person or institution
sija 仕者 incumbent officials
sijŏn 市廛 licensed shops
sijong 侍從 royal attendants
Sijonggwan 侍從官 royal attendants
sikch'ae 食采 prebends
sikhwa 食貨 food and money
sikki seip 食其稅入 collect tax income
sikse 食稅 prebends
siksejiji 食稅之地 prebendal grants
siksejibŏp 食稅之法 prebendal allotments
sikwa 柴科 grades of woodland
sil 實 true, real, actual substance, true facts
silkyŏl 實結 "true land" or taxable land
Silla dynasty 新羅
silli 實理 real principle; the principle that exists in real objects and things of the world
Sillok 實錄 *Veritable Records* of individual kings
silsa 實事 real facts
silsa kusi 實事求事 seek truth from facts (or real events)
silso 失所 landholdings?, places
sim'ŭi 沈衣 ceremonial garment
Simyak 審藥 inspector of medicine
sin 臣 male base person (in the *Rites of Chou*)
sin 臣 subject or official

sin'gong 身貢 personal tribute paid by outside resident slaves to the government

sinhaek t'onggong 辛亥通共 the 1791 "joint-sales" decree, which allowed unlicensed merchants to operate in the capital alongside the six shops (Yug'ŭijŏn or Yukchubijŏn)

sinje 新制 new system; Yu Hyŏngwŏn's term for those military units established after the Imjin War

Sinmyŏngsaek 申明色 local expert for each magistrate

sino 寺奴 official slave

sinobi 寺奴婢 capital bureau slaves

sinp'o 身布 personal cloth tax

Sinsŏn'gun 新選軍 New Select Soldiers

sinyŏk 身役 personal service (including support taxes for soldiers)

Sipchŏn t'ongbo 十錢通寶 Ten-cash Circulating Treasure

Sirhak 實學 Practical Learning

sirhakcha 實學者 Practical Learning scholars

Siwigun 侍衛軍 Attendant Guard Soldiers.

so 序 schools below district level

so (Ch.) 所 local unit (Ming)

sŏ 庶 commoner

sŏ 庶 nothoi, sons of concubines

sŏ 庶 all other sons besides the eldest son of a legitimate wife; see *sŏja*

sŏban 西班 the Western file, i.e., military officials

sŏdang 書堂 elementary schools

soese 衰世 an age of decline

sog'ak 俗樂 popular musicians

Sŏgi 書記 secretary

sog'o 束伍 the Che-chiang system of military organization, or their units

sog'ogun 束伍軍 soldiers of *sog'o* units; often used to mean slave soldiers since slaves were allowed into such units

sŏgyŏng 署經 censorate's right to review candidates recommended for office

Sohak 小學 *The Small Learning*

soho 小戶 smallholder

sŏin (Ch.) 庶人 commoners

sŏin 西人 Westerner faction

soin 小人 "small people," i.e., men of lesser moral capacity

soja 小子 a younger person

sŏja 庶子 nothos or nothoi; sons (or children) of concubines

sŏja 庶子 all other sons besides the eldest son of a legitimate wife

sŏjok 庶族 commoner lineage

sojŏn 小錢 small coin that was one fourth the weight of a "large coin" (*taejŏn*)

sŏk 石 *sŏm*, equivalent to 15 or 20 *mal*, 1 picul, measure of volume

Sŏkchŏn 釋奠 rites to Confucius on 2.8 lunar at the Munmyo shrine

soksin 贖身 purchase of freedom or commoner status by or for slaves

Soktaejŏn 續大典 Chosŏn dynasty law code of 1746

solchŏng 率丁 dependent male adults

solgŏ nobi 率居奴婢 service slaves, not domestic slaves, as previously thought

sŏlgwan-bunjik 設官分職 establishing offices and dividing up responsibilities

sŏm colloquial term for *sŏk*, one picul of grain by volume; 15 or 20 *mal*

sŏmin 庶民 ordinary commoners

sŏng 性 human nature

sŏng 誠 sincerity

Sŏnggyun'gwan 成均館 National Academy

sŏngjok 姓族 surnames and lineages

Sŏngju (p.n.) 星州

Sŏngjung aema 成衆愛馬 Holch'i, or core of the Royal Guards (early Chosŏn)
Sŏngmun 城門 palace gate
Sŏngmyo 聖廟 shrine to the sages
sŏngni (*hsing-li* Ch.) 性理 the philosophy of nature and principle
Sŏn'gonggam 繕工監 Directorate of Construction
Songp'a (p.n.) 松坡 Kwangju area near Seoul
sŏn'gun 選軍 selected soldiers, provided with land grants (early Koryŏ)
Sŏnhyech'ŏng 宣惠廳 Office for Dispensing Benevolence established in 1614 in place of the Taedong Agency (Taedongch'ŏng) to administer the *taedŏng* system and *taedong* tax revenues
Sŏnjo sujŏng sillok 宣祖修正實錄 *The Amended Veritable Record of King Sŏnjo's Reign*
Sŏnjo sillok 宣祖實錄 *The Veritable Record of King Sŏnjo's Reign*
Sŏnjŏn sosik 宣傳消息 see Sŏnjŏn'gwan
Sŏnjŏn'gwan (Sŏngjŏn sosik) 宣傳官 royal messengers (est. Late Koryŏ)
sŏnmu kun'gwan 選武軍官 specially selected military officers
sŏnsa 選士 selected scholars
Sŏnsan (p.n.) 善山 in Kyŏngsang Province
sŏnsang nobi 選上奴婢 slaves selected from the province for duty in the capital
sŏnyong 善用 managing things in the right way
sŏŏl 庶孽 nothoi or sons of yangban or *sajok* by slave concubines
sŏri 胥吏 clerk
Soron 少論 Disciple's Faction, a Westerner splinter group
sŏryangmi 西糧米 the Western provision tax, or the Mao or Chinese provision tax (*moryangmi*, *tangnyangmi*) of 1611, a rice surtax of 1.5 *mal/kyŏl* to provide rations for the troops of the Ming general, Mao Wen-lung
Sosa 小使 Boy Servants
sŏsa 署事 signed concurrence to a proposal, decision, or royal appointment usually by members of the Censorate
Sosŏ 少西 Young Westerner faction
sŏwŏn 書員 low-level clerks in the bureaus
sŏwŏn 書院 private academy
Sŏwŏn *hyangyak* 西原鄉約 Sŏwŏn Community Compact
Ssu-ch'uan (Ch.) (p.n.) 四川
Ssu-hsien. (Ch.) 司險 map official (Chou)
Ssu-k'ou (Ch.) 司寇 Minister of Punishments (Chou)
Ssu-kung (Ch.) 司空 Minister of Land and production from land; or Minister of Works (Chou)
Ssu-lo (Ch.) 司樂 grand master of music
Ssu-ma (Ch.) 司馬 minister of war, the chief military official in the capital of the Chinese Chou dynasty (Kor., Sama)
Ssu-men hsüeh (Ch.) 四門學 Schools of the Four Gates
Ssu-shih (Ch.) 司事 personnel officer, a subordinate in the Office of Summer (Hsia-kuan) (Chou)
Ssu-shih (Ch.) 司市 Market Agency (Chou)
Ssu-t'u (Ch.) 司徒 minister of education (Chou)
Ssu-t'u-fu (Ch.) 司徒府 Personnel Bureau (Wei)
su (see *hyang*) 遂 local government unit

subu 水夫 sailors, river transport workers
such'a sŏkp'o 水車石砲 water-wheel rock cannon
such'ŏl 水鐵 pig iron
Such'ŏlkye 水鐵契 pig-iron association
sugi ch'iin-ji-do 修己治人之道 self rectification (as the means to) the governance of others
sugun (*chusa*) 水軍 marines or maritime soldiers
Sugun chŏltosa 水軍節度使 Provincial Navy Commander
sui (Ch.) 歲 age; see *se*
Sui dynasty 隋
sujinjang 水鎭將 naval garrison commander
Sujŏng 隨從 attendants
suk 塾 a watchtower used also as a local school in ancient China
Sukchong sillok 肅宗實錄 *Veritable Record for King Sukchŏng*
suktong 熟銅 wrought iron (also annealed copper or brass)
sulka 術家 practitioners of shamanism, acupuncture, and geomancy
Sunbyŏnsa 巡邊使 mobile border commander
Sunch'alsa 巡察使 concurrent mobile inspectors, dispatched from capital to command troops in the field
Sunch'ŏn (p.n.) 順天
sŭng 升 (Kor., *toe*); .1 *mal*, a measure of weight used for grain.
sŭng 升 see *sae*
sŭng 丞 assistant magistrate
Sung dynasty 宋
Sung-shih (Ch.) 宋史 *History of the Sung dynasty*
sŭngjach'ong 勝子銃 *sŭng*-type gun
Sŭngbal 承發 assistant to a magistrate
sŭngho 陞戶 promoting support taxpayers to duty soldiers
Sŭngjŏngwŏn 承政院 Royal Secretariat
sŭngmok 升木 type of cloth
Sŭngmunwŏn 承文院 Office of Diplomatic Correspondence
Sŭngsang (Ch'eng-hsiang, Ch.) 承相 prime minister
sun'gyŏng kunsa 巡警軍師 capital constabulary
sunhaeng 巡行 periodic rounds of inspection by a governor of all districts in his province
sunjang 巡將 patrol officers
sunwi 巡衛 capital constabulary
Suŏch'ŏng 守禦廳 Defense Command, at the Namhan fort
Suŏsa 守禦使 Defense Commander of the Defense Command (Suŏch'ŏng) stationed at the Namhan fort
sup'o 收布 cloth taxpaying military officers (*kun'gwan*)
sup'o kun'gwan 收布軍官 cloth taxpaying military officers
suryŏng 守令 generic term for district magistrate
Susa 水使 provincial navy commander
Susayŏng (Suyŏng) 水使營 Provincial Naval Commander's Headquarters
susŏnggun 守城軍 walled town defense troops
Suwŏn (p.n.) 水原
Suyŏng 水營 Susayŏng, Provincial Naval Commander's Headquarters
Szechwan (p.n.) 四川 Chinese province

ta-chen (Ch.) 大鎭 large garrison
ta-ch'uan (Ch.) 大錢 large cash
Ta-ch'üan wu-pai (Ch.) 大泉五百 500-cash coin (Wu)
Ta-fu (Ch.) 大夫 official (Chou)
ta-hsüeh 大學 adult schools
Ta-kuo (Ch.) 大國 largest fief in the Chou dynasty

ta-pi (Ch.) 大比 the triennial census of population and property (Chou)
Ta Ssu-k'ung (Ch.) 大司空 grand minister of works (Chou)
Ta Ssu-ma (Ch.) 大司馬 grand controller of horse (Chou)
Ta Ssu-t'u (Ch.) 大司徒 grand minister of education (Chou)
Ta-tsung-kuan-fu (Ch.) 大總管府 Superior Area Commands
tae 隊 eleven-man squads of the *sog'o* system; or platoon
taebi 大比 a grand triennial evaluation of worthy and able men
taebu 大府 see Tohobu
taebu (*ta-fu*, Ch.) 大夫 middle-rank officials
taebusa. (*ta-fu-shih*, Ch.) 大夫士 officials
Taech'ong 隊總 squad leader
taedong 大同 replacement of tribute with a grain surtax on land, 17th C.
Taedong chŏrmok 大同節目 *taedong* regulations
Taedong River 大同江
taedongbŏp 大同法 *taedong* law
Taedongch'ang 大同倉 Taedong Granary
Taedongch'ŏng 大同廳 Taedong Agency, established 1608
taedongmi 大同米 *taedong* rice tax that replaced tribute in kind
Taegu (p.n.) 大邱
Taegun 大君 Grand Lord, Prince
t'aegŭk 太極 Great Ultimate
taeho 大戶 grand household
Taehŭng fort 大興
Taejang 大將 general, commander, or division commander
taejok 大族 great families
Taejol 隊卒
taejŏn 大錢 large coin
Taejŏn husongnok 大典後續錄 Supplementary Law Code of 1543
taenap 代納 substituting rice and cloth levies for tribute in kind or substitute payments
T'aengniji 擇里志 book by Yi Chunghwan
Taesahŏn 大司憲 inspector-general
Taesama 大司馬 grand controller of horse
taesin 大臣 high officials, of rank 1A-3B
T'aeŭiwŏn 太醫院 Agency of Supreme Physicians
T'ai-hua 5-shu 太和五銖 coin (Northern Wei)
t'ai-shou (Ch.) 太守 district magistrate Ch'in and Han)
tai-t'ien (Ch.) 代田 crop rotation system
T'aip'ing Rebellion 太平
t'ajak 打作 sharecropping
t'ajo 打租 see *t'ajak*
Tamyang (p.n.) 潭陽
tang (Ch.) 黨 unit of 500 families (Chou)
Tang-cheng (Ch.) 黨政 local official in charge of moral education (Chou)
tang ch'ien-ch'ien (Ch.) 當千錢 1000-cash coin (Wu dynasty, 3rd c.)
T'ang-shang (Ch.) 堂上 chief officials (Ming)
tangha 堂下 officials below third rank
tangnyangmi 唐糧米 the Chinese or Mao provision tax (*moryangmi*); see *sŏryangmi*
t'angp'yŏng 蕩平 King Yŏngjo's policy for equal opportunity for all men for office
t'angp'yŏngch'aek 蕩平策 the *t'angp'yŏng* policy of King Yŏngjo
tangsang 黨庠 Yu's subdistrict; see *yŏsuk*
tangsang 堂上 commissioner; also see *tangsanggwan*
tangsanggwan 堂上官 "officials of the

upper end of the hall," high-ranking officials of first, second, and part of the third ranks
T'ang-shu 唐書 *History of the T'ang Dynasty*
tao (Ch.) 道 circuit
taphŏm 踏驗 on-the-spot crop damage inspection for the purpose of tax reduction or exemption
ti 敵 one equal or less than 10 years younger or older than ego
t'i (Ch.) 體 see *ch'e*
tiao (Ch.) 調 the T'ang capitation tax for tribute; household tax in cash
t'ien (Ch.) 甸 well-field unit
T'ien-kuan (Ch.) 天官 Officer of Heaven (Chou), equivalent of a prime minister
T'ien-ch'i (Ch.) 天啓 a Chinese coin
T'ien-tzu ssu-jen (Ch.) 天子私人 private men of Emperor Hsüan-tsung (T'ang); Inner Prime Ministers
ting (Ch.) 亭 watchtower, a subdistrict unit in the Han dynasty
Ting-wei (Ch.) 廷尉 Minister of Punishments (Han)
to 道 circuits
to (or *kye*) 徒 a community compact
to 道 the Way
T'o-pa 拓跋 non-Chinese tribe
Toanch'ŏng 都案廳 office of the palace guards in charge of military support revenues
Tobu 都府 battalions of 1,000 men each (early Chosŏn)
Toch'ebu 都體府 see Toch'ech'alsa
Toch'ech'alsa 都體察使 supreme commander of the Office of the Supreme Commander (Toch'ech'alsabu, or Toch'ebu)
Toch'ech'alsabu 都體察使府 Office of the Supreme Commander
Toch'ŏngbu 都摠府 Supreme Headquarters
toch'ŏp 度牒 monk certificate
t'odan 土團 resettlement of educated elite in the villages; see *t'u-tüan*.
toga 都家 warehouses of private merchants
Togam 都監 General Directorate or Directorate; also short for Hullyŏndogam, the Military Training Agency
togo 都賈 wholesale monopolies
Togwan 都官 Slave Agency
Togyejang 都契長 general *kye* chiefs in Yulgok's *kye* system
tohak (Tao-hsüeh, Ch.) 道學 the learning of the Confucian Way
Tohobu (or Taebu) 都護府 strategic prefecture; largest of four units of local government in Yu Hyŏngwŏn's plan
Tohobusa 都護府使 magistrate of a Tohobu
tohoe 都會 collection center; see Tohoegwan
Tohoegwan 都會館 Tax Collection Centers
Tohundo 都訓導 a superfluous local military official
tojang 導掌 steward
Tojejo 都提調 supreme commissioner, for the Royal Division or Border Defense Command.
toji 賭地 fixed, lower-rate, longer term leaseholds
tojo 賭租 fixed rent
toju 道主 the "lord of the province"
tŏkhaeng 德行 virtuous behavior
toksŏ ch'ulsinjibŏp 讀書出身之法 an examination of reading knowledge
Toksŏdang 讀書堂 Book Reading Hall
Tollyŏngbu 敦寧府 the Agency for Royal Relatives
Tollyŏngbu Yŏngsa 敦寧府領事 director of the Office of the Royal Clan
tong 洞 administrative village
t'ong 統 5-family unit in Yu Hyŏngwŏn's plan

tong si ch'ŏnmin 同是天民 What we have in common is that we are all Heaven's people.
tongban 東班 the Eastern File, i.e., civil officials
tongbok 童僕 slaves
t'onggong parmae 通共發賣 joint sales, i.e., permission for unlicensed vendors to operate alongside the licensed merchants
Tongguk 東國 Eastern Land, Korea
Tongguk chungbo 東國重寶 a Korean coin
Tongguk t'ongbo 東國通寶 coin proposed by Yu Hyŏngwŏn, the Circulating Treasure of the Eastern Country
T'ongguk t'onggam 東國通鑑 The Comprehensive Mirror of the Eastern Land
Tonggwan 冬官 officer of winter
T'onggwan 統官 regional naval commander; see T'ongjesa
tonggye 洞契 village *kye* in Yu Hyŏngwŏn's plan for local government
tonggyu 洞規 ground rules for the Golden Orchid *kye* in Mokch'on, 1641
Tonghak rebellion 東學亂 1894-95.
Tongho mundap 東湖問答 Yulgok's "Questions and Answers at the Eastern Lake"
tong'in 東人 Easterner (faction)
t'ong'in 通引 boy servants; see *kongsaeng* and *ch'ŏngjik*
T'ongjang 統長 chief of a *t'ong*
Tongjasŭp 童子習 *Training Manual for Children*
T'ongjesa 統制使 regional naval commander; see T'onggwan
T'ongjeyŏng 統制營 Regional Naval Headquarters
T'ongju 統主 10-family head in Yulgok's Haeju village granary of 1577
t'ongmyŏng ch'ŏnsa 通明薦士 enlightened selected scholars
Tongmong hunhoe 童蒙訓誨 instructors for children
Tongmong kyogwan 童蒙教官 instructors of the youthful benighted
Tongnae (p.n.) 東萊 in Kyŏngsang Province
T'ongnyewŏn 通禮院 Comprehensive Rites Agency
Tongnyŏngbu expeditions 東寧府征伐 Two expeditionary forces sent into the Liao-yang region of Manchuria in 1370 to recover territory for Koryŏ
tongp'o 同胞 brothers
Tongsa kangmok 東史綱目
T'ongsinsa 通信使 ambassador
T'ongyŏng 統營 Naval Command for the two southern provinces of Chŏlla and Kyŏngsang.
t'op'um 土品 local influentials of rank
Top'yŏng'ŭisasa 都評議使司 Supreme Council of State, the supreme civil deliberative council of the late Koryŏ and early Chosŏn period to 1400, replaced by the Ŭijŏngbu
Tosa 都事 inspector; assistant to a provincial governor, often functioned as magistrate of the provincial capital
tosim 道心 the mind of the Way (see *ch'ŏnsim*)
Tosunbyŏnsa 都巡邊使 General Circuit Defense Commander, dispatched from the capital
Tosunch'alsa 都巡察使 supreme mobile inspector, dispatched from the capital to command troops in the field
Tosŭng 渡丞 ferry-station official
Tosŭngji 都承旨 chief Royal Secretary
Towŏnsu 都元帥 supreme field commander, dispatched from the capital
Toyakchŏng 都約正 general compact head of community compacts
toye 道藝 ability and skills in the arts
Tsai-ch'en (Ch.) 宰臣 state councilor
Tsai-hsiang (Ch.) 宰相 councilor of

state (T'ang)
Ts'ang-shih Ts'ao (Ch.) 常侍曹 Office of Constant Attendance
Tso-chuan (Ch.) 左傳
tsu (Ch.) 租 land tax or rent (see *cho*); unhulled rice, vs. *mi* 米, hulled rice
tsu-pi (Ch.) 自辟 see *chabi*
Tsu-shih (Ch.) 族師 local educational official (Chou)
Tsu-yung-shih (Ch.) 租庸使 special commissioner for taxation
tsu-yung-tiao (Ch.) 租庸調 triple taxes (T'ang)
ts'un (Ch.) 村 village (T'ang)
tsun (Ch.) 尊 respected elder, one twenty or more years older than ego
Ts'un-cheng (Ch.) 村正 village chief
Tsung-kuan (Ch.) 總管 regional governor
Tsung-po (Ch.) 宗伯 minister of rites in *Book of History*
Tsung-tu chün-wu (Ch.) 總督軍物 supreme commander for military affairs
Tsushima (island) 對馬島
Tu (Ch.) 徒 runner (Chou)
Tu-hu-fu (Ch.) 都護府 Grand Protectorate
T'u-mu Rebellion 土木之變 of 1449 (Ming)
Tu-tu (Ch.) 都督 commander-in-chief (Ming).
t'u-tüan (Ch.) 土斷 resettlement of educated elite in the villages (Wei); (Kor., *todan*)
tu-wei (Ch.) 都尉 commandant in the T'ang *fu-ping* system; aide or assistant magistrate (Han)
t'uan-lien (Ch.) 團練 local militia
Tumen River (Tuman'gang) 豆滿江
tun (Ch.) 屯 military colony; see *tunjŏn*
T'ung-chien kang-mu 通鑑綱目
Tung-kuan (Ch.) 冬官 officer of winter (Chou), in charge of industry and public works
T'ung-tien 通典
tŭngwi 等位 ranked position
tunjŏn 屯田 military colonies
turak 斗落 the amount of land on which 1 *mal* could be planted as seed, 0.163 acres (ca. 1910)
tusŏk 豆錫 brass
Tzu-chih t'ung-chien 資治通鑑.
Tz'u-shih (Ch.) 刺史 regional inspector

Uch'amch'an 右參贊 state councilor
Uch'ang 右倉 Right Granary; see Kwanghŭngch'ang
Uhu 虞候 aides of provincial army and navy commanders
ŭi 義 righteousness, righteous obligation, duty
Ŭibin 儀賓 princes
Ŭibinbu 儀賓府 Office of Royal Sons-in-law
Ŭich'ang 義倉 Righteous Granaries
Ŭigŭmbu 義禁府 Office for the Deliberation of Forbidden Affairs or State Tribunal
Ŭihak 醫學 School of Medicine
Ŭihŭng ch'in'gunwi 義興親軍衛 Righteousness Flourishing King's Personal Guards
Ŭihŭng samgunbu 義興三軍府 Righteousness Flourishing Three Armies
Ŭinggo 義盈庫 Storehouse of Overflowing Virtue
Ŭijŏng 議政 member of Yu's State Council
Ŭijŏngbu 議政府 State Council
Ŭiju (p.n.) 義州
Ŭisa 醫司 Bureau of Medicine
ŭisaeng 醫生 medical student, i.e., the post of a medical doctor in the provinces
ŭlmyo waebyŏn 乙卯倭變 The Japanese rising of 1555

Ulsan (p.n.) 蔚山
ŭm privilege 蔭 the right to office without examination for sons of high officials
ŭmgŭp 蔭及 grant of the protection or *ŭm* privilege
ŭmjŏn 蔭田 land grant to someone holding a "protected" (*ŭm*) post
ŭmsa 淫祀 "lewd sacrifices," i.e., a pejorative term for Buddhist, animist, and other non-Confucian rituals conducted in rural villages
ŭn 銀 silver
Un'am (p.n.) 雲巖
ŭnbyŏng 銀瓶 silver jar money
Ŭnggun 鷹軍 Falconers
ŭnggyo 應教 expectant candidates "awaiting instruction," i.e., appointment to office, in Yu Hyŏngwŏn's proposed Yŏngyŏnwŏn (Hall of Invitation to the Brave)
Ŭngyangwi 鷹揚衛
Unjŏnsa 運轉使 transport commissioner
ŭp 邑 district, or district town
ŭphak 邑學 Yu's district schools
Urimwi 羽林軍 Winged Forest Guards, military unit of the Dragon Tiger Regiment or Yonghoyŏng of the Forbidden Soldiers
Usŏ 迂書 book by Yu Suwŏn
Uŭijŏng 右議政 councilor of the right, or third state councilor

Wai-fu (Ch.) 外府 Outer Agency or treasury (Chou)
Wakō (J.) (*waegu*) 倭寇 pirate raids; mostly but not necessarily Japanese
Wan-li t'ung-pao 萬歷通寶 Wan-li Circulating Treasure
wang 王 king; prince
Wang-chih 王制 section of the *Li-chi* (*Book of Rites*)
Wang-kuo (Ch.) 王國 kingdom
wangbŏp 王法 the laws of a virtuous king
wangjŏn 王田 the king's land
wanho 完戶 complete household
Wansan-gun (p.n.) 完山郡
Wasŏ 瓦署 Tile Works
wei (Ch.) 尉 assistant magistrate (Han)
wei (Ch.) 衛 guard units on the frontier (Ming)
Wei dynasty (Ch.) 魏 3rd century A.D.
wei-so (Ch.) 衛所 system of military organization (Ming)
Wen-hsien t'ung-k'ao 文獻通考 Encyclopedia by Ma Tuan-lin 馬端臨
Western Chin dynasty (Ch.) 西晉
wi 僞 falsities
wijang 衛將 guard commanders of the Five Guards
wisangjiin 爲上之人 the man (or men) at the top of the government; the ruler (and his advisers)
wŏnbu 原夫 Tasan's basic farmer family
wŏn'gong 元貢 general tribute
wŏnho 元戶 basic household, a man who served on military duty
wŏnjong 原定 basic assignment of a soldier
wŏnjong kongsin 原從功臣 minor merit subjects
Wŏnju (p.n.) 原州 in Kangwŏn Province
wŏnsa 元士 lower-rank officials
Wŏndang 原黨 Original Faction of Wŏn Tup'yo
Wu dynasty (Ch.) 吳 third century A.D.
Wu-chün tu-tu-fu 五軍都督府 Five Armies Command (Ming)
wu-li (Ch.) 物理 the principle of (material) things
wu-wei (Ch.) 無爲 do nothing (and yet everything is done)

Yakchang 約長 head of a community compact

Yakchŏng 約正 head of the compact, chief official of Yu Hyŏngwŏn's subdistrict community compact (*hyangyak*)

yakho 弱戶 weak household

yaksok 約束 pledges, commitments? among soldiers in the field?

yain 野人 men of the fields, ordinary peasants (vs. scholars)

yang 兩 *liang* (Ch.). 1 tael or 1 ounce; a measure of weight

yang 良 good (status)

yang'an 量案 land registers (Chosŏn)

yangch'ul wiip 量出爲入 determining taxes in advance to finance what the government felt it was necessary to spend

yamen (Ch.) 衙門

yang'in 良人 persons of good status

yang'ip wich'ul 量入爲出 pay-as-you-go, adjusting expenditures to revenue received

yangjŏn 養田 supporting land system

yangjŏng 良丁 adult males of good status

Yangju (p.n.) 楊州 suburbs of Seoul

yangmaek 兩麥 double wheat and barley crop

yangmin 良民 people of good status (commoners)

yangmin 養民 support of the people

yangnoyŏn 養老宴 annual banquet for the elderly

Yangtze River 揚子江

yangyŏk 良役 military service tax for men of good status

Yangyŏk sajŏngch'ŏng 良役查整廳 Commoner Service Investigation Bureau

ye 禮 rites, ritual etiquette, principles of social usage (*li*, Ch.); the six arts or skills of the classics

Yean (p.n.) 禮安 in Kyŏngsang Province

Yebinsi 禮賓寺 Ritual Guest Agency

Yemun'gwan 藝文館 Office of Royal Decrees

yemyŏng 禮命 courtesy appointment, plan of Ch'eng Hao; (*li-ming*,-Ch.)

Yen-t'ieh-shih (Ch.) 鹽鐵使 regional commissioner for salt and iron production

Yen-ying yüan 筵英院 Hall for Inviting the Brave, proposed by Ch'eng Hao (Sung)

Yenching (p.n.) 燕京 old name for Beijing

yesong 禮訟 mourning rite controversy

yin (Ch., Kor., *ŭm*) 蔭 protection privilege, allowing appointment to office of sons of officials

Yin (Shang) dynasty 殷

Ying-chiang 營將 garrison commander in Ch'i Chi-kuang's organization system

yung-hui era 永徽 650-56 (T'ang)

yŏ 閭 a group of 25 households

yŏbok 女僕 female servants

yŏbu 餘夫 other males in Tasan's land distribution system

yŏgaek 旅客 commision agents

Yŏha ilgi 熱河日記 *Diary of My Trip to Jehol*, by Pak Chiwŏn

yŏjang 閭長 head of a 30-family unit under Tasan's land system

yŏjŏn 閭田 Tasan's [Chŏng Yagyong] program for national ownership and egalitarian land distribution

yŏjŏng 餘丁 extra personnel or extra adult males

Yŏk 驛 Post-station

yŏkka 役價 service fee, a fee paid to hire someone to perform labor service

yŏkkunjŏn 役軍田 service-soldier land; see *kunbojijŏn*

yŏkp'o 役布 substitute cloth taxes to pay for labor service, such as the repair of official vessels

Yŏksŭng 役丞 post-station clerk

yŏllip 連立 hereditary succession of military households (Koryŏ)

Yŏllyŏsil kisul 燃藜室記述 Yi Kŭng'ik's private history of the Chosŏn dynasty

Yŏmch'och'ŏng 焰硝廳 Nitrate Bureau

Yŏnbaek (p.n.) 延白

Yŏng 營 governor's yamen; battalion-sized units of 1,000 men each (early Chosŏn); regiment under the *sog'o* system, consisting of five battalions of 2,475 men; command center; regiment

yong (*yung*, Ch.) 用 utility

Yŏngbu 營部 Division-Regiment

Yŏngbu p'yoha pyŏltaegun 營部標下別隊軍 the aides and soldiers of the division-regiments of the Military Training Agency's Special Unit

Yŏngbyŏn (p.n.) 寧邊 in P'yŏng'an Province

Yŏngch'ŏn district 永川 in Kyŏngsang Province

Yŏngdollyŏng 領敦寧 chief officer of the Bureau of Royal Relatives

Yŏnggwan 領官 warehouse manager

Yŏnghak 營學 Yu's Governors' Schools

Yonghoyŏng 龍虎營 Dragon Tiger Regiment of the Forbidden Soldiers

Yong'in (p.n.) 龍仁

Yŏngjang 營將 garrison commanders

yŏngjik 影職 honorary "shadow posts"

yŏnjik 硯直 boy servants recruited from sons of official slaves

Yŏngjosa 營造司 Bureau of Construction in Yu's version of the Ministry of Works

yŏng'ŏpchŏn 永業田 permanent land grant (portion of the Northern Wei-T'ang dynasty equal field systems)

Yŏngsa 領事 chief of the Tollyŏngbu

Yŏng'ŭijong 領議政 chief state councilor

Yŏng'un'gwan 領運官 transport officials

Yŏnsan (p.n.) 燕山

Yŏnyŏngwŏn 延英院 Hall of Invitation to the Brave

yŏoe chŏngbyŏng 餘外正兵 extra-quota regular soldiers

yŏsuk 閭塾 Yu's subdistrict schools

yoyŏk 徭役 miscellaneous labor service requirements

yu 幼 one more than 20 years younger than ego

Yü Kung 禹貢 the tribute of Emperor Yü (Hsia)

yu saminjibyŏl 有士民之別 there is a distinction between scholars and common people

Yü-shih 御史 imperial scribe (later censor)

Yü-shih-tai (Ch.) 御史台 censorate

Yüan dynasty 元

yüan-chia (Ch.) 元嘉 year period of the Liu Sung dynasty, A.D. 424-54; Later Han, A.D. 151-53

Yüan-feng (Ch.) 元豐 year period, A.D. 1078-86 (Sung)

Yüan-wai-kuan (Ch.) 員外官 supernumerary officials (T'ang)

Yüan-wai-lang (Ch.) 員外郎 undersecretary (T'ang)

yüan-yu (Ch.) 元祐 year period, A.D. 1086-94 (Sung)

yubang 留防 guard duty

yuch'in 有親 close relatives of the royal family

yuch'ŏng chapsaek 有廳雜色 miscellaneous military officers or guards assigned to government agencies

Yug'ŭijŏn 六矣廛 the six licensed monopoly shops of the capital

(Yukchubijŏn)
Yugwi 六衛 Six Guards
yugyosaeng 儒教生 students or Confucian students
yuhak 幼學 unofficial term meaning "youthful student" that has been interpreted by Shikata Hiroshi and others as indicating yangban status, but Song June-ho believes that while the term was assigned to men who later passed the *munkwa* examinations and became officials, not all did so; thus, some, but not all men designated as *yuhak* could be deemed members of the yangban
yuhun 遺訓 testament
yuhyang p'umgwan 留鄕品官 local men with official rank or local scholars; see *hyangjungji saryu*
Yuhyangso 留鄕所 local self-governing bodies organized primarily by the local elite
yujigyŏkcha 有職役者 anyone who held a post or performed service for the state
Yukpang 六房 the six major magistrate's bureaus
yukchin 六鎮 six garrisons in North Hamgyŏng Province
Yukcho 六曹 Six Ministries
Yukchubijŏn 六注比廛 see Yug'ŭijŏn
Yulp'o (p.n.) 栗浦
yulsaeng 律生 legal student
Yün-nan 雲南 province in China
yunan 留難 practice whereby clerks and official slaves reaped illicit profits by rejecting tribute items or keeping them in storage without issuing receipts to the district tribute clerks (*kongni*)
yundae 輪對 round-table discussion
yung (Ch.) 庸 labor service tax (T'ang)
yun'ŭm 綸音 royal instructions to the people
yup'o 遊布 cloth tax on men of leisure
yup'o 儒布 Confucian scholar cloth tax
Yusa 有司 subordinate official in Yulgok's *kye* system; heads of the Golden Orchid *Kye* in 1641
yusaeng 儒生 Confucian student
yuse 留税 the portion of national taxes kept on reserve in the magistrate's yamen
yusin 維新 (dynastic) restoration
Yusu 留守 special mayor
yut'ong 流通 liquidity and circulation in the flow of goods
yuŭm 有蔭 sons of high officials with the protection privilege

za 座 guild in feudal Japan

List of Kings of the Chosŏn Dynasty

King	*Reign*
T'aejo 太祖	1392-98
Chŏngjong 定宗	1398-1400
T'aejong 太宗	1400-18
Sejong 世宗	1418-50
Munjong 文宗	1450-52
Tanjong 端宗	1452-55
Sejo 世祖	1455-68
Yejong 睿宗	1468-69
Sŏngjong 成宗	1469-94
Yŏnsan'gun 燕山君	1494-1506
Chungjong 中宗	1506-44
Injong 仁宗	1544-45
Myŏngjong 明宗	1545-67
Sŏnjo 宣祖	1567-1608
Kwanghaegun 光海君	1608-23
Injo 仁祖	1623-49
Hyojong 孝宗	1649-59
Hyŏnjong 顯宗	1659-74
Sukchong 肅宗	1674-1720
Kyŏngjong 景宗	1720-24
Yŏngjo 英祖	1724-76
Chŏngjo 正祖	1776-1800
Sunjo 純祖	1800-34
Hŏnjong 憲宗	1834-49
Ch'ŏlchong 哲宗	1849-63
Kojong 高宗	1863-1907
Sunjong 純宗	1907-10

List of Names

Ai, Emperor (Former Han) 哀帝
An Chŏngbok 安鼎福
An Lu-shan 安祿山
An Pyŏngt'ae 安秉珆
An Tang 安瑭
Andong Kim 安東金氏
Arai Hakuseki 新井白石
Ashikaga (shogunate) 足利

Ch'ae Chegong 蔡濟恭
Chang Ch'ang 張敞
Chang Ch'i-hsien 張齊賢
Chang Chiu-ling 張九齡
Chang Chü-cheng 張居正
Chang Heng 張衡
Chang Hsien-chung 張獻忠
Ch'ang, King 昌王
Chang, Lady [Chang Hŭibin] 禧嬪張氏
Chang Man 張晚
Chang Pung'ik 張鵬翼
Chang Sun-p'ing 長孫平
Chang Tsai 張載
Chang Yu 張維
Chang Yüeh 張説
Chang Yung 張詠
Chao K'uang 趙匡
Chao Kuo 趙過
Chao Pien 趙抃
Ch'ao Ts'o 晁錯
Chaŭi (Dowager) 慈懿大妃 chaŭi-daebi (Dowager)
Che-tsung, Emperor (Sung) 哲宗
Ch'en Ching-chih 陳慶之
Ch'en Fu 陳旉
Ch'en Liang 陳亮
Ch'en Shen-yu 陳舜俞
Chen-tsung, Emperor (T'ang) 真宗
Cheng. Writer of subcommentary to *Shu-ching* 鄭
Ch'eng, Emperor (Former Han) 成帝
Ch'eng Hao 程顥
Cheng Ho 鄭和
Cheng Hsüan 鄭玄
Ch'eng I 程頤
Cheng Ssu-neng 鄭司農
Cheng-t'ung (Ming era) 鄭統
Ch'i Chi-kuang 戚繼光
Ch'i Chin 戚金
Chia I 賈誼
Chia Shan 賈山
Ch'ien-lung, Emperor (Ch'ing) 乾隆
Ching, King (Chou) 景王
Ching, Emperor (Former Han) 景帝
Ching P'u 黥布
Ch'iu Chün 丘濬
Ch'iu Shih-liang 仇士良
Cho Chibin 趙趾彬
Cho Chin 趙珍
Cho Chinhui 趙鎮禧

Cho Chun 趙浚
Cho Hŏn [Chungbong] 趙憲（重峰）
Cho Hyŏnmyŏng 趙顯命
Cho Ik 趙翼
Cho In'ok 趙仁沃
Cho Kwangjo 趙光祖
Cho Munmyŏng 趙文命
Cho Sanggyŏng 趙尚絅
Cho Sasŏk 趙師錫
Cho Sik 曺植
Cho Sŏgyun 趙錫胤
Cho T'aegu 趙泰耇
Cho T'aeŏk 趙泰億
Cho Wŏnmyŏng 趙遠命
Ch'oe Ch'unghŏn 崔忠獻
Ch'oe Hang 崔恒
Ch'oe Hojin 崔虎鎮
Ch'oe Hŭngwŏn 崔興源
Ch'oe Husang 崔後尚
Ch'oe Musŏn 崔茂宣
Ch'oe Myŏnggil 崔鳴吉
Ch'oe Sŏkchŏng 崔錫鼎
Ch'oe Sŭngno 崔承老
Ch'ŏlchong, King (Chosŏn) 哲宗
Chŏn Noksaeng 田祿生
Chŏng Ch'ihwa 鄭致和
Chŏng Ch'ŏl 鄭澈
Chŏng Ham 鄭諴
Chŏng Inhong 鄭仁弘
Chŏng Inji 鄭麟趾
Chŏng Ingnyang 鄭羽良
Chŏng Kwangp'il 鄭光弼
Chŏng Manjo 鄭萬祚
Chŏng Munbu 鄭文孚
Chŏng Pal 鄭撥
Chŏng Sanggi 鄭尚驥
Chŏng Sŏksam 鄭錫三
Chŏng Sunmyŏng 鄭順明
Chŏng T'aehwa 鄭太和
Chŏng T'ak 鄭拓
Chŏng Tojŏn 鄭道傳
Chŏng Uju 鄭宇柱
Chŏng Yagyong [Tasan] 丁若鏞〔茶山〕
Chŏng Yŏrip 鄭汝立
Chŏng Yugil 鄭惟吉
Chŏng Yusŏng 鄭維城
Chŏnghŭi wanghu (King Sejo, Chosŏn) 貞禧王后
Chŏngjo, King 正祖
Chŏngjong, King (Chosŏn) 定宗
Ch'ŏngp'ung Kim 清風金氏
Chŏngsun (Dowager Regent) 定順王后
Chou, Duke of 周公
Ch'ŏyŏng 處英
Chu Hsi 朱熹
Chu-kuo Liang 諸葛亮
Chu Sebung 周世鵬
Chuang Kuei 張軌
Chung Chang-t'ung 仲長統
Chung-tsung, Emperor (T'ang) 中宗（唐）
Chung Yu 鍾繇
Chungjong, King (Chosŏn) 中宗
Ch'ungnyŏl, King 忠烈王
Ch'ungsŏn, King 忠宣王
Ch'ungsuk, King 忠肅王
Crown Prince Sado 思悼世子
Crown Prince Sohyŏn 昭顯世子

Fan Chung-yen 范仲淹
Fan T'ai 范泰
Fan Tsu-yü 范祖禹
Fan Yeh 范燁
Fu Hsüan 傅玄
Fu Sheng 伏生

Ha Yŏn 河演
Ha Yun 河崙
Han Changsŏk 韓章錫
Han Hsien-tsung 韓顯宗
Han Hsin 韓信
Han Hŭng'il 韓興一
Han Ijo 韓頤朝
Han Myŏnghoe 韓明澮
Han Ŏn'gong 韓彥恭

Han Paekkyŏm 韓百謙
Han Wu-ti (Emperor Wu, Former Han) 漢武帝
Han Yü 韓愈
Han Yüan 韓瑗
Hideyoshi. See Toyotomi Hideyoshi 豐臣秀吉
Hŏ Chŏk 許積
Ho Hsiu 何休
Hŏ Hyŏp 許協
Hŏ Kyun 許筠
Hŏ Mok 許穆
Hŏ Pu 許傅
Hŏ Ŭng 許應
Hŏ Wu 何武
Hoeŭn, Prince 懷恩君(李德仁)
Hong Ch'ijung 洪致中
Hong Kugyŏng 洪國榮
Hong Kyehŭi 洪繼禧
Hong Kyŏngnae 洪景來
Hong Myŏngha 洪命夏
Hong Naksŏng 洪樂性
Hong Ponghan 洪鳳漢
Hong Sŏm 洪暹
Hong Taeyong 洪大容
Hsi Shen 郤詵
Hsia Sung 夏竦
Hsiao-ming, Emperor (N. Wei) 孝明帝(北魏)
Hsiao-tsung, Emperor (Sung, Ming) 孝宗(宋,明)
Hsiao-wen, Emperor (N. Wei) 孝文帝(北魏)
Hsieh Ch'ien-kuan 薛謙光
Hsieh T'ien 薛田
Hsien-tsung, Emperor (T'ang) 憲宗(唐)
Hsüan, Emperor (Former Han) 宣帝(前漢)
Hsüan Hsüan 桓玄
Hsüan, King 宣王
Hsüan-tsung, Emperor (T'ang) 玄宗(唐)
Hsüan-wu, Emperor 宣武帝(北魏)
Hsün, Emperor (Later Han) 順帝(後漢)
Hsün Hsü 荀勗
Hsün Yüeh 荀悦
Hu An-kuo 胡安國
Hu Hung 胡宏
Hu Chih-t'ang 胡致堂
Hu Wei-yung 胡惟庸
Huan, Duke (Ch'i) 桓公(齊)
Huang Tsung-hsi 黃宗羲
Hung-wu (era, Ming) 洪武(明)
Hwang Chonghae 黃宗海
Hwang Hŭi 黃喜
Hwang Ŏk 黃億
Hwang Sayong 黃嗣
Hwang Sin 黃慎
Hwang Yun 黃玧
Hwang Yun'gil 黃允吉
Hyojong, King (Chosŏn) 孝宗
Hyŏnjong, King (Chosŏn) 顯宗
Hyujŏng (Monk) 休靜

I Fu 易祓
Im Kyŏngsa 任慶思
Im Pok 林福
Inhyŏn, Queen (King Sukchong, Chosŏn) 仁顯王后
Injo, King [Prince Nŭngyang] 仁祖(綾陽君)
Iryŏn 一然

Jen-tsung, Emperor (Sung) 仁宗(宋)
Jui-tsung, Emperor (T'ang) 睿宗(唐)

Kang Chunhŭm 姜浚欽
Kang Hang 姜沆
Kang Hongnip 姜弘立
Kang Kamch'an 姜邯贊
K'ang-hsi, Emperor (Ch'ing) 康熙
Kang Sŏkki 姜碩期
Kao-tsu, Emperor (Han) 高祖

(漢)
Kao-tsung, Emperor (T'ang) 高宗 (唐)
Katō Kiyomasa 加藤清正
Keng Shou-ch'ang 耿壽昌
Ki Chun 奇遵
Kija (Ch'i-tzu) 箕子
Kim An'guk 金安國
Kim Chaero 金在魯
Kim Chajŏm 金自點
Kim Ch'angjip 金昌集
Kim Changsaeng 金長生
Kim Chi 金墀
Kim Chip 金集
Kim Ch'ŏm 金瞻
Kim Chongjik 金宗直
Kim Chunmin 金俊民
Kim Chwamyŏng 金佐明
Kim Hongdŭk 金弘得
Kim Hong'uk 金弘郁
Kim Hyoson 金孝孫
Kim Ik 金釴
Kim Ikhun 金益勳
Kim Inbŏm 金仁範
Kim Iso 金履素
Kim Iyang 金履陽
Kim Koengp'il 金宏弼
Kim Ku 金構
Kim Kŭn'gong 金謹恭
Kim Malli 金萬里
Kim Man'gi 金萬基
Kim Man'gil 金萬吉
Kim Mindo 金敏道
Kim Minhaeng (Kim Mindo?) 金敏行
Kim Myŏn 金沔
Kim Sanggyŏng 金尚絅
Kim Sanghŏn 金尚憲
Kim Sangsŏng 金尚星
Kim Sejŏng 金世鼎
Kim Seryŏm 金世濂
Kim Seryŏng 金世龍
Kim Sik 金湜
Kim Sin'guk 金藎國
Kim Sŏkchu 金錫胄
Kim Sŏng'il 金誠一
Kim Suhang 金壽恒
Kim Suhŭng 金壽興
Kim Sumun 金秀文
Kim Tŏgwŏn 金德遠
Kim Tongp'il 金東弼
Kim Uch'ŏl 金遇喆
Kim Ŭngsŏ 金應瑞
Kim Ŭngsun 金應淳
Kim Uong 金宇顒
Kim Yangno 金若魯
Kim Yejŏng 金禮正
Kim Yu 金瑬
Kim Yuk 金堉
Kojong, King (Chosŏn) 高宗
Kongmin, King (Koryŏ) 恭愍王
Kongyang, King (Koryŏ) 恭讓王
Konishi Joan 小西如安
Konishi Yukinaga 小西行長
Ku Ch'igon 丘致崑
Ku Kung-yen 賈公彥
Ku Sŏnggyo 具聖教
Ku Suŏn 具修溫
Ku Yen-wu 顧炎武
Kuan-chung 管仲
Kuang-wu, Emperor (Later Han) 光武帝
Kuan-tzu 管子
K'ung An-kuo 孔安國
K'ung I 孔顗
K'ung Lin 孔琳
Kung Ying-ta 孔穎達
Kung Yu 貢禹
Kungye 弓裔
Kwak Chaeu 郭再祐
Kwak Sunsŏng 郭純誠
Kwanghaegun, King (Chosŏn) 光海君
Kwangjong, King (Koryŏ) 光宗
Kwŏn Chŏk 權樀
Kwŏn Ch'ŏl 權轍
Kwŏn Kŭn 權近
Kwŏn Pun 權盼

Kwŏn Taejae 權大載
Kwŏn Taeun 權大運
Kyŏnhwŏn 甄萱
Kyŏngjong, King (Chosŏn) 景宗

Li An-chi 李安期
Li Chi-fu 李吉甫
Li Chung 李重
Li Ju-sung 李如松
Li Kou 李覯
Li K'uei 李悝
Li Lin-fu 李林甫
Li Pi 李泌
Li Tzu-ch'eng 李自成
Li-tsung, Emperor 理宗（南宋）
Lin Chiung 林駉
Lin Hsün 林勲
Ling, Emperor (Later Han) 靈帝（後漢）
Liu, Mr. (commentator, *Li-chi*) 劉氏
Liu Chih 劉秩
Liu Chih-chi 劉知幾
Liu Hsiang-tao 劉祥道
Liu Hsing-cha
Liu I 劉毅
Liu Pa 劉巴
Liu Ting 劉綎
Liu Yao 劉嶢
Liu Yen 劉弇
Lo Ju-fang 羅汝芳
Lo Shang-chih 駱尚志
Lu Chih 陸贄
Lu Hui-shen 盧懷慎
Lü K'un 呂坤
Lü Shang (T'ai-kung, Chou) 呂尚（太公，周）
Lü Ta-chün 呂大鈞
Lü Ta-lin 呂大臨
Lü Tsu-ch'ien 呂祖謙
Lu Yü 盧毓

Ma Chou 馬周
Ma Tuan-lin 馬端臨
Maeng Sasŏng 孟思誠
Mao Tse-tung 毛澤東
Mao Wen-lung 毛文龍
Master Cheng 程氏
Mencius 孟子
Min Chinhu 閔鎮厚
Min Chinwŏn 閔鎮遠
Min Chŏngjung 閔鼎重
Min Ŭnghyŏng 閔應亨
Min Ŭngsu 閔應洙
Min Yujung 閔維重
Ming, Emperor (Wei) 明帝（魏）
Minhoe, Princess 愍懷嬪
Mok Naesŏn 睦來善
Mu-kung (Duke Mu) 穆公
Mun Ikchŏm 文益漸
Munhwa Yu clan 文化柳氏
Munjong, King (Koryŏ) 文宗
Munjŏng, Queen 文定王后
Myŏngjong, King (Chosŏn) 明宗

Nabeshima Naoshige 鍋島直茂
Nam Hyoon 南孝溫
Nam Igong 南以恭
Nam Kon 南袞
Nam Kuman 南九萬
No Susin 盧守慎

O Toil 吳道一
Oda Nobunaga 小田織長
Ou-yang Hsiu 歐陽修

Pae Ikkyŏm 裵益謙
Pae Ki 裵紀
Paek Munbo 白文寶
Paekche (Kingdom) 百濟
Pak Chega 朴齊家
Pak Chiwŏn 朴趾源
Pak Chŏnghŭi. See Park Chung-hee 朴正熙
Pak Hongno 朴弘老
Pak Hyosu 朴孝修
Pak Kwŏn 朴權
Pak Kyusu 朴珪壽
Pak Munsu 朴文秀

Pak Sech'ae 朴世采
Pak Sedang 朴世堂
Pak Sŏ 朴遾
Pak Sun 朴淳
Pak Susin 朴守真
Pak T'aehang 朴泰恆
Pak Tansaeng 朴端生
Pan Ku 班固
Pang Saryang 房世良
Pan'gye [Yu Hyŏngwŏn] 磻溪
P'ap'yŏng Yun clan 坡平尹氏
Park Chung-hee 朴正熙
P'ei Hsing-chien 裴行儉
P'ei Kuang-ting 裴光庭
P'ei Tsu-yeh 裴子野
Pi Shu 薛淑
Po Chü-i 白居易
Po I 伯夷
Poksŏn'gun 福善君
Pongnim, Grand Prince 鳳林大君
Prince Poksŏn. See Poksŏn'gun
P'ungyang Cho clan 豐壤趙氏
Pyŏn Ijung 邊以中

Queen Inhyŏn 仁顯王后
Queen Insŏn 仁宣王后

Sado seja 思悼世子
Sejo, King (Chosŏn) 世祖
Sejong, King (Chosŏn) 世宗
Shang, Lord [Shang Yang] 商君
Shen Chi-ch'i 沈旣濟
Shen Pu-hai 申不害
Shen Wei-ching 沈惟敬
Shen-tsung, Emperor (Sung) 神宗（宋）
Shen Yüeh 沈約
Shih Hsing 石星
Shih Huang-ti (Ch'in) 始皇帝（秦）
Shih Tan 師丹
Shih-tsu, Emperor [Qubilai] 世祖
Shih-tsung, Emperor (Later Chou) 世宗（後周）
Shuang Chi 雙冀
Shun [sage emperor] 舜
Shun-chih, Emperor (Ch'ing) 順治
Sim Chiwŏn 沈之源
Sim Kiwŏn 沈器遠
Sim Sugyŏng 沈守慶
Sim Suhyŏn 沈壽賢
Sim Sunmun 沈順門
Sim T'aekhyŏn 沈宅賢
Sin Ch'ŏsu 申處洙
Sin Hŭm 申欽
Sin Ki 申耆
Sin Kyŏngsin 申景慎
Sin Myŏnggyu 申命圭
Sin Rip 申砬
Sin Sachŏl 申思喆
Sin Sang 申商
Sin Sukchu 申叔周
Sin Ton 辛盹
Sin Wan 申琓
Sin Yonggae 申用溉
Sŏ Chŭngpo 徐曾輔
Sō family of Tsushima 對馬島 宗家
So Fu 索輔
Sŏ Hu 徐厚
Sŏ Kŏjŏng 徐居正
Sŏ Kyŏngdok [Hwadam] 徐敬德〔花潭〕
Sŏ Myŏnggyun 徐命均
Sŏ Myŏngsin 徐命臣
Sŏ Myŏngyŏn 徐命珽
Sŏ Ŏm 徐崦
Sŏ P'ilwŏn 徐必遠
So Sŏng 徐渻
Sŏ T'aebo 邵台輔
Sŏ Yugu 徐有榘
Sō Yoshitoshi 宗義智
Sŏae [Yu Sŏngnyŏng] 西涯〔柳成龍〕
Sohyŏn, Crown Prince 昭顯世子
Son In'gap 孫仁甲
Son Sunhyo 孫舜孝
Song Chaegyŏng 宋在經

Song Chinmyŏng 宋真明
Song Ching'ŭn 宋徵殷
Sŏng Chun 成傪
Song Chun'gil 宋俊吉
Sŏng Hŏn 成渾
Song Inmyŏng 宋寅明
Song Kwangyŏn 宋光淵
Song Sanggi 宋相琦
Song Sanghyŏn 宋相賢
Song Siyŏl 宋時烈
Sŏngho [Yi Ik] 星湖〔李瀷〕
Sŏngjong, King (Chosŏn) 成宗
Sŏnjo, King (Chosŏn) 宣祖
Ssu-ma Ch'ien 司馬遷
Ssu-ma Chih 司馬芝
Ssu-ma Kuang 司馬光
Ssu-ma Yen 司馬炎
Su Ch'o 蘇綽
Su Shih 蘇軾
Su Wang-chih 蕭望之
Su Wei 蘇威
Sukchong, King (Koryŏ) 肅宗
Sukchong, King (Chosŏn) 肅宗
Sun Ch an 孫權
Sun Lung 孫龍
Sung Meng-kuan 孫夢觀
Sung Ying-ch'ang 宋應昌
Sungsŏn, Prince [Sungsŏn'gun] 崇善君
Sunjo, King (Chosŏn) 純祖

T'aejo, King (Koryŏ, Chosŏn) 太祖
T'aejong, King (Chosŏn) 太宗
Taewongun [Taewŏn'gun] 大院君
T'ai-kung (Ch.) (Chou) 太公（周）
T'ai-tsu, Emperor (Sung, Ming) 太祖
T'ai-tsung, Emperor (T'ang, Sung, Ming, Ch'ing) 太宗
T'ang, Emperor (Shang) 湯
Tan'gun 檀君
Tanjong, King 端宗
Tasan [Chŏng Yagyŏng] 茶山〔丁若鏞〕
Te-tsung, Emperor (T'ang) 德宗（唐）
Teng T'ung 鄧通
T'oegye [Yi Hwang] 退溪〔李滉〕
Toyotomi Hideyoshi 豐臣秀吉
Ts'ai Ch'en 蔡沈
Ts'ai Hung 崔鴻
Ts'ai Liang 崔亮
Ts'ai, Mr. 蔡氏
Ts'ao P'i 曹丕
Ts'ao Ts'ao 曹操
Tso Hsiung 左雄
Tu Mu 杜牧
Tu Yu 杜佑
Tung Cho 董卓
Tung Chung-shu 董仲舒

U Chŏnggyu 禹禎圭
U, King (Koryŏ) 禑王
U Hyŏnbo 禹玄寶

Wang An-shih 王安石
Wang Ch'eng 王澄
Wang Chien 王儉
Wang Fu-chih 王夫之
Wang Kŏn [King T'aejo of Koryŏ] 王建
Wang Li-hsin 汪立信
Wang Mang 王莽
Wang Yang-ming 王陽明
Wang Yü 王璵
Wei Hsiang 韋驪
Wei Piao 韋彪
Wei Hsüan-t'ung 魏玄同
Wen, Emperor (Former Han) 文帝
Wen, Emperor (Wei) 文帝
Wen, King (Chou) 文王
Wen, Marquis, of Wei 文侯
Wen-tsung, Emperor (T'ang) 文宗
Wi Sep'ung 魏世風
Wŏn Ho 元豪
Wŏn Inson 元仁孫
Wŏn Kyun 元均
Wŏn Tup'yo 元斗杓
Wŏnsŏng, King (Silla) 元聖王

Wu, Emperor (Former Han) (Wei) 武帝（前漢，魏）
Wu, Empress (T'ang) 武后（唐）
Wu, King (Chou) 武王
Wu Ching 吳競
Wu San-kuei 吳三桂
Wu Wang-bi 吳王濞

Yang Ch'eng 陽城
Yang, Emperor (Sui) 煬帝
Yang Hao 楊鎬
Yang Kuan 楊綰
Yang Kuei-fei 楊貴妃
Yang Kuo-chung 楊國忠
Yang Shang-hsi 楊尚希
Yang Sŏngji 梁誠之
Yang Taebak 梁大樸
Yao [Sage emperor] 堯
Yeh Meng-te 葉夢得
Yejong, King (Koryŏ) 睿宗
Yejong, King (Chosŏn) 睿宗
Yen Shih-ku 顏師古
Yen Ying 晏嬰
Yi Changson 李長孫
Yi Chehyŏn 李齊賢
Yi Chŏng'am 李廷馣
Yi Chŏngje 李廷濟
Yi Chŏngp'il 李廷弼
Yi Chongsŏng 李宗城
Yi Chongyŏng 李宗英
Yi Chunggwan 李重觀
Yi Chungho 李仲虎
Yi Chunghwan 李重煥
Yi Chun'gyŏng 李浚慶
Yi Hae 李海
Yi Haeng 李行
Yi Hang 李沆
Yi Hangbok 李恒福
Yi Huwŏn 李厚源
Yi Hyŏnbo 李賢輔
Yi Hyŏnsŏk 李玄錫
Yi Ik [Sŏngho] 李瀷〔星湖〕
Yi Ikhan 李翊漢
Yi Il 李鎰
Yi Ilche 李日躋
Yi Imyŏng 李頤命
Yi Inhwan 李寅煥
Yi Injwa 李麟佐
Yi Inyŏp 李寅燁
Yi Kŏnmyŏng 李健命
Yi Kŭkki 李克基
Yi Kŭkpae 李克培
Yi Kung'ik 李肯翊
Yi Kwal 李适
Yi Kwangdo 李廣道
Yi Kwangjwa 李光佐
Yi Kwi 李貴
Yi Kyŏngmyŏng 李景明
Yi Kyŏng'ŏm [Prince Yŏnch'ŏn] 李景嚴（延川君）
Yi Kyŏngsŏk 李景奭
Yi Kyŏngyŏ 李景輿
Yi Kyugyŏng 李圭景
Yi Man'un 李萬運
Yi Man'ŭng 李萬雄
Yi Minsŏ 李敏叙
Yi Ŏn'gang 李彥綱
Yi Pohyŏk 李普赫
Yi Pongnam 李福男
Yi Pongsang 李鳳祥
Yi Pyŏngsang 李秉常
Yi Saek 李穡
Yi Samyŏng 李師命
Yi Sangjin 李尚真
Yi Sebaek 李世白
Yi Sehwa 李世華
Yi Siae (rebellion) 李世愛
Yi Sibaek 李時白
Yi Sibang 李時昉
Yi Sigyŏng 李蓍慶
Yi Sik 李植
Yi Sŏ 李署
Yi Sŏnggye [King T'aejo of Chosŏn] 李成桂
Yi Sugwang 李睟光
Yi Sukchu 李叔疇
Yi Sunsin 李舜臣
Yi T'aejwa 李台佐

Yi T'ak 李鐸
Yi Tanha 李端夏
Yi Tŏkhyŏng 李德馨
Yi Ut'ae 李宇泰
Yi Wan 李浣
Yi Wŏn'ik 李元翼
Yi Wŏnjŏng 李元禎
Yi Yangwŏn 李陽元
Yi Yŏbal 李汝發
Yi Yu 李濡
Yi Yut'ae 李惟泰
Yŏ P'iryong 呂必容
Yŏhŭnggun [Prince Yŏhŭng] 驪興君
Yŏn Kaesomun 燕蓋蘇文
Yŏnch'ŏn, Prince [Yŏnch'ŏn'gun, Yi Kyŏng'ŏm] 延川君 李景嚴
Yŏngjo, King (Chosŏn) 英祖
Yŏnsan'gun, King (Chosŏn) 燕山君
Yü, sage emperor (Hsia) 禹
Yü Chi 虞集
Yu Chib'il 俞集一
Yu Cho [Sŏbong] 柳藕（西峰）
Yu Hŏn 俞櫶
Yu Hyŏgyŏn 柳赫然
Yu Hyŏngwŏn [Pan'gye] 柳馨遠（磻溪）
Yu Kye 俞棨
Yu Manjung 柳萬重
Yu Myŏnghyŏn 柳命賢
Yu Ok 柳沃
Yu Ponghwi 柳鳳輝
Yu Pongmyŏng 柳復明
Yu Sŏngnyŏng [Sŏae] 柳成龍（西涯）
Yu Suwŏn 柳壽垣
Yü-wen family 宇文
Yüan, Emperor (Former Han) 元帝
Yüan Tsai 元載
Yang Kuo-chung 楊國忠
Yulgok [Yi I] 栗谷（李珥）
Yun Chihwan 尹趾完
Yun Chŭng 尹拯
Yun Hŏnju 尹憲柱
Yun Hwijŏng 尹彙貞
Yun Hyu 尹鑴
Yun Ido 尹以道
Yun Im 尹任
Yun In'gyŏng 尹仁鏡
Yun Kae 尹漑
Yun Kwan 尹瓘
Yun Kwangch'an 尹光纘
Yun Kwang'ŭi 尹光毅
Yun Kye 尹堦
Yun Pan 尹攀
Yun Pang 尹昉
Yun Pin 尹彬
Yun Sim 尹深
Yun Sun 尹淳
Yun Sunji 尹順之
Yun Wŏllo 尹元老
Yun Wŏnhyŏng 尹元衡
Yun Yangnae 尹陽來
Yung-cheng, Emperor (Ch'ing) 雍正
Yung-lo (era, Emperor, Ming) 永樂

Bibliography

ABBREVIATIONS

CSS Chōsen sōtokufu [Government-general of Chōsen]. *Chŏsenshi* [History of Korea]. 35 vols. in 6 series. Keijō: Chōsen insatsu kabushiki kaika, 1932–40.

Han Woo-keun, KGTJ Han Woo-keun [Han Ugŭn], Yi Sŏngmu, Min Hyŏn'gu, Yi T'aejin, and Kwŏn Oyŏng, eds. *Yŏkchu Kyŏngguk taejŏn* [Translated and annotated Great Code for managing the state]. Sŏngnam, Kyŏnggi Province: Han'guk chŏngsin munhwa yŏn'guwŏn, 1985.

ILSN *Ilsŏngnok* [Record of daily reflection].

KGTJ Chōsen sōtokufu chūsuin, ed. *Kyŏngguk taejŏn* [Great code for managing the state]. Preface dated 1469; subsequently revised four times by 1485. Keijō: Chōsen sōtokufu chūsuin, 1934.

KRS *Koryŏsa* [History of the Koryŏ dynasty]. 3 vols. Seoul: Yŏnhŭi taehakkyo ch'ulp'anbu, 1955.

KRSCY *Koryŏsa chŏryo* [Essentials of Koryŏ history]. Seoul: Asea munhwasa, 1973.

KSDSJ Yi Hongjik, ed. *Kuksadaesajŏn* [Great dictionary of national history]. 2 vols. Seoul: Chimun'gak, 1963.

MGYR *Man'gi yoram.* 2 vols. *Chaeyongp'yŏn* [Handbook of government affairs: Finance]. Keijō: Chōsen sōtokufu chūsūin, 1937. *Kunjŏngp'yŏn* [Handbook of government affairs: Military affairs]. Keijō: Chōsen sōtokufu chūsūin, 1938.

MHBG *Chŭngbo munhŏnbigo* [The *Munhŏnbigo,* supplemented]. 250 *kwŏn.* Seoul: Hongmun'gwan, 1907.

PBSDN *Pibyŏnsa tŭngnok* [Record of the border defense command]. 16 vols. Seoul: Kuksa p'yŏnch'an wiwŏnhoe, 1949.

PGSR Yu Hyŏngwŏn. *Pan'gye surok.*

Sillok All footnote references to Kuksa p'yŏnch'an wiwŏnhoe [National Historical Compilation Committee], ed., *Chosŏn wangjo sillok* [The veritable records of the kings of the Chosŏn dynasty], 48 vols. (Seoul: Tongguk munhwasa, 1955), will be noted according to the *Sillok* or Veritable Record of each king, and the page reference will be to the original folio edition, not the page number of this 1955 edition. E.g., *Hyŏnjong sillok* 16:10a. Frequently this will be followed by the date in the form: year of reign of king.month.day in the sixty-day cycle, as in Hyŏnjong 2.6.imjin. The index to this edition of the *Sillok* was added in 1963.

SJW *Sŭngjŏngwŏn ilgi* [Records of the Royal Secretariat].

TJHT *Taejŏn hoet'ong Kyōshu Taiden kaiden* [The emended and annotated edition of the *Taejŏn hoet'ong*]. Keijō: Chōsen sōtokufu Chūsŭin, 1939.

PRIMARY SOURCES

An Chŏngbok. *Tongsa kangmok.* [Major and minor points about the history of Korea]. 3 vols. Edited by Chōsen kosho kankōkai, apparently photographically reproduced. Seoul: Kyŏng'in munhwasa, 1970.

_____. *Kugyŏk Tongsa kangmok* [Korean translation of the *Tongsa kangmok*]. 10 vols. Seoul: Minjok munhwa ch'ujinhoe, 1977.

_____. "Kun'guk ch'ongnok" [Total national statistics]. In *Chaptong san'i* [Miscellaneous information]. 4 vols. Seoul: Han'gukhak munhŏn yŏn'guso, Han'gukhak kosajŏn ch'ongsŏ series, 1981.

Ch'i Chi-kuang. *Chi-hsiao hsin-shu, Wan-yu wen-k'o* series. Edited by Wang Yün-wu. Shanghai: Commercial Press, 1938.

Cho Kwangjo. *Kugyŏk Chŏng'am Cho Sŏnsaeng munjip* [The collected works of Cho Kwangjo, trans.]. Seoul: Chŏng'am Cho Sŏnsaeng kinyŏm saŏphoe, 1978.

_____. "Chosŏn kyŏnggukchŏn, sang" [Institutes for management of the state of Chosŏn, Part 1]. In idem, *Sambongjip, Sang* [Collected works of Chŏng Tojŏn, part 1], pp. 204–32; *Ha* [part 2], pp. 233–53. Seoul: Kuksa p'yŏnch'an wiwŏnhoe, 1961.

Chŏng Tojŏn. *Sambongjip* [Collected works of Chŏng Tojŏn]. Seoul: Kuksa p'yŏnch'an wiwŏnhoe, 1961.

Chŏng Yagyong. *Chŏng Tasan chŏnso* [The complete works of Chŏng Tasan. Edited by Yun Set'aek. 4 vols. Seoul: Munhŏn p'yŏnch'an wiwŏnhoe, 1960, 1961.

_____. *Mongmin simsŏ* [Essays from the heart on governing the people]. In *Chŏng Tasan Chŏnsŏ* [The complete works of Chŏng Tasan], vol. 3. Seoul: Munhŏn p'yŏnch'an wiwŏnhoe, 1961.

_____. *Tasan nonch'ŏng* [Collected essays of Chŏng Yagyong]. Translated by Yi Iksŏng. Seoul: Ŭryu mun'go, 1972.

Chōsen Sōtokufu Chūsūin, ed. *Kyŏngguk taejŏn* [Great Code for management of the state]. Keijo: 1934.

_____. *Soktaejŏn* [Great Code, continued]. Keijō: Chōsen Sōtokufu Chūsūin, 1935.

_____. *Taejŏn hoet'ong* [Comprehensive collection of the Great Code]. Keijō: Chōsen Sōtokufu Chūsūin, 1939.

Chōsenshi [History of Korea]. 35 vols. Keijō: Chōsen insatsu kabushiki kaika, 1932–40.

Ch'un-ch'iu Kung-yang chüan-chu-shu [Spring and autumn annals, in the Kung-yang tradition]. Ssu-pu pei-yao ed. Vol. 16. Shanghai, 1936.

Chung-hua shu-chü, ed. *Tz'u-hai*. Shanghai, 1947.

Chŭngbo munhŏnbigo [The *Munhŏnbigo*, supplemented]. 250 *kwŏn* Seoul: Hong-mun'gwan ch'anjip kyojŏng, 1907.

Han Paekkyŏm. *Kuam yugo* [The leftover writings of Han Paekkyŏm]. Seoul: Yŏrhwadang, 1972.

Han Woo-keun [Han Ugŭn], Yi Sŏngmu, Min Hyŏn'gu, Yi T'aejin, and Kwŏn Oyŏng, eds. *Yŏkchu Kyŏngguk taejŏn* [Translated and annotated Great Code for the management of the state]. Sŏngnam, Kyŏnggi Province: Han'guk chŏngsin munhwa yŏn'guwŏn, 1985.

Kim Yuk. *Chamgok chŏnjip* [The complete works of Kim Yuk]. Seoul: Taedong munhwa yŏn'guwŏn, Sŏnggyun'gwan Taehakkyo, 1975.

Koryŏsa [History of the Koryŏ dynasty]. 3 vol. Seoul: Yŏnhŭi taehakkyo ch'ulp'anbu, 1955.

Koryŏsa chŏryo [Essentials of the History of Koryŏ]. Seoul: Asea munhwasa, 1973.

Kuksa p'yŏnch'an wiwŏnhoe [National Historical Compilation Committee], ed. *Chosŏn wangjo sillok* [The veritable records of the kings of the Chosŏn dynasty]. 48 vols. and index. Seoul: Tongguk munhwasa, 1955. Index, 1963.

Kyŏngguk taejŏn [Great Code for the management of the state]. Preface dated 1469; revised four times by 1485. Keijō: Chōsen sōtokufu chūsuin, ed., 1934.

Legge, James, trans. *Chinese Classics*. 5 vols. Oxford: Clarendon Press, 1893–95.

Lü Tsu-ch'ien. *Li-tai chih-tu hsiang-shuo* [Detailed discussion of institutions over the ages]. 15 *chüan*. In *Hsü Chin-hua ts'ung-shu*. Vols. 29–30. N.p., 1924.

Man'gi yoram. 2 vols. *Chaeyongp'yŏn* [Handbook of government affairs: Finance]. Keijō: Chōsen sōtokufu chūsūin, 1937. *Kunjŏngp'yŏn* [Handbook of government affairs: Military affairs]. Keijō: Chōsen sōtokufu chūsūin, 1938.

Morohashi Tetsuji, comp. *Daikanwa jiten* [The great Sino-Japanese dictionary]. Tokyo: Taishū-kan shoten, 1955–59. 12 vols.

Pak Chega. *Chŏngyujip: pu Pukhag'ŭi* [The collected works of Pak Chega, with the essay on learning from the north appended]. Seoul: Kuksa p'yŏnch'an wiwŏnhoe, 1971.

Pibyŏnsa tŭngnok [Record of the border defense command]. 16 vols. Seoul: Kuksa p'yŏnch'an wiwŏnhoe, 1949.

Shang-shu [The book of documents]. Edited by Ikeda Sueri. *Zenyaku kambun taikei* ed., vol. 11. Tokyo: Shūeisha, 1976.

Ssu-ma Kuang, comp. *Tzu-chih t'ung-chien*. Shanghai: Shang-mu yin-shu-kuan ts'ang-fan, 1926.

Soktaejŏn [Great code, continued]. Keijō: Chōsen Sōtokufu Chūsūin, 1935.

Song Siyŏl. *Songja taejŏn* [The great works of Master Song] 258 *kwŏn*. Taejŏn: Namyun chongsa, 1927. 112 vols. (double leaves).

Taejŏn hoet'ong, Kyōshu Taiden kaiden [The emended and annotated edition of the *Taejŏn hoet'ong*]. Keijō: Chōsen sōtokufu Chūsŭin, 1939.

Tu Yu, comp. *T'ung-tien*. 4 vols. Taipei: Hsin-hsing shu-chü, 1966.

U Chŏnggye. *Kyŏngje yaron* [Views from a rustic on the management of the country]. Translated by Yi Iksŏng. Seoul: Ŭryu munhwasa, 1973.

Waltham, Clae, ed. *Shu Ching: Book of History. A Modernized Edition of the Translations of James Legge*. Chicago: H. Regnery, 1971.

Wang Yün-wu, ed. *Wan-yu wen-k'o* series. Shanghai: Commercial Press, 1939.

Yi I. *Yulgok chŏnsŏ*. Seoul: Sŏnggyun'gwan taehakkyo, Taedong munhwa yŏn'guwŏn, 1958.

Yi Ik. *Sŏngho saesŏl*. Vol. 1. Seoul: Kyŏnghŭi ch'ulp'ansa, 1967.

_____. *Sŏngho saesŏl ryusŏn*. Edited by An Chŏngbok. Seoul: Kyŏngmunsa, 1976. Reprint of Keijō: Chōsen kosho kankōkai, 1915.

_____. *Sŏngho sŏnsaeng chŏnjip* [The complete works of Master Sŏngho]. 70 *kwŏn*. Seoul: Kyŏng'in munhwasa, 1974. 2 vols.

Yi Kŭng'ik. *Yŏllyŏsil kisul*. 33 *kwŏn*, *sok* (additional) 7 *kwŏn*. Keijō: Chōsen kosho kankōkai, 1912–13. 6 vols.

Yi Kyugyŏng. *Oju yŏnmun changjŏn san'go*. 2 vols. Seoul: Tongguk munhwasa, 1959.

Yi Sugwang. *Chibong yusŏl*. 1614. Seoul: Kyŏng'in munhwasa, 1970.

Yŏnsan'gun ilgi [Daily record of Prince Yŏnsan]. Vols. 12–14 of the *Chosŏn wangjo sillok*.

Yu Hyŏngwŏn. *Pan'gye surok, Purok p'oyu* [Jottings of Yu Hyŏngwŏn, Supplement added]. Edited by Kojŏn kanhaenghoe [The Classic Publication Society]. Seoul: Tongguk munhwasa, 1958.

_____. Translation by Han'gukhak kibon ch'ongsŏ, ed., no. 10, *Chŭngbo pan'gye surok* [Supplemented edition of the *Pan'gye surok*]. 6 vols. Seoul: Kyŏng'in munhwasa, 1974.

_____. Translation by Chosŏn inmin minjujuŭi konghwaguk kwahagwŏn kojŏn yŏn'guso kojŏn yŏn'gusil [Classics study room of the Institute for Classical Studies of the Institute of Science of the People's Democratic Republic of Korea]. *Pan'gye surok*. 4 vols. Pyongyang, 1960, 1963.

_____. *Pan'gye chapko* [Miscellaneous writings of Yu Hyŏngwŏn]. Seoul: Yŏgang ch'ulp'ansa, 1990.

Yu Sŏngnyong, *Sŏae munjip* [Collected works of Yu Sŏngnŏng], Taedong munhwa yŏn'guwŏn, ed. 1958.

_____. *Pan'gye sŏnsaeng yŏnbo*. Seoul: Tongguk munhwasa, 1961.

_____. *Sŏae sŏnsaeng munjip* [Collected works of Master Yu Sŏngnyŏng]. 20 *kwŏn*. N.p., 1894.

_____. *Kugyŏk Sŏaejip* [The works of Yu Sŏngnyŏng translated into Korean]. 2 vols. Seoul: Minjok munhwa ch'ujinhoe, 1977.

_____. *Chingbirok*. In Sŏnggyun'gwan, ed., *Sŏaejip, pu Chingbirok*. Seoul: Tong'a munhwa yon'guso, 1959.

_____. Sŏnggyun'gwan, ed., *Kugyŏk sŏaejip*. Seoul: Kyŏng'in munhwasa, 1959.

Yu Suwŏn. *Usŏ*. Seoul: Sŏul Taehakkyo ch'ulp'anbu, 1971.

Yüan-shih [History of the Yüan dynasty]

SECONDARY SOURCES

Ajia rekishi jiten [Encyclopedia of Asian history[. 10 vols. Tokyo: Heibonsha, 1962.

An Pyŏngt'ae. *Chōsen kindai keizaishi kenkyū* [A study of modern Korean economic history]. Tokyo: Nihon hyōronsha, 1975.

Arii Tomonori. "Richō Hojūgun-kō" [A study of the Poch'unggun of the Yi dynasty]. *Chōsen gakuhō* 21–22 (October 1961):295–338.

Asao Naohiro. "The Sixteenth-century Unification." In John Whitney Hall, ed., *The Cambridge History of Japan* 4:40–95. Cambridge: Cambridge University Press, 1991.

Ernest Barker. *Greek Political Theory: Plato and His Predecessors. 1918.* London: Methuen and Co., 4th ed., 1951.

_____. *The Politics of Aristotle*. New York: Oxford University Press, 1958.

Beattie, Hilary J. *Land and Lineage in China: A Study of T'ung-Ch'eng County, Anhwei, in the Ming and Ch'ing Dynasties*. Cambridge: Cambridge University Press, 1979.

Behrens, Betty. "Government and Society." In E. E. Rich and C. H. Wilson, *The Cambridge Economic History of Europe*, vol. 5, *The Economic Organization of Early Modern Europe*, pp. 573–620. Cambridge: Cambridge University Press, 1977.

Bielenstein, Hans. "The Institutions of Later Han." In Denis Twitchett and Michael Loewe, eds., *The Cambridge History of China* 1:491–519. Cambridge: Cambridge University Press, 1986.

Bloom, Allan, trans. *The Republic of Plato*. New York: Basic Books, 1968.

Bodde, Derk. "The State and Empire of Ch'in." In Denis Twitchett and Michael Loewe, eds., *The Cambridge History of China* 1:20–102. Cambridge: Cambridge University Press, 1986.

Bol, Peter K. *"This Culture of Ours": Intellectual Transitions in T'ang and Sung China*. Stanford, Calif.: Stanford University Press, 1992.

Bottomore, Tom, ed. *A Dictionary of Marxist Thought*. Cambridge: Harvard University Press, 1983.

Braudel, Fernand. *Civilization and Capitalism, 15th-18th Century*. 3 vols. New York: Harper and Row, 1981–84.

_____. Vol. 1. *The Structures of Everyday Life: The Limits of the Possible*. New York: Harper and Row, 1981.

_____. Vol. 2. *The Wheels of Commerce*. New York: Harper and Row, 1982.

_____. Vol. 3. *The Perspective of the World*. New York: Harper and Row, 1984.

Bray, Francesca. *Science and Civilisation in China*. Edited by Joseph Needham. Vol. 6, *Biology and Biological Technology*. Part II: *Agriculture*. Cambridge: Cambridge University Press, 1984.

Buck, John Lossing, Owen L. Dawson, and Yuan-li Wu. *Food and Agriculture in Communist China*. New York: Frederick A. Praeger, 1966.

Ch'a Munsŏp. "Imnan ihu ŭi yangyŏk kwa kyunyŏkp'ŏp ŭi sŏngnip" [The *yangyŏk* system from the Imjin Wars and the establishment of the equal service system]. *Sahak yŏn'gu*, pt. 1, 10 (April 1961):115–30; pt. 2, 11 (July 1961):83–146.

_____. "Chosŏnjo hugi ŭi yŏngjang e taehayŏ" [The *yŏngjang* of the late Chosŏn dynasty]. *Sach'ong* 12–13 (September 1968):495–518.

_____. "Sŏnjojo ŭi Hullyŏn-dogam" [The military training agency of Sŏnjo's reign]. *Sahakchi* 4 (November 1970):11–30. Reprinted in idem, *Chosŏn sidae kunje yŏn'gu* [Studies of the military system of the Chosŏn period], pp. 158–78. Seoul: Tan'guk taehakkyo ch'ulp'anbu, 1973.

_____. "Hyojongjo ŭi kunbi hwakch'ung" [The military defense build-up of King Hyojong's reign]. In idem, *Chosŏn sidae kunje yŏn'gu* [Studies of the military system of the Chosŏn period], pp. 254–341. Seoul: Tan'guk taehakkyo ch'ulp'anbu, 1973.

_____. "Kŭmwiyŏng yŏn'gu" [A study of the royal guard regiment]. In idem, *Chosŏn sidae kunje yŏn'gu* [Studies of the military system of the Chosŏn period], pp. 342–431. Seoul: Tan'guk taehakkyo ch'ulp'anbu, 1973.

_____. "Sŏnch'o ŭi Naegŭmwi" [The inner forbidden guards of early Chosŏn]. In idem, *Chosŏn sidae kunje yŏn'gu* [Studies of the military system of the Chosŏn period], pp. 52–89. Seoul: Tan'guk taehakkyo ch'ulp'anbu, 1973.

_____. "Sŏnch'o ŭi Ch'ung'ŭi, Chungch'an, Ch'ungsunwi" [The loyal and righteous guards, loyal assistant guards, and loyal and obedient guards of the early Chosŏn period]. In idem, *Chosŏn sidae kunje yŏn'gu* [Studies of the military system of the Chosŏn period], pp. 90–135. Seoul: Tan'guk taehakkyo ch'ulp'anbu, 1973.

_____. "Chungjongjo ŭi Chŏngnowi" [The Jurchen quelling guards of Chungjong's reign]. In idem, *Chosŏn sidae kunje yŏn'gu* [Studies of the military system of the Chosŏn period], pp. 136–57. Seoul: Tan'guk taehakkyo ch'ulp'anbu, 1973.

_____. "Sogogun yŏn'gu" [A study of the *sog'o* soldiers]. In Ch'a Munsŏp, *Chosŏn sidae kunje yŏn'gu* [Studies of the military system of the Chosŏn period], pp. 179–228. Seoul: Tan'guk taehakkyo ch'ulp'anbu, 1973.

_____. *Chosŏn sidae kunje yŏngu* [Studies of the military system of the Chosŏn period]. Seoul: Tan'guk taehakkyo ch'ulp'anbu, 1973.

Chaffee, John. *The Thorny Gates of Learning in Sung China: A Social History of Examinations.* Cambridge: Cambridge University Press, 1985.

Chan, Wing-tsit. *A Sourcebook in Chinese Philosophy.* Princeton, N.J.: Princeton University Press, 1963.

Chance, Roger. *Until Philosophers Are Kings: A Study of the Political Theory of Plato and Aristotle in Relation to the Modern State.* New York: Oxford University Press, 1929.

Chang, Carsun. *The Development of Neo-Confucian Thought.* 2 vols. New York: Bookman Associates, 1957, 1962.

Chang Kukchong. "Sipch'il segi kŭmsok hwap'e (tonghwa) ŭi yut'ong e taehayŏ" [Circulation of metallic currency in the seventeenth century]. *Yŏksa kwahak* 6 (1961):44–55.

_____. "Sipp'al segi ŭi tonghwa chujo wa chŏnhwang munje" [The minting of copper cash and the problem of the shortage in money supply in the eighteenth century]. *Yŏksa kwahak* 1 (1963):40–55.

Cho Kyŏngnam. *Nanjung chamnok* [Miscellany on the Imjin War]. Seoul: Minjok munhwa ch'ujinhoe, 1977.

Choe, Ching Young [Cho Chingyang]. "Kim Yuk (1580–1658) and the Taedongbŏp Reform." *Journal of Asian Studies* 23, no. 1 (November 1963):21–35.

Ch'oe Hojin. *Han'guk hwap'ye sosa* [Short history of currency in Korea]. Seoul: Sŏnmundang, 1974.

Ch'oe Idon. "Simnyuk segi Nanggwankwŏn ŭi hyŏngsŏn kwajŏng" [The process of the formation of the rights of *nanggwan* in the sixteenth century]. *Hanguksaron* 14 (February 1986):3–50.

Ch'oe Yŏnghŭi. *Imjin waeranjung ŭi sahoe tongt'ae* [Social dynamics during the Imjin Japanese invasions]. Seoul: Han'guk yŏn'guwŏn, 1975.

Choe, Yong-ho [Ch'oe Yŏngho]. "Commoners in Early Yi Dynasty Civil Examinations:

An Aspect of Korean Social Structure, 1392–1600." *Journal of Asian Studies* 33, no. 4 (August 1974):611–31.

_____. "Yuhak, haksaeng, kyosaeng-go" [A study of *yuhak, haksaeng*, and *kyosaeng*]. *Yŏksa hakpo* 101 (March 1984):1–21.

_____. *The Civil Examinations and the Social Structure in Early Yi Dynasty Korea: 1392–1600*. Seoul: Korean Research Center, 1987.

Ch'oe Yun'o. "Sipp'al-shipku segi nong'ŏp koyong nodong ŭi chŏn'gae wa paltal" [The expansion and development of agricultural hired labor in the eighteenth and nineteenth centuries]. *Han'guksa yŏn'gu* 77 (June 1992):57–88.

Chŏn Haejŏng. "Kado ŭi myŏngch'in e kwanhan sogo" [A short study on the name, Ka Island]. *Seoul taehakkyo nonmunjip*, inmun sahoe kwahak, no. 9 (1959).

_____. *HanJung Kwan'gyesa yŏn'gu* [Studies in the history of Korean-Chinese relations]. Seoul: Ilchogak, 1970.

Chŏn Hyŏngt'aek. "Sipkusegich'o naesinobi ŭi hyŏkp'a" [Changes in government slaves in the early nineteenth century]. *Han'guksaron* 4 (March 1978):189–260.

_____. *Chosŏn hugi nobi sinbun yŏn'gu* [A study of slave status in late Chosŏn]. Seoul: Ilchogak, 1989.

Ch'ŏn Kwan'u. "Pan'gye Yu Hyŏngwŏn yŏn'gu: Sirhak parsaeng esŏ pon Yijo sahoe ŭi iltanmyŏn" [A study of Yu Hyŏngwŏon: One aspect of Yi dynasty society as seen from the birth of practical learning]. Part 1, *Yŏksa hakpo* 2 (October 1952):9–83; part 2, ibid. 3 (January 1953):87–139. Revised and reprinted in idem, *Chosŏn kŭnsesa yŏn'gu* [Studies in the recent history of Korea], pp. 227–336. Seoul: Ilchogak, 1979.

_____. "Chosŏn ch'ogi Owi ŭi pyŏngjong" [The five guards of early Chosŏn]. *Sahak yŏn'gu* 18 (September 1960):59–95. Reprinted in idem, *Kŭnse Chosŏnsa yŏn'gu* [Studies in the recent history of Korea], pp. 88–119. Seoul: Ilchogak, 1979.

_____. "Han'guk t'oji chedosa, ha" [The Korean land system, part 2]. In *Han'guk munhwasa-daegye* [A grand outline of Korean cultural history], pp. 1381–1516. Seoul: Koryŏ taehakkyo minjok munhwa yŏn'guso, 1965.

_____. *Han'guksa ŭi chaebalkyŏn* [The rediscovery of Korean history]. Seoul: Ilchogak, 1974.

_____. "Chosŏn hugi Sirhak ŭi kaenyŏm chaeron" [Reconsideration of the concept of Sirhak in the late Chosŏn period]. In idem, *Han'guksa ŭi chaebalkyŏn* [The rediscovery of Korean history], pp. 107–85. Seoul: Ilchogak, 1974.

_____. "Pan'gye Yu Hyŏngwŏn." In idem, *Han'guksa ŭi chaebalkyŏn* [Rediscoveries in Korean history], pp. 186–231. Seoul: Ilchogak, 1974.

_____. *Kŭnse Chosŏnsa yŏn'gu* [Studies in the recent history of Korea]. Seoul: Ilchogak, 1979.

_____. "Pan'gye Yu Hyŏngwŏn yŏn'gu ŭibo" [A corrigenda to my study of Yu Hyŏngwŏn]. In idem, *Kŭnse Chosŏnsa yŏn'gu* [Studies in the recent history of Korea], pp. 337–47. Seoul: Ilchogak, 1979.

_____. "Sirhak ŭi kaenyŏm sibi" [The controversy over the general concept of Sirhak]. In idem, *Kŭnse Chosŏnsa yŏn'gu* [Studies in the recent history of Korea], pp. 379–83. Seoul: Ilchogak, 1979.

_____. "Sirhak kaenmyŏm sŏngnip e kwanhan sahaksajŏk koch'al" [A historiographical investigation of the establishment of the concept of Sirhak], pp. 392–410. In idem, *Kŭnse Chosŏnsa yŏn'gu* [Studies in the recent history of Korea]. Seoul: Ilchogak, 1979.

Chŏng Hyŏng'u. "Taedongbŏp e taehan il yŏn'gu" [A study of the Taedong system]. *Sahak yŏn'gu* 2 (1958): .

Chŏng Iksŏp. "Pak Chiwŏn ŭi saeng'ae wa sasang" [The life and thought of Pak Chiwŏn]. In Honam munhwa yŏn'guso [Institute of Chŏlla culture], ed., *Pak Urho paksa chŏngnyŏn kinyŏm Sirhak nonch'ong* [Collected essays on practical learning in honor of the retirement of Dr. Pak Urho], pp. 475–83. Kwangju: Chŏnnam taehakkyo ch'ulp'anbu, 1975.

Chŏng Kubok. "Pan'gye Yu Hyŏngwŏn ŭi sahoe kaehyŏk sasang" [Yu Hyŏngwŏn's ideas for the reform of society]. *Yŏksa hakpo* 45 (March 1970):1–53. English summary, pp. 55–60.

Chŏng Manjo. "Chosŏn hugi ŭi yangyŏk pyŏnt'ong non'ŭi e taehan kŏmt'o: Kyunyŏkpŏp sŏngnip ŭi paegyŏng" [A study of the debate over reform of the commoner service system in late Chosŏn: Background to the establishment of the equal service system]. *Tongdae nongch'ong*, vol. 7 (April 1977):5–29.

Chŏng Sŏkchong. "Chosŏn hugi sahoe sinbunje ŭi punggoe: Ulsanbu hojŏk taejang'ŭl chungsimŭro" [The break-up of the social status system in late Chosŏn: The Ulsan district household registers]. *Taedong munhwa yŏn'gu* 9 (1972):267–357.

_____. *Chosŏn hugi sahoe pyŏndong yŏn'gu* [A study of the social changes in the late Chosŏn period]. Seoul: Ilchogak, 1983.

Chŏng Tuhŭi. "Chosŏn ch'ogi samgongsin yŏn'gu: kŭ sahoejŏk paegyŏnggwa chŏngch'ijŏk yŏkhwarŭl chungsimŭro" [A study of the three merit subject lists of the early Chosŏn period, in particular their social background and political role]. *Yŏksa hakpo* 75–76 (December 1977):121–76.

Chŏng Yŏnsik. "Sipch'il-sippal segi yangyŏk kyunilhwa chŏngch'aek ŭi ch'uui" [The trend in policy toward uniform labor service tax on men of good status in the seventeenth and eighteenth centuries]. *Han'guksaron* 13 (August 1985):121–82.

Chōsen sōtokofu, Chūsūin, ed. *Richō no zaisan sōzokuhō* [The property inheritance laws of the Yi dynasty]. Keijō, 1936.

Chōsenshi [History of Korea]. 35 vols. Keijō: Chōsen sōtokufu, 1932–40.

Ch'ü, T'ung-tsu. *Han Social Structure*. Edited by Jack Dull. Seattle: University of Washington Press, 1972.

Chun Haejong [Chŏn Haejong]. "Sino-Korean Tributary Relations in the Ch'ing Period." In John K. Fairbank, ed., *The Chinese World Order*, pp. 90–111. Cambridge: Harvard University Press, 1968.

Cole, David C., and Princeton N. Lyman. *Korean Development: The Interplay of Politics and Economics*. Cambridge: Harvard University Press, 1971.

Crowell, William Gordon. "Government Land Policies and Systems in Early Imperial China." Ph.D. diss., University of Washington, 1979.

_____. "The Land Limitations of Emperor Ai – A Reexamination." Paper presented at the Asian Studies on the Pacific Coast Conference at Eugene, Oregon, June, 1977.

Cumings, Bruce. *The Origins of the Korean War*. Vol. 1, *Liberation and the Emergence of Separate Regimes*. Vol. 2, *The Roaring of the Cataract, 1947–1950*. Princeton, N.J.: Princeton University Press, 1981, 1990.

_____. "Corporatism in North Korea." *Journal of Korean Studies* 4 (1982–83):269–94.

David, Paul A., Herbert G. Gutman, Richard Sutch, Peter Temin, Gavin Wright. Introduction by Kenneth M. Stampp. *Reckoning with Slavery: A Critical Study in the Quantitative History of American Negro Slavery*. New York: Oxford University Press, 1976.

Davis, David Brion. *The Problem of Slavery in Western Culture*. Ithaca, N.Y.: Cornell University Press, 1966.

de Bary, Wm. Theodore, Wing-tsit Chan, and Burton Watson, compilers. *Sources of Chinese Tradition*. 2 vols. 1960. New York: Columbia University Press, 1964.

_____ and the Conference on Seventeenth-Century Chinese Thought. *The Unfolding of Neo-Confucianism*. New York: Princeton University Press, 1975.

_____ and JaHyun Kim Haboush, eds. *The Rise of Neo-Confucianism in Korea*. New York: Columbia University Press, 1985.

_____. "Chu Hsi's Aims as an Educator." In Wm. Theodore de Bary and John Chaffee, eds. *Neo-Confucian Education: The Formative Stage*, pp. 186–218. Berkeley and Los Angeles: University of California Press, 1989.

Deuchler, Martina. "'Heaven Does Not Discriminate': A Study of Secondary Sons in Chosŏn Korea," *Journal of Korean Studies* 6 (1988):121–63.

_____. *The Confucian Transformation of Korea: A Study of Society and Ideology*. Cambridge: Harvard University Press, 1992.

Duby, Georges. *The Early Growth of the European Economy: Warriors and Peasants from the Seventh to the Twelfth Century*. Translated by Howard B. Clarke. Ithaca, N.Y.: Cornell University Press, 1974.

Duncan, John Breckenridge. *The Koryŏ Origins of the Chosŏn Dynasty: Kings, Aristocrats, and Confucianism*. University of Washington Press, forthcoming.

_____. "The Social Background to the Founding of the Chosŏn Dynasty: Change or Continuity?" *Journal of Korean Studies* 6 (1988–89):39–79.

Eckert, Carter J. *Offspring of Empire: The Koch'ang Kims and the Colonial Origins of Korean Capitalism 1876–1945*. Seattle: University of Washington Press, 1991.

Elisonas, Jurgis. "The Inseparable Trinity: Japan's Relations with China and Korea." In John Whitney Hall, ed., *The Cambridge History of Japan* 4:235–301. Cambridge: Cambridge University Press, 1991.

Elvin, Mark. *The Pattern of the Chinese Past*. Stanford, Calif.: Stanford University Press, 1973.

Fairbank, John K. "A Preliminary Framework." In John K. Fairbank, ed., *The Chinese World Order*, pp. 1–9. Cambridge: Harvard University Press, 1968.

Fingarette, Herbert. *Confucius: The Secular as Sacred*. New York: Harper and Row, 1972.

Finley, Moses I. *The Ancient Economy*. Berkeley and Los Angeles: University of California Press, 1973.

_____. *Ancient Slavery and Modern Ideology*. New York: Viking Press, 1980.

_____. "Was Greek Civilization Based on Slave Labour." In idem, *Slavery in Classical Antiquity*, pp. 53–72. Cambridge: W. Heffer, 1960.

Fogel, Robert William, and Stanley L. Engerman. *Time on the Cross: The Economics of American Negro Slavery*. Boston: Little, Brown and Co., 1974.

Fox-Genovese, Elizabeth, and Eugene D. Genovese. *Fruits of Merchant Capital: Slavery and Bourgeois Property in the Rise and Expansion of Capitalism*. New York: Oxford University Press, 1983.

Genovese, Eugene D. *The Political Economy of Slavery*. New York: Vintage Books, 1967.

_____. *The World the Slaveholders Made*. New York: Pantheon Books, 1969.

_____. *Roll, Jordan, Roll: The World the Slaves Made*. New York: Vintage Books, 1976.

Gerth, H. H., and C. Wright Mills. *From Max Weber, Essays in Sociology*. New York: Oxford University Press, 1946.

Gouldner, Alvin W. *Enter Plato: Classical Greece and the Origins of Social Theory*. New York: Basic Books, 1965.

Ha Hyŏn'gang. "Hojok kwa wankwŏn." In Taehan min'guk Mungyobu, Kuksa p'yŏnch'an wiwŏnhoe, ed., *Han'guksa* [History of Korea], vol. 4. *Koryŏ kwijok sahoe ŭi songnip* [The establishment of Koryŏ's aristocratic society], pp. 104–52. Seoul: T'amgudang, 1974.

Haboush, JaHyun Kim. "A Heritage of Kings: One Man's Monarchy in the Confucian World." Ph.D. diss., Columbia University, 1978.

_____. *A Heritage of Kings: One Man's Monarchy in the Confucian World*. New York: Columbia University Press, 1988.

Hall, John Whitney, ed. *The Cambridge History of Japan*. Vols. 4–6. Cambridge: Cambridge University Press, 1991.

_____. "The *bakuhan* System," in John Whitney Hall, ed., *The Cambridge History of Japan* 4:128–82. Cambridge: Cambridge University Press, 1991.

Hamaguchi Shigekuni. *Tō ōchō no sennin seido* [A study of the system of base people in the T'ang dynasty]. Kyoto: Tōyōshi kenkyūkai, 1966.

_____. "Zenkan no Nambokugun ni tsuite" [The southern and northern armies of the former Han]. In idem, *Shin Kan Zui Tō shi no kenkyū* [Studies in the history of the Ch'in, Han, Sui and T'ang dynasties] 1:251–67. Tokyo: Tokyo daigaku shuppankai, 1966.

_____. "Fuhei seido yori shinheisei e" [From the *fu-ping* system to the new-soldier system]. In idem, *Shin Kan Zui Tō shi no kenkyū* [Studies in the history of the Ch'in, Han, Sui and T'ang dynasties] 1:3–83. First published in *Shigaku zasshi*, vol. 41 (1930).

_____. *Shin Kan Zui Tō shi no kenkyū* [Studies in the history of the Ch'in, Han, Sui, and T'ang dynasties]. 2 vols. Tokyo: Tokyo daigaku shuppankai, 1966.

Han Sanggwŏn. "18 segimal—19 segich'o ŭi changsi paltal e taehan kich'o yŏn'gu: Kyŏngsangdo chibang'ŭl chungsim'ŭro" [A basic study of market development in the late eighteenth and early nineteenth centuries: The Kyŏngsang Province area]. *Han'guk saron* 7 (December 1981):179–237.

Han Woo-keun [Han Ugŭn]. *Yijo hugi ŭi sahoe wa sasang* [Society and thought in the late Yi dynasty]. Seoul: Uryu munhwasa, 1961.

_____. "Sŏngho Yi Ik ŭi sasang yŏn'gu" [A study of the thought of Sŏngho Yi Ik], part 1, pp. 135–200; part 2, pp. 201–324. In idem, *Yijo hugi ŭi sahoe wa sasang*. Seoul: Uryu munhwasa, 1961.

_____. *Sŏngho Yi Ik yon'gu: In'gan Sŏngho wa kŭ ŭi chŏngch'i sasang* [A study of Sŏngho Yi Ik: Sŏngho the man and his political thought]. Seoul: Sŏul taehakkyo ch'ulp'anbu, 1980.

_____, Yi Sŏngmu, Min Hyŏn'gu, Yi T'aejin, and Kwŏn Oyŏng, eds. *Yŏkchu Kyŏngguk taejŏn* [Translated and annotated Great Code for the management of the state]. Sŏngnam, Kyŏnggi Province: Han'guk chŏngsin munhwa yŏn'guwŏn, 1985.

Han Yŏngguk. "Hosŏ e silsi toen taedongbŏp, sang" [The Taedong system in Ch'ungch'ŏng Province, part 1]. *Yŏksa hakpo* 13 (October 1960):77–108; ha (part 2), ibid. 14 (April 1961):77–132.

_____. "Honam e silsi toen taedongbŏp, sang" [The Taedong system in Chŏlla Province, part 1], *Yŏksa hakpo* 15 (September 1961):31–60; I (part 2), ibid. 20 (April 1963): 29–80; Sam (part 3), ibid. 21 (August 1963):67–100; Sa, Wan (part 4, completion), ibid. 24 (July 1964):91–118.

_____. "Chosŏn chungyŏp ŭi nobi kyŏlhon yangt'ae, sang: 1609 nyŏn ŭi Ulsan hojŏk e nat'anan saryerŭl chungsimŭro" [Marriages of slaves in mid-Chosŏn, part 1: Examples in the Ulsan household register of 1609]. *Yŏksa hakpo* 75–76 (Dec. 1977):177–97; ha [part 2]. *Yŏksa hakpo* 77 (March 1978):105–25.

_____. "Chosŏn hugi ŭi kogong: 18–19 segi Taegu-bu hojŏk esŏ pon kŭ silt'ae wa sŏnkyŏk" [Hired labor in late Chosŏn: The real situation and character of hired labor as seen through the household registers of Taegu in the eighteenth and nineteenth centuries]. *Yŏksa hakpo* 81 (March 1979):81–124.

Han Yŏng'u. "Chosŏn ch'ogi ŭi sanggŭp sŏri 'Sŏngjunggwan,'" [On the collective posts of high-level clerks in the early Chosŏn period]. *Tong'a munhwa* 10 (September 1971):1–89.

_____. "T'aejong, Sejongjo ŭi taesajŏn sich'aek: Sajŏn ŭi hasamdo igŭp munje rŭl chungsim ŭro" [The policy of Kings T'aejong and Sejong toward *sajŏn*: The problem of the transfer of *sajŏn* to the lower three provinces]. *Han'guksa yŏn'gu* 3 (March 1969):39–88.

_____. "Yu Suwŏn ŭi sinbun kaehyŏk sasang" [Yu Suwŏn's ideas about the reform of social status]. *Han'guksa yŏn'gu* 8 (September 1972):25–62.

_____. *Chŏng Tojŏn sasang ŭi yŏn'gu* [A study of the thought of Chŏng Tojŏn]. Seoul: Han'guk munhwa yŏn'guso, 1973.

_____. "Chosŏn ch'ogi sahoe kyech'ŭng yŏn'gu e taehan chaeron" [A reconsideration of studies on social strata in early Chosŏn]. *Han'guk saron* 12 (February 1985):305–58.

Handlin, Joanna. *Action in Late Ming Thought*. Berkeley and Los Angeles: University of California Press, 1983.

Han'guk sahoe, in'gu wa palchŏn [Korean society, population and development]. Seoul National University Press, 1978.

Han'guk ŭnhaeng [The Bank of Korea]. *Chŭngbo Han'guk hwap'yesa* [Revised edition of the history of currency in Korea]. Seoul: Han'guk ŭnhaeng, 1969.

Hayami, Yūjirū and Saburō Yamada. "Agricultural Productivity at the Beginning of Industrialization." In Kazushi Ohkawa, Bruce F. Johnston, Hiromitsu Kaneda, eds. *Agriculture and Economic Growth: Japan's Experience*, pp. 105–35. Princeton, N.J.: Princeton University Press, 1970.

Higashi Ichio. *Ŏ Anseki simpō no kenkyū* [A study of the new laws of Wang An-shih]. Tokyo: Kazama shobo, 1970.

Hiraki Makoto. "Shipch'il segi e issŏsŏ ŭi nobi chongnyang" [The attainment of commoner status by slaves in the seventeenth century]. *Han'guksa yŏn'gu* 3 (March 1969):89–121.

_____. "Jūshichi-hachi seiki ni okeru nuryōsai shosei no kisoku ni tsuite" [On the status of offspring of male slaves and commoner wives in the seventeenth and eighteenth centuries]. *Chōsen gakuhō* 61 (October 1971):45–76.

_____. *Chosŏn hugi nobije yŏn'gu* [A study of the slave system of the late Chosŏn period]. Seoul: Chisik san'ŏpsa, 1982.

Hishimoto Chōji. *Chōsen-mai no kenkyū* [A study of Korean rice]. Tokyo: Sensō shobo, 1938.

Ho Ping-ti. *The Ladder of Success in Imperial China: Aspects of Social Mobility, 1368–1911*. New York: Columbia University Press, 1962.

Holderness, B. A. *Pre-Industrial England: Economy and Society, 1500–1750*. Totowa, N.J.: J.M. Dent and Sons, 1976.

Hong Isŏp. *Chŏng Yagyong ŭi chŏngch'i kyŏngje sasang yŏn'gu* [A study of the political and economic thought of Chŏng Yagyong]. Seoul: Han'guk yŏn'gu tosŏgwan, 1959.

Hong Sŭnggi. *Koryŏ sidae nobi yŏn'gu* [Slavery in the Koryŏ period]. Seoul: Han'guk yŏn'guwŏn, 1981.

_____. "Koryŏ sidae kongnobi ŭi sŏnggyŏk" [The nature of official slaves in the Koryŏ period]. *Yŏksa hakpo* 80 (December 1978):27–57.

_____. *Koryŏ kwijok sahoe wa nobi* [The aristocratic society of Koryŏ and slavery]. Seoul: Ilchogak, 1983.

Hopkins, Keith. *Conquerors and Slaves: Sociological Studies in Roman History*. Vol. 1. Cambridge: Cambridge University Press, 1978.

Hori Toshikazu. *Kindensei no kenkyū* [A study of the equal-field system]. Tokyo: Iwanami shoten, 1975.

Hsiao, Kung-chuan. *Rural China: Imperial Control in the Nineteenth Century*. 1960. Reprint. Seattle: University of Washington Press, 1967.

Huang, Ch'ing-lien. "The Recruitment and Assessment of Civil Officials under the T'ang Dynasty." Ph.D. diss., Princeton University, 1986.

Huang, Ray. *1587, A Year of No Significance: The Ming Dynasty in Decline*. New Haven, Conn.: Yale University Press, 1981.

_____. *Taxation and Governmental Finance in Sixteenth-Century Ming China*. Cambridge: Cambridge University Press, 1974.

_____. "The Lung-ch'ing and Wan-li reigns, 1576–1620." In Frederick W. Mote and Denis Twitchett, eds., *The Cambridge History of China*, vol. 7, *The Ming Dynasty, 1368–1644*, Part 1. Cambridge: University of Cambridge Press, 1988.

Hucker, Charles O. *A Dictionary of Official Titles in Imperial China*. Stanford, Calif.: Stanford University Press, 1985.

Hurwitz, Edith F. *Politics and the Public Conscience: Slave Emancipation and the Abolitionist Movement in Britain*. London: George Allen and Unwin, New York: Barnes and Noble Books, 1973.

Hymes, Robert P. *Statesmen and Gentlemen: The Elite of Fu-chou, Chiang-hsi in Northern and Southern Sung*. Cambridge: Cambridge University Press, 1986.

Inaba Iwakichi. *Kōkaikun jidai no mansei kankei* [Manchurian-Korean relations in the age of Kwanghaegun]. Keijō: Osakaya goshoten, 1933.

Ishi Yoshikuni. *Kankoku no jinkō zōka no bunseki* [An analysis of population growth in Korea]. Tokyo: Keiso, 1972.

Johnson, David G. *The Medieval Chinese Oligarchy*. Boulder, Colo.: Westview Press, 1977.

Johnson, Wallace, trans. *The T'ang Code*, vol. 1. Princeton, N.J.: Princeton University Press, 1979.

Kameda Keiji. "Kōrai no nuhi ni tsuite" [The slaves of Koryŏ], part 1. *Seikyū gakusō* 26 (1936):100–124; part 2, ibid. 28 (1937): 18–73.

Kang Chinch'ŏl. "Han'guksa ŭi sidae kubun e taehan ilsiron" [An attempt at the periodization of Korean history]. *Chindan hakpo* 29–30 (December 1966):175–98.

_____. *Koryŏ t'oji chedosa yŏn'gu* [A study of the land system of Koryŏ]. Seoul: Koryŏ taehakkyo ch'ulp'anbu, 1980.

Kang Chujin. *Yijo tangjaengsa yŏn'gu* [A study of the history of factionalism in the Yi dynasty]. Seoul: Seoul Taehakkyo ch'ulp'anbu, 1971.

Kang, Hugh. "Institutional Borrowing: The Case of the Chinese Civil Service Examination in Early Koryŏ." *Journal of Asian Studies* 24, no. 1 (November 1974):109–26.

Kang Man'gil. "Chosŏn chŏn'gi kongjanggo" [A study of artisans in the early Chosŏn dynasty]. *Yŏksa hakpo* 12 (September 1961):1–72.

_____. "Punwŏn Yŏn'gu: 17–8 segi Chosŏn wangjo kwanyŏng sugong'ŏpch'e ŭi unyŏng silta'e" [A study of the branch pottery centers: The operation of the handicraft manufacturing system of the Chosŏn dynasty in the seventeenth and eighteenth centuries]. *Asea yŏn'gu* 8, no. 4 (December 1965):79–116. English resumé, pp. 117–20.

_____. "Chosŏn hugi sang'ŏp chabon ŭi sŏngjang: Kyŏngsijŏn Songsangdŭng ŭi Toga sang'ŏb'ŭl chungsimŭro" [The growth of commercial capital in late Chosŏn: Wholesaling by the licensed monopolies in the capital and the merchants of Kaesŏng]. *Han'guksa yŏn'gu* 1 (September 1968):79–108.

_____. "Chosŏn hugi sang'ŏp ŭi munjejŏm: *Usŏ* ŭi sang'op chongch'aek punsŏk" [Problems in commerce in the late Chosŏn period: An analysis of the commercial policies contained in the *Usŏ*]. *Han'guksa yŏn'gu* 6 (September 1971):53–74.

_____. *Chosŏn hugi sang'ŏp chabon ŭi paltal* [The development of commercial capital in the late Chosŏn period]. Seoul: Koryŏ taehakkyo ch'ulp'anbu, 1973.

_____. "Sugong'ŏp" [(Handicrafts]). In Kuksa p'yŏnch'an wiwŏnhoe, ed., *Han'guksa*, vol. 10, *Chosŏn: Yangban kwallyo kukka ŭi sahoe kujo* [Chosŏn: The social structure of the yangban-bureaucratic state], pp. 355–89. Seoul: T'amgudang, 1974.

_____. "Wimin ŭisik kwa chŏngch'aek panyŏng" [Concern for the people and its reflection in policy]. In Chŏnnam taehakkyo, Honam munhwa yŏn'guso [The University of South Chŏlla, Institute for the Study of the Culture of the Honam Region], *Yi Ulho p'aksa chŏngnyŏn kinyŏm, Sirhak nonch'ong* [Commemorative volume in honor of Dr. Yi Ulho; Essays on practical learning], pp. 159–79. Edited by Ko Chaegi. Kwangju: Chŏnnam taehakkyo Ch'ulp'anbu, 1975.

_____. "Chosŏn hugi koripche paltal" [The development of the late Chosŏn hired labor system). *Han'guksa yŏn'gu* 13 (July 1976):59–84.

_____. "Sang'ŏp kyoyŏngnon" [Theories of commerce and trade]. In Taedong munhwa yŏn'guwŏn [Taedong Institute of Culture], ed., *Han'guk sasang taegye* [Grand outline of Korean thought], vol. 2. *Sahoe kyŏngje sasang p'yŏn* [Social and economic thought], pp. 489–565. Seoul: Sŏnggyun'gwan taehakkyo, 1976.

Katō Shigeshi. *Shina kodensei no kenkyū* [A study of the ancient land system of China]. Kyōto: Kyōto hōgakkai, 1916.

Kawashima, Fujiya. "The Local Gentry Association in Mid-Dynasty Korea: A Preliminary Study of the Ch'angnyŏng *Hyangan*, 1600–1839." *Journal of Korean Studies* 2 (1980):113–38.

_____. "A Study of the *Hyangan*: Kin Groups and Aristocratic Localism in the Seventeenth-and Eighteenth-Century Korean Countryside." *Journal of Korean Studies* 5 (1984):3–38.

Kim Chaejin, "Chŏn'gyŏlche yŏn'gu" [A study of the system of land measurement]. *Kyŏngbuk taehakkyo nonjip* 2 (January 1958):75–113.

Kim Chinbong, Ch'a Yonggŏl, and Yang Kisŏk. "Chosŏn sidae kunyŏk chawŏn ŭi pyŏndong e tae han yŏn'gu: Hosŏ chibang ŭi kyŏng'urŭl chungsimŭro" [A study of the changes in the sources of military service taxes in the Chosŏn period: The case of Ch'ungch'ŏng Province]. *Hosŏ munhwa yŏn'gu* 3 (1983):55–113.

Kim Ch'ŏlchun. "Ch'oe Sŭngno ŭi simu isipp'alcho" [The 18-point memorial of Ch'oe Sŭngno]. In Hyosŏng Cho Myŏnggi paksa hwagap kinyŏm Pulgyo sahak nonch'ong kanhaeng wiwŏnhoe [Publication committee for essays on the history of Buddhism in honor of the sixtieth birthday of Dr. Cho Myŏnggi], ed., *Pulgyo sahak nonch'ong* [Essays on the history of Buddhism]. Seoul, 1965. Also included in Kim Ch'ŏlchun, *Han'guk kodae sahoe yŏn'gu* [Studies in ancient Korean society] (Seoul: Chisik san'ŏpsa, 1975).

_____. "Han'guk kodaesahoe ŭi sŏnkyŏkkwa Namal yoch'o ŭi chŏnhwan'gi" [The nature of ancient Korean society and the transition between Silla and Koryŏ]. Han'guk kyŏngjesa hakhoe, ed., *Han'guksa sidae kubunnon* [Theses on the periodical divisions in Korean history], pp. 29–56. Seoul: Ŭryu munhwasa, 1970.

Kim Ch'ungnyŏl. *Koryŏ yugyosa* [A history of Koryŏ Confucianism]. Seoul: Koryŏ taehakkyo ch'ulp'anbu, 1984.

Kim Chunhyŏng. "Sipp'al segi ijŏngbŏp ŭi chŏn'gae" [The development of the village responsibility system in the eighteenth century]. *Chindan hakpo*, no. 58 (1984):69–96.

Kim Chunsŏk. "Yu Hyŏngwŏn ŭi pyŏnbŏpkwan kwa silli-ron" [Yu Hyŏngwŏn's view of legal reform and his theory of real principle]. *Tongbanghak chi* 75 (June 1992):69–114.

Kim, Ellen. "The Enduring Institution: A Case Study of Slavery in Traditional Korea." B.A. thesis, Harvard College, 1991.

Kim Okkŭn. *Chosŏn hugi kyŏngjesa yŏn'gu* [A study of the economic history of late Chosŏn]. Seoul: Sŏmundang, 1977.

Kim P'iltong. "Chosŏn hugi chibang sŏri chiptan ŭi chojik kujo, sang" [The structure of organization of the group of local clerks in the late Chosŏn dynasty, part 1]. *Han'guk hakpo* 28 (Fall 1982):79–116; Ha (part 2), ibid. 29 (Winter 1982):87–116.

Kim Seyun, "Koryŏ hugi ŭi oegŏ nobi" [The outside resident slaves of late Koryŏ]. *Han'guk hakpo* 18 (Spring 1980):63–81.

Kim Yongdŏk. "Sohyŏn seja yŏn'gu" [A study of Crown Prince Sohyŏn]. *Sahak yŏn'gu* 18 (Sept. 1964):433–89.

_____. *Chosŏn hugi sasangsa yŏn'gu* [Studies in the history of thought in late Chosŏn]. Seoul: Uryu munhwasa, 1977.

_____. *Hyangch'ŏng yŏn'gu* [Studies of the local self-government office). Seoul: Han'guk yŏn'guwŏn, 1978.

Kim Yŏngmo. "Chosŏn hugi sinbun kujo wa kŭ pyŏndong" [The social status structure and its change in late Chosŏn]. *Tongbanghak chi* 26 (1981):53–153.

Kim Yongsŏp. "Yang'an ŭi yŏn'gu: Chosŏn hugi ŭi nonka kyŏngje" [A study of the land registers: The peasant households in the late Chosŏn dynasty]. Part 1. *Sahak yŏn'gu* 7 (May 1960):1–95; part 2, ibid. 8 (December 1960):59–119. Reprinted in idem, *Chosŏn hugi nong'ŏpsa yŏn'gu: Nongch'on kyŏngje, sahoe pyŏndong* [Studies in the agricultural history of late Chosŏn: The village economy and social change], pp. 78–188. Seoul: Ilchogak, 1970.

_____. "Chosŏn hugi sinbunje ŭi tongyo wa nongji soyu" [The shakeup of the status system and the ownership of agricultural land in late Chosŏn]. In *Chosŏn hugi nong'ŏpsa yŏn'gu: Nongch'on kyŏngje, sahoe pyŏndong*, pp. 336–444. Seoul: Ilchogak, 1970.

_____. *Chosŏn hugi nong'ŏpsa yŏn'gu: Nongch'on kyŏngje, sahoe pyŏndong* [Studies in the agricultural history of late Chosŏn: The village economy and social change]. Seoul: Ilchogak, 1970.

_____. *Chosŏn hugi nong'ŏpsa yŏn'gu: Nong'ŏp pyŏndong, nonghak sajo* [Studies in the agricultural history of late Chosŏn: Changes in agriculture and trends in agricultural studies]. Seoul: Ilchogak, 1971.

_____. "Chosŏn hugi ŭi sudojak kisul: Iyangbŏp ŭi pogŭp e taehayŏ" [The technology of rice culture in late Chosŏn: The spread of transplantation]. In idem, *Chosŏn hugi nong'ŏpsa yŏn'gu: nong'ŏp pyŏndong, nonghak sajo* [Studies in the agricultural history of late Chosŏn: Changes in agriculture and trends in agricultural studies], pp. 2–18. Seoul: Ilchogak, 1971. Originally published in *Asea yŏn'gu* 7, no. 1 (March 1964):51–76. English resumé, pp. 77–78.

_____. "Chosŏn hugi ŭi sudojak kisul: To, maek imojak ŭi pogŭp e taehayŏ" [The technology of wet rice agriculture in late Chosŏn: The spread of rice/barley double cropping]. In *Chosŏn hugi nong'ŏpsa yŏn'gu: nong'ŏp pyŏndong, nonghak sajo* [Studies in the agricultural history of late Chosŏn: Changes in agriculture and trends in agricultural studies], pp. 40–71. Seoul: Ilchogak, 1971. Originally published in *Asea yŏn'gu* 7, no. 4 (December 1964):125–46. English resumé, pp. 147–48.

_____. "Chosŏn hugi ŭ sudojak kisul: Iyang kwa suri munje" [The technology of wet rice agriculture in late Chosŏn: The problems of transplantation and irrigation]. In *Chosŏn hugi nong'ŏpsa yŏn'gu: Nong'ŏp pyŏndong, nonghak sajo* [Studies in the agricultural history of late Chosŏn: Changes in agriculture and trends in agricultural studies], pp. 72–103. Seoul: Ilchogak, 1971. Originally published in *Asea yŏn'gu* 8, no. 2 (June 1965):281–305.

_____. "Sipp'al segi nongch'on chisig'in ŭi nong'ŏpkwan" [The views on agriculture of rural intellectuals in the eighteenth century]. In idem, *Chosŏn hugi nong'ŏpsa yŏn'gu* [Studies in the agricultural history of the late Chosŏn] 1:4–25. Seoul: Ilchogak, 1970.

_____. "Sipp'alku segi ŭi nong'ŏp silchŏnggwa saeroun nong'ŏp kyŏngyŏngnon" [The agricultural situation in the eighteenth and nineteenth centuries and the new managerial agriculture]. In Kim, *Han'guk kŭndae nong'ŏpsa yŏn'gu* [Studies in the history of modern agriculture in Korea], pp. 2–175. Seoul: Ilchogak, 1975.

_____. "Chosŏn hugi kyunyŏkche ijŏng ŭi ch'uri wa hop'obŏp" [The reasoning behind reform of the military service system in the late Chosŏn period and the household cloth system]. *Sŏnggok nonch'ong*, no. 13 (1982), pp. 7–46.

_____. "Chosŏn hugi kunyŏkche ŭi tongyo wa kunyŏkchŏn" [The shake-up of the equal service system of late Chosŏn and military-service land]. *Tongbanghak chi*, no. 32 (September 1982), pp. 97–147.

Koh, Sung Jae [Ko Sŭngje]. *Kunse Han'guk san'ŏpsa yŏn'gu* [A study of industrial history in recent times]. Seoul: Taedong munhwasa, 1959.

_____. "Myŏn'ŏp" [Cotton textiles]. In Kuksa p'yŏnch'an wiwŏnhoe, ed. *Han'guksa*, vol. 10, *Chosŏn: Yangban kwallyo kukka ŭi sahoe kujo* [Chosŏn: The social structure of the yangban-bureaucratic state], pp. 320–35. Seoul: T'amgudang, 1974.

Kolakowski, Leszek. "Mind and Body: Ideology and Economy in the Collapse of Communism." In Kazimierz A. Poznanski, ed., *Constructing Capitalism: The Reemergence of Civil Society and Liberal Economy in the Post-Communist World*, pp. 9–23. Boulder, Colo.: Westview Press, 1992.

Kracke, E. A., Jr. *Civil Service in Early Sung China, 960–1067*. Cambridge: Harvard University Press, 1953.

Kramers, Robert P. "The Development of the Confucian Schools." In Denis Twitchett and Michael Loewe, eds., *The Cambridge History of China* 1:760–61. Cambridge: Cambridge University Press, 1986.

Kuksa p'yŏnch'an wiwŏnhoe [National Historical Compilation Committee, Ministry of Education, Republic of Korea]. *Han'guksa.* 25 vols. Seoul: T'amgudang, 1973–81.

Kwŏn Yŏng'ik. "Pukhakp'a ŭi hwapye sasang e kwanhan yŏn'gu" [A study of the thought on currency of the northern learning scholars]. *Han'guk kyŏngje* 4 (September 1976):23–41.

_____. "Yu Hyŏngwŏn ŭi hwap'ye sasang e kwanhan yŏn'gu" [A study of Yu Hyŏngwŏn's thought on currency]. *Taedong munhwa yŏn'gu* 11 (1977):55–78.

Ledyard, Gari. *The Dutch Come to Korea*. Seoul: Royal Asiatic Society and Taewon Publishing Company, 1971.

Lee, Hoon K. [Yi Hun'gu]. *Land Utilization and Rural Economy in Korea*. Shanghai, Hong Kong, Singapore: Kelly and Walsh, 1936.

Lee, Ki-baik [Yi Kibaek]. *A New History of Korea*. Translated by Edward W. Wagner. Cambridge: Harvard University Press, 1984.

Lee, Thomas H. C. *Government Education and Examinations in Sung China*. Hong Kong: Chinese University Press, 1985.

Lenski, Gerhard E. *Power and Privilege, A Theory of Social Stratification.* New York: McGraw-Hill, 1966.

Levenson, Joseph R. "Ill Wind in the Well-field: The Erosion of the Confucian Ground of Controversy." In Arthur F. Wright, ed., *The Confucian Persuasion*, pp. 268–87. Stanford, Calif.: Stanford University Press, 1960.

Levinson, Ronald B. *In Defense of Plato.* Cambridge: Harvard University Press, 1953.

Liang Fang-chung. *The Single-Whip Method of Taxation in China.* Cambridge: Chinese Economic and Political Studies, Harvard University, 1956.

Loewe, Michael. "The Former Han Dynasty." In Denis Twitchett and Michael Loewe, eds., *The Cambridge History of China* 1:103–222. Cambridge: Cambridge University Press, 1986.

_____. "The Structure and Practice of Government." In Denis Twitchett and Michael Loewe, eds., *The Cambridge History of China* 1:463–90. Cambridge: Cambridge University Press, 1986.

Ma Tuan-lin. *Wen-hsien t'ung-k'ao.* Reprint. Taipei: Hsin-hsing shu-chü, 1959.

McLellan, David. *Karl Marx: His Life and Thought.* New York: Harper and Row, 1973; Harper Colophon edition, 1977.

Masubushi Tatsuo. "Spring and autumn period." In *Ajia rekishi jiten* [Dictionary of Asian history] 4:343a-b. Tokyo: Heibonsha, 1962.

Metzger, Thomas A. *Escape from Predicament: Neo-Confucianism and China's Evolving Political Culture.* New York: Columbia University Press, 1977.

Michael, Franz. *The Origin of Manchu Rule in China.* Baltimore: Johns Hopkins Press, 1942.

Michell, Tony. "Fact and Hypothesis in Yi Dynasty Economic History: The Demographic Dimension." *Korean Studies Forum*, no. 6 (Winter-Spring 1979/1980), pp. 65–93.

Min Hyŏn'gu. "Kŭnse Chosŏn chŏn'gi kunsa chedo ŭi sŏngnip" [The establishment of the early modern military system in the early Chosŏn period]. In Yukkun sagwan hakkyo Han'guk kunsa yŏn'gusil, *Han'guk kunjesa: kŭnse Chosŏn chŏn'gip'yŏn* [The history of the Korean military system: The early modern Chosŏn period] 1:1–197. Seoul: Yukkun ponbu, 1968.

_____. "Sin Ton ŭi chipkwŏn kwa kŭ chŏngch'ijŏk sŏnkyŏk, sang" [Sin Ton's administration and its political nature, part 1]. *Yŏksa hakpo* 38 (August 1968):36–88, *ha* (part 2) 40 (December 1968):53–119.

_____. *Chosŏn ch'ogi ŭi kunsa chedo wa chŏngch'i* [The military system and politics in the early Chosŏn period]. Seoul: Han'guk yŏn'guwŏn, 1983.

Miyahara Tōichi. "Chōsen shoki no dōsen ni tsuite" [Copper cash in Chosŏn]. *Chōsen gakuhō* 2 (October 1951):75–101.

_____. "Chōsen shoki no choka ni tsuite" [Paper money in early Chosŏn]. Tōyōshigaku kenkyūshitsu, Tokyo Kyōiku Daigaku, *Tōyōshigaku ronshū*, 1954, no. 3, pp. 369–82.

_____. "Jūgo-roku seiki Chōsen no kokō ni tsuite" [Hired labor in fifteenth and sixteenth century Chosŏn], *Chōsen gakuhō* 11 (1957):93–116.

Miyazaki Ichisada. *Kyūhin kanjinhō no kenkyū* [A study of the nine-rank system]. Kyōto: Tōyōshi kenkyū, 1956.

_____. "*Shidaifu*" [*Shih-ta-fu*]. In *Ajia reikishi jiten* [Dictionary of Asian history] 4:174a. Tokyo: Heibonsha, 1962.

Moore, Barrington Moore, Jr. *Social Origins of Dictatorship and Democracy: Lord and Peasants in the Making of the Modern World*. Boston: Beacon Press, 1967.

Morohashi Tetsuji, ed. *Daikanwa jiten* [Great Chinese-Japanese dictionary]. 12 vols. Tokyo: Daishūkan shoten, 1955.

Nakamura, James I. *Agricultural Production and the Economic Development of Japan, 1873–1922*. Princeton, N.J.: Princeton University Press, 1966.

Niida Noboru. *Shina mibumpōshi* [The history of the law on personal status in China]. Tokyo: Tōhō bunka gakuin, 1943.

_____. *Chūgoku hō seishi* [A history of the Chinese legal system]. Tokyo: Iwanami zensho, 1952.

_____. "Chūgokuhō ni okeru dorei no chii to shujinken: Doreihō shoshi" [The position of slaves and the rights of masters in Chinese law]. In idem, *Chūgoku hōseishi kenkyū: Dorei nōnohō, kazoku sonrakuhō* [Studies in Chinese legal history: Slave and serf law, family and village law]. Tokyo: Tōkyō daigaku shuppankai, 1962. Originally published in idem, *Chūgoku hōseishi* [A history of the Chinese legal system]. Tokyo: Iwanami zensho, 1952.

Nishijima Sadao. "Chūgoku kodai nuhisei no saikōsatsu" [Another investigation of the ancient slave system in China]. In *Kodaishi kōza* 7 (Tokyo: Gakuseisha, 1963):162–73.

O Such'ang. "Injodae chŏngch'i seryŏk ŭi tonghyang" [Trends in political forces in King Injo's reign]. *Han'guk saron* 13 (August 1985):49–119.

Ohkawa, Kazushi, Bruce F. Johnston, and Hiromitsu Kaneda, eds. *Agriculture and Economic Growth: Japan's Experience*. Princeton, N.J.: Princeton University Press, 1970.

Okamoto Keiji. "Gendai no doreisei ni tsuite" [The slave system of the Yüan period]. *Tōkyō kyōiku daigaku bungakubu kiyō* 66 (1969):49–50.

Pak Chonggŭn. "Tasan, Tei Jyakuyō no tochi kaikaku shisō no kosatsu: kōsaku (nōryoku ni ojita) tochi bunpai o chushin to shite" [A study of Tasan, Chŏng Yagyong's ideas on land reform: Distribution of land in accordance with labor]. *Chōsen gakuhō* 28 (July 1963):75–111.

Pak Han'gwang, ed. *Chŭngbo Han'guk hwap'yesa* [The history of Korean money, supplemented]. Seoul: Han'guk ŭnhaeng, 1969.

Pak Kwangsŏng. "Kyunyŏkpŏp sihaeng ihu ŭi yangyŏg'e taehayŏ" [Commoner service after the adoption of the equal service system]. *Sŏnggok nonch'ong* 3 (1972):129–84.

Pak Nouk. "Chosŏn sidae komunsŏsang ŭi yong'ŏ kŏmt'o: t'oji nobi mun'girŭl chungsim'ŭro" [An investigation of the use of terms in old documents of the Chosŏn period]. *Tongbanghak chi* 68 (October 1990):75–121.

Pak Pyŏngho. *Han'guk pŏpchesa t'ŭksu yŏn'gu: Yijo sidae ŭi pudongsan maemae kŭp tambobŏp* [Special studies on the history of the Korean legal system: Sale and guarantee of immovable property]. Seoul: Han'guk yŏn'guwŏn, 1960.

_____. "Han'guk kŭnse ŭi toji soyukwŏn e kwan han yŏn'gu" [A study of landownership rights in recent Korean history]. *Sŏul taehakkyo pŏphak* 8, no. 1 (1966):63–93; 8, no. 2 (1966):78–104; 9, no. 1 (1967):157–85.

Pak Sŏngsu. "Kogong yŏn'gu" [A study of hired labor]. *Sahak yŏn'gu* 18 (September 1964):527–54.

Pak Yŏnggyu. "Chosŏnjo Hyŏnjong kyŏngsin yŏn'gan ŭi kikŭn e taehayŏ" [Famine in 1670–71 during Hyŏnjong's reign in the Chosŏn dynasty]. *Hyangt'o Sŏul* 19 (December 1963):5–35.

Palais, James B. *Politics and Policy in Traditional Korea*. Cambridge: Harvard University Press, 1975.

_____. Review of Han Yŏng'u, *Chŏng Tojŏn sasang ŭi yŏn'gu* [A study of the thought of Chŏng Tojŏn]. Seoul: Han'guk munhwa yŏn'guso, 1973. *Journal of Korean Studies* 2 (1980):199–244.

_____. Review of Yi Sŏngmu, *Chosŏn ch'ogi yangban yŏn'gu* [A study of the yangban in the early Chosŏn period]. Seoul: Ilchogak, 1980. *Journal of Korean Studies* 3 (1981):191–202.

_____. Review of Song June-ho [Song Chunho], *Kwagŏ* [The examination system]. Edited by Yŏksa hakhoe (Seoul: Ilchogak, 1981). *Journal of Korean Studies* 3 (1981): 202–12.

_____. "Land Tenure in Korea: Tenth to Twelfth Centuries." *Journal of Korean Studies* 4 (1982–83):73–206.

_____. "Confucianism and the Aristocratic/Bureaucratic Balance in Korea." *Harvard Journal of Asiatic Studies* 44, no. 2 (December 1984):427–68.

Pan Ku. *History of the Former Han Dynasty*. Translated by Homer H. Dubs. Baltimore: Waverley Press, 1938.

Pang Kijung. "Sipch'il-sipp'al segi chŏnban kŭmnap chose ŭi sŏngnip kwa chŏn'gae" [The establishment and development of money taxes in the seventeenth and first half of the eighteenth centuries]. *Tongbanghak chi* 45 (November 1984):117–201.

Patterson, Orlando. *Slavery and Social Death: A Comparative Study*. Cambridge: Harvard University Press, 1982.

Perkins, Dwight H. *Agricultural Development in China, 1368–1968*. Chicago: Aldine, 1969.

Peterson, C. A. "Court and Province in Mid-and Late T'ang." In Denis Twitchett and John K. Fairbank, eds., *The Cambridge History of China*. Vol. 3, part 1, *Sui and T'ang China*. Cambridge: Cambridge University Press, 1979.

Population and Development Studies Center, Seoul National University, ed. *The Population of Korea*. Seoul: Seoul National University, 1975.

_____. *Han'guk sahoe, in'gu wa palchŏn* [Korean society, population and development]. Seoul: Seoul National University Press, 1978.

Pulleyblank, Edwin G. *The Background of the Rebellion of An Lu-shan*. London: Oxford University Press, 1955.

_____. "The Origins and Nature of Chattel Slavery in China." *Journal of the Economic and Social History of the Orient* 1, part 2 (April 1958):18–220.

_____. "Neo-Confucianism and Neo-Legalism in T'ang Intellectual Life, 755–805." In Arthur F. Wright, ed., *The Confucian Persuasion*, pp. 77–114. Stanford, Calif.: Stanford University Press.

Sakai Tadao. "Yi Yulgok and the Community Compact." In William Theodore de Bary and JaHyun Kim Haboush, eds., *The Rise of Neo-Confucianism in Korea*, pp. 323–48. New York: Columbia University Press, 1985.

Salem, Ellen. "Slavery in Medieval Korea." Ph.D. diss., Columbia University, 1978.

Sansom, George. *A History of Japan*. 3 vols. Stanford, Calif.: Stanford University Press, 1961.

Santangelo, Paolo. *La Vita e l'opera di Yu Suwŏn Pensatore Coreano del XVIII Secolo*. Naples: Istituto Universitario Orientale, Seminario di Studi Asiatici, 1981.

Scalapino, Robert A. and Chong-sik Lee. *Communism in Korea*. 2 vols. Berkeley and Los Angeles: University of California Press, 1972.

Schlesinger, Jr., Arthur. *The Age of Jackson*. New York: Book Find Club, 1945.

Schwartz, Benjamin. *The World of Thought in Ancient China*. Cambridge: Harvard University Press, 1985.

Shikata Hiroshi. "Richō jinkō ni kansuru ichi kenkyū" [A study on Yi dynasty population]. In *Chōsen shakai hōseishi kenkyū* [Studies in the social and legal history of Korea], pp. 257–388. Tokyo: Iwanami shoten, 1937.

_____. "Richō jinkō ni kansuru mibun kaikyūbetsuteki kansatsu" [An investigation of Yi dynasty population in terms of status and class]. In Chōsen teikoku daigaku hōgakkai, ed., *Chōsen keizai no kenkyū* [Studies in the economy of Korea] 3:363–482, appendix, pp. 1–33 and attached charts. Tokyo: Iwanami shoten, 1938.

Shin, Susan. "The Social Structure of Kŭmhwa County in the Late Seventeenth Century." *Occasional Papers on Korea*, no. 1 (April 1974), pp. 9–35.

Sin Chihyŏn. "Yŏm'ŏp" [The salt industry]. In *Han'guksa*, vol. 10. *Yangban kwallyo kukka ŭi sahoe kujo* [The history of Korea, the social structure of the yangban-bureaucratic state], pp. 389–412. Seoul: T'amgudang, 1974.

Sin Sŏkho. "Haeje" [Explanatory note]. In Pak Chega, *Chŏngyujip: pu Pukhag'ŭi* [The collected works of Pak Chega, with the essay on learning from the north appended], pp. 1–5 at the end of the volume. Seoul: Kuksa p'yŏnch'an wiwŏhoe, 1971.

Skocpol, Theda. *States and Social Revolutions: A Comparative Analysis of France, Russia, and China*. Cambridge: Cambridge University Press, 1979.

Smith, Thomas C. *The Agrarian Origins of Modern Japan*. Stanford: Stanford University Press, 1959.

Song Ch'ansik. "Pak Chiwŏn ŭi *Yŏnhaengjip*" [The travelogues of Pak Chiwŏn's trips to Yen-ching]. In Yŏksa hakhoe, ed., *Sirhak yŏn'gu immun*, pp. 177–217. Seoul: Ilchogak, 1973.

_____. *Yijo hugi sugong'ŏp e kwanhan yŏn'gu* [A study of manufacture in the late Yi dynasty]. Seoul: Sŏul Taehakkyo ch'ulp'anbu, 1973.

_____. "Chosŏn hugi haengjŏnnon" [The circulation of cash in the late Chosŏn period]. *Han'guk sasang taegye* [Grand outline of Korean thought]. Vol. 2, *Sahoe kyŏngje sasangp'yŏn* [Social and economic thought], pp. 747–929. Seoul: Taedong munhwa yŏnguwŏn, Sŏnggyun'gwan taehakkyo, 1976.

Song June-ho [Song Chunho]. "Chosŏn sidae ŭi kwagŏ wa yangban mit yang'in" [The civil service examinations of the Chosŏn period and yangban and commoners]. *Yŏksa hakpo* 69 (March 1976):101–35.

_____. *Kwagŏ* [The examination system]. Edited by Yŏksa hakhoe. Seoul: Ilchogak, 1981.

_____. "Kwagŏ chedo rŭl t'onghaesŏ pon Chungguk kwa Han'guk" [China and Korea as seen through the examination system]. In *Kwagŏ* [The examination system], pp. 195–223. Edited by Yŏksa hakhoe. Seoul: Ilchogak, 1981.

_____. "Chosŏn ŭi yangbanje rŭl ŏttŏk'e ihae halkŏsin'ga?" [How should we understand the yangban system of Chosŏn?]. In idem, *Chosŏn sahoesa yŏn'gu* [Studies in the social history of Chosŏn], pp. 118–64. Seoul: Ilchogak, 1987.

_____. "Chosŏn yangban'go" [A study of the yangban of Chosŏn]. In Song, *Chosŏn sahoesa yŏn'gu* [Studies in the social history of Chosŏn], pp. 165–259. Seoul: Ilchogak, 1987.

_____. "Namwŏn e tŭrŏonŭn Ch'angp'yŏng ŭ Wŏlkusil Yu-ssi: Yangban segye e issŏ hon'in i ŭimi hayŏttŏngŏt" [The Wŏlkusil Yu clan of Ch'angp'yŏng that moved into Namwŏn: The meaning of marriage in the yangban world]. In idem, *Chosŏn sahoesa yŏn'gu* [Studies in the social history of Chosŏn]. Seoul: Ilchogak, 1987.

Spence, Jonathan, and John E. Wills, Jr. *From Ming to Ch'ing*. New Haven, Conn.: Yale University Press, 1979.

_____. *The Search for Modern China*. New York: W. W. Norton, 1990.

Stampp, Kenneth M. *The Peculiar Institution: Slavery in the Ante-Bellum South*. New York: Vintage Books, 1956.

Sudō Yoshiyuki. "Sensho ni okeru nuhi no benrei to suisatsu to ni tsuite" [On the investigation and adjudication of slaves in the early Chōsen period]. *Seikyū gakusō* 22 (November 1935):1–61.

_____. "Kōrai makki yori Chōsen shoki in itaru nuhi no kenkyū" [A study of slavery from late Koryŏ to the early Chosŏn period], 3 parts. *Rekishigaku kenkyū,* pt. 1, 9, no. 1 (January 1939):6–45; pt. 2, 9, no. 2 (February 1939):57–76; pt. 3, 9, no. 3 (March 1939):23–66; pt. 4, 9, no. 4 (April 1939):64–94.

_____. "Kōraichō yori Chōsen shoki ni itaru densei no kaikaku" [Land reform between the Koryŏ and Chosŏn dynasties]. *Tōagaku* 3 (1940):115–91.

_____. "Kōrai makki yori Chōsen shoki ni itaru orimonogyō no hattatsu" [The development of the textile industry in the late Koryŏ and early Chosŏn period]. *Shakai keizaishigaku* 12, no. 3 (February 1942):245–306

_____. *Chūgoku tochi seidoshi kenkyū* [Studies in the land systems of China]. Tokyo: Tokyo daigaku shuppankai, 1954.

_____. "Hokusō ni okeru hōden kinseihō no shikō katei" [The process of the adoption of the square-field equal-tax system in the Northern Sung]. In idem, *Chūgoku tochi seidoshi kenkyū* [Studies in the history of Chinese land systems], pp. 434–509. Tokyo: Tokyō daigaku shuppankai, 1954.

_____. "Nansōmatsu no kōdenhō" [The public field system of the Southern Sung]. In idem, *Chūgoku tochi seidoshi kenkyū* [Studies in the land systems of China], pp. 537–602. Tokyo: Tokyo daigaku shuppankai, 1954.

_____. "Sōdai no tochi seidoron: Seidenron gendenron o chūshin to shite" [Land system proposals of the Sung period: Proposals for the well-field and limited-field systems]. In idem, *Tōsō shakai keizaishi kenkyū* [Studies in the social and economic history of the T'ang and Sung], pp. 233–320. Tokyo: Tōkyō daigaku shupankai, 1965.

Suh, Dae-sook. "Communist Party Leadership." In Suh Dae-sook and Chae-jin Lee, eds.,

Political Leadership in Korea, pp. 159–91. Seattle: University of Washington Press, 1976.

Tabana Tameo. *Chōsen kyōyaku kyōkashi no kenkyū* [A study of the history of the community compact as moral education in Chosŏn]. Tokyo: Chōhōsha, 1972.

Tagawa Kōzō. *Richō kōnōsei no kenkyū* [A study of the tribute system of the Yi dynasty]. Tokyo: Tōyō bunko, 1964.

_____. "Richō no kyōkyu ni tsuite" [Local regulations in the Yi dynasty]. Part 1, *Chōsen gakuhō* 76 (July 1975):35–72; part 2, 78 (January 1976):45–88; part 3, 81 (October 1976):179–210.

Tashiro Kazui. *Kinsei Nitchō tsūkō bōekishi no kenkyū* [A study of the Japan-Korea trade in recent times]. Tokyo: Sōbunsha, 1981.

Tawney, R. H. *Land and Labor in China*. 1932. Boston: Beacon Press, 1966.

Tillman, Hoyt Cleveland. *Utilitarian Confucianism: Ch'en Liang's Challenge to Chu Hsi*. Cambridge: Harvard University Press, 1982.

Toby, Ronald P. *State and Diplomacy in Early Modern Japan: Asia in the Development of the Tokugawa Bakufu*. Princeton, N.J.: Princeton University Press, 1984.

Tsukiyama Jisaburo. *Tōdai seiji seido no kenkyū* [A study of the T'ang system of government]. Osaka: Sōgenshi, 1967.

Twitchett, Denis. "Lu Chih (754–805): Imperial Adviser and Court Official." In Arthur F. Wright and Denis Twitchett, eds., *Confucian Personalities*, pp. 84–122. Stanford, Calif.: Stanford University Press, 1962.

_____. "Hsüan-tsung." In *The Cambridge History of China*, vol. 3. Cambridge: Cambridge University Press, 1979.

_____ and Michael Loewe, eds. *The Cambridge History of China*, vol. 1. Cambridge: Cambridge University Press, 1986.

_____ and John K. Fairbank, eds. *The Cambridge History of China*, vol. 3. Cambridge: Cambridge University Press, 1979.

Vlastos, Gregory. "Slavery in Plato's Thought." *Philosophical Review* 50 (1941):289–304. Reprinted in M. I. Finley, ed., *Slavery in Classical Antiquity*, pp. 133–49. Cambridge: W. Heffer and Sons, 1960.

Wada Sei. *Chōsen no tochi seido oyobi chisei seido chōsa hōkoku* [A report of an investigation of the land and land tax systems of Korea]. Keijo, 1920.

_____. *Chūgoku chihō jiji hattatsushi* [History of the development of local self-government in China]. 1939. Tokyo: Kyūko shoin, 1975.

Wagner, Edward Willett. *The Literati Purges: Political Conflict in Early Yi Korea*. Cambridge: East Asian Research Center and Harvard University Press, 1974.

_____. "The Ladder of Success in Yi Dynasty Korea." *Occasional Papers on Korea*, no. 1 (April 1974), pp. 1–8.

_____. "Social Stratification in Seventeenth-Century Korea: Some Observations from a 1663 Seoul Census Register." *Occasional Papers on Korea*, no. 1 (April 1974), pp. 36–54.

Wakeman, Frederic Jr. *The Great Enterprise: The Manchu Reconstruction of Imperial Order in Seventeenth-Century China*. 2 vols. Berkeley and Los Angeles: University of California Press, 1985.

Wakita Osamu. "The Social and Economic Consequences of Unification." In John Whitney Hall, ed., *The Cambridge History of Japan*, vol. 4. Cambridge: Cambridge University Press, 1991.

Watanabe Manabu. *Kinsei Chŏsen kyōikushi kenkyū* [A study of the history of education in the recent Chosŏn period]. Tokyo: Yūsankaku, 1969.

Watt, John R. *The District Magistrate in Late Imperial China*. New York: Columbia University Press, 1972.

Weber, Max. *Economy and Society*. Edited by Guenther Roth and Claus Wittich. 2 vols. Berkeley and Los Angeles: University of California Press, 1968.

Wechsler, Howard J. "The Founding of the T'ang Dynasty: Kao-tsu (Reign 618–26)." In Twitchett and Fairbanks, eds., *The Cambridge History of China*, vol. 3. Cambridge: Cambridge University Press, 1979.

Westermann, William L. *The Slave Systems of Greek and Roman Antiquity*. Philadelphia: The American Philosophical Society, 1955.

Wilbur, C. Martin. *Slavery in China During the Former Han Dynasty, 206 B.C. – A.D. 25*. New York: Russell and Russell, 1943.

Williams, Eric. *Capitalism and Slavery*. Chapel Hill: University of North Carolina Press, 1944.

Wills, John E., Jr. "Maritime China from Wang Chih to Shih Lang." In Jonathan Spence and Wills, eds., *From Ming to Ch'ing*, pp. 201–38. New Haven, Conn.: Yale University Press, 1979.

Wilson, C. H. "Trade, Society and the State." In *Cambridge Economic History of Europe*, vol. 4. Cambridge: Cambridge University Press, 1967.

Wŏn Yuhan. "Yijo Sukchong sidae ŭi chujŏn e taehayŏ" [Minting of cash in Sukchong's reign]. *Sahak yŏn'gu* 18 (1964):627–74.

_____. "Yijo Sukchongjo ŭi chujŏn tonggi" [The motive for minting coins in Sukchong's reign]. *Tongguk sahak* 9–10 (1966):37–52.

_____. "Sippal segi e issŏsŏ ŭi hwap'ye chŏngch'aek: Tongjŏn ŭi chujo saŏp chungsim'ŭro" [Currency policy in the eighteenth century: The minting of copper cash]. *Sahak yon'gu* 19 (April 1967):49–88.

_____. "Yijo hugi ch'ŏngjŏn ŭi suip yut'ong e taehayŏ" [Circulation of imported cash in the late Yi dynasty]. *Sahak yŏn'gu* 21 (September 1969):145–55.

_____. "Sŏngho Yi Ik ŭi pujŏngjŏk hwap'yeron" [Yi Ik's negative view of cash]. *Yŏksa hakpo* 48 (December 1970):53–72.

____. "Pan'gye Yu Hyŏngwŏn ŭi kŭngjŏngjŏk hwap'yeron" [Yu Hyŏngwŏn's positive views on currency]. In Hyeam Yu Hongnyŏl paksa Hwagap kinyŏm saŏp wiwŏnhoe, ed., *Yu Hongnyŏl paksa hwagap kinyŏm nonch'ong* [Essays in commemoration of the sixtieth birthday of Dr. Yu Hongnyŏl], pp. 287–301. Seoul: T'amgudang, 1971.

_____. "Chosŏn hugi hwap'ye chŏngch'aek e taehan ilkoch'al: Koaekchŏn ŭi chuyong non'ŭirŭl chungsimŭro" [A study of late Chosŏn currency policy: Proposals to mint multiple-denomination cash]. *Han'guksa yŏn'gu* 6 (September 1971):75–101.

_____. "Chosŏn hugi hwap'ye yut'ong e taehan ilgoch'al" [A study of currency circulation in late Chosŏn]. *Han'guksa yŏn'gu* 7 (March 1972):131–50.

_____. "Chosŏn hugi ŭi kŭmsok hwap'ye yut'ong chŏngch'aek: Sipch'il segi chŏnban ŭi tongjŏn yut'ong sidogirŭl chungsim'ŭro" [Metallic currency policy in late Chosŏn: The attempt to circulate copper cash in the first half of the seventeenth century]. *Tongbanghak chi* 13 (December 1972):97–134.

_____. *Chosŏn hugi hwap'yesa yŏn'gu* [Studies in the history of currency in the late Chosŏn period]. Seoul: Han'guk yŏn'guwŏn, 1975.

_____. "Sirhakcha ŭi hwap'ye sasang palchŏn e taehan koch'al: Kŭm ŭnhwa ŭi t'ongyongnon'ŭl chungsimŭro" [A study of the development of practical learning thought on currency: In particular the idea of circulating gold and silver currency]. *Tongbanghak chi* 23–24 (February 1980):141–66.

_____. "Sirhakcha ŭi hwap'ye kyŏngjeron" [Theories of a cash economy by Sirhak scholars]. *Tongbanghak chi* 26 (March 1981):155–221.

Wright, Arthur F., and Denis Twitchett, eds. *Confucian Personalities*. Stanford, Calif.: Stanford University Press, 1962.

_____. *Perspectives on the T'ang*. New Haven, Conn.: Yale University Press, 1973.

Yang, Lien-sheng. "Notes on Dr. Swann's *Food and Money in Ancient China*." In idem, *Studies in Chinese Institutional History*, pp. 85–118. Cambridge: Harvard University Press, 1961.

Yi Chaeryong, "Chosŏn ch'ŏn'gi ŭi nobi yŏn'gu" [A study of slaves in early Chosŏn]. *Sungjŏn taehakkyo nonmunjip* 3 (1971):169–88.

Yi Chongyŏng. "Chosŏnch'o hwap'yeje ŭi pyŏnch'ŏn [Changes in the currency system of early Chosŏn]. *Inmun kwahak* 7 (1962):295–338.

Yi Chun'gu. "Chosŏn hugi yangban sinbun idong e kwanhan yŏn'gu: Tansŏng changjŏg'ŭl chungsimŭro, sang" [A study of the movement of yangban status in the late Chosŏn period: The Tansŏng registers]. Part 1, *Yŏksa hakpo* 96 (December 1982):139–84; part 2, *Yŏksa hakpo* 97 (March 1983):1–29.

Yi Hŭisŭng, ed. *Minjung kug'ŏ taesajŏn* [Great dictionary of the national language for the masses]. Seoul: Minjung sŏgwan, 1961.

Yi Hongjik, ed. *Kuksadaesajŏn* [Great dictionary of national history]. 2 vols. Seoul: Chimun'gak, 1962, 1963.

Yi Hongnyŏl. "Mankwa sŏlhaeng ŭi chŏngch'aeksajŏk ch'ui: Chosŏn chunggirŭl chungsim'ŭro" [Trends in policy behind the establishment of the *mankwa* examination in the mid-Chosŏn period]. *Sahak yŏn'gu* 18 (September 1964):207–46.

Yi Hyŏngsŏk. *Imjin chŏllansa* [History of the Imjin War]. 3 vols. Seoul: Sinhyŏnsilsa, 1974.

Yi Kawŏn, Kwŏn Odon, and Im Ch'angsun, eds. *Tong'a Hanhan-daesajŏn* [The great East Asia Sino-Korean dictionary]. Seoul: Tong'a ch'ulp'ansa, 1982.

Yi Kibaek [Lee, Ki-baik]. "Silla t'ong'ilki mit Koryŏ ch'ogi ŭi yugyojŏk chŏngch'i inyŏm" [Confucian political ideas in the Unified Silla and early Koryŏ periods]. *Taedong munhwa yŏn'gu* 6–7 (1969):141–61.

_____. "Koryŏ sidae sinbun ŭi sesŭp kwa pyŏndong: Han'guk chŏnt'ong sahoe e issŏsŏ ŭi sinbun" [Changes in status inheritance in the Koryŏ period: Status in Korean traditional society]. In idem, *Minjok kwa yŏksa* [The nation and history], pp. 91–100. Seoul: Ilchogak, 1971.

_____. "Silla kolp'um ch'ejeha ŭi yugyojŏk chŏngch'i inyŏm" [Confucian political ideas in Silla under the bone-rank system]. In idem, *Silla sidae ŭi kukka pulgyo wa yugyo* [State Buddhism and Confucianism in the Silla period], pp. 153–85. Seoul: Han'guk yŏn'guwŏn, 1978.

_____. "Koryŏ kwijok sahoe ŭi hyŏngsŏng" [The formation of Koryŏ aristocratic society]. In Kuksa p'yŏnch'an wiwŏnhoe, ed. *Han'guksa*, vol. 4, *Koryŏ kwijok sahoe ŭi sŏngnip* [The establishment of Koryŏ's aristocratic society], pp. 152–212. Seoul: Taehan min'guk munkyobu, Kuksan p'yŏnch'an wiwŏnhoe, 1974.

Yi Kwangnin. "Yijo ch'ogi ŭi chejiŏp [Papermaking in the early Yi dynasty]. *Yŏksa hakpo* 10 (Sept. 1958):1–38.

_____. "Kyŏngjuin yŏn'gu [A study of the district's capital agent]. *Inmun kwahak* 7 (June 1962):237–67.

Yi Kyŏngsik. "Simnyuk segi chijuch'ŭng ŭi tonghyang" [Trends in the landlord stratum in the sixteenth century]. *Yŏksa kyoyuk* 19 (April 1976):139–83.

_____. "Simnyuk segi changsi ŭi sŏngnip kwa kŭ kiban" [The establishment of markets and their basis in the sixteenth century]. *Han'guksa yŏn'gu* 57 (June 1987):43–91.

_____. *Chosŏn chŏn'gi t'oji chedo yŏn'gu: t'oji pungŭpche wa nongmin chibae* [A study of the land system in the early Chosŏn dynasty: Land distribution and control of the peasantry]. Seoul: Ilchogak, 1986.

Yi Pyŏngdo. "Kwanghaegun ŭi tae Hugŭm chŏngch'aek" [Kwanghaegun's policy toward the Later Chin]. *Kuksasang ŭi chemunje* [Problems in national history] 1 (March 1959):135–73.

Yi Sangbaek. "Sŏŏl ch'adae ŭi yŏnwŏn e taehan ilmunje" [A problem relating to the origin of discrimination against nothoi]. In *Han'guk munhwasa yŏn'gu non'go* [Studies in the cultural history of Korea], pp. 171–204. Seoul: Uryu munhwasa, 1947.

_____. *Han'guksa, kŭnse chŏn'gip'yŏn* [The history of Korea, early modern period]. Seoul: Uryu munhwasa, 1962.

_____. "Ch'ŏnja sumogo" [A study of the inheritance of the mother's status by slaves]. *Chindan hakpo* 25, no. 7 (December 1964):155–84.

_____. *Han'guksa: Kŭnse hugip'yŏn* [History of Korea: Late recent times]. Seoul: Published by Uryu Munhwasa for the Chindan hakhoe, 1965.

Yi Sŏngmu. "Sŏnch'o ŭi Sŏnggyun'gwan yŏn'gu" [A study of the National Academy in the early Chosŏn dynasty]. *Yŏksa hakpo* 35–36 (December 1967):219–68.

_____. "Chosŏn ch'ogi ŭi hyanggyo." In *Hansŏng Yi Sang'ok paksa hwagap nonmunjip* (1970), pp. 235–54.

_____. "Chosŏn ch'ogi ŭi hyangni" [The *hyangni* of the early Chosŏn period]. *Han'guksa yŏn'gu* 5 (March 1970):65–96.

_____. "Yangban." In Kuksa p'yŏnch'an wiwŏnhoe, ed. *Han'guksa*, vol. 10, *Chosŏn: Yangban kwallyo kukka ŭi sahoe kujo* [Chosŏn: The social structure of the yangban-bureaucratic state], pp. 549–94. Seoul: T'amgudang, 1974.

_____. *Chosŏn ch'ogi yangban yŏn'gu* [A study of the yangban in the early Chosŏn period]. Seoul: Ilchogak, 1980.

Yi Sugŏn. *Yŏngnam Sarimp'a ŭi hyŏngsŏng* [The formation of the Sarim group in the Kyŏngsang area]. N.p.: Yŏngnam taehakkyo minjok munhwa yŏn'guso, 1979.

Yi T'aejin. "Chung'ang Ogunyŏngje ŭi sŏngnip kwajŏng" [The process of the establishment of the central five division system]. In Yukkun sagwan hakkyo Han'guk kunsa yŏn'gusil, ed., *Han'guk kunjesa* [The history of the Korean military system]. Vol. 2, *Kŭnse Chosŏn hugip'yŏn* [Early modern period: Late Chosŏn dynasty], pp. 41–162. Seoul: Yukkun ponbu, 1977.

_____. *Chosŏn hugi ŭi chŏngch'i wa kunyŏngje pyŏnch'ŏn* [Politics and changes in the army division system in the late Chosŏn period]. Seoul: Han'guk yŏn'guwŏn, 1985.

_____. *Han'guk sahoesa yŏngu* [Studies in the social history of Korea]. Seoul: Chisik san'ŏpsa, 1986.

_____. "Sarimp'a ŭi Yuhyangso pongnip undong" [The movement by the Sarim group to restore the Yuhyangso]. In *Han'guk sahoesa yŏn'gu: nong'ŏp kisul paltal kwa sahoe pyŏndong* [Studies in the social history of Korea: The development of agricultural technology and social change], pp. 125–85. Seoul: Chisik san'ŏpsa, 1986. Published originally as "Sarimp'a ŭi hyangyak pogŭp undong," *Han'guk munhwa* 4 (December 1983):1–38.

_____. "Simnyuk segi ch'ŏnbang (po) kwan'gae ŭi paltal: Sarim seryŏk taedu ŭi kyŏngjejŏk paegyŏng iltan" [The development of irrigation dikes in the sixteenth century: Part of the economic background to the emergence of the power of the *Sarim*]. In idem, *Han'guk sahoesa yŏngu*, pp. 274–88. Seoul: Chisik san'ŏpsa, 1986.

_____. "Sarimp'a ŭi hyangyak." In idem, *Han'guk sahoesa yŏngu*, pp. 274–88. Seoul: Chisik san'ŏpsa, 1986.

_____. "Yŏnhae chiyŏk ŭi yŏnjŏn kaebal: Ch'ŏksin chŏngch'i ŭi kyŏngjejŏk paegyŏng iltan" [The development of reclaimed fields along the coast: Part of the economic background of the consort-relative regime]. In Yi, *Han'guk sahoesa yŏngu*, pp. 222–52.

Yi Usŏng, "Ch'ogi Sirhak kwa sŏngnihak kwa ŭi kwan'gye: Pan'gye Yu Hyŏngwŏn ŭi kyŏng'u" [The relationship between early Practical Learning and the Learning of Nature and Principle]. *Tongbanghak chi* 58 (June 1988):15–22.

Yu Kyosŏng. "Soŭl Yug'ŭijŏn yŏn'gu [A study of the Seoul six licensed shops]. *Yŏksa hakpo* 8 (1955):377–434.

Yu Sŭngju, "Chosŏn hugi kunsu kwanggong'ŏp ŭi palchŏn" [The development of mining for military purposes in the late Chosŏn period]. *Sahakchi* 3 (July 1969):1–35.

_____. "Kwang'ŏp" [Mining]. In Taehan min'guk Mungyobu, Kuksa p'yŏnch'an wiwŏnhoe, ed.*Han'guksa*. Vol. 10, *Chosŏn: Yangban kwallyo kukka ŭi sahoe kujo* [Chosŏn: the social structure of the yangban-bureaucratic state], pp. 335–55. Seoul: Taehan min'guk mungyobu, Kuksa p'yŏnch'an wiwŏnhoe, 1974.

Yu Sŭngwŏn. *Chosŏn ch'ogi sinbunje yŏn'gu* [A study of the status system of early Chosŏn]. Seoul: Ŭryu munhwasa, 1987.

Yu Wŏndong. "Sang'ŏp" [Commerce]. Taehan min'guk Mungyobu, Kuksa p'yŏnch'an wiwŏnhoe, ed.*Han'guksa*, vol. 10, *Chosŏn: Yangban kwallyo kukka ŭi sahoe kujo* [Chosŏn: the social structure of the yangban-bureaucratic state], pp. 278–320. Seoul: T'amgudang, 1974.

_____. *Han'guk kŭndae kyŏngjesa yŏn'gu* [Studies in the recent economic history of Korea]. Seoul: Ilchisa, 1977.

Yukkun sagwan hakkyo, Han'guk kunsa yŏn'gusil [R.O.K. Army Military Academy, Research Hall for Korean Military History], ed.*Han'guk kunjesa* [The history of the Korean military system]. 2 vols. Vol. 1, *Kŭnse Chosŏn chŏn'gip'yŏn* [Recent times, the early Chosŏn period]. Seoul: Yukkun ponbu, 1968. Vol. 2, *Kŭnse Chosŏn hugip'yŏn* [Recent times, the late Chosŏn period]. Seoul: Yukkun ponbu, 1977.

Index

Korean, Chinese, and Japanese terms are defined in the Glossary.